NEW ENGLAND
NEW YORK, NEW JER
SEY and PENSILVANIA
By H. Moll Geographer.

Note. The Towns to which Missionaries
are sent are marked thus ⟂ 1730.

THE CHURCH OF ENGLAND IN

PRE-REVOLUTIONARY

CONNECTICUT

NEW DOCUMENTS AND LETTERS CONCERNING THE LOYALIST CLERGY AND THE PLIGHT OF THEIR SURVIVING CHURCH

Edited by

KENNETH WALTER CAMERON

TRANSCENDENTAL BOOKS—DRAWER 1080—HARTFORD 06101

COPYRIGHT 1976 BY
KENNETH WALTER CAMERON

TO

RUTH A. DOREY

OF SOUTH WINDSOR, CONNECTICUT,

HOUSEWIFE, MOTHER, CREATIVE TYPIST,

AND SHAPER OF THIS VOLUME,

WHICH REVEALS HER CHARACTERISTIC

PRECISION AND DEDICATED INDUSTRY.

IT ALSO BEARS

THE EDITOR'S THANKS FOR

HER WISDOM AND HELP

THROUGHOUT SEVENTEEN YEARS.

COMPANION

STUDIES IN AMERICAN HISTORY

American Episcopal Clergy: Registers of Ordinations in the Episcopal Church in the United States from 1785 through 1904--with Indexes. Edited by Kenneth Walter Cameron.

The Anglican Episcopate in Connecticut (1784-1899): A Sheaf of Biographical and Institutional Studies for Churchmen and Historians with Early Ecclesiastical Documents. Edited by Kenneth Walter Cameron.

The Catholic Revival in Episcopal Connecticut (1850-1925). By Kenneth Walter Cameron.

Centennial History of Trinity Episcopal Church, Bridgeport, Connecticut, Missionary of the Catholic Faith 1863-1963. By Kenneth Walter Cameron.

The Church of England in Pre-Revolutionary Connecticut: New Documents and Letters, with a Detailed Index. By Kenneth Walter Cameron. [In progress.]

Connecticut Churchmanship: Records and Historical Papers concerning the Anglican Church in Connecticut in the Eighteenth and Early Nineteenth Centuries. Edited by Kenneth Walter Cameron.

Documentary History of the Protestant Episcopal Church in Connecticut, 1704-1789. Edited by Francis L. Hawks and William Stevens Perry. [Originally published in 1863.] (Re-edited by Kenneth Walter Cameron, 2 vols. in 1.)

Early Anglicanism in Connecticut: Materials on the Missionary Career of Roger Viets, Samuel Seabury's Communion Office, and Aids for Scholarly Research. Edited by Kenneth Walter Cameron.

Facsimiles of Early Episcopal Church Documents (1759-1789). Edited by Kenneth Walter Cameron.

The Genesis of Christ Church, Stratford, Connecticut: Pre-Revolutionary Church of England; Background and Earliest Annals... With a Detailed Index. By Kenneth Walter Cameron. An Appendix by Carolyn Hutchens.

Historical Resources of the Episcopal Diocese of Connecticut. Edited by Kenneth Walter Cameron. Index by Carolyn Hutchens.

Index of the Pamphlet Collection of the Diocese of Connecticut. By Kenneth Walter Cameron.

Letter-Book of the Rev. Henry Caner, S.P.G. Missionary in Colonial Connecticut and Massachusetts until the Revolution. A Review of his Correspondence from 1728 through 1778. By Kenneth Walter Cameron.

The Life of Eben Edwards Beardsley, Connecticut Churchman and Ecclesiastical Historian (1808-1891). By William Agur Beardsley. (Edited by Kenneth Walter Cameron.)

The Works of Samuel Peters of Hebron, Connecticut, New-England Historian, Satirist, Folklorist, Anti-Patriot, and Anglican Clergyman (1735-1826). With Historical Indexes. Edited by Kenneth Walter Cameron.

TRANSCENDENTAL BOOKS—DRAWER 1080—HARTFORD 06101

TABLE OF CONTENTS

INTRODUCTION

The first significant collection of early papers on the Anglican tradition in Connecticut was issued in two small volumes in 1863 under the title, <u>Documentary History of the Protestant Episcopal Church...in Connecticut</u>, edited by Francis L. Hawks and William Stevens Perry. Its importance for historians during the past one hundred and fourteen years cannot be overemphasized. No Anglican study of Colonial times or of the earliest parishes has escaped its influence. Produced during the Civil War under distressing conditions and high costs, it is a remarkable example of the best scholarship of that period, whatever may be its limitations by modern editorial standards. One laments, of course, the fact that it printed only excerpts instead of complete letters and that it provided no index of names, places, institutions and subjects; but the scope and quality of its contents attest to the historical acumen of its compilers, who knew exactly what was required in their day to advance the cause of historiography then and now.

Though an independent work, the present volume, the only large collection of early Anglican papers to appear in more than a century, may be regarded as extending "Hawks and Perry" and supplementing it. Benefiting from modern editorial techniques and committed as far as resources have permitted to the editing of complete manuscripts, it is indebted principally to the resources of the Archives of the Diocese of Connecticut, the holdings of which have only in our own times been sufficiently calendered to be accessible and useful. Although Colonial-Church-of-England materials predominate herein, I have included a few papers of the Dissenters--for example, the Stratford petition of March 7, 1669--for the light they throw upon the Anglican situation. Because historiography depends as much upon documents as upon letters, I have here edited for the first time a block of ecclesiastical papers in the Connecticut State Library-- chiefly petitions or "memorials" to the General Assembly--and planted here and there in my chronological sequence a will, a deed, or a relevant business memorandum.

With regard to the surviving eighteenth-century manuscripts from which the present collection is derived, the scholar should be aware of the impossibility, in every instance, of handling what might be called the <u>letter as posted</u>. Occasionally he must settle for a good summary, a rough draft, a copy sent to the New England Commissary or to Dr. Caner or to Dr. Johnson or to the Archbishop of Canterbury--the original having been directed elsewhere and, perhaps, lost. Sometimes, when the writer believed his polished communication to the S. P. G. had failed to arrive, he would send an emended duplicate months or even years later--modified in accordance with new circumstances. Both forms have occasionally come down to us. (For the custom of dispatching a letter simultaneously to two addresses, see pages 133 top and 137 top. For variations between the rough draft and the final copy, see pages 119, 123, 208, 219-222.) Some letters included herein have survived, it appears, only in nineteenth-century transcripts--as in Bishop John Williams's blotting book of historical papers which he used in his lectures at the Berkeley Divinity School. Because of their importance, I have included a few incomplete pieces in the hope that they may serve a good purpose until better texts may be discovered. About twenty others in this gathering are amplifications of materials which, by our modern standards, Hawks and Perry badly mangled. (To restore the omitted portions I have had recourse to the S. P. G. papers on filmstrip in the Library of Congress.) If the exact character of the text I have edited herein be required--whether rough draft, final copy, variant, or late transcript--the scholar ought to visit the Archives of the Diocese of Connecticut and handle the material himself, helpfully calling to the attention of the Archivist any better or different redactions known to him. The effective writing of eighteenth-century history, especially in the area covered by the present volume, I am convinced, requires a large measure of such cooperation to atone for the general indifference toward ecclesiastical bibliography during the last century.

In a compilation of this sort, drawn from a variety of uneven materials, I am aware of the possibility of editorial inconsistency. When dealing with letters-as-posted or with rough drafts, I have tried to reproduce the misspellings and errors (without the use of <u>sic</u>), relying upon the index to regularize names, places, and institutions. Though I cannot hope to have corrected all my own mistakes, I have carefully double-checked everything edited, except on page 53, column 2, where "Northampton [Conn.]" should, of course, read "Northampton [Mass.]." Whatever the limitations of this enterprise, I hope they may be mightily outweighed by the benefits--the stimulation of new research both in Connecticut and throughout the United States.

I wish here to express gratitude to all who have preceded me in the office of Historiographer (sometimes called "Registrar"), to the forgotten hundreds who during the last century helped gather the rich collection the Diocese now possesses, and to twentieth-century donors to the growing collection of manuscripts, typescripts, photostats and films. Among the institutions that graciously permitted me to edit a few of their letters I must mention (besides the Connecticut State Library) Yale University Library, the Historical Society of Pennsylvania, the Massachusetts Diocesan Library, and the Archives of the Episcopal Church, in Austin, Texas. My largest and most conscious debt is to the Church Missions Publishing Company ("C. M. P. C."), of Hartford, for its encouragement under the presidencies of two bishops-- the Rt. Rev. Walter H. Gray and the Rt. Rev. J. Warren Hutchens--interested students of the history of the Diocese and alert conservators of its manuscript resources.

KENNETH WALTER CAMERON

July 4, 1976.

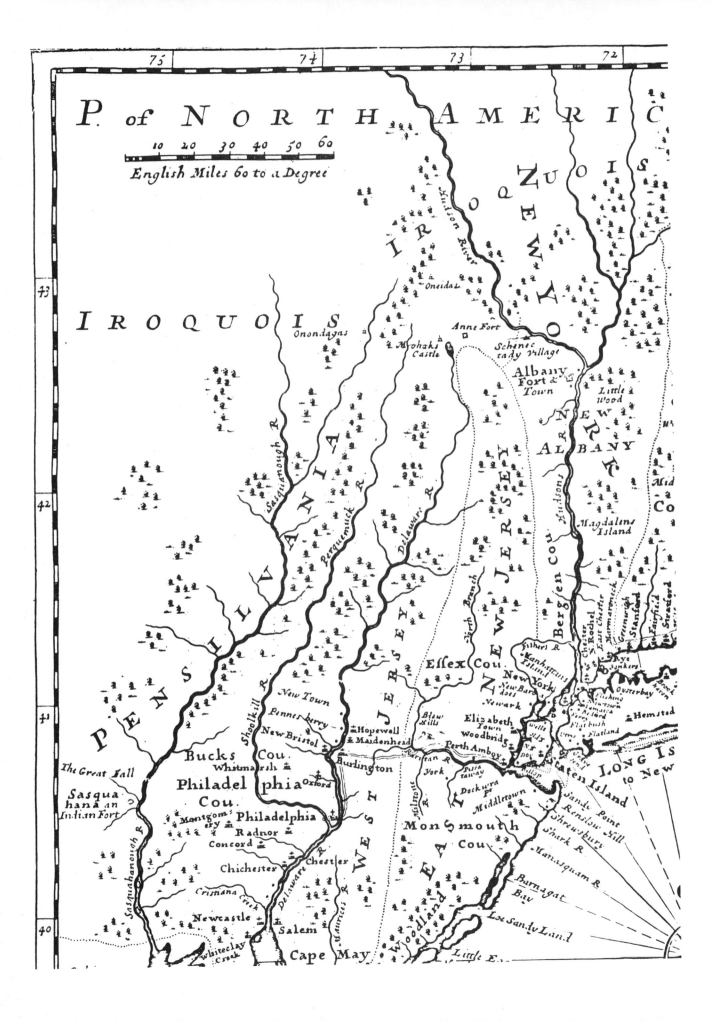

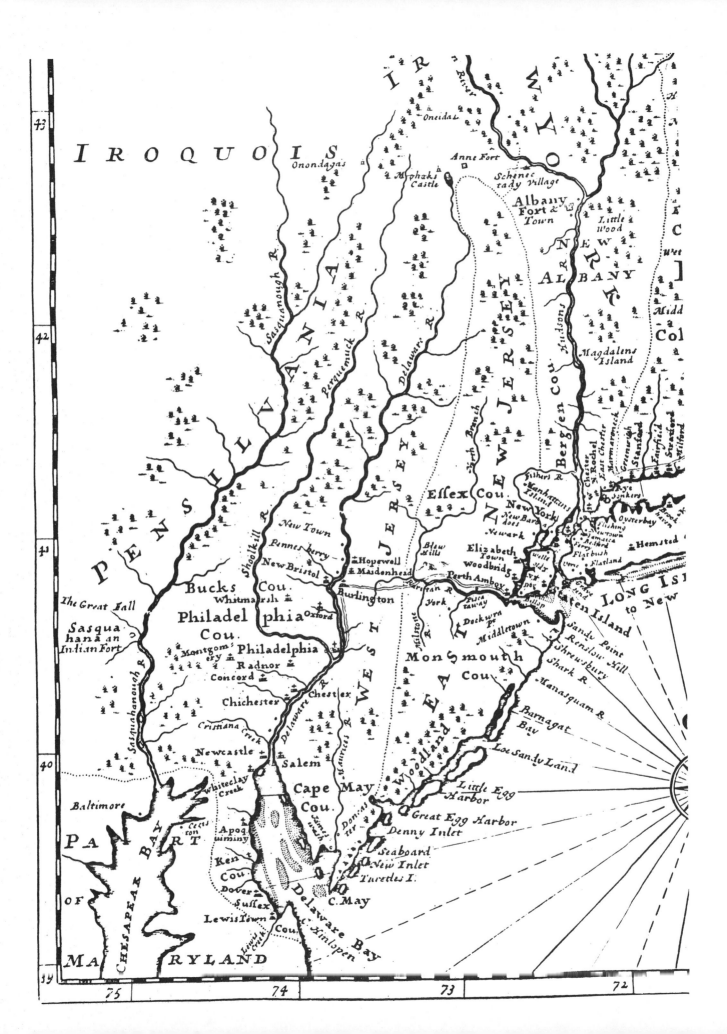

WILLIAM the Third, by the Grace of God, of *England, Scotland, France,* and *Ireland,* King, Defender of the Faith, &c. To all Christian People, to whom these Presents shall come, Greeting.

I. Whereas We are credibly Informed, That in many of Our Plantations, Colonies and Factories beyond the Seas, belonging to Our Kingdom of *England,* the Provision for Ministers is very mean, and many others of Our said Plantations, Colonies and Factories are wholly Destitute and Unprovided of a Maintenance for Ministers, and the Publick Worship of God; and for lack of Support and Maintenance for such, many of our Loving Subjects do want the Administration of God's Word and Sacraments, and

A 2

A
COLLECTION
OF
PAPERS,

Printed by ORDER of the

SOCIETY
FOR THE

PROPAGATION of the GOSPEL
in FOREIGN PARTS.

VIZ.

The Charter,
The Request, &c.
The Qualifications of Missionaries.
} { Instructions for the Clergy.
Instructions for School-Masters.
Prayers for the Charity-Schools.

LONDON,

Printed by *Joseph Downing,* in *Bartholomew-Close* near *West-Smithfield,* 1706.

[4]

and seem to be abandoned to Atheism and Infidelity; and also for want of Learned and Orthodox Ministers to Instruct our said Loving Subjects in the Principles of True Religion, divers Romish Priests and Jesuits are the more encouraged to pervert and draw over Our said Loving Subjects to Popish Superstition and Idolatry.

II. And whereas We think it our Duty, as much as in Us lies, to promote the Glory of God, by the Instruction of Our People in the Christian Religion; and that it will be highly conducive for accomplishing those Ends; that a sufficient Maintenance be provided for an Orthodox Clergy to live amongst them, and that such other Provision be made as may be necessary for the Propagation of the Gospel in those Parts.

III. And whereas we have been well assured, That if We would be graciously pleased to erect and settle a Corporation for the receiving, managing and disposing of the Charity of Our loving Subjects, divers Persons would be Induced to extend their Charity to the Uses and Purposes aforesaid.

IV. Know ye therefore, That We have, for the Considerations aforesaid, and for the better and more orderly carrying on the said Charitable

That a Maintenance for an Orthodox Clergy and other Provision may be made for the Propagation of the Gospel in the Plantations beyond the Sea.

His Majesty Incorporates the Arch-bishop of Canterbury, and 93...

[5]

ble Purposes, of Our special Grace, certain Knowledge, and mere Motion, Willed, Ordained, Constituted and Appointed, and by these Presents, for Us, Our Heirs and Successors, Do Will, Ordain, Constitute, Declare and Grant, That the most Reverend Fathers in God, *Thomas* Lord Archbishop of *Canterbury*, and *John* Lord Archbishop of *York*; the Right Reverend Fathers in God, *Henry* Lord Bishop of *London*, *William* Lord Bishop of *Worcester*, Our Lord Almoner, *Simon* Lord Bishop of *Ely*, *Thomas* Lord Bishop of *Rochester*, Dean of *Westminster*; and the Lords Archbishops of *Canterbury* and *York*, the Bishops of *London* and *Ely*, the Lord Almoner and Dean of *Westminster* for the time being; *Edward* Lord Bishop of *Glocester*, *John* Lord Bishop of *Chichester*, *Nickolas* Lord Bishop of *Chester*, *Richard* Lord Bishop of *Bath* and *Wells*, *Humphrey* Lord Bishop of *Bangor*, *John Montague* Doctor of Divinity, Clerk of our Closet, *William Sherlock* Doctor of Divinity, Dean of *St. Paul's*, *William Stanley* Doctor of Divinity, Arch-Deacon of *London*, and the Clerk of the Closet, of Us, Our Heirs and Successors; the Dean of *St. Paul's*, and Arch-Deacon of *London* for the time being; The two *Regius* and two *Margaret* Professors of Divinity of both Our Universities, for the time being, *Thomas* Earl of *Thanet*, *Thomas* Lord Vis-

others, by the Name of, The Society for the Propagation of the Gospel in Foreign parts.

count

[6]

count Weymouth, Francis Lord Guilford, William Lord Digby, Sir Thomas Cookes of Bently, Sir Richard Bulkley, Sir John Phillips, and Sir Arthur Owen, Baronets; Sir Humphrey Mackworth, Sir William Pritchard, Sir William Russel, Sir Edmund Turner, Sir William Hustler, Sir John Chardin, and Sir Richard Blackmore, Kts. John Hook Esq; Serjeant at Law, George Hooper Doctor of Divinity, Dean of Canterbury, George Booth Doctor of Divinity, Arch-Deacon of Durham, Sir George Wheeler Prebendary of Durham, William Beveridge Doctor of Divinity, Arch-Deacon of Colchester, Sir William Dawes Baronet, Thomas Manningham, Edward Gee, Thomas Lyford, Nathaniel Resbury, Offspring Blackhall, George Stanhope, William Hayley, and Richard Willis, Doctors of Divinity, and Our Chaplains in Ordinary; John Mapletoft, Zacheus Isham, John Davis, William Lancaster, Humphrey Hodey, Richard Lucas, John Evans, Thomas Bray, John Gascarth, White Kennett, Lilly Butler, Josiah Woodward, Doctors in Divinity; Gideon Harvey, and Frederick Slare, Doctors of Physick; Rowland Cotton, Thomas Jervois, Maynard Colchester, James Vernon Junior, Joseph Neal, Grey Nevill, Thomas Clerk, Peter King, Rock, John Comins, William Melmouth, Tho. Bromfield, John Reynolds, Dutton Seaman, Whitlock Bulstrode, Samuel Brewster, John Chamberlain, Richard King, and Daniel Nicoll, Esqs; Benjamin Lawdell,

[7]

Lawdell, John Trimmer, Charles Toriano, and John Hodges, Merchants; William Fleetwood, William Whitfield, and Samuel Bradford, Masters of Arts, and Our Chaplains in Ordinary; Tho. Little, Batchelor in Divinity; Tho. Staino, Henry Altham, William Lloyd, Henry Shute, Tho. Frank, and William Mecken, Clerks, and their Successors; to be Elected in manner as hereafter directed, be, and shall for ever hereafter be, and by Virtue of these Presents, shall be one Body Politick and Corporate, in Deed, and in Name, by the Name of, *The Society for the Propagation of the Gospel in Foreign Parts*: And them and their Successors by the same Name, We do by these Presents, for Us, Our Heirs and Successors, really and fully Make, Ordain, Constitute and Declare, One Body Politick and Corporate in Deed and in Name.

V. And that by the same Name, they and their Successors shall and may have perpetual Succession. *To have perpetual Succession.*

VI. And that they and their Successors, by that Name, shall and may, for ever hereafter, be Persons Able and Capable in the Law to Purchase, Have, Take, Receive, and Enjoy to them, and their Successors, Manors, Messuages, Lands, Tenements, Rents, Advowsons, Liberties, Priviledges, Jurisdictions, Franchises, and other Hereditaments whatsoever, of whatsoever Nature, *To Purchase 2000 l. per Ann. Inheritance, and Estates for Lives or Years, Goods and Chattels of any Value.*

Kind

B

Kind and Quality they be, in Fee and in Perpetuity, not exceeding the yearly Value of Two Thousand Pounds, beyond Reprizals; and also Estates for Lives and for Years, and all other manner of Goods, Chattels, and Things whatsoever, of what Name, Nature, Quality, or Value soever they be, for the better Support and Maintenance of an Orthodox Clergy in Foreign Parts, and other the Uses aforesaid; And to Give, Grant, Lett and Demise the said Manors, Messuages, Lands, Tenements, Hereditaments, Goods, Chattels, and things whatsoever aforesaid, by Lease or Leases, for Term of Years, in Possession at the time of Granting thereof, and not in Reversion, not exceeding the Term of One and Thirty Years from the time of Granting thereof; on which, in Case no Fine be taken, shall be Reserved the full Value; and in Case a Fine be taken, shall be Reserved at least a Moiety of the full Value, that the same shall reasonably and *Bona fide* be worth at the time of such Demise.

And to Grant or Demise for 31 Years in Possession only without Fine at the full Rent, or with Fine at the Moiety of the full Value.

VII. And that by the Name aforesaid, they shall, and may be able to Plead and be Impleaded, Answer and be Answered unto, Defend and be Defended, in all Courts and Places whatsoever, and before whatsoever Judges, Justices, or other Officers, of Us, Our Heirs and Successors, in all and singular Actions, Plaints, Pleas, Matters and

And by that Name to Plead and be Impleaded.

and Demands, of what Kind, Nature or Quality soever they be: And to Act and do all other Matters and Things, in as ample Manner and Form as any other Our Leige Subjects of this Our Realm of *England*, being Persons able and capable in the Law, or any other Body Corporate or Politick within this our Realm of *England*, can, or may have, purchase, receive, possess, take, enjoy, grant, set, let, demise, plead and be impleaded, answer, and be answered unto, defend and be defended, do, permit and execute.

VIII. And that the said Society for ever hereafter, shall and may have a common Seal, to serve for the Causes and Business of them and their Successors: And that it shall and may be lawful for them and their Successors to change, break, alter, and make New the said Seal from time to time, and at their Pleasure, as they shall think best.

And that the said Society shall have a Common Seal.

IX. And for the better Execution of the Purposes aforesaid, We do give and grant to the said *Society for the Propagation of the Gospel in Foreign Parts*, and their Successors, That they and their Successors for ever, shall, upon the third *Friday* in *February* yearly, meet at some convenient Place, to be appointed by the said Society, or Successors, in all the Major part of them, who shall be present at

And Yearly meet on the third Friday in February between 8 and 12 in the Morning. To chuse a President, one or more Vice-Presidents, one or more Treasurers, two or more Auditors, one

B 2

[10]

Secretary, and any General Meeting, between the Hours of Eight and Twelve in the Morning; and that they, or the Major part of such of them that shall then be present, shall choose one President, one or more Vice-President or Vice-Presidents, one or more Treasurer or Treasurers, two or more Auditors, one Secretary, and such other Officers, Ministers and Servants as shall be thought convenient, to serve in the said Offices for the Year ensuing: And that the said President, and Vice-Presidents, and all Officers then elected, shall, before they act in their respective Offices, take an Oath, to be to them Administred by the President, or in his Absence, by one of the Vice-Presidents of the Year preceding, who are hereby Authorized to Administer the same, for the Faithful and due Execution of their respective Offices and Places during the said Year.

X. And Our further Will and Pleasure is, That the first President of the said Society, shall be *Thomas*, by Divine Providence, Lord Archbishop of *Canterbury*, Primate and Metropolitan of all *England*; And that the said President shall, within Thirty Days after the passing of this Charter, cause Summons to be Issued to the several Members of the said Society herein particularly mentioned, to meet at such Time and Place as he shall appoint: And that they, or the ma-

jor

[margin: Secretary, and other Officers for the Year ensuing, shall take Oath for due Execution of Office.]

[margin: That Thomas, Lord Archbishop of Canterbury be the first President, who, in 30 days after the Charter passed, shall issue Summons to meet and elect Vice-Presidents, Treasurers,]

---

jor part of such of them as shall then be present, shall proceed to the Election of one or more Vice-President or Vice-Presidents, one or more Treasurer or Treasurers, two or more Auditors, one Secretary, and such other Officers, Ministers, and Servants, as to them shall seem meet; which said Officers, from the time of their Election into their respective Offices, shall continue therein until the third *Friday* in *February*, which shall be in the Year of our Lord, One Thousand seven Hundred and One, and from thenceforwards until others shall be chosen into their Places in manner aforesaid.

XI. And that if it shall happen, that any of the Persons at any time chosen into any of the said Offices shall Die, or on any account be removed from such Office at any time between the said yearly Days of Election, that in such Case it shall be lawful for the surviving and continuing President, or any one of the Vice-Presidents, to Issue Summons to the several Members of the Body Corporate, to meet at the usual place of the Annual Meeting of the said Society, at such Time, as shall be specified in the said Summons; and that such Members of the said Body Corporate who shall meet upon such Summons, or the Major part of them, shall and may choose an Officer or Officers into the room or place of such Person or Persons, so Dead or Removed, as to them shall seem meet.

XII.

[margin: Auditors, Secretary, and other Officers to continue till the 3d. Friday in Feb. 1700.]

[margin: And if any Officer die, or be removed, the President, or one of the Vice-Presidents, may Summon the Members of the Society to meet and choose another in his place.]

[12]

And that the said Society meet to transact Business on the third Friday in every Month, or oftner if need be. And at such monthly Meeting, may Elect such Members of the Corporation as they see fit.

XII. And We do further Grant unto the said Society for the Propagation of the Gospel in Foreign Parts, and their Successors, that they and their Successors shall and may, on the third Friday in every Month yearly, for ever hereafter, and oftner if need be, every Month yearly, for ever hereafter, and oftner, if occasion requires, meet at some convenient place to be appointed for that purpose, to transact the Business of the said Society, and shall and may at any Meeting on such third Friday in the Month, Elect such Persons to be Members of the said Corporation, as they or the major part of them then present, shall think beneficial to the Charitable Designs of the said Corporation.

But no Act of the Society shall be valid, unless the President or some Vice-President, and seven other Members, be present,& the Major part of them consenting hereto.

XIII. And Our Will and Pleasure is, That no Act done in any Assembly of the said Society, shall be valid, unless the President or some one of the Vice-Presidents, and seven other Members of the said Company at the least, and the Major part of them consenting thereunto.

And at the first or second Meeting of the said Society, and any on the Meeting on the Third Friday in November, February, May, and August, for ever, the

XIV. And We further Will, and by these Presents for Us, Our Heirs and Successors, do Ordain, and Grant unto the said Society for the Propagation of the Gospel in Foreign Parts, and their Successors, That they, or their Successors, or the Major part of them who shall be present at the first and second Meeting of the said Society, or

at

[13]

major part present, may make By-Laws, and execute Leases.

at any Meeting on the third *Friday* in the Months of *November, February, May,* and *August,* yearly for ever, and at no other Meetings of the said Society, shall, and may consult, determine, constitute, ordain, and make any Constitutions, Laws, Ordinances and Statutes whatsoever; as also to Execute Leases for Years, as aforesaid, which to them, or the Major part of them then present, shall seem reasonable, profitable, or requisite, for, touching or concerning the Good Estate, Rule, Order and Government of the said Corporation, and the more effectual promoting the said Charitable Designs: All which Laws, Ordinances and Constitutions, so to be made, ordained and established, as aforesaid, We Will, Command and Ordain by these Presents, for Us, Our Heirs and Successors, to be from time to time, and at all times hereafter, kept and performed in all things, as the same ought to be, on the Penalties and Amerciaments in the same to be imposed and limited, so as the same Laws, Constitutions, Ordinances, Penalties, and Amerciaments, be reasonable, and not repugnant, or contrary to the Laws and Statutes of this Our Realm of *England.*

And the said Society at any Meeting may depute fit Persons to

XV. And We do likewise Grant unto the said Society for the Propagation of *the Gospel in Foreign Parts,* and their Successors, that they and

their

[14]

take Subscriptions, and collect Money contributed for the Purposes aforesaid.

their Successors, or the Major part of such of them as shall be present at any Meeting of the said Society, shall have Power from time to time, and at all times hereafter, to depute such Persons as they shall think fit to take Subscriptions, and to gather and collect such Monies as shall be by any Person or Persons contributed for the purposes aforesaid.

And may cause publick Notification of this Charter.

XVI. And shall, and may remove and displace such Deputies as often as they shall see cause so to do, and to cause publick Notification on to be made of this Charter, and the Powers thereby granted, in such manner as they shall think most conducible to the furtherance of the said Charity.

And shall yearly give Account to the Lord Chancellour or Keeper, and two Chief Justices, or two of them, of all Moneys received and laid out.

XVII. And Our further Will and Pleasure is, That the said Society shall yearly and every year, give an Account in Writing to Our Lord Chancellour, or Lord Keeper of the Great Seal of *England* for the time being, the Lord Chief Justice of the King's Bench, and the Lord Chief Justice of the Common Pleas, or any two of them, of the several Sum or Sums of Money by them received and laid out by Virtue of these Presents, or any Authority hereby given, and of the Management and Disposition of the Revenues and Charities aforesaid.

[15]

And Lastly, Our Pleasure is, That these Our Letters Patents, or the Inrolment thereof, shall be good, firm, valid, and effectual in the Law, according to our Royal Intentions herein before declared. In Witness whereof, We have caused these Our Letters to be made Patents. Witness our Self at *Westminster* the Sixteenth day of *June*, in the Thirteenth Year of Our Reign.

Per Breve de Privato Sigillo

COCKS.

The Names of Members Elected since the Incorporating of the Society.

THE Right Honourable *Thomas* Earl of *Pembroke* and *Montgomery, Nathaniel* Lord Bishop of *Durham, Peter* Lord Bishop of *Winchester, William* Lord Bishop of *Landaff, Jonathan* Lord Bishop of *Exeter, Gilbert* Lord Bishop of *Sarum, John* Lord Bishop of *Coventry* and *Litchfield, John* Lord Bishop of *Norwich, Richard* Lord Bishop of *Peterborough, John* Lord Bishop of *Bristol,*

And

C

[16]

Briſtol, James Lord Biſhop of Lincoln, William Lord Biſhop of Oxford, William Wake Doctor of Divinity & Dean of Exeter, Charles Trimnel Doctor of Divinity, and Arch-Deacon of Norfolk, George Verney, Henry Godolphin, John Younger, and Roger Altham, Doctors of Divinity; Alex. Torriano Batchelour of Laws, Col. Francis Nicholſon Governour of Virginia, George Wright, Robert Nelſon, and Ralph Snow, Eſqs; Col. Joſeph Dudley Governour of New-England, Col. Lewis Morris, Doctor Samuel Freeman Dean of Peterborough, Col. Robert Quarry, Sir Paul Whitchcott, Doctor John Jeffery Arch-Deacon of Norwich, Edward Waddington Maſter of Arts, Robert Hardeſty, Richard Ruth, John Hanger, and John Evelin, Eſqs; George White, John Evans, William Parrot, Henry Loe, Merchants; Joſhua Walker, B. D. Samuel Barton Doctor of Divinity, Sir Nathaniel Johnſon Governour of Carolina, Nicholas Trot Eſq; Attorney Gen. in Carolina, Philip Stubs Maſter of Arts, William Gore Eſq; Humphrey Prideaux Doctor of Divinity and Dean of Norwich, Thomas Plume Doctor of Divinity and Arch-Deacon of Rocheſter, George Thorp Doctor of Divinity and Prebendary of Canterbury, Thomas Amy Eſq; Samuel Lowe B. D. John Langbarne Eſq; William Lord Biſhop of Carliſle; Richard Leech, William Nichols, Doctors of Divinity; Edward Colſton, Francis

[17]

Francis Windham, Eſqs; Thomas Gilbert Gent. Sir John Cook Dean of the Arches, J. F. Oſtervald Profeſſor of Divinity and Paſtor of the Church of Neufchatel, L. Tronchin, J. A. Turretin, Profeſſors of Divinity at Geneva; Francis Gaſtril Doctor of Divinity, John Sharp Eſq; Vigerus Edwards Gent. John Laughton B. D. Prebendary of Worceſter, Ralph Barker, Thomas Paget, John Millington, Doctors of Divinity Thomas Railton; Eſq; The Right Honourable Charles Earl of Berkley, Francis Barker Merchant, George Keith M. A. John Meller Eſq; Mr. Henry Hoare, Colonel Caleb Heathcote, Thomas Dent, Edmond Gibſon, Doctors of Divinity; Richard Bull Merchant, John Hancock Doctor of Divinity, Benedict Pictet Profeſſor of Divinity in Geneva.

C 2

The

[18]

The Request of the SOCIETY *for the Propagation of the Gospel in Foreign Parts, concerning fit Ministers to be sent Abroad for that good Purpose.*

THE SOCIETY for the *Propagation of the Gospel in Foreign Parts,* having been Incorporated by a ROYAL CHARTER under the Great Seal of *England,* dated *June* 16. 1701. and thereby empowered to Ask, Receive, and Dispose of such Monies, as shall be contributed by charitable, devout, and zealous Christians, towards carrying on so great and pious a Design, have already, by what hath been given by themselves and others, not only laid the Foundation, but made considerable Progress in it; having sent, besides Books and other things, several Ministers of the *Church of England* into Her Majesty's Dominions and Colonies in the *West-Indies.*

But understanding by Letters since come from thence, that there is great need of many more,

[19]

more; to Instruct the *English,* and such *Indians* as live among them, or near them, in the Principles of the Christian Religion, to administer the Word and Sacraments, and perform all such Offices as are necessary to the Support and Furtherance of the Gospel in those Parts, did in a general Meeting of the said *Society,* held *January* 15. 1702. agree, That all the Bishops of the Realm, who are Members of the *Society,* should be earnestly desired to recommend it to their Arch-Deacons and their Officials, that publick Notice may be given in their next Archidiaconal Visitations, that such Clergymen as have a mind to be employed in this Apostolical Work, and can bring sufficient Testimonials, according to the Form hereunto annexed, that they are duly qualified for it, may give in their Names to their respective Bishops in whose Diocese they live, or to their Arch-Deacons, to be communicated by them to the *Society,* which will consult with the Lord Bishop of *London,* in order to sending them to such Places as have most need, and where they may therefore, by God's Assistance and Blessing, do most good.

And if any shall be sent to Places, where there is not a sufficient Maintenance already settled, the SOCIETY will take care, that they may have not only a competent Subsistence; but all the

[20]

the Encouragement that is due to those who devote themselves to the Service of Almighty God and our Saviour, by Propagating and Promoting his Gospel in the Truth and Purity of it, according to the Doctrine, Discipline, and Worship Established in the Church of England.

THE SOCIETY Erected by ROYAL CHARTER, for the *Propagation of the Gospel in Foreign Parts*, taking into serious Consideration the absolute Necessity there is, that those *Clergymen* who shall be sent abroad, should be duly qualified for the Work to which they are appointed, desire that all Persons, who shall Recommend any to that Purpose, will testifie their Knowledge as to the following Particulars; *Viz.*

I. The *Age* of the Person.
II. His *Condition of Life, whether Single or Married.*
III. His *Temper.*
IV. His *Prudence.*
V. His *Learning.*

VI. His

[21]

VI. His *Sober and Pious Conversation.*
VII. His *Zeal for the Christian Religion, and Diligence in his Holy Calling.*
VIII. His *Affection to the present Government.* And,
IX. His *Conformity to the Doctrine and Discipline of the Church of England.*

And the said SOCIETY do request and earnestly beseech all Persons concerned, that they recommend no Man out of Favour or Affection, or any other Worldly Consideration: but with a sincere Regard to the Honour of Almighty God and our Blessed Saviour; as they render the Interest of the Christian Religion, and the Good of Mens Souls.

[N. B. It is moreover a standing Order of the Society, *That if any Clergy-man, who offers himself for this Service, shall have a Cure, be shall, besides his other Testimonials, have the Approbation and Consent of his Diocesan, signified under his Hand and Seal.*]

INSTRU-

[22]

INSTRUCTIONS for the Clergy employ'd by the Society for the Propagation of the Gospel in Foreign Parts.

Upon their Admission by the Society.

I. THAT from the Time of their Admission they lodge not in any Publick-House; but at some Bookseller's, or in other private and Reputable Families, till they shall be otherwise accommodated by the Society.

II. That till they can have a convenient Passage, they employ their Time usefully; in reading Prayers, and Preaching, as they have Opportunity; in hearing others Read and Preach; or in such Studies as may tend to fit them for their Employment.

III. That they constantly attend the standing Committee of this Society, at St. *Paul's* Chapter-House, and observe their Directions.

IV. That

[23]

IV. That before their Departure, they wait upon his Grace the Lord Arch-Bishop of *Canterbury*, their Metropolitan; and upon the Lord Bishop of *London*, their Diocesan; to receive their Paternal Benediction and Instructions.

Upon their going on Board the Ship designed for their Passage.

I. THAT they demean themselves not only inoffensively and prudently; but so as to become remarkable Examples of Piety and Virtue to the Ships Company.

II. That whether they be Chaplains in the Ships, or only Passengers, they endeavour to prevail with the Captain or Commander, to have Morning and Evening Prayer said daily, as also Preaching and Catechizing every Lords-Day.

III. That throughout their Passage, they Instruct, Exhort, Admonish, and Reprove, as they have Occasion and Opportunity, with such Seriousness and Prudence as may gain them Reputation and Authority.

D

Upon

Upon their Arrival in the Country whither they fhall be fent.

First, *With Refpect to themfelves.*

I. THAT they always keep in their View the great Defign of their Undertaking; *viz.* t° promote the Glory of Almighty God, and the Salvation of Men, by propagating the Gofpel of our Lord and Saviour.

II. That they often confider the Qualifications requifite for thofe who would effectually promote this Defign, *viz.* A found Knowledge and hearty Belief of the Chriftian Religion; an Apoftolical Zeal temper'd with Prudence, Humility, Meeknefs, and Patience; a fervent Charity towards the Souls of Men; and finally that Temperance, Fortitude, and Conftancy, which become good Soldiers of Jefus Chrift.

III. That in order to the obtaining and preferving the faid Qualifications, they do very frequently in their Retirements offer up fervent Prayers to Almighty God for his Direction and Affiftance; converfe much with the Holy Scriptures; ferioufly reflect upon their Ordination Vows; and confider the Account which they are

16

are to render to the great Shepherd and Bifhop of Souls, at the laft Day.

IV. That they acquaint themfelves thorowly with the Doctrine of the Church of *England*, as contain'd in the Articles and Homilies; its Worfhip and Difcipline, and Rules for Behaviour of the Clergy, as contain'd in the Liturgy and Canons; and that they approve themfelves accordingly, as genuine Miffionaries from this Church.

V. That they endeavour to make themfelves Mafters in thofe Controverfies, which are neceffary to be underftood in order to the preferving their Flock from the Attempts of fuch Gainfayers as are mixt among them.

VI. That in their outward Behaviour they be circumfpect and unblameable, giving no Offence either in Word or Deed; that their Ordinary Difcourfe be grave and edifying; their Apparel decent, and proper for Clergy-Men; and that in their whole Converfation they be Inftances and Patterns of the Chriftian Life.

VII. That they do not board in, or frequent publick-houfes, or lodge in Families of Evil Fame; that they wholly abftain from Gaming, and all vain Paftimes; and converfe not familiarly with lewd or prophane Perfons, otherwife than in order to reprove, admonifh, and reclaim them.

VIII. That

D 2

VIII. That in whatsoever Family they shall lodge, they persuade them to join with them in daily Prayer Morning and Evening.

IX. That they be not nice about Meats or Drinks, nor immoderately careful about their Entertainment in the Places where they shall sojourn; be contented with what Health requires, and the Place easily affords.

X. That as they be Frugal in Opposition to Luxury; so they avoid all Appearance of Covetousness, and recommend themselves according to their Abilities by the prudent Exercise of Liberality and Charity.

XI. That they take special Care to give no Offence to the Civil Government, by intermedling in Affairs not relating to their own Calling and Function.

XII. That avoiding all Names of Distinction, they endeavour to preserve a Christian Agreement and Union one with another, as a Body of Brethren of one and the same Church, united under the Superior Episcopal Order, and all engaged in the same great Design of Propagating the Gospel; and to this End keeping up a Brotherly Correspondence, by meeting together at certain Times, as shall be most convenient for mutual Advice and Assistance.

Second-

Secondly, *With Respect to their Parochial Cure.*

THAT they conscientiously observe the Rules of our Liturgy in the Performance of all the Offices of their Ministry.

II. That besides the stated Service appointed for Sundays and Holy-days, they do, as far as they shall find it practicable, publickly read the daily Morning and Evening Service, and decline no fair Opportunity of Preaching to such as may be Occasionally met together from Remote and Distant Parts.

III. That they perform every part of Divine Service with that Seriousness and Decency, that may recommend their Ministrations to their Flock, and excite a Spirit of Devotion in them.

IV. That the chief Subjects of their Sermons be the great Fundamental Principles of Christianity, and the Duties of a sober, righteous, and godly Life, as resulting from those Principles.

V. That they particularly preach against those Vices, which they shall observe to be most Predominant in the Places of their Residence.

VI. That they carefully instruct the People concerning the Nature and Use of the Sacraments

[28]

ments of Baptifm and the Lord's-Supper, as the peculiar Inftitutions of Chrift, Pledges of Communion with him, and Means of deriving Grace from him.

VII. That they duly confider the Qualifications of thofe adult Perfons, to whom they adminifter Baptifm; and of thofe likewife whom they admit to the Lord's-Supper, according to the Directions of the Rubricks in our Liturgy.

VIII. That they take a fpecial Care, to lay a good Foundation for all their other Miniftrations, by Catechizing thofe under their Care, whether Children or other ignorant Perfons, explaining the Catechifm to them in the moft eafie and familiar Manner.

IX. That in their Inftructing *Heathens* and *Infidels*, they begin with the Principles of natural Religion, appealing to their Reafon and Confcience; and thence proceed to fhew them the Neceffity of Revelation, and the Certainty of that contained in the Holy Scriptures, by the plain and moft obvious Arguments.

X. That they frequently vifit their refpective Parifhioners; thofe of our own Communion, to keep them fteady in the Profeffion and Practice of Religion, as taught in the Church of *England*; thofe that oppofe us, or diffent from us, to convince and reclaim them, with a Spirit of Meeknefs and Gentlenefs.

XI.

[29]

XI. That thofe whofe Parifhes fhall be of large extent, fhall, as they have Opportunity and Convenience, officiate in the feveral Parts thereof, fo that all the Inhabitants may by turns partake of their Miniftrations; and that fuch as fhall be appointed to officiate in feveral places, fhall refide fometimes at one, fometimes at another of thofe Places, as the Neceffities of the People fhall require.

XII. That they fhall, to the beft of their Judgments, diftribute thofe fmall Tracts given by the Society for that Purpofe, amongft fuch of their Parifhioners as fhall want them moft, and appear likely to make the beft Ufe of them; and that fuch ufeful Books, of which they have not a fufficient Number to give, they be ready to lend to thofe who will be moft careful in reading and reftoring them.

XIII. That they encourage the fetting up Schools for the teaching of Children; and particularly by the Widows of fuch Clergy-Men as fhall die in thofe Countries, if they be found capable of that Employment.

XIV. That each of them keep a Regifter of his Parifhioners Names, Profeffion of Religion, Baptifm, &c. according to the Scheme annex'd No. I. for his own Saitsfaction, and the Benefit of the People.

Thirdly,

[31]

No. I. Notitia Parochialis; To be made by each Minister soon after his Acquaintance with his People, and kept by him for his own Ease and Comfort, as well as the Benefit of his Parishioners.						
I. *Names of Pa-rishioners.*	II. *Profession of Religion.*	III. *Which of them Baptized.*	IV. *When Ba-ptized.*	V. *Which of them Communicants.*	VI. *When they first Communicated.*	VII. *What Obstructions they meet with in their Ministration.*

[30]

Thirdly, *With Respect to the Society.*

I. THAT each of them keep a constant and regular Correspondence with the Society, by their Secretary.

II. That they send every six Months an Account of the State of their respective Parishes, according to the Scheme annex'd, Nº. II.

III. That they communicate what shall be done at the Meetings of the Clergy, when settled, and whatsoever else may concern the Society.

Nº. I.

[32]

Nº. II.

Notitia Parochialis; Or, An Account to be sent Home every Six Months to the Society by each Minister, concerning the Spiritual State of their respective Parishes.

I. Number of Inhabitants.	II. No. of the Baptized.	III. No. of Adult Persons Baptized this Half Year.	IV. No. of Actual Communicants of the Church of England.	V. No. of those who profess themselves of the Church of England.	VI. No. of Dissenters of all Sorts, particularly Papists.	VII. No. of Heathens and Infidels.

[33]

Instructions for Schoolmasters Employ'd by the Society, &c.

I. THAT they well consider the End for which they are employ'd by the Society, viz. the Instructing and disposing Children to believe and live as Christians.

II. In order to this end, that they teach them to read truly and distinctly, that they may be capable of reading the Holy Scriptures, and other pious and useful Books; for the informing their Understandings, and regulating their Manners.

III. That they instruct them thorowly in the Church Catechism, teach them first to read it distinctly and exactly, then to learn it perfectly by heart, endeavouring to make them understand the sense and meaning of it, by the help of such Expositions as the Society shall send over.

IV. That they teach them to Write a plain and legible Hand, in order to the fitting them for useful Employments; with as much Arithmetick as shall be necessary to the same Purpose.

V. That they be industrious, and give constant attendance at proper School-hours.

VI. That

E 2

[34]

VI. That they daily use, Morning and Evening, short and proper Prayers with their Scholars in the School, and teach them Prayers and Graces to be used by themselves at home.

VII. That they oblige their Scholars to be constant at Church on the Lord's-Day, Morning and Afternoon, and at all other times of publick Worship; that they cause them to carry their Bibles and Prayer-Books with them, instructing them how to use them there, and how to demean themselves in the several parts of Worship; that they be there present with them, taking Care of their reverent and decent Behaviour, and examine them afterwards as to what they have heard and learn'd.

VIII. That when any of their Scholars are fit for it, they recommend them to the Minister of the Parish, to be publickly Catechiz'd in the Church.

IX. That they take especial Care of their Manners, both in their Schools and out of them, warning them seriously of those Vices to which Children are most liable, teaching them to abhor Lying and Falshood, and to avoid all sorts of Evil-speaking; to love Truth and Honesty; to be Modest, Gentle, Well-behav'd, Just, and Affable, and Courteous to all their Companions, respectful to their Superiours, particularly towards all

[35]

all that Minister in holy things, and especially to the Minister of their Parish; and all this from a sense and fear of Almighty God, endeavouring to bring them in their tender Years to that sense of Religion which may render it the constant Principle of their Lives and Actions.

X. That they use all kind and gentle Methods in the Government of their Scholars, that they may be lov'd as well as fear'd by them; and that when Correction is necessary, they make the Children to understand that it is given them out of kindness, for their good, bringing them to a sense of their Fault, as well as of their Punishment.

XI. That they frequently consult with the Minister of the Parish in which they dwell, about the Methods of Managing their Schools, and be ready to be advised by him.

XII. That they do in their whole Conversation shew themselves Examples of Piety and Virtue to their Scholars, and to all with whom they shall converse.

XIII. That they be ready as they have opportunity, to teach and instruct the Indians and Negroes, and their Children.

XIV. That they send to the Secretary of the Society, once in every six Months, an Account of the State of their respective Schools, the Number of their Scholars, with the Methods and Success of their Teaching.

PRAY.

PRAYERS for the Use of the Charity-Schools in *America*.

A Morning Prayer for the Master and Scholars.

PRaised be the Lord from the rising up of the Sun, to the going down of the same. Thou art our God, and we will Praise thee; thou art our God, and we will thank thee.

Thou hast made us after thine own Image; thou daily preservest and providest for us; thou hast redeemed us by the precious Blood of thy dear Son; thou hast given us thy holy Word for our direction, and promis'd thy holy Spirit for our assistance; thou hast rais'd up to us Friends and Benefactors, who have taken care of our Education and Instruction; thou hast brought us together again this Morning to teach and to learn that which may be profitable to us.

For

For these and all thy favours Spiritual and Temporal, our Souls do Bless and Magnifie thy holy Name, humbly beseeching thee to accept this our Morning Sacrifice of Praise and Thanksgiving, through *Jesus Christ* our Lord.

And do thou, O Lord, who hast safely brought us to the beginning of this day, defend us in the same by thy mighty Power; and grant that this day we fall into no Sin, neither run into any kind of danger; but that all our doings may be ordered by thy Governance, to do always that which is righteous in thy sight, through *Jesus Christ* our Lord.

Particulary we beg thy Blessing upon our present Undertaking. Prevent us, O Lord, in all our doings with thy most gracious Favour, and further us with thy continual Help; that in these and all our Works, begun, continued, and ended in thee, we may glorifie thy holy Name, and finally by thy Mercy obtain everlasting Life, through *Jesus Christ* our Lord.

Enlighten, we pray thee, our Understandings, strengthen our Memories, sanctify our Hearts, and guide us in our Lives. Help us to learn and to practise those things which are good, that we may become serious Christians, and useful in the World, to the Glory of thy great Name, the Satisfaction of those who have so kindly provided

[38]

provided for our Souls and Bodies, and our own preſent and future Well-being.

Let thy Bleſſings be abundantly beſtow'd upon all our Friends and Benefactors, particularly on *the Society Erected for the Propagation of the Goſpel.* Proſper thou the Work of their hands, O Lord, proſper thou their handy-Work.

Theſe Prayers both for them and our ſelves, we humbly offer up, in the Name of thy Son *Jeſus Chriſt* our Redeemer, concluding in his moſt perfect Form of Words ; *Our Father,* &c.

An Evening Prayer for the Maſter and Scholars.

ACcept, we beſeech thee, O Lord, our Evening Sacrifice of Praiſe and Thankſgiving for all thy Goodneſs and Loving-kindneſs to us, particularly for the Bleſſings of this Day, for thy gracious Protection and Preſervation, for the Opportunities we have enjoy'd for the Inſtruction and Improvement of our Minds, for all the comforts of this Life, and the hope of Life everlaſting, through *Jeſus Chriſt* our Redeemer.
Forgive,

[39]

Forgive, moſt merciful Father, we humbly pray thee, all the Errors and Tranſgreſſions which thou haſt beheld in us the Day paſt, and help us to expreſs our unfeigned Sorrow for what has been amiſs, by our care to amend it.

What we know not, do thou teach us, inſtruct us in all the particulars of our Duty both towards thee and towards Men, and give us Grace always to do thoſe things which are good, and well-pleaſing in thy ſight, through *Jeſus Chriſt* our Lord.

Whatſoever good Inſtructions have been here given this day, grant that they may be carefully remember'd, and duly followed : and whatſoever good deſires thou haſt put into any of our Hearts, grant that by the aſſiſtance of thy Grace they may be brought to good Effect, that thy Name may have the Honour, and we, with thoſe who are aſſiſtant to us in this Work of our Inſtruction, may have comfort at the day of Account, through our Lord and Saviour *Jeſus Chriſt.*

Lighten our Darkneſs we beſeech thee, O Lord, and by thy great Mercy defend us from all Perils and Dangers of this Night, continuing to us the Bleſſings which we enjoy, and helping us to teſtifie our Thankfulneſs for them, by a due uſe and improvement of them.

Bleſs,

F

[40]

Bless, O Lord, we beseech thee, all our Friends and Benefactors, particularly that *Society* for which we are bound in especial manner to pray. Direct and prosper all their pious Endeavours for the Propagation of thy Gospel in the World.

These Praises and Prayers we humbly offer up to thy divine Majesty, through the mediation of thy Son *Jesus Christ* our Lord, in whose holy Name and Words we Sum up all our desires;
Our Father, &c.

A Morning Prayer to be used daily by every Child at Home.

GLory be to thee, O Lord, who hast preserved me from the Perils of the Night past, who hast refresh'd me with Sleep, and rais'd me up again to Praise thy holy Name.

I humbly Worship thee, O God, my heavenly Father, through *Jesus Christ* my Redeemer, and I do again devote my self to thee, desiring to serve thee faithfully this and all the days of my Life.

Help

[41]

Help me to remember thee, my Creator, in the days of my Youth.

Preserve me from those Errors and Follies, to which the frailty of my Age does most expose me, and keep me innocent from every great Offence.

Deliver me from the Vanity of mine own Heart, and from the Temptations of evil Company.

Incline my Heart to all that is good; that I may be modest and humble, true and just, temperate and diligent, respectful and obedient to my Superiors, that I may fear and love thee above all, that I may love my Neighbour as my self, and do to every one as I would they should do unto me.

Let thy good Providence defend me this day from all Evil; let the Grace of thy holy Spirit continually prevent and assist me.

Bless me, I pray thee, in my Learning, and help me daily to increase in Knowledge, and Wisdom, and all Virtue.

I humbly beg thy Blessing upon all my Relations and Friends [* particularly my *Father* and *Mother*, my *Brothers* and *Sisters*, and every one in this House;] Grant to them whatsoever may be good for them in this Life, and guide them to Life everlasting.

Let these Words be=added, or omitted, or changed, as occasion requires.

I hum-

F 2

[42]

I humbly commit my self to thee, O Lord, in the Name of *Jesus Christ* my Saviour, and in the Words which he himself hath taught me;

Our Father, &c.

An Evening Prayer to be used daily by every Child at Home.

GLory be to thee, O Lord, who hast preserved me the Day past, who hast defended me from all the Evils to which I am constantly expos'd in this uncertain Life, who hast continued my Health, who hast bestow'd upon me all things necessary for life and godliness.

I humbly beseech thee, O heavenly Father, to pardon whatsoever thou hast seen amiss in me this day, in my Thoughts, or Words, or Actions. (*particularly*) &c. *

Assist me, I pray thee, in making it my constant endeavour to resist and conquer every evil Inclination within me, and every Temptation from without.

Help me daily to increase in the Knowledge and Love of thee, my God, and of my Saviour *Jesus Christ.* Shew

* *Here let the Child mention any particular fault which he knows himself to have been guilty of.*

[43]

Shew me the way in which I should walk, whilst I am young, and grant that I may never depart from it.

Bless to me, I pray thee, whatsoever good Instructions have been given me this day, helping me carefully to remember them, and duly to improve them; that I may be ever growing in Knowledge, and Wisdom, and Goodness.

I humbly commit my Soul and Body to thy Care this Night, begging thy gracious Protection and Blessing.

And all these Blessings which I ask for my self, I heartily desire for my Relations and Friends, and every one in this House. Let it please thee to guide us all in this life present, and to conduct us to thy heavenly Kingdom, through *Jesus Christ* our only Lord and Saviour, in whose Words I conclude my Prayers. *Our Father*, &c.

[44]

A Short Prayer for every Child, when they first come into their Seats at Church.

LORD, I am now in thy Houfe; affift, I pray thee, and accept of my Services. Let thy holy Spirit help my Infirmities, difpofing my Heart to ferioufnefs, attention, and devotion, to the Honour of thy holy Name, and the Benefit of my Soul, through Jefus Chrift our Saviour. Amen.

———

Before they leave their Seats, thus ;

BLeffed be thy Name, O Lord, for this opportunity of attending thee in thy Houfe and Service. Make me, I pray thee, a Doer of thy Word, not a Hearer only. Accept both us and our Services through our only Mediator Jefus Chrift. Amen.

[45]

A Grace before Meat.

SAnctify, O Lord, *I befeech thee, thefe thy *we. good Creatures to †my Ufe, and *me to†our. *us. thy Service, through Jefus Chrift our Lord. Amen.

———

A Grace after Meat.

BLeffed and Praifed be thy holy Name, O Lord, for thefe and all thy other Bleffings beftow'd upon *me, through JefusChrift our *us. Lord. Amen.

———

F I N I S.

[1664, Oct. 17, Hartford and Windsor?]

To the Hon^{le} the Gen^{ll} Assembley of the Corporation of Connecticott in New-England / The Humble Address and Petition of Sundry persons of and belonging to the Same Corporation / Sheweth,

That whereas wee whose names are subscribed, Beeing Proffessors of the Protestant Christian Religion, Members of the Church of England, And Subiects to our Soveraigne Lord Charles the Second by Gods Grace, King of England &c: And under those Sacred tyes mentioned and conteined in our covenant Sealed with our Baptism. Haveing seriously pondered our past and present want of those Ordinances w^{ch}: to us and our Children as members of Christs vissible Church ought to bee administered. Which wee apprehend to bee to the Dishonour of God and the Obstruction of our owne and our Childrens good (Contrary to the Pious will of our Lord the King in his maine purpose in Settling these Plantations As by the Charter, and his ma^{ties} Letter to the Bay June 20th 1662 and otherwayes is most evidently manifest.) to our great greife, The Sence of our Duty towards God, The relation wee stand in to our Mother the Church: our gratefull acceptance of his Maties Royall favor, The edification of our owne and our Childrens Soules and many other good, Christian and profitable ends (as allso at a Late Session of this Hon^{le} Assembley haveing received a favorable incouragement from the Wor^{ll} Dep: Govr:) Hereunto moveing us. Wee are bold by this our Address to declare our Agreiveance and to Petition for a redrese of the Same.

Our Aggreiveance is that wee and ours are not under the Due care of an Orthodox Ministry that will in a due manner administer to us those ordinances that wee stand capeable of, as the Baptizeing of our Children, our beeing admitted (as wee according to Christs order may bee found meete) to the Lords table. And a carefull watch over us in our wayes and Suteable Dealing with us as wee do well, or ill. With all whatsoever benifitts and Advantages belong to us as members of Christs vissible Church, which ought to be dispenced by the officers of the Same. of w^{ch}: wee beeing Destitute

We humbly request, That the Hon^{le} Court would take into Serious Consideration our present State in this respect that we are thus as sheep Scattered haveing no shepheard, and compare it with what wee conceive you cannot but know both God and our King would have it different from what it now is. And take Some Speedy and effective Course for redress herein. And put us in a full and free capascity of inioying these forementioned Advantages which to us as members of Christs vissible Church doe of right bellong. By Establishing Som wholesome Law in this Corporation by vertue whereof wee may both claime and receive of Such Officers as are, or shall bee by Law Set over us in the Church or churshes where wee have our abode or residence these forementioned privilidges and advantages.

ffurthermore wee humbly request that for the future no Law in this corporation may bee of any force to make us pay or contribute to the maintaineance of any Minister or officer in the Church that will neglect or refuse to Baptize our Children, and to take care of us as of Such members of the Church as are under his or thair Charge and care.

Thus in hopes that yor carefull and Speedy consider-

ation and Isshue hereof will bee answerable to the weight of the matter and our nessesity, and that Matters of less moment may bee Omitted till this bee Ishued wee waite for a good answer And for this Hon^{le} Court wee shall ever pray &c:

October 17th: 1664

W^m: Pitkin	James Enno
Michaell Humphrey	Robert Reeve
John Stedman	John Moses
	Jonas Westover

[1669, Mar. 7, Stratford]

To The Hon^d Gen^{ll} Court, Assembled at Hartford May 14th 1669.

The petition of the Church of Christ at Stratford with many of the Inhabitants, humbly sheweth, That uncomfortable Differences have too too long bin and yet remain amongst us in Stratford, to our no small affliction and to the greife of many of our freinds, and that many of your Worships have bin acquainted with, and some of you (which we cannot but thankfully acknowledge) with great seriousness have travelled in to your no small trouble; and seing Diferences still remain notwithstanding some essayes for redresse, we cannot but account it our duty to be humbly and solicitously urgent with this Hon^d Court at this time that you will please to looke upon our condition and see our state, and be pleased to hear us with patience for to whome should we come but to your Worships, as such under Christ appointed for that end by him to releive the oppressed &c and such we take ourselves to bee, and therefore Again beseech you to hear and take our matters into your Juditious Consideration, and doe something for our settlement, and you will thereby (we hope) give us occasion to glorify God in you, and shall not cease to pray that the Wonderful Counsellour may be still with you, and the spirit of Counsel upon you in the great and weighty affaires that are under your handes, and that you may be repairers of the breach, and restorers of paths to dwell in / your unworthy petitioners

Stratford / 7th (3) 69

	John issak 1st
Israel Chauncy	John bostick
Philip Criste	John Birdsey Junr
Richard Boothe	eliasaph preston
William Churh S^r	John Curtis
Joseph Hawley	John birdsey sen^r
Izaack Hittall	John Peatte sen^r
John Brinsmead sen^r	Adam hurd
Moses Whelle	Henry Tomlinson
Thomas Kimberlye	John peacoke
Francis Hatt	Joseph bearsdly
John Willcocksone	Nathaniel porter
John Hakitt Senr	Thomas ffairechild junior
John beach	Samuell Beardsly
John Hurd Junr	Benjamin Beach
James blackman	Stephen Burrit
Zekiell preston	Tho Burritt
Timothy wilcockson	John Brinsmead Junr
James Clarke	Jonas Tomlinson
John Hulls	Daniell Beardsly
Beniamen peat	Daniell Brendsmed
Jabez hargan	John Pickitt Junr
israel curtis	James pickitt

[1710, Jan.-Feb.]

[The following is from the Journal of the Rev. John Sharpe, chaplain to H.M. forces in the Fort at New York, 1704-1717, now in the Historical Society of Pennsylvania, Philadelphia.]

[January]

6 Epiphany day. Fryday I left York & went as farr as new Rochelle on my way to Stratford where I was sent for by the members of the Church of England there to preach I had a fall from my horse but thank God rec^d no hurt.

7 Snowed Coll Heathcote was at N Rochelle I went w^t him to his house

8 To Rye Church I preached a.m. p.m.

9 To New Rochelle I inducted Mr Bouder

10 To dinner at Mr Vallane's. at night Mr Bouder & I to ye Coll

11 It rained.

12 Set out from Coll Heathcots w^t him we lay at Maj^r Sellecks at Stratford that night

13 To Norwalk We lay at Beldens.

14 To Fairfield we were met by Mr Johnston Mr Dunlap & Mr Blackleech You[nger] went to Stratford that night.

15 I preached twice forenoon psl. 31·26. pm. Rom. 2·4.

16 dined at Mrs Edwards Choice of Vestry & Church Wardens

17 dined at Mr Blackleeches

18 dined at Mr Dunlaps it rained. at Night he [?Mr. Blackleech] & Mr Dunlap & I rode to Fairfield & lay at Mr Lewes I was much wett

19 I went to Visit the Deputy Govr & Mr Web the Min^r of the place I preached at Mr Lewis's and lay that night at Mr Sturges' a publick house. Coll Heathcote Dunlap Nisbet Johnston

20 Coll Heathcote went away Wee came to Stratford back.

21 Stayed at home all day.

22 I preached twice and gave notice of the Sacr^t. Tex. 1 Cor 15.55 both parts.

23 Visited M^r pitman Mrs Laborie & m^{rs} Edwards.-- Mr Bridge called

24 Snowed hard. Visited Mr Nisbet

25 Mr Bridge went forward to Rye. I went to Mr Janes.

26 to Longhill. preached Eph. 5.15.16. a Congregation of 200. the greater part wherof had never heard the Common prayer.

27 Baptised Isaac Styles the first male child born in the Colony of Connecticut. a man of 80 years of age. Visited one Zachary a sick person. dined at Lt Johnsons--and returned to Stratford.

28 I stayed at home at Study I recovered my illness

29 I preached. a.m. Math 6. & Admin^{ed} the Sacr^t to 25 Communicants p.m. preached Luke 16.2 & Christned three Children.

30 K. C. Martyr'd. I preached Rom. 13.1. & p.m. Visited.

31 I bought my horse darling set out & noon & preached at Stratford Math. 11.39. I rode to Greens farm's & lay at Simon Couches.

February

1 Came to Norwalk there met Mr Bridge wee came thence in Company w^t the Deputy Govr & Mr Davenport to Stanford

2 Candlemass. To Snowfields it rained very hard Mr Dunlap overtook us. wee rode in the rain to Coll Heathcots y^t night

3 Stay'd all day.

4 A fair day Stayed at Manaranack

5 Septuagesima. Mr Bridge preached at Rye a.m. Jo. 21.15.16. I preached p.m. Math. 11.34

6 Came to New Rochelle. Queens birth day

7 I came to York. Glory be to God.

Baptised In my Voyage to Stratford Janry 1710.

Janry

15 Hannah the wife of James Dickson at Stratford adult

19 Sarah the wife of George wood at Fairfield ad.

26. At Long Hill dorcas the grand daughter of Isaac Styles ad. Elias the son of Sam^{ll} Davis. and Phebe the daughter of Jonathan Gilbert. Children

27. Isaac Styles. aged abt 80.

29. At Stratford. W^m the son of W^{ill} Smyth Jo[s]hua the son of John Mercy & Elizabeth the daughter of archibald Dunlap

[1710, Apr. 25, Stratford]

To the Honble Gurdon Saltenstale Govr of Her Majesties Collony of Connecticut The Petition of the Church wardens & Vestry in behalf of themselves & the members of the Curch of England Inhabitans in the Town of Stratford and Else where in this Collony. Humbly Shueth That wherras severall of us & others professing ourselves members of the Church of England as by Law Established, have lately suffered imprisonment of our bodies & distress of our Goods for not paying such rates as have been assesed towards the Support of Ministers of a different persuation from the Establish^t Curch: we humbly Conceive ourselves to be under no such obligation neither by the Laws of England nor the Charter grant of this Collony & have therefore appealed to the next General Court for their Judgement in our Case.

We therefore humbly intreat your honour will be pleased to put a Stop to all Such proceedings against us till such time as the determination of the Court therein; & to grant us the protection of your authority in the free exercise of our religion; and y^r petitioners shall ever pray &c;

Stratford apr^l 25.th <u>1710</u>

Timothy Titharton	William Smith	} Church Wardens

Willm Ronoldson	William Jeanes	)
Richard Blacklach	Arch:^d Dunlop	} Vestry
Jonat. Pitmann	Hugh Nisbitt	men
John: Johnson	Daniell Shilton	)

[1722. Wrexham, Denbighshire, England]

[This transcript of the will of Elihu Yale (1649-1721) is to be found among the papers of the S.P.G. (MSS. A,

XVI, 22-24). Yale, born in Boston, visited London in 1652 to be educated. From 1671 onward he held high office in the East India Company in Madras. After 1699 he resided in England, whence, in 1714 and 1718, he made gifts of books and goods to the Collegiate School then located in Saybrook, Conn. In his will he mentions that he is a "Member & Son of the Church of England" and leaves £500 to the "Connecticote Colledge," which soon took his name. His tomb is in Wrexham.]

Copy of the last Will of Elihu Yale Esqr

     E Regǫ Curiae Praerogativae Cantuar⌐ Extract.
In the Name of God I Elihu Yale of Place Grono in the Parish of Wrexham in Denbighshire Esqr now in Queens Square in Westminster & praised be the Almighty in very reasonable health & understanding, but that & life being uncertain think it Convenient to settle my affairs & dispose of the Estate God in mercy has blest my long industrious endeavors with & therefore do hereby make my last Will & Testamt Revoking all others whatsoever or wheresoever made or done, & first [I] being a Christian & an unworthy Member & Son of the Church of England As by Law Established, wch I hope God will prosper & increase to ye Worlds end & So humbly recommend my Soul to God that Gave it relying upon his gracious mercy & ye Meritorious Blood & Death of my dear Savior & Redeemer ye Lord Jesus Christ for a free pardon & forgiveness of my Great & many Sins of Omicon & Comision [Omission and Commission] & my Body decently Interr'd with my Ancestors at Wrexham Church Yard in the Ground I appointed at ye West end of that Church with a handsome Black raisd Tombstone with the Epitaph I long since made for it & after my debts & funerall Charges are paid by my Executors or overseers & trustees hereafter named I do hereby give & bequeath the remainder of my Estate according to a Schedule hereunto anext to the following persons & Uses Vizt

     Imprimis I give ffor a Stock to Employ the

	£
poor of Wrexham parish in their work house to be managed by the parson for the time being & such Trustees as that Vestry shall make choice of . . .	200
To Christs Hospitall in London	100
To St Bartholomews Hospital	100
To St Thomas Hospitall	100
To that very Charitable Workhouse in Bishopgate Street	100
To other Charitable Schools for ye poor to be divided among them by my Trustees	100
To the Corporation for propagating ye Gospel in foreign parts	100
To my Godson Elihu Gibson.	100
To ditto Elihu Frenchfield	100
To Elihu [ ] at St Helena	100
To ditto Elihu Pirdock	100
To dǫ William Brown India.	100
To dǫ Ben Hoadley.	100
To dǫ Elihu Nicks	
Denina Nicks	
To Ursula Nicks	
To dǫ Elizabeth Nicks	
To Mrs Katherine Nicks	
To Mr Dudley North & his wife each	
To his two Children each	

To Lord James Cavendish & Wife each & Children	
To Ursula Yale	
To my wicked wife	
To Charles Almanza India	
To David Yale my Godson now in England . . . Wales	
To St Stephen [?] and Stock	
To Mr Will Hales	
To Mr Wm Perkins	
To Elihu Yale & Sister in New England	1000
To Coz Thomas Yale & ffamily dǫ	500
To Coz Nathaniel Yale & ffamily dǫ	500
To Coz James & ffamily	200
To Connecticote Colledge &c	500

                 Hen. Farrant Register Deput⌐

[1722, Apr. 23, New York]
Gentlemen,
     I take this Opportunity by your own Townsman of informing You of the Society's great Care of You, who have been pleased to appoint Me, a mean yet willing Watchman, over You for the Lord. I chose to settle among You, because my Family might be more easily transported from Road-Island (where They now reside) to Your Town, than to any other vacant Mission in America. It is expected from You, that You will make some Provision for Me & Mine; that I may not be necessitated to settle elsewhere, as the Society have promised, if You do not take Care accordingly. I am now waiting for a Passage to Road-Island, from whence, after Settlement of my Affairs, You may expect / Your hitherto Unknown / And very Humble Servant
     New-York / Apr: 23d 1722   George Pigot
[To the Church Wardens at Christ Church, Stratford]

[1722, Sept. 13, New Haven]
     To the Reverend Mr Andrew and Mr Woodbridge and others our Revd Fathers and Brethren present in the Library of Yale Colledge this 13th of Sep: 1722:

Reverend Gentlemen
     Having represented to you ye Difficulties which we labour under, in Relation to our Continuance out of the visible Communion of an Episcopal Church, and a State of Seeming opposition thereto, either as private Christians, or as Officers, and so being insisted on by some of you (after our repeated declinings of it) yt we should Summ up our Case in Writing; we do (though with great reluctance fearing the Consequences of it) submitt to and comply with it. And Signifie to you that Some of us doubt of the Validity, and ye Rest are more fully Persuaded of the Invalidity of the Presbyterian Ordination, in Opposition to Episcopal. And should be heartily thankfull to God and Man, if we may recieve from them Satisfaction herein, and shall be willing to embrace your good Counsells and Instructions in Relation to this important affair, as far as God shall direct and dispose us to it.   Jared Eliot

     Timothy Cutler.   James Wetmore
     John Hart.   Samuel Johnson
     Samuel Whittelsey   Daniel Brown
A true Copy of the Original Testi by Daniel Brown.

[1723, Feb. 15, London]

London Feb. 15. 1722/23

Dear Brother

This is to let You know, that through the Goodness of God, we arrived safe in England the 15th of December, having been 5 weeks and 4 days upon the Sea. The passage was longer than is usual at that Time of the Year, by reason of the contrary and Stormy winds we had, for a considerable time together. We went ashore near the mouth of the River Thames, and went to Canterbury a very ancient City, where is a very famous Old Church which we spent some time to view; and indeed it is a very wonder[ful] Building, both within and without. From Canterbury [we went] through the City of Rochester, in the Stage Coach to London, on the 20th of Decembr. We have all had our health very well since our Arrival, except Mr Cutler who has been Sick of the Small Pox, but is now recovered; He had the Distemper favourably, and was attended by a very good Physician, who was particularly kind to him, and has promised to do the same for Mr Johnson & myself if there be Occasion. We were not with Mr Cutler when he took the Small Pox, and we have been from him 23 days, [so] that we have no reason [at] all to think that we have it and we may escape it [entirely if] we meet with throngs in [the fields and] all Ches, that have [never] been visited with that Distemper: however we are not greatly [con]cerned about it, leaving the matter to the divine Disposal. We have been treated with all possible Kindness by the Bishops and other Ministers of the Church of England, who we find are not such frightfull People, as You in that Country are made to believe. The Honourable Society for propagating the Gospel, have granted all our Requests; and have appointed me to be their Missionary at New-Bristol where there is a very pretty Church built, and a very promising Congregation. We do not intend to make a long stay here, but shall prepare for a Return as fast as we can: I hope to be at home by the middle of May or ye Beginning of June. Shew this Letter to my Honoured, & Dear Mother, to whome I here present my Duty, and my Dearest Love to You, and Isaac, & Mary: I pray God preserve You all in Unity and Peace, especially in the Affairs that are upon Your hands. Pray for me that I may be preserved from every Evil here, and in due time may be returned to You. Give my Kindest Respects to all Friends: I am / Your Affectionate Brother

Daniel Browne

[1723, June 3, London]

Dear Sr

I have two letters to thank you for, one of Septr, & the Other of Novr last. You have heard before now of the death of Mr Brown, the youngest of the three Ministers who came over here from your Colony, & you have probably Seen it in the prints that his death was much lamented. I must needs say it was by me, for his good nature, modesty & ingenuity. Our News papers have told us that Mr Cutler is made a Doctr of Divinity at Oxford, & Mr Johnson Master of Arts, but I think it is not true, tho' it's very probable it may be true in a little while for they are gone to the University with that view. When these Gentlemen came first over, I shew'd them the Civility of a Countrey man, but resolv'd not to meddle in their Affairs, & accordingly

I did not accompany them to any Bishop or other great person of my acquaintance. I was the more cautious in my Carriage towards them, because I understood by letters from Boston that their defection from the religion of their Countrey was owing to the Library I had Sent over, with this particular Slander, that I had fill'd the Library with every book for the Church & not one of the Other Side. You, Sr, that have Seen the books, know that the reverse of this is true, & that there never was an Eminent Dissenter & Author whose works are not in that Collection. Unless some of the books are lost or Stollen (which indeed I hear) You'l find Goodwin, Owen, Baxter, How, Bates, Carryl, Manson, Charnock, Pool, Henry, Calamy; & Others who have learnedly oppos'd the Ceremonys & Hierarchy of the Church, such as Didoclavius, Ames, Peirce & Others. And Yet I find I have bin reproach'd, as before Mention'd, which will discourage me from sending any more books, At least 'till I hear from you about it. As to the matter of Your Charter, I hope it is Safe. Colo Shute has not bin able to move any thing this session of Parliament, & what he proposes to do in the next is pretty much a Secret between him & his Friends (I mean friends to that design) For as to my Selfe tho' I may Stand Neuter as to the Massachusets, who won't let me Serve them, yet I shall be very Active for Connecticut, if any bill for regulating the Charter Governments Should again be brought into the House of Commons.

The Validity of Mr Yale's will is not yet determin'd, but is depending in Doctor's Commons, & I beleive will not be brought to an Issue till October Term.

The King sets out this morning for his German Dominions, the Plot being wholly defeated inasmuch as the Bishop of Rochester, who is thought to have bin the life & Soul of it, has bin convicted, & sentenc'd to perpetual banishment. The Act for his Banishment makes it felony without Clergy for any person to Correspond with him unless they have leave under the King's sign Manual.

Europe at present enjoys a general peace, nor is there any prospect of war, unless the Turk & Czar of Muscovy should fall out about the latter's new Conquests in Persia. And should this happen, it would do us no harm, but rather confirm our tranquility, as it will find the Czar work[ing] at a distance, & thereby prevent his creating new troubles in the Baltick, which will always embroyl us.

I put this letter under Cover to my Brother, & design, if I can meet with any passenger to Send you some prints & pamphlets.

I am with great regards / Sr / Yr Very humble Servt

Jer. Dummer

Middle Temple / 3d June 1723

Mr Woodbridge

[1724, Apr. 3, Stratford]

Stratford April 3. 1724

Dear Sr

I Have this Day Recd a Great Deal of Satisfaction In Your kind Letter of ye Last of March, for Which I thank You, & my pleasure is the greater, because You therein seme to Retain a Kindness For that Glorious Church, Whereof I Have the Honour & Commfort to be a member, & it Would yet add Vastly to my Joys If You were not onely almost but altogether such as I am, I find it impossible

for me under the Multiplicity of my affairs, to think of Coming up Next Election, & therefore I shall hope for the Pleasur You seem to promis me of seeing You Here upon ye Latter End of May. It is always uncertain when I Shall be at Hom & therefore Suffer me to Point out to You the Time when I will Expect You, which If You Pleas let be ye Sunday or munday After the Assention i.e after ye 14th of May. In the menetime I will Suggest to You Whether it Might not be Consistant for you under Your Apprehensions, (by no Means to be ordained in the Presbyterian way but Rather) to think of Serveing the Church at Newtown where Mr Towsey is Leaving them, & where I believe You may Quickley Have the whole Town, a pritty Pleasant New Country Town & where I Can Assure You good Encouragem^t, for I know their Eyes are upon You, & I Doubt not You May Have a good settlement of Land, & an Handsom acknowledgment from the People. I am of opinion it Is ye Most Promising Place in ye Country. If You Cant think of going over for orders Yet I Will presume to advise You to Read Prayers & Preach For a While till Your way is Plain, & I Assure You of admission to ye Societies Favour & Support, when You Pleas, & will write to them & to ye Bishop in Your name. but I Hope in God wee shall in a few Years Have a Bishop over here this I Suggest for You to think of But when You Come I will Contrive Any thing Else for You that Lies in my Power. In the Mean time I am--
Dear Sr Your Sincear Friend & Humble Servant
Veria Copia   Samuel Johnson
     [To John Beach]

[1724, Oct. 10, Boston]
My Lord,

     Your Lordship hath assured your Clergy here of your Readiness to assist us, & to contribute what you can to the Advancement of Religion among us, which, as it is a great Comfort to us; so it emboldens me to trouble your Lordship again with a further Account of the State of things here, especially having the Oppertunity of so good an hand.

     My Lord, There are indeed a Number of very worthy Clergymen here in New England, But yet many things occurr from time to time which make it very apparent how extremely unhappy we are, for want of an Ecclesiastical Governour to have an immediate Inspection over us.

     Among other Instances of this kind, the Conduct of Mr Harris of Boston is a very flagrant one. The Malice wherewith, he hath all along persecuted good Dr Cutler is very extraordinary; & for no other Reason, but because the good people of Boston were desirous, & are so happy as to obtain, that the D^r should be Incumbent of thier New Church, which it seems Mr Harris had an Expectation of. Your Lordship will, I beleive, be sufficiently sensible by looking into the Drs Sermon, how farr it is from the least favourable Aspect upon Popery; & yet this Gentleman would persuade people that the D^r is a papist, & that Sermon at the same time, is all he pretends for a foundation for it. It is from the same Fountain of Envy & Malice, that the False Report originally derived, which represented us to your Lordship as Disaffected, when we had the Hon^r to be in your presence. But we should be glad of an Oppertunity to Submit all our Conduct to your Lordships immediate Inspection, if the thing were possible.

     Another Instance, My Lord, of what I was mentioning,

is, The Injuries which our people suffer from the Governments here. Since my last Letter to your Lordship, notwithstanding my humblest Addresses to the Government of the Colony of Connecticut; yet Sundry of my People have been persecuted for their Taxes to the Independent Teachers, & that notwithstanding that the Honble Society have obliged them to pay to the Support of the Established Church. One man has had above fifty pounds first & last thus injuriously taken away from him; & we have as yet no Mitigation, so that many people are almost discouraged. I beg my Lord, if possible we may have some Relief, for all their Conduct towards the Church has been a direct Abuse of their Charter priviliges.

     Since my last, I have been with M^r Mc Sparran, & have seen your Lordships Order relating to our Communion Furniture, wherin I find your Lordship permits us to represent the Reasons for which we conceive ourselves not bound in Justice to deliver them. I have nothing further to say concerning them. I only submit it to your Lordship to determine, whither the late Queen who gave them, appropriated them to Narraganset or not. (& I can find no body that can give any Light to that matter but General Nicholson, to whome I have written,) & whither (Supposing them not to have been appropriated,) Bishop Comptons ordering them to Stratford does not give us a Right to them, without which we desire not to keep them. As to Bishops Compton's ordering them to Stratford, I have nothing to evidence it but the Revd Mr Myles's Testimony inclos'd, for the papers & Records of the Church at Stratford are, many of them, lost. If we are mistaken as to the Title of them, & must Resign them, we are very unhappy, for such is o^r poverty, that we are utterly unable to provide for our selves another Sett, having been at so much Charge in building a Church. I shall hope to know y^r Lordships pleasure by Mr Salmon, my Church Warden, who, I hope, has before now paid his duty to y^r Lordship.

     I am, My Lord, / y^r Lordships most dutiful Son & Servant.

     Boston Oct. 10. 1724.   Samuel Johnson

[1725, June 15, Stratford]

                   Stratford Jun. 15. 1725
S^r

     I am very thankful to you for yours of Feb. 24 which I received with the Sermons inclosed & wherewith I am very much gratified, & shall be glad if in any thing I can oblige you on this side of the water.

     I ask your pardon for not writing to you before now, which I should not have neglected to do, had I presumed that giving you the Trouble of a Letter would have been acceptable; for I should be very proud of a Correspondence with you, & shall be always glad to hear of your Wellfare, retaining a grateful Remembrance of your kindness & Civility to me when I was in London.

     You desire me to inform you about Mr Lorings Affair with Mr Chappel. He desired one Mr Salmon who is now in England to pay that Money, & I hope it is done before now, but I have promised him if Mr Salmon dont do it I will & you may assure Mr Chappel that the Money shall be faithfully paid, & beg his Pardon for Mr Loring that it has not been done before, the Reason of which was not

want of Justice or Gratitude in M.r Loring, but meerly
the Difficulty which He has laboured under, & which he
is now in some good way of gaining the Ascendant of.

You hope I live in Unity & peace with o.r Dissenting
Bretheren. S.r I live in Love & peace with them & cultivate a friendly Correspondence with them as far as I am
able. & that we are not in Unity one with another, is I
think their Fault & not mine. My humble Service to Good
M.r Newman.

I am S.r your most humble & obliged Servant

Samuel Johnson

P.S. S.r I should have told you that I cant help thinking it
a very great hardship which the poor people of the Chh of
England suffer here in many places in that they are continually persecuted & halled to prisons for their Rates to
y.e Dissenting Ministers, when the Society have obliged
them to Contribute to y.e Support of the Established Church.
But notwithstanding, we have always Conducted our Selves
towards them in the Spirit of Meekness. & should be
obliged to you if you should think proper to say any thing
to our Government in our favour upon this Subject for I
can find nothing in their Charter that justifies these practices, but rather much the Contrary.

[1725, Nov. 25]

My Lord

Finding yo.r Lordship engag'd this Even. I take leave
to cover the enclosed as one of my Errands, and to request M.r Pawlet may give me a line of yo.r L.dps pleasure
therein, there being a Ship now going to Rhode-Island by
whom I can write.

I have advice that the Letters yo.r Lordship was
pleas'd to trust me w.th a few months since for several
Gov.rs in America got safe to Boston.

I should be glad to know yo.r L.dps inclinations to
favour M.r Hopkin's Son according to his desire sometime
since. The good man has wrote again to me, but the days
are so short & I have so much to do at home that I have
not been able to wait on yo.r L.dp unless at an unseasonable
hour as I do now.

The Church of Eng.ld Miss.y at Connecticut hopes by
yo.r L.dps favour that the people who resort to the Chh of
Eng.ld there shall not be oblig'd to pay double Taxes; I am

My Lord yo.r most obed. humble Servant

Henry Newman

[1726, Jan. 25, Stratford]

Stratford Jan.ry 25 1725

Rev.d S.r

I have Rec.d yours, & take this Oppertunity to return
you my Thankful Acknowledgments for your kindness in
informing me of the hopeful Success of our Addresses. I
pray God Almighty grant the desired Event! I hope he has
some such mercy in Store for his Church in this part of
the World. It is but little progress, comparatively, that
the Church can make, till we have Authority that will bear
down the malice of our Enemies. My L.d of London assures me that he shall do the best he Can to procure Bps
for us, & releif for our people about paying Rates, concerning which, as it appears from his Letter to me, Gov.r
Shute has given them a very different Account from what

I ever took to be the Case in any part of N. England.

In the mean time, in spight of all the Endeavours of
the Churches Enemies to blacken her, The Lustre of her
inward Glory is so conspicuous, that a good opinion of
her, daily gains ground upon the minds of people here,
very visibly: tho' it is but Seldom that any new proselytes are intirely gain'd over to our Side, by reason that
all imaginable discouragements from this World lie in
their Way, & all Arts that can be devised are used to
prevent those whose hearts are with us from discovering
themselves. But I hope in Gods good time the Scale will
turn. In the mean time Their Minds are so fast preparing, that, when a favourable Juncture shall happen, They
will I am perswaded, by Sholes come into the Bosom of
the Church.

My humble Service to Madam. I am S.r / your very
humble & obedient obliged / Servant

Samuel Johnson

[1727, Feb. 8, New London]

New London Feb.ry 8.th 1726/7

Right Reverend Father In God,

We the Subscribers Inhabitants of New London in his
Majes.ties Colony of Connecticutt in New England and the
Vicinage thereof, having Never Since our first Settlement
had the Gospel of Christ nor its comfortable Sacraments
Administered to us by any Episcopal Minister resident
among us, whereby sundry Persons, bred up in the Church
of England at Home, others that have been Baptized here
and become Conformists, and a greater Number still
strongly enclined to Conformity do labour under that last
and Most grevious Unhappiness of being left to ourselves,
and leaving our Posterity in this Wilderness excluded as
Wilde uncultivated Trees, from the Saving Benefits of a
Transplantation, into that soundest Part of the Holy Catholick Church, which deservedly distinguishes your Lordship with the Sacred Character of One of her principal
Guides, beg your Lordships Fatherly Compassions on our
truely pitiable Cercumstances.

[We are...miles] from the Church of Narraganset,
the nearest Church of England to us, but by the frequent
Visits of the Rev.d M.r M.cSparran the Incumbent of that
Place (who by the Space of four years last past hath Visited us at least four times in each Year) there have been
Several adults and Infants baptized, a Considerable Auditory gathered and a Church raised and already enclosed in
the Center of New London Town, which wee hope to have
finished by the Next Fall. Wee have, by an address of
this Date, lay.d our Case before the Honourable Ecc. Society for the Propagation of the Gospel in Forreign Parts
for their Charitable Assistance towards the Support and
Encouragement of such Clergyman as Your Lordship
shall think to send us; and we beg y.r Lordships Countenance to these our Proceedings.

But if (as we are given to fear) the Honourable Society
should reject our Prayer because we have not transmitted
a Particular of what we are able and willing to Contribute
Annually towards the Support of a Missionary, we beg
Leave to assure your Lordship that as Soon as the Burthen
of building our Church (which lyes heavy upon our small
Number) is a little lightened, nothing shall then retard
our perfecting and transmitting such a Subscription as

shall at least Manifest how earnestly we covet the Happiness we now pray for. In the Meantime, we crave the Favour of yᵣ Lordships Motion to the Society, that Some Small Encouragement and Instructions be given to the most contiguous Missionary to officiate occasionally among us, till we are made happy with a Resident One of our own. We pray yᵣ Lordship to take our Case into your Compassionate Consideration and beg yᵣ Blessing upon yᵣ distant, but dutyfull Sons & Servants.

	Paul Fraysse
James Smith	Walter Butler
John Merrett	Samuel Fairborn Sᵣ
John Braddick Jnᵣ	Lambeth Tree
George Smith	Richard Wyatt
Robert Whitwill	Thomas Mumford Junᵣ
John Sharkmaple	Jarrard Pell
John Braddick	James Tilley
Thos. Mumford	Joseph Hofman
Moses Parnell	Samˡˡ Burrnes

[1727, Sept. 25, Stratford]

Stratford in N. Englᵈ Sept. 25, 1727

May it please your Lordship,

I have received a Letter from the Honourable Society, wherein I am informed that they have added 10ˡᵇ per anᵣ to my salary, for which as I am very thankful to them, so I am particularly thankful to your Lordship, for what Influence you may have had in procuring this Favour for me, which indeed I had need enough of, having never received near the Vallue of 5ˡᵇ Sterling per anᵣ of my poor people. I shall always reflect on this Kindness of my Generous Benefactors towards me as a fresh Motive to exert my Self with the utmost Zeal & Industry, in endeavouring to answer their Expectations from me & their pious Designs in Supporting the Mission in this place.

Mᵣ Caner, whom the Honᵇˡe Society had appointed School Master at Fairfield, has, I conclude, by this Time, offered himself to their Service; And I hope he will be found in some measure acceptable to them. It will, I am persuaded be of good Service to Religion for him to be sent Missionary to Fairfield, where they have from their Experience of him entertained a great Regard to him, & impatiently hope for his Return to them. He would not have gone so soon but that the depressed State of his People was such, that they were impatient till something could be done for their Releif, & Stood in great need of a Minister Steddily resident among them.

But since the Honᵇˡe Society have been pleased to allow 10ˡᵇ per anᵣ for a School Master, I should be very glad it might be fixed in this Town of Stratford, for it would be of great Service to have a School here: And the rather because when any Young Men, who have had a Liberal Education in the College here, come over to our Communion, they are rejected from all Business by the Dissenters: An Instance of which, I have now, in one Mᵣ Bennet, a very likely young man, & more I expect from time to time. And if there were a Church-of-England School fixed here, it would be a good Resort for them Successively, till they are qualified for higher Business. This is an Affair which, I humbly conceive, with Submission, may deserve your Lordships Notice, because I beleive it will be highly Serviceable to the Interest of Religion here.

I am, My Lord, your Lordships most humble / most thankful & most Dutiful Son / & Servant

Samuel Johnson

[1728, Sept. 13, New London]

New London Septembᵣ 13 1728

My Lord

When I was last at london, I had yᵉ honᵣ of wa[iting] upon Your Lordship relating to a missionairy for yᵉ church at new london I allso took yᵉ libertty to presᵗ a memorial to yᵣ Ld[sp] relating to yᵉ abuses & injustice done to those who adheres to yᵉ church of England wᶜʰ wee hope in due time Yᵣ Lordship will endeavour to redress I have glased our church & yᵗ of Mᵣ Conner at Fairfeild, & have reserved enough for to suply yᵗ at Westerley the subscriptions for yᵉ misionairy of new London amounts to above fourty pounds per anᵣ this cu[rrency] severalls more will come in but affraid of being persecutted & oprest the reasons yᵗ those subscriptions have not been remitted to yᵉ honᵇˡe societty is not known to me but my Lord how can wee assure & make good the subscriptions when our properties are take away at pleasure & have not yᵉ beneflt of yᵉ act of Toleration tho' wee are yᵉ Establish't church, nay yᵉ natives I mean yᵉ infidelles have a greater previl[ege] for they can chuse 6 out of 12 of their own for a Jurie. in short I assure Your Lordship that that it is a dishonᵣ to yᵉ crown under pretence of a charter & libertty this is only a Receptacle of perjurie rebellion & theft I beg Your Ldsp will pardon me if I take yᵉ libertty to send a book wherein their Laws are contained and since wee have yᵉ haplness to be under pastoral care Wee hope our deliverance will be obtained by Yᵣ Ldsp aplication

I most humbly beg Leave to ask Yᵣ Lordships benediction and to Sub[s]cr[i]be my Self / Your Lordships most Humble & most devoted / & obedient Servant

Peter Burr

[1728, Sept. 21, Stratford]

Stratford in N England Sep. 21. 1728

My Lord

Notwithstanding that a Considerable Number of my former Hearers & Communicants are gone off to make up Mᵣ Caners parish, yet my Church is considerably fuller this Summer, than ever it was before, & I have yet fourscore Communicants who constantly attend the Communion here at Stratford.

Seven whole Families have been reconciled to the Church, & besides two of the Native Indians there is one large Family who have always lived like Heathen, are now become serious Christians and are all baptized.

Two Jews have been of late here induced to embrace the Christian Religion, both Serious & Sensible persons, One of them was Baptized last Easter, & the other is preparing to be baptized now in a Short time. So that by the Blessing of God the Interest of Religion considerably advances among us.

I continue to preach with Success at New-Haven, & hope there will be a Church there, in time, tho' they labour under great Opposition & Discouragement from the people of the Town, who will neither give nor sell them a peice of Land for them to build a Church on.

The Difficulties & Oppressions that the people of our Church have suffered under this Independent Government, have been, & are, so great, that no less than Seven Families have removed hence into New York Government, since I came into these parts, of which three removed this year. At present, indeed, we have a little better Quarters with them, by Reason of the Terror they are under from Mr Winthrops Complaints against the Government: & I wish they may be taught a better Temper towards the Church.

I will not trouble your Lordship any further at present than Humbly to ask your Blessing & Subscribe my Self

May it please y^r L^{d}ship / Your Lordships most humble obedient & / dutiful Son & Servt.

Samuel Johnson

[1729, June 10, Stratford]

Stratford June ye 10th 1729.

My Lord,

We yet labour under so much uneasiness in this Government of Connecticut, that Several people have lately removed hence into New-York Government, of which four Families have removed since my Last: & but three new families are become steddy Converts to the Church.

But there are many, & the Number of them, I hope daily increasing, whose Minds are intirely reconciled to our Communion, but dare not declare themselves, for Fear of the Displeasure of the Government. However it is evident that a more friendly & charitable Temper towards the Church, is visibly increasing among the people in this Country.

Among the Converts to the Church since my last, (two whereof are native Indians, & two Negroes,) one Mr Mordecai Markes, a Jew, a very worthy proselyte [&] constant Communicant, the second Jew who has be[come] Christianized in my parish within these two years.

I have met with much Trouble among my [people] occasioned by my Delivering the Communion pl[ates to] the Church of Narraganset, which I was at [last convin]ced, it was my Duty to do, by a Letter of t[he] Reverend Mr Bridge to the Revd Mr Myles late [of   ] from which, with other concurrent proofs, it app[eared] that the original property was truly vested in the Church of Narraganset. I was obliged to use a great deal of Resolution & Selfdenyal on this Occasion, but I hope Time will by Degrees compose the Temper of those of my people who have been greatly exasperated on this Account.

I beg your Lordships Blessing, & am / My Lord, your Lordships / most obedient humble Ser[vant] / & Dutiful Son

Samuel Johnson

[1729, July 1, Stratford]

Stratford in Connecticut

(3)

QUERIES

To be answer'd by every Minister.

How long is it, since you went over to the Plantations as a Missionary? May it please your Lordship, I arived upon my Charge on November 1st 1723.

Have you had any other Church, before you came to that which you now possess; and if you had, what Church was it, and how long have you been remov'd? Answer, I was a Teacher in the Presbyterian Method at West-Haven about 10 Miles off from this Town, but never was in the Service of the Established Church till the Honble Society admitted me into their Service as Missionary.

Have you been duly Licens'd by the Bishop of <u>London</u> to officiate as a Missionary, in the Government where you now are? Answer, I was Licenced by your Lordship to officiate as a Missionary in this Colony of Connecticut

How long have you been Inducted into your Living? Answer, I was admitted into the Honble Societies Service in the beginning of January 1722/3.

Are you ordinarily Resident in the Parish to which you have been Inducted? Answer, I am Constantly Resident at Stratford excepting the Time that I am Riding about to Preach in the Neighbouring Towns that are destitute of Ministers.

Of what Extent is your Parish, and how many Families are there in it? Answer, The Town is nigh 10 miles Square, & has about 250 or 300 Families in it, nigh 50 of which are of the Established Church. But indeed, the Episcopal People of all the Towns adjacent, esteem themselves my parishoners, as at Fairfield about 30 Families, the like Number at New-Town, at West-Haven, about 10, & sundry in other Places.

Are there any Infidels, bond or free, within your Parish; and what means are us'd for their Conversion? Answer, There are nigh 200 Indians, in the bounds of this Town, for whose Conversion, there are no means used, & the like in many other Towns, & many Negro's that are Slaves in particular Families, some of which go to Church but most of them to Meeting

How oft is divine Service perform'd in your Church? And what Proportion of the Parishioners attend it? Answer, Service is performed only on Sundays & Holidays, & many times an 100 or 150 people attend it, but sometimes not half So many, & sometimes thrice that Number, especially upon the three Great Festivals, & when I preach at the neighbouring Towns, especially at Fairfield & Newtown, I have a very Numerous Audience which places as the[y] very much want, so they might be readily Supplied with ministers from among our Selves, & those the Best y^t are educated here, if there was but a Bishop to ordain them.

(4)

How oft is the Sacrament of the Lord's Supper administer'd? And what is the usual Number of Communicants? Answer, I administer the H. Eucharist on the first Sunday of every Month to about 30 & Sometimes 40 Communicants, & upon the 3 great Festivals to about 60, But there are nigh an 100 Communicants here & in the Towns adjacent, to whom I administer as often as I can attend them.

At what times do you Catechise the Youth of your Parish? Answer, I catechise every Lords Day immediately after Evening Service & explain the Catechisme to them.

Are all things duly dispos'd and provided in the Church, for the decent and orderly Performance of divine Service? Answer, We have no Church, have begun to build one, but such is the poverty of the People that we get along but very Slowly, Neither have we any Furniture for the Communion save that which Narraganset people lay Claim to, concerning which I have written to your Lordship by my Church Warden.

Of what Value is your Living in Sterling-Money, and how does it arise? Answer, I have 60 pounds Sterling Settled on me by the Honble Society & Receive but very little from my poor people save now & then a few Small presents.

Have you a House and Glebe? Is your Glebe in Lease, or let by the Year? Or is it occupied by your self? Answer, I have neither House nor Glebe.

Is due Care taken to preserve your House in good Repair? And at whose Expence is it done? [No answer.]

Have you more Cures than one? If you have, what are they? And in what Manner serv'd? Answer, There are Fairfield 8 Miles off, Newtown, 20 Repton 8, West-Haven 10, & New London 70 Miles off, to all which places I Ride, & preach & Administer the Sacraments as often as I can, but have no assistance, save that one Dr Laborie an ingenous Gentleman does gratis, explain the Catechisme at Fairfield, but all these places want Ministers extremely.

Have you in your Parish any publick School for the Instruction of Youth? If you have, is it endow'd? And who is the Master? Answer, The Independents have one or two poor Schools among them, But there are no Schools of the Church of England, in the Town nor Colony, for which Reason I have Recommended my Church Warden to your Lordship & the Honble Society--

Have you a Parochial Library? If you have, are the Books preserv'd, and kept in good Condition? Have you any particular Rules and Orders for the preserving of them? Are those Rules and Orders duly observ'd? Answer, we have no Library save the 10 pounds Worth which the Honble Society gave, which I keep Carefully by themselves in my Study in the Same Condition as I keep my own. I am My Lord, / y.^r Lordships most humble, obedient & / dutiful Son & Servant

    July 1. 1729.   Samuel Johnson

[1729, Oct. 27, Stratford]
         Stratford in N England Oct. 27 1729
May it please y.^r Lordship

The only Occasion of my troubling your Lordship at this time is the Request of Sundry of the good people of Boston, who are desirous that I should Succeed the Revd Mr Harris at the Kings Chappel.

My Lord, I am very well contented in the Service of the Honourable Society, & very thankful for their Generous Encouragement, & Support of me therein: & therefore, (considering withall, the great Improbability of my being thought a proper person for it,) I should not have thought of this Station, were it not for the Importunity of Sundry of the Gentlemen of the Chappel at Boston who assure me that there is a very great Majority that are very desirous, I should apply my Self to your Lordship on this Occasion.

Indeed considering how vastly expensive, living in Boston is, beyond living in the Country, I cannot propose to my Self any Temporal Advantage by Such a Remove: So that the only Motive that could induce me to it is a prospect of being more Serviceable in promoting the Interest of Religion, if I should be thought in any measure qualified for it.

However, whither it shall be thought best that I should be removed thither, or abide where I am, I intirely Submit, with the Disposal of my Self, to your Lordships Judgment

& remain, May it please your Lordship / y.^r Lordships most dutiful Son / & most obedient humble Servant
              Samuel Johnson

[1730, Sept. 18, Fairfield]
     Fairfeild in N: England Sept.^{br} 18.º 1730
My Lord,

I Presume to acquaint You, that I have laid before the Honble Society the Inability of my People to Comply with the Expectations of that venerable Board; and withal the Scheme formed among us for future Support: if we may be favour'd with the Honble Society's Benefactions till that Design arrive at Some Maturity. The People do Seem to have a just Sense of matters, and as they are Sensible of the Necessity, so would willingly if they were able, render my Salary equal to that of other Missionaries in these parts. Whether I Shall ever see the Time I cannot determine; I am however well pleased at the Prospect of a good Support for my Successors Such as may enable them to attend the Business of their Function without Cares and Distractions. The People I am persuaded will from them and me by this means Reap Such Advantages, as may in some Measure Ballance their Preparations and Labours for us which can never I think be more effectually brought about than by a diligent and Industrious Care of that Charge committed to us: in the Execution of which I venture to assure my Self Your Lordships Prayers and Blessing will not fail to attend.

I am my Lord / with the utmost Veneration / Y.^r Lordships much oblidged / & most dutiful Servant
              Henry Caner

[1731, June 4, Stratford]
     Stratford in N England June 4. 1731
May it please y.^r Lordship,

I take this Oppertunity humbly to thank your Lordship for your two excellent Letters to your Diocess, which you have so kindly sent among us & are every where received with the greatest Thankfulness, tho' we very much lament the sad Occasions that have made it necessary for your Lordship to employ your Vigilance in such a Manner: May the Success of them be proportioned to the Excellency of the Performances!

My Lord, there are two things that have occasioned some Dispute among the Clergy & people in these parts, about which I humbly presume to beg your Lordships Directions:

One is, relating to the Exhortation after Baptism to the Godfathers to bring the Child to the Bishop to be confirmed: Some wholly omit this Exhortation, because it is impracticable: others insert the Words, (if there be oppertunity,) because our Adversaries object it as a meer Jest to order the Godfathers to bring the Child to the Bishop, when there is none within a 1000 Leagues of us, which is a Reproach that we cannot answer.

The other Dispute is about employing young Schollars that are Candidates for the Ministry in Villages & destitute places, in reading Sermons & Prayers, (omitting everything that is proper to the Preists Office,)-- This, I own, is what I and some others have earnestly recommended, as excusable by reason of the necessities of the Country,

& have in several Instances, found highly useful in keeping up a Sense of Religion, & propagating it where resident Ministers cannot be had: & tho' I have always let the Honble Society know of my proceedings herein, they have never intimated the least disapprobation of this Method, but on the other hand have practically approved of it, in receiving once & again into their Service those who had been so employed.

Notwithstanding this there are Some of our Brethren who with great Zeal & importunity cry out against this practice as a betraying of the Church & giving up the necessity of Ordination, &c, to the great mortification of those poor destitute people who have no other way of keeping up the Worship of God among them.

My Lord, I humbly submit to y.^r Lordships Correction if in this or any other Instance my Conduct has been faulty, & earnestly beg your Direction & Benediction, who am / with the greatest Veneration / May it please y.^r Lordship, / your Lordships most obedient / & most dutiful Son, / & humble Servant

Samuel Johnson

[1732, Mar. 25, Stratford]
Stratford in Connecticut March 25. 1732
May it please y^r Lordship,

We beg leave to acquaint your Lordship that we have presumed to address the honourable Society in favour of the Bearer hereof, Mr John Beach, who now waits upon your Lordship & the Honourable Society for holy Orders & a Mission, which as you will find in our Letter to the hon.^ble Society, He & We unitedly desire may be at Newtown or Reading which are two small Towns about twenty Miles northward of Fairfield & Stratford, & about seven from each other, encompass'd with some other small Towns as Danbury Ridgefield New Milford & Woodbury, all within the Compass of twelve or fourteen Miles from these in each of which places there are some professors of the Church of England, whom by reason of their Distance from us we can very rarely attend; & neither of the two places above mentioned have any Teacher at all of any Denomination.

There is likewise at the Distance of about three Miles from Newtown a small Village of Indians who indeed are the greatest Number in the County, about 200 souls & being above twenty Miles from the Sea are more temperate, & consequently fitter to be wrought upon, if a Missionary were settled so near as that he might with any tollerable Convenience attend upon them. & we are ready to beleive that they might by a Diligent & proper Instructer be brought to the knowledge of Christianity, if it were recommended to the Govern.^r to oblige them to attend upon his Ministrations.

As to Mr Beach, he had his Education at Yale-College, where he made uncommon proficiency in Learning & hath since he left it taken Care to improve himself in Divinity & other useful Studies; And, (which was indeed almost the unavoidable Consequence of his Education, & want of proper Books,) when he entered into the Dissenting Ministry, he was thought the most proper person to oppose the growth of the Church in Newtown on Account of the Good opinion that every one had of his Learning & piety, & was accordingly placed there, (tho' he never did any thing to the Churches prejudice;) But having since, by his Neighbourhood to some

of us, had the Advantage of better Books, & Information, he hath found it his Duty to quit their Service & come over to our Communion, whereby he hath done great Service to the Church in these parts, &, we doubt not, will always be an Honour to it, if your Lordship shall think fit to Ordain Him & the Honourable Society to admit him into their Service: And as we are well assured his Labours will be of great use here; So we beg leave to assure your Lordship of his firm Attachment to the present Government as established in the illustrious House of Hannover.

Upon the whole therefore we humbly hope y.^r Lordship & the Honble Society will think fit to impower & employ him, who for the peace of his Conscience, hath left the possessions he enjoyed & now taken a long & dangerous Voyage, melancholly in it self, but rendered more so by his leaving his Wife & Children. And we further Trust that it will not displease your Lordship & the Honble Society, that we do from time to time recommend young Men of bright parts & good Abilities, to your Lordship's & their kind Notice & Regard, as well as those who seeing the Error of their Ways, are willing to embrace Truth & peace & submit to our excellent Church. We beg an Interest in your Lordship's prayers & Blessing & are, with the utmost Respect & veneration, / May it please y^r Lordship, / your Lordships most obedient & / dutiful Sons, & humble Servants,

Samuel Johnson   J. Wetmore   Henry Caner

[1732, Apr. 6, Fairfield]
Fairfeild in New-England April 6th 1732
Rev^d S^r

I Presume to Recommend to your kind Notice and Regard the Gentleman who is the Bearer hereof Mr John Beach, now design'd to wait upon my Lord of London and the Honble Society for Holy Orders and a Mission. The Gentleman is an Entire Stranger to your City, and will therefore need the favour of every Gentleman in whose Power it may chance to be, to forward his Business. He had a Liberal Education, and hath taken care to furnish Himself for the Service He desires, and as We hope here He will prove very Serviceable at his Return   Should be very glad his Business might Soon be accomplished

Sr Your goodness to me in particular, Emboldens me to apply for those Favours which, I persuade my Self do naturally flow from You; I only therefore beg Pardon for this freedom Who am / Rev^d S^r / Your most Obedient / Humble Servant

Henry Caner
P.S. The Revd Mr Johnson's Service is hereby tender'd with my own, which please to accept.

[1732, Oct. 12, New Haven]
At a General assembly Holden at New Haven 12th Day of October Anno: Dom 1732

Whereas the Committee appointed by this assembly in may Last to hear the Contending parties in Guilford first Society and to Report the State of that affair with their opinion thereupon to the assembly at their present Sessions have Laid thir Report before the assembly Accordingly which Report this assembly Do accept allow of & approve & Do order and apoint that (at the motion &

Cost of the minor part of the Society in S:d Guilford) the Rev:d Elders hereafter named that is to Say: M:r Seth Shove M:r Anthony Stoddard M:r Jonathan Marsh M:r William Russell M:r Be[n]jamin Lord M:r George Griswould M:r Eleazer Williams and m:r Tho:s Clapp with messengers from their Respective Churches (or So many of them as Shall there assemble & Convene) be a Council to meete at Guilford to hear Consider and finally Determine a Case heretofore moved & Laid against forty Six persons in S:d Guilford & members of the Church in S:d Society before a Council there and upon which the S:d Council gave Sentance against S:d forty Six persons March 10:th 1731 and it is further Resolved that the minor party in S:d Society Shall not be Rated or Taxed the Current year for y:e Settlement or Support of the Rev:d M:r Ruggles and with Respect to the Rates that have been made by y:e S:d Society on the minor party Since y:e Contention and not yet Collected it is Resolved that said Rates or a Rearages Shall be Duly Colleted & paid according to y:e votes of S:d Society--

A True Copy of Record / Exam:d /
New Haven Oct:r 1733   per George Wyllys Secret[ary]

[1732, Nov. 6, Fairfield]
Fairfeild in N: England Nov:r 6:th 1732
My Lord

Having Acquainted the Hon:ble Society with the particular State of my Parish at this Juncture, which is tolerably prosperous; I ventur'd to add my Desire, in very Humble manner, that the State of my Salary might likewise have a Share of their Notice; which is 10:lb Per Ann. less than the least of those that have been allow'd to Missionaries in these parts.

My Lord it is not only my own Humble Request who feel the want of it, but the Desire also of my Brethren, who are afraid the Example will prove a Discouragement to Young Men who are willing to go for Orders, when they See a Diminution in the Accustom'd Salary.

I beg leave to promise my Self your Lordship's Indulgence in this Point, as well as your Prayers and Blessing.

I am with the utmost Veneration / My Lord / Your Lordship's / most Dutiful and Obedient / Son & Humble Servant

Henry Caner

[1733, Apr. 19, Stratford]
Stratford in N England April. 19. 1733
My Lord

Besides what I have written in Conjunction with my Rev:d Brethren, I beg leave to add with Respect to these Young Gentlemen, That I could wish it practicable that the Charge of their Voyage home might be defrayed by the Honourable Society, & especially M:r Browne's, who has for several Years been doing good Service in several destitute places, by teaching Children their Catechism, & to read & write, & Reading prayers & Sermons: And this I the rather presume to ask in his Behalf, because the Society have given me Encouragement by a Letter that some allowance shall be made to him upon the Score of his past Services.

My Lord, I have once & again applyed to the Society for a School in this Town, & it was said in one of their Abstracts that they had come to a Resolution to provide a School Master for this place: If it can be done, I should be very thankful; for here is great need of One, & there is not so much as one in all this Colony. Now here is an Ingenious person that would willingly undertake it, who is brother to this M:r Browne & very well qualified in every respect for that Business, & he may be the more easily provided for by the Society, in Regard, that if this M:r Browne should be sent to Brook-Haven, where they were pleased to grant 70:lb per an:, to M:r Campbell, he would be content to forego that 10:lb which was added in favour of M:r Campbell, & take up with 60:lb especially provided that the 10:lb might be allowed towards a School for his Brother in this Town: And indeed he could the better afford it, especially for several Years at first, because there are two or three wealthy Gentlemen in Brook-Haven, by whose means that Parish is of better ability than some others: Be sure they are able to do much more for him than my People here, who are generally of the poorer Sort, can do either for me or for a School here: I should therefore be much obliged to the Hon:ble Society if they would please to settle that 10:lb pound upon his Brother M:r Joseph Browne for a School Master here at Stratford, & if they could add 5:lb per an: more, so as to make him 15:lb per an: it would indeed be a great Obligation both upon Him & us.

One thing more, My Lord, I will presume to lay before your Lordships Consideration, respecting these Countrys, & that is this: There are considerable numbers of the members of the Church of England scattered up & down in various parts of this & the neighbouring Governments at great Distances from any Parish Church, for whom it is impossible for us that have parishes; to provide, consistent with our several Duties at home; this makes it very needful that there should be an Itinerant Missionary appointed to minister to all these scattering people: And here is a very worthy Gentleman, One M:r Arnold, who is very well qualified for it, & would undertake it, if the Society should think fit to employ him. I should therefore be very much obliged to your Lordship for your Interest with the Honourable Society, that they would be pleased to inform me whither they would be disposed to establish such a Mission; Because this Gentleman, having a good Fortune of his own, & therefore no other veiw in undertaking it, but meerly to do what good he can, would not willingly undertake a Voyage to England without being first acquainted whither the Society would think fit to employ him in such a Mission provided he should come sufficiently recommended.

I am / May it please y:r Lordship / y:r L:dships / most obedient & / dutiful Son / & humble Servant

Sa. Johnson

[1734, Feb. 5, North Groton]

Proceedings against M:r Punderson

Att a Councill held at North Groton Feb:ry 5:th 1733/4 Called by the Church & Soc:ty in that place

Present y:e Rev:d ⎰ M:r Elphalet Adams ⎱
                  ⎱ M:r Salmon Treat   ⎰ Elders
                  ⎩ M:r Jabez: Wright ⎭

$$\left\{\begin{array}{l}\text{M}^r \text{ Josh: Hempst}^d\\ \text{M}^r \text{ Hez}^k \text{ Clark}\\ \text{M}^r \text{ Nath Gideons}\\ \text{M}^r \text{ Sam}^l \text{ Story}\end{array}\right\} \begin{array}{l}\text{Lay}\\ \text{Messengers}\end{array}$$

The Revd Mr Eliphalet Adams was Chosen moderator and Mr Jabez: Wright Scribe

After Supplication to Heaven for Direction and Guidance in the affair, to be laid before us, the letter was read from the Society to the Churches: after wch Mr Ebenezer Punderson gave in to us by writing his declaration for his conformity to the Established Church of England as Followeth.

North Groton Feby 5th 1733/4

After the most serious and impartiall Search and Inquiry (in the fear of God made by me) [I] cannot but think the E[s]tablish'd Church of England in her doctrine Government and Worship to be most agreable to the Sacred will of God; and most conducive Unto Edification; and Consequently do now declare my Conformity to that Church As wittnesseth my hand

Ebenez^r Punderson

And after reading the Said Declaration the Committee spake something to the Letter, and Informed ye Councill of the present Circumstances of the place.

And we do hereupon give it as our Judgm^t that Mr Ebenezer Punderson by his aforesd declaration has render'd himself incapable further to serve this Church and people, and that he is fallen from his ministry and Consequently that this Church & people are released from all obligations to him as their pastour--

And we do Entreat our Neighbouring Elders (as divers of them have already) to take their turns to preach Unto this people, and even a second time (if it be necessary) till they can have an opportunity to look out for some meet person to settle among them in the work of the ministry by the advice of the Neighbouring Elders.

We are heartily Concerned for the Dificulty and Distress that is come Upon this people on this Occasion, and would recommend as a very fit & proper Expedient, that a Day of fasting and prayer be observed as soon as Conveniently may be, by this people with the assistance of some Neighbouring Elder or to humble themselves before God under this great affliction that is brought upon them, and to seek of a right way for their being happily resetled, according to the order of ye Gospell and the good Constitution of these Churches--

All which Judgment and advice we follow with our prayers, that God would Graciously please in this day of temptation to keep this people, and Every Particular person among them Stedfast in the good profession, which they have made at their first being settled in this Church State, and that in his own good time, he would furnish them with a Pastor after his own Heart who may feed them with Knowledge and Understanding--

Signed by Order of Councill
Eliphalet Adams Mod^r
Jabez: Wright Scribe

A True Copy

[1734, after Feb. 5, North Groton]

Petition and Subscription of the People of North Groton in New England deliverd by Mr Punderson, 1734--

Revd Sir

The fame of the Glorious design of the Hon: Society for the propogation of ye Gospell in foreign parts having reached us the Underwritten we beg leave to throw our Selves as Charitable objects upon their Compassionate Concern of the Souls of men:

Humbly representing

That some Years since, that many of us Committed under God the Conduct of our Souls unto Eternity to ye Care & Charge of the Bear^r Mr Punderson in the Presbyterian or Independent way--

That upon a strict & serious Enquiry into ye Nature of his power, for the Exercise of the Ministerial function Mr Punderson found them Defective, and in Consequence himself under a Necessity, from that work to Desist untill his power were strengthened or renewed, and upon Viewing and Examining the frame of the Church of England, in her articles & Government, and seeing the one to be agreable to Scripture & truth and the Other to the primitive pattern and Apostolick Constitution, as well as her Manner of worship tending to Edification, soon determine[d] to Joyn her communion and offer his Service there

That we being moved by his reasons and our own Inclinations; accompanyed with a Strong Sencere and valuable affection for his person, raised in us by his Zeal, for the Glory of God and diligent application in promoting, the true interest of men; as well as his own vertuous and Exemplary Life & Conversation are resolved to adhere unto him promiseing that if he is Encouraged by the Patrons of religion in England, to return us our Minister to Contribute annually to his Support the Sums in our money annexed to our respective Names and to Conclude--

That God would prosper the designs and pour down his richest blessings upon every Member of that Honourable Society are the Sencere and fervent prayers of your Most Obedient and / Revd Sir / Your Most / Humble Servants

	£. S. d		
Thos Rose	1.10.0	Ralph Stoddard	0.15.0
Robt Geer, Senr	1.10.0	John Weed	0.10.0
Robt Stodd^d Senr	1.10.0	Jon^n Williams	1.00.0
Walter Capren	2.00.0	John Perkins	0. 5.-
Henly Peton	1.00.0	Danl McClanton	0.10.0
Wm Spiver	0.15.0	Thomas Minor	1.00.0
Joseph Rose	1.00.0	John Allyne	0.10.0
Thos Mumford	2.00.0	John Safford	2.00.0
Edm^d Fanning	1.10.0	John Amos	0. 5.0
Christ^n French	1.00.0	Matthias Button	0. 5.0
Lawr^ce Powers	1.00.0	Thos Kist	2. 0.0
Wm Williams	1.00.0	Clodius Delus	1.00.0
Joshua Bill	0. 6.0	John Parke	0. 3.0
	£16. 1.0		£10. 3.0
			16. 1.0
			£26. 4.0

The Doctrine of Faith assented unto
by the N: Church at Groton
We Beleive that there is only one true Living and eternall

God Infinite in all the Attributes and perfections of his Divine Nature as holiness, wisdom, Justice, and goodness and other moral perfections. Distinguished into and Subsisting in three undivided persons and Subsistencys being the same in Essence and attributes Yet Distinguished by relative and personall propertys, The Father begetting The Son begotten, The holy Ghost proceeding from Both That this Supream being is the Almighty creator of all things and the Infinitly wise and just Govern.ͬ and Disposer of them.

We Beleive that man was Created after his Image in a State of Integrity and Blessedness and by his disobedience and consequent disunion from God hath suffered the Loss of Both and has such and has such a depraved & vitiated Nature which naturally leads him in the Path to Misery and Wretchedness--

We beleive that the ever blessed God viewing with pity and a tender Compassion Sinfull man in this wretched and Lapsed Condition in the fullness of time sent his true only and beloved Son (equall in glory and honour with him) to take humane nature in Conjunction with his Divine Nature that so Subsisting in and Consisting of two Distinct natures, and one undivided Person he might be a fitt Mediator between God and Man and a Reconciliator of them each to Other and Efficassiously redeem Man by Price and Power; And that this son of God being anointed Prophet, Priest, and King of his Church did execute these offices by Making a revelation of God's mind & Mans Duty, in the Gospell of peace, by his obedience unto the Law, and suffering the Death; even that Death of the Cross, And in his now presenting before his Father his Death and Meritts and in sending his holy Spiritt to Enlighten, cure, and sanctifye all that come Unto him under A sense of their Impotency; and want of Pardon and Divine favour And those that believe in his Name and Conform their Lives to the Gospell precepts and Our Saviours Example by the Spirit of God being enabled therunto shall be judged to Eternall Life & Glory in the Days when God shall exert his power in raising all men from the Dead to Judge them according to their works And all those that have resisted the motions and Suggestions of his holy Spiritt and Defeated the methods and Designs of his Grace Upon their Souls and rather Chose Satans Service and their own misery he will in Justice Judge to Everlasting punishment according to the Scriptures of Truth which we believe to be the word of God & the only rule of Faith & manners--

		Ebenez.ͬ Punderson
William Morgan	⎞	John Morgan
Edward Averey	⎬	Rich.ᵈ Williams
Humph Averey	⎬	Christ.º Averey
John Spicer	⎠	John Dean

[1734, Mar. 14, Fairfield]
Mess.ͬˢ Johnson, Wetmore, Caner, and Browne in behalfe of M.ͬ Punderson, to y.ͤ Secret.ͬʸ

Fairfield N. England Mar: 14: 1734
Rev.ᵈ Sir

M.ͬ Ebenezer Punderson who is y.ͤ bearer hereof, being bound to England, with design to apply himself to the Hon.ᷞ Society and the Bp. of London, for holy Orders, & a

mission; we humbly beg leave to offer to the Hon.ᷞ board our Recommendation of this worthy Gentleman. He has been for above four Years a Settled minister in the Dessenting Way, to a parish near New London Called North Groton, and, as he has a good prospect that a very Consideration [considerable] Numb.ͬ of that Parish, will Conform to the Church with him, he has a Solicitous Desire to return back in holy Orders, to his people, with whom he has So long dwelt, and among whom he is greatly respected, as to the Circumstances of the people our Distance from them; Renders us Uncapable of Saying any thing of them, whose Case we Conclude will be represented, by those of our Brethren, who live near them, But as to the Gent: himself, we having well known him for the Space of Seaven Years, are able with Truth, to assure the Hon.ᷞ Society, that he has always been, remarkable, for a person of good parts, earnestly Inquisitive after truth, and indefatigably Studious in the pursuit of it; That he has read many of our English divines, & has made as great a proficiency in Learning, as can be Expected from his age & Circumstances, And that he has ever been Esteemed a Sober Virtuous, & Devout person; & Remarkable for his contempt of the world, and we are perswadᵈ that it is from a Serious & Impartiall Examination of things, & the Sencere love of the truth, & Sense of Duty, that he has declared himself for our Excellent Church & Come over to Our Communion and he is Sencerely well affected to y.ͤ pres.ͭ Governm.ͭ

We humbly therefore beseech the Hon.ᷞ Society that he may be accepted & Sent back to his people aforesaid whom he is well qualified to Serve--

We are, may it please y.ͤ Hon.ᷞ Society, Their most Dutifull & obedient as well as S.ͬ / Your hum.ᷞᵉ Servants

| Henry Caner | ⎫ | | Sam.ᷞ Johnson |
| Isaac Browne | ⎭ | | J. Wetmore |

[1734, Mar. 30, Stratford]
M.ͬ Johnson to the Secretary

Stratford N England Mar: 30.ᵗʰ 1734
Rev.ᵈ Sir

Since my last, two of the Gentlem.ᷢ I then mentioned have declared their Conformity to the Church, they are M.ͬ Arnold & M.ͬ Punderson, the Bearer Hereof, the Clergy here have now recommended this M.ͬ Pund.ˢ.ᷢ to the Hon.ᷞ Society as very well qualified for their Service, and he has so good hopes of his people, that he Earnestly desires to be sent back to them in holy Orders, as soon as Possible: for the Conditions of things whith them is Such, that he Could not wait, till we could hear from the Hon.ᷞ Society, on which acct. he is Necessiated to apply to my L.ᵈ of London for Orders; that he may return to them again with all speed possible; which he would gladly to even tho it Should not be in y.ͤ Society.ˢ power to provide a Sallary for him; and 'tho he can Expect but a very Slender Support among his people; He however resign's himself with an Implicit faith in Providence concerned for nothing but to Do his Duty & to do good: & I humbly hope that So Disinterested & self denying a disposition will if possible meet with Some Encouragment from the Society tho it be but Small--.

As to Mr Arnold, he has met with great opposition from these about him, who have used so many arts & Endeavours among his people, that there are not so many of them that have appeared to Joyn with him in Conforming to the Church as he Expected he hopes however that they will in the Compass of half a Year, return to what appeared to be their former Resolution, and in the mean time he will Endeavour in a private Capacity to do all the good he can among them, and still Humbly Desires with me to be Informed, if by the fall of the Year, there should appear a Comptnt numbr in New Haven, West Haven, & Milford (which all are within the Compass of 8 or 10 miles) to Subscribe towards his Support as it is probable there will, whither the Honl Society would be Disposed to Encourage his Coming over with a view at his being taken upon the Mission, for those places where there are Considerable Number already to whom I frequently preachd or if they fail whither there might not be provided for him a Mission at Norwalk & Ridgefield which are 2 places near one another about 20 miles to ye westwrd of this Town, where we have all of us been frequently preaching to a Considerable Number of people who are about Building a Church

I Still Continue to preach with good Success at Ripton and Darby, besides West Haven where Mr Arnold is, and there have Severall families lately Conformed to the Church, I have since my last baptized 26 Infants and Six adult persons and admitted 8 Communicants one whereof is a Negro man of very good understanding & Serious Understanding & Piety so that my Notitiæ Parochialis is as follows--(viz).--

No 1: Number of Inhabitants in this Town about families of which Conform to ye Church besides Severall others in the places adjacent — 270 / 57

2 No of the Baptized since the Mission of which since my last 28 & of them 2 adults — 347

3 No of Communicants here & in places adjacent of wch admitted this 1/2 year 8 & one of them a Negro — 110

4 No of those that profess the Church of England here and in the places adjacent under my Care — 250

5 The rest generally Independents
No of those that have been Converted from a loose & Careless way of living to a Serious Sense of Religeon — 2
No of the Heathen Scarce any Fixed inhabitants here, tho Severall Stroll about in a very unsteady manner--

I am / Revd Sir / Your most / Obedient & most / Humble Servant

Sa: Johnson

[1734, May 2, Newport, Rhode Island]
Mr Honeyman to ye Secretary

Newport Rhode Island May 2nd 1734
Revd Sir
I have Carefully Enquired into the Character & Conduct of Mr Ebenezer Punderson who will wait upon You with this; & find that while he was Disenting Minister He Behaved with So much prudence among the people where

he lived, that he is in Such high Esteem with them that a great part of them will Come over to ye Church and Joyn our Communion with him, if the Hon: Society will be pleased to return him as their Missiony unto them and there is no room to Doubt but the Encouraging him in that Station, would be of considerable Service to Religion and the Church in that part of the Country--

As to my own Church it is in a very thriving way I thank God I am Enabled to discharge my Duty with that Diligence & Infidelity [sic] that is Expected and can with Joy assure the Hon. Society that providence is pleased to Bless my Endeavours with Success. If I had them I could Disperse in the Country to great advantage, Bibles, prayer books, Bp. Beveridges thoughts of Religion, whole duty of man &ctr; I present my humble Duty to my Honourable Patrons assureing them that I am with the greatest respect their most Obedient / As I am / Revd Sir / Your most / humble Servant

James Honeyman

[1734, May 7, Boston]
Dr Cutler to the Secretary

Boston N: England May 7th 1734
Sir
It is with a great deal of pleasure, that I joyn with my Reverend Brethn in presenting Mr Ebenezer Punderson to the worthy Society for the Propogation of the gospell

I need not insist on his good Character so well attested by those who live nearest to him; and better acquainted with him then my Self: I only add I know none that Contradict it, and have recied the Confirmation of it from Sundry other hands, and as I presume the preserving affection of his people towards him, further recommends him to the Society, He going over for orders, at the desire of many of them, to whom in his own house as a Layman he has read the prayers of our Church, and Some good Discourses on Sundays for severall months past. So I hope this will Engage the Society's Compassion towards them, Especially when it is known how Convenient a Place Groton is for another Mission: at Sundry Miles distant from New London; and a large & troublesome River between them, & I Suppose at 50 miles distant from any Other Church & towards ye Borders of the Narragansetts where ye People remain wild, & Religion is almost lost in the variety of Sects for want of our ministers to Enlighten and assist them

I hope this Convert to our Church will be followed by another Dissenting Teacher of Good merit & Charactr Mr Jonathan Arnold, who has lately Conform'd to our Excellent Church; and God increases the oppertunity's so he will Encrease abilities of the Society to do good There is our obligation & Dependance under God; and should their favours in these Necessary Instances be withdrawn or Deny'd Us, I Tremble to think how poor a proficiency we should make after it.

That I may not be too troublesom in my Letters to the Society; I beg leave to forestall my half yearly acct to ym by one month; and to acquaint them That from Decr 3d to this Instant I have Baptised 15 Infants 2 adults English, and one adult Indian Female of the Natives amongst Us, who has left the Barbarity of her Kindred which She was

Educated in & has very Seriously Embraced the Christian
Revelation and Dedicated her Self to the Duties of it; I have
also admitted Seaven persons to our Communion whose
lives have been, & I hope will be agreable to their profession: at Christmas I had about 100 Communicants & at
Easter I had 94 belonging to this town & Severall adjacent
ones

    I shall always seek the Countenance of the Society in
a faithfull Discharge of my Duty and shall Remain while
I live / Their most Humb.! Servant

                                  Timothy Cutler

[1734, May 9]
To the Honourable General Assembly now sitting at Hartford May 9th AD 1734. The Petition of the West Parish
in New Haven Humbly Sheweth

    That Your poor Petitioners did some Years ago under
the Countenance & Favour of the Honourable Gen.ll Assembly, Settle a Minister of the Gospel [Samuel Johnson]
among them, approved of by the Elders of the neighbouring
Churches; Who in a few Years so far deserted the Principles of the Churches of New England, as to account his
Ordination a Nullity, & so resigned his Pastoral Care of
us. In our then destitute and broken State we proceeded
to y.e Settling of another Minister [Jonathan Arnold], hoping that He who is y.e Lord of the Harvest, would provide
us one that Should approve Himself Faithful & Steady to y.e
Principles of our New English Churches.--But in this we
have found our Selves disappointed, our Second Minister
relinquishing his Charge upon the Same Pretences the former had done. And we presume it is not unknown at least
to Many of this honourable assembly, that Some of our Society have been influenced to desert our Communion, by
those Who deserted their Ministry with us; whereby we are
rendered Less able to Settle another Minister among us,
and Pains are not Spared to Weaken us farther, by drawing away more, with arguments Suited to our Low Circum-
stances--Sc.t That if we will but accept of an Episcopal
Missionary for our Minister he will Serve us, for little or
No Maintenance from us; which Arguments (tho' Temptations to those of Low & strained Circumstances especially)--We hope may never prevail upon any of us, to forsake
the Purity of the Gospel Worship & administrations and
Submit to a Yoak of Ceremonies our Fathers were not able
to Bear.--In this our Destitute Broken, and Distressed
State, we have our recourse under God, to this Honourable
Assembly for the Exercise of its Compassions towards
us. As it has Cherished the Churches of y.e Colony, as a
Nursing Father,--so we firmly perswade our Selves of its
tender Care of us, and that it will not be wanting, in doing
what Lies w.th them to prevent (if it may be) our being torn
in Pieces, & so the suffering of the whole Body by the Suffering of one of its Members. As we are earnestly desir-
our that we & ours after us, may enjoy a pure Gospel Ministry & Ordinances, & are ready to lay out our Selves to
the utmost under all the Discouragements, we are attended
with, So we are sensible we greatly need Assistance y.rin.
We asked not any of this Honourable Assembly when we
settled our first Minister,--Nor when we Settled our Sec-
ond--But being so deserted by the one & the other in So
short a Space, and w.thall other ways weakened, as we
feel very sensibly we want some Assistance, So we cant

but hope this Honourable Assembly is very apprehensive
of it, & will in their Goodness extend it to us. Either
by giving us a Sum of Money out of the Treasury, or the
Country Rates of the Town of West haven, for two or three
years or untill this Assembly shall see Cause to call for
them; & so order it That where they shall be collected &
paid into the Treasury, they may be thence received by
y.e society to be improved for & towards the Settlement
and Support of Such a Gospel Minister with us, or shall
be approved of by the Associated Elders in the County of
New Haven,--and allso recommend our loss to y.e charity
of sum of y.e Naibouering towns or in some other way, as
this Honourable Assembly in their Wisdom and Goodness
shall Think best. And your poor Petitioners as in Duty
bound shall ever pray

        Sam.ll Smith   ⎫
        Thomas Trowbridge ⎬ Com.te In behalf
        Peter Robourts   ⎭ of S.d Society--

In the Upp.r House The Prayer of this Memoriall granted
Viz that if the Said Society procure a Minister as therein
Exprest that then the Sum of two hundred pounds be drawn
out of the Colony Treasury and Improved towards the Said
Ministers Sett[le]ment--&c and that a Bill be drawn in
form

                  Test Hez: Wyllys Secret.ry
Concurred with in y.e Lower House
                  Test, Jn.o Russell Cle[r]k

Upon the Memoriall of the Inhabitants of the West parish
In the town of New haven showing to this assembly that
they have Settled two Ministers of the gospill In their Said
Society Who both of them one after the other Some time
after their Setling With them So farr desented from the
principles of the Churches In Newengland as to account
their ordination void, and So Resigned their pastoriall
Care of them So that they are now left destitute having no
gospill Minister and being a small Society and being much
Impoverished by the Settling the aforesaid Ministers who
have deserted them they are not able to Settle another of
their own means--and therfore praying this assembly to
Releave them under their poor and low Circumstances--
It is therfore Resolved by this assembly that if the Inhabitants of the Said Society do Call and Settle among them a
authordox--Minister of the gospill (that is to Say) one who
shall be approved of by the elders of the Neighbouring
Churches that then the sum of two hundred pounds shall
be drawn out of the publick Treasury and be Improved
towards the Said Ministers Settlement
    May 1734   Past in the Upper House
                  Test G Wyllys Cler: Concil:
        Concurred with in y.e Lower House
                  Test, Jn.o Russell Clerk

[1734, July 17, London]
                  London July 17.th 1734
To the Venerable & Honourable Society for the propoga-
tion of the Gospell in forreign parts   The petition of
Ebenezer Punderson Clerk Humbly Sheweth

    That he hath been a dissenting Teacher in a Congre-
gation at North Groton in New England for the Space of
4 Years: but by y.e good providence of God after Serious

Examination & Enquiry into the doctrines, Government, & manner of worship of the Church of England was convinc'd that they were most agreable to the will of God; and that it was his duty to Embrace the Establish'd Church, and accordingly did So and declared it unto his Congregation the Sunday Before last Christmas: Since that time he has Continued to read prayers & Sermons in his own house, to Such as were disposed to attend that manner of divine worship: and upon the Labours of y^r Humb^l Petitio^r there was So great a Blessing as that the number of his Congregation has been from 80 to 100 Souls the most of them Serious & Devout persons.

That upon application to the Lord Bishop of London his Lordship was pleased to Conferr holy orders upon him.

That he is very desireous of being employed as a Missionary of the Society, and particularly to the people of North Groton there being great reason to think they will by his Labour & Industry, in Instructing them daily grow into a more favourable opinion of the worship of our excellent Church: their regard for him (tho' unworthy of it) being very great, which has also created in him a reciprocall tenderness for them; and encreases By considering that almost every One of them by Gods blessing upon his Instructions have been reconciled to the Church

It is therefore the Sencere and hearty prayer of Your Humble Petitioner that he may be Sent as a Missionary thither, with Such encouragement as to the wisdom and prudence of this Honourable Society Shall Seem proper:

And that Your Petitioner may be dispatched with as much Expedition as the Nature of the thing will admitt of: The Circumstances of his people and Small family requiring it and also his not having had the Small pox which So often proves fatall to New-England People when they Take it here

Ebenezer Punderson

[1735, May 16, ?London]
Att a General Meeting of the Society for the Propagation of the Gospel in Foreign Parts

16 May 1735

The Society took into Consideration a Letter Signed William Williams Moderator in the Name of the associated Ministers of ye County of Hampshire dated Hatfield September 10th 1734 & another Signed Benjamin Coleman dated Boston New England September 13th 1734 both directed to the Lord Bishop of London; And the Society observed from several Paragraphs in those Letters, that it is represented y^t ye professed End of the Charter granted to the Society & the Design of the Donors is not answered by supporting Missionaries in several Places in New England or if some Sea Port Towns did want assistance there can be no Pretence for it out of the Fund of the Society but ought to be provided for some other Way & not by alienating a confined Charity. In Answer to which the Society remarked, First, That the Fund is not a confined Charity or restrained to any Place otherwise than as specified in the Charter. His Majesties Plantations, Colonies & Factories beyond the Seas belonging to the Kingdom of England. & 2^{ly} that it is the Plain Design of the Charter to impower the Society To support learned & Orthodox Ministers to instruct his Majesties Subjects in the true Religion where there is not a sufficient Provision for Ministers to live

among them. And tho' it may be alledged that the Presbyterians & independents were provided with Ministers according to their own Perswasion yet there were considerable Numbers of People in several Places who could not join with the Dissenters there in their Form of Worship but were desirous of joyning in Communion with the Church of England and were wholly unprovided of Ministers & that in such places only the Society have supported Missionaries upon the earnest Desire of the People & their promising to contribute to the utmost of their Ability towards their Support; & Whereas it is objected that Missionaries are sent where there are dissenting Teachers, The Society remarked further in Answer thereto that it is Notorious that here in Great Britain several dissenting Teachers are sent to many Market Towns & other Places where there is a legal incumbent which Teachers are also partly supported by a Friend [?fund] raised in London.----And whereas it is represented that the Design of the Donors is not answered by supporting Missionaries in several Parts of New England, The Society here remarked that they print yearly an Account of the Places where Missionaries are sent their Reasons for sending them and that such accounts are distributed to all the Benefactors who therefore cannot be unacquainted with this Matter of Fact; & consequently the Society have good Reason to Think that the s^d Donors are so far from disapproving this Method of the Society that they would not contribute did not the Society send Missionaries to such Places.----The Society observed also y^t it is represented in two Paragraphs in the Letter signed William Williams Moderator that the Missionaries that come among them shew a very uncharitable & unchristian Spirit by insinuating y^t their Ministry is no Ministry not having had Episcopal Ordination & by endeavouring to render the Government of their Chhs Insignificant, by receiving into the Communion & Protection of the Chh of England such as lye open to or are under Cesure in them for immoral Behaviour which things tend to breed Disorder in their Churches by cherishing a small Number of disaffected Persons in several Places to the ill example of a Whole Town & further that some Missionaries sett themselves to lay Blocks in the Way of their having Synods convened for the reforming such Evils as have a threatening Aspect upon 'em In Answer to this the Society remarked that they give their Missionaries Directions to meddle as little as possible with any Matters of Controversy, but only to preach the Gospel & administer the Sacraments according to the Doctrine & Discipline of the Chh of England & it hath not yet appeared to the Society that their Missionaries have demeaned themselves contrary to these Directions but when any of the above Mentioned Facts shall be charged & proved upon any particular Person the Society as far as it is in them will be ready to take proper Cognizance of it And the Society['s] no more distinct Answer can be given till they are acquainted, First, with the Names of those Missionaries who insinuate that their Ministry is no Ministry, 2^{ly}, with the Names of those Missionaries who receive into the Communion & Protection of the Chh of England such Persons as lye open to or are under Censure in their Chhs for Immoral Behaviour, 3^{ly}, with the Names of those Persons who have been received into the Chh of England & lay under Censure in their Churches, & 4^{ly}, till it is further explained what is meant by cherishing disaffected Persons

in several Places. And whereas in the same letter it is represented that they have Reason to fear that the Prospect of a better Salary than what their Ministers generally have hath induced some of their young men to goe over & receive Orders:-- In answer to this the Society remarked y^t it is very uncharitably said inasmuch as the Society have received none but such as have come over with ample Recommendation from the best People wher[e] they have lived with great Expence to themselves & Danger of their Health & upon f[ull] Examination have appeared to be duly [qualified] for the Ministry. With Respect to Part of the foregoing Letter signed by Mr Williams wherein it is expressed by him [in the] Name of the associated Ministers (so called) that it hath been often openly declared to the world that their Fathers left their Native Land & at a vast Expence purchased & Subdued a Wilderness that they might in a Place of their own Serve God according to their Consciences in Peace; It appeared to the Society that by the Charter granted by the late King William to the Province of the Massachusets Bay in New England It is established & Ordained that for ever hereafter there shall be a Liberty of Conscience allowed in the Worship of God to all Christians (except Papists) inhabiting or which shall inhabit or be resident within the s^d Province or Territory & therefore the Society concluded y^t ye Members of the Church of England are at least equally intitaled to the Priviledges & Immunities with his Majestys Protestant Subjects of any other Denomination. And upon looking into the Laws of the Massachusets Bay the Society could not but observe that there are many Laws w^h tend to establish a Particular Sect & one at least extending so far as to oblige Persons of every Perswasion even those of the Church of England to pay towards the Maintenance of the Minister of that particular Sect in direct Contradiction to their Charter which expressly restrains them from ye Power of making Laws repugnant or contrary to the Laws of Great Britain.

    A true Copy   David Humphreys Secretary

[Endorsed:] W^m W^{ms} of Hatfield [?Mass.] Moderator

[1735, Aug. 15, Stratford]
              Stratford in N. England Augst 15. 1735
S^r.
    At 10 Days Sight of this my Second Bill of Exchange, my first & third not paid be pleased to pay or cause to be paid to Mr William Beach of Stratford in New England Merch^t, on Order the Sum of Twenty pounds Sterling for value received, & place it to the Account of
           S^r / y^r most humble Servant / Sa. Johnson

To Wm Tryon Esqr Treas^r to the hon^{ll} Society for propagation of the Gospel &c

[1735, Sept. 11, New Haven]
        [To Edmund Gibson, Bishop of London]
May it please Your Lordship,
    Whereas a considerable Number of well disposed people, living remote from any Church in the Towns of New-Haven, Derby, Milford, & Waterbury, whose case we think very pitiable, as destitute of ye Necessary Means of instruction, for their families; have expressed a very earnest desire to be provided for, as well as their circumstances will permit, by having an Episcopal Minister to officiate among them at ye Several Towns where they live, Alternately; and for that purpose have address'd Your Lordship: Particularly requesting that Mr Jonathan Arnold, ye bearer hereof, may be admitted to holy Orders, & receive Your Lordships Licence that he may become ye regular Pastor of their Souls: And Whereas ye Said Mr Arnold has made known to us ye Subscribers his pious resolution to undertake a Voyage to London in order to receive Your Lordships Benediction, & holy Orders that he may be qualified to serve ye interest of ye Church & comply with ye earnest desires of those people whose humble address he is ye bearer of to Your Lordship, Altho' he has no manner of incouragement to hope for any Other Subsistance than the Small contributions of those people We think it our duty to Accompany his pious & Charitable undertaking with our hearty prayers & good Wishes, & to let your Lordship know we have been many years intimately acquainted with Mr Arnold, who was very well esteemed & respected in ye Country here, while he was a dissenting Teacher at New-Haven: And we cannot surmise Any Motive, but conviction of Conscience, could be ye foundation of his Conformity to ye Church of England, the communion of which he imbraced About Eighteen Months Ago & has ever since shewed himself forward to Serve ye interest of ye Church according to his Ability in A Lay-Capacity. We know him to be a person of an unblamable Life & conversation; Well Attached to his Majestys Person & Government according to ye present establishment & well qualified as to his Learning, Age, & Abilities to be admitted to holy Orders, and to serve ye great interests of Religion & our holy Church in these parts. He has a Wife & three Children, and we think it a great argument of his disinterested Zeal & Piety that he is Willing to spend his own fortune & at his own expence, serve ye Church of God & do good to ye Souls of Men: Which disposition we highly applaud in him, and beg leave Most affectionately to recommend him to your Lordship's favour. And tho' we can't presume to address ye Honb^l Society to erect A new Mission after having been informed of their not being in a condition to make New Missions, Yet, as it will be very hard for him to spend his Estate, as well as his strength, in ye Service of ye Church, & as we Judge him highly deserving of ye Society's kind Notice, We humbly beg Your Lordships Interest with that venerable Body that they will take those places on ye Mission as soon as they Shall be in a condition for it: & as he goes over at his own Charge, we should be very thankfull, in his behalf, if ye Honb^{le} Society will grant him some Gratuity for defraying a part of his expences in his present Laudable & most disinterested undertaking. All we think needfull to add further, is, that his circumstances are such that we hope he will be able in the mean time to support himself tolerably by his own Means With ye small assistance those people will afford him. And, tho' this be an unusual Method of addressing Your Lordship, Yet we humbly hope, that considering ye necessity of ye Case, Your Lordship will Judge that small subscription, with their address, to be a sufficient title.
    We Are, May it Please Your / Lordship, Your Lordships Most Obed^t / Sons, & very humb^l / Serv^{ts}
    New-Haven Septr 11. 1735

Samuel Johnson   John Beach
J. Wetmore Jr   John Pierson
Henry Caner   Isaac Browne.
Samuel Seabury

[1735, Sept. 25, New Haven]
[To Edmund Gibson, Bishop of London]
New Haven in New-England Sept.r 25 1735
May it please your Lordship

We the Subscribers, Members & Professors of the
Church of England, & Inhabitants of the Towns of New-
Haven, West-Haven, Milford, Darby, & Waterbury, humbly beg leave to represent to your Lordship our most venerable Diocesan the Condition & Situation we are in as to
our Religious Concerns & to implore your Lordships Favour & Assistance.

We are above fifty Families scattered about on a considerable Tract of Ground, some ten, some fifteen, some
twenty or thirty Miles from the Church of England in Stratford; and tho' the Rev.d M.r Johnson hath been so kind as to
minis[ter] to us as often as the necessary care of his parish would permit; (for which we are very thankful,) and
tho' we as to our own persons, can sometimes, & do as
often as we can, attend on the public Worship at Stratford;
yet, as this is attended with considerable Difficulty to us,
partly on account of a very troublesome Ferry, & partly
on account of the great Distance; so it is scarcely at all
practicable to our Families, who must therefore be obliged
either to attend on the meetings of Some Sectaries or other,
or else be destitute of public Worship.

To prevent which Difficulties, we presume to become
humble petitioners to your Lordship, that you would be
pleased of your paternal Goodness to compassionate our
Case, & to send us a minister who may alternately officiate at the several places above mentioned, & take the pastoral Charge of our Souls & our Children.

And for as much as the Bearer hereof M.r Jonathan Arnold is a Gentleman whose excellent Character & Abilities,
we have long had the Knowledge, & most of us the Experience of, & in whose ministrations we should take unspeakable Satisfaction, & is willing to take the pastoral Charge
of us, being so situated as that he can, with tolerable Conveniency, take the Charge of us all, we most humbly beg
of your Lordship that he may be admitted to holy Orders
& sent over to take care of us.

Our poverty indeed is such, (being generally but
Tradesmen or new planters in an uncultivated Country,)
that we shall be but very indifferently able to provide for
M.r Arnold's Support, especially if it be with all considered
that we shall be obliged to build at least two, if not three
Churches: For which reason we should have humbly presumed to address the Honourable Society for propagation
of the Gospel, for an Interest in their noble Charity, had
we not been informed by the Reverend M.r Johnson, that
they are not at present in a Condition to provide for a new
Mission.

However, as we cannot content our Selves any longer
without the steddy Administrations of the Church of England, & since M.r Arnold is so very condescending & self-
denying as to be freely willing to accept of the best we can
do for him, & to spend & be spent in the service of our
Souls, we shall be glad to lay out our Selves to the utmost

of our power in providing for him, & do hereby promise
to your Lordship, for our Selves & Heirs, to pay him
yearly the several Sums affixed to our names, amounting to £60 per annum of our Currency, which yet as the
Exchange now is, is not more than £12 Sterling.

After all, therefore, as our Necessity will be very
great, & it being a great pity that so worthy a Gentleman
as M.r Arnold is should not be better provided for than
our Ability will admit of; and as we humbly hope & pray
that it may, in due time please God to enlarge the Ability
of the Honourable Society that they may be in a Condition
to add something towards his Support; so we humbly beg
leave to hope for an Interest in their Charity when, & so
soon as they shall be in a Condition for it, & beseech your
Lordship's Interest with that venerable Body for that purpose.

We earnestly beg of God to prolong your Lordship's
most valluable Life & Health, & intreat an Interest in
your Fatherly Blessing & prayers for us & our Children,
& remain,

May it please your Lordship, / your Lordship's /
most obedient & dutiful Sons / & humble Servants

For Darby & Waterbury living within about 15 or
18 miles, & from 10 to 25 miles from New Haven

Samuel Hall	£ 3: 0:0
Abel Gunne	3: 0:0
Jonathan Miles	1:10:0
Samuel Plumb	1: 0:0
John Harger	1: 0:0
Jonah Smith	1:10:0
James Browne	1: 0:0
James Browne jun.r	0:10:0
Nathanael Gunne	1:10:0
Job Pearson	0:10:0
Richard Welton	0:15:0
Samuel Humphries	0:15:0
Anthony Wiersbury	0:15:0
James Blakley	1: 5:0
Jonathan Williams	1: 0:0
Benjamin Warner	1:10:0
Enos Smith	1: 0:0
Benjamin Warner jun.r	0:10:0
James Williams	0:15:0
Andrew Smith	2:10:0
Samuel Tolles	1:10:0
Eliphalet Stephens	0:10:0
Daniel Bristoll	1: 5:0
Thomas Stevens jun.r	1:10:0
Richard Burton	0:15:0
	£30: 5:0

For New-Haven[,] West haven & Milford living
within about 10 or 12 miles

Thomas Stevens	£ 3:10:0
William Leece	0:15:0
Thomas Clinton	2: 0:0
John Smith	2:10:0
Shuball Clinton	1:10:0
Joseph Collins	0:10:0
Daniel Thomas	1:15:0

Daniel Thomas jun.r ------------------ 0:10:0
Stephen Thomas --------------------- 0:10:0
Daniel Hodge ----------------------- 1: 5:0
Henry Tolles ----------------------- 1: 0:0
Ebenezer Thompson------------------ 1:10:0
Timothy Bontecou ------------------- 2: 0:0
Nathanael Browne ------------------- 2: 0:0
James Vandermark ------------------ 1: 0:0
Aaron Tuttle ----------------------- 0:10:0
Ebenezer Blakesley ----------------- 0:10:0
Nicholes Manvil -------------------- 1: 0:0
Allen Nisbett ---------------------- 1:10:0
Laurence Clinton ------------------- 1: 0:0
William Walter --------------------- 0:15:0
Thomas Walter --------------------- 0:10:0
John Humphreville ------------------ 1:10:0
John Thomas ----------------------- 0:10:0
Abraham Blakesley ----------------- 0:10:0
                                   £30: 0:0

My Lord,

The above Address is a true Copy of the Original which M.r Arnold has with him, and I can certifie to your Lordship that besides these there are five more who will be M.r Arnold's Hearers, heads of Families, that had not opportunity to subscribe

I am, My Lord, / y.r Lordships most dutiful Son / & humble Servant

Sa. Johnson

[Addressed:] The Right Reverend Father / in God / Edmund Lord Bishop / of / London

[1735, Oct. 9, New Haven]
To the Hon.rble General Assembley of the Coloncy of Connecticutt Holden at Newhaven on the second thursday of October A:D: 1735

The memoral of Sam.ll Smith of Newhaven West parish Agent of said parish In behaf of said parish Humbley sheweth yt ther Late minister viz: mr Arnold sum time since declared for the Church of England, and hath Left the pastoral Care of said parish which was at is founding very small, not butt about two mills square, and sundery of the Inhabitance: have with said minister declared for the Church and are gone from us with our said minister, by which means we are Lefft very Low and not able to support the preaching of the Gospell with us with out Gratte Difficulty, and we by reason of those Difficultys ware Just ready to give out any Endeavers of doing it by our selves untill yowr Honners did Inceriage us by your Late help for which we are thankfull, yet that not withstanding it is very hard for us to Keep united under so Gratte a burden, and the moreso for that our Late minister holds on preaching to those yt went off with him, and we by yowr Honners Act of may Last dericting yt the Lands in any parish the owners wherof Lived in any other parish, Should be payed for in yt parish wher the owner Lived, are futher burdened, for yt by said Act a Grate part of the Lands yt are ratteable pay to the first society in Newhaven, and so as by yt Act, and the Lads yt do belonge to those yt are gone from us as afforesaid do take off full one half of the Lands in our small parish, which fact Indeed is difficult to shew to your Honners butt by view of a Commity which we pray may by

yowr Honners be appoynted for yt End, and upon it so appearing we pray yt yowr Honners would order and In Act yt the Lands In our parish yt belong to persons Liveing in any other parish, be rated in our said parish for the support of the gospell ther, and futher we pray yt (considering our difficultys above named, viz: yt of our smallness &c, & yt we might not sink under our burden &c) yowr Honners would be pleased to Grant unto us on Good seeurity for the princable, the sum of one thousand pounds more or less for the Term of ten years, and yt Intrest free, yt we may Let the same on Intrest and therby Get a sum of money to Let out the Intrest of which may help us support the charge of maintaning the gospell amoungst us (which we desier only on our saveing the countery saffe from all charges and harm by Leting us have the money &c or releive us in any other way & Manner y.r Hon.rs in y.r Wisdom shall think fit) and we as In duty bound shall Ever pray &c--

Dated In Newhaven   Sam.ll Smith ⎰ Agent for said
October : 1735   ⎱ west parish

In y.e Lower House, on this memorial Edmond Lewiss, Esq.r Cap.t. Jn.o Riggs, Cap.t. Nathan Baldwin are appointed a Com.ttc to view, y.e Circumstances of y.e Society, and make report to y.e assembly in may Next,

past, Test, Jn.o Russell Clerk
and y.t a bill be Drawn in form
Concured with in the Upper House
Test George Wyllys Secret.ry

Upon the memoriall of Cap.t Samuell Smith of Newhaven west parish as agent for sd parish shewing to this assembly the broken surcumstances of sd parish by Reson of there ministers one after another declaring them selves to be of the Church of England principles & Carying from them Considerable Estate & inhabitanc whereby thay are uncapable to maintain the gospell among them & praying to this assembly for sum Relefe
Upon Consideration whereof this assembly do appoint Edmond Lewis Esq.r Cap.t john Riggs & Cap.t Nathan Baldwin a Committee & att the Request of of the sd Smith or others of sd parish to Repair to the sd parish to vew, here observe & Consider the whole surcumstances of them & to make Report to this assembly in may next what is nasessary to be done for there Releafe

past in y.e Lower House
(Oct 1735)   Test, Jn.o Russell Cl[e]rk

[1736, May 10 and Sept. 1, Stratford]
[To Edmund Gibson, Bishop of London]
Stratford in New England May. 10.th 1736
May it please your Lordship

The Rev.d D.r Cutler, who is a Friend that I have a very great Vallue for, & who hath been many years a very faithful & useful Servant of the Honourable Society, having at length bred up a Son who, I presume, may be not undeserving of your Lordship's Notice; I beg leave to joyn with others of my Brethren in recommending him to your Lordship's Favour & patronage.

M.r John Cutler, the Bearer hereof, was bred up at Harvard College in Cambridge, & has been admitted to the Degrees both of Bachelour & Master of Arts, & has

ever had the Character of a virtuous & religious youth with
all that knew him: He has been very inquisitive & laborious in his Studies, & has attained to as much Learning as
can be expected in one of his years, under such Advantages
as this Country affords: He has particularly taken much
pains, by reading a variety of the best Authors, to furnish
himself thoroughly for the Defence of Christianity against
Infidels, & of the Orthodox Doctrines of the Church against
the several Heresies that oppose them: And as He understands the Church of England very well; so he is prepared,
I doubt not, with an Heart truly serious & zealous, to devote his Life to be spent in her Service, & is sincerely
well-affected to the present Government.

I speak knowingly, My Lord, what I say concerning
Him; for I have been well acquainted with him from his
youth up, & have conversed with him frequently, not only
at Boston, but also in these parts, where he passed some
part of the time between his Degrees, a portion of which he
spent with me at my own house.--He is indeed, at present
of age only for Deacon's Orders, but is desirous for his
further Improvement, to spend a year in England, till he
is of Age for the Order of priesthood.

In the mean time, since the D.r having a large Family
to provide for, is not so well able as I wish he was, to support him in England, without some Business which might,
at least in a good part, afford him a Subsistence; I humbly
beg of your Lordship, if it be practicable, that you would
provide some small Curacy for him, for a few Months, till
he shall be of age for priest's Orders; & moreover that
your Lordship will be pleased to use your Interest with the
Society, that as soon as he is in priest's Orders he may
have the first Vacancy or Mission that shall offer it Self
in this Country, to which he may be sent when he returns
to us again.

I am, may it please y.r Lordship, / your Lordship's
most obedient / & most dutiful Son / & humble Servant
                                        Sa. Johnson
To My Lord of London

                              Sept.r the 1.st 1736.

P.S. My Lord. M.r Cutler, not going as I expected in
the Spring, & being now about to embark in a short time,
I beg leave, to what I wrote then, to add my most humble
Thanks for your Lordship's Favour to M.r Arnold, & Interest in his Behalf with the honourable Society, who have
done for him beyond what we could have expected. I am
glad to be informed by him that he obtained hopes of the
Rev.d M.r Dean Conybear of Oxford, that it might be in his
power to provide for M.r Cutler.

[1737, Nov. 4, North Groton]
        [To Edmund Gibson, Bishop of London]
                    N Groton Nov.br 4. 1737
My good Lord
        next To Almighty God, I cant but esteem myself prin-
cipaly oblidgd To your Lordship, for your kind assistance,
and great goodness To me in London: but especialy y.t you
thought me worthy, and was pleasd To put me in y.s Sacred
Station, in which I trust y.t I am instrumental of promoting
knowledge, and virtue, among men; and the interest of our
most excellent Church. and as Tis my particular business
so I hope it will be always my delight: of w.c I shall trouble

your Lordship with a few Lines.

It is now exactly 3 years since I enter'd upon my
pastoral charge; & altho we have here the feircest opposition made against the Chh of Eng.d, yet by the blessing
of God upon my unwearied Labours (I have preachd almost
every Sunday & every other wednesday) in this and the
adjacent places, we have now fourty Seven in our comunion: but 2 of w.h ever receid y.e Sacram.t in the Chh of England before, and such as are of a Sober conversation. I
have Baptizd 86. 15 Adults. and we have in North Groton
erected the frame of a good timber Chh and provided materials To cover it, to the building of which I have contributed 25£ our curency,

I have been 3 times at a Town calld Brimfeild about
54 miles from my house, and To very good excepta[n]ce,
and success; a more particular account of w.c I have sent
the Hon.l Society in my Letter of July last. I have since
upon the repeated desires of a number of Conformits in
Hebron, attended divine service there, & altho they had
but a small space of time To give notice of my being there;
yet upwards of 80 attended and behav'd very devoutly, and
seriously: I am perswaded were that place added To the
Rev.d M.r Seaburys Mission it might be of excelent service
untill by the blessing of God y.e Hon.l Society &c, Should
be in circumstances of providing better for them.

My Lord I shall at present trespas no farther upon
your better imployd time but conclude with my earnest
prayers To Almighty God, that he would long continue
your Lordship in the Station you now are, or a more exalted one to serve and Adorn his Chh.

I am my Lord your Lordships most Obedient / Son &
Serv.t

                              Eben.r Punderson

[1738, April-May]
        To The Honourable, The Governour Council & Repre-
sentatives of His Majesties English Colony of Connecticutt
in General Court to be assembled at Hartford in the s.d
Colony, on the second Thursday of May, next, being in the
year of our Lord 1738- The Humble Address of the Members & Professors of that part of Christ's Church called
The Church of England, living in & under the Government
of the s.d Colony.

May it please your Honour & this Honourable General
Court,

We the Subscribers, Members & Professors of the
Church of England, living in this His Majesties Colony of
Connecticutt, being His Majesties most dutiful & loyal
Subjects, & sincerely well attached to the Constitution of
this Government, do humbly beg leave to lay an Address
before your Honour & this Assembly, relating to An Affair, which, as we apprehend, does very nearly concern
us.

And that this our Address may meet with the more
favourable Reception, we would in the Enterance thereof,
assure your Honour & & this Assembly, That, (however
we may be misrepresented,) we are in no wise disaffected
to this Corporation as it is incorporated by Royal Charter,
but do bear an hearty Affection to it's Constitution & the
priviliges thereof; & do therefore beg that nothing we have
to offer may be interpreted as savouring of any Disaffec-

tion, or any Aim at undermining it, or interrupting the peace of it, in the peace whereof we seek our peace.

In this good Opinion & Cordial Affection to the Constitution & Government of this Corporation, we have been much confirmed, from the Consideration of that impartial Justice observable from time to time in the Members of this Assembly, constituting the Legislative power of this Colony: A particular Instance whereof, we have experienced in that generous & just Act of Assembly, passed in May, in the year 1727.--whereby the Professors of the Church of England are exempted from contributing to the Support of the Ministers of the Congregational or Presbyterian Persuasion, which are those that are peculiarly countenanced by the Laws of this Government, & from paying towards Building Meeting Houses, where such Proffessors of the Church of England have the Advantage of Attending Divine Service according to the Rules & Methods of public worship established in England: And the same Act provides for the support of their own Ministers & their own Method of worshipping God.

From whence we conclude, that it is the Opinion of the Legislature of this Government, That it is, not only, not Right to compel people to the Support of that worship & Ministry which they soberly differ from; But also, that it is Just & Right for every one to have the Benefit of his own Way of Worship, & of his own Labour & Estate to support that way of Worship which he sincerely beleives to be right: And therefore we persuade our Selves, that it is inconsistent with the received & allowed principles of this Legislature to oblige us, by any ways or means to contribute to the Support of the Churches or Ministry peculiarly countenanced by the Laws of this Government.

That therefore which gives Occasion to this Address, is, That we have been informed, that an Act was passed in the Last Assembly held at New-Haven, respecting the Seven Townships laid out in the Western Lands belonging to this Corporation of which we are Members, whereby the Monies to be raised from the Sale of those Lands, were appropriated either to the Use of the Schools, or to the Support of the Ministers of the Presbyterian or Congregational Persuasion, (being those that are peculiarly countenanced by the Laws of this Government,) to be divided to the several Parishes in proportion to their several Lists; & this, in such a Manner, that we of the Church of England, cannot lay claim to any Share of them for the Support of our Ministers or Schools: And that there was a Bill prepared & passed in the Lower House, which, we are told, may probably pass through the whole Legislature at this Assembly, whereby the Public Monies arising from the Loan of the Last Emission, were also to be appropriated to the Support of the Ministers afores^{d}, peculiarly countenanced by the Laws of this Government, in a Manner that would exclude us from having any Share in the Same for the Support of the Ministers of the Church of England.

Now these proceedings of the last General Assembly, are what we humbly beg leave, with all due Defference to your Honour & this Assembly to object to.--Not that we are in the least invidious towards our Brethren of the Congregational Persuasion, or would aim at Hindering the Passing of the Bill last mentioned into an Act: So far from this, that we do heartily applaud so good & generous a Disposition in that Assembly, in being concerned to provide a certain & Sufficient Support for the Ministers of Religion in this Colony: But because it appears to us that it would be a manifest Injustice for us to be denied our Share in those Public Monies for the Support of our Ministers; And that therefore, according to the known & received principles of this Legislature, (as appears by the Act abovementioned,) the s^{d} Act & Bill ought to have been formed in such a manner as to secure to us our proportion in the s^{d} Public Monies, as well as to our Brethren of any other Denomination.--And that for these Reasons:

1. Because the Doctrines & Principles of the Church of England do professedly & most certainly tend, (at least equally with those of any other Persuasion,) not only to fit & prepare men for Eternal Happiness in the Life to come, but also to promote the Public Good of Society in this World, by teaching them to be Sober, Virtuous & Industrious in their Callings, Serious & Devout towards God, & Just & Charitable towards Men, & in every respect to be good Christians, kind Neighbours, Upright Magistrates, Dutiful Subjects, & faithful & Conscientious in every Relation & Condition of Life: And consequently Her Professors ought to have the like equitable & favourable Treatment with those of any other Denomination of Christians.

2. Because the Church of England is that Profession & Persuasion which is established at home in our Mother Country, & which His most Sacred Majesty professes, & hath bound Himself by Oath to maintain, from whom we received, & under whom we hold our Charter Priviliges, & who therefore, with those in the Government & Administration under Him, will be apt to resent any Unequal Treatment which the Members of that Church may receive from the Provinces abroad under His Majesties Government & Protection: And we should be very Sorry to have any thing done among us that may tend to bring his Majesties Displeasure upon this Corporation.

3. Because the Welfare & Happiness of this, as well as all other Governments, depends upon the Union & joynt Endeavours of all the Members of it, in promoting One & the Same Common God & General Interest; whereas an unequal Treatment of different Denominations of Christians, is apt to breed Envies, Animosities & Contentions, which necessarily tend to weaken the Hands of Government, destroy the public Tranquility, & procure a great many Disadvantages to the General Weal & Prosperity of the Government.

4. Because it has been once & again delivered as the Judgment of the Attorney & Solicitor General at Home, & by the Lords Justices, (during the Kings Absence in the year 1725) in their Letter to the Leiutenant Governour of Boston, (all which we are ready to produce,) that there is not & cannot be any such thing as a regular Establishment of any one Denomination of Christians to the Exclusion of the Rest, without an explicit Consent of his Most sacred Majesty: (the same also appears from the late Letters of the Bishop of London & Society to the Ministers of Hampshire:) And consequently, We, standing at least upon an equal Foot with our Brethren of any other Denomination, have an equal Right with them in any Common Interest, & particularly to have our Proportional Share in any Public Monies that have, or may be granted for the Support of the Ministry or Schools.

5. Because, (as we humbly presume,) we have equally a Right in Equity, to our Proportion in those unoccupied Lands with our Brethren of any other Denomination. For-

asmuch as all the Lands within the Bounds of this Government, being purchased or conquered by our common Progenitors or Ancestors, were by the Royal Charter, alike granted & confirmed, according to their several Proportions of Right, to the whole Corporation, consisting of the Body of the People; that is to all that are free of this Government with their Successors & Assigns, to be held for their common use & Benefit: & this, without limiting them to those of any particular Sentiments in matters of Religion; & consequently those unoccupied Lands are their common Estate & Interest: So that none of their Descendants or Assigns can be equitably excluded from the Benefit of any Sale or Disposition to be made of them, whatever Denomination they are of in matters of Religion.

6. Because We bear an equal Proportion of the Public Taxes for Supporting the Government & for paying the Members of the Assembly which are our Common Representatives, & that, while they are consulting & passing Acts for the public Weal; Yea, even while they are consulting Measures for the Disposing of this very Money, as also for defraying of the Cost of any Emissions of the public Bills of Credit, & for supporting of the Credit of them: (which Taxes we have always been chearfully willing to pay;) and consequently, the Loan of any Emission of them, being a Common Interest; we presume we have a Right to an equally proportionable Share in the Benefit accruing therefrom, with those of any other Denomination, according to that just Maxim in the Law, Qui sentit Onus, sentire debet & Commodum, i.e. He that feels a Share in the Burthen, ought also to enjoy his Share in the Advantage. --And

7thly And lastly. That which gives us the greater Reason to insist upon this, is, That the sd Act & Bill appear to us to have a Manifest Inconsistency with the Intent of the Act first above mentioned, passed in the last year of his late Majesties Reign, whereby the Members of the Church of England, were exempted from paying to the Support of the Ministers of the Congregational Persuasion, & provision was made that their Proportion of the Ministers Rate should go to the Support of their own Ministers: Whereas, according to the Tenor of the Act & Bill above mentioned, we should be obliged to contribute our Proportion towards the Support of the Congregational Ministers, from which, by this Act we had been exempted. --And by the way, we would take this Occasion to observe, that the like Inconsistency we humbly apprehend there is between the Intent of the sd Act & the Grants that have been made by some late Acts of Assembly of certain Sums of Money out of the Treasury of this Colony to the Parishes of West-Haven & North-Groton, of which we are laid under a Necessity of paying our proportion by paying our Country Rates. --Not to mention the Contrivance that has been made use of in some places to elude the Intent of this Act by comprehending the Minister's Support in the Towne Rate; & thereby obliging us to contribute to the Support of the Congregational Minister by paying our Towne Rates.

Upon the whole, therefore, what we humbly intreat, & for these Reasons beg leave to expect from your Honour & this General Assembly, is, That some Alteration may be made in our Favour of the Act above mentioned, & that some Amendment may be made of the Bill proposed by the late House of Representatives, if it should again come under Consideration; So that we may be secured of our proportion of those public Monies towards the Support of

our Ministers, & that our Schools also, where we have any peculiar to our Selves, may have their Proportional Benefit of the sd Act, as also of the 40 shillings on the £1000, which has hithertoo been denied to the School of the Church of England at Stratford.

And, to conclude, As we should be very sorry to be laid under any Temptation to complain of any unequal Treatment from the Government under whose protection we live, so we do most humbly intreat that not only on this, but all other occasions that may at any time occur, your Honours would be pleased to consider us as a part of your Selves, & that we may have equal Justice done us, & the like Favours shewed us, with the Rest of our Brethren with whom we desire to live in Peace & Charity & to joyn heart & hand in promoting the public Weal of this Government (on which that of our Selves & posterity does also depend,) as being Fellow members of this Corporation, & Fellow-Subjects of His Majesty, under the Jurisdiction of this Colony. -- In hopes of which, (as in Duty bound,) we shall ever pray for the Health & Happiness of your Honour & all the Members of this Assembly & for the Peace & Prosperity of this Colony.

The Names being Subscribed in the Lists hereunto annexed as follows to the Number of about. 636.

May 1738 In the Upper House The Consideration of this Memorial is Referred to the General Assembly to be holden att New-Haven in Octr next
    In the Lower House Test George Wyllys Secretry
        Concurred wth Test Jonathan Trumble Clerk.

Under the care of ye Rd Mr Wetmore

The subscribers belonging to Greenwich & Stanford, to be annexed to the General Address of the Members & Professors of the Church of England in the Colony of Connecticut. To the Honbl Genll Court in May. 1738. Which address having been communicated to us the subscribers we hereunto sign our names. --in no 50

Gershom Lockwood	Jno Burley
Saml Mills	Nathel Hubbard
Caleb Knap	Peter Demill
Abm Nicholds	John Finch
Theo Jno Lockwood	Benjamin Day
William King	John Hicks
Henry James	Miles Riggs
Ben Knap	Isreal Knapp
James Knap	Charles Southerland
Jos. Knap	Richd Chalton
Jeremy Peck	Saml Morine
Hezekiah Lockwood	Isac Quintard
Jonathan Lockwood	Joseph Barton
Jonathan Austen	John Kirkam
Thos Johnson	Thos Roberts
Thos Bullis	Abm Rundal Junr
David Reynolds	Nathl Lockwood
John Avery	Nathl Worden
John Johnson	James Anderson
John Hall Jr.	Jeremiah Anderson
Samuel Willson	John Slaughter
Benj: Young	Joseph Galpin
Robt Arnold	William Anderson

Joseph Anderson   Thomas Youngs

John Lloyd   Abraham Everet

Under the care of yᵉ Revᵈ Mʳ Ebenʳ Punderson Minsᵗʳ in Groton to the number. 104.

Ephraim Minor	Ezra Hide
Thomas Rose	Benjamin Lee
Thomas Minor	Benjᵐ Hide
William Hide	Peter Waterman
William Fountain	Alexander Doyle
William Williams juʳ	John Basset
John Waterman	Robert Rose
Thomas Grist	Wilb. Rouse --20
Robert Geer	Alpheus Dickwine
Robert Geer junʳ	Joseph Willoughby
Ebenʳ Geer	Bliss Willoughby
Henry Pelton	Adam Cranmer
Christopʳ Thiton	Thomas Pelton
James Forsee	Christopʳ Houghton
James Forsee juʳ	Joseph Malason juʳ
Philip Turner	Moses Stodard
Will— Spicer	Zachariah Rude
Ignatius Barker	Barzillai Dean
Samˡˡ Dickinson	Samˡˡ Hutchison
Samˡˡ Minor --20	Jeremiah Spicer
Samˡˡ Ranger	Willᵐ Spicer juʳ
Edward Hancock	Walter Capron
John Larkin	John Ames
Robert Williams	Mathias Button
Joseph Bondish	John Killam
Samˡˡ Capron	Joseph Rude
John Davis	Willᵐ Meach
Thomas Starkweather	Jacob Park --20
Benajak Starkweather	Joseph Rose
John Ames juʳ	Adam Park
Daniel Ames	Phineas Killam
Daniel Starkweather	Oliver Rude
Calvin Barnard	John Wilkinson
Edmund Fanning	John Wilkinson juʳ
Christopʳ Crouch	Jedidiah Frink
Thomas Leeds	Jonathan Raynalds
Richard Crouch	Josiah Park
Robert Stodard	John Ashcraft
Gershom Holdridge	Jacob Rude
Benjamin Holley --20	Stephen Rude
Jonathan Williams	Jonathan Downing
Jonathan Williams juʳ	Edward Clevland
John Williams	Danˡˡ Mᶜclaughton
John Samson	Joseph Parish
Ebenʳ Norton	John Wood Juʳ
Robert Lancaster	Philip Gray
Joshua Weeks	Ebenʳ Norton
John Allyn	Paul Pelton --20
Jonathan Randal	Ebenʳ Waterman
Willᵐ Turner	Robert Stodard juʳ
Ebenʳ Welsh	Samˡˡ Totley
Joseph Lee	Danˡ Bennet

The Original of this Subscription is in the hands of Capᵗ Avery

Under the pastorall Care of the Rever'd Mʳ Samˡ Seabury of New London--to the Number 85

Peter Tanor	James Parker
Thos Mumford	Joseph Latham
Chs: Stewart	Philip Bill
Samˡˡ Edgunnbe	Benjamin Bill
Jnᵒ Thackmaple	James Parker Juner [Jr.]
John Braddick	John Parker Juʳ
Isaac Ledyard	John Roberttes
Richard Wells	Jonathan Turner
Giles Goddard	Pain Turner
Guy Palmes	Israel Fulsom
Merrett Smith	Samˡˡ Boroughs
John Seabury Junʳ	George Jeffires
Nathaniel Seabury	John Hobart
Wetherell Denison	Daniel Tutel
John Mumford	Joˢ Tallman
John Jeffrey	James Smith
Joseph Purvess	Samˡˡ Powers
Ichabod Powers	Thos Manwaring
John Haley	Elisha Wright
John Haley Juʳ	John Dixson
Joshua Haley	John Wiat
Thomas Eldredg	

There were 10 more rhat had not Opportunity to subscribe

Inhabitants of Hebron and places adjacent Under the pastoral Care of the Reverend Mʳ Samˡˡ Seabury of New-London

John Bliss	John Knox
Samuel Curtice	Johanis Dale
John Taylor	L. Wortly Water
Abraham Clancher	Laurance powers
Richard Curtice	John Chamberlin
Richard Curtice Juneʳ	Samuell Ingham
Thomas Brown	Nathan Rowle
William Slade	Seth Sutton
Ebenezer Haughton	Jonathan Brown
Samuell Water	Robert Cocks
Joshua Tillotson	Moses huchisson
Daniel Jones	Benjamine Neeland
John Chamberlin Jr	Hazakiah hutc[h]isson
Jonathan Wood	Edmund Wells
Thomas Wells	J. Adam Water j[r.]
Samuell Penick	John Bliss juner

Under the Revᵈ Mʳ Arnold Nᵒ 73

Samˡ Clark Junʳ	Ephraim Warner
Edward Allen	James Humphris
John Smith	Samuel Humphrys
Thomas Stevens	Nathanson Woorster
Shubal Clinton	John Hargen
Ebenezer Thompson	Jonathan Mills
Thomas Clinton	Jonah Smith
Henry Tolles	Abel Gunn
Daniel Thomas	John Holbrook
Thomas Stevens Junr	John Whelan
Eliphelet Stevens	Antony Wisbery
Joh[n] Thomus	Benjamin Fairchild
Daniel Hodg	Joseph Smith
Ephraim Gillit	Thomas Barns
Mordecai Marks	Samˡˡ Brown
Samuel Hull	ephraim Isreel
Samˡˡ Blum	Robᵗ Johnson
Ebenezer Chatfield	James Browne

James Browne Jur
Joseph Browne
James Blakeslee
Abraham Warner
William Leece
John Gund
Peter Pond
Nath. Johnson
Daniel Thomas
John Humphrevile
Samuel Toals
Daniel Bristol
Timothy Bonteron
Nathaniel Browne
James Vandermarke
Ebenezer Blakeslee
Abraham Blakslee
Nicholas Manvel
Aaron Tuttle

William Walter
Thomas Walter
Enos Smith
Thomas Ives
John Mackey
Daniel Porter
Moses Brownson
Samuel Lewes
Caleb Thompson
Richard Welton
Jonathan Scott
Ephraim Warner
Beniamin Warner
Thomas Walstone
David Naughty
James Williams
Nathaniel Merit
North Ingham

Under the pastoral care of ye Rev.d M.r Beach to the number 92

Daniel Sherman
Stephen Burwell
James Hordice
Thomas Pears
Benoni Sherman
John Hoatt
James Heard
Lemuel Camp
Benjamin Curtiss
Benj.in Glover
Ebenezer Sanford
Thomas Northrup
John Sanford
John Beers
Henry Glover
Nehemiah Seely
John Glover
Job Sanford
Robert Seely
Robert Seley iun.er
Dan.ll Glover
Daniel Jackson
Abner Hard
John Hard
Sam.ll Brown
Samuel Brown jr
James Hard j.r
Joseph Hard
John Brown
Samuel Sherman
John Foot j.r
Nathan Foot
William Lyon
Moses Lyon
Benjamin Burt
Joshua Lobdell
Richard osburn
James Wallis
Daniel Sherwood
alexand.r Resseguie
peter Resseguie

abraham Resseguie
Samuel Lobdell
Jabez Northrup
Joshua Lobdell jun.r
John Lobdell
David Osburn
Seaborn burt
Benjamin burt j.r
Caleb Lobdell
Ebenezar Lobdell
Gabriel Morehouse
Lemuel Morehouse
John Rikit
Alexand.r Resseguie J.r
Moses Knap
David Knap
Jonathan Knap
fransis kanatide
Daniel Lyon j.r
Jonathan Squier
Zacariah Squier
Ruben Squier
Thomas Taylor
Asa hall
Samuell Henryx
Icabod Squier
Jonathan Lyon
Jonathan Squie[r] iuner
Benony Henryx
David Henryx
Adam Clarke
[Na]than Lyon
Daniel Crofeet
Stephan Morehouse
Nathaniel Henerix
Josh: Hall
Israel Rowland
Tho. Rowland
W.m Stephens
W.m Hill
Dan: Adams j.r

Ben: Slurge
Hen: Vaughan
Jeremy Turner
John Herris

Henry Garlick
John Seely
Ben. Vaughan
Peter Easeman

Under the pastoral Care of the Rev.d M.r Johnson of Stratford, to the number of 102

Church Wardens
Samuel Fairchild   James Laborie   Charles Lane

Vestry

William Beach
Gershom Edwards
Miller Frost
Thomas Latte
John Benjamins
Abraham Beardsley
John Kees
Samuel Blagge

Samuel French
Will. Wilcockson
Joseph Browne
William Smith
Eliphalet Curtiss
Francis Barlow
Zechariah Clarke

The other people

James Wakeley
John Wilcockson
David Wakeley
Ebenezer Wakeley
Israel Bardsley
Edmund Booth
James Fairchild
Samuel Fairchild Jun
Ephraim Fairchild
George Tyley
Paul Maverie
Samuel Hawley
Edward Hinman
John Mitchell
Richard Burton
Zechariah Baldw[in]
Andrew Beardsley
John Lane
Jacob Lane
Timothy Tittarton
Timothy Tittarton Jun.r
Jehiel Beardsley
Joseph Wilcockson
Charles Curtis
Benjamin Blackman
Timothy Blackman
John Hawley
Thomas Stratton
En Tree
D. Loring
Beniamin Pearce
Thomas Silby
Francis Barlow
William Smith
William Smith jun.r
William Beardsley
William Beardsley ju.r
Ebenezer Beardsley
Samuel Beardsley
Enos Beardsley
John Wheeler
Ebenezer Hubbel
David Peat

Joseph Peat
Samuel French jun.r
Jeremiah French
Thomas Salmon
Thomas Scudamore
Will. Stannard
John French
Jonathan French
Isaac Clarke
John Clarke
Samuel Preston
Stephen Frost
Matthew Horn
Richard Hubbel
Richard Blackleach
Robert Wheeler
John Mallit iuner
George Wyldman
Joseph Shilton
Daniel Shilton
Thadeus Shilton
Samuel Shilton
James Shilton
Josiah Shilton
Ichabod Clarke
Ebenezer Sherman
Caleb Beardsley
John Beardsley
Francis Hawley
Jonathan Hawley
Jacob Baldwin
Benjamin Cogswell
Abraham Pulling [?Tulling]
Elisha Blagge
Joseph Collens
W: Nicoll
Benj.am Edwards
Ben Nicoll
George Clarke
Nathaniel Linus
Joseph Nichols
Hugh Curley

(Those on this and the next paper are under the care of Rev. Mr Caner at Fairfield and Norwalk, to the number of 124)

At Norwalk

Josep[h] Hitchcock	Joseph Ketchum Junr
Joseph Lockwood	Nathan Nash Senr
Isaac Browne	George Sanders
Ralph Isaac jr	Sam^ll Jarvis
Jonathan Camp	Sam^ll Jarvis Juner
Nathaniel Fitch	Jonathan Atherton
Lindle Fitch	John Sherwood
James Betts	John Beears
John Williams	John Bears Junr
Nathan Smith	Andrew Mills
Hugh Stone	Nathan Burill
William pearson	William Jarvis
Nathan Olmsted	John Banks
Anthony Bers	Micaiah Nash
Edward Nash	Thomas Gellis
Nathaniel Hayes	Richard partrick
James Hayes	John partrick
John LeHiel	Benjamin Keeler
Joseph Ketchum	Ephraim Lockwood
Haynes Hanford	David Whelply
Joseph Hitchcok Junr	David Keelog

At fairfield

Nathan adams	Daniel Thomson
James Linesay	Abigail Thompson
David Sturgis	Abraham Pulling
Josiah Gilbert	William Hill
Joshua [Jennings]	Thos Turney
Benjemen Turney	Nathaniel Whitehead
John Knap	Nathan Meker
Daniel Knap	Ebenezer Hall
Calab Lyon	Samuel Jennings
Richard Caner	Luke Guire
Jonathan Cutter	Ebenez^r Guire
Stephen Addam	Abigail Whitlok
Jno Whiteor	Sam^ll Adams
Ignatius Nicol	Ebenezer Lyon Junr
Ben^ja Sturgis Junr	George Barlow
Samuel Davis	Abraham Whitlock
Eben^z Hubbel	Buckland Williams
Zabulon Waklon	Ephraim nicolls
Jno Sturgis Junr	Elnathan Sturgis
Sarah M^kenzy	Daniel Adams
Robert Lord	George McEuen
Jno Mathews	Sam^ll Hill
Moses Downing	Elnathan Loyn [Lyon]
Peter Coley	John Nicela
Sam^ll Squire	Chas Duncombe
Alex^r Green	George Stewart
Samuel Barlow	John Jenings
Moses Ward	Nathan Jennings
Sam^ll Lyon	Bochun Lindsay
Joseph Beers	David Bostwick
Eben Lord	Nathan Thompson
Sam^ll Ward	Hester Lines
Will: Taylor	Jno Pound
William osburn	Benjn Lines
John Bell	Sam^ll Barlow Jun
David Bostwick Junr	Joseph Barlow

Joseph Lockwood	Ebenezer Lyon
Joseph Beers Juner	John Smith
David Beers	Mathew
Nath^ll Adams	Nathen Adams Junr
Jno Whitlock	David Adams

Gen^ll Assembly New Haven Octr 1738

The Memorial of the Members and Profess^rs of the Church of England, being now read &c

In the Upper House, The Question was put whether any thing should be granted thereon and resolved in the Negative

Test George Wyllys Secret^ry

In ye Lower House ye above Question was put & Resolved in ye Negative

Test And^w Burr Clerk

[1738, May 11]

To the Hon^bl the Governour, Council & Representatives of his Majesties English Colony of Connecticot, in Gen^ll Court to be assembled at Hartford in the s^d Colony; on the second Thursday of May next being in the Year of our Lord 1738.

The humble Address of the Members & Professors of the Church of England living in Greenwich & Stanford in s^d Colony. May it please Your Hon^r & this Hon^bl Gen^ll Court.

We the subscribers, Professors of the Church of England, living in Greenwich and Stanford, in the Colony of Connecticot, being his Majesties most Loyal & dutifull subjects; and sincerely attached to the Constitution of this Government, in all the Valuable Priviledges granted by the Royal Charter; humbly begg leave to lay this Address at the feet of your Honour & this Hon^bl Assembly, to acknowledge the Justice and Equity of this Legislature, in the Act passed in May 1727. to exempt the Members and Professors of the Church of England from paying Taxes for the support of any other Ministers, but those of the Church of England; where they live so near to a society of the Church of England, with a Minister in Orders among them, that they conveniently can, and do attend divine service with that Society:

The Reason and Equity of which Act, although to us it seems plain, that it ought not to be interpretted in such a sense as to exclude any of the Inhabitants of the Colony from the Benefit, who are qualifyed according to the Restrictions of the Act; yet, some have raised Scruples and Doubts about the Intention and Design of the s^d Act or Law; whether the Benefit thereof ought to extend, to those who live upon the Borders of the Colony within the same, and have no opportunity to enjoy the Means of Religion in a way agreeable to their Consciences, but by associating with some of their own Persuasion living near to them in a Neighbouring Colony, to support a Minister whose Labours they may mutually enjoy the Benefit of; This being our Case in particular; We Begg leave humbly to pray this Hon^bl Legislature, to declare the sense of the before mentioned Act, in such manner that we may not be excluded the Benefit of it, merely because we live in the extreem Parts of the Colony, and are obliged to associate with our fellow Christians & fellow Subjects next adjoyning to us, in the Colony of New-York, to enjoy the Benefit

of a Ministry and Worship, according to the National Constitution, which our Consciences best approve. For,

1: We humbly conceive no exceptions can, or will in the least, (especially by this Hon^bl Assembly) be taken, against our joyning in that Worship established by the Legislature of our Nation, with fellow Christians and fellow Subjects, altho' of another Colony; seeing, that thereby we dont in the least infringe the Rights or Laws of this Corporation, any more than the Priviledges of Towns are infringed, when the Inhabitants of the extreem Parts of two Towns lying contiguous, are orderly united into a society for the Conveniency of attending Gods Worship; which is often done, with Approbation.

2. Among all the Restrictions of the beforementioned Act or Law, there is no mention, that the Minister who shall receive the Proportion of Taxes shall live and reside in this Colony: And therefore, we conceive that the plain & evident Reason and Equity of the Law or Act, can be the only thing in dispute, to govern the Interpretation thereof.--The very making of a Law always and necessarily supposes, something equitable in the Nature of things, fitt to be incouraged by a Law; this Fittness in the Nature of things, upon which the Law is made, we conceive to be the Equity and Reason of a Law; and seems to us plainly intimated in the preamble of this present Act, so as fully to extend unto us, under the circumstances above related.-- What, this Hon^bl Legislature upon good Reason thought equitable, and in the Nature and Reason of things fitt to be incouraged by a Law, was a granting Relief to the Professors of the Church of England in this Colony, under a hardship that some of them complained of; viz. being obliged to pay taxes to support a way of worship different from the established Church of the Nation; Which established Church, seeing they can find no good Reason to dissent from, they think themselves obliged out of Conscience towards God, as well as from a Principle of Loyalty to the Kings Majesty to adhere to the Communion of. The Equity of this Act then, must be the Removeal of this Grievance; which was thought fitt by the Legislature to be so limitted only, that no Persons might be incouraged by a universal Exemption, to profess themselves of the Church of England upon so base a Motive, as that only of being exempted from Ministerial Taxes, and so abandoning themselves to a state of Irreligion, where they could have no Conveniency to attend a Regular Worship of the Church of England: Which is far from being our Case; Nor do we wish for such Exemptions.--But, as those who are in the extreem Parts, are yet in the Colony; We think the Reason for Exempting Any, will extend to All under like circumstances: that is, who have opportunity and Conveniency to attend that Worship which their Consciences approve and are willing and desireous to expend their Money for the Maintainance of such Religious Worship.--And, the Convenience of attending being the same, when a regular Minister resides and officiates near us in another Colony; as when he resides and officiates at the same Distance in this Colony; We conceive, the Colony in which the Minister resides, is to be out of the Question in determining the sense of this Act according to the Reason and Equity, as well as the Letter of it. especially if we conceive rightly, that the Ministers Power to receive and recover of the Collectors, by the said Act, is only the particular Form or Method prescribed for the Peoples Relief; & Not any original Privi-

ledge designed for the Ministers themselves; who, must be supposed to give the full value unto the People in their Labours, for the Taxes they are impowered to receive & demand: And then, the Case will be the same in Equity, whether a Minister living in another Colony, should have Right to receive a just Reward for his good Labours among us in this Colony; or, any other Man living in another Colony have a Right to receive his just Debts & dues in this.--

3: When by the Grant of our Proportion of the Ministerial Tax, according to the Provision of the s^d Act or Law, we can have the Priviledge of choosing our own Pastor, & enjoy the Labours of a Minister whom we like and approve, and whose Ministry we find most edifying to us, To have such a Construction put upon the Act, or to take this Priviledge from us, by disabling of us to contribute to the Incouragement of such Minister whom we well like and approve, is most effectually to establish such Impositions as the first settlers of this Countrey groaned under and complained of at home, as a Yoak of Bondage which neither they nor their Fathers were able to bear: that is, the Imposition of Ministers without the Peoples Choice: which must be a Burthen fixed upon us as inevitably as by any national Establishment is done; if, by any Misconstruction of this Act, we are excluded from the Priviledges of it. And therefore we humbly Request, upon all these Considerations; Your Hon^r and this Hon^bl Assembly in your Legislative Capacity, would declare the said Act passed at Hartford in May 1727. relating to the Ministerial Taxes of the Professors of the Church of England & for exempting &c--ought to be so construed & understood that such Professors of the Church of England, who live in this Colony near the Borders thereof, and do associate, for the more convenient attending the Worship of God, with a regular Society of the Church of England near adjoyning to them in a Neighbouring Colony and do attend the Worship of God in the said Society according to the Restrictions of the said Act, shall be intitled to the Priviledges and Exemptions of the said Act or Law; And such Minister of the Church of England whose Ministry they attend, shall have Right to receive and demand such Proportion of the Taxes, as in the said Act is mentioned, although his Residence be in a Neighbouring Colony. Provided always, that the said Ministers settled abode and Residence be within five Miles of this Colony--and that by officiating alternately in Each Colony, he performs divine service at least twelve times in the year in this Colony, among those who then associate with the Society of the Church of England where he has a regular and fixed Residence.--or to the like effect according to the Wisdom of your Honour and this Hon^bl Assembly. And we shall ever pray &c.--

Gershom Lockwood	Jonathan Austen
Saml Mills	Tomas Johnson
Caleb Knap	Jonathan Lockwood
Ab^m Nicholds	David Reynolds
William King	Thos Bullis
Theo John Lockwood	John Avery
Beniamin Knap	John Hicks
Joseph Knap	John Johnson
James Knap	John Hall Jr
Jeremy Peck	Samuel Willson
Henry James	Robt Arnold
Hezekiah Lockwood	Isreal Knapp

John Matthews	Sam.l Morine
Banjamin Day	Joseph Barton
Char.s Southerland	John Kirkam
John Burley	Tho.s Roberts
Benjam.n Young	Ab.m Rundal Jun.r
Miles Riggs	Nath.ll Worden
Pet.r DeMill	Nath.ll Worden Jun.r
John Finch	Nath.ll Lockwood
Rich.d Chalton	

In the Lower House
    The Prayer of this Memoriall Negative
                  Test Sam.ll Willard Clerk
In the Upper House
    The prayer of this Memorial Negative
               Test George Wyllys Secre.ty

[Endorsement:]
Address / Church of England Profess.rs in / Stanford &
Greenwich / May 1738 / M.r Fitch

[1738, Nov. 22, Fairfield]
        [To Edmund Gibson, Bishop of London]
        Fairfeild in Connecticut New England
                   Nov.r 22.d 1738
My Lord
    I take this Opportunity by the Rev.d M.r Arnold, (the
Circumstances of whose Parish determine Him for England) to acquaint your Lordship that my Parish is in a
preety Good State: That besides Fairfeild I have attended
the Care of Norwalk a place about 12 Miles from me, and
where there are now forty Families professing the Ch.h of
England. This Increase makes them long very much for
a Missionary. I have therefore wrote to the Venerable
Society in their behalf praying some Consideration of so
promising a Church. I have a Broth.r Richard Caner, who
has had a liberal Education, & is preparing for Holy Orders, Who is industrious in teaching Thirty poor Children
for a very Scanty Allowance, & who assists me in Chate-
chizing, & performing such other Offices as in a Lay Capacity he is qualifyd for; And indeed without his Assistance I should be much less able to serve the Necessities
of so large a Parish than at present I am. I have applyd to
the Hon.ble Society by this Opportunity praying their Con-
sid.rtion of this Case, either allowing Him Some further
Support for his Services, or enabling me to Support Him,
or doing what may appear to them most meet in the affair.
    I humbly beg your L.dships Interest & Influence / with
leave to Subscribe my Self / my Lord / your Lordships /
most Dutiful & Obedient / Humble Servant
                        Henry Caner

[1738, Dec. 14, New Haven]
          New Haven in New England
             Decemb.r 14: 1738:
My Lord
    It is with grief that I have heard, Your Lordship's at-
tendance upon the Honourable Society for Propogating the
Gospel is not as usual, but since I have reason to think
Your Lordship's Ears are open to the cries of the needy, I
humbly beg leave to Spread, & plead my necessitous case
before You: Earnestly beging Your Lordship's interest for

my Relief: My labours and travels in my Mission are
most arduous & most Expensive, by reason of the distance of the Towns where I officiate, I have been repeatedly call'd to Several Towns in Hartford County where
there is no Clergyman, fourty or fifty Miles distant, to
preach & Baptize, I have Spar'd no pains Since I have
been in the Society's Service to Serve the interest of the
Church, but my growing charges, & Sinking Circumstances obliges me to beg for an addition to my Support,
and If The Honourable Society Should compassionate my
State, & put me under Equal circumstances with the Rest
of my Brethren, I may be the better able to answer the
good Ends of Their designs & mine Office, for which I
intreat an interest in Your Lordship's prayers & Blessing and remain
    May it please Y.r Lordship / Yo.r Lordships Most
Dutifull Son / & Most Obedient Humble Servant:
                        Jonathan Arnold

[1739, May 28, Boston]
       [To Edmund Gibson, Bishop of London]
My Lord
    I am very sorry that I have given so long an Exercise
to [you]r Patience as to the Enquiry you were pleased to
make of me; but my [utm]ost and faithfullest Endeavors
laid out in the Case could not command [q]uicker Intelligence. Tho' indeed I have been of late suspended from
[my] Business and Care by the most distressing Sorrow
that ever God dis[po]sed to me in my whole Life; in the
Death of my youngest Son, too dear [to me] and dear
enough to all that knew Him, who sail'd into the Mediter-
ranean [for] the Recovery of his Health, for which, I am
sure from his religious and [vir]tuous Life, God has
given Him an happy Exchange in a better world, where
[lo]ng to be with Him.
    But I shall be tedious enough without such Digres-
sions, thinking [it b]etter to be lengthy than slighty in my
Narrative. And, my Lord, I am personally [acq]uainted
with M.r [Jonathan] Edwards of Northampton, [Connecti-
cut,] who is now in Town, and has made [me] a Visit:
but as I expected no more light from Him than what his
Book [con]tain'd, we kept clear of that Subject. Nor was
I an entire Stranger to his [Gra]ndfather, M.r Solomon
Stoddard, his Predecessor there.
    That Gentleman was of no great Learning and Read-
ing, but of a [stro]ng Brain and Thoughtful, and withal
sober and Religious, grave and pru[dent] in Conversation. He was also narrow and odd in his Sentiments,
Self-opin[ioned,] haughty, assuming, and impatient of
Contradiction, and encreased a Stiffness [li]ving remote
from those He could improve by, or dared to oppose Him,
so [that] He was many years the Oracle of the Country,
especially in those parts [wher]e He lived long, had a
numerous Family, and where a great number [of] Ministers were related to Him by Bloud or affinity. I am an
Instance of [his] severity at my first arrival here from
England, who then sent me a Letter [of R]eproof for my
Departure into the Church of England, which I answered
[as m]odestly as I could, and with particular Consideration of his age: but He [repli]ed to me with that Indecency,
that I thought it best to leave Him the [last] word. But I
durst not be so troublesom to your Lordship as to present

you [the] Copies of those Letters.

His notions about Conversion were very peculiar: one was, That [eve]ry man not culpably careless, knew when He was converted: and according[ly] Edwards in his Book, mentions his Grandfather Stoddard as speaking [of] five Harvests He had among his People in above fifty years of [his d]welling with them, which comes out in Ten or Twelve years, when [one] Generation of young People grows up: and Mr Edwards seems to [have] got into this Period: for the Conversions He speaks of were about Two years after his Settlement in Northampton. But Mr Stoddard was oftentimes [de]ceived about his Converts, and many were known, after a Shew of Piety, [to] relapse into, and persist in grievous Sins.

And his Sence of the Operations of Grace, very much resembles wha[tever] we find in his Grandson's Book (which I ask your Lordship's acceptance of) and H[e has] spread the same among many in the Country, his Relations particularly who [uni]versally adhered to Him. A few years agoe I was credibly informed of an Ins[tance] very much akin to ye Narrative, in one Mr Bulkly Teacher in Colchester, and [of] my particular acquaintance, a man of excellent Understanding, and good Imp[rove]ments in Divinity and Physick, who languished under great Disorders, that al[most] ended his Life. Under his Illness, there being no Physitian near whom He cared to con[sult] He sends to one Mr Mix, a Teacher, and Practitioner in Physick, a man of good U[nder]standing, and of his acquaintance, and Son in Law to Mr Stoddard, living 30 or [40] Miles from Him, desiring to see Him. Mr Mix enquires of the Messenger about [his] Condition, and upon the whole concludes, That the work of Conversion was the[n just] beginning in Him, and takes no other care of Him but to send Him a Treatise of Stoddard's called A Guide to Christ, and so Mr Bulkly, distant, from any agre[eable] Physitian, was left to conflict with his Distemper till it overcame Him.

Mr Edwards was brought up under my care at Yale College, a Person [of] good Abilities, Diligence, and Proficiency in Learning, and continues his Applic[ation] to this time, and in such a degree, that He is very much emaciated, and impair'd in his Hea[lth] and it is doubtful to me whether He will attain to the Age of 40. He was Critical, sa[d] and peculiar, but I think not very solid in Disputation. Always a sober Person [he was] withal pretty recluse, austere and rigid. Presently after He left the College, He r[emo]ved to Northmapton to assist his Grandfather, and was intirely formed by Him, a[nd] now has the care of a People at a great distance from the promiscuous Conve[nticles] and the Infection of our Sea-ports, generally regular and sober, uniform in Le[arning] but remarkably train'd up in self-conceit, to Disputation, and a Fondness for [Mr.] Stoddard's own School-Divinity.

About the time of this remarkable appearance at Northampton a[nd] the parts adjacent, there was a number of Visionaries at Cambridge, and in [the] College there. It began in one Langloiserie, a Refugee from Canada, [who] dwell't in Cambridge to teach the Scholars French, and insinuated himsel[f into] the Esteem of many, by a sober Life, and demure Behavior mixed with [some] Enthusiasm, tho' He refuses to attend any Public Worship, and has privately [utt]ered, and laboured to propagate gross Corruptions in Religion. He is [said t]o be an Arian, to believe two Messiahs, Ben David and Ben Ephraim, and

[to] have given out that the World would come to an end within a year or two [of] that time. One of the Tutors of the College, with several of His Relatio[ns] who are Teachers, appeared much affected by it, and remarkably careless a[bout] Temporal affairs; at which the College was alarmed, and warned the Se[niors ag]ainst any Conversation with this Langloiserie, and brought the Tutor of the [Co]llege to some Reflections; and so this matter stopt there. But the Perswasion [th]at the World would soon come to an end got up to Northampton-parts, and wrought [mu]ch on the People's Spirits, and what engaged the Indians thereabouts I cannot [te]ll, but they are also said to have at that time conversed with the English [mo]re seriously, and to have been more abstemious than was common for them.

The New-England Teachers referr'd to in Mr Edwards's Narrative, tho' [ma]ny of them, I hope, very honest men, are not sufficient to set it beyond Contradictio[n.] [S]o Dr Colman to whom the Narrative is directed, He is more noted for easy Expres[sions] than for thorough Judgement, and his well known Foible is to encourage [and c]ourt Public Salutation and Applause, and to be smoothed into a good opinion [by] whatever comes to Him in that manner.

The Four Teachers of Boston who recommend the Narrative, are men [of t]he lowest Form in Learning and Judgment, contracted in their Thoughts, and [ver]y apt to fall in with any thing whimsical and visionary. But for Learning I [ex]cept M^r [Thomas] Prince, tho' his Oddity has got much the upper hand of it, joyn'd with a [stro]ng Disposition to say every thing that He thinks will give Reputation to his own [bo]dy, and leave the Church of England much behind it, as appears from his [own] New England Chronology.

I know all the Teachers upon Connecticut River save one who have [give]n their attestation to ye Narrative, and believe them to be honest men, but [easi]ly led away by whimsical appearances and fantastic Shows, and one of [the]m is a Son in Law to Mr Stoddard, and the other a Descendant.

I also know Twelve of the Teachers referred to in it, Five whereof were rela[ted t]o Mr Stoddard, all byast by his schemes, all weak men, and some of them in [the] lowest degree: and with such only was Mr Edwards industrious to catch up as [many suc]h as would make up a Book, and I can now find none other that do commend [it.] As Mr Edwards takes Stratford into his Reports, I wrote to my Revd Brother [John]son about it, who answers me, That the Humor began in his Parish (where [Mr.] Gould, is Teacher) but never prevail'd as He expected. In the North Parish [whe]re Mr Mills is Teacher, it began with an old whimsical Maid, crazed with Love [for] a young man belonging to his (Mr Johnson's) Church, which she assign'd to [a] Courtship, and complain'd of Him to Mr Johnson, who was not able to find [any]thing culpable in the man, and therefore dismissed the woman with some [pi]ous suggestions and Exhortations. And this gave her (who as well as Mr Mills [ent]ered upon ye Seat of these Schemes) a turn towards this imaginary Relig[ion] and set her to crying for she knew not what, and thereby made others cry for [they] did not know what, especially little Girls.

In Mr Johnson's Parish the Humor did not take with

more than 4 or 5 young women, who in the time of it used to get together and cry, and they continue p[retty] serious, but two of them married soon after these religious Raptures, and h[ad] each of them a Child in 6 or 7 months. Mr Johnson knoweth nothing of th[eir] having been remarkably vicious before or serious since.

And there are many more of whom I have enquired personally, or b[y] assistance of Friends: and some appear very frank in their Narratives, and ot[hers] as shy of giving their sence of Facts, for fear of prejudicing them in that [part] of the Country, by their Contradicting what is there counted very sacred. [Sun]dry young Gentlemen brought up at Harvard and Yale Colleges, some [of] whom are Candidates for Orders among them, say it is all a Whim: Tho' a[ll] that I have spoken with give in to the Truth of ye Narrative: but all say [that] it is now over, and generally add, that many are become as bad as ever.

Several inform me, That their Imaginations were much wrou[ght,] some pretending to have seen very strange Sights, some surprizing Lights[, and] one an Hawk on a Stump of a Tree. A Friend of mine who travelled into [those] parts asked a Teacher there, whether He thought the thing was not catching[. He] answered He did. Another Teacher of those parts, and a very worthy sensible [man] told me upon Enquiry formerly, That He thought there was something remarka[ble] in it, but it was too much magnify'd and strain'd, and proposed to give me a [book] and to discourse more upon the Subject, but I was disappointed. I have si[nce] written to Him upon it, and received no answer, but know not why, unless that H[e is] shy at this juncture, being hotly charged with Arminianism. A Prea[cher] said He had two Sisters who had gone through the work (a favourite Phr[ase] on the Subject) but they were no better than before. I laboured to gain a Visit fr[om] Him, but that stirred up his Jealousy, and He will not see me. A man of Hatf[ield] says, His Minister Mr Wm Williams, (tho' He is one that attests the Narrative) wi[shes] Mr Edwards had not been so full and forward in the matter, and I have [come t]o doubt it, because such things are frequently hurryed on among us by [in]judicious Zeal, and it is scandalous to be slack and deliberate, and beca[use] good information perswades me He is a very honest man: He also thinks th[at] so much in it as is pretended, but is glad He did not see me, as I laid out for [him.] From others I find that Children of about 12 years old would run about [the] Streets, and say, they were bound to Zion, and would enquire the wa[y to]ward, that they would assemble to pray and sing in the Meetinghouses, a[nd] were admitted to the Communion, that the Height of this Paroxysm [was] within two months, and as all others say, now for a considerable time entirely o[ver] and that the sober Anabaptists in those parts take it for a whim, and so[me] others question the nature and tendency of the thing, but conceal th[ems]elves for fear of Displeasure.

It is credibly reported by sundry, That one Mr Hawley han[ged] himself at this time, because what He had been seeking for, and had [not] found in fourty years, others had found in a few days, and that another [cut] his Throat upon it, but the Wound proved not mortal

I employed a Dissenting Friend of mine in this Town to a[ppoint en]quiries; and He finds two Persons who have studiously examin'd the matter; one is a Teacher, who

finds it had it's Rise from a Report that the World would [sho]rtly come to an end, strengthened by Mr Whiston's Prediction of a Co[met, so] that many of the Converts have relapsed, and He thinks there is no[thing] in it: Another is a very consciencious discreet Dissenter, greatly reverencing [and] respectful towards his Teachers, and whom I should rather expect to fall [for] the Scheme than not. He, after strict Enquiry cannot find the Rise to be [from] Preaching, or any thing Providential; He thinks there were [valid] Impressions among some, but much chaff among the wheat. And He re[lates] this Story as very credible: A Certain Person in Northampton wanted [to sup]ply his Pile of Firewood which was low, and bad his Son go into the Woods and [cut s]ome Firewood, who said He could not. Whereupon his Father argued [with] Him, and bad Him observe the need they were under; but He continued saying, [He wo]uld not go. At length his Father told Him that unless He was ill He would [call f]orth his Authority, and make Him go. And then his Son took up his Axe [and] went into the Barn, where He made an hideous Mourning and Noise, that [awak]n'd the Neighbours and they went to Him, and then called his Father. At [last] it was moved to send for Mr Edwards their Minister, before whom He conti[nued] in this manner, who thereupon advised the Father to forbear urging his [son,] telling Him that He was under some extraordinary Influences of the [Spiri]t, and was getting through; a Phrase much apply'd to such cases.

Upon the whole, My Lord, I find it to be the sence of People in general [that] in this great Appearance of Religion there is reason to think many were real, [that] others were led by Example, that many remain serious and unblemisht, & [perh]aps as many who were bad have relapsed in to yr former state; and that [peop]le in those parts any thing unbyast by yr popular Schemes, think there was [a gre]at deal fantastical and foolish in those shows, but find it not for their [inter]est to speak disparagingly of them; that the meanest of the Teachers, here [& elsew]here, and scarce any other Teachers, fall into them; and that the Talk of these [things] is now generally dropt.

I hope your Lordship will have full satisfaction to your Enqui[ry fr]om this Account, which I fear has been too prolix, if not too triffling, at the [same] time that I chose rather to exceed than to be scanty in my Obedience: but [whate]ver further Service your Lordship shall lay on me in this, or any other affair, none [will] be readyer to undertake it.

And now, My Lord, I do in the humblest manner beg your Pity, and [your] Prayers to God for me, under his Hand which presseth me sore, though [most j]ustly, that I may honour Him more in the Bereavement than I have in the [pay]ment of his Favors; and I also beg a Portion in your Lordship's Compassion[ate in]structions to my only Son whenever He has the Honour to come into [your] Lordship's Presence. I shall ever think your Lordship's Life a [grea]t Blessing to the Church, and be glad of making full proof that I am / your Lordship's / most obedient Son & Servant

   [Bos]ton May 28. 1739   Timothy Cutler

[My Lo]rd, your Commands are an entire Secret to [every]body but my Self here, & so will be.

[1739, June 18, Groton]

Groton 18 June 1739.

Rev.d Sr

There is not any more considerable alteration in the Parishes under my Care than that of the Spirit & temper of our Dissenting Brethren many of which from being revilers & haters of the Chh, are brought to have a good oppinion of it and occasionally attend our Worship, I beleive that at the Last Christmas and upon a Lords Day Since there meet in our Chh upwards of 400 persons who behavd Soberly & Devoutly many of wc had been our bitterest enemies, wc to me is an unspeakable Comfort. Upon the earnest desire of a considerable number I have made a Journey to Middletown about 40 miles from my Home and preach'd to a Sober body of people near, 100. two of wc have Since come and joynd to our Communion. the State of My Parishes is nearly as follows.

1 No Inhabitans.		2400
2 No Baptized of ye Chh of Eng.d		218
3 No Baptiz'd Since my last.	3 Adults.	
	15 Infants	
4 No Actual Communicants		70
5 No of Professors of ye Chh of Eng.d about.		200
6 No Dissenters Independents		1800
	Baptists. 1 & 7 Day.	250
	Quakers	90
7 No Heathens		150
8 No Converts from Vice to Virtue	I hope many.	

Rev.d Sr I am your's & the Societys
most obedient Servt.
Ebenr Punderson

[Addressed:] The Rev.d Dr. Humphrys / In Warwick Court Warwick Lane / London
[Endorsed:] Read 15th Octr. 1739.

[1739, Oct., Colony of Conn.]

Oct. 1739

An Act in Addition to an Act, Entitled An Act in Addition to an an Act, Entitled An Act for The Encouragemt. & better Supporting The Schools that by Law ought to be Kept in the Several Towns & Parishes in This Colony; Wch Act was Made in May 1733--

Whereas in Said Act it is provided That In Case any of The Towns or Parishes as afors.d, Shall by Their Major Vote, in any of Their Meetings Regularly Assembled, Shall Well and Truely Sequester Their proportion of Money Raised by The Sale of ye Seven townships in the Western Lands to The Support of The Gospel Ministry, as by The Laws of This Colony Established; & Shall Continue to Improve it To That End, The forfeiture in The first Act Respecting The Encouragement of Schools Shall Not be Taken; and Since The Resolve of ye Assembly as afores.d The Members of The Church of England have Shewn Themselves grieved at The Said Act, Wherefore,

It is now Declared and Resolved &c That whensoever any of The s.d Towns or parishes Shall by Their Major Vote as aforesaid, Sequester Their Money Raised as afores.d, To The Support of The Gospel Ministry as by The Laws of This Colony Established; In That Case The Members of The Church of England within Such Town or Parish Shall Have a Right to and Shall Receive Their Quota of Such Money according To Their Lists of Toles & Rateable Estate at The Time of The Grant of s.d Money in The Year 1733, to be Used and Improved by Them for The Support of Their Ministry, where There is a Person in Orders according To ye Cannons of ye Church of England, Settled and abiding among Them and Performing Divine Service So Near To Such persons as have Declared them selves of ye Church of England, That they Can Conveniently & Do attend The Publick Worship There: and in Case Such Members of The Church of England Shall Neglect To Improve Their Money as afores.d for The End afores.d They Shall forever Loose The Benefit Thereof; and The Treasurer of The Colony Shall Recover The Same Quota as afores.d for ye Use of Ye Colony.

past in ye Lower House
Test, Jno. Russell Clerk

In the Upper House
The Consideration of this Bill is referred to the Genl Assembly in May next
Test George Wyllys Sccrctry
Concurr.d with in ye Lower House
Test, Jno. Russell Clerk

[1740, Wallingford]

[To Edmund Gibson, Bishop of London]

May it Please your Lordship
We the Church wardens & Parishioners of Wallingford & adjacent parts in ye Colony of Connecticut in New England beg leave to offer our Humble duty to your Lordship

We are A Church but newly Planted & however content we are at present to have the service of the Church only once a Quarter by a Minister & on every Lords day besides we perform the service as far as is proper for lay men But in that part we are some thing defecient for want of sermon books &c which we cannot easily procure in this Country We are sensible the Reverend Mr. Theo Morris cannot leave his other Parishes oftener yet we hope God in his providence will so order it that we may at last be oftener attended there are many ready to joyn in our Communion & have nothing to object to it but our having service so sildom by a Minister. We greatly rejoyce that we are assisted in Learning to know which is the true Church of Christ & the Manner how we Ought to worship. But with Malincoly hearts we crave your Lordships Patience while we recite that divers of us have been Imprisoned & our goods from year to year distrained from us for taxes levied for the Building and supporting Meeting Houses And divers actions are now depending in our Courts of law in the like cases And when we have Petitioned our Governour for redress Notifieing to him the Repugnance of such Actions to the laws of England he hath proved a strong Opponent to us, but when the other party hath applyed to him for advise how to proceed against us he hath lately given his sentence to Enlarg the Goal & fill it with them (that is the Church) But we supplicate both God & man that our Persecutors may not always prevail against us

And now that God may Bless your Lordship and the Charitable Endeavours of the Honourable society & Enable them to send more Labourers to a Harvist truly

Plentifull is the sencere prayer of / your Lorships / Most dutifull & Obedient serv^{ts}

Thomas Ives }
North Ingham } Church wardens

Mathew Bellamy	Sahdrick Seagar
Ebenezer Blakslee	John Belamy
Enos Smith	Thomas Dewhittle
John Meky	Waitstill Abinather
Thomas Williams	Aaron Tuttle
George Fisher	Phineas Ives
Ebenezar Wainwright	

[1740, May 8]

To the Honourable the Governour, the Deputy Governour and the rest of the members of the General Assembly, to be holden at Hartford, on the Eighth Day of May in the Year of our Lord 1740.

May it Please your Honours,

We the Subscribers Ministers of the Church of England, beg leave to represent to your Honour and this Assembly, that whereas there was a Petition relating to the seven New Townships and Several other matters laid before the Honourable the General Assembly in May 1738. by all the Members of the Church of England in this Government, and also another from the People of Horseneck, &c. relating to their Ministers Rate, upon neither of which Petitions there has as yet been any thing done to our Satisfaction, which has appeared a matter of Greivance to the Said Members of the Church of England; And whereas We being obliged by the Honourable Society to represent any matters of Greivance that may occurr to the Church of England in the Plantations under our Care, have accordingly represented these; and received order from the Board that one of us should come home to solicit and Support those Affairs: We have hitherto delayed to do it at the Instance and by the Advice of some who were members of the Assembly at that Time, persuading us that we might expect, there would yet be something done on this Side the Water in our behalf; and because we are very unwilling to be laid under a necessity of representing any thing home that might Issue to the Prejudice of our Country, and Should take much more pleasure in having opportunity of informing the Society of the redress of our Greivances than in being oblidged to Support our Complaint there, tho' we have by another Letter this Spring, been again put in mind that it is expected one of us Speedily come home with it. On these Considerations we would humbly intreat your Honour and this Assembly again to take those Petitions into your Consideration, to which we beg leave to referr you, and to grant them a favourable hearing; or otherwise do for us what in your Wisdom and Goodness shall be thought most conducive to the publick Tranquility, and preserving of Brotherly Love and Unity among us; In hope of which We Shall ever Pray for the Weal and Prosperity of this Government, and remain,

Your Honours, / Most Obedient, and / Most Humble

Servants	John Beach
Sa. Johnson	Jon^a Arnold
J: Wetmore	Sam^{ll} Seabury
Henry Caner	Eben^r Punderson

[1740, June 3, North Groton]

N: Groton 3. June. 1740.

S^r

Soon after my last Notitia Parochialis a Box of Books from the Honourable Society came Safe to hand, which I have distributed to Such as I am perswaded will make a good use of them; and by me they desir'd their thanks might be transmited to the Hon.^l Society for this instance of their extraordinary Goodness, and care for them--

I find it so very dificult (living out of the post road) to convey Letters to the Society, that I hope they will excuse me with sending anually a Notitia Parochialis. Since my last besides a constant attendance upon Divine Service in the places more imediatly under my charge, I have preach'd at Brimfield, Distant 50 miles. Stafford 40- Middletown 40- and twice at Canterbury 24. where we have 7 or 8 Comunicants-

1 N^o Inhabitants in { Groton { Preston
     { Norwich { Stonington
     are computed to be about   4,500

2 N^o Baptizd of ye Chh of Eng^d--about.   240

3 No. of Baptizd Since my last--   4 Adults &
                    30 Children.

4 N^o of Actual Communicants of y^e
    Chh of Eng^d   77

5 N^o of Those who profess themselves
    of the Chh of Eng^d   210

6 N^o of Dissenters--the most of them Independents Some Quakers many Baptists scarce any Papists

7 N^o of Heathens & Infidels--Heathens about
               200 Adults
               --No profesd infidels.

8 N^o of Converts &c--I trust there are many

I am S^r / your'n & the Societys Freind & Servt
Eben^r Punderson

[Addressed:] Doc^r Humphrys Sec^r to the Hon^{ll} Society / In Warwick Court warwick Lane / London
[Endorsed:] Read 13th Octr 1740

[1741, May 25, Groton]

Groton 25 May. 1741-

Notitia Parochialis

	Groton }	
	Norwich }	
1 Number of Ihabitants in	Preston }	About
	Stonington }	1500 familys
	& Westerly)	
2 N^o of the Baptiz'd		The greater part
3 N^o of Baptiz'd ye year past.		2 Adults
		17 Infants.
4 N^o of Actual Comunicants &c		71
5 N^o of Profesors of ye Chh of Eng^d		About 185
6 N^o of Dissent^{rs}		

   1 of ye Chh y^t they imagine establishd here about 1000 fa[milys]

   2 Baptists about   200 familys

   3 Quakers   100

   4 Papists   none openly & profesedly

7. Nᵒ. Heathens	About 200 of the orig[in]al natives of yᵉ Land.
8. Nᵒ. of Converts	7 or Eight

Sᵣ

I would inform the Venerable Society &c whose Missionary I am (tho unworthy) That there is not any of our Communion, or yᵗ attend my Ministry; but Such as receiv'd their education in the Independent way, excepting one: and by consequence have interwoven in yʳ Constitution some Regard for it, and are more likely to attend to, & be influenc'd by the Independant Ministry & their own Relations, & freinds; than Such persons who have been educated in, or for a Long time accustomd to, yᵉ worship of our Church.

There are many additional Disadvantages wᶜ this Mission is attended with as My people's great Distance from each other, that I can scarcely visit them twice a year without constant Riding--Since Mᵣ Whitefeild. Tenant, Mills &c. have been About into whose Surprizing Scheme many of the Independent Min' in This Neighbourhood have gone, there seems to be a general Combination of Min', & people here to terrify, Allure, or by some means or other totally to Subvert the Chh here, wᶜ is but in its Infancy; my fear & concern is Indeed very great; Tho' I can't but hope yᵗ Almighty God who has so Signally built up this Chh in the mids't of its most violent enimies, will never suffer it totally to fail altho' the endeavours of the Independents are such now as if it were possible would deceive yᵉ most confirm'd:

We have at yᵉ Cost of near 500£ This Currency built a good timber Chh near the Center of the Conformists to wᶜ I have given 60£ and procur'd of my freinds near 200 more In wᶜ I have preach'd constantly for 2 years past excepting 4 Sund[ays] in the year at Charlestown, or Westerly, & some few in the remote parts of my Mission

I have frequently Receivd earnest invitations some of wᶜ I have complyd with to preach at verry remote places, particly last Sepᵣ I went from my House on wednesday morning travel'd 45 Miles to Stafford, preach'd the next Day to their Min' & people in the meeting House; in wᶜ town I had preachd twice before--the next Day I preachd at Brimfeild 10 miles farther where I had preachd 5 times before--the Day following I travaild 45 or 50 miles, and upon yᵉ Lords Day preach'd at Symsbury to a large Congregation Tho' a very rainy Day; the next Day I rode 25 miles To Middletown where I had preach'd twice before.

This almost constant traveling and preaching in Season & out of Season, has much impaird my Constitution which was never verry Strong; and renderd me verry infirm yet (God be prais'd) I preach 2 Sermons upon every Sunday for near 3 quarters of yᵉ year & 1 almost every other week in Some Distant place--

I am Determin'd (by Divine Assistance) perseveringly to continue my Labours in this uncomfortable Situation where the greatest Degrees of uncharitableness and Enthusiastic Rage prevail, trusting Almighty God will not always permit the interest of truth and virtue to be Thus obscurd and born down; I would not only entreat the prayers of The Honble Society for me and my people, but yᵗ one or more of the members of yᵗ venerable body might be desird to take the inclosd Bill of exchange and Receive its contents 7£ 10/ Procure with it a number of the best Books to vindicate the Docᵗ Govᵗ & Worsp. of the Establish'd Chh from yᵉ unreasonable Cavils and objections of its Adversaries, Suited to the Capacitys of the comon people, to be Distributed. By wᶜ my obligations

To you & the Venble Society will be increasd, and I trust always graetfully acknowledgd by your'n & yᵉ Societys / Real Freind & Servᵗ

Ebenʳ Punderson

[Endorsed:]   Read 16 Novᵣ 1741

[1741, July 12, Warwick, R.I.]

Coeset [Coweset] Church in Warwick July 12. 1741. These are to verify that His Majesty's Order in Council of the 29ᵗʰ of January 1740, directing the Form of Prayer for the Royal Family; with the Vote of the General Assembly of His Majesty's Colony of Rhode-Island & thereon dated the 4ᵗʰ Monday in June A.D. 1741, were this Day read at the Church above mentioned, and the Form in said Royal Order used in the proper Places in the Liturgy, by me

James Macsparran Cler[ic]

Sic quoque testamur presentes,

Lodowick Updike   Edward Cole   Samuel Chace

[1741, Oct. 20, North Groton]

N: Groton, 20ᵗʰ Octᵣ 1741.

Revᵈ Sᵣ

I receivd your's yᵉ 17 of this Instant and shall cheerfully conform to the Contents. until now have receivd no particular Instructions, saving what came in a Letter with my Notititia parochialis, Dated 15ᵗʰ Decemᵣ 1737. Since than, and before I have endeavourd to send a particular Acct. of yᵉ State of my Parish, every year: and for the future will do it every 1/2 year- I hope the Sett of Bills Due yᵉ 25 of Septᵣ last will not be refus'd since sent before I Receivd your Letter. the Collection of papers are not yet sent me. Inclosd I send a Notitia Parochialis for yᵉ half year past, and I would inform the venerble Society &c that Enthusiasm exceedingly rages in the parishes under my Care but especially this. the most amazing Screitchings Screamings, faintings, Convulsions, and Visions attend it and are made the inseperable marks of Conversion and the New Birth. and 2 persons in this parish have been so wonderfully wrought upon in this manner: as to become actually posses'd by yᵉ Devil as all Grant, and one of them who by yᵉ good providence of God is restor'd to yᵉ use of reason confesses. the Spirit in these Demoniaks and Enthusiasts is extreamly violent against the Establishd Church; and both I and all under my care: are often declard both by Teacher and people to be unconverted, and going Straight Down to Hell. tis amazing how this wild Scene prevails and how it will end God only knows. It increases my Labour to yᵗ degree that I can scarce Spend a whole Day in my Study or family. I have twice been desir'd to preach to a Large congregation of 7ᵗʰ day Baptists in Westerly and complyd with yʳ Desires

I hope the Society will accept of the Bill for £7=10=0 which I have drawn upon the Treasᵣ sent in my Last Letter wᶜ Sum I shall deduct out of my next sett of Bills Due in March. and. Send me the Books as soon as possible, and especially Such Books & Pamphlets as may be an Antidote against this Spᵗ of Gidiness, & Enthusiasm:

and Some Small Comon prayer Books with Tate & Bradys version of yᵉ Psalms.

    I am Your's & the Honᵇˡᵉ Societys / Real Freind & Servᵗ

                     Ebenʳ Punderson

      1741. Notititia Parochialis; or an Accᵗ &c.

I	Number of Inhabitants	Groton 200 familys
		Norwich 400.
		Preston 300
		Stonington 350
II	Nᵒ of yᵉ Baptiz'd	About 3/4 of the above
III	Nᵒ of the Baptizd this half year.	5 Adults
		10 Children
IV	Nᵒ of Actual Communicants of yᵉ Chh of Engᵈ	80 {We had 50. at the Communion the 1st Sunday of this Insᵗ
V	Nᵒ of those who profess themselves of yᵉ Chh of Engᵈ	200 Persons.
VI	Nᵒ of Dissenters of all Sorts &c	Presbiterians 400. familys Independents. 300 Qakers 100 Baptists 1 Day-50 7 Day-100 other Sects unknown in Engᵈ 50
VII	No of Heathens & Infidels	Heathens-100 familys Infidels. not many profesedly such--.
VIII	Nᵒ of Converts from a Prophane &c.	A very great Number.

[1741, Dec. 12, North Groton]

              Nᵗʰ Groton 12: Decʳ 1741
My Lord

    The Dutys and Labours of my Mission are exceedingly encreas'd, by yᵉ Surprizing Enthusiasm: or what is worse: yᵗ Rages among us; the Center of wᶜ is the place of my Residence. a Short account of wᶜ I Shall trouble your Lordship with

    Since Mʳ Whitefeild was in this Country, there has been a great Nᵒ of vagrant preachers the most remarkable of wᶜ is Mʳ Davenport of Long Island, who came to N: London, in July: pronound yʳ Minˢ unconverted, and by his Boisterous Behaviour, and vehement crying Come to Christ. many were <u>struck</u> as the phrase is, and made the most terrible and Affecting noise; that was heard a mile from the place--he came to this Society acted in the Same manner 5 Days was followd by innumerable, Some could not endure the House saying that it seem'd to them more like the infernal Regions; than the place of worshiping the God of Heaven. many after the amazing Horrour and Distress yᵗ Seizd them receiv'd <u>Comfort</u> (as they term it) and 5, or 6, of these young men, in this Society are contnnally going about especially in the night converting as they call it their fellow men, 2 of yᵐ as their Minisʳ and they Affirm, converted above 200 in an Irish town about 20 miles back in the Country- their meetings are almost every night in this and the neighbouring Parishes, and the most astonishing Effects Attend them. Screitchings, faintings, Convultions, visions, apparent Death for 20 or 30 Hours-

actual possessions with evil Spirits as they own themselves, this Spᵗ in all is remarkeably bitter against the Chh of England--2 who were Struck and proceeded in this way of exhorting and praying untill actually possesd came to me: ask'd the same Quesᵗ - are you born again have you the witness of yᵉ Spirit &c as they all do. us'd the same texts of Scripᵗ, taught the same Docᵗ. calld me Bellzebub yᵉ prince of Devills & in yʳ possesion burn't above 1200£--they have Since both been to me Askd my forgivness, and bless God that he has restord them to the Spᵗ of a Sound mind.

    There is at least 20 or 30 of these Lay holders forth, within 10 miles of my house who hold their meetings every night in the week in some place or other exceepting Saturday night, and incredible pains is taken to Seduce and draw away yᵉ members of my Chh, but Blessed be God we Still rather encreas---

    I have Sent a Bill wᶜ I trust the Honᵇˡᵉ Society have receiv'd, for 7£10ˢ-00 to be laid out for Books such as are most proper and Seasonable to stop if possible this growing madness.--my Parishioners are very Scattering yᵗ in visiting and Lecturing among them my whole time is employd and that my Labours may not be in vain I entreat an interest in your Lordships prayers who am my Good Lord.

        Your most Obedient Son & Servᵗ
            Ebenʳ Punderson

[1742, Mar. 30, North Groton]

           N: Groton. 30, March. 1742
Revᵈ Sʳ

    According to my instructions I take this opportunity to inform yᵉ Venerable Society for propagating the Gospell in Foreign parts, that I have drawn the Sett of Bills due the 25ᵗʰ of this Instant; bearing Date with this Letter, in favour of yᵉ Person who procures yᵗ of me, he having a good Freind bound for London. and more especially to forward the Box of Books I have troubled the Venᵇˡᵉ Society &c. to procure, if they are not Sent already, there never being more pressing need of Good Books among us than in this astonishing Season: in wᶜ the Wildest Enthusiasm & Superstition prevails, and is attended with the most bitter Fruits of uncharitableness and Spiritual pride. an instance or two of wᶜ I shall trouble the Honᵇˡᵉ Society with- Sometime Since immediatly after I had preachd a Sermon in Norwich; one of these Enthusiasts came to me demanded my Experiences, (wᶜ is verry Common) his Request being deny'd, He pronouncd me Unconverted, and not only going My Self, but leading all under my Charge down to Hell, Soon After he was attended with a Dumb Spirit, and utter'd nothing for 5, or 6, Days unless 2 or 3 Blasphemous expressions (viz) <u>Go tell the Brethren I am Risen</u> at another time <u>Suffer Little Children to come unto me</u> &c There also came another of these Exhorters, (as they are calld here) to my House, attended by many; declard me as Upright and as exemplary a person as any he knew in the world, yet he knew I was unconverted and leading my people down to Hell, he affirmd that he was sent with this Message from God, and felt the Spᵗ upon him &c, he seemd Sincere. Soon After Mʳ Croswell the Dissenting Teacher in this Parish with 2 Attendants came Singing to my House, pronouncd me Unconverted, yet at the same time declard that he did not know me guilty of

any Crime- I assurd him y^t In my oppinion it was a greater crime for him thus to murder my Soul, usefulness, and
Reputation in the world; than for me to attempt his Natural Life, and that he certainly must be a worse man Thus
in cool blood and under a Religious pretence to pronounce
Damnation against me than for a comon Swearer to say to
another God Dam you; Since this he is not So feirce as
before

At ye first Rise of this enchanting Delusion, I was
under melancholy Apprehensions, that the Infant Chh of
England in this and the Adjacent places would be Crushd:
these being the center of ye Religious Delirium. Some
have gone after it, but more Added, and I am more and
more convincd of the promise of our Blessed Lord y^t <u>y^e</u>
<u>Gates of Hell shall never prevail &c</u> My Labours abun-
dantly encrease And I have Scarce been at home a week
together the past winter, Sometimes I preach 2, or 3
Sermons a week besides constantly upon the Lords day,
and I have good hope that my Labour is not in vain--

I Shall trespas no Longer Rev^d S^r upon your'n and
the Ven<u>ble</u> Societys better employd time but conclude
  Your & The Hon<u>ble</u> Societys / Real Freind & Servt
                        Eben^r Punderson

[Addressed:] To The Revd Dr Bearcroft Secretary &c /
At the Charterhouse / London
[Endorsed:] Read 13th Septr 1742

Notitia Parochialis--from Sepr to March 30th 1742.

1	Number of Inhabitants in Groton Stonington Norwich & Preston.	About 1500 familys
2.	N^o of the Baptized	About 2/3^{ds}
3.	N^o of the Baptized by me	6. Adults. 8 Infants.
4.	N^o of Actual Com- municants of the Chh of England	82.
5.	N^o of those who pro- fess themselves of ye Chh of Eng^d	About 200 persons.
6.	N^o of Dissenters of all Sorts.	Independ^{ts}. 800 or 900 fam^s Baptists. 1 & 7 Day 200 fam^s Quakers. about 100, Papists none profesedly. { by much the greater part fall in with Methodism in these towns
7.	N^o of Heathens and Infidels.	About 200 Hundred Heathens
8	N^o of Converts &c	To Appearance many.

[1742, May 13]
To the Honble the Governour and General Court assem-
bled in Hartford this 13th of May 1742. The Memorial of
Sundry persons in Symsbury and places adjacent humbly
Sheweth.

That your Memorialists have for above two years
past seen as we apprehend abundent Reason to conform to
the Church of England as it is Established in our Mother
Church; and have accordingly united and combined together
to promote the Worship and discipline of that Church
among us; and have put our selves under the Conduct of
the Ministers of that Church; who have several of them
agreed to perform Divine Service among us once a month
for Eight months in the year; and particularly we have
put our selves under the pastoral Care of the Reverand
m^r Theophilus Morris who is appointed By the Society for
propagating of the Gospel to be an itinerant Missionary
to officiate to the members of the Church of England dispersed in various parts of this Colony, who accordingly
visits us as often as his other obligations will admit of:
and have moreover by his direction in concurrence of the
Rest of the Clergy of our Church for some time past and
to come hired m^r Ebenezer Thompson as our catechist
and a candidate for the ministry among us; In consequence
of all which most of us, have not at all or but seldom attended upon any other worship for nigh two years past,
and have (with a view at our being setled in the way of the
Church of England) been preparing, and have actually got
timber in order to build a Church of our own.

Notwithstanding all which, our neighbours and brethren of the first parish in this town have insisted that we
chiefly being within the bounds of it pay our rates not only
to the support of the minister there, but also towards the
building of their Meeting house, and sundry of us have
been confined in the Jayl for our Rates, and the rest are
threetned, and daily Expect the same; and a Lawsuit hath
been commenced, in which we have been nonsuited, and if
we should proceed in that method we can Expect nothing
but a tedious course in the law, at the Expence of a very
considerable sum, which it will be difficult for us to raise,
and which we would much rather should be Expended upon
our Church; and shall be Exposed to a very great hazzard
of loosing our Case at last; because tho' we humbly apprehend that in Equity we come within the intent of the
law made in favour of the Church of England, it may bear
some Dispute whether we come within the precise letter
of it.

On all which Considerations, and to prevent any further trouble, we humbly apply our selves to your Honour,
and this Legislature for a redress of our greivance, and
earnestly intreat that we may be allowed to be an Ecclesiastical Community within our selves, and may be Exempted from contributing, both for the two years past and for
the future, towards any other Meeting house or worship
besides that of our own--

We Desire nothing but to live in perfect love and
peace and charity with all our neighbours and Brethren;
and in all dutiful submission to this government, and only
Beg that we may enjoy the benifit of our own estates for
the support of that method of worship that to us appears
most agreeable to the word of god, and in Humble hope
and confidence of your Honours countenance and indulgence, and particularly with regard to our above mentioned Request, We as in duty bound shall Ever Pray, &c

William Case	Thomas Bacon
Willm Enos	Josiah Lumas
Gillet Addams	Samuel beman
Abraham Piney	Danel Tuler
Andrew Moor	Joseph Alderman
Sandars Moor	Timothy Adams
James Tuller	Rana Cosat

benone Grafing   Stephen Griffen
Wiliam Roberts   Joseph addams
Nathanel bacon   John Tuller
John Enos   Rob.ᵗ Brough
Richard Roberts   Thᵒ Stephens
Richard Roberts Jⁿʳ   James Crozier
Ephraim Adams

Connecticut Ss, Hartford / Gen.ˡ Assembly May 1742 /
In the upper House
    The Question was put whether the prayer of this
Memorial should be granted, Resolved in the Negative
               Test George Wyllys Secretʳʸ
    Concurred in yᵉ Lower House
               Test Jnᵒ Fowler Clerk

[1742, Sept. 5, Stratford]
        [To Edmund Gibson, Bishop of London]
      Stratford in New England. Sept. yᵉ 5. 1742.
May it please your Lordship.
    This Letter accompanies another to your Lordship
from my Brethren of the Clergy in this Colony, wherein
they humbly represent the Necessity or at least the great
Advantage of of a Commissary to be resident among us,
by reason of our great Distance from Boston, which at a
Medium is between a 150 & 200 Miles. On this Occasion,
I humbly beg leave to joyn my Voice with theirs to the
same purpose; for I do beleive, with Submission to your
Lordship, that it would be a very considerable means for
the promoting the Interest of Religion & Order among us;
especially considering how much the Church has increased
here within these few years.--When I came here there
were not a 100 Adult persons of the Church in this whole
Colony; whereas now there are considerably more than
2000, & at least 5 or 6000 young & old: & since the progress of this strange Spirit of Enthusiasm, it seems daily
very much increasing.
    My Brethren have indeed done me the Honour to men-
tion my Name to your Lordship.--As to this, I must beg
leave to assure your Lordship, that it is meerly from their
own motion, & not in the least owing to any influence of
mine that they have so done: & that, if your Lordship shall
think fit at all to appoint a Commissary in this Colony, I
shall be very well satisfied to submit to any other person
whom your Lordship shall think proper to appoint to preside over us.
    I am heartily greived for the great Affliction with
which it has pleased God to exercise your Lordship of late
in the Loss of your Lady & Son, which the News-writers
give us an Account of: And I humbly presume on this Occasion to express my most affectionate Condoleance; & do
earnestly pray God to support your Lordship under these
heavy afflictions, & to preserve your most Valuable Life
& Health, that you may have Opportunity to be yet further
serviceable to his Church & the Interest of true Religion,
not only at home, but also in these remote plantations.--
This is the hearty prayer of,
    May it please your Lordship, / your Lordships most
dutiful / & most obedient Son & / humble Servant
                   Samuel Johnson

[1742, Sept. 29, North Groton]
             N: Groton. 29 Sep.ʳ 1742.
Revᵈ S.ʳ
    After having acquainted yᵉ Venerable Society &c. of
my having drawn for my Salary, bearing date with this
Letter: I begg leave in my own, and in behalf, and at the
Desire of my Parishioners: to return our most gratefull
thanks to yᵉ Honᵇˡᵉ Society. for yᵉ Liberal & kind present
of usefull Books; which not long Since came to hand: and
according to my best Discretion have been distributed.
And as there never was more need of Good Books in this
part of the Government than now, I would hope yᵗ a Blessing from Almighty God may attend yᵉ use of them; to the
abating yᵗ Bewitching Enthusiasm, which has prevaild
more abundantly in this; and the Neighbouring Towns: Instances of the Ridiculousness & madness of which it would
be as Endless as needless for me to mention. Many of
these wild visionaries have come publickly to oppose me
in my Ministrations, 2 of yʳ Teachers: I have heard nothing of their boasting Since. At Midsumer I went back in
the Country about 60 miles: preach'd at Canterbury to a
considerable congregation--On Wednesday preachd to a
numerous Assembly in Brimfeild. a Congregation of People was conven'd yᵉ Same day to hear 4 New Light teachers famous in yᵗ way. When divine Service began with us,
the people Left yᵐ & came to Chh, their 4 teachers came
also: I preachd from Eph VI. 10, 11. they seemd very
uneasy, but made no Objections untill I was gone, having
promisd to preach the next day at Stafford 10 miles distant. Imediatly they began to hold forth in the Same House
(a Baptist meeting House wᶜ yᵗ Day we had yᵉ use of) but
(which was admir'd at) they could do nothing in yʳ way;
and instead of holding meeting as in yʳ usual custom until
9 or 10 of yᵉ Clock, sometimes the whole of the Night,
they broke up in great Confusion in less than 1/2 an Hour;
they came to Stafford, and instead of preaching 3 Sermons
there as they had promis'd, they preachd but 1 short one,
and left yᵉ Town. the Next day I preachd at Ashford about
8 miles distant. In yᵗ week I rode about 120 Miles preachd
4 Sermons. And Since my Last have preachd 2 Sermons
upon every Sunday, and sometimes on tuesdays, Wednes-
days, & thursdays, in the same week, and tho I am the
meanest of those imploy'd by the Venerable Society &c
yet I would hope my Labours may be usefull in these dark
corners of yᵉ Earth.
    I really beleive had it not been for The Chh of Engᵈ
wᶜ Methodism seems designd to destroy in this Land; yᵉ
people would almost universally have fallen under the Delusion. The Chh is remarkably preservd from the Infatu-
ation to the Astonishment of its Adversaries. And may
God in his own time make it (by blessing the pious and
Charitable designs of all yᵗ are employd for her good &
especially those of the Venerable Society &c.) the praise
and glory of yᵉ whole Earth thus prays
    Revᵈ S.ʳ Your's & yᵉ Society's / Most Obedient &
Oblidgd / Freind & Serv.ᵗ
              Ebenʳ Punderson

[Addressed:] To The Revᵈ D.ʳ Bearcroft Secretary &c /
at the Charterhouse / London
[Endorsed:] Read 11ᵗʰ April 1743--

[1743, Mar. 29, North Groton]

N: Groton 29 March 1743

Rev^d S^r

The winter having been favourable, I have since my last Visited; & preach'd at the places under my care, together with Canterbury no less than 23 Sermons, (besides constantly upon Sundays) to considerable Congregations. And as the Remarkable Enthusiasm which has Rag'd in these Towns seems to Abate those people who have hapily preserved in ye Spirit of a Sound mind; entertain more favourable thoughts of ye Establishd Chh: And I hope in time may be prevaild upon to Embrace it.

I think it my Duty to Recommend to ye more Special Consideration of ye Venerable Society, the Case of Charles: Town & Westerly: as there appears a better Disposition amongst them, and a greater prospect in time, of A Considerable Chh there; than since I have been on ye Mission: 4 times have I preachd there since my last: 2 Sundays upon one of which I administer'd the Sacrament to 6 Communicants. the better to enable ye Honble Society to provide them a missionary I could willingly forego 10£ of ye Salary allow'd me, altho my Family & Charges are much encreasd.

Inclos'd I send a Notitia Parochialis, in w^c I would only observe that 3 of the Adults were Negro men, and were Admited to ye Communion, and behave with Remarkable Sobriety Dutifulness & Devotion in the worship of God--

I have drawn a Quarter bill for my Salary At Christmas, in favour of Mr Mathew Stewart of New: London. and for the last Quarter bearing Date with this Letter. in Favour of Dr Joshua Babcock I Add no more but my Earnest prayer to Almighty God that he would hasten the time when our Nation may be united in glorifying God with one mind and one mouth; for ye Effecting of which that he would always continue to Bless & Prosper ye Pious and Charitable Endeavours of ye Venerable Society and all who conspire with them to advance the Unity & peace of Christs Chh.

I am with great Respect Rev^d S^r / Your's & the Societys Freind & Servt

Eben^r Punderson

Notitia Parochialis   29 Decr 1743 [1742].

I	Number of Inhabitants	15 or 1600 Families
II	N^o of Baptizd	Upwards of 2/3^{ds}
III	N^o of Actual Commu^{ts} of ye Church of Eng^d	86
IV.	N^o of those who profess themselves of ye Chh.	70 families
V	N^o of Dissen' of all Sorts &c	As in my former Acc^{ts}
VI	N^o of Heathens &c	About 200. Infidels none
VIII	N^o of Converts &c	4 or 5 persons

[1743, May 12]

To the Honble the Governour and General Court assembled in Hartford this 12 May 1743

The Memorial of Sundry persons in Symsbury and places adjacent Humbly Sheweth

That your memorialists have for above three years past Seen as we apprehend abundant reason to Conform to the Church of England as it is established in our mother Church and have accordingly united and purchased a Gleabe for a parsonage and also erected a frame for a Church and are carrying it on toward finishing and have put our Selves under the Conduct and care of the Clergy of the Church [of] England who have Several of them agreed to perform divine Service amongst us once a Month for eight months in the Year and particularly we have put our Selves under the Pastoral care of the Reverend Mr Theophilus Morris who is appointed by the Society for propagating of the Gospel to be an itinerant missionary to Officiate to the members of the Church of England dispersed in Various parts of this Colony who accordingly vissits us as often as his other obligations will admit of and have at Sundry times Severall of the Clergy of the Church of England in this Colony who in care of us are So good to come amongst us and preach and with the advice of Mr Morris and other of the Clergy of our Church for Some time past and to come have hired Mr Ebenezer Thompson as our Catechist who is making preparation to go over to England for Holy orders to Officiate in the Ministry and are in hopes of his return again to us as our Minister and during his absence the neighbouring Clergy belonging to the Church has Severally promis'd to Supply us as Pastors by turns til he return in Consequence of which most of us have not at all or but Seldom attended on any other way of publick worship for nigh three Years past and have with a View at our being Setled in the way of the Church of England been preparing and made Such Progress as before recited by your memorialists which by the Charitable Benefactions of Several well disposed Christians toward the Church have little reasons to fear the finishing of it in a Short time So as to perform divine Service therein

Notwithstanding all which our Neighbours and Brethren of the desenters have insisted on our paying rates not only to the Support of the ministers of the parishes whereunto we formerly did belong but also towards the building of their meeting houses and Sundry of us have been confined in the County Goal for our rates and the rest are threatned and daily expect the Same unless reliev'd by this Honble Assembly.

In all which Considerations we apply our Selves to your honor^r and this Legislature Earnestly intreating that we may be exempted from paying rates for these two years last past or for Such time past as to your Hon^{rs} may appear reasonabl & allso for the future and that wee may enjoy the priviledges of the Said Church and the Benefitt of our Estates for the Support of the Same and in hopes of your hon^{rs} Countenance and indulgence your memorialists as in Duty bound Shall ever pray

	Robt Brough	Church
	William Case	Wardens
Cal^v Sydenvelt	James [ ]	
Daniel Murphey	Sylas x [his mark] Jackson	
John Murphey	Phillip Harris	
Danel Tuler	John Rose	
James Tuller	Richard Lilley	
Wiliam Robert	James Crozier	
John Phelps	Abraham Piney	
Ramsay Garston	Josiah Lumas	
Joseph alderman	Gillet Addams	

William Enos	John Fullar
Samuel Enos	Samuel Beman
Andrew Moor	Thomas Bacon
Sandars Moor	Joshua holcomb
Richard Robertts J^r	Joseph Alderman
Eliabeth pinny	Richard Robertts Senr
Reid Cook II	John Enos
Joseph adams	Tim^o Addams
Nathanel Braken	Jo: Christian Muller
Willm Enos	Thomas Stephens
Asa Phelps	Ephraim adams
Rane Coset	Jon Higley

In the upper House

The Question was put whether The Things prayed for in this Memorial should be granted

Resolved in the Negative

Test George Wyllys Secret^{ry}

Concurred in ye Lower House

Test Jno Fowler Clerk

[1743, Sept. 29, North Groton]

North Groton 29 Septr 1743

Rev^d S^r

The extraordinary Spirit of Enthusiasm that has had such a marvelous Spread in this land; and especially prevaild in this and the neighbouring Towns, has so unsetled people in Gen^{ll} from all Sober and Steady principles; and those in particul^r who have been under the immediate influence of it; as makes me tremble to think of the consequences that will probably follow it, and w^c do already in some measure appear (viz) great prophaneness and disregard of all the instituted means of Religion: for when persons who have been under such Strong sensible Affections & Impressions discover y^t they are but Dreams, they very naturally conclude there is nothing real and substantial in Religion at all.

Altho I have been constant in the Labours of my Mission since my last, preachd twice every Sunday, and once or twice almost every week; yet ye visible success has not been equal to what it us'd to be, under which I am comforted with this consideration that it must be a great work to preserve such a Chh, & Congregation (so lately raisd from nothing, so perpetually exposd to Difficulties, and temptations, and so utterly unable to Strengthen, & support each other being Scatterd far and wide) from being crumbled into nothing again.

Notwithstanding I have trouble more than sufficient in the discharge of the duties of my own Mission, and in the Care of those comited to my Charge: yet I would beg leave to say this in favour of New London Chh, the people of w^c I am well acquainted, that in my oppinion they are in gen^{ll} a generous worthy, & deserving people; who have a very gratefull Sense of the vener$\underline{ble}$ Societys goodness to them, and care in providing a Missionary for them. And as for their zeal in opposing the Revd Mr Morris of w^c I presume the Society have been acquainted, I think I can safely say this in their favour y^t it was not from any prejudice conceivd against his person, or Abilities for the Discharge of ye Ministerial Office; of w^c I have heard many of them speak well before they knew he was appointed for their Missionary; but purely from the Reports of his prophaness

& Imorality the truth or falshood of w^c reports I suppose will before long be made to appear before our Revd Commissary. in the mean time I would beg leave to Entreat that venerable Society to put the most candid Construction upon every branch of their Conduct that may be rendred blameable before y^t Honourable board. and continue their favours to y^t Society which so much need the same. I add only y^t I ha[ve] drawn for a quarters Salary in favour of Math^w Stewart Esqr and shall proba[bly] also at Christmas next.

I am with great Respect / Revd Sr Your's & ye Societys / Freind & Servt

Eben^r Punderson

[1744, Apr. 9, North Groton]

N: Groton. 9 April. 1744

Rev^d S^r

Altho' my Labours have been for the half year past exceedingly Abundant yet the visible Success has been but small as will appear by ye inclosd Notitia parochialis–– Since Brother Seaburys removal I have preachd various times in the Chh at New London and Administer'd the Holy Sacraments----The people of this Country have conceiv'd a very ill oppinion of ye Removal of ye Clergy in General; and Brother Seaburys in particular hapning at a most unfavourable time has been of great disservice to ye growth & Interest of our Chh–– As also the Lamentable Consequences of New Light w^c leaves people as I always feard in a very great disregard of all Instituted Religion, as well as of ye Eternal obligations they lye under to the practice of truth & Virtue.

The Congregations where I officiate are considerably larger at present than they have been sometime past, w^c encourages my hopes, that when the empty dreams of Enthusiasm have more Subsided, and given place to reason & Sober Reflection we shall have an Encreas of our Chh in some measure Answerable to my Daily prayers & Endeavours, and y^t the Sacred institutions of our Blessed Lord will be in greater Esteem and veneration.

As I am at present the only Missionary in this half of ye Government and part of Rhode Island I would earnestly recommend it [to the venerable Board, as soon as possible, to supply the vacancy at New-London, and, if possible, to erect a mission at Stonington and Charlestown, where the harvest would, undoubtedly, be very plenteous, were there a resident labourer of a virtuous character. I preached at Charlestown last Sunday to a considerable congregation.

I am, Reverend Sir, yours, / And the Society's real friend and servant,

Eben^r Punderson.]*

―――

*Supplied from Doc. Hist., I, 207.

[1744, Apr. 22, Waterbury]

To the Honourable General Assembly of the Colony of Connecticut to be held at New haven October eleventh day 1744

The Memorial of the Subscribers being Professors of the Church of England & inhabitants of the Town of Waterbury in New Haven County by their Agent Doc.

Benj. Worner of S^d Waterbury Humbly Sheweth

That whereas your Honours Memoriallists being Professors of the Church of England, and bound in Deuty to carry on the Worship of God amongst us from which there Arise Considerable Charges that are Necessary in Order thereunto, As Building A Church and Keeping it in Repair with many Other things of the Like Importance. Which Charges (as we Your Humble Memoriallists think) Could be Defrayed More Conveniently by a Tax upon Each person According to their List, As Such Charges are in the Parrishes Established by the Laws of this Colony--
And there being no Law of this Colony Enabling us to Lay and Gather Such Taxes, Humbly pray that your Honours in your Great goodness would be pleased to Grant us Parrish Previleges in Every perticular (the School only Excepted) As the Parrishes have which are Established According to the Constitution of this Government,
And Your Memoriallists As in Deuty bound Shall Ever pray
     Waterbury Apriel 22^d 1744

	james Browne ^{ju}
Jonathan Scott	Joseph Browne
John Barns	Daniel How
Gershom Scott	John Brown
Gamaliel Ferrie	Thomas barns
robert johnson	Moses browne
Thomas Welton ju	Dan^{ll} Porter
Timothy Porter	Benjamin Worner
Nathan hubburd	John Judd
Beniamin prichard	Obadiah Worner
Thomas Wellton	Jonatha prindle
Nathan prindel	J S^m Selkrig
Ebenezer Judd	Nathaniel Merrick
Doc. Ephraim Worner	Richad Wellton
Stephen Welton	Joseph Judd
Zebulon Scott	Richard Wellton ^{Jun}
Eliakim Welton	Edmun Scott ^{ju}
John Alcock	Ebenez: Worner
Joseph Bronson	George Nickols
james Browne	Josiah Worner

New Haven ss Genl Assembly Oct^{br} 1744
In the upper House
     The Prayer of this Memorial, Negative
            Test George Wyllys Secret^{ry}
In ye Lower House
     The Question was put Whether they will Grant ye prayer of ye Memorialists
         Answered in ye Negative
            Test John Fowler Clerk

[1744, Sept. 14, New Haven]

            New Haven Sepr 14 1744
Rev^d sir

In my last I give an account of my suspending Sam^{ll} Plumb of Darby and some of the Reasons, with my grievances and the uncivilized Treatment received since Decem^r last; but as I perceive that many vile Plots have been laid to ruine me, and invalidate his suspension; I therefore beg leave to give you a fuller account of my Reasons for forbidding his partakeing of the holy Eucharist. He reported as I can Prove that I keep misses at Boston and at your house and that bad Stories always Come after me where

ever I went. That I offered violence to a young woman in Darby, and that her Father Delivered her out of my hands; and tho' after a litle time none would Confess the Story; yet he not withstanding went about, reporting that he firmly beleived that it was true, asserting that her father was against me for that reason. Reporting also y^t I was rude and immodest with Mrs Beach in New Haven, and tho' she told many it was false and give under her hand all such reports were groundless, thereby certifieing & declareing they were so, yet he still went about insinuating they were true hinting at the same time that I had been guilty of immoralities in Pensilvania directing to one Finlay a new light for my character, viliefying me upon that account: chargeing me often with a lie for saying I heard that he had drawen up Articles against me, tho' he was Convinced it was so, and after I had given him Authors for my information that owned it: Frequently useing me in a rude uncivilized manner, and often in my Lodgings [as]serting he could not wrong me or say too bad of me; ofteen telling lies with a vein to deceive me & others reporting that I took sermons out of the whole Duty of Man; and by many vile arts unworthy of your notice endeavouring to scandalize me, asserting he would never be at Peace while I was in Darby, that he would clear the town of Irish Jeans [hu]nting all ye Country round for Scandal, and reporting wherever he [we]nt that he did not like my life and Conversation; these are the reasons [for] wch I suspended him; and the most of them I mentioned at the time, [but I] would have offered them all had not his rudeness prevented me: [Hear] at the time he assaulted my person dregging me through his house, tear[i]ng my Cloathing, and pushing me out with ye utmost violence, [he] said be [g]one you dog you are but a Feaze at the best; kicking and Spiting upon the man that was with me as I informed you in my last Letter.

And ever since he has assaulted my character belieing, Slandering, Revileing and Backbiteing me in an Inhuman manner: and tho' he has attempted to prove these things, or to fix some thing upon my charecter, in hopes to help himself, as is evident from the number of witness in the sommons I sent you before this; yet he now denies the charges, and in order to palliate and abate his villanie, sommons two witnesses the one a young apprentice boy of no Charecter, the other a man of the vilest charecter, whose oath severals endeavoured to prevent, to whom I believe no other Justice would ad[m]inister an oath; but what farther discovers the villany they were in an [oth]er Room, and did neither hear all the accusations, nor swear right to [an]y of those they pretended to have heard: as I can prove by a man of an [un]exceptionable charecter, that was all that time in the Room, and co[uld not] but hear what passed between us: but him he would not som[mon] Because he knew he could swear the truth. however the night I suspended him I wrote the Questions I proposed to him, and Mr Chatfield y^t had all the time been present signed the Paper before Evidence, and will at any time swear that I not only proposed such questions to Plumb, but also y^t Plumb told him all of y^m

They have consulted the most of the justices round about, and could not find one y^t would Countenance y^r villanies but Sam^{ll} Riggs brother by the law [went] to ye Independent Teacher in Darby, who I find will do any thing to weaken my Interest, in order to support his brother, as

is plain from his last writ [which] was served on me about sunset on Saturday wherein he has made suspension a charge, as also his refuseing to write my interrogations, and ye witnesses answers to them, wch would plainly have shewed y^t they did swear they knew not what.

Besides that their holding this Court was a vile plote to clear himself of my charges against him, and wch he attemped to prove against me at the first appears from my offering to him and before ye Court i[n] writing my reasons for suspending him, wch Reasons he would not accept, as also from my offering to Join in a letter with him and his party, for you to Come & judge between us, wch they refused saying you had no more Power than any other minister resolveing to send y^r complaint to ye Society asserting the Clergy advised them that method to send y^r complaint to ye Society & to hold such Courts, pleading the Case of Mr Morris [in] their Favour, and y^t you accepted of And approved of it; boasting how we [expelled] him &c. I have heard of his geting a Paper signed by some (to this purpose that they do not know y^t he is openly Scandalous) as I never saw it, I presume [to give] nothing further at present about it, than y^t the su[b]scribers Conf[ess they] know he deserves to be suspended; and y^t many of y^m signed it beli[ev]ing it could be no service to him, y^t most of y^m y^t signed it are no[t offended] with me for suspending him, and y^t one of the church warde[ns] and several others have not signed it, and are offended with him [very] much, Particularly the Girls Father above described, but [I doubt] not but he will affixe their names to it, for he has gote dissenters [to] seign it, and in a word no regard is to be paid to it; or what they say [because] he has been suspended twice before and is so guilty of st[urdy] lieing, so rude and unchristian in his behaviour, and [so] contentious with all my Predecessors, and ye dissenting Fear [him and] know it is impossible to live peacably with him, (espe[cially] a Forreigner with whom he will certainly at the first proclaim war [as I can] prove he did with me before ever he saw me) and if his suspensio[n be by] you Confirmed it will be impossible for me to live among y^m and [yet I am] satisfied y^t he deserves it, nay y^t it would be for ye good and Inte[rests] of ye Church if a sentence of excommunication was passed upon him; and I must assure you y^t if he does not make an open acknowledgem[ent] & satisfaction for his misconduct since he was suspended y^t I would suspend hi[s backers] haveing in my last mentioned many of their irregularities; and my [constant] Readiness to assist them in geting a Glebe, and how often they have refused my Advice, designedly Concealing ye societys Letter, declar[ing] that they have no business to Consult me, without applying to m[y] Church Wardens since Easter for a regular vestry, appointing [one] of y^r own; and at y^m abuseing me and any y^t appear for me [and act]ing without me, and contrary to me, to make out a poor Gle[be of (?)] acres only and not all good, wch belongs to a man y^t pr[omises to] assist in geting a Glebe unless it be Confined to his...
[James Lyon, cleric of Derby, Conn., to Roger Price, commissary in Boston.]

[1744, Oct. 12, Groton]

          Groton. 12. Oct 1744
Rev^d S^r

    the extraordinary and wonderfull appearances, that

have for the three years past, attended the marvelous Spirit of Enthusiasm w^c God in Righteous judgment; has been pleasd to let loose in our Nation & this land especially, have abundantly disappear'd. Yet the same root of Roteness continues Still, and disposes them to uncharitableness & Rancour.

I Hope in God that by these Delusions, which are now so manifest: that many serious persons may be brought to the knowledge and obedience of the truth, and the Communion of our most excellent Chh; which is the only unmoveable one in this Land.

Since my last of Ap^l we have had a considerable encrease, the Congregation in the Chh in Groton being generally near 200. and very considerable in all the places under my Charge: And as I administer the Eucharist the first sunday in every month, excepting 2, in my own Chh: we have had the Summer past between 40 & 70 Communicants each Sunday. the 1st Sunday in Sepr we had Sixty. the first of this Instant 56. five Sober devout persons have been added to our Communion and 24 Children have been Christned; and I flatter my self y^t I shall yet more & more see the happy fruits of my Labour and patience.

If the venerable Society are in circumstances to furnish me with a Doz, of the English man directed in the Choice of his Religion; with some small tracts of Devotional, and practical Religion, I am sure they would be most gratefully receivd, and in all probability be of great Service at this season especially.

We are now building a School House near the Chh and if it was in the power I could not but Hope y^t that Venerable board will assist us in maintaining the Master; Mr Sam^ll Hutchison a Native of London; and a Communicant in our Chh. if it were but with 5£ Per Annum: it would add to our great obligations to y^t venerable Society, and I presume to the Glory of God, w^c I earnestly pray G^d the Society may long be continued & enabled to promote, who am / with ye greatest Regard Rev^d S^r / Your & ye Societys / Freind & Servt

          Ebenezer Punderson
P.S. I have drawn for this Quarter in Fav^r of Mathew Stewart Esqr

	Notitia parochialis.	Oct 12. 1744.
I	Number of Inhabitants.	1600 Families
II	N^o of Baptiz'd	About 3/4.
III	N^o of Adult persons Baptizd this 1/2 Year.	2. only
IV	N^o of Actual Communicants &c.	85.
V	N^o of those who profess themselves of y^t Chh	near 300 persons.
VI.	N^o of Dissenters of all Sorts, &c.	1/2 Indep^ts. Bap: Quak. Method. Rogerenes. &c.
VII	N^o Heathens--2 or 3 Hundred Infidels profesedly none.	
VIII	N^o of Converts &c.	Some few.

[1745, Apr. 10, North Groton]

       N: Groton. 10. Ap^r 1745
Rev^d S^r

    Altho I have a very poor State of health probably in-

troduc'd and much agravated by ye extraordinary fatiegues w^c the Care of my Mission necessarily exposes me to; As also the frequent Itinerations that I take beyond the bounds imediatly Assign'd me: Yet thro Divine Goodness I am able to attend constantly upon the Dutyes of my Mission. I was much rejoic'd by receiving a Letter from Mr Seth Payne who has been many years a Dissenting Teacher in Stafford about 45. miles to the Northward of Groton in whose meeting House I have read prayers and preach'd twice, and 4. or 5. times in y^t Town. He informs me not only of his own Conformity and that of a considerable number of people; but also y^t he has great Hopes of a large Harvest; I am not certain y^t he has any Design to enter into Holy Orders. About ye midle of March I visited Hebron, where at present Mr Cole attends, and is a person of a good Character, and highly acceptable to y^t People; and I beg leave to give it as my oppinion that there is no place in N: England. where a Mission is more wanted; the Adjacent Country being plentifully inhabited and no Missionary within 30 miles. I preachd 5 Sermons in four Days and Administred the Sacrament to about 40 Communicants.

Since the Venerable Society have signifid their pleasure to ye Congregation in N: London, y^t in order to have their Mission renewd they must procure a House for their Missionary I shall urge them to a Spedy accomplishment of it. Since B^r Morris's Resignation I have constantly every 5. or 6. weeks attended them by ye Revd Comissarys advice and Administred the Sacrament.

I Advise the Ven^ble Society that I have drawn a sett of Bills bearing Date with this letter in favour of Mr Sam^ll Mason. and shall in June next in favour of Math^w Stewart Esqr also for 2£10. to ye Honble Society for promoting Xtian Knowledge.

Since my last of Octr Some in our Communion have dy'd, others remov'd, and some have been admitted: and many have embrac'd our most excellent Chh who I hope will be ornaments unto it. I add only y^t I am
Revd Sr Your's & ye Societys / Real Freind & Servt
Eben^r Punderson

[1745, Oct. 8, Groton]
                                                    Groton 8 Octr 1745
Rev^d S^r
By these I would inform ye Venerable Society, that I have drawn in favour of Math^w Stewart Esqr; for 15£: the remaining 50^s I have made a present to ye Society for promoting Xtian Knowledge, as a testimony of ye gratefull Sense I have of the Honour, & Advantage they have conferd upon me, in Electing me a Corresponding Member. Also y^t I Shall draw at Christmas in Mr Stewarts favour, excepting 5£ for Mr Thom^s Sandford.

Since my last I have been to Stafford, preach'd and Baptiz'd some Children; Mr Payne of whom I acquainted ye Society in my last, purposes by Divine permission (having obtained leave from the Society) to come Home next summer   he has only a Wife and 2 Children, and there is no missionary within near 50 miles and the Country pretty well Inhabited.

The third Sunday in Sepr I preach'd at N: London, desird the Congregation to meet upon the next day, w^c they did and Voated, to procure a House as soon as possible for their next Missionary: One of ye members of y^t Chh

has given a Convenient and valluable Spot of land for y^t purpose; they have generously subscribed to ye Building of s^d House, which I hope will be fitt to live in by ye begining of next Summer. I verilily think it a peice of Justice due to y^t Congregation in Gener^ll to Assure ye Society that according to their abilities they are a generous good sort of people, they continue firm & unshaken: And I beg leave in the most earnest manner to request the Society to supply y^t place with with a Pious & learned Minister as soon as may be. and also Charlstown and Westerly, the Congregation being much encreasd; and there is 40 Acres of good land procurd for a Glebe adjoyning to ye Chh- Copies of both w^c Deeds we shall soon transmit to ye Society.

I add only y^t if y^t Venerable Board are able and Disposd to send me some Books of Devotion, and religious instruction to be dispersd among ye poor & Ignorant; I should esteem it a great favour, and would have them put into the Packet that annually will be sent me from the Society for promoting Xtian Know^dg And y^t GOD Almighty will be pleasd long to preserve, prosper and bless those Illustrious Societys is the hearty and fervent prayer of
Revd Sr Your's & the Societyes
most Obed^t & Oblid^d Servt
Eben^r Punderson

[Addressed:] To The Revd Dr Bearcroft Sec^r / at ye Charter House / London
[Endorsed:] Read 12 May 1746

[1745, Oct. 10, Redding]
To the Honourable the Governour & Council with the Representatives, in General Court assembled, in New Haven Octo^r 10th 1745.

The humble Petition of the Members of the Church of England, in Reading-Parish:

Whereas the ministerial Charges in this Parish from the Beginning, have been So heavie, that this Honourable Assembly out of their Zeal & tender Concern for the public Worship of God, have charitably & piously exempted, those of the presbyterian Persuasion from paying their Taxes annually due to the Support of the Government of this Colony, for the Space of about 14, Years last past; all which Term, We your Petitioners have chearfully, tho with Difficulty paid our Dues to the Government; Yet by a Law of this Colony we are taxed in the Same Proportion to the Support of the Ministry with our Brethren of that Denomination; And besides having paid for Some Years a Land-Tax, for the Building for them a Meeting House; We did Some Years past begin to Build a Church for the Worship of God according to our Consciences; which to this Day we have not been able to finish; which makes the Burthen upon us much heavier than that which your Honours were pleas'd to lighten to our Neighbours. Your Honours will therefore excuse us, if now, after twice Seven Years distinguishing Hardships, we presume to Begg your Charity, & pray that you would make us Partakers of the Same Relief with our Fellow-Parishioners-- We are not Sensible, that the worshipping God according to the Establishment in Our Mother-Country, is a Transgression of any Law of this Colony; & we are conscious to ourselves that we have been peaceable Subjects of the

Government, seeking its Wealth; & have to the utmost of our Power Oppos'd the late Attempt to introduce Anarchy & Confusion in Religion: And therefore hope our religious Sentiments will not render Us unworthy of your charitable Notice. But tho' our Merits Should not, yet our Hardships may intitle us to Compassion----And tho' our Minister be in Part Supported by the Charity of the Society for Propagation of the Gospel, yet that we hope will be no Bar to your extending Charity to us; Seeing the presbyterian Minister in this Parish is likewise maintained in Part by the Interest of money arising from the Sale of Parsonage Lands; in which (as we conceive we had an equitable Right, but are entirely excluded----If your Honours Should be pleas'd to Grant our Petition, & let your Charity appear to be without Partiality, We believe it will be a Satisfaction to Many, as well as a Relief to, & an Obligation of Thankfulness upon----Your Honours Most Obedient & Humble Servants,

Joshua Hall	Peter Malary
Moses Knap	Oliver fairchild
Benjamin Sturgis	Zachary Squire
Nathan Lyon	Israel Rouland
John Mallory	Thomas Rouland
Enos Lee	Stephen Burwel
John Pigot	James Morgan
Daniel Lyon Juner	Obediah Plat
Daniel Adams j^r	Adam Clark
Gershom Morehouse	Eben^r Hall
Daniel Lion	Samuel Fairchild
John Sanford	Eb^{nr} Beardsly
Nehemiah Seeley	Stephan Morehouse
David Knap	William Hill
Jonathan Squire	Robert Seeley
daniel Croofoot	William Stephens
Jonathan Knap	

[1745, Nov. 20, London]
To the Revd Mr Punderson Itinerant Missionary in
    New England

London Charterhouse Novr 20th 1745.
S^r

Y^r Letter of Octo^r 12th 1744, hath reached the Society which are well pleas'd with the great Pains you take in y^r Laborious Mission, and as a Mark of it they have granted y^r Request in Favour of Mr Hutchinson to allow him £5, Per Ann: as their Schoolm^r & have order'd that it should commence from Mich: last, I must request you to be so good as to acq^t him with it, & to shew him from the Collection of Papers of the Society, a Copy of which you have, in what Manner he is to send over his Notitia Scholastica half Yearly & to draw for his Salary, the Society hath likewise order'd you twelve Copies of the Englishman instructed in the Choice of his Religion, and some other small Tracts, which I propose to send by Mr Dean who is to be the Bearer of this, & is appointed Itinerant Missionary in Connecticut in the Place of Mr Lyons, who is removed to Brookhaven, most heartily praying for Gods Blessing on y^r pious Labours.

I am P: B:

[1745, Nov. 20, London]
To the Revd Dr Johnson Missionary at Stratford in

Connecticut in N. England.

Ditto Date.
Rev^d S^r

This waits upon you by Mr Dean, whom the Society have appointed to Succeed Mr Lyons in the Mission of Derby, Waterbury &C^a he being removed for Peace Sake to Brookhaven, Y^r Letters of Feb: 12th Mar: 30th & Sep^t 2^d are now before me, Mr Lampson is I hope returned safe, the Society having granted his Request, but their meaning is, that none for the future should be sent over to them with Recommendations upon any Occasion, without Leave previously obtain'd from the Society, nor will they for the Future provide for any other; the Church at New London I have once more acquainted that when they shall have Settled on their Church a good convenient House for their Minister, & renew'd under their Hands their Subscriptions according to the best of their Abilities the Society will appoint them a new Missionary.

I have discoursed Mr Davenport about Mr Prince, and his Character of him with proper Testimonials will satisfy the Society both of his Morals & Orthodoxy, & if he will accept of the Mission to the Moskito Indians with a Salary of £50 Per Ann: together with a Subscription of 45 Spanish Pistoles wch the Clergy of Jamaica have already paid into the Commissary of Jamaica for the Use of such Missionary, the Society will further recommend him to the Governor of Ja[maica]....

[P: B:]

[1746, Mar. 10, Stamford]
To all Christian People to whom these Presents Shall come Greeting &^c Know ye that John Lloyd of Stamford in the County of Fairfield within his Majesties English Colony of Connecticut in New England for and in Consideration of the Sum of Five Hundred Pounds Currant Money of the Colony of Connecticut to Me in hand well and Truly paid before the Ensealing hereof by Nathanael Hubbard and Thomas Youngs both of Said Stamford and Sundry Other persons all professors of the Church of England as by Law Established who are all Inhabitants of the Towns of Stamford and Greenwich the Receipt whereof I do hereby Acknowledge and am therewith Fully Satisfied and Contented, have and do by these Presents Give Grant Bargain Alienate Convey and Confirm the Lands hereafter Mentioned Intending the Same with the Appurtenances for the first Gleebe Lands to Endow a Certain Parrish Church called Saint Johns in the Township of Said Stamford by them the Said John Lloyd Nathanael Hubbard and Thomas Youngs and with the Advice and Concurrence of the Rest of their Neighbours Concerned There allready Founded and Still Erecting for Divine Service According to the Usage of the Church of England Now know ye that the Said John Lloyd Nathanael Hubbard and Thomas Youngs with the Advice and Concurrence of the Rest of their Neighbours Concerned herein for the better Accomplishing the Endeavours Aforesaid in Great Reverence and Regard to the Church of England as Established by Law and her Excellent Doctrines--Service Unity and Order Preferable to any Other upon Earth for the Honour of God and the Surest peace and Comfort of themselves their Neighbours and Posterity have Founded the Parish Church Aforesaid for the Use Aforesaid and for the Endowment

thereof do by these presents Freely Give Grant Convey and Confirm to the Society for Propagating the Gospel in Foreign parts A Certain Tract or parcel of Land Situate and lying within the Bounds of Stamford So Called with A Mansion or Dwelling House And Barn thereon Standing, Said Land Contains by Estimation About Seven Acres be the Same More or Less and is Bounded as Followeth Viz.^t South by the High way East by the Land of Jonathan Ferris North by the Land of John Bates and West by the River with all the Rights and Appurtenances   To have and to Hold the Granted premisses with the Appurtenances to Said Society and to their Successors For Ever But in trust and for the Special Interest and purpose hereafter Mentioned: to Say as Soon as there shall be a Rector according to the order of the Church of England by Law Established Instituted and Inducted the premisses shall be and Inure to the Use of Such Rector Incumbent and his Successors as the Glebe Lands of The Said Church in Fee Simple For Ever and the Said John Lloyd Nathanael Hubbard and Thomas Youngs For them Selves and Heirs do Covenant to Warrant And Defend the Above Granted premisses to Said Society and to their Successors for the Use aforesaid Against all persons Laying Any Claim or Demand thereto or to any Part thereof in Witness whereof the Said John Lloyd for him Self &c and the Said Nathanael Hubbard and Thomas Youngs for them selves and the Persons Concerned have hereunto Set there hands and Seals in Stamford this Tenth Day of March in the Twentieth Year of his Majestes Reign and in the Year of Our Lord 1746/7

Signed Sealed and Delivered in Presence of us
    J. Wetmore Jr   John Lloyd
    Ebenez.^r Dibble   Nath^{el} Hubbard
                            Thomas Youngs

fairfield
    County   ss In Stamford on March ye 19th day Ad: 1746/7
There parsonally appeared John Lloyd Nath^{el} Hubbard & Thomas Youngs ye Signers & Sealers of ye above written Instrument & Acknowledged ye Same to be Their free act & deed before me--
            Jonth Hait Justice P [Justice of the Peace]

[1746, Apr. 4, Groton]
                            Groton 4.th Ap.^l 1746
Revd S.^r
    It is with a very sensible pleasure y.^t I can acquaint the Venerable Society with the Almost daily encreas of our Chh; and y.^t the oppinions of most sober, considerate persons grow more favourable towards it: particularly I am rejoyc'd upon Mr John Whiting's embracing the Chh, and resolution by Divine providence & the Society's leave to come over in the fall for Holy Orders; he is a person of an Excellent moral Character, good sense and of a mild Disposition. the people in N: London are very desirous (if they should not be suplyd before) that he may be appointed for them; the Conformists also in Stonington where he lives together with those of Charles Town and Westerly are fond of having him if the Society are able and willing to erect them into A Mission.
    The Harvest is truly great, and at present no Labourer in this 1/2 the Government but my self of the Episcopal Order; and with the most Sincere gratitude I bless GOD

that my Labours are not in Vain: I esteem it a Singular providence that in N: London ye Chh have lost none in their Long Vacancy; but wait with patience. A Deed of ye Land given by a worthy member of y.^t Chh w.^c I Suppose worth 300£ our money will be transmited with my letters, A frame of a House worth 100£ is already got, and they are daily forwarding.
    Capt Mumford in whom Mr Dean Embark'd is not yet arivd, we fear he is taken or founder'd by whom I had expectation of a Letter from the Venerable Society; whom I fervently pray GOD daily to enlarge and make a more extensive Blessing to Mankind in Genl and this Land in particular. I am with the greatest respect Revd S.^r
        Yours & y.^e Societys / Faithful Freind & Servt
                            Eben.^r Punderson
P.S. I beg leave to inform the Society y.^t I have drawn for 5£=12=6 in favour of y.^e Treas.^r of y.^e Society for promoting xtian Knowledge. y.^e remaining 11£.17=6 in favour of Mr Math^w Stewart. in whose favour I shall draw in June, next.

Notitia Parochialis &c	from Oct 1. 1746 To Ap.^l 4. 1747.
I. Number of Inhabitants	About 1500 Families in the 5 Towns (upwards of 3/4
II. N.^o of the Baptiz'd	
III N.^o of Adults Baptiz'd &c	3. 2 of w.^c upwards of 70 years old. 21 Infants.
IV N.^o of Actual Communicants &c	92. 5 Added since my last.
V N.^o of those who profess themselves &c	130 heads of families.
VI N.^o of Dissenters of all Sorts.	Independants. presbyterians Quakers of 2 or 3 Sorts. Baptists 2 Sorts. Methodists many Sorts.
VII N.^o of Heathens & Infidels.	the heathens have mostly embrac'd methodism.
VIII N.^o of Converts &c.	Some considerable number.

[Addressed:] To the Revd Doc.^r Bearcroft Sec.^r / to ye Society for propag &c / at ye Charter: House / London
[Endorsed:] Read 17 Novr 1746

[1746, Oct. 6, North Groton]
                            N Groton 6th Octr 1746
Revd S.^r,
    As I am the only Missionary ye Society at present have in ye eastern half of this Government, I cant think it my Duty in the most pressing manner, to Solicit the Society's farther Assistance to N: London, Charlestown, & Hebron; especially N: London; In Behalf of that People I can plead with great assurance of success; As they have complyd with the Terms on w.^c the Venerable Society Suspended their Assistance, having set up and cover'd a very good House w.^c in a few weeks may be made a Comfortable Habitation.
    With regard to Hebron which I visit about twice a year and administer ye Sacram.^{ts} I have this to observe that when I was there last w.^c was the last day of August, there were about 40 Communcants; and 6 Children Christned: the day following I preach'd them a Sermon after

which [they u]nanimously Subscrib'd 303£ 10 for ye purchace of 30 Acres of exceeding good [land], the Donor gave 30£ a Deed of w^ç I shall transmit with this letter, and begg leave earnestly recommend to y^t Venerable Board the Supply of a people so Stedfast & Zealous, and w^ç have not a Missionary within near 40 miles of them, and I presume there would be as large additions to them as to any Congregation in the Government if they were supplyd with a pious & faithfull Minister. the thursday following I preachd a Sermon in Litchfeild, about 80 miles from my House, where is a considerable number of Conformists, who performd their parts of the Divine Service with propriety & reverence; I furnishd them with some Books and trust their will be additions to them.

I must also beg leave to refresh the memories of y^t Venerable Board with the Melancholy State of Charlstown where there is great need of a Resident missionary the Deed of 40 Acres of good lang [sic] given to y^t Chh I hope has reachd the Society ere this having been sent with my letters of 4th of April, the State of ye Chh in Groton and ye Adjacent Towns remains much in the Same State, but I hope will soon encrease the Independent Teacher in this place having left his People and tis the General oppinion y^t they will not be able to settle another.

I have drawn for my Quarter's Salary and for ye 5£ w^ç was refusd Mr Sandford by reason of a Defect in the Bill; in favour of Mr Stewart: I hope ye Society will pardon my involuntary Slips for with ye utmost Sincerity I can Assure y^m y^t

I am / Rev^d S^r / Your's & ye Societyes / most faithfull Freind & Servt
[Eb]en^r Punderson

[Addressed:] For The Revd Dr Bearcroft Secretary &c / att ye Charterhouse / London
[Endorsed:] Read 11 May 1747.

[1747, Apr. 4, Litchfield]
Litchfield Apriel ye 4th A:D: 1747
Rev^d S^r
Although I am unknown to you yet I hope I may use this boldness viz: to ask you to use your interest with ye Honourable Society for ye Propagation of ye Gospel in foreign parts in my favour. I live in ye South-west corner of Litchfield at a place called ye birch Plain and there is four or five of my neighbours conformists to ye Church we live about Seven miles from ye Town where ye most of us Conformists Dwell what I have given towards ye Support of a missionary may appear by ye information of ye bearer what I would humbly request is this that Mr Samuel Cole if he returns with Holy Order to this Land that his Mission may be in these parts and that he may have Orders to officiate at ye Birch Plain how often I freely Submit to ye wisdom of ye Society--

Rev^d S^r I am your most obedient / and humble Ser^t
John Davies

Rev^d S^r We ye Subscribers inhabitants in Litchfield near to Mr Davis and in other places nearly adjoyning humbly Joyn with him in his Request

Who are Rev^d S^r your most Obliged and humble Servants

Nicolos Masters
Sam Squier
John Handrason
John Sqir
Thomas Bailes
John Handrason Junr
Sam^ll Masters
Thom^as Mathes
Neser Thomas
Willam Bartholomew Sener
Lem[u]el Bartholomew Juner

Thomas Durkee
Caleb Hurlbut
Joseph Hurlbut
Zadock Clark
Nathan Bosert
ye mark B of
Willam Bosart
James argot
Thos Turney
Cherey a Shechen Ingin desiers his [comeing?]

[Addressed:] To The Revd Dr Bearcroft / Secretary to the Society / for Propagation of the Gospel &c / At the Charter House / London
[Endorsed:] Laid before the Committee Septr 14th 1747.

P:S: I: John Davis hereby promise to improve Four Acres at least upon that part of ye Glebe which I gave yearly for ye use of ye Missionary

As Witness my hand [signed] John Davies

[1747, Apr. 4, Litchfield]
Know all Men by these Presents that I Daniel Landon of Litchfield in the County of Hartford and Colony of Connecticutt in New-England in America for and in consideration of the Love and Affection which I have and bear for and towards the People of the Church of England in said Litchfield and for securing and settling the Service & Worship of God amongst us according to the Usage of our most excellent Church within said Litchfield at all Times for ever hereafter; and also for and in consideration of the Sum of one hundred and fifty Pounds Money of the old tenor to me in hand actually paid by Capt. Jacob Griswold and Joseph Kilborn both of said Litchfield in the County and Colony aforesaid Do Give Grant Bargain Sell Enfeoff and Convey unto the said Jacob Griswold and Joseph Kilborn and their Heirs and Assigns for ever to the Use of the Society for the Propogation of the Gospel in foreign Parts and their Successors for ever (which Society were incorporate by Letters Pattent under the Great Seal of England) a certain Tract of Land in Litchfield aforesaid Westward of the Great Pond near a Mountain called little Mount Tom containing by Estimation fifty Acres be it more or less and bounds as followeth the South West Corner being a Heap of Stones by a Highway thence running East one hundred forty seven Rods and an half by John Davies's Land to a Heap of Stones thence North fifty six Rods by a Highway to a Heap of Stones thence West by my own Land one hundred twenty & seven Rods to a Heap of Stones thence South West by a Highway twenty & three Rods thence South thirty & nine Rods by a Highway to the first mentioned Boundary and the said fifty Acres with all the Erections standing on said Premisses with Woods under Woods Meadows and all Water Courses with every other Appurtenance or Privilege of any Sort whatsoever appertaining and the Reversion and Reversions Remainder and Remainders Issues and Profits of all and singular Premisses To Have and to Hold all with every Privilege Commodity & Appurtenance unto the said Jacob Griswold and Joseph Kilborn their Heirs and Assigns for evermore to the Use Benefit and Behoof of the Society for the Propo-

gation of the Gospel in foreign Parts and their Successors for evermore to be by the said Society for ever hereafter applied and appropriated for the Benefit for the Episcopal Minister for the Time being of the Episcopal Church in said Litchfield in said County of Hartford and his Successors for ever and to and for no other Use Intent or Purpose whatsoever. And I the s^d Daniel Landon do hereby for myself my Heirs Executors and Administrators and Successors Covenant to and with the said Jacob Griswold and Joseph Kilborn their Heirs Assigns and also to and with the Society for the Propogation of the Gospel in foreign Parts and their Successors for ever that I am at this present Time and by Right of Indefeasible Inheritance the true lawful and absolute Owner and Proprietor of the said Premises that the same are now free and clear of all manner of Incumbrances whatsoever. And I my Heirs Executors and Administrators now do and for ever shall Warrant and Defend all singular the said Premises with their Appurtenances unto and to the Use of them aforesaid against all Claims and Demands whatsoever. In Witness whereof I have hereunto set my Hand and Seal this fourth Day of April One Thousand seven hundred forty and seven and in the twentieth Year of the Reign of our Sovereign Lord George the Second of Great Brittain &c King

Memorandum. The Sum of One hundred and fifty Pounds being the Consideration Money mentioned in the before written Deed was in our Presence paid by the before named Jacob Griswold unto the before named Daniel Landon after which the said Daniel Landon did in our Presence Sign Seal & Deliver the said before written Instrument of Conveyance as his Act and Deed unto the said Jacob Griswold for and in his own Name and in the Name of the said Joseph Kilborn to the Use of the Society for the Propogation of the Gospel in foreign Parts for the Use and . Intent therein mentioned & immediately thereafter the said Daniel Landon did in Person in our Presence deliver unto the said Jacob Griswold and Joseph Kilborn in Person and put them into full quiet and peaceable Possession and Seisin of the said Tract of Land in the said Deed comprised and the said Jacob Griswold and Joseph Kilborn did enter into and take full quiet and peaceable Possession and Seisin of the same for the Use of the said Society in our Presence all done this fourth Day of April one thousand seven hundred forty and seven

                                        Daniel Landon and Seal

As Witness our Hands
    Abraham Kilborn   William Emens Jn^r
    Isaac Russell   Abiel Smith

Litchfield ss. Hartford County April 4 1747.
    Daniel Landon Ensealer to the within written Instrument acknowleged the same to be his free Act & Deed before me
                            Eben. Marsh Jus^t of Peace
Dated Ap^r 4 1747.

A true Record per Isaac Baldwin Regist^r

A true Copy of Record Exam^{e}d
per Isaac Baldwin Town Clerk

[1747, Apr. 4, Litchfield]

To all People to whom these Presents shall come Greeting Know Ye that I John Davies of Litchfield in the County of Hartford in the Colony of Connecticutt in New England for and in consideration of the Love and Affection I have and bear for and towards the People of the Church of England in the said Town of Litchfield and securing and settling the Service and Worship of God among us according to the Usage of our most Excellent Church within said Litchfield at all Times for ever hereafter and also for the Love and good Will I have for Mr Samuel Cole of Litchfield aforesaid Do therefore Demise Lease and to Farm Lett to the said Samuel Cole his Heirs and Assigns for and during the full Term nine hundred ninety and eight Years to the Use of the Society for the Propogation of the Gospel and their Successors for and during the full Term aforesaid, (which Society were Incorporate by Letters Pattent under the Great Seal of England) Fifty Acres of Land in said Litchfield being part of the Land laid out on the Parsonage Right in said Litchfield; Leased to me by Danl Landon of said Litchfield which Land is bounded North by s^d Landon's Land West by Highway in part and part by Undivided Land South by Moses Staddor's Land in part and part by Josiah Griswold's Land East by Highway. And also about Two Acres of Land laid out to me the said Davies adjoining to the said fifty Acres running from said Fifty Acres West over a Run of Water to a Rock with Stones laid thereon and is bounded East by s^d Fifty Acres in part & partly by Land laid out to John Bird and Westerly by an Highway and South by my own Land. To Have and to Hold said Demised and Leased Premises with all the Privileges & Appurtenances thereunto belonging to him the s^d Saml Cole his Heirs and Assigns for and during the full Term afores^d for the Use Benefit and Dehoof of the said Society for Propogating the Gospel and their Successors to be by the said Society applied and appropriated for the Benefit of the Episcopal Minister for the Time being of the Episcopal Church in Birch Plain in Said Litchfield and to his Successors for and during the full Term afores^d and to and for no other Use Intent or Purpose whatsoever. And I the said John Davies for my self and Heirs Executors and Administrators do Covenant and Promise to and with the s^d Saml Cole his Heirs and Assigns that the s^d Saml Cole shall and may from Time to Time and at all Times for and during the full Term afores^d for the Use and Benefit of the Society afores^d lawfully peaceably and quietly Have Hold Use, Improve, Occupy, Possess, & Enjoy the Premises He or his Heirs yielding and paying therefor one Pepper Corn Annually, at or upon the Feast of St Michael the Arch Angle, if lawfully demanded, In Witness whereof I have hereunto set my Hand and Seal this fourth Day of April in the 20th Year of his Majesty's Reign George the Second of Great Brittain &c. King Anno Domini 1747.

                                        John Davies and Seal

Signed Sealed & Delivered in Presence of
    David Landon   Is^c Baldwin

Litchfield ss Hartford County April 4th 1747.
    John Davies Ensealer to the above written Instrument

acknowledged the same to be his free Act & Deed before me

　　　　　　　　　　　Eben. Marsh Just. of Peace

Dated April 4th 1747.

A true Record per Isaac Baldwin Register

A true Copy of Record / Teste Isaac Baldwin Town Clerk
Litchfield County ss. Litchfield / 5th of March 1770.

[1747, Apr. 7, North Groton]

　　　　　　　　　　　N: Groton 7 Apl. 1747.

Revd Sr

　　the Bearer of these lines Mr. Cole has sustaind a good
Character ever Since I knew him, and if the Venerable Society are in circumstances to Erect a Mission at Hebron
where he has read prayers and sermons for Some time
past, or Charlestown, he might be greatly serviceable
in promoting the Knowledge, & practice, of ye Evelast-
ing Gospel of our Assended Lord: and he would be a considerable Assistance to me in the great Burthen yt lyes
upon me and will soon weer me out.

　　I officiate Steadily at the following places.

N. Groton.	Charlston 4. Sundays
S. Groton.	N. London 8. Sundays
Stonington.	Hebron
Norwich.	Stafford & Brimfield
Preston	Canterbury
	Mansfield. & ·

occasionally at many other places. Surely but little more
from my utmost endeavours can be expected than the preserving the Chh where it is; and the bringing men to a
general acquaintance with the Constitution of our most excellent Chh, the Sowing those seeds of truth & virtue wc I
continually am seeing the good effects of: and hope in time
will spring up into a joyfull Harvest. Inclosd I send a
Notitia parochialis, and also begg leave to inform the
Venerable Society that with my next I purpose to transmit to them a Deed of a Small Gleebe wc is near the Chh
in Groton & that I have drawn for the Last quarter's Salary
in favour of the Bearer.

　　I add only my fervent prayers to Almighty GOD, that
he would be pleasd to encreas and prosper the Society, yt
more Labourers may be sent into a Harvest where they
are so much wanted. I am with great Respect
　　　　　　Revd Sr. Your's & ye Societys sincere
　　　　　　　　　　Freind & Servt.
　　　　　　　　　　　　Ebenr Punderson

[Addressed:] To Dr ---- Bearcroft Secy / at ye Charterhouse / London / per Mr. Cole
[Endorsed:] Laid before the Committee 14th Septr. 1747.

[1747, Apr. 20, North Groton]

　　　　　　　　　North Groton April 20th 1747

Revd Sr.

Inclosed I Send my Notitia Scholastica for the year and half
since my Salary commenc'd as the Revd Mr Punderson Inform'd me: and in the most hearty Sense of ye Honourable
Societys favour to me beg leave to return them my unfeigned thanks resolving to ye utmost of my power con-

stantly to observe the pious Instructions contain'd in ye
Collection of papers, at present in my hands; hoping the
Societys expectation will not be frustrated in employing
me as their Schoolmaster. For as I have long Since
made it ye Sole Buisiness of my life to Instruct Children
and Youth in the Knowledge of what is proper to their age
I Shall for the future esteem my Self under greater obligations to persue this Buisiness with my utmost Zeal, and
hope the Blessing of God may Rest upon my labours. I
Shall Trespass no longer Revd Sr upon your and the Societys patience Save only in informing them that I have
drawn for ye Time past in favour of Mr Dudley Woodbridge

　　and am Revd Sr / Yours & ye Venerable Societys /
most Obedient Humble & Oblig'd Servt

　　　　　　　　　Samuel Hutchinson

Post Script

　　My Revd Pastor　　Recd not his letter until the 15th
of this Instant otherwise the Society should have sooner
heard from me

　　　　　　　　　　　April 20th 1747

Notitia Scholastica

1	Attendance daily given	From 8 A.M. To 4 P.M.
2	Number of children taught in the School	36
3	Number of children Baptized in ye Chh of England	16
4	Number of Indian and Negro Children	3
5	Number of Children Born of Dissenting Parents	20
6	Other Schools in or near the Place	2 in Groton 1.4 Mile Dist. ye other 8 ye Masters Conformist 2 in Preston 1.3 M. ye other 8. 1 Conform
7	Of what Denomination	3 of ye above Masters Conformist
8	Other Employments of the Schoolmaster	None

test / Ebenr Punderson

　　Christopher Newton ⎫
　　David Hulburt 　　　⎬ Chh Wardens

[Addressed:] To The Revd Doctr Bearcroft / Secretary
to the Society &c / Charterhouse London / Per Capt.
Gayton

[1747, May 20, London]

Sr

　　The Society for ye Propagation of ye Gospel in for-
eign Parts have appointed you their Missionary to ye
Church of New-London in the Province of Connecticut in
New-England upon ye Character given you by my good
Lord Bishop of Chester: ye Salary from ye Society will
be sixty Pounds Sterg per annum wth a good new built
House, & a Glebe of thirty Acres of good Land, & Sub-
scriptions from ye Members of ye Congregation yt will

I presume make yᵉ whole worth an hundred Pounds per annum in a good Country, & well setled; your Salary of sixty
Pounds per annum is to commence from Midsummer next,
& yᵉ first half year will be advanced you in London to help
to fit you out for yᵉ Voyage, & twenty Pounds more from yᵉ
Exchequer. It will be proper for you to settle yʳ Affairs,
as soon as conveniently may be, but there is no Occasion
for yʳ coming up to Town, till you hear further from me;
there will probably be no proper Opportunity for yʳ Voyage
till August, or perhaps September, & then you may probably be accompanied by another Clergyman, a very worthy
Person, & I will give you reasonable Notice of yᵉ time, &
recommending you to God's Blessing

  I am Sʳ, Yʳ affectionate Servant / & Brother /
      Philip Bearcroft / Secretary

To / The Revᵈ Mʳ Mat: Graves / in / Chester

London Charterhouse / May 20. 1747

[From a transcript in the hand of Matthew Graves.]

[1747, Sept. 29, North Groton]
      N: Groton. 29. Sepᵣ 1747.
Revᵈ & Dear Sʳ
  Inclosd I send my Notitia Parochialis for the last half
year by which the present State of my large Cure will appear. I fully purposed that a Deed of conveyance of 14
Acres of land for a Glebe, to Assist in perpetuating the
Chh in this parish forever should have accompany'd this
letter; but yᵉ Copy of the Deed by which such lands are
to be given not being at hand I shall endeavour yᵗ it may
soon follow. I have the Satisfaction to inform yᵗ Venerable board that the Ministry House in N: London is near
finish'd. I have contributed something & endeavourd to my
utmost to forward it. --They are Building a Chh in Norwich
the largest and most flourishing Town of any in the Colony;
there are about 30 Families of Conformists- the Town has
always had the Caracter of the most rigid Congregationalists in the Government; tis really surprizing how much
their Dispositions are softned towards the Church, and
Indeed tis so almost every where
  I shall only add that I have drawn a sett of Bills in
favour of Mʳ Stewart & shall also at Christmas & yᵗ I am
    Revᵈ Sʳ yours & yᵉ Societys
     most obedient Humble Servant
      Ebenʳ Punderson

	Notitia Parochialis	Sepᵣ 29 1747
I.	Number of Inhabitants	About 1500 Families
II.	Nᵒ of the Baptiz'd	About 3/4
III	Nᵒ· of Adults Baptiz'd &c	None: but many Children 90
IIII	Nᵒ· of Actual Communi-cants	90
V	Nᵒ· of those who profess themselves Christian.	126 heads of Families
VI.	Nᵒ· of Heathens &c.	About 200 Families.
VII	Nᵒ of Dissenters of all Sorts. &c	Presbiterians. Independants Quakers 2 Sorts Baptists 2 Sorts Some Sects Nameless
VIII	Nᵒ· of Converts, &c.	Some Few.

[Addressed:] For the Revᵈ Docʳ Bearcroft Sec't. /
at yᵉ Charterhouse / London / per Snow Aurora /
Cap Jaˢ Hormbey
[Endorsed:] Read 11 Janry 1747.

[1748, Apr. 26, Stamford]
  Know all Men by these presents, That we, John
Lloyd, Thomas Youngs, Nathanael Hubbard, William
King, George Gorham, Peter Demill, Samuel Jarvis,
Obadiah Seely all of Stamford, in the County of Fairfield
and Colony of Connecticut; & Israel Knap of Greenwich,
in yᵉ County and Colony aforesaid, Church Wardens &
Vestrymen of the Church In Communion wᵗʰ the Estab-
lished Church of England, Composed of the professors in
Said Stamford and Greenwich United, are Held & Stand
firmly Bound and Obliged, unto the Venerable Society for
the propagation of the Gospel in foreign parts, in the Sum
of five Hundred Pounds Sterling; to be paid unto the Said
Venerable Society for the propagation of the Gospel, their
Certain Attorney and Successors to the payment of which
well & truely to be made & Done we bind & oblige Our
Selves & Successors firmly by these presents: Sealed
with our Seals, Dated in Stamford, yᵉ 26ᵗʰ Day of April
in yᵉ Twenty first year of his Majesties Reign in the year
of our Lord 1748
  The Condition of the above Obligation is Such, that
whereas by a Law of yᵉ Colony of Connecticut the Professors of the Church of England are to be rated and Taxed
in Every Parish, in yᵉ Same proportion as the Professors
of Other Denominations approved by the Colony Laws for
the Support & Maintenance of the Ministers of Religion;
and that the proportion of the Tax upon the professors of
the Church of England shall be Gathered by a Common
Collector, & paid unto Such Minister of the Church of
England in Holy orders according to the Cannons of the
Church of England Setled among them, whare they Can &
do attend his Ministry; by which Law, the provision by
Taxing the Professors of the Church of England in Stam-
ford and Greenwich abovesaid, towards Supporting a
Minister in Holy Orders of the Church of England, when
Setled here, amounts at this time, to the Value of Twenty
Pounds Sterling per annum & wheanas, for the Better
Secureing the Sum of Twenty Pounds Sterling, towards
the Support of Such Minister anually, If a Missionary be
Obtained from the above Mentioned Venerable Society,
the Professors of the Church of England in Stamford and
Greenwich Aforesaid, have Obliged themselves by Subscription, to pay Severally & Respectively, Such Sums
anually to the Support of Such Missionary, as do amount
in the whole to the Sum of Twenty Pounds Sterling; Now,
If by the Taxes Collected from Said professors, by the
abovesaid Law of the Colony Aforesaid, the payment of
the abovesaid Subscriptions of the Professors, or by any
Other provision to be Made hereafter, from time to time,
by the associated Professors of the Church of England
as by Law Established, the full Sum of Twenty Pounds
Sterling, anually & Every Year, on or before Lady Day,
shall be well and truely paid unto, & for the Support of,
a Missionary that shall be appointed From Time to time
by the Said Venerable Society, to be the Minister of
Sᵗ Johns Church, in the United Parish of Stamford and
Greenwich, then the above Obligation to be Null and

Void, or Else to Stand and remain in full force power and Vertue.

Signed Sealed and Delivered in presence of

J. Wetmore Jr	William King
Nathanael Lloyd	George Gorum
John Lloyd	Peter Demill
Thomas Youngs	Saml Jarvis
Nathel Hubbard	Israel Knapp

[Addressed:] To The Revrd Dr Bearcraft Secretary / to the Venerable Society for / Propagating the Gospel In / Foreign parts. Charter House / London
[Endorsed:] Read 11 July 1748.

[1748, May 9, Redding]

To the honorable the Governor & Council, with the Representatives, In general Court Assembled, at Hartford May 12th 1748.

The humble Petition of the Professors of the Church of England In the Parish Reading, in the Town of FairField, Sheweth,

That whereas all the Inhabitants of this Parish of the presbyterian Persuasion ever Since it has been erected into a Parish, which is about 20, Years; have by this Honorable Assembly been exempted from paying any Taxes for the Support of the civil Government, upon the Account of the Greatness of their ministerial Charges; And We Your Petitioners being by a Law of this Colony taxed in the Same Proportion with them, for the Support of the Ministry, & having always in Fact paid our ministerial Rates; & therefore being under equal Hardships with our Fellow-Parishioners; yet have ever paid the whole of our Rates due to the civil Government: But Now being under a Necessity to erect an House for the public Worship of God, We therefore humbly pray the honorable Assembly to extend the Same Charity to Us, while we are under the Burthen & Expence of sd Building, as they have in their Wisdom & Piety afforded to our Brethren & Fellow-Parishioners, for near 20, Years past----And tho' We are very Sensible that what we Address your Honours for is not of Debt but of Grace; Yet we cannot entertain So injurious a Thought of the honorable Assembly, as to Suspect that their Goodness will be partial, or their Charity confined to Christians of one Denomination, to the Exclusion of all others. Nor can we Suppose, that their Wisdom will account our Worshipping God in the Manner established in our Mother-Country, Such a Crime as to forfiet & render us unworthy of Enjoying for a Short Season yt Charity, which our Fellow-Parishioners have ever, & do now enjoy----Therefore not doubting but that your Wisdom is of that Kind which St James Says, is from above, & therefore is gentle, easy to be entreated, full of Mercy & good Fruits, & without Partiality. We Shall ever pray, &c

Israel Rowland	Daniel Lyon Jun
Thomas Rowland	James [Tennis?] Morgin
Enos Lee	Nehemiah Seely
Ephrum Meker	Ebenr Hoight
Benia Sturges	Ebenr Bairdly
Robert Meker	William Stevens
Robert Seeley	Abraham Adams

Thomas Tailor	Nathan Lyon
Gershom Morehouse	John Mallory
Obediah Plat	Jonathan Knap
Joshua Hall	David Knap
Samuell fairchild	Daniel Crofoot
Oliver Fairchild	Daniell Hill
Stephen Fairchild	William Hill
John Picket	Adam Clark
Seth Wheler	Joseph Morhous
Ebenezer Hall	Peter Malary
Moses Knap	Daniel Lion
Stephphen Morhous	Daniel Morhous

This may certify, the Honorable Legislature within Addressed that whereas I have been for near 16, Years an unworthy Minister of the Church of England at New Town & Reading, that the Members of the sd Church in the above sd Parish, have punctually paid their ministerial Rates to me: And the Generality of them, to my certain Knowledge have been at considerably greater Expences for the Support of Religion, than our Brethren of the presbyterian Persuasion had any Occasion for---- I thought it a Piece of Justice to make this Declaration; And that to encourage Men to act insincerely in Matters of Religion in Order to Save their Purses, I have in the utmost Indignation----

And am / Honorable Gentlemen / Your most
Obedient / & most humble Sert
Reading, May 9th 1748.   John Beach

In ye Lower House
The Question was put Whether any thing should be Granted in the Prayer of ye within Petition
Resolved in ye Negative
Test Jno Fowler Clerk
In the Upper House
The Question was put whether the Prayer of this Memorial should be granted
Resolved in the Negative
Test George Wyllys Secretry

[1749, Mar. 25, North Groton]

N: Groton 25 March 1749
Revd & Dear Sr

I have the Satisfaction to acquaint the Venerable Society, that the Church in Norwich, (as flourishing a Town as any in the Governt) is of late considerably encreas'd; and by the Charitable Aid of our Brethren we have inclos'd, and glaz'd, an exceeding good timber building: of 35 feet in Breadth, and 45 in length: in which I have officiated the first Sunday in every other month, and administer'd the Eucharist Since my last: and purpose to continue the practice for the future. & earnestly Solicit in behalf of the good people there, that ye Society would Send to that Chh a folio Comon prayer & Bible. Also that there is a better prospect at Charles:town; where I have Baptiz'd 2 Adults and Admitted 4 to the Communion Since my last: I have not the Vanity to Imagine that a particular Account of my Itinerancy, can be a very agreable entertainment to that Venerable Board; whose time is employ'd about the noblest purposes: but I can't forbear mentioning yt Since my preaching last Sepr at Cohabit;

about 8 mile N: of Guilford wch was the first Sermon preach'd in that place by a Clergiman of the Chh of Eng^d they have almost ever Since read prayers & Sermons, to upwards of 40 persons I have promis'd them a Visit the begining of Apr^l

Dear S^r   the parcel of Books you Advis'd me of p^r Brother Graves I have not been able to find: and entreat the Venerable Societys Kind Aid, in Some Comon prayers with the N: Version of pslams; w^c are greatly wanted, as well as other good Books.

I have drawn for my last quarters Salary in favour of Dr Woodbridge of Groton and shall also in June and Am

With the greatest Respect / Rev^d S^r / Your'n & the Societys / Son & Servt

E: Punderson

Notitia Parochialis.   Mar 25th 1749

1	Number of Inhabitants	1500 or 1600 fam.
2	N^o of ye Baptiz'd.	3/4 or More
3	N^o of Adults &c	2.
4	N^o of Actual Com^{ts}	122
5	N^o of those who profess	139 fam^{ls}
6	N^o of Dissent^s of &c	Papipsts none but Dissenterst of allmost all denominations there is in Groton 8 different Sorts.
7	N^o of Heath: &	Near 200 fam mostly in Charlestown.
8	N^o of Converts	7 or 8.

[Addressed:] For The Revd Doc^r Bearcroft / Secrct^y at the / Charterhouse / London
[Endorsed:] Laid before the Commee 17th July 1749.

[1749, June 22, Union]

union aprill ye 20th 1749
Then Received of mathew Pall of union five pounds Eleven shillings and Eighte pence old tenor bils itt being for his proportionable part of a tax Granted by the towne of union in the yeare 1748 of two hundred pounds to be Layd oute towards finishing of ye meting house in s^d union Rcieved by me timothy phelps Colector for s^d rates

union aprill ye 20th 1749
Then received of matthew Pall of union six pounds ninetene shillings and foure Pence old tenor bils itt Being his proportionable part of a tax Granted by the towne of union in the yeare 1748 in order to Pay for preaching in part and in part for other towne Charges I say received By me Timothy phelps Colector for s^d rates

Groton. 22 June 1749.
These may Certifie that Mathew Pall of ye Union upon the first of May in the year of our Lord 1747 declared conformity to ye Establis'd Chh of England Submited himself to my Pastoral Care & has ever Since constantly attended my Ministry.

test.   { Eben^r Punderson
        { Itin^t Miss^y in N: Eng^d

[1749, July 3, Norwich]

To Windham County Sheriff or his Deputy or Either of the Constables of the town of Union In s^d County Greeting.

In his Majesties Name Sumon Timothy Phelps of s^d Union Collector of Raits for s^d Union Chosen in the year ADom̄i 1748. to appear before Luke Perkins Esqr of Groton in the County of New London One of his Majesties [Justices] of the peace for s^d County of New London at the Dwelling House of Capt Thomas Leeds in s^d Groton on the Second Day of August Next at Two of the Clock after noone to answer unto Ebenezer Punderson of s^d Groton Clerk In a plea on one Statute of this Colony in Law Book page 340 intituled An act for the providing how the taxes Levied on Professors of ye Church of England for the Support of the Gospel Shall be Disposed of &c in which Statute it is provided among other things that all persons who are of the Church of England and those that are of the Churches Established by the Laws of this Government that live in the bounds of any parish allowed by the General Assembly of this Colony Shall be taxed by the parrishioners of the s^d Parish by the Same Rule and in the Same proportion for the Support of the Support of the Ministry in Such parish but if it So happen that there be a Society of the Church of England where there is a person in Order according to the Canons of thee Church of England Settled and abiding among them and performing Divine Service So near to any person that haith Declared Himself of the Church of England that he Can and Doth attend the Publick Worship there then the Colecters having first Indifferently Levied the tax as aboves^d Shall Deliver the Taxes Collected of Such persons Declaring themselves & Attending as afores^d unto the Minister of the Church of England Living Near unto Such persons which Minister Shall have full power to Receive and Recover the Same in order to his Support in the Place Assigned to him. As by s^d Statute at Large appears Refference thereto being had and the plan^t in fact Farther Says that before and In the year AD 1748 and Ever Since he was and is a person in holy Orders According to the Canons of the Church of England, Commisioned & Assigned by his Lordship the Bishop of London and the venerable Society for the propagating the Gospel in Foriegn parts an Itenerant Missionary for New England and that within his Limets there was before and in the year AD 1748 and Ever Sence haith been & Still is a Society of the Church of England under his the Plan^t Care and Charge Containing ye towns of Groton, Norwich, Mansfeild, Stafford, and Union, in which and Among whome he was before and in s^d year 1748 Settled and abiding and Ever Since haith and Still Doth Dwell and haith ever Since his being in orders as afores^d and Still Doth faithfully perform Divine Service within his s^d Mission & in s^d Society under his Charage as afores^d and that one Mathew Paul of s^d Union hath before and in s^d year 1748 ever Since Declared himself of the Church of England and hath before in and Ever Sence s^d year 1748 Dwelt in s^d Society under the Plan^t Charge as afores^d & So near to the place of performing Divine Service by the Plan^t as afores^d that s^d Paul would & Did attend Publick worship there in and with s^d Society or Church under the Plan^t Care & Charge as afores^d & the Plan^t further Says that s^d Union is and then was an Eclesiastical Society Established by the Laws of this Colony and the Inhabitance thereof in s^d year 1748

Granted a Rate or Tax on S̲d̲ Inhabitance for the Support of
the Ministry in S̲d̲ Union and also Chose and Appointed the
Deft̲ a Collector to Geather & pay or Dispose of the Same
According to Law and the Deft̲ Accepted of and Took upon
him S̲d̲ Trust and Accordingly on the 20th Day of April
AD: 1749 Collected & Received of S̲d̲ Mathew Paul the Sum
of Six Pounds Nineteen Shillings and four pence in Bills of
Publick Credit of the Old tenor as his S̲d̲ Pauls Proportion-
able part of S̲d̲ Rate or Tax for the Support of the Ministry
Granted in S̲d̲ year 1748 as aforesd̲ and other town Charges
as by a Receipt under the Deft̲ Hand may appear Dated S̲d̲
20th of S̲d̲ Aprill and the plant̲ farther Says that £6=14=0 of
S̲d̲ Sum was by S̲d̲ Union Granted and the Deft̲ Collected and
Recd̲ of S̲d̲ Paul for the Support of the Ministry as aforesd̲
which £6=14=0 did when Collected and Now Doth by S̲d̲
Statute of Right Belong to the Plant̲ and it then by force of
S̲d̲ Statute became the Duty of the Deft̲ to Deliver the Same
to the Plant̲ which the Deft̲ then well Knew yet Nevertheless the Deft̲ being Minded the Plant̲ to wrong hath Never
Delivered the Same to the Plant̲ (tho often Requested) but
always Refuseth which is to the Damage of the Plant̲ as he
Saith the S̲d̲ Sum of £6=14=0 in Said Bills which he Demands
with Cost hereof fail not and make Due Return of this writ
with your Doings thereon dated in Norwich July the 3d̲ Day
AD. 1749. and in the 22nd year of his Majesties Reigne
　　　　　　　　　　　　　　　　Hez: Huntington Assist̲

A true Copy of the Originall Writt on file
　　　　　Test　Luke Perkins　Justice of Peace

[1749, Sept. 25, Groton]
　　　　　　　　　　　　Groton 25 Sepr 1749
Revd Sr
　　It is impossible that any thing Should be an equivalent
to my painfull, & extensive Labours; but a fervent zeal for
ye Glory of GOD & the best good of Immortal Souls, together with the hopes of an exceeding & eternal weight of
Glory, wc the great Shepherd will upon his appearance bestow of his infinite goodness upon his Servants.
　　The first monday in last April, rode to Middletown,
preach'd there on tuesday, after Service rode 6 miles to
Durham, with Mr Camp, who is reading prayers & Sermons in Middletown; on Wednesday preach'd at Cohabit,
and rode 8 miles to Guilford; where I preachd on thursday
& retur'd to Cohabit; on friday preach'd at Middletown.
came to Norwich upon Saturday evening; perform'd Service
& administred ye Sacraments on Sunday and got Home in
the Evening.
　　In May I made another tour to the Union about 45 Miles
from my House preach'd at Mr Lawsons where between 60
& 70 persons were conven'd, 7 than declard Conformity,
and they have ever Since upheld the worship of GOD according to our most excellent Liturgy. in the evening
returd 16 miles to Mansfield preach'd & Administred the
Sacrament of the Lords Supper the next day to 16 Communicants. on friday perform'd Service in the Chh at Norwich. during the Heat of Summer have visited Charlestown Stonington Preston Norwich & S: Groton.
　　Upon the 8th of this Instant I enterd upon a Journey
to my Native place took Hebron in my way, preachd to a
Numerous congregation; Christned 5 Children. & cannot
forbear earnestly to beseech the Venerable Society to have
compassion on them; & give leave for Mr Colton (who
has long been reading Service & Sermons amongst them
to extraordinary acceptance) to come Home: they having
procur'd a good Glebe, & are ready at any time to build
him a House, & Secure to him 20 or 25£ Sterling per annum. there are there 50 Comts the next day rode to
Middleton. christned 2 Children in Colchester. Sunday,
10th Int preachd in the Town House to a congregation of
3 or 400 persons, Administred the Eucharist to 12, &
Christned 2 Infants. the next day preachd at Cohabit,
and the day following at Wallingsford: in the Evening
to New Haven----Preach'd at Cohabit Sunday 17th Inst.
added 10 to the Communion we had 40 in all: I Baptizd
2 Adults, & 9 Infts. Divine Service is there performd
with the greatest propriety, & fervent zeal, they are
peculiarly my Children in the faith, since I am the only
Clergiman that has perform'd divine Service amongst
them. the next day I preachd at Guilford, got home on
Wednesday night as much rejoyc'd as I was fatiegg'd.
I add only my fervent request of an interest in Yours &
the Societys Solicitations at the throne of Grace & am
　　　　　Yours & the Societyes / Faithfull Servt
　　　　　　　　　　Ebenezr Punderson
P.S. I have drawn for my Last quarters Salary in fa-
vour of Docr Woodbridge & Shall also at Christm.̰

Notitia Parochialis	from March 25 to Sepr 25. 1749	
Number of Inhabitans	In Norwich Groton Preston Stonington Chrlstown about 1600 familyes	
No of Baptizd	Upwards of 3/4. 3 Adults Baptizd	
No of Actual Com-municts	Groton & Stoning	60
	Preston & Norwh & Ch	40
	Mansfeild Canterbury Stafford	20
	Hebron- & Middleton	60
	Guilford Cohabit & Wallingford	45
No of those who profess themselves of ye Chh	4 or 500 persons	
No of Dissenters of all Sorts	Papists none openly	
No of Heaths & Infidels	About 200	
No of Converts from a profane.	10	

[1749, Sept. 29, Stamford]
　　　　　　　　Stamford In Connecticut
　　　　　　　　Septembr 29th 1749.
Revd Sir
　　According to the Directions of thee Venerable Society, I Here Inclose my Notitia Parochialis with Advice
that I Acknowledge the Receipt of the Sum of Ten Pounds,
being So much Advanced me by Slingsby Bethell Equre
the Societys Treasurer for my Half Years Sallary due the
24th June Last, and wh will further appear by the Receipt
I Gave him Dated, the 27th August, 1748:--and have the
pleasure to acquaint you that my Labours are Acceptable
to my People, who Shew a forwardness to assist & Support

me according to their ability, and I have Endeavoured to
divide my labours among the Severall parts of my Extensive Mission, So as to be as Serviceable as may be to the
whole. and I Bless God that I have not laboured among
them without some visible Success in Each of the Places
where I have performed Divine Service; I Preach at Horseneck the Second Sunday in each Month--about Six Miles
from Stanford; have had Some Converts to the Ch^h there,
and the People have Zealously Exerted themselves to Build
a Small Chappel of Ease, about 36 foot In Length, & 25 In
Breadth, to Accommodate our Assembling at those Times
which they have Inclosed & Glazed; and If they could be
favourrd with a Bible & Common Prayer Book, for that Ch^h
it would be a very welcome Present, Their Ch^h Wardens
haveing desired me Humbly to Request the Same.----
Greenwich being not above 3 Miles from Stamford, I have
only occasionally officiated there upon Week Dayes, Except two Sundayes the Year Past, and as they have no settled Dissenting Minister among them, they have Invited me
into their Meeting House, and the Inhabitants of all Sorts
generally attend Ch^h when I preach there.--And at Stamford there is a very visible alteration In the Temper &
disposition of the Dissenting Party, Insomuch that Sundry
times when their Meeting House chanced to be destitute of
a dissenting Minister, our Ch^h has been Crowded by the attendance of Dissenters, and many of them Chearfully Unit-
ed In the Service of our Holy Ch^h--w^h together with Sundry
Converts already Obtained, gives me great Incouragement
to hope by the Blessing of God for Abundant Success in my
Ministry: I Had but 16 Communicants (as I inform^d the
Honor^{ble} Society In Mine of ye 18th of Novemb^r Last) at
my first administring the Communion after my Return,
and the Number is now Increased to Forty One--I Preach
Monthly at Stanwich about 8 Miles from Stamford where
I have a Considerable Congregation, and the Last time I
was there more Numerous than at any time before, and at
that time Baptised 2 adult Persons, and 10 Children.----
The people of Norwalk whom I look upon more Immediately Under Mr Lamsons Care; Yet agreable to your Request
& upon their application I have visited them in Sickness
Buried their Dead, and Baptized their Children, as I have
ben frequently Sent for on Such Occasions; and have
Preached Three times there upon Severall Occasions.
And upon Mr Lamsons Request, & the Importunities of the
Poor people at Ridgefield where there are about 30 Heads
of Families professors of Our Holy Ch^h--I Have preached
twice to them on Week dayes; that place being about 16
Miles distant from me, and at much greater distance from
Mr Lamson; and that Mr Lamson might Officate on Sun-
dayes oftner at Norwalk, & keep that flourishing Ch^h from
Crumbling to pieces, untill the Society may be pleased to
provide otherwise for them; I have Encouraged him to
Preach at Ridgefield the Second Sunday In Octob^r & to Afford what Assistance I am Capable off there the Ensue-
ing Winter; I onely add my Humble Duty to the Venerable
Board, with Earnest Prayers to Allmighty God to give his
Blessing to all their Charitable Designs, & Success to all
their pious Endeavours to promote the Interest of true Religion, and with much Respect beg Leave to Subscribe as
I am most Heartily

Rev^d S^r / Your most Obed^t / Most Humble Servt

Ebenez^r Dibblee

The Revd Doct^r Bearcroft
Secret^r to the Venerable Society &c:

Stamford in Connecticut
Septemb^r 29- 1749-

Notitia Parochialis

I	N^o of Inhabitants- about	4500
II	N^o of the Baptized about	3500
III	N^o of Adult persons Baptized last Year	13; Infants 55
IV	N^o of actual Communicants of the Ch^h of England	41.
V	N^o of those who profess themselves of the Ch^h of England	110 Heads of Families
VI	N^o of Dissenters of all Sorts (No Papists) about	760 Heads of Families
VII	N^o of Heathens & Infidels about	150 Negro Slaves
VIII	N^o of Converts &c:	18-

I am / Rev^d S^r / Your most Obed^t / Humble Servt

Ebenez^r Dibblee

[1749, Oct. 4, London]

London Charterhouse October 4th 1749.

Revd Sir

Being lately thro' God's Mercy recovered from a very
dangerous Sickness, I must renew my Correspondence &
acquaint you, that the Society received with great Pleasure
the Accounts of the flourishing Condition of your Church,
and they have granted your Request of a Folio Bible &
Common Prayer Book for the Church of New Milford,
which will come with this, & a parcell of other books
directed to the care of Dr Cutler vizt 100 of Mr White's
first & second answer to the dissenting Genleman, 200 of
Mr West's & Littleton's Discourses, & 150 of the last Anniversary Sermon, some of each of which I make no doubt
he will communicate to you. The Society have heard with
great Pleasure of your Brother Mr Beach's good deeds to
the Church of Stratford, & wishing you all success in your
pious Labours

I remain &c.

[Philip Bearcroft]

To the Revd Mr Beach, Missionary at
Newtown in Connecticut Colony in N. England.

[1749, Oct. 4, London]

London Charterhouse Octr 4th 1749.

Revd Sir

Being lately thro' Good's Mercy recovered from a
very dangerous Sickness, It is time to renew my Correspondence, & to acquaint You that the Society receive with
great satisfaction the account of your Spiritual Labors, &
to help them forward they have granted your Request of a
Folio Bible & Common Prayer Book for the Church of Norwich, & 24 small Common Prayer books to be distributed
as you shall judge proper, they will come with this in a
Box directed to the Care of Dr Cutler, who will I make no
doubt forward them to you, together with some Copies of
the last Anniversary Sermons, of Mr West's & Lyttleton's
Discourses, & of Mr White's first & second answer to
the dissenting Gentleman a large number of all which are

entrusted to his Distribution; wishing you all success in your pious Labours

I am &c.ᵃ

[Philip Bearcroft]

To the Revᵈ Mᵣ Punderson
Itinerant Missionary in New England.

[1749, Oct. 5, London]

London Charterhouse October the 5ᵗʰ 1749.
Revᵈ Sir

The Society to encourage you to perseverance in visiting & instructing occasionally at Taunton, Attleborough & other neighbouring Places, have granted you a Gratuity of twenty Pounds, for which you may draw upon their Treasurer Mᵣ Bethell: wishing you much success in your pious Labors

I am &c.ᵃ

[Philip Bearcroft]

To the Revᵈ Mᵣ Cheekly at
Providence in New England.

[1749, Oct. 12, Colony of Conn.]

To the Honᵇˡ the Generall assembly of His Majesties English Colony of Connecticut in New England to be Holden at Newhaven on the second Thursday of Instant October AD 1749

The Memoriall of us the Subscribers ministers and Church Wardens in behalf of ourselves and the Rest of the professors of the Chh of England all Belonging to the said Colony of Connecticut...[Sheweth?] that whereas this Honᵇˡ Assembly was pleased on the petition of one Moses Ward then Chh Warden in May 1727 to Exempt the professoors of the Chh of England from paying Taxes for the Building Desenting Meeting Houses and paying Desenting Ministers for which Act we take this Oppertunity to Return our publick thanks to this Assembly, which Act in Great Measure Answered the Good purposes for which it was made while the Number of said professors was Very Small But so it is may it please this Honᵇˡ assembly by the Good Hand of God upon us that our Numbers are Greatly Increased and Nothing Doubting but the same pious and Charitable Disposition Still Remains as before in this Honᵇˡ Assembly we take leave to Request of this Honᵇˡ assembly that Some New Act may be made or substituted in the Room or place of said Act which may better Answer the present Circumstances of the professors of the Chh: of England in this Colony and Remove some Hardships which they now Labour under And here we Would Observe that as the Law now Stands Some of the sᵈ professors which Live in Small parishes...the law of this Colony at A Great Distance... of Carrying on publick Services accord[ing] to the Chh of England are Obliged to pay Three times as much as Others althoe Taxed by the same Rule by Reason of the Heavy Taxes for the Support of Ministers in Small parrishes; and secondly we would Humbly Observe that many of the professors of the Chh: of England think themselves Deprived of A natural Right which to them Belong as English Subjects by means of that Act of this assembly passed in May 1746 by which the professors of the Chh of England are all Prohibited from Haveing their Vote or sufferage in any of the society Meetings where Great and Heavy Taxes

are Layd upon them- Whereupon yᵉ Memorialists Humbly pray yᵗ the the professors of the Chh of England may be Exempted from Being Taxed for the Building Desenting Meeting Houses or paying Any Thing for the Support of Disenting Ministers within this Colony and that the professors of the Chh of England may be Incorporated and have the same priviledges of Meeting and Granting Levieing and Collecting Taxes...Churches and for the Support of...[ecclesias]tical Society Established by law of this Colony have...as much as it Can't be thought that Parochial [services] Can be properly Given as is Common to Other parishes we would propose that the severall Ministers of the Chh: of England Within this Colony shall annually Certifie and Give in yᵉ Names to the severall Clerks of the Respective Societyes where such persons do Dwell that are professors of the Chh of England, and under their Respective Care and Charge; and the names of such persons being so Entered that are Liable [by] Law to be Listed may be able to meet from time to time According as the Law directs and allows other Societies to do for the purposes aforesaid. or in some other way Grant to your Memorialists Relief in the Case as you in your Great wisdom shall think fitt and yʳ Honᵇˡ Memorialists as in Duty Bound Shall Ever pray / Samuel Johnson

Samuel Johnson	Joseph Lamson
John Beach	Ebenezᵣ Dibblee
Ebenezer Punderson	Richard Mansfield
Mattʷ Graves.	

In yᵉ Lower house

The Consideration of yᵉ foregoing Memoriall Referred to yᵉ Considera[tion] of this assembly in May next

Test Jnᵒ Fowler Clerk

Samˡˡ Cluckston	
Samˡˡ Jarvis	Church Wardens
Nathᵉˡ Hubbard	
Samˡˡ Jarvis	

Thomas Taylor	Samˡ Hull
John Mallery	Samuel Tomlinson
Isaac Jenings	Edmund Ward
Nathaniel Perry	George Bartlet
Elnathan Peat	John Thomson
[----- Sheldon?]	

[Ca. 1750]

Scheme

For the Settlement of a New Colony to the Westward of Pennsylvania, for the Enlargement of his Majesty's Dominions in America, for the further Promotion of the Christian Religion among the Indian Natives, and for the more effectual Securing them in his Majesty's Alliance.

That humble Application be made either to his Majesty or the General Assembly of Connecticut, or to both, as the Case may require, for a Grant of so much Land as shall be necessary for the Settlement of an ample Colony, to extend from the Western Boundaries of Pennsylvania one Hundred Miles to the Westward of the River Missisippi, and to be divided from Virginia and Carolina by the Great

Chain of Mountains that runs along the Continent from the North-Eastern to the South-Western Parts of America.

That humble Application be made to his Majesty for a Charter to erect the said Territory into a separate Government, with the same Privileges which the Colony of Connecticut enjoys, & for such Supplies of Arms and Ammunition as may be necessary for the Safety & Defence of the Settlers, and that his Majesty would also be pleased to take the said New Colony under his immediate Protection.

That Application be made to the Assemblies of the several British Colonies in North-America, to grant such Supplies of Money and Provisions as may enable the Settlers to secure the Friendship of the Indian Natives, and support themselves and Families till they are established in said Colony in Peace and Safety and can support themselves by their own Industry.

That at least twelve Reverend Ministers of the Gospel be engaged to remove to the said New Colony with such Numbers of their respective Congregations as are willing to go along with them.

That every Person, from the Age of fourteen Years and upwards (Slaves excepted) professing the Christian Religion, being Protestant Subjects of the Crown of Great-Britain, and that will remove to said New Colony with the First Settlers thereof, shall be intitled to a sufficient Quantity of Land for a Plantation, without any Consideration Money, and at the annual Rent of a Pepper Corn:---- Said Plantation to contain at least Three Hundred Acres, Two Hundred Acres of which to be such Land as is fit either for Tillage or Meadow.

That every Person under the Age of Fourteen Years (Slaves excepted) who removes to said Province with the First Settlers thereof, as well as such Children as shall be lawfully born to said First Settlers in said Province, or in the Way to it, shall be intitled to Three Hundred Acres of Land when they come to the Age of Twenty-one Years, without any Purchase Money, at the annual Quit-Rent of Two Shillings Sterling for every Hundred Acres; the Quit-Rent arising from such Lands to be applied to the Support of Government, the Propagation of the Christian Religion among the Indian Natives, the Relief of the Poor, the Encouragement of Learning, and in general to such other publick Uses, as shall be judged by the Legislature of the Province to [be] most conducive to the General Good.

That every Person who is intitled to any Land in the Province, shall be at Liberty to take it up when they please; but when taken up shall be obliged to clear and fence at least Fifteen Acres on every Farm of Three Hundred Acres, within Five Years after the Appropriation of said Land, and also to build a Dwelling House of at least Fifteen Foot square with a good Chimney on the Premises within the said Term, on Pain of forfeiting said Land.

That the said Plantations shall be laid out in Townships, in such Manner as will be most for the Safety and Convenience of the Settlers.

That in order to prevent all Jealousies and Disputes about the Choice of said Plantations, they shall be divided by Lot.

That as soon as possible after a sufficient Number of Persons are engaged, a proper Charter obtained, and the necessary Preparations are made for the Support and Protection of the Settlers, a Place of general Rendezvous shall be appointed, where they shall all meet, and from whence they shall proceed in a Body to the New Colony; but that no Place of Rendezvous shall be appointed till at least Two Thousand Persons able to bear Arms are actually engaged to remove, exclusive of Women and Children.

That it be established as one of the fundamental Laws of the Province, that Protestants of every Denomination who profess the Christian Religion, believe the divine Authority of the Sacred Scriptures of the Old and New Testament, the Doctrine of the Trinity of Persons in the Unity of the Godhead, and whose Lives and Conversations are free from Immorality and Prophaneness, shall be equally capable of serving in all the Posts of Honour, Trust or Profit in the Government, notwithstanding the Diversity of their religious Principles in other Respects: But that none of any Denomination whatsoever, who have been guilty of prophaning the Name of God, of Lying, Drunkenness, or any other of the groser Immoralities, either in their Words or Actions, shall be capable of holding any Office in or under the Government till at least one Year after their Conviction of such Offence.----The Christianizing the Indian Natives, and bringing them to be good Subjects, not only to the Crown of Great-Britain, but to the King of all Kings, being one of the essential Designs of the proposed New Colony, it is a Matter of the utmost Importance that those poor ignorant Heathen should not be prejudiced against the Christian Religion by the bad Lives of those in Authority.

That Protestants of every Denomination who profess the Christian Religion shall have the free and unlimitted Exercise of their Religion, & shall be allowed to defind it, both from the Pulpit and the Press, so long as they remain peaceable Members of Civil Society, and do not propagate Principles inconsistent with the Safety of the State.

That no Member of the Church of Rome shall be able to hold any Lands or Real Estate in the Province, nor be allowed to be owners of, or have any Arms or Ammunition in their Possession on any Pretence whatsoever, nor shall any Mass-Houses, or Popish Chappels be allowed in the Province.

That no Person shall be obliged to pay any Thing towards the Support of a Minister of whose Congregation he is not a Member, or to a Church to which he does not belong.

That the Indians shall on all Occasions be treated with the utmost Kindness and every justifiable Method taken to gain their Friendship; and that whoever injures, cheats, or makes them drunk, shall be punished with peculiar Severity.

That so soon as the Province is able to support Missionaries, and proper Persons can be found to engage in the Affair, a Fund shall be settled for the Purpose, and Missionaries sent among the neighbouring Indian Nations; and that it shall, in all Time coming, be esteem'd as one of the First and Most Essential Duties of the Legislature of the Province, by every proper Method in their Power, to endeavour to spread the Light of the glorious Gospel among the Indians in America, even to its most Western Bounds.

That as the Conversion of the Indians is a Thing much to be desired, from the weightiest Considerations, both of a religious and political Nature, and since the Colony during its Infancy will be unable to provide the necessary Funds for that Purpose, some proper Person or Persons

shall be sent to Europe, duly authorized from the Government, to ask Assistance of such as desire to promote that
great and good Work.

  To all whom these Presents shall come, or may in any-
wise concern. We the Subscribers (being Inhabitants of his
Majesty's Plantations in North-America) having taken the
foregoing Scheme for Settling a New Colony into our most
serious Consideration, and having deliberately weighed the
various Parts thereof, cannot but most heartily approve of
a Design which, when duly executed, would be attended,
with such happy & extensive Consequences to the Crown
of Great-Britain, and all his Majesty's Colonies in North-
America, and which would, at the same Time, open the
most effectual Door for carrying the Light of the glorious
Gospel of Christ among the numerous Tribes of Indians
that inhabit those inland Parts; and as it is the Duty of all
to encourage a Design like this, so we in particular are,
for our Parts, desirous to embark in a Cause we so much
approve of; And seeing it is necessary, for carrying the
Scheme into Execution, that it be seasonably known what
Number of Persons would be willing to remove to the proposed New Colony, we have thought proper to declare, And
we do hereby publickly declare our Willingness to remove
with our Families & Fortunes to the proposed New Colony
upon the Plan of the foregoing Scheme so soon as the Way
is prepared for such Removal agreeable to said Plan and
that we are not only willing, but desirous of doing it if the
said Scheme takes Effect: But that none may mistake our
Intentions, we think it necessary farther to declare, That
however willing we are to remove to a Colony settled on
the foregoing Plan, which we apprehend would secure both
Civil and Religious Liberty as well as private Property to
ourselves and our Posterity, at the same that it would be
doing the most important Service to our King and Country,
we have, nevertheless, too just a Sense of the Value of
our Privileges, as well as of the Duties we owe to our
Children and the future Generations, to entertain the least
Thought of being concerned in Settling a New Colony on
any other Plan than such as would insure these inestima-
ble Jewels, which are of more Importance to their and our
Well-Being and Happyness than all the Treasures of the
Indies.

[1750, Jan. 5, Hebron]

To the Revd Mr Graves at Newlond^n

Rev^d S^r We Expected You at Esqr Jo^s Phelps^s thursday
Last But Your Not being present & Colton as I Supose Being Sent out of the Way Least he Should Be Examin^d Gen^r
Filer & my Self pray^d ajournment & it Was ajourn^d Untill
the Last munday in January they Have Sworn as is Here
Exhibited: But if You Come Up at the Time of the Next
Examination I think We Can make them apear as they are
pray Bring these papers With You When You Come for they
may Be Examined farther and We Shall be able to Shew Y^t
they are But men if they Contradict W^t they Have Sworn
&c--

    Revd Sr Y^r Most
     Humble and obedient Servt
      Ja^s Thompson

Heb^n Jan^r 5th 1750

[1750, Feb. 13, Norwich]

Norwich Ss. Adj^d County Court
       Feb^ry 13th: 1749/50.

  Eben^r Punderson of Groton Clerk, Vers, Tim^o Phelps
of Union, in the County of Windham Collector of Rates for
S^d Union Def^t, In a plea brott on one Statute of this Colony in Law book page 340 Demanding £6=14=0 in Bills of
Public Credit of the old tenor and Cost &c, as per Writt
on file dated July 3^d: 1749. this action was first Brott before Luke Perkins Esqr One of his Majesties Justices of
the Peace for the County of New London where the Defend^t
pleaded in Abatement and the Writt was Ordered to Abate
&c-- thence per Appeall of the Plan^t Came to the County
Court in November Last, where the Defend^t Insisted on
his pleas in Abatem^t And the Partyes were heard thereon,
And the Court were of Opinion that the Writt Ought to
Abate &c, The Plan^t pay^d Cost and Mended thence per
Adjournm^t Comes to this Court,

  And now the Defend^t Says that he is Not Guilty in
Manner and form as the Plan^t in his Declaration hath
Alledged, to which the Partyes are on Tryall, And were
heard at Large by their Council with the Evidences Produced, And the Court are of Opinion the Defend^t is Not
Guilty in Manner and form as the Plantiff in his Dec^l hath
alledged, and thereupon Consider that the Defend^t Shall
Recover of the Plan^t his Cost taxed at £10=13=0 in old
tenor Bills and that Execution &c--

    A true Copy of Record Exam^nd
Copy 3/6   per Daniel Coit Clerk

[1750, Mar. 26, Stamford]
   Stamford In Connecticut. / March 26th 1750.
Rev^d S^r

  Agreable to the Venerable Societies Instructions I
here inclose my Notitia Parochialis, with Advice that I
have this day drawn upon the Treasurer a Set of Bills for
£15 Pounds Sterling Payable at Thirty Dayes after Sight In
Fav^r of Mr John Lloyd Merch^t --Should not have drawn till
the Expiration of my Year, Since I wrote & Sent a Notitia
Parochialis so lately, did not the pressing Circumstances
of my Family oblige me to it.--(and Sincerely acquaint
you that my Labours, so far as I Can judge, are very acceptable to my People; and they Express their gratitude to
the Honr^ble Society, for Appointing me, to their Service,
by Cheerfully Contributeing to my Support, according to
their Ability and they Hope for the future by their Quiet
& Peaceable Behaviour, to preserve their interest, in that
most Charitable Societies Favour; And as ye Interest of
Religion according to the Doctrine & worship of our holy
Ch^h was the great End of my appointment here, so you
may be Assured that I Receive all proper Incouragement
in the Execution of my Office; And my labours are Still
Attended with Some visible Success in Each Part of my
Mission; which is Manifest by the Peoples Zeal for the
Public worship of God, the^r Christian Behavour--and the
Converts y^t are Made to the Ch^h; There has been 4 Heads
of Families of go[od] Reputation lately declared Conformi-
ty &c: Since my last Acco[unt] to ye Honr^ble Society; and
Sundry more y^t Appear disposed to follo[w] their good
Example:--I Preached on Christmas last to a very numer-

ous & large Assembly, great numbers of the dissenters Came to Ch^h who had never ben there before, and be-haved them Selves with great decency, and Some of them Confessed, tha[t] they Never Saw a more Regular & well Ord^red Christian Assembly, alltho the Service of our Ch^h appeard Strange to them. I Still Endeavour to divide my Labours among the Severall Parts of my Extensive Mis-sion, so as to be as Serviceable to ye whole as may be; I Catechised Every Sunday ye last Year for 6 Months to-gether & Shall begin again after Easter & Continue it till September, have a Considerable Number of Children to Instruct--I Preached the Second Sunday in Febr^y last to the Poor People at Ridgefield, which are at about 15 Miles distance, gave the Communion to 31 Communicants; whose destitute Circumstance[s] with ye Poor Ch^h of Norwalk I heartily Compassionate, to whom like wise I lend all the Assistance I am Capable off: and I Pray God to Dispose the Honour^bl Society in their great Charity to Provide for those destitute Churches, assoon as they Judge themselves in a Condition.--I Only Add my Humble Duty to the Ven-erable Society, with Hearty Prayers to Allmighty God to Vouchsafe his Blessing to all their Charitable designs, and Beg leave with much Respect to Subscribe / as I am / Rev^d S^r / your most Obd^t / and very Humble Servt

                                    Ebenez^r Dibb[lee]

[The] Rev^d [Do]ct^r Bearcroft
[Sec]rt^y to the Honble Society &c:

Stamford in Connecticut
March 26th 1750.

Notitia Parochialis

I	N^o of Inhabitants about	4550
II	N^o of the Baptized about	3500.
III	N^o of Adults Baptized Since ye 29th of Sept^br last	3
	of Infants	22.
IV	N^o of actual Communicants of the Ch^h of England	43.
V.	N^o of those who Profess themselves of ye Ch^h of England and are Heads of Families	114.
VI.	N^o of Desenters of All Sorts (no Papists[)] about 756 Heads of Families	
VII:	N^o of Heathen & Infidels about 150 Negro Slaves	
VIII:	N^o of Converts &c: 4.	

Rev^d S^r / Your most Obed^t / Most Humble Servt
                                    Ebenez^r Dibblee

[1750, Mar. 27, Groton]

Groton 27 March 1750

Notitia Parochialis

1	Number of Inhabitants in ye 5 towns more imediatly under my care	About 1600 Familyes
2	N^o of the Baptiz'd	About 2/3
3	N^o of Adults &c	None
4	N^o of Actual Communicants &c under my Care	120
5	N^o of those who profess themselvs of ye Chh &c	About 140 familyes

6	N^o of Disen^r of All Sorts &c.	of every Sort exceepting Pap^ts
7	N^o of Heathens & Infidels	Heath Ab^t 100 Inf: none professedly.
8	N^o of Converts &c	4 or 5

[Ebenezer Punderson]

[1750, June 25, North Groton]

N Groton 25 June 1750
Rev^d S^r

As the venerable Society have appointed me an Itin-crant Missionary in N England the Members of the Chh of England in Middletown, Cohabit, Guilford, Wallingsford, Mansfeild, Stafford, &c have Submited themselves to my Pastoral Care; and whatever Ministerial taxes they have been Assessed to pay, I have order'd to be entirely ap-ply'd towards building their Churches; & maintaining Readers among them: without taking any part of them to my Self. My Discharges they have accepted in Middle-town, Guilford, Wallingford Mansfeild, Stafford Canter-bury &c. But in Branford & Cohabit, they have in the most virulent manner been distressing, & Imprisoning the Mem-bers of ye Chh of Eng^d: the last Winter takeing Encourag-ment from my ill success in indeavouring to recover the taxes taken, about 3 years agoo from one Jonathan Wood, & last year from Mathew Paul of the Union; who had upwards of 12£ our money taken from him, as will appear by the inclosd receipts; great has been the expence, & many the Hardships I have been at in indeavouring to protect ye Chh only in that Liberty w^c Baptists & Quakers universally en-joy, in this Government; & now despair without that Ven-erable Board will Interpose and procure an express Order, that the Professors of the Establish'd Chh Shall enjoy at least the Same Ease & liberty that Dissenters are Indulg'd in. there are So many coming over to the Chh on the one hand, or going over to ye Indepen^ts on the other that the Presbyterians (as they call themselves) imagine oppres-sion & Violence the only method to support their declining Interest. as appears by their taking by distress more than 500£ from the Independants, in a less Space than 15 Miles Sq^r annually, for Some years past; w^c Sufferings greatly excite my pitty, Since both, tho equally involvd in Scism, & Error have or ought to have the Same indulgence from the Act of Tolleration.

Since mine of ye 26 of March ult. upon the 14th of May I set out upon a Long Journey Went to Hartford to forward a Memorial to ye Assembly in favour of the Chh the next day Rode to Middletown 16^m & preachd them a Sermon. the day after went down to Cohabit- 14^m preach'd the day following to a pretty Congregation of Sincere Chh people all brought over to the Chh by GODs blessing my Labours there. the next day & day following preach'd in Guilford christned 4 Children. and went to Brandford. preach'd to at least 300 persons administred the Sacra-ment of ye Lords Supper to about 30 Comt^s Baptizd 4 Children. the next day wrode to Wallingford preachd to a pretty Congregation Bap^d 3 Children. the next day went to Middletown & the day following preachd there. the next

day wrode to E: Haddam where probably there never was a Minist^r of ye Chh of Eng^d before had a congregation of near 100 persons 1 Child Christ^d & 1 Couple marryed added 2 to our Chh. who receivd the Communion the first Sunday of this Instant & are persons of an excellent Caract^{tr} the next day ariv'd at my House. that in the Space of 12 days I traveld near 200⌐ and preach'd 9 Sermons & had near 1000 persons attended divine Service in the Several places. Upon the 12 of this Ins^t I preach'd in Windham, 2 Persons declar'd for the Chh. the next day in Mansfeild cristend a Child. the next day at Hebron to a Large Congregation after Service 20 of them Sign'd a Bond for 30£ Sterling to Mr Colton annually: earnestly entreating the Society that he might have leave to come Home in the fall.

Above all things I earnestly entreat the Venerable Society to have such Compassion upon the members of the Chh of England as to procure immediatly a tolleration for them; from all such unrighteous oppressions, that the Messengers of peace they Send into this Gov^t might not be perplex'd & Harassed by endless law proceedings. I have drawn for 8£ of my last Quarters Salary in Favour of the Revd Mr Broughton & the Rest in favour of Doc^r Woodbridge & am

Rev^d S^r / Your's & the Societys / Obedient Hum^{ble} Servant

Eben^r Punderson

PS. I begg the Societys acceptance of my Humble thanks In behalf of ye Chh in Norwich for their kind present.

[1750, June 25, North Groton]

       Exchange for 8£ Sterling.   25 June 1750

S^r

At thirty days after Sight of this my Second Bill of exchange my first of the Same Tenor not being paid; Pray pay to the Revd Mr Thomas Broughton, or Order eight pounds Sterling, & hereof I have given the Society proper Advice & am

       Your Humble Servt

       Eben^r Punderson

To Slingsby Bethel Esqr Treas^r to ye Society for propagating the Gosp^l

[1750, July 20, New London]

My Lord

To vindicate ye Cause of oppress'd Innocence, & relieve those who suffer for Righteousness Sake, is ye Command of our Saviour & a grand Characteristic of his holy Religion. How far I have succeeded in this noble Design, which now in all Humility sues for Your Lordships consummating Approbation, Mr Copp, ye Bearer hereof is both a Witness & Example. This Gentleman, who has had a liberal Education, according to ye Methods practis'd in this place, descended from Presbyterian Parents, & was brought up in ye utmost Prejudice to our Religion. At my coming to this Mission, I found him ye publick Master of a Grammer & Mathematical School, supported solely by Presbyterian Donations. By Report he was a bigotted Independent, but a strict Moralist. Curiosity at first led me into his Acquaintance, & Conversation inform'd me of his Parts. His Aversion to our Church I easily apprehended arose from Zeal without Knowledge, Zeal to his own Sect,

& Ignorance of our reasonable Service. Hence I apply'd my self to treat with him in an easy manner, & by degrees more closely upon Topics of Religion; & afterwards induc'd him to read some Books wrote in Vindication of our Discipline: ye happy Consequence of which was, he admir'd at, & ingenously own'd his Ignorance, confess'd ye Purity of our Church, & has reason'd & read himself into a conscientious Conformist, as I verily believe. This has so exasperated his bigotted Benefactors, that he is depriv'd of his Office, & ye very house he rented for some Years is hired to another. However, he resolves to persevere in his well-grounded Resolution, & to rely intirely upon ye Providence of that God, who has changed his Darkness into Light: & hence he presumes to cast himself at Your Lordship's Feet, &, if found worthy, to implore ye sacred Imposition of Your Hands. God forbid, y^t I shou'd from any Motives whatever recommend an improper Labourer into Christ's Vineyard; & therefore am humbly of Opinion that this Gentleman will make a very useful Missionary. If it be for his Glory, may God incline Your Heart to add him to our Number, otherwise not.

'Tis reported, my Lord, that you intend to appoint a new Commissary in these parts, & that a Native of the place is to discharge that Office. But I hope Your Lordship (for God's sake pardon my well-intended Freedom) will be pleas'd to consider, y^t as an American is Commissary in ye Western, so to condescend that an European may be empower'd in ye Eastern part of this Continent. For my part I am not at all fit for y^t honourable Post; but will be bold to say, y^t Doctor Macsparran is every way qualified for it.--All Europeans, especially Ministers, meet with a very ungrateful Reception here: & certain I am, y^t there is a Plan already form'd [to] extirpate us entirely. A Plan, which in it's Emb[r]yo I zealously oppos'd, & by ye Help of G^d hit[her]to defeated. A Plan, which I doubt not to affirm wou'd shake ye Foundation of these Infan[t] Churches, by casting us absolutely upon ye Mercy of ye Populace; & reduce us into a servile Presbyterian Dependance. 'Twou'd be too tedious to trouble You with a Recital of ye who[le] Affair, which ye Bearer being perfectly acquainted wth, will, at Your Lor[d]ship's Command, impartially relate.

'Twou'd be too long, as well as tragical to repeat ye several Difficulties, Severities & Affronts, which our Hearers are harass'd with in many parts of this Colony, by rigorous Persec[u]tions, & arbitrary pecuniary Demands, inflicted on ye conscientious Members of our Church [by] domineering Presbyterians, ye old implacable Enemies of Sion's Prosperity & Peace. Here Your Lordship's Sons are imprison'd arrested & non-suited with prodigious Cost, contrary to ye Laws of God & Man. All Professors of ye Church of England, over whom there is not a particular Missionary appointed, are oblig'd to support Presbyterian Teachers & their Meeting Houses, a Cruelty, Injustice & Usurpation impos'd on no other Society. This is solemn Truth. As Your Lor[d]ship is not only Bishop of these parts, but also one of his Majesty's most Honourable Privy Council, I am confident a Letter from You to some of Your Clergy in this Colony, with Your Lordship's Order or Request to our General assembly, y^t all ye Members or Professors of ye Church of England be exempted from all Rates & Demands what-

ever collected for yᵉ Support of other Churches & Ministers than their own, wou'd obtain yᵉ desir'd Effect, & every day gain Proselytes to our holy Communion, who are now restrain'd thro' Fear of additional Taxes.

I cannot, before I conclude, in Justice conceal yᵉ unanimous Approbation Your Lordship's seasonable, pathetic & religious Discourse upon yᵉ two late Earthquakes, met with here, as I am persuaded it did in all other Places & by all Denominations: but greatly lament, yᵗ tho' so many were dispers'd, yet so few came to our Share. I had but one, yᵉ Gift of a Presbiterian Teacher. As I am fully convinc'd, Your Lordship's sole Design was, to revive, instil & impress sincere Religion, & yᵉ Reverential Fear of God in yᵉ Hearts & Souls of a degenerate, licentious Age, so yᵗ Your Generosity will bestow me some of those useful Tracts, & Your Goodness pardon yᵉ candid Freedom, Sentiments & innumerable Faults of this Letter, is yᵉ humble Desire & earnest Request of,

     My Lord, / Your Lordship's, /
         most obedient Servant / & dutiful Son
                 Matt' Graves.

New London July 20ᵗʰ 1750

[Endorsed:] Answᵈ 21ˢᵗ April 1752.

[1750, Aug. 16, Hebron]

Know all Men by these Presents, yᵗ I Jonathan Colton of Hebron in yᵉ County of Hartford in his Majesty's Colony of Connecticut in New England, am holden & stand firmly bound & oblig'd unto John Bliss of Sᵈ Hebron in yᵉ County & Colony aforesaid, in yᵉ full & just Sum of thirty Pounds Bills of publick Credit of yᵉ old Tenor, to yᵉ wᶜʰ Payment well & truly to be made & done I bind my self, my Heirs, Executors & Administrators firmly by these Presents sign'd wᵗʰ my Hand & seal'd wᵗʰ my Seal, dated yᵉ 16ᵗʰ day of Augˢᵗ in yᵉ 24ᵗʰ Year of his Majesty's Reign George yᵉ 2ᵈ of Great Brittain, France & Ireland King &c, Anno Dom: 1750

The Condition of this present Obligation is such, yᵗ if yᵉ above bounden Jonathan Colton, his Heirs, Executors, Administrators, or either of them shall stand ready upon Demand made, to deliver up to yᵉ Sᵈ John Bliss, or his Heirs a Warrantee of an Acre & half of Land, wᶜʰ yᵉ same John Bliss gave to yᵉ Sᵈ Jonathan Colton, or to his Heirs 30£ in Bills of publick Credit of yᵉ old Tenor, then this present Obligation shall be void & of none Effect, but in Default thereof shall remain & abide in full Force, Strength & Power & Virtue

                 Jonathan Colton [Seal]

Sign'd & deliver'd in yᵉ Presence of

Joseph Peters   Andrew Peters

P.S [by Matthew Graves] I assure you I lent yᵉ Money to yᵉ poor Man & Colton refus'd to take it, because it was a fortnight before yᵉ time; & tho' he would not deliver up yᵉ Deed for some Weeks after, yet he made yᵉ poor Man pay Interest for yᵗ very time.

[1750, Sept. 17, Stratford]
May it please your Lordship,

I do, with the utmost Gratitude, acknowledge your

Lordship's most kind & condescending Letter to me of January 23ᵈ which did not come to my hand till late in June. I now take this first Opportunity to lay before you the Duty & Thanks of the Clergy in these parts, as many of them as met at our Commencement which was the last week, to whom I communicated it; who are very glad to understand that your Lordship is so kindly disposed to favour their Request: & I am extremely obliged to your Lordship for your favourable Thoughts & Intentions with regard to me.

Nothing could give us a greater Satisfaction than the Prospect of being under your Lordship's Care: But as there never was so large a Tract of the Earth overspread with Christians, without so much as one Bishop, nor ever a Country wherein Bishops were more wanted, so nothing can be imagined of greater Consequence to the Interest of true Religion than that instead of Commissaries we should have Suffragan Bishops immediately to preside over us, under your Lordship as our Cheif Pastor; that, as London is the Fountain of Trade & Business to the Plantations, it may also be to them the Fountain & Head of Religion: which would be one of the best means to secure our Dependence on our Mother Country, as the Contrary would be apt to have a contrary Tendency.--And very hard it seems, My Lord, as well as not to consist with true Policy, that these large & increasing Dispersions of the true Protestant English Church should not be provided with Bishops, when our Enemies the Roman Catholics of France & Spain find their Account in it to provide for theirs: even Canada has her Bishop which is scarce bigger than some one of our Provinces; not to mention the little whimsical Sect of Moravians who also have theirs. I therefore wish & pray God your Lordship may not be without good Hopes of procuring for us so great a Blessing.--I humbly beg your Lordship's Pardon for my writing with so much Freedom & Earnestness, which, I own, hardly becomes me, but I am urged on to it by my Solicitude for the Interest of true Religion in this my Native Country: I therefore humbly hope your Lordship's Candor will excuse me

When we were together, My Lord, we gave our Testimonials in behalf of three of our Candidates, who proposed this Fall to wait on your Lordship for holy Orders.--Two of them belong to this Province.--And as the Society have not yet been in a Condition to admit of their going with Expectation of any Title from them, the Necessity & Urgency of the people is such, that they propose to beg of your Lordship to accept of such a Title as they are able to make, tho' not without much Difficulty, which is 30 pounds Sterling per ann. & which the young Gentlemen are willing to accept of, at least for the present till the Society can add their Assistance towards their Support.

I pray God long preserve your Lordship's Life & Health which are of so great Importance to his Church, & beg an Interest in your Prayers & Blessing, & remain,

May it please your Lordship, / your Lordship's / most dutiful / & obedient Son, & most / obliged humble Servant,

                 Samuel Johnson

Stratford in New England
Septʳ 17ᵗʰ 1750.

To the Lord Bishop of London

[1750, Sept. 29, Stamford]

Stamford in Connecticut / Septemb.^r 29. 1750.
Revd S.^r

According to the Venerable Societies Direction I here Send inclosed my Notitia Parochialis, with Advice, that I have this Day drawn upon the Treasu.^r A Set of Bills for Ten Pounds Sterling, Payable at Thirty dayes after Sight; In Fav.^r of Henry Lloyd Esqr--Humbly Intimateing my Continuance at Stamford faithfully Endeavouring the discharge of those Important Duties Committed to my trust. Still meeting wth very Suitable Incouragement from ye peaceable Bahav.^r & pious Zeal of the Poor people of my Parish who generally Speaking appear more & more Confirmed in the Doctrine & Worship of our Holy Ch.^h And testify the Same by their Steady Attendance On & their regular & devout performance of the Publick Offices of Religion. So that I confess my Self very Happy and Easy in this respect in my Parish meeting with Suitable incouragement in the Execution of my Office, hopeing by the Blessing of God to be Instrumental of doing much good, & furthering the Pious Ends of that most Charitable Board: My Little flock is Still Increaseing; Have the pleasure to See a more Catholick & Charitable disposition diffuseing it Self among the Dissenters; and the late Conformity of one very Serious good Man Among y^m who has long painfully Laboured to Satisfy himself in the Controversy has Considerably Contributed thereto. I Still Divide my labours among the Several parts of my Extensive Mission to be as Usefull as may be to the Whole; preaching One Sunday in Every Month at Horseneck or Stanwich about 5 Miles distance from me, & Once a month on Week Dayes at one of those Places to Considerable Considerations; there being 52 Heads of Families professors of ye Church In those two places. Have ben prevailed with, by the Importunities of the Poor People at Ridgefield, to Visit y^m four times the Sumer past, twice on Sundayes to Administer the Communion, the last Sunday I was there had 47 Communicants. Mr Lampsons frequent Visits to Norwalk has I Suppose prevented his attending the Ch^h at Ridgefeild the Summer past, & they being much More Contiguous to me than to him, Engage them to Requesting my assistance.

Have Baptized Since Lady Day last 4 Adults, 19 Infants, 7 Added to the Communion. Have performed the Office of Catechist from Easther to Septemb.^r had Near 30 Children who gave their Attendance on Sundays, & Some of Them had allmost Compleated Mr Lewis^s proof Catechism.--Am frequently Sent for 15 or 20 Miles back into the Country to Visit the Sick or Baptize ye Children of poor people who are dispersed about, & destitute of any other Person nearer In ye Ord^{rs} of our Church to administer among y^m: The fatiagues of w^h Service together with the Duties of my own Parish, Occasions Such frequent Absence from my Family, w^h is not Small haveing a Wife, & Six Children, & my Wife an Infirm Person reduces me to Some Straits & difficulties. But If I may be So happy to further the Pious Ends of the Venerable Society, & promote the Interest of True Religion, I Shall think my Self Happy. I Only add my Duty to the Venerable Board, and Hearty thanks for the Valluable Books Sent me w^h I Received by the hands of Doct^r Johnson. (Mr Whites first & Second defence of his Letters comeing very Seasonably, & the pretended Dissenting Gentlemans Answers haveing ben

Industriously dispersed among ye people of my Parish) concludeing with Hearty prayers to Allmighty God to Succeed all their Pious & Charitable Designs Beg Leave with much Respect and in all Humility to Subscribe
Revd S.^r / Your most Obed.^t / Most Humb^{le} Servt
Ebenez.^r Dibblee

The Revd Doct^r Bearcroft Secrat^r
to ye Honorb^{le} Society &c:

Stamford In Connecticut
Septemb.^r 29. 1750.

Notitia Parochialis

1:	N.^o Of Inhabitants about	4600.
2:	N.^o Of the Baptized about	3600
3:	N.^o Of the Adults Baptiz^d last half Year Three of them whites & one Black.	4.
4:	N.^o Of Infants Baptiz^d last half Year	19.
5:	N.^o Of actual Communicants of ye Ch.^h of England	50.
6:	N.^o Heads of Families professing ye Ch.^h &c:	118.
7:	N.^o Dissenters of all Denominations (No Papists) Heads of Families about	770.
8:	N.^o Heathens & Infidels chiefly Negro Slaves about	160.
9:	N.^o Of Converts &c:	7.

I Am / Revd Sr Your / Most Obed^t / Most Humb^{le} Servt
Ebenez.^r Dibblee

[1750, Oct. 24, London]

Charterhouse Octo.^r 24th 1750
Gentlemen

It is with much concern that the Society for the Propagation of the Gospel in Foreign Parts are informed, that you have not yet perform'd your Promise of Setling a good Mansion-house and Glebe on the Missionary of New London, and of Contributing according to your best Abilities to his Support, whose Abilities and good behaviour are such, as right well deserve you should exert your Selves in his Favour, and if you do not immediately make good your Promises in relation to this matter, he will be Removed where his pious Labours will meet with a gratefull acknowledgement, recommending this to your Serious Consideration,

I am &c
P. B.

To the Churchwardens & Vestry }
of the Church of New London }

[1750, Oct. 24, London]

Charterhouse Octo.^r 24th 1750.
Rev^d S^r.

Your Letter dated North Groton 25th June 1750 hath been laid before the Society, which took notice and were pleased with your Diligence in your Propagating the Gospel, and they will do what they can to protect all the Members of our Church from oppression both in Connecticut and every where else, tho' to say the Truth this violent oppressive Spirit shews itself at present only there, and

the several Complaints and Papers relating to it are now under Consideration in order to put the most Effectual Stop to it--

The Petition of Hebron which you recommend hath been considered by the Society, whose low Circumstances will not permit them to fix a Resident Missionary there, but they must be contented to be comprehended within that of New London under the Care of Mr Graves

Mr Honyman of Newport, I find, is gone to his Grave in a good old Age, having obtained a good Report, and is now happy in the Reward of his pious Labours. May we all in our Several Stations do our best Endeavours in the same good Cause, and God grant his Blessing upon them

I am &c
P. B.

To Mr Punderson at North Groton

[1750, Oct. 25, London]

Charterhouse Octo^r 25th 1750
Rev^d S^r.

The Society for the Propagation of the Gospel in Foreign Parts are determined to defend all the Members of the Church of England in Your Colony in all their just and legal Rights, and are now consulting the proper Measures for Redress of those oppressions you complain of, which, it seems, have been audaciously carried as far as Imprisonment in some Neighbouring Places; However it adds to their Satisfaction to find the Church increasing under your Ministration amidst these iniquitous Proceedings, and that God may continue to Bless it and you, is the hearty Prayer of &c

P. B.

To The Revd Mr Mansfield
at Derby in Connecticut.

[1750, Oct. 25, London]
To Mr Dibble at Stanford.   D^o Date. [Oct. 25, 1750]
Rev^d S^r.

Your Letters are come safe, and the Society well pleased with y^r Conduct and Diligence have granted y^r Request of a Folio Bible and Common Prayer Book for the Chappel of Horseneck, The Church of Norwalks Petition, out of Respect to the Largeness of their Number is Granted, and a Missionary will be soon provided for them, in the mean Time you will be so good as to continue y^r Assistance to them, praying for Gods Blessing on all y^r pious Labours.

I remain &c^r
P. B.

This with the Books will
be sent to Dr Cutler.

[1751, Jan. 3, Hebron]

the Testimony of Jacob Ford of Heb^n in Hartford County in the Coloney of Conecticut of Lawfull Age Testifies and Saith Y^t Some Time in Novr Last past I Was in Company With Mr Matt Graves missionary of Newlond^n in Heb^n afores^d & I Told the S^d Graves that Some persons in Heb^n I Had Heard Ware a going to Send Home to the Bishop of England a Complaint against Him the Said Graves for

Treason as I Term^d it or for Speaking Contemptuously of His majesty King Georg & of the Nobility of England at the House of m^r Penock in Heb^n Where I Told Him I Heard that y^r He Should Utter Such Words as these   Speaking Conserning King Georg He Said one Could Seldom See him at His Chapel and of the Nobility of England they Did Not Trouble them Selves much With Relegion   s^d mathew Graves answer^d me the the S^d Ford in these Words--I Could Wish S^d m^r Graves that our King and His Nobility ware men of the temper of Holy David Who Loved to goe Up to the House of God But be it Spoke to their Shame they are Sildom or Never Seen at Church meaning as I Understood Him our Soverangn Lord King George the Second and the Nobility of England   Dated at Heb^n in Conecticut Jan^r the 3rd 1750/51   Jacob Ford--

Heb^n Hartford County Jan^r 3rd 1750/51

True Copy of the origenal attest P^r me--
Joseph Phelps Justice of peace

[1751, Jan. 3, Hebron]

Hebron Conecticut

Wee John Peters and Nathan Rowlee both of lawfull age do testify and say that sume time in the Month of June 1748 Wee heard the Revrd mr Mathew Graves declare that he had Authority over the Church at Hebron some time after wee heard him say that he had Not Authority over the Church at hebron, but turning to a Man he said he would Give him leave to tack of his Eare [take off his ear] if he did not git Author[i]ty over hebron Church In six months

John Peters
Nathan Rowlee

Hartford County Hebron Jan^r 3rd 1750/51

the above is a True Copy of the origenal attest P^r me--
Joseph Phelps Justice of Peace

[1751, Jan. 3, Hebron]

Heb^n in Conecticut

We Joseph man and Willm Penock Boath of Lawfull age Do Testifie and Say Some Time in June in the Year 1748 We Heard the Rev^d m^r Mat_ Graves misionary at Newlond^n Utter these Words viz a man Wou^d have Good Luck to See the King at His Chapel intemating plainly to our Understanding that He Went But Sildom to the publick Worship of God and as for the Great men in England He Said they Did not Trouble their Heads about Relegion: farther We heard m^r Graves Say, Y^t if he Should apear in favour of our Having a minister at Heb^n He fear^d he Should Loose Ten pounds of His Salary Which Was aded to m^r Seaburys Salary for oficiating at Heb^n and farther he Said that in Case We Wou^d Give Him a Bond to pay the Ten pounds our Selves if the Society Should Take it from Him Y^t then He Wou^d Serve Us in any form Y^t We Could Desire & farther m^r Graves put in Jno Bliss a Church Warden at Heb^n Who Was Never a Comunicant--

Heb^n Har[t]ford County
Jan^r 3rd 1750/51

Joseph man
Willm Penock

the above is a True Copy as Attest P^r me
Joseph Phelps [Justice of Peace]

[1751, Mar. 26, Stratford]

May it please your Lordship

The Bearer hereof is M: Thomas Bradbury Chandler whom a number of us joyntly recommended to your Lordship last Fall to be admitted to holy Orders, & he has now Leave from the Society to go for that purpose: concerning whom I need add nothing to what is contained in our joynt Testimonials, to which therefore, I refer your Lordship, & doubt not but he will prove a very worthy Missionary, & continue to deserve well that Recommendation.

On this Occasion, I write my most thankful Acknowledgment of your Lordship's kind Letter of Sept. 19th last, (which came not to my hand till this very month,) & would humbly inform your Lordship how extremely thankful we all are for the tender care you express for our Churches, & the solicitous Endeavours you are using to procure Bishops for these remote parts; & we earnestly pray God they may be attended with the desired Success: And I herewith send your Lordship a Copy of our joint Answer to a paper of proposals which have been sent into these parts, (signed by as many as could have opportunity,) if peradventure it may be of some use, tho' it may probably now be too late.--

As to what your Lordship desires in your letter to the late Bishops Commissaries, I must humbly beg to be excused, & to refer your Lordship to the Answers they will give to it; because I have no Copy of his late Lordship's patent, nor ever had more than a very transient Sight of it, & by reason of my Distance & extensive Care here, I have not for many years been at any Convention of the Clergy, nor was there ever any juridical Act carried on when I was present, besides Inquiries into the Condition of our parishes; so that I am unqualified to give any Light that can be of any use to your Lordship on this Subject.-- I could wish the Bishop or Commissaries might be impowered or directed to require an annual Account from the people of their punctual performing their part towards the Support of their Ministers, & that some provision could be made of a moderate Discipline purely Spiritual, in pursuance of the Rubric to suspend open & notorious evil livers from the H. Sacrament.--But I doubt not but your Lordship will do the utmost you can for us, if at all any thing can be done.--There are two more Candidates to whom we gave our Testimonials, who I beleive will shortly imbark, by whom, if any thing further occurs to me that can be of any use, I shall write further to your Lordship; mean time I remain,

My Lord, / your Lordship's most dutiful / & most obedient Son / & humble Servant

Samuel Johnson

Stratford in New England
    March 26, 1751.

To My L:d of London

A Copy of what was sent to a Member of the Society

As there hath been sent over, by some Members of the Society, to these parts, a Scheme of proposals relating to providing Bishops for these Countries, & some Account is desired concerning the State of things here, & the Sense of the people, & what other Objections there may be that are not already obviated; & one of those papers hath

been sent to the Rev:d M: Dibble, one of our Number, we humbly beg leave to give our joint Testimony relating to this affair; which is as followeth.

1. That we should have been glad if an Episcopate could have obtained among us, in it's full Vigor as at home; but such is the distressed & sinking Condition of Religion for want of a regular Episcopacy, that we should be glad above all things in this World, that a true Episcopate might obtain in these Countries in any Shape.

2. That we humbly apprehend our Dissenting Brethren are, really their own greatest Enemies as well as ours, in opposing Bps being sent into this Country; for their Case is very deplorable among themselves, since the late Enthusiasm hath thrown them into so many Feuds, Contentions & Separations, which the cho[ic]e of a Bishop would, we beleive, tend much to abate; & reduce them to a better State of unity in their own way, (as well as to reclame many of them,) for which reason, we do, from Conversations we have, some of us had with them, know it to be inwardly the hearty wish of several of the wisest & most moderate of them, both of Clergy & Laity, that Bishops were sent into America.

3. That we know of no Objection they can have but what would be sufficiently obviated by such a Scheme as is proposed, besides the general Notions they have against the Church, by which we humbly hope the Government at home will not be influenced even for their own sakes as well as our's, for the reasons above given--

4. That the very Cause of Christianity in general suffers, & will suffer more & more extremely, to the great Advantage of Infidelity, for want of the Influence of some great & worthy person in such a superiour Station to stem the Torrent, whose wise & good Conduct would in such a Country as this be of great Weight--

5. That we verily beleive the Dissenters would, in a little time be intirely easy under such a Scheme as is proposed, & that it would be every way of vast Advantage to the Church & the Interest of Religion in general, as well as the political Interest of the Nation.

6. That there are some Imprudences, to say no worse, & some little Controversies obtaining among some of our own Clergy, that very much hurt the Church & Religion in General, which the Awe of a worthy Bishop, would, we beleive, intirely put an end to, as well as Controversies & Disorders among the people.--And indeed, it is beyond Imagination to conceive how much weight an Episcopal Visitation would have to promote the true Interest both of Religion & Government, even if it were but once in 5 or 7 years.

Samuel Johnson	Joseph Lamson
John Beach	Ebenezer Dibble
James Wetmore	Richard Mansfield

[Endorsed:] Answ:d 21:st April 1752.

[1751, Apr. 2, Stamford]

Stamford Connecticut
New England Apr:l 2. 1751.

Rev:d S:r

Have according to Ord:r of the Venerable Board Inclosed my Notitia Parochialis with Advice that I have this

Day drawn upon yᵉ Treasuʳ a Set of Bills for Ten Pounds Sterling payable at thirty Dayes after Sight In favʳ of Mʳ John Lloyd Merchᵗ.

Have Received Your favʳ of yᵉ 25th of Octobʳ Last; and thank you for the kind Intimation, yᵗ my Conduct and Diligence in attending upon yᵉ Duties of my Office, meets with yᵉ Acceptance of the Honrᵇˡᵉ Society, and with the poor People of Horsneck Return our Hearty thanks for the Books In their great Charity Sent (tho not Yet Received) for yᵉ Use of the Chappel they have Erected.

The Chʰ of Norwalk appear very thankfull that the Society are pleased to Determin in their Favʳ & to grant them In Conjunction with Ridgefield to be a Mission. At their Instance & request, I preached In yᵉ Chʰ of Norwalk, yᵉ 4th Sunday in March last to a large Congregation & gave yᵉ Communion to upwards of Sixty persons. Have appointed Sunday after Esther to be at Ridgfield, where yᵉ poor People have been Entirely destitute of yᵉ publick Administrations of Religion the Year past Excepting, Once a Quarter on Sundayes and oftner on Week Dayes, I have Officiated Among them Sunday after Christmas I gave yᵉ Communion at Ridgefield to Upwards of Forty Persons. Truly Sʳ The Harvest is plenteous but the Labourers are few, And our Earnest prayers to yᵉ Lord of yᵉ Harvest, is, yᵗ a Door may be opened for a further Supply of faithfull Labourers, Have been Obliged In a great Measure to Act yᵉ Part of An Itinerant Missionary Ever Since my Return in Holy Ordʳˢ by Reason of the destitute Circumstances of the Poor people Scattered Abroad as Sheep without a Shepherd, as there are many 20, or 30 Miles back into the Country, who frequently Send for me. Broᵗ Lampson has taken yᵉ principle Care of yᵉ Chʰ of Norwalk for yᵉ Year Past, Excepting visiting them on Special Occasions, In Case of Sickness &c: on wʰ Occasions I have been frequently Sent for--Have Complied with the Request of Sundry poor People liveing back on yᵉ Oblong So Called, a Tract of Land lying as it were between yᵉ two Governments yᵗ of Ney York & Connecticut; 20 or 30 Miles have Engaged to travel up Amongst them yᵉ first week In May Next, where there is no Settled Minister of Any Denomination Among them, and I Am Informed many of them are professʳˢ of our Holy Chʰ but Destitute of yᵉ Means of Salvation & Seldom have an Oppertunity to Devote their Children to God In Covenant, have Appointed to preach at three different places yᵗ week on yᵉ Oblong[.] My Parish Remains by yᵉ Blessing of God on My Labours In Peace & Unity, have Sundry Accessions to yᵉ Chʰ Since my Last of yᵉ 29th of Septembʳ Preached last Christmas to a Large & Numerous assembly- multitude of the Dissenters Came to Chʰ & behaved with great Decency, 7 Heads of Families have declared Conformity Since my Last Accᵗˢ In Stamford & Some at Horseneck & Stanwick: Baptized but 1 Adult, 26 Infants white, 1 Black, 3 Added to yᵉ Communion.

The Duties of my Parish being Considerable, together with yᵉ Additional Duties wʰ in Compassion I have performed Among yᵉ poor people at Ridgfield & at other Places as I have been Occasionally Sent for, has Rendered my family Circumstances difficult, that yᵉ principle Discouragement I Labour Undʳ is with Respect my Support, My People truly Contribute According to their Abillity for my Support--but there are many whose Circumstances Are So Indigent yᵗ I Am Obliged to Remit their

Taxes or Suffer them to be distressed by the Dissenting Collectʳˢ for by yᵉ Laws of this Government the Professors of the Chʰ are Taxed, as there Dissenting B[r]ethren are, yᵉ Tax gathered by a Collectʳ of their Appointing, & he Generally by a too great Remissness in doing his Duty, or too Unreasonable Severity upon yᵉ professors of yᵉ Chʰ Endeavours to distress yᵉ Chʰ & hurt the Ministers of it-- & In Some parts of my Parish I have been no Small Sufferer In this Respect. If The Venerable Board Should find them selves in a Condition, & be So Charitably Disposed as to make Some Addition to my Salary--it would Enable me to go through yᵉ Important Duties of my Trust with much Less difficulty & pleasure, for I humbly beg Leave to Intimate That Since my Return, Endeavouring to Disengage my Self as much as possible from Secular Concerns yᵗ I might Devote my Self to yᵉ Service of God & yᵉ good of his Chʰ My Annual Support has not defrayed the Necesary & Unavoidable Expences of my Family, haveing a Wife & Six Children--But I mention my Case with no Small Reluctancy, knowing yᵉ Continual Applications from all Quarters to yᵉ Honourable Society for their Charitable Assistance, and with the Blessing of God on my Labours hope my Parish wʰ is gathering Strength may In Time be Able to Rendʳ my Circumstance[s] Easy & Comfortable.

Only Add my Humble Duty to the Venerable Board with Hearty & Earnest Prayers to Allmighty God the farther of Mercies to Prosper and Succeed All their Charitable Designs, and with much Respect to Your Self Beg Leave to Subscribe

An[d] I Am most Sincerely Reveᵈ Sʳ / Your most Obedᵗ / Most Humble Servᵗ

                                    Ebenezʳ Dibblee

To The Revᵈ Doctʳ Bearcroft
Secratᵗ To the Honʳ Society &c:

                            Stamford Aprˡˡ 2. 1751.
                            Connecticut in New England

            Notitia Parochialis

1. Nᵒ of Inhabitants about		4600.
2 Nᵒ of the Baptized about		3650
3 Nᵒ of Baptisms last half Year 1 Adult, 26 Infants white 1 Black totⁱⁿ		28
4. Nᵒ of Actual Communicants of yᵉ Chʰ		53
5 Nᵒ of Heads of Families professing yᵉ Chʰ		135
6 Nᵒ of Heads of Families dissenters of all Sorts, but no Papists about		780.
7 Nᵒ of Heathens & Infidels chiefly Negro Slaves		160.
8 Nᵒ of Converts &c:		3.

            Am Sʳ / Your / Very Humble Servᵗ
                            Ebenezʳ Dibblee

[1751, Apr. 29, New London]
My Lord

I hope Yʳ Goodness will excuse my Presumption, & impute this repeated Trouble to my Fondness of Decency & Order, & yᵉ present Necessity I am under of Yʳ Lordship's Advice. 'Tis my Misfortune, in the Parish where I reside, to have a Pair (to add no more) of remarkably

wicked men. One of them has married his Wife's Brother's Daughter, tho' I not only privately & separately discourag'd yᵉ affair, but publickly preach'd against such Cohabitations, both being present, before they were married. The Ceremony was perform'd, according to yᵉ Practice of this Country, by a Justice of yᵉ Peace, yᵉ Laws of this Colony permitting it. The other is an old Sea-Captain, who was never baptiz'd, a swearing, bullying Wretch, & in yᵉ Heathen's Phrase, nullâ Virtute redemptum.

These Persons, My Lord, as formerly, so on last Easter Monday were put up, by some of their iniquitous Brethren, to be Officers in yᵉ Church, which I always strenuously oppos'd; yᵉ former, because he lives in Incest: yᵉ latter, as believing it inconsistent to permit him an Officer of Christ's Church, who is not one of Xᵗ'ˢ Members. As Your Lordship's Advice & Direction are really necessary, so Your Encouragement to persevere, if right, will greatly relieve my present persecuted Condition.

I am, My Lord, by Order of yᵉ Religious Society appointed Missionary of the Parishes of New London & Hebron; in yᵉ latter of which one Mᵣ Jonathan Colton has officiously acted as Lay reader, & now intends to present himself for holy Orders. As I presume he's very unworthy that sacred Depositum, I thought it my Duty to inform Yᵣ Lordship,

1ˢᵗ That his Practice has been to preach his own Sermons or Crudities; & has taken upon him to expound, in Hebron Church, by glossing & adding, yᵉ Scriptures & Matter of Doctrine, tho' I strictly forbid him, & sent him (for he wou'd do Duty in my Absence) the Homilies already set forth to study, read & apply for yᵉ Confirmation of yᵉ true Faith, & Edification of yᵉ People, according to yᵉ 49th Can:, but he absolutely refus'd my Injunction.

2ˡʸ In or about Sepᵣ last he gave Notice in Church for a Parish-Meeting, to be held at one Doctor Shipman's on yᵉ Friday following, where his whole Study & Design were, to pick up what Accusations yᵉ Council cou'd recollect against their lawful Minister; & accordingly got three of them on yᵉ 3ᵈ of last Janʸ to swear against me for some words, said to be utter'd by me in Sᵈ Hebron in June 1748. By which affidavits my Life was struck at, they intending I shou'd, as they said, be try'd for High Treason. But the Wraths of Man did God restrain. The originals I have presum'd to inclose.

3ˡʸ On yᵉ 28th of Janʸ last he swore before a Justice of Peace in my hearing, yᵗ he heard me say on yᵉ 24ᵗʰ of Sᵈ Insᵗ yᵗ I was not afraid of one Eben: Horton (whom I was oblig'd to bind over to his good Behaviour) but omitted, in his Affidavit, these words, which I then added, viz in a publick, but a private Capacity, lest he shou'd shoot me, or knock out my Brains with a Club, behind my back.

4ˡʸ Instead of preparing himself for Orders, he is a Merchant, an Apothecary, a Farmer, & I may add an Extortioner, for which he will soon be prosecuted.

5ˡʸ He has procur'd an Obligation from about twenty Persons in Sᵈ Hebron for the Payment of 30£ Sterᵍ per Ann for his Ministerial Duties there. As I know yᵉ people, I'm persuaded 15 of them cannot pay him 10£ Ster: per Ann. But let me assure Yᵣ Lordship yᵉ Obligation is to be cancell'd whenever he returns. This he own'd, & they told me: & 'twas solely calculated to impose upon Yᵣ Lordship. 'Tis a Contract & Promise made directly by himself with yᵉ People, with his Knowledge & Consent, to pro-

cure & obtain yᵉ Ecclesiastical Place, Office or Living of Hebron; which sᵈ Obligation, Contract, or Promise, made by his Knowledge & Consent he is, when ordain'd, to make null & void, & therefore in my humble Opinion guilty of Simony, Can: 40: but I understand yᵗ he do's not expect yᵗ Oath will be administerd to yᵉ American Candidates. Yᵣ Lordship's known Penetration will easily see & detect yᵉ vile Design & Knavery of that Deed: by it he may, at pleasure, levy an Execution for yᵉ whole Sūm on what particular persons he thinks fit, & exempt yᵉ rest. Besides, they have no Copy of yᵉ Deed, nor any Security yᵗ ever he will resign it. And moreover some of yᵉ most substantial Persons in yᵉ Parish foreseeing yᵉ Intention have not sign'd, & many, that have, condemn themselves of Rashness, & complain'd to me of their Folly.

'Tis not long since I gave one a Discharge for three Years Rates, without any Recompence; & was lately requested by another of yᵉ Principal Signers to forgive him his Rates. So yᵗ I doubt not to pronounce yᵉ whole to be a Cheat, contriv'd to steal into Orders. Thus I have faithfully laid before Yᵣ Lordship yᵉ Impediments & notable Crimes, for which he ought not to be admitted into yᵉ Ministry. The Glory of God, & yᵉ Advancement of his holy Church have been yᵉ true Motives of this tedious Letter from,

My Lord / Yᵣ Lordship's / most obedient & / most dutiful Son, & / very humˡᵉ Servᵗ

Matt' Graves

New-London / Apˡ 29th 1751

[1751, July 17, Hebron]

Hebron Hartford County July 17ᵗʰ AD 1751 I Jonathan Colton of sᵈ Hebron Come to John Phelps Esquᵣ one of his Majestys Justices of the peace for Hartford County and do Complain and say that some Evil minded person in night season next after the sixteenth Day of this instant July did turn out of my inclosure being my proper Estate two Horses which Horses I put in there to pasture which Horses were turned out without my Consent and knoledge out of my pasture which lieth near to the Dwelling House of John Bliss of said Hebron which Horses being so turned out and straing away is to my damage the sum of ten shillings proclamation money and I do vehemently suspect that one John Bliss of sᵈ Hebron turned out said Horses as aforesaid and father I desire that the said John Bliss may be Caused forthwith to answear sᵈ Complaint and be father dealt with as the Law directs--

Jonathan Colton

A true Copey Examined by me
John Phelps Justice of yᵉ peace

[1751, July 17, Hebron]

At a Court for the triall of small Causes held in Hebron in Hartford County July yᵉ 17: 1751 present John Phelps Justice of the peace for said County to hear and try a Complaint brought by Mᵣ Jonathan Coulton of said Hebron against John Bliss of said Hebron for being suspisesly [i.e., suspiciously] gilty of turning out his Horses out of his parster in the night seson next after the sixteenth day of this instant July as by Complaint on file may apear

baring date July yᵉ 17: 1751   now said Bliss being brought
before this Court to answer to said Complaint and be ex-
amened as the Law directs said Bliss pleaded not gilty
this Court having examined the said Bliss and heard the
Evidencees and plees ofered in said Case and Considered
the same is of opinion that the said John Bliss is not gilty
Wheare upon tis Considered by this Court that mʳ Jonathan
Colton of said Hebron plaintiff pay the Corst of this suit
Corst alowed at Eighteen shillings

A true Copey Examined by me
                              John Phelps Justice of yᵉ peace

[1751, Sept. 25, Stratford]
May it please your Lordship,

   As the Ships are now going, I make my most humble
Acknowledgments for your Lordship's kind Condescention in your Letter to me of March yᵉ 6ᵗʰ which I do, by
Messʳˢ Camp & Colton, whom, according to your Instructions, we have recommended for holy Orders for Middletown & Hebron, who engage each 30£ per anⁿ towards their
Support.--I wish the Society could make some small Addition, but if they are not able, I humbly hope your Lordship will accept of this for a Title for the present.

   I am very thankful, as we all are, for Your Lordship's patience & perseverance in soliciting for us, & that
when you wrote you did not yet despair. May God incline
the Hearts of those who oppose it, yet to favour so reasonable & necessary an Establishment!--I am, I must own,
my Lord, the more solicitous, (which is also the Case of
several others,) as I have a Son preparing for Orders, of
whom I have good Hope, if he lives, that he may be of
some good use in the Cause of Religion: But it is somewhat shocking to me that he must go a 1000 Leagues for
Orders, when of 25 within my knowledge, who have gone
that Voyage on that Errand, 5 have died of the Small pox
or been lost at Sea, so that if he goes, it should seem
there are but 5 to 1, whether ever he returns.--

   I humbly hope my Anxiety on this Account, as well as
for the general Interest of the Church & Religion, will be
considered by your Lordship as some Apology for my being
too forward in troubling you on this Subject; & that you will,
for the same reason be so candid as to excuse me, if I
humbly venture to suggest, in case an Establishment cannot be obtained, whether one or other of the younglest &
ablest of the Bishops of the smaller Diocesses, might not
be disposed, & have a Commission, to visit these parts
of the World, & spend a year or two among us; & so from
time to time, once in about seven years, till a Settlement
could be had: Duty being in the mean time done for the absent Bp, by one of the neighbouring Bishops?--This might
answer many good Ends if nothing else could be done.--
Pardon this presumption, my Good Lord, & permit me &
mine still an Interest in your prayers & Blessing, who remain, My Lord,

                        your Lordship's most dutiful Son
                        & most obedient humble Servant
                                    Samuel Johnson.

Stratford in New-England,
   September yᵉ 25ᵗʰ 1751.

My Lord of London

[1751, Sept. 30, Stamford]
                     Stamford Connecticut In
                     New England, Septʳ 30. 1751
Revᵈ Sʳ
   May it please the Honourable Society, That I Inclose
my Notitia Parochialis, with Advice, that I have this Day
drawn upon yᵉ Treasuʳ a Set of Bills for Ten Pounds Ster-
ling; payable at thirty dayes after Sight in favʳ of Henry
Lloyd Esqʳᵉ
   And through yᵉ Blessing of God, on my weak, but I
trust Sincere Endeavours to promote the Interest of True
Religion & Vertue, can truly acquaint yᵉ Venerable Board,
that my Labours in this part of our Lord Vinyard, is Still
Attended with Some visible & desireable Success; more
Especially at Stamford yᵉ Seat of my Extensive Mission.
Our holy Chʰ daily gains ground & Credit among Dissenters who have been Edeacatad In Strong prejudices against
it; and notwithstanding yᵉ Endeavours wʰ are Still Used to
deter Men from Conformity to its Excellent worship, Doctrines & Government: And Blessed be God, yᵉ Chʰ Under
my Pastoral Care continues to Increase In Number; &
what is Still more Comfortable, I Charitablee hope, In
true Piety & Godliness- There has been yᵉ Accession of
5 Heads of Families to yᵉ Chʰ Since my last &c: & Some
of them persons of Note & as good Reputation as any among
the Dissenters- and 5 Added to yᵉ Communion- 40 Infants
Baptizᵈ It is allmost Three Years Since I Returned to my
Cure, Since wʰ Time I have Baptized; 174 Infants: 22
Adults: at my first administring yᵉ Communion had but
16; yᵉ Number is now Increased to fifty Eight;--I Continue
to discharge yᵉ duties of my Parish as formerly.--In May
last, at yᵉ Earnest Instance of Some poor people, about
30 Miles Distance who live back upon yᵉ Borders of yᵉ
two Governments Connecticut & New York, I made them
a Visit; preached four Dayes Successively at different
places, to Numbers of People & Baptized Eleven Children:-
Have Continued to Visit yᵉ Poor people at Ridgefield as
formerly, & Once have Administred the Communion to yᵐ
Since Easter, to upwards of 40 Communicants: hope they
may Now be otherwise happily Supplied In Conjunction with
Norwalk:- Have performed yᵉ Office of Catechist, Since
Easter, on Sundayes after Evening Service to a Considerable Number of Children, Some of yᵐ have made Such
proficiency as to be perfected In Lewisˢ Explanation of
our Excellent Chʰ Catechism.--The want of Prayer Books
& other pious Tracts is very Considerable among many
poor people In my Parish & others Contiguous to me,
those wʰ yᵉ Venerable Board Sent by me were Soon disposed off- And if yᵉ Honourable Board In their great &
Extensive Charity Should be pleased to Supply them with
farther helps to Devotion & Instruction, as In their great
wisdom they Shall See Meet, it would be most thankfully
Received.
   I Only Add my Duty to yᵉ Venerable Board, and
Hearty Prayers to Allmighty God to Succeed all their
Charitable Designs, & beg leave with much Respect to
Your Self to Subscribe as I am In All Humility
   Revᵈ Sʳ / Your most Obedᵗ / Most Humble / Servᵗ
                                    Ebenezʳ Dibblee

To the Revᵈ Doctʳ Bearcroft
Secrataʳ To the Honourable Society
for Propagation of yᵉ Gospel &c:

Stamford In Connecticut
Septemb.^r 30. 1751.

Notitia Parochialis

1. N.^o of Inhabitants about   4650.
2. N.^o of the Baptized about   3700
3. N.^o of Adults Baptized last half Year
   of Infants   40
4. N.^o of Actual Communicants of y^e
   Ch^h of England   58.
5. N.^o of Heads of Families professors
   of ye Ch^h &c: 141.
6. N.^o of Dissenters, Heads of Families,
   No Papists, about   790
7. N.^o of Heathens and Infidels chiefly
   Negro Slaves   160
8. N.^o of Converts &c: 3

I am / Rev^d S^r / Your most Obed^t / Humble Servt
                    Ebenez.^r Dibblee

[1751, Oct. 20, Stratford]
                    Stratford N. E. Oct. 20. 1751
My Lord
    Since writing my other Letter by Messrs Camp &
Colton, I have thought it might not be amiss to obviate an
Objection, that may perhaps fall under your Lordship's
Notice, against each of them.--The only Objection against
Mr Camp will be obvious to your Lordship, & that is a
Defect in his left Hand, which may seem to render him not
so capable of administering the Sacrament with so much
Decency as might be wished, with regard to his holding
the Patten: But as to this; he has by practice acquired such
a Dexterity in the use of it, that I humbly think there will
be no Difficulty attending it that should be a sufficient Reason to debar him, (of which however your Lordship will
readily make a Judgment,) especially since he is so much
esteemed by his people, & there is so good Reason to
think he may do much good Service among them.--
    As to Mr Colton, the only Difficulty with regard to
him, is, that tho' he has the universal Esteem of the rest
of the Clergy in this Colony, & of all his people except one
or two troublesom persons, he has not the good Fortune to
be acceptable to the Revd Mr Graves; (who it is said will
oppose his obtaining orders;) the sole Occasion of which
has been, that he having been chosen by the people of Hebron for their Minister, before Mr Graves came to the
New-London Mission, (to which Hebron had heretofore
been an Appendage,) they were very tenacious of him, &
desirous of having him for their resident Minister, as being 30 Miles distant from New-London, & for that reason
were unwilling to come under Mr Graves, or be accounted
as a part of his Cure.--This occasioned a Sharp Contention between him & them, & some few of them, (on whose
Account it is pity the rest should suffer,) may have treated him indecently, who on his part also, may have carried
his Resentments too far.--This however hath occasioned a
Disaffection in him towards Mr Colton, being aprehensive
of his taking part with those people against him.--But I
cannot find he has any just Grounds for these Apprehensions. On the Contrary he has endeavoured as far as he
could to be at good terms with Mr Graves, & I believe he

has conducted with as much Caution & Discretion as
could be expected under his Circumstances.--So that I
can truly say, I know of nothing in his Conduct that can
be any just Objection against his being admitted to holy
Orders, in which your Lordship sees the Clergy here
are all the rest united.--I am My Lord,
            your Lordship's / most dutiful Son /
                & most obedient humble Servant
                            Samuel Johnson

My L^d of London

My Lord
    to the truth of the Doc^{rs} Letter on the former page
I can safely Subscribe and am
            My Lord / Your Lordships /
                most dutifull Son & Servant
                            Ebenezer Punderson

[1751, Dec. 17, New London]
Good Sirs
    I was hoping y.^t Time & Reflection wou'd have pro-
duc'd some proper & expected Alteration in ye minds of
these People; but despair, while Mr Steward & Capt. Durfey so inflexibly unite in their malicious Principles & infidel Practices. In all other Instances no Persons are at
greater Variance, but in persecuting ye Ministers of
Christ, like Pontius Pilate & Herod, they become Friends.
How indefatigably they have strove to confirm this Assertion, Mr Colton will demonstrate to a tittle. No base
Arts or Devices have been spar'd (during his Continuance
here, where he embark'd) to deceive him in my Character, in order to paint me to my Patrons & Superiors in
ye most frightful Shades. But whilst I can engage Jehova
Nisi on my side, I will not be afraid of what Man can do
unto me.--I formerly laid before you my Objections to
Mr Colton's Designs, & am convinc'd in my Conscience
he's a most improper person for holy Orders--On ye 7th
of July last he procur'd two Boys, one aged 15, ye other
not so old, to swear against one of my Parishoners at
Hebron; but happily ye Justice saw thro' ye horrid Design, & prevented Perjury. I examin'd the elder & ask'd
him, how he cou'd know ye person exactly at nine O Clock
in a dark Night & at a great Distance? He said he thought
it to be him.--The poor man was arrested upon ye Night-
Law for turning Horses out of Mr Colton's Land; tho' by
two aged Witnesses upon Oath it was prov'd he had not
been out of his House y.^t Evening & y.^t Night.--As M.^r
Colton says he go's for holy Orders from an inward Call,
independant of ye Society, I have sent ye original Papers,
relating to this Fact, wrote by ye Justice, to his Lordship; before whom I have also laid an Original Bond,
drawn & sign'd by Colton, a true Copy whereof you have
here inclos'd. The wicked Design you'll easily perceive;
only let me observe, y.^t it's computed he has taken about
10£ for ye Loan of 20£ for half a Year. I cou'd lay before
you several other enormous Crimes, wilful, deliberate
Perjury against me before a Justice I was an Eye-witness
of, wth many other particulars, too numerous to write,
too offensive to be heard. But God's Will be done!
    I have little to say of ye Progress of these People
in Virtue, or ye Good I do among them. I have however
regularly prepar'd & lately baptiz'd five Whites, & two

Negroes, all adults, & have others under proper Instructions, in order to initiate them into Christianity. Certainly
this Congregation wou'd flourish exceedingly were two of
it's Members of another Persuasion, or rather of a more
Christian Spirit. I desire to know how my last Requests
were accepted by yᵉ Venerable Society. Their Will shall
always be agreeable to me, So my sole Study shall be
to promote yᵉ true Religion of Christ & yᵉ Glory of his
Church. When you are at Leisure to honour me with a Letter, be pleas'd to send it to Mʳ James Honeyman. I hope
an Order for this, in Favour of Mʳ Slone of this place, &
of Mʳ Honeyman for next Quarter will meet with proper
Encouragement. Your condescending to present my Duty
& Service to my Venerable & August Patrons is yᵉ earnest
Request of their sincere Missionary & / Good Sirs / Yʳ
most grateful, / humˡᵉ & obedient Servt

                      [Matthew Graves]

My Sister & I beg our Compliments
may be acceptable to yʳ Lady & You.

In yʳˢ dated June 22ᵈ 1749 you were pleas'd to write thus,
I have taken down yᵉ Name of yᵉ Person you mention to
me, & shall remember it upon a proper Occasion.

N. London Decʳ 17ᵗʰ / 1751

Be pleas'd to favour me wᵗʰ some Abstracts, having not
receiv'd any since those publish'd 1749.

[1751, Dec. 23, New London]
My Lord

    I hope my Zeal in a good Cause will plead my Excuse
for writing again upon yᵉ same ungrateful Subject--I suppose Mʳ Colton has already presented himself a Candidate
for holy Orders. About four days ago he brought one to
my House to intercede with me not to write against him,
but yᵉ Honour of yᵗ Religion, wᶜʰ you have so long & eminently adorn'd, obliges me, as to do Justice, so to prevent
yᵉ Encrease of false Prophets. I have already laid before
Yʳ Lordship yᵉ Impudence of Mʳ Colton in persevering to
officiate in my Church in Opposition to my Orders; in
preaching his own Sermons; in holding Parish-meetings
cited in yᵉ Church, & assembled in private Houses without
my Knowledge; in perjuring himself wilfully & deliberately
before a Justice of yᵉ Peace, in order to blast my Character; in procuring an illegal Obligation for 30£ Ster Per
Annum from yᵉ people, which he & they told me he's to
return, when ordain'd: for he expects, as well as others
from these parts, to escape yᵉ Oath of Simony, yᵉ Guilt
whereof he will certainly incur: for yᵉ whole Obligation
& Design thereof are expresly against yᵉ 40 Canon; & by
imposing on yʳ Lor[d]ship's Sagacity to steal into Orders.
However as Matters of Fact are Demonstrations, I have
inclos'd yᵉ Copy of a Bond (whose Original I have sent in
a Letter to Yʳ Lordship Decemʳ 10ᵗʰ) form'd & wrote by
himself, whereby Yʳ Lordship will see, as in Miniature,
yᵉ Extortion & Vileness of yᵉ Man. I presume it might
easily be prov'd yᵉ Principal was but about 22£, consequently yᵉ Interest included & paid was 8£, for six Months
Loan of 22£. The other two Papers are Copies of Originals wrote by yᵉ Justice, before whom he su'd a poor, but
very worthy Man upon yᵉ Night-Law, & brought two Boys,
one aged 15, yᵉ other younger, to swear to yᵉ Identity of

yᵉ Man, seen by them at a considerable Distance about
nine O Clock in a dark Night; tho' by two aged Men 'twas
prov'd, yᵉ poor Man was not out of his House yᵗ Evening
& yᵗ Night.--I hope Yʳ Lordship's Goodness will pardon
me, at this time particularly, for desiring yᵗ You will be
pleas'd to discourage in Candidates from this place the
Confidence they put in yᵉ Meritoriousness of their Works.
Let yᵉ Papists glory in yᵉ prevailing Efficacy of their
Performances; but I hope our Church will always preach
up yᵉ Necessity of Faith, as well as Works; & yᵗ as yᵉ
former is yᵉ mere Gift of God, so yᵉ latter is acceptable
only thro' yᵉ Merits & Intercession of Jesus Christ. Were
I present I wou'd enter my Objections against Mʳ Colton's
Ordination; but tho' I'm prevented yᵗ Opportunity, yet they
are wrote & enter'd in yᵉ Presence of God, whose unworthy
Minister I am. Yʳ Lordship's Prayers on my Labours are
earnestly desired by, My Lord

              Yʳ Lordship's most dutiful Son
                 & most obedient Servt
New-London Decʳ 23ᵈ 1751)   Matt Graves

[1752, Apr. 20, Reading]
               Reading in Connecticut
               N. England, Apˡ 20ᵗʰ 1752.
Reverend Sʳ
    To yᵉ inclos'd I have Nothing to add, but yᵗ I perform
divine Service at Three Churches; New-Town & Reading I
serve every Sunday Alternately; in each of which Churches
I have commonly between 2, & 3, Hundred Hearers, &
near 100, Communicants at a Time: The Church at New
Milford on Some holy Days, where I have about 100, Hearers. Several other Places I Preach at, as often as I can;
But there are other Places back in yᵉ Country, lately Settled, at which I am much importuned to perform divine
Service, but my want of Health will not permit me. And
in deed I dread yᵉ Thoughts of continuing in this laborious
Mission another Winter, altho it would be a Pleasure to me
to perform yᵉ Duties of it, if I had but a common Measure
of Health; which is a Blessing I never expect at enjoy. But
I resign to yᵉ Blessed Will of God & yᵉ Directions of yᵉ
Venerable Society, not being willing to be troublesome to
them by importuning for a Removal,
    & remain Revᵈ Sʳ their & / your most obedient /
humˡᵉ Serᵗ

                  John Beach

[Addressed:] To the Reverend / Dʳ Bearcroft / Secretary to yᵉ Society for / yᵉ Propagation of yᵉ Gospel / in
Foreign Parts / at yᵉ Charterhouse, London

    Notitia Parochialis of New-Town & Reading.

                 Apˡ 20ᵗʰ 1752.

I. Nº of Inhabitants.	/	About 360 Families.
II. Nº of yᵉ Baptized.	/	All are Baptized excepting about 10.
III. Nº of Adul[t] Persons Baptized this Half Year.		/ None.
IV. Nº of actual Communicants of yᵉ Chᶜʰ of England		/ 206.
V. Nº of those who profess them-selves of yᵉ Chᶜʰ of England		/ About 370.

VI. No. of Dissenters.   / About 700.
                                          / No Papists.
VII. No. of Heathens & Infidels.   / None.
VIII. No. of Converts from an   / No Remarkable
      unchristian Life, &c   / Instance.

[1752, May 4, Fairfield]

To the Sheriff of the County of Fairfield his Deputy
or to Either of the Constables of Newtown in said County
Greeting &c

In his Majestys Name you are hereby required to give
Notice unto Thos Tousey Esqr one of the Principal Inhabitants of said Newtown and to the rest of ye Inhabitants of
said Town that they appear before the General Court to be
holden at Hartford on the second Thursday of this Instant
May that is to say that they appear on ye first Tuesday
after said second Thursday if they pleas to shew Rasons if
any they have why the within Memorial of the Professors
of the Church of England of said Newtown and the Prayer
therein contained should not be heard & granted   You are
hereby Required likewise to leave a true and attested Copy
of ye said Memorial and ye Names of ye memorialists
thereto Annexed and of this Citation with Mr John Northrup
Town Clerk of said Newtown or at ye usual place of his
abode hereof fail Not and Make Due return of ye within Memorial and of this writ with your Doings thereon as ye Law
Directs

Dated in Fairfield ye fourth Day of May A:D 1752
                              Andw Burr Assist

Newtown May ye 6th 1752

then the within Memorial was read in ye hearing of
ye above Named Thos Tousey Esqr and likewise ye above
Citation   I allso on ye said sixth of May left a true and attested Copy of said memorial and of ye Names of ye Memorialists thereto annexed and, also a true and attested
Copy of ye above Citation with ye above Named John Northrup Town Clerk of said Town
                              Per me Abel Judson
                                   Constable of Newtown

In ye Lower house

On ye Prayer of ye foregoing Memorialists Granted yt
ye Memorialists have Liberty to meet together and Chuse
a Clerk and a Committee and have power to Levy a Tax or
Taxes among themselves from time to time to support
their Ministry & for ye defraying ye Charge of building or
repairing their Meeting house, and to Chuse a Collector or
Collectors to Collect & gather ye same, and ye Memorialists have Liberty to bring in a bill in form thereon Accordingly

                              Test Jno Fowler Clerk

In the upper House

The Consideration of this Memorial is referred to the
General assembly to be holden at New Haven in October
next
                              Test George Wyllys Secretry

In ye Lower house

Concurred with ye vote of ye Honble upper house In
ye Referring ye Consideration of the foregoing Memoriall

to the Assembly to be held in N. Haven in Octobr next
                              Test Jno Fowler Clerk

This may certify ye Honourable the General Assembly,
that I concur with my Brethren as to ye Prayer within
                                        John Beach

[1752, May ca. 4-10, Newtown]

To the Honourable Generalle Court to be Holden att
Hartford In & for ye Colony of Conectticut on the Second
thursday of May Instant

The Memorial of the Professors of the Church of
England In & of The Town of Newtown in sd Colony Humbly Sheweth

That Your memoriallists by the Blessing of God Have
had a Parson in orders Acording to the Cannons and articles of the Church of England Settled abiding and Performing Divine Service among them according to the Littergy
of sd Church Constantly for about Twenty years past (and
we hope is Like so to Continue) and your Memoriallists
have to the uttmost of their abilitys been att the Expence
of Building Two Churches or Houses for Publick worship
the first of which being too Small the Second Finished only
on the outside and whereas we Ever have & Still do Labour
under the Disadvantage of being unable to Levie and Colect
any Taxes among our Selves for the Equal Carrying on of
sd Buildings and whereas itt freequently happens in Town
meetings in sd Town that many Vouts are Nessaryly passed
Relating to Parrish or Society affairs in which Though Your
Memoriallists are Equally Interested acording to their
Numbers and List of Estate which is at Least one third
part in sd Twoun yet by the Late act of this assembly in
May 1746 are barred and Secluded from voting or otherwise acting in sd Affairs (which is not agreeable to English
Men) Whereupon Your Memoriallists Humbly beg Leave to
apply them selves to this Honourable assembly whome (we
trust may Justly be Stilled the firnds [friends] of Lebirty)
and Pray that they would take our Case into their wise
Consideration and Grant unto us and our adherants Parrish
Privilidges and full Power within our selves to Meet and
Legally to Chuse a Clerk Comittee Colector &c and to
tax our Selves for the Suport of our Minister and finishing
of our Church and to act in all other nescesary affairs Relateing to sd Society as free and Natural Subjects in the
Same maner and that we may be Governed by the Same
Laws as the Societys of the Presbyterian Perswation in
this Colony are Governed by or that you would in Some
other way Releive your Memorialists as you in your great
wisdom Shall think fitt & and your memorialists as in Duty
Bound Shall ever Pray

John Glover	Ebenr Sanford
John Lake	John Sanford
John Glover Junr	Nathaniel nichols
Abel Hawley	Ebener Bristell
Lennon Sherman	Joel Sherman
Benja Curtiss	Thomas Chambers
Stephen Burwell	Abneer Hard
James Heard	Josiah Faxon
Thomas Skidmur	John Blackman iunr
Nathaniel Sanford	Agur fairchild
Leml1 Camp	John fabregue

Tho: Leavenworth
Samuel Beers
Jabez hurd
Nehemiah Skidmur
James: Stilson
John: Beers
Tho Sharp
Mathew Shermen
Joseph Heard
Abrah^m Beers
Abel Duning
John Camp
Jonathan Booth
Peter Ferris
John Farriss
Benjamin Glover
Richard Hubbell
John Foot
David Crook

Moses Sanford
Abraham Bristol
Abraham adames
Moses Lyon
hezekiah Lyon
Daniel Beers
John Bristoll
John Hooff
Bennoni Hendryx
Ephraim Lake
Jehosephat Prindle
Justin Sherman
Henry Glover
Benjn Haley
Enos Bristoll
Abraham hard
James hard iun^r
Saml adams
Amos Hard

Richard Burtin
Richard Hall
Joseph Sebly
John Nicholls
Zechariah Jenings
Peter Moynot

Gabriel Jackson
Samuel Beardslee
Jacob Tradewell
Josiah Smith
Jeremiah Bennitt
Hezekiah Bennitt

[1752, May 7, Stratfield]

To the Honorable Gen^{ll} Assembly to be held at Hartford on ye second Thursday of instant May the Memorial of Jno Nicolls, Joseph Sealy Richard Hall and others Subscribing here unto Inhabitants in the society of Stratfield in the County of Fairfield and Members of the Church of England humbly sheweth

That The Executor of the last Will and Testament of the Reverend Mr Sam^{ll} Cook late Minister of s^d society obtained a Decree of this Honble Assembly in October last for a large sum of Money against Messrs David Sherman and Hezekiah Odle Inhabitants of said society and the rest of the Inhabitants of s^d society which Decree purporteth that the same sho'd be made up by a Tax on ye Inhabitants of s^d society whereby a Tax being levy^d accordingly Your Memorialists are included in the same and are thereby obliged to pay our Proportion according to our List of said Decree which we think not to be reasonable since all of us have come upon the stage of action since any Contract made with the said Mr Cook and not in Justice holden to make good such Contract & since also to oblige us to pay as aforesaid is contrary to the true Intent and meaning of the Statute of this Assembly made in favour of Churchmen in the 13th Year of King George the first intitled: an Act for providing how ye Taxes levied on professors of the Church of England for ye support of the Gospel shall be disposed of befor exempting s^d professors from paying any Taxes for ye Building Meeting Houses for ye present Established Churches of this Government We having a Church among ourselves and under ye Care of the Revd Mr Joseph Lamson whose Ministry we can & do constantly attend--And Your Honours Memorialists are the rather imboldened to ask because we have been Credably informed that had our Circumstances been in Your Hon^{rs} View we sho'd have been exempted in said Decree wherefore we humbly pray this hon^{ble} Assembly to enact and order that we & our Brethren of ye Church of England be exempted from paying any thing towards satisfying said Decree & Your Memorialists as in Duty bound shall ever pray

Dated in Stratfield this 7th Day of May AD 1752

To ye Sheriff of the County of Fairfield his Deputy or either of the Constables of Stratford or Fairfield in s^d County Greeting--

In His Majesties Name you are hereby required to summon Jno Wheeler of the Society of Stratfield in s^d County and Clerk of s^d society and the rest of the Members of s^d society to appear before ye Gen^{ll} Court to be held at Hartford on ye second Thursday of Instant May and that they appear on ye first Tuesday after ye s^d Thursday to shew reason if any they have why the Prayer of the forg[o]ing Memorial sho'd not be granted and you are to leave a true and attested Copy of the foregoing Memorial & this Citation with the said Wheeler or at ye place of his Usual abode and make due return according to Law   dated in Fairfield this 7th Day of May AD 1752
                                    Eben^r Silliman Assist^t

Fairfield May 7 / 1752   Then ye within and above Memorial and Citation was served by Leaveing a True and An Attested Copy of Each of them with ye above named John Wheeler Clerk of ye Society of Stratfield
          Test Robt Wilson Constable of Fairfield

[1752, May 11, Newtown]

A Town meeting of the Inhabitants of Newtown In ye County of Fairfield: Leaugaly warned to be held on munday ye 11th Day of Instant May 1752
----Put to vote at above s^d Meeting whether they would make Choise of any meet person to be an aigant to appeare at hartford on ye second thursday of Instant may of the General Courts siting to opose or Give Resons why ye professors of ye Church of England in newtown should not have there prayer Granted unto them   voted on y^e negitive: a true Copie Test John Northrup Town Clerk
----Also voted att above s^d Meeting that we have no Reasons to offer against the moshon of y^e Professors of y^e Church of England in Newtown [concerning] y^r prayer to the asembly = voted in y^e afirmative = Test John Northrup Town Clerk

[1752, May and Oct., Newtown]   Oct.
                                         ~~May~~ 1752

Upon the Memorial of Henry Glover of y^e Town of New Town and others of said Town professors of the Church of England versus the Inhabitants of the said Town of Newtown. Complaining that by the Law of this Government they are Debarred and Secluded from voting or otherwise Acting in those affairs about which votes are Necessarily passed in ye Town meetings of said Town wherein the Memorialists are Equally interested in proportion to their Number and Lists of Estates with ye Rest of the Inhabit-

ants of said Town Complaining also that they Labour under Disadvantage for want of the poweres and Priviledges of Levying and Collecting Taxes among themselves for ye purposes in said Memorial mentioned and thereupon praying for such Powers and Priviledges to be granted them or that this Assembly would in some other way Relieve them as this Assembly shall think fit as per their Memorial presented to this Assembly at the Session in May last and from thence Continued to this Time appears

Resolved by this Assembly y^t those of the Professors of the Church of England Living in the said Town of New Town who by the Laws of this Government are exempted from Contributing to the support of the Ministry setled and Established by the Laws of this Government and for that Reason are Debarred voting for Raising such support shall be and they are hereby exempted from being taxed with the Rest of the Inhabitants of said Town in all such Rates or taxes as they shall make for the support of the Ministry established therein as aforesaid And the Inhabitants of said Town are hereby fully authorized and impowered exclusive of such Professors therein to grant such Rates or taxes, in their Town Meetings, as they shall from Time to Time Judge Needful for the support of their Minister and other society Disbursments as fully as other societies in this Government by Law are enabled to do--

Provided nevertheless that when and so often as the Major Part of such Professors of the Church of England shall Request the said Town in any of their Town meetings to tax the said professors of the Church of England in said Town together with the Rest of the inhabitants thereof then and in that Case the said Town shall when they grant a Rate or tax for the support of their Minister tax the said Professors with them selves and proceed therein as by Law is provided in such Cases and the said Town are hereby impowered to act accordingly any thing before in this act contained to the Contrary in any wise Notwithstanding

    past in the upper House
     Test George Wyllys Secret^ry
Concurred in ye Lower house
     Test Jno Fowler Clerk

[1752, Oct. 12, New Haven]
Att a Generall Assembly held at New-Haven
Octo^r ye 12th Anno Dom 1752

    In ye Lower house

On ye prayer of this Memoriall Granted y^t ye Memorialists have Liberty to meet together and chuse a Clerk and a Committee & power to Levy a Tax or Taxes on themselves from time to time to support their Ministry and for ye defraying ye Charge of building and Repairing their meeting house, & to Chuse a Collector or Collectors to Collect & gather ye same, & that a bill in form may be brot in thereon accordingly,

    Test Jno Fowler Clerk
Noncurr^d with in the upper House
    Test George Wyllys Clerk

[1753, Mar. 29, London]
    London. Charterhouse March 29th 1753
Revd Sir
  The society much approving of your reasons for your Continuance in your present station hath added 10£ per ann.' to your Salary to commence from Xtmas last in token thereof; not doubting of your perseverance in well doing, & of your diligence & watchfulness over your flock[,] recommending them & you to God's blessing
    I remain / Your faithful & affectionate Servt /
     & Brother in Christ
      P. B.

James Henderson Esqr in Deans yard Westm^r is elected Treasurer of the Society in the room of Mr Bethell who quitting Business desir'd to resign

To the Revd Mr Dibble Missionary at⎞
Stanford in Connecticut   ⎠

[1753, Mar. 29, London]
    London. Charterhouse March 29th 1753
Revd Sir
  The Society much concern'd at your ill treatment hath given you leave to remove to Taunton, if you continue to desire it, by a Letter from Mr Punderson it appears as if the spirit of oppression were got to persecution among you, for such as the fact is stated, appears to be the Case of Mr Pitts being whipt for non attendance at the meeting; I have wrote by order for authentic Vouchers of the fact & for the future whenever any Complaints are made, it is requir'd, that authentic proofs of those Compl.ints come with them, recomending you & your people to God's Blessing
     I remain &c
     [P. B.]

To the Revd Mr Gibbs Missionary at⎞
Simsbury in Connecticut   ⎠

[1753, Oct. 23, London]
     Charterhouse Oct 23 1753
My Lord
  The bearer Mr Samuel Seabury is appointed Missionary to the Church of New Brunswick in New Jersey, if your Lordship shall find him worthy, & be pleased to admitt him into the Holy Orders of our Church; & with him Mr William Smith recommended to your Lordship by the Clergy of New York & New England proposes to pay his Duty to your Lordship
    I am My Lord with all Respect /
     Your most obedient / Servant
      Philip Bearcroft.

[To the Bishop of London]

[1753, Nov. 3, New Haven]
     New Haven Novr 3 1753
Good Sir
  As by divine Providence, & also the Appointment of

the venerable Society for the Propagation of the Gospel in foreign Parts, I am the Incumbent of this Town, I desire it may not be denied to any belonging to the College, whose Parents or Guardians are Professors of the Chh of England, and who desire & have Leave from their Parents or Guardians to attend the Service of the established Chh of England, when performed in this Town, by Rev<u>d</u> Sir,

Your very Humble Servant
Ebenezer Punderson

To the President of Y. College
[Thomas Clap]

[1753, Nov. 5, New Haven]

New Haven Nov<u>r</u> 5 1753
Rev<u>d</u> Sir

I received yours of the 3<u>d</u> Inst and am willing to gratify you, & other Gentlemen of the Church of England, in all Things consistent with the Constitution, Laws, & good Orders of this College. But am of Opinion that this Demand is not. And suppose that you, and others, upon a full Understanding of the Case, will be of the same Mind.

This College was founded in 1701 by 10 Principal Ministers in the Colony of Connecticutt, with the License & Sanction of the General Assembly, the legislative Power of the Colony: who gave about £60 Sterling Per Ann. for its Encouragement. And the rest of the Incomes or Estate came by particular or private Donations.

The Founders of the College & their Successors (chosen by themselves) always have been, & still are the Governors of it; in whom the Power of making Laws, for the Regulation of it, is vested.

These Founders were of the Denomination called Presbyterian, or congregational (for we make no Difference or Distinction between them in this Colony). And their main Design in that Foundation, was to Educate Persons for the Ministry in these Churches, according to their own Doctrine & Discipline & Mode of Worship; their Doctrine being the same with the Doctrines contained in the Confessions of Faith of all Protestant Reformed Churches in general, & the Doctrinal Articles of the Church of England in particular, "taken in the literal & grammatical Sense, in the plain & full Meaning of them," according to his Majesty's Declaration

The Founders of this College & their Successors the Governors of it have always been free to allow the Children of Protestants of all Denominations as Episcopalians, Presbyterians, Congregationalists, Baptists & Quakers, the Privilege & Advantage of an Education in it; they conforming (as they always have done) to the Religion, Rules & Orders of it, while they were here. And accordingly for many Years past, there have been as many of the Children of Episcopalians educated here, as of those of other Denominations, in Proportion to the Numbers of each Denomination inhabiting in the Colony.

The Laws of the College established by the Founders & their Successors (so far as they relate to the present Case) are in the Substance these. --- That the President, or in his Absence, one of the Tutors shall pray in the College Hall Morning & Evening; and shall read a Chapter, or some suitable Portion of holy Scripture; except on the Lord's Day, when there shall be a Sermon, or Exposition, or some theological Discourse. And every Member of the

College, Graduate or Undergraduate, whether residing in the College or in the Town, shall attend upon those Exercises, upon Penalty that every Undergraduate for Neglect, without sufficient Reason, shall be fined one penny Sterling, and every Graduate shall be deprived of the Privilege of the Library. --- That the President is desired, as often as his Time & Business will permit, to deliver in the College Hall Sermons, Expositions, & such other Discourses, as he shall think proper, for the Instruction of the Students; which being publickly notified, every Student shall attend, on the Penalty aforesaid. --- That on the Lord's Day, every Student shall constantly & religiously attend the public Worship of God, with the President & Tutors in the Meeting House, on Penalty of four Pence Sterling for Absence on either Part of the Day.

These Laws, obliging all the Students to attend upon these religious Exercises, on the Lord's Day & other Days, together in one Place, in & under the immediate Direction & Inspection of the Officers of the College, we apprehend to be just & reasonable, necessary for every Society founded for religious Purposes; and agreeable to the common Sense & Practice of Mankind, & the Universities, Colleges & Hospitals in Great Britain. And should these Orders be given up, the religious Exercises appointed by the Laws of College be neglected, & the Students suffered to disperse to various Places for Worship, the Governors of College, considered as Governors of that Society, could have no sufficient Security that the Students attended anywhere, or in any proper Manner: and the religious Design of the Founders be wholly defeated; which, in Fidelity to the Trust committed to us by our Predecessors, we cannot willingly permit.

And tho' Parents & Guardians have a natural Right to dispose of their Children & Minors, to judge of the Laws of any Society so far as relates to their own Conduct, and to send their Children & Minors to such Societies as they, upon the whole, shall approve, & not to commit them to such Societies as they upon the whole think to be disadvantageous: yet Parents & Guardians, as such, have no Right to infringe upon the Rules of any Society, or to give their Children or Minors any License or Dispensation to break the Laws of that Society, of which they are Members. And to allow of this, we think would be to give up the essential & fundamental Rules of all Society & Government.

And as it is a general Rule in all Societies, that the minor Part should give Way to the major, and the Number of Students which have been educated in the Modes of Worship practised in the Church of England being to the rest, but as 1 to 8 or 10, we cannot but think, that all rational & ingenuous Parents & Guardians are willing that their Children & Minors, while here, should be present at such Modes of Worship, as they think less convenient & less eligible, for the sake of the general Good & Benefit of the whole Society, according to the Intention of the Founders.

And on the other side, as the Executive Authority of College do sometimes, upon special Occasion, at Discretion, give Liberty to the Students to be absent from Morning & Evening Prayers, Recitations, & public Worship on the Lord's Day: and the Governors of College would continue to be, as they always have been, as complaisant to the Gentlemen of the Church of England as may be, we shall be willing to give Liberty to those Students, who have been Educated in the Worship of the Church of England, & are of that Communion, to be absent at those

Times when the Sacrament is administred in that Church, & at Christmas, & such other Times as shall not be an Infraction upon the general Order & standing Rules of College, and as shall be found, by Experience, not to be attended with any considerable Inconvenience to the Society.

Hopeing that this may be satisfactory to You, and that the good Harmony & Correspondence, which has hitherto subsisted between the College & the Gentlemen of the Church of England, may still continue, I remain, Revᵈ Sir,
Your Humble Servant
Thomas Clap

Revᵈ Mʳ Punderson

[1754, Mar. 13, London]
                                    London March 13ᵗʰ 1754
£37.10.0
Nine Months after date I promise to pay Mʳ Andrew Millar on Order the Sum of Thirty Seven pounds ten shillings Value reꞓed by me-- Samˡ Seabury Jʳ
                                    Missionary at Brunswick New Jersey

[Indorsed on the back: And: Millar]

[1754, Apr. 4, Hebron]
I Ruben Hutchison of Hebron--in the Coloney of Conecticut in New England of Lawfull age Do Testifie and Say that mʳ Jonathan Colton who was our Lay Reader in the Church at Said Hebron Some Time on or about the Year 1750 and at Sundry other times while He Lived in sᵈ hebron the Said mʳ Colton Tryed to perswad me Not to Hear the Revᵈ mʳ Graves preach when He Came from Newlondon to Hebron & Said Colton Told me that He wondred I went to Hear Said mʳ Graves & Told me mʳ Graves Had no Busness at Hebron more than an indian and was not fit to preach nor to be a minister & Deservᵈ to Have his Head Broke for going into Hebron Church & if He Saw mʳ Graves their again he would brake His head out Doors--& Some time in the Year 1751 as I Remember the Said mʳ Colton Talkᵈ of going to England for Holy Orders He asked me with Some others to Sign a bond Conditioned to pay him thurty pounds Sterlling Pʳ Year as a Title to introduce Him into Orders I being Something Loath the Said Colton & mʳ punderson and Ebenezar Norton Told me it Should Do me no Hurt & Said mʳ Colton & Said Noughton Told me that the Bond Should be So Discharged that no money Should be Recovered By it & that if mʳ Colton Returned with orders the Bond Should be given up & mʳ Colton would Depend upon the Law of this Coloney for Rates in another form. So being over perswaded I Signed Said bond & thought it no more then a formal thing to introduce Said mʳ Colton into orders and Supose those men that Signed Said bond with me obtained a Discharge of mʳ Colton Touching the bond At the time it was Delivered &c   Hebron April the fourth 1754
                                    Reuben Huchisson

Coventry windham County ssᵗᵗ april Yᵉ 4ᵗʰ AD 1754 then the above Named Ruben Hutchison personaly apeared and made oath to the Truth of the above written Before me
                           Silas Long Justice of yᵉ peace

[Addressed:] To The Lord Bishop of London

[1754, Apr. 4, Hebron]
I John Tompson of Hebron in the Coloney of Conecticut of Lawfull age Do Testifie and Say that mʳ Jonathan Colton many Times while He Lived in this Town Came to me and Tryed to perswad me that the Reverend mʳ Graves was unwilling that Hebron Should Have a missionary and was Trying to Bring and keep us in the mision of New London for the Sake of our Rates & Told me mʳ Graves Talkᵈ of writing to the Society in favour of Hebron provided Hebⁿ people would give Him Ten pound Sterling pʳ annum and to Confirm me that mʳ Graves was an Enemy to all Riteousness Told me that He Had Spoken agaᵗ the King. & Sundry times mʳ Colton Desired me to write agaᵗ mʳ Graves to mʳ Caner & others and then Suposing mʳ Colton Spoke True I wrote to mʳ Caner and Represented maters that mʳ Colton & others his favourrites Had Told me of but it was not Long before I was Satified that things ware misrepresented to me & I Took ocation to inform mʳ Caner and as near as I Could gave Him the True State of the afare. whether He Recᵈ my Leter I Canᵗ Say for I Had no Return from Him--But mʳ Colton Dureing the Time He Lived in Hebron Took pains to insinuate into peoples minds that mʳ Graves Had no Busness at Hebron--which was a means to Set people agaᵗ Him--Some time in the Year 1751 mʳ Colton askᵈ me to Sign with others a Bond Conditioned to pay Him thurty pound Sterling pʳ anum that He might therby obtain Holy orders, and I Suposing it Simonaical Refused to Sign it. He Signified to me if I would Sign it I might Have a Discharge from it imediately, or if I would Sign it He Told me it was in order for a Title that He might Have orders & I might keep it in my own Hands if I would give Him a Certificate that their was Such a bond that He might be introduced into Holy orders But I Told Him I would Not Deceave the Bishop but I was informed by Sundry that Did Sign Said bond that they ware to Have the bond gave up at mʳ Coltons Return from England--and I was Told by one of the Signers that mʳ punderson obtained orders by a bond in the Same form that mʳ Colton Did & by all I Could understand by mʳ Colton and those that Signed sᵈ bond He Had no Expectation of their paying Him any money on accᵗᵗ of the bond. but Depended to Recover of His Hearers Rates by way of Colectors by vertue of the Coloney Law--   April Yᵉ 4ᵗʰ AD 1754
                                    Jnᵒ Thompson

Coventry Windham County ssᵗᵗ May Yᵉ 4ᵗʰ 1754   then the above said Jnᵒ Thompson personaly apeared & made Solemn Oath to the Truth of the above written Before me
                           Silas Long Justice of yᵉ peace

[1754, Apr. 22, Hebron]
I John Bliss of Hebron in the County of Hartford and Coloney of Conecticut of Lawfull age Do Testifie and Say that I paid mʳ Jonathan Colton Late of said Hebron the Summ of Nine pounds and Twelve Shillings old Tenor intrest money for the Use of thurty pounds money old Tenor aboat Six months which said Summ or intrest I was obliged to pay By Vertue of a Deed or Bond Drawn by Said Colton Wherby He fraudulently Designed to Have Deprived me of an acar and Half of Land as may Evidently apear by a Coppy of the origenal and I farther Testifie and Say that the Bond that Hebron Church people gave sᵈ mʳ Colton Conditioned

to pay Him thurty pounds Sterling p͟r͟ anum was for No
other Design but to get Said Colton into Holy orders &
was at Said Coltons Return from England with orders to
Be Void to all intents and purposes this I understood by
information of Some of those that Signed said Bond--

Heb͟n͟ April y͟e͟ 22n͟d͟ 1754
                                                John Bliss

Hebron Hartford County ss͟t͟t͟ April 22nd 1754   then the
above named John Bliss personaly apeared & made Solemn
Oath to the Truth of the above written Before me

                                                John Phelps Justice of y͟e͟ peace

[1754, May 29, New London]
My Lord

    The true Reason, why I answer'd not Your Letter long
ago, was, because I waited for y͟e͟ Opportunity of y͟e͟ Rev͟d͟
Doctor Macsparran; who, perhaps, may raze out of Your
Mind some of those Apprehensions, You have conceiv'd of
my Temper, particularly my Allegations against M͟r͟ Colton. Tho de mortius & absentibus nil nisi bonum; yet self-
Defence, & to endeavour y͟e͟ Restoration of my Character,
is both necessary & just--That I wrote nothing but y͟e͟ Truth
about M͟r͟ Colton, I appeal to y͟e͟ Searcher of Hearts, before
whom I shall be justify'd for all y͟t͟ I then wrote at y͟e͟ last
Day. I hope I may be permitted to say, y͟t͟ y͟e͟ Affidavits deliver'd with this are a more corroborating Evidence of my
Assertions, than any thing y͟t͟ has yet appear'd in M͟r͟ Colton's Favour of his Innocence. I cou'd mention one, perhaps y͟e͟ Principal of his Recommenders, who before now
did not only himself, but persuaded others also to certify
for y͟e͟ Morality of one of y͟e͟ most profane & openly disso-
lute Men in y͟e͟ Age. His Name was Prince, not unknown
to y͟e͟ Bearer. What ever Your Lordship may conclude of
me, I presume to say, y͟t͟ I am better pleas'd to have suffer'd Your Censure innocently by declaring necessary
Truths, than y͟e͟ Reflections of a guilty Conscience, by
concealing them. Let me lay before you a certain Truth,
knowing y͟t͟ I only oppos'd, or rather durst oppose M͟r͟ Colton's Views, & believing y͟e͟ Recommendation of many wou'd
prevail against y͟e͟ Objections of one, I tho't of y͟t͟ sorrowful
Man of God, who, y͟e͟ Night before Arius's design'd Consecration, fasted & pray'd, y͟t͟ y͟t͟ grand Heretick might be
disappointed; accordingly I often pour'd out my Soul to y͟e͟
Almighty, humbly beseeching him either to prevent his
Ordination, or bless him with a new Heart & pious Soul--I
believe my Prayers were heard, & hope he dy'd in y͟e͟ Love
of God. If my Expressions were, as Your Lordship observes, too passionate; yet as they were not founded on
Prejudice, but on y͟e͟ Glory of God, & true Zeal (according
to Knowledge) for his Church, I hope they are not to be accounted blameable--'Tis possible one may [be] right, &
several wrong about y͟e͟ same Matter. Had Your Lordship
demanded other Reason[s] than my own, I wou'd readily
have produc'd them. But alas! I was not only censur'd by
my Diocesan, but Your Letter to Doctor Johnson, condemning my Objections against M͟r͟ Colton, publickly read, & I
publickly expos'd at y͟e͟ Commencement in this Colony--But
I suffer all for y͟e͟ Sake of Christ, whose Church's Glory &
Credit was my sole Aim; as to deliver my Sentiments then
was my particular Province, he officiating in my Parish
without my Leave & against y͟e͟ Rubricks & Canons of y͟e͟

Church--Had I permitted Lay-readers to have been fix'd
by Law in vacant Parishes in this Colony, I had not incurr'd Doctor Johnson's Censure & y͟t͟ of his Adherents--
Let Doctor Macsparran tell y͟e͟ whole Story; & I pray God
y͟t͟ he may tell You y͟e͟ whole Truth of my Life, Doctrine &
Conversation here since I left England; & then, possibly,
you may conceive a more favourable Opinion of him, who
as he will, by y͟e͟ best Application of his Powers, a conscientious Discharge of Duty, & an unshakeable Perseverance in Integrity, endeavour to approve himself worthy
y͟e͟ Notice & Love of his Diocesan & y͟e͟ Religious Society;
so particularly of the Euge [i.e., well done] of y͟e͟ Great
Bishop & Saviour of Souls; whose Servant I am, & in whose
Vineyard I'll work faithfully & diligently, whilse his Mercy
& Goodness are pleas'd to employ me

    I hope Your Lordship will throw a Vail of Charity
over y͟e͟ Plainness of my Style--I have had y͟e͟ Honour to
serve in y͟e͟ Church of Christ many Years, & & to be personally acquainted with some Bishops, now with God, who,
were they alive, wou'd have prevented my Apology, & restor'd my Character. However, Submission is my Duty,
& I trust my Sovereign Lord & Master will continue his
Assistance, & multiply his Grace upon, My Lord

    Your Lordship's / most obedient Servant, / most
dutiful Son, tho' / unworthy Minister of / Jesus Christ

                                                Matt Graves

New London May 29t͟h͟ 1754

P.S Y͟r͟ Lordship's Letter was open'd &⎫
publickly known, before I receivd it. ⎭

To the R͟t͟ Rev͟d͟ the Lord Bishop of London

[1755, Oct. 25, New Brunswick]
                                New Brunswick Oct. 25t͟h͟ 1755
Sir

    Some time ago I rec͟e͟d a Letter from you to y͟e͟ Care
of M͟r͟ Smith. I sho͟d͟ have wrote to you before now, but in
Short Sir, the Shame that I have not been able to answer
my Obligation to you has prevented me. I am very Sensible of what you tell me, that you can obtain your Money
of the Society, but the consequence of that to me at this
Juncture wo͟d͟ [be] beggary. I must therefore intreat your
patience 'till the Spring Shipping. then do as you shall
think proper. my expectations have been greatly dis-
apointed; but begin now to mend. And I hope I shall soon
be in a Condition to make you ample Satisfaction. The
Bearer of this M͟r͟ Johnson, who comes for Orders & will
probably want some thing in your way. I shall conclude
with assuring you that in the Spring you shall have a bill
on the Society from your most Obed͟t͟ & very Humble
Serv͟t͟
                                                Sam Seabury J͟r͟

To M. A. Millar Bookseller
Opposite Catherine Street the
Strand London

[1756, May 4, New York]
                                                N Y. May 4 1756
Dear Son

    We have had a great Satisfaction in M͟r͟ Winslow's
Visit. He is indeed an excellent performer both in read-

ing & preaching, & it is an unspeakable Satisfaction to me
that you sit under so good a Minister. I wish your Business could admit of more Leisure to enjoy his Conversation, & that you could inspire the people there with such
Generosity & good Conduct as may make his Continuance
among you agreeable to him, as it cannot fail being happy
to themselves.-- He seems very dubious whether they
will purchass my house unless our Subscriptions may be
deducted out of 400 p^ds This I think would be very hard
since it has been estimated at 450 Whether you think we
can comport with this I must leave to you. I should think
at least they should be contented that your's be included,
& if you cant do otherwise I will forego the use of 200 p^d
for a year or two. But it must at least be called 400 p^d
good to me or y^r. Mother will never be easy.

As I was interrupted when I had wrote thus far, &
M^r. Winslow is come to take his leave, I can only now add,
that I have no new Intelligence from y^r B^r (whom God preserve) & that I have made one Revolution more since I
broke ground at Stratford, being now got to the New House
at Spring Garden & seaded much to my mind, & that we
are all well (thank God) & send our most affectionate Love
to you & yours, & am

                              Dr Son / your's most tenderly
                                            S. Johnson

[To William Samuel Johnson in Stratford, Conn.]

[1756, Oct. 6, New Haven]
To the Hon^bl. General Assembly to be held at New Haven
on the Second thursday of Octr. 1756.

The Petition of Enos Alling & Isaac Doolittle of New
Haven Humbly Sheweth that Y^r Peti^rs in behalf of themselves & the Rest of the Members of the Society in New
Haven professing a Conformity to the Established Church
of England s[ome]time in July 1752, purchased of Mr Sam^ll
Mix late of New Haven Dec^d twenty Square rods of Land
for the building a Church for publick worship Lying & being in said New Haven ye Same on which ye Church in s^d
New Haven now stands, & agreed to give for said Land the
Sum of two hundred pounds old tenor unless Certain men
by the Parties then mutually Chosen for that purpose viz
Capt Joseph Trowbridge & Mr Wm Greenough Should Judge
the said Land was not worth so much, & in Case they
should Estimate the Same Lower then what they should so
Judge & Determin to be ye price & thereupon s^d Mix on the
28th Day of July afor^d made & Executed by Signing Sealing
&c a Deed of s^d Land to Y^r Peti^rs, but omitted to acknowledge the Same inasmuch as the afor^d matter of the price of
ye Land was not Issued & Determined & so the matter Lay
for some time viz until Septr Last when Y^r Peti^rs agreed
with said Mr Mix to give the £200. absolutely, & so to
have no Judgment of s^d Trowbridge & Greenough about the
matter & accordingly paid said Mix said sum & thereupon
said Mix Undertook to Compleat said Deed according to
Law, but Soon after Sickened & Died & that without ever
acknowledging said Deed, having Left his Estate to his two
Daughters his only Children & heirs being Minors under
the Guardianship of their Mother Mrs Abigail Mix, Whereupon Y^r Peti^rs Say that they have honestly bought said Land
of s^d Samuel Mix & it was his full Intent to have fully Executed & Compleated said Deed but was prevented by Sick-

ness & unexpected death Y^r Peti^rs therefore pray that
Y^r Hon^s would Decree & order that Y^r Peti^rs have Liberty
to have said Deed Recorded in the Records of s^d Town of
New Haven & to Use & Improve the Same & that the Same
Shall be & be Esteemed to be as good & Effectual for the
passing the Estate therein Contained as if the same had
been Compleated & fully Executed according to Law or
Some other way Grant Relief in ye premiss & Y^r Pet^rs
as in Duty bound Shall Ever pray

                                            Enos Alling
New Haven Octr 6: 1756.   Isaac Doolittle

To the Sheriff of ye County of New Haven his Deputy or
Constable of New Haven in said County Greeting

In his Majestys name you are hereby Required to
Summon & give Notice unto Mrs Abigail Mix of s^d New
Haven Widow & Relict of Mr Sam^ll Mix late of said New
Haven Dec^d & Guardian to Rebecca Mix & Mary Mix two
minor Children of s^d Sam^ll Mix Dec^d that She appear if
She see Cause before the General Assembly to be held
at New Haven on the Second thursday of Octr 1756 that is
that she appear on the Tuesday next after s^d thursday
to shew reason if any be why the prayer of ye foregoing
Petition should not be granted & you are to Leave a true
attested Copy of s^d. Petition & of this Citation with s^d
Abegail Mix or at the usual place of her abode at Least
twelve Days before s^d Tuesday hereof fail not   Dated
at New Haven Octr 6th 1756.

                              D Edwards Assistant

Octr 1756
     then I Left a true Attested Copy of ye within Petition
& Citation with ye within named Abegail Mix
               Test Tim^o Alling D Sheriff

In the upper House
     The Prayer of the foregoing Petition is granted, and
the Petitioners are allowed to bring in a Bill in form accordingly

               Test George Wyllys Secret^ry

Concur'd in the Lower House
               Test Elihu Chauncey Clerk

[1756, Dec. 27, New Haven]
                                   New Haven 27 Decr 1756
My Very Good Lord
     This day I receivd 10 of the first Vol^ms of Your
Lordships Discourses, and have great expectations of
their being of very great Service, to the great purpose
of promoting Truth, & virtue in my Laborious Mission,
in w^c have 4 good Timber Chh^s and 2 other Congregations
to Each of those I purpose to Distribute one & order it to
be read on Such Sundays as I am not There. and shall endeavour to my utmost to make them as usefull as possible.
in Behalf of all my Parishioners, intreat your Lordship to
accept my hearty and unfeigned Acknowledgment for this
Singular goodness & Generosity in this Seasonable present
and beg leave to implore your Lo[r]dships interest with
the Venerable Society for the Propagation of y^e Gospel &c
that as there is but one of the four Chh^s under my Care
Supplyd with a Fol: Bible & Comon prayer the other 3 may

have them also; and could y^t venerable Body send us some comon prayers w^c are extreamly wanted among the poorer sort of people (who are not able to purchase them) the Charity would be most gratefully receivd, have Baptizd 7 Adults, & admitted 20 to our Communion in ye 12 Months past. I beg an interest in your Lordships Prayers & am with the greatest Respect

    Your Lordships most Dutifull / Son & Servt

                Eben^r Punderson

To Thomas Lord Bishop of London

[1757, Dec. 27, Derby]

               Derby Decr 27th 1757.

Revd Sir,

    There hath been no Material Alteration in the State of my Mission, since my Last of June 27th. I continue constantly to Preach & Perform divine Service in several Parishes, in each of w^h the Number of Hearers & Communicants is considerably Large for these Parts. In my Mission (exclusive of Northbury) there are more than one Hundred Families of People, Professors of the Church of England, & above a Hundred & 50 Communicants, who with Thousands more in this Colony, all must have been destitute of any Christian Ministry & Sacraments that they could in Conscience Join with, were it not for the truly Christian Charity, & Assistance afforded them by the Venerable Society.

    In Decr 1756. I drew a Two Bills of Exchange forty-10 Ster. in Favour of Mr Abel Beach, dated the 27th day of Decr 1756. w^h he sold to Wm Sam^ll Johnson Esqr of Stratford, who Informs me that he sent them Inclosed to Thos Wilcox Bookseller in London, & that as he has had no Advice of their Arrival, he thinks they must have fallen into the Hands of the Enemy, or some Way miscarried. I have therefore drawn a 3^d 4th 5th & 6th Bill of Exchange for £7-10. shilling sterling, in Favour of Mr Beach of the same date with the two former thought to have miscarried.

    I hereto Annex my Notitia Parochialis for the Last Half Year, & have drawn upon the Societies Treasurer, Fifteen Pounds sterling towards my support, & am Revd Sir,

    The Societies & Your / Most Obliged & most Obedient / Humble Servant

                Richard Mansfield

In Derby & Oxford

Number of Families	68.
Baptized last Half Year	20.
Actual Comm: of ye Chh: of Eng:	83
In Waterbury	
Number of Families	48.
Actual Comm: of ye Chh: of Eng:	80

[To Philip Bearcroft, S. P. G., London]

[1759, May 9, Stanford]

    To the Honble Gen^ll Assembly of the Colony of Connecticut in New England in America to be held at Hartford in s^d Colony on the second Thursday of May Inst^t the Memorial of the Rector Church Wardens & Vestry of the Chh: of England in Stanford in the County of Fairfield in behalf of themselves & the other Professors of the Chh: of England in s^d Town humbly sheweth

    That y^r Hon^rs Memorialists being desirous to Enjoy the Worship of God according to the Liturgy & Discipline of the Chh: of England to which we conscienciously tho't it our Duty to Conform did several Year's ago undertake to Build a Church for divine Worship & engaged our present Worthy Incumbant then not in Orders to read Prayer's to us & afterwards sent him home to England for Orders who accordingly went & soon returned In Orders to us, we haveing laid ourselves under Obligation to pay him a considerable sum annually towards his support & for his Expences In going Home; all which undertakings laid us under a considerable Burthen which however we very chearfully endured, but soon finding we were unable to advance the Monies requisite to carry on these designs, we ventured to borrow a considerable sum of Money in New York for the purposes afores^d which together with some benefactions procured for that End we laid out in building our Church hoping we sho'd be able in [a] few Years to repay the same; as indeed had nothing unforeseen happened we should. But soon after these Transactions the Nation became involved in a Dangerous & Expensive Warr whereof this Country unfortunately became a principal seat in consequence whereof the public charges were so encreased (to which nevertheless we very chearfully submitt) that we soon found ourselves unable to pay our Taxes & pursue our designs afores^d or refund s^d borrowed sum, & our Church still remains unfinished & our Debts unpaid; & we are scarcely able to support our Incumbant (who has a numerous Family) & pay our Taxes to the public; & the Interest of s^d Money so borrow'd encreasing y^r Hon^s Memorialists are like to be Involved in great Trouble, & inextricable Difficulties: being absolutely unable to raise Money among ourselves by subscription; & not being impow[er]ed by Law to Tax ourselves for any purposes of this Nature-- Wherefore we humbly take the Liberty to request the favour of y^r Hon^s to Grant us Liberty to set up and Draw a small Lottery of about £2000-0- lawful Money subject to a Deduction of 15 p^r Cent: for the purpose aforesaid & for defraying the Charges of such Lottery--subject to such regulations & inspection as y^r Hon^rs shall direct. Which y^r Hon^rs Memo^ts humbly pray y^r Hon^rs to Grant in Consideration of the afores^d difficulties in which y^r Memor^ts are involved & for That they are strongly encouraged & almost assured if we can obtain this fav^r of y^r Hon^rs that they shall be able to sell the most of the Ticketts in New York Boston & Philadelphia & consequently bring Money into the Colony rather than carry any out & they conceive there is no danger of its being a Prejudice to the Public or to any particular Person: and y^r Memorialists as in Duty bound shall ever pray. Dated in Stanford this 9th Day of May AD 1759.

        Ebenez^r Dibblee Cl^k

Ephraim Smith } Samuel Jarvis }	Church Wardens
John Lloyd } Peter Demill } Ebenezer Holly } John Bates }	Vestry

In the lower House

The question was put wheather the prayer of this memorial Shall be granted, Resolved in the Negative

Test Jz Huntington Clerk

In the upper House

The above Question was put and Resolved in the Negative

Test George Wyllys Secret^{ry}

[1759, May 10, Simsbury]

To The hon^{ble} ye General Assembly of ye Colony of Conecticut to be held att hartford on ye 2^d thursday of may A:D: 1759   The memorial of us The subscribers of ye Town of simsbury and County of s^d hartford & Colony afore said humbly sheweth--   That whereas we the said subscribers being of ye Church of England and Living much scattered within four societys in s^d simsbury & each of Them Raising Different sums for ye suport of Their ministors & neither of Them agreeing with ye sum y^t we must Raise For ye seport of our ministor and it seems not worth Troubleing prisbyterian societys Colt^r to Colect mony for to suport our ministor seing it will not gather our mony in Equal proportion on our Rateable Estate nor make a payment to him according to our agreement   We also Inform y^t we have agreed with a ministor to settle amongst us & that our Rateable Estate on ye grand list amounts to a little more then £3000   We Therefore pray this hon^{ble} assembly to grant us by Their act y^t we the said subscribers of s^d simsbury & so many as shall joyn with us for ye futre & entering their Names with the Town Clerk of s^d Symsbury shall be one destinct society and to grant unto us society privilidges Viz y^t Capt. James Case & m^r Joshua holcomb be appointed a Com^{tee} to Call a society meeting and Lead to ye Choice of a moderator who shall have power to Lead to ye Choice of a Clerk and Com^{tee} for said society & y^t Com^{tee} to call a meetings in ye month of December to Chuse a Clerk and standing Com^{tee} Colt^{rs} or ajents to Raise such sums of mony as may be wanted for ye suport of a ministor or other nessary Charge and y^t our society meetings from december anually may be held by ajournment or ye standing Com^{tee} att any Time here after when Need Require call a society meeting to doe any buisness proper to be done by said society & to be under the Regulations of the Laws of this Colony respecting Societys Which privedge we ask with Great great submission first: because of your hon^{rs} Indulgence in Time past to the Professors of ye Church of England 2^{ly} it does not Disintrest nor will prejudice any society in simsbury 3^{ly} it will prevent ye Colt^{rs} of a great Deal of Trouble and will be of great service to your memorialists who as in Duty Bound Shall ever pray

Subscribed by us   Dated in simsbury May ye 10th 1759

Derias Pinney	John Christin Millan
John Chick	Josiah Holcomb
John Slater Jr	Hez: Holcomb
Hez: Phelps	John Terry
Henrey Molton	Timothy adams
Benony Griffin	Solomon Terrey
Joshua Holcomb Jn^r	Ruben Slater
Ranny Coset	Jeremiah Case

frances Garrit	Amos Case
Joseph adams	Richard Cas
James Helgor	Richard Case jr
Return Holcomb	Isaac Tuller
Stephen Holcomb	Benj^a Dyar
Abr^a Piney Jr	Amasa Case
Jonathan Piney	James Case
William Tuller	Abr^a Piney
Wm Case	francis Loomis
Joshua holcomb	Samuel Enos
Joshua moses	James Tullar
Wm Enos	a[br^a] Enos
Josiah Loomis	Eliphalet Mitchelsone
andrew Robe	math. adams
John Kater	Joseph Alderman
Josiah Case 2	Joseph Alderman Jr

(Negatived in both houses)

[1759, Aug. 1, New Milford]

1 August 1759

Revd Sir;

Your Letter of the 12th of April 1758, I received the 8th of November following (which is the only one that I have had from you) together with the Books therein mentioned, which I have distributed where I thought they were most needed, and would be best improved; the folio Bible and Common Prayer Book I have presented to ye Ch^{hh} of Roxbury to which they were directed; for which they have desired me to return their humble and hearty thanks to the society. There is great want of Common Prayer and other good Books here, a supply of which, I am perswaded would be an happy means to encrease the Church, and advance real piety in the Hearts and Lives of Men; I hope therefore, that as the Society have bestowed many favours of this kind upon their Elder Missions, So they will be further mindfull of this their new one--And as I have been desired by the Church of Roxbury, the most flourishing Branch of my Mission, I would in a particular manner, humbly request some Prayer Books for them: This Church from a Small number, is increased to thirty five Famolies, and is continually encreasing; & the last Sunday forty and two Persons there received the Holy Sacrament of the Lords Supper. And as they have Sufficient Subscriptions--So they purpose to have their new Church finished before next Winter.

I heartily thank the Society for granting my petition respecting the limits of my Mission, and inform inform them that the end I proposed in it, has thereby been entirely answered, So that now no Churchman within the limits of Litchfield County meets with any trouble about his Ministerial Rate from his Dissenting Brethren there.

And as to the Prosecution &c: I have according to the Societies desire Sent over an account thereof in the enclosed Papers. At the Adjourned Superior Court referred to in the Coppy Certifyed p^r G: Pitkin Clerk of said Court, the Plantiffs obtained a judgment against me for fifteen Pounds Lawfull Money Damages, & Cost of Courts, from wch both they and I reviewed to ye Court where the decisive judgm^t upon the Case was given, as p^r s^d Coppy. And y^t I did not appear there to prosecute my Said review, may perhaps Seem Strange to ye Society,

till they know ye reason of it, which was, because in the
Interval of these Courts, the Plantiffs and I Setled ye Business in a Publick Town Meeting—and mutually agreed to
withdraw our S^d Reviews, and so proceed no further in y^e
Law.—I was to answer the judgment of the Court, and they
to wait untill ye first Day of September next then coming,
as 'tis exprest in ye Coppy taken from Cornwall Records.
Test^d by John Patterson Town Clerk, that is, they were
not to take out Execution against me before then, when
I was according to agreement to pay them the Money—But
they not at all regarding this agreement, fraudulently appeared to prosecute their review, and so put me to the Cost
of y^t Court: And as if y^t was not enough, they Sought for
an Execution against me; and Obtained it 12^ve Days Sooner
than was agreed upon between us at S^d Town Meeting, as
will appear by comparing the Copies which I have Sent;
which they instantly put into the hands of the Officer, who
Stood ready to receive it, and without delay came and levelled it upon me, when I thought of no disturbance from
that quarter, whose fees were two Spanish Dolars, and the
execution 1/6 Lawfull Money. Here I would observe, y^t
it was in pursuance of the Advice of my Attorney (who was
by Profession a Churchman) that I entered into ye above
agreement who told me that considering the Prejudice of
the Court and their being judges in their own Case, tho'
they had neither Law nor reason on their Side if I proceeded—I must not expect a more favourable judgment
than had been given, and only to have cost added to Cost.

A Coppy of the Covenant upon which their Prosecution
of me was founded, and which they Say was broken by my
leaving them, I have thought needfull to Send y^t ye whole
Affair might be rightly understood which is all the Covenant and agreement y^t I entered into with that People,
before I became a Teacher among them, and in which all
the Salary and Settlement that I was to have from them is
Specifyed and exprest, and there are no other Records or
writings between us relating to that Affair: this I have Observed lest the Society should imagine y^t ye fifty Pounds,
at my request granted to be added (as it is exprest in the
Covenant) to my settlement, did relate to Something not
mentioned in S^d Covenant; which fifty Pounds was requested and allowed in consideration of its being frontier Town,
& exposed to danger in time of war, which happened Soon
after I Setled there, when we kept a Garrison, and had
frequent Alarms. And an Infant Plantation, 20 m: distant
from any old Setled Towns, nearer than which no provisions were to be had for my Famolies Support for the
three first years I dwelt among them, and which were obtained at a great expence; Every thing being new there,
the People were Scarcely able at first to raise provisions
for their own Famolies; And for their ease in paying my
Salary, ye General Assembly Granted a Tax of five pence
p^r Acre upon the Lands of the nonresidents, who were
many of them rich, wch continued, I think, five Years,
after which they were able themselves to pay my my Salary, and are Still a prosperous People, amongst whom I
could have been well Supported, and lived peaceably to
this day, could I have had peace in my own Conscience.
And thus I have given a Genuine account of ye matter which
I doubt not will be fully Satisfying to ye society, with whom
I leave it which I should sooner have Sent to them had I not
met with a disappointment in getting a Coppy of the judgment, ye Records from whence it has been taken being

fifty miles distant from ye place of my residence, to
which I made one journey on purpose for it but could not
obtain it by reason of ye absence of the Clerk, and so
waited till I had an opportunity of getting it without any
further expence, but the Cost of ye Coppy. After which I
performed a journey of 50 m. to the Notary publick &c—.

Those Bodily disorders y^t I mentioned in my last Still
remain upon me, and tho' I have almost constantly attended my Several Congregations at their proper turns, yet it
has been with no Small pain and difficulty and having but
little hope of a Cure, and so of ever being able to perform
ye duties of an Itinerant Mission, I would beg leave humbly to renew my former request to the Society, that they
would remove me to a Mission consisting of but one Congregation, or if more, where they are not so distant from
each other, as those that I have now ye care of. Had I y^t
health of Body which I enjoyed when I first came here, I
could not wish for a more pleasant Sictuation than I am
now in: I live amongst a sober, Religious & peaceable
People, where with the Societies assistance I am pretty
well Supported. What alone influences me to desire a
removal is for ye sake of Religion, and that the laudable
and truly pious design of ye Society in Erecting Missions,
Sending Missionaries here, and granting them Salaries
might be answered, which by my keeping my present Station would in some measure be frustrated, for instead of
a Valetudinarian, it requires a Man of a Robust Constitution, and a great flow of Animal Spirits to go thro' the
fatiegues, and perform the duties of this extensive Mission, which hitherto, by ye grace of God assisting me, I
have done as well as I could; But now I am not able to do
as I have done, and as I desire to do. My Physitions advise me to ride but a little as I would ever have a Cure,
which they Speak doubtfully about: I would therefore pray
the Society to take these things into consideration, and
order me as they think best. I think that I am Sincerely
disposed to Serve God and my Generation in the Work of
the Gospel Ministrey, and to improve my weak abilities
in doing all the good I can this way; and y^t to ye performance of which I might be under better advantages than
otherwise I could be, I have an earnest desire Still to
continue in ye Societies Service, and to be appointed to
such a Mission as I can do the duties of, but if this cannot
be done, I choose to desist their Service, and Seek for a
livelihood some other way, for I would not be pertaker of
the Societies Charity, but to use it to the Charitable purposes for which it is designed, Viz. That by means thereof the glory of God, and Salvation of immortal souls might
be promoted.

Sience I have been in this Mission the Church here
has greatly encreased, is now in a good State, and is continually encreasing; for besides the three Congregations
to which at first I were particularly appointed, I have
three more, Viz: At Roxbury, Cornwall and Judea, the
two last consist of fifteen famolies each. And there are
Subscriptions raising for the Building a Chu[r]ch in Kent
(which they design to forward as fast as they can) at a
place convenient for about fifty famolies to meet from
Several different Towns; these are all in Litchfield County. And Sience April ye 16th 1758. I have Baptized an
hundred and twenty two Children.

Sir; As I know not the time of my Admission into y^e
Societies Service, and So not when to Date my Bills for

my Salary, I would beg the favour of being advised of it by a line: I have hitherto dated them the first of March, if I mistake not. The last I dated March 1ˢᵗ 1759 for one years salary, Viz £30. which I should have given an account of when I sent my Bills, if I could have had Matters prepared for writing.

The Obligations, yᵗ we, on this Side the Seas are under to the Society for their generous and truly Christian Charity in Sending their Missionaries amongst us, and granting them Salaries in order yᵗ yᵉ Gospel of our Lord jesus Christ (by an Orthodox Clergy) might almost freely be Preached to yᵉ poor, cannot be Sufficiently acknowledged; wᶜʰ Charity, in my oppinion might be better disposed than it is, had yᵉ Society a right understanding of our Scituation, and of the Circumstances of their Missions here: Sure I am yᵗ yᵉ People belonging to some of them are well able of themselves to give their Ministers a generous Support, for far poorer Societies or Parishes of the Dissenters Maintain their Teachers with ease; And why should those of yᵉ Church of England here that are rich, be benefited by, and made pertakers of the Charitable Benefactions of Some poor People in England? I must confess I see no reason for it, nor justice in it; and I am perswaded, if they knew exactly how things are amongst us they would think that no longer a duty which now they do upon Religious Motives and Principles. I believe yᵗ we have many amongst us of the Church who pay not a Crown Sterling a year to their Ministers yᵗ are better able to pay ten pounds, those many of the Societies good and pious Benefactors at home, are able to Contribute a Crown, wᶜʰ to me appears both unreasonable and unjust; I am therefore humbly of the oppinion (not yᵗ I would be So bold as to prescribe----) yᵗ the Society would do well to demand of their Missionaries an account of the circumstances and abilities of their respective Missions, and what Money they Annually receive from them, that So they might know how the better to proportion their Charities, which no doubt would greatly Contribute, not only to the Credit of the Church, but put a stop to such Clamorous complaints as have been so frequently made, by Dissenters at home and here &c: which for my part, I must confess that I don't think have been altogether without cause; tho' I know that here the malice of many against the Church is such yᵗ they would Scarcely Stick at any thing yᵗ should bring an Odium upon it.

I could mention one or two of the Societies Missionaries, who receive no more than about £10 Sterling a Year from their People, who are able enough to pay £60; and others who receive from their People no ways proportionable to their abilities, which their Ministers being enobled from the Society to live without, indulge them in, which is an Error that needs to be Corrected, and which I perswade my Self will be done.

I hope that the Society will pardon me for this long Epistle, and if, they Shall look upon any thing that I have Said in it impertinent yᵗ my Sincerity will Attone for the weakness of my judgment, Who am in all respects,

Sir; Yours, and their / most Dutifull and Humble, / faithfull and Obedient Servant,

Solomon Palmer.

Newmilford
August the 1ˢᵗ
A:D: 1759.

P:S: The Cost of Courts, and Damage   £21=10=7.
Execution and Officers fees---------------   00=13=6
And my own Cost in feeing my Attorneys and waiting upon yᵉ Courts I kept no account of & therefore am not able to tell, but I am pretty certain that it was not less than £4=10=0 ----   £ 4=10=0
All wᶜʰ is what we call Lawfull Money, which we reckon at Silver after the rate of Six Shilling pᵉ ounce.   £26=14=1

I continued a Teacher at Cornwall in the Dissenting way fourteen years: and when I Setled there twenty eight Shillings of our money would buy but an ounce of Silver; & after this rate they paid me all yᵉ money yᵗ I received frᵐ them--

Solomon Palmer.

To the Revᵈ Doctor Bearcroft Secretary to the Society for the Propogation of the Gospel in foreign Parts.

[1759, Sept. 29, Stamford]

Stamford Connecticut in
Ncw England. Septembᵣ 29. 1759
Reverend Sir

I Beg leave to give advice to the Honourrable Board that I have drawn a Set of Bills for 15£ Sterling in the Usual form this day upon their Treasurer Edward Pearson Esqᵣ in favour of Mᵣ John Lloyd Merchant or Ordᵣ--

My people continue in a peacefull united State, in all parts of My Extensive Mission, and I Constantly attend the duties of My Office in the various parts of My Mission as formerly. there hath been no late Accessions to the Church from the Dissenters. the Sound of the Trumpet and the Alarums to war together with a concern for the events thereof principally Engrose the atention of People. Indeed the Church of Stamford is rather Weackned than Strengthned of late by Enlistments into Publick Service and by the Surpriseing Removal of a Number of heads of Families through a very Malignent Disroder that has prevailed among my People. in less than a Year past I have Buried 12 heads of Families 7 Males, some of them the best Ornaments of Religeon and Zeal for the Church and the Support of it among us & of good Esteem among our Dissenting Brethren. June yᵉ 24ᵗʰ Second Sunday after Trinity last I preached in the lower District of Salem to a very Considerable Auditory, Judged, between Three and Four Hundred People Old and Young who behaved very Devoutly and attentively and I gave the Communion to 39 Communicants. there is a hopefull Prospect of the increase and flourishing state of Religeon among that Scattered Poor People and no Endavours of mine are wanting to serve them in in their best Interest. I Preached to them about two weeks before upon a special Fast apointed in that Province to implore the Smiles and Blessings of Divine Providence to attend his Majestyˢ Arms the Ensuing Campaign. upon which occation also that People gave a Religeous & Devout attendance. I Bapised the last half Year 21 Infants and 1 Adult the present Numbᵣ of actual Communicants of the Church in Stamford and Grenwich 70. Heads of families in both Towns 155.

With my humble duty to the Venerable Board and Earnest prayers to Almighty God Still to Bless and prosper

all their Pious and Most Charitable designs together with
all due Respect to your Self I am Revd Sir your
                    Most Obedient Most Humble
                    Servt and Brother in Christ
                    Ebenez^r Dibblee

The Revd Doctor Bearcroft Secretary to the Venerable
Society for Propagation of the Gospel &c.

[Addressed:] To The Reverend Doctor Bearcroft / Secre-
tary to the Venerable / Society for Propagation of the /
Gospel in Foreign Parts / Charter House London
[Endorsed:] Read at a Comm[itt]ee Decr 14th 1760.

[1759, Nov. 23, New London]
Rev^d & good Sir

The Favour of y^rs by Mr Scovil shou'd have been duly
answer'd; but I was prevented by a very tedious Sickness,
wch commenc'd in a tertian & terminated in a burning
Ague; whose dismal Effects I have yet hardly surmounted: The Orders from ye Venerable Society shall be faithfully observed. Mr Peters arriv'd at Boston ye 15th of
November.

I understand Mr Fearweather is appointed to Narraganset. God's Will be done. Sure I am had ye naked Truth
been laid before you, my Request had been preferr'd: I
believe y^t none, but Mr Merret wou'd have presum'd to
impose upon such a glorious Society, in counterfieting a
whole Parish's Design, asserting a glaring Falsehood &
condemning ye Innocent. May God grant him true Repentance! Did they know ye Man, I realy believe, tho' he's
of a great Family & very rich, they, as well as well as
all considerate Independants here, wou'd de[s]pise him.
This is ye second time, y^t he has falsely represented a
Parish, viz y^t of Providence & y^t of Narraganset. Had I
been a Proselyte of Clarke's Arianism, he had been my
sure Friend. But as it was in ye Beginning of Christianity,
so it is now, ye great Men of ye World are always ye greatest Opposers of Christ & his Disciples. The Prospect of
ye Recompence of Reward is, & will, I trust, be my abiding Comforts in all ye Vicissitudes & Disappointments of
Life

I drew my last Bills in Favour of Mr Gibson & shall
my next in Favour of Mr Van Vleck of New-York.

Pray recommend my Duty & Service to my Religious
Patrons, whose pious Esteem I'll study to gain by preaching & living ye sacred Truths of God's holy Word-- That
ye Blessing of ye Almighty may attend y^r Labours & reward y^r serious, paternal & affectionate Advice is y^e
hearty Prayer of
Good Sir / Y^r most oblig'd, grateful / & obedient
Servt
                    Matt Graves

N. London Novr 23^d 1759

To the Revd Doc. Bearcroft

[1760, Mar. 1, Litchfield]
Revd Sir;
According to the Societies desire; in my last, Dated

August -- A:D: 1759. and papers enclosed; I Sent over an
account of the Prosecution of me for leaving the Dissenting Congregation, & Charges &c: which I hope they have
received: Sience which time I have as Steadily as I could,
attended my respective Congregations, tho' with no Small
pain & difficulty, being Still grievously exercised with
those Bodily Ailments that I have heretofore Several times
mentioned--viz: the Gravel, and a degree of the Strangury;
which renders me utterly uncapable of performing the duties of this Mission, wch requires the Fatiegue of So many
long journeys; than wch nothing could be more exercising
to me, & prejudicial to my health; I would therefore, with
earnest importunity, beg leave once more, to pray the Society a little to Animadvert upon my case; & (if they Shall
think y^t ye interest of Religion may be Served by it) to
remove me to Some other Mission where I can have rest.
There is a Vacancy at Groton, at Rochel, and at Chester;
the two last occasioned by the Late Deaths of the Rev^d
Mr Stouppe, and Standard: In either of which I Should be
contented to be placed; and would do ye best that I could
to be usefull, and Serviceable-- But if Such a favour cannot be obtained of the Society, I would humbly ask their
leave (till my Physitions, who forbid me to ride, have
tried their utmost Skill to cure me) to officiate only in y^e
Towns of Litchfield and Cornwall, which lye near to each
other. Were I in a State of health; it would be with the
utmost reluctance y^t I should leave my present Station,
where I am in ye midst of a Religious, Peaceable and
Industreous People; and with ye Societies Benefaction,
generously Supported; & where alone my temporal interest lies, viz: House and Lands; As also Friends and Relatives; Yet considering my infirmity of Body, (which I expect to carry along with me to the Grave) I am willing to
part with these comforts and advantages, & be Ordered
by the Society to any Cure where I may be freed from the
Business of Itinerancy, and in a Capacity of doing good to
the Souls of Men.

The Churches under my Care, are in a truly flourishing State; That at Roxbury increases daily; where there
being a great Scarcity of Common Prayer, and other good
Books--have therefore particularly desired me to beg the
Society to Supply them. Other places are not much better
furnished; which I hope the Venerable Board will consider, and a little turn their Attention to this their Infant
Mission; and let it Suck from their Breasts the Milk that
others have done before it, and be Satisfyed. I would
particularly request a Folio Bible, and common Prayer
Book for the Use of the Church at Litchfield. And inasmuch [as] there is no Library belonging to this Mission,
and I being poorly furnished with Usefull Books; would
pray the Society according to their own order to Allow
Ten Pounds worth &c:--And I will be accountable to the
Society for them, and answer for all damages they may
Sustain, thro' my fault, whilst they are in my care.

Sience the Date of my last I have Baptized 36 Infants.
And not knowing the time when my Salary Commences,
I have hitherto drawn for it by Bills of Exchange, Dated
March &c; and now accordingly, my last Years Salary
being due, I have Drawn a Bill of Thirty Pounds,--Dated
March, 1st A:D: 1760.

Be pleased, Sir; to acquaint me, by a line, when
my Salary Commences, that I may know when to Date

my Bills; Who am, and always Shall be, with profound
respect, Sir; Your, & the Societies,

> Most Oblidged, most Dutifull,
> and Humble Servant,
> Solomon Palmer.

New-England, Litchfield
County, Connecticut
March 1st A:D: 1760.

To the Revd Dr Bearcroft Secretary to the Society for
the Propagation of the Gospel in Foreign Parts.

[Addressed:] To the Revd Doctor Bearcroft / Secretary
to the Society for / the Propagation of the Gospel / in
Foreign Parts / Charter House / London
[Endorsed:] Read at the Committee Jan. 12. 1761.

[1760, Apr. 1, Stamford]

> Stamford Connecticut
> In New England April, 1, 1760

Reverend Sir

I thank you for your Favour of the 3^d of May Last,
which came to hand long since mine of ye 29th of Septemb^r
last in w^h I mentioned the heavy frowns of divine provi-
dence upon my Church, in the Removeal of Sundry of its
principal members and supports. Agreable to ye direction
of ye Venerable Board I have once and again recommended
it to them, to appoint in their Wills such Guardians to their
Children as will be proper to take care of their Religious
Education; and y^t they ought not to be so backward to Stand
Sureties for their brethrens children as occasion offers;
and being backed with so good Authority was in hopes they
would have been better reconciled to their duty; and in regard also to publick order. but that unhappy affair hath
so sowered the tempers of my People, (together wth y^e
tryumphs of their Adversaries, upbraiding them wth their
vain promises, when they see they have no power to fulfill
them) that but very few are to be perswaded to stand Godfathers or Godmothers for others Children, even where
they stand in ye nearest Relation. this Creates me much
trouble, as we have but few publick Baptisms, and Obliges
me to Visit them in all their dispersions, they liveing
very Scattered, and most of them many Miles distant, to
give their Children private Baptism. Under all our discouragements there hath ben lately an Accession of three
Heads of Families declareing conformity to our holy
Church; poor people, but honest frugal and of good Reputation among their dissenting Neighbours: two of them
are become Actual communicants with us.

If I should live to see an End of ye present War, and
this Ch^h should be able to free it self from some perticular Embarresments, I make no doubt of its future Increaseing and flourishing state. But one Considerable
discouragement they labour und^r is this, anticedent to y^e
late National Troubles, and before our country was made
ye Seat of War they had Run themselves in Debt about One
Hundred Pounds Sterling towards finishing their Church.
and the Burden of publick Taxes, Voluntary Enlistments
into publick Service, and the Death of many of its most
Considerable Professers, hath so weakened them, that
they Still lie under the Burden of y^t Debt. This Induced

the Ch^h Wardens and Vestry, with their Minister In October last, to prefer a petition to the Generall Assembly of
ye Province for Liberty to draw a Lottery in their fav^r,
not to Endow ye Church, but to free ye poor people from
those troubles w^h were brought upon them by ye pure
providence of God. But Alas! no such favour could be
obtained, not even to draw a Lottery in ye Government,
if we should not offer a Ticket to sale in it. And why?

Not because it is repugnant to their principles, for
they have given Countenance to publick Lotteries even to
repair the broken fortunes of private persons, and to help
to build up and Establish an Independant Colledge in the
Jerseyes, when they could obtain no such favour in their
own Province. But Alas this was too great an Act of Fav^r
to the Established Church.

No Endeavours of mine are or shall be wanting still
to promote ye pious design of the Venerable Board in Appointing me to this Mission so long as I am continued in
it. I Continue to do ye duties of it in ye same manner as
formerly, I Preached again in ye Upper District at Salem
on Sunday Octob^r 11th, last, to a very Crowded Auditory,
and Baptized Sundry Children, and gave the Communion
to 18 Communicants; & there is the same encourageing
prospect of being very Useful to them in their most Important Interests.

I have passed thro' a Scene of trouble the winter past,
The small Pox by the Providence of God has ben sent into
my family, and proved fatal to one of my Children, a
promiseing youth between 12 & 13 Years Old. the more
distressing as not one of my Family ever had it before,
three other of my Children have ben Inoculated Since and
by the blessing of God, Recovered. we are Still apprehensive of danger the Rest of us, may God preserve us,
and reconcile us to his dispensations. Notwithstanding
our troubles, I have not Neglected the Duties of my Parish. I Baptized t[he] last half Year 24 Infants and one
Adult, and thre[e] have ben add[ed] to the Communion.

I beg leave to Add, that I have this day drawn upon
the Honourable Societies Treasurer, a set of Bills for
£15 Sterling in Usual form, in Fav^r of Doct^r Platt Townsend of Oysterbay in the Province of New York. with my
Humble Duty to the Venerable Board, and devout prayers
to God Almighty to bless and Reward all their pious and
most Charitable Engagements. with my Humble Complement to your self,

I Am Most Worthy and Reverend / Sir Your Very
Humble / Servant and Brother / In Christ

> Ebenez^r Dibblee

The Rever^d Doctor Bearcroft Secretary to the Venerable
Society for Propagation of the Gospel &c

[1760, June 19, London, England]

My Lord

I waited on Doct^r Avery, a few Days Since, upon his
request, in order to give Some Information relative to a
Complaint or representation made to ye Society for propagating the Gospel in foreign parts, by the Revd Mr Palmer
an Episcopal Clergyman in the Colony of Connecticut, the
Subject matter of which Complaint I perceive, is a Certain
Lawsuit which Mr Palmer has Lately had with a People

there, over whom he had, before that time been placed as
a Minister or Teacher according to the Constitution or Usage of that Colony.--this application to me by Mʳ Avery
for information as aboveṣd, I Understand by him, was in
Consequence of the like application made to him by Your
Grace for Such Lights as he Should be Able to give relative
to that Affair.--as I was not altogether unacquainted with
the Subject of Mʳ Palmers Complaint, not only as having
been born & brought up in the Colony & bred to yᵉ Law
there, by which means, I became of Course Somewhat Acquainted with the general Course of Law proceedings &
Customs in the Colony, but as I have had Some personal
knowledge of yᵉ beforementioned Cause or Lawsuit between
Mʳ Palmer & his People, having been myself present at the
Trial of yᵉ Same[.] Some little time before my Coming to
England, I was able to give a pretty full & particular Account of the whole affair this I did to Mʳ Avery & thought
myself happy in having an oportunity So to do--the intelligence, I hope may be of Some Service--Mʳ Avery will be
able to Communicate the Same to Your Grace & which I
Doubt not he will do with all possible Candor & uprightness-

This waits on Yʳ Grace to Let you know the Sense I
have of Yʳ Graces' goodness & Condesention, in this par-
ticular--this humane Endeavour in Yʳ Grace to Obtain Some
light & information, from the Friends of the Accused, in
a matter So Delicate to their honour, hath made So Sensible an impression upon me that I Could not Content myself
without Expressing my Sentiments to Yʳ Grace in Some
proper way, & as I have not the honour of being personally
known to Yʳ Grace, I take the Liberty by this method to
return Yʳ Grace my most humble Acknowledgment, & Sincere thanks, as well for myself as in behalf of the said
Colony, which I have the honour at present, to represent
as their Agent at the Court of Great Britain for this Instance of Your Graces prudent Care, & impartial goodness.--I also beg Leave to ask the favour of Yʳ Grace as
often as Such Complaints Shall Come from that Colony, to
Communicate the Same to the agent for the time being of
yᵉ Sᵈ Colony, as Such Agent from the nature of his Office
will most Likely be Always able to throw Some lights upon
the matters--the Agents name & place of abode may always be known by Enquiring at the office of yᵉ Board of
Trade & Plantation where his Commission is Registred.

as to Mʳ Palmer, tis too much for me to take upon me
to Say, he has met with no Abuse whatever in that Colony,
but this I will Venture to Say & Dare answer for it, that
he has met with none from the Laws nor any from the Administration of Justice, in that Colony, & had he Suffered
from any Individuals in it, I am Sure upon proper application made there, he would have been Seasonally & properly
Redressḍ

Should Yʳ Grace have yᵉ least Desire to Learn from
me any particular relative to the beforementioned Complaint of Mʳ Palmer's, or any other matter respecting the
transactions in the aforesᵈ Colony, I Shall not only think
it my Duty, but shall Esteem it as a particular happiness,
whenever Yʳ Grace Shall Call on me for that purpose, to
wait upon Yʳ Grace & give all Information in my power, &
that with all possible frankness & openess

I am with great Esteem / Yʳ Graces Most Obedᵗ &
Most Devoted / Humbḷ Servᵗ

                                        Jared Ingersoll

N: Palace Yard / 19ᵗʰ June 1760.
for his Grace yᵉ Arch Bishop of Canterbury

[1760, June 20, Lambeth]

The Archbishop of Canterbury sends his Compliments to Dʳ Avery, & desires him to make Inquiry, when
he hath Opportunity, concerning the Case of Mʳ Solomon
Palmer: who saith, that on his conforming to the Church
of England, and quitting the Office of Minister to a Congregation at Cornwall, to which he had not engaged himself for any certain Time, he was sued at Law by the People of the said Congregation, and that Judgment was given
against him for a Sum of Money & Costs of Court, which
together with his own Charges amounted to above 30ˡˡ
Sterling; but that on his suing them in the same Court for
Arrears of his Salary legally due, he could not obtain Relief: and who saith further, that after he had come to an
Agreement with them March 31. 1756, that they should
wait till the first Day of September following, on which
Day a final Determination of the Dispute between them and
Him should be made, they did notwithstanding, in Breach
of that Agreement, bring on the Cause at a Court, held at
Litchfield on the last Tuesday, save two, of August, 1760;
and on his not appearing then, Execution was granted
against him, Aug. 19.

The Archbishop would also be glad, if Dʳ Avery could
procure him Information, whether it be true, that some
Dissenters at Pinner, Trustees for four Acres of Land,
left by one Tyndal to the Preaching Minister of Pinner, let
them for 2ˡˡ5.0. a Year, whereas the Minister could let
them for twice as much at least: and if it be true, what
is the Reason.

Lambeth, June 20. 1760.

[1760, Sept. 2, Litchfield]

                        Connecticut Colony, Litchfield
                            September, 2ᵈ A:D: 1760.

Revᵈ Sir,

Being Still grievously exercised wᵗʰ yᵒˢ Nephritick
Disorders mentioned in Several of my last Letters, I am
very unable to perform yᵉ duties of this extensive and
laborious Mission, which indeed is a task too hard for a
Man of the Strongest constitution, and greatest flow of
Animal Spirits to do. According to my Abilities, and yᵗ
measure of grace God hath given me, I have, ever Sience
I have been in the Societies Service, endeavoured to discharge my duty as one who must give an account; and
been beyond expectation Successfull; having now four good
Timber Churches, Subscriptions for a fifth, and two in
private Houses; and as I have been able, have Ministed
to all on Sundays, and occasionally upon other days, tho'
lately, not So frequently as in time past, by reason of
those Bodily infirmities which So constantly attend me;
which are much provoked by riding, and wᶜʰ my Physitions
have advised me to forbear, as ever I would expect a Cure;
In consideration of which, and for my ease, the Church
People belonging to yᵉ Towns of Newmilford, Woodbury,
wᶜʰ includes the Church of Roxbury, and Sharon, have
consented yᵗ I should omit my duty to them, during yᵉ
Winter Season, and Cold weather; and have by my approbation and Advice, for yᵗ time, agreed with a young Gentleman of a Liberal Education, & good Moral Character,
to read Service for them; [by] name Thomas Davies, a
Native of Great Brittain, and Grand son to Mʳ John Davies,
lately Deceasᵗ; who Sometime Sience, gave to the Venerable Society, fifty Acres of good Land, as a Glebe, lying

in ye Township of Litchfield; And who having business of his Fathers in England to do, designs, (God willing) to come over for yt purpose next Spring, & then to take Holy Orders, with a view of becoming a Teacher of ye Church People belonging to ye above mentioned places; if the Honourable Society, shall in their wisdom see fit so to order it; the which if done, I am Sincerely of the mind, would be a happy means of advancing ye interest of Religion, and greatly encreasing ye Chh of England in these parts; there being no other place yt I know of, where there Seems to be so hopefull and promising a prospect of promoting these great and good purposes. The remaining duties of this Mission would be Such as I could perform; and ye People being very desirous of my tarrying with them, and willing to do to ye utmost of their Abilities for my Support amongst them; makes me unwilling to leave them, and Strongly inclined to tarry where I am, provided ye Venerable Society Shall consent to have the Mission divided, and appoint Mr Davies, when he comes home, to one part of it; otherwise it is my earnest request that I might be removed to Some other Mission where I might be freed from ye fatiegue of so much riding; As there are Such Vacancies enough, both in New England, & the Province of New York, I heartily thank the Society for the provision they have hitherto made for me, which has been the best half of my Salary, and Shall always make it my concern to manifest my gratitude, by being faithfull in their Service, and endeavouring to ye utmost of my power to discharge ye duties of my Mission.

I would beg leave to renew my request of a folio Bible & Common Prayer Book for the Church of Litchfield, which consists of a Body of sober and orderly People; truly Catholick in their Principles, and constant in their attendance upon ye publick Worship and Service of the Church; as also of some Smaller Prayer Books, & pious Tracts for ye Use & Benefit of ye Chh People here in general; where they are much needed, and not to be purchased for Money. And, Sir; I would once more beg the favour of being advised by a line when my Salary Commences, yt I may make no mistake in drawing for it as I am conscious of none &c tho' one- of Thirty Pounds- has been lately returned, protested- and for what reasons I know not.

According to ye Societies desire, as soon as I could, after I received their Letter, I sent over an account of a Process in ye Civil Law against me, ---which I hope they have received; concerning which I have lately heard that our present Agent in England has been consulted, Viz: Mr Ingersole, who was one of ye Plfs Attorneys in the Case; and well understood it, however he has represented it; I would hope from his very good Character, not so extremly different from ye true State of the case, as ye report goes here. If there Still remains a difficulty about it, I pray to be informed where it lies, yt I may have an Opportunity to clear it up, as I am perswaded yt I can do. A Coppy of the Covenant, pretended to be broken by my leaving the dissenting Congregation, and conforming to ye Church of England; I Sent over with ye other papers, wch [was] all ye Stipulation, Writing or agreement yt was ever Mutually entered into between me, and yt People: Neither by my setling amongst ym as a Teacher, did I become entitled to any other interest of theirs, than in Sd Covenant Specifyed and exprest, whatever insinuations or pretences may have been, or shall be made to ye contrary; Nor indeed was ye judgment of Court grounded upon, or relative to any thing else; the Conditions of which Covenant, (if it may be said to be a Covenent) I fulfilled when I become their Minister, and continued a Teacher with ym so long, Viz: about fourteen Years in that way; and where indeed I have to this day continued to Preach, having a Church in that Town, and therefore, I think it must be granted yt the judgment of Court against me was without Law; and deemed to be So till a Law can be produced for it; which I am Sure was not done, nor any one referred to in all the Pleas of the Plfss [i.e., plaintiff's] Attorneys, who confessed the Action to be Singular; and without example. And Mr Ingersole himself, in his concluding Plea allowed ye Law to be Silent in the case; whose Letter, which I referred to in my last, has Sience been communicated to ye general Assembly, at yir Session October last, (but I am Still a Stranger to ye contents of it) and his Honour ye Governour, to whom it was directed, (who for many Years was an Attorney at Law, and the best accomplished of any amongst us) was appointed to Write to the Honourable Society----who undoubtedly will Say the best yt can be Said, and make the matter appear as well as possible on their Side tho' I am perswaded, by all yt he can Say, he cannot make it appear that ye judgment of Court against me, was according to Law; whose Letter, I humbly ask the priviledge of answering, if there shall be any need of it, and for yt purpose of being indulged a Coppy of it: But I leave ye whole affair with yt Venerable Body, begging their most Charitable Constructions,

Who am, theirs, and your / most faithfull, most / obedient & humble Servt,

Solomon Palmer.

To Doctor Bearcroft
Secretary to ye Society &c:

[Addressed:] To the Revd Doctr Bearcroft / Secretary to the Society for / the Propagation of the Gospel / in Foreign Parts / London
[Endorsed:] Read at a Committee June 15th 1761

[1760, Oct. 14, Sharon]

To all People to whom these Presents shall come, Greeting; Know Ye that I Joel Harvey of Sharon in the County of Litchfield in the Colony of Connecticut in New: England For the Consideration of thirty Pounds lawfull Money, Recd to my full Satisfaction of the Honourable Society, for Propagating the Gospel in foreign Parts, do Give, Grant, Bargain, Sell and Confirm Unto the sd Society and to their Successors in the Capacity aforesaid, for the Use of the Church of England in sd Town of Sharon, thirty Acres of Land, Yet to be laid out and already Granted to be laid in the sd Township of Sharon, Being part of the Eleventh and all the twelfth Divisions Granted to be laid out on my own Right of Land in sd Township, Being pitch'd in the North East Part of sd Township, 'tho' not yet actually Surveyed.

To Have And To Hold the above Granted and Bargained Premisses with the Appurtenances thereto to sd Society and to their Successors as aforesd for the Use aforesd, forever, and Also I the sd Joel Harvey do for myself, my Heirs, Executors and administrators, covenant with the sd Society, and their Successors as aforesd that at and Until the Ensealing of these Presents I am well

Seised of the Premises as a good indefeasible Estate in
Fee Simple, and have Good Right to Dispose of the Same
in the Manner, and Form as is above written; and that the
Same is free of all Incumbrances Whatsoever. and Far-
thermore I the s^d Joel Harvey do by these Presents Bind
myself, and my Heirs forever, to Warrant and Defend the
above Granted and Bargained Premisses to the s^d Honourable Society and to their Successors as afores^d, against all
Claims and Demands whatsoever. In Witness whereof I
have hereunto set my Hand and Seal this fourteenth Day of
October in the thirty fourth Year of his Majesty's Reign.
Annoque; Domini 1760. Sign'd, Seal'd and D^d In Presence
of

    Samuel Lewis   ·Joel Harvey
    John Williams

Litchfield County ss. Sharon October the 14th 1760   then
Mr Joel Harvey the Grantor of the foregoing Instrument
personally appeared and acknowledged the Same to be his
voluntary Act and Deed.

                Coram John Williams Jus^s Pac^s

Rec^d Octr 14° 1760. and Entered at large in Fol: 59, 60.
of the fifth Book of Records for Deeds in Sharon.

              per John Williams Register.

[1760, Nov. 25, Stamford]

          Stamford Connecticut In
          New England Novr 25, 1760
Reverend Sir.

In Mine of October 1st 1760, I gave advice to the Venerable Board, that I had that day drawn upon their Treasu^r
Edward Pearson Esqr a set of Bills for fifteen Pounds Sterling, payable at thirty dayes sight in favour of Mr Daniel
Starr Merchant or Order. that there was no Material alteration in the religious state of my Parish, but they continue in their Attachment to our Excellent religious Establishment, in a pious attendance on the publick Offices of
Religion, and I charitable[e] hope in a uniform practice of
the duties of the Christian life. and I have the pleasure to
find my services among them meet with a general Approbation and acceptance. on Sunday ye 29th of June last I
preached to the poor people of Salem, in the lower district,
to a very Numerous Auditory, who conducted with decency,
and performed their parts of the publick officces of Religion, with great appearance of devotion; and I baptized
5 Children. I baptized in all, last half Year 40 Infants
white, 2 blacks, and two were added to the holy Communion. I gave advice also of the Death of the late pious and
worthy Mr Wetmore, whereby a Vacancy was made in the
Parish of Rye. the Church Wardens and Vestry of that
Church signified to me their unanimous Inclinations that I
would supply the Vacancy made by the death of their late
worthy Incumbant. the straitness of my family circumstances and a prospect of being useful there, would have
induced me, with the leave of the Hon^ll Board, to accept
the invitation. but the distreess it was likely to give to the
poor people of my Parish and the disserviice it was thot, it
would be to the Interest of Religion, and our holy Church,
and to avoid the Reproach that we seek not the Church^s
good, but our own, influenced me wholly to decline their
Invitation. but withal have engaged dureing their destitute

state to lend them what assistance I can consistant with the
duties of my more Immediate Mission; and have preached
one Sunday and a lecture to them since the death of their
worthy Incumbant, and gave them the holy Communion.

To the above duplicate, I beg leave to Add, that by
Advice from the Revd Doctor Johnson, and by a letter you
wrote to the late worthy Mr Wetmore Deceased dated May
ye 14th 1760, I find the Honourable Society in their great
Charity hath ben pleased to Augment my Salary to £50 per
Annum from Lady last, with leave to draw my Bills Accordingly; for w^h Instance of Favour I Return my most
Sincere and hearty thanks. And as their pious design is
to encourage worth and Usefulness, tho' bestowed on me,
I shall endeavour by the grace of God, to improve this additional encouragement, to the pious purposes for which
it is bestowed. and can Assure the venerable Board that
no endeavours of mine shall be wanting, to revive and
propagate a true spirit of primitive Christianity, and to
build up and Edify the Church of God. and as above all
things, I am concerned to to approve my Self to almighty
God, by sincerely endeavouring to promote the true interest of Religion; so I am not Insensible of my Obligations to the venerable Board; and I pray God to prosper
all their pious designs, and Reward them sevenfold into
their Bosoms. It affords us likewise a pleasure to find
that the Conduct of the Missionaries, Relative to the affair of Mr Beach^s is so acceptable to the Hon^ll Society.

permit me to add my Humble Duty to the Venerable
Board, and humble Acknowledgements to your Self for
your kind good Offices in my fav^r. And with much Respect I Am Reverend Sir
    your Most Obed^t / Most Humble Servt / Unworthy
but Affect^nt / Brother in Christ
                  Ebenz^r Dibblee

The Reverend Doct^r Bearcroft
Secretary to the Venerable Society &c:

[Addressed:] To / The Reverend Doctor Bearcroft /
Secretary to the Venerable Society / for Propagation of
the Gospel / In Foreign Parts   Charter House / London
[Endorsed:]   read at the Committee April 13 1761

[1760, Dec. 4, Litchfield]

          Connecticut, Litchfield,
          December the 4th A D: 1760
Revd Sir;

My Bill of Exchange for £30. Sterling, Dated, March
the 1st or 2^d A:D: 1759, has been protested- and returned;
The reason whereof I understand was, because Mr Pearson, ye Societies Treasurer, mistook it for a Coppy; As
I writ, Signed against my Name: and this by a Coppy of
part of a Letter from Mr Gyles Lone, Not Pub Sent to
me from Boston, in ye following words, -- 'Afterwards
on the 21st Day of the same Monthe & Year, I ye said
Notary presented the Said Bill to the said Edward Pearson
and demanded payment thereof, He answered, that he was
ready to pay an Origional Bill of the same sum, but as y^e
s^d Bill was only a Coppy, he would not pay the same, y^r
fore I ye said Notary, at ye request afores^d, do hereby
persist to protest ye said Bill, for want of payment, in
Manner & form afores^d

          Gyles Lone Not Pub-

I have therefore drawn for yͤ said sum of Thirty Pounds Sterling, by a Bill of the same Date with this Letter- & Send my humble request to yͤ Venerable Society (the expences of this Mission being very great, as it requires So many long journeys to perform yͤ duties of it) to consider me with respect to yͤ Interest, Costs, and damages which I have Suffered for want of payment of said Bill.

Who am Revᵈ Sir, Yours, / and the Societies most Oblidged, / most humble & obedient Servant,

                     Solomon Palmer

[Addressed:] For the Revᵈ Doctʳ Bearcroft / Secretary to the Society for / the Propagation of the / Gospel in Foreign Parts / Charter House / London

[1760, Dec. 13, New London]
Revᵈ & Good

I am persuaded, yͤ warlike Commotions, wᶜʰ have existed by Sea, as well as by Land, have not only prevented me from yͤ Pleasure of hearing from you, but also suppress'd yͤ Accounts, wᶜʰ I sent you of my Mission. As it is my Duty, so I gratefully embrace all proper Opportunities of laying before You yͤ State of my Parish, & yͤ Success of my Ministry. We have now enlarged yͤ Number of our Pews on yͤ Floor, & erected an handsome Gallary, & yet have not Room for all yͤ Families, yͭ frequent our Church. The Communicants encrease & I have reason to believe have a due Sense of their renew'd, ratify'd Covenant, & yͤ great Importance of being in full Communion. My Parishoners have dug me a Well, wᶜʰ yͤ Goodness of God has supply'd wͭʰ Plenty of good Water. I have publish'd & marry'd several Dissenters, some publish'd by their own Teacher: lately baptiz'd an Adult Anabaptist, well prepar'd for yͭ divine Ordinance, & gain'd a large, growing Family of yͭ Sect to my Hearers, whom I'll study to bring regularly into our Church. Surely no Man was ever better regarded by his Hearers, or belov'd by all Denominations, than I am. They often attend my Service, frequent my House, & by Presents demonstrate their good Will. For wᶜʰ praised be yͤ Lord!

I have lately had an Opportunity of shewing a Christian Resentment to Mʳ Merrett. Hearing of yͭ Letter to Mʳ Caner, I ventur'd to wait upon Mʳ Merrett (hic Murus aheneus esto &c) reason'd with him yͤ Affair concerning yͤ Difference between him & my Brother, & reconcil'd them next Day in yͤ Church, in yͤ Presence & to yͤ great Satisfaction of all yͤ Congregation; as you have or will see by yͤ Votes of yͤ Parish, sent by Mʳ Caner to yͤ Venerable Society. As I undertook this Affair at his own Request, I executed it without any servile Concession. He has long since own'd, yͭ he is sorry for having wrote any thing to my Disadvantage, conscious, yͭ he was influenc'd by Passion, not by Reason. He receiv'd me with a Flood of Tears. But we are all good Friends, & I hope yͤ God of Peace will confirm yͤ triple Unity.

Pray recommend my Duty & Love to my August Patrons, whose pious Designs, by GOD's Assistance, I'll endeavour to perform. My Sister joins wͭʰ me in Compliments to yͭ good Lady, of whose Welfare & her happy Consort's I'd rejoice to be inform'd by yͭ friendly Pen. If you think proper, pray send me some Prayer Books wͭʰ yͤ

Articles, & some Tracts of Wall's infant Baptism, contracted by himself. As yͤ Anabaptists are very numerous & rigid, I presume one of Owens's Pieces againts Gate wou'd be very serviceable to each Missionary.

Pray pardon this Freedom. I shall draw in favour of Mʳ Van Vleck of New-York for my next Quarter's Bill, & perhaps yͤ succeeding, as my Brother did for yͤ last. My Labour being truly very great, & Abilities small, be pleas'd to remember,

Good Sir / Yͭ most obedient, / most grateful & / very humˡͤ Servͭ & / very affͭͤ Brother / in Christ
                     Matt Graves

New-London
Decemʳ 13ᵗʰ 1760

P.S. I hear Mʳ Peters behaves very well, is very laborious, & gains yͤ Approbation of all religious Societies. Yͭ Commands, Sͭ oblige my most chearful Obedience according to my Capacity.

To the Revᵈ Doctor Bearcroft at yͤ Charter-House London

[Endorsed:] read...April 13 1761

[1761, Mar. 2, Litchfield]
         Litchfield, March the 2ᵈ A:D: 1761.
Revᵈ Sir;

Your Letter of August the 4ᵗʰ 1760. I have received, and to which this is humbly presented as an Answer. I heartily thank the Society for the Books they have directed to be Sent to me; which are not yet arived; And for the encouragment they give me of being removed to ⌐ Setled Mission upon a proper opportunity; which I will wait for; and in the meantime, endeavour faithfully to improve those Small abilities that God has given me, in their Service, and for yͤ advancment of true Religion. And as to the Prosecution &c: By the Papers already transmitted, and those which I now send, the Cause of it will clearly appear; So yͭ the Society can no longer be at any loss about it. The Right of Land that I became entitled to on my being Setled Teacher to the Dissenting Congregation at Cornwall, was given and Granted by the Government, as an encouragment to the first Minister, that should so far deny himself, as to Settle amongst a poor People in Such a distant uncultivated Wilderness: Of which, after Some Years labour among them I, in common with the rest of the Proprietors, obtained a Patent; and neither by the Said Grant or Patent was I liable to any forfiture, Damages, or deprivation upon any account whatsoever. By my Setling among them as a Teacher, I, by Act of yͤ Assembly, became a Proprietor in common with yͤ other Proprietors; and yͤ said Patent, was, and is absolute and unconditional; So yͭ even the Power that gave it, could not Legally, and I am Sure not justly reassume it, or require Damages;- for so great was yͤ Expence, fatigue and hardships that I endured, for the three first Years--that I would not Suffer them again for the whole Township. I continued with that People before, and after my Setling among them fifteen Years, till I had Spent an Estate of my own more valuable than yͤ Right of Land &c: and 'till yͤ People had got thro' all the difficulties of Setling a New Town, and they and I began to live pretty well. By reason of the great Expence

the first Setlers were put to, most of them run clear out, (which is commonly the case with those y^t Settle new Towns) and were obliged to quit their Possessions, and leave the Town; tho' they came wth pretty good advantages; and had I not had an Estate of my own to Spend, for all y^t they did, or could have done for me, I must have Suffered the same Fate. And yet, when I left them nothing but Prosecution and Damages would Satisfie them; when a few Years before, a Minister in a Neighbouring Town, Setled a Year before I was, and under the Same circumstances, was dismissed, by a regular Counsel, for the immoderate Use of Inebriating Liquors; and another about two Years after for Lasciviousness; and yet concerning y^m, there was no Prosecution made, nor Damages required; which had their been, it would have been both Illegal & cruel, for they had well Merited their Lands: But Conformity being in the oppinion of our Dissenters, a greater crime than those Enormities, and a more notorious breach of Covenant,--that some some Special mark of disgrace must be put upon Such as do it, and some Signal punishment inflicted: Prosecution must be made, and the Civil Law must bend and Truckle so Serve a turn. My Title to the Lands &c: was never disputed, and concerning which I have never been molested. That for the Use of the Ministrey, I lay no claim to; neither have I Sience my Conformity, reaped any benefit from it. And respecting the Expences, I was put to,--I am not able exactly to compute them, neither can I give a better account, than I did in my former Writing. The Damage, and Costs of Courts is to be Seen in the Coppy of the judgment &c: Which said Lawsuit and Costs happening Soon after I had been at great expence in Prosecuting my Voyage to England, and without any incomes for twelve Months, put me to a great deal of Trouble and difficulty, not only in procuring the Money- but to maintain my Famoly, which was then, and is now Numerous, wch otherwise I could well enough have done. And to add to my distress, and make my case Still more difficult, the Rates of the Church People at Cornwall, were witheld from me, and went to the Support of their Minister, to y^e amount of £64=15=3. Proclamation Money; and no relief could be obtained, till at my request the Society was pleased to confine my Mission chiefly to Litchfield County, tho' in order to it, £11=10=0 Proclamation Money was Spent in the Law, and they were under my Pastoral Care, and to whom I Ministred four times a Year on Sundays, and frequently Preached Lectures to them.

And with reference to y^e information I gave the society concerning the State of their Missions here, of which I am required to give a further account. It had for some time lain with considerable weight upon my mind, and I did it with an upright heart, and truly honest design, for the honour of Religion, and Credit of the Church of England, (whose prosperity I shall always rejoyce at, and which I hope may long be continued and upheld amongst us) & not to hurt any of my worthy Brother Missionaries, but rather to help them, who are good oeconemists, and prudent in their Methods of living; None of whose Salaries are more than Sufficient for the Support of themselves and Famolies; but that ye society might know the true State of their Missions here (which I imagined they did not) and so, if they should in their wisdom think it expedient, come into some resolves whereby to Oblidge the People of such of their Missions, as are rich, to contribute according to

their Abilities towards ye Support and Maintenance of their Ministers; and not Suffer such of their Missionaries as have large salaries from ye society, and so enabled to live without the assistance of their People, to indulge them in Paying so little: And if they should, (not to direct) judge it advisable, withdraw part of their salaries from their rich Missions, erect new ones where they are needed, and bestow it upon them; The doing of which, as it would in it self be highly just and reasonable, so I doubt not but that it would in the long run, however it might opperate at first, turn out to ye benefit and advantage of the Church in these parts, and be best upon all Accounts: Certainly it would remove those Popular reflections of the Dissentors, Viz: That such of our Clergy whose People are able to afford y^m a Sufficient Maintenance, and yet have large salaries from ye society, are not honest in the Use of their Money. That they act with a Party Spirit, and are carrying on a Party design; that those who turn from them to us, do it, as they express it, to save their Money, and the like. Mr Beech, whose People are both rich and numerous, and of themselves well able to give him an honourable Support, pay Scarcely any thing to him; who I had principally in view, when I said in my former Letter that I could mention one or two of the societies Missionaries, who received Yearly from their People not more than ten Pounds sterling &c: which Sum I much question whither he thus receives, and what he does is only in little Perquisites as his People please, they not being oblidged to pay any thing by way of Rate or Tax. Rhoad Island Mission is more than Sufficient to answer all Ministerial Charges. That which Mr Camp lately left is able enough. And doubtless there are Such instances in other Governments. And I much question whether any pay in proportion to their abilities: some I know do not, whose Ministers can Scarcely live so as to Support ye honour of their Character, and maintain a decency in their Famolies in respect of Meats and Cloathing; As that of Mr Windslow's, who as I have been told, have lately assisted him by way of Quarterly Contributions. Mr Mansfields, And I might add this of mine, where the People are so encreased, that their ability is greater than their Liberality. The People of these Missions, as the[y] can, so they ought to do more for the encouragment of their Ministers than they do; Scarcely any of whose Ministerial Rates are more than Eight shillings Sterling per annum, and most not half so much. And I know not of one of the societies Missions, but that can easily enough, with what Assistance they have from them, Maintain their Ministers: Much more Eligible, therefore in my oppinion would it be, for that Venerable Body to Erect new Missions where they are needed, than to grant ye requests; of adding to old Salaries; for by means hereof, the Church might take a more general Spread, and the interest of it, by the blessing of God, be better served, Religion more Effectually promoted, and the pious design of the Venerable society more fully answered. I, last May, moved my Famoly from Newmilford to Litchfield, where there is a Regular and Uniform Church, to which there has lately been an addition of seven good heads of Famolies, and I have the most Sanguine hopes, from fair probabilities, of a greater encrease in a short time; they are worthy of the societies Notice, & I would, with Submission, once more, request the favour of a present from the society,

of a Folio Bible, and Common Prayer Book for them. Who am in all Respects,

Rev.<u>d</u> Sir, Yours, & the Societies, / most Obedient, most faithfull, / and Humble Servant

Solomon Palmer.

P:S: The number of Communicants at Litchfield have much encreased of late: Eleven new ones appeared at ye Communion the Sunday after Christmas. And I beg leave to observe that ye Dissenting People at Litchfield, by order of their Minister and the Church, kept Christmas Day last past, as a Fast, where three of the Neighbouring Ministers were present and assisted in the affairs. They pretended that it was upon account of the small Pox, of which there were two Persons y<u>t</u> Dyed. But it is evident that they did it to prevent Peoples coming to Church to hear a Chrismas Sermon, for it might as well have been a week before, as then, and better, for at that time there was dangerous appearances. One thing more I would add, that ye jewry, who passed the judgment in the Case that I have been giving an account of, said in the time of it that they had no reference to y<u>e</u> Lands I became entitled to upon my Settlement &c: and that whereas it is said in the Writ, that those Lands were then and now are well worth two hundred Pounds Lawfull Money, certain it is that they were not then more worth than Twenty, and that a little before private Rights were sold for less Money. I have writ in great hast, not having time to Methodise things, I hope therefore that all defects may be overlooked, and that what I have writ will be to the satisfaction of the society, Who am,

their most Humble Serv<u>t</u>
Solomon Palmer.

To Doctor Bearcroft Secretary to the Society for the propagation of the Gospel in Foreign Parts. Charter House London

[Endorsed:] Read...Sept. 14. 1761

[1761, Mar. 12, Colony of Conn.]
Rev<u>d</u> Sir

As We understand That The Rev<u>d</u> M<u>r</u> Palmer, the Society's Missionary at New Milford & Litchfield, has signified to the Society, That He finds the Duty of so extensive a Mission, too laborious for his advancing Years, & present State of Health, & has requested either, that He might be removed, or if the Society should be so pleased, His Mission might be divided; And, As a considerable Number of the people in this Mission, have made Application to the Bearer M<u>r</u> Thomas Davies, who is at present, & has been some Time, employed as a Reader, among them, to become their Minister, & have exerted themselves to make what provision they are able for his reputable Support, We therefore take the Liberty to introduce Him to you, as a Person, whom, If the Society should think fit to appoint, either to succeed M<u>r</u> Palmer, or, to the Care of any particular part of that Mission, we are in Hopes may prove greatly serviceable to the Interest of Religion- He has had a liberal Education, & been graduated at Yale College in this Colony, & has supported the Character of Soundness in principles, & Integrity of Life, & is generally esteem'd to have made proficiency in usefull Knowledge, & has render'd Himself universally acceptable & engaging to the Peo-

ple, whom He is desirous to serve- He has been some Time ago mention'd to you by D<u>r</u> Johnson, & would have waited to have known the Society's pleasure, before He presented Himself to them, but that He has Relations, in England, & some private Affairs to transact there, which have induced Him to make his Voyage, somewhat earlier, than He would otherwise have done, hoping at the same Time in the Society's Goodness, & that it may comport with the Condition of their Affairs, to favour his Design, & the real Necessities & Circumstances of a great Number of people, conscientiously attached to the Communion of the Church, as the happiest & most scriptural Method of all needfull Improvement in christian Knowledge & practice, but who are labouring under great Inconveniences & Difficulties, themselves & their Families, for want of the more frequent, regular Administration of religious Offices, occasioned by their remote & dispers'd Scituation.

We are / Rev<u>d</u> Sir, / The Society's, And, / Your, most dutiful, & obed<u>t</u> Serv<u>ts</u>

Ebenezer Punderson   Richard Mansfield
John Beach   Edward Winslow.

Colony of Connecticutt. March. 12th. 1761.

Rev<u>d</u> D<u>r</u> Bearcroft.

[Endorsed:] Read...Aug<u>t</u> 17, 1761

[1761, Mar. 25, Stamford]
Stamford Connecticut in
New England March 25th, 1761.

Reverend Sir.

Agreable to leave granted in yours to the late Worthy Mr Wetmore, Dated London Charter House May ye 14, 1760. I presume to draw this day in usual form a Set of Bills upon the Honourable Societies Treasu<u>r</u> Edward Pearson Esq<u>r</u> for thirty five Pounds Sterling, which includes the late most Charitable addition to my Salary from Lady day 1760. payable at thirty dayes sight in fav^r of Mr Stephen Platt Merch^t. and beg leave to repeat my humble thanks, for ye enlargement of my Salary, and I hope to deserve the continuance of the fav^r of the Venerable Board, by a persevereing diligence & fidelity in the duties of my Office.----My Parish continues in a peaceable good state, in all the parts of my Extensive Mission. Notwithstanding the many discouragements and embarisments w^h ye Ch<u>h</u> of Stamford labours under, the hopes of my poor parishioners are much revived, in expectation of the future growth & prosperity of the Ch<u>h</u> and they now seem determined and animated to do their utmost to free themselves from those incumbrances which the Church has laboured Under, since the commencement of our National troubles, and w^h has proved so prejudicial to the prosperity of it for Years past. and what has Revived their spirits, more than barely seeing their Minister provided for better than their ability allowed, is, a late smile of divine providence in their fav^r, which I have leave to communicate to the Venerable Board. ----In compliance with repeated requests, I preached on Sunday y^e 7th of Decemb^r last to the destitute people at Westchestchester, to a very considerable Congregation. the Even following I paid my Respects to y^e worthy good Mr St George Talbot, who appears to be a Gentleman of

great piety Zeal and Charity. and he desired me to Mention to the Hon^ll Society the very gratefull sense he has of the late unexpected Honour done him, in being admitted & made a Member of the venerable Society. his principle concern in the decline of Life, is to promote the interest of true Religion, the Church of Christ Militant, until it shall please God to translate him to the Church Tryumphant. And he desired me to intimate, that beside the benefaction to the Ch^h of Rye, of w^h Mr Wetmore gave advice; he hath also given six Hundred Pounds New York Currency for the incouragement of Religion, Among the poor people at North Castle, Ratified ye 6th of June 1759. delivered into the hands of Col^l Mac'Donald Jonathan Ogden, Caleb Fowler, and Charls Hait by ye Approbation of the late Mr Wetmore and Security given.----to the Church at Flushing on Long Island, in Mr Seaberry Ju^rs Mission, in hopes of Reviveing a Spirit of true primitive Christianity, he hath also given the like Benefaction, made over ye 5th of Novemb^r last, Security given by Mr John Aspinwall, and Captn Greenall. And haveing laid before him the many frowns of providence and discouragements which the Church of Stamford hath of late Years been under, he freely Engaged to bestow the like Noble Benefaction upon my Church, and with Divine leave proposes to make us a Visit at Whitsuntide to confirm the same. the whole of the forementioned Benefactions, he proposes finally to be improved, after his, and his housekeepers Decease, as he shall direct in his last Will and Testament, or otherwise as the Venerable Board in their great Wisdom shall Judge proper and most conducive to the best Interest of the Respective Churches.---- I preached at Salem in ye upper district on Sunday the 22^d of Feb^r last to a very large Congregation. and the poor people scattered about in the Wilderness, are, I am Informed concerting measures to build a small Church, as a private House will Seldom contain the people y^t resort to Church when I preach among them. which is as often as the Duties of my Extensive Mission will admit. the Church of Stamford now mainly Consists of young Families. the greater part of those Heads of families which composed the Church when I entered into their Service, are removed by Death, and the most of them in the prime of Life.----the present Number of Heads of Families in Stamford professors of the Church are about 112. I Baptized the last half Year 30 Infants, 3 Adults; 2 added to the holy Communion. ----when the Hon^ll Society shall please in their Charity to send me any Books to distribute, I desire they may principle consist of Bibles & common Prayer Books, and Catechisms; as they are most wanted. Sundry poor Families to my knowledge not haveing a Bible in their Houses. those w^h have been heretofore sent me haveing long since ben distributed. permit me to Add my Humble Duty to the Venerable Board, and Earnest Prayers to Allmighty God, Still to prosper and Succeed all their most pious designs. and with my Humble Complement to Your Self, I Am Reverend Sir

Your Most Obed^t / Most Humble Servt / An Affect^nt Br^r In Christ

Ebenez^r Dibblee

The Revd Doct^r Bearcroft
    Secreta^r to the Venerable
    Soceity for Propagation
    of the Gospel &c:-

[1761, Apr. 2, Cornwall]
    The following is an accout of the useage of the Presbyterians towards the Church of England Profesers In Cornwall written upon the desire of the Rev^d mr Solomon Pammer: In the year 1754 after mr Pammer went for orders, the Pris^ans Voted in there meeting that if the Church people would not act with them, that for the time to Come they should not pay any Rates to the[m] towards their minister which proposals they did Comply with and the Pris^ans settled a min^er and Immeadatly assesed the the Church people for there Rates and obliged them to pay them before mr Pammer Returned home and after his Return they made their Rates as a town Rate and took out thereof to pay their minister and there by keept themselves free from the statute made for the Releaf of Church of England in this Colony and used all the artifice to make them pay Rates to there minister that they Could untill they took from the Curch people the sum of £64-15-3. prock^on [i.e., Proclamation] money to pay there minister and the curch people Expended £11-10-0 in the Law before they Could Git any Releaf or be Released from paying the Prisby^an minister and the Pris^ans brought an action of Dammage against mr Pammer for Conforming him self to the Curch of England and Recoverd £15-0-0 Dammage and there Costs against him   all the above facts appear by Record but would be to Large to Inclose in this paper and burdensome to send with the same
    Dated at Cornwall
    april 2^d, 1761

Sam^ll Dean	Exam^ed by us ye Subscribers
Wil^m Tanner	being Eviden^cs, unknown Errors
Ethan Allen	Exepted.
Elihu Allen	
Heman Allen	

[1761, Apr. 2, Litchfield]
        Litchfield, April the 2^d A:D: 1761.
Revd Sir;
    Mr Davies, the bearer--with my consent and approbation, and upon my desire, has for five Months past, been employed as a Reader to the Churches of Newmilford, Roxbury and Sharon, whereby, together with a good Conduct, he has So far recommended himself to their esteem, that they are very desirous (my present State of health being Such as renders me unable Steadily to officiate in all parts of this Mission, which has been much encreased Sience I came into it, and So to give Satisfaction to the whole) that he Should become their Teacher; These are therefore; at their request, to Signifie their desire to the Venerable Society, wishing that it might be granted; & in order to which, that this Mission might be divided, the Said Mr Davies, who is truly worthy of the Society's Notice and encouragment, received into their Service, and appointed as their Missionary to ye above mentioned places, with the allowance of Such a

Salary, as their Fund will permit, and they in their wisdom and Charity shall shall judge to be needfull. But if the Society Shall not consent to divide this Mission; It would be very pleasing to me, and I should, most gratefully resent it, if they would remove me to a Setled Mission (but I will wait their opportunity) and Send M<u>r</u> Davies here, which I know would be highly pleasing, and much to the Satisfaction of this People. I add no more, but my my hearty Prayer to Almighty God, for the Success of the pious designs of that Venerable Body, to whom presenting my humble Duty, I beg leave to Subscribe,

    Rev<u>d</u> Sir, / Your most Dutifull, / most Obedient Humble Serv<u>t</u>,

                     Solomon Palmer.

To the Rev<u>d</u> Doct<u>r</u> Bearcroft
Secretary to the Society--

[Addressed:] To the Rev<u>d</u> Doct<u>r</u> Bearcroft / Secretary to the Society / for the Propagation of the / Gospel in Foreign Parts / Charter House, / London
[Endorsed:] Read...Aug<u>t</u> 17, 1761

[1761, May 5, Fairfield]

To the Honourable General Assembly of the Colony of Connecticutt to be holden at Hartford in s<u>d</u> Colony on the Second Thursday of May AD 1761

The Memorial of the Church Wardens and Vestry-Men of Trinity Church so called standing in the First Society in Fairfield in the County of Fairfield humbly sheweth

That Your Hon<u>rs</u> Memorialists together with those that belong to the aforesaid Church profess to observe and perform and do observe and perform Publick Worship in the Manner and according to the Cannons of the Church of England so called and that Your Hon<u>rs</u> Memorialists some Years ago with great Difficulty did erect and set up with the Aid and Assistance of our Friends abroad a House or Church for the Purpose of celebrating and performing publick Worship in the Manner afores<u>d</u> and that your Memorialists have had for many Years past and now have a Missionary resideing with us who was sent from the Society in England for propagating th[e Gospel] in foreign Parts to preach the Gospell to your [Memorialists], hath constantly a Salary paid to him for [preaching to] s<u>d</u> Society and your Memorialists together with those [belonging] to our s<u>d</u> Church as the Laws of this Colony now stand are yearly and every year taxed by the Societies in whose Limits [we] dwell and obliged to pay the same Rate and Tax to the Support of s<u>d</u> Missionary which the Inhabitants of those Societies pay to their respective Ministers and that we have by Law no Right or Privilege of Voteing in those Societies in their Society Meetings, nor by Law have We any Just Way or equal Method to tax ourselves for repairing and puting in order the Meeting House or Church which we now have which is now much decayed and stands in great Need of being speedily repaired.----And Your Hon<u>rs</u> Memorialists Would further beg Leave to inform Your Honours that We with those that belong to our Church are and always have been good Loyal and obedient Subjects to his Majesty and to his Majesty's Government as established by Charter in this Colony and as good, Loyal, honest and faithfull Subjects have always behaved ourselves in this Colony and have always paid a ready and willing Obedience to all the Laws

of this Colony and do highly esteem and greatly value our Privileges which we in Common with the Rest of his Majesty's Subjects in this Colony do enjoye in the present happy Form of Government which this Colony enjoyes by s<u>d</u> Charter.

We Your Hon<u>rs</u> Memorialists would therefore humbly pray your Honours to releive us from the present Difficulties under which we Labour with Respect particularly to our Meet[ing House] or Church for Publick Worship and that y[our Hon<u>rs</u> woul]d enable us and those that belong to our [s<u>d</u> Church as] often as occasion may require to repair our Ch[urch or] Meeting House and especially that we may now [be] enabled to repair the Meeting House which We now have and which stands in great Need of it, and that for these Purposes Your Hon<u>rs</u> would grant us Liberty in some proper Manner by ourselves to make and Lay such Taxes and Rates upon ourselves as we shall find necessary from Time to Time and that We may have for these Purposes as full and ample Powers and Authority to do and transact all Matters relateing to the repairing our House for the purpose of Publick Worship and as Effectually to collect and gather such Tax as Ecclesiasticall Societies within this Colony by Law have or in some other Way releive Your Memorialists as your Hon<u>rs</u> in your great Wisdom shall Judge best, and Your Memorialists as in Duty bound shall ever pray   Dated in Fairfield the 5<u>th</u> Day of May AD 1761

      Nath<u>l</u> Perry   ⎫
      Jn<u>o</u> Whitour ⎬ Church Wardens

      John Bolt   ⎫
      Jonathun Coley ⎬ [Vestrymen]
      John Williams   ⎪
      zaccheus more   ⎭

In the upper House

The Prayer of the Memorialists [is granted.] Memorialist[s] have Liberty to bring [in a bill] accordingly

            Test G[eorge Wyllys, Secret<u>y</u>]

Concurred in the Lower Ho[use]

            Test Abr<u>m</u> D[avenport, Clerk]

[1761, May, Hartford]

On the Memorial of Nath<u>ll</u> Perry and Zaccheus Morehouse &c Church Wardens and Vestry Men of Trinity Church so called within the first Society in Fairfield shewing to this Assembly the great Difficulties the professors of y<u>e</u> Church of England belonging to s<u>d</u> Church labour under with respect to repairing their s<u>d</u> Church or Meeting House for divine Worship for want of power and Authority to tax themselves for Such purpose praying for Relief in the premises

Resolved by this Assembly that y<u>e</u> Church Wardens & Vestry men of s<u>d</u> Church or y<u>e</u> Major part of them be and hereby are (on five Days Notice) fully authorised and impowered to call y<u>e</u> Members and Professors of y<u>e</u> Church of England belonging to s<u>d</u> Church to meet at such Time and place as they shall appoint when and where being so met they shall be and hereby are fully Authorised and

impowered by their Major vote to grant such Rates and Taxes to be Levyed and collected from such Professors as afores^d as shall be necessary for ye purpose of repairing such Meeting House or Church and they are also hereby further Authorized and impowered to choose a Com^tee to manage the repairing of such house and to appoint a Collector to collect such Rate or Tax who shall have ye same power and Authority to collect such Rate or Tax and be accountable therefor in the same manner as other Collectors by Law are and any one Assistant or Justice of ye Peace is hereby impowered and directed on application to him made by such Com^tee to issue such Warrant for collecting such Rate as by Law they are impowered and directed for collecting other Rates and Taxes

/May 1761/   past in the upper House
                          Test George Wyllys Secret^y

                          Concurred in the Lower House
                          Test Abr^m Davenport Clerk

[1761, Sept. 29, Stamford]
                          Stamford Connecticut In
                          New England Septemb^r 29th, 1761
Reverend Sir.

    In my advice of Apr^ll 1, 1761, upon the desire of the worthy Mr St George Talbot, I mention^d his Noble and pious Benefactions to the Churches of North Castle and Bedford, and to the Church of Flushing. Agreable to the encouragement given, he made us a Visit on Whitsuntide last, and very devoutly received the holy Communion with us on that festival Occasion. after a thourough Acquaintance with the Circumstances of the Church of Stamford, from its first Rise to its present State, he judged us worthy of his Notice and Charity and for the future encouragement of my Poor People, hath made a free donation of Six Hundred Pounds, New York Currancy, in Addition to the present Charity of the Venerable Society, to be improved after his & Housekeepers Decease, for their Ease in supporting a Minister, or the Schooling of their Children, as the Honourable Society in their wisdom shall direct, or as he shall prescribe in his last Will and Testament. they behaveing in such manner as to Continue to deserve the Charitable Notice of the Venerable Board.----That good Gentleman also in his great Zeal for Religion hath encouraged us to hope for a present of two Pieces of Plate, for the Decent administration of the Holy Eucharist. May it please God to reward him and all the pious Benefactors of his Church, Sevenfold into their Boosom.----I hope to improve every encouragement I meet with me, in the duties of my Office, by labouring to be as extensively useful as may be; and my Parish continue in a peaceable united State, paying in general a due regard to the publick offices of Religion in all parts of my Extensive Mission. but I meet with some difficulties in giting my Just Dues in some of my Parishes, perticularly at Horsneck, thro' the Slackness in part of the people, but more thro' the perverseness of the Dissenting Collectors, who by the Law are appointed to Collect the Taxes of the Church, and are willing to distress as as much as they Can unless we Sue them at Common Law; w^h I am afraid will be attended with mischief to the Interest of Religion, and prejudice to the

Church.----The People in the first Society of Greenwich, who have ben long destitute of any Dissenting teacher among them, from the extraordinary pains I've lately taken, seem to be animated with a more proper Zeal for Religion. and the Chief Body of the Dissenters, in concurrance with the professors of the Church have requested my Attending Divine Service on Sundays, as often as is consistant with the extensive Duties of my Cure. which good disposition I have, & shall endeavour to Cultivate, & improve to promote their their best Interest. beside Lectures and funeral Occasions, I have preached to them about one Sunday in Eight for Six Months Past; and have met with proper encouragement. I have once, & propose for the future, as often as may be, to go & attend Evening Service and Preaching to them on Sundayes after Evening Service at Stamford. and so long as I am able to attend three Services on Sundays, am willing to do it, if I may be Serviceable to them, and to prevent their families from being brought up in the habitual Neglect of the publick offices of Religion. I Preached a Lecture at North Castle ye 12th of August Last to a great Congregation. The[y] have Erected a New Church and at their desire, and the Request of Mr St George Talbot the worthy benefactor of our Churches, whom I expect to Meet with, I have Consented to Preach to them ye 2^d Sunday in October Next, In their Church,----August ye 19th at the earnest request of some poor people settled on Philips^s Patten, I preached a Lecture to a large Auditory. and find a great want of a Regular Clergiman to officiate in those parts; to prevent those Confusions in Religion which hath too much obtained. and their seems a general good disposition to the Church, if they could be favoures with a settled Teacher.----Permit me Sir, to add that I have this day drawn a set of Bills in Usual form, upon the Honourable Societies Treasurer, Edward Pearson Esqr for Twenty five Pounds Sterling, payable at thirty dayes Sight, In fav^r of Mr Samuel Farmar Merchant at New York.----The present Number of Heads of Families in Stamford, and Greenwich, and the Parishes belonging thereto, by Reason of Deaths and Removeals, Consists but of 152: N^o of Actual Communicants 53. Baptised last half Year 26 Infants; 1 Adult; 2 added to the Communion.----with my Duty to the Venerable Board, and Prayers to Almighty God, to Smile upon, and reward all their pious and Most Charitable Endeavours to Propagate the Gospel of his Dear Son; I Subscribe with great Esteem, and Humble Regards, to Your Self.
    Reverend Sir / Your Most Obedient / Humble Servant / And Most Affec^t Brother / In Christ
                                    Ebenez^r Dibblee

The Reverend Doctor Bearcroft,
Secretary to the Venerable Society
for Propagateing the Gospel &c:

[1761, Oct. 1, Simsbury]
    To the Honourable the General Assembly of the Colony of Connecticut in New England to be held at New Haven on the Second Thursday of October Anno Domini, 1761.----
    The Memorial of William Case, Joshua Holcomb Church Wardens, and the Rest of the Members and Proffessors of the Church of England, at Simsbury, Humbly Sheweth; That notwithstanding the favourable provision this Honourable Assembly hath hertofore made by a Statute

Law of this Colony in Law Book page 169. &c. Intitled
"an Act for provideing how the Taxes Levyed on the professors of the Church of England, for the Support of the
Gospel Shall be Disposed of; &c.--among other things It
is Enacted that all persons who are of the Church of England, and those who are of the Churches Established by the
Laws of this Government Shall be Taxed by the Parishioners of the Said Parish, by the Same Rule, &c.--and Such a
Tax being Indifferrantly Levyed and Collected of the professors of the Church of England &c: the Collector to pay
the Same to the Minister of the Church of England Liveing
Near Such person, &c--But if Such proportion of Taxes be
not Sufficient in any Society of the Church of England to
Support the Incumbent there, then Such Society may Levy
and Collect of them who profess and Attend as aforesaid,
greater taxes at their own Discretion for the Support of
their Minister,----Yet notwithstanding the favours intending to be Granted by Said Statute, Your memorilists are
Labouring under many Diffialties and Discouragements
which said Statute doth not remedy, that is to Say, Your
Memorilists are Inhabitants within the Limits of Several
Eccleciastical Societies in Said Town of Simsbury, and
Said Societies Tax themselves very differantly according
as their general List arises, for the Support of their Ministers, By means whereof Some of us professors of the
Church of England, are burthened with Very High Taxes,
while others are but Small. And altho' the Said Statute
gives us Liberty to Tax our Selves for an Additional Support for our Minister, Yet there is no provision made how
we may Incorporate, or form our Selves into a Society, to
Raise Taxes as aforesaid.----

Therefore Your Memorilists Humbly pray this Honourable Court to take our Case and Circumstances into
their wise Consideration; and Some way or other provide
for our Relief,--and by an Act Grant that we the professors of the Church of England Inhabitants of said Town of
Simsbury, (and any others liveing adjacent that Shall or
may Join themselves to us if this Honourable Court Shall
think fit) may be Incorporated into a Society Eccleciastical, by the Same Rules, and with the Same priviledges as
are Granted by Law to other Eccleciastical Societies in
this Colony, with full Power to form our Selves into a Society in the Same manner that other new Societies in this
Colony are first formed and Directed to hold Society Meetings, and to Raise Such Sum, or Sums of money among our
Selves, to Repair, or Build our Church House, or Houses;
and to pay our Minister or Ministers as we Shall think
Needfull from Time to Time, and to Chuse proper officers,
and Collectors to Collect Such Rates or Taxes so Granted
as aforesaid; as the other Eccleciastical Societies in this
Colony have by Law Granted unto them:--And that it may
be better known who are professors of the Church of England, and Members of our Society formed as aforesaid,
Your Memorilists pray this Honourable Court further to
Enact, That every professor of the Church of England
among us who Desires to be a Member of our Society thus
formed, shall Enrole themselves by Subscribeing his or
her Names in the Clerks office of our said Society, and
also enter his or her Names in the Clerks office of Such
other Society such person Shall go from, with his or her
Declaration that Such person belongs to the Society of the
Church of England----These things being So reasonable in
themselves, and agreable to the English Constitution, and

the Sentements of all Protestants; Your Memorilists Humbly hope and Pray that this Honourable Assembly will Take
this affair into their wise consideration, and Act and do
their in, as they in their Great Wisdom Shall Judge will
Tend to Remedy the aforesaid Difficulties, and Grant Said
Request, for which favours Your Memorilists look on
themselves bound in Duty to ever Pray. Dated in Simsbury October the first Day Anno Domini, 1761.--

Subscribed to by--   Joshua holcomb
                            William Case

Resolv^d by this Assembly that ye foregoing Memorial &
Matter therein Contain^d be & they are hereby referr^d to
ye Consideration of the Gen^{ll} Assembly att their Session
att Hartford on the 2nd Thursday of May Next--

            Past in the Lower House
            Test Abr^m Davenport Clerk

            Concurr^d in the upper House
            Test George Wyllys Secret^y

[1762, Mar. 26, New Haven]
                            New Haven 26 Ma^{ch} 1762
Respected S^r
      ever since I have been in this Mission w^c is 8 years
& 1/2 I have to ye utmost of my power been endeavouring
To promote ye Religion of our assended Redeemer as professed by our most excellent Chh & blessed be GOD my
Labours have been Attended wth uncomon Success notwithstanding ye continual endeavours of ye numerous & powerfull as well as Subtle adversaries of our Chh to disquiet
my life & render my endeavours Abortive.

      Many young Gentlemen (as there is a Colledge in this
place) have I been serviceable to in reconcileing To our
Communion who I trust will do GOD & his Chh great Service in their Day & Generation. The 3 young Gentlemen
who lately went Home for Holy Orders, safely returd y^e
End of Jany are very acceptable to their people, & I doubt
not will answer the Societys expectations; & desire y^t
venerable board to accept my hearty Thanks for the kind
notice they took of them being greatly rejoycd that my former Mission is now so Hapily [su]pplied; & I am Easd of
North Haven a Chh almost intirely of my rais[ing] up: &
w^c I preachd in the Sunday after Christmas & dedicated to
s^t [Joh]n as it was his Day: had upwards of 20 Com^{ts} altho excessive [cold] 21° in extreme. And I have Mr Hobart an ingenious Young man a Candidate for Holy Orders
reading in the 2 Chh^s of Guilford y^t I now officiate Steadily 2/3 in the Chh in this Town where not long since I
christned 3 Adults. at West Haven every 9th Sunday and
Brandford every 9th, & Northford (about 16 miles from
this Town) every 9$\underline{th}$ where they are now about errecting
a Small Chh.

      There is one favour I would entreat of y^e Society viz
That they would Ellect Joseph Harison Esqr Coll^r for this
port a Member of y^e Society He being a man of y^e greatest probity & ingenuity & will be helpfull to the Society in
prossecuting The glorious designs in w^c they are engagd
& y^t Heaven would bless & prosper them in the work until
ye Knowledge of Jesus & his Gospel shall cover the whole

Earth is ye hearty prayer of Rev^d S^r
    Yours & ye Societys / Humble & faithful Servant
                                    Ebenez^r Punderson
P.S^t I have drawn for my last Quarters Salary in favour
of Roger Sherman Eq^r.

[Addressed:] To / The Secretary of the Society for /
propagation of the Gospel &c / London
[Endorsed:] Read...July 12 1762

[1762, Apr. 10, Judea]
                    Connecticut,
                        Judea in Woodbury 10th of April 1762
Rev^d S^r
    The Circumstances of the Church in Judea are as fol-
lows (viz) We are in Number 21 Famolies: and it is impossible for our present Miss^y to be with us more than 3
or 4 Sundays in a Year, by Reason of the largness of his
Mission and the Number of Churches contain'd in it: Our
Wives and our Children are obliged to neglect the Publick
Worship of God for want of the preaching of God's Word
among us: and Considering the apparent Necessity there
is that the Mission Should be Divided. We togather with
The Towns of Litchfield and Cornwall pray that we might
be Set off as a Mission and that the Revd Solomon Polmer
might be continued among Us. As he is a Man that gives
good Content; and is likely to be more Servisable to the
Interest of the Church than any other Man. Mr Davies
our present Miss^y has Consented that Mr Polmer Should
preach among us. his Words are these: To the people of
Judea Society. Gen^t as to y^r propositions you present me
with;--I have Consider'd them Cursorily; and can do no
further therin; than permit you to pay y^r Rates unto M^r
Polmer for the Time Mr Polmer may preach among you,
and for So long Time, I entirely exempt you from paying
any Thing unto Me. Wishing &c   Signed. Thomas Davies
dated at New Milford March 27th 1762   We therfore
pray that the Society Would take our Circumstances into
Consideration and Relive Us if they Can. for it is to be
fear'd that the Church will decrease if We can have no
order among Us; and there is a great prospect that the
Ch^h will encrease if Mr Polmer is Continued among Us.
We are
            Revd Sr Y^r Humble Serv^ts

            friend Weeks ⎧Ch^h Ward^n
                          ⎨ and Comtt^e
    Abraham Thomlinson   ⎩ Comtt^ee

[1762, Apr. 13, New Milford]
                    New Milford ye 13th of April 1762.

    I beg leave to inform You, and the honorable Society
of my safe arrival to America; after a long & dangerous
Passage; and that I found my Parishoners United, and joyfull upon my success and happy return: joining with me in
grateful acknowledgments to the venerable Society in appointing me as Missionary among them: a prospect opens
for largely encreasing the Church, haveing since my return, had pressing invitations to officiate in some of our
most populous Towns, and where the greatest oppossion

was made against the Church, they having no Pastors, I
have complied; and preached at Hartford, and Woodbury,
to a very large concourse of People; where they seem to
have lost their ancient bitter Temper, and think that
Christianity is clearly taught in our Church: and are
resolved to erect Churches in each of the above named
Places; These Avocations can by me be very seldom complied with; my stated Mission being exceedingly extensive;
and one part of my Mission, being now in bad Circumstances on account of the Revd Sol^n Palmer's removal
from among them viz. Litchfield and Cornwall, who are
particularly fond of him, and engaged in detaining him;
as continual additions are making to those Churches and
in Litchfield a virulent Dissenting Preacher opposing the
Church's grouth; not only so, but I find it almost impossible to attend the Duties of my Mission as on Mr Palmer's
remove, no other missionary being in this large County,
and every Town has persons belonging to the Church, who
constantly sollicit my preaching among them;- if therfore
the honorable Society in their wisdom should think fit, to
detain Mr Palmer at Litchfield and Cornwall; we in these
parts shall always remember it with thankfulness; as it
appears the only probable means wherby the Churches in
both parts may be preserved from falling to decay; and
also greatly augmented as the present Time is exceeding
critical, and mankind seem eager in pursuit of Christian
knowledge;- Sharon one of my Parishes, being of long
standing, and are now a repairing their Church beg leave
with me to sollicit the honorable Society for a Bible and
Prayer Book for the Use of their Church, at the same
Time we all unite in gratfully acknowledging the favours
already receiv[ed] particularly those to Your's and the
honor[able] Societie's
            Most Obliged Obedient / & Humble Servant
                                    Thomas Davies

To The Secretary of The honarable Society for the
propagation of the Gospel in foreign Parts.

[Addressed:] To / The Reverend Dr Burton / Secretary
to the Society for Propagation / of the Gospel in /
Bartlet's Buildings / London
[Endorsed:] A Letter from the Revd Mr Davies, /
Itiner^t Miss^ry in Litchfield / County & Parts Adjacent....
Read / at the Committee Oct. 11. 1762

[1762, Apr. 13, Litchfield]
                    Litchfield, in Connecticut,
                        April the 13th Anno Dom' 1762.
Revd Sir;
    Mr Davies, by the kind providence of God, is lately
returned from England with H: Orders, & Instructions to
Succeed me in this Mission; and tells me that I am appointed at Amboy. I heartily thank ye Society that they
have granted my request of a Setled Mission, tho' it would
have been much more agreeable to me to have been continued where I am, had they consented to a Division of
this; as I imagine y^t my usefulness & influence here would
have been much greater than perhaps at any other place;
and especially as these People are extreamly desirous
of it, & much grieved at ye thoughts of my leaving them.
Sience I have lived in this Town, which is not quite two

Years, twelve Sober, regular and well disposed Famolies,
have upon principle, & not out of prejudice come over to
ye Church; and at present there Seems to be a most hopefull & promissing prospect of a Still greater encrease; &
which I am pretty certain will happen, if I might be continued; otherwise I fear not, tho' Mr Davies is well affected by these People, & has been received by them will all
Suitable Tokens & Demonstrations of respect, and will,
I hope by the blessing of God, be instrumental of doing
much good; he takes a pleasure in Preaching, has been
very laborious Sience he came into ye Missn, & his Services abundantly acceptable: But ye County is large, &
Churches at a great distance from each other, and So
many that there can be but Seldom Preaching at each of
them by one Man; and Preaching being wt the People desire, & wch if they cannot more frequently have, than one
Man can give, I very much fear yt ye present Current of
things will turn, and ye Chh in these parts (which is now in
a flourishing condition) pine and languish; I would therefore pray the Venerable Society to take these things into
consideration, and humbly, but yet earnestly, (begging yt
they would not be displeased) request yt this Missn might,
after all be divided, and I appointed to ye Towns of Canaan,
Norfolk, Goshen, Torrington, New Hartford, Harwinton;
But more particularly to the Towns of Litchfield and Cornwall, where ye main body of the Church People are; and
where alone I shall Officiate at present; who are willing to
Contribute even beyond their Abilities for my Support; but
wch after all, must must in order to make it Sufficient,
depend upon ye good will and Assistance of the Society,
which if their Fund will admit of, and they will be pleased
to afford, I doubt not will be a means greatly to advance
Religion, and encrease the Church here. If the Mission
should be divided, (as there is ye greatest apparent need
of it) there will be more than two thirds of ye Famolies of
Church People in Mr Davies's part--and who will be almost
as able of themselves to maintain him as those that will
belong to my Mission will me, with the additional help of
30£ Sterling Annually; which if a Division should be made,
and as this is a County Town, and a place of great resort,
where I must unavoidably have much Company and be at
great expence, I hope ye Society will consider; otherwise
my Salary will not be equal to my necessary expence. My
former Salary, with what ye People are willing to pay, wth
a Small interest of my own, and the labour of my Famoly
would Suffice, tho' wth all these helps I should Scarcely be
able, with the best oeconomy to live above want, & keep
wt I have; my Famoly being large; however I should most
thankfully receive it, and be entirely Satisfyed with it, as
I am willing to deny my Self, and in a good measure forego
my interest for the Sake of these People, and the pleasing
views I have of being peculiarly usefull among ym. But if
upon the whole the Honourable Body will not consent to a
Division; I must let them know that I am not able to move
my Famoly to Amboy, and furnish them, and a House, So
as to make a decent appearance wn we are there; it being
the Governours Seat, the Court, and a place where ye
People greatly affect Gentility and Politeness.--As there
is a Vacancy at Rey, I should be greatly pleased, with the
Societies consent, to go there.

If I may be continued here; As the Society allow Ten
Pounds worth of Books to Each Mission for a Library, and
five Pounds worth of pious small Tracts &c: Sience this
Allowance has never been made to this Mission, I would
pray the Venerable Board that it may now be made, as
my Library is Small & I am not able to enlarge it; And
particularly I would request the favour of a Folio Bible
& Common Prayer Book, for the use of ye Church here,
Who am, Revd Sir. Yours and the Societies.
                        Most Oblidged & Humble Servant,
                                    Solomon Palmer.

[Addressed:] To / The Reverend Dr Burton / Secretary
to the Society for Propagation / of the Gospel in Bartlet's
Buildings / London
[Endorsed:] Read at the Committee Oct. 11. 1762

[1762, Apr. 13, Litchfield]
                                    Connecticut, Litchfield,
                                    April the 13th A:D: 1762
Revd Sir,
    We ye Professors of ye Chh of England in Litchfield,
beg leave to Exhibit a short Narrative of things relating
to our Conformity to the Established Order, hoping thereby to obtain ye Charitable Assistance of the Venerable
Society in our present State, as we greatly stand in need
of it, (to whom we return our most Sincere, and hearty
thanks for what they have already done for us) and wthout
wch we much fear yt our flourishing Church will Essentially Suffer.

    About 18 years ago ye Revd Doctr Johnson came into
this Town and Preached, accompanied with two other
Gentlemen, who only bore their part with him in ye Service; Consequent upon wch, some were put upon consideration, & enquiery about ye Order of ye Chh of England;
So yt two years after, being desirous to be further informed with respect to ye Sd Constitution, a number of
our inhabitants for yt purpose, requested a visit of ye
Revd Mr Beech, wch he readily complyed with, & came
and Preached among us, gave us good Advice, and good
Instructions; soon after wch, upon principles of reason
and Conscience twelve of us declared for Conformity in a
publick Town meeting, upon which we left ye Dissenting
Congregation, and met together on Sundays in a private
House, assisted by one Mr Cole, then a Candidate for the
Ministrey--who we hired to read Prayers & Sermons--and
in this state we continued four Years, during wch Term
we encreased to ye Number of near 20 Famolies, which
was too many to meet in a private House, we yrfore began to build a Chh, wch wn we had done So much to it, as
to make it convenient to meet in, we invited Mr Mansfield
to come and Preach a Dedication Sermon, which he did,
and gave it ye name of St Michaell's Church: And being
encouraged, by ye above Gentlemen, and particularly, as
assisted by ye good Mr Gibb, who came and Preached 3 or
4 times a year for Several Years Successively, we kept
along under many discouragements; till Mr Palmer, by
our desire, and ye appointment of ye Society, became our
Missionary, together with ye Churches of Newmilford and
Sharon; Soon after wch the Town of Cornwall, where Mr
Palmer had been a Dissenting Teacher, and ye Parishes
of Roxbury & Judea in Woodbury, where he frequently
Preached Lectures, abounding with Churchmen, they petitioned for their proportion of Preaching on Sundays according to their Number, which we readily consented to,

out of a tender regard to ye good of ye C^hh; which was
an happy means of greatly encreasing it in those places,
for from a Small Number at Roxbury ye C^hh there is encreased to about 40 Famolies, and at Judea to 22. Whereupon Mr Palmers task becoming too great, and his burden
too heavy, especially as he laboured under peculiar Bodily
difficulties, wch rendred him incapable of performing the
duties of his Extensive, fatieguing & very laborious Mission; He moved his Famoly to this Town, being Strongly
Sollicited by us to do it, where he purchased a small living,
in hopes, upon Such representations as should be made, y^e
Honourable Board would have divided ye Mission, and continued him here, the prospect of which was very pleasing
to us, and upon which plan, if it had Succeeded, we should
have been in a most happy & flourishing State; but as things
now are (tho' we well esteem Mr Davies) in a pining, discouraging & disconsolate one, As we can have Preaching
on Sundays but about 10 times in a Year, being in Number
50 Famolies & 300^d Souls; We therefore earnestly desire
y^t Mr Palmer might be continued among us, whose labours
have been abundantly acceptable to us, and attended with
equal, if not greater Success, for ye time of his Incum-
bancy, than perhaps any other Missionary in ye Coloney:
The Church in these parts has greatly encreased under his
Administrations, and he has laid a good foundation for a
still greater encrease, which he will be able better to
build upon, than perhaps, any other Man, having by his
good life & Preaching obtained the esteem and good will of
all Parties, so y^t Numbers of whom do every Sunday attend ye Service of our Church, and Seem to be inclined to
come over to us, which if Mr Palmer should be discontinued, these prospects would fail, and those of us y^t are
already conformed, greatly discouraged: We therefore
humbly pray the Venerable Society to take these things into
consideration, and grant our request, of Mr Palmers continuance. We are not able of our Selves, Cornwall C^hh
joyning with us, to Support him, tho' willing to do what we
can, & even beyond our abilities towards it; he having a
Numerous Famoly, Six of w^m are Small Children, And
besides, he must, as this is a County Town--be at great
expence. And as we shall not be a third part of the Number of Famolies--provided ye Mission should be divided,
we beg for the proportionable Assistance & help of the Society, if they are able. Men Women and Children of our
Selves, together with a considerable Number of our Dissenting Brethren & Neighbours, who are all unwilling y^t
Mr Palmer should leave us, are Subscribing and Contributing for his Support, untill ye Matter shall be Setled,
which we hope will be in our favour, Who are

   Revd Sir, Yours & ye Societies, / most gratefull,
most obedient, / & Humble Servants,

      Jonathan Bishop J^r } Church Wardens in the
      Daniel Landon J^r   } name of the Church.

N:B: When we were but 12 Famolies, we purchased a
Glebe of Land, consisting of an hundred Acres, of which
we gave a Deed to ye Society, hoping thereby to encourage
them to help us. Said Land was then, and is now rough
and Uncultivated, but good. It lies at some distance f^m
the Town, so y^t our present Missionary can reap no benefit from it. It may be leased out for a Number of years
and made very profitable.

We have been oblidged to pay equally with the Dissenters here, for for ye reparing and sweeping their
Meeting House, till this Year, when they have excused
us. As also to bear our Proportion of ye Charge for the
Preaching of their present Minister, before his Ordination, and his Ordination Charges.

                              Jonathan Bishop J^r
                              Daniel Landon J^r

[Addressed:] To / The Reverend Dr Burton / Secretary
to the Society for Propagation / of the Gospel, in Bartlets
Buildings / London
[Endorsed:] Read at the Committee Oct. 11. 1762

[1762, June 28, New Milford]
                              New Milford in Connecticut
                              June ye 28th AD 1762.
Revd Sir.
   In April I informed the hon^l. Society, of my safe Arrival, and of the circumstances of my Mission; I now desire to acquaint you; that my Parishes are all happily United in Love and Peace, and express their most grateful
Acknowledgments to the Society, in appointing me over
them as their Minister; and for the seasonable present of
small Tracts; which were committed to my Charge; which
I have carefully distributed, among my People, where I
have reason to beleive they will be of much service: My
health being preserved, I have (besides Officiating every
Sunday in My Mission, and in the week Time preached
Lectures) been frequently at other Towns adjacent and
remote to preach and baptize, particularly in New York
Province, which lies contiguous to the northern part of my
Mission, where the People are either wretchedly ignorant, of Religion in general or else mad with the fervour
of Enthusiasm; altho' many expressed themselves well
pleased with my Instructions, and would rejoice at my
coming among them: In my Parishes of New Milford
Sharon & Roxbury, where I attend whilst Mr Palmer
hears from the Society; there is a fair prospect of the
Growth of the Church; which has moved the Dissenting
Teachers to some unprecedented Steps, to stop the progress;- I have not yet been Able to collect the whole Account, for a Notitia Parochialis, according to the Form
in an Ancient Abstract, Which I hope to do by Christmas;
And can only inform, that I have had four additional Communicants, and have baptized twenty four Infants, in the
last half Year: Agreable to my Instructions I have Drawn
my Bill for the last half Year, upon the Societys Treasurer, which I hope will be accepted, as herin and in all other
things I have behaved agreable to the Intent of the Society
In sending Me here:
             I am Revd Sir Your's & the hon^l. Society's
                       Hum^le Servt.
                                        Thomas Davies

[Addressed:]
To the Revd Doct^r Dan^ll Burton
Secretary of the Hon^l. Society for propagation
of the Gospel in Foreign Parts
In Bartlets Buildings   Holborn,
                              London.
[Endorsed:] Read at the Committee Oct. 11. 1762

[1762, July 6, Stamford]

Stanford Connecticut New England
6th July. 1762

Reverend Sir.

I greatefully Acknowledge the Receit of your Favour, of the 20th of January last and the pleasing Intimation of your being Apointed Secretary to the Venerable Society; Since the removal of the late worthy the Revd Doctr Bearcroft by Death: We that have the Honour to be Missionaries in these Remote parts think our Selves happy, in finding that important and Most Charitable Office Supplyed by a Gentleman of your Distinguished Merrit, well known Zeal & Attachment to our Holy Church and the Pious designs of the Venerable Board.----And with My Humble Duty to the Society present my Tribute of gratitude, for the Books they were so very good to send me, which came with Mr Davis and the Other Young Gentlemen lately Returnd in Holy Orders, also for the Bibles, Common prayer Books & Catechisms; much wanted which shall be Discretionarily Distributed.----And with Submission beg leave to Mention an Error I find in the Societys Abstract of 1761, in which they Mention under the Head of Advices from thier Missionarys, that by My Letter Dated Sepr 29. 1760, and Notitia Parochialis, the Number of My Communicants in Stamford & Greenwich Amounts to 155. Conscious of my Own Integety, I should not have Mentioned this Error, provided I was certain it was in my Self, as I think it must Manifestly have appeared an Involuntary Mistake, by the immediate preceeding, & Subsequent Advices of the State of my Mission. but the Enemies of Our Holy Church, and to thee most pious designs of the Venerable Society are Ready to improve the least Error, and to Aggravate it in the highest Maner, to Obstruct thier most Charitable Views, and to blast the Characters of thier Missionarys, that by so doing, they may prejudice thier Hearers against their Persons, and prevent thier Usefullness; and thier Peoples Conformity to the Church. the Credit and growth of which I fear they Observe with a Jealous & Evil Eye. this proseeds from no spirit of bitterness, for I have as yet had the pleasure to live upon very good Terms with ye Dissenters and thier Teachers in the two Towns, and parishes included in my Extensive Mission. but it Manifestly appears from thier Controversial writings Among us, & thier Attacks upon the morral and Religeous Carectors of Sundry of the Societys worthy Missionarys; the Fathers and first founders of the Church in this Goverment----that Account no way agrees with the Coppy of my Letter of Advice; which was Dated Octobr 1. 1760. and I find was taken from my advice of Sepr 29. 1759, and by that Coppy I suppose thro Mistake the Number of Heads of Families professing the Church in both Towns, which was 155. in the Abstract is said to be Communicants. the utmost number of Communicants hath never Exeeded I think 70, and by a surprising Number of Deaths in my parish within a few Years and the Removal of some others the Number of Actual Communicants hath Rather Diminished than Increased, for by my advice of ye 25. of March Last ye Number of Actual Communicants in both Towns was but 54----The furst Sunday after Easther last I preached in St Georges Church at North Castle to a large Congregation who behaved very decently. & on ye 7th of May last I attended a publick Fast apointed by the Goverment of New York on Acct of the War in the Uper District of Salem, where a great Number of

people gave a very Religeous & Devout Attendance. On the 29th of June last at the Request of the Church Wardens & Vestry of the Parish of Rye I preached a Lecture in their Church to a Considerable Congregation & Baptized 10 Children. & wish to see yt Parish Supplyed with a worthy Zealous Incumbent. permitt me to add, my best Regards to your Self, and prayers to Almighty God to succeed all the pious Designs of the Venerable Society and Subscribe Revd Sir

Your very much Obliged / Humble Servant / and Affectionate Brother / In Christ

Ebenezr Dibblee

The Reverend Doctr Burton &c
Secretary to the Venerable Society &c.

[Addressed:] To / The Reverend Doctor Burton / Secretary to the Venerable Society / for Propagation of the Gospel / In Foreign Parts. / Bartlet Buildings Holbourn / London
[Endorsed:] Read at a Committee Mar. 14 1763

[1762, Sept. 3, Simsbury]

Know all Men by these Presents, that we whose Names are underwritten are held, and firmly bound to pay, or cause to be paid unto Roger Viets A.B. of Symsbury in the County of Hartford and Colony of Connecticut, in New-England, the Annuity or yearly Sum of Thirty Pounds of good and lawful Money of Great Britain at and upon the Feast of the Nativity of Christ by even & equal yearly Payments; the first Payment to begin and be made, on the Feast Day of the Nativity of Christ which will be in the Year of our Lord one Thousand Seven Hundred and sixty three. And for which Payment well and truly to be made we bind ourselves severally and each of us by himself, our Heirs, Executors and Administrators; and of each of us firmly by these Presents; sealed with our Seals. Dated the third Day of September in the second Year of the Reign of the Lord George the third, by the Grace of God of Great-Britain, France & Ireland King, Defender of Faith &c And in the Year of our Lord 1762.

The Condition of this Obligation is such, that if the above named Roger Viets A.B. being a Candidate for holy Orders, shall assoon as conveniently may be transport or cause himself to be transported to Great Britain and there receive holy Orders according to the Usage and Ceremony of the Church of England, and assoon as conveniently may be, after his having thus received holy Orders shall return to Symsbury aforesaid and there officiate in the Office of a Minister, according to the Rites and Ceremonies of the Church of England; then, so long, and untill orderly or providentially dismissed or removed from said Charge, this Obligation to remain in full Force and Virtue; or else to be void and of none Effect.

Micah Miller	Thomas Rowlee
Thomas Griffem	Nathll Holcomb 3d
Daniel adlerman	Jeremiah Case
Joseph alderman	Nathll Griffin
Elnathan alderman	Joshua Holcomb
athinel moses	Henry Viets
John Terey	John Griffem
Reuben Slater	Wm Moor

Consider Holcomb Junr
Josiah Case 2nd
Jonathan Higley
Joseph alderman Jr
Samuel Enos
Amasa Case
Elijah addams
Hezekiah Holcomb
Consider Holcomb
John Viets
Zebulun moses
Jno Christan Müller Jr

Nathl Hillyer
Ranna Cossit
fransway Cossit
Abraham Dibol
Othnel Gisset
Joseph Addams
Simeon Holcomb
Jonas [James?] Hillyer
Josiah Holcomb
Jno Christian Müller
Seth Viets

[1762, Sept. 29, Stamford]

Stamford Connecticut In
New England Septemb^r 29. 1762

Reverend Sir.

I have this day presumed to draw a Sett of Bills for 25£ Sterling upon Edward Pearson Esqr, Treasurer to the Venerable Society, payable at thirty days sight, in favor of Mr Samuel Farmer, Merchant at New York. The number of Inhabitants in Stamford and Greenwich by a late computation is about 4767 Whites & 108 Blacks: the N^o of heads of Families in both Towns professing the Church 165. the N^o of Actual Communicants of the Church in both Towns about 55. I Baptized last half year 56 Infants white, 2 Blacks One Adult.----I continue my wonted care and diligence in doing the Duties of my Office & Mission; and by the blessing of God, have the pleasure to find my Church in an increaseing and flourishing State. there hath been an Accession of Sundry Reputable Heads of Families to the Church in Stamford since my last advice. My Chappel of Ease at Horsneck where I attend Divine Service the Second Sunday in Each Month is often much Crowded. And I hope my Extraordinary Duty at Greenwich where I have Attended an Evning Service & Preaching on every Sunday Since Eas[t]her Excepting Communion Days, after Evning Prayers & Preaching at Stamford, may be of Singular service, the people both Church & Dissenters having given a very good and devout attendance, and Express an Earnes[t] desire of my Continuing to Officiate among them as often as the Duty of my Extensive Mission will Admit. thro the Charitable Assistan[c]e of St George Talbot Esqr notwithstanding the many discouragements the Church of Stamford hath lain under my People have been induced to Exert themselves to finish thier Church, and I hope before Christmas, to see it decently compleated, with a front Galery, which we saw Necessary (agreeable to Mr Talbots advice) to Erect. the Church is 50 by 35 with a handsome Steeple.----And Blessed be God who is the great Author of Peace & lover of Concord my parishoners continue in peace & Unity among themselves and with thier Minister, Except one person, well known to be of an uneasy & Malevolent disposition; who lately in a surprizeing Maner out of personal pique, as is supposed at one of the most considerable of his brethren, hath ineffectually endeavoured to disturb thier peace and raise disturbances among us. since my last Advice, the 21st of July at the request of the People at white Plains in the Parish of Rye I preached a Lecture in thier Court House to a Numerous Congregation and Baptized 12 Children.----I hope soon to see that Vacant Parish supplied by the Revd Mr Punderson whom the good people of Rye have

unanimously invited to supply the Vacancy, and he hath Intimated to me his Inclination to Remove there if Leave may be obtained from the Venerable Board.----Assureing that no Endavours of mine, shall be wanting to be as Extensively Usefull as may be, I only beg leave to Add my Compliment of Duty to the Honorable Society with prayers to God to continue his Blessing upon their endeavours to propagate the Gospel of our dear Redeemer and finally Reward thier great Piety and Charity with an immortal Crown of Glory.--and with great Estem and Most Humble Regards to your Self Subscribe

Reverend Sir / Your Most Obed^t Servt / And Affec^te Brother / In Christ

Ebenez^r Dibblee

The Reverend Doctor Burton
Secretary to the Venerable Society &c:

[Addressed:] To / The Reverend Doctor Burton / Secretary to the Venerable Society / for Propagation of the Gospel in Foreign / Parts. Bartlet Buildings Holborn / London
[Endorsed:] Read at a Committee Mar. 14 1763

[1762, Dec. 28, New Milford]

Revd Sir

I beg leave to acquaint You, and the hono^l. Society, That notwithstanding my punctual Attendance, upon the Duties of my extensive Mission, which has thro' Divine Favour, been attended with Approbation and Success; I have Improved the Time I could spare in Riding thro' different Parts of the back Settlements in This, New York, & Boston Goverment's, and have officiated according to our Lyturgy; and Preached, to great Numbers, of almost all Denominations of People; In these migrations have Preached more than, one Sermon Every Week, since my Arrival. by the Advice of Revd Mr Caner of Boston, a few Families in Barrington, the westlemost Settlement in that Province; sent their earnest Desire, I would come and visit them; accordingly in Sepr last, I went, (it is 60 Miles) and Preached, to a large Concourse of People, and bap^d some Children; I Instructed them into the Meaning, Use, and Propriety, of the common Prayer Book; They informed Me, That many of them, had long been dissatisfied, with their Dissenting Instructions, being constantly taught, "ridgid Calvinism, and that Sin was of Infinite advantage, and has advanced happiness greatly in the World:- "that If the Church was introduced there they must Pay Tythes:- "That the Church was just like the Papists,- "that the Service Book was taken from the Mass book. &c &c: I chose a Clerk, a very regular & Pious Man, long acquainted in the Church, to read Prayers with them as they could not in conscience go to Meeting; one of the most steady among them being Imprisoned last Summer, for non attendance: and they all should if they did not meet among themselves: there are near 40 sober Families, Conformists in this Town, People of worth and good Fame;- Whilst I was in England Dr Bearcroft informed Me that New-Fairfield a Town contiguous to New Milford, was Included in My Mission; but in The Order I received, no mention was made therof; that Difficiency I could wish the hon^l. Society would supply, as the Dissenters have taken, and Sold, the Church People's Effects,

this Winter, to Pay the Dissenting Minister, and will ever
do the same, they tell me; In the last half Year I have bap:d
2 Adults, and, Fourty Children; and In all Respects endeavoured to fulfill the Intent, of my Ministry; My Parisheners
beg me to Express the deepest sense of Love & Gratitude,
for them; to their Rev:d Fathers, and the Rest of the hon:l
Society for the kindness shewn them, and Pray God to
abundantly reward their Charity: I have according to Instruction drawn my last half Year's Bill, upon the Society;
and am Rev:d Sir

    Yours and the honorable Society's / most Obliged
Obedient / & humbe Servant

                      Thomas Davies.

New-Milford
Dec:r 28. AD. 1762.

[Endorsed:] Read at a Committee May. 16. 1763

[1763, Feb. 20, New London]
Rev:d & Dear Sir

    My Ignorance of y:r very worthy Predecessor, now ex-
ulting, I trust, in Hallelujahs to his God, occasion'd my
last Letter to be directed to y:e Treasurer. Permit me to
say, my Loss in his Death was y:e Loss of a Counsellor--a
Friend--a Father. May y:e Lord shew Mercy to his House,
& prepare them for his Glory!

    My Parishoners increase, & wou'd be much more nu-
merous, but are not yet able to enlarge y:e Church, w:ch
is, I presume, in greater Esteem here, than in any Part
of New-England, by all Denominations. This is evident
not only by their constant Attendance on my Lectures, of
w:ch they are very fond, but by coming often upon Sundays,
& liberally rewarding y:e Preacher.

    As I visit y:e Dissenters in Sickness & in Health, it
has gain'd their Love to my Person, & founded a most perfect Harmony of Unity & Love.

    Since my last my Communicants have encreas'd, who,
w:th those added since I came, are rubrical in y:e Church,
& have Prayers at Home; w:ch religious Performance I always enjoin them, especially, to observe. I have married
two Couple, baptiz'd four Children, & buried three Persons.

    My Contributions these four last Years have come to
near fifteen Pounds Ster:g, w:ch they never before amounted
to: on w:ch w:th my Salary I barely subsist. I have only a
small Garden, tho' they promis'd in a fictitious Deed to
y:e Society, y:t I shou'd have 30 Acres of good Land, as appears by Doctor Bearcroft's Letter to me, before I left old
England where every Necessary of Life was far cheaper
than here, y:e dearest Part of New England. But I can truly
say, y:e Salvation of Souls is my only Concern, & to feed
my Flock w:th y:e sincere Milk of y:e Word, as exhibited in
our truly Apostolic Church, is & shall be my Study & Delight. My Ordination Vows recur often to my Mind, & how
to be preserv'd from being cast away causes many Tremors in my Soul, & makes me constantly petition for His
Grace, w:ch is sufficient for me. "Si unus quisque pro se
die Judicii respondebit, quid de Sacerdotibus fiet, quibus
pro omnius Animabus respondendum est? As S:t Austin
truly says. I earnestly desire one Petition, in my behalf,
may be inserted among your own at y:e Throne of Grace.
Evangelic Charity for y:e Successor of my good & sincere,

deceased, Friend, sweetly engages my Compliance to y:e
same divine Exercise.

    Pray, S:r, present my Christian Love & Complements
to my Venerable Patrons; to answer whose pious Designs,
& render my self worthy y:r Regard, shall be my conscientious Endeavors.

    That y:e Spirit of GOD may direct, & his Power enable
you to fulfil your great & important Trust, is, & shall be
y:e frequent Prayer of,

    Rev:d & Worthy S:r / Y:r very hum:le Serv:t & / Aff:te
Brother in / Christ

                      Matt Graves

New-London Feb:y 20:th 1763.

PS. I have drawn, w:th my Brother for last Quarter's ⎞
Salary, as we shall for next, in Favor of M:r Lord,   ⎬
Merc:t in Norwich.   ⎠

To the Rev:d Doctor Dan:l Burton
Secretary to y:e Society &c

[1763, Feb. 20, New London. Same with variations]
S:r

    My Ignorance of your worthy Predecessor's Dea[th,]
now exulting, I trust, in Hallelujahs to his GOD, occasion'd my last Letter to be directed to y:e Treasurer.
Permit me to say, my Loss in y:e Death of Doctor Bearcroft, y:e sincere Patron of Europeans, was y:e Loss of
a Counsellor--a Father & Friend. May y:e Lord shew
Mercy to his House here & hereafter!

    My Parishoners increase, & wou'd be much more
numerous, but are not yet able to enlarge y:e Church, w:ch
is, I presume in greater Esteem here than in any other
place of New-England, by all Denominations. This appears, not only by their constant Attendance on my Lectures, whereof they are very fond, but by coming often on
Sunday, & liberally rewarding y:e Preacher. As I visit y:e
Dissenters in Sickness & Health, it has gain'd their Esteem to my Person, & founded a most perfect Harmony of
Unity & Love.

    Since my last my Communicants are increas'd, who
with those, added since are rubrical in y:e Church, & have
Prayers at home--I have marri[ed] four Couple--baptiz'd
six & buried three Persons. My Contributions last Year
came to near £15 Ster:g, w:ch they never were before; w:ch
with my Salary I barely subsist on. I have only a small
Garden, tho' y:e People promis'd in a fictitious Deed to
y:e Society, y:t I shou'd have 30 Acres of good Land, as
ascertain'd by y. Secretary's Letter to me, before I
left West-Chester, where all Necessaries of Life were
far cheaper than here, y:e dearest Part of New-England.
But I can truly say, y:e gaining of Souls is my only Concern, & feeding my Flock with the sincere Mik of y:e
Word, is & shall be my Study & Delight. My Ordination
Vows recur often to my Mind, & how to be preserv'd
from being Cast away causes many Tremors in my Soul,
& makes me constantly petition for that Grace, which is
sufficient for me. "Si unus quisq´ pro se vix [exi]sterit
in Die Judicii Rationem reddere--quid de Sacerdotibus
futurum est quibus sunt omnium Animae requirendae?
As S. Austin says. I earnestly beg one Petition may, in
my behalf, be inserted among y:r own at [y:e] Throne of

Grace. Evangelic Charity for yᵉ Successor of my good, sincere, deceased Friend will sweetly engage my Compliance to yᵉ same divine Exercise.

Pray present my Christian Love & Duty to my Venerable Patrons; to answer whose pious Designs, & render my self worthy your Regard shall be my conscientious Endeavors.

That yᵉ Holy Spirit of GOD may direct, & his Power enable tyou to fulfil your great & important Trust, is & shall be yᵉ frequent Prayer of

Revᵈ Sir / Yᵗ very hum.ˡᵉ Servᵗ & / Affectionate Brother in / Christ

                                        Matt Graves

New-London Feb. 20ᵗʰ 1763

P.S I have drawn for my last Salary, as I shall for my next, in Favour of Mʳ Lord [Mercᵗ] in Norwich

To Doctor Burton Secratary to yᵉ Religious Society &c
Lond[on]

[1763, Mar. 25, Stamford]
                        Stamford Connecticut In
                        New England March 25ᵗʰ, 1763
Reverend Sir

I beg leave to give advice to the Venerable Society that I have this day drawn a set of Bills, for Twenty five Pounds Sterling, upon Edward Pearson Esqʳ their Treasurer, payable at thirty dayes sight, in favʳ of Mʳ Samuel Farmer Merchant at New York. ---- The happy harmony that subsists between me & my Parishoners in general, their due attendance upon the Publick Offices of Religion, in all Parts of my Extensive Mission, Encourages me to hope, that I Am very Serviceable in promoteing their best Interest. By the blessing of God on my labours, my Church is in an Increaseing & flourish State. -- The Number of Inhabitants in Stamford & Greenwich, by a late Computation, were about 4767 White; and 108 Black. about 166 Heads of Families in both Towns make a profession of our Holy Church, and there are 56 Actual Communicants. I Baptized last Half Year 24 Infants. Thro' yᵉ Charitable Assistance of Sᵗ George Talbot Esqʳ I have the pleasure to see my Church at Stamford decently finished, with a front Gallery Erected. And hope to see my People make Answerable improvements in Virtue, & yᵉ practice of true Religion, to the advantages they enjoy, thro' the Charity of the Venerable Board, & other pious Benefactors. As my Sight begins to fail, I would Again Ask the favʳ of a Folio Bible & Common Prayer Book, for Use in my Chapel of Ease at Horsneck, where I constantly officiate yᵉ 2ᵈ Sundy in each Month to an agreable Congregation. The late Revᵈ Doctor Bearcroft once intimated that the Honˡˡ Society had granted me the favʳ, but not mentioning by what ship they were sent, I have ben apprehensive, that thro' mistake, they probably were never Sent. ---- Purposeing by the Grace of God, to persevere in my Endeavours to be as Extensively Usefull as I can, I Only Add my Humble Duty to the Venerable Board, and Earnest Prayers to Almighty God, to Bless, succeed, & Reward All their Pious and Most Charitable Endeavours to Propagate the Gospel of our dear Redeamer. And Am Reverend Sir,

with Most Sincere Esteem & Humble Respect to Your Self,

Your Most Obedient / Humble Servᵗ & Affecᵗ Brʳ
                                        Ebenezʳ Dibblee

The Reverend Doctor Burton
Secretary to the Venerable Society &c-

[Addressed:] To / The Reverend Doctor Burton / Secretary to the Venerable Society / for Propagation of the Gospel / In Foreign Parts. Bartlet Buildings / Holborn London
[Endorsed:] Read at a Committee July 11. 1763

[1763, Mar. 30, New Haven]
                        New Haven March. 30ᵗʰ 1763.
Reverend Sir

The Reverend M. Punderson, having from some mutual Uneasiness here, entertained an Intention of removing from hence, by the Society's Leave; He was advised by the Clergy to visit the People of Rye, To whom, He has happily been so acceptable, That, They have very unanimously, chosen Him for their Minister, & addressed The Honourable Society to appoint Him over Them; Since which, They have received Notice of the Appointment of The Revᵈ Mʳ Palmer, for Rye, which has proved the Occasion, of much Uneasiness among Them, as They were so entirely united in Mʳ Punderson -- By the Advice of The Revᵈ Dʳ Johnson, We have, under these Circumstances, desired a Visit, from Mʳ Palmer, who hath accordingly been with us, & officiated for three Sundays, His Preaching & Conversation have been to our entire Satisfaction, & His good & amiable Character, We have known, many Years; Wherefore, gratefully acknowledging, The Society's great Favour & Bounty towards us hitherto, We beg Leave, to acquaint That venerable Body, That, If It shall seem good to Them, to appoint Mʳ Palmer to succeed Mʳ Punderson here, It will be entirely agreable to Us, & what, with Submission, We most humbly & earnestly request; To this Proposal Mʳ Palmer has likewise consented, & Four of our principal Members, have given Him a Bond, to pay Him, Twenty Pounds Sterling per Annum & with the adjoining Village of West-Haven, who We trust will add Ten pounds more, We engage to make up Thirty pounds Sterling per Annum- We have also purchased a Lot for a Glebe, with a good new House & Barn, which We doubt not will be agreable to our Minister- Humbly hoping We may succeed in this Application, & with our fervent Prayers for our great & good Benefactors, We are

Revᵈ Sir / The Society's, / And / Your, most obliged & obedient Servᵗˢ

                    Timᵒ Bonticou ⎫ Church
                    Isaac Doolittle ⎬ Wardens

[Addressed:]
                    To
The Reverend Dʳ Burton
Secretary To The Society for The Propagation
of The Gospel, In Forreign Parts:
        Bartlett's Buildings, Holborne
                    London

[1763, May 4, New Haven]

Connecticut, New:Haven, May 4ᵗʰ A:D: 1763

Revᵈ Sir;

Considering the flourishing State of the Church at Litchfield, the harmony & good agreement that has Sub-sisted between me and that People, their great desire of my continuance among them, and grief at the thoughts of my leaving them; it would have been highly pleasing to me to have had my appointment there; but inasmuch as the So-cieties circumstances would not admit of it, I am entirely Satisfyed; And return them my most Sincere and hearty thanks for the various expressions of their kindness, and generosity to me; and particularly, for the liberty they have granted me of going to Rey [i.e., Rye, N.Y.], which I would gladly accept of; were there no Embarrasments in the way: The Revᵈ Mʳ Punderson has at times been there Since September last, and by his good behaviour, and frequent Preaching among them, has obtained their high-est esteem; and Such is their fondness for him, that they will be pleased with no other Man; So that it is the Revᵈ Dʳ Johnson's advice, who very well knows their circum-stances, that (with the Societies consent) he Should pro-ceed there, and I Succeed him in his Mission here; where I have officiated Some times, to their general acceptance; who have accordingly given me a call to be their Minister; and for my encouragment, purchased a Glebe House, and Glebe for my Use; and engaged to give me an Annuity of £30. Sterling, which, together with the Societies Salary of £50. will be an handsome Support even in this Populous Town; I would therefore, with due Submission to the So-ciety, humbly request that my appointment may be here, where I hope, by the blessing of God upon my endeavours, I may be instrumental of promoting the interest of true Religion, and peace of the Church, which shall always be the chief Object of my attention; Who am,

Revᵈ Sir, yours & the Societies,

most oblidged & humble Servant,

Solomon Palmer.

To the Revᵈ Doctor Burton.

[1763, June 8, Litchfield]

Connecticut, Litchfield, June the 8ᵗʰ A:D: 1763.

Revᵈ Sir,

Had I been able to have endured the Fatigues of an Itinerant Mission, I should contentedly have remained in that to which I was first appointed; a harmony & good agreement constantly Subsisting between me & the People there.----I return my thankfull acknowledgment, to the Venerable Society for their goodness to me, in consider-ing my Bodily infirmity, and removing me to yᵉ Setled Mission at Amboy; tho' for Special reasons, with their consent, I chose not to go there.----And I likewise re-turn the Society my most hearty & unfeigned thanks for their Appointment of me at Rye, where I would gladly have gone, had I not been intercepted by the Revᵈ Mʳ Punderson's being there before that designation was made known or expected: However I Should have made them a visit, and offered my Self to be chosen by them, had they not taken a Seasonable precaution to prevent it, by writing, and Sending me a Letter of the following con-tents, which I received in less than a Week after yours of the 6ᵗʰ of Novʳ last came to hand, which gave me the first notice of my appointment to that Mission.

Revᵈ Sir, We the Justices, Church Wardens and Vestry of the Parish of Rye, having greatly at heart the preser-vation of an happy Union that Subsists in our Church, pre-sume Sir yᵗ you, a Preacher of the Gospel of Peace, will highly commend this good disposition, and readily concur with us in oppinion, of the absolute necessity of guarding against every event yᵗ threatens to impede its continuance. Ever Since the decease of the Revᵈ Mʳ Wetmore, our late worthy Pastor, an unhappy Spirit of discord about a Suc-cessor to yᵗ Office, very unfortunately prevailed among us till the coming here of the Revᵈ Mʳ Punderson in Septem-ber last, when by his unwearied endeavours & Successfull Preaching in the Several parts of this Parish, it pleased God to reunite yᵉ minds of the People in Mʳ Punderson, and we did then with one general voice give Mʳ Punderson an invitation to be our Pastor, & he to our great Satisfac-tion, favoured us with his acceptance of it, and in conse-quence whereof, a Petition was immediately drawn, and lodged in the hands of the Honᵇˡᵉ Daniel Horsmander Esqʳ in New York, to be presented, at a proper time, by him, and the Revᵈ Doctʳ Berclay, to his Exellency our Gover-nour, to Induct the Revᵈ Mʳ Punderson into our Church; And on the 5ᵗʰ of October last, the Vestrey, attended by a Number of Parishioners, wrote a Letter to yᵉ Honourable Society, acquainting them with these proceedings, and requested their consent to Mʳ Punderson's Establishment among us, and which was transmitted to yᵉ Revᵈ Doctʳ Johnson in New York....

All which I hope the venerable Society will accept as a sufficient apology...for my going to New Haven.... Yet after all (tho' New: Haven is a pleasant Scituation & would be quite agreeable to me) I should, upon my own account, be content to go to Rye, and, if all things con-sidered, the Society Shall think it best to order me there, I Shall be well Suited. But then I should be concerned for the Church at New Haven, which in yᵉ latter part of Mʳ Pundersons time there, was really in a pining, and lan-guishing State; and should he return to them again (tho' he obtains a good Character, and is truly a valuable Man) I fear he would have the Mortification of Seeing it expire in his hands: This Sir, I hint purely wᵗʰ regard to the good People at N: Haven, who we think are not much to blame. I will particularly give you the Revᵈ Doctʳ Johnson's oppinion of this matter, as I have it in a Letter--Dated, February, 7ᵗʰ 1763. in yᵉ following words----"I Sent you a Message by Mʳ Punderson, which I concluded you had received, yᵗ the Society could not make Litchfield a Mis-sion, and have appointed you to Rye, this I am Sorry for, as He, I doubt can do no more good at New Haven, and is very acceptable, & actually chosen at Rye"----

During my residence in my former Mission, my Task was enough for two Men to perform, It being 20 Miles from New-Milford (where I resided five Years) to Litch-field, to Sharon 30, to Cornwall 25, and to Roxbury and Judea 8. At all which places, I officiated at their proper turns on Sundays, besides frequently Preaching occasion-ally on other Days, at yᵉ constant importunity, of the Peo-ple, not only in, but out of the County, and Government, 30, 40, 50, & 60 Miles distant, both in the Provin[c]e of New York, and Boston----Mʳ Davies has now taken the Same Task upon him, which (tho' a Young Man of a robust

constitution) he complains of as almost an insupportable
burden; Yet ye importunity of the People, being such, as
he cannot refuse, who has indeed been very faithfull, and
Scarcely failed Preaching, once every Week besides Sundays, ever Since he came into ye Mission. For the performance of which duty, & other Services, I was oblidged
to keep 2. Horses at the Yearly expence, at lest of £10.
And the last Year tho' I mostly officiated at Litchfield and
Cornwall; I twice visited the Vacant Church at Simsbury
35 miles--as I had usually done before. Twice I went to
Great Barrington a County Town in Boston Government
35 m. to ye Northward; where I spent some time, and
Preached on Sundays, & Lectures, to crouded Auditories,
and administred the two Sacraments of Baptism and the
Lords Supper. I took a great deal of pains with that People, to instruct them in the Principles, Doctrines & Government of the Church of England, and with good Success;
for at both Visits 36 Persons, most of them heads of Famolies, declared for Conformity.--who, I have good reason
to think will be Stedfast in their Profession, and adorn the
Same by a Suitable Conduct, and where there is the fairest
prospect of a Still plentifull encrease: And on my return
the last time, I Preached, (as desired by many) at Sheffield, a Town in the Same Government, to a large Congregation of Devout People, and Baptized a Woman of good
understanding, & a Sober life, and 12 Children. Once I
visited the C^hh at Noble Town, formed by my Self, eight
Years ago, consisting of 20 Famolies, where no other
Minister of the Church of England had Preached, before
Mr Davies came into these parts; who has visited them
once: this is in the Province of New York. And I have at
the repeated, and very urgent request, of Some People
at a Town called Hartland in this Government 35 miles,
been there twice, where no other Church Minister had
been before, and the first time Baptized one Adult, the
principal Man of the Town (who was born of Baptist Parents, & brought up in that way) of good Principles, and
Sufficient knowledge in Religion, and 5 Infants, when Ten
Persons, all of them heads of Famolies, declared for the
Church, and three the next, who had never before I visited
them, been at all instructed in ye Discipline and Doctrines
of it: & I purpose this Week to make them my last visit.
All which duty I have done, and the latter part of my time
under very grevous Nephritick Disorders, which are so
obstinate that no Medicines can remove them; but yet
Scarcely ever failed to do my duty in every part of my
Mission, besides almost innumerable other journeys.
This I did as long as I was able, that I might further the
Charitable, Generous and most noble design of ye Society,
and hope, by the blessing of God upon my weak endeavours,
my end has in a good measure been answered, for whilst I
was in that Mission, the C^hh there encreased more than
twofold, mostly with Such Persons whose Conversation is
an ornament to their Profession--, the number of Communicants more than proportionably encreased, and I
Baptized 435 Children, and 5 Adults. And as I shall be
able, I purpose, by Divine Aid, to use the Same diligence,
faithfulness and industrey wheresoever the Society Shall
Send me, and do all that I can to advance consistent Notions of God,--and promote real Religion, free f^m Entheu-
siasm and Fanatecism, which Seems of late to have taken a
new turn in these parts. And Sir, as I have been unsetled,
in a g^rt measure, for about two Years, my Perquisites

(being always Small) have very much failed me, by reason of which (having had a large and expensive Famoly,
most of them Small Children, to maintain) I am brought
into Such a Condition that I can Scarcely Assert the honour of my Character, with ye best Oeconomy I can use;
so that I should esteem it a great favour to hear from the
Society as Soon as may be, and know where I am Sent,
that I may have opportunity of moving my Famoly before
Winter, for every Source for a Support now fails me.
And lest the Society Should think me to blame, and y^t I
have brought this trouble upon my Self, in not going to
Amboy,----I must here Say, that I should have gone
there, had I not been discouraged by the Revd Dr Johnson, who in a Letter to me Soon after he heard of my
appointment to that Mission, Wrote me thus,----
"Dear Sir, I give you joy, if it be agreeable to you, upon
your being appointed at Amboy, but I imagine Rye, as I
hoped, would have Suited you better"----"I doubt they will
be a little Shagrine, as I am told they have applyed for
M^r M'Kean Minister of Brunswick"----And in another,
thus,----"You will be as unwelcome to Amboy, as they
to you, because they have Sent home by Doct^r Smith,
who is a Member, to Sollicit for M^r M'Kean"----"I will
desire you may be appointed to Rye"----"I have already
Suggested to ye Arch Bishop ye unsuitableness of your
Appointment at Amboy, & ye greater fitness of Rye for
you, near a Month ago."----Which I have thought needfull to let the Society know, in order to vindicate my
Conduct before them, and by no means to reflect the
lest blame upon the good Doct^r, who, I believe did it out
of Friendship and kindness to me, and I am perswaded,
it is best y^t I was governed by his Advice, though in
consequence thereof, I am at present under some difficulties, which by favour of the Society, I hope Soon to
be extricated from.

 How the Doct^r can reconcile his Conduct in recommending me, and a few Months after, Mr Punderson to
ye Same Mission, i.e. to Rye, I cannot tell: I believe
this Mistake came thro' forgetfulness, or, presumption
of my being continued at Litchfield, or from the goodness
of his Natural disposition, which is to please & Oblidge
every Body: But whatsoever it proceeded from, it has
been greatly to my damage, and the cause of an unhappy
jumble, wch I hope the Society will overlook, and for the
future admit of no exchange of Missionaries, unless there
be the greatest apparent Necessity for it; which indeed
they cannot very well know, at the distance of more than
3000^d Miles, tho' we always endeavour to make the best
representation of things that we can.

 As ye Society allow Ten Pounds worth of Books to
each Mission for a Library,--I hope, if they shall appoint
me to N: Haven, that such an allowance may be made to
that Mission; for tho' I have been in their Service more
than Nine Years,--have never been indulged that priviledge, which then I shall Stand in more need of than before, as there is ye Court the College, and many Gentlemen of Polite Taste and Learning, who, as well as y^e
lower Rank, I would gladly please. And I would ask
leave, particularly, to request a folio Prayer Book for
the use of that Church, begging the Societies forgivness
of all past failings and defects, and promising for the
time to come faithfully and punctually to observe all
their Instructions,

Who am, Rev:d Sir; / Yours, and their most Oblidged, / most Obedient, & Humble Servant,

Solomon Palmer.

June the 16:th A:D: 1763

P:S: Last Week I visited my little Flock at Hartland, Preached there on Sunday and Baptized two Children: And on Monday, Rode to Simsbury--Preached to a full Congregation, and Baptized 4 Children, which probably is y:e last time &c--   Solomon Palmer.

[1763, June 25, New Milford]

New Milford in Connecticut June 25:th 1763

Rev:d Sir,

Your Letter of Nov:r 6:th 1762, came safe to hand last Feb: which has so far, silenced the Uneasiness of People, that they determine to wait, with patience, until their Circumstances, may be sufficient, or the hono:l Society will be pleased to assist, to Support another Missionary among them; I may Assure The hono:l Society, I have nothing more at heart, than to promote the wellfare of the Church; and Diligence is exerted accordingly; but as I cannot be more than Once, in four, and somtimes five, and six Sundays, at each Church, there is very little probability, of the Churches growth; when People are Zealous of steadily attending public Worship somwhere: I have visited the People in the Frontiers of New York, & Boston, Goverments, at Barrington I preached on Sunday, to a very numerous Congregation, who expressed their satisfaction, Urged me to Visit them as often [as] I could, and beg'd Me to reccommend them to the hono:l Society, for some Common Prayer Books and small Tracts; They Read Prayers and Printed Sermons, (which I sent them) every Sunday, but The Dissenters, threaten if they will not come to Meeting to send them to Jail; because say the Dissenters, they are not under any Missionary;--I have baptized in the last half Year thirty four Children; and two Adults, after proper Examination and Instruction; who had been educated Quakers; and the divine Goodness, has so far favoured Me, that neither Storms, nor Distance of Place, nor Ill Health, have hindered my officiating at the different Places, in the stated Periods; and have great Reason to beleive that my diligence is not in vain-- I have drawn upon The hono:l Society, for my last half Years Salery; have not heard of the Books mentioned in Your's-- I am Rev:d Sir,

The hono:l Society's / and Your most Obedient Faithful Servant

Thomas Davies

[Addressed:] To / The Reverend Doct:r Daniel Burton / Secretary to the hono:l Society for propagation / of the Gospel in foreign Parts, / Bartlets Buildings Holborn / London.
[Endorsed:] A letter from the...Itin:t / Miss:ry in Litchfield County / & Parts Adjecent.... / Read at a Committee Dec. 12, 1763

[1763, July 20, New London]

Rev:d S:r

I herewith send you a Copy of my last, lest, having heard nothing from my Venerable Patrons, it has miscarry'd. The Alterations in my parochial Charge, since I wrote, are few. The Communicants are twenty seven. Perhaps they might have been numerous; but I'm very cautious of encouraging Persons to partake of y:t most solemn Ordinance, without previously acquainting me, & due Preparation-- Four Children have been baptiz'd-- We have no Papists; & to come at y:e Knowledge of y:e Number of Dissenters here (y:e only Colony, where they are solely encourag'd, & y:e Professors of our Church solely prohibited all Offices) wou'd be a very arduous Undertaking. Notwithstanding this unchristian Discouragement y:e Churh of England flourishes, & will triumph in Opposition to all their Devices.

Had we more Pews in our Church, I know professing Hearers, w:ch are above 120, wou'd soon encrease; but they are poor, & not able to enlarge y:e Churh. I wish I cou'd say y:e Infidels were as few, as y:e Heathens, w:ch in these parts are growing fond of Religion, & outdo many Christians in Morality.

In y:e Absence of a neighbouring, dissenting Teacher I was ask'd to do Duty in his Meeting-house; I said, provided I might officiate according to y:e Liturgy of y:e Church of England, I woud: to w:ch all his Hearers consented, & I, by Permission given in a former Letter from y:e Society, perform'd to y:e Satisfaction of all. As this was in one of y:e New-light Societies, our glorious & uniform Service has gain'd Ground, & their Bigotry & Prejudices sensibly decay.

My Duties last severe Winter were greatly increas'd; for besides preaching each Lord's Day in my Churh, I preach'd a third time at a private House about 4 Miles off, where a Member of my Charge was confin'd to his Bed. 'Tis true y:e traveling was difficult; but y:e spiritual Exercise was most agreeable, being attended upon with a crouded Audience of various Denominations, whose Presence & Behaviour demonstrated their Satisfaction. But what crown'd all, was, my Labour was not in vain: after a tedious Sickness he died full of Faith--full of Hope, & enter'd into y:e Joy of his Lord.

I occasionally do Duty about 20 Miles hence, preaching--baptizing--churching &c & design in a few days to sail to an Island 15 Leagues off, where I sometimes officiate, & among which People I find a very sincere Reception. Besides these I officiate at other places; resolving thro' divine Aid to answer y:e Christian Design of my religious Patrons, during y:e short Remainder of my Days.

Be pleas'd to present my Duty & Love to y:e Venerable Body, & tell them, I gratefully receiv'd M:r Pilkington's laborious Harmony--Doctor Berriman's pious & evangelical Sermons, wherein y:e true Doctrines of y:e Church of England are so learnedly defended & beautifully display'd. Wou'd to GOD they were more sincerely believ'd, & openly avow'd! The Opposition of Preachers is y:e Bane of Religion, & Errors in Fundamentals y:e Delight of Satan. The pious Doctor's Sermons, so quickly succeeding those divine Discourses of Bishop Sherlock, have done great Honour to our Church, & irrefragably asserted y:e Essentials of our most holy Faith. I also most gratefully acknowledge y:e Receipt of some Common Prayer Books & Dr Wall's infant Baptism. If you have time a few Lines wou'd be very acceptable to

Rev:d S:r / Y:r most Obedient Serv:t & / Affectionate Bro:r in Christ

New-London July 20:th 1763   Matt Graves

[1763, Sept. 29, Stamford]

Stamford Connecticut In
New England Septr 29, 1763

Reverend Sir.

Being still dependant upon the Venerable Board for their Charitable Assistance, I have this day drawn a set of Bills for Twenty five Pounds Sterling, upon their Treasurer Edward Pearson Esqr, payable at thirty days sight, in fav^r of Mr Thomas Ellison Merchant at New York.

I Continue to do the duties of my Extensive Mission, in all the Parts thereof in my wonted manner, and in the usual course I've so often mentioned. And I've good Reason to believe that neither ye Societies Charity is here misapplied, nor my labours, by the blessing of God, in vain, whatever our Restless and implacable Enemies suggest; but that ye Morral and Religious state of the People is much bettered thereby. Tis true that a spirit of Gall & bitterness is remarkable shed abroad among our dissenting Brethren, of late; and most Surrilous and abusive measures taken, by some Crafty and Designing writers, to prejudice the minds of their people against our Holy Church, Ridiculeing its Divine offices, and Causelessly, I Charitable trust, Insulting Her Ministers; nor neglecting even to Arraign the Conduct of ye Venerable Board themselves. But from whence it arises, I know not, unless it proceeds from Envy & Jealousy and ye Increaseing and flourishing State of our Churches; which tis true from Small beginings, are become Considerable. But it hath ben principally oweing, to their own Religious Confusions, and disagreements among themselves, In Doctrine, Discipline and Worship, w^h hath removed the prejudices their people hath ben Educated in, & disposed the minds of many to take sanctuary in our Holy Church As ye only Centre of Christian unity, in ye Nation, and where they may be Instructed and Edified in true genuine Christianity. My Parishoners in all Parts of my Mission continue to behave themselves peaceably & Religiously, are Steadfast in their Religious profession. Except one, who hath lately forsaken the Church, not on a Religious account, but out of personal pique & Resentment, and haveing behaved so Ill as to be Judged unworthy of the Holy Communion, until he declared himself to have Repented of his abusive unchristian Treatment of me, with a promise to behave in a more Christian manner for the future. As I was personally Concerned in his Case, the Reve^d, Mr Leamings advice and Interposition was desired; who sincerely laboured to convince him of his Error, to no Effect:

The Number of Heads of Families professing the Church in the two Towns of Stamford and Greenwich are 167; Actual Communicants 57. I Baptized the last half Year 56 Infants.--

May the smiles of Heaven, and the grace of God, continue to attend & succeed all the Pious and Most Charitable designs of ye Venerable Board; To whom I beg leave to present my Humble Duty; and with Sincere Regards and Respect, to your Self Subscribe

Reverend Sir Your Most Obedient
Humble Servt
And Affect^t B^r In Christ
Ebez^r Dibblee,

The Reverend Doctor Burton
Secretary to the Venerable Society &c.

[1763, Dec. 1, New Haven]

Connecticut, New:Haven December 1st A:D: 1763.
Revd Sir,

After the disadvantage of being for Several Years past in an uncertain Situation, and without a Sufficient Support; I have lately, by a line from the Revd Doctor Johnson, had the agreeable News of my Establishment here by the Soceity; for which instance of their favour, I take this opportunity to return them my unfeigned thanks, and let them know, that I hope, by the help of God, to improve it to greater diligence in their Service, and faithfulness in the discharge of all Ministerial duties.

Tho' the Revd Mr Punderson has been So unhappy as not to make himself agreeable to this People, & the uneasiness between them----So great as to occasion his removal from hence; I do not look upon them to be contentious, or difficult to please: From my first coming among them, they have Shewn me all the kindness & respect that is due to my Character and Office; and done every thing they could for my comfort, the prosperity of the Church, & advancm^t of Religion: They have, tho' but few in number, and at lest, half of them of contracted fortunes, purchased a piece of Ground, in a convenient place, with the frame of an House upon it, which they have in a beautifull manner, at the cost of about four hundred Pounds Lawfull Money, compleatly finished; which they design for the Use & Benefit of the Church for ever. They have likewise made a number of New Pews in the Church, wch Seems to fill apace, as some of those, who by reason of a disaffection to the good Mr Punderson, had left it, & gone back to the Dissenting congregations, are returned, and others returning; and four heads of Famolies newly Proselyted; So that now, as they Say, the congregation is augmented to as many more as it was a Year ago; which gives me reason to hope, that after all, there will be a full and flourishing Church here: And tho' perhaps these People have not been altogether without fault in the case of Mr Punderson, I hope the Society will continue their Notice of them, and as a Token of which present them with a folio Prayer Book, which they have never yet had, and which they humbly request may be done. A Bible has been given them by a Gentleman at New York. And Since there has been no Library granted to this Mission, where there is great need of it, I would beg leave to ask for Such an one as the Society allows, and a few Small Prayer Books, with which I find the poorest of the People are not Supplyed, and are daily coming to me for. And having been told by the Revd Messrs Andrews & Beardsley, when they returned from England, that the Society had granted me the Sum of 30£ Sterling in consideration of Cost & Damages I Sustained by a Legal Prosecution upon account of my leaving my Dissenting Congregation, which they Say, they Saw recorded in their Book, and having had no other Advice about it, which I Suppose has been by reason of ye Revd Doctor Bearcroft's Exit a little before they came away: my request is, if it be So, that you would be so good as to let me know it, and whether I may be permitted to draw for it; which, as ever Since I have been removed from my Mission at Litchfield, I have had but a lean Support, and lately been at Some expence in moving my Famoly here, would be a great relief to me.

I would take leave to inform the ven.ᴸᵉ Society that M.ʳ Jervies & Hubbard, who are coming over for Holy Orders, are both of them in Single life: and recommend them as Persons of a good Natural Genius and Temper, prudent in their Behaviour, Sober in their conversation, & Sound in their Principles; well instructed in the Arts and methods of Human Litrature, firmly Attacht to yᵉ present Government, Strictly conformed to the Established Order, and Such as bid very fair for great usefulness in the Church; and request for them that they may be admitted into the Societies Service, and have their desire, in being placed among those People who have Sent them, & would be greatly pleased to have them for yʳ Ministers, being peculiarly fond of them.

I have only one Favour more to Ask, Viz: that you would be pleased to let me know the Limits of my Mission, & the time of my appointment to it.

Who am, Revᵈ Sir, / Yours; & the Societies / most Oblidged, & Humble Serv.ᵗ

Solomon Palmer

To the Revᵈ Doctor Burton.

[1763, Dec. 28, New Milford]

New Milford, Connecticut Dec.ʳ 28ᵗʰ 1763. Revᵈ Sir.

I Return my hearty Thanks for Your Letter of May 21ˢᵗ 1763, which I received yᵉ 28ᵗʰ Oct: last: and also with the Vestry of Litchfield and Sharon, my sincere Acknowledgements to yᵉ hono.ᴸ Society, for the two 4.ᵗᵒ Bibles, and two Folio Prayer Books, which came safe to hand in last Sep.ʳ: but of yᵉ Books, You Mentioned in yᵉ two Letters I was favoured with, have not heard a word; I hope the hono.ᴸ Society will not be offended at my humbly requesting, yᵉ Favour of a Lybrary, for this Mission, as most of my own books, are scattered among my Parishioners. The People of Litchfield feel very Uneasy, in their presant scituation being anxiously engaged for the Church, yet cannot attend the Duties thereof but seldom:--The People at G. Barrington, feel themselves grozly injured, and can breath their Complaints no where, unless to yᵉ hono.ᴸ Society, having Tried yᵉ Courts of that Goverment: at considerable Cost; and are Obliged after all to sit down under their burthen, to Support a form of Religion, they Abhor: I have visited them once since I wrote last. In N. Milford are 72 Family's and 42 Communicants; in Litchfield are 61 Families, and 57 Com.ᵗˢ; belonging to Roxbury are 34 Families and 24 Com.ᵗˢ; belonging to Sharon 22 Families and 19. Com.ᵗˢ; Total 189: Families and 142, Actual Communicants: My business since last winter has been nearly double, to what M.ʳ Palmers was when in yᵉ Mission: 30. I Officiate nearly every 5ᵗʰ Sunday at Roxbury, and every 5ᵗʰ at Sharon which is 30. Miles distant: besides Lectures about once in yᵉ Week in other Places remote. many poor People have desired my requesting yᵉ hono.ᴸ Society for some Church books; and a few I would beg yᵉ favour of, against Deism. I have baptized 42 Children yᵉ half Year past: and drew for my last half Years Salery:

I am Revᵈ Sir Your hum.ᴸ Serv.ᵗ

Thomas Davies

[Addressed:] To / The Revᵈ Doct.ʳ Dan.ᴸ Burton / Secretary / To the honorable Society, for propagation / of the

Gospel in foreign Parts, / Bartlett's Buildings, London. [Endorsed:] Read at a Committee April 9. 1764

[1764, Mar. 26, Stamford]

Stamford, Connecticut in New England March 26. 1764

Reverend Sir-

I hope it will not be disagreable to the Venerable Board, to Receive advice that I have this day drawn upon their Treasurer. Edward Pearson Esq.ʳ in Usual form, a set of Bills for £25 Sterling, in favour of M.ʳ Thomas Ellison Jun.ʳ Merchant at New York.----I continue to do Duty in all parts of my Extensive Mission as Usual, and by the Blessing of God have the pleasure to find my labours Acceptable and my Church in a peaceable, Increasing, and Flourishing State.

Great pains, indeed hath been taken by a late Member of our Church, as I hinted in my last, both to stir up strife & Division among yᵉ Members of the Church, Relative to the Publick Expences which they have been at in building thier Church &c and for the support of Religeon, but being disregarded, he is now very busy Among Dissenters, who in general of late are spirited up against the Church, beyond what is Usual; but I see no prospect of his being able to disturb our peace or prevent my Usefullness.----The Number of Inhabitants in Stamford and Greenwich are about 4850 Whites. 110 Blacks. Heads of Families professors of our holy Church, in both Towns 170. Actual Communicants of the Church in both Towns 57, two added to the Communion on Christmas last. I Return my Humble thanks to the Venerable Board for a Folio Bible & Common Prayer Book directed to me and newly Receiv.ᵈ, presuming it was design.ᵈ for my Chapel at Horseneck.----I Baptized the last half year 26 Infants, within the Year 82. Purposing by the Grace of God to continue as Extensively Usefull as I can, in promoteing the gracious End of the Gospel, Agreeable to the pious design of the Venerable Board; and the sacred Obligations I am under, And with Humble Duty, and Earnest prayers that God would bless all the Multiplied Instances of their Charity. I am Reverend Sir with High Esteem and due Regard to your Self

Your Very Humble Serv.ᵗ

And Most Aff.ᵗ Br.ʳ In Christ

Ebenez.ʳ Dibblee

The Reverend Doctor Burton Secret.ʳ to the Venerable Society for Propagation of the Gospel in Foreign Parts

[Endorsed:] Read at a Committee July 16, 1764

[1764, May 5, New Haven]

Connecticut, New-Haven May the 5ᵗʰ A:D: 1764. Revᵈ Sir;

Your Letter bearing Date, Nov.ʳ 6ᵗʰ A:D: 1763. is this Day come to hand. The others which you therein mention, I've not received. Doct.ʳ Johnson, about half a Year Since, informed me of my appointm.ᵗ to this Mission; to which I Soon after removed my Famoly; where I am happily Setled: And I hope, by the blessing of God upon my endeavours, to be instrumental of Some Spiritual good to this People, to whom I have had the Satisfaction

hitherto of making my Self agreeable, and of living in Harmony, & good Friendship with the Dissenters.

I return my most Sincere & hearty thanks to the Society for the Charitable assistance they have afforded towards my Support ever since I have been in their Service: And especially for their late favour in removing me from my former expensive, Laborious, & very Fatigueing Mission, to this, where is less duty to be performed, & a larger Salary both from them, and the People here.

The State of this Church is pretty much the Same it was when I last wrote; flourishing & encreasing: Divers straying Members, have returned, & Stedfastly adhere to us; and Several respectable heads of Famolies, been newly proselyted. And from the present view of things, there Seems to be a foundation of hope for a Still greater encrease.

The Church People here have been wanting in nothing that their Abilities could do, for the honour of their Profession: They've, though but few in number, and most of them of but moderate Fortunes, b[uilt] an handsom Church. And Since my coming among them've purchased about an Acre of Land in the midst of the Town, with the frame of an House on it; which they've in an Elegant manner compleatly finished, at the cost, as near as it can be Assertained of 460£ Lawfull Money; which they design to Secure to the Society, as an acknowledgm.t of their favours, for their Use for ever; as Soon as they have Setled their accounts, and got Matters in readiness for it.

The Church in these parts is furiously attacked by her Enemies, the Dissenting Teachers chiefly, who are most industreously putting forth their Strongest Efforts to bring her into contempt, & prevent her encrease. They are Striking at the root, the Society mostly, which they hope, one day, to See overthrown; as knowing it is owing alone to their influence and encouragment, that the Church is become So reputable, and has got So Strong footing here; and God grant that the Gates of Hell may never prevail against it. The invidious D.r Mahew of base Principles, and it is to be feared a dishonest heart, has raised a dust to blind Men's Eyes, and Stir up a Popular clamour. They are very liberal in their Satires, and ready to impute faults where there are none. We are as narrowly watched by them, as a Cat watches a Mouse; & every peccadillo is taken notice of, & made a great crime. They would be glad to find Something to accuse us with, but blessed be God, that Setting aside the frailties & imperfections common to Human Nature, they can find nothing, tho' they are carping at every thing: And to escape the Slanders of their Virulent tongues, we had need to have the perfection of y.e pure Angelick Nature. They are restless to find Some evil thing to Say of us; And Seeing that [they] could find nothing else, they [have] thrown out their In[vectives against] one or two, for giving, (as they Say) too large accounts of their labours & Success &c:--as they Stand in the Societies Abstracts: In which, tho' perhaps, they may have a little exceeded, I am confidently perswaded, have not been wilfull Impositions. These things I mention, because, as they are made publick, they will probably cross the Seas, and reach the Societies Ears,---- which I hope will have no other influence upon that Venerable Body, then to Stir them up the more vigorously to exert themselves for the good of their Missions, & encouragment of their Missionaries; None of whom are

quite So faulty as their Enemies would make them; I think indeed Scarcely at all So; For to Say Truth, I know not of one in New: England, but who behaves with Ministerial prudence, is blameless in his life, and faithfull in y.e discharge of all Ministerial duties. And I verily believe, if the Society exactly knew the Conduct of each, not one would fall under their Censure. It might perhaps, however, have a good influence, if the Society had a larger number of honest hearted, faithfull and upright Members here: A Gentleman in this Town, of a Liberal Education, & affluent circumstances, Viz: M.r Enos Alling, to whom Such a Character justly belongs; I would beg leave to recommend, as well worthy of Such an honour, & to which, I heartily wish He might be advanced. He is truly Catholick in his temper, has been the greatest Benefactor to this Church, and would, I doubt not do all that he could for the interest of the Society, and the furtherance of their pious and charitable designs; And as he is Childless, tho' a Married Man, would at last leave them a valuable Legacy. M.r Harrison, who has lately been made a Member, is coming Home, and will I doubt not if He should be enquired of, confirm what I've Said, and Strongly recommend him too.

I thank the Society for the Library they have granted me, & the folio prayer Book for the Use of my Church: And would Advise them, that (tho' I know not the time when my Salary here commenced) I have by the Advice of Doct.r Johnson, drew for one Year, Viz: 50£. And for 20£ more, which M.r Jervies in a Letter lately received, assures me, he had authority from you, to tell me I might do; It being Some years Since granted by the Society, on account of Costs and Damages I Sustained by a Lytigious Lawsuit &c:

I am not So well acquainted with the State of things here; nor even with that of my own Church and People; as to be able to transmit a regular Notitia Parochialis-- This I hope to do the next time I write, Who am, Rev.d Sir,

Yours, and the Societies, / most Humble Servant,
Solomon Palmer.

P:S: There are a few Scattered Books at West-Haven, the remains of an old Library that was granted to the Mission there &c: which if Some care be not taken of them, will in a little time be quite lost: With the Societies leave I will collect, & add them to the Library they have granted me, & So Secure them for the use of their Succeeding Missionaries.

Sol.m Palmer.

To the Rev.d Doct.r Burton-.

[1764, June 1, New Milford]

New Milford June y.e 1. 1764
Rev.d Sir.

Your Favour of Feb: 10, 1764 I have received, but the Letter mentioned therein is not arrived; as to the Dissenters, Threatning at G. Barrington; it was because the Church People did not go, to the Dissenting Meeting, which has not been executed, the Dissenters, being better advised, altho', they did imprison 15 Days, two Persons of good Character, before I wrote my Letter, for no other Cause; the one educated in the Church, and the other a Lutheran; as to their ministerial Tax, they are obliged

to pay without hesitation, to the Dissenting Teacher; altho'
in almost all his Sermons (as the People inform me) casts
yͤ bitterest Sarcasms against yͤ Church, as a Church:
According to the Instructions contained in your Letter, and
with yͤ approbation of all my Parishioners; I should be
greatly pleased, to have The Towns of New-Milford Woodbury, Kent, and New-Fairfield, included in one Mission:
in which, I should choose to reside, haveing purchased a
small Inheritance, in New Milford, where my Family now
live; in this part, there will be three Churches to officate
in on Sunday; viz. New Milford, in the Center, where,
the Old Church is to small, we have gathered most of yͤ
Materials, for erecting a new One next Spring; Roxbury
a parish in Woodbury, where is a pretty Church neatly
finished; New Preston a parish in Kent, where they have
collected most of yͤ materials, with which they will Erect
a Church next Spring 45 feet by 35: this part propose to
contribute Thirty Pound Sterling pͬ An:---- Litchfield
Cornwall and Sharon, are the Towns in the other part
where a Missionary will Officiate at upon Sunday, Litchfield most probably the place of his residence, where is
a Church: In Sharon is a small Church, which since I
attended there is incapable to contain my Audience, they
have at my Desire, and considerable Expence, both to
them, and me, erected this Spring a new One, 45 feet
long, and 35 feet Wide, which is now a finishing: for to
help build this Church and the two I mentioned above, I
procured of the Gentlemen in New York a Gratuity of 124
Pound York Currency: This part Propose to contribute
Thirty Pound Sterling pͬ An: there are a number of Towns
besides, in this County, which naturally are included in
that part of yͤ Mission, viz Goshen, Torrington, Warring-
ton, New Hartford, Norfolk, Salisbury, Canaan, in which
Places, are a few Church People, who desire to come
under the Society's protection; Hartland, where are a
considerable body of Church People, lying contiguous to
Symsbury, and very remote from Litchfield, would Choose
to be included in Mͬ Viets' Mission: If the honorable Society should be pleased, thus to divide this Mission; or in
any other form, as shall seem most expedient; it will be
easing me of a burthen, which at present is exceeding
heavy, and which long my constitution will not permit me
to bear; it will be doing great good to yͤ Souls of many
People; it will be a means of greatly promoting the Interest of the Church in these back and new Settlements; it
will be a great and inexpressible Favour to us in general,
and in Perticular to yours and the honorable Societys most
Obedient and Faithful Servant

Thomas Davies

P.S. haveing no Opportunity to send away this Letter until
this Date June 25. 1764; I beg leave to Add that in the preceeding half Year I have faithfully and punctually attended
the Duties of my Mission, making that and that only my
Study, my business and Concern; I have baptized 39 Children, and One Adult, have had Considerable Additions to
my Congregations, have received sundry serious Communicants; and God be praised, thro his blessing Peace
Love and harmony prevails, thro yͤ whole; haveing a
great many serious people among my Parishioners, who
are very fond of reading good books of the Church of England which are very scarce here, I therefore Lend them
all I can spare, out of my small Lybrary, that would be
serviceable unto them; and should be very greatly rejoiced

if the Society would Favour this Mission with a Lybrary,
which would supply my wants, whilst I obliged others; to
gather with a few Peices against Deism, and some small
religious Tracts, and small Common Prayer Books for yͤ
benifit of such as are not able to buy them: That God will
abundantly bless and reward our kind benefactors, is the
hearty Prayer of the Societys humble Servͭ

Thomas Davies

[Addressed:] To the Revͩ Doctͬ Daniel Burton / Secretary to the honorable Society / for the propagation of the
Gospel / In foreign Parts / In Bartlett's Buildings / Holborn / London. / pͬ Harriot packet
[Endorsed:] Read at a Committee Nov. 12. 1764.

[1764, July 30, Middletown]
Reverend Sir-

The Reason I did not write by the last Post, was that
I arriv'd too late in the Week before, which was the only
Consideration that made an Excuse to myself, and as such
I hope it will be receiv'd by you-- I would choose not to
be troublesome and therefore I shall only take the Liberty
in general to mention what I have the greater Reason to
judge will be the more acceptable-- We were ordain'd by
the Bishop of Exeter Deacons, and Priests by the Bishop of
Carlisle: the former Gentleman is I think not very graceful or pleasing in his Mien, but seems, if I may venture to
judge, too much elated with his sudden, and as we were inform'd unexpected Promotion; and more affected with the
Grandeur of his Station than attentive to shine in the Character of his Office. The other appear'd more agreable in
his Person, whose Courtesy of Behaviour, and open Readiness to assist us; rendered him as justly meriting our
Thanks, and imprinted in our Minds an Idea of his Worth
and Goodness-- The Behaviour of the Bishop of London,
we found exactly to correspond to the height of what was
previously reported to us-- It was no small Pleasure to
find the Secretary truly a benevolent and friendly Man,
disposd without Reserve to advise and assist us, and that
with all the Appearance of his being welsuited with his
Business, with Marks of Satisfaction that he could oblige
and help us. He was so good, altho' unask'd and even
unexpected, as to meet us at Lambeth, to introduce us
to the Archbishop, whom we found in Appearance to possess, (to speak in the Simplicity of Truth) every Character that serves to compleat the great and the good Man;
which, the Greatness of his Dignity seems only to contribute to render more illustrious-- He convers'd in the
most friendly Manner upon our Business and the Contents
of your Letter, with the expressing of many hearty Wishes
that Matters had been so circumstanc'd that they could
have answered our Requests and done for us to the Ful-
ness of our Desires: but that Prudence seem'd to point
out, as the wisest Part, to desist a little 'till the prevailing malicious Bitterness of Spirit was in some Measure
laid aside--which he was in hopes the Piece wrote in England would have a Tendancy to effect.----And thus all
Hopes of Success for Guilford was cut short at once: and
upon finding that Part of Middletown Mission was establish'd with some adjacent Places, and therefore to re-
establish it, would be like making a new Mission, they
could do Nothing to assist it, so appear'd to suggest that

he accounted the Salary transfer'd to Wallingford.--
However Dr Burton afterwards inform'd us of the Ready
Disposition of the Society to divide Litchfield and make
a new Mission there, as requested by Mr Davies, on the
Reason of its Extensiveness and the Duty required in it,
too great and worrying for one Person to perform-- That
the Want of Money was not the Reason, that influenc'd the
Society in their present Resolutions, (altho' he was willing
it should be so received) for the Subscriptions, and Gra-
tuities were never larger, nor perhaps so large as they
were the Year past-- The Archbishop, when we went to
take our Leave of him, after some friendly and important
Advice, was so good as to discourse freely upon ecclesi-
astick Affairs in America, let us know that there was
still talk about a Bishop for America, but that the settling
Things in the State went on slowly-- That the Dissenters
were not averse to a Bishop's being placed here upon the
Plan as propos'd: as he was particularly assured the Day
before, by Dr Chandler, who waited on him, by Appointment, in Company with Dr Smith of Philadelphia; with
whom he talk'd more largely upon the Subject and the Affairs in general of the Society, and told him he was sorry
to see such bitter and injurious Things, the Product of
meer jealous Ill-Nature, publish'd against the Society,
and askd him whether he himself, could or did approve of
them; to which Dr Chandler replied he was truly sorry to
see what Dr Mahew had publish'd, and had wrote to him
signifying the same with his Desire that he would desist--
With Regard to a Bishop he hoped they would not settle one
in the N. England Colonies, or so as to have any Concerns
with, or any Jurisdiction over them-- As to that the Archbishop observ'd to him the Dissenters had no Cause to
Fear, for it was not propos'd that a Bishop should have
any Concern in civil Matters, but what immediately belong'd to the Church, and the Members of the Church of
England to ordain, and confirm, and to preside over the
Clergy, to direct and govern in Affairs of the Church,
that it might be put on such Footing as is necessary for
the good Regulation, Purity, and Perfection of it, which
was reasonable for those in America to ask and expect,
as their Privilege in Justice and Equity both from Church
and State-- To which Dr Chandler replied, if that was
the Scheme and [full] Intent, for his Part he could have
Nothing to object, but tho[ught it a]ltogether reasonable
and right--and that the Dissenters here could have no just
Pretentions to oppose it.-- He also imformd us, as did
Dr Burton the same, of the Society's having some Thoughts
of appointing a Number of the Clergy, at a suitable Distance from each other, to receive and inspect the Representations and Accounts of the different Churches, to be by
them transcribed to the Society: but not so as to abridge
the Correspondance of Particulars, as that they would
mean to have continued-- He desired us to make his Compliments acceptable to you, and acquaint you, that the Reason he did not write, was that he had not recover'd from a
late severe Fit of the Gout, so far as to be able, for he
chose not to write unless with his own Hand-- Beging your
favourable Excuse for the ill Dress of my Letter, I am
your much oblig'd and very humble Servant

                                        Abraham Jarvis

Middletown July 30th 1764
To the Reverend Dr Johnson

[1764, Aug. 12, Stratford]
            Stratford in Connecticut Augt 12 1764
May it please your Lordship,
    With my humblest and most dutiful Congratulations on
your Lordship's most deserved advancement to the See of
London, I humbly beg leave to recommend to your favourable Notice, the Bearer hereof, Mr Ebenezer Kneeland, as
a very hopeful Candidate for holy Orders. He was bred and
graduated Master of Arts at Yale College in New Haven in
this Colony, and has made very good proficiency in Learning for these parts of the World, and has ever been remarked for a Person of much seriousness, piety & virtue,
and is firmly attached to Our most Gracious King, and the
Constitution both in Church & State. He is a single Man
and will be of the Age of Twenty four years next Spring,
and I am persuaded he will be a very faithful and useful
Missionary in the Society's service, if they shall think
proper to employ him, and your Lordship to ordain him,
and I doubt not but the Society will give him a sufficient
Title-- I humbly beg an Interest in your Lordship's
prayers and Blessings; and that you may long continue a
great blessing and Ornament to your exalted Station, and
at length receive a Glorious Reward of all your faithful
Services, is the earnest Prayer of, my Lord, (with great
veneration,)
    your Lordships / most dutiful Son / & most obedient
humble Servant

                                        Samuel Johnson

[To the Rt. Rev. Richard Terrick, Bp. of London]

[1764, Aug. 15, Norwalk]
            Norwalk in Connecticut Augt 15th 1764.
May it please Your Lordship,
    We the Subscribers, after manifesting our greatest
Joy for Your Lordship's most deserved Promotion to the
See of London, Humbly beg leave to recommend, the Bearer, Mr Ebenezer Kneeland, as a Candidate for Holy Orders. He has been Educated, and graduated Master of
Arts at Yale College in New Haven in this Colony. He is
esteemed a good Scholar in this part of the world: He is
a person of much Seriousness, Piety, and Virtue, Since
our Acquaintance with him, which is three Years: and by
Information, he has borne that Character all his Life. He
is firmly attached to our most Gracious King, and to the
Constitution both in Church and State. He is a Single man,
and will be twenty four Years old, next Spring. We hope,
the Society will give him a Title. And if Your Lordship
finds him qualified for Holy Orders, and ordains him, we
make no Doubt, he will be a very Labourous and Useful
Missionary in the Society's Service.
    We Humbly beg Your Lordship's Blessing, and Prayers
for us: May You long continue a Shining Ornament to Your
Divine and Exalted Station: and in God's Time, through the
Merits of Christ, receive a Crown of Glory for all Your
faithful Services, is the Humble and Earnest Prayer of
Your Lordship's / Most Dutiful Son / and most obedient /
Humble Servants
                                        Ebenezer Dibble
                                        Jeremiah Leaming.

[To the Rt. Rev. Richard Terrick, Bp. of London]

[1764, Sept. 14, New Haven]
To the Right Reverend Father in God, Richard, Lord
Bishop of London.

May it please your Lordship,

We the Episcopal Clergy of the Colony of Connecticut
in New-England, humbly beg leave to offer our united &
most hearty Congratulations, upon your Lordship's truly
deserved advancment to the high and important See of London; which we the rather presume to do, as the Church in
these Provinces hath heretofore been considered as under
the Care and Jurisdiction of that See.

But as the Church is become very numerous in these,
now, wide and vastly extended Countries, Subject to his
most gracious Magesty's Dominion, at so great a distance
from our Mother Country; We humbly hope, especially at
this important Conjuncture, that it is reserved for one
of the Glories of your Lordship's Episcopate, that these
Countries may be provided for with Bishops residing in
Some of these Colonies, to have the more immediate inspection & Government of us; and we humbly implore your
Lordship's best Influence that this blessed Event may now
at length be accomplished.

We earnestly pray God long to preserve your Lordship's most important life and health, to be a great Ornament and blessing to that Illustreous See, and at length to
give you a glorious reward of all your faithful Services in
the Life to come: And humbly recommending our Selves
and our Churches to your Lordship's Prayers and Benediction, We are, with the utmost Veneration, May it
please your Lordship,

Your Lordship's, / Most dutiful Sons, / and most
obedient Humble Ser^vts,

Signed in the Behalf & at the Re-
New-Haven,   quest of the Clergy of this Colony,
Sep^tr 14- 1764.   Samuel Johnson-

To my Lord of London [Richard Terrick]

[1764, Sept. 24, New Haven]
              Connecticut, New-haven Sep^tr 24. A:D: 1764.
Revd Sir;

The Library and folio Common Prayer Book mentioned
in your Letters of the 6th of November, and April last,
(which lay long unknown to me in Doct^r Berclay's care) I
have lately received; for which I return my most hearty &
Sincere thanks. I also thank the Society for the Gratuity of
£20 they gave me at their meeting in Sep^tr 1761, which being Assured of by a Letter from Mr Jervies, when he was
in London, by Authority from you, I immediately drew
for: And not long before by the Advice of Doct^r Johnson
& others, for £50 more as Salary, by a Bill Dated March
29th 1764. just a Year from the time I began to Officiate
here; which by your last Letter, I find was almost three
months before I should have done, however I hope it will
not be protested, but favourably accepted.

I shall for the future draw according to the time of
my appointment to this Mission, Agreeably, I have now
drawn for the first quarter of the Second Year by a Bill
dated September 24th 1764. And as there is of my Old
Salary one quarter due, I have likewise in the Same Bill
drawn for that.

The places where Mr Punderson Officiated after He
left Groton, were here, and at West-haven, At Branford
and Northford, Alias Pauge, a Parish belonging to Branford; And at Guilford, & Cohabit, a Parish belonging to
Guilford: But inasmuch as the People here and at West-
haven invited me to Settle among them, and have purchased
a Small Glebe, & built an House upon it, to the amount of
£382:10 Sterling Cost, I have Officiated only at these two
places, excepting occasionally at Branford and Gui[l]ford,
before Mr Hubbards return from England, when it was expected that he would take the care of them, & is now willing to do it, who cannot otherwise be Supported where he
is, nor even then but poorly.

And Since the Church in this great Town is really of
very great importance, and the growth and encrease of
it depends upon my Officiating pretty Steadily here and is
now in a flourishing way; and in consideration of the fatigues and hard Service of my former Mission which my
Successor, who is a Strong and healthy young Man, already complains, is a Task too great for him to perform;
I earnestly beg the Society to excuse me from going to
Branford, who can otherwise be better provided for, &
confine my Mission only to New-haven which includes the
Parish of West-haven. Mr Hubbard can much better go to
Branford, than I, there being between me and that Town, a
difficult Ferry to pass, especially in the Winter Season;
and the distance being near equal, about ten miles. I
heartily wish that Branford, and Guilford might be made
a Mission, with a Small Salary; at each of which places,
upon Such encouragment. I doubt not but that the Church
would Soon greatly encrease. They have for many years
continued firm in their Profession, under many dark &
discouraging circumstances. Before Mr Punderson's coming, they had only occasional Preaching,--and after, he
did but Seldom visit them, and yet I know not of one in
either of these Towns that has forsaken the Church. I
esteem them well worthy of the Societies regards, and
as Such I hope they will be considered by them; Who am,
Revd Sir,

Yours, & the Societies, most / obedient, & humble
Servant,

                                        Solomon Palmer.
To the Revd Doctor Burton.

P:S: Septr 25. 1764. This Day the Melancholy News of
the Revd Mr Punderson's Death came to Town; He departed this life, after a short Sickness, on Saturday last, and
was decently Interred yesterday, whose death is much lamented by his People.   Solomon Palmer.

Notitia Parochialis.

1. Number of Inhabitants in New-haven.		6000.
2. No. of those who profess themselves of the Church of England in New-haven Town, about,		265.
3. No. of those who profess themselves of the Church of England in the Parish of West-haven, about,		150
4. No. of Actual Communicants belonging to ye Church at New-haven.		38
5. No. of Actual Communicants belonging to ye Church at West-haven.		28

6. No. of Adult Persons Baptised the last Year.   1
7. No. of Children Baptized the last Year.   32
8. No. of Heathens & Infidels,   2
9. No. of Papists   0
10 People of all denominations are generally orderly walkers.

[Addressed:] To the Reverend Doct.ʳ Daniel Burton / Secretary to the Society for the / Propagation of the Gospel in Foreign / Parts, Bartlet's Buildings, Holborn, / London.
[Endorsed:] Read at a Committee. Jan. 14. 1765.

[1764, Oct. 4, Stamford]

Stamford Connecticut In
New England Octobᵉʳ 4, 1764

Reverend Sir-

I beg leave to give you advice, that I've this day drawn a set of Bills for Twenty five Pounds Sterling in usual form, upon Edward Pearson Esq.ʳ Treasurer to the Venerable Society, In Fav.ʳ of M.ʳ Thomas Ellison Ju.ʳ, Merch.ᵗ in New York.--

It may be tho't Needless perhaps so often to repeat the number of Inhabitants, and their several professions in my Extensive Mission.---In the Preceeding Half Year, I have Baptized 41 Infants White 1 Black. Adults 6 White, 1 Black. 4 Added to the Communion.---My Parish continues in an Increaseing, peaceable, religious State. And nothing affords me greater pleasure, than by the grace of God to be instrumental in promoteing Christian knowledge, and the practice of true Religion among them. and whatever our adversaries wo'ud suggest to the Contrary, we have good Reason to think, both the Moral & Religious state of our People are much bettered by our Ministry thro' yᵉ Charity of the Venerable Board:---The Parish of Rye is become Vacant again, by the Death of good M.ʳ Punderson, who departed this Life after a Short Illness the 22 of last Month; I Preached & attended his Funeral yᵉ 24ᵗʰ, at the Request of his bereaved Consort, and Parish by whom he is much lamented. It seems, he was Generally very Acceptable to his People, as appeared from the Numerous Concourse of People yᵗ Attended yᵗ Solemnity, and yᵉ tender Sense they Expressed of their Loss. M.ʳ Timothy Wetmore agreable to advice, is so good as to Read Divine Service and Sermons again among them, and as he is a very Sober deserveing Son of a very worthy Father, we wish the Parish might be United in his fav.ʳ, and make Choice of him for their Minister. The last Sunday, I Preached in a New Church, to a very large Congregation in yᵉ Upper District of Salem; the Church is but little more than Covered and Closed, but the Poor People in that Quarter, and upon Courtlands Mannor, purpose to Pursue yᵉ finishing of it as they are able, hopeing in future time to be Qualified for the Honᵉ Societies fav.ʳ, and better supply of their spiritual wants, thro' their most Charitable Assistance. Permit me to Add my Duty to the Venerable Board, to whose Piety and Charity we are so much indebted, Under God, for the Invaluable blessings we Enjoy; Praying God to accept and Reward their work and labour of Love; And with my Humble Compliment to Your Self to Subscribe Reverend Sir

Your Most Obedᵗ / Most Humble Servᵗ And B.ʳ
Ebenez.ʳ Dibblee

[Addressed:] To / The Reverend Doctor Burton / In Bartlets Buildings Holborn / Secretary to the Venerable Society / for the Propagation of the Gospel / in Foreign Parts. / London
[Endorsed:] Read at a Committee Jan. 14. 1765

[1764, Oct. 9, New London]

Revᵈ & Worthy Sir

Your most friendly & agreeable Letter wrote last Decem.ʳ, I receiv'd yᵉ latter of Ap.ˡ following, & wou'd have answerd directly, had not a Mast-ship, order'd to this Port, met wᵗʰ Misfortunes at Sea. Soon after I heard of 'Squire Harrison's design for England, by whom, having known me these many Years, I concluded to write. I rejoice he is added to y.ʳ Number, as knowing him to be a Gentleman of strict Honor, Integrity, & Sense.

It gives me great Pleasure, yᵗ my Conduct is pleasing to yᵉ Venerable Society. As a conscientious Discharge of Duty is their Will, it shall be my Study. How I go on yᵉ learned Bearer can well inform you. Nothing, but Poverty, prevents yᵉ Growth of my Hearers. My Communicants increase, but slowly. Since my last I baptiz'd 16 Children & three Adults, able to give Account of their Faith. Four new Floor pews have been built: they were engag'd, as soon as laid out, & so wou'd a dozen more. My Duties extraparochial are very numerous. I attend occasionally two Societies, wholly Dissenters, about 18 yᵉ one, yᵉ other 22 Miles distant from y.ˢ, & was lately desir'd to officiate in another 25 off-- also two or three places on Longisland, cross an Arm of the Sea--besides two Indian Tribes, yᵉ one 9--yᵉ other 7 Miles off, who are very ambitious of my coming. One of them has a Preacher, ordain'd in yᵉ dissenting way, resident among them--a discreet, understanding Man of their own Tribe, [Samson Occum] muc[h] under my Unfluence, as indeed yᵉ whole Tribe is. Pray, S.ʳ, present my Du[ty] to my Venerable Patrons, & tell yᵐ, I desire to know, if they wou'd encourage this Indian Minister (if I may so call him) to come home for holy Orders, & settle him over these & the neighbouring Tribes of Indians. My zealous Endeavors shall be exerted: And I am sure Sir Willᵐ Johnson, whom his Majesty has appointed Chief over all his Indians, will heartily concur wᵗʰ me. Besides, this wou'd obviate all yᵉ trifling, impious Objections of yᵉ Socinian Doctor [Mayhew], who has wrote as scurrilously against yᵉ Religious Society, as rebelliously on yᵉ 30ᵗʰ of January, for wᶜʰ he shou'd have emblazon'd a Pillory with his Ears.

In a Lett.ʳ, dated May 20ᵗʰ 1747 from y.ʳ Predicessor, directed to me, residing in Chester in England, are these words--"Y.ʳ Salary from yᵉ Society will be £60 Per Ann̄ wᵗʰ a new-built house, & a Glebe of 30 Acres of good Land." The Deed I never saw--my whole Land only half a Quarter of an Acre within 2 Rods: & tho' I repeatedly wrote to yᵉ Society, I never heard, yᵗ my Complaint was observ'd before. I was, when sent here, desir'd, now & then, to visit Hebron, 30 Miles off, wᶜʰ I did & officiated twelve times in the same Number of Months for some Years, for wᶜʰ I had no Recompence, tho' it cost me several Pounds, & I was a fixt Missionary: And I can truly say I have rode 100--sometimes 120--sometimes

above 200 Miles to propagate yͤ Gospel at my own Expence; tho' others, who have wrote largely of their Performance, have been generously rewarded: but as I did
not--cou'd not agree wᵗʰ some of my Brethren's Proceedings, [I] oppos'd yͫ in wᵗ I tho't wrong, & was also a
Stranger, I incurr'd their Displeasure, & [thr]o' their
Writing gain'd very little Ground wᵗʰ my Superiors.
However Truth appears, & will shine in time, & blaze
in Eternity. Unless my Heart grosly deceives me, I
preach & practise for Eternity.

That yͤ Society got a Deed of 30 Acres of Land, is
unquestionable: I understand it was sent by Mͬ Stewart
of this Town, once a Member; who impos'd yͤ Deed of
another Parish for yᵗ of New-London, tho' he equivocates
about it; all yͤ rest of yͤ Parishoners absolutely deny it.
If Mͬ Punderson pleases, he can unravel yͤ whole dark
proceeding; for I understand he receiv'd yͤ Deed from yͤ
Parish of Hebron (wᶜʰ was for several Years under yͤ
Inspection of yͤ Minister of New-London) & deliver'd it
to Mͬ Steward, & yᵗ they two contrived yͤ Plot, for wᶜʰ
I am a Sufferer. Had I that Land here, my Income wou'd
be worth £100 Per Anñ, as yͤ Secretary's Letter said it
was; whereas, 'till of late, I have not had above £10--now
I have about £15. Sterᵍ, instead of £20 promis'd, yearly;
but I prefer a Contribution to an Obligation. The Society's
frequent Losses, & small Donations for several Years,
after I came, were yͤ true Reason, why I did not request
a Bounty, wᶜʰ wᵈ be very acceptable, if my Pious Patrons
tho't fit.

To Support my self I taught Boys from yͤ West Indies,
where above 500 Dollars are owing to me above ten Years,
& I almost despair of. Death depriv'd me of a Negroe &
Mulatto, worth £30. These Providential Losses have kept
me low; but, praised be GOD, I owe no Man any thing, but
Love.

I understand you were pleas'd to send me some Books,
wᶜʰ came to Mͬ Winslow at Stratford, who took them to
Brantree, whence it's very difficult to get the[m.] But as
a Parcel, directed to Doctor Millar, late of Brantree, was
sent to my Brother, I desire I may have them in stead of
yͤ others.

I drew for my last half Year's Salary in Favor of a
Merchant in New-York, & doubt not of it's honorable Acceptance.

Pray, Sͬ pardon this Prolixity. The next shall be
shorter. May yͤ Holy Spirit of GOD direct & assist you!
I beg an Interest in yͬ Prayers, wᶜʰ all my Religious
Benefactors share in those of Theirs &

Good Sͬ, / Yͬ most humˡᵉ Servᵗ & / affectionate
Brother / in Christ

Matt Graves

P.S. The Length hereof prevents me from adding an odd
Affair, wᶜʰ lately happend to our Churh: yͤ next, please
GOD, shall discover it

New-London Octͬ 9ᵗʰ 1764

To the Revᵈ Doctor Burton Secretary &c

P.S
Sͬ As every thing here is extravagantly dear, I have
sent for some Articles to England, for yͤ Payment of
wᶜʰ I have drawn on yͤ Treasurer for my last Quarter

due Sepᵗ 25ᵗʰ 176[4], wᶜʰ I hope you'll forward In favor
of Mͬ Thoˢ Cox Mercᵗ in London

Sͬ Be pleas'd, if you send by Way of N. York, to direct
to me to yͤ Care of Mͬ Hen: Van Vleck Mercᵗ; if by a
Vessel to Boston, to yͤ Care of Mͬ Willͫ Hubbard Mercᵗ;
then I can depend upon receiving yͬ Letters, & so may my
Brother. Pray excuse this necessary Freedom from

Yͬˢ &c
MGs

[Addressed:] To / Doctor Burton, Secretary to the Reli- /
gious Society for propagating yͤ Gospel / in foreign Parts, /
Barlets building / Holborn / London / Per Favor of 'Squire
Harrison / Q D C
[Endorsed:] Read at a Committee Feb. 11. 1765

[1764, Dec. 24, New Milford]
New Milford Decemͬ 24ᵗʰ 1764

Revᵈ Sir:
I acknowledge the receipt of the two Letters You favoured me with, that of Decemͬ last, came in Octͬ and
that of May last, in Novᵗ; I have already sent Answer, to
yͤ contents of Each of those Letters; the favourable Account of Books excepted. the which I now gratefully, and
heartily, Acknowledge, to have received safe, and in good
Order; and Return my sincerest Thanks, to the, benevolent Society, for the same, viz for the Lybrary for this
Mission, for which I have given a Bond to the Church Wardens, According to Order: for Mͬ Lelands Review &: for
50 small common Prayer Books, for the poor of this Mission, which I have proportioned to Each Town, and shall
carefully, distribute to the properest Objects: for a bundle
for the People of Great-Barrington, which I shall carry,
and distribute.

In this half Year, altho' grievously afflicted with the
Rheumatism, occasioned by being, so often in the Wet,
and Cold; I have besides punctually officiating at each of
my Churches, in their proper turns where I always Preach
Two Sermons each Day;) preached twelve Week Day Lectures, mostly in other Places, particularly at G. Barrington, which I visited in October, and the Parts adjacent, and
if God permits shall set out directly for that Place, in Order to Open an elegant, and Large, Church: Which those
People have Erected, at great Expence, and whilst labouring under the severest ill-treatment, from their brethren
the Dissenters.--have baptized 47 Children, and 2 Adults;
some reputable Families, have joined to the Church; have
admitted some sober Persons to the Communion; harmony
and Peace universally prevails among my People; and mutual Charity with the Dissenters in this Town especially;
my People are willing, to exert themselves to the utmost
to Support another Missionary, as specefied in my last
Letter, earnestly wishing for a favourable Answer, from
the honored Society, to that: with my fervent Prayers,
cordial Thanks, and sincere Prespects, I am Yours, and
the honoˡ Society's most Obedient and humble Servant

Thomas Davies

[Addressed:] To, / The Revᵈ Doctͬ Daniel Burton / Secretary to the honorable Society / for the propagation of

the Gospel / in foreign Parts / In Bartlett's Buildings,
Holburn / London.
[Endorsed:] Read at a Committee April 15. 1765

[1765, Apr. 1, Stamford]
                          Stamford Connecticut
                          In New England Apr^l. 1, 1765
Reverend Sir.
    I have this day drawn upon Edward Pearson Esqr
Treasurer of the Venerable Society, a Set of Bills for
Twenty five Pounds Sterling, in fav^r of Mr Thom^s Elli-
son, Merch^t in New York, in usual form.
    Blessed be God, the Author of Peace, and lover of
Concord, my Parish continues to Increase in Number; and
I Charitable hope in Piety Devotion and Charity, as they
behave in a Christian manner in general, and are Steady,
Zealous and devout, in attending the Publick Offices of Religion.---The Heads of Families in the two Towns of Stam-
ford and Gree[n]wich, Professors of the Ch^h are about 186.
Actual Communicants 62. I Baptised last half Year 33 Infants.---Our late Noble Benefactor, Mr St George Talbot,
hath not only ben so good, as to bestow a fine Bell upon
our Ch^h and some other favours, as a Silver Tankard and
Salver, for the Administration of the Holy Comunion, but
hath ben pleased to Order the enlargement of our Glebe
Lot, by adding the Purchase of upwards of four Acres of
Choice Land Joineing to it. and of better than Eighteen
Acres within about threescore Rods of that, all contiguous,
at least within half of a Mile of the Ch^h; and is by his Ord^r
Purchased and Paid for out of his Late Benefaction of Six
Hundred Pounds; and by Deed on Publick Record, made
over to the Venerable Society, in trust for the use of their
Missionary for the time Being, and as Glebe Land for the
use of the Minister of the Ch^h for Ever. Reserveing to
himself the Interest of his Money Dureing his Life, and
three and half p^r Cent, dureing the Life of Mrs Gould,
after his Decease, in Case she survives Him. To Answer
which purpose, and for the future benefit of the Ch^h I've
agreed to take the present use of the Land, and to pay the
afores^d Rent. knowing that in future time it will greatly
redound to their advantage in the support of the Gospel
among them. neither do I think his benefaction cou'd be
improved and directed to better purpose.--
    As I meet with suitable Encourgement in the duties of
my Office, so by the Grace of God my constant endeav^r
shall be, to be as Extensively useful as I can, to mankind
in their most important Interest.---May my Humble Duty
be acceptable to the Venerable Board, and with best Regards to your Self I beg leave to Subscribe, Reverend Sir
    Your Most Obed^t / Very Humble Servt / And Brother
in Christ

                          Ebenez^r Dibblee
The fav^r of some Common Prayer Books and other Pious
small Tracts, still much wanted among my Poor people,
and parts adjacent, wou'd be very thankfully Accepted.

[Addressed:] To / The Reverend Doctor Daniel Burton /
Secretary of the Venerable Society / for the Propagation
of the Gospel / in Foreign Parts; in Bartlet's / Buildings,
Holborn / London
[Endorsed:] Read at a Committee Sept. 16, 1765

[1765, June 5, Hebron]
    Hebron in Connecticut New England 5. June. 1765
Most Gracious Sovereign,
    We Your Dutiful and Loyal Subjects, the Clergy of the
Church of England in Connecticut convened, Beg Leave with
all Humility and Reverence, to present our warmest Sentiments of Dutifulness and Loyalty, to Your Majesty's Person
and Government, the Benign Influences whereof we have experienced in these remote parts of Your Majesty's Dominions.
    We Being destitute of ecclesiastical Government and
many other Priviledges, which Christians enjoy, in all other
Protestant Countries, Beg Leave, with due Submission to
Your Majesty, to implore Your Majesty's more particular
Attention to the Religious State of this Country, That there
might be such wise Measures concerted, as that one or
more Bishops might be appointed to reside in these Your
Majesty's Plantations, with Authority to govern the Clergy,
to confirm those whom we baptize, and to perform other
Episcopal Acts, conducive to the well Being of Religion.
    We Earnestly and Humbly entreat Your Majesty to
consider whether, if our Request was granted, it would not
very much conduce to the Promotion of Loyalty, the Interest of Religion in general, and the Advantage of the Church
of England in particular.
    We Believe the Religion of the Nation, as by Law es-
tablished, to be agreable to the Will of our Great Master,
therefore we humbly conceive, we behave like Loyal Subjects to Your Majesty, and true Sons of the Church, to
address Your Majesty in this manner, That we may have
it entire. Not to Seek for this, in a Lawful way...
    [The remainder of this MS. appears to be lost.]

[1765, June 5, Hebron]
    Hebron, in Connecticut New England 5th June. 1765
May it please Your Lordship,
    We the Clergy of the Church of England in Connecti-
cut, being convened at Hebron, take this public Opportunity,
humbly to acknowledge the Receipt of [Your] Lordship's
most Christian, kind, and obliging Letter dated the 18.
February 1765; and we earnestly entreat Your Lordship to
accept of our most profound Gratitude for so particular a
Mark of Your Condescention, and Favour: and more particularly for Your condescending to grant us Liberty, to
lay before You any particulars relative to ye State of Religion, that may appear to be of Service to the Church in
these Parts.
    And as we humbly conceive nothing could be more
conducive to the Interest of America, both in a Civil and
Religious Sense, than the Appointment of one, or more
Bishops to reside here; so we are very desirous, that
there may be an Apostolical Bishop sent here, with power
to govern the Clergy, confirm those whom we baptize,
and perform other Episcopal Acts, that may be conducive
to ye well being of the Church here: to which End, we
have enclosed a Petition or Address to our Gracious King,
(who, You acquaint us, is most Sincerely inclined to Promote Religion) that He would be pleased, in his Wisdom
and Goodness, to send us a Bishop.
    We leave it to Your Lordships wisdom, to present
this Address, to his Majesty, or Suppress it, as You

think best. A Copy of which we have sent to His Grace, the A. Bishop of Canterbury, desiring him to make what use of it, he thinks proper.

We annually meet on Wednesday in Trinity week, and Shall gladly receive any Orders, or Directions Your Lordship may be pleased to send, which Shall carefully and punctually be observed.

We humbly beg Your Lordship's Blesing, and Prayers for us; may You long continue a Shining Ornament of Your Divine and exalted Station; and in God's time, thro' the Merits of Christ, receive a Crown of Glory, for all Your faithful Services; this is the humble and earnest Prayer, of

May it please Your Lordship, / Your Lordships, / Most Dutiful Sons, / and most obedient, / Humble Servants

Joseph Lamson	Samuel Andrews
Ebenezer Dibblee	Thomas Davies
Jeremiah Leaming	John Beardsley
Solomon Palmer	Abraham Jarvis
Christopher Newton	Bela Hubbard
Samuel Peters	Roger Viets
James Scovil	

This Copy was ordered to be Drawn and sent, by

                  Jeremiah Leaming
                  Clerk of the Convention

[1765, June 15, London]
Revd Sir

The acc^t you sent me of your good Health and of the florishing State of your Church, gave me the utmost pleasure; And so long as the Society continues to employ such Missionaries as are Educated among your selves, we cannot doubt of their Success.

I shall continue to recommend such Books as are most apt to reconcile, or to Silence the Dissenters, particularly the following pieces wrote by Dr John Nalson in 1677 & 1678, vizt) The true liberty and dominion of Conscience Vindicated from the usurpations and Abuses of opinion and perswasion.

The Countermine; or a Discovery of the Dangerous principles & practices of the Dissenting Party.

The Common Interest of King & People; shewing the Excellency of Monarchy compared with Aristocracy and Democracy.

The Project of Peace; or Unity of Faith and Government, the only Expedient to preserve these Nations from Popery, & Arbitrary Tyranny.

I have given Mr Avery Sir Chas Wolseley on Justification which he has undertaken to get Printed in New England. I am obliged to you for recommending him, and have had great pleasure in his conversation--

I thank Dr Johnson for his favourable opinion, and have sent him another short proof of the true Quantity of a Tropical year.

And now Sir I wish you all Success and happiness, and I am

                  y^r most obliged
From my House in   humble Ser^t
Bolt Court in Fleetstreet   Wm Rivet
       London   15 June 1765

[To the Rev. Abraham Jarvis, Middletown, Conn.]

[1765, June 25, New Haven]
            Connecticut, in New England,
            New-haven June 25. 1765.
Revd Sir,

The Church here, Since I came into this Mission, has been gradually Encreasing; and is in a respectable & flourishing condition. Numbers of Dissenters meet with us every Sunday at Church; And my own People, as they constantly attend Divine Service, So outwardly they behave with a becoming Decency, Seriousness & Devotion, which I doubt not proceeds from inward motives of Piety. I live Amicably with the Dissenters of every Denomination, and in Sweet Harmony with my own People; which gives me reason to hope, that by the blessing of God, my weak and imperfect Administrations, may be of Some Spiritual good & Advantage to them.

I most gratefully resent the Societies kindness to me in the generous provision they have hitherto made for my Support; and particularly in their appointment of me to this most agreable Mission; it being one of the pleasantest Scituations of any upon the Continent; and which I should prefer to any other, were it not for the great Surplussage of Expence I am necessarily put to.

New-haven is a Populous Town, lying upon the Post Road, by the Sea Side, between Boston & New-York, where is the Court, and the College, and which is the Center where most People of Note, meet: So that as my acquaintance is not Contracted, I unavoidably've much Company; Some of which deserve a decent & handsome entertainment; which, as I have a large and expensive Famoly, Two sons and one Daughter in their Infancy; and five Daughters grown to Mature Age, & in the prime and gaiety of life, I am not, with my present Income, able to give, and yet upon the doing of which my credit and influence very much depend; tho' the half of what I receive, almost any where in the Countrey, from the Sea Side, would be Sufficient; where it would be needless & impertinent for my Famoly to make ye like appearance, where they would be freed from giving and receiving so many Complaisant visits, and could be more profitably employed in Domestick Affairs; where Syder, or common Beer would answer instead of Wine, & a less Elegant Table Suffice. But here, as the case now is, with an oeconomy Adequate to the best that can be used, as I am able to Demonstrate, my Famoly cannot be Supported, but must soon become indigent, & unavoidably fall into disgrace, which will have an unkind influence upon this Church, now in a State, far from being despised: I am therefore from these considerations, contrary to my own inclination, constrained, humbly, tho' earnestly, and with ye greatest importunity, to request Such a Gratuity as the Society shall See fit in their wisdom and prudence to bestow, which tho' it be never so small, I shall most thankfully receive.

My tarrying So long in my former Mission, at the importunity of the People there, after the Appointment of Mr Davies to it, though they were very kind, was greatly to my damage, and who after all upon my leaving them, were So far disgusted, that a number of them refused to pay up the Subscriptions they had liberally made; besides which loss, the expence of moving my Famoly & Goods, &c: (part of which these People generously paid) was considerable.

I cannot, considering my extraordinary expence, So

well Support my Famoly here, with my present Salary, as
I did with that of my former Mission, which was but little
more than half So much, So y^t all the Advantage I have obtained by being removed from thence, is an easier Mission,
and a pleasanter Scituation! I would therfore humbly hope
that the Society will consider my case, and grant my above
request, which I would beg leave farther to Urge from the
hard Service, and great fatiegues I endured in my other
Mission, which my Successor, tho' young and healthy,
complains of as an insupportable burden, and indeed it
is a task quite enough for two Men to perform.

I should not have troubled the Society about this matter, knowing they are too often Sollicited upon the like account, did not necessity which has no Law Oblidge me to
it! And my People being unable (tho' willing) to help me,
having lately been at the expence of about £400. Sterling
in purchasing a Small Glebe, & finishing their C^hh, and
Glebe House; which they being but weak handed, & few in
number, has Straitned them very much, tho' they have
chearfully done it; so that I have not an heart, & it would
[be] cruel to request any further Assistance from them,
than they have oblidged themselves to give, wch they are
very punctual in paying.

Of Actual Communicants, but one has been added,
Since I last wrote; And I have Baptized 28 Children. I have
drawn by a Bill, Dated June 25 1765. for £12-10 Sterling,
which for value received, - I have Sold to Roger Sherman
Esqr.

In my last Letter but one- I requested the favour of
being informed, as to the extent of my Mission, to which-
you, in your last to me Said I should have an answer when
I had informed you where Mr Punderson Officiated after he
left Groaton, & came here, & where I had done &c: which
I did in my last, but as yet have received no answer. And
lest you should not have had the Account, I would again tell
you that ye Places where Mr Punderson did duty, & which
were looked upon as parts of his Cure, were, bsides Newhaven, & West-haven, ye places where only I have Steadily
Officiated; Branford & Northford, Alias Paug, - a Parish belonging to Branford: And Guilford, & Cohabit, a Parrish belonging to Guilford; where at their request I have occasionally Preached Lectures, & Baptized Children: This before
the Revd Mr Hubbards coming to Guilford, and Since, at
Branford, besides Seven Sundays Service, till the People
here began to grow uneasie, and desired me to refrain going there any more, which I accordingly did; So that they
have been destitute of any publick Service in the way of the
Church for some time, & are like to be So till ye Society
orders it to be otherwise.

Mr Hubbard is at Guilford, and Officiates only there;
& at Killingworth, where fifteen heads of Famolies have
lately been proselyted to the Church of England; at both
which places they are extreamly fond of him, & he of them.
Guilford is the place of his Nativity & Killingworth contiguous to it, Eastward; which two places he hopes will be So
far considered by the Society, as to be made a Mission, &
he as their Missionary appointed to it; the duty of which,
being not of a Robust Constitution, he imagines will be as
much as he can perform: But then what will become of
Branford where there are near 40 Famolies of Church People, who have continued firm in their Profession for near
20 years, under ye most discouraging circumstances; &
who therefore I am perswaded, as much as any People,

deserve the Societies Notice. They are very desirous of
being under my Pastoral care, and have repeatedly urged
me to write to ye Society on this account, and blame me
that I have not done it before now. As Branford is the
Town where I & my Wife were Born, and where almost all
our near Relatives live, I am very fond of doing them all
ye Service I can; and if I could go there without greatly
disoblidging & frustrating the expectations of the People
here, where it is of importance that Divine Service should
be pretty Steadily performed, it would be quite agreeable
to me; but this cannot be done; and therefore I should be
glad to please these People especially, who have done all
they could for me, are very kind to me, & upon whom is
all my dependence. However, if Branford cannot be better
provided for, if it shall be the pleasure of the Society, I
shall be willing, and indeed desirous to go there, & do the
best for them I can, Who am, Revd Sir,

    .yours, and the Societies, most / faithful, Oblidged &
Humble Servant,

                         Solomon Palmer.

To the Revd Doctor Burton.

[Addressed:] To the Reverend Doct^r Daniel Burton /
Secretary to the Society for the / Propagation of the Gos-
pel in Foreign / Parts, Bartlet's Buildings, Holborn.
[Endorsed:] Read at a Committee Nov. 11. 1765

[1765, June 25, New Milford]
Rev^d S^r

I informed the ho^l Society in my Letter dated June
1764. that we were about erecting three Churches in this
Mission; I would now Add, that, That, at Sharon is so far
compleated, that we can now very conveniently Assemble
in it for publick Worship: and that, That, at N. Milford
was raised this Spring, which when finished will be a very
commodious and handsome Church, haveing a Steeple,
and Chancel; to put forward this Church, I have taken unwearied pains, and expended not only what Money I could
Spare; but what I could get: yet am fearful considering
my further incapacity to help and ye presant distressing
Curcumstances of this Country, that after all, it will not
be fit for Service in some Years. another I mentioned as
intended to be erected this last Spring at New Preston, in
Kent. is laid aside until ye next Spring. on Christmas
Day, I opened the new, and handsome Church, at G. Barrington, with a nemerous Congregation; Administred the
Sacraments: of the Lord's Supper to about 15: and of bap-
tism to 4 Children: if the Society considers them as in my
Mission, I would take the liberty, (at their earnest importunity) to request a Bible, and Common Prayer Book, for
the Use of that Church; Mr Gideon Bostwick a Candidate
for holy Orders, continues to Read Prayers, and D^r
Warners Collection of Sermons to the People there; the
Dissenting Teacher seems highly exasperated, at the
Church People, and Me- and said he would write to the
Society, about something that has Offended him in one of
my Letters:---have Baptized 41 Children this last half
Year: and have faithfully endeavoured, to perform all
the Duties of my Office, to Each part of my Mission;
notwithstanding the Distances of Place, and Inclemency
of Seasons; to ye emaciating of my body, and lessening
my Support; and considering These Difficulties, I should

have rejoyced, with the Societys Liberty and Approbation; to have accepted, an Offer made Me, of removing to Heampstead; had not I, at the same time, been very conscious, my removal would have been greatly detrimental to the Interest of the Church, in these back Settlements. This solely induced me to refuse, and to remain here, where my Labour is fourfould, more; and my Income, not half so much: indeed where Parsimony only keeps me even with the world: however blessed be God, and thanks to the Society, notwithstanding my Difficulties, it rejoyces my heart, in being Instrumental in the propagation, of the just Principles, of the Gospel among a large body of People, where the wildest freaks of Enthusiasm, on the one hand; and professed Infidelity on the Other, in Degrees abound: That Allmighty God would continually strenghten the Hands, and Reward the Labour of all my generous Benefactors, is the fervent Prayer, of the honorable Societys, and Your

                    faithful and humble Servant,
New-Milford   Thomas Davies.
June 25. 1765.

P S. I hope my Letter of June 1764 came safe, wherein I informed, That we should be greatly rejoyced to have New Milford[,] Woodbury, Kent and New-Fairfield in one Mission; And Litchfield, Cornwall, and Sharon, with the Towns in ye Nothern part of the County in the Other, and Each Part Promise when that takes place to Pay 30£ Sterling pr Ann: Each: altho' I have not had the pleasure of hearing on that head any thing from England as yet:--

[Endorsed:] Read at a Committee Oct. 14. 1765.

[1765, July 15, Stratford]
May it please your Lordship,

I humbly take this Opportunity, with the utmost Gratitude, to acknowledge the Kindness of your Lordship's most condescending Letters of Feby 22d, both to the Clergy & me. Theirs I sent to them at their Convention, which I could not attend, by reason of the Distance & the badness of the Roads, & I hear they have also most gratefully acknowledged it in a joint Letter to your Lordship.--I am very glad your Lor[d]ship is pleased with the very worthy Mr Harrison's Account of the Clergy of this Colony, which I hope they will be the more emulous to deserve.

It is, my Lord, a kind Condescension in your Lordship that you are pleased to desire of me an Account of the State of Religion in these parts of the world. It is with much Difficulty that I write, having a trembling hand, so that I can be but brief.-- The true State of Religion in America, with respect to the several Denominations is this:-- The Independents, or Congregationalists, as they call themselves, here in New England, especially in the Massachusetts & Connecticut, without any regard to the King's Supremacy in matters of Religion, have established themselves by Law, & so are pleased to consider & treat us of the Church as Dissenters; but are miserably harrased with Controversies among themselves, at the same time that they unite against the Church.-- One great Cause of their Quarrels are the Arminian, Calvinistical, Antinomian & Enthusiastical Controversies, which run high among them, & create great Feuds & Factions, & these chiefly occasion the great In-

crease of the Church, at which they are much inraged, tho' they themselves are the cheif occasions of it.

As to the Presbyterians, my Lord, they chiefly obtain in the Southwestern Colonies, especially in those of N-York, Jersy & Pensylvania, where they have flourishing Presbyteries & Synods in full Vigor: while the poor Church of England in all these Colonies, is in a low depressed & very imperfect State, for want of her pure primitive Episcopal form of Chh-Government.-- We do not, my Lord, envy our Neighbours, nor in the least desire to disquiet them in their several ways. We only desire to be upon at least as good a foot as they, & as perfect in our kind, as they imagine themselves in theirs: & this we think we have a Right to, both as the Episcopal Government was the only Form at first universally established by the Apostles, and is moreover the Form established by Law in our Mother Country. We therefore can't but think our selves extremely injured, & in a State little short of persecution, while our Candidates, are forced, at a great Expence both of Lives & Fortune, to go a Thousand Leagues for every Ordination, & we are destitute of Confirmation & a regular Government.

So that unless we can have Bishops, especially at this Juncture, the Church, & with it the Interest of true Religion must dwindle & greatly decay, wyile we suffer the Contempt & triumph of our Neighbours, who even plume themselves with the Hopes, (as from the Lukewarmness & Indifference of this miserably apostatizing Age, I doubt, they have too much occasion to do,) that the Episcopate is more likely to be abolished at home than established abroad. & indeed, my Lord, they are vain enough to think that the Civil Government at home is it self, really better affected to them than to the Church, & even disaffected to that; otherwise, say they, it would doubtless establish Episcopacy here as it is there.-- Pudet hæc opprbria, &c--*

I humbly thank your Lordship for having said so much in our behalf in your very excellent Sermon before the Society-- Would to God a due notice might be taken of it! I do also most humbly thank you for your kind Prayers & Blessing, & beg the Continuance of them; nor shall I cease to pray earnestly for the long continuance of your Lordship's very important Life & Health, being truly my Lord, with great Veneration,

Your Lordship's / most dutiful & / most obedient Son / & very humble Servant
    Stratford in Connecticut   Samuel Johnson.
    N. England July 15- 1765.
P.S. Pray, my Lord, would there be any impropriety in it, if the Society as a Corporation should address the King that we may be provided for?

To my Lord of London [Bp. Richard Terrick].

*From Ovid's Metamorphoses, I, 758: "It shames us that these charges can be made...that they cannot be rebutted."

[1765, July 20, Norwalk]
          Norwalk in Connecticut 20 July 1765
May it please Your Lordship,

I write this Letter to beg Your Lordship's Direction concerning a Case of Conscience, which I am not able to solve.

The Case is This.

A Sailor married a Womon, and soon after went to Sea, and in the former War was taken by the Enemy and confined in Prison; a little time after his Capt was released, and supposed the Sailor, who was very sick when the Capt left him, to be dying: The Capt when he came home reported that the Sailor was dead. The wife Supposing herself to be a widow; married, three Years after her husband left her; Six Years after She was married She rec^d a Letter from him, being the first Notice She had, that he was alive. And three Years after this the Sailor came home, but he would not live with her, as She had Children by the last man, but none by him: so he went away Eight Years ago, and has never been heard of Since.

Now the man and Woman being in my Parish, desire to be admitted to the Lords supper; and are very worthy people, Except the Affair above mentioned. I earnestly beg the Advice of my spiritual Rulers, that I may know, whether I ought to admit them or not. If Your Lordship can attend to give me orders what I am to do in this Case, they Shall be carefully observed, by,

may it please Your Lordship, / Your Lordship's / most dutiful Son / and most obedient, / Humble Servant
Jeremiah Leaming.
Miss^y at Norwalk

[Leaming again wrote Bp. Richard Terrick concerning this affair in almost the same words on June 6, 1766.]

[1765, Sept. 5, Stratford]
Stratford, N. England Sept. 5. 1765.
My Lord,

The Bearer hereof is one Mr Giles of New-York of whom I gave some Account to the Society about the middle of last April, as a Person, the Clergy there tho't suitable to succeed Mr Ogilvie at Albany. -- He had learned considerable Latin in his Youth, but had intermitted other Studies, except Mathematics (as a School Master) in which he excelled, till about seven years ago, when he made himself known to me, & appeared to have a great Thirst after Knowledge, & desired my Direction about Books & Studies; & after some time, he was intent on the Study of Latin & Greek, that he might qualifie himself for holy Orders.

In order to this, he put himself under Mr Cuttings Direction in Latin & Greek, & under mine in Philosophy & Divinity, & made so good a proficiency, that he was admitted to the Degree of Master of Arts about two years ago, since which he has read many of our best English Divines, & made some beginning in the Hebrew; & He is very studious of the Holy Scriptures, as well as of a good Religious & Moral Character.

His Design was to offer himself for the Mission at Albany; but we hear Mr Brown is fixed in that Mission. And as Mr Inglis of Dover is chosen an Assistant Minister at New-York, & about moving thither, he is desirous that Mr Giles should succeed him there; where, I doubt not, he will be a faithful Missionary, if the Society shall think proper to employ him. I am, my Lord, with great Veneration, / your Lordships most dutiful / & most obedient humble Servant,
Samuel Johnson.
[The Rt. Rev. Richard Terrick, Bp. of London.]

[1765, Sept. 24, New Milford]
New-Milford ye 24 Sep: 1765.
Reverend S^r

I am credibly informed by some Persons, who lately were My Parishioners, but now removed to ye new settlements in New-Hampshire-Goverment: that the Lands sequestred for ye honorable Society in the New Towns lately patented by Governour Wentworth, and now surveying and setling, are so laid out by the Agents, as renders the Governor's Good Design insignificant, and the sequestration Useless:-- For in most of the Towns the Agents being Dissenters, They in the Division of the Land, contrary to all Rule in similar Cases, lay out (as the term is) the Societys Right or Lott, in some remote swamp; or rockey barren, and mountainous part; wherby the Society's Land is not worth Acceptance: And This they inform Me is ye Case in all the Towns they are acquainted with, Arlington excepted, in which one Jehiel Hawley, lately One of my Parishioners was Agent, who would I beleive very willingly, (being a very sensible and well disposed Man) without any reward, Assist in laying out and taking Care of the Society's Land, had he any Authority from the Society; for that purpose.

It is with pleasure I can Assure the honorable Society, that All my Parishioners, continue by Word and Deed, quiet peceable and loyal; whilst too many of the Dissenters of the various Denominations, by Word and Action Condemn and Oppose the late Act of Parliment: in a word there is such a Fermentation in the Country, as tho' some mighty Change was taking place: In public and private I have shewn the various Obligations we are Under, of Subjection and Obedience to our rightful and gracious Sovereign King George: &c: &c:

Mr Avery informs me this Mission is divided, with the additional Salary of 30£ p^r An: for which I humbly Thank the Society; yet at This Juncture it will be considerable Time before another can be sent Home for holy Orders. so long I must continue to Officiate to all the Places, and yet give up a part of my Income to a Candidate Reader. I would therefore bespeak the compassion of the hol. Society, and humbly request, that until a Missionary can come for the half of This Mission, I may have liberty to draw for ye whole Salary.-- An Account of This, or any thing else, that the hono^l Society, shall see fit to transmit, will be very acceptable to the honorable Societys and Your, most Obliged, Obedient,
and Humble Servant,
Thomas Davies.
P.S. I should be glad to be informed of the hono^l Society's Liberty, for the People of This Mission, sending a proper Person for the hono^l Society's Instructions, and for holy Orders.

[Endorsed:] Read at a Committee Jan. 13, 1766

[1765, Oct. 9, New London]
Oct 9. 1765
Rev^d & Good Sir

Your Letter dated ye 1st of last March was wth Pleasure receiv'd, & is gratefully acknowledg'd.

As to ye Indian Preacher, I presume, from my own Knowledge, to recommend him as a very worthy Person

--of unblemish'd Life & Conversation--as well qualified,
as most y͡t go over; tho' only taught in a private Academy,
where Indians alone are instructed. Shou'd he consent
to be epsicopally ordain'd, I believe 'twou'd be from a
Principle of Conscience; but now fear he will not, as my
Scheme is publish'd, w͡ch I shou'd have desir'd you to
conceal. S͡r W͡m Johnson & several of our Clergy wou'd
heartily recommend him, if ask'd, upon y͡t Occasion.

A Copy of y͡e Letter wrote by D͡r Bearcroft to me
in Chester I herewith send you, wherein you may easily
see a Deed was sent over, from which, tho' wrote by
y͡e Secretary, according to y͡e Society's Orders, I never
had any Advantage. I told you, my Venerable Patrons
were impos'd upon, & my yearly Loss very great. However neither y͡t, nor my fix'd Mission ever prevented me
from doing all y͡e Honor & Service I cou'd to our best of
Churches in distant, as well as adjacent Places.

What with y͡e Loss of Contributions, when absent, &
y͡e Expence of traveling to spread y͡e Gospel, I have many
Years spent several Pounds, having never receiv'd y͡e
least Recompence for my Trouble from y͡e People, neither do I think I ought to expect, tho' others practice y͡e
reverse.

My Acknowledgements & Thank[s] humbly & gratefully
present themselves, thro' your Admission, to y͡e hon͡le
Society for y͡e 10£:, for w͡ch w͡th my last half Year's Sal-
ary I shall, draw in Favor of M͡r Way Merc͡t here. As y͡e
Anabaptists abound in these parts, a few Pieces on y͡t
Subject, particularly Burkit's, who wrote on y͡e N. Testa-
ment--a few Common Prayer Books, & some of B͡p Kenn's
Tracts wou'd be very acceptable.

Since my last I have baptiz'd 18 Children--one Adult
Negroe--preach'd to a young Congregation 30 Miles off--
to a Tribe of Indians 30 Miles off (tho' but 12 out of my
way, as I went to see my Brother) Also I went to y͡e Island over an Arm of y͡e Sea, where, besides other Duties,
I baptis'd 3 Children--to another Tribe of Indians 15--to
another 8--& to another twice, 9 Miles off, at w͡ch latter
place I continued preaching both to Indians & other Congregations several times for two days; besides officiating
several times in our Jail & Neighborhood. I do truly say,
my Blessed Master's Work is my Delight, & while he
gives me Strength & Will, I'll spend & be spent.

I hear y͡e New-England Clergy have form'd some
new Scheme, as no Europeans, but one, living near y͡e
place of convening, above 200 Miles hence, were consulted or desir'd to attend, I hope 'twill not oblige y͡e
absent.

I'm very sensible European Clergy are unwelcome
Guests in N. England, & had not I, tho' alone, oppos'd
some of thier Designs, a Foreigner wou'd have had no
Business here. This cost me much trouble. I communicated y͡e Whole, to y͡r Predecessor, who was well
acquainted with Novanglian Cant (as he call'd it), commended my Resolution, & rejoic'd at my Success.

I pray, dear Sir, for GOD's sake, they may never
have any Power over us. [May] y͡e Constitution of our
truly Apostolic Church, & Instructions from the Venerable & Religious Society be my sole Directory. To these
I freely, conscientiously submit. I cou'd say much, &
were I present, wou'd: but who can stand before Envy;
w͡ch I have severely suffer'd by offending one Person,
tho' in an incumbent Discharge of Duty, & Obedience to
my Superiors Command.

My Brother, as well as I, are sorry he did not remove to Hamstead, seeing Westchester so near, is also
vacant. They wou'd have been very agreeable, only 7
Miles distant. Our pious Patrons have been pleas'd to
repeat their Promise of bringing us nearer to each other,
Opportunity presenting, & tho' I fear we have miss'd
this, & my Brother is asham'd to renew his Request for
Hamstead, yet we hope y͡e LORD will enable us to discharge our Duty faithfully, & so merit y͡e Continuance of
their Favor & y͡r Countenance.

'Tis something melancholy, as we are only two
Brothers & one weakly Sister, to be so far asunder in a
strange Land, & advancing Years. O y͡e ineffable, Comfort of good Relations, when visited by Sickness--on y͡e
Verge of Eternity! I have had some very good Offers,
but too far from my Dear Brother. But my heavenly
Father's Will, not mine be done.

I told you, S͡r, how rarely I see an Abstract &c,
w͡ch I hope y͡r future Direction will prevent & regulate--
I most heartily & sincerely thank you for y͡r kind Letters. May GOD reward y͡r temporal w͡th eternal Love, &
give me Grace to merit my Patrons Favor, & y͡r Interest,
w͡ch I'll study to deserve. Be pleas'd to present to them
y͡e Christian Love & Duty of theirs &,

Good Sir / Y͡r most oblig'd, hum͡le Serv͡t / & affectionate Brother in / Jesus Christ

Ma[tthew Gra]ves

New-London Oct͡r 9͡th 1765.

To D͡r Dan: Burton &c

[Addressed:] To / The Rev͡d Doctor Burton, Secre- /
tary to y͡e religious Society for propa / gating y͡e Gospel
in foreign Parts, in / Abingdon Street Westminster /
London

[1765, Oct. 9, New London]
    [Referring to the S.P.G. letter of appointment dated
     May 20, 1747, q.v.]
Rev͡d S͡r

The above is a true Copy; if my good Patrons wou'd
have it attested, it shall be done. Upon Encouragement
hereof I left England purely to do good in this Wilderness. I really had above £100 per an͞n in Chester; I
communicated my Design to his Grace y͡e Archbishop of
Canterbury, who sent my Letter & recommended me to
y͡e Society; from whom I desir'd to have a fix'd Mission,
& know what I was to depend upon: to which D͡r Bearcroft wrote y͡e above Letter. How much I am disappointed, you may jud[g]e. I have one half a quarter of
an Acre within a Rod; & one year w͡th another I have not
had £12 per A͞n in Contributions. I have complain'd
frequently, but never had any Redress--I have got some
Candidates for holy Order to lay it before y͡e Board, but
they own they have not done it. And now y͡t GOD has
put it into y͡e Society's heart to reflect upon my great
Losses, & you condescend to pity me, & comfort me, I
pray God continue to influence y͡r Hearts in my Favor.
I verily believe my People exert themselves in their
Contributions to y͡e utmost.

Were I to die to Morrow, I cou'd not, beside my
Household Goods, leave my poor weakly Sister £20.--

Whereas had my Expectations been answer'd I cou'd have left her some tolerable Support. We live as frugally as we can in a very dear Place. But my GOD is omnipotent, & my Savior's All-sufficiency my only & true Comfort. He will not leave us, nor forsake us. To gain ye House, y^t is eternal, & ye Treasure, y^t can never fail, is I trust, our sole Endeavor--our ultimate View. That You & I may meet & enjoy each other in those Pleasure[s], y^t shall never cease, is & shall be ye daily Prayers of

Rev^d & Good Sir / Y^r most obedient / most grateful Servt / & affectionate Bro^r in / JESUS CHRIST

N. London Octr 9th 1765   Matt Graves

P.S. Pray pardon my Prolixity. The LORD reward y^r Labors of Love to y^r unworthy Fellow Laborer in Christ's Vineyard!

To Doctor Danl Burton, Secretary to ye Religious Society

[1765, Oct. 22, Groton]

                    Groton in Connecticut Octr 22^d 1765
Revd Sir

The very Grievous Afflictions God in his wise providence hath been pleased to Visit Me with in depriving me of my Dear Husband Mr Eben^r Punderson by Death in Septr 1764 Did so greatly affect me as prevented my Acquainting the Venerable Society therewith myself,--I am now Compelled by the narrow Circumstances I am left in whereby I am deprived of those Comforts of Life I before Enjoy'd to Make my humble Petition to that Venerable Society who hath been so Bountifull In their favours to my Deceas^d Consort when living That they would be pleased to Compationate my present Distress (which Arises In a great Measure from Insolv^t Debt^{rs} & other Misfortunes) by bestowing upon me their Usual favour to the Widows of their Deceas^d Missionary's which will greatly relieve Revd Sr Your very

                    Affectionate Humble Servt
                    Han^h Punderson

[Addressed:] To / The Revd Dr Daniel Burton / In Bartlets Buildings, Holborn / London / Secretary To the Venerable / Society for the Propagation / of the Gospell &c--
[Endorsed:] Read at a Committee Mar. 17, 1766

[1765, Oct. 28, Stamford]

                    Stamford Connecticut
                    In New Englad Octob^r 28, 1765
Reverend Sir

I have this day drawn a Set of Bills for Twenty five Pounds Sterling in usual form, upon Edward Pearson Esqre Treasu^{re} of the Venerable Society, in fav^r of Mr Thomas Ellison Merch^t at New York.----My Parish is in a good state, I still meet with suitable Religious Encouragement in attending the Duty of my Extensive Mission. I Baptized last Half Year 32 Children, 2 added to the Communion. Sunday Augst 25 last I attended Divine Service in the New Church in the upper district of Salem, and preached to a numerous congregation, and gave the Communion to upwards of thirty Communicants, and

Baptized thirteen Children: I have for many Years performed Divine service Occasionally among them, in pure Compassion to their destitute Circumstances, & spiritual wants, without any temporal Reward.----At the Request of the most Charitable M^r St George Talbot, Still Zealous to encourage and Assist our Weak and destitute Churches, I lately went to Danbury, about 30 Miles distant, In company with the Rever^d Mr Leaming, where we had the pleasure of Meeting wth Mr Talbot and ye Revd Mr Lamson: and on the 16th Instant I Preached a Sermon at the Opening of their New Ch^h--w^h thro' Mr Talbots Assistance is Covered and Closed, with a Handsom Steeple, A good Congregation of People gave devout attendance, among whom were Many Dissenters, and some of best Characters among them. they are an Inquisitive People after knowledge, Serious and well disposed, but much divided of late in their Religious sentiments, thro' ye Corrupt Doctrines lately preach'd among them, whereby they are divided into three distinct Religious Assemblies, very Censorious and uncharitable toward each other. Cou'd the few Zealous professors of our holy Ch^h there be blessed with the more constant and settled Administrations of Religion, agreable to their wishes, it might greatly conduce to the interest of true Religion, and it's hopeful the most Rational & sober part among the dissenters, wou'd bethink themselves, and return to the Unity of that Ch^h--which their forefathers thro' mistaken Zeal endeavoured to pull down, and unjustifiable seperated from; and restore them to Peace unity and concord. I Preached a Lecture ye next day also in a private House of my Brothers who is a sober Zealous Dissenter, about 5 Miles distant from the Town (Danbury being the place of my Nativity) where we had also a much greater Number than was Expected to attend Divine service, and their devout behav^r and engaged attention, was highly agreable. Mr Talbot Returning with me, I waited upon him the Next week to North Castle & ye 24th Instant Preached a Lecture in the Ch^h there, to a good Congregation considering the short Notice, and Baptized sundry Children. Mr Avery happily Settled at Rye, tells me he shall be ready to afford them his pious Assistance as often as is consistant with his more immediate Cure.----In this time of general discontent & disturbance in this & ye other Provinces, portentious of Unhappy Consequences to their welbeing, I endeavour both in Publick and private to Inculcate the great Duty of Obedience & Subjection to the Government in being, and Steadfast Adhereance to that well tempered frame of Polity upon w^h this Protestant Ch^h of ours is built; a Constitution happily ballanced between Tyranny and Anarchy. I am not alone in the Opinion, that the Protection, support and encouragement of the Church in the American Colonies, is the highest Wisdom, even in point of Civil Policy, and the best Security of this peoples Allegiance, and Attachment to the Mother Country.----Permit me to Add, my Humble Duty to the Venerable Board, and Earnest prayers to God, for his blessing to accompany all their pious most Charitable designs. And with high Esteem, and Regards to your Self I Am Reverend Sir

    Your Most Obed^t Servt / and Brother In Christ
                    Ebenez^r Dibblee

The Reverend Doct^r Burton / Secret^r to the Venerable Society / for Propagation of the Gospel &c:--

[Addressed:] To / The Reverend Doctor Daniel Burton /
In Bartlet's Buildings Holborn / Secretary of the Venerable
Society / for Propagation of the Gospel In / Foreign Parts.
London
[Endorsed:] Read at a Committee Mar. 17. 1766

[1765, Dec. 26, New Haven]
          Connecticut, New-haven, December 26. 1765.
Revd Sir,
     Notwithstanding I am fixed in a most agreable situ-
ation, where I live peaceably with my own People, and in
perfect friendship with my Neighbours, the Dissenters;
and have had the happiness of Seeing a considerable Increase of this Church, which is now in a more flourishing Condition than ever it has been: Yet, tho' these are
pleasing considerations, there is one thing wanting, extreamly necessary, both to my comfort and happiness, &
to my further usefulness & continuance here, Viz: an Income Sufficient for the Support of my Numerous Famoly,
& to answer my other Necessary Expences, which by full
experience, with the most prudent managment, and best
Industrey of my Famoly, I have found my present one,
is not; and that without some farther Assistance I shall
soon be reduced to want; which, my People not being able
to give, having quite exceded their abilities in finishing
their Church, Building a Glebe House, and purchasing a
Small Glebe, for which they are Several Hundred Pounds
in Debt; I have no where else to apply my Self, but to the
Venerable Society for relief: And Since I have the Honour
and happiness of being in their Service, and must Stand or
fall at their pleasure, I would with all the earnestness I
am capable of using, and yet with the greatest Submission,
beg of them, in a Method they shall think best, to help me;
without which, I can truly say, I see no way how my Famoly shall be provided for, & the honour of my Character
maintained, for poverty and want will almost as certainly bring disgrace, as Vice & Immorality.
     There is no other Mission, that I know of, in which my
present allowance would not be equal to all my demands;
But here, as this is a place of as great Trade & Concourse
as any in the Government, and where by reason of my many
Friends, and acquaintance, with whose Company, wch cannot be escaped, I am quite overburthened, it falls very
short; my Incidental Charges being at least, a quarter
part as much as my Famoly ones; which has caused me
already to consume a considerable part of my little Estate; and must, so long as my circumstances are the same,
be Spending upon it till all that I have is gone: The consideration whereof fills me with much uneasiness, and
greatly unfits me for the discharge of the duties of my
Office.
     Having thus truly represented things, I submit the Mat-
ter to the Societies wise determination, trusting that according to their accostomed goodness, they will some way
or other help me; whose former Favours, I most thankfully acknowledge, and shall always endeavour so faithfully to Serve them, as not to forfit their continuance.
     In looking over the List of the Members of the Socie-
ty, in their latest Abstract, I was pleased to find Mr Enos
Alling amongst them, and am thankful to the Society for
the Honour they have done Him.
     He is truly a Worthy, Valuable, and good Man, firmly

Attach't to the Church of England, and a great Friend to
the Society; whose Interest & Credit, I doubt not but that
he will to the utmost of his Ability, promote; and thus
prove a Useful Member. And as a Testimony of his regards to that Venerable Board, for the honour they have
done him, and in Token of his future purposes, as occasion shall offer, he has told me that he will make a
present Benefaction of Ten Pounds Sterling, and pay it
to me, as part of my Annual Salary, as soon as the Society shall give me Orders to receive it.
     He has been a generous Benefactor to this Church.
By his influence and Money, it has grown into its present respectable State; and to him, I imagine, in a great
measure, is owing its present Existence.
     It may well be Said of him, he hath loved our Church;
And as it was of the Centurion, He hath built us a Syna-
gogue. Upon every Religious occasion, he hath contributed Liberally; And upon my coming into this Mission, when
the Church was about to purchase a Glebe, and build an
House upon it, to further the good Design, he Subscribed
£37-10- Sterling; and by his care and Managment, the
House has been finished.
     This Church flourishes, & is in Peace and Credit.
Some of the Dissenters of every Denomination, do almost every Sunday attend its Publick Worship; amongst
which have been those of the first Repute. Yesterday
the Chief Dissenting Minister of the Town, and almost
all the Gentrey, together with a great number of other
Dissenters, came to Church, and behaved with the utmost Decency.
     Since my last, I have Baptized one Adult, and a num-
ber of Infants. Only two New Communicants have been
added.
     I have Drawn by a Bill of Exchange Dated December,
25--1765 for £12-10 Sterling &c:----Who am, Revd Sir,
Your, & the Societies, / most Humble Servant
                                        Solomon Palmer.

[Endorsed:] Read at a Committee April 14. 1766

[1766, Mar. 25, Stamford]
                    Stamford Connecticut New England
                              March 25, 1766
Reverend Sir,
     Notwithstanding, the late unhappy tumult of the
Times, of which we hope soon to see a Period thro' the
Wisdom and Conciliateing temper of the supreem Legislative Power of the Kingdom; (for it appears Incredible
that an Internal Tax upon the Subjects of these Provinces,
sho'ud be the foundation of all those Publick disturbances)
My Parish continues in its Increaseing and flourishing
state. I Baptised last half Year, 42 Children, 4 Adults,
and four were added to the Holy Communion. I have this
Day drawn a set of Bills for £25 Sterling in usual form
upon Edward Person Esqr Treasu^r of the Venerable Society, In fav^r of Mr Richard Jackson Merch^t or Order,
Resideing in this Place. some Common Prayer Books,
Catechisms and other Pious small Tracts, is much wanted among the Poor of my Parish, and the destitu[t]e
Place[s] I Annully Visit, and wou'd be thankfully Accepted. by the Grace [of] God, I shall Continue with
diligence and fidelity to do the Duties of my Office [and]

to be as Extensively Usefull as I Can. Praying God to pro-
tect his Church, and succeed every Pious design of the
Venerable Board I Am with my Humble Duty; and Great
Respect to Your Self;

Reverend Sir / Your Most Obedient / Very Humble
Servt / And B^r

Ebenez^r Dibblee

The Revd Doctor Burton Secretary of the Venarable So-
city for the Propagation of the Gospel &c:

[Addressed:] To / The Reverend Doctor Burton / Secretary of the Venerable / Society for the Propagation / of
the Gospel in foreign Parts / Abbingdon Buildings / Westminster London
[Endorsed:] Read at a Committee May 12. 1766

[1766, May 28, Wallingford]

Minutes of Convention of Clergy of Connecticut Held at
Wallingford, Connecticut, May 28, 1766

May it please your Lordship,

We the Clergy of the Chh. of England in Connecticut,
in a volentary Convention, beg leave with all Humility to
recommend Mr. Abraham Beach, to Your Lordship, as a
proper Candidate for Holy Orders.

He has been educated in Yale College in this Colony,
has rec^d a Degree of Master of Arts, and made as good
profiency in Learning as can be expected in this Country.
He is well affected to the Constitution in Chh. and State,
and is of full Age for Holy Orders: And if Your Lordship,
upon Examination, finds him qualified for Holy Orders;
we beg he may be admitted thereto.

We understand the Rev^d Mr. Beach will give him a
Sufficient Title.

Next Convention to be at N. Haven on y^d Wednesday
in Oct.--

Mr. Newton to preach.
Mr. Scovil if in case of failure.
M. S. and Diblee to go to the Jersey--

[On the back of this paper is written:]
1. Voted; That a Letter be wrote to the Bishop of London to acquaint him concerning the Conduct of ye Chhs. in
these difficut times: and also concerning ye taking away
Children from the God Fathers.

2. That we are very desirious to unite with ye Clergy
of New Y. and ye Jersies.

[1766, ca. May 30, Litchfield]
Rev^d S^r

These will inform you, of the Death of ye Rev^d M^r
Davies, the Societies Missionary in Litchfield County,
who Departed this Life May the 12: 1766 to the inex-
pressable greif of his Family, and People; and as we
are Administrators, on the Estate of the Deceased,
have Drawn for half a year Salary; and ask the favor
of the venerable Society; that they would grant to the
Bereaved Widow and Fatherless Children half a years
Salary; after Mr Davies Decease; for their Support and

give us information, that we may draw for the Same and
you will ever oblige

your Obedient Humble Servants
Joel Hervey
Mary Davies

[1766, Aug. 25 and Oct. 22, New London]
Rev^d S^r

I hope my last came safe & ye Contents agreeable to
my Venerable Patrons, to whom be pleas'd to present my
Compliments & christian Love.

This Summer I twice visited ye Narraganset Indians,
& find them very capable of Instruction, & ready to embrace ye Christian Faith. I also visit ye other four adjacent Tribes; in each hoping there are many pious Souls.
As their Confidence is very great in me, I'll study to
improve it to their spiritual & temporal Advantage, tho'
my Endeavors are very laborious & attended with Cost;
besides y^t I preach without Notes to their feeble Capaci-
ties. They are all truly pitiable, being daily spoil'd &
plunder'd of their Lands, in wch Sr Willm Johnson privately informs me he designs to serve them.

My Hearers behave well, & are an Ornament to
their Profession. The Number of Communicants are y^e
same. I have baptiz'd, 14--one Adult--marry'd three
Couple--buried five Persons; & preach'd six Sermons,
having regularly read our uniform Service, in dissenting
Meeting Houses, since my last.

As ye Anabaptists abound (owing much to their Exemption from ministerial Rates) be pleas'd to send me
some good Pieces, besides Dr Wall's, upon y^t Subject.
I hear y^t one of ye Wesleys has publish'd an excellent
small Tract on infant Baptism against Dr Gill. If agreeable to my religious Superiors, I wou'd be glad of some
of them; & one of those, wrote by ye pious Mr Burket,
wou'd be very useful, in my humble Opinion, to each
Missionary. A few common Prayer Books wth ye Articles, & B^p Kenn's retir'd Christian are much wanted.
As You were pleas'd to favor me with ye two first Volumes of ye learned & truly orthodox Dr Berriman's Sermons, I wou'd be very glad to read ye rest of those excellent Discourses. Pray, S^r, order me some Abstracts
& appoint ye Number.

On ye 7th of this Instant, Aug^t, I rec^d y^r very wel-
com Letter dated ye 1st of last Ap^l, & will exert my
self faithfully to transact y^r truly charitable Intention.
The Directions of my Honble Patrons wth y^r friendly Advice shall always be gratefully acknowledg'd & conscientiously regarded by their &

Rev^d S^r / Y^r most obedient, / most oblig'd, /
hum^le Servt & aff^te / Bro^r in Christ

Matt Graves

N. London Aug^st 25th 1766

P.S. Since I wrote ye above Letter, I was sent for &
visited a place between 30 & 40 Miles hence--continued
there three days preaching to a very large & attentive
Audience--baptiz'd nine Children--church'd one Woman,
& founded & incorporated a Church, several openly declaring for our blessed, orthodox Establishment, at w^ch
ye bigotted presbyterian Teacher was so enrag'd, y^t he

sent me a long, abusive, defamatory Libel, wch I answer'd
by Silence. I am to revisit them within a few days, & hope
to present you wth an agreeable Account of my Proceedings.
I am

Rev^{d} S^{r}

N. L. Octr 22^{d} 1766.   Y^{rs} M Graves

I have drawn on ye Treasurer for ye last half Year, ending
ye 25th of last Sep^{r}.

[1766, Oct. 7, Stamford]

Stamford Connecticut New England
October, 7, 1766

Reverend Sir.--

With Pleasure, I can inform the Venerable Board,
As through the protecting care of Heaven, our Churches
have Rid out the late Storm and tempest, and something
of a Calm Ensues the happy Repeal of the Stamp Act;
without any undue Influence, there hath lately ben an
Accession of Sundry Heads of Families of Reputation in
Stamford to my Parish. whose Christian deportment I
doubt not will do Honour to their profession, and still
recommend the best of Churches more to the Esteem of
our Dissenting Brethren.----with whom we desire and
study to live, in Peace, (though it be difficult) as far as
we can with a good Conscience toward God and toward
man; i e, with that Dutiful Obedience and Subjection we
owe to Church and State. Principally through the Piety
and Charity of the Honourable Society, we have ben
brought to the knowledge and profession of one of the
best and most Apostolick Churches upon Earth; and we
hope to deserve their future Concern Support and Encouragement; notwithstanding the utmost Efforts of the
profest Enemies of our Religious National Establishment, to deprive us of it. We Envy not our Dissenting
Brethren, the full Enjoyment of their Religious Professions, worship and Church Government, but think our
selves very unhappy in being deprived of Equal Priviledge
for the want of the Appointment of a Bishop or Bishops to
Reside In the American Colonies; for the Ends of Ordination, Government &c'. and we flatter our Selves the Venerable Society will Interest themselves, with the Government in being, in our Favour, as far as in their Wisdom
they think proper; for the Establishment of Episcopacy
in such a manner as will support the Credit and Dignity
of the Office, and prevent its falling into Contempt. Our
Peacable deportment under the late Grievances, and
dureing the Popular Tumults, and Indignities offered to
the Government in Being; even at the Hazard of all that
is dear to us in Life; and for which we are Stigmatized
now with Oblique & Reproach, as Enemies to our Country
and the Liberties of the Colonies; we flatter our Selves
might Merit future Encouragement, Effectual safety,
Religious Liberty Protection and defence.----I Preached
One Sunday in August in the New Church in the Upper
District at Salem, to a Numerous Devoutly behaved Congregation, and gave the Holy Communion to about thirty
Communicants; and Baptized fifteen Children. In Compassion to their Circumstances, and the People of Ridge-
bury and Ridgefield who are Contiguous upon the borders
of Connecticut; Mr Leaming and I have Recommended to
Read divine service and Sermons to them, Mr Epinetus

Townsend, a very Exemplary, sober, worthy Young
Gentleman, graduated at Kings College in New York,
who is very Acceptable to the People. Whom we wish to
have Settled Among them, provided, upon their Qualifying themselves, they might be so happy as to Obtain the
Honourable Societies Encouragement. Co[n]tiguous to
Salem is Courtlands Mannor and Philips's Patten, where
Numbers of Poor People are Settled, and stand in great
need of proper Instruction; many already professing, and
others well disposed to our Holy Church. Notwithstanding
their distance, it being about 25 Miles to the upper district of Salem, as no other Missionary is Contiguous; to
be as Extensively Useful as may be, and in tenderness to
their Spiritual Wants, I have afforded them what Assistance I could consistant with the duties of my particular
Cure, for fifteen or Sixteen Years past; to the Prejudice
of my Family, my Income for twelve Years being too Inconsiderable to my Necessities.----Mr Townsend, who
I think is very deserveing, would think himself Happy to
be provided for at Salem, or Else where as the Venerable Society in their Wisdom shall think proper.----I Baptized the last Year twelve Adult Persons, Eighty Seven
Children, and Six added to the holy Communion.----I
have this day drawn a Bill of twenty five Pounds Sterling, in Usual form, in favour of Mr Thomas Ellison Ju^{r}
Merch^{t} at New York, Upon the Hon^{ll} Societies Treasurer Edward Pearson Esqr.----With Most Dutifull Respect
to the Venerable Board, trusting in God to protect and
defend his Church, to disappoint the Crafty devices
of her Enemies, direct the Counsels and prosper the
most Charitable designs of her Pious Benefactors; I
Am Reverend Sir, with great Regards to Your Self

Your Most Obed^{t} / Humble Servt / And Brother
In Christ

Ebenez^{r} Dibblee

The Reverend Doctor Burton Secretary to the Venerable
Society for Propagation of the Gospel &:

[Addressed:] To / The Reverend Doctor Daniel Burton /
Secretary of the Venerable Society for / Propagation of
the Gospel in Foreign / Parts. Abbingdon Street--West-
minster / London.
[Endorsed:] Read at a Committee Feb. 16. 1767.

[1766, Oct. 8, Stratford]   [Convention of Clergy]
May it please your Lordship,

We the Clergy of the Church of England, met in Convention at Stratford, in the Colony of Connecticut in New
England, humbly beg leave to return our most dutiful and
affectionate thanks to your Lordship for your very kind &
condesending Letter of May ye 10th in answer to what we
presumed to write to your Lordship.----As your Lordship rightly observes could those of us who were then together, have foreseen to what a height the Disturbances
then beginning to arise, would have reached, we should
hardly have thought of addressing his Majesty at such
a juncture, And we can't but acquiess in his Grace's &
your Lordship's reasons for not presenting it.----All
that we can presume to do, is to suggest in the humblest
manner, what we apprehend may be of importance to
the interest of Religion in these parts of the World, &

humbly submit it to his Grace & your Lordship, as the only proper Judges what use can with propriety be made of it; nor can we reasonably doubt of his Grace's or your Lordship's zeal & best endeavours, if it were possible, to procure for us the great & Important Event, that the Interest of Religion in America so vastly suffers for want of.----We cannot however, on this Occasion, but bitterly lament the deploreable Condition of this miserable degenerate & apostatizing Age, that it should not be in the power of his Grace & your Lordship & all the other friends to the Church & true Religion that are left, to have so much Interest & influence in it, as to procure a worthy protestant Bishop or two, in some of these Colonies; especially since the Roman Catholics are so happy as to be indulged with a popish one, & the Moravians with theirs, & the presbyterians &c, have the full enjoyment of their way of Government & Discipline, & the poor Church of England is considered by them with contempt, that she cannot enjoy hers,--nor indeed so much as a shadow of any thing that can be called Ecclesiastical Government; to say nothing now of the vast want of ordaining & confirming powers.--That there should be such a glaring partiality against the Church of England (one half of the national Establishment,) is quite beyond our Conception, it being, in our low apprehension, as utterly inconsistent with all true policy, as it is with Religious Liberty & the very being of any Church of England in America, & indeed even in England itself.-- We are sadly sensible, may it please your Lordship, that some of the principal Colonies are not desirous of Bishops, and we have heard that there are some persons of loose principles, nay some even of the Clergy of those Colonies, where the Church is established, that, (insensible of their miserable Condition,) are rather averse to them; but this is so far from being a reason against it, that it is the strongest reason for sending them Bishops: because they never haveing had any Ecclesiastical Government, or Order, (which ought indeed to have obtained above 70 Years ago) the Cause of Religion for want of it, is sunk & sinking to the lowest Ebb, while some of the Clergy, (as we are credibly informed but are greived to say it) do much neglect their duty, & some of them, on the Continent, & especially on the Islands, are some of the worst of men; and we fear there are but too many that consider their sacred Office in no other light, than as a Trade or means of getting a livelyhood, & many of the Laity, of course, consider it only as a meer Craft, & deploreable ignorance Infidelity & vice greatly obtains; so that unless ecclesiastical Government can so far take place, as that the Clergy may be obliged to do their duty, the very appearance of the Church will, in time be lost, and all kinds of Sactaries will soon prevail, who are indefatigable in making their best Advantage of such a sad Condition of things.----It is therefore we humbly conceive, not only highly reasonable, but absolutely necessary that Bishops be sent, at least to some of these Colonies, (for we do not expect one here in New England,) and we are not willing to despair but that earnest & persevering Endeavours may yet bring it to pass----We humbly beg your Lordship's Candor with regeard to the warmth, our Consciences oblige us to express, on this malancholly Occasion; and with our humblest Thanks to your Lordship for your

prayers and endeavours in our behalf; and our earnest prayers for the health & long life of his Grace & your Lordship, we beg leave, with the deepest Veneration & esteem, to subscribe ourselves, may it please your Lordship, Your

       Lordship's most dutiful Sons, and most
          Obedient humble Servants'.--
             Samuel Johnson, president

Stratford in the Colony   of the Convention.
of Connecticut, New-   Samuel Auchmuty
England Octob.ʳ 8.ᵗʰ 1766   John Beach
                    Joseph Lamson
                    Jeremiah Leaming
    Roger Viets   Solomon Palmer
    Bela Hubbard   Christopher Newton
                    James Scovil
                    Samuel Andrews
                    John Beardsley

[1766, Oct. 10, Stratford]

               Stratford Oct.ʳ 10. 1766
S.ʳ

   I herewith send you the little pittance of money collected for your School only from 5. or 6. of us, in my Church. I am ashamed it is no more, because I am greatly solicitous for the Conversion of the Heathen, & do think you are fallen on the right method, (if any will do without Miracles,) to bring it about.-- What makes people backward in these parts is, partly the great Scarcity of money; & partly a great prejudice aginst the Indians, occasioned by their having lately stolen, & barbarously abused, a child in these parts; & partly by an idle story industriously handed about, that you were seeking y.ʳ own profit by their labour. & among our people many alledged that you would prejudice the Indians against o.ʳ Chh. I have done what I could to answer those Objections.-- As to this last indeed, I am grieved & ashamed that the Heathen should be led to imagin or know that there are any differences, & different Sorts, among Xtians, than which, together with our vices, nothing can more tend to prejudice them against Xtianity, for which reason o.ʳ B. Saviour so earnestly prayed that <u>we might all be one</u>, &c--. <u>that the world may know that thou hast sent me</u>, to which this would indeed be a strong inducem.ᵗ that <u>we all say the same thing</u>, & that <u>with one heart & mouth</u> we join in glorifying our common heavenly Father.-- I say this then rather, because the Society on which we depend, are about contriving to set up two such Schools as your's in the Westward Colonies, & I pray God we may not teach different Doctrines.
   To which purpose I here inclose a little Catechism, which I hope you may approve of for the very first plain Rudiments, to see if we cant agree upon a common Catechism for the purpose, & desire you to let me know your Sentiments whether any thing needs to be added or altered to that which is Corrected, according to which I wish it to be reprinted. Some such thing translated into their language is very necessary.-- If my name would be a prejudice with any of y.ʳ friends let it be blotted out. but neither your public Catechism nor ours, would do well for our purpose, for the young Indians. To this Catechism I have annexed the first Rudiments of a little Grammar applied to the English Tongue, & may be applied to any other,

which may perhaps be of some use to your Design, especially for such as would get some Learning that may qualifie them for Teachers.-- I would write more but a bad tremor in my hand makes it very difficult: I hope you may pick out my meaning. & I pray God prosper y.ʳ faithful Endeavours to make the great Redeemer known to the Heathen! & remain dear S.ʳ

                    your sincere Friend & humble serv.ᵗ
                    Sa. Johnson.

To the Rev.ᵈ M.ʳ Wheelock, the Money £1.13.5.

[Addressed:] To / The Reverend M.ʳ [Eleazar] Whee-lock / at / Lebanon

[1766, Nov. 17, Stratford]
                    Stratford in New England Nov.ʳ 17.ᵗʰ 1766
May it please your Lordship
    The Bearer hereof is M.ʳ Richard Clark who being about to embark on a Voyage to London, for holy Orders, and a Mission from the Society, We beg leave to give Your Lordship the following Account of him, as our Testimonial in his behalf. He hath been bred up by worthy parents of the Church of England in a Zealous and firm Attachment, to the Doctrine, Government and Liturgy of that Church; as well as to the present Government. He was educated at Yale College in New Haven, and has been graduated Bachelour and Master of Arts, both there & at King's College in New York. He is a single Man above twenty five Years of Age, and as he has read service these two or three Years at several places to good Acceptance, and Always behaved with prudence, and Temper, and in a truly religious and virtuous manner, We have good reason to beleive that if your Lordship shall think proper to Ordain him, and the Society to employ him, he will prove a Worthy and Useful Missionary. We are my Lord with great Regard.
    Your Lordship's / most dutiful / & most obedient humble Servants

                                        Samuel Johnson
    N.B. the persons that have   John Beach
signed this Letter, are a Com-   Joseph Lamson
mittee appointed to do it by the   Jeremiah Leaming
Clergy in Connecticut.   Ebenezer Dibblee
                                     Richard Mansfield

[Endorsed:] Read at a Committee Feb. 16. 1767.

[1766, Dec. 15, New Haven]
                    Connecticut, Newhaven, December 15- 1766.
Rev.ᵈ Sir,
    Your Letter of the 26.ᵗʰ of May last, I have received, but that of the 7.ᵗʰ of December, which you therein mention, has failed coming to hand.
    I have been much benefited by the Gratuity of Ten Pounds,--which I have drawn for by a Bill Dated September the 25.ᵗʰ 1766. And by the present of M.ʳ Allings's Benefaction, which according to the Venerable Societies desire, he has paid into my hands: For both which, I take this opportunity to return them my most Sincere and hearty thanks. But after all, I am not able, (my

Expence being So Enormous) to maintain the honour of my Character and Support my Famoly here in credit: Therefore, having the Societies consent, and Doctor Johnson's advice, I've concluded to return again to Litchfield; (from whence I was very unwilling to remove) and relinquish this Mission at Christmas: hoping for Some alteration in that Mission, for as it now Stands the division is quite unequal; Great Barrington being 35 miles distant from Litchfield, Sharon 23, Cornwall 13, and Goshen 8, and the way to each very bad: Whereas on the other hand, Roxbury Church is but 7, and a new Church in Kent 7 miles distant from Newmilford and the Road to each pretty good; Sharon therefore at least, ought to be Annexed to Newmilford Mission, it being but 25 m: distant from Newmilford; and Goshen to Litchfield, to w.ᶜʰ it is contiguous; where there is a greater number of Episcopal Professors than at Sharon: which, when done; Litchfield Mission will be the most fatigueing; Yet there will be but little more than half the duty to be performed in it, that lay upon me when I was there, & the Mission remained entire: So that notwithstanding Some Bodily Disorders attending me, I presume I Shall be able, with this division to perform with pleasure the Duties that Shall be incumbent upon me; which if made, I am perswaded would be for the interest of Religion, and the Benefit of the whole: But if it must remain as it is, the Church at Litchfield, which is the oldest in the County, & consists of as regular, Steady, and well disposed Members as any among us, will be quite discouraged, Sink in her credit, & be triumphed over by the Dissenters, because, by reason of the great extensiveness of the Mission, She can but Seldom have Preaching on Sundays, and Goshen, where upon due encouragment, there is a most promissing appearance of a great encrease of the Church, none at all; and so of course must dwindle into nothing. These People being late Conformists,--and living far up in the Countrey, where Prayer Books are not to be had, and meeting together constantly on Sundays to worship God according to the Liturgy of y.ᵉ Ch.ʰʰ of England, have desired me to request a present from the Society, of a few for them. And the Same favour, I would beg leave to request w.ᵗʰ respect to Great-Barrington, who are Still farther to y.ᵉ Northward. This would be a mighty encouragment to these People; and I think it greatly behoves the Venerable Society, to do every thing they can, to forward the growth, & Encrease of the Church here; as it tends to make better Christians, more Loyal Subjects, and better Members of Society than other Professions among us do; for Notorious it is, the Professors of the Church of England, in this Colony, in y.ᵉ late Tumults & Commotions, occasioned by the Stamp Act, have distinguished themselves by a quiet and peaceable behaviour, and as far as I can find, very few, if any of them have been concerned in any of the Mobb's, or Riotous proceedings which have happened in Consequence of it: But this is a Subject too delicate to be dwelt upon, I shall therefore dismiss it, by only Saying, I wish the Disposition of our Dissentors, with respect to the Authority of the Brittish Parliament, as it relates to them, and the Civil, & Ecclesiastical Establishments, was as well known in England, as it is here.
    As the Venerable Society allow Ten Pounds worth of Books to every Mission for a Library &c: I hope they

will not in this respect, be unmindfull of Litchfield, the first Episcopal Church in the County, who laid the foundation for a Mission there more than tweny Years Since, by purchasing an hundred Acres of good Land for a Glebe, & giving it to the Society. And the Seeds of Infidelity, being lately, by an Arch Infidel, Sown in that County, So that Some amongst them begin boldly to dispute the truth, and Divine Authority of the Sacred Scriptures; That I might be furnished with Arguments against them, by whom I know I shall be often attacked, I would request of the Society, the Priviledge of Some Authors, who have best, & in a most Compendious way, confuted those unhappy Principles.

A most agreeable Harmony has Subsisted between me and this People, ever Since my first coming among them; who have treated me with all the respect that becomes the Relation I have Stood in to them: And as we have lived together in love and peace, So we Shall part, I would therefore recommend them to the Societies further Notice and Care; Whishing Success to their most Pious, & Charitable Designs; Who am; with great Respect, Rev^d, Sir,

                    Your, and the Societies most
                         Dutiful & Humble Servant,
                              Solomon Palmer.
N:B: I have Leland's view of the Deists: Him against Tindal I would particularly ask for.   S: P:

For the Revd Doctor Burton.

[Addressed:] To / The Reverend Dr Burton Sec^ry. / To the Society for Propagation of the Gospel &c^a / In Abingdon Street / Westminster
[Endorsed:] Read at a Committee Mar. 16. 1767.

[1767, Mar. 24, Middletown]
Revd Sir,

The Cause of the Church in America is so sacred and interesting a Point, that every faithful Friend to it, who even ventures to wish himself able to contribute the least in its favour, discovers a well affected Zeal to express his Affection, and intreat the Promotion of it. This indeed more evidently appears in the Clergy, where it ought to appear; having the Concurrence of all, from whom the best Wishes, and their religious Needs in the present imperfect State they enjoy the Church, can only be expected to strengthen and enforce the common Plea; and also the adjuvant Agency of others, that are conspicious enough to afford some Encouragement from their Endeavours. Spirited by that ardent Affection for the Church, which the Faith of the invaluable Treasure She contains in her divine and apostolic Authority and Constitution, and the wholesome Doctrins She dispenses, in the Language and Genius of the Scriptures, animates: the Clergy of several of the Provinces have respectively transmitted Addresses to the Throne, and some of the chief Dignitaries of the Church, and the incorporate Society, for an american Episcopate. To engage as extensive an Interest in the Affair as might be practicable, Particulars have thought it expedient, and have applied to such Persons as might, and from whom they have had good Grounds of Hope would, be useful in a Cause so greatly beneficial to us, and the Act

so highly charitable in them. Solicitous to bear a Part in every Effort of this kind, joint as well as seperate; I take the Freedom to propose the Subject to you, as what, I am persuaded, must be esteem'd by you sufficient to merit your closest Attention. The Cause is sacred to the Honour of God, and the Souls of Men: we also apprehend it so to the Health of the Constitution; a Consideration proper to be attended to in these distant Parts of his Majesty's Dominions: and what is conceived may be advantageously improved, as the Arguments in Favour of it, may be more pointedly urg'd and enforced upon the Minds of different Persons as they shall be inclin'd to regard the Church, in a religious, or civil View, or both together. Your Connections with some of the Nobility, and with his Majesty's Chaplains, is apprehended to place you in a Situation kind to this Purpose: and this cherishes Hopes of your Readiness and Ability to be useful among those in this particular Business.

If the important Affairs of the establish'd Church could be properly laid before, and submitted to, the Consideration of the Duke of Chandois and the Earl of Carrnarvon, in a Point of View just and necessary, their Interest in the Dignities & Prerogatives of the Crown, and the royal Government of the Kingdom, exclusive of a pious Regard to the true Church of Christ, might possibly excite their Deliberations, and lead them to do that essential good Service, their superiour Discretion may deem practicable, to a Cause that supplicates every charitable Aid and Assistance; and which is impregnated with such Principles, as is most likely, in its Fruits, richly to reward the Exertions of those, in the Security of their Dignity and Peace, who labour to promote it. By such an Attempt, executed by you, as shall appear judicious and suitable, it is imagin'd may be discovered, how they are dispos'd, or by that Means, may be stir'd up to a Disposition, previously languid and wanting; and also what Notice and Help, we in these Parts may expect or receive from that Quarter. Upon Tryal, if any good Encouragements are offerd, that will give Licence for an importunate and respectful Address, I dare venture to say, it will be most eagerly embrac'd; and you yourself be waited upon in a Manner more respectable. -- Should you think it proper to do this, it is most earnestly to be wish'd, you would also use your Endeavours to influence the rest of his Majesty's Chaplains, to bestir themselves among the Circle of their respective Acquaintance, to render the Cause diffusive, and spirit as many as may be, seriously and conscientiously to weigh the sacred suffering Cause of the Church of God, which even a cursory Reflection will openly shew how it needs must do here; while we are in a State imperfect, and destitute in a great Measure of that Office and Administrations, which our Lord has appointed in his Church.

It must be suppos'd they, agreeable to the Divine Commission they have received in our most excellent Church, were led to do holy Service at her Altar, from the Dictates and Persuasions of a well directed Conscience: how then, with Deference I observe, can they, in the Faith of Christ's Authority, administer in her Appoinments, as faithful Stewards, unless they extend their Attention and Service to her general Interest, where She is propagated under the Protection of his Majesty's Government? As the Faith is founded on the Christian Constitution, and the Cause is common, not confin'd to this

or that particular Place or Congregation, the Ministers of our common Lord, owe a general Respect to accommodate all, however dispersed, for the Advancement of that Religion, in the Orders that support it, which they think expedient for themselves to embrace.

The Earnestness of my desire, makes me the less reserv'd in beseeching you to do all in your Power in this Case. And there is no small Cause for such a Desire, as it is apprehended, that not only the Church, but even the Well Being of the civil Polity in America, depends in a great Measure, upon the Settlement of Episcopacy here: for republican Principles in Religion, naturally engender the same in civil Government, which of late have been avowedly very rife in these Parts, and have appeared in open and alarming Light, in many melencholly Instances. indeed Sir, if some Methods are not taken more effectually to fix and confirm, the Church here, which nothing but sending a Bishop will do, Things wear a Face, that will bear a shrewd Conjecture, that Opposition and Insolence will grow so sturdy, as, by the Help of the Disaffected with you, which as they always have been, so they ever will be, ready to afford, under the Aid of their Brethren of Scotland; to bring even the Church & Bishops in England into Danger. This, however extravagant it may at first appear, the more Discerning have fear'd from the Spirit on [?at] Work.-- In these Circumstances let me beg you to consider also, how many thousand Souls really languish for lack of Vision, or spiritual Food, in this low Ebb of the Church; and then you will assuredly, be sufficiently sensible, with how much Propriety we implore, and how much christian Charity presses you, and every one, assiduously to use the best Services, in behalf of our Exigency, which so clearly recommends itself, by every possible Urgency.-- I am

Reverend Sir.
Your humble Servant
and Brother.
Middletown in Connecticut
March 24th 1767   Abraham Jarvis.

The Revd Alexander Jacobs.

[1767, Mar. 25, Stamford]
Stamford Connecticut in
New England March 25th, 1767.
Reverend Sir

I have this day drawn a set of Bills for twenty five Pounds Sterling upon Edward Pearson Esqr, Treasur of the Honll Society &c: payable at thirty days sight, In favour of Mr Richard Jackson Mercht, lately resideing in this Place.----Please to accept my grateful Acknowledgements to the Venerable Board, for the Common prayer Books, a number of the Englishman directed in the choice of his Religion, and other pious small tracts, they were pleased to send me. they were soon distributed, and thankfully accepted, by such as wanted either ability or oportunity to provide for themselves.----Thro' the divine blessing on my labours, I am encouraged to persevereance in Duty, with the more chearfulness and Alacrity, from the good peaceable religious State of my Parish, the still frequent Accessions to the Church, from a thourough conviction of the Excellency of its Doctrine Worship and Government; and their more Zealous Atten-

tion to their Christian Duty, manifest, by the Increaseing Number of devout Communicants:----I Baptized last half Year, Seven Adult persons, three of whom were white, and four black; Forty three Children; Admitted six New Communicants.----Every repeated Effort to confirm our dissenting Brethren in their prejudices against our holy Church, seems to fail of its intended effect; disposes many to a more free enquirry after truth, and terminates in the growth of the Church.--In Consequence of the removeal of the worthy good Mr Davis by Death; the professors of the Chh at Sharon, about 75 Miles distant, by their Chh Wardens, Requested my attention to their destitute Circumstances. I made them a Visit, and Preached there in a fine Church newly built, almost finished, on thirsday ye 20th of Novembr last, a Colony thanksgiveing day, to a numerous devout Congregation; also the sunday following, and gave the holy Eucharist to about thirty Communicants, who behaved in a most Christian devout manner. I also Preached a Lecture about 8 Miles distance, on the borders of New York Province, where the poor people, needful of Instruction, have no settled teacher of any denomination, Except a Moravian occasionally resideing, whose Ministry but few attend. upon earnest Sollicitation, I preached also a Lecture at Salsbury an adjacent Town to a considerable Congregation; in which several places, I Baptised, two white Adults, four Black; seventeen Children white, one Black. Dissenting Ministers are Settled in the Towns of Sharon and Salsbury, but the professors of our holy Chh can by no means be reconciled to attend their Instructions; and no wonder as many of their own People are dissatisfied with their Doctrines, and Intemperate Zeal.----The state of Religion there, and upon the Borders of New York Province is truly deploreable, for want of more regular Instructions, and Stated Administration of Divine Ordinances. and the good People Assured me, they wou'd willingly Contribute to their utmost, if they cou'd meet with any Charitable Assistance, to enable them to attain their End. I there heard of Mr Palmers removeal to Litchfield; but that being abut 20 Miles from sharon, and a bad Road, the People can expect no Assistance adequate to their Spiritual Wants. and from a Minister at New milford they can Expect less, that being 30 Miles distant. Mrs Davis, removed under the protection of her Father, Mr Joel Harvey at Sharon, desires me to give Advice to the Venerable Society, That the Books, or Library given to Mr Davis, for his Use only, belonging to New Milford Mission, she had deposited in the Chh Wardens hands there, to be kept in reserve for a Successor, not knowing what better to do with them.----With Humble Duty to the Venerable Board, and all due Esteem and regard to Your self,

I Am Reverend Sir / Your most Obedt / Humble Servt / And Brother in Christ
Ebenezer Dibblee

The Revd Doctor Burton Secretary of the Venerable Society for Propagation of the Gospel &c:--

[Endorsed:] Read at a Committee June 8. 1767

[1767, Apr. 18, New London]
Good Sr
Your's of ye 5th of last February I receiv'd ye 16th

of this Inst., & am heartily thankful to Gd for inclining &
enabling me to be serviceable to ye poor Indians, & also
gratefully acknowledge ye Venerable Society's Notice of
my Attention. My Duty to GOD & my King are ye Springs
of my Endeavors, which, as they shall not be wanting, I
persuade my self, will conduce, to ye Interest of their
Souls, & their stronger Attachment to our Church & his
Majesty's Goverment. May they both grow, as ye Lilly,
& smell, as Lebanon! The last Books were very acceptable; especially I thank you for ye Black-smith--ye best
Piece, yt ever appear'd here for staggering & silencing
all Dissenters--many are their Confusions, wch a Book,
call'd ye Seabrook Platform, lately reprinted at ye Expence of our Colony, has much aggravated. The Power
therein to ye Teachers is highly offensive to their Hearers. The inclos'd is an Original--a Specimen of their
Jealousy, prevailing every where in these Parts. I leave
you, Sr, to remark. I'll endeavor to out-preach them &
out-live them. And tho' I tenaciously adhere to our Doctrin & Disciplin, I am invited into & often accept of their
Pulpits.

I lately spent a Week upon Long-Island; but parochial
Avocations demanding my Attendance, must soon revisit
it & an adjacent Island, whither I am requested to bap-
tize & preach. I preach to, & visit all Denominations.
I lately prepar'd for & administred Baptism to a young
Woman (& her Child) of Credit & Fortune, brought up in
Quaker-principles, who, with her Husband, educated a
Dissenter, comes constantly to Church, & behave very
devoutly. The Poverty of my Parishoners hinders ye
Enlargement of my Church & therefore of my Hearers.
Since my last baptiz'd eight--buried three--my Com-
municants ye same.

I have drawn upon ye Treasurer for last half year's
Salary in favor of a Gentleman of New-York. My Duty &
Christian Love wait upon my religious Patrons, whose
Designs & Commands, the LORD enabling me, shall be
zealously & conscientiously prosecuted by their &
                    Good Sr
                         Yr most oblig'd humle Servt
New-London   & Affectionate Brother in
Apl. 18th 1767   Christ
P.S.   Matt Graves
The narraganset Indians having been deluded by an art-
ful, whining, canting Fellow, have not accepted your
pious Offer; but I hope ye Goodness of ye Society will
not cast them off: As they are fond of my Doctrin, &
desirous of my Advice, I hope their Eyes will be open'd
to see into ye Delusion.

To the Revd Doctor Burton   London

[Endorsed:] Read at a Committee Aug. 17.

[1767, Apr. 20, Westminster]
Revd Sir,
    I have recd your letter of the 8th of Decr last, & have
the satisfaction of informing You, that the grateful sense
which You express for the Socty's last favour, & the Acct
which You send of the good disposition of your People is
very acceptable; but am sorry that You think, You stand
in need of a good Solicitor at our board, who has perfect

knowledge of the circumstances of your station: The Society are not unacquainted with the state of your Case, nor
in the least inattentive to it; & heartily wish, that their
circumstances would enable them to provide Missries
throughout the whole British Empire of America, which
by its Extent calls for more & more Ministers daily: But
as their Income is far too scanty for so extensive & beneficial a Scheme, & the impropriety of crowding a dispro-
portionate number of Missries in one Province, while others have scarce any at all, hath been frequently insisted
upon by friends as well as Enemies; this therefore necessarily restrains them from doing many things, which they
most heartily wish: However, I should be glad to know exactly, what allowance the Gentlemen of your Parish give
You annually, & what other profits & advantages You have.
I am,
                    Your Affectionate Brother
                       & humble Servant
Abingdon Street,   D Burton.
Westminster
April 20th 1767.

[Addressed:] To / The Reverend Mr Jarvis / at Middletown / in Connecticut / New-England

[1767, May 20, New York]
        To the Wardens, Vestry & Congregation of
            St Peter's Church Spotswood--
Gentlemen,
    The Bearor hereof, Mr William Frazier, having of-
fered himself to Us, the Clergy of New York & New Jersey
in voluntary, united Convention assembled--as a Candidate for Holy Orders, & produced ample Testimonials of
his good Life & Conversation, & desiring that we would
mention him to the Venerable Society as a Person preparing himself for their Service, & that till the Society's
Pleasure should be known, we would direct him to some
proper Place, where he might be of Use, & exercise himself in reading Prayers & Sermons--the Convention having
taken the Premises into deliberate Consideration, unanimously agreed to recommend Mr Frazier to the Society
accordingly, & as your Church is now vacant, they do also
recommend him to you to read Prayers & Sermons in your
Church, till it shall be proper for him to go Home-- You
will observe that it is not at present designed that he be
your Missionary, as perhaps another worthy Gentleman,
now in England may be appointed; but if that should not be
the Case, & Mr Frazier prove agreeable to you, we shall
gladly give you all the Assistance in our Power in bringing about the Settlement of such a deserving Person among
you-- With the most ardent Prayers for the Prosperity of
your Church, we are, Gentlemen,
                    Your sincere Friends,
New York,   & humble Servants
May 20, 1767.
                         Richd Charlton President
    R McKean   Samuel Auchmuty
    Charles Inglis.   Isaac Browne
    Harry Munro.   Jeremiah Leaming
    Leo. Cutting   Myles Cooper.
    Saml Provoost   John Ogilvie
    Saml Bennett.   Samuel Seabury

[1767, Oct. 9, New Milford]

New Milford Oto^{br} 9th. 1767

Reverend Sir,

As Mr Hubbard will take his Appointment at New Haven, if the Society do not provide for him at Guilford; so according to the Society's Order, I came to New Milford, and the People have kindly received me: as a Missionary was, as much wanted here, as in any Place.

I have not yet been able to take an Account of the Number of Families professors of the Church; or of the Communicants, but as soon as I have, shall transmit it to the Society.

Since I came to the Mission, (which was the first of last June) I have baptized 26 Infants and one adult. There is at present a very hopeful Prospect of my being serviceable in the Mission; as several have conformed to the C^{hh} since my being here.

The new C^{hh} has been lately dedicated, a Sermon suitable to the Occasion: was preached to a numerous Audience. a new folio prayer Book is much wanted in S^d C^{hh} as the old one is almost gone to Peices, & for the same we shall be very thankful to the Society.

      I am Reverend Sir your, & the Society's
           faithful Missionary, & most obedient hum^{le}
           Servt

To   Richard Clarke
Doc^r Daniel Burton.

[Endorsed:] Read at a Committee Jan 11. 1768

[1767, Oct. 19, Simsbury]

Simsbury Octob^r 19th 1767..

Worthy, rev^d Sir

I have not yet found Time to finish copying the Piece which I promised to send you; however, I have begun it and hope to finish and convey it to you within a few Weeks; perhaps when you shall see it you will think the Subject bad or trifling, perhaps think the Performance mean, or the Arguments sophistical; if you think either of these the case I can't help it; all I can say is that the Affection & Esteem, which I deservedly have for you induced me to write it as well as I could.

I shall take as a Favor that you will become acquainted with Forward, Hilyer, and Cossit, Collegians, the two latter educated in the Church, the former a good Friend, all three worthy young Gentlemen and likely to become useful to our Fraternity.

It would perhaps be well to invite these Young Gentlemen to your Lodgings, when you have Leisure and confirm them (especially Cossit & Hilyer) in the Principles of the Church and encourage them to lead the rest of their Lives according to their good Beginning; you will find them tolerably knowing according to their Age and Advantages; and should it please God to bring them safe to their first Degree I shall be glad to get them immediately recommended for holy Orders, which makes it necessary that some of my Brethren should be acquainted with them.

Our Bro^r Abr^m B--ch is returned safe. The first Sund. after his Return he went in the Forenoon to the South-Hartford Meeting in the Afternoon to the North (a fine Improvement of his Time!) when he might have gone to Church at Middletown 14 Miles or to Simsbury 10 Miles.

He has now been in Hartford more than 3 Weeks, but has not visited his Classmate Peters, or Your Classmate Viets, but has taken much Pains to visit many Dissenters; indeed I would not blame him for visiting Dissenters, would he give some Share of his Time to his own Brethren. Br^r B--ch has many good Properties but in these Things he cannot be commended. We cannot hope to see a Church built at Hartford 'till a worthy Set of Men rise up who will not go to hear Dissenters preach, nor have any Thing to do with Dissenters; and whether M^r B's Conduct is promotive of such laudable Zeal, judge Thou. M^r B's good, moderate Temper, penetrating Genius & remarkable Scholarship make one the more sorry that he cannot be more sincerely & earnestly engaged in the Cause of the Church.

I flatter myself that You will make very good Progress in your holy Function at Newhaven, & will have the Happiness to see your Congregation increase. I wish and desire & pray (if it be not too meddling) that your good Parishioners may be persuaded to keep both their Glebe Houses.

I hope the next News I hear from you will be that you are happily married; Therefore, wishing Yourself, your Spouse and all your Friends God's Blessing

I remain / Rev^d, good Sir / Your most loving Bro^r / And humble Servt

                    Roger Viets.

Revd Bela Hubbard N. Haven

[The people referred to are Abel Forward, Andrew Hillyer, Abraham Beach and Rene Cossit. Taken from the Hist. Mag. of the P. E. Church, III (1934).]

[1767, Oct. 21, New London]

Reverend Sir

As your's of ye 5th of last Feby was thankfully receiv'd, I hope mine of ye 18th of Ap^l following came safe to hand. I am still going on in my Ministry, & hope my Labor is not in vain. I have within twelve Months rode above 300 Miles to one Place, (besides others I frequently officiate at) where, as I told my Venerable Patrons, I had united two small Congregations, & can, wth Thanks for divine Assistance, assure y^m, y^t every time I visit them, I gain daily Additions to our Church. They are fond of our Disciplin, much more of our Apostolic Doctrins.

It's as true, as observable, tho' ye Dissenters have been bred up in ye inexplicable, unedifying Labyrinths of Predestination, yet they admire Subjects of universal Redemption, & ye comfortable Invitations of an irrespective Savior.

I meet wth great Opposition from some of their Teachers in Middlehaddam & Mudus; ye Teacher of ye latter [Dr. Boardman] told me, in much Warmth & ignorant Zeal, I had no business to come into any of their Parishes without their leave, & prov'd it from St Paul, saying--he built not upon another man's Foundation. I told him of his Abuse of Scripture, & ye Authority I acted under, y^t all their Rights & Privileges were secur'd to them by our Church--y^t I deriv'd my Power for preaching in New-England from our King & Parliament (who he said made Bishops & Ministers) & y^t he must not expect y^t ye Master wou'd ask leave of ye Servant.

The religious Society may depend on my unshakeable

Perseverance in their Direction, & yͤ incumbent Duty of my divine Master, & yͭ nothing shall intimidate me from preaching yͤ everlasting Doctrins of Jesus Christ.

If yͤ Society pleas'd, I wou'd be glad they wou'd send some Essays upon universal Redemption, lately publish'd by one Smith, whose Arguments are illustrated from our Articles & Homilies. As Predestination & Anabaptism are yͤ general Doctrins here inculcated, I presume, yͭ Essay of Smith & Westly, on infant Baptism against Gill wou'd be very serviceable to undeceive yͤ Ignorant, & enlarge our Church, to wͨʰ yͤ nervous Black-smith greatly contributes. [He here refers to the Blacksmith's Letters.]

I baptiz'd one Child at Middlehaddam & four here since my last--buried two Corpses my Hearers, tho' poor, are enlarging my House, & Love & Peace rule in our Society-- my Communicants yͤ same.

I have drawn for my last half Year's Salary in favor of Mͬ Stewart, our Collector, who with his Lady & Servants attends our Service, wͨʰ yͤ late Collector, being a Quaker, did not.

My christian Love, Gratitude & Complements wait upon my pious Benefactors, whose Favors I thankfully acknowledge from your memorable Goodness, & whose Instructions I'll endeavor to obey. That yͤ Spirit of GOD may direct & preside over all yͬ Designs, is, as in Duty bound, yͤ sincere, constant Prayer of their &

Revᵈ & Good Sͬ

Yͬ most oblig'd

New-London Octͬ 21ˢᵗ   most thankful &
          1767   humˡͤ Servͭ
                                                    Matt Graves

P.S. I hope you receiv'd yͤ original Manuscript directed to me, when at Middlehaddam

To the Revᵈ Doctor Burton,
Secretary to yͤ religious Society &c

[Endorsed:] Read at a Committee Dec. 14. 1767

[1767, Nov. 20, New London]
Revᵈ & Good Sͬ

The Indian, who presents this Letter, is of the Narraganset Tribe, whom, for his Prudence & Sobriety I doubt not to recommend to yͬ Notice & Regard. He is, tho' young, sent over with full Power from yͤ best & Majority of yͭ Tribe to complain of yͤ Abuses of yͤ Assembly of yͭ Government, yͤ Affront offer'd to Sͬ William Johnson's espistolary Advice, & yͤ Disloyalty publickly enacted & given to his Majesty's peremptory Directions & Commands at St James's yͤ 9ᵗʰ of Decemͬ 1761, intitled--Additional Instructions concerning yͤ Indians in North-America &c.--wͨʰ were never regarded, but shamfully suppres'd, & whereof I had been ignorant without Sͬ William's Benevolence.

I declare, Sͬ, unless yͭ Tribe is reliev'd from yͤ cruel Votes of yͤ Assembly, wͨʰ yͤ Bearer has a true Copy of, they must seek their Bread in desolate Places; & our just & righteous King lose a very large Body of those very Indians, who first (in those part[s]) submitted to yͤ Crown, & assisted one of yͤ Predecessors of yͭ Mason, who is now soliciting in London, with an hundred Wariors to destroy yͤ Piquatonic Tribe, who livd & were

totally routed within four Miles of my dwelling.

The young Man is very intelligible & thirsts after Learning. Cou'd he be encouraged wou'd continue in London, 'till qualified & episcopally ordain'd to preach yͤ Gospel to yͤ Indians.

One of yͤ former Sachems of his Nation gave 40 Acres of good Land there to yͤ Church of England, upon wͨʰ a Church was built, & wherein Service was frequently perform'd; but as I am told yͤ itenerant Missionary exchang'd [it] for equal Quantity of bad Land; since yͤ Missionary's death, yͤ very Church was pull'd down, & is metamorphos'd into a Tavern & all yͤ Land converted to his own Use, I mean yͤ Use of yͤ Landlord. This was done before yͭ Tribe desir'd my Assistance, else I had pervented yͤ Desecration of yͤ Church. If my Patrons please to give me any Power or Order, I'll exert my self in this Affair. Tho' some may be afraid of displeasing some great Men, yet I am not. I beg leave to add, yͭ yͭ Church was never glaz'd, (Shame prevents me from discovering yͤ Reason) but yͤ Glass was bought & sent to yͤ Parish but put into a great Man's House, who promis'd to restore it or as good, to yͤ Church, when demanded.

Since my last I baptiz'd seven Children & young Persons in Houses about 28 & 30 Miles off. I have spent near twelve days to yͤ united Congregations of Millington & Mudus, where I spend four days at each Visit, preaching always once, sometimes twice a day, & have great Encouragement by new Members frequently added. But am sorry I have reason to complain that yͤ Dissenters rage furiously against me & persecute them seizing their Goods, driving & pounding their Cattle for their Teachers Rates, because there's no resident Missionary among them, tho' they frequently attend my Church or Mͬ Peter's wͨʰ is fourteen Miles distant. Alas! yͭ yͤ Anabaptists are exempt from these Abuses by order of Council, & his Majesty's Religion be daily subject to independant & congregational Iniquity & Depradation. The Law, favoring our Religion, is imperfect & I think, rather a Snare, than a Security to our Establishment. Had our Religion yͤ same Privilege thro' out this Colony yͭ yͤ Babtists have, we wou'd flourish & encrease like yͤ Lilly of yͤ Valey, & yͤ Cedars of Lebanon. But we are totally discourag'd & discredited. Deus dabit his quoꝗ Finem.

My Communicants are yͤ same in Number, have christned five, buried three, married none since my last.

Pray present my christian Love & Duty to yͤ Religious Society, whose Instructions & Advice I'll study to obey. As yͤ Blacksmith has been very serviceable to our Church, so I am persuaded an Essay upon universal Redemption by one Mͬ Smith formerly a Baptist, wou'd open yͤ prejudic'd Eyes of many Predestinarians here. Fas est et ab hoste doceri.

An Interest in yͬ Prayers, & also Pardon for this tedious Epistle are earnestly desir'd by

Revᵈ & Good Sͬ / Yͬ very humˡͤ Servͭ & / Affᵗͤ Brother in / Jesus Christ

New-London Novͬ 20. 1767   Matt Graves

To Doctor Burton Secretary to yͤ Society &c

[Addressed:] To / Doctor Burton Secretary &c
[Endorsed:] Read at a Committee Septͬ 12. 1768.

[1768, Jan. 6, Groton, etc.]

The humble Petition of yͤ united Parishes of Groton Stoningtown & Preston to yͤ Religious Society for propagating yͤ Gospell in Foreign Parts; Humbly sheweth

That as Children under yͤ Care of Parents & Guardians fly to them in times of Troubles & threatning Dangers so We your Spiritual Children fly to You for Relief since yͤ Blessings of yͤ Gospell are likely to be taken away from us And we left a Prey to those whose Communion our Consciencͤˢ obliged us to forsake We are very sensible of & sincerely thankfull for your encouraging & continuing an Episcopal Church among us somany Years but greatly concerned least yͤ little Foxes shou'd spoil yͤ Vines by crafty Misrepresentations of things & we be deprived of our Vineyard. As therefore we have been unjustly represented to yͤ Venerable Board & accused of detaining yͤ Revᵈ Mͬ Beardsleyˢ just Reward and so breaking our Covenant with him We humbly crave you of your Clemency to hear us solemnly declaring to you nothing but yͤ Truth & accordingly to have the Bounty restored or your Displeasure confirmed.

Janͬ 16ᵗͪ 1759 The Parishoners met at Groton Church & 24 Sponsible Men all Parishoners Drew up & signed a Bond of £20. on yͤ June following yͤ Chh. Wardens & Principal Men went to Norwich & yͤ Members of that Chh agreed also to give £20 Yearly towards yͤ Suport of a Missionary.

On yͤ 14 of Janͬ 1761 Mͬ Beardsley came to Groton; being assembled at yͤ Chh we agreed to give him £20 pͬ Annum which he accepted of & we promised to pay should he obtain Episcopal Ordination & be appointed Minister to Groton Stonington Preston & Norwich he Preaching alte[r]nately at Groton & Norwich with this Condition in favour of Groton Society that if any shou'd in yͤ Destricts of Grotⁿ Stoningtⁿ & Prestⁿ conform to yͤ Chh. their Rates shou'd be accepted as part of the sᵈ £20 and yͭ Mͬ Beardsley shou'd not Discharge any without Informing yͤ Clerk of yͤ Vestry And for his further Encouragement as he had no Money We wou'd advance one Year's pay & also contribute £5 to defray yͤ Charge of Inoculation before he went to England all which was agreed to & ratified; yͤ £25 was raised & he Left us yͤ 1ˢͭ of Aplͭ 1761

Febͬ 26ᵗͪ 1761 we purchased a Glebe for £83.S4. for Him the 14 Acres of Land left by yͤ Revᵈ Mͬ Punderson being insufficient for a Minister.

Febͬ 22ᵈ 1762 the Revᵈ Mͬ Beardsley returned with Orders Took possession of yͤ 14 Acres & yͤ Glebe we bought for yͤ Ministͬ That which we bought Contains 18 Acres of Choice Land with good Fire wood The amount of the two Glebes according to his own Estimate came to £22 in 6 Years more than his yearly Payment. He also discharged some new Conformˢͭˢ in Preston whose Money came to £10.13.9 for which he rendered no Acctͭ contrary to Contract.

Augˢͭ 16ᵗͪ 1763 The Clerk paid him & took his Recptͭ for the two first years & half Service & so continued 'till 1764 in yͤ Fall at which time we supose he wrote Home & complained of our Deficiency but in Novͬ following we discharged the Year before You'll be pleased to believe Us when he Complained to your Honors we owed but [ ] tho he had yͤ Use & profits of yͤ two Glebes & recᵈ sᵈ £10.13.9 & have reason to believe he recᵈ more tho' we cannot prove it.

In Febͬ following we met at his Request & found we owed him £4 Exclusive of yͤ Glebes & yͤ £24.3.9 which he discharged without accounting for contrary to Agreement for in 1764 he had given recptͭˢ to new Comers to our Chh. amounting to £13.10 which with yͤ £10.13.9 before Mentioned makes yͤ £24.3.9 as above.

In May 1765 We were surpris'd & sorry at your Letter blaming us for non performance of Payment £4 only due from us and he having upon Adjustment recᵈ £24.3.9 over & above yͤ £20 contracted for Yearly.

June 12ᵗͪ 1765 We met & Mͬ Beardsley wou'd own only £1.5.0 recᵈ from Preston. And tho' he complained of our breaking Contract we know neither can he deny it he did not preach half yͤ time to Us but was generally gone two Months Yearly to the Westward and in sᵈ Year preached to us only thrice in three Months Requiring yͤ full Tale of Brick without giving us Straw.

Novͬ 1766 At a Parish Meeting he told us he designed to remove but would not shew his Orders said he Could remove or shou'd remove or cou'd stay. We ask'd if he wanted Money he said he did always & now if we would advance £100 he wou'd stay he threatned to sue us for £20. We said he recᵈ above that sum from Preston & offer'd to prove it upon which he said he wou'd write a Lettͬ of Complaint to yͤ Society & so left yͤ Parish not regarding the Sheep.

Having recᵈ yͬ Lettͬ in 1765 we In our Ansͬ to yͤ same requested the Continuance of yͬ Favors but concealed those Facts now Mention[ed] Unwilling to bring the Missionary under your Displeasure For which Tenderness to him we now suffer but hope Truth will prevail and Matters be brought into a right Chanel.

Now with the most profound Submission we beg yͤ Religio[us] Society will first consider yͤ Extent of those Parishes alway[s] connected with us the Contract then yͤ Payments the Value of yͤ Glebes the Sums advanced & Discharged & Judge if we are Deficient; We presume we have paid above £20 to Mͬ Beardsley more than we contracted for.

As Groton (which had a Chh long before Norwich & which that People frequented being 5 Miles distant) Stoningtⁿ Preston & Norwich were one Body We beg we may not be disinherited of our Birth Right but if You please Let us at Least have one third of yͤ Benefit of Chh Ordinances Norwich a Third & Preston a Third Each pay his proper Dividend or third par[t] but this as you please. As these Affairs are we presume Represented in two very opposite Lights and as we are likely thro' a false Representation to have our Candlestick remov'd we humbly Desire yͭ you'll be pleased to appoint yͤ Revᵈ Mͬ Grave[s] who lives next to us with some others to Examine into yͤ whole affair & Return you a true state of yͤ Case & your Petitioners will as in Duty Bound pray &c

                                        Chh. Wardens
                                        Vestry Men

Christopher Newton }
Samuell Newton   } Chh Wardens

Joseph Rose Jͬ   }
Willͫ Billings   } Vestry Men
Theopˢ Avery   }

Having at yͤ Request of yͤ Parishoners of Groton examin'd

& compar'd this Petiton to ye original one sent to ye religious Society, I find it to be a true & literal Copy thereof: given under my hand this 6th of Jany 1768

Matt Graves

[1768, Jan. 14, New London]

Sirs

I most gratefully acknowledge your very signal Favor of ye 19th of last Sepr, which shou'd have been sooner observ'd, had not a new, unprecedented Machination been devised again[s]t ye poor Narraganset Indians by ye Assembly; wch was in few words, to sell as much of their Lands, as wou'd clear their Sachem of all his Debts. It was mention'd--voted--executed. They apply'd to me, I sent ym to Mr Robinson, their Lawyer, who, as I told them about three years ago, is their real & worst Enemy. I never lik'd his dark Letters, told them to take care of him, & yt I wou'd hav[e] nothing to do with him, nor them if, they were directed by him. In short he deluded them so much, yt they wrote very improper Letters to me, telling me they only desir'd me to preach.

However seeing ye Storm gathering they came & own'd their Error, & desir'd my Advice. Go, said I, to Mr Robinson, desire him to consider yr Grievances & draw up ye State of yr Case. They went, & he refus'd. They then acknow'd ye Equity of my Opinion & left themselves to my Direction

Hearing ye Collector of Newport, Squire Robinson commiserated their Misfortunes & spoke friendly to them, I wrote a Letter of thanks to him for his Humanity & desir'd his Interest in their behalf. He told me [he] wou'd serve them. Permit me to transcribe his own Words--Mr Johnston (a Lawyer in Newport) has upon my Recommendation undertaken ye Affair. When he has prepar'd a State of their Case, I will peruse it, & adapt it as near as I can to ye Temper & Genius of ye great, before whom it is to go. Having been for some time past pretty conversant with ye iniquitous Proceedings of this Governmt I shall not fail to expose to view their Oppression of this People.

With this agreeable Letter ye Indians brought me one from their Lawyer, stuft wth Equivocations, Falsehoods & Lies, wch I scorn'd to answer. I read it to them, gave them a Charge not to go near their old Lawyer, to get ye State of ye Case, Mr Robinson's Assistance, give a full Power to Tobias Shattock, who waited lately upon yr Honr, & as you advis'd to go home wth ye Affair He is now here going to New-York, whence ye Ship sails in three or four Weeks. I have recommended him to Mr Ogilvie, to whom I send this Letter to be convey'd to Johnson-hall.

I need not tell you how very necessary a Letter from you will be in behalf of ye distress'd Indians, & what seasonable Relief it will procure to their Case (to use yr own Words) to mention ye Case to his Majesty's Ministers, & recommend it to their Attention.

I receiv'd a Letter lately from Mr Occom, & begin to be jealous of him--his Words are few & cool. Besides he has given ye Petition, I drew up to ye King & Council for ye Nahantic Tribe, to General Lyman, a great Favorite to this Colony, therefore no Friend to ye plunder'd Indians. I wrote a long, sharp Letter to Mr Occom, & told him plainly, he seem'd to be more studious to get Money, than to vindicate his People, & yt unless he gave better proofs of his Integrity to them, I wd pray for him, but drop his Correspondence & our Intimacy. Besides he says ye Bishops wou'd not ordain him; I believe ye reverse, for ye Secretary told me, he shou'd, if he sincerely desir'd it. But I wish I may be wrong, & Occum prove faithful. I hope you'll pardon my Prolixity, arising from my conscientious Concern for his Majesty's Subjects, harrass'd, plunder'd & abus'd by a seditious, mutinous & iniquitous People. O for a King's Governor for Rhode Island & Connecticut, & a Bishop to direct & support his Clergy! That ye LORD may bless & preserve his Majesty, direct his Honle Council, restore & establish Peace, Unanimity & Love at home; & also bless you with sound Wisdom Wealth & Health is ye hearty Prayer of

Sr
Yr Honr's most dutiful, obedient &
very humle Servt
Matt Graves

New-London Jany 14
1768

To ye honle Sr Willm Johnson &c

[1768, Feb. 1, New London]

Sirs

The growing Troubles of y. Indians oblige me to write to you again-- The Honble Mr Robinson, while Collector at Newport, had engag'd one Mr Johnson to draw out a State of ye Indian Case, & had Assurance of his Integrity: this he acquainted me of-- I told him, Mr Johnson was able, but unsteady-- He said he had fixt him, & it shou'd be immediately done. His Words are--"He has undertaken ye Affair. Besides ye strongest Professions of Sincerity I have his further Security for his Attachment to them (ye Indians) yt their Interest wth respect to this Colony is one & ye same."-- In short I sent an Indian to Mr Johnson, who waited four days, but in vain, then ye indian School master, who waited as long in vain--in short Mr Robinson left Newport & Johnson ye poor Indians. I advis'd to take ye papers out of Johnson's hands, whence ye Case was to be drawn, wch were got after much trouble, all worn & scarce legible. I must add, this Johnson was King's Attorney, & now he thinks to be reinstated by his Treachery to ye Indians, & base Friendship to several of ye great (I had almost said wicked) Men at Newport & others his Neighbors, & Mr Robinson having remov'd he has laid aside all his Promises. However I have order'd Tobias Shattock to sail by New-York fo[r] London, assuring him I wou'd write to yr Honr, who wou'd consider ye Affair & endeavor to relieve them. Now Sr as several dread ye Indian's going home & do all they can to embarrass the design--as they know yr Influence & will unite & strengthen their European Forces, I hope you'll condescend to send ye State of their Case home with a Letter to some of ye Nobility. This will rout out their Allies & settle ye poor Indians on a solid Foundation.

I have dispatch'd an Indian with a Letter to Mr Robinson, & press'd ye Continuance of his Interest, & to write in their Favor. I wish I had proper Power. My Bowels yern for ye plunder'd Indians--they are plunder'd of their Land, we of our Glebe & our Church torn down & converted into a Tavern by ye same people. The Indian waits to carry this with ye other to N. York. I pray GOD continue

you for yͤ Good of his Church, yͤ Interest of his Majesty, & yͤ Relief of yͤ distrest; & yͭ you'll pardon this scrole & Freedom is yͤ earnest Request of

Sͬ

Yͬ Honͬ's most obedient &
most oblig'd, humᶫᵉ Servͭ

N. London Febͬ 1ˢͭ 1768   Matt Graves

To yͤ Honᶫᵉ Sͬ William Johnson &c

[1768, Mar. 21, Westminster]
Revᵈ Sir

I have received your Letter of the 21 Novͬ last; & assure you, that We are very sensible of the difficulties you must be under from the incompetent maintenance which you receive from your people, & the more so, because It is not thought a prudent measure in us to make an establishment in your Town; on which subject I wrote so fully in my last that I can add nothing farther to it. The Society however have given you a Gratuity of £10, for which you have leave to draw. Mͬ Pearson our late Treasurer being dead, Mͬ Symondson is appointed in his room. Your Bill must be drawn on him. Direct to him at the first fruits Office in the Temple.

You need not be under Solicitude about any expressions in your last letter: There was nothing in it to give the least Offence; & I trust you will have Candour enough not to put any misconstruction on my answer to it.

I am Revᵈ Sir

Abingdon street   Your affectionate
Westminster   humble Servant
March. 21ˢͭ 1768.   D Burton.

[Addressed:] To / The Revᵈ Mͬ Abraham Jarvis, / at Middletown in Connecticut / New-England. / To the care / of Dͬ Auchmuty / of New-York.

[1768, Apr. 6, Stamford]
Stamford Connecticut Colony
New England   April 6, 1768
Reverend Sir, ---

I received your favour of the 26 of June last. --- Notwithstanding the goodness of the Venerable Society in appointing two Missionaries, one for the Nothern, & the other for the Southern District in the late Mͬ Davis's Mission: It seems some little dispute arose, concerning supplying the Church of Sharon, & to whose Alotment it belonged. at the importunity of the Church of Sharon, complaining of Neglect, I set forward about the middle of November last to make them another Visit; but being stopt on my Jorney by Illness, sent for Mͬ Clark, communicated to him the contents of your Letter; and let him know the expectation of the Society, that he & Mͬ Palmer should supply the necessities of the Church in that County, at Sharon as else where, in the best manner they were able. Mͬ Clark (who is very acceptable to the people among whom he officiates, & bids fair to be very Useful) lately gave me advice, that thro' the interposition of the Revᵈ Doctor Johnson, He & Mͬ Palmer had agreed to afford the good People of sharon, what equal Assistance they were able. ---

As in duty bound, we must submit to the superior wisdom of the Society, both as to their Ability, & the propriety of when & Where, they shall open new Missions. and we that have the Honour of being employed in their service, with grateful Acknowledgements for past & continued favours, must remain as extensively useful as we can: ---

for my own part, unless Salem & parts contiguous (where I preached Sunday last before Easter to a numerous, devout, attentive congregation) are better supplied thro' the Societies charitable appointment of Mͬ Townsend to serve them; I see no prospect but of wearing out Life in fateague of publick Duty, which much Increases rather than diminishes upon my hands, for notwithstanding, the late shocking religious Clamours that are raised, to inspire the enemies of our holy Church with groundless fears and Jealousies; by crafty designing men, through Political Views & the lust of Dominion, we have reason to fear, more than an honest Zeal for Religion. Our Churches continue to increase and flourish, is an Ark of safety for the honest inquisitive unprejudiced enquirer after truth and concord. It is a Critical day in the Provinces of America-- may we deserve the protection & blessing of Heaven, the smiles and defence of our Superiors in our Mother Country, both in Church and State; our only Guardians, protectors & benefactors under God. ---

Mͬ Clark engaged to give Mͬˢ Davis Advice, That the Society expected a Catalogue of the Books deposited in the hands of the Church Wardens at New-Milford. ---

I acknowledge with gratitude your repeated Advice of the Societies gratuity of ten Pounds for extraordinary service out my cure, which I thankfully accepted and drew for in my last Bill. ---

Notwithstanding party Rage and Malice, my Parish in all parts continue in a peaceable united increaseing State, and we live as inoffensively as we can, toward those that are without. ---

I baptized last half Year two Adults, Seventy Children; and three were added to the communion. ---

I have this day drawn a set of Bills in usual form for twenty five Pounds Sterling upon the Venerable Societies Secretary, Edward Pearson Esqͬ, in favour of Mͬ Thomas Ellison Juͬ Merchͭ in New York.

Praying for Gods blessing upon our pious benefactors, and to give success to all their pious designs, I beg leave, with Humble Duty to the Venerable Board, and high Esteem and regard to your Self, to Assure you, I am Reverend Sir,

Your Most Obedͭ

The Reverend Doctor Burton   Most Humble Servͭ
Secretary of the Venerable Society   and Affectͭ Brother
for Propagation of the Gospel, &c.   Ebenezͬ Dibblee

[Addressed:] To / The Reverend Doctor Burton / Secretary of the Venerable Society / for Propagation of the Gospel in / Foreign Parts. Abingdon Street / Westminster.- London
[Endorsed:] Read...July 11. 1768

[1768, May 2, Stratford]
To the Honourable the General Assembly of the Colony of Connecticut in New England in america to be holden at Hartford In sd Colony on the Second Thirsday of May 1768

The Memorial of James Clark of the Parish of New Stratford and Elihu Thompson of Ripton parish both of the town of Stratford in fairfield County Church Wardiants and the Vestremen and the Rest of the parrisheners and Profesers of the Church of England who Live in the parish of Ripton and Part in North Stratford and part in New Stratford Humbly beg Leave to observe to your Hon^{rs} there is and for a Longe time has been of the Profesers of the Church of England a Society and Church Regerlerly Imbodyed and a Minister of the Gospel Setteled and abideing amoung them (viz; the Reve^d Mr Christopher Newton) and attending upon and Carying on divine servis according to the Cannons of the Church of England, alternately in Sd Ripton and North Stratford parrishes and your Hon^{rs} Memoralst and others of our Bretheren are Constant attendants on the Ministry of the Sd Mr Newton and we being willing and desierous to Releave and free our Bretheren who are of the Ecclesastical Constitution of the Goverment Esstablished by the Laws of ye Colony from the troble and Burden of Taxing us and Collecting our Rates while we have No Liberty to act in and about the Same [--] we humbly Conceeve it unconstitutional to be taxed without our Consent [--] and should be Glad & are desireous to enjoy the Liberty and previledges of [loyal] and faithfull English Subjects in Taxing our Selves and Gathering the Same for the Support of the Gosple which we are willing to do In such Manner as is agreable to our Contionce^s and your Hon^{rs} Memorialst further observes that the parishonors afore Sd haveing Lately set up a House in Sd Ripton for publick worship and find it to be very difficult to Carry on and finish the Same haveing No Method to Compell any person to do his part and Equil proportion towards the same without being Enabled by this Honor^{bl} Assembly and we haveing agreed with our adjatiant Brethren the profesers of the Church how far and to what Limits and Lines the Sd profesers as afore sd ought to Contribute there proportion for the Support of the Sd Reveren^d Mr Newton and Building and finishing s^d house for worship that is to Say to begin at the Mouth of the furnivll Mo... River where it falls on to the Cove So Called Near the dwelling house of Col^{ll} Jos: Wooster and from thence a Line westerly to the house where Sam^{ll} Blogge in his Lifetime Lived and from thence South Westerly in the Common Rhode to North Stratford untill it Comes to tha[t] of the home Lott of Dan^{ll} Fairchild Esqr Near his dweling house Where the Rhode turns and from thence still Something Westwardly with Sd Rhode to the Corner by the dweling house of John Hinman and from thence in the Rhode Called Newtown Rode untill it Comes to the River Called poquanock River at the going over neare the dweling house of oliver Howley in North Stratford and from thence Northwardly by Sd River untill it Comes a little below or S:wardly of Searses Mill So Called standing on Sd River where there is two Branches of Sd River Meets and these Runing by the East-branch of Sd River Northwardly and So Continuing that Genal Corse to the North Line of Sd Stratford town Ship which Includs the whole of Ripton parish and some part of North Stratford and some part of New Stratford parrishes as afore sd: whereupon your Humb^l Memoril^{sts} Humbly pray this Honour^{bl} Assembly to Grant Liberty and Inable and fully Impower all the afore Sd profesers of the Church of England Liveing within the above described Lines and Limits to tax themselves for the future from time to time as ocation

May Require for the Support of their Minister that is or May be Settled there according to the Rules and order of the Cannons of the Church of England and building and Repairing of a house for publick worship and to Chouse Collector or Collectors for Gathering and Collecting the Same and to Chouse Com^{tee} or Com^{tees} to take Care of Manage and Carry on the prudential Ecclisastical affares amoung us with priviledges and powers to Inforce the Same as Societies Esstablished by the Laws of the Goverment have or Some other way Grant us Release and help for Carrying on the publick worship that all who Joyn with us may be Compeled to have their proportion thereof and we as In duty Bound will Ever pray

Dated in Stratford this 2^d day of May AD 1768

James Clark } Church
Elihu Thompson } Wardens

Joseph Bostwick ⎫
John Laborie ⎪
John Yeats ⎬ Vestry
Jeremiah Hubbel ⎪ Men
Sam^{ll} Shelton ⎭
Elisha Beardslee ⎭ Clerk

General Assembly New Haven Jan^{ry} 1769 In the upper House[:] The Question was put whether the Prayer of this Memorial should be granted Resolved in the Negative
Test George Wyllys Secret^y
In ye lower House[:] The ye same Question, & ye same Resolution thereon was put, & made as above men. in ye vote of ye up^r House Test Wm Williams Cler

We the Subscribers are profesers of the Church of England Living in the Parish of New Stratford

Reuben Lane	Nathan Clark Junr
Ephraim Lane	James Curtis
Elnathan Nichols	Fred^k Hawley
Daniel Beardslee	Silas Nichols
Zechariah Clark	Joseph French

We the Subscribers profesers of the Church of England Living in ye parish [of] North Stratford

Isaac Beardslee	Daniel Shelton 3
Michael Beardslee	Abel Lewis
Ebenezer Hurd jur	David Peet jn^r

We the Subscribers are profesers [of] the Church of England in ye Parish of Ripton

Thaddeus Shelton	John Shelton
Daniel Shelton Juner	Jarsey Waklee
John Hubbell	Clay Waklee
Timothy Hubbell	David Waklee
jonathan french	Abijah Shelton
John french	Ebenezer Shelton
Josiah [?Shel]ton	William Shelton
Sam^{ll} Clark	Joseph Shilton
James Laborie	Jacob Baldwin
Jonathan Thompson	Ephraim Lewis
Edmund Pulford	Elias Baldwin
Samuel Shelton	John Blackleach
James Shelton	Joseph Smith
Willian Perry	Ebenezur Hinman
Dan^{ll} Shelton	Gedeon Seley

[1768, June 29, New Milford]
Rev.d Sir

I have received your Letter of the 1.t of February last.
Since I have been in the Mission, I have preached the one
half of my Time at New Milford the other half equally divided between Roxbury and New Preston, only four Sundays
in a Year, I have reserved for Sharon, two of which I take
from New Milford and one out of each of the other Parishes. As I had no Orders from the honorable Society, how,
I should divide my Time between the several Places (by
them committed to my Care) I took the Advice of several
of the Elder Missionaries who are well acquainted with the
Circumstances of the Church in these Places, and accordingly followed their Advice, which was in the Manner above
described; but if the Society think it is not properly divided,
I shall be very thankful to them for their Instruction, and,
shall likewise obey their Orders. As to Newfairfield there
is but about six Families of the Church, who constantly
attend the C.hh at New Milford as they are but about five
Miles Distant, tho', I propose frequently to visit & preach
Lectures to them on Week Days. I shall be extremely
thankful to the venerable Society (as I am but of a slender
Constitution for so extensive a Mission) if it may be their
Pleasure to let Sharon at present, or till it can be otherwise Provided for, be under the Care of M.r Palmer & myself, as we have already settled the Affair by the Advice &
Direction of Doc.r Johnson and the Convention. In New Milford there are 92 Families of the C.h, about 50 Communicants, at Woodbury about 50 Families of the C.h 35 comuni-
cants, at Kent about 65 C.h Families & about 40 Communicants, since the 9th. of October last I have baptised 60 Infants and 8 Adults one of which was Black, the Church in
these Parts is in very flourishing Circumstances, and, I
am determned as far as the Duties of my Extensive Mission will permit, to embrace every Circumstance that
promises Success to the Cause of true Religion, and the
Advancement of the Church of England for the Advancement of which is my whole Study and Employment, and
am Rev.d Sir your and the

New Milford   Society's faithful Missionary
June 29th. 1768   & most Obedient humble Servant
                                    Richard Clarke

I have drawn upon the Society for my last half years
Sallery in Favour of M.r Josiah Starr of New Milford

I have received the whole of the Society's Library
belonging to this Mission which was lodged in the Church
Warden's Hands

To the Reverend Doc.tr Daniel Burton

[Addressed:] To / The Reverend Doc.tr Daniel Burton /
Secretary to the Society for the Propagation / of the Gos-
pel in foreign Parts / In Abingdon Street, / Westminster
[Endorsed:] Read...Nov.r 14. 1768.

[Clarke had charge of New Milford, Woodbury, Kent,
New Fairfield and Sharon.]

[1768, July 1, Middletown]
Middletown July 1.st 1768   We the Subscribers promise
to pay to Mess.s Philip Mortimer and Richard Alsop the
several sums annexed to our names in lawful money
within Six months from the above date it being for the

purchase of A Glebe for the use of Christ Church in s.d
Middletown as Witness our Hands--

P. Mortimer--twenty five pounds
Rich.d Alsop--twenty five pounds
W.m Johnson--twenty pounds
Jer. Wetmore--ten pounds
John Easton--ten pounds
Ichabod Wetmore   twenty pounds
Jonathan Thorpe   ten pounds
Ashbel Burnham   ten pounds
Benj.a Clark   five pounds
Will.m Hall   Five pounds
Wait Plum   Four pounds
Elisha Fairchild   Five pounds
Nath.l Shaler   Five pounds
George Starr   Five pounds
Asahel Johnson   Six pounds
Mary Alsop   Ten pounds
John Osborn   Three pounds
Rev.d Jer.h Leaming   Ten pounds
Stephen Ranney   Five pounds
William Keith   Three pounds
Robert Warner   Three pounds
Elizabeth Bigelow   Four pounds
Abigail Shaler   Five pounds
George Phillips   Four pounds
Charles Magill   Two pounds
Peleg Sanford   three pounds
Reuben Plum   two pounds
Charles Plum   two pounds
Sanford Thompson   Four pounds
Nath.l G. Ingraham   two pounds
Arthur Magill }
Stephen Clay } Six pounds

Middletown 23.d day of June 1785
These may Certify whom it may concern that we the Subscribers have this day given to the Episcopal Church in
Middletown a deed of a certain piece of land and dwelling
house thereon in which the Rev.d Abraham Jervice now
lives for the use intended by the within Subscribers and
though no pecuniary Consideration is mentioned in said
deed yet the several sums within subscribed was actually
the consideration which induced us to make the conveyance and we hereby declares that the within Subscribers
in proportion to the sums by them respectively subscribed
are equally the Doners with us who executed s.d Deed In
Witness whereof we have hereunto set our hands
                                              Philip Mortimer
July 5th 1785   A true Record   Mary Alsop
Test. B. Fisk Reg.r

T.n Clk.s Off.ce }
Middletown   } May 9. 1809   The foregoing is a true
                                                Copy of Record....

[1768, Sept. 2, Brooklyn]

Brooklyn Sep.t 2 1768
The Inhabitanc of the Society of Brooklyn in Windham
County that are by Law qualifyed to vot in Sociaty meting
are hearby warned to meat at the meting hous in sd Society on Wednesday the 28 Day of September instant at two
of the Clock in the afternoon to choose society officers

for the year Ensuing and to vote the Rever^d Mr Whitnays Sallary for the present year and vote a rate to Defray the School and other Society Charges the Ensuing year and to see how much Schooling the Society will keep the Ensuing year and to see if the Society will Choose Som Parson or Parsons to sue for the School monny that is Due to S^d Society and see if the society will vote that Jacob Stapels shall have his School Rate if he lays it out to School his Children------and to see if the Secity will vote to build a meting Hous in Said Society for Publick Worship by order of

> John Hubbard
> Israel Putnam

[1768, Sept. 24, New Haven]
These are to Certifie the Venerable Society that the Revd Solomon Palmer committed into our hands when he left this Mission the following Books, being the S^d Societies Library &c. which we have Since delivered to the Revd Mr Hubbard, Viz Patrick & Lowths's Commentary &c: upon the Prophets, Whitby in 2 Vol: on the New Testament, Stanhopes Paraphrase 4 Vol: Burnett on the 39 Articles, Echards Ecclesiastical Hystory 2 Vol: Sherlock on Providence, Death, and judgment; Nelson's Festivals, Wall on Infant Baptism, and Blackhall on the Lord Prayer.

Newhaven Sep^tr the 24- 1768.

> Timothy Bontécou ⎫ Church
> Isaac Doolittle ⎬ Wardens

[1768, Oct. 18, Stamford]
Stamford Connecticut New England
October, 18; 1768.

Reverend Sir

I have this day drawn a set of Bills for Twenty five Pounds Sterling upon Edward Pearson Esqr, or the Treasurer of the Society for the time being in fav^r of Mr Thomas Ellison Ju^r Merchant in New York.----

With pleasure I can inform the Venerable Board of the peaceable, flourishing, increaseing state of my Parish; and of their firm Attachment to our happy Constitution both in Chur[ch] & State; notwithstanding party rage never ran higher, and under the specious pretence of Civil & Religious Liberty, every Art is used to throw us into all imaginable confusion, & to prejudice his Majesties Subjects against the conduct of the Governmen[t] in being, & our Religious constitution in particular.----

We hope in God for better times, that the Provinces will obtain redress of Just grievances, and effectual provision be made for the support & encouragement of our National religion in these remote Regions, and the subjects of it delivered from their fines & Insults, and indulged in the full enjoyment of their religious profession & Church Government. May our dissenting Brethren ever enjoy unmolested their religious sentiments & peculiarities, we envy not their happy alotment; but take it tenderly that groundless fears & Jealousies, never to be satisfied, Shall deprive the Loyal and worthy Members of our holy Ch^h equal liberty & indulgence.----

I Baptized last half Year, thirteen Adult persons and Sixty four children. three were added to the Communion.

the whole Number of communicants in the two Towns of Stamford & Greenwich are about Eighty six. They have agreed at Horsneck to enlarge the Chapel there, it being too small in ye beast Season of the year to contain the number of devout Worshippers, who attend.----

My Parish dues, comeing by Law thro' the hands of dissenting Collectors have for some Years back, been very poorly Collected or not paid to me in full; in consequence of w^h Neglect I am put to some disagreable Inconveniences; ever Studious of peace & of avoiding Civil contention. But by the Grace of God it shall ever be my greatest concern to be as extensively Useful as may be, and with fidelity to attend the important duties of my Mission; with gratitude acknowledgeing every favour & encouragement received from the Venerable Board.----

On the 19th of May last, Accompanied by the Revd Mr Leaming, I Preached a Lecture in Salem Ch^h at the introduction of good Mr Townsend, Joyfully received by the poor people of Salem & parts contiguous, and expressed their gratitude to the Society for appointing him their Missionary. I doubt not he will do honour to his profession, and approve himself worthy of his appointment.----

Sunday July 17th I preached in the Ch^h at Danbury, to a numerious Congregation (Mr Townsend being so good as to supply my Ch^h) likewise on the first Sunday Instant Octob^r, (Mr Leaming supplying my Absence) I preached among them. their religious state is truly compassionate, and in all human probability their religious contentions & subdivisions, would terminate in a great increase and growth of the Church, if they could more constantly enjoy the means of better Instruction. Many Dissenters attended, and their prejudices subside.----

In Compliance with repeated Requests, supported by the Intercession of Mr Palmer & Mr Clark unable to supply the spiritual wants of the Poor people at Sharon, Salsbury & the North Preacinct on the Oblong in the Province of New York, I went from Danbury and Visited Each of those places. I Preached second Sunday Instant in Sharon to a more Numerous Congregation than a fine Church could well contain; the peoples attentive devout behav^r was very agreable. I preached also two or three Lectures in Sharon, One in Salsbury, & one in North Precinct on the Oblong so called; where great Numbers of poor people are settled, wholly destitute of proper religious Instruction, upwards of 20 Heads of families already professors of the Ch^h, & many others so well disposed that they are about building a Church, in hopes providence will open a door for a Minister in the Ord^r of the Ch^h of England for their better instruction & Edification. they tell me this seems the desire of most all denominations among them, wearied out with religious seperations. the Circumstances of the people on the borders of the province of New York are truly compassionate. some of the best people in Salsbury have lately declared conformity, and do honour to the Ch^h-- they propose also the building a Church. A Missionary might be most Eminently Useful in those Places, and meet with all the encouragement they were able to give him, if they might be so happy as to obtain one. I Baptized in those several places, thirty four Children and two Adults. May it please the Lord of the Harvest to send forth more Labourers into his Vinyard.

with Most Dutiful regards to the Venerable Board,

& prayers for the blessing of God to Succeed all their designs, I Am Reverend Sir with high Esteem

Your Most / Humble Servt and Brother in Christ

Ebez^r Dibblee

[Addressed:] To / The Reverend Doctor Daniel Burton / Secretary of the Venerable Society / for the Propagation of the Gospel in / Foreign Parts. / Abingdon Street Westminster / London

[Endorsed:] Read...Jan. 16. 1769.

[1768, Nov. 1, Litchfield]

Connecticut, Litchfield, November 1st 1768.

Revd Sir,

Since my return from Newhaven to this Mission, I have (thro' the goodness of God) been favoured with a better State of health, than for Some Years before I had enjoyed, So that I have been able, not only to perform the Stated Duties of it, but occasionally to administer to the Spiritual Necessities of other People at a distance from it. Twice I have officiated at Nobleton, where there is 32 Famolies of C^{hh} People, and an 193 Souls: Twice at New-Concord, where is 37 Famolies & 213 Souls, both in the Province of New-York; the one about 14, the other 20 Miles distant from Great-Barrington: And once at Lainsburrough in the Province of the Masechusetts Bey, 25 miles--where is 19 heads of Famolies and an 100^d Souls. At all which places they constantly meet, and attend on the Service of the Church on Sundays; whose Condition is truly deplororable & calls for pitty & Assistance, they being almost destitute of the proper Administrations of God's House, & by reason of their Poverty, unable to procure to themselves Such a Priviledge, which they earnestly wish for and desire.

Mr Bostwick, (the bearer of this) has for about four Years [p]ast been employed in reading Prayers & Sermons at Great-Bar[rin]gton, and lately occasionally at the above mentioned Places, who has So far recommended himself to their esteem, that they are very desirous he Should become their Minister. He is a Man of an Amiable disposition, Sober, Pious & prudent; Steady in his Temper, Commendable for a close Application to his Studies, and judged to have made good proficiency therein; well Affected to the present Government, truly Conformed to the Doctrine and Discipline of the Church of England, of Single life, and Age Sufficient for Holy Orders. His Qualifications are Such as render him worthy of the Venerable Societies favour & Respect; Who, I hope, will not only receive him into their Service, but appoint him Missionary to the abovementioned Places, with the Allowance of Such a Salary as their Fund will permit, & they in their wisdom, & Charity Shall judge needful, which would, not only be much to his, and their Satisfaction, but an happy expedient, by the blessing of God, of promoting true Religion, where the Means of Christian Knowledge are greatly wanted.

And with regard to my particular Mission; In general, it is in a flourishing way, gradually encreasing in every part of it, and particularly, at Goshen, a Town Contiguous to Litchfield, from Seven Famolies when I came into this Mission, they are grown up to 42, including a few belonging to Several Neighbouring Towns, who constantly attend their Church, which they have lately, with the greatest

Unanimity and dispatch erected, (it being 40 by 30 feet)-- and tho' not finished made convenient to Meet in for Divine Worship.

I have heard nothing of the Library, which you, in your Letter of the 20th of April, 1767 promised to Send me for the Use of the Mission; nor of the other Books you mentioned &c: Which if they have been Sent, I would beg the favour of being acquainted by whom, & to whose care, that I may have them. Common Prayer Books are much wanted in this Mission, especially by the late Conformists--who would be much encouraged, & very thankful if the Venerable Society would be pleased, So far to regard them, as to Send them a Small Supply, tho' hundreds are needed, together with some other good Books; And I would beg leave, particularly, to request a Bible and Prayer Book Suitable for the Church at Goshen, which is truly in a very flourishing way, composed, not only of good livers, but worthy Members. But with relation to the Church in this Town, I found it in a worse condition, than I left it, Some had been turned away from the faith, and others become Scepticks, there being a proud, Self-conceited Arch Infidel at the head of this Mischief; one of which has Since been reclaimed, and brought back to the Lord's Table; the rest remain as they were, I w[ould] therefore beg leave, to renew my Request, for some Books. [When] the deceitfulness of Infidel Principles are discovered, and Infi[deli]ty in the best, & most compendious Manner refuted; by the help of which, I would hope, and endeavour to deliver some of them from the Snare, into which, they have unhappily run themselves.

The number of Communicants in each of my Parishes, I am not able particularly to Ascertain. From January, 4th 1767--to October 9th 1768. I have, after proper Examination and Instruction Baptized 12 Adults; And an 147 Children, two of which had Indian Parents.

The Societies Library at Newhaven, I committed to the Care of my Church Wardens there, when I left that Mission, A Testimonial of which, from under their hands I have here enclosed, which has Since been delivered by them to Mr Hubbard.

I have drawn, by Bills of Exchange, for my Salary &c: to the 25 Day of September last past.

I have nothing further to Add, but my hearty wishes for Success to the Societies pious designs, Who am, Reverend Sir,

both Yours, and their, most obedient humble Servant,

To the Revd Doctor Burton.   Solomon Palmer.

[Addressed:] For / the Revd Doctor Daniel Burton / Secretary to the Society for the / Propagation of the Gospel in / Foreign Parts in Abingdon / Street, Westminster

[Endorsed:] Read...March 13. 1769.

[1769, Jan. 3, Stratford]

To the Honourable The General assembly of The Colony of Connecticut to be holden by adjourndment at New haven on the first Thirsday of January 1769

We being Informed That that our Bretheren of the profestion of The Church of England Liveing in the parrishes of Ripton and New Stratford have a Memorial Now Lying before the s^d General Assembly praying for previledges

of Taxing them Selves & Gathering their own Rates &c We the Subcribers being Sociaty Com^tee in the afore s^d parrishes do here by Shew our desire and willingness that the s^d Memorial should be Granted not onely because we think it to be Reasonable they should Tax themselves and Gather their own Rates as a previledge due to Every English subject but by so doing would Relieve the s^d parrishes from Much Troble and difficulty in Taxing them & Gathering their Rates for them without any Reword for our Troble and pains about the same and we understand that The People off and belonging to the s^d parishes are Generally willing and desirerous for the same to be done and therefore pray that the same May be Granted accordingly

Stratford January 3^d day 1769

Andrew Thompson   ⎰ Society Com^tee for the
Matthew Hawley   ⎱ parish of Ripton

Nathan Booth   John Judson
John Mots   Zechariah Tomlinson ⎰ Society Com^tee
Elijah Adams   Daniel Hawley   ⎱ for the Parish of
Beach Lewis   Sam^ll Blakman   ⎰ New Stratford
Ebenezer Lewis

[1769, Jan. 9, New London]
Rev^d & good S^r

I wou'd have wrote long since to my Venerable Patrons, were it not y^t ye Indian, who waited upon You, wrote, y^t I shou'd soon be favor'd with a Letter from you; w^ch, if you sent, I have not yet receiv'd. Indeed I know very little of w^t ye Society do's, having seen but one Abstract these three last Years, & therefore cannot observe some things, wch might be expected from me. This Loss & Inconvenience, if you please, may be prevented by directing what Parcels are order'd for me to ye Care of Mr Ogilvie in New-York, from whom I shall receive them.

I administer'd clinic Baptism to two Persons, & christned an Adult & her five Children, all brought up Anabaptists & eight other Children, besides nine Children born of dissenting Parents--buryd but one--marryd four Couple, & had two Conformists, since my last.

Mr Byles's Conformity has enrag'd ye dissenters here; & ye tho'ts of an American Bishop drives them almost into distraction throughout New-England.

As I drew in favor of Mr Lotrop of Norwich for last Sep^r, so, I suppose I shall for next March.

Be pleas'd to present my christian Love & Compliments to ye Venerable Society, to obey whom shall be ye Study of their &   Rev^d S^r

Y^r very hum^le Servt &
N. London Jany 9th 1769   Aff^te Bro^r in Christ
P.S.   Matt Graves
A few Christian Monitors &c wou'd be very acceptable--

[1769, Jan. 9, New London]
Revd Sirs

I forgot to mention in my Letter, y^t whereas some Lands were given by some former Sachems of ye Narraganset Tribe to ye Church of England, wch are occupied & every Year much injur'd by a person adjoining, nay, & some of them alienated, & in danger of being for ever lost

to ye Church; & whereas I am at a great deal of Trouble & some Expence in visiting y^t Tribe, above 30 Miles from New-London, I wou'd be highly oblig'd to ye Venerable Society, if they wou'd impower me to set that Land, & receive ye Income for my Trouble. I am told 'twou'd set for about 20 Dollars Per Annum. If my Patrons approve of this Motion, I wou'd endeavor to recover ye Church's Right, & secure it's Interest.

There is a dissenting Teacher, who is hir'd to visit them; but I can truly say, as scarce any do or will attend him, no Minister of any Denomination, except my self, will engage their Attendance or be agreeable to them. Besides, they don't like to be under a dissenting Teacher, & openly declare their Approbation of our Service. By ye Religious Society consenting to my proposal, I shall better be enabled to visit two other Tribes in my way to Narraganset.

Whatever any may say otherwise, a New House, or Tavern was mostly built of ye Church's Timber, & ye Father's glaz'd wth ye Glass given by one Major Buer for y^t Church. I cou[ld s]ay more; but to act impartially, & dischar[g]e my Duty conscientiously shall, ye LORD assisting me, be ye sole Study of,   Good S^r
Y^r very hum^le & obedient
Servt
N. London Jan 9th 1769   Matt Graves

[Addressed:] To / The Revd Doctor Burton / Secretary &c
[Endorsed:] Read...April 17. 1769.

[1769, Mar. 27, Stamford]
Stamford Connecticut New England
March, 27th, 1769.
Reverend Sir.

Permit me to inform the Venerable Board that my Parish remains in a peaceable good religious State, and with usual diligence I give attention to the Duties of my extensive Mission. the number of Heads of families in my Cure much the same, but upon the increase. I baptized last half Year thirty four Children; the Number of Communicants is 87. On Sexagessima sunday last I preached again at Danbury, (distant about 30 Miles) and considering the severity of the season & unfinished state of the Church, the Number that paid a devout attention exceeded expectation.-----

On tuesday following I also attended a Lecture there, when a Number of Dissenters gave attendance; who seem wearied out with their religious contentions, and many appear well disposed to our Church, if they had but a Minister.

Mr Talbot in his day, to induce them to build a Church, with a Steeple, freely gave them One Hundred pound New York money, and under his hand promised them another Hundred to be laid out in Glebe Land for the use of a Minister, and incouraged them to hope for a present of A Bell; but his Death prevented his fulfilling it. He was so concerned to lay a foundation to have them provided for, that a little before his Death he wrote to me to prepare to accompany him again to Danbury, for in compassion to their circumstances, he was determined to bestow two Hundred Pounds more upon them.

The Poor people on the North precinct of the Oblong in

New York Province, bordering on the Towns of Sharon and Salsbury, flatter themselves with hopes of the Societies favour, as soon as they are Qualified therefor. I know of no place where a prudent discreet Missionary would be more eminently & extensively Useful, tha[n] in those back parts, Now full of Inhabitants.

My Bill in usual form, for twenty five Pounds Sterling, is drawn this day upon the Societies Treasurer for the time being in fav.^r of Mr Thomas Ellison Merch^t in New York.

Both Civil & Religious disputes here still run very high, but we hope for more settled and Established times, through the wisdom & Stability of the Government; And a more happy union between our Parent Country and these remote Provinces; and a more effectual encouragement and support of true religion & our holy Church; the best Security to fidelity. Whoever now contends for the faith as it was once delivered to the saints, in opposition to faniticism & independancy, must expect the roughest treatment.

Common prayer Books, some Bibles, Catechisms and other pious small tracts, are very much wanted and would be thankfully Accepted.

Praying God to bless & reward our pious benefactors, and succeed all their charitable designs; with profound Duty to the Venerable Board, and great respect to your self, I Am Reverend Sir

Your Most Obede^t / Most Humble Servt / And Brother in Christ

Ebenez^r Dibblee,

The Reverend Doctor Burton
Secretary of the Venerable Society
for Propagation of the Gospel &c:

[Addressed:] To / The Reverend Doctor Daniel Burton / Secretary of the Venerable Society / for Propagation of the Gospel in / Foreign Parts. Abingdon Street / Westminster London
[Endorsed:] Read...Sepr 11. 1769

[1769, June 25, New Milford]

New Milford, June 25th: 1769
Reverend Sir--

The Reason of my Not Writing to the Society Since the 29 of June 1768, was owing to my being Disappointed in Mr Bostwicks not Going home last fall nor in the Spring.

The Church in all parts of my Mission is in a flourishing State, near a hundred families of the Church in New Milford and 55 Communicants; about 70 at Woodbury and 30 Communicants, & as many at Kent; at Sharon there is about 25 Families; Over in the Oblong in the province of New York there is a Considerable many Church People, under the Most Destitute Circumstances, Not a Clergyman of the Church of England within 30 Miles of them. In this Country Sectaries of all kinds much Abound & Run into the Wildest Errors-- Those amongst them who are of the Established Religion are Erecting of a Church and Qualifying themselves for the Societys favour, if the Society should think proper to Erect a Mission there, I Should be Glad that Sharon and Salisbury (as they Lie Contiguous) might be placed under the Care of that Missionary----
Since the Date of my Last Letter to the Society I have

Baptized 79 Infants, 3 of which were Blacks. I have not as yet Received the prayer Book for the New Church at New Milford, which you mentioned in your Last--

I am Revd S.^r your & the Societys most Obedient Humble Servt

Richard Clarke

I have Drawn upon the Society my two Last Quarter Bills for the year 1768, in Favour of Mr John R. Marshall of Stratford & Mr Josiah Starr of New Milford and I have Likewise drawn for my two first Quarter Bills for the year 1769 beginning at Christmas, in favour of the above named Gentlemen--

To the Revd Doct.^r Daniel Burton,

[1769, Sept. 7, Brooklyn--Pomfret]

Pomfret September 7th 1769
The Inhabitants of the Society of Brooklyn that are by Law Qualified to vote in Society Meetings are hereby Warned to Meet at the Meeting House in S^d Society on Monday the 18th Day of September Instant at two of the Clock PM to Choose Societys officers for the Ensuing Year and see if the Society will vote a tax to pay the Revd Josiah Whitneys Salary the Present Year and also vote a tax to Defray the School and other Society Charges the Ensuing Year and Also to see if the Society Will repair the Meeting House in S^d Society and also to see whether the Society will build a Meeting House in S^d Society for Publick Worship and See how long the Society will Keep School in Each Distrit the Ensuing Year and also to see if the Society will vote that Capt Peirce & others that are in Canterbury that do not belong to any District in S^d Society shall have their part of the Draw Back Money by order of

Benj.ⁿ Peirce   } Society
John Hubbard   } Com^{tee}
Israel Putnam   }

[1769, Oct. 20, Stamford]

Stamford Connecticut In
New England Octob^r, 20th, 1769.
Reverend Sir.

Having received no advice of a New Treasurer, I have this day drawn a set of Bills in customary form for Twenty five Pounds Sterling upon Edward Pearson Esqr Treas.^r or upon the Treasurer of the Venerable Society for ye time being, in favour of Mr Thomas Ellison Ju.^r Merchant in New York----

Notwithstanding the many Rubs we have lately met with, and torrent of abuse thrown upon the whole Church, by our Restless adversaries, whose Jealousies and fears are never to be satisfied, tho' groundless; I have been able by the blessing of God, in a good Measure to preserve my parish in a peaceable good and religious state; as little tinctured, and uncorrupted with ye pernicious principles of ye times, as could be Expected. I Baptized last half Year, Six Adults, and forty two Children, the Number of Communicants in my whole Care, are Eighty Nine.

We hope, through ye Wisdom and Lenity of ye Supreem Legislative Authority of ye Realm, soon to see an End put to our late unhappy Contention about our Civil and religious priviledges; All Just ground of Complaints

removed, our National Religion more effectually Established and protected in ye Colonies, and the best friends of our happy Constitution in Ch^h and State, blessed and Indulged in the full enjoyment of their religious profession and not abridged beyond any other protestant Dissenters. Otherwise the late formidable combinations here in America will afford the members of our holy Church but a Meloncholly prospect. Religion, now is become the tool of party, and subservient to promote the most pernicious Views; unless it pleases God to restore publick tranquility, the consequences are to be dreaded.

Under all ye present Meloncholly Aspects, I shall continue to attend the duties of my extensive Cure with as much chierfulness & Alacrity as possible, and afford, as I still do, what assistance I am able to the destitute, who apply for assistance.

Praying God to Restore peace & a more happy Union among all the parts of the British Empire, prevent the dire Calamities of Civil & religious dissentions, and in a peculiar maner, bless and prosper all the most pious designs, Charitable and kind Offices of the Venerable Board, to whom may my humble Duty and Acknowledgements be acceptable, which, together with due regards and high Esteem to your self; I Am Reverend Sir

Your most Obed^t / Very Humble Servt / And Brother in Christ

Ebenezer Dibblee

The Reverend Doctor Burton
Secretary of the Venerable Society
for Propagation of the Gospel in Foreign Parts.

[1769, Nov. 1, Litchfield]

Connecticut, Litchfield, November the 1st 1769.
Revd Sir,

I have received your Letter of the fifteenth of April last, before which time I had heard of the Library and prayer Books you Sent me in 1767. which came in the Hope, and were Consigned to the Revd Dr Auchmuty, and lately have obtained them; for which I return you, and the Venerable Society my most hearty and Sincere thanks.

With regard to Mr Bostwick, the Bearer of this, who is coming for Holy Orders, and the People who are very fond of him, and greatly desirous to have him for their Minister, to whom he might be peculiarly Serviceable, I need Say nothing, but only refer you to my Letter of the first of November last, wherein you will find a true account given with relation to both, which I hope will be considered by the Society to their Advantage. And Since Sharon in conjunction with Several places in the Province of New-York are Solliciting the Society for a Mission--I would take this opportunity to inform them that Nobleton, and New-Concord in Said Province; and Great-Barrington, and Lainsborough in Boston Government, do upon almost every account, Stand in vastly greater need of their help, as I could easily Demonstrate. The Society have already done much this way, too much indeed for Some of their Missions, & enough for the rest. To Some of their Missionaries they allow £50 Sterling Salary Per Annum whose People are more than able of themselves to Support them & ought therefore to relinquish all claim to the Societies Money, and yet pay but little: whilst to others they allow no more than £20 or 30. which they really Stand in need

of, as they live amongst a poor People, and have the greatest Task imposed upon them. As for my part, I Suppose I perform more tedious, long and expensive journeys and Preach more occasional Lectures than Some five of my Brethren, whose Sterling Salaries are almost double to mine, (which is enough) and whose People are more than twice as able to maintain them, and yet give them no more than mine do me, which I look upon to be an unreasonable Indulgence, and unwarrantable dependence upon the Society. I heartily wish, (which would be much for the Credit of the Society, and the Church of England in these parts) that these Matters were rightly understood, and duly considered and adjusted; and then I am Sure that the Money now given in Salaries by the Society to their respective Missionaries, would not only be enough for each, but that there would be an overplus Sufficient to Supply destitute places that Stand in need of their help, and without which must remain without Setled Ministers, as the places above mentioned, or else give them but a poor Support, Such as would bring their Persons into contempt, and render their Labours unsucseful.

In all parts of my Mission the Church is encreasing and especially at Goshen, a Town joyning upon Litchfield, where from Seven Famolies when I came here they have grown up to near fifty, who, when they were but about 20 in Number, Erected a Church, and in a Short Time made it fit to meet in for Divine Service &c--upon whose desire, I would Ask leave to requ[e]st for them, a Bible and prayer Book, Such as the Society shall be pleased to give.

Since my last, being just a Year ago, I have Baptized Seven Adults, and an hundred and Seven Infants. Actual Communicants are pretty much the Same.

I am Revd Sir, / your, and the Societies / most dutiful & Humble Servant,

Solomon Palmer.

[Addressed:] For / The Reverend Doctor Daniel / Burton Secretary to the Society / for the Propagation of the Gospel / in Foreign Parts, / In Abingdon Street, / Westminster.
[Endorsed:] Read...Feb^ry 12. 1770

[1769, Nov. 20, New Milford]

New-Milford Novr 20[t]h 1769
Reverend Sir,

There are ma[n]y well dispos'd Church Families within the Limits of this Mission (especially at the Parish of New-Preston) whos Necessities plead the venerable Society's Favour in sending of them some Prayer Books & other small pious Tracts, they being really unable to supply either their Families or themselves.

Within this Mission several Families, besides single Persons, have conformed to the Church since my first coming into it, tho' at the Time, I cant say the Congregations are much Larger (excepting at New Milford which is conside[rably] larger) by Reason of many Families moving from hence, back into the new settled Countries.

I have baptized since the 25 of June Ult 21 Infants and one Adult who was educated a Quaker. The church People in this Mission seem to adorn their Profession by a suitable Conduct.

As I am not of a robust Constitution but quite the re-

verse, I find the Dutuies of so extensive a Mission rather too severe, tho', by the Grace of God, I hope faithfully to discharge the Duties of the Mission

I am Reverend Sir your / and the Society's most obed.^t humble / Servt

Richard Clarke

I have drawn upon the Society for my third Quarter Bill for the y.^r 1769 in Favour of Mr Gideon Bostwick

[Addressed:] To / The Reverend Doctor Daniel Burton / Secretary to the Society for the propagation / of the Gospel in foreign Parts / Abingdon Street / Westminster
[Endorsed:] Read...Feb.^{ry} 12. 1770

[1769, Dec. 13, New London]
Rev.^d & Good S.^r

I woud have wrote much sooner to my Venerable Patrons, but resolv'd to obey their prudent Directions, their cautionary Advice. Accordingly I procur'd a Copy to be taken off ye Records, containing ye following Words.

One Deed, given by Geo: Ninegret to ye Church of England in Charlestown & Westerly in ye County of King's County in ye Colony of Rhode-Island, & for securing & setling ye Service & Worship of GOD amongst them, according to ye Usage of y.^t most excellent Church within ye s.^d Charles Town: wch Deed contains by Estimation 40 Acres of Land, & is bounded as follows, viz beginning at a Stake w.th stones about it--then running South 38º E 45 Rods & 1/4 to Stone & Heap of Stones by ye Country Road, & from thence easterly as ye Road runs 128 Rods to a Stake w.th Stones about it--from thence North 14º. W. 40 Rods to a stake w.th stones about it--from thence North 14º W 40 Rods to a small white Oak Tree, mark'd on two sides--from thence S.^o 50º. W.^t 12 Rods to a heap of stones --from thence N.º 75º W. 12 Rods to a Stake & Stones-- from thence a straight line to ye first mentioned Corner. The Consideration in S.^d Deed is five Shill.^{gs} Old Tenor & is dated ye 14.th of Jany AD 1745/6

Attested per John Horsey Town Clk
Novr 21.st 1767

Now if ye religious Society wou'd think proper to write to Ja.^s Honeyman Esqr, living in Newport in ye Colony of Rhode Island, Son of their old faithful Missionary there; desiring him to examin into ye Affair, & send his Opinion, they may expect a full & satisfactory Knowledge of ye Deed. Permit me, S.^r, by you to inform ye Society, y.^t there were two Deeds, ye first granting 40 Acres of Land, 20 on one side of ye high Road, & 20 on ye other, opposite to it, lying towards ye Sea--these latter 20 Acres one Mr Champlain w.th ye Approbation of ye Revd Mr Punderson, then Missionary at Grotton, appointed to preach occasionally in those parts, got exchang'd by Act of Assembly at Newport for 20 adjoining ye former 20, tho' ye latter 20 were worth 60 Acres more y.ⁿ ye other, those for wch they were exchang'd. This I know, having frequently seen ye Lands; as I also have ye Church built upon ye former 20 Acres, wch Mr Champlain of his own accord had taken down, tho' divine Service had been often perform'd in it: & when it was taken down, I'm told, he had it valued, & built a Tavern w.th ye Timber. I know ye very spot ye Church stood on; for on ye high road, adjoining ye Fence

next ye Church, Trees grew, wch were since cut down, & ye small Stumps are there yet. If you write to Mr Honeyman, desire him to consult Mr Mumford ye old Post [rider], who can & will inform him of every particular, relating both to ye Land & Church, & also y.^t ye Glass bought & given by Major Buer (if I remem[b]er right) was by s.^d Champlain converted to his own Use, promising y.^t ye Church shou'd have it again; but 'twas never done. Mr Honeyman will chearfully grant any favor you desire; he is a Gentleman of Fortune, an honest Lawyer, & a faithful Friend to our Church. If I can do any thing in ye affair, direct, command, & I'll obey.

My Parishoners, S.^r, rather increase amidst ye Strifes & Contentions raging in these Parts. I have buried five & baptiz'd 12, beside an adult Negroe whom I instructed before hand, & have since admitted her to ye LORD's Supper. My Communicants, except ye last one, remain ye same. I crossed ye Sea, preach'd several times, & am invited both by ye Ministers & People to renew my Visit. I have rode above 200 Miles, since my last, on ye Island & places about 30 Miles off. Tho' Bills are 5 Per C.^t below Par, I must draw on ye Treasurer, & doubt not of it's acceptance in March next-- My Duty & Compliments beg leave to wait on ye religious Society, whose Approbation I'll study conscientiously to obtain. That ye Blessing of GOD may attend their Designs & y.^r Study is ye constant Prayer of their &

              Rev.^d & Good S.^r
N. London   Y.^r most oblig'd & very hum.^{le}
Decem.^r 13. 1769   Servt, & Aff.^{te} Brother in Christ
                  Matt Graves

The last Books came very seasonably, & shall be distributed according to ye very pious Intention of ye religious Donors. Excuse me for asking a few late Abstracts.

To the Revd Dr Burton Secretary

[1769, Dec. 20, Norwalk]

To promote the Gospel among the Indians, the 2.^d thing I propose is, That all the Missionaries shd be single men, & marry into some chief family of the Tribe to w.^h they are sent. 3.^d thing proposed is, That only one sort of christians shd be allowed to go among them, for if there be more, neither will succeed.

My zeal for the cause I wrote upon must be my apology for laying my mind so freely open to your excellency in an affair unsolicited.

I understand the convention of the Clergy of this Colony have wrote to you in fav.^r of Patrick Thacher Esqr the Bearer of this, who I have been informed waits upon your excellency for advice in matters of great importance. You will find him a plain, honest man, a thorough Churchman, and a good Man; In short he has been trained up in our spiritual slanders where he has learnt the use of every weapon, & always ready to defend religion from the perpetual attacks of Dissenters & Infidels.

     I am may it please y.^r excellency &c
Norwalk in Cont.^t⎫   Jeremiah Leaming
Decr 20. 1769. ⎬   Miss.^{ry} at Norwalk
          ⎭

[Extract from letter to Sir Wm. Johnson in the Library of Congress.]

[1770, Feb. 6, Pomfret]

1770-

Whereas, at a Society Meeting this day convened in the Parish of Brookline, in the Township of Pomfret and Colony of Connecticut, it hath been voted and Resolved to demolish the Present meeting House appropriated to publick, Religious Worship and in the Place thereof to erect a new one, the expence of which is to be paid by an Assesment on the parishioners, conformable to their Lists given in to the Assessors; We the Subscribers; Inhabitants of said Parish, do hereby dissent and Solemnly protest against the said Vote and Resolutions for the Reasons following

1st We deem the Present House, with a few Trifling Repairs, altogether Sufficient, proper and adequate to the Purpose for which it was Originally designed; It being in noways antiquated, and with a very small Expence, may be Render'd equal to what it was when first finished, but about Thirty years ago, and full as decent as the Situation of the Parishioners will admit, and certainly much more Suitable to our Circumstances, in general, than the Costly, unnecessary Fabrick proposed to be erected; God Almighty not being so much delighted with Temples made with Hands, as with meek, Humble and upright Hearts

2d If the building a new Meeting House shoud have been really necessary, from the destruction of the one we have, at Present by any Act of Divine Providince, it would be prudent to postpone it, rather than Burthen the Inhabitants at this very distressfull Time when there is scarcely a Farthing of Money circulating among us, and those who are esteemed the most wealthy are obliged to send their Produce to markets far distant, selling it at a very under Rate to raise a sufficiency for the Payment of Taxes for the support of the ministry only. And the Generality, with their families scarce able (altho We pay no Provinc Tax) to Live a poor, miserable, wretched Life; And some (qualified only by being Members of the meeting) who have now joined in this Vote, are excused, by Reason of their extreme Poverty, from the Payment of any Rates at all, and, notwithstanding, their Voices, most unfairly, have equal Weight with those among us who must bear the greatest Proportion of this very unnecessary Burthen, which appears to be, and is absolutely, undertaken rather from a Ridiculous, despicable Spirit of Ostentation, Levity and Wantonness, than from an Inclination to serve God.

3d The Sole Point[?] which was, or could possibly be urged, with the Least Shadow of Reason, in support of this measure at our Last Society meeting on the 18th of September past, which was the Incapacity of the present meeting House to Contain the number of Hearers, is now entirely removed by the Charitable Benevolence of Pious and Well disposed Persons; who considering our general Inability to accomplish so Laudible a Purpose of ourselves, have freely and Voluntarily, contributed a Sufficient Sum to erect a Church for the Publick worship of God, according to the use of the Church of England, in which we have already made a very Considerable Progress, and, when Compleated, which We Reasonably hope will be by the end of next summer, We propose to form a distinct Congregation by ourselves, which leaving Room in the meeting in proportion to the number of Families that draw off to the more rational Worship of the Church, will, consequently save the absurd, unnecessary, extravagant and Ill Judged Expence which by this Vote, must be Charged upon the Parish.

4th The Meeting being Called at this unusual Time of the Year Which is very uncommon; as the sense of the Parish, upon this Occasion, hath been Twice before Taken, Viz. in September 1768, and again so lately as in September 1769, and a Question of this nature being not customarily, renewed untill the Return of the Year, makes it appear plainly to us that this extraordinary Effort hath been made, merely from a Spirit of Enmity and opposition to the Progress of the Church, which some of you, led by a blind Zeal and mistaking the means for the End of Religion cannot bear to see erected amongst you, as you know and are convinced, from all experience, that it cannot but thrive and prosper, to the Diminution and weakning Your own Establishment; wherefore you would burthen the members of it, Who by Law would be exempted before the anual Return of the Time of holding your society meetings, with every possible expence in order to defeat and destroy their Pious and Commendable design by which Conduct, as we are to form a Judgement of the Tree from the Fruit that it Bears, it seems Suspicious that ye are not actuated merely by a motive of Religion, but that ye are a People that Honour Almighty God with your Lips, while your Heart is far from Him. Otherwise ye, most wrongly, Conceive that he can be pleased with a Sacrifice made up by downright cruel Oppression

For all which Reasons, We do again, in the most Publick and Solemn manner, hereby repeat our Dissent and do, absolutely, protest against this Vote and every part of this procedure, and all Damages, Costs and Charges, which in Defence of our Just Rights and Liberties may be Consequent thereupon. In Testimony whereof we have hereunto Set our hands at Pomfret this Sixth Day of February 1770.

Godfrey Malbone   Nehemiah Adams
William Walton   Jedidiah Ashcraft
Noah Adams   Benjamin Cady
Jabez Allyn   Thomas Adams
Joseph Hubbard

[1770, Pomfret]

1770

[Endorsed:] Narrative of what pass'd at the Church Meeting at Pomfret in Connecticutt respecting the Building a New Meeting house.

When the Meeting was opened and the Warrant, declaring the Purpose for which they were assembled, had been read, Mr Malbone Stood up and informed the Moderator, That He and a Number of others had agreed to form a Congregation to Worship the Divine Being according to the Manner of the Church of England and that very great Progress was already made towards Building the Church, and as this was notoriously the Case He demanded the Sense of the Meeting whether or not, the Churchmen as He Should now call them were to be affected by any Vote or Resolution of their's-- For if such a Thing was not meant they would all of them withdraw, and not interrupt the Business of their Meeting-- But, if on the contrary, the Design of the Meeting, as it appeared very Suspicious, was particularly levelled against them, He and they were determined to oppose it with the most calm but determined Resolution-- It was determined, that as they were not by Law e[x]emptd by any Resolution of a future Mode of Worship

which had not then an Existence that they were affected--

After Some Debate, Upon the Question, the Vote was put and there were 77 Voices for and 24 against the Meeting. Every Person in the Parish the Lame, the Halt & the blind being collected on the Occasion to vote against a Bishop, for it had been given out, that building a Church was tantamount to introducing a Bishop and this Bishop would take to Himself the Tenth Bushell of all the Grain &c they raised &c And if we can make these People who are going to join the Church first pay towards Building a Meeting H[ouse]--we will not Care a Farthing what becomes of a Church and the Matter will of Course fall through-- But as this was not enough the Teacher from the Pulpit (preaching from I Kings 18 Chap 21 V. How Long will ye halt between two Opinions? If the Lord be God, follow Him: but if Baal, then, follow Him) thundering out His Anathemas, in three different Discourses upon the Same Words, against all those who Should not exert themselves to defend their Religious Liberties which were now so violently invaded, and I dare say much more of the Same Stuff of Nonsense. This Spirited up some of the Principles [Principals] to the Use of Bribes, Threats, Promises &c. to the effectual Accomplishment of what they So much desired--

Malbone complained to the Moderator of the Injustice of the Vote, which must very much affect the Property of a Sett of Men, who might now be considered, to all intents & Purposes, as of a distinct Congregation and who, most unjustly, must be made to pay and very dearly, not only for what was really unnecessary, but for what they could not, in the Nature of Things, even in the Least benefited and He begged them to consider How improper Such a Conduct was, just at this Juncture, when they themselves were Loudly complaining and remonstrating, petitioning &c against the Same Conduct in Mother Country, which they themselves did not in the Least Scruple so violently to practice. He desired Him not to adjourn the Meeting, but give Time to the 24 Objectors to Sign a Protest which, upon a Certainty of their Resolution, He had ready drawn in His Pocket. The Moderator, with out taking the Opinion of the Meeting, consented. Malbone drew off to a Seat in the Corner of the Meeting to Sign this Instrument & almost immediately but Nine Heads having Signed it, He had a Message from the Moderator to come up to the Table, When T. Williams a Justice of the Peace objected to the Protests being received as altogether unprecedented &c and asked why He thought it necessary or what Service it could possibly do Him. He answered He conceived Himself much grievously imposed upon by the Vote & for Himself & the others who formed the Church He was determined to proceed in the Opposition against this manifest Invasion of their Rights & Liberties (which Words He Studiously employed upon every possible Occasion) with all possible Regularity and a most determined Resolution to persevere in His Defence of His own & their R[ight]s & L[ibertie]s to the very utmost of His Abilities, and that if He could not find Relief in this Colony, that He would Seek it, where He was most certain to find it from the Head of the Church, Our most gracious King-- His Studied Affectation of the Words Rights and Liberties and His Declaration of appealing to the King, very apparently affected their Countenances-- Anger and Disdain Seemed to dart from their Eyes-- One of them replied He was Surprized that He, a Gentleman whom every Body meaned to treat

with the utmost Respect, Should Seek occasion to make Such frequent Mention of the R--s & Lib's, which no Body meant to hurt, nor that there was one Man in the Parish who wanted to deprive Him of a Single Farthing; why then will you threaten us with this Protest and the King & Council-- All Faces expressing the utmost Resentment were now fixed upon Him pressed with the Surrounding Crowd-- Sir, Says He, After a three year's Residence among you, I should have imagined that you had discovered So much of my Temper & Disposition as to know with Certainty, that I never mean to threaten-- I always mean to educate, and I now repeat that as my Ri--s & L--s and the R--s & L--s of those who form the Church with me are most violently invaded, that I have drawn up this Protest against it, which as Soon as Signed I mean to declare to you all Publickly by reading it in this Meeting, and then to deliver it to your Moderator, to be by Him delivered to the Clerk to be placed upon Record, that from this I may have a certified Copy on which I purpose to found my Opposition to this most unjust & arbitrary Measure & that if the Government of Connecticut will not relieve me, rely upon it, I do not mean to threaten you, if I am not most amazingly mistaken, the King will, to whom I will, as certainly appeal, as God Spares my Life and I will also interest the whole Church upon the Content in the Cause, which I think, upon good Grounds, I shall most certainly be able to do-- Therefore Gentlemen, Do not mistake the Matter so far, as to think that I mean to threaten, I will give my word and Honour and my Estate into the Bargain if I do not really execute, which ye may soon find out to your Sorrows--

There was a considerable Juggle & as He knew they would not receive His Protest He waved His Motion--

N.B. The Meeting have been called, purposely, to burthen those who had left them to join the Church, with their Proportions of the Expense of building the Meeting House; whether it would not be practicable to obtain an Order from the Throne, upon the Representation of G. Malbone, W[m] Walton & others, to this Government to relieve them from this intolerable Oppression? If it could, it would be a glorious Point gained & would redound to the advantage of the Church, in a very Singular Manner, throughout the Colony.

It is a great Pity, that what may be productive of Such general good Consequences Should excite in any particular Person the Least Spirit of Envy, Contention or reviling. I trust that We, who are to form the Church will so demean Ourselves towards God and our Neighbours as not to give the weakest Brother of you all the Least Offence. As for my own Part, [I] am determined, at Least, not to deserve your Ill-Will. I flatter My Self that the Example will be followed. If you, then, on your Parts, will Set up the Same Resolution and endeavour to recommend Your Selves to the Divine Being by every possible good-office to your Brethren----What a glorious Emulation! How noble a Contention! And How worthy universal Imitation would this be? Let us then not neglect the Opportunity that is now Set before Us; for I humbly conceive that by as much as this Measure may be now disagreable to you, by so much the more acceptable to the Father of Mercies will be your Adoption of a Spirit of Reconciliation & Benevolence. A mutual Striving in offices of Love cannot

but be, from every Warrant of Scripture, a certain Means of recommending Us to the Throne of Grace.

[1770, Mar. 13, Pomfret]
Dear John,

This will be delivered to you by Stephen Hazard, whom I sent for, by John Howland, with an Intention of engaging Him in my Service as an Overseer on the Farm. I learnt by Him & one Knowles, His Companion, who hires the Beaver Tail Farm (Part of it) that Hazard let Himself out for the 8 Seasonable Months at £50 Old Tenor only per Month, which Hazard says Himself is true. I offered Him One Hundred Dollars a Year, for the Service of Himself and His Wife, and to maintain Him & five Children, the eldest but 11 years old, the year round, free of any Expence, except their cloathing. My Terms do not Suit Him-- He requires 160 Dollars, which, however unable I am convinced my Constitution is to undergo the Fatigues of the Business that I am engaged in, I am determined not to give. It is in vain that I have represented to Him that whatever He receives of me at the year's End is so much clear gain; whereas the Maintenance of His Family at His own Expence must infallibly absorb His whole Earnings, be they what they will. I have promised Him that He should not lose his Time or be at any Expence in coming to see me, for which I have engaged that you should pay Him four Dollars, the Expence of Ferriages for Himself and the Retinue He brings with Him included. I have made use of the Opportunity by Him to send down four fat Cattle. I have paid him all the Silver I had in the House 8s / 1 1/4, to bear Expences on the Road to the Ferry-- What ever it comes to more, you are to pay Him over & above His Four Dollars. I fancy my Beef will be tolerably good though nothing equal to what it was the last year. They have been very highly fed the whole Winter, and I am sure 3^d a Pound will scantily make an Amends for the Expence. I am in Hopes they will produce that. Dick Chilcot tells me the Doctor & Major will each of them take a Side & Jonathan Thurston a Side; The other five Sides I imagine you may easily get rid of among our particular acquaintance-- If you do not chose this Trouble, you may sell them to the Butchers, if they will pay you the Ready, on Foot. I had a very great Inclination to follow my Cattle my self, but this is so critical a Season with my Stock, that I am afraid to leave the Farm. We lost one three year old Heifer, by Accident, last Saturday Night. Otherwise We are all in extreme good Order. I shall not be able to keep over so much Hay as I did the last Summer, but I am in Hopes We shall have a Sufficiency to carry us very well through. I have let the Paine & Nantasquet Farms to Joseph Kingsbury and His son, of Scotland upon a Seven year's Lease. For the three first years at £40 & the whole Rent to be paid out in Improvements. For the four last years at £58-- Twenty nine Pounds of which to be employed in Improvements on the Farm & the remaining £29 in Cash. I suppose I have already told you that I have renewed Murdock's Lease at £30 and Ashcraft's at £25; each of them for five years, to be paid one half Cash and the other half in Improvements.

Our Timber for the Church is all cut & except, four Sticks, drawn to the Spot. You must also except what is drawn to the Saw-Mill-- The Non-Cons had a Society

Meeting last Week and voted a Tax of Nine Pence a Pound, on the Last August List, to be paid in, on the first Day of December next. Was ever any Thing so damned-Stupidly-barefaced?-- It is evident to me The Scoundrells are cursed Fools, or they would quit their Nonsensical Practices in Religion-- This Matter Must carry me infallibly to the General Assembly at Hartford in May next, where if We do not get Relief I am determined, So help me God! to appeal to the King in Council, where if I am not an over-Match for the Little Parish of Brookline, Adieu to all Religion, Friendship & every Virtue! To prepare the Way for this important Step, I have Scribbled, already, more Paper in three Months, than ever I did before, I was going to say, in twice as many years.

By Jim's Return Send me a good Lock for the outer Door of the Dairy House-- One of the Barrells Mackarell you sent for me to Providence two Autumns ago, I have received, and it turns out a Barrell of very bad Beef. Whether the Mistake was made at Newport or Providence I know not. Let me know whether I must consume it here, or send it back again. I will not allow one Copper Difference-- Write to Nick. Tillinghast about it. The other Barrell still remains at Providence. Our Bridges are all gone. I suppose I must send my Cheese to Norwich, when the Carts go down for Materials for the Church. You have not sent me one quarter Seed Pease enough. The Season last year was so much against us, that not a Single Pea of our own filled in the Pod.

Give our Duty to our Mother and remember us to our Friends. You need not risque the sending me any Money by Jim, as I suppose Some of our Friends will be travelling this Way before long; or I my self may take a step towards Newport. I remain

Your Affectionate Brother & Friend
G. Malbone

Pomfret 13 March 1770.

[P.S.] N. Governor Wentworth hath endowed the Church at Pomfret with a whole Share or Right in the Township of Lyme, on Connecticut River, free from all past Taxes or Charges whatsoever.

[Addressed:] To / Mr John Malbone / In / Newport / By S. Hazard.

[1770, Mar. 15, New London]
Rev^d S^r

At last I have procur'd two Copies of ye deed, I mention'd in my last: One inclos'd, of wch if you make no mention in y^r next, I will send ye other. If ye Religious Society wou'd be pleas'd to desire James Honeyman Esqr Lawyer in Newport in Rhode Island, to search in to this Affair, he wou'd discover more than I can. If this Advice is acceptable, they wou'd do well to desire him to consult one Mr Mumford, ye old Post-rider, Jo^n Case, Thos Brown & one Willet Esq^{rs} at Tower Hill in Narraganset with some others, yet living, who can tell, where ye original Lands were; for (as Dr. Macsparran told me) 20 of good Land were exchang'd for 20 Acres of bad--ye Church thrown down in my time, & a Tavern built wth part of ye Timber--ye Glass for ye Church, given by one Major Buer, (who also bestow'd Glass to ours) put into Coll: Champlain's

Custody, wᵗʰ wᶜʰ he glaz'd his own house, without Satisfaction to yᵉ Church, as yᵉ old Post [rider] told me-- Service was occasionally perform'd in Sᵈ Church, as yᵉ old Post told me; & on yᵉ high road, adjoining yᵉ Church, severa[l] Trees were planted, & growing, since I came, now cut down, but yᵉ Stumps remain. As yᵉ Coll: is a Person of some Interest; & as his Son (lately deceas'd) was guilty of demolishing yᵉ Church, &, if I'm rightly inform'd, of having yᵉ Lands exchang'd; perhaps yᵉ Coll: will get a certain Person to write in his Favor, & therefore, I humbly Conceive, 'twou'd not be amiss if yᵉ Society wou'd send two Letters, one to Joⁿ Case Esqʳ, who will bequeath a fine Legacy to yᵉ Church; a second to Thoˢ Brown Esqʳ a truly pious & conscientious Gentleman, who gave above £100 Sterᵍ toward purchasing a Parsonage & Glebe these Gentlemen will lead you into yᵉ whole Truth of this Affair. If I can be serviceable, my Patrons may command me.

Since my last I have travell'd near 200 Miles, by Sea & Land, spreading yᵉ Service & Doctrins of our Church, where she was not known before. I have bury'd four Persons, baptis'd seven, & yᵉ Communicants are still yᵉ same. Endeed Religion is almost silenc'd & dethron'd by yᵉ prevailing, factious Politics of yᵉ times. The restless Congregationalists & Independents are ceaseless in defaming our happy, ecclesiastic Constitution, & have adopted Juno's Malevolence--Flectere si nequeo Superes &c. The Blessings of a Bishop to our Churches here wou'd be inconceivable. Perhaps GOD permits these Confusions, because his Vineyard, tho' surrounded wᵗʰ restless E[ne]mies, is neglected. I have drawn for my last Year's Salary in favor of Messʳˢ Russells of Providence. The tedious Severity of yᵉ Winter prevented this from coming sooner. My Duty & christian Love desire to wait on my Religious Patrons, whom to pray for is my Duty, & whom to obey is yᵉ Interst, as it shall be yᵉ Practice of their &

                    Revᵈ & Good Sir
                    Yʳ most obedient Servᵗ &
N. London March   very affᵗᵉ Broʳ in Christ
    15ᵗʰ 1770   Matt Graves

[Endorsed:] Read...Augˢᵗ 13. 1770

[1770, Apr. 10, Brooklyn--Pomfret]
    To the Honll the General Assembly of the Colony of Connecticut convened at Hartford Second Thursday of May 1770

Humbly Shew the Petitioners Subscribers hereunto, Inhabitants of the Parish of Brooklime within the Township of Pomfret and parts thereto adjacent

That your Petitioners desirous of Worshipping God in Publick according to their Own Sentiments and the Direction of their Consciences in the Beginning of October AD: 1769 did Assemble themselves together and enter into Engagements for Building and erecting within the Said Parish of Brooklime a House or Church for the Publick Worship of God according to the Model established by the Name of the Church of England and for the Supplying the Said Church with a Minister duly Qualified and have Since carried the Same into Execution So that Publick Worship will be performed therein in a few Months

That the Publick Meeting House within the Said Parish of Brooklime ever hath been and Still is of Dimensions Sufficient to contain the Congregation that hath been used to assemble therein and with Some few Repairs would be a good and a Decent House

That Soon after it became known that your Petitioners had entered into the Engagements aforementioned, the Inhabitants of Said Brooklime at a Society Meeting holden at Said Brooklime upon the Sixth day of February AD: 1770 did Vote and Order that the publick Meeting House in the Parish of Brooklime Should be pulled down and a New One erected in Stead thereof the expence whereof Should be paid by an Assessment on the Parishioners conformable to their Lists given in to the Assessors, And to precipitate the Said Transaction the Said Society Meeting did afterwards Viz: upon the Ninth day of March then Next following Vote and Resolve that the Assessment aforesaid Should be compleated according to the list of Rateable Estates given in in the Month of September last past altho the Said Tax or Assessment by Said Vote is Not Made payable or Subject to be levied until the first day of December AD: 1770 by which illegal and unprecedented Steps it is Made Manifest that the whole was framed with a design to include Such of your Petitioners as belonged to Brooklime in the Taxation altho the Church Should before that Time be erected in Brooklime and themselves be excused by the Statute of this Colony

Whereupon your Petitioners Humbly Pray that in and upon Condition the Church intended by your Petitioners to be Built in the Said Parish of Brooklime Shall be by them Built So that Publick Worship [may be conducted] before the Said first Day of December that then your Petitioners may Stand accquitted and discharged from Said Tax or Assessment, or that this Honᵇˡ Assembly will otherwise Relieve your Petitioners as in your Wisdom and Justice you Shall think Fitt and your Petitioners as in Duty Bound Shall ever pray

Dated at Brooklime this 10 day of April 1770

Godfrey Malbone	Benjamin Cady
John Allyn	Benjᵃ Jewett
Jonathan Wheeler	Seth Sabin
Henry Cady	Benjᵐ Wiggins
John Wheeler	William Walton
Jacob Gert	Joseph Hubbard
Elihu Adams	Noah Adams
Leonard Cady	Jonas Cleaveland
John Ashcraft	Jesse Cleavland
Jacob Staples	Timothy Lovejoy
Thomas Adams	Benjⁿ Herrick
Isaac Adams	Jabez Allyn
Daniel McCloud	Jedidiah Ashcraft
Benjⁿ Hubbard	Jedediah Ashcraft [?Jr.]
James Aldpedy	Nehemiah Adams
Caleb Spaulding	Ahaziah Adams
James Darbe Juner	Thomas Smith

We the Underwritten Inhabitants of Towns adjacent to the Parish of Brooklime and United in Building Said Church Beg leave to Recommend the aforegoing Petitition to your Honours as reasonable and fit to be granted

J. Aplin	Dudley Wade
Abijah Cady	Morgan Connors

Peter Yost	Sam! Cleaveland
Asa Stevens	Jonatha[n] Downing
Timothy Adams	Edward Cleaveland
William Pellet	Robt Durkee

These Names should have been aded to the Names of those in Towns adjacent

	John Tyler
John Pellet	Phileman Holt
Sam!! Adams	Phineas Tyler
Rich? Smith	Zeb. Tyler
David Pellet	Joseph Pellet
John Pellet Ju.r	David Hide
Caleb Faulkner	Tho.s Pellet

[1770, Apr. 10, Brooklyn--Pomfret]

To the Sheriff of the County of Windham his Deputy or Constable of Pomfret in said County Greeting--

Whereas Godfrey Malbone and others Inhabitants of the Town of Pomfret in the Parish of Brooklime & Parts thereto adjacent brought their Petition to the Hon.! Gen.! Assembly of the Colony of Connecticut to be holden at Hartford on the Second Thursday of May Instant in the following Words Viz.t

Connecticut Ss To the Hon.! the Gen.! Assembly of the Colony of Connecticut conven'd at Hartford second Thursday of May 1770-- Humbly shew the Petitioners subscribers hereunto, Inhabitants of the Parish of Brooklime within the Township of Pomfret and Parts thereto adjacent--

That your Petitioners desirous of Worshiping God in Publick according to their own Sentiments and the Direction of their Consciences in the Beginning of October 1769 did Assemble themselves together and enter into Engagements for Building and Erecting within the said Parish of Brooklime a House or Church for the Publick Worship of God according to the Model established by the name of The Church of England and for the supplying the said Church with a Minister duly qualified; and have since carried the same into Execution, so that Publick Worship will be performed therein in a few months--

That The Publick Meeting House [Congregational] within the said Parish of Brooklime ever hath been and still is of Dimensions sufficient to contain the Congregation that hath been used to assemble therein, and with some few Repairs would be a Good & a Decent House--

That soon after it became known that your Petitioners had enter'd into the Engagements aforementioned the [non-Anglican] Inhabitants of said Brooklime at a Society Meeting holden at said Brooklime upon the sixth day of February AD 1770 did Vote & order that the Publick Meeting House [Congregational] in the Parish of Brooklime should be pulled down and a new one erected instead thereof the Expence whereof should be paid by an Assessment on the Parishioners conformable to their Lists given in to the Assessors; and to precipitate the said Transaction the said Society Meeting [Congregational] did Afterwards Viz.t upon the ninth day of March then next following vote and resolve that the Assesment aforesaid should be compleated according to the List of Rateable Estates given in in the Month of September last past altho the said Tax or Assesment by said Vote is not made payable or subject to

be levied untill the first day of December 1770; by which illegal and unprecedented steps it is made manifest that the whole was passed with a Design to include such of your Petitioners as belonged to Brooklime in the Taxation altho the Church should before that time be erected in Brooklime and themselves be excused by the Statute of this Colony--

Whereupon your Pet.s humbly pray that in and upon Condition the [Episcopal] Church intended by your Petitioners to be built in the said Parish of Brooklime shall be by them built so that Publick Worship be performed therein at or before the said first day of December that then your Petitioners may stand acquitted and discharged from said Tax or Assesment. Or that this Hon.ll Assembly will otherwise relieve your Petitioners as in your Wisdome and Justice you shall think fit. And your Pet.s as in Duty bound shall ever pray--

Dated at Brooklime this 10th day of April 1770--

Godfrey Malbone	Tho.s Adams
Joseph Hubbard	Benj.a Hubbard
Timothy Lovejoy	James Darbe Ju.r
Jese Cleaveland	Benj.a Wiggins
Jedidiah Ashcraf	Jon.a Wheeler
Ahaziah Adams	Jacob Geer
Jacob Staple	Sam.! Adams
Dan.! McCloud	William Walton
Caleb Spaulding	Jonas Cleaveland
Benj.a Jewet	Jabez Allyn
John Allyn	Nehemiah Adams
John Wheeler	John Ascraft
Joseph Pellet	Isaac Adams
Leonard Cady	James Eldridge
Noah Adams	Benj.a Cady
Benj.a Herrick	Seth Sabin
Jedediah Ashcraft J.r	Henry Cady
Thomas Smith	Elihu Adams

We the Subscribers Inhabitants of Towns adjacent to the Parish of Brooklime and united in Building said Church beg leave to recommend the aforegoing Petition to your Hon.s as reasonable and fit to be granted

John Pellet	Caleb Faulkner
Richard Smith	Phineas Tyler
John Tyler	Abijah Cady
Tho.s Pellet	Peter York
David Pellet	William Pellet
Joseph Pellet	Edward Cleaveland
Sam.! Adams	Richard Burt
Jn.o Pelet Ju.r	David Hide
Philemon Holt	Dudley Wade
John Aplin	Asa Stevens
Morgan Connors	Sam.!! Cleaveland
Timothy Adams	Robert Durkee
Jonathan Downing	

And Whereas the Consideration of said Petition is by said Assembly defered intill their Sessions in October next---

These are therefore In his Maj.s Name to command you to summon Seth Payne Ju.r one of the Principal Inhabitants of the said Parish [Congregational] of Brooklime and the Rest of the Inhabitants of said Parish to appear before

the General Assembly of the said Colony to be holden at New Haven in said Colony on the second Thursday of October next to shew reason if any they have why the Prayer of the foregoing Petition should not be granted; and you are to summon them by leaving a true and Attested Copy of this Citation with the said Seth Paine Jur at least twelve days before the first Tuesday after the said second Thursday, that they appear &c on the said first Tuesday-- Hereof fail not and of this Citation with your Doings make due Return--

Dated in Hartford this 25th day of May 1770---
Elepht Dyer Assist

September 14th 1770 then Left A true and attested copy of this original Citation and Memorial With the above named Seth Paine Junr Test Josiah Fasset Constable

In the upper House On this Memorial, Granted, that Colo Godfrey Malbone the first Subscriber hereto, be acquitted and discharged from any Tax or Assesment laid or that may be made or laid on him by said [Congregational] Society of Brookline for or towards the Building a Meeting House in or for sd Society-- And that Bill in fform may be brott in Accordingly-- Test George Wyllys Secrety

[In the] lower House--- The question was put whether [the pra]yer of this Memo should be granted & resolved in ye Negative & Then the [question] whether ye House do concur with ye grant of ye upper House on the same, [when] put was resolved in the affirmative
Test. Wm Williams Cler.

[1770, Apr. 30, Stamford]

Stamford Connecticut
In New England April 30, 1770.

Reverend Sir

I have received your favour of the 24th of October last; as duty obliges me to a diligent attention to the Duties of my office, it affords an additional pleasure to find my labours acceptable to the Venerable Board.

Compassion, and the importunity of destitute people, perishing for lack of knowledge, and the prey of Sectaries, Solicitors of better means of instruction; may induce us to recommend their spiritual wants to the Societies Charitable Notice, beyond what may be tho't proper, which we hope will be forgiven. We can only wish the Societies ability Equal to the goodness of their Hearts.----

If there is a disproportionable increase of Missionaries in New England, it still bears no proportion to the spiritual wants and desires of the people, who seeing no end to their seperations and the mischievous consequences of d[i]visions both Civil and religious, flee into the Church for safety & security. and without Vanity, we hope the good fruit of the societies Charity is conspicuous, in the larger Accessions to ye Church, the best Security to Church & State.

But the North Pre[c]inct on the Oblong is in New York Province, where they have lately Erected a New Church, which will be soon fit to be opened, where the people are destitute of any setled Minister of any Denomination, none in that Province Nearer than 30 or 40 Miles. And as they border upon the Northwest part of Connecticut, we only hoped if a Missionary might be Established there, he might include under his care the good people of Sharon & Salsbury, as they ly contiguous, and are about thirty Miles distant from Mr Clark, whose extensive Cure renders it impossible to supply their wants. Doctor Auchmuty and his Brethren in New York have signified to me, how fully sensible they are of the Necessity of a Missionary there, and it is expected the Doctor or one of his Brethren, goes up to attend the opening of the New Church.---A great opening in my opinion there is in that Quarter of Extensive usefulness, but we must submit to ye superior wisdom of the Venerable Board.

the poor unhappy divided people of Danbury, thro' their request, and intercession of my Brethren, call for all the Attention I can spare from my own Cure. I Preached there Yesterday, being sunday to a Numerous well devout Congregation, And the Church Wardens have desired me to transmit the Inclosed Copey of a paper signed by Mr Talbot, which was the foundation of their undertakeing to build their Church so large, with a Handsom Steeple from the Ground, as they have done. Mr Talbot attended me with sundry of our Brethren at the opening of that Church, was well pleased with their Conduct; and they acknowledge the Receipt of about £100 which has been laid out on their Chh which he freely bestowed without takeing any obligation from them. his sudden unexpected Death prevented their receiving the other £100 to be laid out in Glebe Land, as he promised, and which they think themselves intitled to, in Equity; to lay a foundation in due time for the support of a Minister. they have shown the Original of which the Inclosed is a true Copy to Mr Leaming, but he tells me he dare not presume to comply with the peoples requisition, without the society's Order and Concurrance.

About a Month before Mr Talbots Death, he wrote me to be ready to accompany him again to Danbury after Whitsunday then ensuing, for he purposed £200 more to bestow upon them, to prepare the way to their having a Minister. The Societies pleasure they wou'd gladly know. The Books you advised woud be sent to Doctor Auchmuty's care for me will be thankfully received.

I forwarded Advice immediately to Mr Cole of his agreable Appointment to be the Societies School Master at Claremont. The Revd Mr Leaming is ye Standing Secretary of our Conventions.----

My Parish remains in a good State. I Baptized last half Year one Adult & twenty seven Children-- Actual Communicants in my Cure are Seventy one:--

My Bill in Usual form for last half Years Salary viz for £25 Sterling, is drawn this day upon the Honourable Societies Treasurer Mr William Symondson in favour of Mr Benjamin Hildreth Mercht in New York.

May my Duty be Acceptable to the Venerable Board; and the blessing of God attend their pious & Charitable endeavours, to support his Church and Propagate true uncorrupt Religion. with unfeigned Esteem and Respect to Your Self, I Am

I Am Reverend Sir
Your Most Obedient
Humble Servt
And Brother
Ebenezer Dibblee

The Reverend Doctor Burton
Secretary of the Venerable
Society for Propagation
of the Gospel &c:--

[1770, May 2, New Milford]

To ye honorable General Assembly of ye Colony of Connecticutt to be held at Hartford in s^d Colony on ye Second Thursday of May Instant

The Memorial of those of ye Inhabitants that live within ye Limmits of ye first Society in Newmilford in s^d Colony who are Professors of ye Church of England humbly sheweth: that some Years past they undertook by Way of Subscription to Errect & Build a proper House for publick Worship Call^d St Johns Church & have proceeded so far as to Errect & almost finish ye outside of s^d House in Doing which ye whole Subscription Money has been fully Expended & your Honours Memorialists in Order to Inable themselves to Compleat & finish s^d House have granted Two several Rates or Taxes upon themselves & appointed Collectors to Collect ye Same, one of s^d Rates being granted in ye Year 1767 & ye other in ye Year 1770 Your Mem^{sts} then Supposing themselves by Law to have good Right to grant & Collect Rates for ye purpose afores^d & accordingly a Considerable Number of your Mem^{sts} have paid their full Rates: But so it is that ye greater Part of s^d Rates yet remain uncollected & your Honours Memorialists are advised that they have no legal Right to grant and Collect any Taxes for ye Purpose afores^d & many Persons on that Account refuse to pay ye Same; by Means whereof great Inequality & Injustice will not only be done. But also your Memorialists will be intirely Deprived of ye whole Benefit of s^d House unless Releived by ye Interposition of your Honours: & we haveing by Vote appointed a Committee to make Application to your Honours for Releiff in ye Premises

Whereupon your Honours Mem^{sts} humbly pray your Honours to take their unhappy Case into your Wise Consideration & to Inable and impower them in Some proper Way as to your Honours may seem most [expedient] to Inforce ye Collecting of those Taxes already granted [&] also to Tax themselves for ye future for ye Purpose only of finishing s^d House & keeping ye Same in Repair with Power of appointing Collectors to Collect ye Same according to ye Usual & Ordinary Methods of Collecting Taxes in ye Colony among other Denominations of Christians & they as in Duty bound shall ever pray &c

Dated at Newmilford this 2^d Day of May AD 1770

     Justus Mills   ⎫
     Daniel Pickitt ⎬ Com^{tt}
     Daniel Burritt ⎭

In the lower House The Prayer of this Mem^l is granted Liberty &c   Test. Wm Williams Cler

Concur^d in the upper House
      Test George Wyllys Secre

[1770, May 10? Hartford]

Upon ye Mamorial of Justus Miles, Dan^{ll} Picket & Dan^{ll} Burritt all of Newmilford being Professors of ye Church of England & liveing within ye Limmitts of ye first Society in s^d Newmilford & ye Rest of ye Professors of ye Church of England liveing within said first Society Shewing to this Assembly

That some Years past they undertook by Way of Sub-

scription to Errect a House for publick Worship Call^d St Johns Church & have proceeded so far as to Errect & almost finish ye out side of s^d House in Doing which ye whole of s^d Subscription Money has been fully Expended & that they have gra[n]ted Two saveral Rates for ye purpose of finishing s^d House which have been Collected but in part; praying that they May be Authorized & impowered to Inforce ye Collecting of those Taxes already granted & to Tax themselves for ye future for ye Purpose of Compleating s^d House & keeping the Same in Repair &c

Resolved by this Assembly that ye Collector or Collectors now Chosen or hereafter to be chosen by ye Memorialists to Collect ye Rates already by them granted as afore s^d have Power & they are hereby impowered to Collect ye Remainder of s^d Rates yet uncollected & to be accountable to ye Memorialists or a Committee by them to be appointed for ye Same, & to be under ye Same Regulations & have ye Same Powers as Collectors of other Taxes by Law have: And that ye Memorialists & their Successors (being Professors of ye Church of England) be & they are hereby impowerd from Time to Time as they may find Occation to Tax themselves for ye purpose of finishing s^d House & keeping ye same in Repair & to appoint Collectors for Collecting ye Same which s^d Collectors Shall have ye Same Powers & be Subject to ye Same Rules & Intitled to ye Same Fees as Collectors of other Taxes by Law have and any Meetings of s^d Memorialists for ye purpose aforesaid to be Regulated by ye Same Rules as Society Meetings by Law are

Pass^d in the Lower House
May 1770   Test Wm Williams Cler.
   Concurr^d in the upper House
        Test George Wyllys Secrety

[1770, May 14, New Haven]

To the Honourable General Assembly of the Colony of Connecticut to be holden at Hartford on the Second Thursday of May AD. 1770

The Memorial of Eliphalet Beacher of New Haven in the County of New Haven---humbly sheweth---

That Many Years since, one James Hartford then a soldier in the Army at Albany, about Thirteen Years Last past, delivered to your Pet[itione]r the sum of Fifteen Pounds Lawful Money, to keep for him s^d Hartford until the same should be called for, declaring at the same Time, that if it should not be called for by him he the Mem[orial]ist should be welcome to it--which Money your Mem[orial]ist Loaned on Interest to Capt. Hez. Deforest of Norwalk with a sum of his own Money, & by the failing Circumstances of s^d Deforest the s^d Money is Lost--& your Memorialist begs Leave to observe that s^d Hartford is deceased & without Heir, or being indebted unto any Person whatever, whereby all his Credits have become escheated unto this Colony & belong unto them-- That Constant Kirtland of Wallingford in s^d County hath taken Administration on the Estate of s^d Hartford, to whom your Mem[orial]ist hath given his Note for the s^d Money, by advice of the Honble Judge of Probate for the District of New Haven, with Condition Indorsed of its being to be payable or not agreable as your Honours shall Judge it the Duty or not of your Mem[orial]ist to pay said Monies

under the Circumstances of Receiving the same & on Account of their Loss as afores^d-- Whereupon the Memor[i]alist humbly prays your Honours to decree & Order the s^d Note so given as afores^d shall be given up & destroyed-- Or otherwise Grant Relief as in your great Wisdom shall seem good & as in Duty bound he shall ever pray &c
          Dated at New Haven the 14th Day of May--AD 1770--
                              Eliphalit Becher

In ye Lower House Oct^o 1770 on the Question The Prayer of this Memorial is not granted, nor any thing thereon
                    Test Wm Williams Cler.
In the upper House On the Question, The Prayer of this Memorial is not granted nor any Thing thereon--
                    Test George Wyllys Secrety

[1770, May 19, Wallingford]

To the Hon^l Genl Assembly now setting at New Haven the Memorial of Constant Kirtland of Wallingford humbly sheweth that One James Harford a foriegner having lived sometime in s^d Wallingford & Acquired Estate to the Value of about Sixty pounds Lawfull money he then went away a foreign Voyage & having never returned after many years had Elapsed the Judge of Probate in New Haven District Granted Letters of admenistration to your Mem[oriali]st who having Collected & Inventoried the Estate of s^d Dec^d he being supposed to be dead, holds the same to be disposed of according to Law, the s^d Dec^d James having no known relations or kindred whatsoever

further your Memorialist says that the said James a little time before he went away Declared in serious & solemn manner that in Case he should never return it was his Desire & will that what Estate he should leave should be Desposed of the one half to the Episcopal Church in s^d Wallingford with which he associated & the other half to the poor of said Town of Wallingford at the Descretion of Capt Titus Bracket of s^d Town his particular friend Whereupon Your Mem[oriali]st humbly prays that your Hon^{rs} will Grant & permit that your Mem[oriali]st Despose of the s^d Estate & pay & deliver over ye same to s^d Church & s^d poor accordingly (the same haveing by Law Escheated to this Colony) Upon your Memorialists giving sufficient bond to the Govr & Company that the s^d Estate or the Value thereof shall be Deliverd over & paid to the heir or heirs of ye s^d Dec^d if any shall Appear & he as in Duty bound shall Ever pray
          Dated at Wallingford May 19 1770
                              Cons^t Kirtland

[1770, Oct. 4, Brooklyn--Pomfret]

Zechariah Spaulding of Lawfull age testifieth and Saith that there hath been four Society meetings at Different times within these few Years Within the Society of Brooklyn in the Colony of Connecticut to See whether the s^d Society would build a meeting House in s^d Society for publick worship that at the third Meeting which was in September AD 1769 there wanted but one of a vote there being twenty two that voted against building a Meeting House and forty three that voted for building a Meeting House that at the fourth Meeting which was the begining of Last February I my Self being Moderator of s^d Meeting ordered the voters

to Divide when there was twenty one Lawfull voters that voted against building a Meeting House among whom were Col^l Godfrey Malbone Wm Walton and others Signers to a petition preferd to the General Assembly of the Colony of Connecticut who not only voted against building a Meeting House but Insisted that Ahaziah Adams and Zebulun Tyler who Appeared to vote on the Same side were Lawfull voters that there were 72 voters that voted to build a Meeting House among whom were Jonas Cleaveland & Benjn Herrick
                    Zechariah Spaulding

Israel Putnam and Daniel Tyler & Joseph Scarborough all of Lawfull age Testify and Say that they Did not Know nor Never heard of theire being any Person or Persons in the Society of Brooklyn in Pomfret that have Signed the Memorial to the General Assemby for a Church in said Society before Said Society Voted to build a New Meeting house for Publick Worship in Said Society excepting Coll Godfrey Malbone and Docter William Walton
                              Israel Putnam
                              Daniel Tyler
                              Joseph Scarborough

Windham Sst Pomfret October ye 4th 1770 Personaly Appeared Coll Israel Putnam and Daniel Tyler & Joseph Scarborough Signers to the Above Deposition and made Solem Oath to the Truth of this Deposition the adverce Partie being Present before me
          Ebenezer Williams Justice of Peace

Ephraim Woodard of brookline being of Lawfull Age Testifyeth that About 4 years Past I was at the dwelling hous of David Smith of Said Brookline & doc^r watson was there And as ther was a Society Meet which was to be as I understood the next day In Ord^r to See whether ye Society would Buld A new meeting hous and then Ask^d me whether I would vote to have a new meeting and I then Told him that I Should not be for Bulding At Present and the doc^r then Sayed that he hoped there was noon of the Society of my minde and that I was very Meen for not being of the minde to have a new Meeting house for the Old meeting hous was So Old and Shakling that it was not fit to meet in-- and After Sum time upon further Confersation he Say^d he was agoing a Jorney but if he thought that any Other Persons At the meeting would be of my minde he would Stay and be at the meeting & for me to be So meen as Not to be a minde to Buld a new meeting hous I Ought to have my Ass Kick^d and I the deponant further Say that I was the next day at s^d Society meeting and the doc^r who is now one of the Peticioners In favour of the Church was their and that he then voted to Buld a new meeting hous
                              Ephraim Woodard

Windham Sst Pomfret October ye 4th 1770 Personally Appeared Ephraim Woodward the above Deponant and made Solem Oath to the Truth of this deposition the adverse Present Sworn before me
          Ebenezer Williams Justice of ye Peace

The deponant further Saith that the old meeting House

in s^d Society is 43 feet Long and 38 feat wide that there
are 143 families in s^d Society & about 1040 persons   the
Deponant farther Saith he has Several times Since s^d meeting heard Wm Walton Say that any Person or Men that would
Sign to be a Churchman he the s^d Walton would Clear them
from paying any Rates toward building s^d Meeting House
and that once Sometime Last Winter He heard s^d Walton
Say he would turn the Society tother Side up on his being
asked whether he thot he could turn it the other Side up
he said the Streams run up Hill and he would turn them
into another Channel

                                        Seth Paine Junr

Windham County viz Pomfret October ye 4th 1770   Personally Appeared Seth Pain Jn^r Signs to the foregoing Deposition and made Solem Oath to the Truth of this Deposition
the adverce Partie Present   Sworn before Me
                    Ebenezer Williams Justice of Peace

John Hammond & Ephraim Woodard of Lawfull Age
Testifyeth and sayeth that sum time In April Last wee
with Others was a Working at the High way In Brook Line
In Canterbury and that then & ther was Jesse Cleaveland
one of the non Petesioners In Favour of the Church and sum
Person then ask^d him whether he had signed to the Church
and he then Sayed I have   they then asked him whether he
had been of that Perswasion of any Time he then Say^d no
they then asked him whether he was Ever at the Church
Meeting he Sayed he never was at ther meeting nor never
Read any of the Church Books & no Nothing what the Church
articles are   then they asked him what was the Reason that
you Signed he then Sayed he Signed out of Spight for that
you have Got a vote to Buld a Meeting hous which he be-
leved was not Right
                    John Hammond   Ephraim Woodard

Windham County viz Pomfret October ye 4th 1770   Personally Appeared John Hammond & Ephraim Woodward the
Above Deponants and Made Solem Oath to the Truth of this
Deposition   the adverce Partie Present   The above Mentioned Jesse Cleaveland Neither Notified or Present   Sworn
before me
                    Ebenezer Williams Justice of Peace

Seth Paine j^r of Lawfull age testifieth & Saith that on
the Sixth Day of Feby Last at a Society Meeting in the Society of Brooklyn warned to See whether the Society would
build a Meeting House in s^d Society for Publick Worship
when Capt Zech^h Spaulding who was Moderator ordered
the voters to divide there were 21 voters that voted against
building a Meetinge House among whom were Co^l Godfrey
Malbone Wm Walton Joseph Hubbard and others Signers
to a Petition prefer^d to the General Assembly in May last
& laid over to October present   that the above named Persons not only voted against building a meeting House but
Insi[sted] that Ahaziah Adams & Zebulun Tyler who appeared to vote on the Same side had a right to vote tho the
Moderator tho^t they were not qualified by Law   that there
were Seventy two voters that voted to build a Meeting
House among whom were Mess Jonas Clea[veland] and
Benjⁿ Herrick Signers of the s^d Petition   The Deponant

further Saith that there was a Society Meeting in [the]
Society on the 25th Day of Sep^t 1766 to see whether the
Society would build a Meeting House but did not obtain a
vote   that there was a Society Meeting on the 28th Day of
Sep^t 1768 to See whether the Society would build a Meeting House but did not obtain a vote   that there was a Society Meeting on the 18th Day of September AD. 1769
when they [did] not obtain a vote to build a meeting House
there being twenty two voters against building and forty
three for building a Meeting House

Joseph Holland of Lawful age Testifyeth and Sayth that
Some Short time before the Society Meeting in in Brooklyn
in Pomfret Which was the Sixth Day of February 1770 I
heard Some People in Said Society Say to the following Affect that it was best to endeavour to get a Vote to Build a
Meetinghouse at the Above Said Meeting for if they Should
fail of geting a Vote to build a Meetinghouse til Co^{ll} Godfrey Malbon and Others Should Build a Church that the Society would Loose Said Malbones and Others Rates
    Pomfret October 4th 1770   Joseph Holland

Windham Sst Pomfret October ye 4th 1770   Personally
Appeared Joseph Holland the above Deponent and Made
Solem Oath to the Truth of the above Deposition   the ad-
verce partie present   before Me
                    Ebenezer Williams Justice of Peace
Opened in the General Assembly Newhaven Octr 1770
                    Test George Wyllys Secrety

Noah Adams Jn^r of Pomfret of Lawfull age Testifieth
& Saith that Some time Last Winter before the Society
Meeting in Brookline Parish for to bui[l]d A meeting House
in Said Society for Publick Worship I was in Company with
Coll Israel Putnam, and the Coll Asked me to Sign a Paper
for A Society Meeting and I told him I was not A Voter and
mr Seth Pain jn^r being Present Said that I was a Voter,
then I Said if I was A Voter I Should vote Against it, then
Coll Putnam said if I would not vote Against it or if I would
Vote for it he would pay my Rate for twenty five Shillings
    Pomfret October ye 4th 1770   Noah Adams j^r

Question[:] was You at S^d Society Meeting
Answer[:] Yes
Question[:] Did You vote to build
Answer[:] no I Did note vote at all

Windham S^{ct} Pomfret October ye 4th 1770   Personally
Appeared Noah Adams jnr Signs to the above Deposetion
and made Solem oath to the truth thereof   the adverce
partie present   before Me
                    Ebenezer Williams Justice of ye Peace

Nehemiah Bacon of Pomfret of Lawfull Age Testifieth
and Saith that Some time Last Winter A Little before the
Society Meeting in Brookline Parish for Building a meeting House in Said Parish I was in Company with m^r Seth
Pain Jn^r in Conversation about Building Said House and
m^r Pain Asked me if I would Sign A paper for to Build A
Meeting House, I answered him that I Supposed we Wanted

A Meeting House but my Curcumstances was Such that I was not Able at Present to pay my Part for Doctor Walton Said it would Cost me Six or Seven Pounds, and m^r Pain Said he would Pay my Parte for thirty Shillings and take it in Grain or Pork or beef or in Labour at the Market Prise or in Old Horses

    Pomfret October ye 4th 1770   Nehemiah Bacon

Question[:] was You at the Society Meeting when they vot-
ed to build a Meeting House
Answer[:] no
Question put by mr Seth pain[:] when I ofered to pay Your
parte to Said Meeting House, Did not you think that I
Suposed that would be about Your parte
Answer[:] Yes for you asked how much my List was

Windham S^ct Pomfret October ye 4th 1770   Personally Appeared Nehemiah Bacon the above Depona[n]t and Made Solem Oath to the Truth of this Deposition   the adverce partie being present

        Ebenezer Williams Justice of Peace
Opened in the General Assembly Newhaven Octr 1770
        Test [George] Wyllys Secrety

    Israel Putnam & Seth Pain Jnr of Lawfull age Testify & Say that being in Company with Joseph Hubbard one of the Signers in A Memorial Against Brooklign Parish in Pomfret about the Beginning of Last february we heard Said Hubbard Say he had not Signed to be a Churchman nor had any thoughts of it

    Pomfret October ye 4th 1770   Israel Putnam
                             Seth Paine Junr

Question put[:] was it a Not Said by a Number of People
in brookline Parish aboute the time that they vote to
build a New meeting house [----] that Nov is the time
to get a Vote to build or they will Loose the Church-
mens Money
answered by both[:] no not as I Ever heard

Windham County viz Pomfret October ye 4th 1770   Personally Appeared Coll Israel Putnam and m^r Seth Pain Jnr Signers to the Above Deposition and Made Solem Oath to the Truth of this Deposition   the adverce Partie Present Sworn before me

        Ebenezer Williams Justice of Peace
N Haven General Assembly Octo^r 2^d thursday 1770
        Open^d p^r George Wyllys Secrety

[1770, Oct. 4, Brooklyn--Pomfret]

Godfrey Malbone	£1001--0--0
William Walton	62--0--
Joseph Hubbard	90--13--
Noah Adams	98--0--
Jonas Cleavland	46--2--
Jesse Cleavland	40--7--
Timothy Lovejoye	22--0--
Benjamin Herrick	58--4--
Jedediah Ashcraft	107--9--
Jed Ashcraft J^r	20--
Nehemiah Adams	51--16--
Ahaziah Adams	0--
Seth Sabin	64--6--
John Allyn	97--13--6
Jabez Allyn	109--17--6
Henry Cady	44--0--
Elihu Adams	68--12--
Daniel McCloud	24--0--
Benjamin Hubbard	45--8--
James Eldred	32--0--
Caleb Spaulding	0--0--
James Darbe J^n	65--0--
Benjamin Cady	56--5--
Benjamin Jewet	36--0--
Thomas Smith	72--6--
Leonard Cady	18--12--
John Ashcraft	21--1--
Jacob Staples	0--0--
Thomas Adams	42--5--
Isaac Adams	44--14--
	£2439 : 9 : 0

Theses May Certify that the Sums Annexed to the Several names above is the True Lists of their Ratable Estate for August List 1769

    Pomfret October 4th 1770

                  Sam^ll Wilson } Listers
                  [   ]

[1770, Oct. 11, New Haven]

    At a Gen^ll Assembly of the Colony of Connecticut holden at New Haven second Thurday of October 1770--

    Upon the Petition of Godfrey Malbone and others Inhabitants of the Town of Pomfret in the Parish of Brookline and parts thereunto adjacent setting forth to said Assembly That the Pet^s desirous of worshiping God according to their own sentiments did in the beginning of October 1769 assemble together & enter into engagements to erect a church for worship according to the Model established by the name of the Church of England &c That soon after it became known the Pet^s had entered into said Engagement the Inhabitants of said Parish of Brookline at a Society Meeting holden at Brooklin upon the sixth day of February 1770 voted and ordered a meeting House to be built in said Parish the expence whereof to be paid by an Assesment on the Parishioners conformable to their Lists of the year 1769 to be collected after the first of Decr 1770 &c   praying that the Pet^rs may stand acquited and discharged from said Tax or Assessment as by said Pet^n on file dated April 10th 1770--

    Resolved by this Assembly That the Said Godfrey Malbone be acquitted and discharged from any Tax or Assessment laid or that may be laid on him by said Society of Brookline for or towards the Building a Meeting House in or for said Society

Pass^d in the upper House   Test George Wyllys Secret^y
Concurr^d in ye Lower House   Test W. Williams Cler.

[1770, Oct. 29, New London]
Dear John,

    This Day Fortnight, I acquainted you I was upon my Road to New Haven upon the Subject of the Petition of the

Infant Church Congregation at Pomfret. The Matter was not heard untill Last Tuesday Afternoon, when the upper House kept the Petition untill Thursday Evening, when they sent to the Lower House the following Resolve Viz.

On Col⁰ Malbone's Petition &c.

"In the upper House, granted that Col⁰ Malbone be acquitted and discharged from any Tax or Assessment Laid, or that may be made or Laid on Him by said Society of Brookline, for or towards the building a Meeting House in or for said Society and that a Bill in Form may be brought in accordingly."

In the Lower House the Petitioners met with many very zealous Friends, and Col⁰ Salstonstall, of this Town, made great efforts in our Favour, but to very little Purpose as Puritanic Frenzy prevailed over Right Reason & Justice in such a Manner that their Determination was couched in the following Words, which I received on Friday Afternoon.

"In the Lower House the Question was put whether the Prayer of the Memorialists should be granted, and resolved in the Negative; and then the Question whether the House do concur with the Grant of the upper House on the same being put, was resolved in the Affirmative." I am but ill furnished with Pen & Ink, so shall not comment upon this most unjust & partial Determination I shall only tell you that, after waiting upon the Secretary (who behaved much like a Gentleman) & paying the Fees, I left the Town immediately, after giving Money to Mr Douglass to prepare me a proper state of the Matter which I shall transmit to England as soon as possible. The Lawyers, for, were Ingersoll & Douglass & behaved Well. Against, were Elderkin & Huntington who in the most fulsom Manner dawbed me all over with Flummery at least a Foot thick, and treated my Associates in a very different Manner. The thin Covering may be easily seen through & which I design to make no improper use of.

I stay in Town to Day on Purpose to dine with Thom. Mumford, shall spend the Evening with Mr Stuart & to morrow Morning set out with Mr Chew for Pomfret. Moffatt is in Hartford.

I understand Ingraham is got up to Norwich, and hath some Things for me, I hope I shall find the Window Glass. I remain Dear John

                                              Your Friend
New London 29 Oct. 1770.   G. Malbone

[Addressed:] To / Mr John Malbone / at / Newport

[1770, Nov. 7, Litchfield]
                     Litchfield, November the 7th 1770.
Revd Sir,

Your Letter of the 21st of March last, I have received by the Revd Mr Bostwick; and heartily thank the Society for his Appointment to the Mission of Noble-town, New-Concord, Great-Barrington & Lainsboro', whereby my Labours are much lessened: For besides Officiating at Great-Barrington about ten Sundays in a Year, which is 35 Miles distant from Litchfield, I often Preached Lectures at the three other Towns of his Mission, & in the whole of which have Baptized 8 Adults, & 116 Infants.

I have Still enough Duty for one Man to perform; for besides my Stated attendance on my remaining Congregations of Litchfield, Goshen & Cornwall; I often Preach oc-casional Sermons, on Week Days, at other Places, at the distance of 20 Miles from home, by which means Sundry Religious, well disposed People have been made to declare their Conformity to the Church.

The Congregations of my particular Cure are favoured with a gradual Increase: At Litchfield are 78 Heads of Famolies, and 43 Communicants: At Goshen 47 Heads of Famolies yt attend upon the Service of their Church, a few of which live in other Towns; and 28 Communicants: At Cornwall 8 Heads of Famolies, and 5 Communicants. In my present Mission, in the last Year I have Baptized 4 Adults, & 44 Infants; Married 2 Couple, buried 2 Corpses, and received 11 new Conformists.

There is in this Town (Litchfield) a Glebe of Land belonging to the Society, rough and uncultivated, lying at Such a distance from the Church, that no present benefit can be obtained by it. The Land is good, and would Sell for about £80- Sterling; which Money might be improved in purchasing Land in a far more convenient place, & from which present profit might Accrue to the Church. We therefore beg the Societies leave to make this advantage, which if granted, we do Assure the Society, the Land which we shall purchase near the Church, Shall be Secured to their Use by Such an Instrument as they Shall Advise to. A Coppy of the Deeds of Said Lands upon our Records we inclose, for the Society to inspect, and enable them to give proper directions for conveyance. Pray, Sir, let us know as Soon as possible the Societies determination on this Point; there being a good Opportunity to make Sale of the Land at the present juncture.

I remain with Gratitude & Deference / The Venerable Societies, & Your / most Obedient humble Servt
                                    Solomon Palmer.

For the Revd Dr Burton.

[1770, Nov. 19, Litchfield]
Know all men by these presents that We James Masters & Hezekiah Thompson both of Woodbury in the County of Litchfield & Colony of Connecticutt in New England Do promise to pay unto Mr John Rutgers Marshall of Stratford in the County of Fairfield & Colony Aforesaid the full & Just Sum of thirty pounds in Current Sterling Money of Great Britain on the Eigth Day of April AD: 1771 And so on the Same Sum of thirty pounds Sterling Money as aforesaid Per Annum to be paid on the Eight day of April for and During the Term of the Natural Life of him the Said John Rutgers Marshall to the which payment well and truly to be made, we bind ourselves, heirs, Executors & Administrators firmly by these Presents, In Witness Whereof we have Hereunto Set our hands & Seals this 19th Day of November ADomini 1770 and in the 11 year of the Reign of our Sovereign Lord George the third by the Grace of God, King of Great Britain France & Ireland, Defender of the Faith &c.

Signed, Seal'd & Delivered   Samuel Moody
In Presence of   Charles Whittelsy
                                    James Masters
                                    Hezekiah Thompson

Litchfield County Ss: Woodbury November the 19th AD 1770 James Masters and Hezekiah Thompson the

Signers and Sealers of the foregoing Instrument Personally appeared and acknowledged the Same to be their free act and Deed before me.

                    Gideon Walker Jus^t of Peace

[1770, Dec. 7, New Milford]
                    New Milford Dec^m 7th 1770
Reverend Sir,

I have now received the large prayer Book for the Church of New Milford, and 24 of a smaller sort with a Number of pious Tracts for the Parishioners, and they return their thanks to the venerable Society for their kind Attention towards them.

In the Township of Woodbury there is upwards of 80 Families Professors of the Church who have employed one Mr Marshall educated at Kings College in New York to read Prayers & printed Sermons, who has performed to so great Acceptance, that, they are fond of having him receive holy Orders for them, and have likwise agreed to give him £30 sterling p^r Annum & provide a handsome house & Glebe, in Case he might receive Orders for them; these People earnestly entreate the Society to take them into their Consideration, & think with a small Sallery from the Society they can support a Clergyman in Character; As there is within the Limits of my Mission about 300 Families Professors of the Church, and it being of so large Extent 40 Miles one Way North & South & near 30 East & West, which renders it impossible for a single Clergyman to supply the spiritual Wants of such a scattered People, tho' I hope, faithfully to contribute what lies in my Power towards it, and if the Society in their Wisdom should think proper (as I hope they may) to send Mr Marshall to Woodbury, I believe it would be of emminent Service to the Cause of true Religion, as there now is a very promising Prospect of a flourishing Church in that Part of the Mission: for the Dissenting Teachers th[e]re will not admit the Infants of any to baptism, but the Infants of those in full Communion, by which means Numbers of Infants are in a heathenish State as undoubtedly many grown Persons are. three Parishes in Woodbury it is likely Mr Marshall will Visit, Woodbury town, Roxbury, and Judea, the first of which he will reside at.

The 16^h of July last & the 3^d Instant, I visited the poor destitute People at the North East Precinct on the Oblong preached to [them] 2 Sermons & led them to the Choice of Church Officers, really these People are to be pitied & deserve the Compassion of every well wisher to the truth of Christianity, their Circumstances for want of better Instructions are deplorable, they run into almost all kinds of Errors, not only many heads of Families very Ignorant themselves but their Children most miserably educated, many of them ten & twelve years old (as I am informed) never taught to read a Syllable, by which Means the Sabbath is shamefully disregarded, in short they seem to live as it were without God in the World as two many do. those few Church People amongst them in Conjunction with Sharon & Salsbury have employed one Mr Hillyer educated at Yale College to read Prayers & printed Sermons, & hope the Society will take them into their Consideration, as they will give £30 Sterling annually to the Support of a Clergyman and provide a handsome house & Glebe.

Since the 20^h of Nov: 1769. I have baptized 71 Infants,

two of which were blacks. within this year past several Persons & families have conformed to the Church, & the Addition of Communicants has been Considerable.

I have drawn upon the Society for my last Quarter Bill in the 1769 in favour of Mr Nathan Beers, & I have likwise drawn for my three first Quarter Bills for the year 1770. the first in fav^r of Messrs abel Hine ye second in fav^r of David Baldwin, the 3^d in fav^r of Daniel Merritt.

The 11 of last Month I visited the Church People of Hartford & preached to a large Audience, these People are much grieved by having the Foundation, which was laid for a beautiful Church torn up & converted into a private Building by its Enemies. I am Reverend Sir your most obed^t humble Servt

                    Richard Clarke

[Addressed:] To / The Reverend Doctor Daniel Burton / Secretary to the Society for the propagation / of the Gospel in foreign Parts / Abingdon Street / Westminster
[Endorsed:] Read...Octr 14. 1771

[1770, Dec. 16, New London]
Rev^d & Dear S^r

Having lately troubled You wth a few Lines, I have scarcely any thing new to lay before my Venerable Patrons.

The Number of my Communicants is ye same; but I hope soon to encrease them. Indeed I'm cautious of encouraging any to come to y^t sacred Ordinance, before they are well instructed in ye Importance of ye Duty.

I continue my Visits to Moodus, Millington, East-Haddam & Chatham, 30 Miles off. I have been wth them four times this Year, as I have attended them ye three preceding, preaching five six, sometimes seven Sermons at a Visit from house to house among them. After much Diligence & Labor in acquainting them in ye Nature & Design of ye LORD's Supper, I admin[is]t[e]red to fifteen Communicants, & had about 200 Hearers on ye 25th of Novr last--baptiz'd two Children & one Adult, ye rest of whose Family I had formerly receiv'd into ye Church. Their devout Behavior & Zeal to be instructed in our solemn Worship afford me great Pleasure.

However they have their Troubles from ye independents & congregationalists, false[ly na]m'd here presbyterians, who seize their Cattle to support their Teachers & Meet[in]ghouses: nay some, who have been Professors of our Church near thirty Years ago, are now order'd to pay Rates to their Collectors, but are resolv'd to prefer a Jail. I'm heartily sorry for ye implacable, restless Spirit of our Enemies; & can devise no way to relieve them, unless ye Religious Society wou'd appoint me to attend them. I'm willing & able. I have, as I said, officiated among them for four years, rode many hundred Miles of very bad rodes upon their Account &, except one Bar^l of Flour, never receiv'd any recompense, no, not even for my travelling Expences. They are poor. The Bearer hereof is 'Squire Stewart, his Majesty's Collector of this Port, & my Parishoner--a very worthy, sober, sensible Gentleman--a great Ornament to Religion, & Blessing to our Church. He has exerted himself most incessantly to regulate our Affairs, hitherto in great Confusion, & been very instrumental in making my House

more decent & convenient. To him I presume to refer you for Parochial & American News. I hope to see him enroll'd among y͡e Number of my worthy Patrons, & restor'd to us in health.

M͟r Stewart will, at my request leave 13s / 6 w͟th you for M͟r Pearson Treasurer, w͟ch he paid a Notary public for me, to enable me to defen'd myself against a broken Merc͟t, by whom I shall lose a great deal of money, w͟ch he had in Bills from me. I hope you'll pardon my freedom in desiring you to receive & pay this Sum.

My christian Duty & Compliments wait upon y͡e religious Society. By ordering me a few of next Year's Abstracts & whatever Pamphlets & Books you please, by way of N. York, You will greatly oblige

Good S͟r / Y͟r most obedient Serv͟t / & Aff͟te Brother in / Jesus Christ

Matt Graves

N. London Decem͟r 16͟th 1770

[Addressed:] To / The Rev͟d Dr. Burton Secretary to the Religious / Society for propagating the Gospel in foreign / Parts / Bartlet Buildings / Hoburn / London / Per Favor of / D. Stewarr Esq͟r N͟o 45 Fleet Street / Q D C
[Endorsed:] Read...March 11. 1771

[1771, Mar. 22, London]

Cravenshut, London
22͟d March 1771--

My dear Sir,

I have been just now honored with a long Visit from Doctor Burton, who gave me an account of the Success of your application for a Missionary & left for me two Letters, one from himself & the other from the Bishop of Litchfield & Coventry, to forward to you-- He gives you an account of the Terms on which your application was received; &, indeed, witho't my proposing & in effect-- engaging in the manner set forth in the inclosed Paper, I found it would be impossible to succeed, so that I am in hopes you will not disapprove of what I have done in your behalf-- as it was my wish to get you £40 a year I took every step to accomplish it. Were you to double the Quantity of Land, I think it is very probable that the Society wo͟d in a year or two increase the Salary to £40-- As it wo͟d be difficult, if not impossible, to get a person of Character (& no other will do for you) to embark for America from this Country, you must endeavour to find out somebody in America that has been lately ordained, but can not obtain a Cure-- The Doctor said he mentioned to you one or two such persons; & he named to me some others, particularly your Neighbour Luke Babcock, & M͟r Hopkinson & a M͟r White of Philadelphia-- If you can not meet with any such person, you must send over to England a suitable Man for Ordination.

The Doctor says he remembers you extremely well, & I have to assure you that you owe a great deal to him as well as the Bishop of Litchfield &t.-- He has promised to send me a Collection of Books to be forwarded to you; & you will receive them with this Letter, if they come time enough--

My own affairs are as yet very uncertain-- If I resign my Commission, it will be on Terms to my Mind. My brother T--- is here, & gives out he is to have some

genteel preferment, but it is the opinion of those that ought to know, as well as my own, that he never will have any thing given him, of which you may rest assured, whatever you may hear to the contrary. He has given out that the Gov͟t of Granada &c was offered to him, but it could not be as L͟d H---t has often told me his Sentiments of him, & besides that Gov͟t was engaged to M͟r ---- Leybourn when Melvill went out to the West Indies, where it was resolved he sho͟d resign it.--

Give my best Regards to M͟rs Malbone, & all your family & friends, & believe me to be, Dear Sir
                              very affectionately
                                   Yours &c-
                                        Jn͟o Robinson.
P.S. Capt͟n Miller of the Britannia has undertaken the Care of the Books fr͟t free-- They come addressed to M͟r Watts who is desired to forward them to Doctor Moffatt.

My Lord Mayor & Alderman Oliver are in the Tower for a contempt of the house of Commons--

[To Godfrey Malbone, Pomfret, Conn.]

[1771, Mar. 22, Westminster]
Sir,

The Bishop of Litchfield, & some other of your friends, to whom you have lately sent an account of the oppressive usage you have received from some of the inhabitants in your township, have interested themselves so much in your behalf, that the Society have been prevailed upon to depart from a resolution (which They have for some time taken not to establish any more missions in New England, & which was indeed become necessary on account of the numerous applications & earnest demands from all parts of the Continent) & have consented to make an allowance, tho' a small one, yet the utmost They can possibly afford, & indeed more than in prudence They ought at present, for a Missionary in your township of Pomfret, Plainfield, & Canterbury.-----Our allowance is £30 per an͞n; & We trust that you will, beside the house & the 20 acres of good land at least & conveniently situated, also exert your interest among the church-people, to contribute handsomely towards his support.-- We cannot on this prospect prevail on any Clergyman to go from England; but hope, as there are several young Americans, who have lately come over for holy orders, & have been accordingly ordained, but returned without any appointment, because We were not able to give them One, that you will engage some one of them, of good character & suitable abilities, to take upon him this mission. This seems to be the only scheme to supply you soon with a Clergyman; if This can't be done, you must send over some young man, whom you can recommend, for Orders. --Our Salary is to commence from the time of his entering on his duty.

I shall take care to send you the books which you desire, & am with great respect, Sir,
                         Your very humble Servant
                              D Burton

Abingdon-street,
   Westminster.
March 22͟d 1771.   Godfrey Malbone Esq͟r--

P.S. Your Township, which is full of dissenters [and] those not of the best temper & disposition towards [the] Church of England, certainly requires an able & [.]

It is thought, that if you hope for relief [from] the oppressions you complain of in being comp[elled to] attend that worship which you do not approve [and to] support dissenting ministers, to build or repair meeting-houses &c-- A joint application [should] come directly from the Gentlemen & others [in the] several parts of your province, who are ag[reeable] to his Majesty's privy Council, or to the [Council] of Trade & Plantations, to be forwarded [to us.] The Society are very willing to concur in [such a] matter by occasionally suggesting to pe[rsons in] administration the expedience & even nec[essity of] such a measure, but are unwilling to [take the] lead in that affair, fearing It would n[ot be] attended to as It ought.

[1771, Apr. 10, Stamford]

Stamford Connecticut in
New England April, 10, 1771.

Reverend Sir

With persevering diligence I continue my Attention to the duties of my extensive Cure. the fateaguing Service of my allotment, from my first entrance into this Mission, is alleviated with the hopes, of having, by the blessing of God, been subservient in promoting the most important interest of my brethren by Nature and Grace.----my Parish in all parts, remain in a good state.--I attended divine Service and preaching at Danbury 15th of Novembr last upon a Colony Thanksgiving & sunday following, to an agreable devout Congregation. I hope that much good will come out of their religious confusions. the people are generally disposed to be religious, and inquisitive after knowledge, but most unhappily divided in sentiment.---- Compassion again induces me to set off for Sharon on Monday next to attend a Colony fast with them ye 18th Instant; and having appointed sunday following to perform divine Service in the new Church at Amenia in New York Province. Every mischievous consequence to the interest of Religion, I fear will ensue, upon their being neglected in that Quarter; the most Zealous and well disposed, being discouraged, seeing so little a Prospect of obtaining the setled Administrations of Religion among them.----I Baptized last half Year, but twenty one Children, and one Adult; Actual Communicants within my Cure are but Eighty three. My Bill in usual form for twenty five pounds, is this day drawn upon the Venerable Societies Treasurer, in favr of Mr Thomas Ellison Jur Merchant in New York.----May the Venerable Society have the pleasure to see the good fruit and effect of their great piety and Charity here, in the Prosperity peace and Unity of Christ Church, and thro' the tender Mercy of God be abundantly recompenced hereafter.

I gratefully acknowledg their favr in the Books lately received, which shall be prudently distributed. may God Strengthen their hands and encourage their hearts in so benevolent a design. I am Reverend Sir, with my Duty to the Venerable Board, and with due Esteem and regards to Your Self

Your most Obedient
The Reverend Doctor Burton   Very Humble Servant
Secretary of the Venerable Society   And Brother in Christ
for Popagation of the Gospel &c-   Ebenezer Dibblee

[Addressed:] To / The Reverend Doctor Daniel Burton / Secretary of the Venerable Society / for the Propagation of the Gospel / in Foreign Parts, / In Abingdon Street, Westminster / London

[1771, Apr. 15, Hartford]

To the honorable the general Assembly of the Colony of Connecticut to be held at Hartford in said Colony on the second Thursday of May 1771.

The Memorial of Abel Moses, Moses Cadwell, Thomas Frazier John Hodgkin Daniel Frazier of Hartland in the County of Litchfield humbly sheweth that one Uriel Holmes of said Hartland was by the general Assembly of this Colony holden at Hartford in said Colony on the second Thursday of May A.D. 1768 appointed a Collector to collect a Tax or Rate of three Pence per Acre for four years then to come on all divided Lands in said Township of Hartland of the then present Proprietors of said Hartland, lying east of the River that runs through said Town to be improved for the settling a Minister and building a Meeting House in said Town of Hartland and that the said Holmes having received a Warrant for that Purpose dated the 8th Day of February A.D. 1769 and signed by the late deceased honorable William Pitkin then Governor of this Colony under Pretext of said Warrant in Hartland aforesaid on the 23rd Day of April 1770 he said Uriel Holmes arrested the Body of one of your Memorialists Abel Moses aforesaid pretending to him that his propo[r]tionable Part of Said Tax or assessment for the two first years before mentioned then amounted to the Sum of £3-10s-0d lawfull Money & also commited him to the keeper of the Said Litchfeild County Goal within Said Prison and that your memorialest Abel Moses being unwilling to be Confined in Goal and in order to procure his Enlargement from Prison in Litchfield afore Said on the 24th Day of Apriel 1770 being So in Goal as afore Said Signed a Note of Hand dated the Said 24th Day of Apriel 1770 payable to the Said Collector wherein was included the Said Sum of £3-10s-0d lawful Money together with the further Sum of 23s/8d lawful Money more for his the said Collectors fees making the Sum of £4-13S-8D. Lawful Money in the whole which said Note he the said Holmes to[ok] and there received and thereupon your Memorial[ist] was discharged from Goal.

And the said Moses Cadwel, thomas frazer John hodgkin Daniel frazer your Memorialists were taxed by the Same Rule an[d] the same Proportion as the aforesaid Abel Moses and the several Sums at which they were respectively Taxed were extorted from your Memorialists respectively by the said Uriel Holmes to the great Distress and almost Ruin of your Memorialists. And your Memorialists further say that altho true it is the said Assembly did enact that a Rate or Tax of three pence per Acre should be levied on the divided Lands aforesaid of the then present Proprietors and although your Memorialests then were and Still are Propriators of Said divided Lands yet they Say that the true intent and meaning of Said Act of Assembly must have been that Such Tax as afore Said Should be levied on those divided Lands in Said Township only as did not then belong to Such Persons as then were by law exempted and excused from paying any Taxes for building Meeting-Houses for the present estab-

lished Churches of this Government and not on the Lands the property whereof belonged to those who are by law excused from paying Taxes as aforesaid and that therefore the Said Collector was not by virtue of Said warant impowered to levy nor collect the Said Tax of any Such Persons as are excused as afore Said.

Whereas your Memorialists beg Leave to rem[ind] your Honour's that long Time before and at the Time [of] making said Act of Assembly they were and still are Professors of the Church of England living at said Hartland within a Society or Parish of the Church of England where there was and still is a Parson Viz. the Revd Mr Roger Viets in Orders according to the Cannons of the Church of England settled & abiding among them and performing divine Service so near to your Memorialists who have declared themselves of the Church of England as aforesaid that they can conveniently and for many Years now last past have and still do attend the publick Worship there and are Parishoners of the Church of England and therefore are by the Laws of this Colony excused from the Payment of the said Tax of three pence p^r Acre as aforesaid. And your Memorialists have applied to the County Court of Litchfield [that] held [in] Litchfield in September 1770. who rejected their Petition as judging the Matter not properly coming under their Cognizance. Whereupon your Memorialists humbly pray this honorable Assembly to take their unhappy and distressful Case under your wise & judicious Consideration and abate them of the aforesaid Assessment & order the several Sums of the Money aforementioned which have been extorted from them to be again restored to them together with Costs & to free them from all Taxes of the same Kind for the future. or grant such other Relief as your Honours in your great Wisdom shall see fit. And your Honours Memorialists as in Duty bound shall ever pray-- dated at Hartford this 15th Day of April 1771 And in the Eleventh Year of his Majesty's Reign.

Abel Moses	Daniel Frazier
Moses Cadwell	Thomas Frazier
	John Hodgkin

To the Sheriff of the County of Litchfield his Depu[ty] or either of the Constables of Hartland within [said] County Greeting

In his Majesty's Name you are hereby commanded [to] summon Uriel Holmes of said Hartland to appear before [the] honorable general Assembly of the Colony of Connecticut [to be] held at Hartford in said Colony on the second Thursday i[n May] Anno Domini 1771 if he see Cause then and there [to give] Reason if any be why the Prayer of the foregoing Mem[orial] be not heard and granted-- And you are to leave [an] attested Copy of this Citation and the foregoing Me[mor]ial with the said Uriel Holmes or at the Place of his [usu]al Abode at least Twelve Days before the first Tuesday which shall be next after the second Thursday of may next-- hereof fail not and of this Writ and [the] foregoing Memorial with your Doings thereon make due [Report] dated at Hartford this 16th Day of April A.D. 1771 A[nd] the Eleventh year of his Majesty's Reign

           Wm Pitkin Asses^r

Hartland April the 24 AD 1771

Then I Left A true and an attested Coppy of the Within memorial and Citation at the usual Plac of the Within Named urial holme abode In hartland   Test by me Isaac Burnham Constable of Sd Town   Fee £0-6-0

In ye L. House[:] This Mem^o granted That ye Memorialists should be refunded ye sums They have actually paid [as] set forth, exclusive of any Cost to be repaid by him or them who have fee & who hold ye same & that a Bill in form &c.

      Test W- Williams Cler
Concurr^d in the upper House.
      Test. George Wyllys Secrety

Upon ye Memorial of Abel Moses, Moses Cadwell, Dan^{ll} Frazier Thomas Frazier and John Hodgkin all of Hartland in ye County of Litchfield shewing to this Assembly that they were Professors of ye Church of England & own^d Lands in s^d Hartland East of ye River runing through s^d Town which is divided and that ye General Assembly granted a Tax of three pence p^r acre for four Years on all s^d Lands by Reason of which ye Money of ye Memorealists had been taken from them by Urial Holms Collector of s^d Tax praying for a Reimbursment of ye Money as actually paid & an Exemption for ye future &c

Resolv^d by this Assembly that ye s^d Urial Holms pay & he is hereby Ordered to refund and pay back to ye Memorialists ye Several Sums by them paid towards s^d Tax (vizt) to ye s^d Moses Cadwell ye Sum of £2-14-0   to s^d Abel Moses £3-10-0   to s^d Thomas Frazier £0-5-0 & to ye s^d Daniel Frazier ye Sum of 6s/6d and that within ye Term of Six Months from the riseing of this Assembly, and that all ye Memorialists be and they hereby are freed and Exempted from ye Payment of any part of said Tax for ye future

Pas^d in ye L. House
      Test Wm Williams Cler.
Concurrd, in the upper House
      Test George Wyllys Secre^{ty}

[1771, Apr. 28, New London]
Rev^d & Good S^r

Having wrote lately by 'Squire Stewart, I have ye less to trouble you wth at present.

I hope my very good Parishoner is become a Member of ye Venerable Society, to whom I doubt not his being a great Ornament.

I am told Mr Peters has preach'd his valedictory Sermon, left Hebron & gone to a more lucrative Living.

Mr Brown of Newport is dead: I hope ye Society will drop y^t Mission; The People are are more able to allow £100 Ster^g Per Ann, than ye Religious Society are to allow £20 to a Minister: No Parish in London exceeds them for Dress & Brilliancy. This is Truth; but wth Submission to my Superiors.

I praise GOD for encreasing my Hearers & Communicants, they behave very decently, but are really poor, as Mr Stewart knows.

I have sent my Bills for last Year's Salary to New-York; & tho' I don't yet know ye Purchaser, hope they will be duly accepted.

My Christian Love & Duty beg leave to wait upon y^e

religious Society: to answer whose very pious Designs is
& shall be ye conscientious Study of their &

Rev^d S^r

Y^r most obedient Servt &
affectionate Brother in

New-London Ap^l 28th   Jesus Christ
  1771   To ye Rev^d Dr Burton   Matt Graves

[Addressed:] To / The Rev^d Dr Burton / London
[Endorsed:] Read...Novr 11. 1771

[1771, Sept. 30, Pomfret]
Sir,

    On Friday the 13 ins^t I first had the Pleasure to see
the Bearer Mr Mosely at Pomfret, who came to me charged
with a Letter, from my Friend Mr Lloyd recommending
Him, in the Character of a Clergyman to whatever Civilities I would Show Him. He brought with Him also a Letter
from Mr Shrimpton Hutchinson, by which I am informed
that Mr Mosely told Him He was coming hither upon Your
Recommendation. This last Circumstance, together with
the Subject, I hope will sufficiently apologize for the Trouble of this Letter as well as the inclosed Copy from D^r
Burton, Secretary to the Society, wherein You will perceive that the Care of Supplying this Mission is principally
left with me. Mr Mosely hath given universal Satisfaction
by His Performance of the Service at Church to a full Congregation for the three Sundays last past; which together
with His agreable private Behaviour & Conversation, in-
titles Him to my particular Esteem, and I myself think
Him well qualified to become our Incumbent. But, that I
may not be thought wantonly to Sport with the Sacred Trust
committed to my Charge, as the Gentleman is a perfect
Stranger to me; and I have never heard of nor saw Him
until this Visit, and the Business is of too delicate and important a Nature for me to act upon of my own Head, and
I might incurr the Disapprobation of the Society, as well
as the Displeasure of my own particular Friends, should
I rashly venture upon a Step of such Consequence without
the Sanction of Some Gentlemen of Eminence among our
own Clergy, I must beg the Favour of You, provided You
have discovered by a Residence of Eleven Months of M^r
Mosely at Boston, that His moral Character and Qualifications perfectly correspond with the Rules established by
the Society, that You will be pleased to recommend Him
to me in Form as a proper Person to fill up this Mission.
I shall be highly obliged to my Friend Troutbeck if He also
will Subscribe a like Recommendation, which I shall think
Sufficient Ground for the Establishment of the Gentleman,
according to the Power vested in me by the Society. If
neither You, nor Mr Troutbeck should be well acquainted
with Mr Mosely's moral Character, I hope You will give
Your selves the Trouble to enquire into it, and not refuse
me the Satisfaction of knowing the Result; for without this,
or an equal Warrant, I shall never presume to act, and it
is of great Importance that this Mission be immediately
Supplied. If every Thing turns out in Favour of this Gentleman, as I sincerely hope, I must intreat You both that You
will be So kind as to give Your Promise that you will Subscribe a joint Letter to Dr Burton, informing Him of the
Steps that have been taken; which may confirm what I myself shall write upon the Same Subject.

I have the Honour to be with the greatest Esteem and
Respect--

Sir, Your very Hble Servt
Godfrey Malbone

Pomfret 30 September 1771.
  To The Revd Dr Caner at Boston

[1771, Oct. 9, Stamford]

Stamford in Connecticut
New England, Octob^r, 9, 1771.

Reverend Sir
    I have this day drawn a set of Bills for twenty five
pounds sterling upon the Treasurer of the Venerable Society in favour of Mr Thomas Ellison Ju^r Merchant, in
New York; or Order.----I Baptised last half Year, two
Adults, and forty four Children. Two were added to the
Communion. There are about Eighty five communicants,
and upwards of One Hundred and thirty heads of families,
in the two Towns, under my Cure. I continue my attention
to the duties of my Office, and am happy in the peaceable,
increasing and flourishing state of my Parish.--Enjoying,
by the blessing of God a good share of health, shall persevere in being as extensively useful as may be; esteeming
the reproach of Christ greater riches than the treasures
of Egypt.
    Who ever contends earnestly for the faith, must ex-
pect to pass through evil report, and good report.----The
rise and progress of our holy Church, out of the Ruins of
Fanitacism, is view'd by every Sect with a Jealous Eye;
like rising Christiany. They gladly combine and lay their
Heads together, to prevent if possible our enjoying the
privileges of our Birthright; cruelly upbraiding us with
the want of that perfection in Government, which they
vainly Claim, and boast of in Virtue of the gracious Act
of Tolleration. We hope to see a check to their thirst
after Dominion by an effectual support and encouragement
of our National Religion.----We envy not our dissenting
Brethren, in the liberties they are indulged, and only wish
and Pray for like indulgence in our religious profession,
and full enjoyment of the blessings of y^t Church, of which
we have the happiness to be Members.
    I preached at Sharon on a Colony Fast ye 18 of April
Last, and sunday following to a good devout Congregation,
and gave the Communion to upwards of thirty Communicants. Wednesday following attended a Lecture at Salsbury, and the next sunday performed divine Service in the
New Church upon the border of New York Province. A Numerous Congregation attended and behaved devoutly. their
Religious State for want of more constant and better instruction is truly compassionate. I Baptized in those several places, Two Adults, Twenty two Children White, two
Blacks. By Advice, they have employed at present, to
read Divine Service and Sermons among them, a deserving
young Gentleman lately graduated at Kings College in New
York; Mr William Hubbard who is pursuing his Studies
with a View to enter into holy Orders.
    Sunday ye 28th of July last I attended at Danbury, and
had a much larger Congregation than was expected, considering the badness of the Weather. the good people are
very thankful, for that intimation in your favour to me of
ye 14th of November last, Viz- that the Society think they
have a fair claim to some part of the late Mr Talbots

Legacy; hoping the Society in their wisdom will duly consider them when his intricate affairs are Setled. I have
been a sufferer by being obliged to pay during Mr Talbots
Life an extravigant interest for the Money laid out by his
Order in Glebe Lands, an encumbrance upon which continues during Mrs Goolds Life. my only inducment was,
to secure his benefaction in the best manner for the future
benefit of this Ch^h; tho' rather a burden to me, yet will be
of great advantage to my successor, and enable the Parish
to support a Minister less dependent upon the Societies
Charity

I Am Sir Obliged to you, for the assurance of the Societies approbation of my conduct in my occasional Visits
to Danbury, and for their good wishes. I heartily thank
them for past favours, and hope to deserve the continuance of their Notice; and pray God their Ability may be
enlarged, equal to the goodness of their hearts. With my
Humble Duty to the Venerable Board; believe me to be with
great Esteem an Repect to Your self, Reverend Sir

    Your Most Affectionate / Most Obed^t Humble Servt
                    Ebenez^r Dibblee

To the Revd Doctor Burton, Secretary of the Society for
Propagation of the Gospel &c.

[Endorsed:] Read...Janry 13· 1772

[1771, Oct. 14, Boston]
Sir

    Your Favor of Septr 13th by Mr Mosley I received, &
communicated the Contents to Mr Troutbeck, who, as well
as my self would be glad to oblidge you, in the affair you
desire to be satisfied in, but neither of us know more of
Mr Mosley, than you your self may know by a fortnights
conversation. He has met with the fate of all Strangers
that come among us (how deservedly I know not) to be censured for a freedom & openess, which do not exactly correspond with our manners, or the taste of the Country. For
my own part, as I have been much confin'd of late by frequent Infirmities, I have had little opportunity to learn the
public opinion, & less to form one of my own; for which
reason, as I should be cautious of recommending him, so
neither shall I presume without more particular knowledge,
to except to his character. 'Tis true, as he inform'd me
that he had nothing at present to employ him, I did suggest
to him, that he might be usefully employed for a few of the
Winter Months in some of the vacant Country Churches, &
mentioned to him Taunton Pomfret & Almsbury, & I must
confess, I still think so; but as to recommending him as a
settled Incumbent at your Church, it is what neither M^r
Troutbeck nor I, are qualified to do, either by our own
personal knowledge, or by any inquiry we should be able to
make here-- If you have any thoughts of that kind, your
best & safest method perhaps, would be that of writing to
your friend the Bishop of Litchfield, who might soon learn
his Character from the Archbishop of York, & give you the
satisfaction you desire.

    I am with much Respect / Sir / Your Most Obedient
& / Most Humble Servant

                      H. Caner
Boston Octr 14th 1771   J^{no} Troutbeck
To Godfrey Malbone Esqr

[1771, Oct. 15, Boston]
Sir

    I perceive by your Letter to Mr Lloyd, which he
communicated to me, & which I also communicated to
Mr Troutbeck, that you are desirous I should write to
Mr Fogg, (if not already too far engaged) to invite him
to remove to Pomfret.--But the conditions it seems are,
that Mr Troutbeck & I recommend him to you & to the So-
ciety--As to his moral Character we can, & have heretofore done it, when he first offered himself as a Candidate
for Orders; nor have we since met with any thing, that
should alter our opinion of him, but very much on the contrary. We likewise suppose that his prudence Abilities,
& other ministerial qualifications, intitle him to expect a
kind reception at Pomfret, yet as the fancy's of people are
often capricious, we cannot pretend to recommend him as
a person who will infallibly be agreeable to your People;
That will very much depend upon the taste & fancy of the
Hearers. With this reserve, we think he will prove, a
useful exemplary, & worthy Man; And as such shall be
ready to join with you in recommending him to the Society.

    Mr Troutbeck has seen, & fully concurs with me as
above, altho' not at this time present to sign it with
                            Sir
                  Your Most Obedient &
Boston Octr 15th 1771   Most Humble Servant
                        H. Caner
P.S. For your further Satisfaction in regard to Mr Fogg,
I have transcribed & inclos'd a Certificate given him by
the whole Convention when he was a Candidate for Orders,
& was about to travel to the Southward intending to embark from thence for England
                          Y^{rs}   H. C

[To Col. Godfrey Malbone, Pomfret, Conn.]

[1771, Nov. 2, Pomfret]
Sir,

    I am exceedingly obliged to you for the Favour of
your two Letters by Mr Mosely, as well as for the Trouble which, by Mr Lloyd's Information, you have been kind
enough to take upon another Account, which, I think, I can
very plainly discover hath had it's proper Effect.

    I am informed, by several ways, that Mr Fogg is very
desirous of returning from North Carolina to N. England.
Upon the first Intelligence of this, as Mr Leaming had, before, given me His Character, I wrote to Mr Lloyd telling
Him that We would gladly receive Him at Pomfret Church.
This, it seems, produced your second Letter, inclosing
me His Certificate signed by the Convention, which, together with what you write to me concerning Him, is much
more than sufficient to justify me to the Society for establishing Him in this Mission. I am told by Mr Lloyd that
you expect such a Letter from me as I now mean to send
you previous to your writing to Mr Fogg, that He may be
made acquainted with the Terms He is to expect from the
Church, which I with great Pleasure, undertake that the
Gentleman may not be surprized in to a Conduct which
He may, afterwards, have Occasion to repent.

    Both you and He have undoubtedly so very frequently
heard what first gave Occasion to the Rise of this Church

that it might be impertement to repeat it, but it may be very proper to hint that it is, as yet, but very imperfectly formed, & I cannot pretend to say with the least Degree of Certainty what are the Principles of a great Many of the Members who now pretty generally attend the Service. That some of them come from a Motive of Curiosity only, I believe may be depended upon. A few others, on the contrary, are the highest Church-Men you ever knew, whose impetuous Zeal, I am very confident, will greatly disserve the Interest of the Church notwithstanding my utmost Care to restrain them within proper Bounds. A very few there are who are actuated with a proper and becoming Spirit, and I flatter myself they will do great Honour to the Cause which they have lately espoused. Besides this very general Character of the Members, you must understand that our small Congregation, at present, is not made up of the wealthiest Men in the Neighbourhood, but I will venture to pawn my Reputation and Estate, that, by the constant Observation of a proper Conduct on our side, it will hereafter become as flourishing a Church as any in this Colony; the Incumbent may, therefore, reasonably expect such an Increase of His present Salary as may, by & by, amount to the Summit of His moderate Wishes. The Sum total of His present Encouragement stands thus, the whole of which is not alltogether certain; particularly, what I have mentioned from M.ʳ Commissioner Burch is not in Consequence of any Letter from Him, but a verbal Message only delivered me by M.ʳ George Mills Comptroller of the Custom at New-Haven.

From the Society £30 Sterling in Currency	£40--
From M.ʳ Paxton, for five years only, one Guinea	1--8--
From M.ʳ Burch .... one Guinea	1--8--
G. Malbone	10--
D.ʳ Walton	2--10--
M.ʳ Aplin, probably, ...	2--10--
From the other Members, uncertain, I think the Probability is on the side of more, rather than less, but to even the sum I carry out only	10--4--
	£68--

The above Sum of £68, equal to £51 Sterling, is what, I think I have the greatest Reason to expect will be punctually paid; it certainly cannot fall very short, and if there should be any Delinquents, We may, perhaps, some how or other contrive to make up the Deficiency.

We have no Glebe. I my self live in a Hutt, in which, however, God be praised! We have hitherto found very comfortable Provision, of which my Parson shall be heartily wellcome to His equal Share and shall be considered as one of my Family, as long as We each of us shall prove good-natured, I, on my Part, continue to live in Pomfret, and He, on His Part, continues to live single, for He cannot find Room wherein to cram a Wife, and if He could, as I have no Brats of my own I am determined to have no Plague from those of other People. The Society, with the greatest Reason, expect a Glebe House and at least Twenty Acres of good Land. This Circumstance shall ever be uppermost in my Mind until We shall have atchieved it,

but We must be Silent for the present. Perhaps, before either of the above mentioned Events take Place, We shall be in a fair Way.

I think I have now mentioned every Circumstance without the least Disguise, with which if M.ʳ Fogg is content, I, on my Part, shall be very ready to receive Him as our Missionary, and I flatter my self that He will be equally wellcome to every other Person of our Parish.

I remain with very great Esteem and Respect,
Sir, Your most obedient &
very humble Servant
Pomfret 2 Nov.ʳ 1771.   Godfrey Malbone

To The Rev.ᵈ D.ʳ Caner at Boston.

[1771, Dec. 26, Simsbury]

Exchange for 10£. Sterling
Simsbury, Connecticut 26ᵗʰ December 1771.
Sir
At Thirty Days Sight after this my second Bill of Exchange, my first & third of the same Tenor not being paid, pay to M.ʳ Peter Verstille, or Order the Sum of Ten Pounds Sterling: And hereof I have given the Society proper Advice
Roger Viets.

To M.ʳ William Symondson at the First-Fruits Office in the inner Temple, Treasurer to the Society for the Propagation of the Gospel in foreign Parts.

[1772, Feb. 13, Pomfret]
Dear Simon;
Permit me herewith to present You with a Dozen Copies of the Sermon preached at the Dedication of Trinity Church in this Township, the very being whereof was greatly owing to your Successful Assiduity in procuring the Subscriptions of the benevolent and charitable Gentlemen at Newport; a Step which justly entitles You to the Esteem of all honest and good Men, whether they are those who are, or may be, immediately benefitted by it, in Consideration of their Proximity, or those whose Situation may be howsoever distant from it. It is certainly a melancholy Truth that the Professors of the Independent Congregational Worship, who are Inhabitants of our Settlements remote from large Towns (where their Tempers and Morels are free from Observation, and are neither corrected nor restrained by Examples, which frequently occurr in large Cities; but, on the contrary, where their Imaginations are so lost and bewildered that they reduce the Understanding and honesty of every Man, of whatsoever Condition, or howsoever situated, to a level with their own, and positively determine Him to be wrong who doth not readily do as they do, and think as they think) are so lost to the Practice of Religion & Virtue in the general Conduct of their Lives, that however diligent they are to maintain specious Appearances, there is scarcely the Shadow of Morality left among them. I mean & hope to be understood with some few Exceptions. Was this my Assertion to be made publick, I am very sure I should be charged with that Bigotry to the Religion I adhere to, which I think is so natural to them in their's, as to constitute their peculiar Characteristick; but in the

Circle of your Acquaintance, where I have the Honour to be more intimately known, I flatter myself that I shall be [?by no] Means obnoxious to so severe a Censure; for it certainly hath ever been a fixed Principle with me, that the true Believers of revealed Religion, let them be of whatsoever Persuasion, will find Acceptance with their Master provided they sincerely use their Endeavours to imitate the Example & obey the Precepts and Injunctions of the blessed Author of it; but I am much afraid, and am sorry to say I can scarce help believing that in such Parts of this Colony, where I have had any Opportunity of Observation, this is not the Rule of Practice; The Teachers, far from recommending & enforcing the obvious Precepts of the Gospel, do but amuse themselves and their deluded Auditors with Speculative Notions & metaphysical Subtleties, taking the subject of their Discourses from those mystical Parts of it, which have been, long since, let alone and neglected by the most able and approved Divines, as far surpassing the Limits of our very narrow Conceptions. Hence the numberless Quacks in Divinity that abound in these Colonies. Every Cobler or Tinker, that does not understand five sentences of common English, pretending to a Nostrum that will conduct his wretched Hearers, by a secret, sure & easy guide to Heaven, which He discovers by unfolding to them certain Mysteries, which Men, of the greatest Genius & Learning in the World have hitherto deemed inexplicable! Hence also are they taught to form very inadequate Notions of the Deity, very exalted ones of themselves, a thorough Contempt and fixed Hatred of every Body who differs from them in Opinion, and almost a total Neglect of every Thing that is valuable in the Conduct of their Lives and Practices. Such Fanaticism, God be praised! is very infrequent among the Professors of the Church of England; the more extended therefore and general she becomes, by so much the greater must be the Reformation of our Manners; since by Her are we taught to shew our Belief by our Practice, in Order to recommend Ourselves to the Throne of Grace. Words, frequently, are, and will be false. Actions alone cannot lie.

I have been led into this Train of thinking, or rather, have been induced to express these Sentiments from the Conduct of a Committee of this Society of Brookline, who, yesterday paid me a Visit, which I imagine You will think very extraordinary: Ever since the Church was about to be erected, they omitted no Practices, however dirty or mean, to impede or entirely prevent it. It was no sooner compleated, contrary to their most sanguine Expectations, than they redoubled their Efforts to restrain & check the Growth of it. They made no Scruple, industriously, to propagate that as soon as ever any of them should be freed from their Meeting and received and acknowledged as Churchmen, that I should bring them in to pay their full Proportions of the whole Expense of building the Church; and, also, that whatever Letters I pretended to have received from the Secretary of the [Society] or my Friends in England relating to the Establishment of a Mission here, were counterfeited by me, and read to the Members of the Church as genuine. I am told, and have reason to believe, that [they] have employed Bribes to buy off, and Menaces to intimidate those whom they suspected to have an Inclination to leave their Meeting and become Churchmen. But these practices, whether open or concealed, in Addition to their oppressive and arbitrary Rates, are not likely to avail them. The Church, left entirely to Herself, must,

at Length, triumph over the Genius of Independancy, assisted by all Her low Cunning and infamous Arts. I am further told that they themselves have been obliged to own that the Sermons which they have occasionally heard at Church (where some of them sometimes will come, were it only to try to pick Holes) are much better and more calculated for the Benefit of Mankind than what they hear at their Meetings; but still, they say, We will not attend them as it would be a Departure from the Religion of our Fore-Fathers, and that, finally, it may be the Means of the Introduction of the Bush-hups. To prevent so terrible an Evil, every Method they can put in Practice, appears to them to be justifiable. Upon this noble Principle Calumny and Slander cease to be vicious, and at once become virtuous, and they have not failed to bestow them very liberally, upon poor Mr Mosley, whom they have bespattered in a most plentiful Manner. This Gentleman, a Relation of Sir Edward Hawke, came out of England, upon his Appointment as Chaplain of the Salisbury Man of War, and when his Ship left Boston upon her Return, He obtained his Discharge and came up to Pomfret, about the middle of September last, upon the Recommendation of Dr Cauer, with Letters to me from Harry Lloyd and Shrimpton Hutchinson. He is one of my Family, and I can sincerely say, I take Him to be One of the best natured Men I ever knew in my Life. His Behaviour hath been, in every Respect, entirely correspondent with his Profession, and both at Church, and out of it, He hath given universal Satisfaction to His Parish, as well as to every one of at least a Dozen of my particular Friends, who have been kind enough to visit me at my Hermitage since his Residence among us. Notwithstanding all this, Our Opponents, not contented with their former Behaviour, of which there had not been the least publick Notice taken either by Him or by me, were so ignorant and so stupid as to attempt to add personal Insult to their Invectives and had the Assurance to come to my House, in Form, to demand the Inspection of His Letters of Orders; and also, if they found Him properly qualified, to know by what Right or Authority I pretended to establish Him at Pomfret. I was luckily apprised of their Intention a few Days before they came, and concluded with Mr Mosley, that the best Method of Treatment We could fall upon, was to receive them with the utmost good Nature and Civility as Neighbours, but as Inquisitors to shew them the greatest Contempt and Disdain & to turn...matter into a Jest, He himself not to appear in the Scene, and I...even bitter... to hold his Tongue, &...Mosele[y]s.

Upon this Plan I drew up the inclosed Paper, purposely making it as ridiculously formal as You now see it, in Order to open their Eyes and to expose them to Themselves, and by what I have since heard it hath had a very thorough Effect. I did not produce it until after above an Hour's..., wherein, I give You my Word, I did not spare them, but...to them, in the most explicit Manner, the Whole of their Conduct; Part of which they owned and Part they denied. There was an Incident which, I have been since informed, aggravated my Reception of them to a very great Degree; This was the Arrival of two entire Strangers, upon a Visit to Mr Mosley, who were Spectators of the whole Scene. They happened to come into the Room, not long after the Arrival of the first Comittee Man, Williams, who came alone, and immedi-

ately preceeding that of the other two. Conscious of their own Demerit, they said, immediately upon their Return, they could have forgiven me the Schooling had they been by themselves, but to give them such a severe Lesson before so many strangers was very monstrous and schocking; not considering that if any Thing was amiss they brought it upon Themselves. From the opening to the Close of the Scene, there passed at least two Hours. The whole Time, I was happy so to keep my Temper as not to omit a single Circumstance in the Conversation which I have since recollected might have been an Advantage. When they left their Chairs to go off, I told them that since they did not chuse to purchase the Gratification of their Curiosities at the Expence of signing the Declaration I had drawn up, there was still one Alternative; if their Minister, M̲r̲ Whitney, would come and pay M̲r̲ Mosley a Visit as a Christian and Gentleman, and by Consequence a Friend, that I, on my Part, would show Him all the Politeness of which I was capable, and from that inexhaustible Fund of good Nature, with which M̲r̲ Mosley was possessed, I would take upon my self to promise that He would not only shew Him his Orders, but give Him every other Information which lay in his Power, and that as He was a Man of such little Knowledge and Experience of the World, they might tell Him from me that it would be well worth his while to cultivate the Acquaintance, which if He thought proper to do, they might perceive that their Visit would not be all-together fruitless.

I am afraid You will be heartily tired with this tedious detail, and sick of the Trifle which, when I began, I was in Hopes would afford You some Amusement at this very dull and severe season, but I hope I shall readily meet with Your Pardon if I am mistaken in what was certainly well intended.

The best Wishes of the Sett at Pomfret-Hall attend You, Your Lady, the Tuesday and Friday Clubs which concluded....

                                        Godfrey Malbone.

Pomfret 13 February 1772.

To Simon Pease Esq̲r̲ at Newport

[Enclosure:]

We the Subscribers, appointed a Comittee by the Society of Brookline, In the Township of Pomfret, In the Conty of Windham, In the Colony of Connecticut, for the Inspection and Transa[c]tion of the religious Concerns of said Society, do hereby certify, declare and make known to all Manner of Persons; That to prevent, as much as in Us lies, every Possibility of Chicanery, Fraud, or Collusion in those who have seceeded from our Independant Congregational Meeting (where the Worship of God is singly, simply, truely and spiritually performed, according to the very sensible and righteous Manner which was framed and HERE established as the glorious Fruit of the great Sagacity, Wisdom and Policy of the Religion of our pure, holy and renowned Fore-Fathers) and declared themselves Conformists to the Church of England, and have invariably acted agreable thereto since the Month of October 1770, We, in Consequence of that high and great Authority, the utmost they could possibly bestow delegated to Us by the said Society of Brookline; Or which We, being very active and zealous Members, assumed of Ourselves, it is no Matter which,

called upon Richard Mosley, Clerk, who presumes to stile Himself Legis Legum Baccalaureus, a Degree of Honour, conferred upon Him by the University of Cambridge in Great Britain, in Consequence of his Studies and Literary Merit during a seven Year's Residence at S̲t̲ John's College; and pretends to have been, legally and duely, ordained a Deacon and Priest, according to the Cannon-Law of the said Church of England, and to have lately been employed in the Service of his Majesty George the third, by the Grace of God King of Great Britain France and Ireland, as Chaplain on Board of His ship Salisbury, of Fifty guns, commanded at Boston by the Honorable Commodore James Gambier; and also to have frequently and publickly, officiated as a Priest in each of the several Churches of the said good Town of Boston, the several Rectors, or Ministers of which may, for aught We know, have been such negligent, stupid, idle and irreverend Blockheads, as to have been very indifferent and careless whether they received and admitted into their Desks and Pulpits an Impostor, Or not, provided they might have their Business performed without any Care or Trouble to themselves. The Lords of the Admiralty, also, may have been equally to blame in suffering themselves to be imposed upon by appointing to the Cure of a national Ship a worthless, vagrant Person, without a due Inquisition into his Qualifications and religious Character, previous to such His Appointment: Nay, who knows but that the pretended Bishop who ordained Him, that Bishop's Predecessor and the whole Series of them up to the very Founder of their Order Himself, may have been, all of them, Impostors, and their Religion a Cheat? And yet, notwithstanding this very reasonable Presumption, the said Richard Mosley, in Virtue of this aforementioned pretended Power, with great Effrontery (not having, before hand, consulted our Will & Pleasure and obtained our gracious Consent for the same) claimeth a Right and hath absolutely exercised the five Months last past, the said Office of Priesthood, according to the Rites & Ceremonies of the said Church of England, in this very Parish of Brookline; the like whereof hath never before been practised, or heard of, in all Windham County. Wherefore, as of our invaluable and indubitable Right, & not to derogate from the high Office, Trust, and Authority committed to our Exercise and keeping by the said Society of Brookline, We were not abashed, shame-faced nor mealymouthed; but, impertinently, boldly and peremptorily demanded of Him the said Mosley the Inspection and Examination of His said Letters of Orders which He (undoubtedly influenced by the Religion He professeth, which, He saith, ordaineth that if a Man take away thy Coat to let Him have thy Cloak also) took not the least Offence at, but in a most becoming, humane & condescending Manner, upon our Solemn Promise of signing, with our Christian and Sur-Names, this present Acknoledgement, Declaration and Certificate, immediately produced. And it appears to us that the said Reverend Richard Mosley is, really, what We thought, or said We thought, He only pretended to be, and that He is truely and absolutely charged with the Orders, both of Deacon and Priest, granted by His Grace Robert, by Divine Providence, Lord Arch-Bishop of York, which We have employed our best Faculties to enquire into, and to the very utmost of our Skill, Knowledge and Judgement proceeding from the

small share of light that is within Us, pronounce them
to be valid and genuine; and do hereby acknowledge Ourselves to be therewith fully & duely satisfied.

In Testimony whereof We have hereunto signed Our
Names, at Brookline aforesaid this 12 Day of February
1772.

The Comittee were Joseph Holland, Samuel Williams
& Josiah Fassett, who attended at my House on the Day of
the Date, and upon their persisting upon the Propriety and
Necessity of being satisfied in Relation to Mr Mosley's
Orders, and also to the Right with which I was invested to
place Him in the Church as a Minister, I told them that if
they would sign to the above Instrument in acknoledgement
of their own Ignorance and Folly, that I would give them
every Kind of Satisfaction in my Power, even to the Perusal
of my own private Letters, as well as Mr Mosley's publick Orders and read to them the above Writing, as distinctly and emphatically as I was able, in the Presence of
Mrs Malbone, William Temple, Esqr Peter Maxfield and
two Strangers who happened to call here upon a Visit to
Mr Mosley; Their Names, La-Peire, of Boston, and Turner of Medway.

Godfrey Malbone

[1772, Mar. 25, Norwalk]
            Norwalk in Connecticut March 25. 1772
Reverend Sir,
    The last half year, I have baptized 38 Children three
of which were negros. And have admited Six persons to
the Lords supper who not having joined in that Ordinance
before. I have upwards of 150 Communicants.
    I have been to Pomfret 160 miles to supply that Church
before Mr Mosley was appointed. Mr Godfree Malbone with
what he collected from his friends, and his own money has
built a neat Church there, and a very decent Congregation
appeared that Sunday I officiated. Mr Malbone has taken
unwearied pains to instruct the people to use the Service;
and they carried it on with the Appearance of true Devotion, and with a striking Solemnity.
    I have been to sharon, Salisbury, and Armenia 80
miles, and preached in those places four days Successively to large numbers of people, who are in great want of Instruction. I been to Hartford also 70 miles to assist them
in their destitute State.
    I have acquainted you before of the Death of Doctor
Johnson. I now herewith send you a Copy of the Sermon
which was preached at His Funeral.
    I have drawn a Bill of £25 Sterling, in favour of Mr
Thomas Ellison, upon the Treasurer.
    As I live in one of the Sea port Towns, if the Society
direct the packets for any of the Clergy of this Colony to
my Care, I will take Care that they receive them. Any
Directions of the Society shall be punctually obeyed.--
By their and your Humble Servant
                                    Jeremiah Leaming
P.S. If the Society could favour my poor people with a
number of prayer Book, it would be kindly accepted, and
I believe properly bestowed.

The Revd Doct Daniel Burton

[1772, Apr. 24, Stamford]
                            Stamford Connecticut
                        New England April 24th 1772
Reverend Sir.
    My Bill for twenty five pounds Sterling, is this day
drawn in usual form upon Mr William Symondson. Treasurer of the Venerable Society, in favour of Mr Thomas
Ellison Jur Merchant in New York.-
    I Baptized last half Year thirty seven Children. the
number of Communicants in the Towns under my Cure, is,
Eighty two.- of Heads of families professing the Church,
two Hundred and Nineteen.----My Parish in all parts,
continue in a good State. notwithstanding my advanced
state of Life, thro' the blessing of God, I am still able
with unremiting diligence to attend the duties of my Extensive Cure.
    I have again visited the destitute in the interior parts
of the Country. on Sunday the 27th of last October, I attended Divine Service & Preaching at Sharon. Tuesday
following a Lecture at Salsbury. thirsday following a
Lecture at Cornwall. Sunday, 3d of November, in the
New Church on the borders of New York Province. and
the fifth of November at Sharon. A Numerous and devout
Congregation attended in all those places (except Cornwall,
where they had not timely Notice) and behaved with great
decency. I Baptized among them Sixteen Children. They
are under no small discouragement, in seeing no prospect
of being provided with a Setled Minister, and being so remote from any Established Missionary, and unable to provide for themselves. In Consequence of which, Mr Hubberd whom they lately employed to Read Prayers & Sermons among them, hath left them. Mrs Palmer, who with
her Children, was lately Recommended to the Societies
notice and Charity, is Married again, to a Dissenter in
good Circumstances, with in the space of four Months
after Mr Palmers Death. His Children are left under uncomfortable Circumstances, and are proper Objects of
Charity, in case the Society is pleased to confer a gratuity.
    Purposing by Gods Grace to continue as Extensively
useful as may be; with my Compliment of gratitude & Duty
to the Venerable Board, and best Respects to Your Self.
I Am Reverend Sir
    Your Most Obedient / Very Humble Servant / and
Affectionate Brother
                                    Ebenezer Dibblee

To the Reverend Doctr Burton Secretary of the Venerable
Society for Propagation of the Gospel in Foreign Parts.

[Endorsed:] Read...July 13. 1772

[1772, ?May, ?Pomfret]
[Godfrey Malbone to the Secretary of the S.P.G., Westminster, England, referring to letters of Mar. 22, 1771,
now available in the Doc. Hist. of the P.E. Church in
Conn.]

Revd Sir,
    I have so long deferred to return You my unfeigned
Thanks for the very great Obligation You have conferred
upon me, in countenancing the Establishment of a Mission

at Pomfret, that I find myself too much at a Loss for a sufficient Apology for not answering Your Letter of the 22 March, of the last Year, which I received the 9 July following, together with One from my Lord Bishop of Litchfield, under Cover of my Friend Mr Robinson. At the same Time, I received, in very good Order, the Books which You were pleased to forward from the Society; of which I have taken great Care in the Distribution, excepting the 50 Copies of the Version of the Psalms by Tate and Brady in a single Volume, not one of which have I parted with, lest these People, who are more fond of Psalm singing than of any other Part of Divine Worship being furnished with the Means of gratifying this particular Passion might be induced to neglect providing them selves with Prayer Books, and consequently ever continue in their Ignorance of the Beauty and Holiness of our Method of Worship. I hope this Reason will be esteemed sufficient to justify me to the Society for an Attempt, though unsuccessful, to exchange them with the Booksellers for some pious Tracts which I had the Presumption to conclude would be more useful. Had I succeeded I should have given You the Information; and had I met with your just Reprehensions for perverting the Intentions of the Society, I was resolved to replace them at my own Expence. As it now is, I reserve them to bestow in such a Manner as to do no Injury; being very certain that a further Increase of our Congregation will furnish me with sufficient Occasion.

The Omission of my Acknoledgements for the Receipt of the Bishop's and your Letter, which, certainly, gave me the highest Satisfaction, of the Kind, I ever met with in my Life, is vastly unaccountable, and I have such a thorough Sense of the Neglect that in Vain should I attempt to search for sufficient Reasons to justify my self. Nothing therefore is left me but humbly to implore Your Pardon and sincerely to promise that I will never give just Cause for an Imputation of the like offence for the future. I further esteem my self reprehensible that I have so far presumed to invade the sacred office of Preisthood as to read the entire service of the Church (the Absolution, substituting in lieu thereof a Prayer in the Commination, and the Benediction excepted) together with a Sermon every Sunday, to a moderate Number of Hearers, for near Ten Months; the last seven of which, owing to the Increase of the Audience, in the Reading Desk at the Church; the former Part of the Time at my own House. It was some Time before I could bring myself to determine upon this step, but upon Consideration that our future Congregation were as ignorant of the service as so many of the Iroquois, not above two or three of them having ever seen a Common Prayer Book until my Removal hither, I thought, however averse I am to Lay-reading in general, the Intention of keeping these People together and instructing them in the Service, previous to the Establishment of a Missionary might, possibly, be justifiable.

I no sooner received your Letter than I dispatched Copies of it to Dr Caner at Boston, and Mr Leaming at Norwalk (as I was informed that Dr Cooper of New York was about to embark for England) and requested the Favour of them to exert themselves, one to the Eastward, the other to the Westward to pick up a vacant Clergyman to supply this Mission. In Consequence of this Application, at the Instance of Dr Caner, Mr Richard Mosley, who came out of England Chaplain to His Majesty's Ship Salisbury, made his Appearance at Pomfret on the 13 September last, at a Time when the Independent Teacher happened to be absent at a Commencement at New Haven College. The Church, on the two following Sundays, was much crowded by this Man's Auditors, who came thither, upon a Principle of Curiosity, to hear a Sermon from a <u>Boatswain of a Man of War</u>, as they termed Him in Derision. His Performance in the Desk, the Regularity of the Congregation in making their Responses (a plain Proof that the Pains taken to instruct them had not been ill bestowed) together with the Sermons that He delivered from His Pulpit had an extreme good Effect. Their Tone was changed and many of them thought seriously of the great Solemnity and Beauty of that Form of Worship which they had never before seen; and had thought of, only since my Undertaking to build the Church, by hearing it frequently mentioned, with the greatest disrespect by our violent Opposers. Our Houses, here, are so scattered and many of them so distant that between the services We, none of Us, think of retiring to our own Homes; but wait our Dinners until both are concluded. I each Day spent the Hour of Intermission in familiar Conversation with One or other of these People, who were as variously affected as their Complexions were different. Upon the whole, I plainly discovered that a large Majority were highly satisfied not only with the Substance and Manner of our Addresses to the Almighty, but also with the Doctrines, which had been delivered, in a very pleasing Manner, from the Pulpit. That Mr Mosley would be a very popular Preacher was certain, and I thought my self happy in the Opportunity of showing Him Your Letter and telling Him that I should be glad to appoint Him to the Mission of Pomfret if, for this Purpose, He could get a Recommendation from Dr Caner and Mr Troutbeck, the only two Clergymen, with whom I had the Honour to be acquainted, in Boston. He answered----He did not think such an Application necessary as He was determined not to stay above a Year or two in America, but that if I would admit Him to continue One of my Family, He would tarry with Us, upon any Terms, during the Winter. I assured Him I should be much pleased with the Honour of His Company, but [as] I thought my self responsible to the Society for the well-being of the Church, until We had a Missionary established [and] as He was a perfect Stranger to me, and was then going to Boston to give Orders about His own private Affairs, if He meant to continue to Serve the Church, He must be the Bearer of my Letter to those Gentlemen which I had already wrote and which I desired Him to peruse. He did so & presented it to Dr Caner who, with Mr Troutbeck, returned me for Answer, of which He Himself was the Bearer the 14 October, "that though He might be usefully employed a few of the Winter Months in some of the vacant Country Churches, they would not think of recommending Him as a Settled Incumbent at our Church, either by their own personal Knowledge or by any enquiry that they should be able to make at Boston; that He had met with the Fate of all Strangers that came among Us, to be censured for a Freedom and Openess which do not exactly correspond with our Manners of the Taste of the Country, and that as they should be cautious of recommending Him, so neither would they presume, without more particular Knowledge to except to His Character." Previous to this Transaction, the worthy Mr Leaming & Mr Nickole who

now assists Mr McGilchrist at Salem, had each of them, with very great Kindness, visited the Church at Pomfret, and had spoken to me highly in Favour of Mr Daniel Fogg, a young Man who had lately received Orders, & who they told me would well supply this Mission. In the Course of Mr Mosley's Journey, I wrote to Dr Caner and, mentioning this Circumstance, requested of Him that provided Mr Mosley should fail He would send one such a Recommendation of Mr Fogg as, in Case of His Establishment, would justify my Conduct to the Society. This was done in most ample Form and sent me by Mr Mosley with the beforementioned Letter, both of which I communicated to Him. On the 2nd of November I wrote again to Dr Caner inviting Mr Fogg, who was at this Time in North Carolina, to the Mission upon the Terms which formed the principal Subject of my Letter. This Invitation being accepted, Mr Fogg quitted His Living at North Carolina and made his Appearance here on the 6 of this Month ["May" struck out].

During the intervening, near, eight Months, Mr Mosley hath continued in the Exercise of His Function with such Ability and such Assiduity that by frequent familiar Visits, preaching Lectures, and composing many particular Discourses which He delivered from His Pulpit to gratify the People and to answer and remove Objections which they had raised in their Private Conversations and had been instructed to make against some particular Parts of our Service, He hath raised among them a wonderful Attachment to His Person. He, on the other Hand, contrary to His own Expectations, was so much pleased with his Situation that He was determined, in Case of Mr Fogg's Refusal, to continue in the Society's Service at Pomfret. To effect this a Step was taken which I cannot commend either for it's Propriety or Regularity. However, for the Good of the Church, and His particular Gratification, I sent a State of the Case to Dr Caner on the 16 of last Month, leaving it intirely to Him either to confirm Mr Mosley and reject Mr Fogg, if it could be done with Justice and Propriety, or to give the Preference to the latter, as He might think the Circumstances required. Mr Fogg by this Time, though unknown to Us, had arrived in New England, and before my Letter reached Dr Caner, had left Boston for Pomfret. Mosley, the best natured Man and the most ready to oblige of any One I ever knew in my Life, though much agitated and chagrined at his Appearance, resigned up the Mission to Him with the greatest Equanimity. The next Day was spent in giving Mr Fogg the necessary Information relative to His Parish, and laying a Plan to conciliate the Affections of His Parishioners, four of whom had refused to sign the Bond for the Support of the Incumbent because I had made the Subscriptions payable to the Church Wardens for the Use and Benefit of Mr Mosley and His Successors, when late in the Afternoon I received the Honour of your Letter of the 25 January nominating and particularly appointing Mr Mosley to this Mission, at the Instance of His Lordship the Bishop of London. This produced a sudden Alteration. Mr Fogg, who had quitted His Bread at Carolina to enjoy this Mission thought it His Duty to give up His Pretensions and not to interfere with the Intentions of the Society and Mr Mosley began to think He had now a more equitable Claim to it. At this Juncture, luckily, came to my House Mr Tyler Missionary of Norwich, with whom the Evening

was spent in the Discussion of this Matter. As the Good of the Church and my Esteem for Mr Mosley on the one Hand, so, on the other did Justice to Mr Fogg keep me so much on the Reserve that I said very little on the Occasion until I found He was about to yield to His Prejudice, when I represented that the Receipt of your last Letter made no Alteration in the Circumstance of His Appointment; that the Society having invested me with a Power which I had already exerted in Favour of Mr Fogg it was become impossible for me to undo what I had done and that the Bishop would, certainly, never had directed me to appoint Mr Mosley to the Mission, could He have known that in Consequence of your former Letter it had actually been disposed of to Mr Fogg; that therefore the Letter of the 25 January ought not, nor could not have any Effect and that if Mr Fogg resigned to Mr Mosley it must be His own voluntary Act and Deed, for that I certainly would not with Justice be any Way instrumental to it. This was too plain to be controverted. Mr Fogg, however, with the greatest Benevolence set out on the Monday Morning, with Mr Tyler for Hebron, in order to consult Mr Peters about the vacant Living of Litchfield, and Mr Mosley who had returned from Norwich, where He went to supply Mr Tyler's Pulpit in His Absence, determining not to be outdone in an Act of Generosity, resolved to give up all Thoughts of sitting down at Pomfret and to try His Interest with the Bishop of London to get an Appointment for Litchfield and immediately wrote to Him a Letter in Consequence. I wish Him the Living which His many good Qualities deserve. Thus ended this generous Contest, which, in my Opinion, doth great Honour to each of the Parties. Mr Mosley having served the Parish, with great Zeal and Fidelity, full eight Months, including the Time that He takes to introduce Mr Fogg to His People is undoubtedly intitled to an equal Portion of the year's Salary which the truely venerable Society have, most charitably, been pleased to allow to this Mission and I hope His Bill for £20 Sterling, the justly merited Reward of His Services will meet with due Honour.

Mr Fogg being now become our Settled Incumbent, You may rely upon my doing every Thing in my Power, not only to make his Situation agreable to Him but also to assist Him in promoting the great and good Work He hath undertaken. The Bond I have drawn for His support payable by the Parishioners on the Monday in Easter Week, wherein the Subscribers are obligated to make up any deficiency that may arise by the Removal of any One of them at such Distance that He cannot attend, is for £28 Lawful Money, equivalent to £21 Sterling. Besides this two Gentlemen in Boston Mr Commissioner Saxton & Mr Commissioner Burch have promised the yearly Payment of one Guinea each in Addition to His Salary; So that with the Society's Bounty His Emolument will amount to the yearly sum of £53--2/ Sterling. It cannot be less and I hope and dare say it will soon be much more. We have not at present a Glebe House even in Embryo, but You may be assured that the Fabrick shall rise. A valuable Lot of 23 1/2 Acres, whereon I at first proposed to erect the Church, near to my own House, is now Known at too great a Distance by my conforming to the Inclinations of the People to place it two Miles to the Southward on the Confines of the Townships of Plainfield, Canterbury & Killingley. This Disposition....

[1772, May 5, Farmington]

To the Honorable the General Assembly of the Colony of Connecticutt to be Convened at Hartford on the Second Thursday of May A Dom 1772.

The Petition of Jonathan Miller Junr of Farmington in said County humbly Sheweth

That the Society of Northington in s.^d Town where the Pet.^r lives on or about the 5.th day of December 1768, granted a Tax to raise among Other things, the Sum of £43-2s-2d 1/4 upon the Inhabitants of said Society for defraying the Charges arisen for the Support of the Ministry within the same and appointed the Pet.^r to Collect the same and pay it over as the Law directs--that the Com.^{tee} of said Society soon afterwards made out a Rate Bill and delivered it to the Pet.^r including also a Rate against Samuel Northaway [for] the Sum of £1:4:0, also against John Northaway for the sum of £1:6:9 1/4 also against Medad Newel for the Sum of £0:10:4 1/4--also against Judah Hutchinson for the sum of £0:1:7 3/4 also against John Fuller for the Sum of £0:17:6--also against Ruth Norton for the Sum of 3/- also against Bulah Buel for the Sum of 16s/1d--all in lawful money amounting in the whole to the Sum of £4:19:3 1/4 all of which s.^d Several Persons last Named live and have rateable Estates within the said the bounds of s.^d Northington Society and are and for a long Time have been professors of the Church of England Deemed & treated as such, towit, long before the granting of said Tax and have for many years before and ever since soberly & Conscientiously attended public Worship within the Town of Symsbury near & Convenient for their attending the same where there is a Society of the Church of England and a Person in Orders according to the Canons of the Church of England Settled and abiding among them and performing Divine Service-- That the Pet.^r soon after receiving s.^d Rate Bill honestly & faithfully Collected and paid all & Every of the several Rates against s.^d Inhabitants of Said Society exclusive of s.^d Professors into the hands of the Treasurer of s.^d Society to his Acceptance, and he also Collected & paid said Rates made out against Professors [of the Church of England] into the hands of the s.^d Incumbent & Person In Orders in s.^d Town of Symsbury as the Law Directs and as Other & former Coll.^{rs} in s.^d Society had done without the least Complaint for Years before--and duely Notified s.^d Com.^{tee} & Treasurer thereof-- Yet notwithstanding s.^d Com.^{tee} & Treasurer with the Advice & Instigation of Joseph Hart Esqr of s.^d Town & Society Contriving together to Vex the Pet.^r and s.^d Professors, Combined together and insisted to have s.^d Professors Rates Collected & paid into their hands (Contrary to all former usuage, and the Pet.^r refusing to do the same unless they would Indemnify him therein, which they refused, the s.^d Joseph Hart Esqr Issued out his warrant against the Pet.^r therefor for the Sum of about five pounds L:money alledging his neglect &c--and Caused his Body to be taken & Imprisoned thereon for the Space of about five days & then tendered him one pist[a]rene for his Imprisonment and Sett him at Liberty, and then immediately Issued Another Precept Against him for the Sum of about £7:6:2d 1/2 alledged his Neglect & refusal to pay the Same into the hands of s.^d Com.^{tee} and Treasurer, on which last Warrant or Distress the Pet.^r was taken & Commited to the Common Goal in said County merely for not paying s.^d Professors Rates into the hands of s.^d Society Treasurer That the Pet.^r procured his Friends and gave Bail to the Sherif of said County for his Enlargment & left the Prison with a View of Obtaining A Remedy at Law for the misdoings of S.^d Society's Com.^{tee} & Treasurer for whose Conduct he Supposed s.^d Society were Answerable-- That accordingly he brot his Action against them therefor, at Common Law but failed of a recovery therein merely because the Society as a Community Could not be Answerable in such Case & y.^r Pet.^r has been putt to immense Cost and Trouble therein & is without Remedy unless by your Honors, and not only so but the s.^d Society by their Treasurer &c have since brot their Action against the Sherif of s.^d County for Suffering the Pet.^r to leave said Gaol & have recovered the whole Sum mentioned in said Last Mentioned warrant with the Interest & Cost thereon amounting in the whole to the Sum of £13:9:0 lawful money And the Pet.^r is holden to pay the same when in fact there was not at the Time of Issuing s.^d Warrant and his Commitment thereon One farthing due to S.^d Society of the Rates Commited to him to Collect either in Law or Equity, exclusive of s.^d Professors, which the s.^d Society could not, by Law, require or Demand and the Pet.^r as well as s.^d professors feel much alarmed at such Oppressive Proceedings and are Obliged to apply to the Righteous Interposition of your Honors-- Wherefore the Pet.^r humbly prays your Honors to take his very Singular Case into your wise Consideration and Appoint a Judicious & Impartial Com.^{tee} to enquire of the matters of his Complaint, and Report the same with their Opinion thereon--and if it shall appear that the Pet.^r faithfully did his Duty as a Collector towards s.^d Society and Discharged his trust in that Respect as the Law required, that he may not only be Discharged from the Cost recovered by s.^d Society against him in the Action brot by him in order to his Relief as aforesaid, but that the Sherif also to whom the Pet.^r is holden may be Excused & Exonerate from paying or suffering the Judgment afores.^d or at least no more than shall appear in Equity due on s.^d Rate Bill if any there be--or Otherwise Relieve the Pet.^r in Some Other way as your Honors in your great Wisdom Shall think fit and he as in Duty bound Shall Ever pray-- Dated at Farmington the 5.th day of May Anno Dom: 1772

Jonathan Miller Jr

Farmington May ye 7.th AD 1772 then the Within Peticin was Read in ye hearing of Barnad Thomson one of the principle inhabitent of the within Sd Society of Northington and a true attested Coppy therof Left with Joseph hart Esq Society's Clark

Fee 3/6   Test   Ichabod Norton Constable of Farmington

May 1773 In ye L. House the Question, whether the Plea offered in abatem.^t of this Petition, was Suffecient, to abate ye Same, was put & resolved in the affirmative

Test Wm Williams Cler.

In the upper House The Question whether the Plea offered in Abatement of this Petition was sufficient to abate the same was put and Resolved also in the Affirmative

Test. George Wyllys Secrety

[1772, May 8, Boston]

Sir

I was yesterday favour'd with your's of April 16.th Whatever my Advice might have been under the Circum-

stances described in your Letter, the occasion for it seems now to be superseded by the appearance of Mr Fogg, who went from hence last Tuesday, & is now I suppose with you. Mr Fogg, as I formerly acquainted you, is a worthy good Man, well known among us, & able to produce sufficient Testimony of his Prudence & Virtue from his Youth upwards; nor do I doubt but he will prove a sound Divine & a useful Minister wherever he may be appointed especially as he increases in Years & Experience. Mr Mosley is cer-[tainly urbane] & more popular in the Pulpit, but I [look upon him as] out of the Question as he never proposed [more than] the spending a few leizure Months of the [Winter with you in] Expectation of a Chaplainship in the Spr[ing & if that has failed] I suppose he will soon embark for Engla[nd for he] must have larger Views, than to [return and settle] himself at Pomfret. The Opportunity [is by no] means lost, since he may be at Boston [in time for any] Man of War which the Admiral may intend to send home.

Had Mr Mosley any thoughts of fixing with you, he ought at least to have acquainted me with his purpose when he was last at Boston, that I might if possible have wrote to Mr Fogg to prevent his return. On the contrary, he asked me when I expected him, & assured me that upon his Arrival he would do every thing in his Power to procure him a kind Reception among the People at Pomfret. From hence you will perceive that I had not any room to imagine he had any Thoughts of fixing there himself.

In regard to your Engagement in point of Honour with M^r [Fogg, he can better] inform you than I can when he received [your letter from me,] & consequently (the Severity of the Winter [and the freq^t delay] of Letters considered) whether you could [have reasonably] expected an Answer earlier than his own [return.]

[If Mr Mosely] is really desirous of settling with you, whi[ch I can scarcely tell] how to imagine, (at least I think it can be [only for a short] time, & till he can provide himself better M^r [Fogg must look out] for another Birth-- In the meantime, you [may do well to co]nsider whether Mr Mosley has a sufficient [Acquaintance a]mong the Clergy in these parts to procure a [recommendation to] the Society-- & further--If Mr Fogg is dismist & Mr Mosley should leave you in a short time, it may be worth considering whether your Church might not remain long vacant to its great prejudice before it may be again supply'd--

I sincerely wish the Success & Prosperity of your Church preferable to any Mans convenience,

& am with much Respect / Sir / Your Most Obedient & / Most Humble Servant

H. Caner

Boston May 8th 1772

[The gaps in the MS. have been conjecturally supplied from the rough draft of this letter, dated May 9, 1772, in the Letter-Book of the Rev. Henry Caner, p. 146.]

[1772, Oct. 23, Stamford]

Stamford Connecticut
New England Octob^r 23^d, 1772

Reverend Sir.

I have received Your favour of the 31st of July last; and have this day drawn a set of Bills in due form upon Mr William Symondson, Treasurer of the Venerable Society, for £35 Sterling, Inclusive of the charitable Donation of £10 for the benefit of Mr Palmers Children; in fav^r of Mr Thomas Ellison Ju^r, Merchant in New York.

I shall take due care to apply the Societies kind Charity agreable to their pious intention.

There is no Material alteration in the state of my Parish. As a happy harmony subsists between me and my Parishiners, and they continue to behave well, it affords the pleasing Prospect, thro' the blessing of God, of being useful in promoting their most important Interest. I attend duty as usual in all parts of my Cure. Occasionally Catechise in different parts; Children in general are well Instructed; and due regard is paid to the Publick Offices of Religion.

I Baptised last Year, 98 Children, One Adult, 2 lately added to the Communion. On Sunday, last of May, I attended divine Service and Preaching at Danbury; Baptized 3 Children. their good disposition to our holy Ch^{hh} increases; the prejudices of many Subside; some Heads of families of good repute, lately declared Conformity; at present they keep up reading of divine Service & Sermons Among them.

I returned Yesterday from Sharon, where I preached on Sunday ye 11th Instant, to a large devout Congregation. On Tuesday following attended Service & a Lecture at Salsbury. On Wednesday at a sick mans House at Sharon. On Sunday last attended divine Service at the new Church on the borders of New York Province, to a numerous well behaved Congregation. In those several places I Baptised 29 Children, and One Adult, well Instructed.

I had the pleasure of meeting with the Revd Mr Mosly at Sharon, who preached there last Sunday to good acceptance; and is highly Esteemed. He appears to be a worthy good Gentleman, Zealous and well Affected, deserving better treatment than he met with at Litchfield. The good People in New York Government, Sharon & Salsbury, would have given him the utmost incouragement in their Power to have obtained his Establishment among them, had he not been previously engaged by Sir William Johnson. The good People in those Parts offer to Purchase a Valuable Glebe, build a House, and Oblige themselves to the Payment of thirty or 35£ Sterling Per Annum to a Minister, if they might be so happy as to obtain one. Mr Mosly is full in Opinion with me, that their Religious state is compasionate, and they deserve encouragement; And that a Minister Established at Amenia or the North Precinct, and to Include Sharon and Salsbury under his care, would be of infinite Service to the interest of true Religion.--

Compassion to their Spiritual wants, is the only inducement of my repeatedly mentioning their unhappy Circumstances; and their inability wholly to provide for themselves-- I Only beg leave to add my Earnest prayers to Almighty God to enlarge the ability of the Venerable Society, and to render it Equal to the Charitable disposition of their Hearts; to whose Judgment of their own Ability, and Superior wisdom to direct, how and where they shall dispose their Charity, it is our bounden Duty to Submit.

With my Humble Duty to the Venerable Board, And great Esteem and regards to Your Self,

I Am Reverend Sir / Your most Obedient Humble Servant, / And most Affectionate Brother in Christ

Ebenezer Dibblee

The Reverend Doctor Burton Secretary of the Venerable Society for Propagation of the Gospel &c-

[Addressed:] To / The Reverend Doctor Daniel Burton / Secretary of the Venerable Society / for the Propagation of the Gospel / in Foreign Parts. In Abingdon / Street, Westminster London

[1772, Dec. 28, Derby]

Derby Dec.ʳ 28th 1772.

Revᵈ Sir

Since my last in Decʳ 26t̪h 1771, I have been assiduous in the Care of my Parishes, having never once failed in that Time, nor indeed within Upwards of twenty Years, to preach & perform divine Service on Sundays, & the principal Holy Days, & not a few of my Parishioners appear to improve much & to be edified by those Means of Religion wʰ the Benevolence & Charity of the Society contributes to furnish them with. Yet I find Cause to lament that there are so many among them who pay but little Regard to the Duties of Religion & those whose Affections seem almost wholly ingross'd by inferiour & less worthy objects; to reclaim whom to a better Sense of their duty, I desire to continue to use my best Endeavours.----I receive yearly of my Parishioners, as much Assistance towards my Support as can well be expected, considering both their slender Abilities, & the Backwardness & Lothness of People of all Professions in Religion, (I mean in America) to part with much of their worldly Substance for their Religious Support. Yet as I have a large Family to support, consisting of a Wife with Eight Children, & as I have had of late, as well as heretofore, the Misfortune of having a great deal of Sickness in my Family wʰ hath been attended with considerable but unavoidable Expence, I stand in Need of more than the whole of my present Income to keep me from falling into Circumstances more strait & less than are in any tolerable Degree becoming a Clergyman. I hope therefore that the Society will favour me with occasional Gratuitie, If ev[en] less I may be allowed to hope that the Length of my Services, will induce them to make me an Addition to my Stated Salary. The Number of Families who are Professors of the Chh. of England in Derby & Oxford &c 124 The Number of actual Communicants 110 21 such have been added to the Communicants, & I have baptiz'd 37 Infants & one Adult since my Letter of Decʳ 1771. I have drawn upon the Societies Treasurer Ten Pounds Quarterly towards my Support & am

Revᵈ Sir The Societies & Your most obliged & most obedient &c

Richᵈ Mansfield

To The Revᵈ Dr Burton}

[1773, Apr. 12, New London]

Revᵈ Sʳ

Having not heard from my Venerable Patrons a long time, I fear my former Letter miscarried, therefore presume to repeat some particulars therein mention'd.

As it is yᵉ Opinion of judicious Persons, who have read yᵉ Indian Deed, (whereof I sent you a Copy) yᵗ yᵉ Donation was not made for a resident Minister, Mʳ Punderson, yᵗ

itinerant Missionary having enjoy'd it for some Years, tho' residing in a distant Parish, as far off yᵉ Indians, as I am; so if I am properly impower'd, I doubt not to recover yᵉ Land to yᵉ Society; & if I do, all I desire for my Trouble & Expence shall be yᵉ profit of yᵉ Glebe, worth about £4.10 yearly, for wᶜh I wou'd visit them several times in yᵉ year: If I lose yᵉ Case, yᵉ Society may allow me what they please. I'm very sorry I recommended them to Mʳ Honeyman; I hop'd better things of him; & am persuaded no reputable Lawyer wou'd corroborate his Opinion. But this wᵗh submission to my Superiors, whose civil & religious Interests 'tis my Duty to regard & defend.

I told you I marry'd three Couple, baptiz'd five Children, & a young Woman by Immersion, educated a Quaker; but whom I carefully instructed in yᵉ Worship & Disciplin of our Church-- That at several Places from seven to twelve Miles off with great Success I officiated, having baptiz'd fourteen Persons from two to seventeen years old in two Families, besides several other children, & rode eighty Miles at several times, all at my own Expence, to serve yᵐ-- To other Places, some 24, some 30 Miles off, I rode last Year 334 Miles, preach'd 23 times & baptiz'd eleven Children--administred yᵉ LORD's Supper in one place to 28 People, in another to 30, all, except yᵉ Horsehire, at my own Charges. I do now wᵗh Pleasure assure yᵉ religious Society my Parishoners at Chatham have, tho' wᵗh much Difficulty, built a small Church, wherein I officiated twice; & also yᵗ I sued yᵉ congregational (falsly call'd yᵉ presbyterian) Collector for Rates forc'd from my Hearers there, & recover'd them, yᵉ Judges having shewn me great Respect. By this very signal Victory I have rescu'd five Parishes (in each of wᶜh I have Converts) from yᵉ rapacious Designs of arbitrary Teachers. I beg leave to observe, if my good Patrons wou'd be pleas'd in yᵉ next Abstracts to take Notice of yᵉ Equity & Impartiality of yᵉ Judges, & yᵉ Civility & Respect, to their Missionary by all yᵉ Lawyers, it might prove serviceable, shou'd any of us be oblig'd to vindicate & rescue our Hearers from Oppression again.

Praised be GOD my Parishoners & Communicants encrease, & wou'd encrease more & more, did not their Poverty prevent them from enlarging yᵉ Church.

I beg yᵉ Venerable Society may encourage yᵉ Church at Chatham by presenting a large Bible, & Prayer Book, & yᵉ Homilies to yᵐ: If they wou'd send them a few pious Tracts, 'twou'd promote their religious Design, & facilitate my Labors. I will draw in Favor of some Mercᵗ (I suppose in New-York) for yᵉ last Year's Salary.

I design to set off to Morrow to visit my distant Parishes, & doubt not but All-sufficient Grace will enable me to give a pleasing Account to yᵉ Society, who are hereby desir'd to accept of yᵉ christian Respects, & to depend on yᵉ conscientious Labors of their faithful Missionary, who is wᵗh all Esteem & Regard their &

Revᵈ & Good Sʳ

Yʳ very humˡe Servᵗ & most

New-London   Affectionate Broʳ in Jesus Christ
Apˡ 12. 1773   Matt Graves

P.S. Be pleas'd to order me a few Common Prayer Books & some pious Tracts, especially yᵉ three Dialogues, &c. I have not had an Abstract, or any Pieces from yᵉ religious Society for some Years.

Pray pardon this Direction, not yet knowing your Name.
To ye Secratary to ye religious Society for propagating
ye Gospel &c

London

[Addressed:] To / The Secretary of ye religious Society
[Endorsed:] Read...July 12. 1773

[1773, Apr. 16, Stamford]

Stamford Connecticut in
New England April, 16, 1773.

Reverend Sir.

I have this day drawn a set of Bills in form, for 25£ Sterling upon Mr William Symondsom Treasurer of the Venerable Society, in favour of Mr Comfort Sands, Merchant in New York.

Through Divine favour, I continue able to attend to the Duties my Office, in all parts of my extensive Cure; and meet with proper encouragement.

Sunday sixth of January last, I attended Divine Service again at Danbury, where, I Baptized three Children; and there is a hopeful prospect of a flourishing Church, if happily they could be provided with a setled Ministry. I Baptized last half Year but 20 Children.

From Danbury I went to New Milford, where some of the late Mr Palmers Children are Setled; more perfectly to enquire into their Numbers and Circumstances; and with a View to distribute the Societies late Charity. He left Nine Children, 4 Sons, & 5 Daughters. He left but 3 unmarried, 2 sons & a Daughter, the Youngest a son about 12 Years Old. By one of his Children, I was informed Mr Palmer had done or confered somewhat in Land, and Household Furniture upon those that were married, except ye last Daughter; She with the three Minors, were left without the lest Inheritance. that the rest live comfortable, without dependence. Hence, I was at a loss how to distribute the Societies Charity among them, as I had received only a general Direction; without regarding the most Necessitous; and as some of the Married did not desire to be interested, thinking the youngest Married Sister and the three Minors who had nothing given them by their Father, should enjoy the benefit; but some others were of the contrary Sentiments. Consequently, It was tho't advisable to lay their State before the Venerable Society, and wait their direction----whether their Charity shall be Equally, or Discretionarily, Distributed; as their circumstances Are so Unequal. Mrs Palmer that was, will think it a favour if the two Months Salary granted after Mr Palmers Decease, might be appropriated to her benefit, during the short space of her Widowhood, as she was driven to straits with her Children, and it will be of no Consequence in setling his affairs-- It was intimated to me, such was the ingratitude and Neglect of the Parish to the Relict Widow & children Necessity Obliged her to such a sudden change of State.

With my Humble Duty, and fervent prayers to God for the continuance of his blessing, and gracious acceptance of all the pious and most Charitable Designs of the Venerable Board: I Am, Reverend Sir; with high Esteem,

Your most Obedient Humble Servt
In Christ Your Affec^t Brother;
Ebenezer Dibblee

To
The Reverend Doctor Burton; Secretary
Or to the Secretary for the time being, of the Venerable
Society for Propagation of the Gospel in Foreign Parts.--

[Endorsed:] Read...July 12. 1773

[1773, Apr. 26, Pomfret]

Revd Sir,

About twelve Months are passed, since I did my self the Honour to write you a very circumstantial Letter relating to the Mission of Pomfret; but I never was so happy as to hear whether it met with your Approbation, or even whether it reached it's Address.

I then acquainted You that the Revd Mr Daniel Fogg, in Consequence of my Invitation to Him, communicated by the Revd Dr Caner, had left North Carolina, had accepted of this Mission, and had entered upon the Exercise of his Function from the 6th May 1772. Immediately after this He wrote to the venerable Society, requesting that they would be pleased to send Him a Confirmation of my Appointment; but He hath, ever since, been waiting their Answer.

The scanty Pittance, which His Congregation Stipulated to pay Him annually, was pretty regularly discharged on the last Easter Monday, but as this small sum was vastly insufficient to Supply his Necessities, which were somewhat urgent, He hath desired me to give you the Trouble of a Letter, assuring you of His very punctual & faithful Discharge of the Duties of His Station ever since the Time of his first entering upon the Exercise of them. As I am able to do this with the Strictest Adherence to Truth, I undertake it with the greatest Pleasure; but, at the same Time, I hope you will not think that there is any Impropriety in my not avoiding to say that I think this Gentleman's Situation is, at present, very particularly circumstanced, as He does not make an Application to the venerable Society for the small Reward of his Labours, but with the greatest Diffidence and Circumspection. I therefore hope, and think it my Duty to request the Favour of you, that you will be pleased to make Application to them that He may be confirmed in His Appointment and furnished with such Instructions as they shall think proper to give Him; that when the Periods appointed for His Draughts, for the Payment of His Salary, are elapsed, He may be able to do it upon the Same Terms with the other Servants of the Society and not conceive Him self to be obliged to make Application to His Friends for Letters in Form of Testimonials of His good Conduct.

I dare say you will not do me the Injustice to imagine that this Request of mine proceeds from a Disposition to favour my own Indolence and to save myself the Trouble, once or twice a year, of blotting a Sheet of Paper as often as my very modest Parson wants to draw for His Salary. That is not the Case I assure you; but I think it but common Justice that He should be invested with this Power from the Society themselves, and be able to do it as a Matter of undoubted Right, without being subject to the disagreable Necessity of making Application for suppliant Letters to any Person whatsoever. Should He unhappily, which God avert! change His Disposition and go counter

to the Intentions of the Society in placing Him here, or be remarkably negligent of the Interests of Religion and the Church, you may rely upon meeting with no Excuses from me for not writing; for I pledge you my Honour that upon such an unfortunate Occasion, I should be as ready with my Complaints as I am now with my Intreaties that He may be put upon the same Footing with the Rest of His Brethren.

I remain with the greatest Deference / Revd Sir, Your much obliged / & very humble Servt

Godfrey Malbone

Colony of Connecticut
Pomfret 26 April 1773.

[Addressed:] The Revd Dr Burton / Secretary to the Society for / propagating the Gospel / London.

[1773, June 25, New Milford]
New Milford June 25.th 1773.
Reverend Sir,

I wrote to the honorable Society June 25.th 1771. (to which I have had no Answer) acquainting the Society, that in Kent there was a Number of late Conformists to the established Church, who had erected a very decent Church with a Chancel about 14 Miles Distant from New Milford. I also asked the Favour of a large prayer Book and Bible for that Church, together with some of a smaller sort to be distributed among the poor People, as many of them are under very needy Circumstances. and, As I now have the happiness to inform the honorable Society, that the Church of Kent is under a very happy and flourishing Scituation; permit me once more to ask for the above Request in behalf of that People.

In New Milford there is about a 100 families Professors of the Church and about 70 Communit.^{ts}-- At New Preston 50 families and 20 Communit.^{ts}-- At Kent 40 families and 12 Communit.^{ts}-- At New Milford several Families have been added to the Church since I have been in the Mission, tho' at the same time they have not encreased as to Numb.^r; by Reason of their continual moving up into the new settled Countries, Allington especially: I have baptized since June 25.th 1771.--129 Infants (2 of which were blacks) and 5 Adults of which one was a Native.

I have drawn upon the honorable Society my Sallery since June 25th 1771 to June 25.th 1773 in fav.^r of Messrs Christopher Kilby abel Hine Jabez Bacon and Isaac Tomlinson.

I am Revd Sir your your most Obed.^t hum.^l Servt

Richard Clarke

[1773, Sept. 29, Stamford]
Stamford Connecticut
New England Sep.^t, 29.th 1773.
Reverend Sir

I beg leave to Advise the Venerable Society, that I have this Day drawn a Sett of Bills for Twenty five Pounds Sterling, upon Mr William Symondson their Treasurer; in favour of Mr Comfort Sands or Order: Merchant in New York.

My Parish continues in a peaceable, increasing and flourishing State; and I have the pleasure to live among a pious well disposed People, who in general pay a due re-

gard to the publick Offices of Religion, and are Zealously Attached to the Doctrine, Worship, and Government of our Holy Church: And do Honour to their Religious Profession-- their hath been lately sundry Accessions of Heads of Families to the Church.

I Baptized last half Year, 39 Children; 1 Adult. Actual Communicants in the two Towns of Stamford and Gree[n]wich, are about Eighty Nine: And the Heads of Families about 220. I attand my Publice Duty in all parts of my extensive Cure in like manner, as I have heretofore intimated; and continue my attention to be as extensively useful as is consistent with the duties of my particular Cure.

After a Short distressing Illness, it pleased Almighty God, On the 13.th of August late, to remove by Death, the Reverend Mr Lamson, the Societies late Pious and worthy Missionary at Fairfield. He hath left a Disconsolate Widow, and Six Children, who will Experience the want of Him.----His Lady was Step Mother to his Children, and it's tho't is left under more disagreable Circumstances than when she Married Him-- His Children unsetled; tho none very Young. If the Society in their great Charity should be pleased to bestow half a Years Salary, the One half for the Widows benefit, the other for the Childrens; it would be very thankfully Accepted: or to be divided among them as in their wisdom they thought Proper.

The unequal Circumstances Mr Palmers Children are under, render the four Youngest who have nothing left to inherit, in my apprehension, the most proper Subjects of the Societies late Charitable Donation; if left discretionary with me; and I could wish for the Societies Direction. His Youngest Son, wanting better Instruction, before he is Put to some Trade, at his Mothers Request, and in compassion to his circumstances, is at present under my Care.

With my Duty to the Venerable Board, And great Esteem and Respect to Your Self; I Am Reverend Sir
Your Very Humble Servt
And Affectionate Brother in Christ
Ebenezer Dibblee

To the Reverend Doctor Richard Hind,
Secretary of the Venerable Society for Propagation of the Gospel in Foreign Parts.

[Endorsed:] Read...Decr 13. 1773

[1773, Nov. 15, New London]
Rev.^d & Good S.^r

Yours dated ye 20.th of July I rec.^d Novr 26.th In Answer to wch according to ye Venerable Society's Orders, I have procur'd a 2.^d Copy of ye Indian Deed, wch I hope will come safe herewith. In a Letter from Dr Burton, Decem.^r 16.th 1768. I have ye Society's Thanks for my Information of y.^t Land, & in March 1770 I understand they receiv'd ye Deed I sent them. I did recommend Mr Honeyman, but am sorry. I was deceiv'd in ye man; but if I am authoriz'd to recover ye Land, be pleas'd to send me sufficient Power under ye Society's Seal, sign'd by You, & corroborated by a Public Notary. I'll undertake to employ a proper Person, not one in League w.th Coll: Champlin, who seiz'd & occupied ye Glebe there several Years as [&] also threw down ye Church erected on it, to build a Tavern for his Son. I have preach'd often to ye Indian

Tribe, who gave yͤ Land; as well as to yͤ other four Tribes about me; for whom I am much engag'd, & have gain'd Sͬ Wᵐ Johnston's Esteem for my Assistance & Advice upon all Occasions. If yͤ religious Society wou'd be pleas'd to bestow a Bible & Common Prayer Book upon yͤ Church, lately erected in Chatham, & accept of what yͤ Copies of yͤ two Deeds cost me towards yͤ charge of them, twou'd be very acceptable. Endeed they are poor & wᵗʰ difficulty built a small House for yͤ Service & Worship of yͤ Church of England: & I hope in time will prove their Regard by Demonstrations of Love. Officiating there & several other Places I have travell'd this Year above 614 Miles—preach'd above 30 times—baptiz'd in one Family there nine Persons, besides five others in yᵗ & other Parishes, wᶜʰ are daily encreasing—all at my own Expence; & without neglecting my own Mission: in wᶜʰ I have christned 15 Children—married 6 Pair—buried 6 Persons; & thro' yͤ Blessing of GOD see yͤ Work of yͤ LORD prosper in my hand by yͤ growing Numbers of Hearers & Communicants

Be pleas'd to send me wᵗ Abstracts &c you think proper to yͤ Care of Doctor Auchmuty in N. York. Sometimes I do, but rarely, get an Abstract, speciali Gratiâ, from Boston. I have frequent Opportunities from N. York, & our Boatmen ready to oblige me gratis.

Be pleas'd to consult some Lawyer about yͤ Deed: for Mͬ Honeyman says it's only in favor of a resident Minister: it was made in Mͬ Punderson's time, an itinerant Missionary—"To yͤ Use of yͤ Society for &c[."] I am sure there's no Mention of Residence, as I am, none can live upon 20 Dollars (yͤ annual Value of yͤ Glebe). It was given just three Years, before I left England, & in yͤ Church, wᶜʰ was built on it, yͤ Ordinances were frequently perform'd; but, as I wrote, was pull'd down & metamorphos'd into a Tavern.

My christian Love, Gratitude & Respects wait upon my Venerable Patrons, whom to serve faithfully in this Affair & especially in yͤ sacred Depositum committed to my pastoral Care, is & shall, by GOD's Assistance, be yͤ daily Study of their &

                Good Sͬ

New London. Novͬ 15ᵗʰ   Yͬ very humˡᵉ Servᵗ & most
    1773   Affectionate Broͬ in
                      Jesus Christ
P.S.   Matt Graves

Since I wrote this Letter, I submitted yͤ Indian Deed to yͤ Judgment of some of yͤ most knowing of our Judges, who assert—yᵗ Residency is not enjoyn'd—yᵗ they may appoint wᵗ Missionary they please, & by sending me an Authority under yͤ Society's Seal, sign'd by yͤ Secretary & a Public Notary, the Lands will be restor'd, & become your Property.

To the Revᵈ Doctor Hind, Secretary to yͤ Society for propagating yͤ Gospel in foreign &c

[1773, Nov. 16, Boston]

                Boston Novͬ 16ᵗʰ 1773
Sir

Sometime before Sir Francis Bernard left this Province he set on foot the reprinting an Edition of the Morning & Ev'ning Prayer of the Church in the Mohawk Tongue, & desired me to oversee the Press. It was done from an antient Copy formerly in use among them, but as I presently perceived, very incorrect. Some few Errors I was able to rectify, but am sensible there must be many more, which for want of knowledge in that Language, I was not able to amend. When Sir Francis left the Province, he gave Orders that the Edition should be put into my hands, & I know not how to apply it more properly to the use intended, than to transmit the Books to your care, who, if they are calculated in any measure to serve the end designed, will make a suitable distribution of them.

    I am with much Respect
        Sir
           Your Most Obedient & Most Humˡᵉ Servant
                    H. Caner

To Sir Wᵐ Johnson

[1774, Mar. 4, New London]
Revᵈ & Good Sͬ

Having answer'd yͬˢ of yͤ 6ᵗʰ of Novͬ last in yͤ following Month, I have little to say about my Mission. My Hearers, being poor, have wᵗʰ great Difficulty erected a South-Gallery, wᶜʰ I hope will in time be a means of encreasing our Number; to promote wᶜʰ my Doctrin & Life shall not be wanting.

The Severity of yͤ Winter has hitherto prevented me from visiting yͤ distant Parishes I occasionally attend.

I hope yͤ Indian Deed arriv'd safe, & it's Contents fully invalidate Mͬ Honeyman's Opinion, wᶜʰ I stand ready to confute, & if my Venerable Patrons give me yͤ Authority I mention'd, I presume yͤ Coll: & his Friend wou'd be asham'd, desist & be mute. As I know all their Strength, or rather Weakness, clothed wᵗʰ yͬ Sanction, I doubt not adire—videre—vincere—&, if GOD spare me, to gather a Church among yͤ poor, neglected, generous Indians, who continue to fear GOD, & honor yͤ King.

Several Inhabitants of Poccatonic have desir'd me to write to yͤ Religious Society in their Favor, about taking down yͤ Church at Groton, about 9 or 10 Miles off. I having consider'd yͤ Affair am persuaded tis for yͤ Interest of our Religion. They have held a Parish Meeting, & unanimously voted to build a Church at Poccatonic with yͤ Materials of yͤ old, contributing what will be wanting to compleat it. Four Families in Groton, who only belong to yͤ Church, are hearty in the Motion, who, tho' 9 Miles from Poccatonic, wᶜʰ is three from Norwich Church, wou'd have frequently yͤ Benefit of our Evangelical Service, whereof they are totally depriv'd, & their Families likely to become a Prey to yͤ Dissenters. Having done Duty there I find a great Probability of gathering a Society, as there is no Meetinghouse within 2 or 3 Miles of it. I beg leave to add, yᵗ as yͤ Church of Groton has for several Years been neglected, it is in a very ruinous Condition, &, if not taken down, must soon tumble down of it self; yͤ consequence will be all yͤ Timbers &c will become a Prey; an Instance whereof happen'd lately to yͤ Eastward to my Knowledge.

Be pleas'd to present my Duty to yͤ Venerable Society, to promote whose pious Expectations & Commands, shall be my Study; as on yͤ due Execution thereof depends

yᵉ temporal & eternal Interest of their &
                    Good Sir

N: London   Yᵗ very humˡᵉ & oblig'd Servᵗ
March 4ᵗʰ 1774   & Affectionate Brother in
                                        Jesus Christ
                                        Matt Graves

[1774, Apr. 12, Stamford]
                            Stamford Connecticut in
                            New England April. 12. 1774.
Reverend Sir

I received your favour of the 17ᵗʰ of July 1773, in November following; and wrote immediately to Doctor George
Hurd of New Milford, who Married a Daughter of the late
Mʳ Palmer, to whose care I had committed the Honˡˡ Societies Charity for his Children; and Ordered the Distribution of it, for the benefit of the four Youngest, the Interest of three Minors, to be put to Loan, till they were
of Age; unless they wanted some Charitable immediate relief.

I also acknowledge your Letter of the 17ᵗʰ of Decembʳ,
73. lately come to hand. I immediately also wrote to Young
Mʳ Lamson, the agreable advice I received from You, relative to the acceptance of his Draft for his Fathers Salary:
Advising him, as the Family expected any farther favour of
the Society, to transmit to me, to be forwarded to the Society, an attested Copy, or Catalogue of the Books belonging to the Library in that Mission, deposited in the hands
of the Church Wardens, for the Use of a Successor &c.--
I have impatiently waited his Andwer, but have received
None. If I receive no Satisfactory Advice soon, will go to
Fairfield and inspect into the circumstan[ce] of the Library
my Self. the two Eldest Daughters of the late Mʳ Lamson
were lately Married, to the satisfaction of their friends,
and are well provided for.

There is no material Alteration in the Religious State
of my Parish. through the blessing of an uncommon share
of hea[l]th in the decline of Life, I am able to attend the
Duties of my extensive Cure. there hath been some late
Accessions to the Chʰ and an agreable Prospect of More:
and an increase of Communicants.

Some disagreable Embarisments I meet with, respecting my Parish Dues, not being well Collected and Paid--
partly owing to negligence, but principally to the Ill temper
of the Dissenters, and perverseness of their Collectors; to
whom, as the Law of the Government stands, I must look
to Collect my Dues. Who are either slack; or if called
upon, exercise unreasonable Severity, in order to promote Dissention in the Chʰ: the increasing Reputation of
the Church, being Viewed with a Jealus Eye. I have also
been too much burdened with interest Money to the late Sᵗ
George Talbot, & now to his Housekeeper Mʳˢ Goold, to
Secure for the good of the Parish a most Valuable Glebe;
which to a Successor will be likely to be a singular benefit,
but to me of no advantage: as 7 per Cent during his life, &
3 1/2 during Mʳˢ Goolds, amounts to more than the clear
profit I have been able to make off of it: Considering the
circumstances of its not being well fenced, and the Parishes Neglect of an engagement, some entered into in their
behalf, to put the Land under good Fence.

I Preached at Danbury on a Colony Thanksgiving in November last to a good Devout Congregation, and Baptised

Sundry Children. Sunday following I Preached at Fairfield, upon a Request, in compassion to their broken Circumstances. (I wish to see that Vacancy supplied with a
very able, Prudent Worthy Missionary, being a County
Town.) I Baptized last half Year, Twenty one Children.

Mʳˢ Buel, the late Mʳ Palmers Widow, begs that her
grateful acknowledgements may be acceptable to the Venerable Society for the two Months Salary granted to her:
And which, at her request; is Included in my Bill of Thirty Pounds Sterling this Day drawn for upon the Societies
Treasurer, in favour of Mʳ Comfort Sands Merchant in
New York or Order.

Permit me only to add, my Humble Duty to the Vener-
able Board, and with great Esteem and Respect to Your
Self, to Subscribe my Self, Reverend Sir;
                            Your most Obedᵗ
                            Very Humble Servᵗ
                            And Brother in Christ
To   Ebenezer Dibblee
The Reverend Doctor Hind
Secretary of the Venerable Society
for the Propagation of the Gospel &c.

[Endorsed:] Read...Aug. 15. 1774

[1774, May 28, Stamford]
                            Stamford Connecticut in
                            New England May 28. 1774.
Reverend Sir

I now inclose an attested Copy of the Library at Fairfield Deposited in the hands of the Church Wardens. how
far it is entire & compleat, you must Judge, as no Catalogue is to be found among Mʳ Lamsons Manuscripts.

If the Society are pleased to grant a half Years Salary,
it may be more satisfactory for them to direct in what
manner it shall be divided between the Widow and Children. If left Discretionary with me, I should think the
Widow entitled at least to one half: and the other half not
improperly, if bestowed upon the three Youngest; a Son
and two Daughters, left under the greatest disadvantage.
the Eldest Son having had considerable bestowed upon him
for his Education; and his Brother about 14, gone to an apprenticeship. the two Eldest Daughters now Married and
well provided for, but the two Youngest in their Non Age,
under the care of their friends. The Family dispersed,
the Widow is left to provide for her self in the decline of
life, not under equal circumstances, or advantage, as
when She Married Mʳ Lamson; as I am well informed.
I've been thus particular, that the Venerable Board may
know their Circumstances, and Direct, as in their Wisdom they think proper.

I could wish for the Venerable Societies direction in
what manner the two Months Salary granted to the late Mʳ
Palmers Widow shall be applied. By her Order I drew for
it, as I advised the Society, inclusive in my last Bill soon
after I received Advice of her Death, which was sometime
before before I drew my Bill of Exchange.----As I think
the Societies Charity ought to be applied for the benefit of
her Children, and 5£ inconsiderable to be divided among
them, I could wish it might be Appropriated for the benefit of her Youngest Son, whose Education through the Misfortunes of his Fathers Family; hath been too much Neg-

lected. On this Condition, and of the Societies concurrance, I have prevailed with Doctor George Hurd of New
Milford, who Mirried his Sister to take the Guardianship
& care of him, and Educate him for the Practice of Physick. He is not of a Robust Constitution for labour at a
Trade, and think this the best that can be done for him.
It hath been thought unnecessary to trouble the Society,
but I choose their direction, in the improvement of their
Charity.

The Church of Fairfield hope for the continuance of
the Societies Charitable Assistance, without which they are
Ill able to Support a Minister in Character: from what I
can learn, 30 or 35£ Sterling Per Annum will Equal their
Ability, and Exceed the Annual Tax the Dissenters pay
their Minister. Fairfield is a County Town, and the Courts
of Judicature held there; of Course it renders the place
more expensive to a Minister, in consequence of Company
extraordinary.----The Neighbouring Missionaries are Attentive to their present destitute circumstances, and lend
them such Assistance as we are able; and are concerned
to find a Person that will fill that Vacancy with Honour and
Credit to Religion & the Church.

As the State of these remote Colonies engrose general
attention, and is the particular object of Government; we
hope from the corrupt Principles which prevail, and the
Political Mischiefs that have happened, that good will arise
to the Church, and a more effectual Indulgence & support
be granted. And as the Establishment of an American
Bishop or Bishops, hath been the great Object of our desires and Requests; So if you Sir, should have the Honour
of being appointed the first American Bishop, permit me
to Assure you from the Amiable Character you Sustain, I
believe it would not be disagreable to the Clergy of the Chh
in this Province, and would be very Acceptable to him, who
with great Esteem begs leave to Subscribe, Reverend Sir
    Your most Obedt / Most Humble Servant / And Brother
in Christ
                                    Ebenezer Dibblee

N.B. A Few Bibles Common Prayer Books, Catechisms
and other small Tracts, are much wanted, and would
thankfully be accepted.

[Addressed:] To / The Reverend Doctor Richard Hind /
Secretary of the Venerable Society for the / Propagation of
the Gospel in Foreign / Parts. St Ann's, Westminster. /
London
[Endorsed:] Read...Octr 17. 1774

[1774, Sept. 20, Norwalk]
    at a Conn of ye Clergy of the Chh of England in Cont
met at Norwalk--Sep. 20. 1774----Taking into serious
Consideration the very alarming State of publick Affairs;
& judging it a Season peculiarly critical, in respect of our
common Interests & Rights: & which is render'd greatly
aggravated by the too predominant Divisions, & Jealousies
that have been disseminated to blow up & increase Parties,
& Violence of Opposition: among which we have not faild to
have much laid to our Charge, & have been industriously
held up to View, as entertaining & propagating Principles,
unfriendly to the Charter Rites & Privileges, & subversive
of the Laws of this Colony-- Induced by these Reasons, &
Reasons of such a Nature only wo[ul]d induce us to publish

our Sentiments relative to Matters political: We think it
may be subservient to wipe off unjust Imputations, &
satisfy the candid & impartial to lay before the public the
Sentiments of this Convention; & to exculpate ourselves
from wt we apprehend unjust Censure laid upon particular Instances of our Conduct----Our known Attachment
to Governmt & Principles that it is our Duty to honor &
obey those that are appointed over, to rule & govern us,
renders it unnecessary to declare that we are Friends to
Governmt in its general Idea: as we avow this, so we are
equally ready unreservedly to assert that we bear good
Affectn & real Attachment to the Government, as it is
settled in, & administer'd accordg to the Charter Rights
& Privileges of this Colony: we warmly wish its Preser-
vatn, & hope uninterruptedly to enjoy it. Every Attempt,
either by our own illegal intestine Commotions, & Broils,
to interrupt the due opperation of Law, or enervate its
Force for the Protection & Security of all in their Persons
& Properties, or any Infringement by Superior Authority
we heartily regret & lament:-- & so far as is consistant
with our Character, & falls within our Province are determin'd from Motives both of Inclinatn & Duty to enforce
by Precept & Example, a peaceable Submission & steady
Adherence to the Legal Constitutn of ye Colony-- Tho we
freely own, in our Opinion we cannot agree, to the Mode
of Proceedure adopted among many, & more flagrantly in
Many Parts, under the Color of assertg our Rights: a Proceedure no less ruinous to ye common Rights of Mankd,
than to the good Subsistance & Welfare of civil Society; &
such as ought to be, & we presume is abhorrent to every
Person, yt entertains just Sentiments, & a benevolent
Mind (to civil Society) & desires to live happy undr ye Influence and Protection of good Laws: Yet any Measures
to redress actual Grievances or ward off impending ones
which the Laws of God, or the Realm, authorize, we believe & maintain are justifiable to be taken. These we
appreh[end] are a constitutional Methd to ascertain &
vindicate constitutional Rights:-- This, so far as we can
judge is warranted by the Wisdom of Governmt, who have
provided Laws to defend the Subject & enable him to obtain Right, agt the male-Administratn of the Executive
Authority, & to resist Encroachment made by the Legislative: If we err in this our Error has the Sanction of that
Wisdom whh has been uniform in all States prohibitg Violence from the Subject, as a Convulsion whh severs & dissolves the Body-- To these Sentiments & Declarations, it
may be thot, Instances of our Conduct are incompatible
(especially a late one, that has been much animadverted
upon, & no small Degree of Obloquy & Reproach dealt out
upon us on that Account) Our not celebrating Divine Service on the Fast, the 31 of Augt last--Whether the Spirit of
the Times will admit of a fair hearing, & give our Reasons
their just Weight, there is perhaps too much Cause for
Doubt: Reasons however we are willing to offer; such as
appear to us, satisfactory, & do not militate agt any Thg
said above-- If the Part that we acted on that Occasn was
a Breach of any of the Laws of this Colony, it was wt we
were then, & still remain ignorant of-- Similar Conduct
in similar Cases, we do not find meets w[it]h that Resentment, as is shown in this. The Dissenters in Engld hold
themselves exempt from observg the Days appointed by
the national Chh. & enjoin by the whole Authority of the
Kingdm: the Rights of Cons[cience] are here pleaded, &

their Brethⁿ in America allow the Validity of the Plea, &
yet will not allow that they are on that Account worse Subjects to the State, or less Friends to the Constitutⁿ of the
Kingdom: & we see no good Argᵗ why the same shod not
be granted in the full Force of it to us, & we exempt from
the contrary Inference;-- We claim in this Case the Rights
of Cons[cience] & the Acceptance of this Claim, rests upon
the common Right we have to be believ'd. But what is peculiar in our Case, & ought to be consider'd, is a Circumstance delicate in its Nature, & attended with a difficult
alternative: The most of us, are Missionaries from the
venerable Society, & all in Subordination to his Lordship
the Bishop of London; Our Conduct has been directed by an
Attention to both of these our Connections in strict Observ-
ance to which, we have adhered to our Clerical Character,
& have not made political Matters, or any of the Controversies now subsisting, our Concernment in, or the Subject of any of our Letters to the Society or any Persons,
in England, in private Correspondence or upon Affairs of
our public Duty & Office-- Firm in our own Integrity, we
are willing to appear in that Point of View, a just Knowledge & Opinion of our Action will place us; for this Purpose, it is, we declare with Frankness, our Innocence as
to the Charge, founded on nothᵍ more than Surmise, of
writing things Home, inflamatory, & obnoxious to yᵉ good
of yᵉ Colony: that we have not made nor are dispose[d] to
make political Matters, or any of the Controversies now
subsisting, our Concernment, but have adhered only to our
Clerica[l] Character, & Office in our Correspondence, public or private.

[This first draft was rewritten the following day, when it
took the following form:]

[1774, Sept. 21, Norwalk]
          At a Convention held at Norwalk Sepᵗ 21. 1774
     We, the Clergy of the Church of England in the Colony
of Connecticut, reflecting on the State of public Affairs,
which we view as portending very serious Consequences to
the common Weal, judge it a Season peculiarly critical, in
respect of our common Interests and Rights. This, in our
Opinion, is render'd greatly aggravated by the Jealousies
and Divisions that are too predominant among us, which
have been indiscreetly fomented to widen Parties and increase the Violence of Opposition: among which, we have
had much laid to our Charge, and have been industriously
held up to view, as entertaining and propagating Principles
unfriendly to the Charter Rights and Privileges, and subversive of the Laws, of this Colony--
     Induced by these Reasons, (and Reasons of such a Na-
ture only would induce us to publish our Sentiments relative to Matters political) we think it may be subservient to
wipe off unjust Imputations, and satisfy the candid and impartial, to lay before the public the Sentiments of this Convention; and to exculpate ourselves from what we apprehend unjust Censure laid upon particular Instances of our
Conduct.
     Our known Attachment to Government, and Principles,
that it is our Duty to honor and obey those that are appointed over, to rule and govern us, renders it unnecessary to
declare, that we are Friends to Government in its general
Idea: As we avow this, so we are equally ready unreservedly to assert, that we bear good Affection, and real At-

tachment, to the Government, as it is settled in, and administerd according to, the charter Rights and privileges
of this Colony; that we warmly wish its Preservation and
hope uninterruptedly to enjoy it.
     Every Attempt, either by our own illegal intestine
Commotions and Broils, to interrupt the due Operation of
Law, or enervate its Force for the Protection and Security
of all, in their Persons and Properties; or any Infringement by superior Authority, we heartily regret and lament.
And so far as is consistant with our Character, and falls
within our Province, are determin'd, from Motives, both
of Inclination and Duty, to enforce, by Precept and Example, a peaceable Submission and steady Adherence to the
legal Constitution of the Colony-- Tho, we freely own, we
cannot agree to the Mode of Proceedure adopted among
Many, and more flagrantly in many Parts, under the Color
of asserting our Rights: A Proceedure no less ruinous to
the common Rights of Mankind, than to the good Subsistance and Welfare of civil Society; and such as ought to be,
and we presume is, adhorrent to every Person that entertains just Sentiments, and a benevolent Mind, and desires
to live happy under the Influence and Protection of good
Laws: Yet any Measures to redress actual Grievances,
or ward off impending Ones, which the Laws of God, or
the Realm authorize, we believe and maintain are justifiable to be taken.
     These, we apprehend are a constitutional Method to
ascertain and vindicate constitutional Rights. And this, so
far as we can judge, is warranted by the Wisdom of Government; which hath at all Times, provided Laws to defend the Subject, and enable him to obtain Rights against
the Male Administration of the executive Authority, and
to resist Encroachments made by the Legislative. If we
err in this, our Error hath the Sanction of _that_ Wisdom
which hath been uniform in all States, prohibiting every
Species of Violence, as a Convulsion which severs and
dissolves the Body.
     To these Sentiments and Declarations, it may be
thought, Instances of our Conduct are incompatible; especially a late one, that hath been much animadverted
upon, and no small Degree of Obloquy and reproach dealt
out upon us on that Account, Our not celebrating Divine
Service on the Fast of the 31. of August last-- Whether
the Spirit of the Times will admit of a fair hearing, and
give our Reasons their just Weight, there is perhaps too
much cause for Doubt. Reasons however we are willing
to offer, such as appear to us satisfactory, and do not
militate against any thing already said--
     If the Part we acted on that Occasion was a Breach of
any of the Laws of this Colony, it was what we were then,
and still remain, ignorant of. Similar Conduct in similar
Cases we do not find meets with that Resentment, as is
shown in this. The Dissenters in England hold themselves
exempt from observing the Days appointed by the national
Church, and enjoin'd by the whole Authority of the Kingdom: The Rights of Conscience are here pleaded, and
their Brethren in America allow the Validity of the Plea;
and yet will not allow that they are, on that Account, worse
Subjects to the State, or less Friends to the Constitution of
the Kingdom; and we see no good Argument why the same
should not be granted in the full Force of it to us, and we
exempt from the contrary Inference. We claim in this
Case the Rights of Conscience, and the Acceptance of

this Claim rests upon the common right we have to be believ'd.

Firm in our own Integrity, we are willing to appear in that Point of View a just Knowledge and Opinion of our Actions will place us, for this Purpose it is, we declare with Frankness our Innocence as to the Charge, founded on mere Surmise, of our writing things Home that are inflamatory and obnoxious to the good of the Colony; That we have not made, nor are we disposed to make Political Matters, or any of the Controversies now subsisting, our Concernment, or the Subject of any of our Letters to the Society, or any Persons in England, with whom any of us have a Correspondence, but have adhered only to our clerical Character and Office.

[1774, Sept. 29, Stamford]

Stamford Connecticut in
New England Sept^r, 29. 1774.
Reverend Sir.

I have this day drawn a sett of Bills in usual form for Twenty five Pounds Sterling, upon Mr William Symondson Treasurer of the Venerable Society, in favour of Mr Comfort Sands Merchant of New York.

My Parish remains in as Peaceable Quiet State, as can well be expected, in this time of general concern for their Civil and Religious privileges, through the Provinces:---- The consequences of those unhappy Disputes that have arisen with our Parent Country; and the mode of Opposition to the supposed late unconstitutional Acts of the British Legislature, grow every Day more and more Serious and Alarming: And bear a very threatning Aspect upon the interest of Religion and the well being of the Church in this Province. May it please God to Avert impending Judgements, and dispose Government to grant such redress of Just Grievances, as may quiet the minds of his Majesties Subjects in these remote parts, and pour down upon us a Spirit of Peace, Unity and Concord.

The Heads of Families within my Cure remain much the same, notwithstanding sundry Emigrations into the interior parts of the Country. I continue my Attention to the Duties of my extensive Cure, and to be as extensively useful as may be: I Baptized last half Year, 1 Adult, 56 Children white; 3 Black. 2 Added to the Communion.

With my Humble Duty to the Venerable Board, and earnest Prayers to God to bless and reward all their Charitable designs to Propagate the Gospel of Peace. I am Reverend Sir, with highest Esteem and Regards to Your Self:

Your Most Obedient / Most Humble Servt, / And Affectionate Brother

Ebenezer Dibblee,

The Reverend Doctor Hind, Secretary of the Venerable Society for Propagation of the Gospel in Foreign Parts.

[1774, Oct. 26, New Haven]

New-Haven, October, 26. 1774. To the Printers-- Sir-- Just before I set out for this town I saw copies of two of Mr Peters's letters, which have since been published-- I had very little leisure, but could not forbare expressing to him my sentiments on the baseness of his apparent intentions, which I did, hastily, in a letter which perhaps may have reached him, and of which the following is a copy. Several respectable gentlemen of the Assembly here, happening to see it, were pleased to express and repeat their desire that it might be made as public as the letters which occationed it. I had not entertained a thought of publishing it before, but consented to submit it to their pleasure, tho' I have no expectation of its making any good impression on the gentleman to whom it is addressed, nor any fear of his unaided efforts; yet it may be one additional testimony to the innocence and virtue of this much abused country.--

10th Octo. 1774
Rev'd Sir--

Altho' you have long been suspected of entertaining sentiments inimical to your native country, and of co-operating with those who have cruelly misrepresented its faithfull and loyal inhabitants, yet I was extremely sorry to hear that an unlawfull assembly (or mob if you please) had lately collected & demanded of you an explanation of your conduct. Such proceedings in such cases I utterly disapprove, as every way wrong and injurious. But no government was ever perfectly free of such Commotions, and it is a happy circumstance, that this colony has had less of them than perhaps any in the world, and far less in proportion than the mother country. And in this instance I have heard they treated you with much more decency than is common for mobs, and even with almost infinitely more than it is said the populace lately shewed his Majesty himself. It is said that you parted on very civil and moderate terms, and having good reason to be satisfied that such conduct was discountinanced and condemned by authority, and almost universally by the people, and that you would be perfectly safe for the future, I concluded you had passed it over as a rash action never to be repeated; but am very sorry I have reason to believe that under the influence of a strang and unnatural ill-will which it is said you have ever shewn towards the land of your nativity, & of resentment for that affront, you are about to cross the Atlantic frought with evil and false representations concerning your country, a country filled with the most virtuous, loyal, friendly, benevolent and peaceable people under heaven, and this from your own reading and acquaintance you know right well. And I dare challenge you and the world to accuse them of any national crime but that of loving English Liberty as they love their lives--(if that be a crime they are guilty indeed)-- But it's the self same crime which took the British crown from the Stewart race, and placed it on the sacred & blessed head of the illustrious George, in which royal line may it long rest secure, by the auspices of benignant heaven. If our gracious King well knew the true state of the Colonies, he would be far from suffering his ministry to deal with us as they have done. He would regard us as the most faithfull subjects that ever king was blessed with, and as having thro' trials more distressing and severe than tongue can utter or language describe, laid a secure foundation for the greatest empire that was ever subject to one earthly monarch, as having immensely contributed to the wealth and strength of his native country & nation and desireous to do so forever; populating at an amazing rate, and every new subject adding stability and glory to his crown, and riches to

the nation, as already almost innumerable, and all united
with one heart and one soul, in long live our gracious King,
and may the illustrious house of Hanover reign over us till
time shall be no more; and as far from being disobedient,
factious, rebellious, aiming or wishing for independence
of the crown of Great-Britain as heaven is from hell. That
this is no fiction, but perfect truth and reality, I trust God
knows, and your own conscience bears it witness.----Is it
then possible that such more than savage cruelty and barbarous treachery can dwell in your breast, towards such
a people, towards the native, and dwelling place of all your
friends, towards your country. Do not the first dictates of
humanity teach us to love our country? Do not the most uncivilized and barbarous of mankind obey this dictate? Do
not the histories of heathen Greece and Rome, and of all
nations, exhibit bright examples of this noble virtue? Does
not the gospel of our common Saviour enjoin this temper
and spirit in the most strong and forcible manner, even to
love our enemies, and bless them that curse us, and call
him even a murderer that hateth his brother? Does not
vengeance belong to God Almighty? and is it not his to re-
pay?----Is it then possible, I repeat it, for one who has
early been taught the principles of morality, had the advantage of a philosophic and liberal education, and well
acquainted with the precepts of the Christian religion and
the awfull sanctions that enforce them, a professor, yea
more, a teacher and a preacher of the religion of the compassionate Jesus, who laid down his life for his enemies,
but will yet reveal himself in flaiming fire, to take vengeance on those who obey not his gospel, (I speak to you in
caracter) Is it possible I say again, for such a one to rise
up and endeavour to augment the fierce anger of the mistaken powers at home, who are inflicting grievous distresses upon us for no other fault, but loving the liberty
which God and the King have given us to enjoy. If you,
Sir, should be instrumental in procuring further evil to
your country, and of blood or additional blood to be shed;
you do not believe the gospel you preach, or you must believe the God of truth and justice will require this blood at
your hands.----If you should endeavour to subdue your anger, & reflect coolly on your errand, you must, I think, be
convinced that it would be far better to give it over, or instead of executing so malicious a purpose to diffuse sentiments of moderation and equity, to proclaim the peaceable, benevolent and loyal temper of this country, their
satisfaction and joy to remain forever the most faithfull
subjects of the King of Great-Britain in the present agust
line and succession of Brunswick, and only enjoy their
constitutional liberties as Englishmen; and that it is impossible for the nation to extort from us by force so much
as they may have by our consent in a more gentle way; that
if we are not oppressed, this country would never be independant if they could; but if we are, the colonies will certainly be lost to them forever.

The sentiments of the renowned and excellent Bishop
of St Asaph, are founded in eternal truth and equity.----
You may believe me when I say, it is not thro' fear, but
for the love I bear my country, my King, and the British
nation, that I write thus. I know the ministry are sur-
prizingly susceptible of evil reports of America, and have
judged and condemned without such hearing and candor
as we think we have right to expect; but if they knew the
truth, they never would have done what they have.----

I know the nation is great and powerfull, and as such I re-
vere them; as just and humane, as our friends and elder
brothers, I love and respect them. They may greatly
injure and distress us, if in spite of justice and policy
they will; but not without drinking deep of the same cup
themselves; and if they could destroy us, it would cost
them immensely dear (so determined is the spirit of this
continent) and it would end in their own ruin.-- Much
more might be said, but I forbear.

If the Right Honorable the Secretary of State can condescend to disperse pamphlets thro' the colonies, to justify the King and parliament, surely a little American may
be allowed to justify his country, and to conjure you, by
the love of God, of the King, and of both countries, for
whose sake alone I write, not to attempt any thing in aid
of the wicked designs of those who by slander and lies
have sought the destruction of this, ande thereby the per-
dition of both countries.----If you are going on this design, it is a base and a wicked one, and your sin will assuredly find you out, the curses of all America will follow, and without deep repentance the blast of the Almighty
will confound you. But I would hope better things of you,
and may the God of heaven bless and succeed you in every
laudable and benevolent undertaking.----If you are a true
friend to your King & country, I am really so to you, and
your hearty well-wisher.

                                   William Williams.

To the Rev. Samuel Peters.

[1774, Nov., Derby]
                                   Derby Novr 1774
Revd Sir
    Since my last of Decr 27th 1774 [i.e., 1773], I have
constantly performed Parochial Duty in Derby & Oxford. I
frequently inculcate the reasonable & necessary Duties of
Peaceableness & quiet Subjection to the King & to those that
are in Authority; & I trust not without some Good Effect
upon my Parishioners, who (with the Rest of the Episcopalians in General in the Colony) are noted for their Loyalty
to the King & dutiful Submission to the Supreme Legislature of the Nation, & this at a Time when it is dangerous
to Profess Loyalty, when Antimonarchical Principles & seditious Practices are prevalent & fashionable, & the most
determined Opposition to King & Parliament (tho' it be thro
a Sea of Blood) is reckon'd to be the most necessary important Duty, & what compleats the Character of an American Patriot. & tho' no Pains have been spared to fill the
Minds of People with fears, & Apprehensions that the
late Parliament & the present Ministry [have] had a fond
Design to oppress & enslave America, yet a considerable
Number of People who are Dissenters, in this eastern Part
of this Colony, together with the main Body of Chh People
seem to be of Opinion that we have much more Cause to
fear Oppression Slavery & utter Ruin from American pretended Patriots than from great Britian, from whom we
have hitherto receivd kind Protection, & on the most easy
& [m]oderate Terms. The Professors of the Chh. of England here, in general heartily wish that the Authority of the
King & Parliament may be again established in the Colony,
apprehending a Design in its Enemies totally to suppress
& even eradicate the Chh. As those who are most violent

in their Opposition to the Legislature of Great Britain are every where the most determin'd inveterate Enemies to the Chh. & seek & endeavour its overthrow & Ruin. But as all Designs formed against the Chh. by its Enemies, whether Popish or Puritanical, have been hitherto frustrated & brought to nought, & some of them by very wonderful Interpositions of divine Providence; the [in]creased Numbers of our Chh. are [an]other happy instance. I think [gap   ] naturally Induc'd to hope & Pray that under their Protection by the Blessing of its divine Friend it may subsist & flourish superiour to all the Attempts & Designs that are made & named against it by its most inveterate & potent Enemies. Number of Families who are Professors of the Chh. of England in Derby & Oxford is one Hundred & thirty The Number of actual Communicants is one Hundred & Nine New Communicants have been added since Decr 27th 1773. I have baptized within s^d Time thirty five Infants one Adult. I have drawn upon the Societies Treasurer ten Pounds [Ste]rling quarterly towards my Support & am Revd Sir

> The societies & Your most obliged & most Obedient servant
> Richd Mansfield

To the Revd Dr Hind

[1774, Nov. 8, Pomfret]
Sir,

On the 12th of the last Month, and not before, I received a Letter from Mr Mosley, dated at New York 13th April, in which He tells me that He had left his Lady a Bill on me for five Pounds; being the Value of a Cot left at my House; and, in the Letter, came a Bill, drawn in your Favour for that Amount, with your endorsement thereon. I conclude, therefore, that you are no Stranger to the Contents of it, and, that you imagine that I had, really, purchased the Cot of Mr Mosley; and, perhaps, in the Agitation of His Mind, at that Time, He, poor Fellow, thought so too, or I think I am certain He would not have acted about it just as He hath done, and given Mrs Mosley Room to imagine, that I was any Way indebted to Him, which, in good Truth, I am not: But it is very true that there is now in my House, which He left here, a Sea-Bed and Bedding, all bound up together in a Cot or Hammock, which, the last Time We saw Him, He absolutely refused to have sent after Him with His other Things; but desired Mrs M. to give it House Room and begged of Her to order some one or other of the Servants, every now and then, to open and expose them to the Sun & Air, which she promised Him she would do and hath faithfully performed: but you may rely upon it He never desired me to buy them, nor should I have done it if He had; for, however serviceable they may be, to those who want them, they certainly can never be either of Use or Value to me. He also left a Wig here, which I believe was never wore. These Things I am ready to deliver either to Mrs Mosley's, or your Order, whenever you think proper. The Draught on me for £5, with your endorsement thereon, I did Design, when I sat down to write, to have returned in this Letter; But I have this moment recollected that, should you have any Postage to pay, which, however, I shall endeavour to save you, it may be making the useless Punctilio rather too expensive

to you. Be that as it may, I now acknowledge the Bill, notwithstanding your Endorsement, to be your Property and not mine, I shall, therefore, preserve it to deliver to your Order, whenever it is demanded.

I am directed to forward the Wig to you, addressed to the care of Mr Kemp, Attorney General at New York, but as I am situated above 20 Miles from the nearest Landing Place, and it must of Consequence go through so many Strange Hands, by Land and by Water, to reach you by this Rout, that I rather think it will be so worn out by the Way, that the last Possessor will not think it worth his while to give it you at all; wherefore it may be best to let it remain where it is with the Cot, until you may give me Orders to send them together to Newport, from whence they may come to you in a more direct Manner, by one of the Coasters that Trade between Newport & the Indies. If this Method is agreable, the sooner you inform me of it the better; for I live in such a retired Nook that there must be a Concurrence of Incidents to get them to you, in any tolerable Season, even in this Manner; which is, certainly the easiest & readiest that I know of.

The Inconsistency of Mr Mosley's Behaviour, since He left Pomfret, is too great for a Comment; and there is little Probability that the Rout which He hath taken will produce a Reformation, which often gives me much Concern; for His Behaviour, while here, was certainly such as to secure Him a Place in my Esteem; which I, now, fear proceeded rather from an Inclination to be fixed here than from any virtuous Disposition. I, sincerely, wish that his future Conduct may prove that my Apprehensions are ill founded.

With a great Regard for your Office & Character I remain,

> Revd Sir, Your most H͠ble Servt.
> G. Malbone

Pomfret 8 Nov. 1774.

To the Revd Mr Isaac Browne Missionary at Newark
In the Province of New Jersey.

[1775, Apr. 5, Stamford]
> Stamford Connecticut in
> New England April, 5. 1775

Reverend Sir

I have this day drawn a Set of Bills upon the Venerable Societies Treasurer, Mr William Symondson, in Usual form, for Twenty five Pounds Sterling; in favour of Mr Comfort Sands Merchant, at New York, or his Order.

I am still permitted in Providence to attend the duties of my Cure in all parts of my Mission. notwithstanding the Meloncholly Aspect of the times, and the Emigration of some Heads of Families, there remains in the two Towns of Stamford and Greenwich about 227 Heads of Families, Professors of the Church; about 90 Communicants. I Baptized last half Year, 2 Adults, and 31 Children, White; 2 Blacks, and 2 were added to Communion.

We view with the deepest Anxiety, Affliction and Concern, the great dangers we are in, by reason of our unhappy Divisions, and the amazing height to which the unfortunate Dispute between great Britain and these remote Provinces, hath Arisen: the baneful influence it hath upon the interest of true Religion, and the welbeing of the

Church.

Our Duty as Ministers of Religion is now attended with peculiar difficulty; faithfully to discharge the Duties of our Office, and yet carefully to avoid taking any part in these Political Disputes, as I trust my Brethren in this Colony have done, as much as possible; notwithstanding any representations, to our prejudice to the contrary. We can only pray Allmighty God, in compassion to our Ch^h and Nation, and the welbeing of these Provinces in particular, to Avert those terrible Calamities, that are the natural result of such an unhappy contest with our Parent State; to save us from the Horrors of a Civil War; and remove all groundless fears and Jealousies, and whatsoever else, may hinder us from godly Union and Concord.

I only add; my Duty to the Venerable Board, Praying God to bless his Ch^h and Still succeed all their most Charitable designs, and with unfeigned Esteem to Your Self; Subscribe, Reverend Sir

Most Obedient / Most Affec^t Servt & Brother / in Christ.

Ebenezer Dibblee

The Reverend Doctor Richard Hind. Secretary of the most Venerable Society for Propagation of the Gospel in Foreign Parts.

[Addressed:] To / The Reverend Doctor Richard Hind / Secretary of the Venerable Society / for Propagation of the Gospel in / Foreign Parts. St Ann's, Westminster / London   Via Falmouth
[Endorsed: Read] Sepr 11. 75

[1775, June 25, New Milford]

New Milford June 25th 1775
Reverend Sir,

I have very lately receiv^d your Letter of Novr 20th. 1773 near 18 Months after the Date, and am thankful to hear the honorable Society have complied with my Request by your sending to me, by the first opportunity a Quarto Bible and Prayer Book for the new Church at Kent, together with ten small Bibles and twenty five small common prayer Books, which Books, I have not as yet received, and when they come to hand, I shall dispose of them according to your Direction.

I wrote to the honorable Society June 25th 1774 in favour of the Church People of Danbury, to which, I have receiv^d no Answer; and least the Letter shou'd have miscarried I now transcribe that part of it from the Copy.

At Danbury about sixteen Miles from home, there is upwards of 70 Families Professors of the Episcopal Church under very destitute Circumstances, who have made Application to me in a very pressing Manner to take them under my pastoral Care (altho my Mission is extensive) yet out of Pity to their destitute Condition, and there being a most hopeful Prospect of a very flourishing Church by being suitably encouraged; I accordingly laid the Matter before the Convention, as it was then near sitting, and the Advice of the Clergy was for me to comply with their Request, as they really needed and deserved Encouragement, and likewise to acquaint the honorable Society and desire their Approbation, which favour, in behalf of that People, I now beg leave to ask the honorable Society in the mean while

assuring the Society, that if they in their Wisdom shall think proper to indulge the Church People of Danbury of being under my Care, I shall endeavour faithfully to discharge my Duty towards them. I hope I may have the Pleasure of hearing from the honorable Society as soon as Convenient.

It affords me Satisfaction to say that amidst the Disorders of a Distracted World, the Church People under my Care are firm in their Principles. At New Milford their is about one 100 families Professors of the Church of England, Communicants 70, at Kent 42 families and 18 Communicants, at New Preston 48 families and 20 Communicants, at New Fairfield 17 families and 8 Communicants.-- Sharon has left this Mission by Joining with the Church People over in the oblong and Salsbury, who had agreed with one Mr Moore, but very unhappily disappointed as Mr Moore afterwards accepted of an Invitation at New York.-- I have baptized since June 25th 1774 65 Infants and 3 adults.

I hope the honorable Society's Approbation of my Conduct for for the future will be more intire, as I am fully determined to be so regular in my Correspondence as not to fail sending my Notitia twice in the year. I have lived under great Disadvantages of conveying my Letters to the Post Office, as there is not any within 40 Miles, and sometimes they have been lodged at particular Houses where they have laid a long time and not sent into the Post Office. I shall Esteem it a favour that you wou'd be pleas'd to direct all your Letters for me to the Revd Mr Leaming at NorWalk

I am Rev^d S^{ir} your and the Society's
faithful Missionary and most Obed^t hum^{be} Servt
Richard Clarke

I have drawn upon the Society my Sallery since June 25th 1774 in favour of Mr Isaac Tomlinson

[Addressed:] To / The Reverend Doc^{tr} Hind / Secretary to the Society for the Propagation / of the Gospel in foreign Parts / St Ann's Westminster.
[Endorsed: Read] March 77

[1775, Aug. 14, Oyster Ponds]

Oyster ponds Augt 14th 1775
Sir,

Your favour of the 10th Instant with the 300^{lb} of powder p^r Cap^n Griffing I receiv'd, and now acquaint your honour that last friday morning a large Sloop of War and two transports sailed round Plumb Island. After they had got through the Gut, I sent one hundred and twenty Men in three boats (which were all the boats, we then had) to s^d Island if possible to get off the Stock; with Orders to return immediately upon the first appearance of the Enimies attempting to bring any of their Shipping betwixt the Island and Oyster pond point, least their retreat might be cut off, it being impossible to support them without Boats--. Before the last boat had got over, the Sloop of War was observed to be returning, wind and tide favouring her, our Boats were therefore obliged to put back again, the hindmost of which had several Cannon fired at her, but at so great a distance they did no dammage. A Cutter came within fifteen or twenty rods of our last boat, but discovering there were armed men in the boat stopped their

pursuit-- Our Soldiers in the Boat and some others on the Beach then fired at them, but I fancy to little effect, as our boat was obliged to make all the sail possible to keep out of the reach of the Cannon from the Sloop of War, which was close behind them-- The Sloop of War then came to Anchor betwixt the point and the Island, and that night took from the Island nine Cattle & then joined the Fleet which came to Sail very early Saturday Morning & I suppose have gone to Boston-- I have since taken from Plumb Island their Cattle & Sheep & the Inhabitants have engaged to thresh out their grain and convey it from the Island as soon as possible. I shall tomorrow go to Gardiner's Island and make such dispositions as shall appear most conducive to the common good-- I expect by thursday to be able to embark for New York-- I am informed that Col. Willart told the people on Gardiner's Island that he intended to pay Long Island a visit before fall & also that the King's Troops had been in-vited to purchase provisions at Brookhaven and Flushing, in consequence of this intelligence, the Committees of Brook-haven Smith Town and the other adjacent Towns have taken and sent to me the Re[v.] James Lyon a Church of England Clergyman--a man of infamous Character but a pretty sen-sible fellow, who they say has corresp[o]nded with Henry Lloyd of Boston-- This Parson Lyon by wha[t] I can learn, is the main spring to all the Tories on that part of the Long Island. He has a considerable money at Interest in differ-ent hands among his neighbours, which gains him ascend-ancy over them, and he has been indifatigable both by writ-in[g,] preaching, and in every other way to gain prosolites and by his connections with those in other parts of the Country who ar[e] inimical to the cause we are embarked in, he will be able to do great mischief. The Committees of the several adjacent Towns, thinking him a very danger-ous person to remain among them, hav[e] desired me to take care of him-- I shall therefore by the first convenient opportunity send him to the care of the Committee of Hart-ford till they can receive your honour's orders concerning him-- I am with the greatest sincerity you[r] honour's most obedient h^{ble} Servt

Dav^d Wooster

P.S. I enclose Col. Willart's Account of the Stock he took from Gardiner's Island--

To the Hono^{ble} Jonathan Trumbull Esqr

[1775, Aug. 16, Lebanon]

Lebanon 16$\underline{th}$ Augt 1775

Sir--

I have your Favour of the 14$\underline{th}$ in[s]tant per James Lockwood Esqr. Am of Opinion that your Return to Har-lem, with your men will be best-- That it is necessary the Stock on Long-Island &c be secured against further depredation--hope the people there will be able to secure the Same--if not, should rather at their desire & Expense furnish some other Companies from the main provided they can be Spared-- Will send your Account to General Washington-- As to the Revd James Lyon you mention shall leave the Disposition of him to your prudent Direction-- Such persons are very pernicious--

My Council will be with me to-morrow, shall then con-sult on the Affair-- Am obliged for your Intelligence, & for the Service you have done the Islanders-- I don't get

any Intelligence of importance that is late to Comunicate

I am with Esteem and Regard / Sir / Your Obed^t Hble Servant

J Trumbull

General Wooster

[1775, Aug. 16, Lebanon]

Lebanon 16$\underline{th}$ August 1775

Sir

I expe[c]t my Council with me to-Morrow, with whom I choose to Advise before I give you an Answer-- Whether you shall Undertake the Risk mentioned--and also whether you may release M^r M^{c}clean-- You shall have our result by Friday Or Saturday next--

I am / Sir- Your Obed^t Hble Servant

[Jonathan Trumbull]

Capt Jere^h Wadsworth--

[1775, Oct. 10, Stamford]

Stamford Connecticut in New England Octob^r 10. 1775.

Reverend Sir.

In answer to Your favour of the 28th of Octob^r last; I should directly have complied with the Societies requisi-tion, but Months before your letter came to hand, the sub-ject matter in Dispute between Mr William Lamson and the Trustees of Mr St George Talbots Donation to the Ch^h of Fairfield, was settled by a Course of Law. the Trustees sued him as Administrator to Acc^t for Said Donation left in trust in his Fathers hands, the Court appointed Audi-tors to adjust matters in dispute, and make Report; which report, (as my Son tells me, who was one of the Referees or Auditors) was accepted and Established, he thinks very equitably, and to the tolerable satisfaction of the Trustees. how they have disposed of the remainder of the Donation, I can't say, but shall enquire and make report in my next.-- Mrs Lamson and the Children, return their Tribute of gratitude and thanks to the Venerable Board for their good-ness in granting to them half a Years Salary: Which Gra-tuity Inclusive of my last half Years Salary, I have drawn for this day, in a sett of Bills for 50£ Sterling, upon the Societies Treasurer Mr William Symondson, in fav^r of Mr Comfort Sands Merchant in New York. I shall bestow one half of the Societies Gratuity upon the poor Widow, whose circumstances are compassionate, the other half discretionarily upon the Children.

I shall continue my attention to my Parish Duty, en-cumbered with peculiar difficulties and discouraging Pros-pects, relative to the unhappy contest of the Colonies with the Parent State; prejudicial in a high degree, at present, to the interest of Religion, the peace and welbing of the Church. may we be inspired with a spirit of primitive Christianity, patiently to suffer, if called in Providence, as well as do the will of God.

I Baptized last half Year, 23 Infants. two were added to the Communion. the Books you mentioned, are not come to hand.

May Infinite Wisdom direct the great Council of the Nation, Infinite Power protect the Ch^h Infinite goodness

pardon our National impiety, heal our unhappy Divisions, and Unite us again in the bond of peace & Charity.

with my Duty to the Venerable Board, I am, Reverend Sir, with great Esteem,

Your most Obed^t Servant
and Brother in Christ
Ebenezer Dibblee

The Revd Doctor
Richard Hind Secretary of
the Venerable Society for
Propagation of the Gospel &c.

[Endorsed: Read] Janry 1776

[1775, Nov. 2, New London]
Rev^d & Good Sir

Hitherto Necessity enjoin'd me Silence. True, I might, perhaps, have wrote, but, perhaps, You never have seen it. To describe my Situation is as dangerous, as awful; & as I have always been strictly silent about Politics, resolve to continue so: & tho' my Patrons might demand Obedience to their Commands, yet I'm persuaded they will excuse my involuntary Neglect.

The Inhabitants of this most beautiful, sea-port Town, having remov'd their Effects & almost all their Families, occasion'd me to follow ye mournful Example, & seek an Asylum in ye Desert. I stay'd, till ye small Number of my Hearers, & threatning Desolation forc'd me into ye Woods; where I have a large Congregation, as poor as Job, to preach to. They furnish me wth House-room & Fire, & I'm free from the daily Din of War, Slaughter &c.-- How long I can subsist here, GOD only knows. I am afraid to draw for Relief, & to live much longer without it, is impossible. For GOD's sake, advise & relieve me. I wish I were off ye Land, but fear to venture between two Fires. My Circumstances are truly deplorable, &, unless Mercy interpose, I fear ye Spring will behold America delug'd wth Blood.

This Town, Boston, Newport & New-york are ye only Places in these Parts subject to be visited by Men of War

I am here now, visiting my Hearers, whom I shall continue to visit, as often as ye Weather & Safety will permit-- My Duty attends my Venerable Patrons. A Letter to me, under Cover to Dr Auchmuty, will come safe, if it [is] deliver'd to some particular Friend, to

Rev^d S^r / Y^r most hum^l Servt & / affectionate Brother in / Jesus Christ,

New-London Novr 2^d 1775   Matt Graves

[Addressed:] To / The Revd Doctor Burton, Secretary / to the Society for propagating the / Gospel in foreign Parts / London
[Endorsed:] July 1776

[1776?, Fairfield]
Mr Holt Sir

The Letter which the Reverend Mr Sayre sent unto the Committee I here send you, as he is very desirous of having it publish'd, to shew the World why he did not sign the Association; and the Committee have agreed it may be, I am Sir

Your very humble Servt
Thaddeus Burr

Gentlemen

Yesterday my Neighbour Mr Lewis called on me with a Paper stiled an Association, which he informed me was sent by your desire with a view that I should subscribe it. Of that Paper I requested a Copy, that I might have time to consider of the propriety of the desired Subscription; and was served with it the same Day about noon, and now beg the candid attention of the Gentlemen of the Committee while I give them my answer to their requisition

I shall first consider the Paper with respect to its particular parts; and then with regard to its general intention.

The first Clause contains a recital of some of those things which are commonly charged against the Mother Country, as unconstitutional, and therefore unwarrantable exertions of power on her part; and the resolutions of the united Colonies on their part, to resist by force of Arms, the measures prescribed by the Parent state, and to die or be free. I beg to be consider'd as a Servant (though unworthy) of the Gospel of Christ, who am taught by one of its inspired Preachers, that "the Weapons of our Warfare are not carnal, but mighty through God, to the bringing every thought to the obedience of Christ." Which Expressions plainly designate them to be Spiritual: I dare not therefore promise to take up and use any carnal Arms at all. The same Apostle teacheth me, that "in whatever state I am, therewith I must be content." If therefore the Providence of God should bring me into a state even of Slavery itself, I desire that his Will may be done, and that I may be content with that Lot however hard, and considering myself at the same time as being the Lord's Freeman may chearfully as well as faithfully discharge my duties in that state, knowing that in Christ Jesus there is neither bond nor free. I dare not therefore resolve I will be free, because I am sensible that many better Men than myself have by the Providence of God been brought into a state of bondage, and that I ought not to complain if I should be made partaker of the same affliction

The second Clause of the Paper before me contains an hearty approbation of the Continental Association, and a resolution faithfully to observe and comply with it without any equivocation or mental reservation. There is one part of that Association (especially as it hath been practised upon here) with which I dare not promise to comply, my Conscience will not permit me to act upon it, and our common Master hath commanded me to "let my Yea be yea and my Nay, nay," and I am also enjoined to speak the truth to my Neighbour in love, I must not therefore equivocate with you.

The part I mean is that which prohibits me from extending the kind offices of humanity and hospitality to any who may refuse to be bound by it. The Saviour of the World (whose Servant I am) hath commanded me to feed the hungry and give Drink to the thirsty; to clothe the Naked; to take in the Stranger or Traveller; to give to him that asketh of me, and from him that would borrow of me not to turn away. Here it may be to no purpose to say that such or such persons are mine Enemies; because our Lord hath expressly, and that too in an especial manner commanded me to extend my good offices to mine Enemies as such; and I beg the Committee to remember that Ministers of the Gospel are in a particular manner commanded to keep hospitality

The first Paragraph of the last Clause in the Association sent me, I have spoken to already; the remainder of it commenceth with a declaration, that we notice and gratefully acknowledge the Divine interpositions in favour of all our Warlike Enterprises, crowning them with most unparallel'd success. I know not Gentlemen that if this is true it is a proper rule for Christians to judge on concerning the goodness or badness of any Cause of this kind in controversy, for History (sacred and prophane) furnisheth us with many instances wherein we shall all agree in saying, that the most unjust Cause did not always meet an overthrow nor the most just prosper. Thus in the first efforts for establishing the Protestant Religion, the Protestants in the [schmalkaldic] League were intirely routed by the Romish Emperor Charles the fifth, when one of the two great Champions in the Protestant Cause, the Elector of Saxony was taken Prisoner, the other the Landgrave of Hesse was forced to surrender himself and beg pardon of Charles

There are sundry Prophecies yet to be fulfilld which declare that the Potentates of the Earth shall have power to make War against the Saints and to overcome them.

I look on the present unnatural War as being a Judgment of God on the People of old England as well as on us Americans, for our many crying offences against his most holy Laws, and a loud call to a sincere and immediate return to him and to our duty. It is therefore a constant part of my Prayers to him who doth not afflict willingly nor grieve the Children of Men, that he would make it effectual to the production of a true and general reformation in both Countries to the Glory of his Mercy.

What follows in the Paper seems to be a recapitulation of the substance of what was said before; it is therefore unnecessary for me to add any further as to the particulars of it; I shall therefore proceed to consider it with respect to its general intention.

I take it for granted that the design of this Association is to make a discrimination between the Friends of America and its Liberties, and the Enemies of both. And I now beg the Committee to believe me when I declare in the presence of him who knows all Hearts, and before whom I am finally to be judged in that awful Day when the secrets of all Hearts shall be revealed, that I am a sincere Friend to both.

America is my native Country; all my Connections are in it; I have enjoyed the Liberty and plenty of it (through the goodness of God) too long and too thankfully not to be sensible of the value of both and to desire a continuance of them if it be his Will.

It can be matter of very little importance to the Community whether I subscribe the Association or not, for I am no Politicion, am not connected with Politicions as such, and never will be either.

Those things belong not to my Profession, and I find sufficient employment for my Head and my Heart in that honourable though arduous employment, to which in the presence of the adorable Trinity I have vowed to devote my whole Life.

After this open Testimony, I cannot fear that you Gentlemen will run any risk of a breach of the ninth Commandment, by advertising me as an Enemy to my Country.

Praying that Infinite Wisdom may guide the Councils of my Country; Infinite Power protect it in all its Lawful Priviledges; and Infinite Love pardon all our misdoings and comfort us here and forever, I subscribe myself Gentlemen

To the Gentlemen of ⎫
the Committee of the ⎬
Town of Fairfield ⎭

Your sincere Friend &
Servt in Christ Jesus
John Sayre

[1776, Feb. 29, Stratford]
Dear Sir

Agreable to your request I have Obtained Dr Johnsons Answer to your several Questions in the Words following--

"The Collectors are the only Persons who are properly accountable for the Rates, & they alone can be sued by the Minister for them. But it is made the Duty of the Society to grant the Tax's & of the Societys Committee to take all proper Care that such Tax's be granted & Collected & to that end to apply to a Justice of the Peace for a Warrant to the Collector to Levy & Collect the Rates-- And on his failure to take out a Distress against such Negligent Collector for the purpose of Leavying such part of the Tax as remains unpaid out of the Estate of such Negligent Collector-- And in Case of the Committees neglect their Duty in taking out a Distress ag^t the Collector & C^h they are made liable to pay such part of the Rate as remains unpaid & also a fine of Three pounds for every Neglect-- All which is to be recovered by Action bro't by the Kings Attorney to the County Court in the same County-- If therefore the Collector has received, or might have received the Money he is to be sued for it-- If the Committee have Neglected their Duty, Complaint should be made to the King's Attorney of the County, and this is the only Remedy provided expressly by the Law, but if he should refuse, or Neglect to prosecute, I will not say, that an Action might not be devised ag^t the Committee or Society in the Name of the Clergyman, which would be Maintainable, tho' I believe no such Action has ever been brought in the Colony"--

You will be good enough to make my Compliments in which also Mrs Van Dyck who is here Joins me in acceptable [form] to Mr Jarvis & I am

Stratford Feby 29th 1776.

Yr Brother & hble Servt
Ebenezer Kneeland

P.S. I beg Dear Sir you will accept of my best Wishes & believe me to be at all times   Yours to Love & Serve
H Van Dyck

[Addressed:] To / The Revd Mr Jarvis / at / Middletown

[1776, May, Middletown]
To the Honble the General Assembly now sitting in Hartford in the Colony of Connecticut

The Memorial of Philip Mortimer & the rest of the Members of the Episcopal Church in Middleton and Mary Alsop of s^d Middletown in s^d Colony, s^d Mary as administratrix of the Goods & Estate of Richard Alsop Esq. late of s^d Middletown deceased, and as Guardian of the Children of s^d dec^d humbly sheweth

That some Years ago the Members of the Episcopal

Church in Middletown agreed to and did purchase a House & Houselot in s^d Middletown as a Glebe for the use of the Minister in Orders according to the Canons of the Church of England then settled abiding & performing divine service among them and his Successors, and a Deed thereof was made and executed to the said Philip and s^d Richard who advanced most of the purchase Mony & were secured therefor by a Subscription or voluntary promise in writing from sundry Persons Members of s^d Church In which they undertook & promised to pay certain Sums to their Names annexed to reimburse them for the sums advanced for s^d House & Land and also took s^d Deed of the same to s^d Phillip & Richard to secure them while s^d subscription money was collecting, Part of which Money hath been collected & paid,

Your memorialists further shew that s^d Richard in his Lifetime never made any Conveyance of s^d House and Land to the s^d Church--and that there is due to his Estate for the Money advanced for s^d House and Land the Sum of £75-0-0 lawfull money, & the Heirs of s^d Richard being all minors & not able by Law to make any Conveyance of s^d Estate they humbly pray your Honours to enable the s^d Mary to convey s^d Estate to s^d Church agreably to the Trust reposed in s^d Richard deceased upon her receiving s^d Sum of £75-0-0 lawf^l Mony from the Members of s^d Church or in some other way grant Relief to your Memorialists and they as in duty bound shall ever pray &c

Philip Mortimer for himself & s^d Church
Mary Alsop

In the Lower House[:] The prayer of this Memorial is granted and that a Bill in fform may be brought in Accordingly

Test Titus Hosmer Clerk
Concurr^d in the upper House

Test George Wyllys Secrety

Upon the Memorial of Phillip Mortimer and the rest of the Members of the Episcopal Church in Middletown, & Mary Alsop of s^d Middletown Administratrix of the Estate of Richard Alsop Esqr deceased & Guardian of his Children who are Minors, shewing that A Deed of a House and Acre of Land in s^d Middletown, which was purchased by s^d Church for a Glebe was made to s^d philip & Richard in Trust to secure them for the purchase Money by them advanced &c & that there is £75 due to s^d Mary as adm^x aforesaid on that Account & no more, praying that she may be authorized & enabled to convey s^d House & Land to the Members of s^d Church upon their pay[ing] s^d Sum due &c as per Memorial on ffile--

Resolved by this Assembly that said Mary Alsop be and she is hereby authorized and impowered, upon Receipt of said Sum of Seventy five pounds to transfer & convey all the Right Title and Interest in and to s^d House and Land vested in s^d Richard by vertue of said Deed to the parson & Parishioners of s^d Church, agreably to the Trust and Confidence reposed in s^d Richard and in Execution of the same.

Passed in The Lower House

Test Titus Hosmer Clerk
Concurr^d in the upper House

Test George Wyllys Secrety

[1776, June 4, Waterbury]
At a Convention of the Clergy of the Church of England, of the Colony of Connecticut, held at Waterbury on Tuesday the fourth day of June. being the Tuesday in Trinity Week in the year of our Lord 1776. Present

Abraham Jarvis President.	Daniel Fogg
James Scovil	Gidion Bostwick
Samuel Andrews	John. R. Marshall
Bela Hubbard	John Sayre
Richard Clarke	James Nichols

Mr Jarvis according to course & an unanimous approbation was Nominated President, and Mr Sayre chosen Secretary pro tempore, the Stated Secretary being absent-- Mr Sayre was also appointed to perform Divine Service tomorrow; & Mr Clarke to Preach, Mr Kneeland being absent. after which the Convention was adjourned by the President to meet again at Mr Scovil's at eight o Clock tomorrow morning--

Wednesday the 5th 8 o Clock in the Morning, Met again according to adjournment. & proceeded to Saint James's Church in Waterbury, where a Sermon was Preached by Mr Clarke Resolved on Motion of Mr Andrews that, the President be requested to return the thanks of this Convention to Mr Clarke for his Sermon preached this day before them; & also to Mr Sayre for his Services, which was accordingly done by the President. Mr Sayre Moved that this Convention should consider of the propriety of their agreeing to supply the Vacant Congregations of the Church of England in this Colony, as often as will be consistent with their other Duties--which motion meeting with their approbation resolved that it be recommended to Mr Scovil Mr Andrews Mr Marshall & Mr Nichols to attend at Litchfield each once in a year at such times as will be most agreeable, they giving proper previous Notice to the People--and that Mr Clarke Mr Leaming Mr Diblee and Mr Sayre be requested to attend in like manner at Danbury and that Mr Bostwick Mr Nichols Mr Clarke and Mr Diblee be requested to attend in like manner at Sharon and that Mr Jarvis Mr Tyler Mr Fogg and Mr Mathew Graves be requested to attend in like manner at Hebron

Mr John Nichols a Gentleman of Waterbury in the County of New Haven having applied to this Convention for recommendatory Letters in his favor to the Society and to the Lord Bishop of London in order to his admittence into Holy Orders in the Church of England--resolved that they be granted accordingly--& the Secretary is therefor ordered to furnish him with them. The Convention was then adjourned till tomorrow morning eight o Clock, to meet at Mr Scovil's--

Thursday 6th 8 o Clock. Met again according to adjournment. Letters in favor of Mr Nichols according to yesterday's Order, were prepared, read, and subscribed by all present-- Ordered that Mr Tyler be prepared to preach before the Convention at their next annual meeting in Trinity Week, & that the Secretary serve him with notice accordingly--& that Mr Sayre do prepare a suitable discourse in case any thing should prevent Mr Tylers attendance-- The Convention then proceeded to appoint a Standing Committee & the following Gentlemen were unanimously agreed to viz. Mr Scovil Mr Andrews Mr Hubbard Mr Jarvis and Mr Sayre--after which the Con-

vention adjourned to meet again at New Cambridge on Tuesday which shall be in Trinity-week next ensuing--

> Abraham Jarvis,} Presid^t
> John Sayre Secre^{ty}

[Endorsed:] " Minutes of a Convention held at Waterbury. 1776. Trinity week June 4th"

[1776, July 23, New Haven]

At a Convention of the Clergy of the Church of England in the Colony of Connecticut, at the house of M^r. Hubbard in New Haven on Tuesday the 23^d day of July in the year 1776 at 8 o'Clock in the evening.

Present

Abraham Jarvis. President	Bela Hubbard.
Richard Mansfield	John Sayre.
Samuel Andrews.	

The Revd Mr Bowden of New York having attended this Convention by invitation, resolved that the President be requested to [extend] their thanks to him for his company on this occasion, and that he be asked to take his seat as a member of this Convention, which he did accordingly--

The standing Secretary being absent, Mr Sayre was chosen to officiate as Secretary, pro hac Vice.

The President then adjourned the Convention, to meet again tomorrow morning at 8 o'Clock, at this place.

Wednesday July 24th 1776. met again according to adjournment, at 8 o'Clock in the forenoon--

At ten o'Clock Mr Clarke and Mr Marshal came in and took their seats--as did also Mr Scovil shortly after

Considering the present critical and alarming situation of the Church of England in America in general, and the Clergy & members of it in this Colony in particular--the Convention in pursuance of the main design of this meeting proceeded to consider what measures will be most proper and prudent for them to adopt for ye promotion & preservation of peace and security of the Congregations under their care.

Mr Andrews moved to collect the sentiments of the Convention on the following question viz. Whether we can go on as usual in the performance of Divine Service in our Churches consistently with the general benefit of the Church and our own personal security, considering the declaration of Independency published by the Continental Congress on the 4th of the present month on which it was unanimously resolved that we cannot.----Mr President then moved for the sense of the Convention whether it is in our power to make or submit to any alterations in the Liturgy of the Church of England as it is now by Law established, consistantly with our duty and our solemn obligations--which motion being deliberated on was unanimously answered in the negative for the following reasons. 1st Because at the time of our Ordination, we solemnly bound ourselves by Oaths, promises and Subscriptions that we would use the form of Prayer and Administration of Sacraments provided in the Book of Common Prayer and none other: as will appear from a perusal of the Oath contained in the offices for the ordination of Priests & Deacons and the three Articles contained in the 36th Canon-- 2^{ly} Because we being only Presbyters in the Church are not by any means invested with authority sufficient to entitle us to make any mutila-

tions or alterations, either in her Government or Worship--and if we should attempt it we apprehend we should attempt a sacriligious invasion of the Authority and privilige of a superior Order. 3^{ly} Because should we make or submit to any alterations as above mentioned we should incur the penalties denounced in the 38th Canon viz. Suspension, Excommunication and Deposition.

The Convention taking into their serious consideration the melancholy situation of the Church in this time of public controversy and distress and most heartily desiring to do all that is left in their power according with the foregoing resolutions, for the spiritual comfort and emolument of their people, do agree that if we should open our churches and read the Holy Scriptures, together with some approved practical Commentaries on them; read the Homilies or other orthodox Sermons published by Divines of our Church, or any pious tracts which may be thought most proper for the present state of the Church; to examine the Children in their Catechism and read approved Lectures thereon, and also to continue all the occasional Services when requisite (except the Celebration of the Holy Eucharist, which we think should only be used for the present in the Chambers of ye Sick) It will have a tendency to promote a great part of ye general intentions of public religious meetings & that the retired devotions of the people may make up in a great measure for the unavoidable deficiencies--and that such a mode of proceedure will preserve us in a conscience void of offence towards God & towards man.

The President then adjourned the Convention, to meet again tomorrow morning at 8, O'Clock at this place--

Thursday 25th July 1776. Met again at 8, O'Clock in the morning according to yesterdays adjournment. The Convention considering that it would be very proper to make our absent Brethren acquainted with the proceedings of this meeting--and that as a fraternal intercourse hath uniformly subsisted between this Convention & that of the Colonies of N York & N Jersey, they also should know our proceedings & the reasons on which they are founded; resolved unanimously that Copies of the minutes of them be presented to both.

The President then dissolved this Convention.

> Abraham Jarvis} Pres^t
> John Sayre. Secr^y

[1776, Nov. 13, Philadelphia]

At a Conference of the subscribers at Philadelphia, Nov. 13, 1776.

Taking into consideration the suffering state of the fund for the relief of the widows and children of Clergymen in the Communion of the Church of England of America owing to the impossibility of holding the last annual meeting at N. Y. agreeable to the rules of the Corporation, and finding that large sums of money remain in the hands of the Treasurers, which cannot be put out agreeable to the said rules, and that the keeping the money unemployed, and in paper of various currencies may be very prejudicial to the fund-- We are of opinion that the treasurers and standing committees with the Secretary, should endeavor to vest the said monies in the purchase of some real estate or estates, using their best judgement and discretion therein, as they would in laying out their own money.

And, whereas through the present difficulty and distress of the times, some of the Clergy have not an opportunity, and others want the ability of paying their annual subscriptions agreeable to the laws, and if the said subscriptions were paid in, it would only add to the risk of the Capital, which cannot be lent out--we are further of opinion, that the Treasurer should not insist on the legal fine for neglect of payment, but that it would be more for the advantage of the fund to leave the subscriptions in the hands of the different subscribers at 6 per. cent. interest, till the treasurers either have an opportunity of laying out the same in a convenient purchase, or letting it at interest agreeable to the laws of the Corporation. And we will endeavor to obtain an indemnification for the Treasurers at the first meeting of the Corporation for acting according to this advice, and will, in the mean time, apply (as occasion offers) to other clerical and lay members for their approbation hereof.

Having further affectionately conferred together on the state of our Churches, some of which have been shut up by the Clergy, while others have been kept open, and being persuaded that both parties have acted agreeably to their consciences, and the different circumstances in which they are placed, we think that this ought to occasion no breach in our brotherly union or christian charity, and that we should be candidly disposed to wait the opinion of our Superiors on so interesting and difficult a matter.

William Smith.	William Stringer.
Jacob Duché.	William White.
Abr'm Beach.	Robert Blackwell.
Th. Coombe.	

[1777, Jan. 12, Newport, R.I.?]

Presented 12th Jany 1777

May it please your Excellency--

The present Application is in Consequence of the Grove of Woods' being cut off the Farm of Godfrey Malbone Esqr at present and for some Time past in Residence in the Township of Pomfret in the Colony of Connecticut a well known Friend to Government and his Brother who with him now addresses Your Excellency, having ever been connected in Business, requests to know in what Manner to apply for Redress, or whether he may expect to receive any Satisfaction for the same, wishing Your Excellency every Happiness--

I am with great Respect your most obed^t & most humble Servt

J. M.

To Sir Henry Clinton, Lieutenant General
commanding his Majesty's Forces at Rhode Island &c.

The above was sent to his Excellency the General a Day or two before his Departure, to which I rec^d no answer, imputing the same to his Excellency's early embarkation.

[1777, May 3, Brooklyn--Pomfret?]

Presented 3^d May 1777

Mr Jno Malbone presents his Compliments to his Excellency Earl Percy and begs Leave to intercede for the Trees growing on the Farm, as he has just left the Fashion Party* who cut down the Avenue Trees of at least two feet Diameter close to the Ground for our Faschion, his Lordship's Interposition will greatly oblige him.

To which Mr Malbone presumes his Ex^y paid some attention as the Party ceased cutting, altho' he rec^d no answer to the said Message

[*The MS. originally read "Fashion Battery." A "fashioning party" was, apparently, a "construction gang" as opposed to a "foraging party."]

[1777? after August; Newport, R.I.]

Major General Sir Robert Pigot commanding his Majesty's Forces at Rhode Island &c. &c.

Humbly sheweth,

John Malbone of Newport in the County of Newport in the Colony of Rhode Island   Gentleman in behalf of himself as well as his Brother Godfrey Malbone Esquire now and long since a Resident in the Colony of Connecticut That they are joint Proprietors of the farms at Newport under the Improvement of Elisha Shelfield and John Anthony, containing upwards of six hundred acres of Land, from which said Farms from the tenth Day of August last to the Close of the said Month, sixty Tons of Hay in Stack were carried off, eight Tons in the Barn, partly taken by Carts for Doctor Paine and Captain Maltsburg the Residue disposed off by others unknown, eight acres of Oats in two Stacks, supposed eight Tons; part of which was taken by the above Persons and others, four Acres of Barley, mostly secured in the Stack the remaining part in Swath and Cock supposed to be four Tons were likewise disposed of together with four Acres of Potatoes and the Cattle brought in from the Island were turned into an hundred Acres of Land, fit for mowing, besides which Your Petitioner hath sustained the Loss of twenty Acres of Indian Corn thirty Pigs and six grown Hogs with two Cows and one Steer which were killed a Calf he was raising above five Months old for which he was offered fifty Dollars and a Calf of five Weeks old: An old Ox Cart, an Horse Cart almost new four Ploughs, six Hoes and four Hay Pitch Forks are totally destroyed and lost and by Estimation four thousand Rails and upwards were taken off that par[t] of the Farm occupied by the said Shelfield, add to which a large dwelling House and Out Houses on the said Farms are almost destroyed, some of the Out Houses being pulled down and totally taken away, the Dwelling House stripped of its Windows Doors and part of the Floor and otherwise much injured, the Barn and Crib almost rendered useless, a large Orchard of Fruit Trees with the like in the Garden, together with part of two other Orchards are cut down and the Garden entirely ruined a large Line of Board Fence wholly supported by red Cedar Posts with the Gates and Bars on the said Farms and every kind of wooden Fence (the Inclosure of the Garden improved for the Benefit of the Hospital excepted) and the greatest part of the Stone Walls with the remaining Avenue Trees are cut, thrown down and destroyed, in Consequence of which the said Farms are rendered untenantable; the whole Amount of which heavy Losses devolve solely upon your Petitioner

Wherefore he most humbly prays your Excellency would
cause an Estimate of his Losses to be made and would in
your great Justice order him such Redress as to your Excellency may seem consistent, considering that his present
Sufferings with those already related in a former Memorial, hath reduced your Petitioner from a State of Ease and
Affluence to that of the greatest Anxiety and Distress, to
which Redress he humbly conceives from his Majesty's
Royal Proclamation assuring all his Subjects of Support
and Protection in their Lives, Properties and Estates upon
their remaining quiet and peaceable Subjects, he hath an
undoubted Right and as in Duty bound he will ever pray &c.
                                    J[ohn] M[albone]

The last Memorial was presented by the s.d Malbone in his
proper person in the Beginning of October last, upon the
Receival of which by the General, he cast the same upon
the Table (after reading a few Lines) declaring the same
too trivial at that Conjuncture for his Attention or Words
to that Import; to which M.r Malbone replied that after the
many Injuries he had received, he as an Individual and good
Subject, thought it Matter of Importance and however trivial
in the Public Eye, was extremely consequential in the View
of M.r Malbone

[1777, Nov. 12, Norwich]
                    Norwich in New England Nov.r 12: 1777
Gentlemen,
    I have been informed that there was a Collection in
England, for the suffering Clergy in America, whose
Churches were shut up--that they had Liberty to draw for
Fifty Pounds sterling each--on whom they were to draw
&c.-- Some of the Clergy have drawn.
    Agreeable to this Advice, my Church having been shut
ever since July 7: 1776, I have drawn Bills of Exchange on
Mess.rs Hoar and Company Bankers in Fleet-Street Lon-
don, for Fifty Pounds sterling, in Favour of John Baker
Brimmer Merch.t dated April 22: 1777----
    From your Friend and humble Servant
                                    John Tyler

To Mess.rs Hoar and Company ⎫
Bankers in Fleet-Street London ⎭

[1778, Feb. 7, Newport, R.I.]
                    Newport February 7th 1778
Sir
    Permit me to lay the inclosed Memorial before your
Excellency, as it is by no means the first or least of our
Misfortunes, having previously suffered greatly both by
Fire, and Water, and other Casualties which altogether
with the present unhappy Times, have rendered one of the
most Opulent and well known Families of this Colony from
moving in their former Sphere of Life. I would also beg
leave to inform your Excellency we now suffer within this
Colony upwards of Fourteen Hundred Dollars in our Annual Rents, which with other Circumstances is truely distressing, otherwise I would not presume to have introduced amidst the many and weighty Publick Concerns,
those of Individuals--which hope will be a sufficient

apology for the present intrusion from
                    sir
            Your mo Obed.t & mo. hb.l sv[.t]
                                    J. M.
M. Gen.l Robert Pigot, &c. &c. &c.

Major General Robert Pigot, Commanding his
Majesty's Forces at Rhod-Island &c. &c. &c.

The Memorial of John Malbone of Newport in the County
of Newport in the Colony of Rhod-Island &c. Gentleman--
humbly sheweth,
    That in the Month of December in the Year of our
Lord one thousand seven hundred and seventy six, a Number of Soldiers and Sailors entered into a certain Dwelling House and out Houses upon a Farm belonging to his
Brother Godfrey Malbone Esq.r (a well known Friend to
Government) formerly a Resident in the said Town, but
now and long since of Connecticut and there wantonly
spilled, wasted and drank a Quantity of Cyder, pillaged
the House of the Kitchen Furniture to the supposed Value
of ten pounds Sterling; in which said Month a Party of Soldiers belonging to the 63.d Regiment broke open his Distill
House carried away Fencing Stuff there deposited with
sundry the Apparatus and Implements of Distillery such
as Copper Cranes, Funnels, Buckets &c. to the Value of
£40. like Money, upon which your Memorialist, entered
in Complaint to an officer, who either from Mistake or
Misinformation of an other officer declined interfering,
the Consequence of which was a Repetition of the same
act in less than three Hours after, add to which the Inclosure of a certain Lot in said Newport bounded by the
Sea, with the Timber, which served as a Buttment against
the Same and prevented said Lot from being overflowed
hath been taken away to the Damage of your Memorialist
as he conceives of at least £36. Money aforesaid. That
some Transports have totally ballasted themselves with
Stones from off his two Wharves, which hath so damaged
the Timber and exposed the same to the Tide as hath occasioned a Loss of at least £100. like Money.
    That upon the Application of Colon.l Campbell, whose
attentive Regard for the Wellfare of his Majestys Forces
foresaw the many Advantages which might arise to the
sick and infirm from the Cultivation and Improvement of
the most capital Garden on the Island receiving repeated
Injuries, Your Memorialist more cheerfully resigned the
same for that sole Intent, reserving to himself free In-
gress and Egress to and from the same, with the Grass
Plots and Grass in an adjoining Orchard, which in the
preceeding year afforded him a Profit of 88 3/4. Dollars,
from which he hath not rec.d the least Emolument or Advantage. That the first & second Party of Men there
placed cut down and destroyed a long Line of Board Fence
with the red Cedar Posts which supported the same,
ripped up the Stable Floor, destroyed the Partition, rendered his Coach & Chaise useless, having taken off both
Cloth & Leather, cut Down his Trees and committed such
other Waste as must at the most moderate Computation
amount to £300.
    That your Memorialist (tho' no Application hath as
yet been made to him) understands the said Garden is

still to be improved the present Year for the same Purpose; for a reasonable Rent for which and for a Prevention of that Waste which must inevitably ensue as the Party there posted, keep two large Fires and are not supplied with Wood, your Memorialist doubts not of your Excellency's kind Interference.

That Your Memorialist reported to the Deputy Commissary General a Quantity of Hay supposed fifty Tons, one hundred Bushels of Corn and one hundred Bushels of Potatoes computed at £100. on the Island of Prudence which was pilfered and taken by some Seamen from his Majesty's Ships, a Part of which Hay was appropriated to his Majesty's Use and the Remainder burned and destroyed.

And permit Your Memorialist with Regret to say, that a fine Grove of Trees which afforded refreshing Shade and the cool Retreat to the Inhabitants, added Beauty to as well as enhanced the Value of the Farm, was cut down: part of which from Information of his Tenant measuring 80 Cords, were for the Use of the Troops; for Payment of which he presented his Bill of 320 Dollars, which said Wood with the other cut down and not mensurated is valued at £200, Sterling.

That many of the Avenue Trees were made use of for the Purpose of Faschines* (and had it not been for the kind Interposition of Earl Percy the whole must have been wasted and the Farm deprived of its chiefest Ornaments). The Damage sustained thereby with the loss of Part of its' Inclosures, cannot be estimated at a less Value than £260. Sterling; beside which from Information some of the People of his Majestys Ships Cerberus or Amazon, upon a Shell Fish Party on the said Island of Prudence, burnt two large Dwelling Houses, a Barn, Cribb, Dairy House and other Buildings thereon the Property of your Memorialist to the Value of £850, by which and the aforerecited acts he hath sustained a Loss of .1950. pounds Sterling.

Conscious of his Loyalty to his Sovereign and Attachment to the British Constitution, he is emboldened to lay the Premises before your Excellency, in full Assurance that Redress will be granted unto him, which to Right and Justice may appertain and as in Duty bound he will ever pray &c--

The subsequent Letter inclosing the aforesaid Memorial was delivered by M.r Malbone at his sisters [M.rs] Hunters to Captain Welch then Aid de Camp to Major General Pigot upon his assurance he would present the same as soon as he saw the General

Both the aforegoing M.r Malbone doubts not the General received as he was informed a few Days after by M.r Paine Apothecary that the General could not allow any Rent for the Garden as [the] aforesaid improved

[*Fascine is defined as "a long bundle of sticks of wood, bound together, used in raising batteries, filling ditches, strengthening ramparts, &c."]

[1778, Feb. 12, Redding]
         Redding February y.e 12.th day AD. 1778
Rev.d Sir.
    We have no dispostion to restrain and limit You or others in matters of Conscience. But understanding that

you in your Public Worship still continue to pray that the King of Great-Britain may be strengthened to vanquish and overcome all his enemies, which manner of praying must be thought to be a great insult upon the [?Laws truth] and People of this State, as you and all others can't but know that the King of England has put the People of these united States from under his protection, Declared them Rebels, and is now at open war with said States; and consequently we are his enemies. Likewise you must have understood that the American States have declared themselves indepe[ndent] of any foreign Power, -- Now S.r in order that we may have Peace and quietness at home among ourselves-- We desire that for the future You wou'd omit praying in Public that King George y.e third, or any other foreign Prince or Power may Vanquish &c. the People of this Land-- Your compliance herewith may prevent You trouble-- We are Rev.d S.r with due Respect Your Obed.t Hum.le Serv.ts

To the Rev.d Jn.o Beach

Lem.ll Sanford W.m Hawly	} Justices

Hez.h Sanford Seth Sanford Thad.s Benedict John Gray W.m Heron	} Select Men of Redding

[1778, Mar. 7, Newport]
         Newport March 7.th 1778
My Lord
    Permit me in behalf of myself & Family to lay before your Lordship the inclosed Memorial humbly requesting your Lordships kind attention to the many and Recapitulated sufferings which they have sustained during the present Troubles by which and the loss of 10 hundred Dollars & upwards in their Annual Rents, a well known Family accustomed to affluence will be scarcely able to live with Decency or Decorum unless your Lordship will kindly intervene in their behalf and order them Payment for at least that Part of their Effects which hath been appropriated to his Majestys use-- I would beg leave to observe that your Lordship's proclamation was early embraced by
    Your Lordships most Obed.t / and most hble serv.t
                J. Malbone

[Reverse side is addressed:] The Right Honorable / Richard Lord Viscount Howe &c. &c. &c.

To the Right honorable Richard Lord Viscount Howe and Sir William Howe Knight of the most honorable order of the Bath, the King's Commissioners for restoring Peace to his Majesty's Colonies & Plantations in North America &c. &c. &c.

The Memorial and Petition of John Malbone of Newport in the County of Newport in the Colony of Rhode Island and so forth   Gentleman Humbly sheweth

    That in the Month of December in the Year of our Lord one thousand seven hundred and seventy six, a Number of Soldiers and Sailors forcibly entered into a certain House and Out Houses upon a Farm belonging to his Broth-

er Godfrey Malbone Esquire (a well known Friend to Government) formerly a Resident in the said Town but now and long since of Connecticut and there wantonly spilled, wasted and drank six Barrels of Cyder, pillaged the House of the Kitchen Furniture to the supposed value of ten pounds Sterling, in which said Month a Party of Soldiers belonging to the sixty third Regiment, broke open his Distill House, plundered the Fencing Stuff there deposited, with Sundry Articles and Implements of Distillery, such as Copper Cranes, Funnels, Buckets and so forth to the computed Value of forty pounds like Money; upon which Your Memorialist entered a Complaint to an Officer who either from Mistake or Misinformation of an other Officer declined interfering: the Consequence of which was a Repetition of the same Act in less than three Hours after.

Since which Your Memorialist is sorry to have the Occasion to observe that all the Inclosure of a certain Lot in the same Newport bounded by the Sea, with the Timber, which served as a Buttment and prevented the overflowing of the Tide was taken and carried away to the Damage of Your Memorialist as he conceives of at least thirty pounds Money aforesaid. That four Transports have ballasted themselves with Stones from off his two wharfs, which hath so damaged the Timber and so forth thereon as hath occasioned a Loss of at least one hundred pounds like Money. That Your Memorialist upon the Attentive Regard paid to the most capital Garden on the Island (which was dayly greatly injured) by and upon the Application of Colonel Campbell of the twenty second, most cheerfully resigned the Use and Improvement of the same for the Benefit of the Naval and Army Hospitals, with a Reservation to himself of the Grass Plats in the same and the Grass in an adjoining Orchard, which in the preceeding Year afforded him a Profit of eighty three Dollars and three Quarters of a Dollar; from which Reservation he hath not received the least Emolument or advantage. That the first and second Party of Men there placed, cut down and destroyed a long Line of Board Fence, supported by red Cedar Posts, ripped up the Stable Floors, destroyed the Partitions, rendered his Coach and Chaise useless, having taken off both Cloth and Leather, cut down his Trees and committed such other Waste as will at the most moderate Calculation amount to three hundred Pounds, which said Garden is now continued and without the least Application or Consent's being asked for the Purposes aforesaid, for a reasonable Rent for which and for a Prevention of that waste which must inevitably ensue for want of sufficient Firing for the Party now posted there, Your Memorialist doubts not of Your Lordships kind Interference. That Your Memorialist reported to the Deputy Commissary General a Quantity of Hay, Corn and Potatoes on the Island of Prudence in the Narrow Ganset Bay, the Property of Your Memorialist, which said Corn and Potatoes were pilfered and taken away by some Seamen from his Majesty's Ships, a certain part of which Hay was appropriated to his Majesty's Use and the Remainder burnt and destroyed, the whole computed at the Value of [estimated at] one hundred and sixty Pounds consisting of fifty Tons of Hay, one hundred Bushels of Corn and one hundred Bushels of Potatoes, and,

It is with Regret your Memorialist must beg leave to say, that a fine Grove of Wood, not only ornamental, enhancing the Value of the Farm, but the cool Retreat, the public Resort of the Town, was cut down part of which Wood from the Information of his Tenant measuring eighty

Cord was for the Use of the Troops, for Payment of which he presented a Bill of three hundred and twenty Dollars to the Deputy Quarter Master General which was refused which said wood with the other cut and not mensurated is valued at two hundred Pounds Sterling. That many of the Avenue Trees were made Use of for the Purpose of Fascining had it not been for the kind Interposition of Earle Percy the whole must have been wasted and the Beauty of the Farm entirely spoiled, the Loss already sustained thereby cannot be reckoned at a less Value considering it stripped of all it's Inclosures, than two hundred and sixty pounds: Besides which from Information some of the People of his Majesty's Ships Cerberus or Amazon, upon a Shell Fish Party on the said Island of Prudence, burnt two large Dwelling Houses, a Barn, Crib, Dairy House, and other Buildings thereon to the Amount of eight hundred and fifty pounds, by which and the afore recited Acts he humbly conceives he hath sustained a Loss Damage of one thousand Nine hundred and fifty pounds.

Conscious of which and of the Uprightness of his own Conduct amidst the Confusion of the Times, Your Memorialist made Application to Major General Prescot for Redress, to which not the least Attention hath been paid: but Your Lordship's Arrival at this Port affords him the pleasing Satisfaction of having the Premises taken into Consideration, not doubting from Your Lordship's exalted and amiable Character due Justice will be administered him for which as in Duty bound he will ever pray &c

Jnọ Malbone

The preceeding Memorial and Epistle were delivered into the Hands of Charles Waller Esq. Deputy Agent Victualler for his Majesty's Fleet at Rhode Island, who informed Mr Malbone he delivered the same to Captain Duncan (of the Admiral Ship) who promised it should be immediately presented, which appears in the Multiplicity of his Lordship's Business to have been mislaid as no Notice hath been taken thereof.

[1778, Oct. 8, Groton]

To the Honorable General Assembly of the State of Connecticut to be held at New Haven in and for Said State on the 2d Thursday of October AD 1778--

The Petition of Theophilus Avery Joseph Rose & Robert Geer Junr a Committee Appointed by the Members & Professors of the Church of England in Groton to take Care of the Lands Belonging to Said Church in Groton & to Remove the Church to a More Convenient Place, Humbly Sheweth that the Revd Mr Ebenezer Punderson who was formerly Minister or Missionary to Said Church Did when he left this Place about 27 Years ago give to Said Church a Tract of Land Containing about 14 Acres in Groton aforesaid well worth five Hundred Pounds L[awfu]ll Money Bounded Easterly on the Highway Leading from Preston towards the North Meeting House in Groton Southerly on a Farm that Said Punderson's Son Ebenezer Sold to Stephen Hurlbertt Westerly on Land of Mark Newton & Northerly on a Highway and Executed a Deed thereof to the Society in England for Propagating the Gospel in Foreign Parts And the Said Mr Punderson at the Time of Giving said Deed was so sound in the Faith and abundantly Orthodox that in Stead of having the Deed Recorded in

Records of the Town of Groton as he ought to have Done he Sent the Same to the Said Society in England to be Recorded there and the Same never was Recorded in Groton, and the Said Land was without Dispute held Let out and Improved for the Benefit of the Church & its Incumbents untill Since the Declaration of American Independence since which one Mark Newton of Groton aforesaid has unlawfully got into Possession of Said Tract of Land and Put the Said Church & Society out therefrom and Deprived them of the Rents & Profits thereof which is worth £30.0.0 and well Knowing Said Deed is not Recorded in Said Groton takes the unrighteous Advantage of holding the Same from your Petitioners & Said Society & Still holds the Same and the Said Church has Ordered the Same to be said of this Manifest tort by the said unjust Doing of said Marke [&] the Said Church hath Wholly lost the Same unless Relieved by your Honors

   Wherefore Your Petitioners Humbly Pray your Honors to take the Matters aforesaid into Consideration and Appoint a Judicious Committee to Enquire into the Matters Aforesaid and Report Make of what they Shall Find to be Facts with thier Opinion & that the Title of said Land may be Established to Said Church & Said Marke Put out of Possession thereof & Compelled to Pay the Rents thereof whilst he has held Said Land, or in Some other way order & Decree the Title & Use of said Land to Said Church that the Same may be had held & Enjoyed by them According to the Design of Said Mr Punderson who is now Deceased or in some other way Grant Relief as your Honors shall Judge Just & Reasonable and your Petitioners as in Duty Bound Shall Ever Pray
      Dated at Groton the 21st Day of Septr 1778
                              Theophilus Avery
                              Joseph Rose
                              Robart Geer 2d

[1779, Sept. 14, Stratford]
         Stratford in New England, Septbr 14th 1779.
May it please your Lordship.

   We the Clergy of the Church of England, beg leave to introduce the bearer Mr Henry Van Dyck to your Lordship, as a Gentleman of ingenuity, of a Liberal Education, Graduated at Kings College New York in the Degrees of Batcherlor and Master of Arts, hath made good proficiency in the Liberal Arts, and for many Years past hath applied himself to the Study of Divinity, is Orthodox in the Faith of our Excellent Church, A Gentleman of unblemished reputation, of a fine Address, and, of Morals unsullied; we are happy to be able to assure your Lordship that we can give this Testimony from a personal Knowledge of Mr Van Dyck of many Years standing.

   He is a married Man & of more than Age sufficient for Holy Orders, and would have sooner Applied to your Lordship for the same, had it not been for the peculiar Difficulties of the Times, he has, however, for several Years read Prayers and Sermons at Stratford and Newtown to good Acceptance, and should your Lordship upon Examination think him qualified for Holy Orders we doubt not he will make a very Usefull Clergyman.

   We have the Honor to be, / May it please your Lordship, / Your Lordship's Most Obedient Sons & Servants,
                              Richard Mansfield
                              Christopher Newton

Saml Andrews
Bela Hubbard
Abraham Jarvis
Richd Clarke
John Rutgers Marshall
The Lord Bishop of London.

[Addressed:] His Lordship / The Right Reverend, / Robert, Lord Bishop of / London

[The contents of the foregoing were also sent to the Rev. Dr. Richard Hind, Sec. of the S.P.G., London, under the same date and with the same signatures.]

[1780, May 23-25, Derby]
At a Convention of the Clergy of the Church of Engd in Connecticut, held at the Revd Mr Mansfield'[s] Derby, in Trinity Week, in the Year of our Lord 1780   Tuesday Eveng May 23d present--
                              Revd Mr Mansfield
                              -- Mr Scovil
                              -- Mr Andrews
                              -- Mr Hubbard
                              -- Mr Jarvis
                              -- Mr Clarke
                              -- Mr Marshal

   The Convention was open'd, and the Revd Mr Clarke chosen to be the President of this present Convention--
   Mr Scovil chosen to be the Chaplin of the same, and Mr Jarvis, was chosen Secretary. Then proceeded to Business--
   Mr Hubbard acquainted the Convention that he had a Letter wrote by the Revd Mr Cossit to the Revd Mr Viets, which he was desired to lay before the Con: The Letter was order'd to be read--and was read accordingly.
   The contents of the Letter being consider'd, the Convention resolved that a Letter be wrote to Mr clement Sumner, in whose behalf the above Letter was written, acquainting him with what the Con: think proper to suggest as its Opinion and Advice relative to the substance of the Application; and that Mr Andrews draw up a Letter for that purpose   It was next proposed, whether the Conven: would take into Consideratn the Sentiments & Doctrins lately adopted by the Revd Mr Tyler, which was agree'd to-- And then the Convention was adjourn'd to 9. of ye Clock to Morrow Morning--
   Wedn. 24. The Convention was open'd-- It was agreed that a conventional Letter be wrote to Mr Tyler, expressive of their Concern at his Deviation from the Doctrins of the Chh. and their Apprehensions of the Tendency and Conseqs that it will have upon the Chh in general, with respect to her Interest & Union and Harmony: and as advisory relative to what is tho't prudential as to his Conduct: and what they as his Brethren in the Ministry desire and expect from him. And that Mr Scovil, Mr Hubbard, & Mr Jarvis be appointed to prepare a Letter for that purpose; who were accordingly appointed. Then the Convention was adjournd to 4 O. Cl. P.M--and proceeded to Chh--where a Sermon was preachd by the Revd Mr Marshal, ----
   Met according to Adjournment-- and the thanks of

the Convention was voted, and given by the President, to the Revd Mr Marshal for the good Sermon that he hath deliver'd this Day before the Convention--

Major Baldwin, Doctr Clarke, and Doctr Thomlinson, waited on this Convent:n and requested that the Clergy would consider the very destitute State of the Chh at Milford, and in their turns visit that vacant Chh. and favor them in Rotatn with a Sundays Service, each, and as often as may be consistent with their stated Duties in their respective Churches, and the Engagements they are already under--

The Convention concurred with the Request, and agreed to visit and officiate at that vacant Chh successively, in the following Order--Mr Scovil in June, Mr Jarvis in July, Mr Marshal in Augt, Mr Andrews Sept., Mr Hubbard, Octr Mr Clark, Novr, Mr Mansfield, December--

Mr Andrews brought in the letter, he was directed to prepare, to send to Mr Clement Sumner, which was read and approved, and order'd to be forwarded to him--

Adjourn'd until to Morrow Morning--

Thursdy 25, met accordg to Adjournmt   The Letter to Mr Tyler according to Direction was prepar'd, and approv'd, by the Convention, sign'd by order of Convention by the Secretary, to be transmited to him. Agreed to meet in our next Convention on Wednesday in Trinity Week 1781-- at Mr Newton's, if convenient, if not there, at Mr Clarkes-- and

The present Convention is concluded--
Signed by
Abraham Jarvis ⎫ Secretary

It was order'd that Mr Shelton be enter'd on the Minutes of this Conventn as a Candidate for holy Orders, under the patronage of this Convention--

[1780, Aug., New York]
Dear Sir:

Your favor of the 11th inst. did not reach me, (owing to a particular reason which it is needless now to mention) until the 23d

I immediately complied with your request, and consulted with the following Clergymen separately, and as I could find them, not having it cleverly in my power, though I much wished it, to get them together. The Rector, Dr. Seabury, Mr. Browne, [?Leaming,] Moore, Odell, Sayre, Beardsly, Panten. All of whom I beleive you well know, and are acquainted with. I cannot say we were unanimous in our opinions on the case. One however only, advised a compliance, and backed his opinion with the respectable authorities of Bps. Bull, Sanderson, Usher and Dr. Hammond in the time of the great Rebellion. One other I call a Neutral. He thought no advice could be properly given by us at this distance, being ignorant of many circumstances which ought to guide and govern us in such cases---that you, yourself on the spot, could be the only competent judge, both of your own feelings, and the propriety of it. The rest were of opinion that a compliance would be wrong, if not sinful.

Thus have I given you, in short, the sentiments of your brethren here. It is needless to adduce the arguments that were used pro and con; and perhaps might not be prudent, as the conveyance of letters is precarious.

I have been just writing to London, and have asked Dr. Chandler's opinion of the case; which if I receive, I will take an opportunity of conveying to you. In the mean time may God direct you for the best-- may he soon bring us out of our present distress, and restore to us those blessings of peace and plenty, which we formerly, with so much happiness enjoyed.

. . .

Dr. Inglis has sent you the last abstract; the present year's being not yet arrived. I have the pleasure to acquaint you that the society's fund is very different at present, from what it was at the publication of this abstract. They have had a general collection throughout England, and the largest ever known since they have been a Corporation amounting to 20000£ sterling, besides a legacy of 2000£ sterling, by one of the London clergy, viz: Mr. Hecksball, Rector of St. Ann's, Aldergate....
Samuel Cooke

[Rev. Dr. Abraham Beach at New Brunswick, N.J.]

[1781, June 12-13, Litchfield]
At a Convention of the Clergy of the Church of England in Connecticut, holden at Litchfield, at the Revd Mr James Nichol's, Wednesdy in Trinity Week, in the Year of our Lord 1781-- Tuesday Eveng June 12. present
Revd Messrs Mansfield
Scovil
Andrews
Viets
Hubbard
Jarvis
Tyler
Clarke
Marshal
Nichols

The Convention was open'd, and the Revd Mr Viets was chosen to be the president of this present Convention-- Mr Andrews was chosen to be the Chaplain of the same-- And Mr Jarvis was chosen to be the Secretary--

Then proceeded to Business,-- The Minutes of the last Con: were order'd to be read, & were read accordingly--

Mr Bostwick being not present, who is expected to preach the conventional Sermon, in Case he comes: on failure it is voted that Mr Andrews preach the Sermon in the Morning. It was agreed that there be a 2d Service, and that Mr Jarvis preach the Sermon, Mr Hubbard to read prayers in the Morning: And that Mr Viets read Prayers in the Afternoon. The President adjourn'd the Conventn until 7. O. C. to Morrow Morning--

Wednesdy Morng Met accordg to Adjournmt-- adjourn'd to attend Church-- After divine Service, Conventn was open,d and the Thanks of the Con-- was voted to be returnd by the presidt to the Revd Mr Andrews for his very good Sermon deliverd this Day-- Thanks accordgly were return'd-- And then Con. was adjourn'd to attend the 2d Service, the Sermon was preach'd by Mr Jarvis, to whom for sd Sermon, the Thanks accordg to Custom, was voted, & return'd by the President--

A Petition was brot in by Mr Nichols from the People

of Cornwal for the Approbation of ye Con-- that Mr Allen
a young Gentleman of that Town should read prayers & Sermons to them; the Con-- approv'd the proposal and gave
Encouragm^t to him, that in Case he qualified himself sufficiently the Con-- would give him their Interest to obtain
a Degree from some College, that he may be properly prepared to be recommended for holy Orders, should the State
of ye public admit of their so doing. The Con-- was adjourn'd to Thursd^y Morn^g--

Thursd^y Morn-- met accord^g to Adjournment--
noth^g com^g before the Conv-- for Entry-- the Convent^n
voted to meet at Middletown on Wednesd^y in Trinity Week
of ye next Year, 1782. Mr Bostwick to preach ye Sermon,
in Case of failure, Mr Nichols is appointed the sec^d to be
prepared. The Con: was concluded

Signd by
Abraham Jarvis } Secretary--

[1781, Aug. 24, New York]
[Dear Sir,]

I told you that about this time twelvemonth I answered
a letter of yours upon a particular subject---sent you the
opinion of your brethren resident in this city, on that subject. I told you that I would ask the advice and opinion of
Dr. Chandler. I accordingly did so, and about five weeks
ago I received an answer dated so long since as October
last, of which the following is an extract.

"The extract from Beach's letter, which you have given
me, is much to his honor; it discovers in him such a principle and disposition as I am always pleased to see in any
of our brethren. He will not enter upon a measure, though
it appears to him of importance, without the approbation or
at least the advice of the clergy in New York. It seems
that you were not quite unanimous in your opinion, and you
ask me for mine. Though the case will have been determined before this can reach you, I think myself obliged to
send you a few observations upon it.

"To depart from a standing rule, established by Legal
Authority, and to which we have promised and sworn conformity, on the supposition of the utility of such a step,
and without a dispensation, must, in an ordinary way, fall
under the condemnation of doing evil, that good may come.
Yet where law and order are totally subverted through the
wickedness of others, and we see an opportunity of giving
support to an unquestionably good cause by such a measure
as would be unjustifiable in other circumstances, I am by
no means such a Casuist as to condemn every compliance
however small. For it may be presumed that our Superiors, were they acquainted with our prospects and motives,
would dispense with, or not condemn a discrete and temperate accomodation of ourselves to the times. But the
danger is, that when we have once departed from established rules, we shall know not where to stop---that compliance in one instance naturally lead to it in a second, and
that omissions are productive of Commissions. The good
therefore in view ought to be great and unquestionable and
the resolution not to proceed from Concession to Concession ought to be inflexibly established, before transgress-
ing the legal boundaries can be warrantable.

"About two years ago I was desired by the Clergy of
Connecticut through Dr. Seabury to consult the Archbishop
and Bishop of London, on this very case, which I accord-

ingly did. I reported to Dr. Seabury, that they did not
choose to give a formal consent or opinion upon the matter, but that if the clergy unanimously thought that the use
of the Liturgy, with only the omission of the prayers for
the King and Royal Family, were expedient, in the present state of things, and should act accordingly, they need
not apprehend the censure of their Superiors here. I suppose that the experiment was tried in Connecticut, and as
it appears from your letter that Messrs Leaming and Sayre
did not wish to see it repeated in New Jersey, I conclude
that it had failed of success.

"On the whole, the clergy in New Jersey are so few
that but little benefit can be expected from a general compliance, and unless it be general and unanimous, it can
hardly be justified; and I would use no unwarrantable steps
even in supporting the tottering Ark, through a distrust in
Divine Providence."

Thus far Dr. Chandler---What use you will make of
his advice must be left entirely to your own judgement
and discretion, who, being on the spot, and best knowing
your own situation, and particular circumstances, must
certainly be better capable of judging for yourself, than
it is possible for us to judge for you. We can only pray
to God to direct you for the best, and to prosper you in
all your undertakings.

Every good man, my dear sir, must lament the fate
of this unhappy war, attended as it is with such ruinous
consequences to both countries---must equally wish for
a restoration of Peace, and that ancient harmony which
once subsisted between them....

Samuel Cooke

[1782, Jan. 11, Brooklyn--Pomfret]

The Revd Daniel Fogg of this Town having made Application to us, the Select Men, representing his desire of
going to New York, in order to recover a considerable sum
of Money, which is due to Him in England: We do not apprehend that the Publick would receive any Injury from
Granting Him, this Favour, as he has conducted Himself
in a peaceable & quiet Manner since our Contest began
with great Britain.

In Testimony whereof We have hereunto affixed our
Names at Pomfret this 11th January 1782

To all Whom it may Concern.

Peter Chandler	Elijah Williams } Select
Ebenezer Weeks	Seth Grosvenor } Men

[1782, Jan. 16, Brooklyn--Pomfret]

To the Honble the General Assembly of the State of Connecticut now sitting at Hartford by Adjournment, the Memorial of Daniel Fogg of Pomfrett in ye County of Windham,
Clerk, humbly sheweth,   That in May 1772, he was appointed a Missionary to & for the episcopal Church in Pomfrett afores^d, with a Salary of Thirty Pounds Sterling per
Annum, by the Society in England for propagating the Gospel in foreign Parts, ---That ever since his said Appointment he hath continued to discharge the Duties of his said
Office to the present Time; That there is now due to him
seven Years Sallary for his said Services, which he is
greatly in Want of, for his Support, as it is almost his

whose Dependance for his Subsistance; and that he knows of no Way in which he can procure the same without going to New York to negotiate the Affair, which he can not do without a Permit from your Hon^rs. Wherefore your Memorialist humbly prays your Hon^rs to grant him the Indulgence of a Permit to go to New York for the Purpose aforesaid, under such Regulations & Restrictions, & in such Way as your Hon^rs in your Wisdom shall judge expedient & the same to bring out in hard money only, & to return as soon as the same is accomplished   And he as in Duty bound, will ever pray. Dated at Pomfrett the 16th Day of Jany AD: 1782

Daniel Fogg

In the lower house
    The prayer of this Mem^l negative[d]
Test S. M. Mitchell Clerk

[1782, Jan. 16, New York]

New York Jan 16. 1782

Sir,
    We the Subscribers have taken into Consideration the Circumstances of ye Chh at Middletown in Connecticut w^h was formerly a Mission: and we wish the Society in their wisdom may think proper to revive it again; otherwise we fear the Chh in y^t part may suffer much. And we imagine ye Society w^d be of our Opinion, if y^y knew of how much importance it is to Support ye Chh in y^t large town: In ye County of Hartford w^h contains upwards of fifty thousand Souls; there is only Hebron and Simsburry beside Middletown y^t have Chh. The good people of this Town have bought a house and Glebe, w^h cost £400 Sterling, and have contributed to the Support of the Revd Abraham Jarvis, for 16 Years past, as far as y^y c^d: but these distressing times render it more difficult than ever.
    We verily believe ye End and Design the Society have in View w^d be as fully answered in every particular, in reviving the Mission in this Town, as in any that are now under their Care.
    And Mr Jarvis, for his prudent Conduct, his faithfulness in discharge of his Office, together with his firm attachment to the British Constitution in Chh and State, is deserving the favour we request for him

Jeremiah Leaming

To the Secretary of the Society
for the propagation of the Gospel
in foriegn parts--

[This is a rough draft; the original letter, doubtless, had other signatures.]

[1782, Oct. 15, Stratford]
    To the Hon^l General Assembly of the State of Connecticut now sitting at Hartford, the Memorial of the Professors of the Church of England in Stratford & Milford in s^d State humbly sheweth
    That they have been long destitute of the regular Administration of Gods Word & Sac[r]aments in the manner in which their Consciences direct them to worship the Father of Spirits. That they are extremely desirous to settle a regular Ordain'd Minister amongst them. And

for that purpose wish for an Opportunity to attend upon the Ministerial Administrations of the Revd James Sayre late of Fredericksburg in the State of New York now resident at Brooklyn on Long Island in s^d State & to Invite him to Preach amongst them on Probation-- The Character of this Gent^n they are advised is that of a pious worthy Clergyman who has never actively Interested himself in the Controversy between Great Britain & the United States of America but was sent within the Enemies Lines in Consequence of certain scruples of Conscience he at that time Entertain'd relative to taking the Oath of Fidelity prescribed by s^d State of N York, & has there kept himself entirely to the Line of his Duty as a Clergyman-- That y^r Memor^ts would not by any means wish to settle this Gent^n amongst them unless it sho'd appear upon experience & Observation that he would probably become a good Citizen of the State as well as a useful Minister of the Gospel & do not therefore at present request a permission absolutely to call & settle this Gent^n amongst them, but only humbly beg the favour of y^r Hon^s to permit the s^d Revd Mr James Sayre (with his Wife Family & Effects) to come into this State & to Preach to y^r Memor^ts on Probation for the space of three or four Months under such Inspection & Observation as y^r Hon^s shall think proper & y^r Mem^ts as in Duty bound shall ever pray &c.
    Dated at Stratford Octr 15th 1782.

Eben^r Allen⎫ Chh Wardens of the Chh at
Eli Lewis ⎬ Stratford

Dav^d Baldwin   ⎫ Chh Warden's Chh at
Abr. Tomlinson⎭ Milford

Negatived in the lower house
Test S. M. Mitchell Clerk

[1782, Oct. 16, Fairfield]
    The Subscriber, being requested by some Gentlemen of Stratford to say what he knows respecting the Revd Mr James Sayers, testifieth and sayeth, that the Revd Mr James Sayers, came to Fairfield sometime in Decr 1774, when he understood that he came directly from England-- That in the Spring 1775 he went to Fredrickborgh where he was setled in the ministry; where he continued in the Ministry to good acceptance (as I have been inform'd) untill sometime in 1776; when some of his discourses on passive obedience and nonresistance gave uneasiness to the people; and in November 1776 he was sent by the Committee of New York State, to Springfield in Massachusetts State where he continued through part of the Winter, & returned by order into New York State, when he was ordered to take a perticular Oath required by their Law, and on refusal to go into the Enemies Lines-- He refusing, the Committee ordered him with his Family to go into the Enemies Lines, with Liberty to take with him all his moveable effects-- Sometime in the Spring 1777, Mr Sayers's Wife being a native of Fairfield, and with her Mother, Mr Sayer requested that she would come to Long Island to him-- in consequence of which application was made to the Governor and council of Safety, for Liberty for her to go in, which, as I understand, was granted; but to be under the inspection of General Silliman and the Selectmen of the Town--who permitted her to carry with her the furnature and effects, she then had with her

at Fairfield-- That, as I am informed by Letters and otherwise he made Brooklyn on Long Island his place of aboad, and officiated in the Ministry at different places, solicitious to do all the good he could; and not with standing he had several offers of being a Chaplain to a Reg^t he refused, upon the principle that he would take no active part in the War-- That from the acquaintance I have with him, he is a Man of a good heart, ever, endeavoring all in his power to promote christianity, and do all the good he can--

Thaddeus Burr

Fairfield Octob. 16. 1782   Personally Appeared Thad^s Burr Esq. & made Solemn Oath to the Truth of ye Above
           Before Me   And^W Rowland. Jus. P^s
Opened in the General Assembly at Hartford Octr 2^d Thursday 1782

Test   George Wyllys Secret^y.

[1782, Oct. 30, New York]
                 New York Oct. 30. 1782
Dear sir,

The 29 Ins^t I rec^d Your fav^r of the 15 Augt with Mr Baxters Sermon. I wish it had appeared in the form of State pamphlet rathar [than] a Sermon, as its maxims were all founded in State policy. As a Sermon, if he would not be tho't a Brimstone preacher, he should have put on a milder Aspect; that when a man Smighteth on one cheek, he may turn to him the other: while State policy dictates Retaliation, true Divinity requires forgiveness.

If Jarvis and Marshall can be provided for, it would be esteemed a favour. I hope You and Dr Chandler may be able to accomplish so desirable an Event--Especially when the Society take a Just View of the State of the Church in North America, they will find that the only hope of the future Support of the Church must be from Connecticut. The Good Seed sown there, by a united Clergy, is now Springing up; and will produce a plentiful Crop, if it is but properly watered. And I doubt not, but the Divine Spirit will accompany the well meant, and Judicious Labours of the Clergy. Whether it is from the Conduct of the Civil Rulers, or that of the Clergy, or both together, the Church is in a prosperous way in Connecticut. The Clergy have Supported their Characters, as honest men, while the Dissenting Teachers, have lost theirs, and have been so devout in praying for their great and Good Ally; after frighting the people out of their Senses, because the Romish Relition, (as they said) was Established in Canady, that the populace now have no Confidence in them. The Church there must have a Bishop in some future day: when a Bishop in England will have so much of an Apostolic Spirit as to give an Apostle to Connecticut. If that Government could have a Bishop for themselves they will Support him; and they would find no dificulty in doing of it-- For the people of that Church believe Religion, and have shewn they believed it, by suffering for it, in these infatuated Times, and have Supported their Characters as honest men and good Christians, against those who forgot humanity, and every amiable Qualification.

You found fault that my last Letter was too short, I Suppose you will find fault with this as too long; unless I had said more to the purpose.

My best regards to your dear Girl-- Phebe Joins in love with Your Sincere friend
               H. Grimael
               [i.e., Jeremiah Leaming]

[1783, May 6, Waterbury]
               Waterbury May 6th 1783
Reverend Sir,

After a long and disagreeable Cessation of Correspondence with the Venerable Society, we the Clergy of Connecticut met in voluntary Convention, embrace with Pleasure this early Opportunity, unitedly to return them our sincere Thanks, for the continuance of their Kind Support, dureing the Progress of the late Dispute, which hath at last, contrary to our Wishes and Hopes, terminated so calamitously as in a total seperation of this Country, from the Government and Protection of the Parent State.-- We are bound in duty to acquiesce in the Alotment of Divine Providence; and it will be our Care to approve ourselves wholesom Members and Peacable Subjects of the Government & Laws in being under which we are now placed: but we can never without Regret look back to the loss of those Days anticedent to ye late unhappy contest, which compleeted the Separation.

By this Event, the Episcopal Church in America, degraded as it is by the loss of its former Head and Protector, seems left to the Mercy of its Enemies, without any spiritual Power in itself to provide for vacant Parishes as it is destitute of Authority to continue the Succession in the Ministry, and indeed, in the Northern States, is unable to support the few Clergymen which are still left to serve it.----In a Condition of a Church so Unprecedented in the Christian World, and so Calamitous as this, what can its Clergy do? After recommending our Case, the Church, and ourselves to the Patronage and Protection of Almighty God, (of whose Care, we hope we have not rendered ourselves totally Unworthy, tho we have been severely Chastised in Rightiousness) to what human Arm shall we apply for Assistance?----In this Exigence of our Church, we want the Advice--we want the Patronage--we want the Charity of all our Friends and Benefactors--and under God, to whom can we complain and make our Distress known?--and to whom can we apply for Assistance with equal Propriety, on an equal Prospect of Success; as to that Venerable Society in England, to whose defusive Charity and more than Paternal Care the Church here, owes its Rise, its Progress, and its present Existance?--permit us then to ask the further Patronage of the Venerable Society--to beg their Interest in procuring an Episcopate for the Church here; which, tho now Unfortunately separated from the National Establishment, yet Boasts her Pedigree from this Society--We conceive there can now be here no Objection against resident Bishops, as they will be purely Ecclesiasticks, and equally with all other Clergymen, Under the Control of Law and the civil Authority of these States: and we are ignorant upon what Principle of Piety or Policy, the Mother Church can, in this State of Things, reject a Petition so Reasonable and just, and so essential to the Existence of the Church in America.--

Suffer us also in our own behalf, to beg the Venerable Society to continue their kind Support to the Missionary Clergy in Connecticut. Tho' we are now seperated (de-

graded) from being a part of the Nation, we have done Nothing to promote the Separation, but have suffered every Indignity, and every Species of Distress for our steady adhearence to our Oaths, and attachment to the Brittish Government.---- We have dureing the late melancholly Contest exerted ourselves in the Societies Service, to promote the Interest of pure Religion & undefiled, solely to attend to ye duties of our Office, interesting our selves as little as possible in ye late unhappy disputes between ye parent State & this country; and hope our conducts, in our critical Scituation may be approved of by ye venerable Board, chusing to cast a vail over every difficulty & danger with wch we have had to contend, & by ye blessing of God, have surmounted in some measure to impress upon the Consciences of our Hearers the Friendly Doctrines of our own Church and the inflexible Loyalty she teaches: and our Labours have been attended with some Success, for not to mention the large Numbers that have joyned the Brittish Army and fled to it for Protection, from our Parishes, very few have been in the Revolt of those who tarryed behind; most of them have suffered patiently for their Attachment to their Prince, and in this trying Time have supported the Character of good Christians, if not of good Subjects to the States--but what exceeds our most sanguine Hopes, and seems to be the special Effect of Divine Interposition, the Work of God alone is, that notwithstanding the Numbers which have gone from our Parishes within the Brittish Lines, very few of our Congregations have decreased--many of them have greatly increased, and tho Nothing but Danger and Rage seemed to await the Professors of the Church, yet some new Congregations have rissen among us since the Commencement of the War.---- Tho the Church here is not in general much diminished in Numbers, it is however so greatly impoverished & distressed by Plunder and a Train of Expensive Mischiefs, that it seems impossible she should either support her Clergy, or even maintain her Existence in this State, without the Continuation, and indeed in some Instances, the further Extention of the Venerable Societies Bounty; and as we are not conscious that we ourselves or that the great Body of our Parishioners have been guilty of any Crime against either the Brittish Church or State, --we intreat, that to all our former Calamities, this insupportable one may not be added, of being discarded by the Society. Suffer us finally to plead for the Societies Charitable Notice in favour of three Worthy Clergymen in Connecticut, Messrs Jarvis, Marshal, and Nichols; dureing these Times, they have been equal in their Labours, and equal in their Sufferings with the Missionaries--and we intreat that, as a Reward of their Sufferings, and of their Indefatigable Labours in the Vinyard of God, to prevent also their own Penury, and the Extinction of the Churches they Serve, they may be admitted into the Venerable Societies Service.----For a more particular Knowledge of the State of the Church here--of its Wants--of its Wishes--and of Every Thing which concerns its well being, we beg leave to refer the Society to the Reverend Doctor Seabury, with whom we have prevailed to represent our Case to that Venerable Board.

We are Reverend Sir the Societies / and your much Obliged and very / Humble Servants, the Clergy / of Connecticut

Signed by Order of Convention

The Reverend Doctor Morice

Endorsed by Jarvis: "Copy of a letter to the Rev. Dr Morrice...in Mr S. Andrew's Hand writing"

[1783, June 1, Stamford]

         Stamford Connecticut
         New England June 1. 1783.

Reverend Sir

God in his providence opening a door of Correspondence; as in duty bound, with pleasure I embrace the earliest opportunity of advising the Venerable Society of my continuance in the discharge of the duties of my Mission; and agreable to my Original Instructions, to be as extensively useful as may be.

My Situation hath been peculiarly unhappy, difficult and dangerous, so near to New York, and this place a thorough fare for Troops, a Hospital Town during the Continentals continuance at New York, & White Plains; and a Garrisond Town during the 3 last Years, bordering upon the Lines between the two contending Powers.

The Society hath been well Informed, of the difficult part their Missionaries have had to Act; the Obsticles in Duty, the dangers to which the[y] have been exposed, and the special interpositions of providence in their favour; which renders it unnecessary to enter into a minute account of my personal dangers & Sufferings, ascribing my own & families preservation, to nothing but the Special interpositions of divine providence in our favour; chusing to cast a Veil over many past Occurrances, which where a reproach to humanity, and our common Christiany.

The Moral and Religious State of the Country is truly deplorable. Never was a greater Corruption of the Principles and Manners of a people; in consequence of the late troubles, and the Lax state of the Laws of Society.

Notwithstanding all difficulties, dangers and discouragements, I continued in the use of our Excellent Liturgy, without alteration, till the declaration of Indepency. From that period my Church was Shut up, and I continued my private Duty of visiting the Sick, Baptizing of Children, Burying the Dead. This service, was fateagueing, sometimes dangerous, and at the hazard of my Life. In 1779 it was thought, the interest of Religion, the preservation and well being of the Church, required an attendance upon the publick Offices of Religion; I opened my Ch^h on Christmas with such Omissions as gave publick Offence. I have occasionally visited Rye, white plains, sometimes on Sundays, chiefly on Lecture occations, Marrying, Baptizing of Children, Burying their Dead. Not long after the burning of Norwalk, and good Mr Leaming was obliged to retire to New York, that large destitute Church applied to me for Assistance, compassion induced my compliance, and I have attended that Church every fourth Sunday above two Years, both the publick and private duties of it; a large Congregation attends.

The people animated with a primitive Zeal, soon Erected a building for Publick worship, much more convenient than a prive house; hereafter to be converted into a Barn, for the future convenience of a Minister, when they shall be able to build a new Church. There are sundry late accessions to the Church, and from Seventy to Eighty constant communicants. The Church itself at Stamford hath suffered considerable damage, but Escaped better than was expected. The Church at Rye is

demolished, the Inhabitants in an unhappy State, while between the Lines. The Church at Horsneck Nodding to Ruin,
but worth repairing, and which they promise, as soon as
they can collet and gather a little Strength-- The broken
State of the professors of the Church at Horsneck, preventing my attendance on Sundays since last October, the
good people at Danbury, about thirty Miles distant, having
obtained repossession of their Church, long detained for
a publick Continental Storehouse, most importunately requested the time I allotted to Horsneck; and I have attended them every fourth Sunday; a large Congregation always
attended. The Church there, and in general Increases in
number and reputation. As soon as the professors of the
Church at Horsnect, gather Streng, can repair the Ch^h,
as I expect in the fall, Shall attend duty there. The members of my Church at Stamford, as in other places, hath
suffered extreemly in the late unhappy troubles, by Taxes,
Retaliations, transportations and imprisonments. Great
numbers fled for refuge under ye protection of Government. Upwards of thirty Families, beside a great number
of Young men. Two Sons of mine, One wth a large family,
now gone to Nova Scotia.--

Some through fear, neglecting the publick worship have
contracted a habit of Negligence, but few have renounced
their profession, or induced to take an active part, during
the late unhappy times. Nevertheless I have a good Congregation, about 50 Communicants, and of late sundry respectable accessions of heads of families; So that, notwithstanding I have almost ran my Race, being almost 69; Yet
as the Church rises in publick Estimation, I hope by the
quiet and peaceable submission of its members to the Will
of heaven, and the new Government in being to see it flourish, praying for the peace thereof, as in their Peace, we
shall have Peace. God grant the late troubles may serve
to promote the refinement and purification of his Church,
and the late fiery trials, revive a spirit of true primitive
Christianity.

I have given the holy Eucharist at Norwalk, once in
eight weeks, have had from about 70 to 80 constant Communicants. Since my last advice to the Venerable Society
I have Baptized 621 Children. Adults 15. Married 61.
Buried 72.

My Parishioners, through Inability in part, and haveing
no taxes laid upon them for the support of Religion nor the
benefit of Law to tax themselves, have contributed little towards my Support, for Years past; My own, and the Glebe
Lands have been in a good measure laid Wast, by the destruction of the Fences, 50£ Sterling would not make good
the damage.

The Intention was to distress me beyond measure, but
by the Charity of the Venerable Society, and the voluntary
contributions of the people among whom I have Officiated,
I have been able to keepe my family together and attend my
Duty; which engroses all my time, and is pretty burdensome in the decline of life.--

For 2 or 3 Years past, I have enjoyed greater peace,
and more indulgence than formerly, in attending my Duty
without the Lines; from the Politeness & humanity of the
Commandants upon the Lines. All such Obstructions are
now removed, by the blessing of Peace, if we are worthy
to enjoy the blessings of it.--

I have this day drawn a Set of Bills for 50£ Sterling
in usual form (which compleats my Salary to Easter term

last) upon John Bacon Esqr the Societies Treasurer, in
Favour of Messrs Willim Fitch & J^o William Holly in
Company, or Order.--

Hoping for the continuance of the Societies Charity,
on which the present support of the best of Churches depends, the greatest bond of unity of Spirit; and praying
God to bless, prosper, Succeed and reward, their most
pious and charitable desings, I am, with my humble Duty
to the Venerable Board, and grateful Acknowledgements
of past favours, --

	Reverend Sir
NB. Never was a few	Your most Obedient
Bibles; common Pray^r	Humble Servt,
Books & more, and	and Brother in Christ
gratefully accepted	Ebenezer Dibblee

The Reverend Docto Morice Secretary of the Venerable
Society for the Propagation of the Gospel in Foreign Parts.

[1783, June 4, New Milford]

New Milford June 4th 1783
Reverend Sir,
It is with the highest Pleasure, that, I write to the
venerable Society acquainting them, that by the Blessing
of God, I enjoy, at present a State of health, and after
shuting up the Church for about 15 Months, at the time
they were generally shut in Connecticut, since which
time, have not been molested in my sacred Employment,
and have constantly devoted myself to the society's Service in the important Duties of my Mission, and in vacant
Parishers, by Request of the People in the several towns
of Stratford, Milford, Redding, Newtown, & Ridgefeild.--
I visited Poughkeepsie Sep^t last at which time I baptized
40 Infants and 2 Adults-- At Salisbury where there is a
large Body of respectable Episcopalians, have frequently
visited as they and Sharon are a United People

I have wrote to the Society since the Commencent
of the unhappy contest, but least the advices contained in
those Letters should have failed, I will give the Society an
account of the Number I have baptized since the year 1776,
Infants 635 Adults 13 and married 38 Couple. my Parishoner[s] being so greatly reduced as to their Wealth and
Numbers having fled to different Parts within Districts of
the Brittish Arms (and from the first of my coming among
them having been very Negligent in making good their Engagements to me) and that Part of my support, which depended on the People, having so long fail'd me, that I am
reduced to a Necessitous Condition, and not able by any
means to support my family under my present Scituation;
therefore, beg the venerable Society would be pleas'd to
give me leave to remove to the Missions either of Fairfield, or Salem, if to Fairfeild with my usual allowance
from the Society, at least, if to Salem withe the former
Sallery to that Mission, suffer me to repeat the earnest
desire I have of being removed to one of the above Places.

I have drawn Bills of Exchange on the Society's Treasurer dated Sep^t 25th 1776 down to Mar 25th 1783 in favour
of Elias Shipman and Cong. Abiathar Camp Elijah Brard-
man and Revd John R Marshall

I am Reverand Sir your / and the Society's much
Obliged and very hum^bl / Servt

Richard Clarke

[Addressed:] The Reverend Doctor Morice / Hatton Garden. / Secretary to the Society for the / Propagation of the Gospel in foreign / Parts. / London
[Endorsed: Read] July 1783.

[1783, June 18, Simsbury]
At a Convention holden at Simsbury in Connecticut on Wensday in Trinity Week June 18th 1783. Present
Messrs James Scovil   John Tyler.
          Samuel Andrews   Gideon Bostwick
          Roger Viets.   Daniel Fogg.
          Bela Hubbard.   John R Marshall
          Richard Clark   James Nicholls.

Voted, the Revd Daniel Fogg President; & the Revd John R Marshall, secretary, to this Convention.

This Convention adjourned 'till to Morrow Morning 8 o'Clock.--

Wednesday Morning, the Convention met according to Adjournment: & proceeded to Business.-- At 11 o Clock. Attended Divine Service at St Andrews Church, w[h]ere a Sermon was preached by Mr Nicholls of Litchfield, & for which he received the thanks of this Convention.

Voted. the next Convention to be held at New Milford, &, that, Mr Fogg be the preacher, & Mr Dibblee the Second.

Business ended, this Convention was Adjourned to Wednesday Next in Trinity Week, at New Milford--
          Tes^{ts} John R Marshall: secretary,

[1783, July 17, Boston]
                                        Boston July 17 1783
Dear Sir
Yours of the 2^d Instant I received sometime since & have replied thereto by a Mr Cady of Plainfield but suspect he is not yet left this Town; having sold a Bill of £25 St^g for Judge Lightfoot, he drew an Order on me for the Amo't in favour of this Cady & believe that he has not yet quite spent all the Money, as soon as this is effected I suppose you will be in the Way of getting my Letter by him. This Morn^g yours of the 14 was handed me, the Affair of your not waiting for me I finished in my last. I am glad to hear that the Matter of an American Episcopate is in such a probable Way of succeeding. You ask my Opinion of the Measure. I answer I like the Plan very well & the Person pitched upon tho' personally unknown to me, from the character I have had of him, is the most proper of any. My fears are a little alarmed by the Circumstance of his being a Refugee; Any Persons coming into New England with complete Orders or in character of a Bishop I fear will alarm our Puritans & put them upon devising Means of preventing his tarrying among us. Will they not then take the Advantage of the present Disposition of the Populace tow^{ds} the Absentees & make Use of that Weapon to keep him away? And therefore if a proper Man could be found for that Office, would it not have been more eligible to have pitched upon one that was not an Absentee? As one Bishop would be sufficient for the New England States & New York, I could also have wished that all the Clergy in the five States had been consulted upon the Choice, as that might have proved the Means of objection arising hereafter from his being rather imposed upon them

than the Object of their free choice. The Dean & chapter of the Diocese with whom the Right of electing a Bishop is vested in England, must be represented in this Country by all the Parochial clergy within his Jurisdiction. However I am far from a Desire to start any Objections to the Plan myself, but only hint these as what might have obviated any Objections that others may hereafter raise. I sincerely wish that the Plan may succeed even beyond our most sanguine Expectations, & that the Doctor may not be obliged to use the Alternative you say he is instructed to do. I have no Doubt in my own Mind that if the Matter is properly conducted he will receive complete Orders from the ArchB^p of Canterbury by a special Mandate from his Majesty. But another Question occurs how will he be supported? He certainly ought to have such a Living at least as will enable him to keep a public Table, for as his House must often be the Resort of other Clergymen, he sh^d be enabled to treat them hospitably, & if he has only the Salary of a Missionary or a common Parish, he will not be in Circumstances to do this. He ought also to have a Curate or chaplain whose Business will be to examine Candidates for Orders & present them as well as to assist him in parochial Duty. The Resolution of this must be an after Consideration.

We had a grand Commencement at Cambridge yesterday when the honorary Degree of Doct^r of Laws was conferred on Mr Bowdoin & that of Doct^r of Physic on Dr Holyoke of Salem. I have had no late Letters from England which I a little wonder at as so many Vessels have lately arrived from thence.

Please to make my best Respects to Mr Malbone & Lady & Niece; I suppose they have received particular Accounts of the Death of Mr Hutchinson which happened the very Day after I was at your House. Miss Betsy Hunter from Newport is now in this Town at Dr Lloyd's & I believe will spend the Remainder of the Summer here-- Nothing special in the political World has occurred lately.
                    I am your friend & Bro[ther]
                              S Parker
PS I expect to have the Fish ready to send by the middle or latter End of next Month--

[Addressed:] Revd Daniel Fogg / at / Pomfret / Hon^d by / Mr Grosvenor

[1784, Jan. 8, Pimlico, London]
                              Pimlico January 8th 1784
I hereby certify that I was at Newhaven in the Colony of Connecticut in Septemb^r 1774 and saw Joseph Pynchon Esqr and many other Gentlemen called Sandemanians barberously insulted by three Mobs (headed by Arnold, Wooster & Mansfield) composed of the Sect called (in their Law Book) sober Dissenters, for refusing to sign the League & Covenant-- the Mobs cried along the streets, that the Sandemanians had proved themselves to be guilty of the damnable Sin of Loyalty to the King of England by not signing the Covenant--" Mr Pynchon had supported a good Character from a Child among the sober Dissenters, had his Education at Yale College, had been Representative in the General Assembly for the Town of Guildford & a Justice of the Peace prior to the year 1770, about which Time, he joined in the religious System (of the Revd Mr Sandeman), which taught Loyalty to the King as a christian Virtue, whereby Mr Pynchon lost

his Reputation with the General Assembly & sober Dissent-
ers--Mr Pynchon strictly adhered to his religious Tenets,
one of which was, to enable the poor (if converted) to live
as well a[s] the rich--he thereby parted with much of his
Property; having been a Merchant & reputed to be a Gentle-
man of Wealth; he moved from Guildford to Newhaven with
Hopes of being better able to support his Religion, Loyalty,
& Integrity, & to render them as conspicuous as were his
Generosity an[d] Piety-- Colonel Fanning at whose Request
I give this Account informed me by his Letter that said
Joseph Pynch[on] with his Wife & Children reside at Shel-
burne in Nova Scotia--

                                        Samuel Peters

[1784, Mar., New York]
Dear Sir,

        Your letter of the 22d inst. I have received, and shall
make no objection to the proposed alteration of the time
and place of meeting; having been taught by woeful experience, that unless some people have their own time and
place on every occasion, there will be no dealing with
them. Thought I feel a little of that obstinacy and perverseness so natural to the human heart, not to indulge
an overbearing character even in the minutest circumstances; yet for the sake of public peace, private resentment should ever be sacrificed, as far as it may be done
with decency and dignity. For I have always been of opinion, (which opinion I have lately had no reason to alter,
that a man may be angry and sin not.

        Would it not be proper to invite our Brethren of Con-
necticut to the intended Convention? Though they have
nothing to do with the "Corporation for the Relief, &c"
yet other matters may come before us in which it will be
expedient to have their concurrence. My great aim and
desire is to preserve uniformity in the Episcopal Church.
It is pleasing in itself, and will be a strong bond in holding us together when so many other ties are rent asunder.

        I do not promise, but I may pay you a visit between
this and the month of May. The Legislature is now debat-
ing upon the business of the Church; while the matter remains in suspense, I cannot well leave the city; there is,
however, too much reason to expect that I shall soon have
"the world before me, where to seek" my place of rest;
and Providence I hope will be my guide.

        There are several vacant Churches in New Jersey, but
can any of them afford bread and meat to a Clergyman?
When we look round, we find the laborers few; while the
harvest, (not the grain but the work of the harvest) is very
plenteous....

                                        Benjamin Moore

[Rev. Dr. Abraham Beach at New Brunswick, N.J.]

[1784, Mar. 1, Mangerville, Nova Scotia]
                        Mangerville. March 1st 1784
My dear Brother.

        Ever since I arrived here I have been confined to my
room, and for the most part to my bed (except that I have
been out very small distances in a Sled two or three times)
with a most distressing disease in my Lungs, which it was
thought for a long time by every body about me would have

finished my pilgrimage; but it has been the good pleasure
of our dear Lord to recover me so far as that I can now
move a little about my room, and have the comfort of
writing to you once more: however I am very far from
being well, and from any idea that I ever shall recover
my usual health.--

        Yet I must acknowlege with gratitude, that thro the
whole of my sufferings I have experienced the nearness
and faithfulness of our Redeemer, in that he comforted
and sustained me constantly; so that when in all appearance my dissolution was very near at hand, I could say,
"tho I pass through the valley of the shadow of death, I
will fear no evil; for thou art with me."--

        If I recover more strength I will give you a longer
Letter at present my weakness compels me to be short.
I will only request you to remember us in the matter of
garden seeds, & if you can send me some by my freind
Mr. Peters who will deliver you this. Farewell my dear
brother & the Lord be with your Spirit, so prays Your
affectte brother

                                        John Sayre

[Addressed:] Reverend Mr Bailey / Annapolis Royal

[1784, Apr. 22, Stamford]
                New England. State of Connecticut
                        April 22. 1784.
Reverend Sir

        I have this day drawn a Set of Bills, in common form,
upon John Bacon Esqr Treasurer of the Venerable Society,
for Twenty five pounds Sterling, in favour of Mr Jacob
Bogardus Merchant in New York.

        No material alteration hath happened within my Cure
since my last. I continue to attend upon the duties of my
Office and Mission, as I have before intimated, both within
and without my Cure. Sundry Accessions have been made
both at Norwalk and Stamford; and some additions to the
holy Communion of the Episcopal Church.

        Thro' the pious Zeal of a few at Horsneck, the Church
is so repaired, that I expect in future to attend divine Service there one Sunday in each Month; hoping they will give
proper attendance upon the publick Offices of Religion, to
the revival of their languishing Zeal, and the promotion of
their future growth and Edification.

        Having been requested very earnestly, by some mem-
bers of the Church, I attended divine Service in a private
house, near North Castle Church, the last sunday in March.
A large Congregation gave a devout attendance; they lament
with good reason their broken destitute state, not having
had divine service, according to the Liturgy of the Episcopal Church, performed among them, since the death of the
late Mr Avery, within whose Cure they formerly were.
Their strength hath been greatly weakened, their number
diminished, by their peculiar unhappy Scituation in our
late troubles; and their Church, within and without in a
ruinous state. They were so animated by having again an
opportunity to unite in the publick Offices of Religion, that
they promised to secure the Church against the Weather,
until they were better able to repair it; and to Associate
with the Chh at Rye, to procure a Reader, until they can
obtain a person in holy Orders.

        I Baptized last half Year seventy six Children; Seven

Adults Married Nine Couple, and buried a number, in and out of my Cure. By the blessing of God I shall continue my attention to the spiritual wants of the people, as I judge will be most conducive to their general good, and as my health and advanced age will permit. Hoping with the blessing of peace to see an enlargement of Christs Kingdom, and a revival of the Spirit of true primitive Christianity. Some Bibles Common prayer books &c were never more wanted, if the Venerable Society according to their wonted goodness, is pleased to bestow them.

Praying for Gods blessing and Rewards to Attend them,
I am with unfeigned Esteem, Reverend Sir
Your most Obed^t
Humble Servant and Brother in Christ
Ebenezer Dibblee

The Reverend Doctor Morris Secretary of the Venerable Society for the Propagation of ye Gospel in Foreign Parts.

[Addressed:] The Reverend Doctor Morice / Secretary of the Venerable Society / for the Propagation of the Gospel / in Foreign Parts / In Hatton Garden / London.
[Endorsed: Read] Oct. 1784

[1784, May, London]
[Dear Sir,]

Had it not been for the change in the ministry, which took place in December last, I should probably by this time have found myself once more in America--either in New Jersey or a little more to the northward. In what manner that change has contributed to delay me, I have heretofore partly informed you, though when I wrote you last, I had no conception that the season would be suffered to advance thus far, before anything was done. But the new ministers have hardly yet ventured to enter upon public business, having but just got through the general Election which has given them for the present, a large majority in the house. The Parliament, however, is now got together, and a farther neglect of those national affairs which call for immediate attention, will appear to be inexcusable.

A plan including a proper general arrangement of the governments of Nova Scotia, Canada, &c has been presented the Administration by Sir G. Carlton, and several Cabinet Councils have already been held upon it. We have reason still to hope that Sir Guy's proposals will be adopted, and that matters will be brought to a decision within ten days or a fortnight. The place proposed for me to fill makes a part of his arrangement; and, it being connected with his plan nothing can be known of it, till the whole is settled. A few days ago I was with the Arch-Bishop. His Grace has lately had a conversation with the present Secretary of State and other ministers, who apologise to him for the delay, and allow that the Church ought to be provided for, in the manner proposed. You see therefore that I have still reason to hope for Success, and this state of suspense will not continue, probably, much longer. Such procrastination is to me mortifying and vexatious; but the most disagreeable part of it is, the apprehension that all the excuses I can make, will not prevent Mrs. Chandler's patience from being worn to tatters, though she seems to have a tolerable stock of that necessary commodity.

There is another important subject which I will venture to mention: I wish that full security could be given me, that this letter shall not fall into improper hands! It is possible that you may know that the Clergy of Connecticut agreed in recommending Dr. S. for Episcopal Consecration, requesting that he might be sent over to take care of the Church in that country, and that he might be allowed to enjoy some part of the Society's funds appropriated to the support of Am. Bishops; On his arrival here last Summer, he opened the proposal to the two Arch-Bishops and the Bishop of London. Upon consideration, they did not then think proper to encourage it, especially as it was apprehended that such a measure would be disagreeable to the State of Connecticut, and might involve Government in trouble. Since that time their legislature have passed an act, allowing to the Church, as well as to other Religious Denominations, a complete toleration, and liberty to enjoy all its institutions. Of this, Leaming, Jarvis, and Hubbard, the Committee of the Convention, have written home an ample account which arrived six weeks ago; but omitted to send a copy of the act which the clerk of the Assembly had transcribed and authenticated, and which was promised to be sent by the same conveyance. Since that, another packet has arrived, but the Act is still due. However, for a month past, I have been of opinion that Dr. S. would succeed so far as to be consecrated, though there is no chance of his enjoying any allowance [?from] our Episcopal Fund, which is insufficient for the support [of] our own Episcopate in Nova Scotia. This want of support for a Connecticut Bp, without any security that he will be supported or prevented from the necessity of returning to his country, in a mendicant capacity, has, within a few days, been started as another insuperable difficulty; and I begin to doubt whether his business will go forward or not. If it fails, he will settle in Nova Scotia....

Thomas Bradbury Chandler

[Rev. Dr. Abraham Beach at New Brunswick, N.J.]

[1784, May, Middletown]
My Dear Sir,

On the first instant, I received your favor of the 15 April; I trust that Mr. Hubbard has answered your letter to him, and acquainted you that it was impossible that any of the Clergy of Connecticut should attend your proposed Convention.

I certainly do join with you in thinking that our Church at this time stands in the utmost need of the firm and efficient exertions of all her true sons. I also think that her true sons should deliberately consider that her affairs require much circumspection and caution. And I will venture to beleive that you will join with me in thinking that the Christian Church is not a mere peice of secular manufacture, indifferently to be wrought into any shape or mould, as the Political potter fancies. We in Connecticut devoutly wish, for ourselves, and for all in the American States professing the same Church, to retain the religious polity--the primitive and evangelical doctrine and discipline, which at the Reformation were restored & established in the Church of England: and to complete and perpetuate that polity in this country, by the obtaining and

fixing among us, a genuine Apostolical Episcopate----
To set out right, and to lay the Foundation of the Church
properly in the beginnings of this new Empire, we judge
to be a matter of the utmost consequence. Accordingly,
that the Church among us, might be complete in all her
members, as a primary object, the Clergy of Connecticut
adopted a measure, and some time past essayed to carry
it into effect, to obtain that desirable end, and we are now
waiting with concern to know the event. If we succeed,
we shall then be able to convene in the full powers of our
Church to consult and endeavor to settle whatever may be
necessary for Union and Uniformity in all the Offices of
Worship and Administrations in the Church. If we fail in
the attempt which remains as yet undecided, we shall be
glad of the united exertions of all who wish well to our religious constitution to accomplish that particular by such
measures as shall be regular and practicable. So far as
I am able to speak the sense of our clergy, it is that we
can take no step to any particular or general measure,
until we know the issue of what we have already done.

I know not that our council or advice, if we had any
to offer, would be of any weight, or if we could be present, could with right act, or have any consideration in the
decisions of a Body of which we should be no part.

May you have wisdom to act, and whatever is done,
God grant may be well done....

Abraham Jarvis

[Rev. Dr. Abraham Beach at New Brunswick, N.J.]

[1784, June 8, New Milford]
At a Convention of the Clergy of the Church of England
of Connecticut holden at New Milford June 8, 1784--at
the Rev^d Mr. Clarke's Tuesday Even-- Present
Revd Messe^rs Jer: Leaming
Richd Mansfield
Roger Veits
A. Jarvis
Richd Clarke
Gideon Bostwick
J. R. Marshall--

This Convention open'd and Rev^d Mr. Leaming was
chosen president-- Mr. Fog, who was appointed at the
last Con: to preach the Sermon before this Con: not being
arrived, it was thot desirable in case of his Failure, to
appoint a Preacher in his place. The Rev^d Mr. L--g was
accordingly chosen to preach the Sermon tomorrow, before the Con--

Mr. Jarvis was appointed to read prayers in the Morning, and if there a 2nd Sermon desired, to preach in the
afternoon. (Insert--Mr. Jarvis being unwel, Mr. Bostwick
read in the Morng.)

Mr. Bostwick was appointed to read prayers-- After-
noon--Mr. Moore preached & Mr. Bloomer read prayers.

The Committee appointed to carry into Execut^n the
Vote of Convent^n at Wallingford in Jany last, made th^t Report to this Convent^n of w^t they had done and read the letter they had written to Dr. S--y, whh was approved by the
Conv: then the Conv: was adjourned by the Presid^t to Wed:

Wed: Morn: Rev^d Mr. Beach from N. Jersey, and
Rev^d Mr. Bloomer & Moore from N. York, arrived, &

joined this Convent^n--which met, and proceeded to Church
--after Morng. Service, Notice was given that there would
be Service in the Afternoon & Sermon w^d be prach'd by the
Rev^d Mr. Moore--

Wed: Even. Con: was opened, and the Thanks of the
Con: was returned to Mr. L--g & Mr. Moore for their ex-
cell^t Sermons this day delivered before them--

The Practice of the Candidates in constantly deliver^g
their own Compositions, when they read divine Service,
was considered, & the conven: came to this Resolution--
that they do not approve of the Candidates deliver^g Sermons of their own compos: oftener than once in a Quarter
of a Year, and that they be previously inspected & approved by a Clergyman--and further that this Con disapprove of the Candidates leaving the read^g Desk in any part
of the Service they perform in public--and that each Candidate be furnished with a Copy of this Resolution--

Convention adjourned by the President to Thursday
Morn^g.

Thursd: Convent: opened, and entered upon Business--

Messrs. Beach, Bloomer & Moore, as a Committee
from a Convent^n of the Clergy of Pennsylvania, N. Jersey,
N. York, held at New Brunswick, to this Convention, communicated the purport of their particular Business, which
was to invite this Con. to enter into a Correspondence with
them, for the setting a Uniformity in ye Epis: Chh, & to
meet them in a Convent^n proposed to be holden at N. Y. on
the Tuesday after the Feast of S. Michael.

To whh this Con: agreed, and appointed Messr^s L--g
(Leaming), M--d (Mansfield) and J--v (Jarvis), the committee to form a Plan, for such Settlement, and to report
the same to the Conven: that will be held at N. H. the Time
of the Commencement in Septem^r--

Then it was agreed to, that our next annual Conven:
sh^d be at the Revd Bostwick in G. Barrington: and Mr.
M--d was appointed to preach the Conven: Serm: in case
Mr. Fogg, and Mr. Dibble who stand the next Preachers
by a former appointment sh^d both fail in th^r Attend--e
And then this Conven: was adjourned by the President.

A. Jarvis, Secretary.

[1784, June 19, New Brunswick, N.J.]
Dear Sir,

I have just returned from Connecticut, where I accompanied Mr. Bloomer and Mr. Moore, and at their desire, am now to acquaint you that the clergy there seem
well disposed to join the Episcopal church in the other
states in forming regulations for the government of it,
and for preserving uniformity of worship. They indeed
made some objections with regard to Lay Delegates. We
informed them in answer to their objections, that it was
thought necessary in some of the states, particularly in
Pennsylvania, to associate some respectable characters
of the laity in order to give weight and importance, to the
Church--but that we meant not to prescribe to other states
the mode of procuring a representation of the Episcopal
Church in their respective states--provided the End was
obtained, we would not differ with them as to the means,
if they were fair and honest. They replied that they
thought themselves fully adequate to the business of
representing the Episcopal church in their state, and
that the laity did not expect or even wish to be called in

as delegates on such an occasion, but would, with full confidence trust matters purely ecclesiastical to their clergy. They accordingly determined unanimously to send a Committee to represent the Episcopal Church in Connecticut at our general Meeting in New York, on the Tuesday after Michaelmas, and engaged likewise to get a representation from the states farther eastward. Thus you see the Committee appointed to attend the Convention in Connecticut have executed the purposes of their appointment; and expect the Committee of Correspondence in Philadelphia will endeavor to get a representation in the more southern states....

                 Abraham Beach

[Rev. Dr. William White at Philadelphia, Pa.]

[1784, Aug. 16, London]

              Old Jewry, London
              16 August 1784
Mr & Mrs Peters

I made all the enquiries that I could of Mr Mauduit, & Mr Bell respecting the subject of your obliging joint Letter dated the 3 July 1783, and I wrote you a full account of the result in my letter dated 1 Septemr 1783, which was addressed to Mr Peters at Middleton agreeable to the direction in your Letter. But as I have heard nothing from you since, I am apprehensive the Letter may have been lost, & has not reached your hands; and therefore I postponed the sending of my Grandfathers Sermons, (mentioned therein) lest they should also be lost for want of a proper direction. Having now an opportunity of sending by a Gentleman (Mr Watson), who is going to America, & intends to land first in New England, I have committed to his care a Parcel addressed to Mr Peters at Middleton, New England; which contains the promised Sermons, & also a Sermon by the present Bishop of Chester, against the Slave Trade, with a Tract also on that subject by a benevolent Quaker, whose Society were likewise at the expence of reprinting the Bishop of Chester's Sermon. In the parcel I have packed likewise a Copy of a Tract which I have lately printed on the ancient Legal Division of the People into Tithings & Hundreds, a form of Government which I recommended in my last. If my Letter of the 1 Septr 1783 should not have come to your hands, be pleased to inform me, & I will immediately send you a Copy of it, which will shew you the state of affairs between you & Mr Bell, whom indeed I have never seen since that time. I would send you a Copy of the Letter by this opportunity but have hardly time to transcribe it before Mr Watsons departure; & besides this would be a needless trouble if you have already received the original.----

I remain with esteem, Mr & Mrs Peters, your freind & most humble Servant

              Granville Sharp
P.S. Mr Watson did not send at the time appointed so that I had time to Copy my Letter of the 1 Septr 1783, which I send inclosed.

[Addressed:] Mr & Mrs Peters / at Middleton / New England / With a Parcel / Per favour of / Watson Esqr
[Endorsed by Samuel Farmar Jarvis that the foregoing letter having been directed to Middletown, Conn., had come into the hands of his father, Abraham Jarvis.]

[1784, Sept. 10, Boston]

              Boston Septemr 10th 1784
Revd Sir

I have the honour to inform you that at a Convention of the Episcopal Clergy held in this Town the 8th Instant it was unanimously concluded that a Letter be sent to the Clergy of the Episcopal Churches in the States of Connecticut New York & Pensylvania urging the Necessity of their uniting with us in adopting some immediate measures to procure an American Episcopate. I now Sir enclose you the Letter voted by said Convention to be sent forward & am instructed to request the favour of you to communicate it to our Brethren in your State in such a manner as you shall judge best. In order for a regular Correspondence upon this Subject with the Clergy of the other States, the Convention have chosen the Revd Mr Bass of Newburypt Mr Fisher of Salem & myself a Committee, & in the Name of said Comtee I beg the favour of you Sir to inform us whether any Steps have been or are taking to settle our Church. We have had no Accounts from the Southern States whether any thing is [in] contemplation among them for the good of the Church, except what has been done at Philadelphia, the Extract from their Minutes has doubtless been communicated to you by Dr White. We have a Rumour also that a Comtee of the Churches from the several States are to convene at New York the first Week in next Month, but are uncertain whether it is really so, Should that be the Case I would by all means endeavour to meet with them, the Convention having done me the honour of choosing me for that Purpose--

We shall be very happy to correspond with you upon this Affair & shall be much obliged for any Intelligence you shall please to favour us with & also for your Sentiments upon that mode of proceeding that you shall think best calculated to promote the Interests of our Church--

Any Letters intended for said Comtee you will please to direct to me as I live more directly in the Line of Communication

         I have the honour to be Revd Sir your
           affectte Brother & very humble Servant
                 Samuel Parker

[Addressed:] Reverend Mr Hubbard / at / Newhaven / Favoured / pr Revd Mr Elliot

[1784, Sept. 10, Stamford]
            Stamford State of
              Connecticut. September 10th, 1784.
My Dear Sir,

I am happy to find by your favour of the 17th of May, the Sunshine of Safety and security in the late Civel Tempest, hath not blotted out of your remembrance your aged Friend and Brother, whose grey hairs will go down with sorrow to the grave.

Many and great, my dear friend, hath been the interpositions of Divine providence, in preserving me and my family, in the late troublesome times, from falling a sacrifice.

Should I enter upon a detail of personal dangers, family troubles, destruction of property, Quartering of Soldiers upon us, laying Waste my own & Glebe lands, the attempts upon my life; the flight of my Sons, and a

great number of my Parishoners; the distresses of them that remained, and were determined to ride out the Storm, or perish in the Ruins of the Church & Country; together with my being cut off from all ye means of my family support for 7 or eight years, except that was handed in, or cast into our Lap by private Charity; it would fill a Volume; it would amaze a disinterested and unprejudiced observer: You can form some Idea of it from a Specimen of Your own unhappy Experience.

I choose to cast a Vail over, rather than, enter upon a partic-recital of past Occurances, many of which were a reproach to a Christian Name & Character, and which the best of Causes, Civil or Religious can never Justify.

Nevertheless, what ever I have suffered personally or relatively; Under God, our preservation hath been owing to some worthy Characters, in Civil Authority, and Officers of the Military Line; from whom, I have received protection from Violence, countenance and encouragement to persevere in attending upon the Duties of my Office, Publick and private, since the opening of my Ch^h on Christmas, 1779; having been shut up from the declaration of Independency to that period.

Great hath been the burden of Duty I have to perform in the decline of Life, but that uncommon share of health I have been favoured with hath enabled me to go through with it; and the Continuance of the Venerable Societys Charity, hath been a temporal Consolation, without which, I must have sunk under reproach. No tax hath been levied and collected for my Support since 1774, in my Cure till ye present year. £50 sterling will not repair the Damage done to my Own and the Glebe Lands, in the destruction of Fence &c. But blessed be God, a Remnant of the Episcopal Ch^h hath been preserved; Since the Peace, it Rises and Increases in Number & Reputation; hath found favour with the Government in being, and by a late Act is placed upon a liberal and respectable Establishment, being Invested with equal power & privilege with ye Presbyterian Established Church, for ye support of Religion the building and repairing of Churches, which opens a prospect to our faith of its future Increase; if an Episcopate may be obtained to support ye Credit of its Authority, Discipline, Doctrine and Uniformity, of which we are not without hopes. Yet the heavy and Dark Cloud, which, in the dispensations of Providence, hangs over my family, oppresses my spirits.

You complain of the Ingratitude, Cruelty and Desertion of Mankind; (my friend, trust in the Lord with all thine heart, lean not to thine own understanding, in all thy ways acknowledge him, and he will direct thy path). I hope you enjoy all ye favour, support and incouragement, under your happy Constitution Your Seal & Loyalty Merits. Notwithstanding my age, if consistent with Duty; I would wish my Self under Royal Protection.

Your concern for your Brethren here unprovided for by the Society, is gratefully acknowledged. But different Towns in this State may unite, as they are impowered in Law, to support a clergyman among them, till such place can support one themselves.

I thank you for the care in forwarding the last Abstracts, and wish to know by what Authority you intimate we may remove into any Parish, upon prospect of greater usefulness, with the continuance of the Societys favour and Charity. Many passages in your letter, wants explanation, which I hope for in your next, hoping you will improve the

Door that is opened for correspondence.

Please to direct to the care of Mr. Bogardus Merchant at New York. You will present my compliments of best respects to Mr. Hubbard and Mr. Jarvis, who make honourable mention of you in their Letters to their Friends. Their Connexions are well.

Brother Leaming fixes at Stratford, to whom I wrote, to present your Paternal regards & blessing to your Son.

The family Join in best wishes and Respect. Farewell Dear Sir; Through the tender mercy of our God, may we have a happy meeting in the world of Spirits.

With unfeigned Esteem, I am. Revd Sir.
Your ever Affect Brother
and Humble Servt
Ebenezer Diblee.

Rev. Mr. Peters.

[Addressed:] The Reverend Mr. Peters / Pimlico / London.
[Endorsed:] Recd Dec. 7, 1784

[1784, Sept. 22, London]
Rev. and Dear Sir,

I have just delivered my letters which are to go by Mr. Ricketts, and lo! yours of Aug 5, has this moment found its way to me. It was enclosed to the care of some person who is now at Chester, near 200 miles distant, and it comes to me from thence as does that from Dr. [William] Morrice, in a parcel sent me by Dr. Ogden. I am very sorry that I have not time to consult the Dr. nor to consider carefully the point of casuistry which you are pleased to refer to me. The inducement is undoubtedly strong for your removal to N. York, and I can have but one objection to it, which is the forlorn state in which the poor church in N. Jersey must be left. I should think it would be in the power of the several congregations with which you have been connected for some time past, if they were properly disposed, by means of parsonage, houses and glebes, and otherwise to make it advisable in you to stay among them; but if they will not, there is nothing more to be said. I am confident you will take the arguments into serious consideration, and act in a manner that is not unworthy of your character. It pleases me to find that you have written to the society on the occasion: for several of their missionaries, when they thought they could better themselves by leaving the service, have gone off, sans ceremonie without consulting them or thanking them for past favors. Such conduct has an ill effect here. Let me therefore advise you, if you should think proper to remove, to let the Society first hear it from yourself, and receive the resignation of your salary from your own hands.

The backwardness here in providing you with an Episcopate, is not so much to be charged upon the Bishops as upon the King's ministers. The Bishops cannot proceed in a consecration for that purpose, without an act of Parliament to authorise them; & such an act will not be brought forward, without the application, or at least the express approbation of some state, for fear of giving umbrage to the Americans, who are supposed to be generally disaffected to the measure. For this reason Dr. S who was strongly recommended by the Conn. Clergy, has

not been able to carry his point with Government; but there are other resources left, & I think it probable that he will obtain the Episcopal Character in a way that will render it perfectly unexceptionable on purely ecclesiastical principles....

Thomas Bradbury Chandler

[Rev. Dr. Abraham Beach at New Brunswick, N.J.]

[1784, Oct. 6, Stamford]

Stamford State of Connecticut
In America. October, 6. 1784

Reverend Sir--

I have this day drawn a Set of Bills in usual form, for Twenty five Pounds Sterling upon Calvert Clapham Esq.r Treasurer of the Venerable Society, in favour of Mess.rs Reed and Bogardus Merchants in New York.

I gratefully acknowledge the receipt of a number of the last Abstracts, and have distributed them among my Brethren in Connecticut.----We think ourselves happy in the continuance of the Venerable Societies notice, and hope to merit their future favor by a diligent attention to the Duties of our Office.

Blessed be God; the Respectable ground upon which the Episcopal Ch.h in Connecticut is placed, by the liberallity of a late Act of the Legislature, enabling them to tax themselves, for the support of Religion, the building and repairing of their Churches, in like manner as the Established religious Societies of the State are; Opens a happy prospect of the future growth and reputable increase of the Church in this State.----More Especially if an American Episcopate can be obtained, the want and necessity of which, more manifestly appears, to maintain Sound Doctrine, Discipline and Uniformity, and perpetuate a regular Ministry.

The Churches among whom I continue to Officiate, remain in a peaceable increasing State. In Stamford & Norwalk especially, greater attention is paid to the publick Worship of God, than in the time of our late troubles; when an Episcopalian & a Tory, were looked upon as Synonimus terms. Every other Sunday I attend divine Service at Norwalk, and Horsneck. Horsneck Ch.h remains in a Lukewarm State, having not recovered their primitive Zeal, and their Church is very unfit to attend divine Service in, in the Winter. The Church of Norwalk in a peculiar manner merits my attention, till they can be otherwise better provided, in consideration of the largeness of their Congregation, and number of Communicant[s]. I give the Communion once in Eight weeks at Norwalk, and the constant Communicants are about Eighty; and at Stamford from forty to fifty.----I Baptised last half Year 58 White Children, 2 Adults. 5 black children, 4 Adults.----Permit me to add my humble duty to the Venerable Board, and grateful acknowledgements for the continuance of their charitable Notice, and concern for the welbeing of the best of Churches, praying for Gods blessing to attend and succeed all their most pious designs, for the enlargement of the Redeemers kingdom; I am with high Esteem and Respect to Your Self, Reverend Sir

Your most Obedient
Most Humble Serv.t & Brother
in Christ
Ebenezer Dibblee

The Reverend Doctor Morise
Secretary of the Venerable
Society for Propagation of the Gospel &c

[Endorsed: Read] Dec.r 1784.

[1784, Dec. 1, Norwich]

Norwich in Connecticut Decem.r 1: 1784.

Rev.d Sir,

I take this Oppertunity of writing to you, by Cp.t Gurdon Bill, a non con. who is about to sail from Norwich Landing, for London. I have heard of several Letters from you since last winter, but have seen none. I heard that in one to Doctor Sutton, of the 1.st of March last you proposed to go to France, and should not correspond with America for some years. Again I heard of Letters from you to M.r Birdsey of Stratford; and this fall past, I heard of Letters received in Hebron from you, in which you mentioned the Receipt of Letters from some one in Hartford, and from Doctor Bliss in Hebron, who were of Opinion that you could not return in Safety: perhaps they did not wish to encourage your Return. However, the vindictive Spirit of the Country is almost totally altered in the space of one year past: and though, if you had returned last spring, some few Curs might have growled a little, and I am confident that would have been all; yet now I can assure you that the fierce Spirit of Whigism is Dead; and it is the general Sense, of the People of Connecticut, Rulers and all, that the old Spirit of Bitterness is now the worst of Policy. Not one word of Whig & Tory appears now in the Newspapers; and even the fiery Darts at general Arnold, which lasted longest, are now tottally out of Fashion; those heretofore call'd Tories, and who were treated with the greatest Bitterness, are now in as good Reputation as any. Doctor Johnson is chosen a Member of Congress, M.r Se[y]mour Mayor of the City of Hartford, and Cp.t Nathaniel Bac[kus?], who was much Harrassed in the War, for being a bold Friend to great Britain, is now the Second Alderman of our City of Norwich. And if you should incline to return, I am sure that not one Dog would move his Tongue against you. And you would be much more at Peace here, than you were even Seven Years before the War. Our Friend Ebenezer Punderson, is return'd to Paucatanoc with his Family, and our general Assembly have restor'd to him all his Estate; & he is well received, not a Mouth opened against him.

In my Letter to you of the 9.th of Jan.y last, which I conclude you must have received, I mentioned a Letter of mine to the Society of the same Date; but I did not send it forward 'till the 20.th of last April; and suppose you have seen it. But I have not heard any Thing from the Society in Consequence of it: and I wish you to write me by the Return of Cp.t Bill, or sooner than his Return if you have an Oppertunity; and inform me all you know of the Matter, that is what Reception my Letter has met with   What you think of my Opinion respecting the final Salvation of all Men I know not; but if you can render me any Services with Doctor Morrice, and will be kind enough to use what Influence you have that I may not be cut off from the Society's Favor, you will merit my sincerest Thanks. After what I have said of my Opinion, in my Letter to Doctor Morrice, of the 20.th of April last, which I suppose you

must have seen, it will be to no Purpose for me to attempt in this Letter, to explain to you the Reasons of my Opinion.

I have not heard how Doctor Seabury succeeds; but expect to hear soon.-- The Motion of the Philadelphia episcopal Clergy with their Lay-Delegates, respecting the Founding of our American Episcopal Church, you have or will no Doubt hear by other Hands: But our Connecticut Clergy look totally askew at their Lay-Delegates, and will never I believe admit those Tobacco Cutters with them. The Pensilvania, New-Jersy & New-York Clergy met lately at New-York, & the Connecticut Clergy sent a Letter & a Representative, to put off Matters 'till we have a Bishop; plead that we cannot act in Founding a Church 'till we have a Bishop, & so are organized, as a Church.-- Our old Friend Cpt Bushnell is dead,--and our good Friend Mr Brimmer died in Boston last Summer-- My Family has been considerably visited with Sickness at Times, for more than a Year and I have lost my oldest Son by Death the Summer past, who was between eleven and twelve Years of Age; which was a grievous Stroak to me, and the Recollection is yet very painful; and my Spirits are low.-- I hear, Mr Man's Son is return'd from you to Hebron, but have not seen him; and have heard very little of the Accounts he brings.-- Mrs Tyler joins me in her Compliments and kind Regards to you, and Daughter.

Sir, I remain your sincere Friend and Brother
John Tyler.

The Revd Samuel Peters ⎞
Pimlico, Charlotte Street ⎬
No 1, London   ⎠

[1785, Apr. 2, Norwich]
Norwich in Connecticut April 2: 1785
Reverend Sir,

It is about ten Days since I received your Letter of the 26th of last July, via Boston: and am not offended at the Freedom with which you write-- By your Letter, I perceive that my Letter went safe to the Society, wherein I declar'd it to be my Opinion that all Mankind will finally be saved. Your Letter is the first & only Intimation I have received of it's Arrival. I thank you for your candid Observation, that My Opinion may be true, although it was not, nor is now the Opinion of the Church universal.-- The first Reformers in England, varied in some Points from the Opinion which had been generally received in the Church universal, for near a Thousand Years.-- As to the Beneficial Consequences of my Opinion to Religion I suppose every sincere Minister of Jesus Christ, will be very apt to think that Gospel most beneficial, which he supposes his Master order'd to be preached to every Creature: and that we read, is The Gospel of Peace--the Gospel, or good News of the Grace of God; but I know not that we any where read of the Gospel of final Misery. St Paul tells us Gals 3:8, The Gospel preached unto Abraham was, In thee shall all Nations be blessed; not part of them cursed. And is the Servant of Jesus to obey Orders, and leave the Consequences to his Master, who is able to take Care of them, having all Power in Heaven & Earth, and being able to turn the Hearts of Kings, and of all other Men, like the Rivers of Water, even as he pleases? or is the Servant of Jesus to be more wise & prudent in Respect of Consequences, than his Master, and a greater Lover of Peace than his Master, who

declar'd that He came not to send Peace on the Earth, but a sword; and by whose spirit we are informed, that The Wisdom of Men is Foolishness with God--and that The Foolishness of God is wiser than Man? I know the Heralds of Good Tidings are to be wise as serpents, as well as harmless as Doves: but if, under the Notion of Wisdom, they persuade the People that they are subject to that very Curse, which Jesus was made for us, (which implies that Justice having already received full "Satisfaction for all the sins of the whole World both original and actual," is still unsatisfied, and will demand Satisfaction over again the second Time) they may one Day be rebuked, and be asked who requir'd this at their Hands? and how they came to make those sorrowful and thro' Fear of Death subject to bondage, with a Sentance already executed, whom Jesus sent them to comfort & edify in Love, with good Tidings of Peace and Reconciliation? And will not those Heralds, who were sent to preach the Gospel--to publish good Tidings of Good Things, and instead of this, became preachers of the Law, of which Jesus fulfilled every Tittle, will they not, I say, be found to have built little else than Wood, Hay, and Stubble on the true Foundation, and suffer Loss by the Distruction of their Works, tho' themselves be saved so as by Fire, seperating the precious from the vile?-- The Wages of Sin is Death: but St Paul Concludes that if one died for all, then were all Dead; and shall the Heralds of Peace, now declare that Death to be endur'd over again?

It is true the Law threatens eternal Death to Disobedience: but Christ is the End of the Law for Righteousness, in the View of every one who puts his Trust in him. And an human Legislator may fall short in Point of Punishment threatned by the civil Law; but God cannot abate the least Iota of what his Law threatens; for his Truth is concern'd in the Fulfilment of his Word, and He will not alter the Thing that is gone out of his Lips;--for He is not a Man that he should repent; otherwise, that bitter Cup might have been removed from the holy Jesus. But why should we talk of Abatements of Punishment, when The Testimony of Jesus which is the Spirit of Prophecy, has taught us, Isaiah 40th:2nd, That our Warfare is accomplished, and our Iniquity is pardoned: for we have received of the Lord's Hand double for all our Sins? Behold the surety the Lamb of God on the Cross, taking away the sin of the World, and listen to his Declaration that It is finished--as the Prophet Daniel foretold, he finished the Transgression, made an End of Sin--. Where then is the Abatement of the Threatening to be found then? has not the just suffer'd for the unjust--the infinite for the finite? Is not the Punishment already double? I know there is a Day coming when every one must receive according to the deeds done in the Body,--every Unbeliever must become guilty before God, even the whole World sooner or later, and the Man Christ Jesus also must receive according to the deeds done in his Body in the Garden & on the Cross--he must receive the Reward of his bloody sweat and Agonies, which was the Price of our Redemption,: we are bought with this Price; & he is The Heir of the World; and in that Day, when every Mouth shall be stopped, and the whole World be found Guilty before God,--then the Lord alone shall be exalted,--and receive the Heathen for his Inheritance, and the uttermost Parts of the Earth for his Possession, Knowing therefore the Terror which the Lord Jesus en-

dur'd in the Garden for our Sake, when the Powers of Darkness buffetted him, and being in an Agony he sweat great Drops of Blood, and pray'd earnestly, --and was heard in that he feared & knowing that he must receive the Reward of his sufferings, --we persuade Men by the moving Eloquence of such bleeding, dying Love, and by all their Feelings of gratitude to love the Lord Jesus, --to put their Trust in him, and to acknowledge him before Men.

My good Friend, you say "The Loveliness of Virtue, --of God & Heaven were not and are not sufficient Motives to deter Men from Sins": but do the Terrors of eternal Punishment, thunder'd abroad by Priests deter Men? Has the Loveliness of God, as our perfectly reconciled Father, and the Love of Christ, our complete Saviour, been sufficiently tried in these last Ages? Christ says This is eternal Life to know thee, the only true God & Jᵉ Christ wᵐ thou hast sent Sᵗ. Paul says of Christians in his Day, The Love of Christ constraineth us-- & Sᵗ. John says, We love him (Christ) because he first loved us. But my dear Sir, are Christ's Ministers, the Ministers of the Law, or the Gospel? The Law worketh Wrath-- The Law is a Ministration of Death--a Ministration of Condemnation--cursing every one that continueth not in all Things, which are written in the Book of the Law to do them: and are not the Threats of eternal Punishment, pure Law--the Ministration of Death? But now we are delivered from the Law, --that being dead wherein we were held, Romᵉ 7:6. And is not the Gospel good News of Peace--good News that one Jot or Tittle of the Law did not pass or fail, 'till all was fulfilled, in the holy Life of him, whose Name is The Lord our Righteousness, and in the agonizing Death of him, who tasted Death for every Man? for all were dead, when one died for all. Sᵗ. Paul says, I through the Law, am dead to the Law--I am crucified with Christ.-- Now to Abraham and his seed were the Promises made, --and to thy Seed, which is Christ, that is, In thee & in thy Seed, shall all the Nations --Kindreds and Families of the Earth be blessed. And this Covenant confirmed of God in Christ, the Law published at Sinai four hundred and thirty years after cannot disannul-- Wherefore then serveth the Law? it was added because of Transressions, 'till the Seed should come. to whom the Promise was made-- Wherefore the Law was our Schoolmaster unto Christ--but after that Faith is come, we are no longer under a Schoolmaster, no longer under the Law-- the Law is dead, being fulfilled, that being dead wherein we were held, --and now speaks de jure, not de facto. Indeed The Law entered, that the Offence might abound-- that it might appear Sin exceeding Sinful-- But where Sin abounded, Grace did much more abound--the Law was given that we might know from how great an Evil we are saved--the greater the Mischief the greater the deliverance from it; and the Remedy was much greater than the Disease--Grace did much more abound. And, As by the Offence of one, even Adam, Judgment came upon all Men to Condemnation, in the Surety, who bore our Sins in his own Body on the Tree; even so by the Righteousness of one, even Christ, the free Gift came upon all Men, unto Justification of Life; all being acquitted, by the Release of the Surety from the Hand of Justice, when he arose for our Justification, as a demonstrative Proof that he had obtained a Tittle to Life for us.

But my dear Sir, as you appear not to me by your Letter to have understood any of the Reasons in my Letter to the Society; why it was my Opinion that all Mankind will finally be saved as for Instance, because Christ has paid the Price of Redemption for all, and obtained: a Thought Occurs, that perhaps you will not take the intended Force; of one single Argument in this long Letter. And we are far from sitting side by side, to compare Ideas, that we may see Eye to Eye. Nor when you read this Letter, shall I be near enough to reply, in any tolerable Season, to the Consequences you may draw from what I say. For Instance, you may say, If that is dead wherein we were held, (viz) the Law, then now we may live as we list; all is atonened for. But very many Things might well be said in Answer to this. However I briefly answer; nay, the Apostle has answer'd for me, Shall we continue in Sin that Grace may abound? God forbid; how shall we that are dead to Sin, live any longer therein?-- What Fruit had ye then in those Things, whereof ye are now ashamed? in the whole 6ᵗʰ Chapter to the Romᵉ. The Law is now the Rule for a Christian to live by; though he cannot obtain Immortality by it: For if there had been a Law given, which could have given Life, then verily Righteousness would have been by the Law. We are not under the Law, but under Grace. What then? shall we sin, because we are not under the Law, but under Grace? God forbid, that we should be so ungrateful to that precious Lamb, that bled in Agonies for us! But he that once tastes of the heavenly Gift, and then gives himself up to sin is harden'd thro' the Deceitfulness of Sin, & quickly makes Shipwreck of his Faith; and returns under Bondage to the Fear of Death, the Wages of Sin; for he grieves that holy Spirit, whereby he is sealed unto the Day of Redemption: and being forsaken of the Spirit of Grace, that dark Cloud of the Apprehension of the Wrath of God returns over him again, and abideth on him--he loses his Joy & Peace in believing --and judges himself unworthy of that eternal Life, which consists in knowing the true God & Jesus Christ--he remains in a fearful Looking for of Judgment, and fiery Indignation, 'till his Works of Wood, Hay & Stubble is burnt up--he judged with Unbelievers--found guilty before God: and though the Book of Life will then be opened, and he saved so as by Fire; yet he must suffer Loss, not shining with the Glory of the Sun--Moon, or any Star near the first Magnitude; for one Star differeth from another in Glory-- So is the Resurrection of the Dead. If all be saved, is it no Matter how we Live, think you? Is it no Matter whether we die in Peace, and sleep in Jesus? or die in Horror or Despair? Or is it no Matter whether we have that Joy unspeakable & full of Glory, which enabled the Martyrs to rejoice in the Midst of flaming Faggots, or remain All our Life Time in Bondage through Fear of Death; because Christ came to deliver even such? But I cannot foresee, nor prevent all the untoward Consequences, that may occurr to your Mind.

The Clergy of our Church here, are generaly so good-natured as to be willing that all Mankind should finally be Saved; and there are many of the Layity of our Church in New England who believe it; more, I fancy, than you have any Idea of; and not a few Presbyterians, all over New-England who profess it, and who therefore wish me well; and who, if the Society should be so kind & liberal as to wink at my Opinion, will love the Church for it's Liberality and no Doubt manifest their Friendship, and afford their Influence in Favor of it, whenever there is an Oppertunity

or Occasion for it.-- Most of them in this Town are my Hearers and pay to my support. But if the Society should deny me their Favor, I cannot well express how much alteration it must make, or how much depends on this Event. The Missionaries must for their own Interest and Safety consider me as an outcast--as an excommunicated Person, and deny me Fellowship--the Lay Members of our Church who are of my Opinion in many different Places, must consider themselves as Outcasts also, and be grieved at the Frown it will appear to look with on them--the presbyterian universalists can no longer behold with Complacence, a Church that will seem to them less tolerant than that they belonged to; who have not yet, that I know of, denied Fellowship with Doctor Chancy of Boston & his Colleague, who have published "Salvation for all Men," in Pamphlets, even a gross purgatorial one, that is, that the Torments of the Damned will cease when Justice is satisfied, and they are Physically purified by Sufferings. Which Scheme introduces "Salvation independent of the Merits of Jesus Christ: whereas my Opinion gives all the Glory to him. And will not a new Thing appear in the ecclesiasti[cal] World,? our Church noted for the greatest Liberality and Charity, of any Denomination, now seeming to have the least of either, in the Eyes of the presbyterian universalists if I am excluded! Doctor Seabury, I have just heard, is consecrated Bishop of Connecticut, to reside at New-London, where the Church are much rejoicing, many of whom are Universalists: but how will the Joy of that Part of them be dashed, if the Opinion is not to be tolerated in our Church I might continue this Theme, but the Subject is too disagreeab[le.] But as you are no Doubt conversant with the Secretary of the Society, it is in your Power perhaps to do me many kind Offices consistent with Truth; and to benefit the Episcopal Church in New-England in Respect of it's Unity: and from the Aspect of your Letter, I cannot doubt your good Will to me, notwithstanding my Opinion.-- I know you consider me as the Sparrow in the Fable, who is represented as sitting on a spray, and seeing a Company of Monkeys, in a cool Evening, putting dry barks and sticks round a Glowworm, to enkindle a Fire for their Comfort; to whom the Sparrow with officious Friendship, says, you are deceived, the supposed Coal of Fire, is a Living Reptile, who emits Light without Heat or Fire; but the Monkeys advised him to mind his own Concerns, and not trouble them with his Impertinence. However, the Officiously kind Sparrow after using many Arguments, alit to pick up the glowworm, and convince them of their Error; but the Monkeys enraged at the Sparrow's obstinately persisting in his Attempt to convince them, of what was so unwelcome, seized on the Sparrow, and deprived him of Life.

I do not mean to intrude my Opinion on you, or any other Person: but the Candour & Friendship of your Letter, inclines me to think, that some Reasons for my Opinion, would at least gratify your Curiosity, & give you no Offence, if it should not incline you to think still more favorably of my Conduct.-- When I preach for any of the Clergy, I do not hint any of my peculiar Sentiments; and we live in very good Harmony: being agreed to differ in this one Point, without any Contention. It was not possible for me to conceal my Opinion; for perhaps one half of my Hearers were of this Opinion before me, on the Point being largely discussed in this Town, and in most Parts of New-England; while I opposed it: but when I was convinced, no Prudence,

consistent with Truth, could hide it from the inquisitive Multitude--if my Parishioners knew it; the World must know it. Now, there is but one of my Parishioners who opposes it; and he a Person of very little Consequence-- This may appear almost incredible to you; but it is a Fact.-- I have taken every Precaution in my Power to avoid Discord in our Churches here--: and have succeeded to Admiration, in Respect to Peace;--I have follow'd the Advice of our Clergy in Respect to the Manner of my proceeding; and have used my utmost Endeavours, not to disturb the Peace of the Church here: and I trust our Clergy here will give me the Credit of it if they should be called on to testify concerning it. The Missionaries in Connecticut were afraid that they should lose their Salaries, if they did not inform the Society of my Opinion; and wrote a very short Letter to acquaint the Society of my Opinion, declaring that I was "unexceptionable as a Missionary of the Society in every other Respect, but this one Opinion":--then told me, on reading the Letter to me, that they were under a Necessity to do this, for their own Safety, unless I would inform the Society myself, which would please them better-- I chose to inform the Society myself: then they desir'd me still to attend the Conventions, which I do. So that I hope to avoid being call'd a disturber of the Peace of the Church. As to being a Novelist Mr. Murdon in England, is openly of my Opinion; I have a Piece of his publishing on the Epistle of St. James and he preaches to a Congregation, I suppose, if now living: and I am informed, is in regular Standing under his Bishop without Offence. And if I do not in Fact disturb the Peace of the Church here, why should I, or how can I, disturb the Peace of it in England? But my Salary from the Society is a Favor that may be withheld at Pleasure; yet it must operate here like an Excommunication here: because our Clergy here are at present Missionaries. I verily believe, that if the Society knew every Circumstance here relating to my Affair, they would not dismiss me from their Service: but how can they know all this at such a Distance?

My Opinion is evidently in perfect Harmony with the 39 Articles, except one E[x]pression in the 17th--"chosen in Christ out of Mankind" which perhaps to some m[a]y seem not quite to harmonize with it; yet even that Expression is more strictly agreeable to my Opinion, it must be confessed I think by all, who understand the Master, than it is to Arminianism, which you know is generally the Doctrine of our Clergy. But for my Part, I am well reconciled to all contained in the 17th Article, .-- I wish you to be so kind as to inform me of whatever Turn my Matter takes with the Society. And if any Part of this Letter, should be, of any kind of Use in my Favor, you may use it, at your Discretion.-- I am confident that none of our Clergy [who attend] our Convention, have wrote to the Society against [me. Whether others have,] who know little of the Matter, I know not. But Those who rehearse Vague Reports, you know are very apt to misrepresent, be they everso honest. But if any Thing has been Wrote to the Society against me, you will be so good as to give me Notice, I trust; for certainly I ought to know it; and not to be Smitten secretly.

You ask, Why should we lessen our great Fort the Punishments eternal &c-- I ask in Return, what Fort Christ's Ministers have, but the Gospel, which shows the Law ful-

filled, and those Punishments already endur'd? What is
Christ's Banner? Is it not Love? We are told that Love is
Stronger than Death. If so, then it is our strongest Fort.
Christ so loved the World as to submit to Death--and how
many Martyrs suffer'd it, not accepting Deliverance? You
say, "If you love me keep my Commandments, is the better,
and more solid Doctrine"--then Love is the proper Motive
of Obedience--and our strongest Fort. But your Views are
not to confute my Doctrine--but to prevent my suffering the
poor Sparrow's Fate. I thank you, my Friend, for your kind
Intention. But what precaution can I take, more than I have
done, consistent with Honesty? Can I renounce what I believe to be true? Would this make me appear a worthy Missionary? Any innocent Prudence I am willing to use. And
what more can I do? For any Fault that I am convinced of;
Repentance & Reformation is my Duty: but to repent of believing what appears true, is a Farce. But after all, I am
at the Disposal of him who over-rules all human Affairs as
he sees fit.

In the Time of the War, while my Church was shut up
not knowing what my future living would be, nor where I
might chance to have my Residence; I turned my Mind much
on Trade: I adventur'd small sums in about 8 or nine different merc[hant] Vessels, the largest Sum which I ventur'd,
was £17 ten shillings sterling, for english Cloths by way of
Holland; and I proved lucky in every one of these Adventures, generally more than doubling my Money; and turned
those Articles which came to me, into Necessaries for my
Family, and to good Advantage, retailing them myself--but
having opened my Church, and afterwards the Peace taking
Place, I desisted from these Adventures, expecting that my
Living would soon become better; but as yet it is no better.
In the Time of the War, most of my Parishioners, who were
in the mercantile Way, did no Business; and lived on their
Interest, and hoped for better and more settled Times.
And the Peace found them much reduced--some of them
moved away, for better Advantages of reassuming [Indus-
try. This] operates yet against my Income from my Peo-
ple. In the....

                                            [John Tyler]

[The Rev.d Samuel Peters
Pimlico, Charlotte Street
N.o 1, London]

[1785, Apr. 4, Pimlico]

                             Pimlico April 4th.1785
Reverend & dear Sir
    your favor of Decemb. 2.d 1784 reached me Feb.y 10th
1785 I received your Letter also dated Jan.y 9th 1784 & answered it-- your Letter to D.r Morice has been read & considered by the Society--& the Secretary has written to you
upon your Opinions not new among the antient Athenians--
you stand condemned for new vamping obsolete Opinions,
which as a Divine I speak, may be true or false without
danger to any Soul, yet Noveltry seems not necessary in
our Days, when the love of money has waxed cold, & the
cry is, who will show us any good? we on this Side the
water stand amazed at the Opinion of, "the final Salvation
of all Men" because we stand on Mount Pisgah, & survey
the World as it is, and compare human actions to the Rule
given by God as the only mode of being saved-- therefore
we conclude no flesh can or will be saved finally, unless

the Americans are better infinitely than we in Europe
Asia & Africa are--which no one beleives--except D.r
Price & other Scepticks totally blind & ignorant of the ten
last years which have disgraced human nature and mur-
dered every divine Law sent down from Heaven to guide
mankind on Earth-- we pray that Peace may be in our
Days, for the following given Reason, "because there is
none other but God that fights for us"-- How happy would
Peace have been for Europe & America the ten last years,
Seeing God fought for neither, nor did our Generals or
yours, nor any other being-- In such a Situation we most
properly pray for Peace, that Murders, Robberies and
all old & new Crimes may not reign as virtues, instead
of Purity the perfect Rule of him "who went about doing
good"-- Can Herod, Nero Caligula, Trumbull, Howe,
George & protestant Bps & Priests of Baal ever get to
Heaven by a Saviour whose Life is despised, & whose
commands are but Trifles? Omnipotence itself cannot
save a sinful Christian if our Revelation come from God
& you may say, he may repent and so be saved--but the
sinners, here & with you, will not repent--and God forces
no one to repent--sinners therefore die sinners, & go to
Hell a place fit for them--as Heaven would make them
miserable, for the same Reasons that Virtue and Religion
did on Earth--as a tree falleth, so it lyeth, & in the Grave
is no Repentance--and no one can reprcave a soul from
Hell--unless the Pope--and it would surprise me to find
the Pope holds more Power than God almighty & Jesus C.t
his Son-- your Charity beleives all things, and more than
all things revealed--we scarcely beleive all things revealed, "that a few will be saved" D.r Mather well said,
if ten souls should finally get to Heaven out of the great
town of Boston, (he might have said America) that number
would surpass my present thoughts & would teach me that
there was another way to save sinners than the Gospel and
the law of st[rict?] Justice-- you say, punishments in justice, cannot be eternal, as sins are temporal--sinners always beleive they shall never die--their hopes lie here below; they dispise the blood of Christ--and will not know
his ways--such sinners deserve such Punishments as they
prefer to God & Virtue--Secula Secularum, is just their
wages--if this is not the Case--then Virtue, Piety, Love
& faith, with the blood of Christ, cannot have more than
temporal Felicity in Heaven--

    I will now quit Divinity--to converse with you my ab-
sent friend on other Matters, after saying I wish every
human being may receive whatever is due to his Piety; and
to his Sins--I beleive I shall live forever in the Heavens,
because of my sincere Belief in the Merits of a Saviour;
and my love of Holiness and integrity of soul in which is
no Enmity, yet could I think heaven hereafter would be
filled with Rebels, & Marauders & Tyrants, I should have
no objection to return & spend my Life in my native Country, where I might learn to enjoy Heaven with greater
Pleasure than such as live with holy & humble Men--

    blessed are the dead--your little son is gone to Heaven
before you--was my son with him, I could quit America and
my Property with Joy--but alas, poor child, he is left to
Evils coming on your World-- Patience & Resignation are
Lessons for you & me to practise as well as teach--without
Tryals, Virtue could not Shine; nor you, nor I could See the
blessed World--like me overcome a World unworthy of a
Saviour, of you and me-- I find the Society were easily to

be satisfied by you, if you droped preaching your opinions--
but now, Dr Seabury having been Consecrated Bp of Connecticut by the nonjuring Bps in Scotland in consequence of
your Petition and Direction; & Sailed from hence to Nova
Scotia the 13th of March last--you Missionaries are Considered as culpable with him--the Society therefore in
Passion Week, passed a Vote, which Cut us, Dr Seabury,
& all Missionaries in the united States, & in England, off
their respective Salaries after the 29th of Septr next; unless the Missionary move into some British Colony--of
this you will all be duely notified by the Secretary-- you
all have the option to become subjects, of our Gracious
King & pious Bishops, again; or to transfer your allegeance
to the virtuous Congress and Bishop Seabury who goes like
titus & his Brother Paul to fight the beast of Ephesus, &
who like St Peter my ancestor, if you find him with a sword,
will cut off the Ear of Malchus, & secure the Adoration of
Asiaboutros, well done Peter" in the Greek Church to this
day, & forever, when that Chapter is read--

    The King gives £70, & the Society £50 per Ann, to such
Missionaries as settle in Nova Scotia &c &c--besides that
the Parishioners must give, & a Glebe; and a Right of Land
as Loyalists-- you will never be considered again as Members of the British Church after you submit to the Episcopal Power of Bishop Seabury--if you abide there, you will
lie at the mercy of your oppressed Parishioners; loaded
with Taxes & Poverty, & want of Generosity--in that awful situation you will need no foes--your friends will be
police, Herod, & pontius Pilate; your Houses will be Dens
& Caves; your Clothing will be Cattles hair & Goat Skins;
your meat will be Locusts & wild honey; & your lodging a
bed of Straw-- Thus you stand on an Air Balloon between
Scylla & Charybdis--God and Baal-- Choose therefore for
yourselves--

    I will give no Opinion--the above is all the favor your
friend could procure for you & the absent Brethern--your
lives were spared six months, in Consequence of an Assertion, that you sent Dr Seabury to be consecrated by
Canterbury; which not being granted there; Dr Seabury
had gone to Scotland without your Knowledge; & that the
Society would act prudently if they waited till the Clergy
of Connecticut accepted Dr Seabury for their Bishop--

    I told the ABP that Mr Marshal went to oppose that
puritanic meeting of the Clergy at New york--and that he
did oppose it--let this be known to all the Clergy--I hope
M^r E- Punderson is happy; to him pray offer my Blessings
& love & Esteem-- my Daughter recollects you and joins
me in every Civility to you, Mr Holden, M^r & Miss^s Lancaster &c Love dear Mrs Tylor and her Children because
they are worthy of it, & of the veneration of dear sir, your
Friend & Brother
    I have Wrote in great haste--
                   St Peter 2us
                   [i.e., Samuel Peters]
Revd Mr Tyler--

[1785, May 3, Stamford]
               Stamford State of Connecticut
               New England May 3^d. 1785.
Reverend Sir
    To my surprize, I lately received advice from Messrs
Reed and Bogardus, Merchants in New York, that my Bill

for £25 Sterling drawn in their favour upon the Societies
Treasurer in Octob^r last, was returned Protested.

    Your favour of ye 22 of November 1784 explains the
reason. But, Sir, I am not conscious of any other irregularity in drawing my Bills, save the dates of my drawing;
which the necessity of the times occasioned. Neither was
it ever my intention to draw for my Salary before it was
due. Anticedent to our late troubles it was my constant
practice to draw my Bills every half year, about Easter
and Michlemas Term. The begining of my Salary I know
was appointed St Johns day 1748--in which Year I was appointed their Missionary. But the term to Easter, to introduce a regular drawing, spring and Autum hath been adjusted long since, and I cannot find or recollect, I have ever
drawn a Quarter Salary of £12:10.----I cannot have a regular recourse back any farther than April, 1776. From
that time my Correspondence and regular drawing for my
Salary of necessity ceased, and from April 1776 to April
1784 is Eight Years. From Minutes I kept before a doore
of Correspondence was opened; and regular advices and
accounts of my drawing my Bills since, to the last mentioned period, exclusive of the last protested Bill, I cannot
find I've drawn for more than my Just Salary. Please Sir,
to see or request of the treasurer, an accurate examination of the late Treasurerers accounts of Bills drawn &
in whose favour by me, and accept'd, some years before
April 1776, and from y^t period to April 1784; and I flatter
my self the Error will not ly in me. Upon the death of
the Revd Mr Palmer, previous to our late troubles, the
secretary wrote to me, that the Society had granted a Be-
quest to his widow and Orphans, about ye sum of £12:10;
directed me to draw for it; I did so, paid it according to
Ord^r, and Receipts were given. In like manner after M^r
Lampsons death, by order of the then Secretary, I drew a
Bill of £25 for his Widow and Children, paid the Charitable donation to them and took their Recepts. These Bills
being drawn according to Order in my Name may possible
have Occasioned the Error.

    Since April 1776, Some Bills for 2 years Salary were
drawn, I cannot ascertain the names of the Gentlemen in
New York in whose Fav^r they were drawn; neither did I
preserve any more, than Minutes of the sums I drew, for;
it was presumption, Situated as I was, to do it. A Bill of
£100 was likewise drawn I think in fav^r of Mr Nathaniel
Peck who in a friendly manner undertook to negociate it
for me. A Bill of £50 in fav^r of Mr Seabury Merch^t in New
York. A Bill of £50 in fav^r of Messrs Fitch & Holly--
Ditto one of £50 in fav^r of the Revd Mr Leaming, April, 83.
One in fav^r of Mr Ellison of New Yor, Octob^r, 83, of but
£25. One also of £25 in fav^r of Mr Bogardus of New York,
Aprill 22. 1784.-- These are all the Bills I can at present
find I have drawn for, Since Aprill 1776 to the 22 of April
1784 which compleats but 8 Years Salary. So that if I am
not in an Error the Bill drawn ye 6 of Octob^r last in fav^r
of Messrs Reed and Bogardus and returned protested is
Justly Due.

    Notwithstanding, the Bills drawn & accepted in the
Secretaries Office, must Illustrate the Matter if Critically
examined; and I shall submit to your correction; and Omit
drawing this spring Bill, and bear the inconvenience of the
Protested Bill, for which I am accountable, till the Irregularity be adjusted; as well as I can: Wishing the earliest
advice you can give me. I shall not draw any more Bills

till Autumn, unless by your permission--

With respect to the other contents of your Letter, I am of the opinion, if the Society come to a Speedy final resolution to withdraw the Salaries of such Missionaries as chuse to continue in the Independent States, it would be attended with unhappy consequences both to them and the welbeing of their Parishes. Their persevereance, through that Sea of trouble, torrent of abuse, personal danger, distress and want, in regard to their Duty, & to prevent the ruin of their Churches & preserve their attachment & Affection to ye English Constitution both in Ch^h & State, Merits in my humble Opinion the continuance of the Venerable Societies Notice and Charity.-- And some of their Parishoners have suffered so amazingly for their Loyalty, by fines, compositions Improsentments &c &c, and have been so diminished by the flight of many, and weakened; that the Episcopal Ch^h must sink, and the fruit of the Societies past Charity be lost, if in future withdrawn.

Some Churches, I am not insensible may be able, almost with equal ability with other denominations, to support their own Minister and they are laudible exerting themselves. The Ch^h of Norwalk have agreed and Setled the Revd Mr Boden among them. And I am relieved from that burden of Duty in part, w^h I have Sustained, too great in the decline of life, being upwards of 70 Years of Age.

The Church in Newtown are so considerable in number & ability, that I am informed, they are providing for themselves. Some other destitute Churches, I am told, in different Towns & parishes are uniting in a commendable manner for the like pious purpose, to procure the regular administrations of religion.

But as I live upon the Western Border of the State, I cannot inform you so particularly as you request; I shall make enquery, and give you the best advice I can.

Neither can I say, to which of the Missionaries it would be most agreable, if called upon, to remove to New Brunswick or Cape Breton, or whether it would be agreable to any; but it appears probable some may be willing to imbrace the proposal, if I may Judge of their affection to the British Constitution, by my own, were I not so farr behind the Noon of Life.

Permit me Sir to recommend my Youngest Son Frederick, to Your and the Venerable Societies charitable Notice. Graduated at Kings College, New York, Obliged to flee in about twelve Months after his Graduation, first under Royal Protection and now with other Refugees Setled at Kingston, St Johns River, New Brunswick; at the peoples request he Reads divine Service to them, and as I am informed, they wish him to take Orders and Settle among them. Number of families there were once under my Pastoral Care.--

As to the alterations in divine Service, I can answer for none but my self. In the Litany I make no alterations, nor omissions, except not praying for the King Royal family & Noblesse.-- In the Communion Service, Instead of praying for the King, before the Collect for the day is Substituted a prayer for the Supreem Rulers in the Government here in being, as conformable to the prayer for the High Court of Parlement as is consistent with our present State. "Humbly beseeching Almighty God, as for the American States in general, and the High Court which presides over the whole, so for the Supreem Legislature of this State in particular, that God would [be] pleased to direct and prosper all their consultations to the advancement of his glory,

the good of his Church, the safety honour and welfare of his people, &c, &c"; in the words of the forementioned Collect.--

In the Prayer for the Ch^h Militant, we pray for all Christian Kings Princes & Governors, only omitting, Specially thy Servant George our King.

In the bidding prayer before Sermon, I only use a Short Collect "Prevent us O Lord in all our doings &c, ["] concluding with the Lords Prayer. Such I am informed is the general practice of the Missionaries. Such omissions & small alterations are Judged necessary as things are now Setled, Contrary to all expectations of the friends of Government in Ch^h & State here.

The Captive Jews were directed by God to pray for the Rulers & Government in being over them, that in the peace thereof, they might have peace. Much more do we think it our Christian Duty, for such, as in providence, are appointed to Rule over us.

I confine my self now principally to the Duties of my particular Cure, Officiating every third Sunday at Horsneck. Have the happiness to live in peace & attend my publick & private Duties without fear or danger; and hope to be Serviceable in promoting the interest of true Religion, and see my Ch^h again rise to a reputable State; though I n[e]ver Expect to see it in Number & Ability equal to what it was before our late unhappy troubles.

I only add my duty to the Venerable Board, hoping for the continuance of their favor and Charity to their Aged Servt, during now, his short pilgrimage, and best endeavours to be useful. And with high Esteem and unfeigned regard to Your Self, I am

Reverend Sir / Your Most Obed^t Humble Servt / and Affectionate Brother in Christ

Ebenezer Dibblee

The Reverend Doct^r Morice Secretary of the Venerable Society for Propagation of the Gospel in Foreign Parts.

[Addressed:] The Reverend Doctor Morice / Secretary of the Venerable Society / For the Propagation of the Gospel / in Foreign Parts. / Hatton Garden / London
[Endorsed: Read] Septr 1785

[1785, May 3, Stamford]

Stamford State of Connecticut
May 3, 1785

My Dear Revd Sir,

I am happy in the receipt of your fav of Feb. 14, 1785. Good Sir, why do you complain of my Silence, I answered with Joy the first advise I received from you, not knowing, only by hearsay, where you were, or how to Direct to you. You'r the only person of the Clergy fled from these inhospitable Regions, Solacing in the Sunshine of Royal fav^r -- that hath ever tho't me worthy of remembrance, neither have I troubled any one with a line but you, to remind them of my Existence.

Let my Brethren answer for themselves. My unhappy Situation in the late troublesome times, hath rendered me a Stranger to my Brethren here, and but seldem do I hear of what is planing in the Clerical Cabinet, or carrying into Execution.

This Spring we had news of the Peace. I was in New

York, had the pleasure to find and approve of Doctor Seabury's intention to go home for Episcopal Orders. By hearsay only, except by you, & since from Brother Hubbard at
New Haven, have I ever heard of the Obsticles he met with,
his final Tryumph over all opposition, by Climbing over
the Wall.

Let me ask you my Friend was there no other way for
him to be Cloathed with his Pontificals but by coming in at
the back Dore. In what Light is it viewed at Home, by the
dignified in Ch^h and State. Why did I say at Home, Gov-
ern^t hath disinherited us, nevertheless I trust we of the
Episcopal Ch^h in America have many friends, who wish
to serve us in our most important interests and Concerns.
And was there no possible way for Doctor Seabury to obtain Consecration but in a Method so obnoxious to Revolu-
tional Principles?

Will not Government with you, the Dignified Clergy &
the venerable Society, think we are all Jacobites? I have
no doubt of his Ecclesiastical Authority, but wish we might
preserve as friends to a union, as close a Connection, and
Uniformity with the Chh of England, as our present dis-
joynted state will admit.

But I am in the winter of life, Old mens Counsel is seldom asked, if it be, but little regarded. The cold climate
of adversity in which I have long been, may make me view
things in a wrong light, (yet) I could have wished Doctor
Seabury had waited a little longer with faith & patience.
I can see no reason why Government should oppose, or be
unfriendly to an American Episcopate in point of policy,
for I am persuaded if it had been granted many years before the late Revolution, it would have been their best security against it.

With respect to Dr. Chandler's Distribution of the
Voluntary Contributions for the suffering clergy, I never
addressed him on that Subject; nor inquired of my Brethren
of their Receipts. I received £50 comparitively with others
you mention, a trifle, if our sufferings could be weighed in
an Equal balance.

You know the former Laws & Constitutions of this
State, not a Rate was made up and Collected for me among
my people from the year 1775 to 1783. Every man did
what was right in his own eyes for the support of Religion.
Fences on the Glebe-Lands (purchased with St. George
Talbot's Benefaction, Subjected to an exorbitant interest
of 7 pr Cent during his Life & 3-1/2 during Mrs. Goolds,
but lately Dead, and for which I am yet greatly in arrears)
burnt up, lying as in common 7 or 8 years. 50 Sterling
will not repair at present the Damages in Fence & [----?]
equally fit for improvement, before my Dore a valuable
plot of three 3 acres of my own. Fences all destroyed,
from 1775 to 1781 like a common, which cost me better
than 10 Sterling to repair. Add to this the flight of my
Eldest Son (unhappy man--would to God I had died for him)
about Christmas 1776, his house plundered, a Wife and 5
children turned out and myself obliged to take them in until Spring, then Sent off to him. Destitute of necessary
bedding and Cloathing, not a grandson, whom I would have
kept, permitted to stay, the Cloathing given him taken
from him.

The Banishment of my Son Frederick in Novr 1776 till
Spring, then lately graduated at Kings College, New York,
to Lebanon (with about 20 of my Parishoners chiefly heads
of families) supported at my cost. Myself Obliged to flee

in March 1777 to my Dauter at Sharon to be inoculated for
smal Pox. The town then a Hospital Town, and the smal
Pox brought in by ye return of Soldiers, prisoners at Fort
Washington. The flight of Frederick (left to take care of
the family in my Absence) to save his life (Occasioned by
ye alarm of his Excellencies Genl Tryons Excursion to
Danbury) to his brothers on Long Island. My Sons looking
to me for Assistance, not daring to enter into Service wh
they might have done to advantage, in regard to my safety;
cost me better than 150 sterling in Bills Drawn and privately conveyed; wanted for my own Support. Add to this
the diminution of my Parish by the flight of numbers, reputable families and (best) support of the Chh. The Dangers
attending my person. One bold attempt on my life being
Shot at as I was going to attend a funeral. Waylaid and
not presuming to return the same way but seldom when I
went to attend the private Duties of my Cure. The bil-
letting and Quartering of Soldiers upon me, sometimes
a Company of a Troop of Horse, or a Militia Company,
Officers and Men. Terrors by night and Day for fear of
the Violence of Lawless Mobs & ungoverned Soldiery.
The Ruin of one of my Daughters by frights, for a long
time wholly Insane; and to this Day not wholly recovered
her former composure & tranquility. Add to this the
Burden of Publick Duty since our Churches were opened
(wh mine was Christmas, 1779) wh I never neglected
within or without our Lines, when permission could be
obtained to pass & repass; and for one or two years before the peace I met with less Interruption.

I have given you some general hints, my Dear Sir,
before of those past occurences; and my preservation, I
can ascribe to nothing but the providential care of Almighty God. I should not have troubled you again with a
repitition of my past sufferings During the unhappy Contest now subsided; were it not for the apparent Difference
between [----?] temporal Notice taken of them, and the
unequal distribution of publick Charity Designed for ye
relief of the greatest sufferers. But I never petitioned,
nor never will.

But my friend, my friend, who hath not forgotten your
Brethren in adversity--The family troubles, that dark
cloud in the dispensations of Providence wh hangs over
my head, overwhelms my Spirit, and will bring my Gray
hairs with Sorrow to the Grave.

"One trouble calls another on; and gathering o'er
    my Head, Falls
  Spouting down, till round my soul, a roaring Sea
    is Spread".

Blessed be God our Candlestick is not yet removed
with out Sceptre [----?]; I hope it will brighten up, and
the very principles for which it was persecuted, are now
in Wisdom Adopted for the Support of Government in Chh
and State.

Permit me to ask a fav^r from your readiness to
oblige, I repose my Confidence. A Bill for £25 Sterling,
Half years Salary, was Drawn upon the New Treasurer
of the Society 4th of October last in favor of Messr Reed
and Bogardus, is returned protested.

When first advised of it I was astonished, concluding
the Society had finally Determined to withdraw their Salaries from such of their servants as have borne the burden
& heat of the day.

Their Secretary, Doctor Morice, hath opened the Secret, and Says the Treasurer informs him, the Bills I've already Drawn & are already accepted amounts to £12, 10^sh last Christmas more than was due to me. Be pleased, good Sir, to examine critically into this affair. It appears to me the error is in the Secretary: If in me, I stand Justly Corrected.

I can have recourse back no farther than April, 1776, my last Draft while a Correspondence was kept open. All my Accounts & Advises to the Society are destroyed (my house having been searched & liable continually to be so as pretended for Illicit Goods) to that period. And I opened no correspondence till since the Peace. If I have drawn for more than was my Due it was since that period. From April 1776 to April 1784, makes 8 years. Two of my first Bills Drawn, of 50 each, were privately drawn for the relief of my children under Loyal Protection, and I cannot ascertain in whose Names they were drawn, my only concern was to know the Bills drawn were Due. I regarded not the Dates of the Bills Drawn at any time provided the Bills were Due. Every half Year at Easter & Michelmas-time for upwards of 20 years past hath been my practice to draw. Now from the minutes I have kept of Bills drawn since April 1776 to April 1784 are 2 of 50 in whose names I know not. 2 of 50 or 1 of one hundred, I think in favor of Nathaniel Peck of Greenwich in this State or for his benefit, who negociated it. 1 of 50 in favr Mr. Seabury Mercht in New York. 1 of 50 for Messrs. Fitch & Holly in Stamford. 1 of 50 in favr of Rev. Mr. Leaming, April, 1783. 1 of 25 in favr of Mr. Thomas Ellison of New York October 8, 1783; 1 Ditto of 25 in favr of Mr. Bogardus, April 22, 1784. Which makes 8 years compleat. The protested Bill in favr of Messrs Reed and Bogardus was dated 6th of October 1784, which so far as I can see at present judge is justly Due. My Salary was originally Appointed to Commence from St. John's Day, but between it and Easter term, was long Since adjusted to render half years drawing convenient. I recollect not that I ever Drew a Quarterly Bill of 12.10. Upon the Death of Mr. Palmer, I was ordered by he Secretary to Draw so far as I can recollect for that Nominal Sum, & pay it to his relict family. In like manner after Mr. Lamsons Death I was Ordered to Draw a Bill of 25 and pay it to ye relict Widow & Children; I did so and took Receipts. Those Bills Drawn in my name possible hath Occasioned the Errors. If I have erred it is through Mistake not intentially. If permitted, please to examin the Treasurer's Accounts, the Bills I have Drawn, the sums and in whose favor, which will Ascertain the matter. If I am in error I hope it will be considered as involuntary.

Frederick by applying to Business upon the Island had acquired to himself in Trade as good as 6 or 700£. New York Money. Married an agreeable Young Lady, but a Refugee of no other fortune but her personal vertues; but towards the Close of the War. Our Whale Boat [----?] found him, plundered him of all his goods, [----?] and even their Wareing Apparel. He is now in St. Johns River, at Kingston, New Brunswick. A number of Refugies are Settled there formerly of my Parish. He writes me [----?] of last month, he reads Divine Service to them. Doctor Morice tells me the attention of the Society is turned to that Province if my Son might be admitted to holy Orders & appointed a Missionary there I believe it would be highly

agreeable to him, as I designed him for the Service of the Ch^h in giving him a Collegiate education. If you can be of any Service in promoting it, it would be gratefully accepted. I have mentioned him to the Society....

Frederick is requested to take Orders and Settle among them.

Doctor Seabury, our right Reverend Father in God is not arrived. I believe he will not be received with that [----?], as if he came in at the right Dore.

If the New England States consulted their own Interest, for they are such the weightiest in the American Scale, they would enter soon into the treaty you mention.

With Family Compliments to You and your Daughter, with my prayers for the best of heaven's blessings to attend you.

I am Reverend Sir,
Your unfeigned Friend
And Affectionate Brother
Ebenezer Diblee.
Reverend Mr. Peters.

[Addressed:] The Reverend Mr. Peters / Pimlico / London.
[Endorsed:] received July 6, 85

[1785, May 5, London?]
Asylum, May 5th, 1785
My Dear & Honoured Madam,

I wrote to you particularly by Capt. Willett & Capt. Frost, and had just Time to add a Postcript to my Letters on the Death of our dear Sister, of which we had just received an Account from Mr Hamilton, but not a Line from any of the Family-- Within this Fortnight we have had two Letters from our Brother Francis, but no Particulars of her Sickness & Death--Dear Soul! She is happy--her Life was spent in Active Goodness, which reaches much higher than Speculation. She did not "understand all Mysteries & all Knowledge," yet she had that Gift, which is superior to all, even the Gift of Divine Charity, the Love of the Lord & the Love of our Neighbour-- Without these all besides is no better than sounding Brass or a tinkling Cymbal--

Dr Chandler sails for New-York in a few Days on a Visit to his Family at Elizabeth-Town-- He spends a Year I believe with them, & returns to England--to be consecrated a Bishop, as it is generally believed here-- By this Time I hope you have seen our good Friend Bishop Seabury, who is gone on the truly Apostolical Plan to be Bishop of ye Episcopal Church in Connecticut. He talked of making a Visit to Philada--and will undoubtedly call on you--

The New Church from above, the Jerusalem of the Revelation, is come down upon Earth--the Number of her Members is yet small--but they will increase-- You will understand my Meaning, if you have read ye Books Mr Adams sent you-- Look henceforward for an Internal Millennium--for that must first come-- The External is the last-- Wonderful are the ways of Jehovah-- Great Things are ripening for Manifestation-- How little & contemptible the Politics of a foolish World-- How idle, how wicked, the busy, bustling, fighting, selfish Contentions, which have lately shaken two unhappy Countries-- Both now sacrificed to ye dirty Views of their pretended Patriots on both Sides-- The Lust of Dominion--not the genuine Love of

Liberty, has at length fully appeared to be their Motives--
The Ring-Leaders are dropping of[f]--and their Tools, tho
now high in Office, will not long continue-- How favoured
have I been, to be torn, from the Worldly Contention, in
which I was too much engaged--& enabled to spend my last
Seven Years in increasing Tranquillity, & Preparation for
yᵉ Appearance of Xt's Kingdom--

We are all well-- My Father never so happy since he
was born-- He has now & then a few Weaknesses & Aches,
that are inseparable from Age-- But in his Health upon the
whole, amazingly improved since his Arrival--& bids fair
for many Years to come-- Betsy makes it her whole Study
to make him & all of us happy-- He is delighted with her
attention-- We have all the Comforts, without the Superfluities of Life-- Our only Wants are for our Friends.
A few Superfluities, if we had them, we could chearfully
spare-- But if Heaven thought proper, he would send them--
When he does, he will. It is our Parts to be content &
thankful--

Pray send us no more good things-- They cost us 6
times their value, to get them into our Hands--

I beg to be affectionately remembered to good Mʳˢ
White, & am pleased to hear, that you reside under the
same Roof-- I have written largely to Dʳ White, by Willett
& Frost, & hourly expect his Answer-- Tell our Brother
Francis, that I am pleased with his continuing the Correspondence thro his sister-- He writes to me & I to him by
yᵉ same Channel-- My Love to Nancy & yᵉ Babes--

All join me in hearty & affectionate Remembrances to
Jenny, and yᶜ Dʳ & Nancy Coalc & their Children-- I am
pleased to hear that our Brother Thomas has taken such an
happy Turn, & is like to be well settled in Virginia-- I have
scrawled you a long Letter, in Hopes of a long & particular
Answer-- This will be sent by Dʳ Chandler--from your
most affectionate Son,
J. Duché

[1785, June 23, Middletown]
To all People to whom these Presents shall come Greeting
Know Ye that we Philip Mortimer and Mary Alsop both of
Middletown, in the County of Middlesex, the said Mary as
Administratrix on the estate of Richard Alsop Esqʳ late of
sᵈ Middletown decᵈ and Guardian of the Minor Heirs of said
estate being hereunto specially impowered &, authorized by
a special act of the General Assembly of the State of Connecticut dated the second Thursday of May AD 1776 for the
consideration of our affection for the Episcopal Church in
sᵈ Middletown, our Zeal to promote its Interest and other
good causes & considerations us thereunto moving; do
give, grant, Bargain, Sell and confirm unto said Episcopal
Church called Christs Church one certain piece of land
lying in sᵈ Middletown containing about one acre and is
Butted and Bounded Northerly and Easterly on Highways
Westerly and Southerly on Land that belonged to Lieuᵗ John
Kents Homelot together with the Mantion House and all the
other Buildings thereon standing-- To Have and to Hold the
above granted and bargained premises with the appurtenances thereof unto the sᵈ Church called Christs Church
forever for the use and support of the Gospel Ministry
therein And we the said Philip and Mary for ourselves
our Heirs Executors & Administrators covenant to & with
sᵈ Church that at & until the ensealing of these presents

we are well seized of the premises as of a good indefeasa-
ble estate in fee simple and have good right to bargain and
sell the same in manner as is above written and further-
more we the said Philip & Mary do by these presents bind
ourselves and our heirs forever to warrant & defend the
above granted and bargained premises unto the sᵈ Church
against all claims and demands whatsoever In Witness
whereof we have hereunto set our hands and seals this
23ᵈ day of June AD 1785--

Philip Mortimer   ⟨Seal⟩
Mary Alsop   ⟨Seal⟩

Signed Sealed & delivered   Middˣ County ss Middletown
    in Presence of   June 23. 1785 Personally ap-
    Asher Miller   pearᵈ Philip Mortimer Esqʳ &
    Abby Alsop   Mary Alsop Signers & Sealers
       of the foregoing instrument &
July 5ᵗʰ 1785 A true Record   acknowledged the same to be
Test: B. Fisk Regʳ   their free act & deed before
       me
       Asher Miller Jusᵗ Peace

NB The Consideration of the above deed is in the
    Subscription at the Right hand

Tⁿ Clkˢ Offᶜᵉ ⎫
Middletown   ⎬ May 9. 1809.
       The foregoing is a true Copy of Record
       Exᵈ By Jnº Fisk Tⁿ Clk

[1785, July, Stratford]
My Dear Sir,
I now acquaint you, that Bishop Seabury is to meet
the Clergy of this state, at Middletown on the 3d of August
next. At which time & place we shall be much pleased to
see you, and the rest of the clergy of your state.

I must wish for a Christian union of all the Churches
in the thirteen states; for which good purpose we must lay
aside all warmth of temper, and allow private convenience
to give way to public utility.

We have no views of usurping any authority over our
Brothers and Neighbors, but wish them to unite with us,
in the same friendly manner, that we are ready and willing to do, with them....

Jeremiah Leaming

[Rev. Dr. Abraham Beach at New York, N.Y.]

[1785, Aug. 2-4, Middletown]
Augᵗ 2, 1785
At a Conventⁿ of the Clergy of the Chh. of England at
Middleton, present,

Revᵈ Messʳˢ Leaming   Jarvis
          Mansfield   Bowden
          Scovil   Clarke
          Andrews   Bostwick
          Hubbard   Tyler

Messʳˢ Ben: Moore from New York & Mr. Parker
from Boston joined us.

The Conven. was opened and the Rev. Mʳ Leaming
was chosen president.

The right reve^d Dr. S. Seabury attended upon this Con. and his Letters of Consec: being requested by the same; they were produced and read, whereby it appeared to this Con: that he hath been duly & canonically consecrated a Bishop by the Bishops of the Epis: Chh: in Scotland.

Augt 3^d

8 o.Clock A.M. Conven: met. after the Address of the Cler: to the Bishop was reconsidered by the Conven: & approved, the Clergy repaired to the Chh. and appointed 4 of their Body to return to the parsonage, & Mr. Jarvis, in the name of the Clergy, declared to the Bp. their Confirmat^n of their former Election of him, & that they now acknowleg^d & rec^d him their Bp.

Then the Bp. return'd his Answ^r of Acceptance & proceeded with them to the Chh-- Being introduced into Chh. & seated in his Chair in the Altar. the Cler at the Rails; their address to him was read by Mr. Hubbard, after whh the Bp. read his Answer--and gave the Apostolical Blessing--then the Clergy retired to th^r pews. And the Bp. began D. Service wh ye Litany, accord^g to the Rubrick in the Office for Ordination of Deacons: The four follow^g persons, Messrs Vandyke, Shelton, Baldwin, of Connec. & Mr. Fergusson of Maryland, being present to be admitted into the Order of Deacons--

The Litany being ended, Mr. Bowden read the first Commun^n Service. The Bishop then read the Service, consecrated the Elements & administered the Bread, Mr. Bowden assisted by administering the Cup. The Commun^n finished, the Bp. then proceeded to the Ordination. Mr. Jarvis officiated as ArchDeacon--after the Ordinat^n a Sermon was preached by the Rev^d Mr. Leaming. The Congregat^n was dismiss'd by the Bp.--from Chh. the Clergy preceeded by the Bp returned to the parsonage. Mr. Jarvis by order of the Conven: gave the thanks of the same to Mr. Leaming for his Sermon delivered before them, with their desire of a copy of it to be printed.

The Bp. then dissolv'd the Convent^n, & directed the Clergy to meet him at 5 o'clock in Convocation-- They met accordingly, & the Convocat^n was adjourned to the next Morn^g Thursday 9 o'Clock--A.M.

Thursd^y 4th--Met--at 11 o'c A.M. went to Chh. Mr. Parker read prayers, and Mr. Moore preach^d a Sermon. after which the Bp delivered a Charge to the Clergy--

P.M. Mr. Parker communicated to the Convocat^n the purport of his Delegation from the Clergy in the State of Massachusets; viz to collect the Sentiments of the Connect Clergy in respect of Dr. Seabury's episcopal Consecrat^n, the Regulat^ns of his episcopal Jurisdict^n, and their thots of connecting themselves with them, under his Episcopal Charge. The Clergy of Conn: expressed th^r warmest Wishes for the Union & concurrence of th^r Breth^rn in Massachusetts und^r Bp. Seabury--

Frid^y 5th. After appointing Mr. Bowden, Mr. Parker & Mr. Jarvis as a Committee to consider & make some Alterat^ns in the Liturgy needful for the present Use of the Chh, the Convent^n adjourned to meet ag^n at New Haven in Sept^r--

Sund^y 7. Mr. Colin Ferguson was ordain'd priest, Mr. Parker, Mr. Bowden & Mr. Jarvis attended the Ordinat^n as presbyters. Mr. Thom^s Fitch Oliver, from Providence, Rhode Island, was ordain'd Deacon on the same Day--

Order of Service

The following mem of the Order of Service is appended to the paper containing the Minutes of the Convention:

1. at 10. the Clerg: proceed to Chh.
2. 4 Cler: deputed to acquaint Bp. S. of y^e of Cler: do now Confirm the form^r Elect^n--to recognize him as th^r Bp.
3. 2 Cler: to return wh his answ^r of Acceptance the other two follow after wh the Bp--
4. the presid^t ye Add of ye Clergy at the Altar--
5. the Bp. return his Answ^r--
6. The Cler:, kneeling receive the apostolic Bless^g--
7. The Bp. proceed to the Litany.
8. Mr. Bowden read the first Commun^n Service.
9. the Sermon.
10. the Offertory & Administ^n by the Bp--
11. Ordinat^n.

Then follows what is evidently the promise of Conformity made by the candidates for Ordination:

I N.M. do declare that the Book of Common Prayer, & Ordering of Bishops, Priests, & Deacons, of the Church of England, contains in it nothing contrary to the Word of God, & that it may lawfully be so used; & that I myself will, so far as shall be consistent with the alteration necessary to be made on account of the civil constitutions of the State in which I shall live, use the form in the said book prescribed, in Public prayer, & administration of the Sacraments, and none other, unless in Obedience to competent ecclesiastical Authority; And I do make & subscribe this declaration willingly & ex animo & in the presence of Alm. God do promise to observe it faithfully.

MS. record of the Address of the Clergy of Connecticut presented to Bishop Samuel Seabury at the Convention of the Clergy held at Middletown, Connecticut, August 3rd, 1785; together with the reply of the Bishop to the same. (Jarvis Papers.)

> To the Right Rever^d Father in God Samuel by Divine Providence Bishop of Connecticut
> The Address of the Episcopal Clergy of the State of Connecticut in Convention Assembled

Rev^rd Father We the Subscribers for ourselves & other Presbyters of the Chh of England embrace with pleasure this early opportunity of congratulating you on your safe return to your native country & on the accomplishment of that arduous enterprise in whh at our desire you engaged.

Devoutly do we adore & reverently thank the great head of the Chh that he has been pleased to preserve you thro' a long & dangerous voyage, that he has crowned your endeavours with success & now at last permits us to enjoy, under you, the long & ardently desired blessing of a pure valid & free Episcopacy. A Blessing which we receive as the precious gift of God himself; & humbly hope that the work which he has so auspiciously begun he will confirm and prosper, & make it a real benefit to our Church not only in this State, but in all the American States in general by uniting them in doctrine, discipline, & worship; by supporting the cause of Christianity against all its opposers, & by promoting piety, peace, concord & mutual affection among all denominations of Christians-- Whatever can be done by us, for the promotion of so good a work, shall be done with united attention, & the exertion of our best

abilities--& as you are now, by our voluntary & united Suffrages, signified first to you, at New York in April, 1783, by the Rev^d Mr. Jarvis, & now ratified & Confirmed in this present Convention, elected Bp. of that branch of the Catholic & Apostolical Church in Connecticut, to which we belong, We, in the presence of Almighty God, declare to the world that we do unanimously & voluntarily accept, & receive & recognize you to be our Bishop, Supreme in the government & administration of all Ecclesiastical Offices in our Church.

And we do solemnly engage to render you all that respect, duty & submission, which we believe do belong & are due to your high office: & which as we understand, were given by the Presbyters to their Bishops in the Primitive Church, while in her native purity, she was unconnected with, & uncontrolled by any secular power.

The Experience of many years had convinced the whole body of the clergy, & many of the Laymembers of our Communion, of the necessity there was of resident bishops among us. Fully & publicly was our cause pleaded, & by such arguments as must have carried conviction to the minds of all candid & liberal. they were however, for reasons which we unable to assign, neglected by our superiors in England. Many of those arguments had been drawn from our being members in the national Church, & Subjects of the British Government. These of course lost their force, upon the separation of this country from great Britain, by the late peace. Our case thereby became more desperate, & our spiritual necessities much increased. Filial affection induced us still to place confidence in our parent Church & country, whose Liberal benevolence we had experienced & do gratefully acknowledge. to this Church was our immediate application directed, earnestly requesting a Bishop to collect, govern & continue our scattered, wandring & sinking Church. And great was, & still continues to be our surprise, that a request so reasonable in itself, so congrous to the nature of government of that church, & so absolutely necessary in the Church of Christ as they & we believe it to be, should be refused. We hope that the successors of the Apostles in the Church of England have sufficient reasons to justify themselves to the world & to God; we however no of none such, nor can our imagination frame any.

But blessed be God! another door was opened for you. In the mysterious economy of his Providence he had preserved the remains of the old Episcopal Church of Scotland, under all the malice & persecutions of its enemies. In the school of adversity its pious & venerable Bps. had learned to renounce the pomps & grandeur of the world, & were ready to do the work of their heavenly father. As outcasts they pitied us; as faithful holders of the Apostolical Commission, what they had freely received they freely gave. From them we have received a valid, & purely ecclesiastical Episcopacy, & are thereby made complete in all our parts, & have our right to be considered as a living, & we hope thro God's grace shall be, a vigorous branch of the Catholic Church.

To these venerable Fathers our sincerest thanks are due; & they have them most fervidly-- May the Almighty be their rewarder, regard them in mercy, support them under the persecutions of their enemies, & turn the hearts of their persecutors, & make their simplicity & godly sincerity to be known unto all men! And whereever the American Episcopal Church shall be mentioned in the world, may this good deed wh they have done for us be spoken of for a memorial of them.

Reply of Bishop Seabury to the Foregoing Address

Rev^d & highly esteemed Gentlemen

I heartily thank you for your kind congratulations on my safe return to my native country, & Join with you in joy & thanks to Alm God for the success of ye important business which your application excited me to undertake. May God enable us to do every thing wth a view to his glory & the good of his Church.

Accept of my acknowledgements for the Assurances you give of exerting your best abilities to promote the welfare of, not only our own Church, but of common Christianity & the peace & mutual affection of all denominations of Christians. I shall most certainly be very apprehensive of sinking under the weight of that high office to which I have been, under God's providence, raised by your voluntary & free Election--did I not assure myself of your ready advise & assistance in the discharge of its important duties--grateful therefore must be to me the assurances of supporting the Authority of your Bp. upon the true principles of the primitive Church, before it was controlled and corrupted by secular connections & worldly policy. Let me intreat your prayers to our supreme head for the continual assistance of his holy Spirit, that I may in all things fulfil his holy will--

The surprise you express at the rejection of your application in England is natural. But where the ecclesiastical & civil constitution are so closely woven together, the first characters in the church for station & merit may find their good dispositions rendered ineffectual by the intervention of the civil authority. And whether it is better to submit quietly to this state of Affairs in England or to risque that confusion whh would probably ensue sh^d an Amendment be attempted, demands some consideration.

The Sentiments you entertain of the venerable Bpps. in Scotland is highly (pleasing) to me. Their Conduct thro the whole business was candid, friendly & Christian, appearing to me to arise from a true sense of duty & to be founded in & conducted by the true principles of the primitive Apostolical Church. And I hope you will join with me in manifestations of Gratitude to them by always keeping up the most intimate Communion with them & their suffering Church.

[1785, Sept. 25, New Milford]

New Milford Connectit. Sepr 25th 1785

Reverend Sir,

I acknowledge the Receipt of your Letter Feb^ry 27th 1785, in which, the Treasurer of the Society accuses me of having drawn on him in Dec^m last when Nothing was due to me, and that before, I had overdrawn £2..10..0: but in Consideration of the Expense attending Protests of Bills, the Draft has been paid. Was this actually the Case. I acknowledge myself under the strongest Obligation to the Treasurer, and the venerable Society and esteem it as a singular Mark of their Favour to me: but as I have endeavourd to keep an exact and regular Account of all my Drafts since or before the Close of the War, have drawn in favour of Mr Isaac Beers of New Haven, and in favour of no other Person, having confered with him on the Subject

not being able to discover any mistake on my Side, must (at present) think the Mistake is owing to the Treasurer.

Notwithstanding necessity has forced me contrary to my Wish, as well as that of the Treasurer to draw Quarterly, yet, had I received your Letter sooner, should have complyed with his Request of only drawing every half year; but your Letter did not arrive till it was out of my Power, according to the Resolution of the Society published in their late Abstract, of withdrawing their Assistance from the Missionaries within the States.

However inconsistant it might have been with their Charter, to continue Missionaries without the Kings Dominion, [I] was in hopes, the Salleries might have continued during the Lives of the present Missionarys, who in the late horrible War for the Sake of their Conscience, King and the Brittish Government endured every scene of Distress; and now the Society's withdrawing their Bounty from us, renders our Scituation (mine in particular) truely deplorable, Notwithstanding, I acknowledge we ought to be truly thankful for, and ever bear in Mind the Charity that has been displayed in these Parts of the World by that venerable Body.

As the Society and Brittish Government propose doing for those Missionaries that will repair within the Dominions of the King, I wish to have the Offer of a Mission in New Brunswick, and shoud hope Joyfully to spend the remainder of my Days under Brittish Government upon the River of S.t John, where I have two very Affectionate Brothers, who in the late troublesome times for the sake of the King left their Habitations and followed their Profession (that of Surgery) in the Brittish Army

As I stand ready to serve the Society within the Brittish Empire, whenever properly encouraged to remove, hope their Compassion will suffer me to draw as usual upon their Treasurer. Wish as soon as possible to know their Pleasure.

Since Mar: 25: 1785 have baptized 100 Infants 13 adult Persons, and married only three Couple. Last Aug.t I visited the Destitute Mission of New Windsor, at which time, I baptized 60 Infants and 13 adults.

I have drawn upon the Societys Treasurer two Quarter Bills £7..10 each dated June and Sep.t 25: 1785 in favour of M.r Isaac Beers of New Haven.-- I am Reverend Sir with every Sentiment of Respect your most Obed.t humb.le Serv.t
Richard Clarke

[1786, Mar. 20, Stamford]
Stamford State of Connecticut
March 20th, 1786.
My Dear Sir,

Your favour of the 20th of July last, I received in October. Upbraid me not with neglect of indifference, it will be cruel. It astonished and confounded me. I knew not what to say. When the Son of Man cometh, will he find faith in the earth? I esteem you for your probity and integrity, and shall be happy in your future correspondence. You say what profit can I receive from your groans and tears. Much every way. Your language speaks the pulse of your heart. It is no small consolation that I have a Brother who regards that Apostolical precept; Bear ye one anothers burdens, and so fulfill the law of Christ. This and the consolations of Religion are my support in this last cloudy por-

tion of life. I thank you for every demonstration of your regards to me & my Son, and your kind endeavours to serve.

I unbosomed my troubled mind but little expected my uncorrected letter would have been laid before that pious, learned, most charitable Body. It was wrote in the bitterness of my Soul. That severe rebuke of providence, (less than my defects) and my age, constrains me to sojourn in Mosoch, and dwell in the tents of Kedar. What delayed my Answers to yours; I could get no answer from my Son in New Brunswick, till within a few days. I gave him the earliest notice of my final determination not to remove, of having recommended him to the Society, wishing to know if he retained his former inclination to enter into Orders. My advises never reached him, till mine of the 25th of last November--tho he had received Mr. Jarvis's wrote by your kind order. Till my last he flattered himself, I might be induced to remove; but in his letter of the 29th of Janr. Just received, he says, it was always his wish to go into the service of the Church, till the unhappy disturbances between the Mother Country and the Colonies began. The rubbers he met with damped his spirits, but by reading of service for the Chh of Kingston his inclination for the service returned. He laments his long necessary seperation from his Studies, the want of books and Cash &c.

He hath met with a kind invitation from Doctor Morice with assurances of being provided for at Kingston by the Society, upon recommendations in his favr & due representation of the propriety of Establishing a Mission there. I have just advised him of it, and doubt not of his resolution to go home for holy Orders, if he can make his way, relying upon the good disposition of the Society to provide for him there, or else where more to his advantage. My finances are so small, I cannot lend him that assistance I could wish. I fear he will be put to difficulty to make his way into holy Orders. If he goes home, you will be so kind as to favour him with your best advice, and take him under your paternal care & direction. What ever service you render him, it shall be gratefully accepted & rewarded--place it to my account. Can no charitable allowance be obtained, to defray the expence of his Voyage, and furnish him with Books? If the Society withdraw their supporting hand from me, I must end my days in want, dishonor and contempt. Happy for me, that the irregularity complained of in the draft of my Bills arose from former mistakes in the treasurer of the Society, not placing to their account the money I drew for Palmer & Lamson families. Doctor Morice, hath in a most friendly and polite manner given me early advice of it, and given me leave to draw for Seventy Pound; twenty-five of which I drew last Michelmas, knowing that to be due; to atone for my protested Bill, and wh was better than £5 New York Money extraordinary expense. But as there was no error in my Drafts, it appears to me £75 must be my due at the closing my account with the Society.

The Character you give some Gentlemen, some of whom I entertained a favourable opinion, is very surprising. Their high opinion of themselves, I have been fully sensible; the unequal distribution of the Charitable Collection for the suffering Clergy is amazing. I never had but fifty pounds assigned me. The Rebuffs the haughty, Proud, Covetous, aspiring Hibernian, Dr. I-g-l-s* hath

met with, to his great mortification; together with the secrets of the other characters, I wish to be let into the knowledge. I envy not their Wealth or Honours. It is too late in life for me to wish or desire undeserved honour or promotion. Mr. Mansfield['s] unhappy dispute with the Laights is compromised and settled by his Son. The Clergys neglect of the Venerable Society in their application for Dr. Seaburys consecration, is the height of ingratitude & unpardonable. Who counselled Doct[r] S-b-y to that unadvised Step to obtain Episcopal Orders, I cannot lean. If my name was exhibited among the rest to the Arch Bishop, it was without my knowledge--I was not in their Counsels--I have no personal Objection to the Bishop but his coming in at the back door of the British Constitution, I have signified my disapprobation of, for which, & my neglect of a congratularly address, hath been Esteemed unfriendly. We are not all Jacobites, however we are esteemed & neglected, for I know of more than One in this State who had no Idea of Dr. S pursuing such a measure to obtain Episcopal Consecration, until it was publickley announced, and think it hard the innocent should suffer with the guilty.

But to his honour be it spoken, the BP conducts with great wisdom and prudence, in the security he hath taken, of such as he hath ordained, of their conformity to the Liturgy of the Chh of England, except where it affects the civil State & Rulers.--and he hath appointed no other alterations in any part of the Service, but in praying for the Governor & Rulers of the State, instead of the King & Royal Family. Having set his foot down I hope it will remain immovable. And that Connecticut Episcopal Chh for the unity prosperity, increase of Edification of which I am deeply interested & concerned, will finally be placed upon as near a footing, in point of Ecclesiastical Polity, Doctrine, Discipline & Worship with the Chh for which we retain the greatest reverence & esteem, as the Civil Constitutions of the respective States will admit.

It hath been a matter of doubt with me, whether by the Revolution, we were released from all obligation in Spiritualities of Canonical obedience & subjection to your Chh. And if in the wisdom of the Gov[m] in Ch[h] & State, it was thought unadvisable to consecrate Bish[p] S-S--Duty, Gratitude & Interest dictated the wisdom & prudence, till in providence an effectual door was opened to obtain a Bishop in a more regular way. And I feared, as it hath in fact proved, where the Episcopal Ch[h] in the United States looked upon themselves released from all obligations of Uniformity conformity and Subjection to our Mother Ch[h] we should make wild work in reforming the Liturgy, and Setting an Ecclesiastical Polity & Constitution. Witness the late grand Convention at Philadelphia last Sept. composed of Ecclesiastical & Lay delegates of the Southern States. They have laid it down as a fundamental principle in their new Constitution, that the Churches should be governed by such a consistery or convention; their Bishop or Bishops if they can obtain such, shall be members only ex officio--not president--and Amenable to s[d] convention for his conduct (a Bishop only in name, & do the drudgery of Ordination). In a high opinion of their own wisdom self sufficienty & importance, they have at a Jirk knocked off the Athe[rn] & Nicene Creeds, [----?] & altered y[e] Apostle's Creed, also the frequent repition of y[e] Lord's prayer, and it is said of y[e] Gloria Patri. Also have altered the Baptismal, Matrimonial, Visitation of the Sick, & Burial Office.

They have Ordered their new Fangled Service, or Common Prayer to be Printed,** and I shall be able to give you a more accurate & Authentic account. What will not men do when loose from restraint?

A form of Service is printed in the Bay State with an intire exclusion of all Divine honour to the Son of God, in the Creeds, & all parts of the Service.***

The Crown is not only despoiled of one of its brightest Jewels, but the Ark of God is in the Dust!

Our compliments wait upon Miss your admirable Daughter & Mr. Jarvis. His connections are well. I have sent to Frederick to be delivered, or forwarded to you, Mr. Leaming's Sermon, & address of the Clergy &c to B-S at there first meeting at Middle Town.

My prayers and best wishes attend you,
I am, Revd Sir, with unfeigned Esteem,
Your Most Affect Brother, in adversity,
Ebenezer Diblee.

Reverend Mr. Peters.

_____

*Rev. Dr. Inglis, later Bishop of Nova Scotia.

**The liturgical alterations adopted by the Convention of 1785 were printed in what was known as "The Proposed Book". It met with so much disfavor that it did not come into common use, and was superseded by the Prayer Book adopted at the Convention of 1789.

***The reference is to the revised Prayer Book issued by King's Chapel, Boston, which reflected its adoption of the Unitarian faith. The title page runs as follows:

```
            A
         LITURGY
Collected Principally From The
 BOOK OF COMMON PRAYER
      For the Use of The
FIRST EPISCOPAL CHURCH
            IN
          BOSTON;
      Together With The
    PSALTER OR PSALMS
            OF
          DAVID.
          Boston
Printed by Peter Edes, in State Street
        MDCCLXXXV
```

[Addressed:] The Reverend Mr. Peters / Pimlico / London.
[Endorsed:] recd June 13

[1786, Apr. 20, Norwich]

Norwich in Connecticut
April 20: 1786
Rev[d] Sir,

Your Letter of July 20th & 26th I received Octo[r] 28th and soon after wrote in Answer to it, which I hope you have received.-- Trade has been on the Decline here, for more than a Year; and is now at a very low Ebb; and in all Appearance, must decline still more.-- I see no Chance of meddling with Trade to any Advantage. We have no Mony here.-- The People of Connecticut are

tearing one another to Pieces, with Executions, for Debt.--
I hear that Scovel, Andrews, Viets &c, are going to Nova
Scotia this Spring. The Livings of the Clergy here, are
miserable indeed-- The People are poorer than ever;--
loaded with Taxes; and no Money to be had. M͛ Fogg has
lately received a Letter from the Society, offering hi[m]
the Mission of Harbour Island & Eleuthera in the Bahamas;
and intimat[es] that the Mission of New Providence was
likely to be vacant. I h[ear] Brother Fogg will go by the
first Oppertunity to harbor-Island; and he wishes to have
me go to New-Prov[idence] that we may be Company for
each other. I am now Writing to [the] Society to know
whether they will give me Liberty to move to [New]-
Providence if the Mission there is vacant; even in C[ase
I] have benefit to continue my Salery here, a few years
long[er I] see no reasonable Prospect of living here. I
am not likely to [earn] so much as thirty Pounds sterling
a Year where I am; which [would] no more than pay for the
Board and Lodging of a single Man But I have a Wife and
six Children living: and to continue here, with the Society's
Assistance, I must spend more than thirty Pounds 11 sterling a Year, of my Wives Estate; and Lands now are in no
Demand here, and the Times are rapidly growing worse.
What then can I do, but Move, if I have Liberty, into the
Kings Dominions, which I should be very fond of: Nova-
scotia I am not fond of; but New-Providence I think would
be agreeable if it is a good Living. I know not what the
Living is; but I am told it is a very healthy Place and suppose the Living must be a good one; & I wish for your Assistance, with the Secretary of the Society, to obtain the
Mission at New-Providence, if [it is] vacant or will be vacant soon. That State of this Country, which you pointed
out, in your last Letter but one, I think, is likely to take
Place. This once ple[ntiful] Country for Provisions, is
now a Country of Scarcity [a] starving Country. N[othing]
but Money will purchase either Bread or Meat or any Necessary of Life for the most Part. And but few know how
to get Money. The Consequence is, that many Families
in Norwich are totally destitute both of Bread and Meat,
for ten Days at a Time which was never the Case here before. Taxes are high, and Nothing to pay the Hard-mony
ones with. Many Peoples Estates are taken for their Taxes: but the Collectors can sell but few of them on Account
of the Scarsity of Money. The Times are grown vastly
worse in six Months past. It is frequently said, that all
the hard Money in Connecticut is not enough to pay for the
Writs, Court Charges, Officers Fees & Executions arising
on the private Debts that are already sued with out paying
one farthing of the Debt. And the Courts sit a great Part
o[f the time;] hence on[e] may Judge of the Situation we are
in. The Congress has lately told us publicly, that all the
Continental Taxes paid since the War, have not been sufficient to pay the Saleries of the public Officers: and if we
do not pay more, we cannot Support our national Credit
and seem to intimate that we must cease to be a Nation.
The Interest of our national Debt abroad is call'd for, and
the first Payment of the Principal is due next Spring. But
we cannot pay the Interest of that part of the national Debt
which we owe among ourselves; so that the Debt is accumu-
lating, & our public Securities, and even the Certificates
for Interest are depreciated from two thirds of their nominal Sum to one half. And instead of paying higher Taxes,
we are not now able to pay Taxes so high as we have paid.

The Taxes that have already been laid, is a Burden that
daily crushes the Estates of many of the People by it's
Weight. I believe this Country, especially New England,
will be very full of Trouble & Confusion, perhaps Riots
and great Convulsions, in two Years Time. And where
the Troubles will End, I have not sagacity to foresee. And
I am willing to be out of [th]e Country with my Family, before the heavy Troubles come on; [wh]ich I am afraid will
be much greater than even those of the late War. Indeed
now [it] is more difficult for most People to live, than it
was at any Time [in] the War: but I apprehend that great
Troubles [will a]rise from party Rage, when Poverty and
Oppression becomes [more] distressing. Most of the com-
mercial Interest have been very [unsucc]essful abroad
since the War; and many of them seem now to be [turni]ng
their Attention to the Estates of their Debtors to make
their Fortunes at Home: and this [tur]n is become fashionable with most People who have outstanding [de]bts. An
Estate lately accounted worth five Hundred Pounds, will
scarcely pay one hundred Pounds of Debts. But since the
sufferers are likely to be much the most numerous Part of
the Community; these Things will bring Us trouble in the
End. I have had no Hand in the Occasion of these troubles,
and I am willing to avoid the Misery of them; which I cannot do without quitting the Country. And therefore I am
ready to move into the Kings Dominions; and wish to be
an useful Missionary of the Society.

 I remain your affectionat / Friend and Brother,
          John Tyler.
Rev͎ᵈ Samuel Peters.

[1786, May 5, New Milford]
      New Milford May 5ͭͪ 1786
Reverend Sir
 I wrote to the venerable Society the 7ͭͪ of last March
acquainting them that I shou'd draw upon their Treasurer
a Bill for £50..0 Sterling to enable me to go as soon as
possible, in Company with Mess͙ʳˢ Scovel and Andrews to
New Brunswick as I with a thankful heart, accepted of the
Appointment to one of the new Missions there, which in
fact was offerd me by what was expressed in your Letter
to M͙ʳ Scovel, the Words of which are as follows "There
will be in this next year's Estimate an allowance for two
more Missions in New Brunswick, which may be a provision for M͙ʳ Clarke unless M͙ʳ Mansfield shou'd prefer
it. But whoever goes must go as early as possible"--
In as much as M͙ʳ Mansfield does not prefer it, the Invitation is to me, and I have readily accepted of it-- M͙ʳ
Mansfield tells me he has wrote to the Society & given
the Reasons of his not inclining to remove.
 I have put of[f] drawing the Bill to this very Day,
hoping to have had the Pleasure of receiving from the Society an Answer to a Letter I wrote the 25ͭͪ of last Sep͙ʳ
for an Appointment in New Brunswick.-- But as I am going on Board to Morrow in Company with M͙ʳˢʳˢ Scovel
and Andrews bound to S͙ᵗ John's in New Brunswick I have
draw'd a Bill of £50, fifty pounds Sterling upon the Society's Treasurer in favour of M͙ʳˢʳˢ Daniel and Elijah
Boardman, to enable me to remove my family to New
Brunswick where I promise myself the happiness of
spending the remainder of my days under the Protection of King George and the <u>wholesome</u> Laws of British

Government.

I shall write to the venerable Society immediately after my Arrival at St Johns, and wish the Answer to this (if [I] may be favour'd with one) may be directed to the Care of Revd Mr Hubbard at New Haven, as I shall be obliged to return in the fall to settle some Affairs here which I have not time now to go thro' with and obey the Order of the Society of "going as early as possible" which Order I chearfully & punctually obey and trust ever shall

I am Reverend Sir with every sentiment of Respect your and the venerable [Society's] most Obed.^t hum.^l Sev.^t

Richard Clarke

Revd Dr Morice

[Addressed:] Reverend Dr Morice Secretary / to the Society for the Propagation / of the Gospel in foreign Parts / Hatton Gardens London
[Endorsed: Read] Septr 1786.

[1786, May 11, Norwalk]
To the Honble the General Assembly of the State of Connecticut to be holden at Hartford on the 2.^d thursday of Instant Maye

The Memorial of John Sanders of Norwalk in the County of Fairfield and said State as Agent for and in behalf of the professors of the Church of England or Episcopal Church in said Norwalk humbly Sheweth.--

That said professors some years since at a very great Expence and with much Difficulty (as their Numbers were few) built themselves in said Norwalk an Elegant and Decent Church and well finished the same at their own Cost and Expence where said professors for many years back had a Minister regularly Settled and performed Divine Service at their Cost and Still have the Gospel preached among them and are now formed into a Society agreable to the privilidge by Statute Law lately given to the Episcopal Church in this State.

That in the Month of July in the year of Our Lord One Thousand Seven hundred and Seventy Nine the Enemy then at open War with the United States of America burnt up and Destroyed said Church to the great Impoverishment and Distress of said professors and that said professors have Ever since been put to great Inconveniences for want of said Church to meet in and carry on Public Worship and whereas said Professors are Subjects of said State and being such have met with said Loss in the Course of the late War which was Estimated by your Hon.^{rs} Committee at about twelve hundred pounds Lawful money; said professors are induced to look up to your Hon.^{rs} for relief or some Assistance towards obtaining or furnishing themselves with a Church again in order to have a place convenient for performing Divine Service.

That said professors are very Desirous to have a Church again to meet in for public Worship but are Unable to build one without the Assistance of your Hon.^{rs} and as the Loss of said Church is a Misfortune in the Course of a Warr said Professors have reason to hope for relief from your Hon.^{rs} in the premises. Wherefore your Hon.^{rs} Memorialist in behalf of said professors humbly prays your Hon.^{rs} to take their Unhappy Case Situation and Circumstances into your Wise Consideration and grant said professors the Sum of Five Hundred pounds Lawful money

for the purpose aforesaid or such other Sum as your Hon.^{rs} in your Great Wisdom shall Judge Suitable or in such other way grant such relief in the premises as shall by you be tho't proper and your Memorialist as in Duty bound shall Ever pray. Dated at Norwalk the 1.st Day of May, AD: 1786

John Sanders Agent

This certifys that the within Named John Sanders was Appointed Agent by the Episcopal Society in Norwalk at a legal Meeting coveyned on 7.th of Octr 1785 for the above and foregoing Purposes

Certified by Hez^{ah} Belden Societys Clerk
In the Lower House
The Prayer of this Memorial is Negatived

Test Jedidiah Strong Clerke

[1786, Aug. 5, Stratford]
[My Dear Sir,]
I suppose it will be impossible to bring the members of our church in this state, to lay aside the English prayer book, and receive a new one. Would there be any inconsistency in our uniting with the Southern Churches, although we continue to use the old prayer book? Our people esteem it next to inspiration, if not actually such.

There seems to be one obstacle in the way, as your constitution now stands. If I remember right you have one article, which prohibits any man from being received by you as a Clergyman, unless he has subscribed your constitution. For the sake of union, might it not be best to relax a little on your part? If we hold the apostolical power, and the same articles of Faith, are we not the same church, and cannot we unite as such? As you represent it, this is the sense of [the] English Bps., upon which they will consecrate your Bps....

Jeremiah Leaming

[Rev. Dr. Abraham Beach at New York]

[1786, Sept., Stratford]
[My Dear Sir,]
By your Constitution as it now is, the 4 July is to be observed as a day of Thanksgiving forever, for the liberty we enjoy. This necessarily implies that before that time, we were in a state of slavery. The Bishops of England would appear in a strange attitude, to set to their hands, that the King, Lords and Commons were a pack of Tyrants, and kept us in a state of slavery, till we threw off the yoke. This is worth attending to in season.

It is my solid opinion that your General Convention will act wisely to lay aside even the thought of a day of Thanksgiving on that account, as it will be an insuperable difficulty in their way, and will, if appointed, in a little time be laid aside.

If you can inspire the members that are to represent the states of New York and the Jersies in the General Convention, of the necessity of laying aside that whimsical appointment, you will ever be pleased with your success.

It must forever be kept private, both in the Southern States and in Connecticut that you and I have corresponded upon these affairs, if we intend, as I have no doubt we

both do, to promote the general good of the whole. Many things may be done where there is no suspicion, that cannot be effected where there is.

There is another thing your general convention ought to take into consideration, that is, the style they have given to the Church, which is, the Protestant Episcopal Church. The Church of England is not called a Protestant Church, but a reformed Church; they never entered any protest against the civil powers; they reformed as a Nation; they never had the title of Protestant given them by any sensible writer unless he was a Scotchman.

It will be a great pity that we should commit any blunders of this sort, at first setting out; for posterity to laugh at, when we are forgotten for everything but the mistakes which we committed, and left behind us, as monuments that we wanted proper sagacity.

Perhaps this may be little thought of, but if we commit any mistakes now, we must bear them forever.

It actually appears to me, that your general Convention proceeded precipitately in many things; or they wanted old soldiers that knew the strength of every fortification, and the method how to defend it....

Jeremiah Leaming

[Rev. Dr. Abraham Beach at New York]

[1786, Sept. 14, London]

London, Mortimer Street, N.° 15
September 14, 1786

My very Worthy & Right Reverend Friend,

I am favoured with yours, dated New London, July 19th & sincerely rejoice to hear of your Health & Welfare. This Letter contained the first satisfactory Account of your Situation that I had received or heard; & as I was exceedingly anxious for your Success, it was the more pleasing. Sorry I am that the temporal Provision for you is not better--more adequate to your Services, Station & Merit. However, I trust you will be able to rub through for the present, & that God, in his good Providence, will by some other Methods, besides those you mention, supply what is wanting. Wealth & external Grandeur are not essentials of the Church of Christ--when it flourished most & was in its greatest Purity, these Circumstances were unknown to it. Yet it is right that it should have a proper Establishment; for those who serve at the Altar, should live by the Altar. No one more sincerely wishes for the Prosperity of the Church of Connecticut than I do; & I have the firmest Trust that if She adheres to that Truth once delivered to the Saints, as She has hitherto, & I hope always will, those Externals which she yet wants, will in due Time be added to her.

You observe that my last Letter shewed some Lowness of Spirits, which probably was the Case; but this was more owing to bodily Indisposition than any other Cause. Last Winter, Peggy was at the Point of Death. Anxiety for her, & Fatigue, threw me into a violent Fever, which brought me very low, & which I did not fully recover from till very lately. This Summer I rode more than usual, & have taken Bark frequently, which have braced me up; & I thank God, I feel stronger & heartier now than I have been since I left New York. Indeed my State of Health has been wretched since I came to England--totally relaxed, & thereby enfeebled, I could scarcely keep awake while in Company; &

at Night could not sleep. These Symptoms were doubtless aggravated by the Disasters & Calamities I had suffered--Time, that kind Assuager of Aff[l]iction, seems to have softened these somewhat; & blessed be God, I have now Reason to hope for more Health in future.

A few Weeks since I received the first Payment of my Compensation, which was greatly inferior to what I had a Right to expect; being only £1468, when my just Claim was upwards of £9,000. But as more than £2,000 of that Sum consisted of Bonds, which at present are not considered; & as some of my Lands had not been sold, which were also thrown out of the Account at this Time; moreover, as I know not on what Principle the Commissioners proceeded, or what is to be further done: It is impossible to know whether I have Reason to complain or not. What I have received is much greater in Proportion, than what has been received by many others; & since this is the Case, & I never am inclined to be querulous, I chuse to say little, & hope the best.

Before this Time, you have probably heard more particularly how the Conventional Episcopate for the Southern States, is circumstanced; at least, I requested D.r Chandler to transmit to you the Information which I was obliged to communicate to him on that Head; & I am persuaded, if he has not done it, that his Indisposition is the Cause.

The first Conventional Letter to the A. Bishops & Bishops, was very decent. It mentioned Nothing of Alterations in the Liturgy, &c but professed a strong Attachment to the Doctrine & Discipline of the Church of England--hinted that an Episcopate could be obtained from Denmark; but spurned the Idea, as the Members of Convention wished to have the Succession from hence; & desired to know, whether Persons sent hither for the Purpose, would be Consecrated Bishops. All this was fair & plausible; but various Reports were circulated here that many Alterations were to be made in the Prayer Book; & D.r Smith in his Sermon before the Convention, hinted that Alterations were intended, without specifying what they were to be. All this roused Suspicions in the Bishops, very justly; & accordingly in their Answer, which I have copied, they declare their Readiness to succour, as far as they are able, the American Church; but as reports prevailed that many Alterations of the Liturgy, Articles, &c were intended, they must in Prudence suspend their Judgment how they were to act, till fully acquainted with those Alterations. This is the Sum & Substance of that Letter, which is very short; & less the Bishops could not do, as the Conventional Letter was very decent, & the Prayer of it was supported by M.r Adams, the American Ambassador, by Dick Peters & other Americans, & even Congress had given its Sanction to the Measure.

In the mean Time, the several Parts of the Prayer Book, as they were printed, came over. Many of the Alterations & Omissions were very much disliked by the Bishops; others seemed trifling & injudicious, & very few for the better. His Grace of Canterbury appeared to be very uneasy & much disgusted. He utterly disliked Smith, & was afraid of his being obtruded; he reprobated many of the Alterations, which he thought injurious to the Essentials of Christianity, although many Things were retained to ascertain the Doctrine of the Trinity. I frequently conversed with him on the Subject; pointed out the Tendency of omitting the Nicene & Athanasian Creeds, when the Rage

for Socinianism was so prevalent, to say Nothing of expunging an Article from the Apostle's Creed; & I exclaimed loudly against their shameful Degradation of their Bishop, whose Barber might shave him in the Morning, & in the Evening join in turning him out of his Office. I also hinted to his Grace, that if he & the Bishops wished to see the Church in those Parts saved from utter Ruin, they should interpose to check those Innovations; for although they could do nothing authoratatively, yet they could withold their Concurrence & not become Parties to such Measures. This was going as far as I could with Propriety or Prudence.

After much Deliberation, the Arch-Bishop drew up a second Letter to the Convention, which went in the June Packet. It was admirably written. The Substance of it was--that the New Prayer Book had been received--that no supposed Necessity could justify many of the Alterations--that the Bishops were willing to do whatever was consistent with their Duty for the American Church; & to shew their Readiness for this Purpose, they would apply for an Act of Parliament to enable them to Consecrate Bishops without requiring Oaths or Engagements inconsistent with the late Revolution--that something however was required on the Part of the Convention to facilitate this Business, & justify the Bishops in proceeding further--that the discarded Article of the Apostles' Creed be restored; that the Ath. & Nicene Creeds be also restored, so far at least as to leave the Use of them discretional--that the Bishops be placed on a more permanent & respectable Foot--& that the Persons who, after this, come for Consecration, do bring the Testimonials (drawn up here & inclosed in the Letter) signed by the general Convention, as well as by the Conventions of those States respectively where the Persons reside. It is impossible to draw up Testimonials more solemn or strict than those are; & I think that Smith never can prevail on the Conventions to sign them for him. This Letter, as I said before, went in the June Packet; but did not reach America till after the Convention broke up. I think it will probably have one or other of these Effects--either to bring the Convention to a right Way of thinking & acting; or else totally knock up the Scheme which was pushed forward on bad principles, by some at least; & in either Case, I trust it will turn out advantageously for you. After this Letter was sent off, the Arch Bishop received the whole of the Conventional Prayer Book, & found, to his Astonishment, that even the Reading Psalms have been altered & mangled--at this he seemed much disgusted, being what he did not by any means expect. I imagine this will produce a fresh Remonstrance from his Grace to the Convention; & as for the Gentlemen that are elected to come here for Consecration, the Letter already dispatched will unquestionably stop their Voyage till there is another General Convention--how the Matter will end, I know not. The Act of Parliament above mentioned, was applied for & obtained.

As to the Nova Scotia Episcopate, there is no saying how it will turn out. His Grace of Canterbury & the Bishop of London presented a Memorial to the King this Summer, praying that due Provision might be made for the Church in our remaining Colonies, & a Bishop appointed to reside there; for it seems the Discovery of what we always believed in America, was made here at last, viz. that the King was fully vested with the Right of appointing American Bishops. His Majesty intirely approved of the Measure, & as is usual in such Cases, referred the Business to a Com-

mittee of Council to be reported on--& there the Matter rests. Sir Guy Carleton (now Lord Dorchester) spoke his Sentiments fully on the Subject, which were such as we could wish; the Members of Administration seemed to acquiesce, & the Arch Bishop was & is zealous: Yet Nothing further has been done. As Dr Chandler seems to have no Hope that his Disorder can be removed, he has explicitly relinquished all Claim to the Episcopate; Mr Boucher has also declined it; & so far as I can learn, I am the Person that is considered as most likely now to succeed. But I am by no means sanguine, having many Doubts whether the Appointment itself will take place, though the A. Bishop thinks it will.--The Will of God be done--& whatever becomes of me, may His Church flourish!

Agreeably to your Desire, I called upon Mr Stone about the Mitre. As no Mitres are worn by our Bishops in England, the Manufacture of them is consequently little known. Neither Stone, nor any other Person I could hear of, had ever made one. However, I told Stone he must try his Hand. He & I have consulted together at least a Dozen Times; & we also called in a very ingenious Embroiderer to assist us. After consulting a Variety of Books, Cuts, Monuments, &c (for no real Mitre was to be found) we at last fixed on the Size, Materials & Manner of Execution; all of which I hope will meet your Approbation. The Size I fancy is large enough. The Materials are Paste-Board covered with black Sattin; a Cross, in Gold Embroidery, with a Glory round it, in Front; & a Crown of Thorns, in Gold Embroidery, on the back Part. The two Lobes, if I may so call them, lined with White Silk; & each pointed with a gilt Cross, such as is usual on the Mitres of Bishops. The lower Part bound with a handsome black Lace, & the Inside lined with black thin Silk. The Ribbons with which it ties down, are Purple & each pointed with a Bit of Gold Lace. My Wish was to have it decent & respectable; without any Thing tawdry, or very expensive about it. What the Expence will be, I known [sic] not, & shall order the Bill to be put up with the Mitre, by which you will learn it--it cannot be very great; & therefore if this Mitre does not please or fit you, the next may be made more to Your Mind.

Give my Love to your Children, whose Welfare I rejoice to hear of. Tell Charles I am indulgent to a small Portion of Laziness in Boys; but it is always with this Proviso, that they double their Diligence afterwards, & bring up their lost Time. I hope he will be a good Scholar, & thereby become an Honour to his Father, & respectable Supporter of the Church. My little Folks are well, & desire to present their Love & Duty to you. Jack gets aHead fast, & has overtaken most of the Latin Scholars at his School, though some had begun Latin 2 or 3 Years before him. He now writes to me in Latin, & although the Latinity is not Ciceronian, yet it is tolerably well for a Boy, not 9 Nine Years old, & who began his Grammar only 18 Months since. Our Friend Duché is well--but over Head & Ears in Swedenborgh. He is likely to draw in Kempe, who seems inclined to change the Gentoos for the Swedish Knight. No Man has a better Heart than Duché; but I often grieve & am astonished at his constant Propensity to unintelligible, paradoxical Systems. This Letter I intend should go by Young Mr Kane--I hope the Mitre will be ready to go with him also--they must go together. There has not been a Moment lost in setting

about the Mitre & having it done since your Letter arrived.-- I wish you would write oftener to your Friends on this side of the Water--I should think it would not be amiss to write to some of the Bishops--particularly to his Grace of Canterbury. It could do no Hurt, & might be of Use. The Bishops wish well to your Church, & Information of its State would, I believe, be well received. That the Almighty may bless you, & prosper your Endeavours for the Furtherance of his Kingdom & Edification of his Church, is the unfeigned Prayer of your ever affectionate Friend

Charles Inglis

R. Rev.ᵈ Bishop Seabury

[1786, Oct., Middletown]

Middletown Oct.ʳ 1786

Dear Sir-

I was very sorry for my disappointment of meeting you in Convocation at Derby. I am fond of being present with the Clergy, tho' my Presence is of no great Importance. The shortness of the Time, the public Services and the unavoidable Interruptions, prevent the doing any considerable Business on those Occasions; will it not be adviseable to have a special Convocation, of which the Clergy only to be notified, that we may be free from all Incumbrances, & so be able [to] pursue & attend only to the particular & general purposes of the Church? Our general Maxim hath been to do nothing,--that our Strength is to stand still. I begin to suspect, that by so doing we shall prove & experience the Truth of another Maxim, that Extreme right is extreme wrong. We are the only Body in America, that are scripturally & cannonically authorised to form Rubricks and Cannons, for the Regulations of the Clergy in their public Ministrations in the Church; yet we do nothing for fear of bad Consequences. But as we now stand are we in danger of no bad Consequences? The Layety, yᵗ is great numbers of them, do, & will think, the ground on which we now stand in regard to ecclesiastical Affairs, is shifted from what it formerly was, and if the Clergy do nothing, to express their Sense of the new State in which our Church is now plac'd by her Seperation from all civil Establishments & in full possession of all the ministerial Characters which complete her Constitution; & let them see us, in the same light, they have been taught to view the Church of England, yᵗ is, as having her public prayers & religious Offices, Articles of Religion, Rubricks, and Cannons, framed and compiled, by the Bishops & Clergy, without any Connection with Laymen, any otherwise than as secular powers, to ratify their doings, as a civil Establis[h]ment.

If the Clergy, I say, do Nothing of this Nature; the Layety, in the present Situation of things, will be more & more drawn off from their first Principles, & begin to think, that we have no Right or Authority to act, & that that is the reason why we do not attempt it, & then they will begin to take up the Affair themselves, will contend for it as their right, dispute every thing the Clergy do, & set up themselves as Principals in ordering & managing the Affairs of the Church. It is a very critical Time, & if we for want of reasonable Care & Vigilance, lose our Ground, no after care or Exertion may be sufficient to recover it. The Tares may be sown & spring up among our People we cannot tell how; amid the Variety of Accidental or concur-

ring Causes to pervert or seduce our people, to keep them from falling off into wrong principals & practices, may be more difficult, require more Labour & pains, than it did to gain them over at first to think & believe right. I doubt not but there are a great number of our people whose Sentiments are such as we would wish them to be, but all are not Israel, that are of Israel; & one or a few mischievous Men may do more hurt than twenty times the number can do good. I could continue to add more Reflections of this kind, to communicate to you the Motives with me to have the Subject taken up, and seriously, & fully discuss'd in Convocation; but if I do, I shall write a much longer Letter than you are fond of----In the Plantation & Growth of the Church in America, I have always understood, that the Church of England was considered as propagated & enlarged,--now as our Church was in her original a part, & is in her Formation the Image & Character of that: if we still adhere to yᵗ worship & Doctrin, which we from Conviction of the Truth & excellency thereof embrace'd, is it not proper, the question may be, whether it be not needful, under the present Circumstances, to declare authoratatively, according to the entire powers we now possess, that we do. Give me leave then to desire you, to weigh the Matter, whether we should not in Convocation pass some resolves of that Nature, & thereby ascertain the ground upon which we stand, & be prepared either for a more firm defence, or to meet those who are taking, & have taken such wanton Liberties wh the Faith & worship of our Church--May not this be done by us, with the same propriety, & I know not why in Reason it ought not to be with the same Force, as what the civil Government hath done in adopting as the Constitution of the State, what were formerly, as a british Colony, their chartered privileges----I would then submit to your Consideration the following particulars

First, that it be recommended to the Bishop for a Convocation to be held as soon as conveniently may be; and that the question be mov'd for a Resolution of the same, that we do adopt, the Liturgy of the Church of England, either entire, except the prayers for the State, & the Offices appointed for State days; or with some few Abbreviations, such as will do no injury to the Sense, order, or Connection of the whole: To be the Liturgy of the Church in Connecticut--

2ᵈˡˡʸ That some particular prayers be added to those for special Occasions viz for sick Children,--for persons under Affliction for the death of Friends, and for persons bound to Se[a] &c--

3ᵈˡʸ That such of the Rubricks as we have found it necessary to deviate from be altered, where some Alteration only is wanting: or others made, that are necessary to render our Service & practice strictly rubrical & uniform.

4ᵗʰˡʸ That there be a revision of yᵉ Cannons & such as are applicable, or may be made so, be selected; & in Matters for which it is needful to provide entire new Ones, suitable to the State & Circumstances of our Church, that such be provided, & confirm'd by act of Convocation-- The length of our Morning Service is of itself a proof that the Compilers, principally attended to one Service in a day; & the commentators on the Liturgy tell us that several Offices, which were anciently performed at different Hours of the Day are combined together into one Service,

as it now stands. This is the reason that the Lords prayer so often recurs, the Collect for the day twice &c   Now as we have statedly two Services in the day; an equal Attention to both is a good reason for a more equal division of the Service; & for omiting the Lords prayer &c where it may be done, in the Morning Service, so as to shorten it to a more convenient length. Tho' every part in its place, is capable of a Vindication & we have done as we ought to do, in strictly adhereing to the use of it, yet it cannot be denied, but that a shorter Service would be better adapted to the depth of Winter, & the heat of Summer in our climate: & if this may be done, without deranging its System, or injuring its perfection, I confess I do not know of any Objection sufficient to decide against it.

The Nature of the Litany as a general Supplication, affords a fair Argument for seperate Prayers to reduce general Petitions to particular Instances; that the Beauty & Energy of the general Petition may not be lost by the Introduction of Specialties--And in respect of the Rubricks, why should we let them stand staring us in the Face, while we are violating them in our practice? While we have competent Authority, what Advantage accrues to us from it, in regard to the regulating & ordering our Church? Notwithstanding we have a Bishop at our Head, nominally presiding over us, is he not a mere cypher as Kings now are; may not every Presbyter take what Liberties he pleases with the public Offices, & what Rule does he transgress? The Rules of the Church of England--Those are not binding; do we not all, in one Instance or other do the same?

[Abraham Jarvis]

[1787, Feb. 25, Stamford]
[My Dear Sir,]
...Bishop Seabury continues to do honor to the Sacred dignity of his office. Next convocation, the Bp. advises me, will be at Norwalk, Whitsun week on Wednesday. We shall be happy to see you on that agreeable occasion....
Ebenezer Dibblee

[Rev. Dr. Abraham Beach at New York]

[1787, Feb. 27-28, Wallingford]
A special Convocation held at Wallingford Feby 27. 1787.-- Present--
Right Reverend Bishop Seabury

Presbyters / Revd Messrs
Leaming
Mansfield
Scovil
Hubbard
Jarvis
Clarke

Marshal
Bowden
Shelton
Baldwin
Andrews
Viets

Deacons / Perry
Ives
Brownson

Upon an Application made by the Church at Ripton to the Clergy in Convocation, that they would supply their Church, which is become vacant by the death of the Revd Mr Newton-- It was agreed to give them the Service of

a Sunday by the Clergy in their Turns--

Wed: 28. Mr Marshall inform'd ye Convocat^n of an Invitation that he had rec^d from the Chh's of Milford & West. H. to remove to Mil: & take the Cure of those Churches, and wish'd to know, in case he sh^d agree with them whether it w^d meet with the Approbation of the Bp. & the Concurrence of the Pres^rs for his removal-- The Bp. & Convoc: declared they had no Objection--

Upon a Motion, agreed that no person shall be admitted to Deacon's Orders, without he has a Title from some particular Church to present to the Bishop, engaging to receive him for their Minister, and to provide for his decent Support--

Upon Motion made--Agreed that the Liturgy of the Chh of England be accommodated to the present Situation of the Church in Connecticut, and Revd Messrs Leaming, Mansfield & Hubbard, were appointed to attend Bp Seabury in order to make the necessary Arrangements, to be laid before the Convocation to be held at Stamford on Wednesday in Whitsunday Week--

The securing the episcopal Succession to the Church of England in Connecticut, was taken into Consideration, and it was agreed that one of this Body be elected to go to Scotland to obtain Consecration, that the episcopal Office may be cannonically transferred. The Convocat^n then proceeded to a Choice. Revd Jer. Leaming was chosen. declined-- They proceeded to 2^d Choice. The Revd Richd Mansfield was chosen. declined-- The 3^d Choice was the Revd Bela Hubbard-- declined-- The 4th Choice was Revd Abraham Jarvis, who suspended his Answer until the next Convocation--

[1787, May, Stratford]
[My Dear Sir,]
...I have concluded that you have a design to give us the pleasure of your company at our Convocation which is to be held at Stamford the 30 inst: at which time and place I shall be much pleased to see you. I hope there will be a number of your clergy with you. The Bishops of England have always been averse to our having Bishops here: and had not the plan been carried into execution by us, before any scheme could be formed to prevent it, we never should have had one. This we knew; and we knew also, that it must take time to form a general union: and if we waited for that, we should not succeed. It must be done then, or never. That was the motive, for proceeding, when we did, and with as little noise as possible....
Jeremiah Leaming

[Rev. Dr. Abraham Beach at New York]

[1787, May 2, Stratford]
Stratford May 2^d 1787.
[My Dear Sir,]
Allow me, my very dear Sir, to congratulate you upon your happy success in your Undertaking for the Service of the Church, and your Safe Return to your Native Land.

I am far advanced in Life; and nothing can give me more pleasure, than to see the Church of England, (for by that Title I wish she may be called) fixed upon a firm Basis, in Unity thro all the States.

May it not be worth consideration to enquire, what method is most likely to produce this effect? Perhaps, there is no Scheme that promises so fair to accomplish the End desired, as keeping, as near as we can to the old Forms. We know these have been tried for Ages, and have always answered the purpose. Why should we make a new Experiment, upon a subject which has had sufficient Trial already?

It seems, that Dr. S.--the last man in the world for such Business, has been the Director; in forming the constitution and service of the Chh, for these States, as he intended. He was one of the Com^{tee}, and you know, they must do what he directed, or do nothing.

It appears to me, that it is unhappy for the Church, That, that man ever came into this land: he has done more harm to it, than any other person.

However, let us lay aside all worldly schemes, and take a View of what will be agreeable to our Great Master's design, in building up his Kingdom which is not of this world. Provided we do this, we shall see the Chh in its native purity.

There is no need to enlarge upon this point, as I have sent you with this Letter, my sentiments, in what Method the Chh of England is to be perpetuated in this land. If I have made any mistake, I shall stand corrected by you.

If your affairs will permit, it would give me unspeakable pleasure to see you at our Convocation, which will be held at Stamford in Whitsunday week.

Remember me kindly to all your Clergy, and to your good Lady, and believe me to be,

Right Reverend Sir,
Your most obedient & hum. Ser.
Jeremiah Leaming

Bp. White.

[Addressed:] The Right Reverend Doctor White / Bishop in Pensilvania / Philadelphia

[1787, May 30, Stamford]
At a Convocation held at Stamford, May the 30th 1787 Present

The R^t Revd B^p Seabury

Revd Messrs

Leaming   Tyler
Dibblee   Marshal
Mansfield Presbyters Bowden
Jarvis   Shelton
Hubbard   Baldwin

Resolved, that it be recommended to the Congregations of Branford, Guilford, Cohabit & Killingsworth to unite, & to give an Invitation to a Clergyman to settle with them,

Resolved, that it be recommended to the Congregations of North Haven, Wallingford, Cheshire & Bethany to associate, & invite a Clergyman to settle with them.

& That it be recommended to the Churches of Reading, Danbury, & Ridgefield to unite for the Purpose of settling a Clergyman.

That it be recommended to the Congregations of New Cambridge & Northbury to associate & settle a Minister.

& That it be recommended to Salisbury, Sharon, Canaan & Cornwal to form a Connection & settle a Clergyman

& That it be recommended to New Milford, New Preston, New Fairfield, Kent & Washington to unite & settle a Minister.

That it be recommended to Ripton to settle a Minister as soon as possible, & to Tashaway to associate with the Church at Ripton, upon the Settlement of a Minister, the Limits of the former to extend to the dividing Line between Stratford & Fairfield.

Resolved that Mr Jarvis & Mr Bowden be a Committee to draw up a Circular Letter, conveying the above Resolutions to the respective Associations.

Resolved that it be requested from these associated Societies to give to the Bishop as speedy an Answer as possible of their Determination, in Respect to the above Resolutions, & also to inform him what Support they will afford a Clergyman, & in the mean time to endeavour to find a proper person to be their minister.

Resolved, That it be recommended to the different Churches to procure Surplices for their Ministers.

The next Convocation to be held at New Lond: on the 20th of Sep^r

[1789, May, Stamford]
[My Dear Sir,]
...Be assured, Wednesday Whitsun Week, is Convocation week. I fear from what Mr. Foot tells me you will not avail yourself of the time: let not your heart fail you; you know not what good you may do.

Mr. Foot officiated last Sunday at Rye. I cannot bear to see so many worthy disciples of the Bishop of Connecticut, boxing the compass, and fishing from state to state, and town to town, for good livings. I think it makes the priest hood in our holy church too cheap in the eyes of the world, if not contemptible....

Ebenezer Dibblee

[Rev. Dr. Abraham Beach at New York]

[1789, Aug. 31, Newburyport, Mass.]
Newbury Port August 31st 1789
Gentlemen
We have been favoured with the Journal of a Convention of the Protestant Episcopal Church in the States of New-York, New-Jersey, Pensylvania, Deleware, Maryland, Virginia, and, South-Carolina holden at Philadelphia from the 28th of July last to the 8th of the Current Month. We cannot but lament that the Churches in these Eastern States had no Representative therein, Especially as it appears that an affair of the highest Consequence to us came under their Consideration; We mean the Election of a Bishop to be set over the Church in this and our Sister State of New-Hampshire. The Manner in which that Election was conducted, and the profound Silence and even Secrecy which has been maintained by the Reverend actors in it, have given us great concern. Disposed as we are to give every Proof in our power of our Veneration and Esteem for our spiritual Teachers, we cannot refrain from ex-

pressing our opinion that in a Matter of that high moment, it would have been but a peice of condescension becoming Ministers of Christ, to have admitted their Brethren of the Laity to a Participation of their Counsels. Neither can we divest ourselves entirely of an apprehension that a System of Ecclesiastical Government is contemplated in these States not perfectly consistent with that Freedom with which it hath pleased a merciful God in his Providence to bless us, and which has been so assiduously supported and cultivated by our Sister Churches in the Southern Governments.

Impressed with these Sentiments we have assembled and deliberated on these Subjects; and in the Result have determined (though young and few in Number) to propose to the several Episcopal Churches in these two Eastern States, to elect one or more Lay-Deputies to attend in our Behalf at the Adjournment of the afore-mentioned Convention to be holden at Philadelphia on the 29th Day of September next. This Measure has appeared to us well-calculated, if not even necessary, to preserve that Union of our Chruch through these United States, which is so earnestly to be desired. We are invited to it by the Convention. The Business to be then transacted is of the first consequence to us. Canons are to be established, the Book of Common Prayer to be revised and altered, and other interesting concerns to come before that Body. We would not for our own part willingly lose our voice on the occasion; and we fear it will be thought disrespectful to neglect it.

Should our Ideas on this Subject meet yours, we beg leave to propose that a Convention of Lay Deputies from the several Churches in these States assemble at Salem in the County of Essex & Commonwealth of Massachusetts on Wednesday the sixteenth Day of September next beforenoon--To elect one or more Lay-Deputies to represent the said Churches at the Convention to be holden by adjournment at Philadelphia on the twenty-ninth Day of September next; To give the said Deputy or Deputies such advice and Instructions as may be thought necessary or proper; and to consider of and recommend any Measures they may think promotive of the Welfare and Improvement of these Churches.

If this Letter should by any Means be delayed on its Passage, so that time be wanting, or should any other cause prevent your Society from adopting our Proposal, We beg leave to Observe that there are now in New-York three respectable Members and [w]e believe sincere Friends of our Churches; viz: The Hon: Mr Dalton The Hon. Mr Gerry-and the Hon Mr Livermore. We cannot doubt but any of these Gentlemen would readily undertake the charge of representing us in Convention; and We hope it will not be deemed too assuming in us to recommend that those Societies, who shall not join in the proposed Convention at Salem, furnish one or more of those Gentlemen with Powers to represent them in the Convention at Philadelphia.

We beg the Favour of you to inform us of your receipt of this, with an Account of your Proceedings; and shall at all times gladly receive from you any communications tending to the benefit of the Church.

We are, Gentlemen, your respectful Friends and Brethren--

Signed   By the Unanimous Desire of the
            Vestry of St. Paul's Church in Newbury Port

Sam. Cutler   } Wardens of
Dudley Atkins } said Church.

The Wardens and Vestry of Trinity Church Boston.

[1789, Sept. 15, Stratfield]

At a special Convention of the presbyters of the Chh of engd in Connect: on Tuesday the 15th of Sepr 1789. at the house of the Revd Mr Shelton in Stratfield-- Conventn open'd 10 o Clock- A.M.-- presen[t] Revd Dr Leaming Mr Mansfield Mr Hubbard-- Mr Jarvis Mr Shelton-- The Revd Dr Leaming was chosen president-- Mr Jarvis chosen, Secretary--

The purpose of calling this Convention, and the Business that comes now before it is, to deliberate upon the Invitation recd from the genll Convention at Philadelphia by the Bishop and Clergy of the Chh in Connect to attend their Con: whh they had adjourn'd for that end to the 27 of Sepr; and to consider on what terms we can cooperate wh yt Body towards forming a general Union in the Chh throughout the united States--

11 o Clock- Revd Mr Bowden, Mr Sayre, & Mr Foot arrived, and join'd the Conven--

Upon Motion of the Revd Mr Hubbard; voted that the Letters and praye[rs] sent for the perusal of this conven: be read-- They were accordingly read on Motion- resolv'd, that such parts of the Journal of the Con. at Philad: be read as related to the subject of a genl Union-

1 o Clock P.M. Revd Mr Clark arriv'd & join'd the Conven--

Mr Bowden made a Motion, whether this Con: will send clerical delegates to meet the Conven at Philadel-- Voted in the Affirmative--

6 o Clock P.M. The Revd Mr Prindle joined the Con[vention.]

On Motion of Mr Bowden, Whether a general Constitution--(as the Word Constitution implies Rules & Regulations for the Exercise of that Government which Ct & his Apostles established in the Church) is necessary for effectuating a Union of all the Churches in the United States; Or whether, it will not answer every essential Purpose for each State to form its own particular Constitution:-- Resolved, That the former is by no Means necessary, and in the present State of the Church impracticable, and tha[t] the latter is sufficient.

On further Motion by Mr B, Whether the Deputi[es] of this Church shall be empowered to confer with the general Convention upon the Subject of making Alterations in the Book of Common Prayer:-- Resolved That they shall; but the Ratification of such Alterations as may be made, shall rest with the Bp & Clergy of this Church.

Wednesday Morng Conven. was open'd according to adjournment. and proceeded to the Choice of Delegates to go to Philadelphia, when the following Persons viz. Revd Mr Hubard, and the Revd Mr Jarvis were chosen--

[1789, Nov. 14, Boston]

             Boston Novemr 14 1789.
Rt Revd & much Respected Sir.

It is but a Debt of Gratitude I owe to you & your amiable Lady to embrace the first Opportunity of acknowledg-

ing the kindness & Attention paid to me under your hospitable Roof, for which I beg you & Mrs White to accept my sincere thanks & to assure you I shall ever retain a grateful Sense of your Politeness--

I have the pleasure to inform you that I arrived at my own Dwelling the Day Se'nnight I left your house & found my family as well as I could expect, & myself very happy in having surmounted the fatigues of Stages & Passages by water-- I have not yet had the pleasure of hearing from Philadelphia since I left it; I hope you wound off the Convention more to your Satisfaction than you expected during some part of its Session. It being a matter in which I felt myself much interested, I am impatient to hear the last of it--

As you are a Member of every useful Institution in Philadelphia, I take it for granted you belong to the Humane Society; I have therefore taken the liberty of sending under Cover to you a Letter & some Publications to Doct^r Jones the President of that Society in your City, requesting the favour that after perusal (for which purpose I have not sealed them) you will seal the Letter & send it with the Enclosures to that Gentleman--

I find my Constituents are generally well pleased with the Account I have given them of the Proceedings of the Convention, & can perceive no Impediment on our part to a permanent Union, & sincerely hope none will arise among our Brethren at the Southward--

Pray make my most respectful Compliments acceptable to your good Lady & family, your Brother Harrison, & all other friends, & receive the same from your

most obliged Friend / & very humble Servant
Samuel Parker

R^t Revd Bishop White--

[Addressed:] Right Reverend / William White DD / Bishop of Pennsylvania / Philadelphia

[1790, Jan. 7, Newtown]
To the Honorable General Assembly of the State of Connecticut now convened at New Haven in the County of New Haven in s^d State   The Memorial of the Members of the Episcopal Society in Danbury in the County of Fairfield by their Agent James Clark of s^d Danbury and of the Episcopal Society in the Town of Newtown in s^d County by their Agents David Baldwin and Andrew Beers of s^d Newtown humbly sheweth-- That s^d Society in Danbury being small in number were at great pains and expence to the amount of about £500 in erecting a house for Public worship in s^d Danbury, which s^d House in April 1777 tho' not entirely finished was so far completed as to be decent and comfortable, at which time the enemy then at Open war with these States came to & burnt and destroyed the Public Stores at s^d Danbury. and s^d house was thereupon taken up and occupied as a Store house for Public Use for about six years in which time s^d building went fast to decay, the floors seats & windows were broken to pieces, and the whole left in ruinous circumstances. the memorialists (for s^d Danbury Society) would further represent, that the tumults and troubles of those times, the general phrenzy that prevailed, with the Destruction by fire in that town and the calamities of the war have lessened the Number, & weakened the Strength of s^d Society, so that notwithstand-

ing the allowances hitherto made, amounting to about £40, they are Still unable to pay their Public Taxes, support the preaching of the gospel among them as formerly, and complete the repairs necessary to make s^d building decent and preserve it from ruin. The Memorialists of s^d Newtown Society would likewise beg leave to represent to your honors that s^d Newtown Society have lately been at great expence in the Settle[ment] of [a] Minister among them in whom they are happily united. that their Church is old and gone to decay & is so small and inconvenient it has become necessary for them to build another provided they can obtain a Suitable place. that the only convenient place to be had and in which s^d Society can be agreed near the Centre of s^d Society, is about two rods East of the Presbuterian Meeting house in s^d Town and where the Town house belonging to s^d Newtown now stands in the mouth of a Cross highway. that the only objection to this place is its vicinity to s^d Meeting-house which stands in the Centre of the main Street which is only Eight rods in width and almost obstructs the same, that if s^d Meeting house was removed West about Six rods where is a suitable and convenient place for the same to stand & the Town house also removed, to which the Town & s^d Presbuterian Society consent, all parties concerned might be happily accomodated, & that harmony preserved which now prevails in s^d Episcopal Society and which is so necessary to enable them to carry their purpose of building into effect. that the only difficulty remaining is the expence attending the removal of s^d buildings, which together with the expence already occurred in Settling a Minister and which must necessarily arise in building a Church is more than they feel themselves at present able to encounter. in these circumstances from a firm persuasion that such a measure would contribute to the interest peace and happiness of s^d two Episcopal Societies without being in any respect Detrimental to the Public your memorialists in behalf of s^d Societies pray your honors to consider of their circumstances and (if you shall judge it expedient) grant them a Lottery to enable them to raise the Sum of £700. three hundred pounds thereof to [be] applied for the use of s^d Danbury Episcopal society in repairing their s^d house & Supporting the Ministry therein & the remaining £400 to be applied for the benifit of s^d Newtown Episcopal Society in removing s^d Town & Meeting houses and erecting a Church, upon their procuring sufficient bonds for a faithful & just management of s^d Lottery and application of the monies arising therefrom in manner as afors^d or in some other way grant them relief as your honors in your wisdom shall think best and they as in Duty Bound shall pray

Newtown   James Clark } Agent for s^d
Jany 7th 1790   Danbury Society

                 David Baldwin } Agents for said
                 Andrew Beers } Newtown Society

In the house of Representatives
    on the previous Question being put--   Voted to do nothing on this Pet^n   Test Uriah Tracy Clerk

[1790, Apr. 30, Norwich]
    To the honorable General Assembly of the State of Connecticut, to be holden at Hartford on the second thursday of May next--

The petition of the subscribers, belonging to the Episcopalian Society in Norwich humbly sheweth-- That the episcopalian society in this town are destitute of a suitable place wherein to worship God, and are totally unable to complete one for so desireable a purpose-- Your petitioners by their exertion, & by donations from some of their friends have raised a frame & covered the same, but can proceed no farther without the aid of your honors-- your petitioners therefore for themselves, and the rest of the said society, pray your honors to grant them a lottery for the purpose of raising one hundred & sixty pounds lawful money, to be applied solely towards the completing a house for religious worship for said episcopalian society and your petitioners as in duty bound will ever pray--

Dated at Norwich this 30^h day of April 1790

In the House of Representatives	John Tyler
The prayer of this Mem$^!$	Eben^r Whiting
is Negatived--	Eben: Huntington
Test. Uriah Tracy Clerk	Phineh^s Holden
	James Christie
In the upper House	Erastus Backus 3
The Prayer of this Memorial	Benadam Denison
is negatived	John Moore
Test. George Wyllys Secret^y	

[1790, Sept. 27, Stamford]

Stamford State of Connecticut
Septemb^r 27. 1790.

Reverend and Dear Sir.

I have received advice, (tho' not officially) that the Society in their great charity & compassion to an old Servant of their Venerable Board, hath been pleased to recommend me to the Honourable Commissioners of American claims for such favour as they in their wisdom might think proper to grant, in consideration of my great Sufferings & losses for my Loyalty to my Sovereign, fidelity & attachment to the British constitution in Church & State.-- For their many former favours, and especially this recent instance of their attention & benevolent concern for me, I beg leave to present (as in duty bound) my unfeigned tribute of thanks & gratitude, for this unme[ri]tted favour.

It is needless to repeat to the Society the personal dangers, & family troubles I had to contened with, during our late troubles; Suffice it to Say; Since the Revolution, I have been blessed with an uncommon Share of personal health, whereby I have been permitted to pay an uninterrupted attendance upon parochial duty for a long course of years; and I have the pleasure to See the Ch^h gradually rising out of its ruinous State, under all its disadvantagous circumstances, which is no Small consolation; but never expect to see it arrive to that State of maturity, respectability in number & ability, as it was before the war;-- But, thro' the adverse dispensations of providence, I am unhappy in my family, Straitned in my circumstances, and unable [to] Support my dependants in decency & public character, in consequence of Sufferings in the time of the late troubles.-- My two Daughters ruinous State of health remains, which originated in the terrors tumults & distresses in the time of the War.-- In that time & ever Since, they have been Subject to Hysterical Affections, which terminates in insanity for a long time.-- A recent instance of which we

have now had in one of them, who for Eighteen Months past hath been a most miserable compassionate object; occupying the constant attention of the family, & her Aged Parents, Sinking under the weight of trouble & the infirmities of Age.-- Words cannot paint the family distress we have been in, & So far as we can judge is like to continue.-- Gods will be done in Earth as it is in heaven.----Bear ye one anothers burdens say's an Apostle and so fulfil the Law of Christ. Incontestible proofs of the venerable Societies being endued with this most excellent gift of charity which never fails are manifest: therefore I lay open my grief with freedom.

Dear Sir-- The unhappy Situation of my family predominated with me more than any other consideration at the Revolution; when I declined accepting your proposal to remove to Digby, Nova Scotia.-- An affectionate concern for my broken dispirited Ch^h and in the Winter of Life to forsake my native tho' ruined country, and form new Connexions, had their proper weight in the Scale; but when I adverted to the reluctant afflicted State of the family, to remove into a new world, distant from all family connexions; when ever I sho'd be called into the world of Spirits, preponderated in my mind; and I thought duty, required a Sacrifice of interest, & the warmest affection to the British Constitution in Ch^h & State; & rely upon providence.-- But if the application to Government in my favour, Supported by so Venerable & respectable a body, Should prove abortive; and the Society in their great wisdom, wonted goodness & charity, are not pleased to restore me to their charitable notice, I must patiently Submit to the Issues of providence, and cast my burdon wholly upon the Lord; as my Ch^h are incapable of affording me a Support adequate to my necessities, & to prevent my falling into contempt.----In truth my attachment to the British Constitution hath been Such, & ever will be, and the unsetled State of both our Civil & Ecclesiastical Polity, which hath undergone, [in] Ch^h & State new Modifications, I wish to flee away & be at rest;-- But-- Heaven forbids it-- the few remaining days of my pilgrimage & usefulness forbid it-- the Evening of life & cold climate of adversity forbid it.--

The adopting of a new form, or constitution of Ch^h Government and correction or omissions & mutilations of the Liturgy in order to promote unity & concord in the Episcopal Ch^h throughout the States; I fear, will rather tend to break the bond of peace; which together with the abounding of Sectaries of every denomination, will entangle us more in error, till divisions are multiplied by endless Subdivisions, and religion & the Ch^h of Christ be a Scene of confusion and a chaos of discordant forms of worship, & inconsistent Systems of faith.-- To Coalesce with the other States, in uniformity of worship & Government, the Ch^h of Connecticut, in my opinion, hath imprudently quitted the firmest & best ground they lately made choice of, to Stand upon; Viz, that of the Church of England, professing themselves, in unity with it, in doctrine worship & Government.-- And dignified themselves with the title & honor of being the Ch^h of England in Connecticut. Which resolution, if abided by, might have been a Solid foundation to have preserved the peace, unity, purity & edification of the Ch^h. But an imagination of Superiour wisdom to that of former ages, and no cement of Christian union, I fear, will eventually prove fatal to

the interest of true religion & well being of the Church.

May my humble duty thankfulness and gratitude, be acceptable to the Venerable Board--with every Sentiment of personal esteem to your Self, believe me to be

most Reverend Sir

Your very Aged, most afflicted

Most Obedient, Humble Servt

and Affectionate Brother in Christ

Ebenezer Dibblee

The Reverend Doctor Morice Secretary of the Venerable Society for Propagation of the Gospel in Foreign Parts.

NB- My Revd Brother in adversity, I Sincerely condole with you in your affliction, in the loss of your excellent Lady.-- May the consolations of Religion be your Support, as they are of mine; adding every Dispensation of providence, conducted by infinite wisdom & goodness, having a happy tendency, tho' grievous.-- I Sincerely notice & thank you for the part you have taken & attention you have paid, to the unhappy, afflicted State of your brother by nature & grace. You will forgive my freedom. You have all the tender feelings of humanity & graces of christianity, to excite compassion, & induce your Sympathy with the unhappy allotment of the afflicted.-- May we, nay I hope to meet with you in the Parid[i]se [of] God, out of the reach of all tempests of [earthly life.] Adieu--

[1790, Oct. 1, Watertown]

To the Honourable General Court of the State of Connecticut to be holden at New Haven Within and for Said State on the Second Thursday of Instant October-- The Memorial of Caleb Matthews of Bristol in the County of Hartford one of the Principal Members of the Episcopal Society of New Cambridge, and the Rest of the Members of the said Episcopal Society of New Cambridge, Jointly With a Number of Episcopalians, Inhabitants of the South East Part of the Town of Harwinton in Litchfield County, and a Number of Episcopalians of the Inhabitants of the North East Part of the Parish of Northbury in the Town of Watertown in s^d Litchfield County----Humbly Sheweth. That almost every Individual member of the said Episcopal Society of New Cambridge Live in the Northwest Part of the said Society of New Cambridge and adjoining Near unto the Said South East Bounds of Harwinton and the said North East Bound of said Northbury and very Remote from the Senter of the Local Bounds of said Society of New Cambridge, and that although they have a very Small Church House Now Built Near the Senter of the Local Bounds of the said Society of New Cambridge, in which the Said Episcopal Society have heretofore usually meet. But that said House is By Age, Greatly Decayed and out off Repare, and the Whole of the Individual members of said Episcopal Society Living at a Great Distance to the Northwest from s^d House Renders it very Burdensome and inconvenient for s^d Society to Meet, for and Perform Public Worship in said House, and as it has become Necessary to Buil[d] a New House for the said Episcopal Church to Meet in for the Purpose of Public Worship, and No Convenient Senter Can be found on Which to Buil[d] said House for Public Worship, unless the s^d South East Part of Harwinton and the said North East Part of

Northbury be Annexed to and Incorporated With the said Episcopal Society of New Cambridge (Viz) Beginning at a Heep of stones being the North East Corner of the Society of Northbury in the s^d Town of Watertown and the South East Corner of the Bounds of Harwinton, and from thence Running Northward in the Dividing Line between the said Harwinton and the Society of West Brittain untill it Comes to the Northside of Jonathan Tylor Farm, and from thence a West Line untill it Comes to the Road Leading from Nathaniel Barnses in said Northbury to Harwintown Meeting House, and from thence Southward in s^d Road untill it Comes to Northbury Line, and from thence Still South in said Road untill it Comes to Aaron Dunbar's House in said Northbury, and from thence East in the Road running by Dodges Mill untill it Comes to said Cambridge Line. Which Limates as above Discribed being Annexed to the said Episcopal Society of New Cambridge, Would form a Very natural & Convenient Senter, (Just Within the Bounds of said Northbury) for the Said Episcopalians Living in the Said Limates Described in the said South East Part of Harwinton, and the Said Episcopalians Living Within the said Limates Discribed in the said North East Part of said Northbury--and your Memorialists Would further Beg Leave to Inform your Honours, That there are Not Less than Ten Episcopalian Families Now Living in said Harwinton Within the Limates afore Discribed Who Live at the Distance of about 4-1/2 Miles from the Church House in said Harwinton over a most intolerably Rough and Mountainous Road, and Who are not at a Greater Distance from the Senter as is herein Proposed, than about 2 miles and the Road feasible and Good, and that in the said Northeast Part of Northbury there is 15 Episcopalian Families Now Living Within the Limates above Discribed who Live at the Distance of about four and five Miles Distant from the Church House in said Northbury, over a very Rough and uneven Road, and not more than one Mile & Half from the senter herein Proposed, and that Scarce any one of the Individual members of the said Episcopal Society of New Cambridge Now Live at a Greater Distance from the senter as herein Proposed, than Two miles and a very Good and feasible Road----Wherefore for the Purpose of accomadating a Large Number of People and rendering it Convenient for them to assemble and to attend upon the Public Worship of God on the Lord's Day &c. your Memorialists Humbly Pray, your Honours to take our Situation into Consideration and Incorporate with and Annex all Persons Living Within the Limates herein before Discribed in the said Harwinton and Northbury Who do Now or hereafter Shall, Profess the Episcopalian mood of Worship to the Said Episcopal Society of New Cambridge, as to your Honours shall Seem Meete and your Memorialists as in Duty Bound shall ever Pray &c

Dated at Watertown the 1st day of October AD 1790--

Caleb Matthews Clerk

of s^d Episcopal Society

of s^d New Cambridge

Stephen Graves	David Curtiss	
Curtiss Hall	Jonathan Tyler	Inhabitants
Calvin Woodin	Asa Smith	of
Chancy Gaylord	Amasa Smith	Harwinton
Jabez Gilbert	Noah Wilton	

Ozias Tyler   Ezra Dodge   ⎞
Moses Coles   Thos Curtis   ⎟
Ira Dodge   Ebenr Coles   ⎟
Isaac Millar   Eliphalet Barnes   ⎬ of Northbury
Samuel Hally   Aner Woodin   ⎟
Daniel Bourn   Jacob Mallory   ⎟
Oliver Loomis   Amos Wright   ⎠
Robert Jerum

[1790, Oct. 1, Watertown]
To the Sheriff of Litchfield County or his Deputy or Either
of the Constables of Harwintown & Watertown in said County
Greeting-- By Authority of the State of Connecticut you are
hereby Commanded to Summon William Merriam of said
Harwinton one of the Principal Members of the Episcopal
Society of Harwinton and a Committee of said society and
the Rest of the Members of sd Society-- and Bela Blaikslee
of Watertown aforesaid one of the Principal Members of the
Episcopal Society of Northbury in sd Watertown and a Com-
mittee of said Society and the Rest of the Said Episcopal
Society of said Northbury to appear before the General
Court of the State of Connecticut to be holden at Newhaven
in Newhaven County, Within and for said State on the Second
Thursday of Instant October, (that is to say) that they ap-
pear before said Court on the Next Tuesday after the said
second Thursday if they See Cause, then and there to Shew
Reasons if any they have Why the Prayer of the foregoing
Memorial Should not be Granted and you are to Leave a
True and attested Copy of the foregoing Memorial and this
Citation With the Clerk of the Episcopal Society of said
Harwinton, and another With the Clerk of the said Episcopal Society of said Northbury at Least 12 days before the
said Tuesday after the said Second Thursday----Hereof
fail not and make Due Return of this Writ With your Do-
ings thereon according to Law   Dated at Watertown the
First day of October A.D. 1790-
                          Eli Curtiss Justice of Peace
a Duty of Twelve Shillings
is Paid on this Memorial
Certifyed per Eli Curtiss Justice of Peace

Harwinton October 4th 1790 Then I read the within Memorial and Citation in the hearing of the within Named
William Merriam and Likewise Left a true and Attested
Copy of the aforesd Memorial and Citation with the Clerk
of the Episcopal Society in Harwinton on the aforesd 4th
day October 1790
                          Test Charles Prindle Constable

Watertown Oct 7th AD 1790 Then I Read the within Memorial & Citation In the Hearing of all the Committee
of the Episcopal Society of Northbury & the Rest of the
Members Legally [assembled, and left a true and attested]
coppy of the aforesd Memorial & Citation with the Clerk of
sd Society
                          Test Bela Blakslee Constable

In the House of Representatives
     Granted the prayer of this Memorial and Liberty of a
Bill in form &c
                          Test L Swift Clerk

In the upper House
     The Prayer of this Memorial is negatived
                          Test George Wyllys Secrety

Mr Cleaveland and Mr Wilton are appointed a Committee
to confer with such Gentlemen as Govr & Council shall
appoint upon the different votes of the Houses upon this
Memorial
                          Test L Swift Clerk

In the upper House
     Heman Swift Esqr, is appointed to confer with the
Comtee of the House of Representatives, on the differing Votes of the Houses on this Memorial--
                          Test George Wyllys Secrety

Genl Assembly Newhaven Decemr 1790
In the upper House
     On Report of the Comtee and Reconsideration This
House do adhere to their first Vote on this Memorial
                          Test George Wyllys Secrety

[1790, Oct. 15, Danbury]
To the Honorable General Assembly of the State of Connecticut now Convened at New Haven in the County of New
Haven in sd State--
     The Memorial of the Members of the Episcopal So-
ciety in Danbury in the County of Fairfield by their Agent
James Clark of sd Danbury humbly sheweth that sd Society
being small in number wer at great pains and expence to
the amount of about £500 in erecting a House for Public
worship in sd Danbury which sd House in April AD 1777
tho not intirely finished was so far completed as to be decent and comfortable at which time the Enemy then at open
war with these States came to and burnt and destroyed the
Public Stores at sd Danbury and sd House was thereupon
taken up and occupied as a Store house for Public Use for
about six years in which time sd building went fast to decay the floors seats and windows wer broken to peices and
the whole left in ruinous Circumstances the Memorialist
would further represent that the tumults and troubles of
those times the general phrenzy that prevailed with the
destruction by fire in that town and the Calamities of the
war lessend the numbers and weakened the strength of sd
Society to such a degree that notwithstanding the allowances made amounting in the whole to about £40--they are
still unable to pay their Public taxes support the preaching
of the Gospel among them as formerly and complete the
repairs necessary to make sd building decent and to preserve it from ruin whereupon your memorialist pray[s]
your Honors to take their unhappy circumstances into your
wise consideration and Grant them a Lottery to raise the
sum of £300, or such other sum as your Honors may think
advisable to be applied in repairing sd House upon their
procuring sufficient bonds for a faithfull and just management of sd Lottery and application of the monies arising
therefrom in manner as aforsd or in some other way
grant relief as your honors in your wisdom shall think
best and they as in duty bound shall pray
     Danbury October 15th 1790
                    James Clark--⎬ Agent for sd Society

Oct 18<u>th</u> In the house of Representatives
    The Prayer of this Mem<u>l</u> is granted with liberty for
a lottery
                        Test Uriah Tracy Clerk

In the upper House
    The Prayer of this Memorial is negativ<u>d</u>
                        Test George Wyllys Secret<u>y</u>

In the house of Representatives-
    M<u>r</u> Edmonds and M<u>r</u> Ingersol are appointed a Com-
mittee to confer with such Gentlemen as the Governor and
Council shall appoint upon the different votes of the Houses
upon this Memorial
                        Test T Swift Clerk

In the upper House
    William Hillhouse Esq<u>r</u> is appointed to conferr with
the Com<u>tee</u> of the House of Representatives, on the differing Votes of the Houses, on this Memorial
                        Test George Wyllys Secret<u>y</u>

In the upper House
    On Report of the Com<u>tee</u> and Reconsideration This
House do adhere to their first Vote on this Memorial
                        Test George Wyllys Secret<u>y</u>

[1790, Dec. 21, Barkhamsted]
    To the Hon<u>ble</u> General Assembly of the State of Con-
necticut to be holden at New Haven on y<u>e</u> 29<u>th</u> Day of December it [be]ing by Adjournment The Memorial of Richard Adams of Berkhamsted in Litchfield County agent for
the Professors of the Episcopal Church in sd Berkhamsted
& y<u>e</u> Rest of sd professors of sd Church humbly Shews that
at a general Assembly of sd State held at Hartford on y<u>e</u>
2<u>nd</u> Thursday of May AD 1790 it was Resolved by sd Assembly that a Tax of three pence Lawfull money per acre
was thereby granted & Laid upon all Lands of y<u>e</u> Resident
& nonresident proprietors Lying & being within y<u>e</u> limits of
y<u>e</u> Society in sd Town of Berkhamsted of what Name & Description soever for the purpose of and to be applied to y<u>e</u>
Building y<u>e</u> meeting House & y<u>e</u> Settlement of the Minister
in sd Society payable by y<u>e</u> 1<u>st</u> day of February AD 1791 and
appointed Israel Jones Jun<u>r</u> of Said Berkhamsted to be a Collector to Collet y<u>e</u> same & appropriate it to the use aforesd
& now the Memorialists beg Leave to Represent to your
Honors that y<u>e</u> Number of sd Episcopalians in sd Town that
are Subjected to pay sd Tax to sd presbyterian Society is
about Thirty & they have for a Number of years past assisted in Supporting an Episcopal Minester who has performed divine Service & preached among them & that they
are willing Still to do y<u>e</u> Same According to their abilitys
However they would observe to your Hon<u>rs</u> that as y<u>e</u> sd
Town of Berkhamsted is New & much of the Land therein
Rough & uncultivated it affords but Little profit to the owners [B]eing in this Situation is very Burdensome for us to
Support y<u>e</u> gospel among us according to our own Profession & at the Same time to be at great Expences in maintaining a differant Denomination will Render it Still more
difficult however under these Circumstances we desire to
ask nothing of your Hon<u>rs</u> more than y<u>e</u> Laws of the State
grant to all Serious professors of every Denomination

where upon your Memorialists pray your Hon<u>rs</u> to take
their unhappy Case into your wise Consideration and
would pray your Hon<u>rs</u> to Reconsider sd Resolve or Vote
or exempt free & discharge us from sd Land Tax or any
part thereof as in your wisdom you Shall see fit and we
as in duty bound Shall ever pray
    Dated at Berkhamstead December 21<u>st</u> AD 1790
        Richard Adams Agent for sd Society

Gen<u>l</u> Assembly Newhaven Decem<u>r</u> 1790
In the upper House
    This Memorial is continued to the General Assembly
to be holden at Hartford on the 2<u>d</u> Thursday of May next
for Consideration
                    Test. George Wyllys Secret<u>y</u>

For want of a proper officer without great Inconvenience
[T]o Alexander Chubb of Berkhamstead in Litchfield Coun-
ty indifferent person to Serve and Return   Greeting
By Authority of the State of Connecticut you are hereby
Commanded to Summons Petatiah Allyn of sd Berkham-
stead Clark of y<u>e</u> Society in sd Town & the Rest of the
Inhabitants of sd Society to appear if they see Cause before y<u>e</u> general assembly of the State of Connecticut to be
Convened at New-Haven in sd State by adjournment on the
29<u>th</u> day of December Instant to wit that they appear on y<u>e</u>
Tuesday next after y<u>e</u> sd 29<u>th</u> day then & there to Shew
Reason if any they have why y<u>e</u> prayer of y<u>e</u> foregoing Memorial Should not be granted and you are to Leave a true
and attested Copy of y<u>e</u> foregoing Memorial and this Citation with sd Petatiah Allyn, Clerk of sd Society or at
the place of his usual abode at Least Twelve days before
y<u>e</u> sd Tuesday Hereof fail not & due Return make
    Dated at Farmington the 22<u>d</u> day of Decem<u>r</u> AD 1790
Duty of twelve shillings paid hereon
                    Certified and signed
                    p<u>r</u> John Treadwell Assess<u>r</u>

Berkhamsted December y<u>e</u> 23<u>d</u> day AD 1790 then I left
a true & attested Copy of the within Memoral & the above
Citation at the usual place of the abo[d]e of the above
named Petitiah Allyn
            test Alexander Chubb Indeferant Person

Litchfield County SS Berkhamsted December 23<u>d</u> 1790
Personally appeared Alexander Chubb and made Solomn
oath to the Truth of the above Endorsement before me
            Joseph Wilder Jus<u>t</u> Peace

[1791, Oct., Winsted]
    it is evident that it is comonly customary in Laying
out New Places to make provision for the settlement of a
minster Some thing for personage, and Some thing for
schooling, and it is their Wisdom and intrist So to do:
but if it be neglected it is no more than resonable, nor on
the whole any thing against their intrest to Lay out some
of their property for such publick usses: as it hath a tendancy to rais or keep up the valew of their Land.
    the Clearing up roads for the necisary traviling of
their own inhabitants must be of great utility to the Land
of the Nonresident proprioters, and the roads and Bridges
are wel Known by the Laws of this state to be suported by

the inhabitant[s]

  our familys are to Supporte our children to school our Houses and barnes are in but Low Situation and therefore we are un able to build a Meeting house without Some help from the nonresident propŗs

  and We would not only plead our poverty and nesessity but the Justice of the Case requires that a Meeting house being a Real Estate of the Society it necisarily ads to the Real Estate of the individuals only and not in the Leas to the polls or pesnal Estate and therefore if the whole of the Lands ware now the property of the inhabitants and the List was Just as it is justice would require that a Meting house should be build in a great measur by a Land tax

  in the [Congregational] Society of Winsted there are eighty 4 familyes Consisting of rising of four hundred Soles. there are twelve yung men prepareing to make Settlements in the parish   of the familys there is but four whose Children are Grown out of the way of Schooling and thirteen their Children are yet too small to Send   Of the family above there are four of the apiscopal order   one of the Seperate order and two of the Baptist order

  the above is a true Statement taken pŗ David Austin by direction of the Societys Committee

A Coppey of Winsted List for the year 1789

Henry Allyn	62-10-0
Petetiah Allyn	23- 0-6
Nathaniel Crow	21-17-0
John Crow	20- 6-0
William Case	2-11-0
Rufus Cleaveland	35- 0-6
Noadiah B Gates	23- 1-0
Seth Goodrich	26- 1-0
Samuel Hoyadon	39-12-6
Noah Kellogg	25-17-0
Daniel Kellogg	21-13-0
Roger Loomis	29- 9-0
William Moore	24- 0-0
Amasa Mallary	35- 0-0
	391-18-6

Non Residents in Winsted Society

Josiah Allyn	£ 2- 4-6
Ephraim Banerst heirs	1-10-0
Jabez Bacon	4- 4-6
Elijah Chapman	3- 6-0
Stephen Chubb	0- 9-0
Timothy Dwight	1-10-0
Mertain Denslows heirs	0-11-6
Silas Drake	2- 5-0
Wilcox Ashbel Eno	0- 2-0
Martin Driggs	1-16-0
Michal Goodwin	0- 8-0
Matthew Gillit	0- 9-0
Chancy Mills	3- 0-0
Selvanus Griswould	6- 9-0
Thomas & Phinŝ Griswould	2- 4-0
John Gillitt	0- 6-0
	30-14-6

Nonresidents in Winsted Society

Thomas Giddings	£ 1-10-0
Daniel Gillit	3-15-0

John Isaac & Abial Griswould	1- 5-0
Amasa Loomis	3-19-0
John Loomis	0-16-6
William Moore	5- 0-0
Oliver Marther	1-16-0
Dŗ Samuel Marther heirs	1- 2-0
Eliakim Mather	1-12-6
Jacob & Isaac Noble	1- 8-0
Joel, John & Jonathan Palmer	1-12-0
Abraham Pettibone	2- 3-6
Cᵒ Noah Phelps & Co	0- 7-0
Simeon Rogers	0-11-0
Oliver Roberts	2-10-0
John Strong	2- 5-0
	31- 2-6

Nonresidents in Winsted Society

Elisha Stoughton	2- 1-0
Ephraim Tucker	2- 8-0
William Thrall	0-18-6
Elihu & Samuel Tuder	2- 4-6
Elisha Wilcox, Elijah Fuller and	
Moses Case	0-14-6
Mary Woster	5- 0-0
Thomas Wills and Wills Diggins	1-18-0
	14-14-6
	62-10-0
	30-14-6
total of nonresidents List in	31- 2-6
Barkhamsted in Winstead parish	£139- 1-6

Elknah & Zerah Phelps	£ 46- 2-0
Paul Roberts	53- 1-6
Seth Spencer	38- 3-3
James Sweet	12-17-0
Reuben Sweet	26-15-6
Elijah Wilder	41- 7-0
Robert Whitford	49-16-3
Jonas Weed	6- 9-0
Dan Weed	23- 0-0
John Waite	18- 0-0
Lemuel Walter	19- 0-0
Jonah Woodruff	23- 0-0
	327-11-6
	391-18-6
	£719-10-0
NB £62-10-0 of this is nonresidents	62-10-0
	757- 0-0

  in the foregoing List there are two included of the Episcopal order viz. Paul Roberts and William Case

[1792, Aug. 6, Stratford]

    Stratford in Connecticut Augŝt 6ᵗh 1792

Dear Sir,

  I wrote to you many Weeks ago, upon the Subject of the present Letter. But, having received no answer, suppose my former Letter miscarried by Reason of a wrong Address. I have been such a Traveller, that I was ignorant, till after I had written, that you were one of the Judges of the supreme Court of Pennsylvania; and there-

fore directed to James Wilson Esq.ʳ-- Perhaps there may
be a Gentleman of the Law of that Name in Philadᵃ-- My
End in writing to you, was, to tell you, That I had handed
the Sum which Mʳ E. Biddle & yourself were so kind as
to lend me before I embarked from Philadᵃ to England for
Orders in the year 1774--to a Servant of my old Friend
Capᵗ: Duncan Campbell, I suppose in the year 1775, or 6,
in Continental Money when at Par, with Directions (to the
best of my Memory) to give it to Col. Cox, to hand it to
you. The Man went to Philadᵃ (from Fredericksburgh in
N. York Governmᵗ where I was then placed as a Minʳ)
probably upon a private Errand for his Master, at a Time
when it might not be prudent for him to be known. I did
not therefore write to Mʳ Cox by him. He reported to me
on his Return, that he had delivered the Money & Message
to Mʳ Cox; and I took it for granted ever since that you had
received the Money, till I was last in Philadᵃ viz. in April
last: When, upon asking Mʳ Cox whether he had received
the Money, he told me that he was clear that he had not. I
have often blamed myself for not asking you about it when
I had the Pleasure of dining with you in Philadᵃ 7 or 8 Yʳ's
ago, in order to ascertain the Matter.

Now, as I thought it possible that my Memory deceived
me about the Person to whom I directed the Money to be
given; & that, therefore, you might have received it, I
write now, to ask the Question. If not, I am sorry that two
of my Friends have been so long without their Right. The
Sum furnished me, was £30 Pennsylvᵃ Money. Bo so kind
as to answer my Question by the 1ˢᵗ Post after Recᵗ of this;
that, in Case of the Money being still due to you, I may inclose you a Bill for it, or, (if I should travel to the Southward in a short Time) bear the Money to you myself. I forgot to tell you, that I called twice at your House, when last
at Philadᵃ--but that you had not returned from N. Castle.

I am, dear Sir, with the old Friendship & Regard,
your obliged &c.

                                        James Sayre

Honble James Wilson Esqʳ

[Addressed:] The Honorable James Wilson Esquire /
Philadelphia / Per Post.

[1792, Aug. 12, Stamford]

                              Stamford, Connecticut
                                  August 12, 1792.
Reverend Dear Doctor.

I gratefully acknowledge the favour of yours of the 18th
of Febʳᵉ which came to hand the 7th of June. Too late in
my apprehension to give you answer, expecting you were
on your passage to your native Country.

Last evening Mr. Samuel Jarvis communicated the advice he just received from you dated in May, intimating
your Stay in London till some time in Septʳ--This prompts
me to thank you for the agreeable advice you gave me of
the Arch-Bᵖˢ gracious goodness in allotting me the gratuity of £40, &c. I received advice also of this from Doctor
Morice Dated the 7th of March, Authorising me to draw
upon him for said benefaction, which I have accordingly
done; Mr. Bates not desiring my Bill, & unwilling to pay
for it, until he could get a letter to you, & advise of its
acceptance; which he judges improbably, & would be too
late.

For every instance of your humanity, brotherly love,
fellow feeling, Services &c, may God reward you Seven
fold into your bosom. God grant I may live to See you before we meet in the world of Spirits.--

Family troubles remain; tho I thank God, alleviated
in some measure. My daughter Polly is more composed,
tho not wholly restored to a State of tranquility. She was
the most melancholy unhappy object you ever saw the last
year. Mrs. Diblee, by Sickness, Age & family troubles,
is quite an invalid. Uncommon health I am favoured with,
& persevere in my course of publick Duty, but the Shadows
of the evening are fast approaching.

Mr. Jarvis will advise you of his brother & Lady's
Safe arrival at Mont Real &c. I must again advise you of
Sally Thorps Marriage (agreeable to her friends) to Elisha Leeds, son to Israel Leeds deceased, of her having
a Daughter; please to notice it to her Father & Brother;
Suspecting, from your mentioning of her, you have not
received advice I gave you of it, above a year past. She
remembers your promise. My best respects wait upon
Henry Lloyd Esq., & his Lady. God bless them & grant
of his unmerited grace, they may go down to the grave in
peace, & receive the reward of their exemplary virtue,
piety & Charity. I should have long since wrote to him, &
endeavoured to have removed any unfavourable impressions he might have received of me or my Chʰ--(Slowly
but gradually rising out of its ruins, & the Chʰ it Self
nedding to ruin, now thoroughly & decently repaired) tending sooner or later to obstruct his intended benefaction to
a Chʰ first founded & encouraged by his Patronage: But it
was too tender a point. I had rather Suffer my Self in his
estimation than hurt his feelings. Off Public intelligence,
I find you know everything here better than I can advise
you. God bless you, my Revᵈ Dear Sir--Prosper your intended Voyage; this is the since [sincere] wish & fervent
prayer of your

                    Most Affecᵗ friend & Brothʳ in Christ
                                        Ebenezer Diblee.

N.B. I am not allowed time to copy or correct; you
must accept of this as you find it. My Son Frederick--
New Brunswick--was admitted to Deacons Orders last Oc-
tobʳ--was to be Ordained Priest 15th instant, or meet the
Bishop at St. John's for that purpose.

[Addressed:] Reverend Doctor Samuel Peters / Pimlico /
London.
[Endorsed:] rec. Oct. 20

[1792, Nov. 7, Aberdeen, Scotland]

At Aberdeen, the seventh day of November 1792.

The Bishop and Clergy of the Diocese of Aberdeen,
take the Opportunity of their being assembled in Synod, to
return their gratefull Thanks to the Society for promoting
Christian Knowledge, for the acceptable present of Common Prayer Books, which the Society was pleased to transmit to the Bishop for the Use of his Diocese.

While the peculiar Situation of the Scotch Episcopal
Church, (surrounded by various Sects, hostile in their
principles to those of Episcopacy, and by many powerfull
Temptations to seduce it's Members from a Communion,
which has no temporal Advantage or Distinction to recommend it) renders the Duties of it's Clergy exceedingly

difficult and laborious, they feel themselves comforted and encouraged by the Countenance and Support they have received from many great and worthy Members of the Church of England, and particularly by the flattering Mark of Attention and Favour conferred on them by a Society, so eminent for it's piety and Christian Zeal.

It has been the Endeavour of the Bishops and Clergy of the Scotch Episcopal Church, to make their people acquainted with those Doctrines which peculiarly distinguish <u>Christianity</u>, from the Philosophy of the World, and which the more they are understood, will secure that piety towards God, and the Exercise of those relative Duties towards Men, without which neither can the Peace of Society be preserved, nor the Happiness of Individuals be promoted. And as their Labours have not been altogether unsuccessfull, when circumscribed in some measure by penal Restrictions, they flatter themselves, that, being now blessed with the Enjoyment of greater religious Liberty, they shall be able, through the divine Assistance, to cooperate more effectually with the Society, in diffusing the knowledge of those heavenly Truths, which can alone make men Wise unto Salvation.--

May the great Author, and Finisher of our Faith be graciously pleased to accept and prosper the pious Labours of the Society, and grant Success to all those, who humbly endeavour to make "his Ways known unto Men, his saving Health unto all Nations."--

John Skinner Bishop of Aberdeen.--

[1793, Feb. 5, Stamford]

Stamford State of Connecticut
Feb. 5, 1793.

Reverend dearly beloved Sir,

I lately received a kind letter from Henry Lloyd Esq in which he Speaks most respectfully of you, and of your benevolent disposition & kind Services to me--Believe me, it will ever be had in grateful remembrance. He makes no mention of his once intended benefaction of a valuable Library to this Ch^h of which I hoped to see the completion; and a Select number given for the use & Benefit of the Rector of St. John's Ch^h for the time being upon Divinity.

Having long experience the adverse Dispensations of providence, in family troubles; alleviated, but not wholly removed, I most heartily compassionate his aged afflicted brother, in the late death of his Son John Lloyd, and Son in law Doctor Coggiel. I thank God, my unhappy Dauter remains better, but greatly deranged & discomposed in her mind. I fear will ever remain so.

In a late Convention of the Bishops, Clerical & Lay Delegates of the United States; a happy Coalition among the Bishops took place Through Bishop Seabury's wise & prudent conduct, all contention for primacy or precedency is laid aside. A happy union we hope will succeed. The new Service is generally adopted in the States, & complied with for peace & unity sake; altho the omissions & verbal alterations, will never be agreeable to the old Tory Church men. We hope the defects in Government will be rectified in a future Convention, & the Church restored to its primitive purity & Episcopal form of Government. Brother Sayer, thro an intemperate Zeal, & imprudent conduct, towards the Bishop & his brethren, hath left Stratford; & how he will Dispose of himself & his future Services, I am not

advised. He hath Sounded an alarm of herisy & levelled his artillery against the impiety & irreligion of the day he would have been more serviceable to the true interest of Religion. For Sectaries of all Denominations abound; Infidelity & Disrespect to all Religion & contempt of all Ecclesiastical Authority; and that it matters not what religious profession a man is of, provided he is a good Citizen; is the prevailing Spirit & temper of the Day. We shall soon be as thorough paced Republicans in Church as in State. The best Preacher, is the best Minister, let him be of what Ch^h & Denomination so ever. The Ch^h begins to catch the contagion, and if the laws in this State for the Support of a public Religion are once abolished, as we have reason to fear, both Ch^h & Presbyterians will be in an unhappy case. I hope your Government in the Ch^h & State stands firm, notwithstanding, our Newspaper [----?] of its tottering State. France hath received the reward of their perfidy, in full measure, pressed down, & running over.

I thank you for your remembrance of me in your letter to Mr. Saml Jarvis, communicated yesterday. The kind Services you have rendered me, will ever be remembered with gratitude. From the goodness of your heart I hope for the continuance of your influence in my favour. I condole with you in the loss of your Grandson, Mr. Jarvis eldest Son, of which I trust you have been advised.

Concerning Mr. Thorp's Daughter Sally, in your letter of the 25th of July, 1790; you was pleased to say, "If Mr. Thorp's daughter maries according to your liking, I will give her a new gown &c". I marryd her the 27 Jan^r 1791 to Elisha Leeds, a reputable, Sober industrious young man & Christened a Daughter of hers, Decemb^r following.

With every sentiment of Respect & Esteem to your self, to the most worthy Henry Lloyd Esq. & Lady, and the Venerable Doctor Breynton, recommending you all to the blessing & protection of Almighty God. I am in the bond of love & charity,

Your ever most Affectionate Brother
faithful friend & Humble Servt
Ebenezer Diblee.

The Revd Doctor Peters

When shall we see him, and honored with the Mitre?

[Addressed:] Reverend Doctor Samuel Peters, / Grosvenor Square, Pimlico. / London.
[Endorsed:] rec^d April 18

[1793, Oct. 12, New Haven]

To the honourable General Assembly of the State of Connecticut, now convened at Newhaven in said State-- the Memorial of the several episcopal Societies in the State of Connecticut, by Isaac Beers, Elias Shipman and Jonathan Ingersoll of said Newhaven, appointed Agents for said Societies, by the Convention of the Clergy & Delegates from said Societies holden at Middletown in the County of Middlesex, on the fifth Day of June AD 1793, humbly sheweth-- That, by the Constitution of the episcopal Church, the Bishop thereof, besides the Duties which he is obliged to perform within the Society, Parish or Church of which he may be a Minister, is obliged to superintend and do various

Duties as Bishop in the several Churches within his Jurisdiction.-- That, the several episcopal Societies in this
State are within the Jurisdiction of one Bishop, and it is the
Practice & Duty of s^d Bishop to visit the same, once or
twice in a Year, in order to perform the Duties pertaining
to his Office.-- That the Duty of s^d Bishop being so laborious, the said Societies have thought it unreasonable, that
he should perform the same, without any Reward, and it
therefore has been their Practice for some Time to contribute towards his Support.-- That, tho they reprobate
the Idea of supporting a Bishop in Luxury and Idleness,
yet they are strongly of Opinion, that the Labourer is
worthy of his Hire.-- That as there are ecclesiastical
Societies in this State formed for the Purpose of supporting
Religion and more particularly the Ministers thereof; they
think it not unreasonable, that a similar Institution be established for the Support or partial Support of s^d Bishop.--
They therefore humbly pray your Honours to pass an Act
appointing certain Persons Trustees with Power to hold any
Estate real or personal, to them & their Successors, which
may be conveyed to them, for the Benefit of the Bishop of
the episcopal Church in Connecticut, for the Time being,
and they as in Duty bound shall ever pray--

Dated at Newhaven the 14th Day of October AD 1793--

> Isaac Beers ⎱
> Elias Shipman ⎰ Agents as
> Jon^tn Ingersoll ⎰ aforesaid

In the House of Representatives
Granted the prayer of this Memorial with liberty of
a Bill &c

> Test T Swift Clerk

In the upper House
The Prayer of this Memorial is Negatived

> Test George Wyllys Secret^y

In the House of Representatives--
Mr Daggett and Mr Austin are appointed a Committee
to confer with such Gentlemen as Governor and Council
shall appoint on the differing Votes of the Houses on this
Petition

> Test T Swift Clerk

In the upper House
Thomas Seymour Esqr is appointed, to conferr with
the Gentlemen appointed (by the House of Representatives)
on the differing Votes of the Houses, on the within Memorial

> Test George Wyllys Secret^y

In the upper House
On Report of the Comittee &c And Reconsideration
This House do adhere to their first Vote on this Memorial

> Test George Wyllys Secret^y

[1795, Oct. 12, New Haven]
To the honorable General Assembly of the State of Con-
necticut, now convened at New Haven in said State, the
Memorial of the several Episcopal Societies in the State of
Connecticut, by Isaac Beers, Elias Shipman and William
McCrackan of said New Haven, appointed Agents for said
Societies, by the Clergy and Delegates from said Societies
holden at Middletown in the County of Middlesex, on the
fifth day of June AD 1793 humbly sheweth--

That, by the Constitution of the Episcopal Church, the
Bishop thereof, besides the duties which he is obliged to
perform within the Society, Parish or Church of which he
may be a Minister is obliged to Superintend and do various
duties as Bishop in the several Churches within his Jurisdiction.-- That, the several Episcopal Societies in this
State are within the Jurisdiction of one Bishop, and it is
the practice and duty of said Bishop to visit the same once
or twice in a Year, in order to perform the duties pertaining to his Office.-- That the duty of said Bishop being so
laborious, the said Societies have thought it unreasonable,
that he should perform the same, without any reward and
it therefore has been their Practice for some time to contribute towards his Support.-- That, though they reprobate
the Idea of Supporting a Bishop in Luxury and Idleness, yet
they are strongly of Opinion, that the Labourer is worthy
of his Hire.-- That, as there are ecclesiastical Societies
in this State formed for the purpose of supporting Religion
and more particularly the Ministers thereof, they think it
not unreasonable, that a similar Institution be established
for the support or partial support of said Bishop.-- They
therefore humbly pray your Honors to pass an Act appointing certain Persons Trustees with power to hold any Estate
real or personal, to them and their successors, which may
be conveyed to them, for the benefit of the Bishop of the
Episcopal Church in Connecticut, for the time being; And
they as in duty bound shall ever pray--

Dated at New Haven the 12th day of October AD 1795

> Isaac Beers ⎱ Agents
> Elias Shipman ⎰ as
> William McCrackan ⎰ aforesaid

In House of Rep^s Octr 27th 1795.
The prayer of the preceding memorial is negatived.

> Test. Saml W. Dana Clerk

[1798, June 8, Norwalk]

Norwalk June 8th 1798-

Sir.
I take the liberty to forward the enclosed address to
you, with a request that you would do us the favour to present it. The episcopal Clergy of this State do not wish to
take any part in the public affairs of government, that is
not immediately connected with their professional character, and not essential to the regular and faithful performance of their office in inculcating on the people of their
charge, the social and moral duties of religion.
They would have acquiesced on common occasions in
being considered as embraced in an address of the government of the State; but on the present alarming and critical
situation of our country, they hope it will not be deemed
improper for them to express in their own behalf, their unfeigned benevolence to the existing government; and their
readiness to do whatever is proper, and within their power,
to promote that unanimity and zeal, which under the blessing of God, is so apparently necessary to preserve and secure those privileges, religious and civil, which it is our
ardent desire and prayer that we may uninterruptedly enjoy.
I am, with esteem, / your obedient / and very hum^le
Servant

> Abraham, Connecticut

[Addressed:] The Honorable / James Hillhouse / Philadelphia

[1798, Aug. 24, Digby, Nova Scotia]
                    Digby in Nov. Scot. 24th August 1798.
Revd & dear Sir,

Your kind Letter of 2nd Ult. came safe to Hand. I thank
you sincerely for the Care & Trouble you have taken of my
Affairs in New England.

Please to charge whatever You have paid or shall hereafter pay for Freight Postage &c to my Acct.

You mention 20 odd Dollars due me for Interest: But if
I rightly remember in the Statement of our former Accounts
there was found your due a much larger Sum. I think about
11 or 12£. In order to bring the Balance in my Favor again
I have endeavored this long Time to save a £25 Bill for you
& then I could send for necessary Articles to Boston. But
as it is I should think it very proper that you should keep
the Six Pounds odd towards Part of Payment of the Sum due
you from me. I have some Hopes within a year to send you
a £25 Bill, and then I can send boldly to you for whatever I
want.

I most sincerely Sympathize with my worthy cordial
Friend Mr Stoddard on the distressed State of his Family.
May God the Source of all solid Comfort give him all req-
uisite Consolation!

Will you take the Trouble to call on Mr Stoddard (He
was formerly & I suppose is still a great Admirer of you)
and give my Wive's and my own tenderest Respects to him,
and tell him that We take the deepest Interest in his extreme Distress! Our heartiest Prayers to God are that he
would give him "Patience under his Sufferings & an happy
Issue out of all his Afflictions"!

I am sorry for the sudden Death of those two worthy
Gentlemen of the dissenting Ministry Mr Clark & Dr Bel-
knap. Not long ago We lost 5 Clergymen in this Province
& New Brunswick in one year. 3 of them very good exemplary Gentlemen, the other 2 not bad Men. Mr Cook formerly Missionary in Monmouth Co New Jersey since at
St Ann's New Brunswick drowned there--Mr Roland died
suddenly at Shelburne--Mr Lloyd of Chester frozen to
Death on a Journey thro' the Woods--Mr Ellis of Windsor
& Mr Delaroche of Guysborough. Our Brethren are all
well in these Parts.--

With sincere Regards to your amiable Consort & good
Children I remain with all Gratitude & Respect your very
obliged Friend & humble Servant and Brother
                                              Roger Viets.
Revd Dr Parker.

[Addressed:] To / The Revd Dr Samuel Parker / Boston /
New England. / Favd by Mr Severio Jones

[1798, Oct. 12, New Haven]
To the Honorable Genl Assembly of the State of Connecticut now sitting at New Haven in said State--the Memorial
of the Protestant Episcopal Societies, in sd State by their
Agents Elias Shipman & Isaac Beers--humbly Sheweth.--

That by the Constitution of the Protestant Episcopal
Churches, it is necessary there should be a Bishop to preside over them--a part of whose business is, to visit the

several Churches, under his care. That however unim-
portant such an Officer in the Christian Church, may be
esteemed by other denominations of Christians--yet to
your Memorialists, it appears a matter of the highest importance. The precepts of the religion, professed by your
memorialists, teach them to be good members of Society;
& in conformity to their precepts, they flatter themselves,
that they have uniformly, as a body, shewn themselves to
be firm friends & supporters of the government of this
State--as well as of the United States. They are of opinion, that they have a right, not only to the protection--but
to the assistance of Government, in the enjoyment of their
religion. They have had for a number of years, a Bishop
to preside over them--& as a partial maintenance for his
services, have made voluntary contributions. They are
induced to believe, there are many well disposed persons,
who would make donations for his support, were there a
body of men vested with Corporate powers, so as to receive & hold such donations, to them & to their successors
& to pay the interest thereof to the support of the Bishop.
They therefore humbly pray your honors, to incorporate a
suitable number of persons as Trustees to receive such
donations--under such restrictions and limitations, as to
your honors shall seem meet--and as they in duty bound
shall ever pray.
          Dated at New Haven Octr 12th AD 1798.
                                        Isaac Beers
                                        Elias Shipman

In the house of Reps Octr Session 1798--
          The prayer of this petition is negatived
                              Attest--John C. Smith Clerk

[1798, Oct. 28, New Haven]
To the honorable General Assembly of the State of Connecticut, now convened at Newhaven in said State, the
Memorial of the Members of the episcopal Society, who
meet to carry on public Worship in Trinity Church (so-
called) in the City of Newhaven, by their Agents Joseph
Bradley, Richard Cutler & John Barker, humbly sheweth,

That your Memorialists living within the Limits of
the first ecclesiastical Society in sd Newhaven, having
taken Advantage of the Law of this State, entituled, An
Act securing equal Rights and Privileges to Christians of
every Denomination in this State, maintain the public
Worship of God in sd Church and by taxing themselves
maintain a Minister who officiates according to the Rites
and Ceremonies of the protestant episcopal Church in
America.

That within the Limits of sd first Society, there are
also, established as ecclesiastical Societies said first Society; and the united Society, the latter being made up of
Whitehaven and Fairhaven Societies. That said Societies
are not distinguished from each other by any Metes and
Bounds. [A]side from their peculiar Situation, it is ques-
tionable, whether all the Inhabitants living within the Limits of sd first Society & belonging to the aforesaid Societies have a Right to form & erect themselves into a School
Society in order, to take any Benifit of the Monies arising
from the Sale of the Western Lands-- That sd first Society claims to be of itself a School Society; according
to which Idea, it becomes very uncertain to what School

Society many of your Memorialists belong.

That under these Circumstances they pray your Honors, that all those who now live within the Limits of s^d first Society, and now belong to s^d episcopal Society as well as such, as hereafter according to the existing Laws of this State shall join s^d episcopal Society (& shall live within s^d Limits) may be formed into a School Society, And thus as in Duty bound shall ever pray-- Dated at Newhaven Octr 28th 1798

                                    Joseph Bradley
                                    Richard Cutler
                                    Jno Barker

At session 1798   The prayer of this Society is granted in the House of Rep^s

                    Attest E Goodall Clerk

Dissented to in the Upper House
                    Test Saml Wyllys Secretary

In the house of Rep^s

Messrs J Pitkin & Jon^n O. Mosely are appointed a committee to confer &c on the differing votes of the houses on this petition

                    Attest J. C. Smith Clerk
In the Upper House
The Honble Thomas Seymour is appointed a Com^te to confer with the Gentlemen appointed by the House of Representatives on the different Votes of the Houses on this Petition

                    Test Saml Wyllys Secretary
In the Upper House
On report of Com^te and reconsideration this House adhere to their first Vote on this Petition

                    Test Saml Wyllys Secretary

[1798, Nov. 9, Norwich]
                              Norwich Novr 9: 1798
Sir,

Three or four Weeks ago, I was in Guilford some Hours--conversing with Cp^t Johnson respecting the Church there, a Thought came in my Mind, that Killingsworth, Guilford, & Cohabit, might perhaps be supplied with a Minister-- Accordingly I mentioned to Cp^t Johnson, that there was a Mr Thompson, a Methodist Preacher, of good Character, esteemed a foremost Man of Abilities among the Methodists, who married in a good Family in Norwich, is now preaching in a Part of Woodstock, a Man of real Piety, I believe, & a firm Supporter of the Doctrines of our Church, & who, for more than a Year past, has been uneasy with his Ordination--has conversed freely with me on the Subject, & has had the Reading of several of my Books on the Subject, & appears convinced of the Necessity of a lineal Succession in the Priesthood. Also I suggested that in the broken situation of the Presbyterian Meeting at Guilford, the Zeal & Manner of Address of one who had been a Methodist, might perhaps be attractive.-- On which Cp^t Johnson said, send him on to see us--I promised to consult Mr Thompson. Accordingly, the next Week Mr Thompson came to see me, & I told him what I had been doing for him, without his Knowledge. He said that he had just undertaken a School, together with Preaching, for five

Months--he wished me to write to some principal People of the Church in Guilford and Killingsworth, & if it should be agreeable to them, he would go & spend Christmas with them, & tarry a Week. I know not whether you would consider yourselves in the three Parishes, able to support a Clergiman, or not. But be so kind as to consult the Church People in your Vicinity, & write me a Line by the Post, as soon as you can with Convenience, & inform me whether it would be agreeable to receive a Visit from Mr Thompson on Christmas Week, & what you suppose the Church People in Killingsworth could contribute towards the Support of a Priest, if suited in the Man, & what you Imagine it probable, might be contributed in Guilford and Cohabit.-- A Methodist Preacher by the Name of Rogers, who married a Wife in Middletown, is about to settle in the Episcopal Church in Hebron, I am told; who has waited on Bishop Jervis, & that the Bishop told him that he would ordain him, if he obtained a Title to a support.-- Mr Thompson has for some Time been Conversant with this Mr Rogers, & has been proposing a Visit to Bishop Jervis. I am now going to write to Cp^t Johnson of Guilford on this Subject;-- & to hear soon from you & him, will oblige your Friend & humble Servant

                                    John Tyler

William Morgan Esqr

[1799, May 15, Hartford]
To the General Assembly of the State of Connecticut, now sitting at Hartford in & for said State.--

The Memorial of the Protestant Episcopal Societies in said State by their Agents Isaac Beers & Elias Shipman, humbly sheweth.-- That by the Constitution of their system of divine worship, it is indispensibly necessary that they have a Bishop to preside over them--a part of whose duty is to visit the respective Churches under his charge-- that some compensation for his services in their duty to render--and that this compensation by way of a partial support for him, has been heretofore raised by means of a voluntary contribution. Your Memorialists beg leave further to state, that by the constitution of the Civil government of this State, they have a right, as firm friends & supporters of this government, & of the government of the United States, to legislative protection & assistance in the exercise of their religion. They have wellgrounded belief that there are many well disposed persons, who have the happiness of their christian brethren at heart, & would willingly ameliorate the condition of them, by making donations for the support of the Bishop, which would relieve them from a considerable burden.--

Your Memorialists therefore pray this Honble Assembly to pass an act of incorporation in their favor, thereby vesting a number of persons with corporate powers, for the purpose of receiving donations, to them & to their successors for the support of a Bishop. Your Memorialist[s] ask this grant under such limitations & restrictions, in regard to the amount of the sum funded, & in every other respect, as to this Honble Assembly may seem proper.-- And as they in duty bound shall ever pray.--
    Dated at Hartford May. 15th   Isaac Beers
         1799   E. Shipman

May Sessions 1799   In the House of Representatives the

prayer of the within Petition is granted with liberty of a
bill &c
                    Test Calvin Goddard Clerk
Concurr^d in the Upper House
                    Test Saml Wyllys Secretary

Upon the Memorial of the Protestant Episcopal Societies in
the State of Connecticut, representing, that by the Constitution of their System of divine worship it is indispensibly
necessary that they have a Bishop to preside over them, a
part of whose duty it is to visit the respective Churches
under his charge--that some compensation for his services
is their duty to render, and that this compensation by way
of a partial support for him has heretofore been raised
by means of a voluntary contribution; and that many well
disposed persons who have the happiness of their christian
brethren at heart would willingly make donations for the
support of the Bishop which would relieve the memorialists
from a considerable burden. Praying for an Act of incorporation to invest a number of persons and their successors
with powers to receive donations for the support of a Bishop

Resolved by this Assembly, that Bela Hubbard, --Jona-
than Ingersoll,--Elias Shipman John Morgan,--Samuel W.
Johnson,--William Herring,--Jonathan Starr, & Evan Malbone, and their successors be and they hereby are incorporated by the name of "The Trustees for receiving donations
for the support of the Bishop with all the powers and immunities incident to an agregate corporation; by which name
to sue and be sued, and to continue its succession by electing such persons as said Corporation shall deem proper to
fill such vacancies as may happen by death, resignation or
otherwise.

Provided that said Corporation shall not have power at
any time to hold property, the annual product of which exceeds the sum of One thousand dollars--and said corporation shall be and continue during the pleasure of the general
Assembly--

Passed in the house of Rep^s
                    Attest John C. Smith Clerk
pass^d in the Upper House
                    Test Saml Wyllys Secretary

Upon the memorial of Bela Hubbard, Jonathan Ingersoll,
Elias Shipman and Jonathan Starr, trustees for receiving
donations for the support of the Bishop of the protestant
episcopal church in Connecticut, shewing to this Assembly
that since the incorporation of the memorialists and the
other trustees for receiving donations for the support of
the Bishop of Connecticut, many attempts have been made
to get together s^d trustees, in order to organize themselves and to do other necessary business, but on account
of the dispersed local situation of said trustees, a majority
cannot be collected, praying for an additional number of
trustees, as per petition on file &c--

Resolved by this Assembly that Philo Shelton, Ashbel
Baldwin, Isaac Beers and Joseph Drake be added to said
board of trustees, and that said board, after the addition
made as aforesaid, be intituled to and invested with the
same powers and privileges, as they had before said addition, and that after they have organized themselves, the
president or chairman of said board, together with five
others of said trustees, shall make a quorum, and in case

of the death or absence of the president, then shall be
seven of said trustees to make a quorum, and a majority
of said trustees shall be competent to meet and choose a
president and otherwise organize said board--

Pass^d in the Upper House
                    Test Samuel Wyllys Secretary
Concurred in the House of Representatives
                    Test N Rossiter Clerk

[1800, May 22, Middletown]
    The subscribers to wit Mary Alsop George Starr &
Ann C Starr his wife the latter being sole heir to the estate of Philip Mortimer deceased--all of the Town of Middletown in the County of Middlesex--hereby signify to all
persons whom it may concern that we acquiese in a sale of
the Glebe so called being the real estate conveyed by said
Mary & Philip to the Episcopal Church in s^d Town by deed
dated the twenty third day of June 1785--& are desirous
that Richard Alsop Jehoshaphat Starr & Josiah Williams
the Committee appointed by s^d Church to sell the same
be empowered by the Legislature or otherwise to convey
a fee simple estate therein to such person as they may
deem proper
    Middletown May 22^d 1800--
In Presence of   Mary Alsop
    Rose Champion   George Starr
    Robert Watkinson   Ann C Starr
    Ezra Bolles
    J. Lawrence Lewis

[1800, Sept. 16, Cheshire]
Dear Sir,
    By a letter from the Rev. Mr. Hart, now at N.Y. I
am informed that Mr. Hobart is elected an assistant in
Trinity Church, and in all probability Mr. Ratoon will
have the offer of St. Marks. These removals will cause
a vacancy in two parishes, one of which he lets me know,
it would be agreeable to him to place himself in; and requests a letter from me to you, in his behalf, as he particularly wishes for your friendship and that of Mr. Ratoon
in this matter. Mr. Hart has been in your city sometime,
in pursuit of an object which his circumstances induced
him to enterprise. A consideration, that with me was his
apology for so long an absence from his parishes, to which
he ministered in Connecticut. During the time he has been
in N.Y. you have had opportunity for some personal knowledge of him, perhaps sufficient to make up your mind, in
regard to his succeeding in an attempt for a settlement in
one of these parishes. I beleive he gave satisfaction to
the people among whom he officiated in Connecticut. One
parish, where he chiefly attended, I know, were fond of
him, and wished him to abide with them.
    I readily concur in his desire, and commend him to
your friendship and likewise to that of Mr. Ratoon, wishing he will do credit to himself, and to those gentlemen
who will aid him in the object of his desires. This letter
is now waited for, and is the cause of my not writing to
Mr. Ratoon, to whom, please to make my regards....
                    Abraham Jarvis
[Rev. Dr. Abraham Beach at New York]

[1800, Oct. 13, Danbury]
To the honorable Genl Assembly of the State of Connecticut now conven'd at New Haven in the County of New Haven in sd State--

The memorial of the Episcopal Society in Danbury in the County of Fairfield by their Agent Comfort S Mygatt humbly sheweth, That sd Society being small in number were at great pains & expence in erecting a House for public worship in sd Danbury which sd House in April 1777, tho not entirely, was so far compleated as to be decent & comfortable, at which time then at open war with these States came to & burnt and destroyed the public Stores at sd Danbury & sd House was thereupon taken up & occupied as a Store House for Public use for about six years in which time sd building went fast to decay, the floors, seats and windows were broken to pieces and the whole left in ruinous circumstances-- The memorialist wou'd further represent that the tumults and troubles of those times, & the general phrensy that prevailed with the destruction by fire in that Town and the calamities of the war have lessened the numbers and weakend the strength of the Society to such a degree that notwithstanding the allowances hitherto made amounting in all to about £40. They are still unable to pay their public taxes, support the preaching of the Gospel among them as formerly & compleat the repairs necessary to make sd building decent and to preserve it from ruin.-- Whereupon your memorialist[s] pray your honors to take their unhappy circumstances into your wise consideration and grant them a Lottery to raise the sum of $2000, or such other sum as your honors may think advisable, to be applied in repairing sd House, upon their procuring sufficient bonds for a faithful and Just management of sd Lottery, and application of the monies arising therefrom in manner as aforsd or in some other way grant relief as your honors in your wisdom shall think best and they as in duty bound shall pray &c.

Comfort S Mygatt } Agent for sd Society

Danbury Oct. 13th 1800.

General Assembly Oct Session 1800
In the House of Representatives The Prayer of the within Petition is granted, with liberty of a Bill &c
Test Timo Pethrap Clerk
In the Upper House
Granted on this Memorial that the memorialists have liberty to raise by lottery the sum of Eighteen hundred dollars inclusive of all expence & that a bill &c.
Test Samuel Wyllys Secretary

In the House of Representatives on reconsideration concurrd with the Governer & Council in their Grant on this Memorial & that a bill &c
Attest Danl N Bronprad Clerk

[1800, Oct. 15, New London]
At a Convocation of the Right Revd Bishop & Clergy of Connecticut, holden at New London on the 15th of October 1800.

Clergy Present
Right Revd Bishop Jarvis

Revd Doctr John Bowdain   Daniel Burhance
        John Tyler   Revd Charles Seabury
        Daniel Fogg   Alexander Griswold
        Chauncey Prindle   ----- Green
        Reuben Ives   Evan Rogers
        Truman Marsh   Joseph Warren
Revd Doctr Walter from Boston
        Bethuel Chittenden [from] Vermont
        Ammi Rogers [from] State of New York

Convocation was duly opened by the Right Revd Bishop Jarvis presiding Ex Officio.
Voted, that Truman Marsh be appointed Secretary of this Convention.
Resolved, in Convocation of the Bishop and Clergy of the Church of Connecticut, that the Revd Ezra Bradley in deserting the Ministry of Christ's Church, to the faithful discharge of which he bound himself in the Most Solemn and awful manner at his Ordination, without assigning any reasons to his Ecclesiastical Superior, when Called on, for taking a step which has such serious influence on the Character of the Clergy, and on religion, has acted an unworthy and unchristian part,--and the Convocation do therefore call on Mr Bradley to deliver to the Bishop, or to the person whom he shall appoint, his letters of Deacon's Orders--
Resolved, the Clergy recommend Revd Evan Rogers to the Bishop as a Candidate for Priest's Orders and that Revd Messrs Tyler Burhance and Seabury be appointed as a Committee to examine Mr Rogers.

[1800, Late Oct., New Haven]
Upon the Petition of the Episcopal Society in Danbury in Fairfield County, Shewing to this Assembly, that said Society had been at Great expence in erecting & building a House for Public Worship in said Danbury & that during the late war, after the British Troops had destroyed and Burnt the Public Buildings, & Stores in said Town; said House was taken up and occupyed as a Store for Public use, for about Six Years, during which time said Meeting House went fast to decay and was greatly injured, and that said Society have become so reduced in numbers and in property that they cannot repair said House without aid--and praying for a Lottery as by Petition on file--& the Petitioners having been hea[r]d thereon
Resolved by this Assembly that the Memori[a]lists have Liberty to raise by Lottery the sum not exceeding Eighteen hundred Dollars including costs, for the purpose of repairing the Episcopal Meeting House in said Danbury-- and this Assembly do Constitute and appoint James Clark, William Heron, Timothy Taylor Junr Esqrs and Nathan Cornwell or any three of them managers of said Lottery, with Liberty to form a Scheme for said Lottery, and said Managers or such of them as shall undertake the Trust, before they enter upon the execution of the Same, shall become bound to the Treasurer of this State in the Sum of three thousand Dollars, conditioned for the faithful discharge of the duties of their said Trust, and that they will pay the respective prizes to the fortunate adventurers in said Lottery and will account for the avails thereof with the Committee of said Society--and the Attorney for this State for Fairfield County, is hereby directed & impowered

to take said bond and to keep the Same in his hands, untill the purposes for which the same shall be given shall be answered--

Passed, in the House of Representatives,
                                    Test Tim⁰ Pethrap Clerk
Concurr^d in the Upper House
                                    Test Samuel Wyllys Secretary

[1802, May 12, Cheshire]
    To the Honb^l the General Assembly of the State of Connecticut to be holden at Hartford in s^d State on the second Thursday of May AD. 1802--
    The Memorial of the Trustees of the Episcopal Academy of Connecticut humbly sheweth--
    That the Academy since the period of it's establishment, at Cheshire in the Year AD 1795, has generally had from Sixty to Seventy Students, --That with a view to accommodate, with the means of Education, the less wealthy classes of people, the price of tuition, is moderate; owing to which, & the small funds of the Academy amounting only to about Two Thousand Dollars, the Salaries of the Instructors have been, and still are, in part, dependant upon the voluntary Contributions of the friends & patrons of the Institution;--That to Assist such Students as are desirous of an Education in the higher branches of Literature, large and very expensive Additions are necessary to be made to the Library & Philosophical Apparatus--which your Memorialists, are unable to do from the present situation of the funds of the Academy-- Wherefore your Memorialists pray your Honors to grant them liberty to raise by Lottery the sum of Fifteen Thousand Dollars to be preserved as a perpetual fund for the use and benefit of the Academy, the Interest whereof may enable your Memorialists to ensure permanent Sallaries to the Instructors, make the necessary Additions to the Library and Philosophical Apparatus, discharge the important duties and accomplish the great object of the Institution, the advancement of Literature & Science-- And your Memorialists as in Duty bound will ever Pray--
    Dated at Cheshire this 12th day of May AD 1802--

        For the Trustees   Abraham Jarvis President
                            Burrage Beach Secretary

General Assembly May Session 1802
    In the house of Rep^s The prayer of the foregoing Petition is granted with Liberty &c
                            Attest E. Goodrich Clerk
In the upper House
        the prayer of the foregoing Petition is negatived
                            Test Samuel Wyllys Secretary

[1802, May 15, Greenwich]
    The testimony of Capt John Hobby of Greenwich of lawfull age testifieth and saith that in the year 1776 at the time the American troops retreated from Newyork a great number of sick soldiers were brought into this town to be accomodated with barracks at this time the seats of the church was taken up and sick soldiers were put in the church after this it was made use of as a public store--

in February 1779 General Tryon came into this town with a detachment of the British Army and destroyed the pulpit reading desk, windows, doors, part of the floor and considerable of the siding on said House in consequence of the above injurys done to s^d house and being exposed to the weather since I am of the opinion the house will not answer to repair

    Bezaleel Brown agrees with the above deponent excepting he does not remember the sick soldiers being put in the Church but thinks it is likely to be so

    Fairfield County ss In Greenwich May 15th AD 1802 personally appeared John Hobby and Bezaleel Brown the above deponents and made oath that the above depositions concerning the cause in question is the truth the whole truth and nothing but the truth before me
                            Jabez Fitch Justice of peace

[1802, May 15, Greenwich]
    Eben^r Mead of Greenwich of Lawfull age deposeth and saith that in the month of February 1779 General Tryon came up to Greenwich with a body of British troops and plundered the Inhabitance of Greenwich West Society and did damage to the buildings & perticularly to the Episcopal Church in s^d Society by removing the seats pews desk and pulpit out of the house and tore up the flours and carried them out--broke the windows and the sides of the house very much

    Fairfield County ss In Greenwich May 15th AD 1802 personally appeared Ebenezer Mead the above deponent and made oath to the truth [of] above deposition agreeably to Law before me
        15th May   Jabez Fitch Justice of peace

[1802, May 15, Greenwich]
    To the Honorable General Assembly of the State of Connecticut, now in Session at Hartford.
    The Repre[se]ntation & Petition of the Episcopal Society of the Town of Greenwich, in said State, by their Agent, Jabez Fitch Esquire of said Greenwich, Most respectfully Setting forth, ----That previous to the American Revolution, the said Society bid fair to be in flourishing & eligible circumstances to support & maintain public worship, & to enjoy, in common with other religious Societies, in the State, the benefits resulting from the benign influence of the Sabbath, and of those religious institutions and Ordinances, so essential to the infusion of moral & virtuous principles, & so friendly to Social Order. But this pleasing prospect vanished during the Revolutionary War; a considerable number of the members of said Society (as is the case in other Societies) were in a condition below mediocrity, & by the frequent incursions & Depredations of the enemy on the small property they possessed, they were reduced in their circumstances, & still continue unable to contribute to the present pressing exigency of the Society, destitute of a comfortable House to accom[m]odate the Congregation; for, by the injuries their House of worship sustained in said war, by being in the year 1776, occupied by the American Army as an

Hospital, & afterwards for the Storage of their provisions, whereby the Seats & Pews were destroyed; and in the year 1779, when Gen! Tryon with his Army, made an incursion into sd Greenwich, their said House of worship was improved as a Horse-stable whereby the Pulpit, windows & Doors were destroyed--by which dispensations, the Society are laboring under embarrassments arising from the mutilation of their House of worship, & the inability of many of its members.

At the close of the war, however, anxious to support the public worship of God, the sd Society engaged a worthy Clergyman to lead them in Divine Service, & made such partial repairs, as their circumstances would admit, not being able to effect thorough repairs, which, on examination of the materials, was found to be impracticable by reason of their Decay. The Society still maintain & Support public worship, sometimes in private Houses, which is found to be inconvenient. They therefore contemplate to erect a new House of worship, a Task to which they are incompetent without Legislative aid, upon which they rely from the many instances of liberal encouragements heretofore granted by the Legislature of this State to promote moral & religious habits.

Wherefore your Petitioner humbly prays your honors to take the Premises into your wise Consideration, and to extend your fostering hand to said Society, by a Grant of such a sum of money out of the State Treasury, as, on consideration of their sufferings above represented, & the importance of their Object at the present conjuncture, may appear in your honors judgment to merit; or in some other way grant them such relief, as to your Honors, in the exercise of your wise Deliberations may think proper, and your Petitioner as in Duty bound shall ever pray.
Dated at Greenwich May 15th 1802
            Jabez Fitch Agent for Society

In the Upper House
    The Prayer of the foregoing Petition is negatived
            Test Sam¹ Wyllys, Secretary

[1802, Oct. 19, New Haven]
    To the Honorable General Assembly of the State of Connecticut now sitting at New Haven, The Memorial of the Trustees of the Episcopal Academy, humbly sheweth,
    That the Academy aforesaid was in the year 1796 established at Cheshire in said State for the instruction of youth in the sciences generally, or in any science in particular, and from that period to the present time has had in a course of education about Sixty Students annually and this number is rapidly increasing. That to the Trustees aforesaid, An acre of Land with a brick building thereon was given by certain Inhabitants of Said Cheshire, to be improved to the purposes of academical instruction, the building aforesaid consisting of two Stories, & being Sixty feet in front & about thirty feet in width; Your Memorialists State, that the funds of said Academy amount to Seventeen Hundred dollars only; That the building aforesaid is in want of present repairs, and considerable enlargement to accommodate the Students; That the Said Academy is destitute of a Library & of an apparatus Mathematical & philosophical, of which it is in present Necessity; That a house is Much wanted for the accommodation of the Principal of

sd Academy, and funds to compensate an additional assistant instructor, That for these various important purposes, of a nature highly interesting to the public, the Trustees aforesaid are in want of at least $15,000 Dollars, & to obtain this sum their only resource is in the Munificence & wisdom of your honors; They therefore request of the honorable assembly to grant them a Lottery whereby they May raise the afores¢ Sum of $15,000 Dollars, or in Some other way to grant relief, & as in duty bound they will pray &c.
    Dated at New Haven this 19th day of October AD 1802.
            Abraham Jarvis - Princ¹ of s¢ Academy,
                in behalf of the Trustees.

Gen¹ Assembly Octr session 1802
    In the House of Rep$ the prayer of the foregoing Memorial is granted with liberty of a Bill &c.
            Albert Jon^a Moseley Clerk
Concurr^d in the Upper House
            Test Sam¹ Wyllys Secretary

[1802, Oct. 19, New Haven]
    Upon the memorial of the trustees of the episcopal academy shewing to this assembly,
    That the Academy aforesaid established at Cheshire, in this State for the instruction in the sciences is in want of buildings, library, and apparatus, mathematical and philosophical and a fund to support an Instructor &c, praying the honorable Assembly to grant them a lottery whereby they may raise the sum of fifteen thousand dollars for the purposes aforesaid, as per Memorial on file--
    Resolved by this Assembly, that a lottery of one or more classes to raise the sum of fifteen thousand dollars exclusive of the expences of managing said lottery, be and the same is hereby granted to the memorialists, and the same is hereby put under the direction of Timothy Phelps, John Barker, Isaac Mills, Nathan Smith Naphtah Daggetts, and Stephen Twining of Newhaven and Rufus Hitchcock and Burrage Beach of Cheshire and Samuel Woodruff of Wallingford, or any five of them, who are hereby appointed and constituted managers thereof; and the said managers before they enter on the execution of s^d trust shall be sworn to a faithful discharge thereof and shall give bond to the treasurer of this state in the sum of Thirty thousand dollars for a like discharge of their said trust, pursuant to the directions of this act, and to such other orders and directions as they shall receive from time to time from the General Assembly, or in their ruin from the Governor & Council, and to render their accounts when required

pass^d in the Upper House
            Test Samuel Wyllys Secretary
Concurred in the House of Rep^s
            Albert Jon^a Moseley Clerk

[1803, Oct. 27, New Haven]
To the honorable General Assembly, now sitting at Newhaven, The memorial of Bela Hubbard, Jonathan Ingersoll, Elias Shipman and Jonathan Starr, trustees for receiving donations for the support of the Bishop of the protestant episcopal church in Connecticut, humbly sheweth,

That your memorialists, together with John Morgan, Samuel W. Johnson, William Heron and Evan Malbone have been appointed trustees, and made a body corporate, for the purpose of receiving donations as aforesaid.-- That various attempts have been made since s^d incorporation to get together a majority of said trustees, in order to organize themselves and to do other necessary business, but all to no purpose. For which reason the object of s^d incorporation hath been hitherto unobtained.-- That from the dispersed local situation of said trustees, it will be very inconvenient for a majority of them to be convened either for organization, or to do any business whatever.-- They therefore humbly pray your honors, that an addition be made to s^d board of trustees of three or four persons, to be taken from Newhaven or places thereto adjacent, in order the more easily to answer the ends of s^d incorporation, or in some other way to grant relief-- As your memorialists in duty bound shall ever pray--

Dated at Newhaven Octr 27th 1803

      Bela Hubbard   Elias Shipman
      Jon^th Ingersoll   Jon^th Starr

[1805, May 1, Roxbury]

To the Honorable General Assembly of the State of Connecticut to be holden at Hartford in & for s^d State on the second thursday of May 1805--

The Petition of Amos Squier & the rest of the Inhabitants of the Episcopal Society of the Town of Roxbury in Litchfield County Humbly sheweth--

That about fifty years since the Episcopalians of s^d Roxbury formed themselves into a society and built a small house in which they might convene to perform divine service That s^d house was built about Twenty years previous to the revolutionary War & from the Troubles that then existed the smallness and inability of the society to repair the house (though the society did something in repairs) the house went to decay and is now almost intirely useless the Timbers being rotten & the covering poor, and not worth repairing Yet, s^d society have met in it for Divine Worship ever since it was built except in the winter season it being so open & decayed considered it too uncomfortable. Your Petitioners would further state to your Honors that under these [cir]cumstances they have had it in contemplation to build a new house for Divine Worship but on examination of the Abilities of your Petitioners they were fully satisfied they were Unable & that their local situation was such that it would be extreemly dificult for them to attend at any other place any Episcopalian Congregation the roads & Hills being extreme[ly] bad leading in every direction from s^d Town & the distance from five to Eight miles Your Petitioners therefore prays your Honors to take their unhappy case into your wise consideration and grant them a Lottery under such restrictions & regulations as your Honors may think fit to enable them to Build a house for Divine Worship or in some other way grant relief as to your Honors shall seem Just & right & as in Duty bound we shall ever pray

Dated at Roxbury this 1st day of May 1805

      Amos Squier for himself & the rest
      of Episcopalian Society in Roxbury

[1805, May 3, Roxbury]

A List of the Polls & Rateable Estate of the following Persons / viz /.

Eli Booth	$ 98.30	Brot up	$2911.61
Samuel Booth	124.36	Adna Mallory	179.33
Enos Beacher	75.91	Victory Shelton	20.20
Stephen Beacher	97.00	Benja^m Shelton	10.20
Elias Bates	145.36	Amos Squire	360.00
Peter Castle	137.43	Nathan Squire	111.51
David Castle	139.63	Solloman Squire	151.68
Abraham Castle Jr.	72.50	Benjamin Squire	92.91
Booth Castle	169.25	Thomas Squire	143.39
Abraham Castle	238.92	Elisha Shelton	47.17
Peter Castle Jr.	147.77	John Sherman	79.30
Truman Coggshal	67.00	Samuel Thompson	190.79
Ezeria Eastman	176.59	Daniel Wakeley	154.28
Nathaniel Flowers	183.87	Daniel Wetler	139.78
George Graham	237.48	David Warner	382.68
Daniel Gorham	227.37	Macock Ward	20.01
Buel Hough	67.79	Macock Ward Jr.	124.78
Benajah Hawley	153.29	Eli Ward	107.67
Benajah Hawley Jr.	178.35		$5227.29
Lemuel Nichols	109.44		
Daniel Mallory	64.00		
	$2916.61		

This is a true Copy of the List of the Polls & Rateable Estate of the above named person for the Year 1804--

Certified by us { Benjamin Squire / Amos Squire / Adna Mallory } Comm^ttee for the Episcopal Society

Roxbury May 3rd 1805--

[1805, May 6, New Milford]

To the Honb^le Genl Assembly to be holden at Hartford on the 2^d Thursday of May 1805--

The petition & Memorial of Jeremiah Platt, James Jessup, & Ebenezer Trobridge of New Milford in Litchfield County, Wardens of the Episcopal Church, in the Society of Bridgewater in s^d town, in behalf of themselves & the rest of s^d Church & Congregation, humbly sheweth--that your memorialists, since the recent establishment of the present located Society of Bridgewater aforesaid, have never had any Church edifice in which to meet for the celebration of Divine Service; & that from the smallness of their numbers, & the scantyness of their means, they are utterly unable to erect or procure such Edifice, without public aid by means of a Lottery or otherwise-- Trusting therefore, to the beneficence of the Legislature so often & so justly exercised towards others in similar situations, they pray your honors to grant them permission to raise by means of a lottery the sum of three thousand dollars, to be appropriated to the building of a Church in s^d Society, which sum with such exertions as your Memorialists are enabled to make would, in the apprehension of your Memorialists, be sufficient to enable them to erect & compleat a suitable building for the purpose aforesaid; & without which aid so desireable an object cannot be accomplished--

Your Memorialists therefore pray your Honors, to take their case into your wise consideration & upon being

satisfied of the foregoing facts, that you would grant the prayer of your memorialists, upon their entering into the usual stipulations in such cases imposed--& your Memorialists as in Duty bound will ever pray--

New Milford
6th May 1805--

Jeremiah Platt
Jas Jessup
Ebenr Trobridge

[1805, May 13, Greenwich]

I Bazaleel Brown of lawful age deposeth and saith that in the year 1776 there was a great number of Sick Soldiers brought from the American army, into the town of Greenwich and this deponant being one of the Selectmen of said Greenwich at that time, was call'd on to furnish quarters for said sick Soldiers While this deponant was in pursuit for quarters for said sick he found the offecers who had charge of said sick had broken up the Seats of the Church for the purpose of making a hospital of the same and had fill'd it with said sick soldiers, soon after the sick had left said church it was taken by the public for Storing Provisions for the Army and in the year 1779 General Tryon with a detachment of the British Army made an incursion into said Greenwich the dragoons under his command destroy'd the Pulpit, reading desk, seats and doors and did great injury to the floor and out side covering, and appropriated it as a Stable for their Horses the House lay in this situation untill the close of the War, at w[h]ich time the Society were so reduced by the frequent ravages of the Enemy that they were not able to make any repairs on said church before it was so injured by being Exposed to the weather that the Society Judg'd it prudent to put but small repairs on the same the Society have been under the necessity to attend public worship at private Houses in the cold season of the year in consequence of the injury the church sustain'd as above the church before the seats were broken up in 1776 was in good repair--

Sworn before me
Ebenr Mead Justice of peace

May 13th 1805

[1805, Oct. 1, Durham]

To the Honorable Legislature of the State of Connecticut to be convened at New Haven on Thursday the 10th Day of Inst October

The Memorial of the Protestant Episcopal Church in Durham humbly sheweth.----That your Memorialists are destitute of a House for publick Worship, and that their numbers are greater than their resources for providing stated, and constant preaching, and also for building a House necessary for the purpose.----That hitherto they have been able to convene in a School House, or a private dwelling House; but that their numbers having considerably increased, they find themselves under the necessity of having a Building erected for the purpose; and feeling unable to accomplish the undertaking, they are induced to pray your Honors to grant them a Lottery sufficient to aid them in erecting a Building wherein they may meet for publick Worship, secure from the inclemency of the Weather, and wherein they may enjoy the smiles of the God of All Mercies.----That the said Lottery be under such restrictions, and limitations as the Legislature in their wisdom may deem proper; or in some other way to grant relief.----

And Your Petitioners as in Duty bound shall ever Pray--
Dated in Durham October 1st 1805--

Manoah Camp ⎫ Committee in behalf
Lemuel Camp ⎬ of Durham Episcopal
John Scarrit ⎭ Society

At a Meeting of the Episcop. Society in Durham legally warned holden at the Quarry School House (so called) in said Town, on the 1st day of October 1805--

Voted that Manoah Camp, Lemuel Camp, and John Scarrit be a Committee in behalf of said Society to sign the Petition to be preferred to the General Assembly, to be holden at New Haven on the 10th day of Inst October.

The above is a true Copy extracted from the Durham Episcopal Society's Records--

Attest John Scarrit, Clerk
Durham October 1st 1805

In the House of Representatives, the Within petition is referred to Messrs Cleaveland, David Smith, Latham Hull, Goddard & Eliphalet Terry, to join such gentlemen as the Governor & Council may appoint to take the same into consideration & make report by bill or otherwise

Test N Webster, Clerk
In the Upper House

The Honble Roger Newberry is appointed to Join the Gentlemen mentioned in the above Vote of the House of Representatives to take into Consideration this Petition &c

Test, Saml Wyllys Secretary

In the House of Representatives, the consideration of the within petition is referred to the General Assembly to be held at Hartford on the second thursday of May next

Test N Webster, Clerk

[1805, Oct. 19, Durham]

The number of Families contained in the Episcopal Church in Durham is Sixty Two, the number of Souls belonging to said Congregation is Three hundred & eight--

The above is a correct statement of the number of Families, and souls belonging to the Episcopal Congregation in Durham--

As extracted from the Parish Records--

Attest--John Scarrit Clk Epl Chh
Parish Office Durham 19th October 1805--

To the Honorable Committee appointed to Report on the Merits of the Petition in favor of the Episcopal Congregation in Durham

Signed Pr order of the Committee of said Church
John Scarrit Clerk

[1805, Oct. 20, Milford]

At a Meeting of the Wardens, Vestry and other Members of the Episcopall Chh in Milford October 20th 1805. Voted that Abm V H DeWitt Esqr be appointd Agent for the Episcopal Society in Milford to present a Memorial to the general Assembly now in session at new Haven for the purpose of obtaining $2500 by Lottery or otherwise to repair & finish the Chh in Milford.

Attest Abm Tomlinson Clerk.

[Supporting Records:]

Bond	£400-00	
Interest	165-10	
	£565-10-0	
	96-15-10	
Due	£468-14-2	

Rec^d on the Bond viz

Shingles & siding	£37-14-9
Nails	7- 5-8
Glass & Paints	38- 8-9
Mr Clarks Bill	13- 6-8
	£96-15-10

In the Spring of 1777 This Money was paid in to David
Baldwin in Continental Money in its depreciated State by
Ab^m Davenport Esqr of Stamford, he the said Baldwin not
daring to refuse the same, for fear of being illtreated on
that Account.

        Certified by Ab^m Tomlinson Clerk of the Episcopal
                         Society in Milford.

Remarks, the C^{hh} people exerted themslves, got Timber
for, framed & raised the C^{hh} in expectation of aid from
Mr Talbots Donation, they thought it best not to call on
Mr Talbot for his Money untill his decease, when the Interest on the Bond would add considerable to the sum to be
rec^d they obtained forbearance from the various Workmen
and for other Bills, 'till the Money should fall due, that
when it was rec^d ou[r] Debts could be cancelled with it.
In consequence of which, they were obliged to sell a Gleeb
Lot (the Donation of Mrs Rebeca Allen) to exonerate themselves from the Debts then incured. Also that by Deaths,
Removals and other unavoidable Accidents they have not
been able to repair their C^{hh} to this Time, which is in a
ruinous State, and must soon be lost, unless aid can be obtained. For further Information inquire of Ab^m V H Dewitt
and Elias Clark Esq^{rs}.

     Amount of Lists of the Episcopal Society for the Year
1805 $3183:$\frac{27}{100}$.

[1805, Oct. 21, Milford]

     To the Honorable General Assembly of the State of
Connecticut now in Session at New Haven in said State--

     The Episcopal Society in Milford in New Haven County,
by their Agent Abraham V H DeWitt, Humbly beg leave to
Represent-- That a number of years since--relying on the
Honorable payment of a certain bond they then held demanding about Twelve Hundred Dollars--combined with exertions
of the Society--they Commenc'd building a Church of Fifty
Feet by Thirty Seven, wherein they might Assemble for Public Worship-- They progress'd so far as to get the building
erected & Cover'd--when much to the surprise of your Pe-
titioners--a Tenury in Continental bills was made on said
bond which was by said Society unfortunately reciev'd &
by the rapid depreciation theirof--became an almost Total
loss-- Thus disappointed in their pleasing prospects--they
erected Temporary seats for the accomodation of said So-
ciety--without anything more being done to the inside--in
this situation it has remain'd to the present time in Conse-

quence of the inability of s^d Society
     They would now suggest--that it is now much out of
repair & unless immediately Cover'd--must go to ruin--
while your Petitioners--from the smallness of their number & also their list--amounting to about Three Thousand
Dollars only--must with regret--remain silent spectators
--unless reliev'd by your Honors-- They therefore, fond-
ly believing--that the same measure of Justice will be
meted out to them as has been to others in similar Cases--
Humbly solicit your Honors to grant them leave to raise by
Lottery Twenty Five Hundred Dollars--for the purposes of
repairing & Finishing said building or in some other way
Grant relief--& they as in duty bound will ever pray--

                Ab^m V H DeWitt } Agent for
                                 s^d Society
Milford Octr 21- 1805

[1806, May]
To the Honourable the General Assembly

     The joint Committe to whom was refered The Petitions
of the North Society in Canterbury of Eastford Society in
Ashford of the Episcopal Church in Durham and the Episcopal Society in Milford praying for Lotteries &c
     haveing taken the Same into consideration beg leave to
report that said Petitions be refered to the General Assembly to be holden at Hartford in May next att which is submitted

                Signed per Order Roger Newberry

In the House of Representatives, the foregoing report is
accepted & approved.

                Test N Webster Clerk
Concurr^d in the Upper House

                Test Saml Wyllys Secretary

[1806, May 9, Hartford]
To the Hon. General Assembly of the State of Connecticut
now in session--

     The Petition of Benjamin Slater Nathl Dickenson and
Oliver Sage a Commitee of the Episcopalian Society in the
Towns of Wethersfield and Berlin humbly sheweth--

     That they the said Society for the purpose of having a
more convenient place to assemble for the public worship
of God did about five years ago set about to erect a building for that purpose that altho they are not numerous yet
by uncommon exertion together with the aid of some generous individuals not of the Society they have been able to
raise and cover the outside of [a] building of decent sise &
dimentions with a steeple duly proportioned near the dividing line of the s^d towns of Wethersfield & Berlin that not
being able to secure said building by painting the outside
or to complete the inside thereof having already made
great sacrifise of private property--your petitioners for
and in behalf of the said Society pray your Honors to take
their case into your deliberate and wise consideration and
to lend them your generous aid by granting a Lotery sufficient to raise one thousand dollars which shall be laid
out in painting the out side and in doing off the inside of
the said building or church so that it may be a decent and
convenient house in which to assemble for the all important purpose of the public worship of God or that your

Honors would in some other way grant them aid and relief

And your petitioners as in duty bound shall ever pray--

Dated at Hartford May 9th 1806--

Benjamin Slater }
Nathl Dickinson } Committee
Oliver Sage }

In the House of Representatives

The consideration of the aforegoing Petition in referred to the Committee appointed on the Subject of Lotteries

Test Jh. Y. Seymour Clerk

Concurrd in the upper House

Test Saml Wyllys Secretary

[1806, May 21, Durham]

James Arnold	189.38	Richard Robinson	129.95
James Arnold Jr	56.06	Charles Robinson	87.08
Jesse Atwell	164.38	Ebenezer Robinson	214.07
Jeremiah Butler Jr	124.53	Stephen Robinson	126.54
Richard Barrit	100.06	Ebenezer Robinson Jr	21.88
Ebenezer Belknap	13.02	Seth Strong	289.42
John Camp	26.48	James Robinson	124.58
Lemuel Camp	143.50	Medad Strong	101.11
Luke Camp	71.42	Thomas Strong	67.76
Gad Camp	101.48	Ichabod Scrantom	60.00
Manoah Camp	161.59	Elizur Spelman	16.79
Abial Camp	25.00	John Spencer	186.46
George Galpin	40.40	William Swathel	81.38
Asher Gillum	97.73	Robert Smithson	82.36
Wido Sarah Gurnsey	78.01	Elizabeth Spelman	17.50
Henry Hall	112.52	James Tibbals	200.45
Day Hall	51.86	Job Wheler	60.00
Eliakim Hull	60.00	Samuel Woodsey	79.70
Eliakim Hull Jr	167.00	Richard M. Nary	71.40
James Hinman	26.07	Camp Robinson &c	84.00
Daniel Hickcon	113.92	Hezekiah Camp	186.98
Thomas Lyman	436.78	Asa Chamberlain Jur	50.00
Abel Lyman	139.67		2339.41
Titus & Richard			3741.86
Loveland	312.37		$6089.33
Ezra & Isaac			
Loveland	179.85		
Titus Loveland Jur	121.80		
Benjamin Pickitt	225.28		
Aaron & Curtiss			
Parsons	281.49		
James Robinson Jr	30.71		
John Reed	69.50		
	$3741.86		

Durham May 21st 1806

This May Certify that the Within is a true Copy taken from the Grand[list] for the year 1805

Attest James Robinson Clerk

No. of Soules belonging to the Episcopal Society in Durham - - - 240

Attest. J Robinson Clerk

[1807, May 12, Wethersfield]

To the Hon General Assembly of the State of Connecticut to be holden at Hartford in sd State on the 2nd thursday of May AD 1807--

The Petition of Benjamin Slater John Goodrich 2d and Nathl Dickinson a Committee of the Episcopalian Society of Wethersfield and Berlin in County   Humbly sheweth   That your petitioners together with other individuals of the sd Society have lately at their own cost near the dividing line between the sd Towns of Wethersfield & Berlin erected a meeting house or church for the accomodation of the sd Society in which to meet for the public worship of God-- And your petitioners further state to your Honors that altho' they have been able by great exertions and sacrifises to cover the outside of sd building yet they cannot without too great sacrifise of private property do off the inside of sd house and paint the outside thereof-- And your petitioners further State that they preferd a petition a year ago to the Honorable Assembly; of the purport of the above and that by some means it was mislaid and lost--

Whereupon your petitioners pray your Honors to take their case into your wise consideration and if upon the foregoing facts being proved--you deem it expedient to grant them a Lottery to raise the sum of one thousand dollars to be appropriated for the purpose of doing off the inside of sd house and of painting the outside therof-- or in some other way grant them relief--

And they as in duty bound shall ever pray

Dated at Wethersfield May 12th 1807

John Goodrich 2nd }
Benjamin Slater } Committee
Nathl Dickinson }

In the House of Reps: The consideration of this Petition is refered to the Committee appointed to take into consideration the subject of granting Lotteries to report by bill or otherwise--   Attest E Goddard Speaker

[1807, Oct. 12, Hartford]

To the Honourable the General Assembly of the State of Connecticut now sitting at New-Haven.--

The Petition of John Morgan of Hartford in the County of Hartford, a Member of the Episcopal Parish of Christ's Church in Hartford, in behalff of himself and the rest of the Members of said Parish, humbly sheweth, that several years since in pursuance of the Statute for forming, ordering, and regulating Societies they formed themselves into an organized Society, and afterwards held their annual Meetings on Easter Monday according to the Usages of their Church; but not adverting to the first paragraph of said Statute, they omitted to fix the said time for their said annual Meetings by Vote, and by reason of the premises they are advised that their proceedings in Strictness of Law are not valid. They therefore pray your Honours to authorize them to hold a Meeting of said Parish according to the Provisions of the fifth paragraph of said Statute; and at such meeting to confirm the proceedings of their Meetings holden as aforesaid, in such manner that the effect thereof may be the same as if their said Meetings

had been holden at the times specified in said Statute Or in some other way grant relief to the Petitioners; and they as in duty bound shall ever pray--

Dated at Hartford the 12th day of October AD 1807--
John Morgan for himself & the
rest of the Members of Christ Church--

In the house of Representatives
Granted the foregoing Petition, with liberty of a Bill
Test L Law Clk
Concurr^d in the Upper House
Test Saml Wyllys Secretary

[1808, May 7, Greenwich]

To the honorable General Assembly of the State of Connecticut to be convened at the City of Hartford on the second Thursday of May 1808.

The Representation and Petition of the Episcopal Society of the Town of Greenwich in said State, by their agent William Knapp of said Greenwich Respectfully Sheweth

That previous to the American revolution the Society flattered themselves that their circumstances were in so flourishing a condition, that they would be enabled to enjoy the benefits resulting from the exercise and maintainance of Public Worship, so essential to the promulgation of virtuous principles; and so congenial to social order, but this pleasing prospect vanished by the intervention of the revolutionary War and by the injuries their house of Worship sustaincd in the year 1776 being then occupied by the American Troops as an hospital, and shortly after appropriated as a place of Storage for provisions &cc, and in the year 1779 when General Tryon with his army made an incursion to said Greenwich, it was converted into a horse stable, which completed the ruin of it, by the demolition of the Pulpit, Windows and doors. At the conclusion of the War the society once more anxious to assembly together to support the worship of God, made such partial repairs to it, as their circumstances would admit; and had occasional service performed therein, however since that period it is found that the materials of the Church are so much impared and decayed as to render any farther repairs useless. They therefore contemplate the building of a new Church an undertaking to which their resources are inadequate, without Legislative aid, upon which they solely rely, and are more especially encouraged, from the many instances of Liberallity, manifested heretofore by the Legislature of this State to promote Moral and Religious institutions.

Your Petitioners pray your honors therefore to take the premises into your serious and wise consideration, and extend your protection and aid, by granting them the power, to raise by Lottery under proper regulations the sum of four thousand Dollars clear of charges, for the purpose of erecting in said Greenwich, a suitable house of Worship for said Episcopal Society; or in some other way grant them such relief, as to your honors may seem fit; and your petitioners as in duty bound shall ever pray.

Dated at Greenwich   William Knapp
May 7. 1808.   agent

[1809, May 9, Middletown]

To the honorable the General Assembly to be holden at Hartford in & for the State of Connecticut on the 2nd Thursday of May AD 1809---- The Memorial of Jehosaphat Starr Richard Alsop & Josiah Williams all of the Town of Middletown in the County of Middlesex in s^d State humbly sheweth--

That in the year 1785--sundry persons members of the Episcopal Church in s^d Town by voluntary contribution purchased a certain piece of land containing about one acre & its appurtenances situate in s^d town bounded northerly & easterly by highway southerly & Westerly by land then owned by John Elert now owned by Thomas Mather & the heirs of Stephen Clay dec^d & the same was on the 23^d day of July in the year afors^d conveyed by Philip Mortimer & Mary Alsop to s^d Episcopal Church "called Christ's Church" to have & to hold the same forever--for the use & support of the Gospel Ministry therein--to which use s^d land & the dwelling house thereon called the Glebe have been applied--

Your Memorialists would further state that at the Annual Meeting of the Members of s^d Society on the first Monday of April last it was unanimously voted by s^d Society to sell s^d Glebe & invest the avails thereof in other estate for the use before Mentioned & s^d society appointed the Subscribers a committee for that purpose & authorized them so far as s^d Society could confer authority in that respect to sell & convey s^d Glebe--s^d society were induced to s^d vote by the decayed condition of s^d house fences & outhouses--the same being wholly unfit for the residence of their clergyman & the prospect of obtaining a large price for the same--

In pursuance of s^d vote your memorialists did at s^d Town on the 4th day of April last contract for the sale of s^d Glebe for the sum of fifteen hundred Dollars & have stipulated to convey by a warranty deed a fee simple estate in the Same so soon as they shall be empowered thereto by the General Assembly--

Wherefore your Memorialists pray the General Assembly to enquire as to the facts afors^d & empower them to convey the premises to such person as they may deem expedient by a warrantee Deed in usual form & thereby to vest in their Grantee a fee simple estate therein any law or usage to the contrary notwithstanding all in conformity to s^d vote or in some other way grant relief in the premises--And your memorialists as in Duty bound shall pray &c   Dated at Middletown the 9th day of May AD 1809--

Jehos^t Starr   ⌈Committee of
Richd Alsop   ⟨Christ Church
Josiah Williams ⌊in Middletown

In House of Rep. May Sess. 1809   Prayer Granted
Test S Rowland Clerk

[1809, May Session]

Upon the Petition of Jehosaphat Starr Richard Alsop & Josiah Williams of the Town of Middletown, stating that in the year 1785 Philip Mortimer & Mary Alsop conveyed to the Episcopal Society in said Town a certain piece of Land with the buildings thereon situate in s^d Town, bounded Northwardly & Eastwardly by highway, Southwardly by land owned by Thomas & Elizabeth Mather & westwardly by land lately owned by Stephen Clay deceased & that the

same was granted & given for the use & support of the Gospel Ministry therein--also that s^d Society at their annual Meeting in April last did Vote to sell the same & appointed the Petitioners a committee for that purpose, which facts have been proved to this Assembly & also that the heirs of said Philip Mortimer deceased to Wit--George Starr & his Wife Ann C Starr & said Mary Alsop did by a written instrument, dated at s^d Middletown on the 22^d Day of May 1809, by them subscribed, express their Consent to a Sale to be made by s^d Petitioners & request this Assembly to empower them to convey a fee simple Estate in the same

Resolved by this Assembly, that the af[ore]said Jehosaphat Starr, Richard Alsop & Josiah Williams be & they are hereby empowered & authorized to convey the said real Estate to such Person or persons as they may judge expedient in Conformity to the aforesd Vote, by a Deed will executed in usual form to convey a fee simple Estate & thereby, their Grantee shall be invested with a fee simple Estate in ye said Glebe, any law or Usage to the contrary notwithstanding----And that the Avails of the Estate aforesaid be paid over to the said Society & the same to be by them vested in Real Estate Bank Stock, or loaned on Mortgage Security so that the Avails thereof shall remain & forever be a permanent fund, the Income or Interest of which may annually be appropriated to the same purposes for which the annual Income of the Estate afores^d was by the Grant to be appropriated

pass^d in the Upper House
Test   Samuel Wyllys   Secretary

In H. of Rep. May Sess. 1809   Concurred
Test   S. Rowland   Clerk

[1809, May 20, Norwich]
Norwich in Connecticut   May 20: 1809
Gentlemen,

Since I wrote you last Septr I have disposed of

1 Life of Jarratt	$1
1 Fowlers Exposition	1
1 Edwards on Baptism	.38
2 Common Prayer Books	1.60
3 Catechisms	.30
2 Hymns	.50
	$4.78

The small Sale of Books since last fall has been owing partly to the Embargo, but more to my Want of Health during the Winter & this Spring. Very few People come to me for Books; but I go round among my People, and tell them that such & such Books they ought to have: and frequently they will take them.--I believe that I have Books enough on Hand, at present unless Something new & interesting should appear,--I remain with Esteem, your Friend and humble Servant
John Tyler

N.B. I send you by Cp^t Roath $5, J.T.

T and J. Swords, Printers / New-York / By Cp^t Roath

[1810, May 16, East Windsor]
To the Honorable General Assembly of the State of Connecticut now in Session.

The Petition of the subscribers inhabitants of the Towns of East Windsor, Windsor and Ellington, resideing at and in the vicinity of that part of East Windsor called Ware House Point humbly sheweth. That your Petitioners did, in the year 1809, by subscription erect a large and elegant Church at said Ware House Point for the convenience and accomodation of the East Windsor Episcopal Society and that they have completed the outside of said Church. That the money subscribed not being equal to the amount actually expended for said purpose, the Committee appointed to superintend the building of said Church have been obleiged to advance a large additional sum of money in order to fulfil their contracts. And your Petitioners would further represent to your Hon^s that the said Church is not in a situation to be used for Public worship, and the society not being able to contribute further toward the completion thereof, the said Church must remain unfinished and useless to said Society without the special interposition of your Hon^s

Your Petitioners therefore pray that your Hon^s to take their Case into your wise consideration and on finding the facts stated in this petition to grant a lottery thereby enableing them to raise the sum of four thousand dollars to pay the arrearages now due and to complete said Church, or such other sum as your Hon^s may think meet, or in some other way grant relief   And Your Petitioners as in duty bound shall ever pray--

Dated at East Windsor the 16th day of May AD 1810--

Joel Hoskins	Charles Jencks	Bethuel Phelps
Abner Norcott	John Abbe	Horace Barber
		Levi Palmer

[1810, May Session]
To the Hon^l The House of Representatives now in session

The Committee to whom was referred the Petition of Charles Jencks & others praying for a lottery to enable them to finish the Episcopal Church lately erected at Ware house point in the town of East-Windsor   Report   That during the last year the Petitioners & others by private subscription erected a large Church at the place above mentioned & expended thereon the sum of 3500 Doll^s-- that the whole amount of subscriptions for that purpose was 2672 Doll^s, that the building Committee are liable for the deficiency amounting to the sum of 828 Doll^s-- The subscriptions were liberal; & in the opinion of the Committee no more money can in that way be raised for the purpose afores^d-- The Committee are satisfied from the facts disclosed on the enquiry, that the Society at present possess no adequate means of completing the building which they have begun & which in it's present state is represented as wholly useless-- They deem it highly important, to the welfare of the settlement at Ware house point & it's vicinity, that the means of regular instruction in Religion should be provided--The Inhabitants of that village appear willing to exert themselves to the extent of their ability for the attainment of this object-- Although the Com^{ee} doubt the expediency of granting Lotteries for any purpose & particularly for purposes such as are contemplated in this Petition, yet as they find that this Assembly have in repeated instances granted lotteries

for these objects in cases no better entitled to legislative favor than the present, they recommend that the prayer of the Petition referred to them be granted

Hartford--May session 1810   Ch^y Whittelsey
Ch^s Denison   } Com^{ee}
David Belden

In the House of Rep^s, This Report is not accepted
           Test W. I. Williams Cl^k

[1810, Oct.]
To His Excellency the Governor and the Honourable Council. The Committee to whom was referred the memorial of the Trustees of the Episcopal Academy, Report,

That the Object of the Memorialists is to obtain an Act of the Legislature granting to the Academy authority to confer degrees in the Arts, in Divinity Law and Physick, and to invest it with the rights immunities & privileges of a College by the name of the Episcopal College of Connecticut. One reason assigned in this memorial, is that to confer literary honours on young men educated at the Academy, would gratify a laudable ambition, and add to the respectability of the institution. This Academy is permanently established at Cheshire about fourteen miles from Yale College. The Trustees state the funds at about fourteen thousand dollars, & to be rapidly increasing.

The Committee are impressed with the importance of cherishing literary institutions, of giving them such aid as is consistent with the finances of the State, and with sound and liberal policy, and thus of advancing the interests of Literature. In the first settlement of the State, when few seminaries of science existed in this Country, & none in Connecticut, it was wise to commence the establishment of a College, with such inconsiderable endowments as inconsiderable means could furnish. At this day when there are more than Twenty Colleges in the United States, and eight in New England, and several, of distinguished rank, it is obvious that to render a College respectable in the view of the publick, and that it may in any good degree meet the wishes of its friends, it is indispensible that it be extensively endowed. Buildings, libraries, apparatus in the various departments of science, and instructors of eminence must be procured. The advanced State of literature demands it. Where are the resources competent to these attainments?

The population of Connecticut is nearly stationary in consequence of rapid emigrations,--its situation forbids the expectation of great oppulence; and perhaps its best interests do not require it. Should the prayer of the Memorial be granted, and the College established, it would be reasonable & proper that it should be patronized by the State with liberal endowments. Its founders would, with just expectations, look to the Legislature for such endowments, and they could not be withholden.--

Is it then wise to erect another College within so small a distance of that already established? Is the Legislature prepared to afford it such munificence as policy & good faith would require? Can Colleges in the vicinity of each other in such a small State, flourish so as either to gratify their friends or promote the welfare of literature? And can any thing short of an establishment of the first rank &

character; equally honourable to the State & its founders, answer the liberal views of the Memorialists? It is believd that these questions must be answered in the negative. No State in the Union affords an example of Colleges thus situated. New York has two at the distance of about two hundred miles from each other. New Hampshire & Rhode Island has each one--Massachusetts has three about one hundred & fifty miles apart.--

The Committee also notice that the memorialists state that their great & primary object in the erection of this Academy was the instruction of youth in the doctrines of their Church. It is doubted whether the objects of a College should not be instruction in the Arts & sciences & literature generally, rather than the propagation of the principles of any particular denomination of Christians, and it is believed that the association of young men of different denominations in the same College, pursuing the same general objects would rather tend to promote that spirit of liberality so much desired by men of enlarged minds.

Did the present College exercise any illiberality towards those youths of the episcopal Church who are also members of that College, or if it was true that the children of parents of any religious denomination had not an equal opportunity to acquire knowledge, and receive academic honours, with those of any other denomination, doubtless a College or Colleges ought to be established whose government would be more just & more conformable to the wishes of all enlightened men. No complaints against Yale College, or against any sister College, so far as the Committee are informed, on the grounds above mentioned, exist. In this State of things the Committee believe that in the establishment of a College, it would be inexpedient to confine its superintendance instruction & government to any class of Christians.

With these impressions the Committee deem it not wise to grant the prayer of this Memorial.--All which is respectfully submitted
     Octr 1810   Roger Griswold
                          David Daggett

[1813, Oct. 28, New Haven]
To the honourable General Assembly, now sitting at New Haven, the memorial of Jonathan Ingersoll Elias Shipman, John Morgan and Nathan Smith, trustees for receiving donations for the support of a bishop of the protestant episcopal church in the state of Connecticut, humbly showeth--

That by the charter of incorporation of said board of trustees, it is provided, that the president of such board with five trustees, shall constitute a quorum to transact all business relative to the business of their appointment. That by a bye law of said board, it is provided, that there shall be a meeting of said board of trustees at said Newhaven, on the wednesday next after the fourth tuesday in October every year, for the purpose of chusing officers of said board, to wit, a president, secretary and treasurer, and to fill up vacancies in said board, if any such there should be.----That by reason of the death of two of said trustees, who resided in said Newhaven since the last annual meeting, and by reason of the extreme inclemency of the day on which said board was to meet, to wit, on the wednesday next after the fourth Tuesday of the present

month of October, a quorum of said board could not be collected for the purpose of doing the business of the day, but that your memorialists met (the said Ingersoll being president of said board) and chose the president, secretary and treasurer for the year ensuing, and chose two persons trustees instead of the two trustees deceased as aforesaid.-- They therefore in behalf of said board of trustees humbly pray your honours to ratify and establish said election so made as aforesaid and to establish said meeting to be a legal meeting, or in some other way grant relief, as in your great wisdom shall seem meet, and they as in duty bound will ever pray-- Dated at Newhaven October 28th 1813

Jon.th Ingersoll   John Morgan
Elias Shipman   Nathan Smith

General Assembly October Session 1813

In the Upper House. The prayer of the foregoing Petition is granted with liberty of a bill in form &c.

Attest. Thomas Day Sec.y

In the House of Rep.s   Concurred.

Attest Ch.s Dawson Clk

[1818, Apr. 15, Fairfield]

To the Honourable Gen.ll Assembly of the State of Connecticut to be Holden at Hartford in s.d State on the Second thursday of May Next, the Petition of Abram Bulkley Walter Sherwood Hull Sherwood Jessee Banks & David Jennings Wardens & Vestry of Trinity Church in the Town of Fairfield in Fairfield County & the Rest of the Subscribers hereunto, Members of Said Church Humbly Sheweth, that the Church in S.d Fairfield togeather With the Parsonage House, Barn and Out Houses Was Burnt by the British in the Revolutionary War at the time that the Town of Fairfield was Burnt in July in the year 1779 and that the Plate to a Considerable Amount belonging to S.d Church was at the Same time Carried Away by the Enemy, Now your Petitioners would further inform the Honb.ll Gen.ll Assembly that with the funds they heretofore held and the Small Grand List of less than Six Thousand Dollars they have been about Twenty Seven years Engag.d in the Building of Another Small House for Public Worship, but have been Unable to Complete the Same; and in doing it they have been Oblig.d to Dispose of all their funds and Sell the principal part of their Glebe Lands, which was heretofore Appropriated for the Support of their Clergiman, which altogeather has proved a loss and Burthen to Said Church, in Consequence of Which the Members with all their Zeal and Exertions find it Verry Difficult and Almost Impossible for them to finish Said Church and at the Same time to pay their Clergiman for the One third part of his Services he being paid for the Remaining Two thirds of his Services by the Parrish of Bridgeport-- Now your Petitioners would further inform the Honb.ll Gen.ll Assembly that Notwithstanding all Individuals and many Ecclesiastical Societies that suffered Losses by the fire of so Barbarous an Enemy in the Revolutionary War, have Since by the Bounty of the Honb.ll Gen.ll Assembly in Some Measure been Remunerated, and knowing that all Societies and Individuals who Suffered Losses by the fire of the Enemy are Equally Entitled to the Bounty of the Honb.ll Legislature whare None have Appeal.d in Vain, your Petitioners never intended nor would they Ask for any

Indemnity for their Loss Could they possibly Surmount it by their Own Exertions--

Whareupon your Petitioners Appeal to the Honb.ll Gen.ll Assembly as thier Only Resource from Which they Can Expect Any Relief for their great Loss and Burthens and pray your Honours to take their Case into your Wise Consideration and grant them a Lottery to Raise the Sum of ten Thousand Dollars as a Remuneration for thier Loss or in some other way grant Relief and as in Duty Bound will Ever pray.   Dated at Fairfield this 15th day of April 1818--

Abram Bulkley	Jeremiah Sturgis
Walter Sherwood	W.m Robinson
Hull Sherwood	Benjamin Sherwood
Jesse Banks	Abel Beers
David Jennings	

[1818, May 7, Fairfield]

At a Meeting of the Inhabitants of the first Society [Congregational] in Fairfield Legally Warned & held at the Town House in s.d Fairfield on thursday the 14 day of Nov.r AD. 1782 Voted that Coll. Elijah Abel be instructed to Petition to the General Assembly at thier Next Session for a Grant of the Sum of One thousand pounds or more out of the Confiscated Estates of the Town of Fairfield to Build a Meeting House

at A Meeting of the Inhabitants of the first Society [Congregational] in Fairfield had by an Adjournment at the Town House in s.d Fairfield on thursday the 27th day of Feb.y AD. 1783 Voted that Jonathan Sturges Esq. & Coll. Elijah Abel be a Committee to find Out and Ascertain so much of the Confiscated Estates in the County of Fairfield that are Unsold as will be sufficient to Raise the Sum of Six Hundred Eighty pounds Seventeen Shillings Lawfull Money and to Request the Assemblys Committee to sell the same and to Raise s.d sum of s.d Committee & pay the same to the Committee of this Society to be Applied toward Building a Meeting House for this Society

at A Meeting of the Inhabitants of the first Society [Congregational] in Fairfield Legally Warned & held at the Town House in s.d Fairfield on Monday the 10th day of November AD. 1783 Voted that the Society instruct the Committee that is appointed by the Judge of Probates for Fairfield District to make Sale of the Confiscated Estate of Joseph Lyon & Peter Guyre in this Town, be sold upon Credit with good security, on[e] quarter part of s.d monies arising from s.d Sale be paid April Next. Another quarter part be paid November Next following the afore s.d April all to be paid in four Successive payments,

at a Meeting of the Inhabitants of the first Society [Congregational] in Fairfield Legally Warned & held at the Town House in s.d Fairfield on thursday the 17th day of June AD 1784 Voted that the Society appoint a Committee to Confer with Norwalk & Greenfarms Committee on the subject, the Late Resolve of the General Assembly Relative to the Grant made to Accomodate this & Greensfarms Societies to Build Meeting Houses & to Call Out the Assembli's Committee to Apprise such Confiscated Estates as they shall find & if on such Apprisal they shall think best to get Deeds from the Treasurer of this State agreeable to s.d Resolve--

at a Meeting of the Inhabitants of the first Society

[Congregational] in Fairfield Legally Warned & held at the Town House in s^d Fairfield on the 16th day of Septr AD. 1784   Whereas the Committee of this Society appointed to Call Out the Committee Appointed by the Gen^ll Assembly to Apprise the Confiscated Lands granted to this Society Greensfarms & Norwalk for Building Meeting Houses & to procure Deeds of the Treasurer of this State, have Reported to this Meeting that they have procured Deeds of the s^d Treasurer to this Society so much of the Confiscated Lands As to satisfy s^d Grant which Deeds are now laid before this Meeting, that Norwalk & Greensfarms have similar Deeds & that they have agreed With the Committees of s^d Norwalk & Greensfarms to Share in loss & Gain with s^d Norwalk & Greensfarms in the sale of those Lands provided thare is a Uniformity pursued in Mode & Terms of Sale this Meeting Accepts the Report of said Committee and Direct[s] the Treasurer of this Society to Recive ye Deeds & Cause the same to be Recorded in their proper offices Voted & agreed that Mr Davis Allen be and is hereby appointed a Commitee to make sale of all the Confiscated Lands Granted to this Society-- Voted & agreed that the afore s^d Committee be Directed to make sale of the afore s^d Lands in the Manner following / viz / one third part to be pay^d April Next   One third part November following the Other third part to be pay^d Ap^ll Next following Said November Except whare s^d Committee Can Make Sale of s^d Lands up to the Apprisement by giving a shorter time of payment for s^d Lands

at a Meeting of the Inhabitants of the first Society [Congregational] in Fairfield Legally War^d & held at the Meeting House in s^d Society on the 31st day of March AD 1786-- Voted and agreed that Jonathan Sturges Assist^t and Mr David Allen be appointed a Committee to prefer a Petition to the Hon General Assembly at their Next Session at Hartford to make up the Loss this Society have sustain^d and are likely to sustain by the sale of the Confiscated Lands Granted to this Society for Building their New Meeting House--

I Certify the above & foregoing Votes are True Extracts from the Records of the first Society [Congregational] in Fairfield
                        David Burr Clerk of said Society
Fairfield May 7. 1818

[1818, May 9, Fairfield]

We Benjamin Sturges & Nathaniel Perry of the Town & County of Fairfield being duly sworn do testify & say that in the Month of July 1779, the Episcopal Church in said Town of Fairfield was burnt by the British Troops under Tryon, that said church was completely furnished, & painted inside & out & in good repair; and had therein an excellent bell & was at the time it was burnt, with said bell, according to our best Judgement of the Value of twelve Hundred pounds, lawful Money; and we further testify that said British Troops, also burnt at said time a large & elegant Parsonage, House barn & out houses, which we now estimate to have been worth four Hundred pounds lawful Money, and that said British Troops robbed said Church of a very large & elegant set of Plate which had been previously presented to it for the use thereof, which we, though not very conversant with the value of such articles, estimate to have been worth one Hundred & fifty pounds, lawful Money. And further the deponents say not.
                Benj^m Sturges   Nathaniel Perry

[1818, May 11, Bridgeport]
Fairfield County Ss Bridgeport
On this 11th day of May AD 1818 before me Joseph Backus Justice of the Peace for said County came Ozias Burr of Fairfield in said County and Elijah Burritt of Stratford in the County aforesaid who being duly sworn &c depose & say that in the year 1779 Trinity Church in said Fairfield was burnt by the British Troops under General Tryon and that said Church before being so burnt was completely finished & painted inside and out & in good repair furnished with an excellent Bell the whole being in their opinion and according to their best judgement at the time when the same was burnt of the value of four thousand Dollars

The Deponents further say that at the time when said Church was so burnt the parsonage house barn & outhouses belonging to the members of the Congregation belonging to said Church were all well finished in good repair & the house indeed elegant were also burnt by said British Troops And that there was also in said parsonage house belonging to said Congregation a valuable library burnt with said house and that the value of said house barn & out houses was at least three thousand dollars and said library of the value of two hundred Dollars And that at the same time the said British Troops robbed said Church of a very large & Elegant sett of silver plate belonging to it and in the same And that these Deponents though then both belonging to said Congregation do neither of them now belong to it

                                        Ozias Burr
Sworn as above and before me   Elijah Burritt
   Joseph Backus Justice of the Peace

[1818, May Session]
The Committee appointed by the Honourable General Assembly now in session, to consider the Petition of Abram Bulkley and others of Fairfield, praying that a lottery be granted to raise a Sum for the relief of Trinity Church in said Fairfield--make the following report: That they have examined the merits of said Petition, and find the following facts, as proved by the attestation of respectable witnesses.

That said Church, the Parsonage-House and library, and the barn & outhouses, all belonging to said religious Society, were burnt by the British troops during the revolutionary war, in July 1779, at the time of the conflagration of Fairfield; and that a very valuable set of Church-plate was carried away by the enemy--the whole loss being by some estimated at six thousand, and by others, at nearly eight thousand dollars.

That, under the pressure of great pecuniary difficulties, said Society has laboured for twenty seven years, in order to complete the building of a small house of public worship--the interior of said house being yet in an unfinished state.----They have failed to accomplish this object, after having expended their funds, and the principal part of their glebe-lands for that purpose.

That the taxable property of the members of said Society is less than six thousand dollars upon the grand list, and that said Society are unable to pay a clergyman for the performance of his ministerial duties among them, except for one third part of the time--he being employed at Bridgeport for the remainder.

That the honourable General Assembly have to a considerable extent, re-imbursed individuals and many Ecclesiastical Societies for their losses arising from conflagration by the enemy at that period. The honourable Assembly (as appears on record in the office of the Secretary of State) granted in January 1783 to the first ecclesiastical society in Norwalk, the sum of one thousand, six hundred, sixty six dollars, and sixty six cents--and also to the first ecclesiastical society of Fairfield in conjunction with that of Green's Farms, the sum of three thousand, three hundred, and thirty three dollars and thirty three cents, from the fund produced by confiscated estates, as a compensation for the conflagration by the enemy of their respective houses of public worship.

Your Committee are impressed with the belief that all religious societies and individuals who suffered in the manner aforesaid, have an equally just claim to the bounty of the honourable Assembly, who have not (as far as it is known) rejected any appeals of this nature when well substantiated.

Further, your Committee unanimously concur in the opinion that the sum of Six thousand dollars (being the lowest estimation of loss sustained by said Society) may be equitably granted to the Petitioners, through the medium of a Lottery; more especially as the lowest sum of estimated damages would (if it had been re-imbursed to said society at the time when relief was granted to other ecclesiastical societies & to individuals) have amounted at present to more than thirteen thousand dollars, upon a computation of simple interest only for the whole term.----Indeed, a very partial compensation for the loss sustained by said society, would, if it had been obtained at an early period, have precluded the necessity of the present application. But it appears that said Society have deferred applying for relief, until they at last found that no other resource remained to extricate them from their embarassments.

Wherefore, upon a consideration of all the circumstances of this case, your Committee recommend that there be granted to the Petitioners, for the benefit of the Society of Trinity Church in Fairfield, a Lottery, the net proceeds of which shall amount to the sum of Six thousand dollars.

Respectfully submitted   Signed pr Order
                                Elijah Boardman Chairman
May Session 1818--

[1818, May Session]

Upon the Memorial of the Wardens & Vestry of Trinity Church in the Episcopal Society in the town of Fairfield, by their Agents, Abraham Buckley, Walter Sherwood &c.--showing that in the late Revolutionary war, their Church, Parsonage-house &c. were destroyed by the enemy--and that said Episcopal Society is poor and unable to complete their Church, and to support their minister, without the aid of the Legislature; and praying for a Lottery, as per petition on file:

Resolved by this Assembly that the Petitioners have liberty; and liberty & authority are hereby granted them to raise a Lottery (consisting of one or two classes as the managers hereafter appointed shall prefer, but no more) the net sum of Six thousand dollars, after deducting all necessary expenses for conducting said lottery--the said net proceeds to be applied to the purposes abovementioned:

And be it further resolved that Jeremiah Sturges, Elijah Boardman, Simun H. Miner Ralph T. Ingersol Gideon Tomlinson Nathan Smith & John S. Connor be and they are hereby appointed managers of said lottery, with power to make such scheme of said class or classes as they may deem expedient; and they or such of them as shall accept the trust of being managers as aforesaid, before they enter on the business of their appointment, shall become bound to the Treasurer of the State in the penal sum of Twelve Thousand dollars, with one or more sufficient sureties, conditioned for the faithful performance of their trust, and that they will well & truly pay the prizes to the fortunate adventurers in said lottery, and that they will faithfully account with said Society for the net avails of said lottery--and the Court of Common Pleas for the County of Fairfield are hereby authorised & fully empowered to fill any vacancies that may happen among said managers by death or otherwise; and said managers so appointed shall, before they enter on the business of their said appointment, give sufficient bonds in the manner herein before directed.

And be it further resolved that said managers shall not enter upon the business of their appointment, nor issue any scheme of said lottery, nor offer nor cause to be offered for sale any tickets therein, until nine months from & after the rising of this Assembly.

Genl Assembly May Session 1818
    Passed in House of Representatives
                        Attest J A Foot Clk
Concurred in the Upper House
                        Attest. Thomas Day Secy

[1818, Oct. 6, Norwalk]

To the Honorable General Assembly now in session at New Haven in and for the State of Connecticut

The Petition of Henry Belden and others, Members of the Protestant Episcopal Society of Norwalk in the County of Fairfield humbly sheweth that previous to the Year One Thousand Seven hundred and Seventy Nine, said Society had at Great expence erected a large and valuable house of Public Worship that in July of that Year said house was burned and entirely consumed by the Public Enemy of the United States and that said Society thereby sustained a loss of about Eight Thousand Dollars And your Petitioners would State that the House of Public worship belonging to the Presbyterian Society in said Town of Norwalk having been at the same time and in the same manner destroyed the Honorable General Assembly at their Session holden at Hartford in May One thousand seven Hundred and Eighty-four in consideration of said Loss and as a partial indemnity for the same Granted to said Society the Sum of Five Hundred Pounds Lawfull Money of this State and that simular relief was also granted to Several of the Neighboring Societies in this County who had been in like manner unfortunate Now your Petitioners would State that they have hitherto received no assistance nor has any grant in their favor as yet been made And although by great and uncommon individual exertions a House of Public Worship has been erected yet the same is too small for the Accommodation of said parish and now wants great repairs and an addition thereto, And as the Society has no funds

from which appropriations for the necessary repairs of said House and Said additions thereto can be made Your petitioners therefore pray the Interference of the Honorable Assembly in their behalf Trusting that in consideration of their loss as aforesaid the same aid and assistance will be extended to them which has heretofore been afforded to a Sister Society in the Same Town and to all individuals in this State who suffered in the Same way in consequence of like Misfortunes. Your Petitioners therefore pray the Assembly to take their case into consideration and upon finding the facts stated to be true to Grant for the relief of said Society the Sum of Five Hundred Pounds Lawfull Money for the purpose of Necessary and convenient repairs of their said House of Worship and of Making an addition to the same or in some other way grant relief and your Petitioners as in duty bound shall ever pray   Dated at Norwalk the 6th day of October 1818

> Henry Belden
> Reuben Sherwood
> Benjn Isaacs
> William J. Street
> Enok Kellogg
> Stephen B. St John
>
> agents for the Episcopal Society in Norwalk

House of RepS Octr 1818-- MessS Alsop, Joel Foot, James Stevens are appointed a Committee to whom this petition is refered with leave to report by Bill or otherwise--
                     Edwards Clk
Genl Assembly   Granted in House of Rep the Sum of Five hundred Dollars, with liberty of Bill in form &c
                 Attest   J A Foot   Clk
Concurred in the Upper House--
                 Attest.   Thomas Day, Secy

[1818, Oct. Session]
To the honourable house of Representatives of the State of Connecticut now in session,

     The Committee appointed by said house on the petition of Henry Belden and others, Agents for the Episcopal Society in Norwalk, praying for a grant of Five hundred pounds lawful money, respectfully report,

     That having examined the testimony adduced in behalf of the Petition they find, that the Episcopal Church in Norwalk was burnt by the British troops in the year 1779.-- Said Church was at that time a good building and had belonging thereto a good bell, Church plate, and a quantity of paint, together with a barn then standing on the Church land--which were also destroyed at that time.

     The whole estimated loss was (as appears by different depositions of respectable persons) from Eight to Ten thousand dollars. Said Episcopal Church, it also appears, was at least of equal if not greater value than the Congregational Church in Norwalk which was burnt at the same period, and to whose Society the sum of Five hundred pounds lawful money was long since granted by the General Assembly of Connecticut. Other Congregational Societies, whose churches were destroyed in like manner at the above time, have, also, long since received compensation therefor from our honourable Legislature.-- Indeed, the principle that compensation shall be granted in Such cases, is not only an act of natural justice and of general policy, but it has also been clearly recognised and established by frequent deci-

sions of the legislature of this State; as, so far as we can learn, not a single application of this nature, supported by respectable evidence, has been rejected. It appears further that an addition to the building of the present Episcopal Church in Norwalk and many repairs thereto are necessary which, unless some legislative aid be given, cannot now be effected, as the said Episcopal Society is embarassed by debt and a deficiency of funds.

     Under these circumstances and from the testimony adduced in this case, your Committee are of opinion, that the sum of Five hundred pounds prayed for by the Petitioners is an amount to which they are equitably entitled from the State--but as a grant of the whole sum may not be conveniently made at this time, your Committee, therefore, recommend that, for the present, Five hundred Dollars be granted to the Petitioners; leaving the residue of the sum prayed for, to be allowed them whenever the state of the treasury will permit, and the honourable General Assembly shall deem it most expedient & proper.
           Signed per order   John Alsop   Chairman
October session 1818

Accepted & Approved in House of RepS
              Attest   J A Foot   Clk

[1818, Oct. Session]
     Whereas Henry Belden & others, as agents in behalf of the Episcopal Society at Norwalk, have petitioned this Assembly to grant said Society the sum of Five hundred Pounds, lawful money, in consideration of the loss sustained by said Society in the conflagration of their Church and in the destruction of other articles also belonging to said Society at the time of the invasion by the British forces in the year 1779:

     Resolved, that the Treasurer of this State be and he is hereby directed to pay the sum of Five hundred Dollars to whomsoever the aforesaid Episcopal Society in Norwalk shall duly authorise to receive the same.

October Session 1818   Passed in House of Repr
              Attest   J A Foot   Clk
Concurred in the Upper House--
              Attest.   Thomas Day, Secy

[1819, Apr. 26, New London]
To the Honourable General Assembly of the State of Connecticut to be holden at Hartford within & for said State on the First Wednesday of May 1819--

     The Petition of the Wardens, Vestry and Parishioners of St James' Church in the Town of New London, by Jared Starr & Isaac Thompson their Committee duly appointed for that purpose,--respectfully sheweth,--that during the War of the Revolution, the House of Public Worship then belonging to said Parish was destroyed, in the conflagration of New London by the public Enemy.-- That said Church was at that time in good repair & of the value of more than $3,000 (Three Thousand Dollars) The Parish being without funds, and poor remained for a long time destitute of any House of Public Worship, but by great exertions of the Parishioners in the year 1787 another Church was erected for the accomodation of the Parish

at an expence of about $ Five Thousand Dollars-- This
Building is too small & is also now out of repair & the Parish is destitute of funds and unable to enlarge or repair it
& the Petitioners are advised that in all Cases of destruction or loss of Houses of Public Worship belonging to the
different denominations of Christians in this State remuneration has in some way been made by the Honourable
Assembly & very recently a Grant has been made to the
Episcopal Church at Norwalk which was also destroyed by
the Enemy during the Revolutionary War----Your Petitioners have never received any compensation for the loss of
their Church which was great & sorely felt, but they confidently hope & trust, that neither the late hour at which they
solicit relief, nor the circumstance, that by the blessing
of the Great Head of the Church upon their exertions they
were enabled once more to provide a House of Public Worship will be considered as impairing their claims.--

   Your Petitioners now ask the Honourable Assembly to
take their Case into consideration & on finding the facts to
be truly and correctly Stated to grant to your Petitioners a
meet compensation for the loss of their Church afores.^d or
at least such sum as shall be adequate to the enlargement
& repair of their present Church, that they may enjoy with
their Christian Brethren an equal share of the public liber-
ality--or that the honourable Assembly would grant such
other relief in the Premises as to their wisdom shall seem
just and equitable & your Petitioners as in duty bound will
ever pray--   Dated at New London   April 26th 1819

                    Jared Starr   ⎫
                    Isaac Thompson ⎬ Committee

We the Subscribers, (members of the 1st Ecclesiastical
Society in New London) having been called on by the Committee of the Episcopal Church in said Town, do certify
& make known to all whom it doth or may concern that the
House of Public Worship belonging to said Episcopal Church
was burned in the conflagration of New London in Sep.^t 1781,
by the public Enemy & was in our opinion of the value of
about $2,000--(Two Thousand Dollars) according to our
present & best recollection & belief

                              Guy Richards
                              John Way
                              Amasa Learned

New London County Ss. New London April 29th 1819--
   Personally appeared the above named Guy Richards,
Amasa Learned & John Way Esq.^{ers} Signers of the foregoing Certificate & made solemn oath to the truth of the
facts therein stated
            Before me-- Eben Learned Justice of peace

House of Representatives May Session 1819.
   Passed with Liberty of bill in form & special grant of
five hundred Dollars
                    Attest. A Sterling Clerk
In Senate
   Granted on this Petiton the sum of One hundred Dollars
with liberty of a bill.
                    Attest Wm W. Boardman Clerk
In House of Rep.^r
   M.^{esr} Law & Goddard appointed a Com.^t of conference
                    A Sterling Clerk

In Senate
   The Honble Mr Boardman appointed Committee to join
            Attest. Wm W. Boardman Clerk

Whereas Jared Starr and Isaac Thompson Committee in
behalf of the Wardens Vestry and Parishoners of St James
Church in the town of New London have petitioned to this
Assembly to grant such sum as may be just and reasonable
in Consideration, of the loss by them sustained, by the destruction of their Church, at the Conflagration of New London by the British on the 6th of September in the Year 1781.
Resolved that the Treasurer of the State be & he is hereby authorized & directed, to pay to said Committee for the
Use of said Wardens Vestry & Parishoners, the sum of
three hundred Dollars, or to whomsoever should be duly
authorized to receive the same-- Approved May 26th 1819
                              Oliv.^r Wolcott.

[1820, May 30]
   Resolved by this Assembly that the Trustees of the
Bishops Fund of the Episcopal Church in this State, have
liberty, and liberty and authority are hereby granted them
to raise by a Lottery consisting of one or more classes as
may be necessary, the net sum of fifteen thousand Dollars
after deducting all necessary expences for conducting said
Lottery, provided the same be raised within six years after the rising of this assembly, the said net proceeds to be
applied for the benefit aforesaid.--

   And be it further Resolved, that the County Court for
the County of New Haven are hereby authorized & fully empowered on request of said Trustees to appoint any number
of managers that may be necessary to conduct said Lottery
& at any time to fill any vacancy that may happen among
the managers aforesaid first appointed by death or otherwise:--and the managers so appointed shall have full power to make such scheme of said class or classes as they
may deem expedient:--and every person who shall accept
the trust of being a Manager of said Lottery, before he en-
ters upon the duties of his appointment shall become bound
to the Treasurer of this State with one or more surety or
sureties to the acceptance of said County Court in the penal sum of twenty five thousand Dollars conditioned for
the faithful performance of his Trust, and that he will well
& truly pay the prizes to the fortunate adventurers in said
Lottery and will faithfully account to said Trustees for the
net avails of said Lottery. And be it further Resolved that
no other Lottery shall be granted within five Years from &
after the rising of this Assembly.--

In H of R   passed
                         Attest   A Sterling Clk
In Senate May Session 1820   Concurred
                         Attest   Wm W. Boardman Clk
Approved May 30th 1820.
            Oliv.^r Wolcott.

Diocese of Connecticut # FORMATIVE PERIOD ## 1784-1791 Edited for THE COMMISSION ON PAROCHIAL ARCHICES BY JOSEPH HOOPER PRINTED FOR THE DIOCESE 1913	

PAPERS OF THE REV. SAMUEL PETERS — *A SELECTION*

INTRODUCTION.

The Commission on Parochial Archives has the honor to present to the Diocese and to all interested in the history of the Church in Connecticut its third publication.

The period to which these letters belong was in the Church as in the State, one of experiment, when the independence of the Church, as of the former Colonies, was being tested. Hardship and suffering were the lot of many.

The Clergy of Connecticut were ready to endure all things for the sake of the establishment of the Church upon the best and surest foundations. They had chosen, or rather designated a choice, of a fit person to be their Bishop. The manner in which they met the difficulties of the situation was admirable.

Letters in this series throw new light upon the meeting at Woodbury on the feast of the Annunciation, 1783, and show true loyalty to the ancient and catholic polity of the Christian Church, without regard to the expediency of the hour or following the suggestions in a notable pamphlet by a prominent clergyman to the southward, Dr. White, afterward Bishop of Pennsylvania.

Jeremiah Leaming, Bela Hubbard, Samuel Andrews, John Tyler, and Ebenezer Dibblee, were true confessors of the faith whom we still delight to honor.

William Samuel Johnson stands as a type of the well-instructed, devout layman, serving ably both the Church and the State.

The friend to whom these letters were sent has been greatly misunderstood and misjudged by many of his contemporaries, but his brethren of the clergy were near his heart and they repaid him with affection and respect.

The preservation of the papers of Dr. Samuel Peters through many vicissitudes until they found a permanent place among the archives of the General Convention has made possible a revision and correction of our history.

The editor has prepared the absolutely necessary notes covering the essential facts in the lives of the writers of the letters and a few of the persons mentioned in them. While fuller annotation was desirable it was impossible within the limit set for the appearance of this volume. The notes upon Dr. Bliss and Mr. Mann were courteously furnished by the secretary of the Commission, Mr. F. Clarence Bissell, Deputy Comptroller of the State of Connecticut. He is a recognized authority upon the genealogy of the Peters family and the history of the Town of Hebron.

The half-tone illustrations of Dr. Peters and Dr. Hubbard are taken from the best known likenesses of these worthies.

June 5, 1913.   J. H.

JOHN BREYNTON.

The town of Halifax was laid out in 1748 under the auspices of the Honorable Edward Cornwallis, Captain General and Governor of Nova Scotia. It is situated on the western side of a deep inlet of the sea known as Halifax Harbor. It was named in honor of George Montague, Earl of Halifax, the President of the Board of Trade.

An ample plot opposite the Grand Parade was reserved for a church, and a parish by the name of St. Paul's Church was organized. The frame of a church building was ordered from New England, and it was estimated that it would cost one thousand pounds to set it up. It was said by Governor Cornwallis to have been a copy of Marylebone Chapel, London. Those who know both buildings have declared that it was identical with St. Peter's Church, Vere Street, London. The Rev. William Tutty was sent by the Venerable Propagation Society early in 1750 to be its minister. On September 2 of that year he formally opened the building although it was not finished.

In 1752 the Venerable Society sent the Rev. John Breynton to be his assistant. Mr. Breynton had been a chaplain in the British Navy and was at the siege and capture of the fortress of Louisburg in the summer of 1745. He at once gained a high place in the affection of the people of Halifax. He was earnest, active, sympathetic, and efficient. Mr. Tutty soon after went to England on private business leaving his curate in charge. He never returned and died in 1754. Mr. Breynton was then made Rector of St. Paul's. Few men seem to have left a deeper impression on a community than he did.

He was pastor to all sorts and conditions of men. He went into the forests to show the squalid Micmac Indians the power and beauty of Christian faith and life; he made himself familiar with the German language that he might minister to the poor Germans settled at Lauenburg. He was the friend and adviser of the Loyalists when they came from the former American Colonies to find life in the British Province less ideal than the glowing fancy of British under-secretaries had pictured it, and to be sufferers in purse and person from the unfulfilled promises of the government for which they had left their native land and made many sacrifices.

His friend, Jonathan Belcher, the first Chief Justice of Nova Scotia, calls him "a man of indefatigable labors, experienced assiduity, moderation and perfect good acceptance."

Dr. George W. Hill, the fourth Rector and historian of St. Paul's, says: "He was the personal friend and counsellor of the successive Governor and Lieutenant Governor, the associate and adviser of all others in authority, the friend and helper of the poor, the sick, and afflicted, and the promoter and supervisor of education. He doubtless deserved the high encomium passed upon him during his absence by a brother missionary, the Rev. William Bennett, that he never knew a man so universally regretted by every individual of every denomination."

After his hard and successful work of thirty-three years Dr. Breynton went to England upon a leave of absence in the fall of 1785, leaving the parish in charge of his curate, the Rev. Joshua Wingate Weeks, formerly missionary at St. Michael's Church, Marblehead, Massachusetts.

He fully expected to return but for some unknown reason did not, to the great disappointment of the whole parish.

EXTRACT.   [To Samuel Peters, London, England.]

I have your favor of 5 & 17 feb. & M^r. Weeks informs me I am to expect a thundering Episcopate by D^r. Byles. I found Col. Fanning has a Letter from you of a much later Date by which we are informed of your Successful efforts for the worthy Houseal. That measure will be attended with more salutary Consequences than are to be expected from the *heaven born preacher & military Confessor*—D^r. Seabury or Bishop Seabury stay'd ten Days with us, was treated with great civility by all that I & Col. Hannory could influence. He preached here in my Church & performed very well.

John Breynton.

Halifax Nova Scotia
3 May 1785.

JOSHUA WINGATE WEEKS.

Joshua Wingate, a son of Colonel John and Martha Weeks, was born at Hampton, New Hampshire. He was well prepared for College and graduated from Harvard in 1758. He studied for the holy ministry, and went to England late in 1762. He was made deacon and ordained priest in the spring of 1763, and on April 17 of that year licensed by the Bishop of London to officiate in the Plantations.

He was appointed by the Venerable Propagation Society as Missionary of St. Michael's Church, Marblehead, Massachusetts. He served faithfully and acceptably until the approach of the Revolution. The old seaport was intensely patriotic, with the exception of a few wealthy merchants,

and the fishermen and sailors who made up the greater part of its population tolerated no one who adhered to King and Church. In 1775 he took refuge with his brother-in-law, the Rev. Jacob Bailey of Pownalborough in the District of Maine. He returned with his family in June, 1776. It is understood that he did not open the Church but ministered in private houses and to the sick and afflicted. In the summer of 1778 he was again compelled to flee from the violence of the patriots to Rhode Island, leaving his family in the parsonage. Mrs. Weeks and her eight children were provided with passage to Nova Scotia in the fall of that year. They were courteously received at Halifax and through the generous kindness of Dr. Breynton provision made for their support. Mr. Weeks went from Newport to New York City in September and soon after sailed for England. He was given by the Venerable Society the mission of Annapolis Royal with a salary of one hundred and forty pounds, vacant by the death of the Rev. Thomas Wood in December, 1778. While in England he accused his former friend and neighbor, the Rev. Edward Bass of Newburyport, afterwards the first Bishop of Massachusetts, of disloyalty. As a consequence, after a blameless ministry of twenty-six years, he was deprived of his stipend and dismissed from the Society's service upon the verge of old age. The most impartial testimony shows that he was a friend to the British government although in some particulars Dr. Bass yielded to the request of his parishioners in the conduct of the service; many of them being strong patriots. Mr. Weeks arrived at Halifax July 16, 1779, and found his succession at Annapolis resisted by a strong party having the support of many provincial officials who desired the appointment of the Rev. Nathaniel Fisher who had for two years been Mr. Wood's assistant. A friend, Colonel Rogers, made him Chaplain of his battalion, known as the Orange Rangers. While the controversy over the charge of Annapolis was in progress Mr. Weeks, after paying one or two visits to the town, remained in Halifax, assisting in St. Paul's Church and serving in turn with Dr. Mather Byles as Chaplain to the garrison. In 1781, displeased at his neglect, the Venerable Society dismissed him from their service and offered Annapolis to Dr. Byles or, if he rejected it, to Mr. Bailey. As Dr. Byles refused, Mr. Bailey took up his residence in August, 1782. An unpleasant controversy then took place with his brother-in-law over the Chaplaincy to the garrison which Mr. Weeks contended was his by right. It appears that for some time Mr. Weeks received the salary and Mr. Bailey performed the duties.

In 1784 Mr. Weeks went to England, submitted an apology to the Society and was once more admitted to their favour on condition that he would resign any claim to the Chaplaincy at Annapolis Royal. Mr. Weeks was in charge of St. Paul's Church, Halifax, after the departure of Dr. Breynton for England in September, 1785, until the arrival of Dr. Stanser in 1791.

In 1793 he took charge of the mission of Preston where he remained until 1795 when he was transferred to Guysborough where he died in 1804. Mr. Weeks married in 1763 Mary Treadwell of Ipswich, Massachusetts. They had eight children. One of his sons, Charles William Weeks, became a clergyman and served in 1799 Weymouth, Guysborough, in succession to his father; Manchester from 1834 to 1836, and was visiting missionary from 1837 to 1842. A grandson, Joshua Wingate, a son of the Rev. Charles William Weeks, was ordained priest in 1829 and served Cornwallis and New Dublin. A daughter married October 5, 1789, the Rev. William Twining, the missionary at Rawdon. She was the mother of the Rev. John Thomas Twining, the friend of that Christian soldier, Captain Hedley Vicars.

MATHER BYLES.

Mather, a son of the Rev. Dr. Mather Byles of Boston, Massachusetts, was born in that town January 12, 1735. His father was one of the best known Congregational ministers of his day and noted for his pungent wit and an intense dislike to prelacy and the Church of England. He was well prepared under his father's direction for College and graduated from Harvard in 1751. He studied theology and in November, 1757, became the successor of Dr. Eliphalet Adams in the First Church of Christ, New London, Connecticut. It had been formed in 1650 and had for its first minister Richard Blinman. Mr. Byles was a man of great intellect, a vigorous thinker and a clear and convincing speaker. The people were charmed with him and admired his sermons which were profound, attractive and eloquent. Tradition says that he was "grand and lordly in his ways," but the people were proud of him and fascinated by his brilliant and powerful personality.

There was both incredulity and indignation when he announced in April, 1768, that he had become a convert "to the ritual of the Church of England." There was much denunciation of him by his congregational brethren, and scurrilous songs and lampoons written about him.

He sailed for England in May, 1768, was made deacon and ordained priest by Dr. Richard Terrick, Bishop of London. He was licensed to officiate in the Plantations June 29, 1768. He soon after received from the University of Oxford the degree of Doctor in Divinity. Upon his return he became the Rector of Christ Church, Boston, in succession to the Rev. James Greaton. He was much admired and did an excellent work. In 1775 he was appointed by the Venerable Society to St. John's Church, Portsmouth, but never assumed that position owing to the disturbances of the Revolution. He sailed with his family from Boston for Halifax with the British fleet in the summer of 1776. He became Chaplain to the garrison at Halifax and also assisted Dr. Breynton in St. Paul's Church. Here he gained new friends and a high reputation for his learning and adaptability to new conditions of life. In 1778 he was among a large number of Loyalists proscribed and banished by the State of Massachusetts.

The parish of St. John, New Brunswick, where a church had been erected about 1783, of which the Rev. George Bissett in that year became Rector, was vacant by the sudden death of its first incumbent, March 3, 1788. A new church had been commenced to bear the name of Trinity Church, the cornerstone of which was laid by Bishop Inglis August 20, 1788. Dr. Byles accepted the rectorship in the spring of 1789 and took charge on May 4 of that year.

He remained loving and beloved until his death, March 12, 1814, in the eightieth year of his age.

BERNARD MICHAEL HOWSEAL.

Mr. Howseal had been for many years senior pastor of the Lutheran Church in New York City. In 1776 he was among the signers of an address of welcome to Lord Howe.

He went to Halifax with the British fleet in 1783 and took charge of the German Congregation at Lunenburgh near Halifax. In 1786 he went to England, was made deacon and ordained priest. He was then made Rector of the German Congregation and served with rare devotion and patience until his death, March 9, 1799.

He is described as a worthy man who suffered severely by the Revolution. He was humble, devout and did great good.

EDMUND FANNING.

Edmund, a son of Captain James and Hannah (Smith) Fanning, was born at Riverhead, Long Island, in 1737. His grandfather, Thomas Fanning, had been a prominent resident of Groton, Connecticut.

He graduated from Yale College in 1757, as a Berkeley scholar. He studied law and in 1760 settled at Hillsborough, then Childsburgh, North Carolina. In 1763 he was Register of Deeds and Colonel of the Militia of Orange County. He was highly esteemed and entered largely into the political and social life of the Province. He was appointed by Governor William Tryon in March, 1766, Judge of the Superior Court for the District of Salisbury. He was also elected in that year to the Assembly and sat in that body for five successive terms where he was useful and active. A body known as the Regulators attacked in 1768 his house, claiming that he exacted illegal fees as Register. Consequently he was defeated at the next election as representative of the County. Governor Tryon, however, allowed Hillsborough representation and Colonel Fanning was returned from that town. In September, 1770, the Regulators took Judge Fanning from the bench and after beating him destroyed his house and household possessions.

Upon the removal in June, 1774, of Governor Tryon to New York, Colonel Fanning accompanied him as private secretary. In 1774 the Governor made him Surveyor General of the Province of New York which he held in connection with that of Surrogate of New York City to which he was appointed in 1771.

In 1776 and 1777 he raised a regiment made up of Loyalists, which was named the Associated Refugees or King's American Regiment of Foot. Dr. Samuel Seabury was the Chaplain. It is said by many writers that members of the Regiment were rude, cruel and grasping. He remained in the British service until near the close of the Revolution when he went to Halifax.

He was made Colonel in the British Army in December, 1782, and in September, 1783, was appointed counsellor and Lieutenant Governor of the Province of Nova Scotia. In 1787 he was made Lieutenant Governor of the Island of St. John's, now Prince Edward Island, in the Gulf of St. Lawrence. He was here charged with tyranny. The complaint was brought before the Privy Council and dismissed in August, 1792. In October, 1793, he was promoted to be Major General and in June, 1799, advanced to the rank of Lieutenant General. In May, 1806, he resigned as Governor. In April, 1808, he was made General. His closing years were spent in London. He died February 28, 1818, in his eighty-first year. A widow and three daughters survived him. His only son, who was a captain in the Twenty-Second Foot, died in 1812, leaving his father grief-stricken.

While he is bitterly denounced by writers on North Carolina history and the Revolution, others who knew him at a later period give him a

most exalted character. He was honored in 1774 with the degree of Doctor of Civil Law by the University of Oxford and with that of Doctor of Law by Yale and Dartmouth in 1803. In writing to his classmate, the Rev. Eden Burroughs, asking for the honors, he claimed to have saved Yale College when General Tryon in the summer of 1779 made his famous raid along Long Island Sound, burning and pillaging several towns.

JOHN PETERS.

John, a son of Colonel John and Lydia (Phelps) Peters, was born at Hebron, Connecticut, June 30, 1740. He was a nephew of Dr. Peters. He graduated from Yale College in 1759. He settled at Hebron where he opened a law office. In 1766 he removed to the new town of Bradford, now in Orange County, Vermont. This was supposed to be in the Province of New York. He held a very high position in the community and was much respected by all the people. Governor Tryon made him, in 1770, clerk of the new County of Gloucester and Associate Justice of the Court of Common Pleas. In 1772 he was made Colonel of Militia and in October, 1774, Lieutenant Governor Colden made him Chief Judge of the Court of Common Pleas. He suffered much insult from the Green Mountain boys because he was loyal to his King and in 1776 he fled to Canada leaving his family and home. In 1777 he was made Lieutenant Colonel of the Queen's Loyal Rangers. He took part in the battle of Bennington in October, 1777, after which he escaped to Canada making a perilous journey through the woods. He returned for his family and established them comfortably on Cape Breton Island and then went to London to prosecute before the Claims Commissioners his claim for losses and back pay as Lieutenant Colonel. He spent three years without accomplishing his purpose. He died of gout in the head and stomach, January 11, 1788, in the forty-eighth year of his age. He left a wife, six sons and one daughter.

JOSEPH PETERS.

Joseph, a son of William and Hannah (Cheney) Peters, was born at Dedham, Massachusetts, in that part of the town now Walpole, December 11, 1729. He settled in Mendon and removed to Watertown, Massachusetts. As he was a staunch loyalist he went after the Revolution to Halifax, Nova Scotia. Here he received much consideration and served for many years as postmaster-general of Halifax and afterward Judge of the Supreme Court. He died February 13, 1800, in the seventy-first year of his age. He married Abigail Thompson. Their children were: Abigail, who died in Medfield, Massachusetts, December 30, 1829, at the age of seventy-nine years. She was unmarried. Moses, born at Waterford, Massachusetts, April 26, 1752, died at Mendon, Massachusetts, December 29, 1810. He married Eleanor Penniman.

EXTRACT.

I received your highly esteemed favor of the 19th February, by his Grace the Right Reverend &c Bishop Seabury—whom I have heard Preach, but I fail'd in obtaining what I thought a reasonable Share of his Company, he being perpetually dragged about while he was here—his Preaching is highly esteemed here, and I my self am much pleased with his person as a man, a Gentleman and Divine—God send him success—but I am afraid he will not meet the treatment he hath a right to expect from the blue *Connecticutites.* I wish I may be found in a mistake.

Our Printers are the most dastardly Sycophants I ever saw— I did not chuse to be seen in the affair for some reasons, but I Wrote the matter out and sent it first to one and then (upon) his omitting it) to the other, one being a New England Saint and a disciple of the Holy Sandiman, and the other a Ger-
who professes to be a Saint of Luther;
man, neither of which had Courage to show to the World so innocent a piece of Intelligence—His Grace is gone by Water, to Annapolis and New Brunswick.

                                        Joseph Peters

SAMUEL ANDREWS.

Samuel, a son of Samuel and Abigail (Tyler) Andrews, was born in Wallingford, Connecticut, April 27, 1737. His father's farm occupied a tract of land "about a mile west of the present railroad station in Meriden" near the famous Hanging Hills.

Through the influence of a son, Laban, who had been apprenticed to

Captain Macock Ward, the family had conformed to the Church of England. Captain Ward was a prominent man in the town, a staunch supporter of Union Church, as it was then called, built near the North Haven line so as to accommodate the Churchmen of North Haven, Cheshire and Wallingford.

The family early determined that the youngest son, Samuel, should become a clergyman. He was given as good an education as was then possible in the common schools and graduated from Yale College in 1759. He acted while in College and for two years after as lay reader. He went to England in April, 1761, and was made deacon August 23 and priest August 24 of that year by Dr. Thomas Hayter, Bishop of London, and in October licensed by that Bishop to officiate in the Plantations.

After his arrival home in March, 1762, he took charge of St. Paul's Church, Wallingford, with Cheshire and North Haven. He was already known and respected and under his care the Church in each of the three towns grew.

Mr. Andrews was a Loyalist but when the proclamation was made of a Fast Day in July, 1775, he opened the church and preached a sermon from the text: "I hate, I despise your feast days, and I will not dwell in your solemn assemblies." Amos 5:21. In the course of the sermon he urged his hearers to consider the power and resources of England and beware how they aroused the ministry and people of the motherland. The granting of liberty and equality, he said, is absurd when so many are held in slavery in various parts of the colonies.

The sermon aroused much resentment, although there is in it no violent denunciation but a calm and plain setting forth of political principles which he thought right and just. Only his positive goodness and high Christian character and the regard in which he was held saved him from violence. As it was, he was placed under heavy bonds and confined within limits. No services were held in the Church until 1778, when the Bishop of London allowed churches to be opened and the prayers for the King and Royal Family omitted.

When the Revolution ended, Mr. Andrews with others who had remained true to their convictions found the greater part of their congregation not only in poverty but also enthusiastic adherents of the new Republic. The offers of parishes with ample salaries and glebes in the British possessions were attractive. Mr. Andrews although he loved his home and birthplace thought the needs of his family required him to accept one of them. He removed in the spring of 1788 to the town of St. Andrews on the St. Croix River. From his house he could look across to the shores of Maine. In 1791 he purchased the island of Chamcook in the St. Croix River, where he built for himself a pleasant home. It is now known as Minster's Island and has been greatly improved by Sir William VanHorn, who has a summer home on it.

The parish of St. Andrew's, Charlotte County, New Brunswick, was organized August 2, 1786. A church was built in 1788, fifty-two feet in length and forty in width. After recovery from a severe paralytic stroke which unfitted him for duty for some months he was the busy and venerated pastor of a devoted flock until his death September 26, 1818, in the eighty-second year of his age.

Mr. Andrews married September 13, 1764, Hannah, a daughter of James and Anna (Wheeler) Shelton of that part of Stratford now Huntington. She died in her seventy-sixth year, January 1, 1816. His eldest son, Samuel James, was a graduate of Yale College in 1785, a shipping merchant in Derby, Connecticut, and subsequently a pioneer in the present city of Rochester, where he attained large wealth and great prominence. A staunch churchman he was a founder of St. Luke's Church and carried the sound Connecticut churchmanship into western New York.

Mr. Andrews published several sermons which in style and matter are superior to many of those printed by his contemporaries.

                                        Wallingford May 17th. 1785.
My dear Sir,

I have received your very friendly and obliging Letter of the 27th. of last March by Mr. Killbey—I am very glad to hear of your Health, and that you are settling at Cape Breton, as it is near to Milford Haven on Chiclabucto, where the Company I represented last Summer are going to reside— Should they meet with Disappointments with Regard to that Place, your Patronage would probably lead them to Cape Breton, could they obtain a Settlement there.

With regard to myself, I think it probable that I must soon seek other Quarters, as well thro' a want of Support, as a Wish to enjoy Brittish Government—should this Event take place, Nothing could be more agreeable to me than what you Suggest in a frollic indeed, concerning a Clergyman in your

Settlement, as it would restore me to the Company, and place me under the Protection of an old Friend and Classmate— Should you desire it, you will doubtless be able soon to procure the Clerical Appointment you mention, and you will Essentially Oblige me, if you will Correspond with me upon the Subject, and inform me what Encouragements are to be Expected by a Clergyman both from England and the Settlement itself—is the Country where you Settle all together in its Natural State, or is any part of it Cultivated? will it produce any Grane or Grass? in a Word it is a Land which will eat up its inhabitants, or must they eat *that* for want of other aliment? Excuse these Freedoms, and

believe me to be dear and Respected Sir
your antient and Sincere
Friend and very Humble
Servant.
Sam¹. Andrews.

Col¹. John Peters.

WILLIAM SAMUEL JOHNSON.

William Samuel, the eldest son of the Rev. Samuel and Charity (Floyd) Johnson, was born at Stratford, Connecticut, October 7, 1727. His father was the well-known Rector of Christ Church, Stratford, justly called "the father of Episcopacy in Connecticut," missionary, theologian, educator. He trained the boy very carefully both morally and mentally and at the age of thirteen sent him to Yale College, where he attained a high rank and graduated in 1744 as a Dean Berkeley scholar. Upon leaving College his father directed his further studies. He served for some years as lay reader in St. Paul's Church, Ripton, now Huntington. Determining that his vocation was not the ministry Mr. Johnson turned his attention to the law. He soon became one of the most skilful lawyers in the colony and his reputation went beyond its borders. He served in the General Assembly in 1761 and 1765 and was a member of the Stamp Act Congress which met in New York in 1765. He was made in 1766 a member of the Upper House, known also as the Governor's Council. In October, 1766, he was chosen by the General Assembly as the special agent of the colony at the British Court in the famous Mohegan Case, which involved the legality of its title to the land held by the remaining members of the Mohegan tribe of Indians. The matter had been in controversy for seventy years and involved some very abstruse and knotty legal problems. Dr. Johnson, during his agency, wrote many letters to the Governor of Connecticut, which are models of good English and lucid statements of the difficulties encountered by him as well as vivid pictures of the political state of England. The final hearing was on June 11, 1771, and the decision was given in favor of the colony. Dr. Johnson returned home in the fall of that year and resumed his seat in the Council. In 1772 he was appointed a Judge of the Supreme Court of the Colony but served only a few months. He was appointed a delegate to the Congress of 1774 but declined on account of professional engagements.

He lived in retirement at Stratford during the Revolution and was unmolested, although opposed to a war with England. At the return of peace he resumed the practice of law. He was a member of the Continental Congress from 1784 to 1787. He was placed at the head of the delegation to the Constitutional Convention which met in Philadelphia in October, 1787. In that brilliant assemblage of statesmen and men of affairs, Dr. Johnson was considered as the ablest lawyer and was always accorded a respectful hearing. In several disputed matters his voice was potent. It is largely to his exposition of the Connecticut system that the plan of equal representation of the states in the Senate is due.

The reorganization of King's College, New York City, of which his father was the honored first President, took final shape under the name of Columbia College in the spring of 1787 and Dr. Johnson was in May of that year elected as President. Under his wise administration a university plan was adopted and carried out as far as circumstances would allow. Dr. Johnson was again a member of the Connecticut Assembly from 1787 to 1789 when he was elected the first Senator from Connecticut to the Congress of the United States, his colleague being Oliver Ellsworth, afterwards Chief Justice of the United States.

He resigned the presidency of Columbia College in July, 1800, as his health was seriously impaired. He then went to Stratford where he received with cordial and gracious hospitality in his spacious mansion his friends and all who sought him out. He was consulted by many and his advice was both sensible and sound.

He died November 14, 1819, in his ninety-third year.

Dr. Johnson married November 5, 1749, Anne, a daughter of William Beach of Stratford. She died at New York, April 24, 1796, in her sixty-

seventh year. He married December 11, 1800, Mrs. Mary Beach of Kent, Connecticut. She died in April, 1827.

New York Septr. 22^d. 1788

Rev^d. & D^r. S^r.

At length your Son, after many delays is embark'd with Capt. Woolsey & is to sail tomorrow. I most heartily commending him to the divine Protection, wish him a safe & agreeable Passage, & that you & he may soon have a happy meeting together. The Captn. did not wish me to pay for his Passage, as I should readily have done, but will receive it of you at his arrival in London. He goes off cheerfully, but while he has resided with me here at the College he seems to have contracted some affection for the place, & to wish that it may be agreeable to you that he may return again ere long & receive part of his Education, at least, in this Country. He has asked me very many questions upon the subject, I have constantly referred him to you, assuring him that he may rely upon it that you will certainly do what is best for him. But when he repeatedly pressed me for my Opinion, I could not avoid telling him, as I really think, that if he is to spend his Days here, that it is best he sho'd be chiefly Educated here, & this he earnestly desires me to mention to you, which I accordingly do merely in compliance with his wishes, knowing very well at the same time, that you need none of my suggestions upon the subject.

Eleven States, having adopted the proposed Constitution, our Congress have now published their Ordinance directing the necessary steps towards the Organization of the new Government, & that it commence its Operations in this City on the first Wednesday of March next—Very many are extremely sanguine in their Expectations that we shall derive great Blessings from it, while many, on the other hand, are aiming at, & expecting soon to obtain great alterations & emendations of the plan— Both sides will as usual, probably be in some measure, disappointed, & how it will finally operate is known only to the allwise disposer of all Events.

As M^rs. Kneeland is not now with me, I cannot at present pursue the directions you have favour'd me with, to write to the Abp on her affair. It must therefore be deferr'd to another Opportunity, but indeed, so inattentive are they grown to the calls of Justice, that it seems to little purpose to make any application to them. I am with the sincerest wishes for your welfare

Rev^d. & Dear S^r.
Your most obedient
humble Servant
W^m. Saml. Johnson.

Rev^d. M^r. Peters.
Rev^d. M^r. Samuel Peters
Pimlico
Westminster.

Johnson D^r. W^m. S—
Sept^t. 22—1788
rec^d. Nov—16—
Ans^d. Nov 17—

New York May 5th 1791.

Rev^d. & Dear S^r.,

The Trustees of Columbia College are delicate with respect to granting the higher Degrees, & conceive that many Colleges both in Europe & America, have injured their own Reputation, and done disservice to Literature, by the facility with which they have conferr'd them. They declined granting the Degree of M.D. to D^r. Stearns,

1^ly. Because I could give no Information with respect to the Medical Doct^r who signed the Certificate transmitted to me, & you not being of that Profession, your signature alone, they considered, would not be a ground upon which they could

determine that he had Medical Knowledge sufficient to entitle him to that Degree.

2ˡʸ. Two of the Gentlemen had seen a Publication (which I had not heard of, nor have yet seen) by the Dʳ. of a Tour to France, of which they had conceived a very indifferent Opinion.

3ˡʸ. One of the Corporation, himself a Phyſian of Character, declared that he had known Dʳ. Stearns where he resided during the late War on Long Island, & that neither his Knowledge in that Science, nor his conduct at that time, did in his Judgment by any means qualify him for that Degree. It is highly probable that these Objections might have been obviated, but I had no Information or means, not being aware of them, by which I could do it effectually.

The Georgian & Jacobite Bishops will I trust amicably coalesce, & occasion no Discussion or Controversey in this Country.

I am happy to hear of your Son's health, & that he is to pursue his Studies at Oxford or Cambridge. I pray God he may become an accomplished Scholar, & a good Man, & am with affectionate Compliments to him.

Revᵈ. & Dʳ. Sʳ.
    Your most obedient
        & most humble Servant
Revᵈ. Dʳ. Peters.   Wᵐ. Samˡ. Johnson.

The Revᵈ. Dʳ. Samuel Peters,
        Grosvenor Place
            London—

Johnson Dʳ.
May 5ᵗʰ 1791
reᵈ. June 28—

WILLIAM ABERNETHY DRUMMOND.

William Abernethy was born in 1719 or 1720 at Saltoun, Haddingtonshire, Scotland, where the family had long been established. He studied medicine at the University of Edinburgh and after practicing for some years took a theological course, was ordained, and took charge of a Chapel of the Episcopal Church of Scotland in Edinburgh. He was consecrated Bishop of Brechin at Petershead on September 26, 1787. He was soon after elected Bishop of Edinburgh. His Episcopate was remarkable for its energy and the part he took after the death of Charles Edward Stuart in causing the removal of the disabilities of the Episcopal Church of Scotland. He resigned his see of Edinburgh in 1805 in favor of Dr. David Sanford.

He died at his seat, Hawthornden, August 27, 1809, in the ninetieth year of his age.

Upon his marriage with Mary Barbara, the widow of Robert MacGregor, and heiress of William Drummond of Hawthornden, he took the name of Drummond.

Revᵈ. Sir

Your obliging letter of the 5ᵗʰ came safe to hand, & I take this opportunity of returning my hearty thanks for your kind communication anent our friend Bishop Seabury. The consecration of Madison & the other two Bishops refusing to unite with him in the promotion of Mʳ. Bass, behoved to make him uneasy; but I trust in God, that these gentlemen will soon open their eyes, & see it to be their Duty to promote the peace of their Jerusalem, by a happy agreement with their worthy Brother. Indeed, I think the Archbᵖ. of Cny's answer cannot fail to have that effect: or if not, they must be blind beyond the possibility of seeing, & much will they have to answer for at the Great Day of Accounts—The Chancellor, thro the good Bishop of St. David's means, has at last agreed that a bill be brought into Parliament for the relief of the Scotch Episcopal Clergy, & I expect to hear immediately after the Easter recess, that the Lord Advocate has apply'd for leave to bring One in accordingly. I give you joy of Mʳ. Jarvis's success, and heartily wish you & all your friends health & happiness commending you & them to the Grace & protection of God's Holy Spirit, I am

with the blessing of the approaching high Festival:

R. Sir
    your affect. Brother
        Wᵐ. Abernethy Drummond.

Ednʳ. 20ᵗʰ April 1791.

The Revᵈ.
    Samuel Peters Grosvenor Place
        near   London.

April 20ᵗʰ 1791
recᵈ. 23ᵈ
Thurs.

JOHN TYLER.

John, a son of John and Mary (Doolittle) Tyler, was born in Wallingford, August 15, 1742. The family had been prominent in the town, as Roger Tyler, its ancestor, had been one of the original proprietors in 1638.

As a young man Mr. Tyler conformed to the Church of England. He graduated from Yale College in 1765, having the high honour of delivering the valedictory oration. He pursued a post-graduate course at King's College, New York City, now Columbia University. This procedure was then almost unknown. Its president was the witty and brilliant Myles Cooper. The young scholar then studied theology under the Rev. Dr. Johnson at Stratford and became lay-reader in Christ Church. Some of the congregation were in favor of making him assistant to the Rector, the majority, however, thought him unfitted for such a prominent position. He was recommended by Dr. Johnson to the churchmen in his native town, Guilford, as a suitable successor to Bela Hubbard, the minister who had been reader in Christ Church for some years previous to his ordination in 1764. Mr. Tyler was acceptable and permission was sought for him "to go home for orders." He sailed May 10, 1768, bearing with him a petition for the erection of Guilford into a mission by the Venerable Society. He was made deacon June 24, and ordained priest June 29, 1768, by Dr. Richard Terrick, Bishop of London. The request of Guilford was refused, as the Society had determined to erect no new missions in New England.

Mr. Tyler was appointed to Norwich, from which John Beardsley had removed to Poughkeepsie, New York. Mr. Tyler commenced his work at Norwich, November 1, 1768. Without the brilliance of some of his contemporaries, there was a sweet earnestness and inflexible purpose in all he said or did. He had a most musical voice and in his intercourse with his parishioners and others was mild and benevolent. His knowledge of medicine was freely given to the poor and gained him many warm friends. During the Revolution although threatened by the Committee of Safety and others he was practically unharmed. Traditionally his well was poisoned or attempted to be. The Church was closed from 1776 to 1778 but the Rector of Norwich continued his pastoral work and held some informal services in houses of parishioners.

He fell into disfavor with some of his brethren because of the report that when John Murray, the advocate of universal salvation, visited Norwich in 1778 he declared his acquiescence in his views. Such startling reports of his views and their advocacy by him in sermon and conversation reached the clergy in other parts of the Diocese, that he was in August, 1786, formally cited by Bishop Seabury to appear before the Convocation of the Clergy "at the house of the Reverend Mr. Richard Mansfield, on the twentieth day of September next, to see whether mutual explanations may not remove that offense which your proceedings at Wallingford and Norwich have, we conceive justly given to them and myself." He could not attend at Derby but was summoned to meet the Bishop with Dr. Abraham Jarvis and Dr. Bela Hubbard at New London in October. He appears to have satisfied them that he had not transgressed the authorized liberty of opinion on a matter upon which there was no formal declaration.

His friendly relations with the Bishop and other clergy continued. The sudden death of the first great Bishop of Connecticut on February 26, 1796, brought to Mr. Tyler the sad duty of officiating at his funeral on Sunday, February 28, and burial in the public cemetery at New London.

Mr. Tyler continued his quiet, effective work until past his three-score and ten years. His young friend and assistant, the Rev. Seth Birdseye Paddock, the father of two Bishops, in his declining years took all care and anxiety from the old Rector. Mr. Tyler died January 20, 1823, in the eighty-first year of his age and the fifty-fourth year of his ministry. He was the last survivor of the Connecticut clergy ordained in England.

Mr. Tyler married May 6, 1770, Hannah, a daughter of Isaac and Elizabeth (Bushnell) Tracy of Norwich. She died at Norwich, January 19, 1826, in the seventy-fifth year of her age. A grandson, the Rev. Dr. Alfred Lee Brewer, established on the Pacific coast the well-known St. Matthew's School, first located at San Mateo, California, near San Francisco, now at Burlingame.

Mr. Tyler published several sermons, notably that at the opening of Trinity Church, Pomfret, in 1770, and one adapted from Bishop Secker on Peace. Six sermons on The Law and the Gospel, attributed to him by undoubted evidence, were published in 1798 and 1815, anonymously. They advocated universal salvation.

Norwich in Connecticut Jan.ʸ 9: 1784.

Rev.ᵈ Sir,

I received your kind Letter of August 4, 1783, by M.ʳ Chandler Wattles; who expected to return to Europe in about six Weeks, and was to call on me for a Letter: but contrary to Expectation, he called I think, the very next Week, in Haste, and went unluckily I had no Letter written—I should have wrote long before, had I known where to direct: but now perhaps I may write again.

I have taken the whole Care that has been taken of Hebron Church ever since you left it: though I must confess that I durst not go there for some Time after you went away; so bitter was the Spirit of some People: but since, I have been three or four Sundays there every year.—Your Estate is not confiscated, as by your Letter I see you had supposed: and your Friends in Hebron since the News of Peace expected your Return; and are not a little disappointed.—Strange Alterations have indeed taken Place since you left this Country We are in general become a poor People—the Episcopalians are most impoverished: but all groan under the Burden of heavy Taxes.—And I need not tell you that the Missionaries have suffer'd much most every Way, in Name, Person, and Estate. I have been obliged to sell Bills as low as twenty per cent under par, when I actually purchased Wheat at three Spanish Dollars per Bushel: and even now, the Necessaries of Life are on an Average, one quarter dearer than they were when you left the Country; though Money perhaps was never scarcer than at present—New York was very full of money when the News of Peace came: but the Narrowness of our Policy drove from thence about thirty Thousand Refugees, and with them most of the Money; and the Remainder is gone to Europe for Goods. By this you may have some Idea of the Present State of the Country.

As to the Episcopal Church in America, it has Reason to expect an Establishment; nor can it be Prudence for her to subject herself to a Presbyterian Head: this, I am determined to oppose with all my Might, if any Proposal of this Nature should appear. No: the episcopal Church in America, like primitive Christianity, must be a Kingdom of its own—a religious Polity distinct from the civil. And if she can enjoy equal Toleration or Liberty with other religious Denominations in general, must think herself upon the best Footing she can expect. T'would be absurd to the last Degree, for the episcopal Church to look up to the sons of Jack Presbyter in the civil Chair, as to Nursing Fathers. There is good Reason to hope that the episcopal Church here will be tolerated, considering her Numbers on this Continent; and that civil Policy has so engrossed the Attention of America in general, for eight or nine Years past, that Religion has very little thought of; and the dissenting Clergy, by preaching little else but Politics, have lost their religious Influence past Recovery: and the leading People are now, I believe, much more bigotted to Money, than to any religious Denomination. But what fickle Mortals are a People, when once their Polity is unsettled!—First in Pretence, horribly afraid of Popery—then full of Candour towards it—at last rather indifferent to all Profession.—You can hardly imagine how the People here are altered.

It is the prevailing Opinion here, that the Missionaries now in their Missions, will have their Salaries continued to them during their Lives; though we doubt much of having the vacant Missions continued. But if the Salaries of the present Missionaries should be discontinued, after sacrificing every temporal Interest to their Fidelity, and being unfortunate in the Issue, their Fate would be hard indeed. All the episcopal Clergymen in Connecticut, have been uniform and persevering in their Fidelity, and have thereby kept a good Conscience, if no more; but the Consideration of having one's Virtues immortalized in historic Page, while he lives in Want of the very Necessaries of Life, and must die in Poverty, is but a poor Consolation. I much Question whether Hannibal, who after the Destruction of Carthage, was hunted from Nation to Nation, struggling with the Hardships of Poverty and Contempt, was much comforted by the Prospect of having his military Skill recorded in History. I know it is not uncommon for the World to neglect and despise the Unfortunate while alive, howsoever virtuous they are; and then to speak mighty well of them when they are dead and gone, and can receive no Benefit from it. So the Jews killed the Prophets, and their Sons built their Sepulchres, and decorated them with many ornaments.

The false Papers, you say, we signed *versus* you, I believe you must be under a Mistake concerning them, if my Memory serves me. I never saw them but once, and that was about five months after they were signed. Either you must have been imposed on by a Forgery, or have drawn very remote Consequences. After you left the Country our Clergy were continually threatened, and endured many Violences; and at a Session of the Assembly of Connecticut at New Haven, several of the Members told Parson Hubbard, that the general Opinion was, that our Clergy were in a Combination or Conspiracy with Mr. Peters, to rob the Country of their Liberties; which Combination Hubbard denied. Those Members then advised Hubbard to call in some of the neighboring Clergy, to sign a Denial of any such Conspiracy; and then the Members of the Assembly would use their Influence to pacify the People to desist from Violences towards the Clergy. Accordingly Hubbard called in several of the Clergy; who, in the Presence of many Members of the Assembly, at Hubbard's House, signed Papers the whole Substance of which was, that we, the episcopal Clergy of Connecticut, are in no Conspiracy with the Rev.ᵈ M.ʳ: Peters against the Liberties of the Country. This was, to the best of my Remembrances, all that those Papers said concerning you, and as near as I can remember, in those very Words. I was not present; nor did I hear so much as a Word of it for near Six Months.—I saw your Letter to Doctor Inglis respecting this Matter, and from that strongly suspected that a very fallacious or forged Account of this Matter has been made use of against you. But if those Papers really did contain any thing more than I have said, it is my Mistake.

As to the Petition that Doctor Seabury may be made our Bishop; at the News of Peace, the Clergy suddenly met together, without notifying either Fogg or me, and did as you have heard; and no Doubt as they thought for the best; and I believe, without the least Idea of the Clergy of New York, or any other Place, having any party or personal Views to the Prejudice of the Connecticut Clergy; for you know, those who mean no evil, are apt to suspect none.

As to our Convention signing Petitions by our Secretary, I have several times objected against it, because we are not a Body corporate in Law: but it has been answered that this is common to voluntary Associations; and that thus we have often done, when we have wrote to the Society, without any Appearance of their Disapprobation, and that the Society understand us: and I have replied, that there may be Occasion for showing our Petitions to Persons not acquainted with our Custon of Subscribing, who may ask, how came these Clergymen

to be a Corporation and the Explanation cannot be much to our Advantage, vis. that as Children ape the Adult, so we ape Bodies corporate.—I was not present when the Clergy petitioned for Jarvis, &c. to be made Missionaries.—I am not willing to petition our sovereign States to permit the Residence of Bishops here; because I think we have the same Right to Bishops as to Presbyters; and to ask Permission to enjoy our religious Liberties or Privileges, before we are forbid, looks too much like an Acknowledgment of our Subjection as a Church, to the Control of those civil Rulers who profess a different Religion: and if we seem to acknowledge, that presbyterian civil Rulers have a Right to say, whether the episcopalians shall have Bishops or not; can it be supposed that those Rulers will think that we need Bishops? But if we procure Bishops, the civil Rulers here, cannot refuse their Residence, without a manifest Violation of religious Liberty; which would injure their Reputation in the Eyes of all Europe; and would divest them of all Pretence of patronizing religious Liberty, which is a Character they much affect, since the Alliance with France. So that the best way for the Episcopalians to preserve their religious Privileges, is, I think, to use them freely, without appearing to fear any Control.—But after all, I am of Opinion, that we shall not obtain a Bishop in Connecticut at present; but that there will be a Bishop sent out to Nova-scotia first.

You seem determined not to see this Country again.—I know you was ever fond of a City Life: but possibly when you come to know the State of your Affairs here, which you will learn by the Letters from your Friends at Hebron, you may alter your Mind; at least so far as to make us a Visit—I should be sorry to see you no more.—You have some Inducements to come again, if not to tarry.—You have an Estate at Hebron worth looking after; and a Son at Stratford, who I believe is in good Health.—and whom you must wish to see, and his grand Parents will not be willing to part with for Life.—I should suppose you were by this Time weary of the Hurry and Noise of a City; though in a good Degree compensated by many Things that are agreeable. To this Country, I know you have now two capital Objections, which I need not name.—I will be much obliged to you for a Letter as soon as may be after you receive this. But first I wish you to obtain the Perusal of my Letter to the Secretary of the Society, which is of the same Date with this to you; and which contains Something that very nearly concerns me; and if you can be of any Service to me in the Matter, and will befriend me, you will not doubt my receiving it very kindly of you. And then I wish you to write me, by the first Opportunity, what Reception my Letter meets with, or is likely to meet with. To give you any tolerable Idea of the Matter in this Letter, would render it by far too long. What you will think of the Matter, I cannot conjecture; but I think you cannot doubt my Sincerity.

Our old Friend Mr. Griste is gone to Rest—old Mrs. Lancaster also—Messrs. Holden, Lancaster, Bushnells, Cook, Leffingwell &c. much as usual, except what it common to us all here become poorer, and low spirited.—Many of my Parishioners have moved away, within the four last years, several are dead, and several new ones have conformed.—Mrs. Tyler joins me in respectful Compliments to you and your Daughter.—

I remain your Friend and Brother,

John Tyler.

The Revd. Samuel Peters,)
)
Pimlico, London.   )   Recd. May 14th, 1784.

Norwich in Connecticut December 2, 1784

Revd. Sir:

I take this Opportunity of writing to you, by Cpt. Gurdon Bill, a Non-con. who is about to sail from Norwich Landing for London. I have heard of several Letters from you since last Winter, but have seen none. I heard that in one to Doctor Sutton, of the 1st. of March last, you proposed to go to France, and should not correspond with America for some years. Again, I heard of Letters from you to Mr. Birdsey of Stratford: and this Fall past, I heard of Letters received in Hebron from you, in which you mentioned the Receipt of Letters from some one in Hartford, and from Doctor Bliss in Hebron, who were of Opinion that you could not return in Safety, perhaps they did not wish to encourage your Return. However, the vindictive Spirit of the Country is almost totally altered in the Space of one Year past: and though, if you had returned last Spring, some few Curs might have growled a little, and I am confident that would have been all yet now I can assure you, that the fierce Spirit of Whigism is dead: and it is the general Sense of the People of Connecticut, Rulers and all, that the old Spirit of Bitterness is now the worst of Policy. Not one word of Whig and Tory appears now in the News-papers; and even the fiery Darts at General Arnold, which lasted longest, are now totally out of Fashion. Those heretofore call'd Tories, and who were treated with the greatest Bitterness, are now in as good Reputation as any. Doctor Johnson is chosen a Member of Congress—Mr. Semour Mayor of the City of Hartford,—and Cpt. Nathaniel Backus, who was much harrassed in the War, for being a bold Friend of Great-Britain, is now the Second Alderman of our City of Norwich. And if you should incline to return, I am sure that not one Dog would move his Tongue against you. And you would be much more at Peace here, than you was even seven years before the War.—Our Friend Ebenezer Punderson, is returned to Pamutanoc with his Family, and our general Assembly have returned to him all his Estate; and he is well received,—and not a Mouth opened against him.

In my Letter to you of the 9th of Jany. last, which I conclude you must have received, I mentioned a Letter of mine to the Society of the same Date; but I did not send it forward 'till the 20th of last April; and suppose you have seen it. But I have not heard any Thing from the Society in Consequence of it: and I wish you to write me by Cpt. Bill, or sooner than his Return if you have an Opportunity, and inform me all you know of the Matter, that is, what Reception my Letter has met with. What you think of my Opinion, respecting the final Salvation of all Men, I know not: but if you can render me any Services, with Doctor Morrice, and will be kind enough to use what Influence you have, that I may not be cut off from merit the Society's Favor, you will my sincerest Thanks. After what I have said of my Opinion, in my Letter to Doctor Morrice, of the 20th. of April last, which I suppose you must have it seen, will be to no Purpose for me to attempt in this Letter, to explain to you the Reasons of my Opinion.

I have not heard how Doctor Seabury proceeds; but expect to hear soon.—The Motion of the Philadelphia-episcopal Clergy, with their *Lay-Delegates,* respecting the founding of our American-Episcopal Church, you have, or will no doubt hear by other Hands. But our Connecticut Clergy look totally askew at their lay-Delegates, and will never I believe, admit those Tobacco-cutters with them. The Pennsilvania, New-Jersey,

and New-York Clergy met lately at New-York; and the Connecticut Clergy sent a Letter, and a Representative, to put off Matters, 'till we have a Bishop; pleading that we cannot act in founding a Church, 'till we have a Bishop, and so are organized, as a Church.

Our old Friend Cpᵗ. Bushnell is dead—and our good Friend Mʳ. Brimmer died in Boston last Summer—My Family has been considerably visited with Sickness, at Times, for more than a Year: and I have lost my oldest Son by Death the Summer past, who was between eleven and twelve years of Age: which was a grievous Stroak to me, and the Recollection is yet very painful; and my Spirits are low.—I hear that Mʳ. Man's Son is return'd from you to Hebron; but have not seen him; and have heard very little of the Accounts he brings.

Mʳˢ. Tyler joins me in her Compliments and kind Regards to you and Daughter.

Sir, I remain you sincere Friend and Brother,

John Tyler.

The Revᵈ. Samuel Peters)
)
Pimlico, Charlotte Street)
)
Nᵒ 1, London.   )

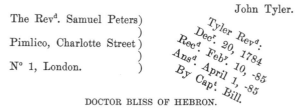

Tyler Revᵈ:
Decʳ. 20, 1784.
Recᵈ. Febʳ. 10, '85
Ansᵈ. April 1, '85
By Capᵗ. Bill.

DOCTOR BLISS OF HEBRON.

Dr. Neziah Bliss of Hebron was a son of Rev. John Bliss of Hebron (first settled pastor of the Congregational Church, afterwards conformed to Church of England, and was one of the founders of St. Peter's Church, Hebron), born March 21, 1737, graduated Yale 1760, one of the most eminent citizens of Hebron, served fourteen terms in the Legislature prior to the Revolution. "To him the American People owe more than suggestion of their common school system; he was its founder in the state of Connecticut where it was first adopted, and where he procured such Legislation in its aid as nursed it through its incipient stages and gave it vigor for the almost sublime descent it has accomplished." (Bliss genealogy.)

He died August 31, 1787.

JOHN AND NATHANIEL MANN.

Rev. Samuel Peters wrote from London, October 24, 1786, to "John and Nathaniel Mann of Hebron." "I have appointed you John Mann and your son Nathaniel jointly and severally to be my attorney and attorneys, not believing that the state of Connecticut is now graced with two other men of equal virtue and honor."

John Mann married Margaret Peters, a sister of Rev. Samuel Peters. Dr. Nathaniel, his son, nephew of Rev. S. Peters, graduated at Dartmouth, completed his education in England as physician and surgeon. Was in business as druggist and physician in Hebron for a time, finally going to Georgia, where he died.

Dr. Nathaniel Mann writes to Col. John Peters at Quebec, September 21, 1783, "Your father and Dr. Sutton and my brother Andrew are become Deists and most of the Church are Universalists, alias Murrianites."

BELA HUBBARD.

Bela, a son of Lieutenant Daniel and Dianna (Ward) Hubbard, was born in Guilford, Connecticut, August 27, 1739. His father died when he was only twelve years old. His mother married for her second husband, Captain Nathaniel Johnson of Guilford, a younger brother of the Rev. Dr. Samuel Johnson of Stratford.

The boy was well brought up and thoroughly taught in the subjects which would fit him for College and graduated from Yale in 1758.

He was under the direction of Dr. Johnson during his course in theology in New York City, as the Doctor was then President of King's College. After a year he returned to his home in Guilford and became lay reader in Christ Church. He sailed for England in November, 1763, in company with his dear friend, Abraham Jarvis, and William Walter of Boston. They were most courteously received, but the petition of Guilford to be made a mission and placed under the care of Mr. Hubbard was refused by the Venerable Society. The story has long been current and rests upon well-authenticated tradition, that when with his fellow candidates he paid his respects, according to custom, to the Archbishop of Canterbury, and was introduced, his Grace in perplexity repeated his name:

"Bela, Bela, I never heard of that name." "Very likely not, your Grace," said the young man, "it is in the Bible."

Mr. Hubbard, with his companions, was made deacon in St. James's Church, Piccadilly, London, February 5, 1764, by Bishop Keppel of Exeter. They were ordained priests by Bishop Lyttleton of Carlisle, February 19, of the same year. He returned to take charge of Christ Church, Guilford, and St. John's, North Guilford, where for three years he labored incessantly and extended his ministrations to the neighboring town of Killingworth, now Madison.

It was with very real grief that the people of Guilford learned in the summer of 1767 that Mr. Hubbard had accepted an appointment from the Venerable Society to New Haven and West Haven. Under the new missionary, Trinity Church grew rapidly and Christ Church increased its strength. Mr. Hubbard was a man who combined great patience and capacity for work with a very high ideal of duty. Simple and guileless in his manners, without the gift of eloquence, his teaching was plain, direct and based upon the true conception of the Church of God. His goodness and sincerity attracted and attached every one to him.

His attitude during the Revolution was most admirable, for while he was firmly attached to the Crown he did not allow himself to be drawn into controversy.

Trinity Church was closed until 1778 but the minister continued his round of visits and consolation to the sick and afflicted. He was one of those who determined that the Church in Connecticut should have an Episcopal head before any change in the English Book of Common Prayer should be made or any united effort made for an independent branch of Christ's Holy Church. As New Haven grew the Church grew and Dr. Hubbard won more and more the good will of all sorts and conditions of men. Under his supervision the negotiations for a new Church building on the Green were conducted.

In 1811 his failing health made an assistant minister necessary and the saintly Henry Whitlock of Norwalk was chosen in June of that year.

Dr. Hubbard survived in great weakness of body until he departed this life, December 6, 1812, in the seventy-fourth year of his age and the forty-eighth of his ministry. His old friend and companion, Bishop Jarvis, lived only four months longer, for he died on May 3, 1813.

Dr. Hubbard married in Fairfield, Connecticut, May 15, 1768, Grace Dunbar Hill of Antigua, West Indies. She was a daughter of Thaddeus and Elizabeth (Isaacs) Hill. She died in Farmington, Connecticut, April 27, 1820, in the seventy-third year of her age.

One of their sons, Thomas, became prominent in the affairs of Syracuse, New York, as a man of public spirit and Judge. Another, Bela, was for many years active in business life in Detroit, Michigan, and a strong and liberal supporter of St. Paul's Church.

New Haven January 21ˢᵗ. 1784.

My very dear friend:

'tis a very long time since, I have been blessed with your very agreeable society & converse, and the late destracted times prevented me writing you—but you have not forgotten me, with pride & satisfaction I received your letter written soon after the peace, the Spirit of which did you honor & gave pleasure to me & your friends, you appear to have had a perfect knowledge of our political Situation, Law providence will determine in the final issue, our Eclesiastical; time will show, but certain it is that the Church in America is more respected than I expected.

The General Assembly now setting in this town seem disposed to give full scope to the toleration of all religious parties, and have in this Session passed some acts, that give equal countenance to each religious denomination, which will help the Church in particular, and was a bishop to come into this government, it is my real opinion, that every thing would be made easy to him on the part of government provided thʳ was no formal application made to them on that score.

Your Estate hath never been, nor will it be confiscated, although I believe the Assembly have availed themselves of the interest of it—your aged mother was alive as young Jones told me at Christmass & sent a letter to be forwarded to you via N York—your son I saw lately at Mʳ. Birdseys, he with Dʳ. Johnson & myself concluded on the whole that your son had better tarry for a season here, good care will be taken of him.

All old things are done away, but your brethren in their conduct in consequence of your going away hath been altogether misrepresented to you, I shall God willing soon convince you by original papers that your brethren have in no instance acted an unfriendly part with you.

A young gentleman I much esteem calls on me going to morrow from this port to London which determined me to write you—the gentleman is Mr Jeremiah Townsend he is in ye marcantile line connected with Mr Jeremiah Atwater a good man uniformily, he goes I suppose to form some connections in trade, is industrious, sensible, & of strict honor, any civilities shown to him by you I shall consider as an honor done me and shall not be forgotten by me—by him I send you Dr Styles Election Sermon—I leave you to make your own remarks upon it—I have another favor to ask & I conjure you by the love I bare you, that you grant it me, which is to give yourself the trouble to enquire out a proper person in London to furnish us a neat good well toned Organ with a decent case for about 100^d Guinea's, we have now a subscription filling up for the purpose and shall probably in the Spring forward the money—you know my Church is small, but if we succeed as I think we shall in filling up our subscription I shall write you more particularly about the matter.

I had written so far & your favor of October 20th 1783 was handed to me, I shall communicate the contents to my brethren, and am obliged to you for your good advice respecting the Interest of the poor Church in this part of the World—we hope not to fall under the leather mitten & be damed up in Utica but yet to stand on good ground & have a bishop among our-selves who are now y^r largest body of Episcopal Clergy in any one Gov^t. in America—what you say about the points N York, whose influence, had ruined y^r clergy of Connecticut. If M^r. Leaming, Jarvis, Andrews & Scovil & myself c^d. have prevailed at the convention & what follows is all a riddle to me wish you to explain it to me, by the return of the bearer of this, and I conjure you to tell me how you live, what are your hopes, this side Jordon, we shall no doubt find better   on the other side of it, pray how does your dear girl Miss Hannah who we are told is much accomplished, speaks and writes French well &c. &c. M^rs. Hubbard the mother of six children & who hath borne 8 desires not to be forgotten by you & your dear girl, she hath a woman's anxieties to know whether or no Miss Hannah is married & whether the Rev^d. Pimlico parson is a single or a married man—tell me in your next all these things & add many like words of things for our mutual curiosity—you mention M^rs. Cargil please to make our kind love to her & husband & if she wishes to know the present State of New Haven Mr Townsend the bearer can fully gratify her—you men-tion still a desire that M^r. Birdseye would send you your son I shall see him probably very soon and I will communicate to him what you say on the Subject, but as I observed before D^r. Johnson thinks it would be better for you with respect to your Estate in Hebron for him to reside here at least for the present, he is truly a very fine child, he looks much like a cherry cheek'd lad by the Name of S P— whom I knew in Y College some 20 years since, I have kissed Grace on your account & my own, & she most cordially saluteth you, as does the worthy Mr Leaming our good brother who happens to be here—the spirit of the people oppressed with the burden of taxes, grows daily more & more mild, hope in a year or two you will come among us & make your abode with us, we are undoubtedly, we allways were, & always shall be undoubtedly the best, the worthyest the

best natured loving & amiable Clergy in the World—it would now give your heart the utmost joy to be with us in one of our Conventions, you shall yet be blessed no doubt with our good Company, & Society, but if Heaven sho'^d. determine otherwise, hope we shall all meet in Heaven, whose King is Just, & among whose subjects, mercy, Justice, peace & love forever reign may we meet there never more to part is ye wish & prayer of my very dear brother, your's affectionately,

Bela Hubbard.

Assembled cordially in Convention at Wallingford at the house of the Rev^d. Peter Lizzard the Rector of Rectors the last week Rev^d. Messrs Leaming, Scovil, Jarvis, Clarke Hubbard—Scovil Andrews will probably go in the Spring to view the Nova Scotia world as agents for a company going thither—Scovil hath 8 children Andrews 5 I have six how they are to be provided for God knows, we are all confounded poor tho' rich in good works & in love to one another. Clarke remains at New Milford poor, Marshall still at Woodbury, but thinks of Milford—Old Milford which place is destitute of ministers of all denominations many of y^e *dissenting* parishes are vacant, & likely to continue so, their Ministers out preached themselves & have very much lost their influence with their people, Viets Roger, Dibblee, Tyler, Fogg, Nichols, Newton, Mansfield & Bostwick are all still above ground, Father Beach Dead—his parish vacant, as is Stratford, Fairfield, Norwalk, N London, Hebron &c. My people are civil to me & my church gains ground daily.

Once more God bless you faith.

Bela your friend.

Rev^d. S^l. Peters.

New Haven March 19, 1784.

Dear Sir:

One good arises from the general evil that is brought on by the seperation of the countries,—a door is opened for a freer intercourse with ones friends, I acknowledge with pride & pleasure that I have received two letters which I have read to hundreds of your friends, to my and their edification, in your last you have been good enough to mark out a plan for the Connecticut episcopate corresponding in the general with the sentiments of your brethren in these *goings down of the sun,* but the grand difficulty appears to lie in your dim climes of light,—the spirit of our New england puritan brethren are mightily cooled & cooling, poverty who can stand before, it hath produced great alterations feeling its pains they are now projecting plans to recal their banished brethren from Nova Scotia, the strife and contention is between the City of N Haven & the City of N London for you must know that both these places have obtained charters from the general Assembly of Connect-icut last January and are Incorporated City's. New Haven ye first with liberal privileges I expect M^r. Elias Shipman com-mon-counselman of the City of N Haven & Capt. W^m. Powel a citizen of the same City will go to London in the course of ye ensuing summer by whome I intend to write you about many things & they will be able to tell you many more than I can write—in the mean season to give you some faint Idea of the spirit of our citizens I enclose a vote of ye Town of N Haven as comprehending its parishes about which I say—The Charter is as I told you a liberal one, & by ye above named gentleman. I propose sending it to you without expense, I wrote you some time since by a Mr Townsend with a Sermon of D^r. Stiles

which I hope you have received also I asked your favorable attention to a matter we have much at heart the procuring an Organ for Trinity Church. Shipman & Powel will I suppose bring with them one Hundred Guineas to procure the Organ & case—they will probably tarry but a few weeks in London & if the business could be forwarded any way beforehand so that they might be able to bring it with them we should be very much obliged—we have at this present writing some 70 or 80 £ lawful raised for yᵉ purpose, pray dont fail writing me by the return of Townsend.

We have had to grappel with the most severe frost the last winter, that the memory of man can furnish us with an account of; our harbour for many months bound with frost but two or three days ago broke up, how cold it hath been at N Carolina the last winter in the course of but a few weeks from Boston to N York it has been said we lost not less than 1500 souls—our commerce as yet is very far from making us rich most of our people have come into the opinion that our Independence is not the one thing needful, unless poverty is that thing, how we are to get money is the grand question—if we go to N Scotia meet we must the difficulties that always attend setlers in N Countrys, if we stay where we are we can but only starve, we shall not perish by the Sword that is Sheathed, in a word we are on the ground and can get no lower—Scovel & Andrews representatives to a company of adventurers to the Eastward set out in the month of April to explore land for their settlement, but I think they will return to their missions and probably stay with them while inhabitants of this lower world & that may be the case of the rest of your brethren of the Episcopal Church in N England.—The dissenting clergy have no cause of triumph the late struggle hath made them cheap & generally dispised and as far as religion is thought of the Church is now by far yᵉ most popular.

Our Clergy of Maryland nominated Dʳ. Smith for their Bishop, but the Assembly, who imagined they should have a voice in that affair would not approve of the candidate—this refusal drew from the Clergy a *Bill of rights* &c.—this disagreement at present retards the setling the Church in that quarter.—Mʳ. White a quondam chaplin to congress Philadelphia, goes on another plan, & endeavors to get a Bᵖ. nominated by the General Vestrys in that State—our *plan* you know but I cannot omit the mention of the favourable attention of our general Assembly to it, they declare they have no objection, but if we can support him they will give us no trouble—hope your bishops will help us at this lift—do you intend to spend all your days in England? You can return soon if you will—your Son at Stratford is well & your friends there. I shall trouble you but a little more, but I must not omit an important matter or two and will dismiss you—first for myself—in your future letters to me pray dont fail to direct to me thus—Rev. B. Hubbard rector of Trinity Church in yᵉ City of N Haven in yᵉ first City of N England—be so good then as to pull off your canonical hat in future to your canonical & important brother of yᵉ City, viz. The Rev. Rector Hubbard of the City of N Haven—& as for my very good wife & of her I have to observe that grace hath & still doth increase & for yʳ very honorable mention made of her makes you one of her best a very low City courtesy & she hath learned to make them for know you that our City furnishes dancing masters, she prostrates herself to the Rev. Mʳ. Peters, pimlico, London begs she may not be forgotten of him, & remembers his daughter & wishes she could mention Mʳˢ. Peters, as likewise she remembers most kindly Mʳˢ. Cargel, Miss Harrison & her good husband in which joins

the rector of the New City, let us all meet again on better terms & in a more stable World.   your old friend, who hath the honor to subscribe himself the rector of &c. &c. your friend.

Bela Hubbard.

Rev. S. Peters.

New Haven Connecticut June 1. 1784.
My dear Sir:

I wrote you sometime since and amongst other things mentioned a matter of business I wished you to transact for my little Church, viz. the procuring for it an Organ.

In an application of this sort I would much sooner consult my friend yⁿ a mere Stranger, partly impelled by necessity to procure an organ we wish it may be a well toned and well made one with such a number of stops as will make it proper for excellent Church musick from the common Psalm tune to the Anthem—Voluntary &c. & we wish you to get an honest unprejudiced organist in London or Westminster to play on this organ and determin whether it will answer our purpose or not before it is sent over.

You know the Church building is but small the inside 40 by 60 feet, the Arch &c but what the maker need to know about this will appear by the little plan of the space of the Church that is to contain it—which is enclosed—150 guineas will be paid for the first cost to the maker of the organ & the case, my meaning is that the organ case & shipping expenses, without the freight should cost 150 guineas, and the case we wish a neat Oak case, neatly varnished, but would have no extravagant work put on it and my good friend Mʳ. Isaac Beers who forwards this business from N York sends you £100 pounds sterling & the remainder will be compleated in smaller sums in six months, at furtherst—a very able gentleman has promised us that as soon as advice is received of its being shipped he will advance us as far as £50 sterling immediately so that we are sure of the money at all events without the aid of the Churches property or rents which also hath secured us the ballance.—

Further, we should wish to have a full direction in writing describing the members & parts of the organ, & how they are to be put together as such an instrument is new to us, also a book containing such instrumental music as is necessary for Churches, & the whole if got ready soon enough to be shipped & sent out by one of the autumn ships to N York that we may hear the sound by Christmass.—and now when our Church *in these goings down of the sun shall rise* in importance & flourish our free City & port may be the seat of an Archbishop should it be his grace *Samuel* not Hugh—pray remember your friend the underwriter & let him be an Archdeacon and let this self same organ do your Grace's choice do your Grace much honor—and further if you should happen to stumble on some poor but yet honest English lad that would come out & bring with him a small venture in Books of Psalms, & that could play skilfully the organ & hath an English School & Musick altho I dare not promise or engage any thing yet I think he might procure a decent support here, think of this my friend and be not backward in this whole business & you may depend upon it that myself and all your musical friends will love & thank you.

Pray let me know what is said & all that is said about an American bishop in these times of unhappiness on your side of the water in my next letter which I intend to write you from N Milford where a meeting of your brethren in Trinity

week will be held I shall give you a picture of our present State & condition both in Church & State till then I must take my leave and beg you to believe me, with M^{rs}. Hubbards best love & to Miss Hannah yours faithfully & most affectionately

Bela Hubbard.

N.B.   Since the writing the above our good friend & Brother M^r. Leaming came to my house from Stratford (where he is building up the ruins of that Church) and brought in with him your little Son who is in perfect health & looks as you did when you was 16 years old—M^r. Birdseye wishes you & daughter to send over to him or any other person a power of attorney to take possession of your & her interest which is not confiscated & is safely yours, but is at present let out by the high Sheriff of Hartford.

Yours as before

B. H.

Revd S. Peters.

COPY.

No.   Exch. £100 " - " - Sterling, New-York, June 10th, 1784 Forty Days after Sight of this draft per Exchange, (second and third unpaid) .... pay M^r. Isaac Beers .... or Order, One Hundred Pounds .... Sterling Value received, and charge the same to Account, with or without advice from

To

John Rivington Esq.   James Rivington
& Sons
London.

New Haven November 25th. 1784.

Reverend & dear brother,

I am sincerely obliged to you for your letter of the 21st. of July handed to me by M^r. Townsend & for your polite & kind attention to him he speaks of it with gratitude—your ideas of D^r. Ezra Stiles & his piece which his Son called *pop-robin* perfectly agree with those generally entertained on this side the water.

The reception his piece met with from the public is a sufficient mortification to the poor man.

I acknowledge with the same gratitude likewise yours of July 14th. via N York enclosed in which was a letter for your friend D^r. Sutton which I forwarded to brother Abraham and doubt not but he hath carefully forwarded it to the Doctor, by the way brother Abraham hath been the Father of one child by Sister Nancy but deceased from after its birth whither this took place before, or since your departure from America I forget, the good old man remains rector of Christ Chh in the City of Middletown & hath the satisfaction of seeing his congregation grow in numbers & importance—tis pleasurable further to tell you that I have been highly delighted with yours of August & the pamphlets and 30 odd pages in manuscript.— you have bought an Organ for £157. Ster: & endorsed the £100 bill to M^r. Henry Holland, we hoped to have had it at Christmass but by M^r. Austin's arrival without it which was at N York on the 14th. of the present month & who left London about the 24th. of September we think whether it will not be too late to send it out this winter, he saith about ten days previous to his sailing he called at your house to see you but did not find you at home, I had been flattered with an expectation of receiving by him a fresh

packet from you—your letter by ye way of Rhodeisland to M^r. Isaac Beers hath not as yet come to hand—I think we mentioned a wish to you to get the Organ ensured out you will be kind enough to do it when you send it.   you mentioned in your last to me that there remained due to the late M^r. Kneeland from the Society £25. Ster. enclosed I send a bill of exchange endorsed to you with Letters f^m D^r. Johnson & Leaming if the bills are honoured by the Society as I trust they will be, wish you to be so good as to pay the contents to M^r. Henry Holland for the organ, & what further will remain due to him, we shall endeavor in the course of the Winter to collect & transmit to you, mean while I hope M^r. Holland will be under no uneasiness for the rest due as he may depend on it shortly, although *Church work* as old S^t. Roger said, is *slow-work*—your humane and polite attention we do not forget but you will hear further on these matters.

I was much surprised to hear that the late M^r. Kneelands character as a Loyalist had suffered with the Society, wish I could know from what quarters the accusation came, to his death you may depend on it he remained a loyal & firm friend to his Majesty & government, no suspicion to ye contrary was ever hinted here.

Brother Bostwick was here in September last he never hinted ye least suspicion of his entertaining a thought of your unfriendliness to him—I doubt on your side the water you have too many stirrers up of difficulty—and with regard to the information you had of the conduct of your brethren here in the late distracted times it was unjust & cruel—when your letters were Seized they were brought to N Haven by Hosmer now no more, who called on me & pretended friendship, I sent for several of the brethren & they were met at my house by more than 60 I believe of ye lower house of Assembly who were clamourous to get us publicly to condemn your conduct & to say that we did not think y^s was a necessity for your going away, we persisted in it to ye last y^t you could not get protection from Govr. Trumbul after an application to him for it, and that therefore we did think you justified before God & man in going away & that we shod have done the like in the like situation, and all that we did in effect say ultimately was that we did not at that time know of it, a short piece of this tenor & importing in short our political creed was inserted in the newspapers wch I have taken pains to get & send you— M^r. Isaac Beers told me sometime since that he had seen it among his papers & would hand it to me, but upon a further search he was not able to find it, but I hope yet to procure it & I will send it you & our conduct will then appear to you in a very different point of light from the representation of it on your side of water possibly by some members of the then Genl. Assembly, t'was but lately we had any hints of foul play in this matter, but if you have any remaining uneasiness, I can assure you with great sincerity that at that time, & at all times your character stood high & altogether unempeached by any of your Brethren of the clergy or laity on our side of ye question & still doth, but enough of this for ye present.

M^r. Leaming has placed himself at Stratford & doubtless gives you information of the condition of your son.—

I send you likewise the doings of a convention & premising that the Connecticut Clergy are no friends to the lay representation, & if we are ever so happy as to have a bishop at our head we shall be able I trust to preserve our Church in Connecticut decent—D^r. Smith always busy hath published a Sermon & written some remarks on the proceedings of the clergy & laity of Maryland for the establishment of a bishop

in that Province I will try to get & send it you.

Lizard Peter, the rector of pauls hath received yours in answer to one written by deacon Scovel & himself f^m Nova Scotia—M^r. Bowden I think will settle himself at Norwalk where y^r remains still a respectable body of Chh people but my dear Sir this country is really poor and will remain so at least through the present generation. I think with you that our best days are gone, I shall endeavor for myself to get through life with as much ease to myself with respect to any Gov^t. as possible. I have been heretofore anxious & distressed I leave it all & hope to meet you where good gov^t. obtains & where friendship will by no means be interrupted—in the mean season I shall always be happy to hear of any good that awaits you & yours & as to support &c., all that I am able to collect is that the Rev^d. M^r. Peters resides at Pimlico in his own hired house & that he entertains all that call on him with much hospitality & elegance—you are not married nor your dear Hannah it shod seem, I wish when that event takes place you & she may be as happy as you wish & that your happiness may increase & multiply upon you continually as long as you wish it, & that at last the fervent S^t. Peter may open to you a gate which will let you in to a scene of happiness too great for description—Grace D. Hubbard my good Spouse yet lives & hath been ye mother of 9 children of which 6 are now living 4 sons & two daughters viz. John James, Nancy, Bela, Elisabeth, Frederic, & Thomas Still, James & Nancy begin to remind us of our old age, this comfort of mine doth not forget you & yours & wishes to see & tell you what a sense she hath of the very kind notice you take of her, she begs her best love to you & Miss Hannah D^e ve Peters, & likewise we present our love to M^r. & M^rs. Cargel whom we wish happy, pray is old M^r. Harrison her uncle yet alive? I wish I could see your daughter touch ye chord of a musical instrument & her feet & fine shape in a minuet tell her still to dance & rejoice! I believe we shall see one-another yet on this side ye grave! Grace wishes you to tell her how Miss Hannah came by her new name she supposes it was given her in her travils abroad you must let her know in your next, we are all as we were poor & if ye Society drops us we are ruined,— I will endeavor soon to write you again, my Brother & Sister Hubbard drove from Guilford in ye fury of ye late times lives here and loves you & N Caldwell who calls ready to laugh & Bless you and your Letters.

Yours affectionately,

B. Hubbard.

New Haven January 29th. 1785.

My dear brother,

I take this method, to introduce to you, my friend & parishioner M^r. Jared Mansfield, a young Gentleman of a liberal education & of a mathematical genius a Son of the late M^r. Stephen Mansfield a quondam faithful Church Warden of mine, now in Heaven, & when on Earth as loyal a subject of his King as he was a faithful one to his God—he is in company with Capt. French another worthy character & excellent parishioner of mine, these men will probably stay in your overgrown City 8 or 10 weeks, and any civilities shown them will be gratefully received by them & not easily forgotten by the underwriter your ancient & present old fashioned friend.

They will I presume be very able to answer any questions you may be disposed to ask them, about pil-garlie in particular, and your own bamboozled brethren in general, in the States in general—bamboozled by both countries—Our affairs are in a very narrow circle, we are considered as of no consequence, as nobody, are poor, contemptible & forgotten—your world is mad!—wish they would recover their senses, but I presume however they will take th^r own way & they must. For myself I intend to meet you in heaven, short of that Country I expect nothing.—But why doth England refuse to meet us on the ground of religion? Why will she not give us a bishop, did they once but open y^r eyes they would certainly see it just & very political, but if they will keep y^r eyes closed we cannot help it!—Your premier I do not like, he appears to be an unfeeling boy, & let D^r. Price be hanged, & go where he belongs, I like him not—as a politician I am afraid he is too much listened to & that the Presbyterian interest is a growing interest—tell me how that is and tell me every thing proper for me to know by ye return of my friends—I believe in my last I told you of the reception of your pamphlets & Lucubations they have afforded me much pleasure & your friends in this part of the world.—

M^r. Leaming I told you was setled at Stratford & Mr Boding at Norwalk, M^r. Leaming hath resided principally with M^r. Birdsey where of course your little Son hath become an object of his attention, he is really a fine child & when I see him brings you to my mind as you looked at the age of Sixteen— I have heard nothing from him some weeks although I presume they are all well as lately I have had a line from M^r. Leaming.

M^r. James Sayre hath settled with the people of Guilford & Branford with a Salary of £80 p^r annum & last Saturday I had a letter from our Brother Mr John Graves signifying a wish to come into Connecticut, so that the old missions are filling up & if we had a bishop at our head the Church would soon be numerous & respectible. I shall add no more at the present but a wish for your & the happiness of your amiable daughter whom God long preserve to you.—M^rs. Cargel perhaps hath ere this been told of ye decease of her good mother M^rs. Harrison at Rhodeisland which happen'd a few weeks since our compliments of condolence to her & partner, and accept M^rs. Hubbards & my familys best love to you & Miss Hannah, which concludes me dear M^r. Peters your affectionate Brother & obliged humble Servant.

Bela Hubbard.

Rev^d. M^r. Peters.

Dear Sir,

Yours of the 6th of September via Boston came to hand, and I wrote you a long letter in answer which I expected to have sent by M^r. Samuel Broome, and after having sealed it & got a bundle of pamphlets & a letter from M^r. Trumbul N Haven which are now on hand to go still I hope before winter is ended perhaps by W^m. Hillhouse, I was disappointed in Broomes failing—if God Spares my life I will add many more words & pamphlets to those already Sealed up which are by me, but of this hereafter—at present I must trouble you with the Postage of this on my own concerns. I have this day a

M^r. Whitlock

letter from one of the wardens of S^t. Johns Church

Cap^n.

by the way poor Camp left this world eleven days after his arrival at S^t. Johns—I am behol^n with a hint you furnished some one at S^t. Johns that Bayley would not be appointed to that living & that I could have it for asking for it—I am here as poor as Jobs hens or Turkeys, but if all other difficulties

were removed, how am I to get my expenses paid in removing my family to that country and will the Society continue the £50 for certain during my life—If I could support my great family at S^t. Johns as I think I cannot here if the Society would be pleased to appoint me their missionary there why I think I would if too, in pity to my moneyless state bare my expenses to the parish, venture to go to that cold country—you know I love and allways shall continue to love that country from which I am now seperated—but M^r. Whitlock says he understands that Bishop Inglis hath wrote a Second letter in favour of D^r. Bayley but if you will try to hold ye parish for me, I will as early as possible, write to D^r. Morice & lay my distressed condition before ye Society & beg an appointment of me to S^t. John—what you wrote about M^r. Dibblee being at S^t. John is altogether a mistake—he has never been there old M^r. Dibblee, and I never learned that he had any thoughts of going there, he has not been there,—my eyes are Sore I cannot write and my thoughts are I know not where,—pray good Doctor Peters will you think Still of Bela & Grace & Nancy & James & Bela 2^d & Frederic & Thomas & Betsey & W^m. Henry &c.—of Grace & all her children—& help the old couple to be in a situation to scramble for them—pray do know of D^r. Morice too, whither the Government Salary will be continued & whither any chaplinships can be tacked to that parish—in short help me if you can, & I will write soon to the Society meanwhile I rest your humble admirer altho' in the

State of Connecticut—with Graces love to you M^r. and M^rs. Jarvis your own & your Grandson I am as ever your real friend & very humble Servant.

Bela Hubbard.

New Haven four days before Xmas—
be the blessings of that Season yours—
I shall write you soon—
Write me by ye first packet.

Rev^d D^r. Peters.

> Reverend Doctor Samuel Peters
> Charlotte Street Pimlico
> London—

Hubbard Bela
21 Decr. 1788
rec^d. March 2-89-

New Haven December 27th 1788

Dear Sir,

A few days since I wrote to you, but as a Vessel sails to morrow for England I must still trouble you with another line on my concerns only, I have weighed as well as I am able my going to S^t. John—and by this conveyance tell D^r. Maurice that I will if the Society say so—and will render permanent the Salary of 150, from Gov^nt. & them, and will be at ye expense of removing me but will you dear Sir, be so good as to trouble y^r self further, & know if there is no chaplinship obtainable to add to ye comforts of a Mission as cold as Greenland, if there is any thing in that way pray help me if you can & I will pray for you & wish you well untill you shall have no need of prayers & wishes,—Grace thanks you,—I shall send you Trumbuls pamphlets with others soon, I can now add no more as the Vessel I now find is going off only that I am yours affectionately,

B. Hubbard

Your kinsman in College Dined with me yesterday is clever—
God bless you all—
Rev^d. D^r. Peters—

SAMUEL (ANDREW) PETERS.

Samuel (Andrew), a son of John and Mary (Mark) Peters, was born at Hebron, Connecticut, November 20, 1735, O. S.

He was educated in the common country school of the village and privately prepared for College. He graduated from Yale College in 1757.

He had conformed to the Church of England and studied theology under Dr. Samuel Johnson of Stratford. He went to England in the fall of 1758, bearing letters of commendation from Dr. Johnson and others. Soon after his arrival he had a severe attack of small pox. The Archbishop of Canterbury and the Bishop of London saw that he was well cared for and personally visited him when the possibility of infection was past. He was made deacon and ordained priest in the summer of 1759. His license to officiate in Plantations was given by the Bishop of London, August 25 of that year.

He made full proof of his ministry, was affectionately regarded by his parishioners and by the clergy of the colony was most highly esteemed. He did much missionary work, notably in the New Hampshire Grant, now Vermont. In a letter to the Venerable Society, he describes one visit when he took his clerk with him, and after prayer upon a hill top, from which an extensive view can be had, he named the region *verd mont*.

Mr. Peters was a thorough and consistent believer in a united British Empire; in conversation and formal argument and in newspapers of the day he showed his bitter detestation of any attempt at independence. So bitter was his pen that in the summer of 1774, when there had reached Hebron copies of the reports sent by Mr. Peters, as they thought, the Sons of Liberty called upon him defiant and angry and demanded the retraction of the malicious libels upon the cause of American freedom. Mr. Peters stoutly refused, was hooted, jeered at and his house and furniture damaged. After a second visit from the same persons he fled from Hebron to Boston after having on Sunday, September 4, 1774, while all men were indignant at the British troops for firing upon Boston. He sailed for England in October, leaving behind him house, land and children. His daughter Hannah joined him in London after some time.

Mr. Peters lived comfortably upon a pension from the Crown, engaging in literary and political work, receiving hospitably the friends who in those troubled times visited England. He hoped that he might be made Bishop of Nova Scotia and friends solicited the honour for him.

The circumstances under which he was elected Bishop of Vermont in February, 1794, were somewhat extraordinary, for Dr. Samuel Bass of Newburyport, Massachusetts, had been elected a few months previously and had not declined.

The efforts to obtain consecration for Dr. Peters in England were unavailing. No request appears to have been made to the American Bishops. The testimonials necessary could not have been furnished, for Dr. Peters seldom officiated anywhere. In the course of the correspondence he suggested a state ceremonial by proclamation of the governor and acknowledgment of him by the clergy, citing passages from ancient writers to prove its legality and feasibility In addition to an epistle to the Church in Vermont which has been printed, there are found among his manuscripts two charges and forms for letters of order and a device for the seal of the Diocese.

A difference of opinion and controversy with William Pitt, the Prime Minister, in 1804 caused that dignitary to strike his name from the pension list. Broken in health, but indomitable in spirit, he returned to the United States in 1805. He spent several years in Washington endeavoring to obtain from Congress a confirmation of a grant of land near the Fall of St. Anthony, now the site of Minneapolis and St. Paul, by the Indians to the famous traveler, Jonathan Carver, who gave it to Dr. John Coakley Lettsom and Dr. Peters. He failed utterly, but still persevered in his attempt to have the Indians ratify it. He commenced a journey to the Northwest for that purpose in 1817, but was taken ill and was tenderly cared for by Indians at Prairie du Chien, Wisconsin, during the winter.

He died in the City of New York, April 19, 1826.

Dr. Peters married, February 14, 1760, Hannah, a daughter of Silas and Elizabeth Owen of Hebron, Connecticut. Two daughters were born to them, Hannah, who died an infant, March 2, 1761, and Hannah Delavan, who was born January 2, 1762. She married, in London, England, William Jarvis, a son of Samuel and Martha (Seymour) Jarvis of Norwalk, Connecticut. Her husband was an officer in the first American Regiment and served in Canada, where he held several civil offices, among them, that of provincial secretary in the administration of Governors Simcoe, Hunter and Gore. He died at York, Canada, August 13, 1817. Mrs. Jarvis died at Queenstown, Canada, September 20, 1845. They had seven children.

Mr. Peters married for the second time, June 28, 1769, Abigail, a daughter of Captain Samuel Gilbert. She died July 14, 1769.

He married for the third time at Stratford, Connecticut, April 21, 1773, Mary, the only daughter of William and Eunice (Benjamin) Birdseye. She died at Hebron, June 16, 1774. They had one son, born at Hebron, June 16, 1774, and named William Birdseye. He was brought up until his fourteenth year by his grandparents and then completed his education in England and France under the supervision of his father. He graduated

from Oxford University, studied law at the Temple, London, practiced in Canada and Mobile, Alabama, where he died in 1817.

Dr. Peters' most famous work, though never formally acknowledged by him, is: "A General History of Connecticut, By a Gentleman of the Province," published originally in London in 1781 and republished in 1829, and in a final edition in 1877 by Samuel Jarvis McCormick. The satirical tone, the sometimes malicious amusement of the writer over the events of Connecticut history, their treatment of all dissenters from Congregationalism, and his printing of certain alleged laws which he called the Blue Laws, holding some of these up to ridicule, brought upon him much vituperation and abuse. Writers upon Connecticut history even to the present day speak of it as untruthful, unfair and exaggerated. It has, however, been shown that the "laws" have a resemblance to some which were enacted in the early days of the Colony.

He also published in 1785, a letter to the Rev. John Tyler on the Possibility of Eternal Punishment and the Improbability of Universal Salvation; A History of the Rev. Hugh Peters, 1807; besides articles in the English magazines and papers.

Rev⁴. Sir

I place my Confidance on your Goodness to pardon me for offering my Sentiments concerning a Clergyman who is by you to be named your Successor at Halifax—your acquaintance with that People & your Popularity in that Country, your Abilities, long Service & Great Merit were Reasons Sufficient to have made you the Bishop of Nova Scotia in any Periods of time before 1788 and after 1788. The Authors of this neglect too late see their Error, and were they not Infidels or Dissenters from our excellent Establishment, they would Mourn for folly and for the Ruin of our Church in Nova Scotia under a Redemptioner whose recent Conduct added to his former compleats his character to the Disgrace of the Mitre—Qui vult perdere &c. &c.—seems applicable to the Society as well as the Civil Powers of Great Britain—they spend great sums of money in their Colonies to support the Church & by ever sending improper Clergymen & civil Rulers displease the Colonists and turn from the Church & State—nothing appears so absurd in my Opinion, as to consult only three or four leading Men about who shall be the Clergyman of a town—this Conduct will never increase the Church in America & it has almost emptied the Churches in England—The Society have appointed D⁴. Byles Missioner at Sᵗ. John's—& by it have made it necessary for the People to shelter themselves under James & Milton Lady Huntingdon's Chaplains—and the rest, in general, will follow—and Sally Criecy or Mother Plantan cannot prevent, them, nor hinder their Belief in D⁴. Califfs Reports.—

If you intend (as I believe you do) the Prosperity of the Church in Halifax; you will not be directed by any Individual in that Town, in appointing your Successor—I know your Character well, and that the People there esteem it highly—& I know of no Man that can succeed to you with half the Reputation you left, unless it be the Rev⁴. Bela Hubbard of Newhaven in Connecticut, whose voice, address, and politeness exceeds all every other Clergyman ever known to me in New England.—His Character is perfectly known to M⁴. H. Loyd, he is a good Scholar, & is Dean Barkley's Greek Examiner at the University of New Haven—he was invited to succeed D⁴. Apthorp at Cambridge, & D⁴. Cutler at Boston but he refused both—he was a disciple of & a Convert of mine from the Dissenters—& excelled in perfections the Rev⁴. M⁴. Kneeland—who was known to you—& me—. If any man besides you can unite the People of Halifax as they were when you left them, M⁴. Hubbard for his own good & that of the Church you have been forty years in building up. He has a large Family & brought up in great politeness in a most delightful Town now oppressed with Taxes & Poverty & discontent with Congress—M⁴. Hubbard has been always loyal, and good policy makes his

wish on December 27ᵗʰ 1788 worthy of Notice,—his views are not made known in Connecticut yet—If you should think proper to recommend him for your successor at Halifax—he Expects to be a Servant of the Society and not a dean to a Redemptioner—One thing more, M⁴. Hubbard has a grateful Heart, an Article understood by only few of the Clergy since the Reformation—

I have the honour to be Rev⁴. Sir
Your affectionate Friend and
Most humble Servant
Feb⁴. 3ᵈ. 1789
Rev⁴. D⁴. Breynton.
Samuel Peters.

• • •

Brother Abᵐ mutters & drops his lip that he is forgotten by you & says he should write you but has never a private conveyance, have pitty upon Abᵐ The *Israelite* at Derby is as you are *wifeless* & will continue so,—Your *Nephew* is a Student of Law he was with me from the North last week on his way to *Hebron* he is clever & bids fair to do honour to the *Name*—Grace remembers you as does Levi, Anna, Caldwell & Clarinda, but I think Clarinda is in a decline and may soon go to heaven—We have been visited in the united States last fall & this spring with the *Influenza* wch in many Instances proved fatal especially to old people, it carried off my old Clerk *Joseph Browne* a good old venerable man in his 89ᵗʰ year, if M⁴. Leavenworth is yᵉ bearer of this he has been to London before perhaps you know him, he is a Lawyer of this Town Son to M⁴. Leavenworth of Waterbury he is a sensible man, if it is Baldwin I dont know him but suppose he is a good man by yᵉ return of yᵉ one or the other whoever it is pray write me, and believe me as long as I live your sincerely attached friend & obliged humble Servant.

Bela Hubbard.
After folding up my letter I find it is probable that D⁴. Baldwin will be the bearer who tho not a man of much address is esteemed an honest worthy man—he may have some questions to ask you on the business he goes upon he is trusty & clever.

Rev⁴. D⁴: Peters.
Hubbard Bela Rev⁴.
5 July 1790
22 August 1790 Rec⁴.
30 Octob⁴. Answr⁴.

New Haven October 30ᵗʰ 1790.

Dear Sir:

This moment M⁴. Broome called on me to let me know that he sets out for Norfolk to morrow morning to embark once more for England, and mentions to me the very kind and gentleman like treatment he hath met with from you, & speaks in yᵉ most handsom manner of you in all companies, as do all our *folks* who visit your World—I wish I had known sooner of this Voige, I would have sent you a New *American prayer book* the *constitutions* to wᶜʰ it pertains I send you with a *catologue* of Yale College, the president of which tells me that if you will send your signature, or rather the Name of the College in wᶜʰ, or, from which, you received your Doctorate he will be careful to do you justice—he is more friendly & is sorry I believe that he ever has written any thing against the Ch⁴. in particular—with regard to our ecclesiastical con-

stitution lately adopted in this & other States I can only say that it is the best we could get for the present—the door being still open for amendments, it may yet be amended and I do believe such as our Church now is it will be increased by large additions from the Congregatiolists who are much pestured by yᵉ Methodists & Baptists who swarm in all parts of this & indeed in most other States & will go near to win them, the consequence will be that the better people who have any wish for order & stability will in their own defence come into the Church—I have been some time since expecting to hear of your appointment to a Bishoprick of a *Trait* of *country* in the Kings American dominions not far from *Canady*—*Scovel* or *Andrews* wrote me last Summer some things about it, but I have heard nothing since, wish most heartily that something may turn up worth your accepting that may bring you once more into yᵉ *Land of your Nativity*—I have dreamed often of seeing you but when I awoke, it was a delusion—I wish it was a reality that you was once more an Inhabitant of this part of it O, I mean I wish so for myself and many many other of your friends:—last week your Nephew Mʳ. Peters Son of Jonathan was at my house from *Sharon* where he keeps a School & read *Law,* and thinks of pursuing that Study more effectually either here or at N Haven or Hartford, he is sensible & I think bids fair to do honor to his Family is highly respected of his friends, told me he had a letter from you in August I think—in which if I remember you told him of your going to France, & of yᵉ ill State of a Mʳ. Peters a relation—you have omitted to write me for a great while I am sorry, but will endeavor to provoke you all I can to renew this business, and if you knew how much satisfaction your letters give me Grace & a circle of your friends in this Town I know your good & benevolent heart would lead you to write oftener than you do—*Jarvis,* complains, bitterly that he is neglected, & says he is incapacitated to write you by means of his situation, his Church is as it was, but a *New Chʰ* is formed at *Chatham* & is on yᵉ growing Land where, Jarvis christened about one hundred on landing, adults & Infants at one stand—at present that Chʰ is connected with *Hebron* where they have a *young man* a Mʳ. *Brownson* educated with your kinsman & put into Orders by Bᴾ. Seabury but believe he will not tarry long with them—Mʳ. *James Sayre* is now at Stratford, in the place of our old Friend Dʳ. I. *Leaming,* created a Doctor by the president of Columbia College *N York* last Commencement, Dʳ. Leaming has with his wife *Phebe* for yᵉ gratification of her friends in New York viz: Aunt *Hannah* & others—removed thither Aunt *Hannah* remains still Aunt *Hannah* & will continue to remain Aunt *Hannah* for ever—*Jarvis's* boy is a fine *boy,* I mean *Isaac* yᵉ Son of Father Abraham & Nancy his Consort—whom not

I have seen for some years—*Nathaniel* of Derby is yet a Nathaniel indeed—a daughter of his is joined with a Mʳ. *Blakesly* in orders at Northhaven in yᵉ neighbourhood of your Friend Trumbull, who *boasts* & *vaunts* himself on being a correspondent with Dʳ. Peters, take care that you do not burst him—Congress you know have left N York for Philadelphia, but wherever yᵉ go, they are not very likely to give much satisfaction to yᵉ good people of yᵉ States, having learned to take care of themselves & forget their constituents the Six Dollars pʳ day wᶜʰ they have secured to themselves does not give our frugal Farmers much affection for them, or *Zeal* for their *patriotism,* from an Aristocracy we may get next a Government more nearly resembling a limited Monarchy, but whatever shall take place it will very little concern me, as I have little further

probably to do in this wayward World being now, an *old man* with many wrinkles a pale face and a consumptive habit—*Grace* my old fashioned & very good wife is in much Yᵉ same condition,—but I hope she will live yet a good while she is ambitious to be thought well of by you and therefore begs me to thank you, and thank you again for your many & particularly truths I mean

your late favors, forced upon you by Mʳ. Broome & Hillhouse I meant for her gowns &c. &c.—Hillhouse is your everlasting friend & yᵉ old Philosopher I Mansfield—Levi & Anna, Caldwell & Clarinda & a number of those old fashioned friends still continue—& still continue your warm hearty & everlasting friends, as do yᵉ present generation in Connecticut—pray did you receive a line from me by yᵉ hands of a brother in law of Mark Leavingsworth Esqʳ. a Mʳ Baldwin—if this reaches you before he leaves England pray let me hear from you—Mʳ. T. Green your friend just this moment begs his love to you & begs you to accept a Sketch of yᵉ life of a certain *Joseph Mountain* & if you can find out after yᵉ reading of his extraordinary life that there is any truth in all, or any of the facts recorded in it, that you would let us know it,—The General Assembly now sits in this Town, a bill for a Divorce preferred by I Strong Esquire, of our upper house of Assembly—and likewise a Bill from his wife who was Susanna Wyllys daughter of old Secretary Wyllys, has occasioned me to attend yᵉ house e several days & will take up possibly two or three days more before it will be finished, yᵉ consequence if a Divorce takes place, will be, that both, will remain, without help meats during life, & yᵉ one dropped from all public entrustments, let them pass—I do not wish you such a wife, but if you ever again change your condition, may you have a better, yet I think her far better than her husband—Our business in State Assemblies grow less & less and will finally come to nothing—All your friends here salute you—especially Levi & Anna, & Wᵐ. G.
& Elizabeth his wife
Hubbard who was Betsey Douglass, daughter of *B. Douglass Esqʳ.*—*Grace Nancy* Hubbard my Daughter & all my family begging the best love to you & your good daughter, Son in Law own Son &c.—& believe me worthy & dear Sir yours unalterably

Revᵈ. Dʳ. Peters   *Hubbard Bela 30 Octb 90 recᵈ. Decʳ. 10—*   Bela Hubbard.

New Haven January 9ᵗʰ. 1791

Dear Sir:

I wrote you some time since by Mʳ. Samuel Broome, and learning this moment that, a Vessel is bound from this port to London I cannot fail writing you, although I have nothing that I can say to you that can afford you satisfaction. I told you before that the Gentlemen from America who have been so fortunate as to be recommended to your acquaintance, all speak, highly of you, as not only a good and benevolent man of a great Stock of Information, but as a *warm friend to your Native Country:* & I think Dʳ. Stiles begins to think more favorably of you, yet he cannot forgive you for 'writing (as he says you did) the history of Connecticut'—but old Secretary *Wyllys* who quarters in the Sessions of the Assembly two doors from me will not be a moment without it, he reads it yᵉ last thing when he goes to bed & the first thing when he arises—but few people now are disposed to laugh with us, if they cry

not, they have the inclination at least to be serious, the expenses of our Government & the duties with which our trade is sadled are enough to make those furious, who expected our Independence would be productive of every good—Our general Assembly are now setting at *New Haven*—& they have permitted a Refugee D^r. Jos. Clarke late of Stratford but of New-Brunswick to collect his debts in this State so that you see that body begins to be inclined to open th^r. Eyes to see things as right & just which but a little while ago was otherwise—I think in a letter sent you by M^r. Broome I forwarded our Ecclesiastical constitution, and before this, I presume you have seen our *New*-common *prayer book*. I would thank you for your candid opinion both on the one & the other—the book is adopted but not as yet gone into general use but suppose it will—if I can send you one of these books I will—I think the Church in Connecticut is on ye whole gaining reputation old prejudices are daily giving way—and dissenters think more justly of religion—Trumball is your friend, has sent you D^r. Edwards piece ag^t Universalism, I think *I'zm* is not encreasing, though Tyler continues to preach it as heretofore and *Murray*, but few of the Clergy in this Country of any denomination have appeared on its side—but Arianism & Socinianism are I think gaining ground in this Country, both to the Eastward & Westward, our Clergy keep Connecticut to ye old orthodox Doctrines—and we have in our Church a worthy set of young Clergymen coming forward who I hope will make good ye ground of the Old-ones, of these there are Perry of Newtown, Baldwin of Litchfield, Ives of Cheshire, Hull of Branford, *Blakesley* of Northhaven, *Shelton* of Fairfield, &c. &c., *Foot* of Rye, & lately *Ogilvie* of Norwalk with others, at hebron & Chatham th^r is a M^r. Tillotson Brunson a Scholar & man of sense but no great preacher—D^r. Walter I hear has left Shelbourn & about to settle at D^r. Cutlars Chh. in Boston & Cambrige—a M^r. Ogden is at Portsmouth an active Clergyman but why do I take up your time in mentioning particular men, we have many in the Country who do well in y^r stations—Old Jarvis wishes you would excuse his Indolence, & believe him at bottom your friend, he is in truth an old man and his son & Nancy to take care of—Scovel & Andrews I suppose you hear of now & then who are forever seperated from me—I wish you was on this side the Atlantuk setled as a Bp. in some Northern Sea & when that shall take place, I intend if *Grace* continues with me & I with her, to do myself the honor to become one of your Presbyters—with her best love in perfect union with mine I subscribe myself dear Sir your very affectionate friend & brother.

Rev^d. D^r. Peters.   Bela Hubbard.

Hubbard Rev^d
9 Jany. 1791
rec^d. April 6,-91
Ans. May 2^d-91

| Reverend Samuel Peters, L. L. D. |
| Grosvenor Place, |
| Favoured by)   London. |
| Capt. Brooks.) |

New Haven April 5th. 1795.

Dear Sir,

The bearer of this is Mark Leavenworth Esquire a Lawyer of New Haven who with his wife an agreeable woman goes to London on some business & to return, he has promised to deliver this & the letter that accompanies it to you, and any little Services you can in your way render him I have no doubt

you will afford him and his amiable companion he is a sensible man & son of M^r. Leavenworth of Waterbury—The occasion of my troubling you now is this, I have lately received a letter from Bishop Inglis inviting me to accept the vacant Mission of Cumberland in N. Scotia—it seems it is an old Mission and worth as he tells me £70 Sterling from Government and £40 Ster. from the Society, I thought these Missions had a larger allowance, it has likewise he says a good Glebe pertaining to it, but no parsonage house built upon it, the mission is but a little better than my allowance from my present Cure, but I believe I cannot engage the people here to fix a Salary for life, and I think with a numerous family rendered poor from a poor Salary & an expensive situation I ought to accept a *Certainty* for an uncertainty—you know I can obtain from the Bishop & Clergy in this State such Testimonials of my good moral character & diligence in my clerical office as will be fully satisfactory to the Society & the Bishop of Nova Scotia as they may think needful—I have accordingly written to D^r. Morice, and asked his assistance with ye Society to add if the Mission is but £40 to add £10 Ster—to it & bare the expense of removal of my family, or, if they have another Mission in that quarter of the World with a larger allowance, that they would appoint me to it—will you deliver the letter that accompanies this to D^r. Morice, and use your influence in my favour, it will be absolutely impossible for me to move to Nova Scotia without the Societies assistance—and if they would be so good as to advance a years salary it would be of great use to me, as I might then lay in a years store of provisions much cheaper here than there, I could have wished the vacancy had been in New Brunswick as those Missions have £100 Ster from Government and £50 Ster—from the Society— but believe me my dear Sir, my poverty calls too so strongly upon me to do something for my family better y^n I can do for them in this place, that I must I think accept of this Missions but I hope that in consideration of my former long Services for about Twenty years the Society will consider me, and in their wisdom & goodness make the Mission at least equal to any other in that Province, you will much oblige me in urging my necessities which are truly pressing—since the receipt of your letter by M^r. Baldwin, our American papers have announced the Rev^d. D^r. Peters Bishop of Canada how is it? let me hear from you as soon as may be, your friends salute & greet you well here, & none more heartily than my old companion—accept our best wishes for you, & present our best love to M^r and M^rs. Jarvis with our congratulations for her happy addition to her family, and enfold in your arms for me your former image & likeness *Birdseye Peters* whom God bless and make him good, useful & happy in this World & Eternally blessed in another thus prays your old friend and most obed^t. humble Servt.

N.B. you recollect the Society allowed   Bela Hubbard.
     Scovel Andrews &c. some back Salaries
Grace wishes you to hint if it will do something
of this for me assist me all you can & God bless you—
The Rev^d. D^r. Peters—

To
     The Rev^d. D^r. S. Peters
       Grosvenor place or Charlotte
   Street Pimlico
Favour'd by   London—
   Mark Leavenworth Esqr.

Hubbard Rev^d
5th April 1791
rec^d 26 May—

JEREMIAH LEAMING.

Jeremiah, a son of Jeremiah and Abigail (Turner) Leaming, was born in Durham, Connecticut, and was baptized by Nathaniel Chauncey, who was the first pastor of the Church of Christ in that town, on May 12, 1717. His father's farm appears to have been near the Middletown line, but the family evidently attended service in the old Congregational Church on Durham Green.

The son probably worked upon the farm in the summer and attended school in the winter as was the custom in New England. He entered Yale College when he was twenty-four and graduated with honor in 1745. Among his classmates was Thomas Bradbury Chandler, afterward one of the most noted of the Colonial Clergy and the pleader for an American Episcopate.

It was while in College that Mr. Leaming conformed to the Church of England as many other young men of ability were then doing. He studied theology under the Rev. Dr. Johnson of Stratford. He became lay reader in St. Paul's Church, Norwalk, very much to the gratification of the Congregation. They were desirous that he should become their minister upon his ordination. But his eminent qualifications as a teacher caused Dr. Johnson to commend him to the Vestry of Trinity Church, Newport, Rhode Island, as a suitable principal for the school founded under the will of Nathaniel Kay and assistant to the Rev. James Honyman.

Mr. Leaming went to England in the spring of 1748. He was made deacon June 5 of that year by Dr. Gilbert, Bishop of Llandaff, and ordained priest June 19, by Dr. Hoadley, Bishop of Winchester.

Upon his return he entered upon his duties in Newport. He was very acceptable and remained for ten years. During a vacancy after the death of Mr. Honyman in 1750, he had full charge of the parish until the arrival of the Rev. Thomas Pollen in 1754. In 1758 he became Rector at Norwalk and missionary in a wide circuit.

To the development of the work in that growing town he gave twenty-one years, in which the parish grew in every way and a new church was built.

The invasion of Norwalk by troops under the British General Tryon, in July, 1779, completed the indignity and suffering he had received from the Sons of Liberty, and the mob masquerading under the name of patriots. He had been confined in a damp room at the jail, compelled to take long midnight journeys to be examined as to his tory principles and endured other outrages.

The disasters of that summer day when General Tryon burned Norwalk were great. The church, rectory, library and nearly all Mr. Leaming's household goods were destroyed. With his family he took refuge in New York City. He officiated in turn with other loyalist clergymen in the City Hall, as St. Paul's Chapel could not hold all the people who desired to attend.

It was during this period that he was offered in April, 1783, by Mr. Jarvis, Secretary of the Convention, which met at Woodbury on March 25, the episcopal chair of Connecticut. His infirmities compelled him to decline, for he had contracted a serious hip disease.

At Easter, 1784, Mr. Leaming became Rector of Christ Church, Stratford. In that time of uncertainty while the Bishop designate was seeking consecration in England his wise counsel and cheering words encouraged his brethren. With Abraham Jarvis, the Secretary of the Convention, he conducted the correspondence with Dr. Seabury. He preached the sermon before the Convention at Middletown on August 3, 1785, when they recognized Bishop Seabury.

When the difficulties in the way of a continental union of the Church in the United States seemed insurmountable, he was asked during a meeting of the Convocation at Wallingford to go to Scotland to be made a coadjutor to Bishop Seabury. He again refused for his infirmities had grown greater.

In 1790 he resigned his parish and lived for some time in the city of New York but spent the later years of his life at New Haven in the home of Mr. James A. Hillhouse, an intimate friend of Mr. Leaming.

He died, September 15, 1804, in the eighty-eighth year of his age.

Dr. Leaming married in 1751, while in Newport, a relation to the Kay family, who died a few months after. He married in 1755, Elizabeth Peck of New York. She was the aunt of Hannah (Peck) Farmar, the wife of Bishop Abraham Jarvis. She died after a few years. A life interest in her large estate was left to her husband. It then reverted to the family of the Bishop.

Dr. Leaming was a forcible writer and sustained well his part in a controversy with Noah Welles upon Episcopal government. The letters were published in 1765 and 1770. His Evidences of Christianity and Dissertations upon various subjects are of value.

Upon his tombstone in the Grove Street Cemetery he is characterized as "well instructed, especially in his holy office, unremitting in his labours, charitable, patient, and of primitive meekness."

Stratford Nov. 8, 1784.

Dear Sir:

I suppose you know, I have consented to take the Care of this Church, which has been for many years, in a very broken, unsettled State. It was supposed, that it was necessary in order to collect this Church together, that an old man should undertake the Task. I am old enough, if that will do, and if I am not too old, I make no doubt, I shall accomplish it.

The Chh. at Norwalk, all wanted me to return there, but that Chh. is able to do without me. It would have been for my advantage to have gone there. But it was supposed that the general Good of the Chh. required me to take the Charge of this Chh.

I suppose you will *take* this, for a *New England Cant:* because you have lately lived, where the Enquiry is, Who will give the best Salary, not where can I do the most Good.

I understand it has been represented to the Society, that M^r. Kneeland, was an Enemy to the British Constitution. This is certainly a very *false report.* And I hope you will rectify the Error.

You must send over a power of Attorney, or come yourself immediately, or you will be in danger of losing your fortune in this State, a word to the wise is Sufficient.

Joseph Peters, Daughter claims an £100 of your Estate; and says you had it, at your Brothers death; and she is about take your land and sell it, to pay the Debt. I am your sincere friend.

J. Leaming

Leaming Rev^d.
Nov. 8, 1784.
rec^d. Jan. 25, 1785.
Ans^d. Feb. 17, 1785.

Society
P.S. I wonder the   have not let me know, that approve of my Endeavor to raise up Doc^r. Johnson, Chh—

We all join in Love to you and Hanah: M^r. Birdseye is much better with whom M^{rs}. Leaming and I live at this time. Your Son is well and has rec^d. your Letter, July 20.

Stratford Feb. 15, 1785,

My dear Sir:

been

The Letters you have sent have   answered. But many of them were a long time before they came to hand. The Letter

'till

you wrote Augt. 11th. did not arrive at New York   the 19

y^e

Jany. this is last I rec^d. altho I had rec^d. two before of a later date. I have rec^d. the Letter directed to M^r. Jarvis and the committee, a few days before. That Letter is not answered. But if you have rec^d. the Letters we wrote before, you have all that you wish to know—If you have not, you may be assured that the Clergy will gladly receive you, in this State, in case you bring Episcopal Authority, from a valid Line. For the Clergy here are resolute to Support the Church, at all Events. And they are upon so good Terms, with the other Denominations, that we have their good wishes that we may succeed. You will think this is strange, but the case is thus, Infidelity is coming in like a flood, and they own that the Chh. is a Bulwark against Infidelity: and say further, that they (the Clergy) of this State will choose a mg^r. for a Bp,

he

that would be as agreeable to them, as   would be to the Chh. That they can confide in the Clergy that will choose one that

is Orthodox in his principles, and regular in his Conduct. This is what I have heard myself from some principal people. The truth is, they have laid down their Arms.

It is a very melancholy thing, to find that some Bps. have lost all their Influence, in matters of a religious Nature. But it will not be long, if this is the case, before they will find themselves in a worse Condition, than the despised Clergy of Connecticut. If they lose their immense Riches, they may be glad to fly to America: But after all the slights they have cast upon us here, we must be very humble indeed to receive them. If they believe that Episcopacy is necessary, they do not act according to their faith.—

If they have Cond to so wisely as to live in friendship and Amity with Each other, and have the love of the Clergy and Laity, of whom they should be afraid, If they have not, every Blast of popular Commotion must frighten them.

But enough of —————

You must not come over without the Episcopal Character.

I have sent money to Miss Maria and I have this day ordered some more, and shall take care of her. I have been cut short in my income by a set of people who went into N. York after the peace; took possession of my houses, lived in them till the Rent amounted to more than £400—and went out without a Copper: indeed nothing could be expected, for they went into the City without any thing. And the City was forced to support with fuel and Bread; and my houses has a tax £100— to support those that lived in them without any Rent, so you see, what is in the world. One third must maintain all the rest.

Adue—dearest heart—

J. Leaming.

The Rev^d. Doc^r. Seabury
To the Care of the)
Rev^d. M^r. Peters   )
Pimlico   )
                 London.

Rec^d. April 23
answe^rd.—23
Ship Minton Capt.
Neutrals.—

[To Samuel Peters:] —————

Stratford Feb. 15, 1785.
Dear Sir:

I now sit down to give you some Advice concerning your Son. There is no Latin School in this Town; and I wished to do something to help him in the Knowledge of the Latin Tongue. But I was disappointed in my View; he does not love his Book, and having no one with him to Stimulate his Ambition, from a disrelish to Learning, he soon contracted an absolute hatred to it. There is no such thing, as you know, as forcing a Child to learn. He is an Active, Sprightly Boy; and if he were placed among a Number of other Lads, his pride would lead him to be one of the foremost of them; and his Abilities would Support him in the Attempt. In this View

of the Affair I sent him back to his Grandfather who is excessively fond of him; and wishes to do every thing in his power to make a man of him: but the old Gentleman, for the troubles he has had have made him *old indeed*. His Son went away after the Law was made, by which his whole Estate was confiscated. And this lay intermixed with his Fathers, in such manner, that the old Gentleman was ruined, unless he bought it. And doing this in his old Age, and no one to help him, he is embarrassed to a great Degree. If he had been able, he would have sent your Son where he might had the best Advantage. It is not want of good will to the Lad, but for want of money. He has expected you would have given a power of Atorney to some one, and that some of the availes of your Estate would have been ordered by you for the Education of your Son. You must see and know, that all M^r. Birdseys hopes are centered in those two grandchildren that are with him. You hurt the old Gentlemans feelings very much, in your last Letter to him, in which you desired him to send you the Account of what Expense he had been at, in bringing up, your Son and you would pay him. He says, he never gave you any Reason, by his Conduct to you, for you to treat him, in such a manner. And therefore was the more surprised to meet with it.

I have sent a Letter, to D^r. Seabury addressed to your care, supposing that the D^r. may have left England before the Letter may reach thither. If that should be the case, make the Letter your own property, my best regards to your Dear Daughter.

Adue, my heart—

J. Leaming.

Leaming Rec^d.
Feby. 15-1785
Rec^d. April 23—
Answ^d. 23—

EBENEZER DIBBLEE.

Ebenezer, a son of Wakefield Dibbee of Danbury, Connecticut, was born about 1715. He graduated from Yale College in 1734. The death in his senior year threw him entirely upon his own exertions for a living. He studied theology and on March 4, 1734-5, the Fairfield East Association licensed him to preach. For ten years he occupied the pulpit of vacant Congregational Churches in Fairfield County, but apparently had no call to settle.

In 1745 he conformed to the Church of England and became lay reader at Stamford. He went to England for ordination in April, 1748, partly at the expense of the parish. He was made deacon and ordained priest in September of that year by the Bishop of London.

In addition to his duties in Stamford and Greenwich he went into Litchfield County and the destitute portion of Westchester County. His ministration at Sharon led to the building of a Church in that town in 1758. He was instrumental in fostering the Church in Danbury and officiated at the opening of a new Church building there in 1763. His work was of the most arduous character but was always done with cheerful content. He had the warm regard of the whole community in which he lived. He remained at his post during the Revolution, and so great was the esteem in which he was held that he was practically undisturbed by mobs or patriot violence. He suffered, however, greatly from the necessary withholding of his stipend from the Venerable Society and the inability of the congregations he served to give him a comfortable support. After the declaration of peace the distress which was everywhere affected him. He, however, continued his ministrations without murmur or complaint until the end of earth came in the eighty-fourth year of his age and the fifty-first of his ministry.

Upon his monument is this eulogium: "He became endeared to all by his unwavering devotion to their best interests, his holy life, and unremitted zeal in the name of Christ and His Church."

Mr. Dibbee married in 1736, Joanna, daughter of Jonathan and Joanna (Selleck) Bates of Stamford.

His son Frederick was for many years a highly honored clergyman in New Brunswick.

It is to be noted that the name is spelled both Dibble and Dibblee. Usually the Rector of Stamford employed two ee's.

State of Connecticut
Stamford Aug^st. 1, 1788.

Reverend and dear
Sir—

I have yours of the 24th of March before me, and note the contents.

The forsaken Miss Sally Thorp, with your approbation, hath this day in my presence, drawn a set of bills upon you for £25 Sterling, payable at ten days sight, in favour of M^r. Moses Rogers merchant in New York. Uppon your honoring the bill, he promises to her the money, with interest, at 5 or 6 p^r cent above par.

Miss Sally wishes me to give you this advice, with her tribute of gratitude.

It is a seasonable favour to Miss, a promising young woman for her years, and manner of Education.—Her parental neglect hath been surprising, as it is reported, her father, through your kind influence, hath a pension and is not under needy circumstances. Her friend's here, are ill able to support her without her own industry. I say no more, in this case, as in many others there is a whele within a whele.

Morice

I received your advice that Doctor had paid you my bill of £25, and advised you that I had drawn a bill upon you for £20 in favour of M^r. Moses Rogers of New York, wishing £5 worth of books might be sent to his care for me; as I have heretofore mentioned; of which, & concerning my son and his prospects, I trust you must have received advice.— Bishop Inglis was expected this month at New Brunswick, and expect soon to hear if Frederick goes into Orders or not.

I am not too much prejudiced in the Bishops fav^r, I have no reason to be, from the character he sustains in many respects, especially from his unpolite treatment of me just before his departure from New York.—Nevertheless since he is honor'd with the Mitre, I sincerely wish and pray he may do honor to religion, the Church of God, and the dignity of the office he sustains. The hearts of Bishops as well as Kings are in the hand of God, and he can turn them as the rivers of water are turned—

Our English Jesuits, I think equal, if not exceed, any in France & Spain—

Great are the expectations, pompous are the representations of the same, of the increasing, flourishing state of the Episcopal Church in genal, in the united States; in New England in particular. Would to God it may be true. The prevailing influence of honor, Power, Reputation, Interest, are against us. Under the present load of public taxes, the unsettled state of our Government I fear not likely to be betterd, by the new revolution or constitution which will undoubtedly take place; together, with the incapacity of the Ch^h to support it self and their dignified Clergy; I can se no such happy & glorious prospect.—

My Church rises but slowly out of its ruins, labours under uncommon obstructions, insufficient for my support, clogged the third time with an expensive law suit, with my good old friend M^r. John Lloyd, demanding *Hundreds,* for what he expended upon it from its infancy to its maturity and to the baneful Independency of the United States—at which period he renounced all connection with me and concern for the Ch^h, and seemingly with as much zeal endeavors to demolish it, as in a laudable manner he endeavoured to raise it up.

The adverse dispensations of providence are great to me and mine. (Gods will be done) Doctor Morice's neglect to answer my last letter to him, and address to the venerable Society, and your Silence, prognosticates; I am in future, in the winter of life, to end my days in want and its constant attendant, contempt.

It is my dear friend, with reluctance I repeat my grievances—I know the goodness of your heart; can no method be devised for my relief, in consequence of my declining, in the winter of life, and cold climate of adversity, to remove to Nova Scotia. Necessity not choice prevents. Heaven forbids it, by my great age & M^rs. Dibble's, now in her 80th year; and in the want of health in the family, the effects of my persevering in that line of duty allotted me during the late Rebellion; out of Loyalty to my Sovereign, and to confirm & preserve his Subjects, and members of my Church in dutiful Obedience to Church and State; at the hazard of all that is dear in life.

I mean not to arraign the conduct of the Venerable Society; but I sincerely thank them for their past favours, and pray God to prosper, & succeed, & reward all their most pious & charible designs, but I see no more merit in fleeing from the storm, than abiding it; nor any more inconsistency, in continuing their vaunted charity to such as remain unable to flee under Royal protection, after the winds & rains abates, but having suffered shipwreck; then in granting their favours to such, as being in the Noon of the life can flee under their Shadow or for the State to continue their Pensions to their Chaplains, residing and officiating as ministers of religion in the United States. Neither can I see why such Loyalists have suffered the loss of all things, for their Loyalty to their Sovereign, and attachment to the british constitution in Ch^h & State, are not equally entitled to Royal favour and recompense, as well as those that fled, not having taken an active part against Government; but were Serving the interests of it effectually, by encouraging persevering Loyalty, amidst the most fiery trials. God bless you my dear Sir, for your past attention to my unhappy Situation, readiness to do good to the suffering State of your countrimen in general, & your brethren in particular.—

But if I am forsaken in my old age, and while I am grey headed, by my best friends and Benefactors, mine integrity I will hold fast, my heart shall not reproach me so long as I live; and the uncommon share of health, I am personally favour'd with, shall be employed in promoting the interest of the best religion, and best constituted Ch^h in the World.—

My time is now short, the fashion of this world will soon pass away; I am sick of this world; were it not for my tender, connexions, am so worn out with trouble, that I could wish to sing good old Simeons nunc dimittis.

All things continue in much in Statu quo.

Doctor Seabury continues to conduct with propriety. No alterations in Ecclesiastical Polity hath taken place.—

Please to make my compliments acceptable to Doctor Morice. No Coalition with B— Seabury takes place. Bishops Provost and White refuse to unite with him in constituting a Bishop for Virginia. Brother Hubberd is meditating a Removal to St. Johns N- Brunswick. Bowdon to West Indies.—

My Prayers & best wishes attend you. Affectionate regards to Mr. Jarvis & his Lady. His friends well. His Sister Levina is addressed by Mr. Todd in Deacons Orders. A likely young Gentleman, a good Speaker. I prophesy a Match.

> Revd. Sir
>
> Yours most Affectionately,
>
> Ebenezre Dibblee.

Revd. Doctor Peters.

Stamford, State of Connecticut
Octobre 22. 1789.

Reverend, Dear Doctor.

The 17th instant Mr. Bates delivered your favor of the 4th of August. I sincerely thank you for the advice you give me, and that the venerable Society in their charity pay any attention to the unhappy incumstanies of your aged brother in Christ, and your most affectionate friend, almost worn out with the troubles of life.

Last May I wrote you a long letter, as soon as I got the affair of Miss Thorps bill setled; with an acknowledgement of the receipt of the books you sent. I have neglected no letter I ever received from you, without a return of my most grateful acknowledgements. I am happy to hear the candle of the Lord Shines bright upon your tabernacle. May the best of heavens blessings always attend you and yours &c.

I am chained down here, to suffer the inflictions of an angry God. Your letter found my family in the greatest adversity.

never

My Daughter Polly, who had fully recovered the steadiness and tranquility of her mind, since by the terrour of our *Sovereign Lords* the Mob in the begining of our late troubles,

of

she was thrown into a state insanity; hath a third time, gradually relapsed into it; for 3 months past I have been confined to close attention to her, scarcely can go out but to attend public duty. She is reduced to the lowest state, her

days

life not expected many; we thot her expiring this morning; but she revived; but still as discomposed. Gods will be done— In this time of life, and scenes of adversity, how could it be that possible for me to remove?

I envy not Mr. Moore, Beach, good Mr. Leaming, their deserved honors. The honour which comes from God, my highest ambition is to obtain.

I can only advert a little to the concerns of the Chn. Bishop Seabury an ornament to the Episcopal character, is gone to

an

Philadelphia, accompanied with Hubbard & Jarvis to adjourned Convention of the Southern States; who have in ample manner recognized his ecclesiastical dignity, a happy Condition we hope will succeed; Unity, Uniformity, in doctrine worship & government be established, without any mutilated Service. But unhappy, Bishop Provost I hear refused to attend P Convention, and treated Bishop Seabury at New York with entire neglect.—I lay down my pen to attend my distressed child.

Mr. Bowden sailed last Saturday week, with his family,

of so

for St. Croix, West Indies, we lament the loss worthy and good a man. Public annimadversions begin to appear, upon the doings of our new Sovereigns the Congress. They treat religion, and the publick support and encouragement of it with neglect. The Chh. must stand upon its own ground: and for the want of a better establishment and support will rise but slowly to a high degree of estimation. Sectaries of every denomination, abound.

Mr. Bates cannot he says furnish me with proper information concerning the power of appointing you my Agent &c. I shall soon forward it.

> Our prayers & best wishes attend you.
> Your ever most affect. Brother
> In adversity.
>
> Ebenezer Dibblee.

Kind compliments wait upon Mr. Jarvis and his Lady.
Reverend Doctor Peters.

Stamford State of Connecticut.
November 6, 1789.

My dear, and Worthy Friend:

Agreeable to the intimation in my last, I have it now in my power to send you my power of Attorney, hoping it may be of service. The kind offices you render me, meets with, and merits, my most grateful acknowledgements.

The melancholy distressed state of my family, in consequence of my Daughter Polly's Insanity, into which she hath relapsed, and continued in ever since, last June, engrosses all my attention, scarce leaves room for parochial duty.

to remove

How could the Venerable Society think it practicable in this time of life, encumbered with a family, ruined by the late Rebellion; and reduced by oppression, for persevering in a line of duty appointed me; or cruelly desert me in this day of adversity and winter of life?

Their charitable interposition and application to Government for the relief of my necessities; which if not successful and the encouragement you give of the renewal of their charity, will merit, and meet with the most grateful resentments.

If there is in your hands or Mr. Jarvis's any money granted by Government, or shall be granted, for the relief of the Widow and children of my unhappy son, I wish it might be stopped and retained for the discharge of a Debt of his to a considerable amount; to the payment of which, I am unexpectedly liable and exposed.

His Widow inherits all the Lands destined to her husband and his effects, &c. &c. &c.

The grand Convention at Philadelphia is broke up, we are to have a federal Chh. as well as State. I have received no particular authentic account of their doings; am only told, mutilations, omissions and alterations in our Service, are inconsiderable & of no importance. As they judged in their superour wisdom. Poor Athanasius is beheaded, his Creed condemned as heretical. Areans Socinians &c. may now fill our Churches.

Bishop Seabury did himself honour, but returned with the loss of a fifth part of his dignity; as four fifths of the lower house of Convocation, made up with lay delegates, will carry any point against the House of Bishops. I suspect this State will not adopt the doings of the general Convention.

The Convocation here, has agreed and unanimously voted, and adopted the Ch^h. of England, as the Standard of Orthodoxy, her form of Government & worship, as the rule of their faith and practice, unconnected with the State.

I may be able, perhaps, in my next to advise you more minutely of the doings of the late council of Trent.

I cannot see how Episcopacy & Republicanism can well coalesce. Bowdon, truly wrote well, as you observed in his first and 2^d. Letter to Stiles; and the Weaver was just and good rod of correction to the pedantick M^r. Sherman. But I cannot see the wisdom of reviving those religious controversies, in our present unsettled state; unless with an evil design to prejudice Government here against the Ch^h. as unfriendly to the united States——— I impatiently wait for your next.

The best of heavens blessings attend you, and yours; is the sincere wish and fervent prayer of,
Reverend Sir

        Your humble Servant
        and most affectionate Brother in Christ.

                Ebenezer Dibblee.
Reverend Doctor Peters.

        Dibblee Rev^d.
        6 Novr. 1789:
        rec^d. March 9-1790.
        ans^d. June 5-90.

            Stamford State of Connecticut
                Semb^r 27, 1790.

My Rev^d. dear Sir:

Your favour of the 5th of June 1790, I received the 25th Instant. In which I have the melancholy advice, that nothing as yet was done for me, either by the Commissioners of American claims, or the Venerable Society—

I am full of anxiety to know my fate. Have you received my power of Atorney &c. &c.? If there be no prospect of relief, I must, at least I can see no other way, to avoid contempt but throw my self upon the Societies Charity, & ask for a living in Nova Scotia, or New Brunswick rather.

Your letter found me, still in the greatest family trouble, Polly is no better, but remains insane, a miserable unhappy object, engaging our whole attention.

The Church slowly & gradually rises out of its ruinous State, but incapable of affording me & dependents an adequate support, & in character, and in this evening of life, & cold climate of adversity to think of removing, it is impossible—Heaven forbids it—I must have my distressed family—The Ch^h under my care will crumble to pieces—No—I hope still, & will cast my burden upon the Lord.

I pray God to still the tumults among the Nations, & prevent the calamities of a general War.

Our Civil & Ecclesiastical Policy is upon no permanent foundation. The bond of peace is broken, and cement to Christian Union—Our new form of Ch^h Government & purification of the Liturgy will take place—but not to the satisfaction of the old English Churchmen—They court B^p. Seabury, but will never coalesce with him in a Consecration of a Bishop. Sectaries abound—Error is multiplied upon Error—Division upon Subdivision—The Ch^h. I fear will become a scene of confusion, discordant forms of worship—Inconsistent

systems of faith—The Lord have mercy upon us,—Make my Compliments acceptable to Harry Lloyd Esqr. & his Lady—Mr. Jarvis & his agreeable Consort; his Connexion^s are well—May you be honord with a Mitre—I hope to meet you in the undisturbed delight of Paradise—My prayers & best wishes attend you—I am with sentiments of unfeigned esteem
        Rev^d. Sir
           Your aged, afflicted Affec^t. B^ro.
                Ebenezer Dibblee.

N.B. I have wrote to the Society & Doctor Morice, Doctor Chandler is gone, for heaven—Doctor Leaming returns to private life—

Sundry of B^p. Seabury's Disciples cannot find Cures.

BELA HUBBARD

SAMUEL PETERS

SKETCHES OF MEMBERS OF THE CONVOCATION

THE RIGHT REVEREND SAMUEL SEABURY, D.D.

Samuel, the second son of Samuel and Abigail (Mumford) Seabury, was born at North Groton (now Ledyard), Connecticut, on November 30, 1729. His father was then officiating as a licentiate of the "Standing Order" in the meeting house of the Second Ecclesiastical Society of Groton located in North Groton, but soon after conformed to the Church of England, was ordained in England and became the first incumbent of St. James' Church, New London. The future bishop was educated by his father and in the common schools of the town until his father's removal to Hempstead, Long Island, in 1742. He entered Yale College in 1744, and graduated with honor in 1748. Mr. Seabury was sent by his father to Huntington, Long Island, as "catechist" in 1748, in which position he was confirmed by the Venerable Society with a salary of ten pounds sterling per annum. He commenced the study of medicine while at Huntington and in 1752 went to Edinburgh to continue his medical course until of age to present himself to the Bishop of London for ordination.

He was made deacon in the Chapel of Fulham Palace on St. Thomas' Day, December 21, 1753, by the Rt. Rev. John Thomas, Bishop of Lincoln, acting for the infirm Bishop of London, Dr. Thomas Sherlock. He was ordained priest in the same chapel on Sunday, December 23, 1753, by the Rt. Rev. Richard Osbaldiston, Bishop of Carlisle.

He was immediately appointed by the Propagation Society to the mission of Christ Church, New Brunswick, New Jersey. In 1757 he went to Grace Church, Jamaica, from which he removed in 1766 to the Rectorship of St. Peter's Church, Westchester County, New York. To add to his small income he opened while at Westchester a classical school.

As the Revolution approached, with his friends Dr. Chandler, Dr. Inglis, and the Hon. Isaac Wilkins, he allied himself with the cause of the united British Empire, which to his mind included the welfare of the Church of England, and wrote strongly in its favor. His "Letters of a Westchester Farmer" are an excellent specimen of his style in political controversy. He was also for several years the Secretary of the Voluntary Conventions of the Clergy of New York and New Jersey which some from Connecticut occasionally attended.

He was roughly treated by the patriots in his neighborhood, compelled at various times to conceal himself and on one occasion was taken to New Haven and treated with much indignity. Upon his release from confinement he returned to Westchester, but was soon obliged, early in 1776, to close the churches in his parish and join the numerous loyalists in the city of New York. After the departure of General Washington from Manhattan Island in September, 1776, he officiated, in turn with other clergymen who had left their parishes, for the refugees in the old City Hall on Wall Street. In 1778 he was appointed to the charge of St. Andrew's Church, Staten Island, but found it unsafe to take up his residence there.

His support for seven years came from the stipend of fifty pounds a year from the Venerable Society, the practice of medicine, and his chaplaincy of the Royal American Regiment of Colonel Edmund Fanning. He was made a Doctor in Divinity by Oxford University in 1778. With his election and acceptance of the Bishopric of Connecticut came a new period in Dr. Seabury's life. He went to England in July, 1783, in the flagship of Admiral Digby. His noble and unceasing efforts to induce the Bishops in England to rise above political and traditional precedents and consecrate him under a special act of Parliament, form a chapter of pathetic interest in our annals. In the summer of 1784 he made a formal application to the Bishops of the Church in Scotland to consecrate him. Upon their favorable answer he journeyed to Aberdeen and was consecrated a Bishop in the Church of God, in Bishop Skinner's chapel in Long Acre, Aberdeen on Sunday, November 14, 1784 by the Primus, Dr. Robert Kilgour of Aberdeen, Dr. Arthur Petrie of Moray and Ross, and Dr. John Skinner, Coadjutor Bishop of Aberdeen. He returned to London immediately after and sailed for America in March, 1785. He spent some weeks among relatives in Nova Scotia and arrived at Newport, Rhode Island, on June 20, 1785. It is unnecessary here to trace the events of his Episcopate, some details of which will be found in the introduction and text of these "Records".

Bishop Seabury died suddenly on February 25, 1796 in the sixty-seventh year of his age.

THE REVEREND BELA HUBBARD, D.D.

Bela, a son of Daniel and Diana (Ward) Hubbard, was born in Guilford, Connecticut, on August 27, 1739. He was prepared for college in the common schools and at home. In his fourteenth year he entered Yale College, from which he was graduated in 1758. He then enjoyed a year of theological study with his relative by marriage, the Rev. Dr. Samuel Johnson, President of King's College, New York.

In 1761 he became lay reader at Christ Church in his native town, under the oversight of the Rev. Ebenezer Punderson, of New Haven, whose missionary circuit included Guilford.

In the fall of 1763, in company with Abraham Jarvis, his life-long friend, and William Walter of Roxbury, Massachusetts, he went "home" to England for ordination.

On Sunday, February 5, 1764, in "the Royal Chapel of St. James, Westminster," he was made deacon by the Rt. Rev. Frederick Keppel, Bishop of Exeter, acting for the infirm Bishop of London, Dr. Richard Osbaldiston. On Sunday, February 19, 1764, in "the parish Church of St. James, Westminster," he was ordained priest by the Rt. Rev. Charles Lyttleton, Bishop of Carlisle, acting for the Bishop of London. Upon his return he took charge of Christ Church, Guilford, and St. John's, North Guilford, to which he soon added a congregation in Killingworth, now Clinton, "a seaport Town 10 miles distant."

He occasionally officiated in remoter places, as Saybrook, Branford, New Haven, Litchfield. His work was fruitful and acceptable. His salary came wholly from his parishioners and was only thirty pounds sterling per annum. The Venerable Society at that time did not think it expedient to form any new missions in New England and would not make any appropriation for Guilford. In 1767 he accepted the joint rectorship of Trinity Church, New Haven, and Christ Church, West Haven, at an increased salary.

He was a resident of New Haven in the critical days of the Revolution. Although a pronounced loyalist, he retained the full esteem of the patriots. His services to the Church in Connecticut at the formative period are great and deserve recognition. His ability as a parish priest and his theological learning were recognized by his alma mater by the degree of Doctor in Divinity in 1804. After an incumbency of forty-five years in one parish Bela Hubbard rested from his earthly labors on Sunday, December 6, 1812, in the seventy-fourth year of his age and the forty-eighth of his ministry.

In the present Trinity Church, New Haven, which his zeal and tact made possible, there is in the chancel an appropriate monument setting forth his excellencies.

THE RIGHT REVEREND ABRAHAM JARVIS, D.D.

Abraham, the sixth son and ninth child of Captain Samuel and Naomi (Brush) Jarvis, was born at Norwalk, Connecticut, on May 5, 1739. He was carefully trained in the district school and at home, and then placed under the tuition of the Rev. Noah Wells, the Congregational minister of Stratford, to be prepared for college. He became a student at Yale when eighteen and graduated with honor in 1761.

He went immediately after to Middletown to officiate as lay reader in Christ Church. He also pursued by himself a course in theology, presumably set forth for him by the learned Dr. Samuel Johnson.

About 1762 it becoming necessary to leave his work to be inoculated for the small pox, he resided for several months at Elizabeth Town, New Jersey, in the family of the Rev. Dr. Thomas Bradbury Chandler, the well-read theologian and acute pleader for an American Episcopate. Under him he probably completed his course in theology.

In the fall of 1763, in company with his intimate friend, Bela Hubbard, and William Walter of Roxbury, Massachusetts, he sailed for England to seek holy orders. His expenses were defrayed by a subscription of the members of the Middletown parish. He was made deacon in "the royal Chapel of St. James, Westminster," on Sunday, February 5, 1764, by the Rt. Rev. Frederick Keppel, Bishop of Exeter.

He was ordained priest in "the parish Church of St. James, Westminster," on Sunday, February 19, 1764, by the Rt. Rev. Charles Lyttleton, Bishop of Carlisle.

Both of these ordinations, at which his companions also were ordained, were by special commission from the aged and feeble Bishop of London, Dr. Richard Osbaldiston, who, as had his predecessors, exercised jurisdiction over the American Colonies. He sailed for America in April and was again at work in June. He had been duly chosen as Rector of Christ Church, Middletown. An annual salary of seventy pounds sterling was pledged to him by the parish. For some reason not now to be ascertained, the Venerable Society declined to continue the stipend of

twenty pounds which had been allowed to the Rev. Ichabod Camp, the first Rector and Missionary. Mr. Jarvis became a true pastor not only for the people in Middletown, but in all the surrounding country. He greatly encouraged the small band of churchmen in Hartford by his presence, his services and his advice. There would have been rapid growth in Hartford had the suggestion to make Middletown and Hartford a mission under Mr. Jarvis met with the approval of the authorities in England.

His energy and success as a parish priest are shown by a memorandum made a few years after his ordination, in which three hundred and sixty-five souls, of whom one hundred and fifty were communicants, are recorded as under his charge. The esteem in which Mr. Jarvis was held by his brethren and the active part he took in the organization of the Church in Connecticut, his wisdom and prudence in all the steps taken for a true General Convention, are detailed in the introduction to these "Records."

With the continued regard and affection of his parishioners he served them in holy things for thirty-five years.

Upon the death of Bishop Seabury, at the special Convention held in Trinity Church, New Haven, on May 5, 1796, he was chosen Bishop. As there had been a diversity of opinion among the clergy and some opposition by prominent laymen, he immediately declined the election.

When Dr. Bowden, who in October, 1796, had been elected, finally declined the Episcopate, Mr. Jarvis was unanimously elected for the third time, by his brethren at the annual convention held in St. James's Church, Derby, on June 7, 1797. He accepted and was consecrated in Trinity Church, New Haven, on the feast of St. Luke, October 18, 1797. The sermon was preached by the Rev. Dr. William Smith, of St. Paul's Church, Norwalk. It is one of the five instances in the history of the American Church when the sermon at the consecration of a Bishop has been by a priest.[1]

[1] The others are: The Rev. Dr. William Smith, Provost of the University of Pennsylvania, preached at the consecration of Dr. Claggett, 1792; Dr. Robert Smith, 1795; and Dr. Bass, 1797. The Rev. Dr. Frederick Beasley preached at the consecration of Mr. Chase in 1819.

The consecrators were the presiding Bishop, Dr. William White, and the Bishop of New York (Dr. Provoost), and the Bishop of Massachusetts (Dr. Bass). Yale College conferred on him, in 1797, the degree of Doctor in Divinity.

The second Bishop of Connecticut was faithful in his administration of the Diocese and saw a moderate but real growth. During his later years he was afflicted with asthma and any clerical duty was done with difficulty, but he never allowed his bodily infirmity to interfere with his official and religious obligations. In 1799 he removed to Cheshire, where the Episcopal Academy, under Dr. Bowden, was coming into favorable knowledge of the people.

The "Records" give particulars of the unhappy incident of his Episcopate, the career of Ammi Rogers in the Diocese, and other events of diocesan life in which the Bishop took an active part.

In 1803 Bishop Jarvis removed to New Haven, where he passed the remainder of his days.

He departed this life at New Haven on May 3, 1813, having lived nearly seventy-four years.

When the present Trinity Church was erected his body was removed from the public cemetery and buried beneath the chancel. An elegant Gothic monument with a classic and affectionate Latin inscription written by his son, the distinguished scholar, Dr. Samuel Farmar Jarvis, adorns the walls of the Church.

The Reverend GIDEON BOSTWICK, M.A.

Gideon, the fifth son and eighth child of Captain Nathaniel and Esther (Hitchcock) Bostwick, was born in New Milford, Connecticut, on September 21, 1742. He was strictly brought up in the pious ways of the "Standing Order." He was educated principally at home and then fitted for college by the celebrated Nathaniel Taylor, the Congregational minister of New Milford. He entered Yale College in 1758, sustained a high rank throughout his course and graduated with honor in 1762. He had, under the influence of an intimate friend and classmate, "declared" for the Church of England. As then there was little prospect of a new mission being erected in any part of New England by the Venerable Society, he went, at the suggestion of the Rev. Thomas Davies, Rector of St. John's, New Milford, and an ardent missionary, to Great Barrington, Massachusetts. A small and vigorous parish had been founded there under the auspices of the Rev. Solomon Palmer and the Rev. Thomas Davies. Mr. Bostwick became the lay reader and opened a classical school, which from the first was successful. The young candidate was not content with merely reading the service on Sunday, but did such

pastoral work as a layman could, and went into the surrounding country to seek out the lost or strayed sheep of Christ.

In 1769 such strength had been developed that it seemed expedient to the clergy of Connecticut, with which the work had always been connected, to make an effort to obtain a grant from the Venerable Society and the erection by it of a mission to include Great Barrington and Lanesborough in Berkshire County, together with Nobletown and New Concord on the New York side of the Berkshire Hills, in what was aptly called "a wilderness country."

A petition from the four congregations was prepared and universally signed, asking for recognition by the Society, a stipend, and the ordination of Mr. Bostwick. With this and a commendatory letter from the clergy of New York, Mr. Bostwick went to England late in 1769. He was successful in his quest. The Society broke its rule, erected the Berkshire Mission, assigned to it a stipend of twenty-five pounds sterling per annum and appointed Mr. Bostwick the Missionary upon his ordination. After due examination he was made deacon by the Bishop of London, the Rt. Rev. Dr. Richard Terrick, on St. Matthias' Day, February 24, 1770, in the royal Chapel of St. James. He was ordained priest by the same Bishop on Sunday, March 11, 1770, "in the Chapel Royal at Saint James's Palace in Westminster."[1]

After a pleasant passage of six weeks, he arrived at New York on May 29, and reached his mission on June 4.

From that day he was abundant in labors laying foundations to be afterward built upon. He made a house to house visitation in the newly settled towns of what is now Columbia County, New York, Bennington County, Vermont, and Berkshire County, Massachusetts. For the earlier years of his ministry his services were almost daily. His letters show him to be active, diligent, and discerning. His influence over those who had moved into this northern portion of New England after the old French war was very great. His private register records in his ministry of twenty-three years the baptism of two thousand two hundred and seventy-four children and eighty-one adults, the marriage of one hundred and twenty-seven couples and the burials of eighty-four persons. There is hardly another record equal to it in the missionary annals of our country. The "Records" show that Mr. Bostwick was honored in the Diocese. Much of his work was ephemeral for many promising settlements never attained maturity, but enough remains to keep green the memory of a true herald of the Cross, notably St. James's, Great Barrington, Trinity, Lenox, and Christ Church, Hudson, New York. Upon his return from the Convocation and Convention at Middletown on June 5, 1793, where he had presented his friend and lay reader at Lanesborough, Mr. Daniel Burhans, for ordination, he rode a hard-trotting horse. When he arrived at his old home in New Milford, he was taken violently and dangerously ill as the result. After lingering in much pain for some days, he entered into the rest of Paradise on June 13, 1793, in the fifty-first year of his age. Over his grave in the lower cemetery at Great Barrington, friends erected a handsome marble monument appropriately inscribed.

[1] Mr. Bostwick's letter of Orders as priest is in the custody of the writer.

The Reverend JAMES SAYRE, M.A.

James Sayre is supposed to have been born in Scotland in 1745. He is said to have come to America with his older brother John, while a boy.

He studied at the College of Philadelphia when that institution was under the presidency of Dr. William Smith. He was graduated in 1765 in the same class with Bishop White.

Removing to New York City, he studied law and was admitted to the bar in 1771. His brother John had been ordained in 1768 and taken charge of an extensive mission on the west bank of the Hudson, which included Newburgh, New Windsor, and Walden. He was laborious and successful. It was possibly through his persuasion and influence that Mr. Sayre abandoned the law and sailed in the summer of 1774 for England. He was ordained in the fall of that year and was licensed to officiate in the Plantations on September 21, 1774.

A manuscript note on the margin of the Book of Licenses of the Diocese of London assigns him to "Fredericksburgh precinct." This term evidently indicates the region bordering on Connecticut east of Poughkeepsie, Peekskill, Fishkill, and other towns on the east bank of the Hudson. It was sparsely settled and spiritually destitute.

There had been intermittent church work in the river towns from 1765, when the Rev. Samuel Seabury made a missionary tour and held the first services. The Rev. John Beardsley became, in 1761, the missionary in Dutchess County, and in 1766 was promoted to the rectorship of Poughkeepsie. Probably it was to assist him by caring for the "back country," as Mr. Beardsley's work was over a wide area, that Mr. Sayre was ordained.

The commencement of actual hostilities with England taking place soon after his return, it is extremely doubtful if he remained long in the precinct.

In 1775 he accepted a commission as chaplain to one of the loyalist battalions raised by Colonel De Lancey. Camp life and the monotony of service in and near the city of New York, to which the British were principally confined, was irksome. His power as a preacher was acknowledged by all who heard him and his reading of the service was impressive and solemn.

He felt that it was a great relief to be asked to officiate for the few churchmen at Brooklyn Ferry, then a hamlet of about sixty houses and less than two thousand people. Previously they had traveled the long distance to Grace Church, Jamaica, or crossed the East River to worship in Trinity Church or one of its chapels.

Mr. Sayre commenced his work in Brooklyn in 1778 and continued it for five years. His success in the little village, now part of a great city, can only be inferred from the fact that in 1787 a parish was organized.

The archives of St. Ann's, the mother parish of Brooklyn, contain the record of only one official act of Mr. Sayre. It is a copy of a baptismal certificate dated August 20, 1783, and signed

"James Sayre, Minister of the Church at Brooklyn Ferry."

Upon the evacuation of New York City by the British on November 25, 1783, Mr. Sayre, with many other loyalists, went under the escort of the fleet to St. John, New Brunswick. Here a tract of land had been assigned him. He does not appear to have had any settled congregation or sought any parish. He evidently was not placed on the list of the Venerable Society's missionaries and the poor refugees were unable to give adequate salaries to their ministers.

After an experience not altogether pleasant, he returned to the United States and seems to have been in Connecticut in the spring of 1784. In June, 1784, he became the minister of Trinity Church, Branford, Christ Church, Guilford, and St. John's, North Guilford. He resided in Branford, giving three-quarters of his time to Branford and Guilford and the other quarter to North Guilford. He was both active and popular. In the following year efforts were made to induce him to live in Guilford, but without success. He resigned in the spring of 1786 and went to live in Fairfield, where the Rev. Philo Shelton was Rector.

In July, 1786, Bishop Seabury recommended him to the vestry of Trinity Church, Newport, one of the important parishes of New England, as "a worthy and prudent man," of "good understanding" who "reads prayers much to my satisfaction."

Mr. Sayre accepted the invitation to visit Newport sent during the summer and removed to that town in October, 1786.

For nearly a year he was beloved and respected by all his parishioners. An unhappy conflict with some of the prominent laymen in the parish then occurred, principally concerning the revision of the Prayer Book, and for two years there was bitter controversy and mutual discontent. Finally, by the intervention of Bishop Seabury, the pastoral relation was dissolved and Mr. Sayre returned to Fairfield in the early days of 1789.

The parish at Stratford became vacant by the resignation of Mr. Leaming in 1790. Its members esteemed Mr. Sayre highly and had endeavored to have him visit them during the Revolution, but permission was refused by the civil authority. They were now glad to call him as their rector. His services were peculiarly acceptable to them and they gave him a loyal and sincere support.

The fixed conviction of Mr. Sayre that the revision of the Prayer Book at Philadelphia was unnecessary and deprived it of essential features; that laymen should never have any influence or authority in the Church, or sit in ecclesiastical conventions, he so strongly impressed upon the people of Christ Church that they determined never to use the new book or to approve the union of the Church in the United States.

The text of the "Records" shows the serious and unpleasant consequences of this course.

The Rev. John Bowden was then living in Stratford. He had the cordial good will and respect of the churchmen of the parish. With the desire of convincing them of their error and leading them to see the absurdity of their position, he wrote in March, 1792, an affectionate and logical "Address" and a "Letter" to Mr. Sayre.[1] His letter to Mr. Sayre

[1] An Address from John Bowden, A.M. to the Members of the Episcopal Church in Stratford, to which is added a Letter to the Rev. Mr. James Sayre. * * * New Haven: Printed by T. and S. Green. n. d. 12mo, pp. 39.

rehearses the manner in which Mr. Bowden was welcomed by Mr. Sayre, and their pleasant relations until Mr. Sayre made his "Protest."

The change that then occurred is noted, Mr. Sayre's abuse of his brethren mentioned, and he is asked to reconsider and pause before leading "a congregation into a separation that must in a few years end in

their ruin."

The effect of the "Address" upon the parish was slowly apparent and Mr. Sayre was compelled to resign at Easter, 1793. He removed to Woodbury and became the rector of St. Paul's Church. Here again he aroused the people of that staid old parish to open defiance of the whole Diocese and refusal to submit to the constituted authorities. But in July, 1794, Woodbury conformed and Mr. Sayre was once more obliged to leave his home. He spent the remainder of his days in Fairfield. It is said that he continued to denounce bitterly the Bishop and clergy, finally renouncing the Church of his fathers. He died in 1798, in the fifty-third year of his age. It was learned after his death, that he had been for some years mentally unbalanced.

His life is a sad instance of perverted energy and misdirected zeal.

The Reverend PHILO SHELTON, M.A.

Philo, a son of Samuel Shelton, was born in Ripton (now Huntington), Connecticut, on May 5, 1754. His ancestors had been churchmen in the days when it meant persecution and much personal abuse. His grandfather, Daniel Shelton, a pioneer of the town and a large land owner, had been one of the founders and benefactors of St. Paul's Church in that village.

Mr. Shelton was carefully trained in the ways of the Church. He attended the district school, where only a slight knowledge of the rudiments of education could be obtained. He also came under the instruction of his pastor, the Rev. Christopher Newton, aand when seventeen years old was ready for college. He was graduated with honor from Yale College in 1775.

He had early determined to study for the holy ministry. His son, the Rev. Dr. William Shelton, states that his theological course was pursued with the Rev. James Scovill, Rector of St. John's, Waterbury, a man of excellent attainments and sound judgment. The condition of Connecticut during the Revolution did not allow any new church work to be undertaken.

As noted in the "Introduction," several clergymen were able to keep open their churches.

It is probable that Mr. Shelton while with Mr. Scovill aided him as lay reader in his widely extended parish, which included Waterbury, Westbury (now Watertown), Northbury (now Plymouth), and New Cambridge (now Bristol). On July 8, 1779, Fairfield was burned by the British under General Tryon, when the church, rectory, meeting houses, and many dwellings were destroyed. The minister of Trinity Church, the Rev. John Sayre, with his family, lost everything and became a refugee in New York.

On August 24, 1779, a meeting of members of the parish was held at the house of Mr. John Sherwood at Greenfield.

It was resolved "to apply to Mr. Shelton at Ripton in order to hire him to officiate for them if Mr. Shelton will please to come."

A regular routine for the three sections of the parish, Fairfield, Stratfield (now Bridgeport), and North Fairfield (now Weston), was made out. Mr. Shelton accepted and for six years faithfully read the service according to the routine, visited the people in every part of the parish and accumulated much experience for his future ministry.

With several other Connecticut candidates, Mr. Shelton patiently waited for the return of the Bishop-designate invested with the Episcopal character.

On August 3, 1785, he was presented in Christ Church, Middletown, to "Samuel, Bishop of Connecticut," to be made deacon. The others ordained at this memorable first ordination by a Bishop of the American Church were: Ashbel Baldwin, of Litchfield; Henry Van Dyck, of Milford, and Colin Ferguson, of Maryland. The evidence of these "Records" and the tradition of Mr. Shelton's descendants and the older clergy of the Diocese show that he was the first deacon ordained in the Church in the United States. Mr. Shelton was ordained priest by Bishop Seabury in Trinity Church, New Haven, on September 16, 1785.

Upon his return home, he entered upon the rectorship of the parish he had served as lay reader. His incumbency continued throughout his life.

The work done by him was large and encouraging.

His "Parochiales Notitiae" show that in the forty years of his ministry he baptized nineteen hundred and seventy-eight persons, four hundred and fifty-four persons were confirmed, five hundred and eighty persons had become communicants, and eight hundred and thirty-eight persons had been buried.[1]

New churches were built in Fairfield in 1790, and in the borough of

[1] The Rev. Dr. Guilbert in his "Annals of an Old Parish" (New York: T. Whittaker, 1898) has printed this valuable document as Appendix I., pp. 183–273. The original is in the possession of Mr. Hamilton Shelton of Bridgeport.

Bridgeport in 1801. Mr. Shelton paid much attention to developing the Church in the new borough, which was rapidly filling up with an intelligent population. He was, however, zealous in maintaining the work in the other portions of the parish.

At Easter, 1824, as he felt the growing infirmities of age, he resigned the charge of St. John's, Bridgeport, and confined his attention to Fairfield. Mr. Shelton died on February 27, 1825, in the seventy-first year of his age. He was buried under the chancel of Trinity Church on Mill Plain, Fairfield. A tablet to his memory was placed in the church.

Subsequently his body was removed to Mountain Grove Cemetery, Bridgeport, where an elaborate monument of Italian marble suitably inscribed has been erected.

Few clergymen were more beloved, honored and trusted. He held many responsible offices in the gift of the Convention and of the Convocation. He was almost continuously from 1795 a member of the Standing Committee, and from 1801 a deputy to the General Convention. During the vacancy in the Episcopate from 1813-1816, he as senior presbyter presided in the Diocesan Convention. In a letter to Mrs. Shelton, Bishop Brownell gives this estimate of his character: "I feel that I have lost one of my best friends and counsellors, and that the Diocese has lost one of its best patterns of ministerial faithfulness and Christian simplicity."

The Reverend ASHBEL BALDWIN, M.A.

Ashbel, a son of Isaac Baldwin, was born in Litchfield, Connecticut, on March 7, 1757.

His father, a graduate of Yale in 1735, had commenced life as licentiate for the Congregational ministry and preached for some time in that portion of Litchfield County now the town of Washington. He abandoned the ministry for farming and became a useful and public spirited citizen of Litchfield.

Mr. Baldwin sent two of his sons to Yale College after they had been prepared in the common schools and under his own direction. Isaac, the elder, was graduated in 1774, and Ashbel, the younger, in 1776. Both achieved distinction in their classes.

It was in the early days of the Revolution and Litchfield County was thoroughly patriotic. The young graduate with several of his classmates was eager to enter the army. Circumstances, however, compelled Mr. Ashbel Baldwin to accept a private tutorship, as have many other of Yale's brightest men. He was pleasantly situated in a delightful home in Dutchess County, New York, near the Hudson River. The family were members of the Church of England. It was at that time customary for the tutors in the old colonial families to conduct the family worship, and when the house was remote from church to read the service and a sermon to the household and neighbors. When called upon for this duty, Mr. Baldwin, who had been brought up a strict Congregationalist, was perplexed, for his ignorance of the Prayer Book was profound. A friendly gardener on the place, whom he consulted, made him familiar with the Book. He then read the service with fervor and intelligence. From admiration of the pure English and devotional fervor of the prayers he advanced to a belief in the doctrines expressed in the Prayer Book. By study and examination, he became thoroughly convinced that the Church of England was a pure branch of the Catholic Church of Christ, and conformed to it.

At the close of his tutorship, about 1778, he secured a position as quartermaster in the commissary department of the Connecticut line of the Continental army, and was stationed at Litchfield in charge of a large depot of stores, many of which had been surrendered at Saratoga by General Burgoyne. Much to his regret, he could not engage in active service, as imprudence in swimming when a boy had brought on a permanent lameness and shortening of one of his legs.

His studies for the ministry were probably pursued by himself with the advice of his friend and neighbor, the Rev. Richard Clarke of New Milford.

He was in attendance as a spectator at the convocation of the clergy at Woodbury, on the feast of the Annunciation, 1783, when the first Bishop of Connecticut was chosen. During the absence of the incumbent, the Rev. James Nichols, in some other part of his mission, Mr. Baldwin read the service at Litchfield. When Mr. Nichols removed to Sandgate, Vermont, Mr. Baldwin was invited to take charge as lay reader. A parish by the name of Saint Michael's Church, Litchfield, was incorporated under the state law in October, 1784.

Mr. Baldwin was invited by representatives of St. John's, North Guilford, and Christ Church, Guilford, in November, 1784, to take the lay readership in those parishes at a salary of eighty pounds, Connecticut currency, which was then equal to forty pounds sterling, and the rector-

ship when ordained. As he had already commenced his work at Litchfield, he felt obliged to decline.

At the first ordination by Bishop Seabury in Christ Church, Middletown, on August 3, 1785, he, with three others, was made deacon. He was ordained priest in Trinity Church, New Haven, on September 18, 1785, by the same Bishop.

He immediately entered upon the rectorship of St. Michael's, Litchfield.

His work was well planned and carefully carried out, both in the parish and county. He went all over the beautiful hills of Litchfield County reviving the courage of neglected and depressed Church folk. He saw that closed churches were opened, officiated in them himself, and, whenever possible, had the parochial organization completed and clergymen provided for them.

With sound wisdom he continued the excellent work of those ardent missionaries, Solomon Palmer, Thomas Davies, and Richard Clarke.

In 1793 he became Rector of Christ Church, Stratford, and spent thirty years of faithful service in that parish, adding to his labors some successful missionary effort in the surrounding region. For many years he took charge of Christ Church, Tashua, which as North Stratford had once been part of the mother parish. As Mr. Baldwin grew older he felt that the work of the parish needed a younger man, and in 1824 he resigned.

But to one full of energy, although verging on old age, idleness was impossible, and Mr. Baldwin began to officiate at Southington and Meriden, where the Church was beginning to make progress. These places quickly felt the benefit of his ministrations.

In 1827 he took charge of St. John's, North Haven, and St. Paul's, Wallingford. After five years of gratifying prosperity for these ancient parishes, he accepted temporarily the rectorship of St. Peter's, Oxford, and Christ Church, Quaker Farms. Here amid rural and pleasant surroundings, he spent two years. In 1834 he found that his eyesight was failing and other marks of old age were so apparent that active work for him must cease. For a few years after his resignation he lived in New Haven, Bridgeport, and Stratford.

To the Convention of the Diocese in 1837 Mr. Baldwin sent a touching and pathetic letter, resigning his office as trustee of the Episcopal Academy, in which he graphically contrasted the condition of the Church in Connecticut when he was ordained and its rapid progress in fifty-two years. "My days of pilgrimage, I know, are almost closed, and I can do no more than to be in readiness by the grace of God to leave the Church Militant in peace. May I be permitted, Sir, to ask the prayers of my Bishop and his clergy that my last days may be happy?"

His closing years were spent in the family of an old friend who had removed from Connecticut to Rochester, New York, and who gladly made cheerful for him the weary hours of inaction. He ended his earthly life on Sunday, February 8, 1846, having nearly reached the age of eighty-nine years. Mr. Baldwin had a clear and logical mind. He was a ready speaker and could put into writing important papers, resolutions, or debates, with accurate rapidity. This made his service as secretary of the Convocation, as secretary of the Convention of the Diocese for thirty years, and as secretary of the House of Clerical and Lay Deputies of the General Convention for twelve years, invaluable.

Mr. Baldwin held nearly every position in the gift of the Diocese and filled each with efficiency and dignity.

At the time of his death he was the oldest clergyman of the American Church and the oldest graduate of Yale College.

The Reverend PHILO PERRY, M.A.

Philo, a son of Dr. Joseph and Ruth (Preston) Perry, was born in Woodbury, Connecticut, on December 22, 1752. His father was a well known physician.

His early education was received in the common schools and under the careful guidance of his father. In his twenty-first year he entered Yale College and was graduated in 1777.

He studied medicine and settled in Stratford, where he built up an extensive practice.

It is probable that he attended Christ Church, then lovingly served by the Rev. Jeremiah Leaming, and through his influence entered upon a course of theology.

With David Belden, "Tilley" Bronson and Reuben Ives, he was recommended for ordination by the Convocation at Derby in September, 1786. The four candidates were made deacons on the feast of St. Matthew, September 21, 1786, in Christ Church, Derby, by Bishop Seabury.

On January 9, 1787, Mr. Perry became the Rector of Trinity Church, Newtown.

This parish, one of the very oldest in the Diocese, had been organized in 1732 by the Rev. John Beach, of blessed memory, whose long and brave witness for the truth as this Church hath received the same, had built up congregations in Newtown and Redding, which were the largest of our communion in the colony.

The four years since the death of Mr. Beach, on March 19, 1782, and the ravages of the Revolution had somewhat impaired its strength.

Mr. Perry entered upon his work with great enthusiasm; by faithful industry, patience and tact he repaired the waste places of the parish. Mr. Perry was ordained priest in St. John's Church, Stamford, on Trinity Sunday, June 3, 1787, by Bishop Seabury, "upon a Title," says the Bishop's Register, "from Christ's Church, Newton, and from the Church at Newberry."[1]

As a pastor Mr. Perry was constant, both in personal appeals for holiness of life and frequent in his visitations of his parishioners. He is represented as a man of genial manners, a modest demeanor, and sufficient learning.

His ability as a preacher can be partly judged by an extract of a manuscript sermon of Mr. Perry in the possession of the writer from the text: "Endeavoring to keep the unity of the Spirit in the bond of peace." Ephesians iv, 3. After considering the circumstances under which the Epistle was written he develops the theme: "We cannot preserve 'the unity of the Spirit' unless we hold to the doctrines taught by the Spirit." In the course of his argument, he insists upon true Christian charity to all men and the duty of Christian forgiveness. In conclusion, he says: "Now, to sum up the whole in a few words: If we have any regard to the welfare of the Church, if we have any regard to our own welfare in the present life, and to our complete felicity in the next, let us all, my friends & Brethren, endeavour, by all the means in our power, 'to keep the unity of the Spirit in the bond of peace.' As to doctrines, let us 'be perfectly joined together in the same mind & in the same judgment,'—unanimously grounded & settled in the truly excellent and apostolical doctrines of our Church;—not being 'tossed to & fro, & carried about with every wind of doctrine by the sleight of men, & cunning craftiness, whereby they lie in wait to deceive; for this never fails to end in schism and separation.

"As to our behaviour one toward another; let it be always such as to show forth that meek & quiet spirit, which in the sight of God is of great price,' that heavenly wisdom which is peaceable, gentle & easy to be entreated. Let us put away all bitterness & wrath & anger & clamour & evil speaking with all malice; & be kind one to another, tender hearted, forgiving one another, even as God for Christ's sake hath forgiven us.' If we will thus be directed & governed by the Gospel law of Charity, it will be no difficult matter to preserve unity, peace, & concord in the Ch[h] which that we may do, & finally be united with the Church triumphant in Heaven, God of his infinite mercy grant, thro our Lord Jesus Christ. To whom &c., &c."[2]

[1] P. 6. *A Reprint in full of the Registry of Ordinations by Bishops Seabury and Jarvis.* As published in the Journal of A. D. 1882, by order of the Convention.

[2] From a collection of manuscript sermons, made by the Rev. Dr. Burhans. This sermon is endorsed: Newtown, Nov[r]. 6, 1791, and Sept[r]. 29, 1793. Another sermon of Mr. Perry from Romans viii, 16, is endorsed: Newtown, Aug[t]. 7, 1796, Aug[t]. 13, 1797, and Brookfield, May 6, 1798.

Within five years after Mr. Perry's settlement in Newtown a new church seemed necessary. It replaced that built in 1746, which was forty-six feet long and thirty-five feet wide.

The new church was considered very spacious and elegant and served the parish for nearly eighty years.

The consecration was on Thursday, September 19, 1793, by Bishop Seabury, it being the fifth church consecrated by him in the Diocese.

Mr. Perry continued for five years more to minister in holy things to the people of Newtown, but in the midst of his usefulness he departed this life on October 26, 1798, in the forty-sixth year of his age.

While still young in his ministry, he had obtained the confidence and regard of his Bishop and brethren of the clergy.

He was secretary of the Convocation, secretary of the Convention, a member and secretary of the Standing Committee, and a deputy to the General Convention.

When the present Trinity Church, Newtown, was consecrated on June 8, 1882, there were unveiled four mural tablets of marble and brass commemorating the founder and three other rectors of the parish. Upon that in memory of Mr. Perry there is this truthful inscription:

"He was the devoted and efficient Rector of this Parish—and a Clergyman of eminence in the Councils of the Church."

THE REVEREND REUBEN IVES, M.A.

Reuben, a son of Mr. Zachariah Ives, was born in Cheshire, Connecticut, on October 26, 1762.

His early life and preliminary education were in his native town. In his twentieth year he entered Yale College, from which he was graduated in 1786.

It had been from boyhood his cherished desire to enter the holy ministry. The lack of clergymen was so great in the Diocese that Bishop Seabury was willing to ordain him without full theological preparation with the understanding that he would give attention to such studies during his diaconate. Mr. Ives was recommended for ordination by the Convocation during its meeting at Derby in September, 1786.

On St. Matthew's Day, September 21, 1786, he was made deacon with three others, in Christ Church, Derby, by Bishop Seabury.

The great privilege was accorded to the young deacon of becoming a member of the Bishop's household and pursuing under his direction a thorough course in patristic and Anglican theology, liturgics and Church history. Mr. Ives also had practical instruction in pastoral theology by acting as the Bishop's assistant in St. James's Church, New London, and during the necessary absences of the Bishop taking charge of the pastoral work.

On St. Matthias' Day, February 24, 1788, Reuben Ives, Tillotson Bronson and Chauncey Prindle were ordained priests, and Edward Blakeslee made deacon in St. James's Church, New London, by Bishop Seabury.

He became at once Rector of St. Peter's Church, Cheshire.

The earliest services of the Church in that town, which was until 1780 "the western society of Wallingford," although the name New Cheshire was given to it from 1720, were about 1750. It formed part of the mission field of the Rev. Ichabod Camp, Rector of Christ Church, Middletown, from 1752 to 1760. It was faithfully served by him for eight years. It then came under the care of the Rev. Samuel Andrews, missionary at Wallingford, who took great pains to implant true Church principles in the people of Cheshire. The first church, which was a square building, forty-two by forty-two feet, and very high, was erected in 1760. Upon Mr. Andrews' removal to Nova Scotia in 1785, there had been only occasional services until Mr. Ives was summoned home to be the first resident rector. By agreement he gave to Cheshire two-thirds of his time and spent the remainder in officiating in the neighboring towns, particularly Wallingford and North Haven.

By his faithful ministrations the congregations were so increased that in 1795 an enlargement of the church was necessary.

There was long current among the elder clergy of the Diocese a story that when Bishop Seabury on a visitation to Cheshire was told by one of the parishioners that the parish was intending to add a steeple to the church, he quickly replied with one of his bright flashes of wit: "You had better build a Church to your steeple."

When the plan for an Academy for the education of the children of the Church was proposed by Bishop Seabury and some of the clergy, Mr. Ives was one of its firmest supporters. He thought that Cheshire possessed many advantages and was instrumental in locating there the Episcopal Academy.

Until 1820 he was diligent in labor and careful in the administration of the parish. The causes of his resignation are only thus alluded to by Dr. Beardsley, the historian of the parish: "Circumstances then, of which it is needless now to speak, led to a dissolution of a connection which had existed for a period of more than thirty years. During this time, the Church had apparently been visited with the love and favor of God."[1]

Mr. Ives' work did not cease in other parts of the county when he resigned the rectorship of Cheshire, and it is the testimony of those who know that several parishes in the county of New Haven were by him rescued from an almost moribund condition and restored to vigor and prosperity.

Mr. Ives died at his home in Cheshire on October 14, 1836, having nearly reached his seventy-fourth year.

He was one of the humble and meek of the earth, whose work and labor of love were indeed appreciated by his contemporaries, but did not make him well known to the Church at large.

[1] P. 10. A Historical Sermon delivered in St. Peter's Church, Cheshire, July 28th, 1839; it being the last Sunday on which divine service was performed in the old Church. By Rev. E. E. Beardsley, Rector of the Parish. * * * Hartford; Printed by Case, Tiffany & Co., Pearl Street, 1839. 8vo, pp. 16.

THE REVEREND CHAUNCEY PRINDLE, M.A.

Chauncey, the only son of Eleazar and Anna (Scovill) Prindle, was born in that part of Waterbury, Connecticut, then called Westbury, now Watertown, on July 13, 1753. After being instructed in the district schools he was carefully prepared for college by his uncle, the Rev. James Scovill, Rector of St. John's, Waterbury. He entered Yale College

in his nineteenth year and graduated with honor in 1776. During the years of the Revolution he remained at home, and like other young men who could not serve in the Continental Army, cultivated his father's farm to supply a portion of the food needed by the troops in the field. It is also probable that he assisted his uncle in the wide missionary circuit assigned to Waterbury.

With Philo Shelton he studied theology under his uncle's direction. After due examination he was recommended for ordination by the convocation at its meeting in Stamford on May 31, 1787. With Ambrose Todd and Bethuel Chittenden he was made deacon in St. John's Church, Stamford, on Friday, June 1, 1787.

His uncle had in the fall of 1785 received an offer from the Venerable Society to settle in New Brunswick, with a competent salary. The necessities of his family by the withdrawal from Missionaries of the Venerable Society remaining in the United States of the stipends they had received induced him to accept. During his absences in New Brunswick, Mr. Prindle supplied his place. When finally Mr. Scovill gave up his temporary arrangement of spending the winters in Waterbury and the summers in his new parish of Kingston, New Brunswick, and in March, 1788, settled permanently in New Brunswick, Mr. Prindle was able to officiate until a rector was called for Waterbury. Mr. Prindle had been lay reader in Watertown for some years previous to his ordination.

On February 15, 1788, he was formally called to be minister of St. Peter's, Northbury (now Plymouth), at a salary of thirty-seven pounds and ten shillings. During the same month he was also called to be minister of Christ Church, Watertown, at a salary of thirty pounds. It was stipulated that his time should be equitably divided between them.

Mr. Prindle went to New London soon after accepting the calls and was, at the same time with Reuben Ives and Tillotson Bronson, ordained priest on St. Matthias' Day, February 24, 1788, in St. James's Church, by Bishop Seabury. His work in Watertown and Plymouth was earnest, judicious, and successful. So rapid was the growth of the parish that the church built in 1765, whose dimensions were thirty-seven by forty-five feet, was too small. A new church was determined upon, a better site procured for it and a building larger and upon "a more elegant plan" was erected. It was occupied in the fall of 1793, and consecrated by Bishop Seabury on November 18, 1794. This served the parish until 1855, when a beautiful Gothic church was completed and consecrated.

At Plymouth the increase was equally gratifying. A church was needed to replace that which had been built about 1740. The only difficulty was in agreeing upon a suitable location; finally the new St. Peter's was built in 1796, and opened during the fall of that year. It was consecrated on November 2, 1797, by Bishop Jarvis, being the second of those consecrated by that prelate. It still stands upon its hilltop and its doors are still open for the service of prayer and praise.

Mr. Prindle continued to be the able pastor and persuasive preacher at Watertown until 1804, when he resigned to give his time more fully to Plymouth, which had felt severely the loss of many of its families who had removed to the "western wilderness," which was then in the neighborhood of Whitestown, a few miles beyond Utica, New York. In his farewell sermon at Christ Church, Watertown, Mr. Prindle stated that thirty families had been added to the congregation, there had been three hundred and eighty-one baptisms, eighty-six marriages and sixty-six burials.

An incident of his pastoral work was long told in Watertown as showing his determination to overcome obstacles. He had promised to preach at St. John's Church and to baptize some children in Waterbury whose parents were about to remove to the West. It was the midsummer of 1795, and there was no clergyman in Waterbury. Between Watertown and Waterbury flows the Naugatuck river, which is about a third of a mile wide. It was usually crossed in a canoe or forded by travellers on horseback. Some distance beyond the village was a bridge. Mr. Prindle expected to cross in the canoe, but upon reaching the place where it was kept he found that the summer rains had so swollen the river that the canoe had disappeared. To retrace his steps and cross by the bridge would make him late for his appointment. He plunged boldly into the rapid stream and swam across in time to meet his friends, baptize their children and send them to their new home rejoicing. In 1806 Mr. Prindle resigned the charge of Plymouth, where he had been able in the two years he devoted to that work to build up again the congregation. During the eighteen years of his pastorate he had baptized three hundred and thirty-nine persons, married seventeen couples, and buried sixty persons.

In 1806 he became rector of St. Michael's Church, Salem (now Naugatuck), and also of St. Peter's, Oxford. His charge of Salem continued until 1814, but he remained at Oxford to the close of his life,

the same clear and sound preacher and good pastor as in his first charge.

A church was soon commenced at Salem, and that in Oxford improved. St. Peter's, Oxford, was consecrated by Bishop Hobart on his memorable first visitation of the Diocese, on October 21, 1816.

Mr. Prindle was a real missionary and in every hamlet near his home was well known and honored. For some years he held services in Amity in Woodbridge, and in the later years of his life Christ Church, Bethany received his ministrations. Until extreme old age he labored in the Gospel without diminution of energy or fervor.

He died at his home in North Oxford on August 25, 1833, in the eighty-first year of his age and was buried in the old cemetery at Gunntown.

The Reverend DAVID FOOTE, M.A.

David, a son of Asa Foote, and a direct descendant of Nathaniel Foote, one of the original settlers of Wethersfield, Connecticut, was born in that part of Colchester now Marlborough, on October 5, 1760. His early years were spent in his native town, where he was fitted for college. In his twelfth year he entered Dartmouth College and was graduated in 1776.

This college in the woods of New Hampshire had under Dr. Eleazar Wheelock, its first president, an enviable reputation for scholarship.

There is no account of his occupations during twelve years after his graduation.

The parish of St. Peter, Hebron, was the nearest to Colchester, and the few churchmen in that town attended its services.

The greater part of St. Peter's congregation were patriots, but its rector, the Rev. Samuel Peters, one of the celebrities of the colony for his missionary zeal, intense dislike of the "Standing Order," and his literary ability, was an outspoken and aggressive loyalist. He went to England in 1774. It is possible that Mr. Foote officiated at St. Peter's although no traditions or records for that period of the parish history have been preserved.

The Rev. John Tyler, of Christ Church, Norwich, went out from that centre into all the surrounding country upon periodical missionary journeys. Mr. Tyler may have encouraged Mr. Foote to study for holy orders and superintended his studies. In June, 1788, the rector of Norwich presented him to the Bishop at New London for examination for the order of deacon. This ordeal was successfully passed, and on St. Barnabas Day, June 11, 1788, David Foote was made deacon by Bishop Seabury in St. James's Church, New London.

Mr. Foote was licensed to preach and was appointed "to serve in the congregations of Hebron and Chatham."

The congregation that is meant in Chatham is evidently that at Middle Haddam, where a parish was formed in 1785 and a church built in 1787; for the parish in the portion of Chatham known now as Portland was not organized until September, 1788. There seems to be no records of Mr. Foote's ministrations in the archives of either parish in the town of Chatham.

Christ Church, Middle Haddam, was until 1791 under the charge of the Rev. Dr. Jarvis of Middletown, as was also Trinity Church, Portland. The first rector mentioned in the annals of the parishes who was resident is the Rev. Tillotson Bronson, in 1791.

Mr. Foote, although he has been almost forgotten, did diligently in Chatham and Hebron the varied duties of the ministry.

From his work of restoration and upbuilding he was called to the ancient parish of Grace (now Christ) Church, Rye, Westchester County, New York.

In this well ordered and settled community he found his efforts for greater temporal prosperity and spiritual growth fully seconded by the members of his new parish. A large increase in attendants and communicants was soon apparent. But as he was maturing plans for the future he was suddenly taken from this world on August 1, 1793, in the thirty-third year of his age.

His brief ministry showed his courage, his endurance, and his patience and held large promise of a brilliant and faithful career.

Mr. Foote retained his interest in the Diocese of Connecticut, attended regularly its convocations and conventions and was reckoned among its clergy. His name is also found upon the clergy list of the Diocese of New York.

The Reverend ABRAHAM LYNSEN CLARKE, M.A.

Abraham Lynsen Clarke is said to have been a native of Milford, Connecticut, but his parentage, date of birth, and the events of his early years do not seem to be known.

He was graduated from Yale College in 1785, and then, according to tradition, became lay reader in St. Peter's Church in his native town.

When the Rev Henry Van Dyck left Milford to assume the rectorship of Christ Church, Poughkeepsie and Trinity Church, Fishkill, Mr. Clarke was left in charge of St. Peter's Church. With Bryan Fairfax, of Virginia, he was made deacon by Bishop Seabury in Christ Church, Stamford, on June 9, 1786. In the spring of 1787 he became rector of St. Paul's Church, Huntington, in succession to the Rev. Christopher Newton, who had died on February 6, 1787. He was also rector of Christ Church, Tashua, to which he gave one-third of his time.

He served these parishes with devotion and discretion during his diaconate. Upon Trinity Sunday, June 7, 1789, in St. Paul's Church, Norwalk, with the Rev. Ambrose Todd and the Rev. Ambrose Hull, he was ordained priest by Bishop Seabury.

A new church was commenced at Tashua in 1789. It was fifty feet in length, thirty feet in breadth, and twenty-four feet in height. The church was finished in 1790 and consecrated by Bishop Seabury on June 8, 1795.

The death in September, 1792, of the Rev. Moses Badger, rector of King's Chapel, Providence, Rhode Island, made a vacancy in that important and desirable parish. The vestry followed the suggestion of the Rev. William Smith, then at Newport, and invited the Rev. John Bowden to the parish. His loss of voice compelled him to decline and he cordially commended Mr. Clarke as a clergyman who would fill admirably the rectorship of that parish. Bishop Seabury wrote to the vestry that Mr. Clarke was "not only a gentleman of good character and understanding, but also of easy and polite manners, and of diligence in his profession."

Mr. Clarke commenced his duties on Easter Day, March 31, 1793, and remained with growing appreciation in Providence for seven years. There was increase in the congregation and general prosperity in the parish during his incumbency. In 1794 the name of the corporation was changed from King's Chapel to St. John's Church.

Mr. Clarke resigned on March 30, 1800, and soon after took charge of St. Michael's Church, Bristol, Rhode Island. This was one of the oldest parishes in New England, having been founded in 1719. The beloved and venerated John Usher was then rector. He was the first child baptized in the parish, and after the death of his father, the Rev. John Usher, in 1775, whose connection with St. Michael's extended over fifty-two years, had kept it alive by reading the service. Mr. Usher in his seventy-third year received holy orders and with all the energy of a young man maintained the services and did his parish work. Feeling in his eightieth year the need of some relief, Mr. Clarke was called to his assistance.

Mr. Clarke's work was commendable and he showed great consideration to his colleague. From some cause not fully ascertainable dissension arose in the parish and early in 1803 Mr. Clarke resigned.

He accepted the united parishes of St. James, Newtown, and St. George's, Flushing, on Long Island, and was inducted into them in the spring of 1803.

The Church of England had been established on Long Island in the beginning of the eighteenth century. Jamaica was the chief parish at the western end of the island. Newtown and Flushing had from their organization been associated with it under the charge of one incumbent.

The blindness and other infirmities of the Rev. William Hammell, rector in 1794, led to a severing of the long connection between Jamaica and the outlying parishes. The Rev. Henry Van Dyck became in 1795 rector of St. James, Newtown, and also officiated at Flushing.

The resignation of Mr. Van Dyck in the winter of 1802-03 led to a formal union of the two congregations at Newtown and Flushing. It was probably due to the knowledge Mr. Van Dyck had of Mr. Clarke that the call was made by the vestries of these parishes.

In the exacting but pleasant and varied duties of a country parson Mr. Clarke spent the remainder of his life. He died at St. James's parsonage, Newtown, on December 31, 1810.

The Reverend AMBROSE HULL, M.A.

Ambrose Hull is, traditionally, a native of Cheshire, Connecticut.

No authentic documents are available concerning his ancestry, early years, and many events of his life.

He is known to have been graduated from Harvard College in 1785, and afterward to have pursued the study of theology. He was recommended by the convocation at its meeting in North Haven on October 22, 1788. The entry in the Bishop's register gives the date of the ordination of Mr. Hull as deacon as "Sunday the 12th day of October, 1788," in Trinity Church, New Haven. The candidate was presented by the

Rev. Jeremiah Leaming. To the entry in his register Bishop Seabury appends this: "NOTE: The following registry of the ordinations of Mr. Foot and Dr. Nesbitt ought to have preceded that of Mr. Hull."[1] The

[1] P. 7. A Reprint in full of the Registry of Ordinations by Bishops Seabury and Jarvis.

exact date of the ordination it is impossible now to ascertain. Mr. Hull was licensed to preach and "appointed to officiate as Deacon at Reading." The parish of Christ Church, Reading, is one of the oldest in the Diocese. Under the fostering care of the Rev. Dr. Samuel Johnson the Rev. Henry Caner established Church of England services there in 1727. The congregation came under the pastoral oversight of the Rev. John Beach, that noble confessor, until his death in 1782. The first church was built in 1732, but as the congregation increased rapidly a larger church was erected in 1750. After the Revolution the Rev. Richard S. Clarke of New Milford officiated occasionally. Mr. Truman Marsh, of Litchfield, acted as lay reader until 1786, when Mr. David Belden was made deacon and began a brief ministry.

On June 7th, 1789, Mr. Hull was made priest in St. Paul's Church, Norwalk, by Bishop Seabury at the same time with the Rev. Abraham Lynsen Clarke and the Rev. Ambrose Todd. Mr. Hull continued in charge of Reading until 1791, when he resigned. It is not certain that he took another parish immediately. In 1792 he was rector of the "Episcopal Church of Brooklyn," afterward St. Ann's Church. He succeeded the Rev. Elijah D. Rattoone, who had become a professor in Columbia College.

The incompleteness of the records of St. Ann's Church for this period is an obstacle to ascertaining the cause of Mr. Hull's sudden resignation early in January, 1793.

Mr. Hull's name does not appear in the Journal of any diocese or of the General Convention after 1792. There is no record of his deposition and there is no reason to suppose any moral delinquency on his part. Like two or three other clergymen of that period, notably the Rev. James Kilbourn, deacon, who became after a brief ministerial career a prominent politician in Ohio, Mr. Hull apparently ceased to execute the priest's office.

His later years are said to have been spent in South Carolina, Ohio, and Florida. He is reported to have won political honors and ascended the judicial bench in East Florida, where it is supposed he died in 1821.

The Reverend TRUMAN MARSH, M.A.

Truman Marsh was born in Litchfield, Connecticut, on February 24, 1768. After completing the course in the common schools he was well fitted for college by the Rev. George Beckwith, the Congregational minister of Litchfield South Farms (now Morris). He was graduated from Yale College in 1786.

It was then customary for Yale graduates to seek employment as tutors in the southern states. Mr. Marsh went to Maryland and became an instructor in Cokesbury College, near Baltimore, under the Rev. Levi Heath. Mr. Heath gave him a full theological course, and probably was his presenter when he was made deacon by Bishop White on March 5, 1789.

After his ordination, in addition to his duties in the college, he assisted Mr. Heath in the parochial work of St. John's parish, Baltimore.

For various reasons Mr. Marsh was desirous to become a clergyman in his native state and on that account refused the principalship of Cokesbury College.

In a letter to Bishop Seabury written from Philadelphia on August 11, 1789, Bishop White refers to the ordination of Mr. Marsh and his work in Maryland, which was earnest and acceptable. The Bishop also says: "I believe him to be a deserving young man and of unblemished morals."*

The ancient and influential parish of St. John's, New Milford, founded in 1742 by the Rev. John Beach, became vacant by the removal of the Rev. Tillotson Bronson, who had been temporarily in charge.

Mr. Marsh was invited in 1790 to become its rector and accepted.

He entered upon his duties soon after his ordination to the priesthood. The *"Records"* show that this service was in the old "meeting house" near the Litchfield Green on June 2, 1790, by Bishop Seabury, and that Mr. Marsh had been recommended by the clergy of Connecticut.

Mr. Marsh's work in New Milford, Roxbury, and New Preston, which were included in his cure, was characterized by tact, zeal and success.

The second church building in New Milford, erected in 1765, had remained unfinished. The sale by the town of "highway lands" and the division of the proceeds among the several "ecclesiastical societies" of the town materially benefited the parish. Ultimately the share of St. John's Church was forty-six pounds. With twenty-seven pounds, which

had been paid in 1793, and other contributions, the church was completed. Among the "improvements" was a front gallery and a high pulpit with winding stairs.

The church was consecrated by Bishop Seabury on September 25, 1793.

In 1799 the Rev. David Butler resigned his charge of St. Michael's, Litchfield.

Mr. Marsh's townsmen appreciated him and he was asked to become the successor of Mr. Butler.

Mr. Marsh removed to Litchfield late in 1799. He there spent the remainder of his life; thirty years of it in hard and exacting work. He was ever punctual in the performance of his duty and went into every nook and corner of the town. He was known and beloved by every one.

As his health and endurance began to fail after 1810, he was obliged to have the help of assistants; among them were the Rev. Dr. Isaac Jones, the Rev. Dr. John S. Stone and the Rev. William Lucas. In 1830, having fallen into a state of nervous hypochondria, he felt obliged to resign, very much to the regret of his parishioners.

It is said that during the later months of his active ministry he became so much depressed that he shrank from officiating. A simple remedy administered by his wife encouraged him. He mounted his horse and attended by his man servant proceeded to church, where he read the

¹ P. 338. *Connecticut Church Documents*, II.

service with dignity and preached with logical power and eloquence two admirable sermons. In his retirement he did not wholly omit clerical duty.

He remained to be the confidant and adviser of many of his former parishioners, the counsellor and friend of his successors in the parish, and a venerable and respected senior among his brethren of the clergy.

Mr. Marsh ended his earthly life on March 28, 1851, in the eighty-fourth year of his age.

His funeral was largely attended from the Congregational church, as the old St. Michael's had been demolished and the new one was not completed. The full Church service was used and a funeral sermon preached by the Rev. Benjamin W. Stone, rector of the parish.

Mr. Marsh was entrusted with various diocesan offices, among them membership on the Standing Committee, trusteeship in several boards, and a clerical deputyship in the General Convention.

In his Convention address in 1851, Bishop Brownell says: "Few of his brethren have surpassed him for clearness of mind, simplicity of character, purity of life, and faithfulness to the trust committed to him. This venerable brother has been taken from us like a shock of corn fully ripe." The Rev. Alonzo B. Chapin in his *"Sketches of the Early Clergy"* gives this characterization: "a fine scholar, an acceptable preacher, an able instructor, a man of pure character and unblemished reputation."¹

The Reverend EDWARD BLAKESLEE, M.A.

Edward, a son of Abraham Blakeslee, was born in North Haven, Connecticut, on June 27, 1766. He was educated in the common schools, and entered Yale College, where he took a high rank, before his twentieth year. He was compelled to leave college in his Junior year on account of the sickness and death of his parents.

From 1786 he had acted as lay reader for St. John's Church, North Haven. The congregation were very much pleased with his manner of conducting the service and wished him to obtain holy orders. At "a meeting in the red school house near Dr. Trumbull's Church," Mr. Blakeslee was requested to ride to New London and be ordained. Three dollars were voted for his expenses.

Mr. Blakeslee went to New London bearing letters of commendation from the Rev. Drs. Mansfield, Leaming, and Hubbard, also the votes of the meeting of the congregation of St. John's Church. He had a pleasant interview with Bishop Seabury and successfully passed the required examinations.

On Sunday, February 24, 1788, the feast of St. Matthias, he was made deacon in St. James's Church, New London, by Bishop Seabury. At the same service the Rev. Reuben Ives, the Rev. Chauncey Prindle, and the Rev. Tillotson Bronson were ordained priests.

Mr. Blakeslee was expected by the people of St. John's to become their minister. He, however, accepted the invitation of Trinity Church, Bran-

¹ *The Calendar*, August 19, 1854.

ford, and for two years worked with faithful diligence in that parish, with which were then associated Christ Church, Guilford, and St. John's, North Guilford. To properly care for them required much riding and constant vigilance.

In 1790 Mr. Blakeslee resigned, returned to his native town, and accepted the pastorate of St. John's and St. Andrew's, Northford. He

was also expected to explore the surrounding country for churchmen and organize new congregations wherever it could be done. During his ministry a parish was formed at Hamden and named Grace Church.

In 1791 Mr. Blakeslee became assistant to the Rev. Dr. Mansfield at Derby. He was to assist in the services, preach occasionally, and also to visit and hold service in remote parts of the town.

On Sunday, July 9, 1793, Mr. Blakeslee was ordained priest by Bishop Seabury at the same time with Rev. Solomon Blakeslee, the Rev. Russel Catling, and the Rev. David Butler in Christ Church, Middletown. In the Bishop's register is noted that he was appointed "to the cure of Woodbridge for one-half his time, the other half as assistant to the Rev'd Dr. Mansfield at Derby."

In this double duty he was diligent and faithful.

In that part of Derby then known as Chusetown, afterward Humphreysville (now Seymour), a parish was organized in February, 1797. With this the congregation worshipping on Great Hill was united and the new corporation took the name of Union Church. Mr. Blakeslee laid the corner-stone of a church building for that parish during the early spring of 1797 which was framed and enclosed before the following winter. It was not fully completed and ready for consecration until 1817, when, on September 2, it was consecrated by Bishop Hobart. The ancient frame still remains sound. Upon it in 1857 a new church was built and consecrated by Bishop Williams on May 11, 1858, as Trinity Church, Seymour.

Mr. Blakeslee died on July 15, 1797, in the thirty-first year of his age. His death was felt as a personal loss by many both in Derby and wherever he was known. His clerical brethren mourned for him and grieved that his earthly ministry had so soon ended, as they had anticipated for him a brilliant future.

This brief extract from a manuscript sermon upon fasting will show his method of sermonizing. His text is from St. Luke v. 34, 35. "Can ye make the children of the bridechamber fast while the bridegroom is with them? But the days will come when the bridegroom shall be taken away from them and then shall they fast in those days."

He first states the circumstances under which our Lord spoke these words and then shows the necessity for joy while the Bridegroom is with His disciples, and the reason for sadness and fasting when the light of His countenance is withdrawn from them. He considers the reasons why Christians should fast and alludes to the practice of the Primitive Church and the obligation resting upon all Christians to follow its example. He then says: "Again this Duty is too often abused by considering yᵉ bare performance of it acceptable to God, without regard to those other Religious exercises wʰ are inseparably connected with it—for Fasting considerᵈ in yᵉ Abstract is but A Colateral Duty, & enjoined for no other Purpose yⁿ to assist us in yᵉ great & essential Duties of Prayer, Almsgiving & an holy life, & is intended to be wholly subservient thereto. If *ergo* we flatter ourselves with yᵉ Notion, yᵗ having modified our Appetites for a little Time, we may yⁿ indulge yᵐ at large, till yᵉ return of the next stated Season of Fasting & Humiliation we grossely Deceive ourselves & add to our own Condemnation, by turning yᵗ wʰ is intended for an Assistant to Virtue & Godliness, into an Instrument of Impiety & Wickedness; since He who lives A good life without fasting, is a much better Man yⁿ He who abstains from Meat only, without regarding those other ends, wʰ yᵗ Abstinence was designed to promote.

Notwithstanding, *ergo*, this as well as many other Religious Duties is often neglected or Abused, yet, let us not, for this Reason lay aside yᵉ Use of it, but Deliberately consider those good Purposes for wʰ it was originally Designed, & yᵉ great advantages yᵗ will arise to us from a regular & conscientious Discharge of it. Fasting, it must be acknowledged, is a very fit & becoming Act of Humiliation to God for our past Offences against his Divine Majesty. The best of us all have abundant reason to pray with yᵉ Devout Publican in yᵉ Gospel, Lᵈ be merciful, &c."¹

The Reverend SOLOMON BLAKESLEE, M.A.

Solomon, a son of Zophar Blakeslee, was born at North Haven, Connecticut, on November 9, 1762. He was educated in the schools of the town and when nineteen years old entered Yale College, where he maintained a creditable rank and was graduated in 1785.

He probably studied theology with the Rev. Dr. Mansfield of Derby, but was, like other candidates of the period, better versed in the practical duties of the ministry than in systematic divinity. The lack of ordained clergymen compelled the students to read the service in parishes which otherwise would be wholly without the ministrations of the Church. His time seems to have been spent largely in Claremont, New Hampshire, where a parish had been formed as early as 1770 and a church commenced in 1773. Among the earliest services in Claremont were those

of the Rev. Samuel Peters, of Hebron, Connecticut, who made a missionary tour in 1770 which included Claremont. The parish then was occasionally visited by the itinerant missionary in New Hampshire, the Rev. Moses Badger, and in 1773 the Rev. Ranna Cositt became rector and missionary. An outspoken loyalist, Mr. Cossit finally became a missionary in Sydney, Cape Breton Island. There is evidence that Mr. Blakeslee was in New Hampshire in the closing months of 1788 and that he officiated until the time of his ordination. Mr. Blakeslee entered heartily into the work and did good service not only in Claremont but also in the new settlements of New Hampshire and Vermont. He is known to have made several journeys to Connecticut, where he officiated at North

¹ Dr. Burhans' Collection of Manuscript Sermons. The sermon is thus endorsed: Amity, March 11, 1792; Great Hill, March 18, 1792; Derby, April 1ˢᵗ, 1792.

Haven and other places after his cousin, the Rev. Edward Blakeslee, had in 1791 gone to Derby. A recent writer upon North Haven says that he was "rather in advance of the older people, and locally known as the man who whistled on the sabbath day."¹

For three years he was in New Hampshire during the greater portion of his time. The last services by him in Claremont are in September, 1792. What he did for the upbuilding of the Church and the searching out of the scattered and uncared for people in the wilderness towns and hamlets merits high praise.

A parish by the name of St. Stephen's Church had been formed at Haddam, on the Connecticut river, under the auspices of the Rev. Dr. Abraham Jarvis of Middletown in April, 1791. Dr. Jarvis in addition to his other onerous duties had cheerfully served it until 1792. On March 1st, 1793, Mr. Blakeslee accepted the charge of it. He was a devoted parish priest and a preacher of sound common sense. He possessed a practical knowledge of men which made him attractive to his parishioners. Mr. Blakeslee was ordained priest in Christ Church, Middletown, on Sunday, June 9, 1793 by Bishop Seabury at the same time with Edward Blakeslee, Russel Catling and David Butler.

A church was planned in February, 1792, which was to be "fifty-four feet long, thirty-seven feet wide, and twenty-one feet posts, with a steeple." This church was not finished and ready for consecration until October, 1795. The consecration was on St. Luke's Day, October 18, 1795. It served the parish for nearly a hundred years until the erection and consecration of the present St. Stephen's, which is nearer the "Landing," in 1890. It still stands, a witness to the zeal of the fathers, and a conspicuous and cherished object to all vessels passing up or down the river.

Mr. Blakeslee in 1803 was one of six clergymen who united in a memorial to Bishop Jarvis concerning the right of the Rev. Ammi Rogers to a seat in the Convention of the Diocese; basing their plea upon the principle that "each parish has a right to choose its own rector," subject to the approval of the Bishop. For one of his parishes the memorial stated Mr. Rogers had obtained approval.²

In thus joining with five of his brethren of undoubted loyalty to the Diocese and conspicuously successful as parish priests, Mr. Blakeslee did not intend to prejudge the case of Mr. Rogers or oppose the decision of the Bishop.

The rector of East Haddam had the pleasure of seeing the church well filled and new families of intelligence inquiring into the principles of the American Church, many of whom became earnest and consistent churchmen.

In 1815 the Rev. Charles Seabury, who had succeeded his father, the

¹ P. 155. *North Haven Annals*, * * * by Sheldon B. Thorpe. New Haven: 1892. The Rev. Wm. Lusk's sketch of St. John's Church.
² P. 31. Dr. Beardsley's "*History*," II. The other clergymen were the Rev. Dr. Mansfield, of Derby; the Rev. John Tyler, of Norwich; the Rev. Ambrose Todd, of Huntington; the Rev. Joseph Warren, of Middletown; and the Rev. Smith Miles, of Chatham.

Bishop, as rector of St. James's Church, New London, resigned. On March 27, 1815, Mr. Blakeslee was chosen as his successor. He accepted immediately and soon after removed to New London. During his three years incumbency there was much activity and abundant life in the old parish. In 1816 the gallery in St. James's Church was lowered and in 1817 a small organ of English manufacture and of excellent tone, was presented to the parish and placed in the gallery. Previously the music had been entirely vocal. This was the first organ in New London. Mr. Blakeslee's advocacy of the deposed priest, Ammi Rogers, in which his neighbor, the Rev. John Tyler, of Norwich, joined, brought him into disfavor with some of his brethren. It seemed expedient for him to resign St. James's Church, which he did early in 1818. East Haddam had been vacant since Mr. Blakeslee's departure for New London and had relied upon him for various clerical offices.

Yielding to the wishes of his former parishioners, he accepted in April,

1818, the call made by them and continued to serve the parish until October, 1821.

Mr. Blakeslee then went to St. James's Church, Great Barrington, Massachusetts, where he did excellent work until May, 1827. In 1828 he returned to Connecticut but without taking any parochial charge, and soon after removed to the state of New York. He made his home at New Lisbon, Otsego County, in that picturesque region made famous by the pen of James Fenimore Cooper. It was that part of the state long blessed with the unceasing labors of that apostolic missionary affectionately known as "Father Nash."

Mr. Blakeslee as he had health and opportunity engaged in mission work in Otsego and Chenango Counties with much acceptance and success.

He died at New Lisbon on April 10, 1835, in the seventy-third year of his age.

Bishop Onderdonk of New York in his Convention address for 1835 says of him: "He had been for several years residing on an estate in Otsego County, and rendered important gratuitous service to the missionary cause in this Diocese. * * * I am personally cognisant of much good which he had done to the Church in our Diocese." The Rev. Dr. Robert Hallam, who was a boy in St. James's in New London during Mr. Blakeslee's rectorship, gives these recollections of Mr. Blakeslee in his valuable "*Annals of St. James's Church, New London*": "He was a man of peculiarly cheerful, genial, and social temperament, an agreeable companion and associate; but was thought to be by many, perhaps not without reason, somewhat deficient in the gravity and seriousness which became his calling."¹

¹ P. 88. *Annals of St. James's Church, New London, for one hundred and fifty years*: by Robert A. Hallam, D.D., Rector. *The Church Press*: M. H. Mallory & Co., Hartford, Conn., 1873. 12mo, pp. v, 120.

The Rev. DAVID PERRY

David, a son of Micah and Grace (Sturgis) Perry, was born in 1747.

His ancestors were well known in Fairfield County and traced their descent from Richard Perry, an eminent lawyer, who had emigrated from England in 1637, settled in New Haven in 1642 and had acquired large tracts of land in Fairfield County.

David Perry studied medicine, and at the age of twenty-five settled in Ridgefield. He soon had an extensive practice in that pleasant town and the surrounding region. He is said to have been both bold and successful in the trial of new remedies. Dr. Perry was a stanch supporter of St. Stephen's Church.

This parish owes its existence to the missionary zeal of the Rev. Dr. Samuel Johnson, who visited the town in 1725. It was faithfully served by the Rev. Henry Caner, the Rev. John Beach, the Rev. James Wetmore, the Rev. Joseph Lawson, the Rev. Richard Clark, and the Rev. Epenetus Townsend during the Colonial period. Mr. Townsend left Ridgefield early in July, 1776. The services were then suspended. The first church had been built in 1740 "directly in front of the Sturtevant lot." It became a storehouse for supplies for the American Army and was burned by the British in April, 1777, on their return from the raid on Danbury. No regular services of the church seem to have been held until after the Revolution, when Dr. Perry acted as lay reader. A meeting to consider the building of a new church was held on June 19, 1784. Dr. Perry seems to have been very active in arousing the latent energy of the parish and his name heads the call for this meeting. It was then determined to build a new church whose dimensions were to be "forty by thirty feet with eighteen foot posts" at "the northeast corner of the Sturtevant lot so called adjoining the town street in the first society of Ridgefield on a piece of ground given by Benjamin Smith for that purpose." While the frame of the church was finished and the building occupied in 1785, it was not fully completed and furnished until 1791.

After the brief incumbency of four months in 1788 by the Rev. David Belden, deacon, Dr. Perry resumed his duties as lay reader, to the great satisfaction of the congregation. At a parish meeting held at the Town House on the first Monday in August, 1789, it was "voted that Doct. David Perry receive Holy Orders for this Society." The "*Records*" give the fact of his ordination as Deacon on June 6, 1790. In the "*Register*" the Bishop records the ordination as "special." The candidate had been recommended by the clergy and was "licensed to preach." ¹

The double duty of priest and physician seems at first to have been performed with much vigor. Three parishes were under his care, Ridge-

¹ P. 8, *Registry of Ordinations*, by Bishops Seabury and Jarvis.

field, Redding, and Danbury. He fully earned the higher office of priesthood to which he was ordained in St. John's Church, Stratfield (now

Bridgeport), on October 16, 1791.[1] His presenter was the Rev. Philo Shelton.

The growth of the congregations made necessary more supervision than such a busy man as Dr. Perry could give. Discontent arose in some portions of the parish. Rumors of it at last reached the ears of the Bishop and his clerical brethren. They had been grieved that he did not attend the meetings of either the Convention or Convocation. Severe comments were made upon his conduct and urgent requests sent to him to show respect and regard for his brethren by attendance.

The Convocation finally took action in 1794, as the "Records" show. To the Bishop's letter of admonition a reply was received from Dr. Perry, in which he declared his intention of resigning immediately his pastoral charge and relinquishing the exercise of his ministry. This letter, as the text of the Records informs us, was laid before the Convocation on June 3, 1795.

There seems to have been no more formal act of deposition than the resolution entered upon the "Records."[2]

Dr. Perry continued in lay communion, devoting all his time to the practice of medicine, until his death on May 8, 1822.

His son and grandson became well known physicians in Ridgefield, where his descendants were for many years faithful members of the parish which he had served.

[1] P. 8, *Registry of Ordinations*.   [2] See pp. 44, 45, 46, 47, *ante*.

THE REVEREND DANIEL FOGG.

Daniel Fogg, the son of a prosperous farmer, was born at Rye, New Hampshire, on August 18, 1743.

The death of his father and mother while he was a child placed him at an early age under the care of his uncle, the Rev. Jeremiah Fogg, who was the Congregational minister of Kensington, a neighboring town.

By him the boy was carefully trained, and in 1760 entered Harvard College. He maintained a high rank in his class and also excelled in all athletic sports, being, it is said, the best football player of his time. Mr. Fogg was graduated with high honors in 1764.

It was while in college that he studied the doctrines and polity of the Church of England, and probably learned much of her excellencies from the energetic young missionary of Christ Church, Cambridge, the Rev. East Apthorp, who was both a scholar and a busy parish priest. Becoming convinced of the primitive truth and apostolic order of the Church, he "declared" for it and studied theology under the Rev. Dr. Henry Caner of King's Chapel, Boston. This course of the nephew is represented as not displeasing to his uncle, who was "one of the small minority of his denomination holding Armenian tenets, thus naturally without any extreme antipathy to that very uncalvanistic body, the Communion of the Church of England in America."[1] To support himself he opened a school of high grade in Newburyport, which was well patronized.

In the spring of 1770 he "went home" to England to receive Holy Orders. He was duly confirmed, passed successfully the Bishop of London's examination, and was made deacon on August 19, 1770, and was ordained priest on August 24, 1770, by the Rt. Rev. Richard Terrick, Bishop of London.

Upon his return he became temporarily assistant to Dr. Caner.

After a brief service in Boston, Mr. Fogg went to North Carolina, where he did faithful work as a missionary and a teacher. Ill health obliged him to seek again a Northern climate, and in May, 1772, he accepted the incumbency of Trinity Church, Brooklyn, in the town of Pomfret, Connecticut.

The story of the building of this church through the determination of Colonel Godfrey Malbone, who owned a large estate in Pomfret, is one of the romantic incidents of our Connecticut Church history.

Mr. Fogg was an industrious and painstaking pastor.

During the Revolution he remained in Brooklyn, which was also the home of the patriot General Putnam, sharing with Colonel Malbone the

[1] The Rev. Thomas Brinley Fogg, in *The Herald*, New London, Archdeaconry Quarterly, March, 1891. Vol. I, No. 3.

odium of being a Tory. Neither was molested. While the church had to be closed, there was no disturbance of the services held at the house of Colonel Malbone.

Mr. Fogg was one of the ten clergymen who, on the Feast of the Annunciation, 1783, met at Woodbury to elect a Bishop for Connecticut. The importance of his letters on the subject has been already noted.

In the quiet discharge of his duty in a parish which was neither wealthy nor able to expand largely, he passed the remainder of his life.

He is described as the kind friend and adviser of his parishioners, fond of society and an agreeable companion. His sermons, it is said, were highly esteemed by persons of good judgment.

Mr. Fogg departed this life on June 29, 1815, in the seventy-second year of his age. The burial was in Trinity Churchyard on July 2. The Rev. Philander Chase came from Hartford to perform this last office for his brother in the ministry.

THE REVEREND JOHN TYLER.

John, a son of John and Mary (Doolittle) Tyler, was born in Wallingford, Connecticut, on August 15, 1742. He was descended from Roger Tyler, one of the original proprietors of Wallingford.

Mr. Tyler was graduated from Yale College in 1765 with distinction and pronounced the valedictory oration. He took a post graduate course at King's College, New York City (now Columbia University), under that versatile, accomplished man, President Miles Cooper. This was then very unusual. He received both the Bachelor's and Master's degrees from that institution. Like many other young men in Connecticut, he abandoned the "Standing Order" in which he had been brought up, declared for the Church, and studied theology under the Rev. Dr. Samuel Johnson, then enjoying a well earned rest at Stratford. He assisted Dr. Johnson on Sundays, and by some of the people of Christ Church was thought worthy to be the successor of that Nestor of the Colonial Church. He had also read the services in Dr. Johnson's native town, Guilford, vacant by the removal of the Rev. Bela Hubbard to New Haven.

Mr. Tyler went to England on May 10, 1768, sailing from New York in the ship Edward. He bore testimonials from Dr. Johnson and the Connecticut clergy to the Bishop of London and the Venerable Society. He also carried a petition from the Wardens and Vestry of Christ Church, Guilford, for the erection of a new mission, of which Guilford should be the central station and the appointment of Mr. Tyler as the missionary.

Upon his arrival in England he sought first the powerful personal aid of the Hon. William Samuel Johnson, a son of Dr. Johnson, then the agent of the Colony of Connecticut in London. By him he was introduced to many persons of influence and the object of his quest facilitated.

He was examined on June 20, by Dr. Carr, chaplain to the Bishop of London. On Friday, June 24, the feast of St. John Baptist, "at nine o'clock in the morning," Mr. Tyler was made deacon by the Rt. Rev. Dr. Terrick, Bishop of London. On Wednesday, June 29, St. Peter's Day, he was ordained priest in Fulham Chapel by the same prelate.

It was a very great disappointment that Dr. Burton, the Secretary, and other authorities of the Venerable Propagation Society would not erect Guilford into a mission. Mr. Tyler was chosen by the Society for the mission at Norwich, made vacant by the removal of the Rev. John Beardsley to Poughkeepsie, New York, with a salary of thirty pounds a year.

Mr. Tyler sailed for New York on August 2 in the same vessel in which he went to England. After a stormy passage and much detention by contrary winds, the Edward reached New York on September 26, 1768.

He made several visits to friends in New York and Stratford, spent some days with his family at the home in Wallingford, and commenced his duties at Norwich on November 1.

A journal kept by him during the six months he spent in obtaining Holy Orders, which give many interesting glimpses of his life on shipboard and sojourn in London, was privately printed in 1894 by Mr. Tyler's grandson, the Rev. Dr. Alfred L. Brewer, the founder of St. Matthew's Hall, San Mateo, California.

Mr. Tyler was an earnest and faithful pastor. When Trinity Church, Pomfret, was ready for use, Colonel Malbone invited Mr. Tyler to preach the opening sermon. It is said that the service of opening "was made as nearly one of consecration as was possible."

During the Revolution the Rector of Norwich remained in his parish. The church was closed from 1776 to 1779, but services were held in the Rector's house. He suffered little indignity from the patriots, although it is traditional that there were attempts to poison his well.

In 1779 Mr. Tyler, after consultation with his parishioners, agreed to open the church and use the prayer for Congress, provided the congregation desired it. The church was then opened, to the great satisfaction of the people. There were no startling events in the parish of Christ Church. Harmony and progress were apparent. As the years went on, Mr. Tyler became more endeared to the people. He practiced medicine freely among the poor, and this often won them to a true religious life.

Upon Sunday, February 28, 1796, Mr. Tyler had the distinction of officiating at the funeral of the first Bishop of the American Church, Dr. Samuel Seabury, at New London. Mr. Tyler died on January 20, 1823, in the eighty-first year of his age.

Two sermons of Mr. Tyler's were printed, that at the "Opening of Trinity Church, Pomfret, April 5, 1771," and one upon "The Blessing of Peace," preached at Christ Church, Norwich, on the "Continental Thanksgiving," February 19, 1795. An extract from the sermon on Peace will show his style:

"I might, indeed, upon this Occasion congratulate with Views of our National Prosperity—of the extensiveness of our Territory—of the various and happy Climates in it—of our rapidly growing Numbers—of the great Increase of New Settlements—of the Security we enjoy by being so distant from powerful and corrupted Nations—of our various great and increasing Resources for Wealth or War. I might remind you that the natural means of our Subsistence are so great, that in a measure we are become the Granary of other Nations—that Knowledge and all useful arts are making great Progress among us—and I might boast of the Liberality and Prosperity of our free and happy Constitution of Government. But what are all these things without the divine Blessing and Protection? And what purpose would all this Adulation serve, but, instead of promoting real Gratitude to God, rather perhaps to excite and encourage pride; which is the great Bane of Man: and it is one great Purpose of God, in national as well as private Judgments to hide *Pride from Man*. I might indeed have said little else, except what would contribute something to promote the Arrogance of National Prosperity. But perhaps I should have fallen under the condemnation of the false Prophets in Judah; of whom Jehovah of Hosts said,—*They have healed the hurt of the daughter of my People slightly, saying Peace, peace, when there is no Peace.* For says the Prophet *There is no Peace, saith my God, to the wicked.* This last is what innumerable Facts in every Age have proclaimed. But more especially this holds true in free popular Governments, like ours. For there must be public Virtue, or they can not flourish with Peace and Prosperity. There must also be private Virtue or there will be no such thing as public Virtue. There must be Religion, or there will be neither public nor private Virtue. There must be true Religion, otherwise there will be generally abundance of false Religion. And there must be attendance on the Worship of God, otherwise there will soon be no Religion at all." [1]

The Reverend AMBROSE TODD, M.A.

Ambrose Todd was born in that portion of the town of Branford, Connecticut, known as Northford, on December 7, 1764.

He was educated in the common schools, studied assiduously to prepare himself for college and was graduated with honor from Yale College in 1786. He spent a year pursuing a course of theology and was made deacon by Bishop Seabury in St. John's Church, Stamford, on June 1, 1787, at the same time as Mr. Chauncy Prindle and Mr. Bethuel Chittenden. [2]

He at once took charge of St. Andrew's Church, Simsbury (now St. Andrew's, Bloomfield), which was vacant by the final removal in 1787 of the Rev. Roger Viets, one of the most accomplished clergymen in the State and Diocese, to Digby, Nova Scotia.

Mr. Todd was ordained priest in St. Paul's Church, Norwalk, by Bishop Seabury, on Trinity Sunday, June 7, 1789, at the same time as the Rev. Ambrose Hall and the Rev. Abram Lynsen Clark. [3]

[1] Pp. 17, 18, The Blessing of Peace, * * * by John Tyler, A.M., 8vo, pp. 20. Printed by John Trumbull, Norwich, MDCCXCV.
[2] P. 6, *Registry of Ordinations.*   [3] P. 8, *Registry of Ordinations.*

Mr. Todd's work in Simsbury, Granby and other places in the vicinity was both conscientious and successful. He was a man of profound earnestness and strict in his attention to all the duties of his ministry. His direct and plain speaking caused Mr. Alexander Viets Griswold, a nephew of the Rev. Roger Viets, to study for the ministry. The whole Church knows the result; a faithful priesthood, followed by an energetic episcopate in the association of dioceses, known as the Eastern Diocese, which revived the Church in the greater part of New England.

After eleven years of hard work, to the great sorrow of his parishioners, Mr. Todd accepted the rectorship of St. Paul's Church, Huntington, Connecticut, where he remained until the close of his earthly life, using all faithful diligence in building up the parish.

Mr. Todd died of consumption, after an illness of three months, on July 25, 1809, in the forty-fifth year of his age.

A writer in *The Churchman's Magazine* describes Mr. Todd as "prudent in his secular concerns, and an active and faithful servant in the vineyard. He was much beloved by his parishioners, heard with attention and treated with respect, and died much lamented. His life and conversation were such as to leave a lasting impression." [1]

Two of his sons entered the ministry. The Rev. Charles Jarvis Todd was for many years a missionary in Illinois, where he died in 1859. The Rev. Ambrose Seymour Todd spent two years as rector of Christ Church, Redding, and St. James' Church, Danbury, and then became the honored and beloved rector of St. John's Church, Stamford, for nearly forty years. He died in 1861.

The Reverend GEORGE OGILVIE, M.A.

George, a son of the Rev. John and Catharine (Symes) Ogilvie, was born at Albany, New York, in 1758. His father, probably the most finished pulpit orator in the Colonial Church, was then the incumbent of St. Peter's Church, Albany, and missionary to the Mohawk Indians. Dr. Ogilvie in 1764 became an assistant minister of Trinity Church, New York City. His son George was very carefully educated at home and in the best schools of the city. He was graduated from King's College (now Columbia University), of which his father was a governor, in 1774.

Great responsibility came to him at this early age, for his father died suddenly of apoplexy on November 26, 1774.

During the Revolution, like many others in the City of New York, it is said that he joined the Royal American Regiment of Colonel Edmund Fanning and became a commissioned officer. It is traditional that at the close of the war he went to England, but his visit could not have been a long one, as he was living in Newark, New Jersey, in 1785, and studying theology under the Rev. Dr. Uzal Ogden, Rector of Trinity Church, Newark. At the second Convention of the Diocese of New Jersey, which was held in St. Peter's Church, Perth Amboy, on May 16, 1785, Mr. Ogilvie was a lay delegate.

[1] P. 374, *The Churchman's Magazine*, September and October, 1809, Vol. 6, No. 5.

At the first ordination held by Bishop Provoost on July 15, 1787, in St. George's Chapel, New York City, Mr. Ogilvie was made deacon at the same time with Mr. Joseph Grove John Bend and Mr. Richard Channing Moore. Mr. Ogilvie became minister of Christ Church, New Brunswick, New Jersey, soon after his ordination. He was a good reader of the service and a preacher of marked originality. He had a pleasant manner, and in person is said to have resembled his father, who was a large, portly man with a highly intellectual countenance.

St. Paul's Church, Norwalk, Connecticut, to its very sincere regret, had accepted the resignation of the Rev. Dr. John Bowden, whose health required a total cessation from work, in the summer of 1789. At the termination of a six months' engagement with the Rev. David Foote in May, 1790, Mr. Ogilvie was invited to the rectorship. Upon his arrival in that pleasant shore town he found some of the congregation who still recalled with pleasure the brief term forty years before when Dr. John Ogilvie had officiated. Mr. Ogilvie was energetic and industrious. The congregation generously seconded his plans for the improvement and completion of the church edifice, which had taken the place of the one burned by the British during the Revolution, and which had been consecrated by Bishop Seabury in 1786, on the first occasion when the office of consecration was used in the United States.

The six years spent by him in this parish were pleasant and profitable to both priest and people.

Mr. Ogilvie resigned the rectorship of St. Paul's in October, 1796. It was accepted by the Vestry with expressions of unqualified respect and appreciation.

Upon October 26, 1796, a call was extended by the Vestry of Christ Church, Rye, Westchester County, New York. This was one of the most ancient parishes in that diocese and had been served by many strong and eminent men, among them the Rev. George Muirson, the first clergyman of the Church who held regularly services in the Colony of Connecticut.

Mr. Ogilvie assumed his new duties in the fall of 1796 and was rapidly gaining the affection of his parishioners when, after a brief illness, he died on April 3, 1797, in the fortieth year of his age and the tenth of his ministry. He was buried in the plot reserved in the old cemetery of the parish for its rectors and sincerely mourned by all his friends.

The Reverend SETH HART, M.A.

Seth Hart was born at Berlin, Connecticut, on June 21, 1763. After his preliminary course in the common schools and privately, he entered Yale College, from which he was graduated in 1784. During his period of waiting for ordination he probably acted as lay reader under the direction of the Rev. Chauncy Prindle. He was made deacon in Christ Church, Westbury (now Watertown), on Sunday, October 9, 1791. [1] He was at once placed in charge of St. James's Church (now St. John's), Waterbury, which served with Salem (now Naugatuck)

until 1793. The *"Records"* give an account of his ordination as priest in St. Paul's Church, Huntington, on Sunday, October 14, 1792.[3]

In 1794 he became Rector of St. Paul's Church, Wallingford, and St. John's Church, North Haven. He served these parishes with abundant zeal. In 1798 he resigned St. John's Church and took charge of the churches in Worthington (now New Britain) and Wethersfield (now Newington). With three parishes to care for, he found leisure to instruct several young men in the classics and mathematics, and prepare them for college. The old Colonial parish of St. George, Hempstead, Long Island, where the Rev. Samuel Seabury, father of the Bishop, had served for many years, became vacant in the fall of 1800 by the resignation of the Rev. John Henry Hobart after a brief incumbency. Mr. Hobart was willing to delay his departure for New York until his successor was appointed. Mr. Hart was commended by Bishop Jarvis, the Rev. Dr. Beach of Trinity Church, New York, and the Rev. Ambrose Hull, to the Vestry of St. George's. Mr. Hart was duly elected, and entered upon his new duties on the feast of St. Thomas, Sunday, December 21, 1800. The parish was an extensive one, its boundaries stretching for fourteen miles in one direction and with two places of worship some miles apart. It was estimated by Mr. Hobart that one thousand souls were under his pastoral care, and the number had increased when the new rector came to Hempstead. During his incumbency, Christ Church, Manhansett, was built and set off as a separate parish, and a new church erected in Hempstead.

In addition to his parish work Mr. Hart continued to receive and educate pupils in his own house. He was considered a successful teacher.

A stroke of paralysis in January, 1829, caused Mr. Hart to resign the rectorship of St. George's on February 16, 1829. He was given a small retiring annuity, and lived in Hempstead until his death on March 14, 1832, in the sixty-ninth year of his age and the forty-first of his ministry.

Mr. Hart was a sound and practical preacher and a careful pastor. He was "a good classical scholar and an amiable man of a cheerful and almost jovial temperament."[3]

[1] P. 8, *Registry of Ordinations.*   [2] P. 43, *ante.*
[3] P. 197, *History of St. George's Church, Hempstead, Long Island, N. Y.,* by the Rev. Wm H. Moore, D.D., Rector of St. George's Church, Hempstead, N. Y. E. P. Dutton & Company. 1881. 12mo, pp. 308.

The Reverend RUSSELL CATLIN.

The personal history of Mr. Catlin is almost unknown. He was born in Harwinton, Connecticut. He became after his ordination the incumbent of St. James's Church, Arlington, Vermont. The Church in that State had received in the Colonial period and after the Revolution the services of several Connecticut clergymen, notably the Rev. Dr. Mansfield, the Rev. Samuel Peters, the Rev. Samuel Andrews, and the Rev. Gideon Bostwick. Arlington was largely settled from Litchfield County. The first Convention of clergymen and laymen was held at Arlington in September, 1790, with the Rev. Daniel Barber of Arlington, who had been ordained by Bishop Seabury, and the Rev. James Nichols of Sandgate, and representatives from eight towns in attendance.

Mr. Catlin was ordained priest on Sunday, June 9, 1793, by Bishop Seabury in Christ Church, Middletown. Mr. Catlin seems to have succeeded Mr. Barber when that ardent missionary removed to Claremont, New Hampshire, and been a laborious and successful clergyman. In the Convention of Vermont Mr. Catlin was prominent, serving upon the Standing Committee, acting as its President, and being appointed upon important committees.

Previous to 1804 Mr. Catlin removed to Hartland, Vermont, and organized a parish at Plainfield, New Hampshire. In 1804 he was recognized by the diocesan convention of New Hampshire and declared to be entitled to the leases of the glebe lands in that town.[1] Mr. Catlin was the preacher at the Convention of Vermont held at Manchester on September 24, 1806.[2] The last mention of Mr. Catlin is in August, 1808, when he is censured by the New Hampshire Convention as acting in "an irregular and improper manner" concerning the glebe lands. The Convention does "not consider him as a clergyman of this State, he not having a parish or curé within the same."[3] This makes it probable that the organization at Plainfield was only temporary.

There appears to be no definite information as to his subsequent life, and there is no record of his deposition.

The Reverend DAVID BUTLER, D.D.

David Butler was born in Harwinton, Connecticut, in 1763. While a very young man he learned a mechanical trade which he abandoned

temporarily to serve in the Connecticut line of the American army

[1] P. 13, *Journals of the first Twenty Eight Conventions of the Diocese of New Hampshire* . . . Tilton: George Burnham Munsey. MDCCCLXXXIII. 8vo, pp. 290.
[2] P. 103, *The Documentary History of the Protestant Episcopal Church in the Diocese of Vermont.* New York: Pott & Amey. 1870. 8vo, pp. 418.
[3] P. 23, *Journals of the first Twenty Eight Conventions.*

during the later months of the Revolution. At its close he resumed his trade with every prospect of success. He had been much impressed with the beauty of the church service, although a member of the "Standing Order," and his intimacy with the Rev. Ashbel Baldwin caused him to examine the claims of the Church, and especially the origin of the Episcopate. He became convinced of the truth of her doctrines and polity, and soon conformed. He became a candidate for holy orders and was made deacon by Bishop Seabury, as noted in the *"Records."* Mr. Butler immediately began his work as incumbent of Christ Church, Guilford, St. John's, North Guilford, and the Church at Killingworth (now Clinton). There are no details of his ministrations available. We only know that Mr. Butler lived in the new parsonage at North Guilford, and that he was diligent in his visiting every portion of his hard and laborious mission field, Killingworth (now Clinton) being sixteen miles southeast of his home.

The Bishop visited the parishes on October 17, 18 and 19, 1792, when seven persons were confirmed in North Guilford, one in Guilford, and five in Killingworth; a second visitation was made in June, 1794, when twenty-four were confirmed in North Guilford, four in Guilford, and twenty-seven in Killingworth. This shows honest and faithful work. Mr. Butler was ordained priest on Sunday, June 9, 1793, in Christ Church, Middletown, at the same time with the Rev. Solomon Blakeslee, the Rev. Edward Blakeslee, and the Rev. Russell Catling.[1]

The parishes felt keenly the loss of such an energetic pastor, when in the fall of 1794 Mr. Butler resigned to accept St. Michael's Church, Litchfield, which had been without a rector for a year, as Mr. Baldwin had gone to Stratford in November, 1793.

Mr. Butler found the people cordial and pleasant, the work exacting and the results gratifying. The secession of some families in 1797 who built a church at Bradleyville (now Bantam) rendered it expedient for him to resign, which he did on February 21, 1799. He had already been called to Christ Church, Reading. In this position he served with great fidelity, doing much missionary work for five years.

In 1804 he received an urgent request from the Hon. Mr. Buel and other churchmen in the new village of Troy, six miles above Albany, New York, to be their pastor.

Mr. Eliakim Warren and other men of ability and wealth were removing from Norwalk to Troy. Mr. Butler was earnestly desired by them to be the pioneer priest in Troy and the region round about. They sailed in a sloop from Norwalk through the Sound, the East River, and the Hudson River to Troy. The services of the Church had been commenced twelve years before by the Rev. Thomas Ellison, Rector of St. Peter's Church, Albany. During his residence with Mr. Ellison, from 1796 to 1798, as a student in divinity, Philander Chase, afterwards Bishop of Ohio, officiated as lay reader.

No parochial organization, apparently, was effected until Mr. Butler arrived, when St. Paul's Church was organized, of which Mr. Warren

[1] P. 9, *Registry of Ordinations.*

became the senior warden. Mr. Butler showed in his labors for the Church in Troy, Lansingburgh and Waterford, sound judgment, patient tact, persevering energy. Under him the Church, both in the growing village and neighboring towns, was firmly established. In 1827 the present spacious Gothic church of St. Paul's parish was built. He became recognized in the town as a leader in every good work and his missionary zeal led him into many places remote from Troy. His intense application had undermined his health, and in 1834 he resigned his rectorship, retaining, however, a fatherly interest in the rapid expansion of the Church in Troy and watching with interest the moral and material growth of the city.

Dr. Butler died in his eighty-first year and the fiftieth of his ministry, on July 11, 1842.

A parishioner who knew him well gives this description: "His personal appearance was at once commanding and attractive. He had a well built, well proportioned frame, indicating a habit of activity and more than common power of endurance. His eye was large and dark, and his whole visage indicative at once of a vigorous intellect and an amiable and genial temper."[1]

Mr. Butler received the degree of Doctor in Divinity from Washington (now Trinity) College, Hartford, in 1832. Dr. Butler published several sermons, including one delivered before a Masonic Lodge in St. Paul's

Church, Woodbury, on the feast of St. John, December 27, 1804.

A son of Dr. Butler, the Rev. Clement M. Butler, D.D., filled many positions of eminence in the Church, and died recently while Professor of Ecclesiastical History in the Philadelphia Divinity School.

[1] Letter of Judge David Buel of Troy in sketch of the Rev. Dr. Butler on p. 390, *Annals of the American Pulpit*, V, by the Rev. William B. Sprague, D.D. New York: Robert Carter & Brothers. 1861. 8vo, pp. xxi, 822.

The Reverend DANIEL BURHANS, D.D.

Daniel, a son of Henry Burhans, an officer in the British army during the "old French war," was born at Sherman, Connecticut, on July 7, 1763. As his father had a large family to support by his work upon a small farm, the only opportunity his son Daniel had for education was in the district school during the brief winter terms. He early showed a desire for knowledge and so impressed his teachers that one of them promised to aid, provided Mr. Burhans would consent to send his son to college. This he finally agreed to do. When seventeen he commenced

[1] This word is abbreviated in the manuscript. It may be "medium."
[2] An extract of a portion of the MS. Autobiography of the Rev. Daniel Burhans, D.D., in possession of the writer.

his preparation for college, combining with it work upon the farm in summer and teaching in the winter. At the end of two years he was ready for college, but upon visiting his old teacher found him dying. This disappointment was severe, but determined him in a newer part of the country to make his own way and secure an education. He went to Lanesborough, Massachusetts, in the heart of the Berkshires. Here at first working for his board he attended a school of high grade and made as rapid progress as the incompetence of the teacher would permit. Finally his natural ability and acquired knowledge was recognized. The teacher was dismissed and Mr. Burhans offered the principalship, which he accepted. The school grew and flourished and a large brick school house was built for him.

Lanesborough was a part of the missionary circuit of the Rev. Gideon Bostwick. During a revival in the Congregational Church, which Mr. Burhans attended, several theological and philosophical questions concerning Regeneration, Election, and the Means of Grace, were brought before him. In his examination of these abstruse subjects he found that his views of them were widely different from those of his fellow worshippers. While his mind was puzzled with the problems, the Thirty-Nine Articles of Religion were put into his hands by a friend, but without his knowing with what body of Christians they originated. Their statements seemed to him forcible, just, and true. When informed of their origin he immediately sought out Mr. Bostwick, found in him a friend and counsellor, became an attendant and soon a communicant in St. Luke's Church. So fully had his thoughts dwelt upon religious matters that he determined to study for the holy ministry.[1] It was, however, ten years before his intention was carried out. In the meantime he had aided Mr. Bostwick by reading the service at Lanesborough on three Sundays in each month. For some months he read the service at Lebanon Springs, Columbia County, New York, on the western slope of the Berkshires, ten miles from his home, then becoming a fashionable resort. After his ordination he became the minister in charge of Lanesborough and Lenox, for Mr. Bostwick had died at New Milford on June 13, 1793.

Dr. Burhans vividly pictures his work in Berkshire County and the surrounding country. It was thorough and faithful. He was ordained priest in Trinity Church, New Haven, by Bishop Seabury on Whitsun-Day, June 8, 1794.

In August, 1799, he accepted the rectorship of Trinity Church, Newtown, vacant by the death of the Rev. Philo Perry. He entered upon his duties in October and began a long course of usefulness. "The church," he records, "was filled to overflowing. I had a large number of candidates for Communion at Easter, & to have all things done decently & in order according to the excellent provision made in the Rubrics I invite[d the Bishop] to hold a Confirmation, & rising of eighty were confirmed. And a great proportion of [them] were admitted [to] the

[1] This religious experience is stated in very nearly the exact words of Dr. Burhans in his communication to Dr. Pitkin, who prepared his funeral sermon.

Holy Communion on Easter Sunday. At this Revival while there was a Jubilee in the Church, the sectarians stared with astonishment! And were ready [to cry] out '[Is] Saul among the Prophets'?"[1]

Dr. Burhans became very active in Diocesan affairs and was honored with many offices. He was especially energetic as an agent in securing funds for the General Theological Seminary, both at its inception in 1817 and when in the Diocese from 1820 to 1822. Upon the verge of old age

he resigned his parish on November 1, 1830. Without accepting another charge he officiated in St. Paul's, Woodbury, Christ Church, Bethlehem, and Christ Church, Roxbury. In 1831 he became rector of St. Peter's Church, Plymouth, where he served six years, when he resigned, as the infirmities of old age were increasing upon him. He temporarily served at Oxford and Zoar for some time, and in 1844 he retired from the active duties of the ministry and spent the remaining years of his life at Poughkeepsie, New York. He retained his vigor of mind and body to the last. In his ninety-first year he commenced his "Autobiography," of which only a portion seems to have been preserved. He was a storehouse of information upon all matters of Connecticut diocesan history, and his recollections of Bishop Seabury and Bishop Jarvis, recorded in Dr. Sprague's *"Annals of the American Pulpit,"* are graphic and lifelike. He departed this life peacefully on December 30, 1853, in the ninety-first year of his age and the sixty-first of his ministry.

He received from Washington (now Trinity) College the degree of Doctor in Divinity in 1831.

While he wrote much he seems to have published only one sermon: *The Scripture Doctrine of the Election of Jacob and the Rejection of Esau Considered.*[2]

The Rev. Dr. Buel, Rector of Christ Church, Poughkeepsie, at the time of Dr. Burhans' residence, says that he was "a man of commanding personal appearance, of a large and well built frame, of a healthy and ruddy countenance, of a nervous temperament and somewhat quick in his movements. His manners, though not highly polished, were simple and natural, and evinced what he actually possessed, a fine genial spirit."[3]

Dr. Burhans was the last survivor of those ordained by Bishop Seabury. During the session of the General Convention of 1853 in the City of New York he was formally welcomed in the House of Bishops.

The Rev. Dr. Burhans has preserved this interesting account of his examination for Holy Orders:

"On the first of June I accompanied the Rev. Mr. Bostwick to Middletown, Ct., to attend the annual Convention of that Diocese, who introduced me as a candidate for holy orders. The next morning I was examined in the presence of the Bishop by the late venerable Rev. Richard Mansfield, D.D., Rev. Dr. Hubbard & Rev. Mr. Fogg. They were courteous & familiar. I was soon at ease & unembarrassed, supporting myself [with] confidence, with becoming humility.

The most puzzling and difficult question was put by Dr. Mansfield as follows: 'Aside from the fulfilment of Prophecy & Miracles, on what ground would you defend Divine Revelation?' By its internal effects upon the external conduct. Contrast the Civilization & Morality of nations who receive & make the Bible the measure (?)[1] of their Council, with the Nations destitute of the Holy Scriptures; you have ocular demonstration of the prosperity of the one & the depression of the other. These with a few of the conclusive arguments of Soame Jennings in his unanswerable defence of Christianity from its Internal Evidence.

This was perfectly satisfactory, & Testimonials were cheerfully signed with many flattering remarks.—In time & due form a Procession of the Bishop, Clergy & Laity proceed to the Church where I was soon robed & presented to the Bishop with his son Charles & received the Order [of] Deacon, June 5, 1793 in the 30th year of my age.

The mingled sensations of joy & fear under the high responsibilities of the office is better realized by the Novitiate properly impressed than by any language he can express.

The next day I parted from the Bishop & Clergy with mutual and Christian wishes."[2]

The Reverend CHARLES SEABURY.

Charles, the youngest son of the Rt. Rev. Samuel and Mary (Hicks) Seabury, was born at Westchester, New York, on May 20, 1770. When he was five years old he was taken by his father to New York City, where the family remained during the Revolution and until Bishop Seabury assumed his Episcopal duties and made his home at New London.

[1] MS. Autobiography of Dr. Burhans.
[2] Vergennes, 1810; reprinted, 1828. 8vo, pp. 32.
[3] P. 414, Dr. Wm. B. Sprague's *Annals of the American Pulpit*, V.

He studied theology under the Rev. Dr. Mansfield and the Rev. Dr. William Smith the younger, then at Narragansett, Rhode Island. With these well read divines he was made ready for ordination. Upon his return to New London he pursued a special course of systematic divinity with his father. He was made a deacon, as the *"Records"* note, on June 5, 1793. He spent the year after his ordination at Ripton (now Huntington) in charge of St. Paul's Church. He assisted his father in

New London during his frequent absences until the fall of 1795, when he was called for six months to Grace Church, Jamaica, Long Island. Here his services were appreciated and he found much parish work to be done. The sudden death of his father on February 26, 1796, summoned him once more to New London.

On March 28, 1796, he was called to the rectorship of St. James's Church, New London, which he accepted. Without the force and grace of his father or the profound knowledge of men and books which made the Bishop preëminent, his son Charles was an excellent parish priest. Few events occurred during his rectorship, which covered the period of depression, financial and spiritual, immediately preceding and during the War of 1812. On July 17, 1796, Mr. Seabury was ordained priest by Bishop Provoost in St. George's Chapel, New York City. In 1814 Mr. Seabury removed to Long Island and became Rector of Caroline Church, Setauket. Here, in pleasant surroundings, in the busy and unnoted cares of a rural parish he spent the remainder of his days. For several years he had charge also of Huntington and Islip.

In 1843 he resigned and accepted a retiring pension from the Aged and Infirm Clergy Fund of the Diocese of New York. His home was still in Setauket, where he died on December 29, 1844, in the seventy-fourth year of his age, fifty-first of his ministry.

Bishop Onderdonk, in announcing his retirement to the Convention, said that he had since he was commissioned to the ministry given himself to his Master's work, "unweariedly, disinterestedly, and with no small share of trial and self sacrifice."[1]

Dr. Hallam says: "His was the fate of too many of our clergy even now, whose life is but the trial of the varieties of starvation, and it is believed that his removal to Setauket brought with it little alleviation of his condition, so that his whole life, that of a good, kind-hearted, sensible and faithful man, was but a long struggle with adversity, which after being maintained for more than half a century with a zeal and ardor which trouble and privation could not abate, and age could scarcely dull, has ended at last we doubt not in a better and enduring substance."[2]

Mr. Seabury was the third in the illustrious line of clergymen in one family, his grandfather, Samuel Seabury, having been the first resident missionary in New London. His son was the well known Dr. Samuel Seabury, editor, theologian, and professor, and his grandson is the present senior professor in the General Theological Seminary, Dr. William Jones Seabury, the eminent canonist.

[1] P. 401, Sprague's *Annals*, V.   [2] P. 83, *Annals of St. James's*, New London.

The Reverend CALEB CHILD.

Nothing seems to be known of the birth or parentage of Mr. Child.

He was made deacon in Christ Church, Stratford, on the first Sunday after Trinity, June 7, 1795, at the last ordination held by Bishop Seabury.[1]

He was placed in charge of St. James's Church, Great Barrington, Massachusetts, where he remained for nearly two years. He seems to have returned to Connecticut and officiated wherever there was a vacancy.

As early as 1800 rumors affecting his character were in circulation and a formal complaint made to the Convocation. The report of the Committee was made at Newtown on June 2, 1801. It had found the charges true and the Bishop was asked to publish his sentence of degradation in such way and manner as he shall judge proper.[2]

The sentence was pronounced on Wednesday, June 2, 1802, by the Bishop of the Diocese and entered on the "*Records*."[3] No details of his subsequent life have been found after a careful investigation of probable sources of information.

The Reverend SMITH MILES, M. A.

Manoah Smith Miles was born in Derby on March 19, 1766. He was educated in the schools of the town and studied by himself and under competent tutors until ready for college. He was graduated with honor from Yale College in 1791. He evidently soon determined to study for the ministry, as the "*Records*" show. He was made deacon on June 7, 1795, in Christ Church, Stratford, by Bishop Seabury, at the same time with Mr. Caleb Childs and Mr. Alexander Viets Griswold.[4]

[1] P. 10, *Registry of Ordinations*.
[2] P. 55, *ante*.   [3] P. 58, *ante*.   [4] P. 10, *Registry of Ordinations*.

Mr. Miles took charge of Trinity Church, Branford, Christ Church, Guilford, and St. John's, North Guilford. His work was difficult and required much effort, as the parishes were several miles from each other. He made here full proof of his ministry. In 1796 he became the minister in charge of Christ Church, Middle Haddam, and Trinity Church,

Chatham. In this field of labor he was most earnest and successful. His charge of Middle Haddam continued until 1810, when he devoted himself wholly to Chatham. He was a good pastor and considered an instructive preacher. Like many of the country parsons he kept for many years a classical school, which gained a high reputation. After a ministry of nearly thirty-four years, he died on January 30, 1830, in the sixty-fourth year of his age.

The Right Reverend ALEXANDER VIETS GRISWOLD, D.D.

Alexander Viets, a son of Elisha and Eunice (Viets) Griswold, was born in Simsbury, Connecticut, on April 22, 1766. His ancestry was distinguished in the annals of the Colony, and his father was a man of high reputation in the community. His mother had the charge of his early education and taught him carefully the rudiments of what was then considered essential for one not designed for the law or ministry. He then came under the instruction of his uncle, the Rev. Roger Viets, Rector of St. Andrew's Church, Simsbury, whose attainments in both literature and the classics were remarkable. It was intended by the family and Mr. Griswold that he should accompany his uncle to Nova Scotia, where he accepted the parish of Digby. Mr. Griswold's early marriage, however, interfered with their plan. He temporarily abandoned the study of theology and commenced to read law. It was the faithfulness of his pastor, the Rev. Ambrose Todd, that brought him to a renewed sense of his duty and led to his becoming a candidate for holy orders. He was made deacon in Christ Church, Stratford, on June 7, 1795.[1]

His first charge was at Cambridge (now Bristol), Harwinton and Northfield. The stations were eight miles distant from each other. He gave to Trinity Church, Northfield, and to St. Mark's, Harwinton, one-quarter each of his time. The remainder he devoted to St. Matthew's, East Plymouth, to which church the people of Cambridge then came. In this work Mr. Griswold was extremely useful. He was honored and respected by every one in a wide region of country. A few months after his incumbency the new church of St. Matthew's was ready for consecration. The Convocation met on October 22, 1795, and, as the *Records* state, the Church of St. Matthew's was consecrated and the Rev. Mr. Griswold ordained priest.[2]

"Then, too, it was, though with no thought or expectation of such a thing, that the clergy proposed to the Bishop and to myself that I should

[1] P. 10, *Registry of Ordinations*.
[2] P. 10, *Registry of Ordinations*. P. 49, *ante*.

be ordained priest, which was accordingly done."[1] Mr. Griswold now redoubled his efforts, and by his long missionary journeys extended a knowledge of the Church to many hamlets very remote from his home. In June, 1804, after much solicitation he accepted the very pressing call of St. Michael's Church, Bristol, Rhode Island. Here, amid happy surroundings, with a parish compact and aggressive, he spent twenty-six years. He was the most prominent clergyman in Rhode Island, although his extreme modesty and self-distrust caused him to shun publicity. In 1810 he was about to accept the charge of St. Michael's, Litchfield, as the Rev. Truman Marsh was unable to do full duty, when, to his surprise, he was informed of his election on May 29, 1810, as Bishop of the Eastern Diocese, that confederation of the existing dioceses of Massachusetts, Rhode Island, New Hampshire and Vermont which had been made necessary by the extreme feebleness of the Church in them.

The consecration of Dr. Griswold took place in Trinity Church, New York City, on May 29, 1811 by Bishop White, Bishop Provoost and Bishop Jarvis. At the same time the Rev. John Henry Hobart was consecrated assistant Bishop of New York. This event was the turning point in the history of the American Church, the end of the period of extreme depression and the beginning of a constant growth and expansion.

It is unnecessary here to follow minutely the details of Bishop Griswold's work as Bishop. It was wise, judicious, fruitful. The Church recovered from her despondency throughout New England. The design of the Eastern Diocese was accomplished. Bishop Griswold became Presiding Bishop of the American Church on the death of Bishop White in 1830.

From 1830 to 1835 he was Rector of St. Peter's Church, Salem, Massachusetts. He then relinquished all parochial cares and removed to Boston, giving himself fully to his Episcopal functions. Upon the morning of February 15, 1843, he made a call upon his recently consecrated coadjutor in Massachusetts, Dr. Eastburn, and fell upon his doorstep and died instantly. He was in the seventy-sixth year of his age and the thirty-fourth of his Episcopate.

Bishop Griswold published a few sermons and charges, among them one before the General Convention of 1817.

He received from Brown University, Princeton University and Harvard University the degree of Doctor in Divinity.

[1] P. 70, Extracts from Bp. Griswold's Autobiography in *Memoirs of the Life of the Rt. Rev. Alexander Viets Griswold, D.D.*, by John S. Stone, D.D. Philadelphia: Stavely & McCalla, 1844. 8vo, pp. xl, 620.

THE REVEREND DAVID BALDWIN.

David, a son of William Baldwin, was born in Litchfield on February 4, 1780. While carefully educated, he did not enjoy the advantages of a college course. He was a student in theology with his cousin, Dr. Ashbel Baldwin, and is known to have been officiating as lay reader in Guilford and North Guilford in November, 1806. In March, 1807, he was called to be the minister of Christ Church, Guilford, but was not made deacon until September 1, 1807.[1] Mr. Baldwin served with great fidelity and unwearied patience the three parishes of Guilford, North Guilford and North Killingworth, sometimes called North Bristol. There are still living those who remember him with gratitude and affection. At Easter

1834 he resigned the charge of Guilford, but retained the other parishes and added Branford until 1838. In 1851 he resigned North Guilford. He continued to serve Zion Church, North Branford, and Union Church, Killingworth, until 1858, when his age and infirmities made his retirement from all active service necessary. Bishop Williams said of him then, that he was "the senior presbyter of the Diocese and carried with him into his retirement the affectionate veneration of his brethren, and the blessing of those to whom he had so long and faithfully ministered." He died at Guilford on August 2, 1862, in the eighty-third year of his age and the fifty-sixth of his ministry.

The present Rector of Christ Church, in his history of the parish, says of him that "he was to all men a model of Christian fidelity, and the members of his widely scattered flock, whom he never neglected in heat or cold, in sunshine or storm, though often exposed as he went to and fro on horseback, to severe hardship, and to whom his house was open for unstinted hospitality, found in him a noble example of that unswerving devotion to pastoral duty which distinguished the early representatives of Connecticut Churchmanship."[2]

[1] *Registry of Ordinations.*
[2] P. 70, *History of Christ Episcopal Church.*

At a TOWN-MEETING holden in NEW-HAVEN, upon the eighth day of March, Anno Dom. 1784.

ON Motion of *Pierpont Edwards*, Efq.

Voted, That *Pierpont Edwards, John Whiting, David Auftin, David Atwater, Samuel Huggins, James Hillhoufe, Jonathan Ingerfoll,* and *Jonathan Dickerman,* be a Committee to confider of the propriety, and expediency of admitting as inhabitants of this town, perfons, who in the courfe of the late war, have adhered to the caufe of Great-Britain, againft thefe United States, and are of fair characters, and will be good and ufeful members of fociety, and faithful citizens of this State, and that faid Committee report to this Meeting.

To the Town of New-Haven, in Town-Meeting affembled.

WE your Committee, appointed " to confi- " der of the propriety and expediency of " admitting as inhabitants of this town, perfons, " who in the courfe of the late war have adhered to " the caufe of Great-Britain againft thefe United " States, and are of fair characters, and will be " good and ufeful members of fociety, and faith- " ful citizens of this State," beg leave to report,

That, by the fœderal Conftitution of the United States, each State, as to its internal police, is fovereign and independent to all purpofes not fpecially excepted in the Articles of Confederation ; and the power of admitting to inhabitancy, is referved unimpeached to each State, liable to no reftriction or limitation, but by its own municipal laws—That there is no law of this State which forbids the perfons pointed out in the vote of the town from coming into or dwelling therein—That by the exprefs provifions of the Statutes of this State, each town has the exclufive right and power of admitting its inhabitants—That by the Articles of the Definitive Treaty, and the Recommendations of Congrefs founded thereon, a fpirit of real peace and philanthropy towards our countrymen of the aforefaid defcription are

moft ftrongly inculcated.

That as thefe United States have by the bleffing of Heaven eftablifhed their independence, and fecured their liberties on that bafis to which their wifhes and exertions were directed, and as the great national queftion on which thofe perfons differed from us in fentiment is terminated authoritatively in favour of the United States, it is our opinion that, in point of law and conftitution, it will be proper to admit, as inhabitants of this town, fuch perfons as are fpecificated in faid Vote ; but that no perfons who have committed unauthorized and lawlefs plundering and murder, or have waged war againft thefe United States contrary to the laws and ufages of civilized nations, ought on any account to be admitted.

With refpect to the expediency of fuch a meafure, we beg leave to report, That in our opinion no nation, however diftinguifhed for prowefs in arms, and fuccefs in war, can be confidered as truly great, unlefs it is alfo diftinguifhed for juftice and magnanimity : and no people can, with the leaft propriety, lay claim to the character of being *juft,* who violate their moft folemn treaties, or of being *magnanimous* who perfecute a conquered and fubmitting enemy ; that therefore the prefent and future national glory of the United States is deeply concerned in their conduct relative to the perfons defcribed in faid Vote. For altho' at the prefent moment, while the diftreffes and calamities of the late war are frefh in our recollection, we may confider a perfecuting fpirit as juftifiable, we muft, when difpaffionate reafon refumes her empire, reprobate fuch a line of conduct, and be convinced that future generations, not being influenced by our paffions, will form their ideas of our characters, from thofe acts which a faithful hiftorian fhall have recorded, and not from our paffions of which they can have no hiftory. That as this town is moft advantageoufly fituated for Commerce, having a fpacious and fafe harbour, furrounded by a very extenfive

and fertile country, which is inhabited by an induftrious and enterprizing people fully fenfible of the advantages of trade ; and as the relative and effential importance and confequence of this State depend on the profperity and extent of its agriculture and commerce, neither of which can alone render it important and happy, we are of opinion that in point of real honour and permanent utility the meafure propofed will be highly expedient.

Voted, That the town accept and approve the foregoing Report of Committee, and that this town will admit as inhabitants thereof, all perfons by faid report recommended to be admitted ; and the Select-Men are directed to regulate their conduct towards fuch perfons accordingly.

Voted, That the Select-Men of this Town caufe the foregoing Votes to be publifhed in the News-Paper.

A true Copy of Record,
Examined by SAMUEL BISHOP, Town-Clerk.

JOHN WHITING,
DAVID AUSTIN,
JONATHAN DICKERMAN,
DAVID ATWATER,
JONATHAN INGERSOLL,
PIERPONT EDWARDS,
JAMES HILLHOUSE,
SAMUEL HUGGINS.

The following sketches of the early clergy were compiled in 1854 by the Rev. Dr. Alonzo Bowen Chapin for the Diocesan newspaper, The Calendar, published weekly on Saturdays throughout the year: [1] Jan. 14, [2] July 1, [3] July 8, [4] July 15, [5] July 22, [6] July 29, [7] Aug. 5, [8] Aug. 12, [9] Aug. 19, [10] Aug. 26, [11] Sept. 2, [12] Sept. 9, [13] Sept. 16, [14] Sept. 23, [15] Sept. 30, [16] Oct. 7, [17] Oct. 14, [18] Oct. 21, [19] Oct. 28, [20] Nov. 4, [21] Nov. 11, [22] Nov. 18, [23] Nov. 25. Files of this newspaper will be found in the Archives of the Diocese of Connecticut and in the Library of Trinity College, Hartford. The issue of August 12, 1854, is extant only at Trinity College.

[1]   **Obituary**

REV. DANIEL BURHANS.

The decease of this aged and eminent servant of God, calls for some particular notice from his surviving brethren ; especially, as being one of the last links connecting the present and the past, in that he was the last surviving Presbyter ordained by Bishop Seabury. Born at Sherman, Conn., July 6th, 1763, and educated in the creed of Calvinistic Congregationalism, he commenced preparation for College under the patronage of Dr. Page, of the same place. He subsequently became melancholy, under the impression that he was of the non-elect, from which condition he was providentially delivered by an opportune acquaintance with the Theology of the Church, which commenced at Lanesboro', Mass., whither his father had removed, and where the Rev. Gideon Bostwick officiated once a month.

The patron of Mr. B. dying without making any provision for him, he relinquished the idea of college, and the ministry, and opened a school in Lanesboro', which succeeded beyond his expectations. At this time he became acquainted with Mr. Bostwick, through whose instrumentality his Calvinistic doubts were removed, and by whom he was persuaded to prepare for Holy Orders. He pursued his studies at intervals, out of school hours, without any intention of relinquishing his school. At length, being found qualified for Deacon's Orders, the Rev. Mr. Bostwick, who was stationed at Great Barrington, about twenty-five miles from Lanesboro', advised his taking Deacon's Orders, which he received at the hands of Bishop Seabury at Middletown, Conn., in 1793.

He returned to Lanesboro', intending to supply that place, and go on with his school. But a mysterious Providence ordered otherwise. In less than a week he was sent for to attend the funeral of Mr. Bostwick. There seemed now, no alternative. The school was given up, and all the parishes in that vicinity devolved upon him, and received his faithful oversight until 1799, when he was called to Trinity Church, Newtown, Conn., where he remained about thirty years.

Mr. B received Priest's Orders in 1794, was admitted Honorary M. A. at Williamstown, in 1804, and to the same, at Geneva, in 1835. He was made D. D., at Trinity College, in 1831. He died December 30th, 1853.

During his residence in Massachusetts, he organized Parishes in Pittsfield, Lenox, Tyrringham, and Williamstown, Mass.; New Lebanon Springs, Cooperstown, Richfield, and Exeter, N. Y. In 1807, he organized Parishes in Sharon and Kent, and in 1816, in Salisbury. In 1810, he made the tour of Vermont, in order to ascertain the condition of the Church lands there ; visiting Canada, and securing the services of the Rev. Sir Charles Stuart, afterwards the Lord Bishop of Quebec, as an agent and advocate of the same. In 1832, Dr. B. took charge of St. Peter's Church, Plymouth, where he remained

five or six years. Leaving Plymouth, he went to Oxford and officiated until 1839, since which time he has had no regular charge, though he has rendered frequent occasional service when there was a call for his labors. His residence has been for some time past, at Poughkeepsie, N. Y., where he married his fourth wife about two years since.

Dr. B. was long a member of the Standing Committee of this Diocese, a Delegate to the General Convention for many years, and a Trustee of Trinity College. He wrote *A History of the Church in Newtown*, in part, which was published in the *Churchman's Magazine* for 1823, and which came to an end with the death, or suspension of that periodical. He has also published several Sermons, the time and titles of which have not been ascertained. A just and beautiful tribute to Dr. B. may be found in Rev. J H. Nichols' " Christmas Eve," first published in the *Token*, and subsequently in the *Chronicle of the Church*.

Indefatigable in purpose, persevering in industry, correct in deportment, sound in faith, impressive and winning in manner, Dr. B. lived to accomplish a vast work for the Church, and unlike most others, was permitted to see the results of his labors.   A. B. C.

BIOGRAPHICAL SKETCHES
OF ALL THE CLERGY ORDAINED BY BISHOP SEABURY.

[2]   BY REV. A. B. CHAPIN, D. D.

COLIN FERGUSON, D. D.

Rev. Colin Ferguson, M. A., of Washington College, Md., 1783, and D. D. of the same in 1787, youngest son of Colin Ferguson, a respectable emigrant from Scotland, was born about three miles from Georgetown, Cross-Roads, Kent County, Maryland in 1755. Where he received his rudimental education, is uncertain. He was, however, sent, at a suitable age, to Edinburgh, to prosecute his studies at the University in that city. In 1782, and probably for some years before, he was an Instructor in Kent County School, a flourishing Academy at Chestertown.

In 1783, at its organization, he was appointed Professor of Languages, Mathematics, and Natural Philosophy, in Washington College, Chestertown, the oldest College, in Maryland. He held this post until he was appointed Principal of the College, in 1793; and in this latter position, he continued until 1804 or 5, when he resigned, and removed to the farm, on which he was born, near Georgetown, Cross-Roads, where he died, and was buried, in March, 1807.

He studied Theology under the Rev. William Smith, D. D., Rector of Chester Parish, and was admitted to Deacons Orders by Bishop Seabury, in Christ Church, Middletown, August 3d, and to Priests Orders August 7th, 1785. On the day of his ordination to the Priesthood, he received a license from the Bishop, "to perform the office of a Priest in the Church of CHRIST, particularly in St. Paul's Parish, in Kent

County, in the State of Maryland." In this, his only Parish, he officiated from his ordination to 1799 ; and probably a year or two longer.

He married a Miss Hyland of Kent County, by whom he had two daughters, who survived him.

As a preacher, he appears, by his sermons, many of which still remain, to have been instructive and argumentative, earnest and faithful.

Dr. Ferguson was distinguished for his literary acquirements. A pupil thus describes his Teacher : "Doctor Ferguson was eminently fitted for a Principal of a College. He was no less distinguished for his knowledge of Mathematical and Physical Science, than his intimate acquaintance with the languages of Greece and Rome. Of the French, he was a perfect Master— and as the writer believes, of the Italian also, as when he left College, he was about to become one of a class in that language, not before taught in Washington College."

"But his greatest qualification consisted in a most matured and excellent judgment, and a well regulated temper. Strict without severity, he administered discipline without giving dissatisfaction even to those whom he thought it necessary to punish. Mild but firm, never under the influence of passion, he commanded the respectful obedience of all under his care. He took real pleasure in explaining to his classes any difficulties, which the most studious *will* encounter, and would proceed, without looking at a book, many lines beyond the difficulty which the pupil *wished* to be explained. He was particularly fond of the Odes of Horace and the Aeneid of Virgil, which, it is believed, he had by heart, though the whole number of the Latin and Greek classics were as familiar to him as his mother tongue. The Doctor was never satisfied with giving a bare translation of a passage in Latin or Greek when consulted by the pupil. He always added explanations and illustrations, by which the meaning of the author, was rendered perfectly plain. His Lectures, during the recitations of the Class of Rhetoric, were more copious than Blair—and his eloquence during the exercises in Physics, especially in Chemistry, was of a character remarkable for the chaste purity of his style, and graceful fluency and strength. I have never seen his equal, in all the parts of a College course."

Dr. F. was also an active and influential member of the general convention of 1789, which formed the federate constitution of the Church, in this country.

AUTHORITIES.—Bishop White's Memoirs of the P. E. Church, 288, 292. MSS. S. R. G. and Dr. P. W.

[3]

HENRY VAN DYKE, M. A.

Henry Van Dyke, M. A., was born in the city of New York, and educated to the Law. After a few years, he relinquished practice, and prepared himself for Holy Orders. During the absence of Dr. Seabury in Europe, he read prayers in vacant

congregations in Connecticut. He was ordained Deacon by Bish. S. at his first ordination, August 3d, 1785, and Priest a few days after. He preached for a time at Milford and Stratford. He was Rector of St. Peter's Church, Auburn, and Christ Church, New Brunswick, for a while, when he was called, in July, 1793, to the Rectorship of St. Mary's, Burlington, which he resigned in August, 1796. In 1797, he was invited to St. James' Church, Newtown, L. I., being the first clergyman that had devoted his entire service to that Parish. He left Newtown in 1802, and probably died soon after, as his name does not appear in the Clergy List of New York in 1803, nor in the list of the Gen. Conv. of 1804. He was a gentleman of good learning and polite manners; but so much of a hypochondriac as to be, in a great measure, but the slave of his imagination.

AUTHORITIES.—F. MSS. VI. 1167. Thomp, L. J. 407. Doane's Hist. Not. Ch. Burl. 44. Stubb's Hist. Ch.—N. B.—13.

REV. ASHBEL BALDWIN.

Rev. Ashbel Baldwin, M. A., of Yale, son of Isaac Baldwin, Esq., was born at Litchfield, March 7th, 1757, and was graduated at Yale College in 1776. Soon after leaving College, he received an appointment in the continental army, which he held for some time, and which, in his latter years, when age had disabled him from every kind of service, afforded him a pension.

He married Clarissa, eldest daughter of Mr. Samuel Johnson, of Guilford, and grand-neice of Rev. Dr. Johnson, of Stratford. Though but a student of theology, he attended the Convocation at Woodbury, 1783, when Dr. Seabury was elected Bishop, and walked with the clergy. He was ordained Deacon August 3d, and Priest September 18th, 1785, and immediately called to the Rectorship of St. Michael's Church in his native place.

In 1793, he was called to fill the place so long and honorably occupied by Rev. Dr. Johnson, the great uncle of his wife, and remained there until 1824. He was long a member of the Standing Committee of the Diocese, delegate to the General Convention, Secretary of the Diocesan Convention for many years, and Secretary of the General Convention several times. After leaving Stratford, he officiated at Wallingford for several years, and a short time at Meriden, North Haven, and Oxford, until 1832, when he became disabled by age from any active duty. He died at Rochester, N. Y., 1846, in the 89th year of his age, having preached about ten thousand times, baptized three thousand and ten, married six hundred couple, and buried about three thousand individuals.

Mr. B. was a sound and well informed theologian, an animated and eloquent speaker, a warm and lasting friend, an agreeable and instructive companion, a humane and benevolent citizen, a faithful and zealous parish clergyman.

AUTHORITIES—F. MSS II. 317—IV. 1080—VII. 1247. Jones 26, 39, 48. Cal. 1846.

[4]

REV. PHILO SHELTON.

Rev. Philo Shelton, M. A., of Yale, was born at Ripton, now Huntington, May 5th, 1754, and was graduated at Yale College in 1775. He was an Episcopalian by birth, education, and choice, and being of a serious disposition, early devoted himself to the ministry. While pursuing theological studies, he read prayers at Fairfield and places adjacent. He was ordained Deacon August 3d, and Priest September 16th, 1785. After having been ordained, he was called to the Rectorship of Trinity Church, Fairfield, with which the small parishes of Stratfield (Bridgeport) and Weston, were for a time united. He married Lucy Nichols, daughter of Philip Nichols, Esq., of Stratford, April 20th, 1780, and died at Fairfield, February 27th, 1825, in his 71st year, having never changed his parish. Previously to July 11th, 1817, Mr. S. had baptized 675 persons, married 225 couples, and buried 314 individuals. He was many years a member of the Standing Committee of the Diocese, Secretary of the Diocesan Convention for a time, Delegate to the General Convention fifteen years, and once Secretary to the House of Bishops.

"As a man, he was distinguished for his virtues, intelligence, and urbanity; as a Christian, he was admired for his sincere piety, and unaffected humility; and as a divine, he was respected for the soundness of his faith, the activity of his zeal, and the correctness of his discipline. Having framed and fashioned himself according to the doctrine of Christ, he was a wholesome example, and pattern to his flock. Being illuminated with the true knowledge and understanding of God's word, he labored earnestly to set it forth, and showed the efficiency of it both by his preaching and living. He was the instructive and agreeable companion, the warm and lasting friend, and the true and faithful monitor; having united in his character, those elements which constitute the gentleman the Christian, and the divine." He leaves two sons adorning that ministry, upon which the father cast so brilliant a gleam of holy light.

AUTHORITIES.—F. MSS. I. 102, II. 344, VIII, 1633 1636. Chur Ch. VI. 139. Corn. Hist. Ch. Fair. 39, 47. Church Mag. 1825, 32. Journ. Am. Conv. Conn.

REV. SAMUEL SPRAGGS.

Rev. Samuel Spraggs of New Jersey, had been a minister of the Methodist denomination for several years, having been admitted preacher in 1776, but becoming persuaded of the necessity of orders from the hands of a Bishop, was ordained Deacon by Bishop Seabury, September 16th, 1785, and Priest on the 18th of the same month.

He officiated at Mount Holly, in New Jersey, about ten years, when he removed to Elizabethtown, in N. J. On the death of Rev. Dr. Chandler, he was called to succeed him, in 1790, where he died in 1794 greatly lamented.

AUTHORITY.—F. MSS. III. 322, 3.

REV. SAMUEL ROE.

Rev. Samuel Roe of New Jersey, was licensed by the clergy of Connecticut in 1784, to officiate as a Lay Reader, and in 1785, he was ordained Deacon September 16th, and Priest September 18th. He was called to the Rectorship of St. Mary's, Burlington, N. J., which he resigned in 1786, and no further account has been obtained of him, unless the name of "William Roe," which stands in the Clergy List of 1792, as the successor of Mr. Spraggs, at Mount Holly, be a mistake for "Samuel Roe."

AUTHORITIES.—Doane's Hist. Church Burl. 43.—Jour. Gen. Conv.

REV. SAMUEL ARMOR.

Rev. Samuel Armor of Maryland, was ordained Deacon September 16th, and Priest September 18th, 1785. No account of this man has been obtained, beyond that furnished by the Bishop's Register, given above. As his name does not appear in the earliest Clergy List, (1792,) he had probably deceased before that time.

[5]

REV. THOMAS FITCH OLIVER.

Rev. Thomas Fitch Oliver, M. A. of Harvard and Brown, was a native of Salem, Mass., and graduated at Harvard, 1775. He was a Congregational minister in Pelham, Mass., for a time, but becoming a Churchman, he officiated as Lay Reader in St. John's Church, Providence, until he was ordained Priest by Bishop Seabury, Sept. 18th, 1785, when he became Rector of that Church. Being invited to Marblehead, Ms., among his friends and relatives, he preached his last sermon in Providence, Sept. 3d, 1786. In 1791, he was Rector of the Churches of Johnstown and Fort Hunter,

N. Y., though his name does not appear in the Clergy List of 1792. In 1795, he was Rector of St. Thomas' Church, Baltimore, where he died January 25, 1797.

AUTHOR.—Dorrance's Rec. Hist. St. John's—Chr. Wit. May, 1843. Updike's 415,419—Jour. Gen. Conv. and Ann. Conv. N. Y.—Tri. Cat. Harv. 1851.—*Amr.* 2, *J. X.* 384, *XV.* 188—*Gen. Reg. V.* 53.

REV. HATCH DENT.

Rev. Hatch Dent, of Maryland, was born in Trinity Parish, Charles co., Md., on the 10th of May, 1751, of pious and respectable parents, descendants of the early settlers of the State. He was educated by Rev. Mr. Campbell, a pious and learned clergyman of the Church, who was for many years the Rector of the Parish.

On completing his education, he became a Private Tutor in the family of Capt. West, of Virginia, and at the beginning of the Revolutionary war, volunteered as an ensign in the American Army. At the battle of Long Island in 1776, he was captured, and remained a prisoner of war for eighteen months, when for his good conduct he was exchanged, and returned home, to the great joy of his friends, beloved and honored by his countrymen. After this, he opened a private school in the Parish, and had the honor of conducting the early education of that distinguished lawyer of the State, Wm. Wirt. He now also commenced the study of Theology, and officiated as Lay Reader during a vacancy of the Parish, occasioned by the death of the Rector. He also served as Lay Delegate in the first Convention of the State, and was thus instrumental in laying the foundation of the Diocese. He was ordained Deacon, Oct. 16th, and Priest, Oct. 18th, 1785, and was shortly after chosen Rector of the Parish. In this capacity he served for several years, when he was called to a parish in North Carolina, which he accepted. In 1796, he was elected the first Principal of Charlotte Hall, a school of much celebrity, in the lower part of this State. At the same time, he was chosen Rector of Trinity Parish also, both of which offices he accepted, and filled with great credit and usefulness. In October, 1799, he resigned his office as Principal, probably owing to declining health, and shortly after this, his death occurred at his place of residence, which is now the glebe of the Parish, and his remains are deposited in the family burial yard, there to await "the general resurrection at the last day." It is a lamentable fact, that there is nothing to mark the place of his sepulture, but a common field stone, on which is "*carved not a line*"! "Sic transit gloria mundi." But what of this?

"Thou shalt lie down
With patriarchs of the infant world—with kings,
The powerful of the earth—the wise—the good,
Fair forms, and hoary seers of ages past,
All in one mighty Sepulchre"—

AUTHOR.—Mss. S. C. D.

[6]

REV. WILLIAM DUKE.

Rev. William Duke, of Maryland, born at Back-Creek-Neck, Baltimore co., Md., was educated in the English branches at that place, and at Charlotte Hall School, St. Mary's county. He instructed himself in Latin, Greek and French, and in his theological studies. At the solicitation of the Methodists, he consented to preach for them until such time as he could obtain Episcopal Ordination. He was admitted preacher among the Methodists in 1775. He was ordained by Bishop Seabury, Deacon, Oct. 16th, and Priest, Oct. 18th, 1785. He was then called to the Rectorship of St. Anne's Parish, Annapolis, and was appointed a Professor in St. John's College in that place. In 1795-6, he was officiating in St. Mary Ann's Parish, Cecil co., and did so occasionally, subsequent to that time, though disabled from performing the full service, by a partial palsy. He died in 1840, in his 83d year. His piety was unquestioned, but he ever retained a leaning towards the Methodist denomination, in which he ministered for a time.

AUTHOR.—MSS. Rev. R. S. G.

REV. JOHN LOWE.

Rev. John Lowe, of N. Y., was ordained Deacon, Nov. 2d, and Priest, Nov. 3d, 1785. No account has been obtained of this man, beyond that furnished by the Bishop's Register.

REV. JOSEPH PILMORE.

Rev. Joseph Pilmore, D.D. of Penn. University, (1807) was an Englishman by birth, and when he came to this country, was a popular preacher among the Methodists.—Becoming dissatisfied with Methodist orders, he applied to Bp. Seabury, and was ordained Deacon, Nov. 27th, and Priest, Nov. 29th, 1785. He was soon called to the Rectorship of the churches of Trinity, St. Thomas, and All Saints, Philadelphia. He was a delegate to the General Convention from Penn., was afterwards Rector of Christ Church, New York city, (1802) and subsequently of St. Paul's, Philadelphia— He died July 24th, 1825, leaving most of his property to various benevolent uses, principally in connection with the Church in Philadelphia. He was a popular and eminently successful laborer in the vineyard of the Lord.

AUTHOR.—Ch. Mag. 1825, 191—Phil. Rec. 1825— Jour. N. Y. Ann. Conv. F MSS. II. 98. Ber. N. Y. 184.

REV. JOHN WOOD, OF IRELAND.

Rev. John Wood (Ireland) was ordained Deacon, January 4th, 1786. The Bishop's Register gives us all the certain knowledge we have of this man. The Fowler manuscripts have "1817" in pencil marks against the name of this man, in the column of ordinations to the Priesthood, probably by mistake for the column denoting the time of death. But they give no clue to the place and circumstances of it.

REV. JOHN PRIEST.

Rev. John Priest was ordained Priest, June 6th, 1786. No account of this man's life or labors has been received.

[7]

REV. JOHN BISSETT.

The history of this man, is involved in considerable doubt. In 1767, Mr. Bissett came to Newport, R. I., as an Assistant to the Rector, and Schoolmaster. The parish records describe him as "Rev. Mr. Bissett," but the abstracts of the society, as "Mr. Bissett." In 1771 the Parish chose him "to be their minister," being the first man, they had undertaken to support themselves. In 1779 he left with the British, and went to New York. He was ordained Deacon, March 12th, and Priest, March 15th, 1786, at Newport, R. I., unless that were a different individual. In 1789 a man of the same name was a delegate to the General Convention from Maryland. In 1792 he was elected both from Delaware and Maryland, but sat as a member from Delaware. In the fall of the same year he was called to be an Assistant Minister of Trinity Church, New York city, where he remained until 1800, when he went to England. He was also a Delegate to the General Convention of 1795, and 1799, and Secretary of that body in 1792, and a prominent, active member of the House of Clerical and Lay Delegates. These facts raise the suspicion, that there was but one man of this name, and that he officiated at Newport, from 1771 to 1779, without being in Orders, as we know some others did, in other places during those troublesome times. It is very possible, however, that the person ordained by Bishop Seabury was son of the person who had been at Newport from 1767 to 1779. If so, he must have been born in England, which is not probable.

AUTHOR.—Updike 402, 3, 475—Berrian 191-193.

REV. BRYAN (LORD) FAIRFAX.

Rev. Bryan (Lord) Fairfax, was the son

of William Fairfax, the Grandson of Henry Fairfax, and Great-Grandson of Henry, 4th Baron of Fairfax, in the Peerage of Scotland, created Oct. 18th, 1627, to which titles and estate he succeeded in 1800, as the Eighth Baron. He was ordained Deacon by Bishop Seabury June 9th, 1786, and Priest on the 11th of the same month. He was a man of simple and unfeigned manners and piety, bearing the distressing illness, which put an end to his life, with the most perfect resignation. He died at Mount Eagle, Alexandria, D C., August 7th, 1802, in the 76th year of his age.— The first volume of the *American Preacher* contains a Sermon of his, "On the Forgetfulness of God."

Author.—Burke's Peerage 385—Dodd's Peerage 111—F. MSS. II. 318.

REV. ABRAHAM LYNSEN CLARKE.

Rev. Abraham Lynsen Clarke, M. A. of Yale, a native of Milford, Conn., was graduated at Yale, 1785, ordained Deacon June 9th, 1786, and Priest, June 7th, 1789.— After preaching a short time at Milford, he went to Huntington, Conn., and was called from thence to the Rectorship of St. John's, Providence in 1792, and commenced his labors there at Easter, 1793. He resigned that Parish in 1800, and after assisting Rev. Mr. Usher at Bristol, R. I., went to St. George's, Flushing, and St. James', Newtown, L. I., in 1803, holding the Rectorship of both churches for six years, (to 1809) from which time to his death, in 1811, his labors were confined to Newtown alone.— Bp. Seabury described him as being "a gentleman of good understanding and character, of easy and polite manners, and of diligence in his profession."

Author.—Upd. 415-442—Thomp. 375, 417. Dormnce's Rec. Hist. St. John's Prov.—Chr. Wit., May, 1843. F MSS. II. 330, III 534.

REV. WALKER MAURY, OF MARYLAND.

Rev. Walker Maury, of Maryland, was ordained Deacon, June 2d, and Priest, June 3d, 1786. Nothing has been found concerning this man, beyond the Register of the Bishop.

REV. WILLIAM SKELLY.

Rev. William Skelly, of Maryland, was ordained Deacon, June 2d, and Priest, June 3d, 1786. He was Rector of Christ Church, Sussex co., Delaware, in 1792 and 1795. His name not appearing in any of the later Clergy Lists, it is probable that he died between 1795 and 1799.

[8]

REV. BENJAMIN LINDSAY.

Rev. Benjamin Lindsay, of North Carolina, was ordained Deacon, July 26th, and Priest, July 27th, 1786. This name does not appear on the Clergy Lists of 1792, and we find no subsequent account of him. He had been a Methodist, among whom he was admitted preacher in 1776; but his name is omitted in the Minutes of Conference, after 1778.

REV. HENRY MOSCROP.

Rev. Henry Moscrop, of R. I., was ordained Deacon, Aug. 27th, and Priest, Aug. 29th, 1786. He was Rector of St. James' Church, Prince George's Co., Md., in 1792, but in 1795 was at All Hallows' Church, Anne Arundel Co., in the same State. In 1797, he was supplying Trinity Church, Newport, gratuitously, but in 1799, and for some years after, was residing in Anne Arundel Co., Md. In 1804 and 1805, his name is not on the Clergy Lists, but in 1811 he was residing in St. Paul's Parish, Baltimore. From 1813, to his death in 1817, he resided in the city of New York. His daughter married Rt. Rev. B. T. Onderdonk. D. D., from whom we had hoped to obtain full particulars of his life. But our application not having met with any response, we give such facts as we have been able to glean from other sources.

Author.—Updike, 408.—Bp. Hobart's Add. 1817.

REV. PHILO PERRY.

Rev. Philo Perry was the son of Joseph Perry, M. D., of Woodbury, Conn., born Dec. 22d, 1752, was graduated at Yale, 1777, and studied Medicine. He pursued the practice for some time at Stratford, where he married Miss Benjamin. He subsequently studied Theology, and was ordained Deacon, Sept. 21st, 1786, and Priest, June 3d, 1787. After his ordination, he was called to the Rectorship of Trinity Church, Newtown, where he remained until his death, which took place in 1789, in the 45th year of his age. He was universally lamented. Nathaniel Perry, M. D., of Woodbury, and Bennet Perry, M. D., of Newtown, were his brothers. He was Secretary of the Convention of Connecticut, Delegate to the Gen. Convention, and member of the Standing Committee.

Author.—F. MSS. vi. 1166. MSS. Dr. Burhans Ch. Ch. v 134. Cothren's Woodbury, 666.

REV. DAVID BELDEN.

Rev. David Belden was graduated at Yale, 1785, and received Deacon's Orders, Sept. 21st, 1786, but appears never to have been advanced to the Priesthood. He resided at Wilton, and died in 1832. Some want of attention to the Canons of the Church, in regard to preaching in the limits of another's parish, brought upon him the censure of the Convention in 1793, and neglect of clerical duty led the Convention to demand his letters of orders in 1801. He was a man of much personal worth, but prevented from exercising the clerical office, mainly, as is supposed, by an excessive and unconquerable diffidence.

Author.—F. MSS. vii. 1252.

[9]

REV. TILLOTSON BRONSON, D. D.

Rev. Tillotson Bronson, D. D. of Brown University, (1813) was born at Plymouth, Conn., 1762, and was graduated at Yale, 1786. He received Deacon's Orders the same year, and Priest's in 1718. While a Deacon, he officiated at Stratford, Vt., and Hanover, N. H., and subsequently to his ordination to the Priesthood for a short time at New London. In 1792, he preached a short time in Christ Church, Boston, but soon returned to Connecticut, and was called to Chatham and Middle Haddam, to which Hebron was afterwards added. In 1795, he was called to the Rectorship of St. John's, Waterbury, where he remained until 1805, when he resigned, and removed to New Haven, in order to edit the Churchman's Magazine, of which he had been chosen the Editor. He was soon after elected Principal of Cheshire Academy, an office which he held till his death, which took place at Cheshire, Sept. 6th, 1826, in the 65th year of his age. The Churchman's Magazine, having been removed to New York in 1809, Dr. B.'s connection with it ceased, and it was subsequently discontinued. It was revived by the Convention of Connecticut in 1821, and Dr. B. again appointed to edit it. The volumes edited by him furnish convincing proof of the soundness of his principles and judgment. He was a good scholar, an able writer, but only an ordinary preacher. He was for many years one of the Standing Committee of the Diocese, and often represented it in General Convention.

Author.—Ch. Mag. 1826, 260-269. Beard's. Hist. Ch. Acad. 21-27.

REV. JOHN COSINS OGDEN.

Rev. John Cosins Ogden, M. A. of Nassau Hall, and Yale, 1782, was graduated at Nassau Hall, 1770. He received Deacon's Orders, Sept. 24, 1786, and Priest's, March 27th, 1788. Our impression is, that he had been a preacher in another denomination, but of this we are not sure. He married the daughter of Gen. Wooster, of New Haven, and labored many years in Vermont and New Hampshire, devotedly and faith-

fully, where his name is still held in veneration. He was Rector of Queen's Chapel, Portsmouth, N. H., 1789. He preached a sermon in Philadelphia, Sunday evening, Feb. 23d, 1800, on Peace, Charity and Toleration, which was published and dedicated to John Adams, President of the United States. He died in 1800. There is a tablet to the memory of his daughter, Miss Mary Wooster Ogden, in Trinity Church, New Haven, where she died in 1839, in the 63d year of her age; and to whose munificence and zeal, the Church in that city is much indebted.

AUTHOR.—Chase, Rem. 19—Wm's. Vermont, 196—F. MSS. ii. 1155. Ch. Ch. iii. 107 Cal. Y. C, and Nev.—C.

REV. DANIEL BARBER.

Rev. Daniel Barber, of Vermont, M. A. of Dartmouth, 1801, was born at Simsbury, Oct. 2d, 1756, and was ordained Deacon, Oct 29, 1786. He officiated in Vermont until 1794, mostly in Manchester and its vicinity, when he went to Claremont, N.H., and became Rector of Union Church, in that place. On the 15th of Nov., 1818, he resigned the Parish, and followed his son, Virgil Horace Barber, into the Romish Church, and spent his days at Georgetown, D. C. He was Secretary of the Convention that elected Samuel Peters, Bp. of Vermont in 1791; there being at that time but one other clergyman settled in Vermont Mr. B's. apostacy was marked by the same duplicity which has characterized later acts of the kind, for within three weeks of his own profession of the Romish faith, he gave Bp. Griswold the most solemn assurances of his soundness in the Protestant faith.

AUTHOR.—Ch. Mag. 1805, 175, and 1807. 231.—Bp. White Mem. 174 A. B. C. MSS.

[10]

REV. CHAUNCY PRINDLE.

Rev. Chauncey Prindle, M. A. of Yale, was born at Westbury, now Watertown, in 1753, and was graduated at Yale, 1776. He was ordained Deacon, June 1, 1787, and Priest, Feb. 24th, 1788. From the time of his ordination until 1804, he preached a part of the time in Watertown, and the remainder in Northbury, now Plymouth, until 1806. During this period he baptized in Plymouth 339, married 17 couples, and attended 60 funerals. After this, he was Rector of the churches in Oxford and Salem (Naugatuc) for several years. He died in 1833, aged 80.

AUTHOR.—Watt. Hist. Plym. in Cal. Feb. 1845.—Prindle, MSS. in Ch. Ch. iii. 236, 237.

REV. AMBROSE TODD.

Rev. Ambrose Todd, born at Northford,

1765, was graduated, 1786. He was ordained Deacon, June 1st, 1787, and Priest, June 7th, 1789. From the time of his ordination until 1801, he preached in Simsbury and Granby, when he was called and removed to Huntington, where he died. He was a member of the Standing Committee of the Diocese, for a time. The following is a copy of the inscription placed over his grave.

"In memory of the Rev. Ambrose Todd, Rector of St. Paul's and St. Peter's in Huntington, who expired on the 25th of July, 1809, in the 45th year of his age, and the 22d of his ministry. This monument is erected by the Episcopal Society, as a testimony of respect and esteem towards him, their clergyman, for his piety and zeal as a preacher, and his benevolence and goodness as a man."

He left two sons, who have entered the ministry, from which he was taken in the midst of his usefulness.

AUTHOR.—Ch. Mag. 1805, 245, and 1809, 370—F. MSS. vi. 1223. Phelps' Hist. Gran. iii. Sims. 74.

REV. BETHUEL CHITTENDEN.

Rev. Bethuel Chittenden, of Vermont, was brother of the Hon. Thomas Chittenden, Governor of Vermont, and both were natives of East Guilford, Conn. Hon. Thomas Chittenden was Governor of that State from its independence in 1777, to his death in 1797, with the exception of a single year. The mother of the Rev. Bethuel Chittenden was sister of the Rev. Samuel Johnson, D. D. He was born at Guilford, about 1737. He was ordained Deacon in 1787, at the age of fifty, and Priest in 1794. He labored in Vermont and New Hampshire, but mostly at Shelburn, in the former State. He was led to take Orders at this late period of life, by the pressing need of Clergymen in that State. He was possessed of a strong mind, and great good sense, but had enjoyed but poor advantages of early training. He was one of the individuals actively engaged in establishing the University of Vermont, and was one of the Trustees, as was also his brother, the Governor. He died in 1809.

AUTHOR.—Allen, 256—Chase Rem. 19.—Wm. Hist. Vermont, 196. Ann. 2, Reg. xiii. 399, 400. Kill. Litch.—Co.—Biog. 89.

REV. REUBEN GARLICK.

Rev. Reuben Garlick, of Vermont, was ordained Deacon, July 29th, 1787. Nothing has been learned of this man, beyond the fact of his ordination to the Diaconate.

[11]

REV. EDWARD BLAKESLEE.

Rev. Edward Blakeslee was born at North Haven, June 27th, 1766. He entered Yale

College, but was obliged to leave in his Senior year, in consequence of the sickness and death of his parents, and consequently did not receive the degree of A. B. He was ordained Deacon, Feb. 24, 1788, and Priest, June 5th, 1793. The first three years after his ordination were spent in North Haven and its vicinity, but in 1790 he was called to Derby, as an Assistant to Rev. Dr. Mansfield, whose daughter he had married two years before. He died July 15th, 1797, aged 31.

By his premature death, his family were deprived of a kind and affectionate husband, father and brother, the Church of a faithful devoted and zealous minister, and the public of a disinterested friend.

AUTHOR.—Scott's Hist. Ch. Derby, 12, and Ch. Ch. vi. 22. Chapin's Ch. N. H., Ch. Ch. vi. 127.—Sund. Vist. 1819, 93·—F. MSS. ii. 116.

REV. REUBEN IVES.

Rev. Reuben Ives was born at Cheshire, Oct. 26, 1762, and was graduated at Yale, 1786. He was ordained Deacon in 1786, but remained with Bishop Seabury nearly two years as Pupil and Assistant. Immediately after his ordination to the Priesthood, 1788, he was called to the Rectorship of the Church in his native place, which he held until 1820. He was a delegate to the Gen. Convention, and member of the Standing Committee. From 1820 to his death, Oct. 4th, 1836, he officiated in the vacant Parishes of the neighborhood, whenever his health would permit, and finally departed in a good old age, after many years of arduous service in the ministry. His wife was the daughter of Rev. J. R. Marshall of Woodbury. He left a son in the ministry, (E. J. Ives) who has since apostatized to Rome.

AUTH.—Beards. Hist. Ch. Cheshire, 10-14. Add. Bp. Brown. 1837.

REV. DAVID FOOTE.

Rev. David Foote, M. A. of Dartmouth, was born at Colchester (now Marlborough) Oct. 5th, 1760, and was graduated at Dartmouth, 1778. He was ordained Deacon, June 11th, 1788, and Priest, Oct. 22d, 1788. He was called to the Rectorship of Grace (now Christ) Church, Rye, N. Y., in 1790, but died Aug. 1st, 1793. He seems to have retained his connection with Bishop Seabury, always attended the Convocations of Connecticut, and was a member of the Connecticut Convention in 1792. His name is entered there as Daniel Foote, and the same mistake occurs in the Register of the Clergy in the Journal of New York in 1791, and also in the Journal of the General Convention of 1792.

AUTH.—Good. Gen. Foote, Fam. 59. Bolton's Hist. West, ii. 75-6.

REV. ADAM BOYD.

Rev. Adam Boyd, of Georgia, was ordained Deacon, Aug. 18th, and Priest, Aug. 19th, 1788. Nothing is known of this man beyond the fact of his ordination.

REV. AMBROSE HULL.

Rev. Ambrose Hull was a native of Cheshire, Ct., and was graduated at Harvard, 1785. He was ordained Deacon, Oct. 12th, 1788, and Priest, June 7th, 1789. After officiating in some of the vacant Parishes in Connecticut, he removed to South Carolina, and was Rector of the Church on St. Helena Island. His stay there must have been short, for at the meeting of the General Convention in 1792, he was Rector of a Church in Brooklyn, N. Y. His stay here was still shorter. Leaving Brooklyn, he went to Ohio, and from thence to East Florida, where he laid aside his clerical profession, and was appointed Judge in the Civil Courts. He died in 1821.

AUTHOR.—F. MSS. vii, 1431. Cat. Harv. 1851.—Journ. Gen. Conv. 1792.

[12]

REV. SAMUEL NISBETT.

Rev. Samuel Nisbett was ordained Deacon Oct. 12th, and Priest Oct. 22d, 1788. He was Rector of St. Thomas' and St. Dennis' Parish, in South Carolina, from 1791 to 1793. From 1793 to 1797 he was Rector of St. Ann's, Brooklyn. In 1804, 1808, 1811, he was residing in New York. No account of his death has been found.

AUTHOR.—Dalcho. 293, 485. This name is erroneously printed "Bissett" in the Report of the Con. Journals, when recording his ordination as Deacon.

REV. SOLOMON BLAKESLEE.

Rev. Solomon Blakeslee was born at North Haven, Nov. 9th, 1762, and was graduated at Yale 1785. He was ordained Deacon, June 3d, 1789, and Priest, June 5th, 1793. He preached a short time in North Haven, one year in Claremont, N.H.; for twelve or fourteen years was Rector of St. Stephen's Church, East Haddam, and three years (from 1815 to 1818) of St. James' Church, New London. After his resignation of the Church in New London, he does not seem to have had any Cure.— He died in Otsego County, N. Y., April 10th, 1835, aged 73. He was a man of easy address, zeal and eloquence. He published an Address delivered before the Peace Society of East Haddam, Dec. 30th, 1819.

AUTHOR.—Chap. H. C. N. H. in Ch. Ch. vi. 127.—Hal. H. C. N. L. 28.—Ch. Mag. 1805, 177.

REV. ROBERT FOWLE.

Rev. Robert Fowle, of New Hampshire, graduated at Harvard, 1786. He was or-dained Deacon, Dec. 17th, 1789, and Priest June 29th, 1791. He was one of the earliest settlers of Holderness, N. H., was a Lay Reader in the Church before his ordination, was called to the Rectorship of the Parish there immediately upon his receiving Orders, and labored faithfully and zealously in that place until within a short time of his death, which took place Oct. 16th, 1847, in the 82d year of his age. The Sermon preached by Bishop Seabury at the Ordination, gave great offence to some of the Sectaries there, and led to much abuse of the Bishop, in consequence of which the Sermon was published.

AUTHOR.—Ch. Rev. i. 147.—Adv. to Ord. Serm. Rev. R. F.—Cat. H. C., 1851.

REV. TRUMAN MARSH.

Rev. Truman Marsh was born at Litchfield, Conn., Feb. 22d, 1768, was graduated at Yale, 1786, ordained Deacon by Bishop White in 1790, and Priest by Bp. Seabury, June 2d, 1790. He was Tutor in Cokesbury College, Baltimore, before he received Orders, and was elected to the Presidency of the same, but declined it. He was Rector of the Churches in New Milford, New Preston, and Roxbury, from 1790 to 1799, when he was elected Rector of St. Michael's Church, Litchfield, which he held until 1830, though his health had required an Assistant after 1810. He died March 28th, 1851, in the 84th year of his age. He was a Delegate to the General Convention, and Member of the Standing Committee. Mr. M. was a fine scholar, an acceptable and successful preacher, an able instructor, a man of pure character, sincere piety, and an unblemished reputation. He published an Exhortation to Early Piety, A Sermon on the death of Nathaniel Bosworth, Sept. 18, 1801.

AUTHOR.—Jones' Hist. Ch. Litch. 37—Cal. Apr. 1851, 116—Ch. Rev. iv. 318.

REV. DAVID PERRY.

Rev. David Perry, M. A. of Yale, was graduated at Yale, 1772, studied medicine, and settled at Ridgefield, as a physician. He was ordained Deacon, June 6th, 1790, and Priest, Oct. 16th, 1791, and took charge of the Parishes of Reading, Ridgefield, and Danbury. Neglecting to attend the Convocations of the Clergy, and the Conventions of the Diocese, (probably because of his practice as a physician) he fell under censure, and finally resigned his letters of Orders, and relinquished the clerical profession, June 3d, 1795. He continued the practice of medicine, and died in 1817.

AUTHOR.—F. MSS. vi.

[13]

REV. GEORGE OGILVIE.

Rev. George Ogilvie, a native of New York, son of Rev. John Ogilvie, D.D., was graduated at King's (Columbia) College in 1774. He was ordained Deacon by Bishop Provost, and Priest by Bishop Seabury, Oct. 3d, 1790. He was Rector of Christ Church, New Brunswick, from 1787 to 1790, and of St. Paul's, Norwalk, from 1790 to 1796, when he was called to Christ Church, Rye, N. Y., where he died in March or April, 1797. His wife was the daughter of the Rev. Dr. McWhorter, the Presbyterian Minister of Newark, N. J.— He was a tall, noble-looking man, a pleasant companion, a good reader, and a very acceptable preacher. A daughter of Mr. O., who married Thomas Belden, of Fairfield Co., died Jan. 16th, 1846, in the 68th year of her age.

AUTHOR.—F. MSS. v. 969.—Ch. Mag. 1806, 469.—Ch. Ch. iv. 209—Cal. 1846, 19. The name of this man being entered by Bp. S. as "Mr. Ogilvie," it was mistaken for "Wm. O." by the Editors of the Reprint of the Conv. Journals, 141.

REV. JOSEPH WARREN.

Rev. Joseph Warren, a native of Mass., M. A. of Harvard, graduated at Harvard, 1790. He was ordained Deacon, Nov. 28, 1790, and Priest, Sept. 18th, 1792. He is said, in Updike's History of the Narragansett Church, to have been Rector of St. Paul's Church, Narragansett, from 1794 to 1805. It appears, however, from the Records of Christ Church, Middletown, that he was called to the Rectorship of that Church, Oct. 6th, 1800, and remained there "two years, seven months and twelve days," when he resigned, to return, as his letter of resignation says, "to the Parish from which he came." In 1806, 7 and 8, he was at Peekskill and Phillipstown, N.Y. In 1808, he removed to South Carolina, and ministered on Edisto Island until 1811, when he was chosen Rector of St. Thomas' and St. Deny's Parishes in that State. He died in 1815, in North Carolina, where he had gone for his health. He was a plain man, both in manners and dress, and an accomplished scholar, both in Latin and Greek.

AUTHOR.—Updike 302—Journ. N. Y. Conv.—Dalcho. 391, 394. 552. Epis. W. 1831, 118.—F. MSS. vi. 1071, 1193.

REV. SETH HART.

Rev. Seth Hart, born at Berlin, June 21st, 1763, graduated at Yale, 1784, was ordained Deacon, Oct. 9th, 1791, and Priest, Oct. 14th, 1792. He preached first at Waterbury, and from 1794 to 1798, was Rector of the Churches in Wallingford and North

Haven. Some difficulty having arisen in the Parish at North Haven, growing out of a story, that while absent on a journey, he had been seen playing cards, he resigned it, and in 1801 was called to St. George's Ch., Hempstead, L. I., where he remained until his death, March 16th, 1832. He was a good classical scholar, an amiable, sociable, benevolent man, a successful teacher, and acceptable preacher. The Rev. William Henry Hart, his son, died July 28th, 1852, aged sixty-two years. He was graduated at Columbia, 1811—ordained Deacon by Bishop Hobart in 1814, and Priest by Bp. White, at a suitable time thereafter. He was Rector of Christ Church, Richmond, Va., from 1850 to 1820, and of one in Walden, N. Y., from 1830 to 1836. From 1836 to 1842, he was again in his first Parish. He then returned north, and after preaching at Fishkill, returned to his old Parish at Walden, which he held until 1851. His death was caused by paralysis, as was his father's also.

AUTHOR.—Thomp. 356—F. MSS. ii. 238.—Chap. H. C. N. H. in Ch. Ch. vi. 127.—Ch. Mag., 1807, 173. Ep. W. 1832, 183.—Church. 1852, 103.

REV. RUSSEL CATLIN.

Rev. Russel Catlin was graduated at Yale, 1784. He was ordained Deacon, June 10th, 1792, and Priest, June 5th, 1793. He officiated but a short time in Connecticut, when he secularized himself for a time. He subsequently removed to Vermont, where he came to an end that did him no credit.

AUTHOR.—Wm's Vermont, 196.

[14]

REV. DAVID BUTLER, D. D.

Rev. David Butler, D. D. of Trinity, 1832, was born at Harwinton in 1763. At an early age he was apprenticed to the shoemaker's trade, which he left for a time to serve as a soldier in the war of the Revolution. On arriving at the proper age, he commenced business for himself, and was successful in its pursuit. Having married a wife, and settled down, his condition might have been considered as determined for life. But he was fond of books, and pursued a course of reading in his moments of leisure, especially in the evenings. He thus became a Churchman, for he had been educated a Congregationalist, and at length, having qualified himself for the ministry, was ordained Deacon, June 10th, 1792, and Priest, June 5th, 1793. He officiated first at Guilford and Killingworth. In June, 1794, he became Rector of St. Michael's Church, Litchfield, which he resigned in Feb., 1799. He went from thence to Reading, having Danbury and Litchfield in con-

nection, where he remained until 1804, when he was called to St. Paul's, Troy, N. Y., which age and ill health compelled him to resign, about 1833. He died July 11th, 1842, aged 79. The sermon of Mr. B. at the Institution of Rev. Mr. Van Horne into the Rectorship of the Church at Ballstown was published. He also published a Sermon on 1 John, ix., in the *Churchman's Magazine* for July, 1807, and a Sermon of his, preached before the Masons in Woodbury, on the Festival of St. John the Evangelist, 1804, was also published by them. He was a member of the Standing Committee in Conn. a while, and a Delegate to the General Convention from New York. He was a man of strong mind and lively imagination, active, zealous and prudent, wise in the wisdom of the Church; he conquered in her might, and now wears the crown of her glory.

AUTHOR.—Jones' H. C. L. 31. Bp. Doane's "Catholic Pastor," Sermon preached at Dr. B.'s funeral. Ch. Ch. vi. 119. F. MSS. vii. 1278 and 1371.

REV. DANIEL BURHANS, D. D.

The *Calendar* published an account of Dr. B. at the time of his death, a few months since, taken from these sketches, and hence is not repeated.

REV. CHARLES SEABURY.

Rev. Charles Seabury, son of Rt. Rev. Samuel Seabury, Bishop of Connecticut, was born at West Chester, N.Y., May, 1770. He was ordained Deacon by his father, June 5th, 1793. He was Rector of St. James' Church, New London, from 1796 to 1803, and from 1814 to the time of his death in 1844, in the 75th year of his age, he was Rector of the Church in Setauket, L. I. His second wife was the widow of Rev. Henry Moscrop, the mother of Bishop B. T. Onderdonk's wife.

AUTHOR.—Up. 144 —Cal. 1845, 11.—Hall. H. C. in N. L. 28.—Thomp. H. L. I. 274.

REV. JOHN USHER.

Rev. John Usher, of Rhode Island, M.A. of Harvard, 1746, and of Brown, 1794, born at Bristol, R. I., 1722, was graduated at Harvard, 1743, ordained Deacon, July 28th, and Priest, July 31st, 1793, just fifty years after leaving College, was admitted Master of Arts, ad eundem, at Brown University, 1794. He was the son of Rev. John Usher, who was graduated at Harvard, 1719, and died 1775, after having been Missionary of the Venerable Society for Propagating the Gospel in Foreign Parts. in Rhode Island, *fifty-three years.* Mr. John Usher, Jr. was the first person baptized by his father in Bristol, and after his father's death,

continued the service of the Church, and the organization of the Parish, even when compelled to do it secretly, and never failed of a Parish meeting on Easter Monday, though there were not more than two or three to attend. He commenced reading Service when he was *fifty-three years old*, and continued it *eighteen years* before receiving Orders. He was ordained in 1793, and was Rector of the Parish until 1800, when he resigned it, being *seventy-eight years old*. He died in 1804, aged *eighty-two*, having lived long enough to see the fruits of his faith and labors, in the establishment of a large and flourishing Parish. It is a curious fact, that the Rev. Mr. Usher, who had been a lawyer before his ordination, was succeeded from 1803 to 1829, by Bp. Griswold, who had studied law before his ordination, and that from that time to the present, the Rector of the same Church has been Rev. John Bristed, for many years a successful practitioner in the same profession, in the city of New York, so that for *seventy-five* years, the Rectors and Clergy of St. Michael's Church, Bristol, were or had been lawyers.

REV. WILLIAM GREEN.

Rev. William Green, B. A. of Dartmouth and Yale, 1791, a native of New London, was graduated at Dartmouth and Yale the same year. He was ordained Deacon Oct. 18th, 1793. In 1796 and 7, he was officiating in Waterbury, but subsequently went south. He afterwards returned to New London, and engaged in teaching. He remained there until his death in 1801.

AUTHOR.—Ch. Mag. iv. (1807) 173. Cat. Yale. Col. 1850.

REV. CALEB CHILD.

Rev. Caleb Child, of Massachusetts, ordained Deacon, June 7th, 1795, preached in Salisbury until 1799, when being accused by rumor of teaching doctrines contrary to the Church, a committee was appointed to investigate the matter, and he was degraded from the ministry in 1800.

[15]

RT. REV. ALEXANDER VIETS GRISWOLD.

Rt. Rev. Alexander Viets Griswold, D.D. of Brown and Nassau Hall, 1811, and Harvard, 1812, was born at Simsbury, April 26th, 1766, and received his early education and training from the Rev. Roger Viets, the brother of his mother, but the pressure of the times, and the straitness of his father's means, prevented him from receiving the University training. His mind was early turned to the study of law, but weakness of voice prevented him from offering

himself for admission to the bar. He married Miss Elizabeth Mitchelson, and settled in his native place. Here, first as leader to the choir, then as Lay Reader, he made himself useful to the Parish, until the time of his ordination as Deacon, June 7th, and Priest, Oct. 1st, 1795, at Bishop Seabury's last Ordination. He was immediately called to Harwinton, East Plymouth and Northfield, where he remained until 1804, when he was invited to the Rectorship of St. Michael's Church, Bristol, R. I. In 1810, he was elected Bishop of the Eastern Diocese, but retained his connection with the Parish of Bristol, until 1829, when he removed to Salem, Mass., and was Rector of St. Peter's Church until 1835, when he relinquished parochial duty, and removed to Boston. He died Feb. 15th, 1843.

Bishop Griswold was so well known, and his departure was so recent, and the means of learning his history are so abundant, that it cannot be necessary to add more to the eulogies that perpetuate the knowledge of one whose memory is embalmed in the hearts of the Church, and all Christian people. The following is a list of his publications, so far as they have come to our knowledge :

Discourses on the most important Doctrines and Duties of the Christian Religion. 1830. 8vo. pp.
The Apostolic Office, being some brief remarks on the different Orders of the Christian Ministry. 1843. 12mo. pp. 18.
The Reformation, a brief exposition of some of the Errors and Corruptions of Rome. 1843. 12mo. pp. 130.
The Doctrine of Justification, being a Pastoral Letter, (published after his death) 12mo. pp. 22.

REV. (MANOAH) SMITH MILES.

Rev. (Manoah) Smith Miles, born at Derby, March 19th, 1766, was graduated at Yale, 1791. After leaving College, he read Prayers for a time in Barrington, Salisbury, Canaan, and Sandersfield. He became a Candidate for Holy Orders in 1793, and pursued study with such intensity as to produce great debility of body, and some occasional derangement of mind. For this cause the Convocation in Sept., 1794, declined recommending him for ordination, until his health and mind regained their accustomed vigor. This had been done before June, 1795, and he was accordingly recommended and ordained Deacon, June 7th, 1795. He received Priest's Orders from Bishop Provost, of New York, July 31st, 1796. About 1797 he was called to the Rectorship of Trinity Church, Chatham, now Portland, which he retained until his death, Jan. 31st, 1830, having been Rector of that Parish thirty-three years. He preached in Chatham only one-fourth of the time, until 1814, from which time to 1820, he preached three-fourths of the time, when his services were confined to that Parish alone. He was married to Abigail Isaacs of Branford, Oct. 8th, 1796, born Nov. 4th, 1774.

AUTHOR.—MSS. S. M. E.

BIOGRAPHICAL SKETCHES
OF ALL THE CLERGY ORDAINED BY BISHOP JARVIS.
REV. CALVIN WHITE.

Rev. Calvin White was graduated at Yale, 1786, and received Orders in 1798 and 1799. After having been a Presbyterian minister in New Jersey for some years, he conformed to the Church, and was ordained as above. Mr. W. officiated in Middletown about nine months. In 1801, he was Rector of St. John's, Stamford, but in 1804, was called to Christ Church, Derby. He seems to have labored under some difficulty in regard to Baptism, as early as 1805, but remained in the Church, and at Derby, until 1819, when he renounced the Protestant Faith, and soon after joined the Romanists, and was displaced from the ministry in 1822. He died March 21st, 1853, aged ninety.

AUTHOR.—F. MSS. ii. 345.—Scott's H. C. D. 12.—McVickar's, Prof. Years of Bp. Hobart, 114.

[16]   #### REV. BETHEL JUDD.

Rev. Bethel Judd, M. A. of Yale, D. D. of Trinity, 1831, born at Watertown, was graduated at Yale, 1797, and ordained by Bp. Jarvis in 1798. He preached a couple of years at Woodbury and Roxbury, when he was called to Hudson, N.Y., and became Rector of Christ Church in 1802. In 1808 he was chosen Principal of St. John's College, and Rector of St. Anne's Parish, Anne Arundel County, Md., where he remained several years. He then went to Fayetteville, N.C., and was Rector of St. John's Church there, laboring successfully for the revivifying of the Church in North Carolina, until 1818, when he was chosen Rector of St. James' Church, New London, where he remained until 1832. This year he was elected Principal of Cheshire Academy, and soon after Rector of St. Peter's Church, Cheshire, which office he held until 1835. After leaving Cheshire, he resided at Norwalk, and officiated at Wilton, until 1838, when he removed to Ithaca, W. N. Y., where he remained until 1844. From that time to the present, he has resided in that region. He was a Delegate to the General Convention, and a member of the Standing Committee in Connecticut. He published—

Presbyterian Ordination doubtful,—A Letter in two parts, being a reply to (Rev. Mr. Han's) Plain reasons for relying on Presbyterian Ordination. 1819. 12mo. Part I pp. 44. Part II. pp. 30. Two thousand copies of this work were printed at the expense of the Convention.
Baptism not Regeneration. A Sermon preached in St. James' Church, New London, 1820.

AUTHOR.—Miller's Early Ch. N. C. in Church Rev. iii. 309. Jour. Conv. N. Y. and Gen. Conv.—Hitch. H. C. W. in Ch. Ch. iv. 171. Beards. H. C. Acad. 28. H. C. C. 13.

REV. EZRA BRADLEY.

Rev. Ezra Bradley, born at Hamden, was graduated at Yale, 1797. After his ordination in 1798, he preached at Great Barrington, Mass. two or three years. He was degraded in 1804, at the request of Convocation. He subsequently studied law in Baltimore, but some difficulty in regard to a duel induced him to return to his native place. He lived for a time at Hamden, and then removed to West Springfield, where he died in 1853.

AUTHOR.—Murdock's Sketch Class of 1797, 20, 21.

REV. AMOS PARDEE.

Rev. Amos Pardee, born at East Haven, 1770, was graduated at Yale, 1793, ordained Deacon by Bp. Bass of Massachusetts, 1795, and Priest by Bp. Jarvis, 1798. After officiating as a Missionary in Vermont for a few years, he was settled in Lanesboro', Mass., where he continued from 1802 to 1818. From that period until his death, Dec. 21, 1849, he was mostly employed as a Missionary in the Northern and Western part of New York.

AUTHOR.—Ch. Rev. iii. 158.

REV. JOHN CALLAHAN.

Rev. John Callahan, a native of Charleston, S. C., was graduated at the college in his native city about 1796. He was appointed Tutor in the same College soon after graduating, which office he filled for a year or two, when he studied divinity, and was ordained in 1799. Immediately upon his ordination he was called to the Rectorship of St. Mark's in the Bowery, N. Y.— While on a visit to his friends, he was thrown from a carriage and so badly wounded that he died the same day, April 14th, 1800, in the 24th year of his age. He was universally admired as a preacher, was possessed of high intellect and uncommon judgment. A monument was erected to his memory, in the church from which he had been taken.

AUTHOR.—Hist. Col. S. C. in Am. Q. R. xii. 166.—F. MSS. ii. 346.

                                            [17]

REV. EVAN ROGERS.

Rev. Evan Rogers was a native of Hebron. The repulsive doctrines of a high-toned Calvinism in which he was educated, drove him from the Congregationalists to the Methodists, among whom he was a preacher for some time, and by whom he was very highly respected as a man of piety

and Christian zeal. After his ordination in 1799 and 1800, he officiated in Hebron until 1802, when he was called to Christ Church, Rye, where he died January 25th, 1809, in the 42d year of his age, greatly lamented by all who knew him. He was once a Delegate to the General Convention from Connecticut.

AUTHOR.—F. MSS. v. 882, 1017, vi. 1050. Bolton's West. ii. 80. Dow. Journ. 21.

REV. ABRAHAM BRONSON.

Rev. Abraham Bronson, M.A. of Columbia, 1809, and of Middlebury, 1817, the oldest officiating Presbyter in the United States, until his death a few months since, was born at Waterbury, April 11th, 1778. He pursued his studies for a while with the Rev. Mr. Prindle of Watertown, and subsequently at Cheshire Aademy. In 1799, he was Assistant to the Rev. Dr. Bowden. In April, 1800, he was elected Assistant Minister of Trinity Church, Newport, R. I, where he remained till 1803, when he went to Vermont and took charge of the Parishes in Manchester and Abington, in that State. He was active in procuring the formation of the Eastern Diocese, composed of Massachusetts, New Hampshire, Rhode Island and Vermont, and made the first draft of a Constitution of the same, by which an union was entered into for Episcopal purposes, reserving to each Diocese its own Diocesan privileges and independence. In 1805, he commenced a series of efforts for the recovery of the Church lands in Vermont, which had been seized by the State. After twelve years of unremitting perseverance, and with the assistance of some other friends of the Church, power was given to certain Churchmen in Vermont to act as agents of the Society for Propagating the Gospel, to whom the lands were given, to prosecute and recover them for the benefit of the Church in Vermont. Suits were immediately commenced and property recovered to the value of about *three thousand dollars a year*. In 1826, he resigned the two Parishes he had held for twenty-three years, and attempted to establish a manual labor school in that State. Not succeeding in this, he accepted the appointment of Missionary to Ohio, and in 1835 was called to the Rectorship of the Church in Boston, Ohio. At the end of ten years, he resigned this Parish, and settled at Norwalk, in the same State, officiating in the Parishes in the vicinity as there was need. The Parishes at Wakeman, Union and Lyme have thus been enabled to gather strength sufficient to sustain a resident clergyman; and in his seventy-fifth year, (1852) he was at-

tempting to raise a Parish in Plymouth, in the same State, twenty miles from the place of his residence. Mr. B. has also been a Delegate to the General Convention, and one of the Standing Committee of Vermont. A sermon of his, preached before the Convention of Vermont in 1807, is printed in the Churchman's Magazine for that year.

AUTHOR.—MSS. A. B.

REV. JASPER DAVIS JONES.

Rev. Jasper Davis Jones, M. A. of Nassau Hall, 1806, received Orders in 1800 and 1802. For some time preceding 1804, until subsequent to 1808, he was Rector of St. Peter's Church, Perth Amboy, N. J. He subsequently went to Simsbury, where he preached awhile, and where he had married his wife. He continued to reside there for several years, in bad health. He removed from there to Cheshire, where he died very suddenly in 1824.

AUTHOR.—MSS. A. B. C.

REV. GAMALIEL THATCHER.

Rev. Gamaliel Thatcher, of Massachusetts, ordained in 1800 and 1801, was called to the Rectorship of the Church in Ballstown, and vicinity, immediately after his Ordination to the Priesthood. In 1804 he was employed as a Missionary at large, in the western part of New York, but died in 1806.

AUTHOR.—F. MSS. ii. 348.

REV. NATHAN B. BURGESS.

Rev. Nathan B. Burgess, born at Killingworth, (as is supposed) ordained in 1801 and 1802, officiated at Guilford and in the vicinity, and in 1808 he was at Hebron. In 1811 he was on Long Island, and in 1817 residing at Milford. He continued in Connecticut until 1834, at Glastenbury and Preston, and some adjacent places, and then took letters dimissory to New York, where he resided until his death in 1853, officiating as he had ability, and there was need.

[18]
REV. JAMES KILBORN.

Rev. James Kilborn was born at Berlin, Oct. 19th, 1770. His father having been very much reduced in property by the Revolution, and its attendant consequences, advised his son, at the age of sixteen, to commence life for himself, as nothing could be expected by inheritance. Leaving him at that age, without friends, money or education, Providence directed his steps to Granby, where he became acquainted with

Alexander Viets Griswold, and was subsequently an apprentice to Mr., afterwards Bishop Griswold's father. During the evenings of his apprenticeship, he pursued the study of the English, Latin and Greek languages, and several of the branches of Mathematics, under the direction of Mr. A. V. Griswold, making very rapid progress in all of them. A short time before young Kilborn arrived at the age of twenty, Mr. Griswold resigned the business of the shop to him, and he began life as a clothier, and soon after married Lucy, daughter of John Fitch, Esq., the inventor and builder of the first steamboat. By incessant toil and well-directed skill, Mr. K. realized a very handsome fortune in a comparatively short period, a fair proportion of which he expended from time to time in such public improvements as tended to advance the civil, literary or religious condition of the people about him.

The severity of labor, which at first was unheeded, undermined the foundation of a naturally robust constitution, and Mr. K. found it necessary to relax his exertions, which easy circumstances enabled him to do with comfort. Before this, he had become a communicant in the Episcopal Church, though educated in the Congregational faith, and had occasionally officiated as Lay Reader in the Parish Church, which he had materially assisted in building. At the solicitation of several of his friends, he became a Candidate for Orders, and was ordained Deacon in 1802.

Soon after this he removed to Ohio, as the head of the "Sciota Company," and began the settlement of Worthington, Ohio, and founded St. John's Church, in that town. He was the officiating minister of the same for some years, but the needs and necessities of a new colony, made such frequent calls upon the time and labor of Mr. K., that he found it requisite to relinquish the Parish, or refuse other calls, important and pressing in a new colony. He decided upon the former, and has since been engaged in various public and private enterprises and employments.

In 1806 he was appointed a Trustee of Ohio College, at Athens; in 1808 was one of the Commissioners to locate Miami University, and has been President of the Corporation of Worthington College from its organization in 1812 to his death in 1850. He has been a Representative in the Ohio Legislature several times, and was a Member of the House of Representatives from that State in the 13th and 14th Congresses. Having embarked his property in woollen

manufactures during the last war, his shared the fate of similar enterprises, and at the age of fifty (1820) he found himself penniless, and again took his surveying apparatus and went into the woods to obtain a livelihood, and by it once more secured a comparative independence. He has been extensively known in Ohio as a politician, and as a friend of education, has presided at a very large number of public meetings, delivered hundreds of public addresses, and has published several public speeches and addresses.

AUTHOR.—Kilborn's Mem. 66–78.

REV. CLEMENT MERRIAM.

Rev. Clement Merriam, M. A. of Columbia, 1805, was Assistant Minister and School-master in Trinity Church, Newport, from his ordination as Deacon, April 14th, 1802, until called to the Rectorship of Christ Church, Middletown, April 2, 1804. He was ordained Priest, June 6th, 1805, and continued there until June, 1806. As his name does not appear in the Clergy Lists subsequent to this, he probably died soon after.

AUTHOR.—Upd. 107 M. R.

REV. HENRY WHITLOCK.

Rev. Henry Whitlock graduated at Williamstown, 1798, was ordained Deacon [by Bp. Provost,] Oct. 12th, 1800, and Priest, 1802. He was settled at Norwalk and Wilton from 1804 to 1811, when he was called to be the Assistant of Rev. Dr. Hubbard, of New Haven. He died in the winter of 1814–15, at Fayetteville, N. C., on his way further south, for his health, at the age of thirty-seven. He married Euhalia Bartram, and left five children, the eldest of which married the Rev. William L. Johnson, at the early age of 17, and died May 19th, 1848, aged 43 years. A sermon by Mr. W., preached before the Connecticut Convention in 1806, is in the *Churchman's Magazine* for 1807.

AUTHOR.—Cal. June 17th, 1848. Panoplist, 1815, 142.

REV. JOSEPH PERRY.

Rev. Joseph Perry, son of Rev. Philo Perry, was born at Stratford about 1778.— After his ordination, (1802) he officiated a short time in Connecticut, and then at New Stamford and Ballstown, N. Y., from 1804 to 1819. From 1820 to 1826, he was Rector of the Churches at West and East Haven. He died at New Haven, Dec. 13th, 1829, aged 51.

AUTHOR.—Journ. N. Y. Conv.—Chap. H. C. W. H. 18.—Epis. Watch. 1829, 320.

REV. GALEN HICKS.

Rev. Galen Hicks, M. A. of Brown University, educated a Congregationalist, was graduated at Brown University, 1799, and ordained Priest in 1803. He was Assistant and afterwards Principal of the Academy at Taunton, Mass. He was Rector of St. Helena's Parish, Beaufort, S. C., from Jan. 1, 1804 to Oct. 1811, and taught a select school there for some time after. In 1814, he was Rector of Trinity Church, Baltimore. He was residing at Taunton, Mass., 1826, where he probably died.

AUTHOR.—F. MSS. 357. Dalcho. 381.

[19]

REV. SAMUEL GRISWOLD.

Rev. Samuel Griswold, brother of Bishop Griswold, was born at Simsbury, and ordained in 1803 and 1805. Immediately after his ordination, he was called to Great Barrington and Lenox, where he remained until 1820, when he went to Granby and Simsbury, where he officiated till 1823, but without connecting himself with the Diocese of Connecticut. He subsequently removed to the West. Whether living or not, we have not learned.

REV. ASA CORNWALL.

Rev. Asa Cornwall was born at Chatham, [Portland] April, 1782, and graduated at Cheshire Academy, both in the Academical and Theological department. After his ordination, 1804 and 1807, he was Rector of the Churches at Simsbury and Granby, was subsequently at Woodbridge for a time, where he was elected Assistant Principal of Cheshire Academy, 1820, and subsequently Rector of St. Peter's Church in that place. These offices he resigned in 1828, and was able to do only occasional duty until his death, Jan. 28th, 1838. Mr. C. was a member of the Standing Committee of the Diocese for several years, and received many tokens of the respect and confidence of his brethren. He was a devoted and faithful Christian minister, a laborious and successful Parish Clergyman, and an unusually successful teacher. He has a son laboring faithfully, acceptably and successfully in the cause of the same Divine Master.

AUTHOR.—Ch. Ch. ii. 47.—Beards. H. C. C. ii.

REV. TIMOTHY HILLIARD.

Rev. Timothy Hilliard, M. A. of Harvard, was graduated at Harvard, 1793, and ordained Priest, 1805. He was minister of the Church in Portland, Maine, until about 1810, when his name disappears from the

Clergy Lists for several years. In 1832, he was at Gorham, Maine, and continued there until about the time of his death, which took place at Claremont, N. H., Jan. 2d, 1842.

AUTHOR.—Cat. Harv.—Bp. Gris. 1821, Journ Gen. Conv.

REV. RUSSELL WHEELER.

Rev. Russell Wheeler, graduated at Williamstown, 1803, ordained 1805 and 1807, Rector of Christ Church, Watertown, from 1805 to 1814. After resigning this Parish, he went into the Western part of New York, where he continues his labors to the present day.

AUTHOR.—A. B. C. MSS. and Journ. Conv.

REV. BARZILLAI BULKLEY.

Rev. Barzillai Bulkley was ordained Deacon in 1805, and soon after removed from the Diocese. From 1805 to 1808 he was minister of the Churches at Poughkeepsie and Fishkill, and from 1809 to his death, March 29th, 1820, Rector of St. George's, Flushing. He was forty years old at his decease.

AUTHOR.—Ch. Journ. 1820, 127.—F. MSS. vi. 1030. Thomp. H. L. i. 376. This name is erroneously printed Burzillai Blakeslee in the reprint of the Conn. Journals, p. 142.

REV. VIRGIL HORACE BARBER.

Rev. Virgil Horace Barber was son of Rev. Daniel Barber, already mentioned — Immediately after his ordination, 1805 and 1807, he was called to St. John's, Waterbury, where he remained until 1814, when he was elected Principal of Fairfield Academy, N. Y., and Rector of the Church there. About 1817, he declared himself a Romanist. He had previously signalized himself by an application to the General Convention in 1811, to procure a resolution of that body, affirming the invalidity of Lay Baptism, and finally joined that Church which carries the practice to the greatest extent.

AUTHOR.—F. MSS. vi. 1072.—Cal. Feb. 1848.— White M. P. E. C. 211.

REV. JOHN LYNN BLACKBURN.

Rev. John Lynn Blackburn graduated at Queen's College, Oxford, was called to the Rectorship of St. John's Church, Providence, immediately after his ordination, 1805 and 1806. His views and habits not being in accordance with the wishes of his Parishioners, he resigned the Parish in 1807, and returned to Europe.

AUTHOR.—Updike's Hist. Ch. Nar. 423. F. MSS. i. 101.

REV. ROGER SEARL.   [20]

Rev. Roger Searl, M. A. of Middlebury,

1807, appears to have been a native of Coventry, born about 1772, where he was converted, and joined the Methodists in 1791. He was an intimate friend of Lorenzo Dow in his youth, who was a native of the same place, and a second cousin of Mr. S. At the age of nineteen he had resolved to enter the ministry, which he did among the Methodists at that early age. A few years' experience as a Methodist preacher, together with some knowledge of the Episcopal Church gained in his itinerancy, led him to conform to the Church, which he did in 1805.

He first preached about two years, in a Parish in Durham and Berlin, which soon after became extinct, by the removal of the principal inhabitants to the West. From this period, he went to Plymouth, and took charge of the churches there. In 1817 he went to Ohio, and labored faithfully and successfully until his death, Sept. 26th, 1826, in the 55th year of his age. He once represented the Diocese of Connecticut in General Convention.

AUTHOR.—Dow. Jour. 12, 13, 45, 71.—Ch. Mag. 1826, 256.—F. MSS. iii. 371.

REV. ELIJAH G. PLUMB.

Rev. Elijah G. Plumb was ordained in 1806 and 1808. From 1807 to 1818, Mr. P. officiated in East Haven, North Haven, Branford, North Branford and Wallingford.

REV. SALMON WHEATON.

Rev. Salmon Wheaton, D. D. of Trinity, 1835, born 1783, was graduated at Yale, 1805, and ordained 1807 and 1808. After preaching a short time at Stamford, he was called to Newport, R. I., and was Rector of that Church for thirty years, 1810 to 1840. Resigning that parish, he was called to St. John's Church, Johnstown, N. Y., where he died Nov. 24th, 1844, aged 61. A man of eminent piety, deep devotion, sound learning and untiring zeal, he was universally respected and beloved. His wife was sister of Bp. Dehon.

AUTHOR.—Ch. Ch. viii. 382. Up. H. C. Nar. 408.

REV. BENJAMIN BENHAM.

Rev. Benjamin Benham was born at Waterbury, July 21st, 1773. After his marriage in 1790, he was a teacher of vocal music in Dutchess County, N. Y., and subsequently in his native place. In 1802, while teaching in Harwinton, he became intimately acquainted with Rev. Mr., afterwards Bishop Griswold. and in 1803 commenced the study of Theology with him. He accompanied Mr. G. on his first visit to Bristol, R. I., when called to that place, and

spent the following winter with him there, after his removal. He then returned to Waterbury, and pursued study with Rev. Dr. Bronson, going with him to Cheshire when he removed to that place to take charge of the Episcopal Academy. Before his ordination, Mr. B. had read prayers in New Milford and Preston, the first of which he retained twenty years after his ordination in 1807 and 1808. Other Parishes were generally united ;—first New Preston and Roxbury ; then Washington instead of Roxbury, and afterwards Brookfield and Bridgewater, in lieu of New Preston and Washington. In 1821 he resigned Bridgewater, in 1827 New Milford, and in 1828 Brookfield. Deeming his health insufficient to continue clerical duty, he purchased a small farm in Brookfield, and resided there until his death a few days ago.

AUTHOR.—MSS. BB.

REV. DAVID BALDWIN

Rev. David Baldwin was educated a Congregationalist. After his ordination in 1807 and 1809, he was called to Christ Church, Guilford, and St. John's Church, North Guilford, which he retained until 1834. From that time to the present, he has officiated in North Guilford and places in the vicinity.

[21]

REV. JOHN WARD.

Rev. John Ward was a native of Litchfield, perhaps the same as John Y. Ward, who was graduated at Columbia College in 1800. In 1803 and 4, Mr. Ward had charge of the school in Newport, and officiated as Lay Reader in Trinity Church there, during the absence of the Rev. Mr. (afterwards Bishop) Dehon. He was invited to take Orders, and become Assistant Minister of the Parish, but declined. After having been ordained Deacon in 1805, he was again elected to the same office, and accepted it, Nov., 1805. In 1807, he received Priests' Orders He was in the same place until after 1808. His name then disappears from the Clergy Lists of the Gen. Convention until 1829, when he appears as Principal of a Female Academy in Lexington, Ky. He was present, however, at the Annual Convention of Pennsylvania in 1813, but not being in possession of the Diocesan Clergy List for that year, we are not able to determine his location.

AUTHOR.—Upd. 407—Bp White's Abrd. Penn. Jour. Ch. Rev. iii. 125—Kill Litch. Co. Biog. 149.

REV. JOSEPH DAVIS WELTON.

Rev. Joseph Davis Welton, educated at Cheshire, was called to St. Paul's Church,

Woodbury, in connection with Bethlehem and Roxbury, as soon as ordained Deacon, Dec. 18, 1808, Priest Dec. 10, 1810, and retained the first until 1816. He then went to Weston, which ill health soon compelled him to resign. After a long and painful illness, he died at Waterbury, Jan. 16th, 1825, in the 42d year of his age. His character combined those graces which make the Christian lovely, the man holy, and the minister mighty.

AUTHOR.—Hitch. H. C. W. in Ch. Ch. iv. 169. Ch. Mag. 1825, 32.

REV. STURGES GILBERT.

Rev. Sturges Gilbert, educated at Cheshire, officiated in Kent, Sharon, Salisbury and Canaan until 1816, when he succeeded Mr. Welton at Woodbury and Roxbury, where he remained until 1827. From Woodbury he went to Great Barrington, Mass., where he remained until 1840.— From there he went to Hobart, N. Y., and then to Westford, where he died, Sept. 3d, 1847. He was ordained Deacon, Dec. 18, 1808, and Priest, Dec. 28, 1810,

AUTHOR.—Hitch. H. C. W. in Ch. Ch. iv. 171.— Ban. Cross. Sept. 1817.

[22]

REV. SAMUEL FARMAR JARVIS, D. D., LL. D.

Rev. Samuel Farmar Jarvis, D.D. of Pa. Univ. 1819, LL. D. of Trinity, son of Rt. Rev. Abraham Jarvis, D. D., born at Middletown, Jan. 20th, 1787, was graduated at Yale 1805, ordained by his father, Deacon, in Trinity Church, New Haven, March 18, 1810, and Priest in the same place, April 5, 1811. He died at Middletown, March 26, 1851. Dr. Jarvis, having filled so large a share in the public councils of the Church, and being so universally known as a man, a Christian, a scholar and a Priest, and his life and character having been so recently described, (Church Review, July, 1851), it is not necessary that we should, nor would our limits permit us to go into any detailed account of his life and labors. The following is a list of the offices he has filled, and the works he has published, so far as they have come to our knowledge. In 1811 and 12, he was Rector of St. Michael's Church, Bloomingdale, N. Y., and from 1812 to 1819, of St. James' Church, New York City, in connection with it. From 1820 to 1826, he was Rector of St. Paul's Church, Boston. From 1826 to 1835, he was absent in Europe. After his return, he was Professor of Oriental Literature in Trinity (Washington) College. From 1837 to 1840 he was Rector of Christ Church, Middletown, and subsequently did Missionary duty

in the vacant places in that vicinity. He was Delegate to the Gen. Convention and a Member of the Standing Committee, nearly the whole time from his return to this country until his death. He was appointed "Historiographer of the Church," by the Gen. Convention of 1838, the results of which have been —

A Chronological Introduction to the History of the Church. London and New York, 1845 ; 8vo. pp. 618. And,

The Church of the Redeemed, or the History of the Mediatorial Kingdom from the fall of man in Paradise to the rejection of the Jews, and the calling of the Gentiles. 1850, 8vo. pp. 622.

He was one of the Editors of the Gospel Advocate from 1821 to 1826, and published many valuable papers in it during that time, among which his Review of Webster's Plymouth Rock Oration, deserves especial notice. He also published—

1806. An Oration before the Phi Beta Kappa Society of Yale College.
1811. A Sermon on the death of Mrs. Hart.
1814. An Address at the laying of the corner-stone of Trinity Church, New Haven.
1815. A Thanksgiving Sermon for the Restoration of Peace.
1816. A Sermon on "the Unity of the Church" before the New York Convention.
1817. A Letter to the Chiefs of the Onondaga Indians, to convert them to Christianity.
1820. A Discourse on the Religion of the Indian Tribes of North America, delivered before the N. Y. Hist. Society, Dec. 1819.
1822. A Sermon preached on the 3d Anniversary of the Auxiliary Education Society of the Young Men of Boston.
1822. A Sermon on Regeneration, before the Mass. Diocesan Convention of 1821, with copious and valuable appendix.
1825. Narrative of Events connected with the acceptance and resignation of the Rectorship of St. Paul's, Boston. (Printed for private circulation only.)
1835. Sermon preached before the Church Scholarship Society, Hartford, 1835.
1836. An Address to the citizens of Hartford on the Birth day of Linnæus.
1836. Sermon on "Christian Unity" before the Board of Missions.
1838. Easter Address of a Rector to his Parishioners.
1838. The Long Home of Man ; a Sermon preached at the Funeral of the Rev. Stephen Beach, 1838, (printed 1839.)
1841. Address to the citizens of Middletown, occasioned by the death of President Harrison.
1843. Two Discourses on Prophecy, with an Appendix, being a refutation of Millerism.
1843. No Union with Rome.
1844. Worldly and Christian Education compared ; a Sermon preached in St John's Ch, South Hackney.
1844. "The Holy of Holies seen through the Sanctuary," pr. in the Church & All Souls, St. Mary Le Bone.
1844. T. H. Horne, B. D.'s Mariolatry corrected and enlarged from the 2d London edition, and edited by the Rev. Dr. Jarvis.
1846. "The Promise is to you and your Children," a Sermon on Infant Baptism, Oct. 11th, 1846.
1846. A Synoptical Table of Egyptian and Sacred History.—[In connection with this; were written four Lectures on the same subject, delivered in Utica, but never published. He wrote and prepared a work on a larger scale for the Press—embracing the matter contained in the Lectures.]

1846. The Colonies of Heaven, a Sermon preached before the Diocesan Convention of Conn., 1846.
1847. The Presence of God in His Church, a Sermon preached at the ordination of Rev. Prof. Jackson ; with a Vindication of the Chronological Introduction from the aspersions of Prof. Kingsley.
1847-9. Five Articles in the Church Review—
    1. Vindication against Prof. Kingsley.
    2. Review of Kenrick on the Primary. (1)
    3.   do.   do.   do.   (2)
    4.   do.   do.   do.   (3)
    5. Egyptian Antiquities (Review of Dr. Hawks.)
1849. A Voice from Connecticut, occasioned by the late Pastoral Letter of the Bishop of N. Carolina.
1847. Reply to Bp. Milner's End of Religious Controversy.
1850. The Church of the Redeemed, vol. 1.

In addition to the above, he had prepared for the press, a Chronological Harmony of the Four Gospels, on the plan of that annexed to the Chronological Introduction. He began Vol. II. of the Church of the Redeemed, but had proceeded only as far as *two chapters*, when it pleased God to end his labors on earth. He had also commenced a series of sermons on Sacrifice, intended for Lent, but we do not know whether it was completed.

[23]

REV. DANIEL MACDONALD, D. D.

Rev. Daniel MacDonald, D. D. of Columbia 1821, after his ordination was Assistant Preceptor of Cheshire Academy, until 1813, when he was called to St. Peter's Church, Auburn, N. Y. In 1817, he was chosen Principal of Fairfield Academy. When that was made into a College, he was appointed one of its Professors, which post he filled until his death in 1830.

AUTHOR.—Sermon by Rev. J. C. Rudd, 1836.

REV. NATHANIEL HUSE.

Rev. Nathaniel Huse, M. A. of Dartmouth, born at Methuen, Mass., was graduated at Dartmouth, 1802, and ordained Deacon by Bp. Griswold, at Bristol, R. I. He was at Warehouse Point several years, when he went to Simsbury, and remained there about four years. From thence he went to the western part of New York, where he still continues his labors.

REV. FREDERICK HOLCOMB, D. D.

Rev. Frederick Holcomb, D.D. of Trinity, 1838, born at Granby, Oct. 13th, 1786, graduated at Williams College, 1809. He was called to the Rectorship of Christ Ch., Watertown, in 1814, and resigned it in 1838, having performed the duties of the office faithfully, acceptably and successfully for a period of twenty-four years. Since then he has been Rector of some of the neighboring Parishes, most of the time.— He is still living and active in his Master's

service. A Sermon of Dr. H.'s, preached before the Diocesan Convention in 1841, was printed in the *Chronicle of the Church* for that year. Dr. H. was for many years a member of the Standing Committee of the Diocese, and has also represented it in General Convention.

REV. REUBEN HUBBARD.

Particulars not obtained.

REV. BIRDSEY G. NOBLE.

Particulars not obtained.

REV. STEPHEN JEWETT.

Rev. Stephen Jewett, M. A. of Trinity, 1833, born at Lanesboro', Mass., was educated at Cheshire. He was ordained Deacon, Sept. 15, 1811, and Priest by Rt. Rev. J. H. Hobart, Oct. 5, 1813. He officiated from this time until 1821, in Hampton and Granville, N. Y., and some of the adjacent towns in Vermont. From Dec., 1821 to Nov., 1833, he was Rector of Christ Church, Derby, and Union Church, Humphreysville. He soon after removed to New Haven and performed Missionary duty in the neighboring Parishes, as long as his health would permit. St. James' Church, Westville, and St. James' Church, Fair Haven, may be said to owe their existence to his labors, as also the first attempt to resuscitate the old and dilapidated Parish of Christ Church, West Haven. During his residence in Derby, he was employed as a teacher most of the time, and many young men looking forward to the ministry, received his instruction then, as others have his patronage since, by enjoying the benefit of Scholarships in Trinity College, created by funds which he has given. A Sermon on Duelling was published in 1820, without name, which was from his pen. His health has disabled him from ministerial labor for some time past.

REV. ORRIN CLARK.

Rev. Orrin Clark, M. A. of Union, 1817, and D. D. 1827, was ordained Deacon, ******, and Priest, by Bp. Hobart, between the New York Conventions of 1812 and 1813. He was Rector of Trinity Church, Geneva, N. Y., from 1814 to his death, which took place Feb. 24th, 1830, in the 41st year of his age. He died after a long and trying illness, greatly lamented, having exemplified by his own patient endurance of suffering, in private, the principles he inculcated in his public teachings.

AUTHOR.—Epis. Watch. i. 408.

EXCOMMUNICATION, 65, 136; rubric
  on, 85; Samuel Plumb, of Derby, 64
EXETER, ENGLAND, Dean of, 12
EXETER, N.Y., 303
EXHORTATION to bring a child to a
  bishop for Confirmation, 35
EXHORTERS, 59
EXPLANATION OF THE CHURCH CATE-
  CHISM (LEWIS)
EXPOSITION OF THE XXXIX ARTICLES
  (BURNET)
EXPOSITORY NOTES...ON THE NEW
  TESTAMENT (BURKITT)

F

FAIRBORN, SAMUEL, SR., 33
FAIRCHILD, AGUR, 91
FAIRCHILD, BENJAMIN, 49
FAIRCHILD, DANIEL, 152
FAIRCHILD, ELISHA, 153
FAIRCHILD, EPHRAIM, 50
FAIRCHILD, JAMES, 50
FAIRCHILD, OLIVER, 67, 73
FAIRCHILD, SAMUEL, 50, 67, 73
FAIRCHILD, STEPHEN, 73
FAIRCHILD, THOMAS, JR., 27
FAIRFAX, REV. BRYAN (LORD), 294;
  sketch of, 305
FAIRFAX, HENRY, 306
FAIRFAX, WILLIAM, 306
FAIRFIELD, CONN., now Southport,
  28, 35-36, 53, 73, 91-92, 187, 189,
  197, 208-209, 211, 238, 274-275,
  282, 290; a county town with courts
  of judicature, 190; glass put into
  church windows at, 33; Churchmen
  in, 34; list of Episcopalians at, 51;
  Dr. James Laborie catechizes at,
  35; Henry Caner schoolmaster at,
  33; problem of Caner's salary there,
  37; Revolutionary Committee of, 198;
  trustees of St. George Talbot's donation to the church there, 196; Memorial of Trinity Church to the General
  Assembly, 111; Congregational Society at, 263; Episcopal Society in,
  263; First Congregational Society,
  262; First Ecclesiastical Society,
  264; Trinity Church, 262-264, 290-
  291, 304
FAIRFIELD, N.Y., Episcopal church
  in, 312
FAIRFIELD ACADEMY, FAIRFIELD,
  N.Y., 312, 314
FAIRFIELD COUNTY, CONN., 68, 91
FAIRFIELD EAST ASSOCIATION, 284
FAIR HAVEN, CONN., 249; St. James's
  Church, 314
FALMOUTH, ENGLAND, 195
FANATICISM, 122, 157, 175, 178
FANNING, EDMUND, Governor and

Colonel, 38, 49, 213, 267, 298;
  sketch of, 268
FANNING, HANNAH (SMITH), 268
FANNING, CAPT. JAMES, 268
FANNING, THOMAS, 268
FARMAR, HANNAH (PECK), 283
FARMAR, SAMUEL, merchant, 112,
  118, 120
FARMINGTON, CONN., 183, 244, 274
FARRANT, HENRY, 29
FASCHINES, 203-204
FASHION BATTERY, 201
FASHION PARTY cuts trees from Col.
  Malbone's farm, 201
FASSETT, JOSIAH, 165, 180
FAST DAYS, 190-191, 269
FASTING, 295
FAULKNER, CALEB, 164
FAYERWEATHER, REV. SAMUEL,
  102
FAYETTEVILLE, N.C., 312; St.
  John's Church, 310
FAXON, JOSIAH, 91
FEAZE, 64
FEBREGUE, JOHN, 91
FEMALE ACADEMY, 313
FERGUSON, REV. COLIN, 228, 290;
  sketch of, 303
FERRIE, GAMALIEL, 64
FERRIS, JOHN, 92
FERRIS, JONATHAN, 68
FERRIS, PETER, 92
FERRY (FERRIES), 44, 129, 162
FEVERS, 102
FILER, GENERAL, 79
FINCH, JOHN, 48, 53
FINLAY, MR., 64
FIREWOOD, 55
FIRST FRUITS OFFICE, 151, 177
FISHER, MR., of Salem, Mass., 216
FISHER, GEORGE, 57
FISHER, REV. NATHANIEL, 268
FISHKILL, N.Y., 289, 294, 309, 312
FISK, B., 153, 227
FISK, JOHN, 227
FITCH, MR., 53
FITCH, JABEZ, 253-254
FITCH, JOHN, 311
FITCH, LINDLE, 51
FITCH, LUCY, 311
FITCH, NATHANIEL, 51
FITCH, WILLIAM, 211
FITCH & HOLLY, MESSRS., mer-
  chants of Stamford, 223, 226
FLECTERE SI NEQUEO SUPERES,
  163
FLEETWOOD, WILLIAM, 7
FLOWERS, NATHANIEL, 255
FLUSHING, LONG ISLAND, N.Y., 110,
  112, 196; St. George's Church, 294,
  306, 312
FOGG, REV. DANIEL, 176-177, 182,
  184, 186, 199, 208, 212, 215, 232,

252, 272, 275, 297, 300; petitions
  the General Assembly regarding a
  salary seven years in arrears, 207;
  desires permission of the Select-
  men of Pomfret to go to New York
  on business, 207
FOGG, REV. JEREMIAH, 297
FOGG, REV. THOMAS BRINLEY, 297
FOOT, J. A., 264-265
FOOT, JOEL, 265
FOOT, JOHN, 50, 92
FOOT, NATHAN, 50
FOOTE, ASA, 293
FOOTE, DANIEL, 307
FOOTE, REV. DAVID, 238-239, 282,
  293-294, 298; sketch of, 307
FOOTE, NATHANIEL, 293
FORD, JACOB, 84
FORSEE, JAMES, 49
FORT HUNTER, N.Y., 304
FORWARD, ABEL, student at Yale, 147
FOUNTAIN, WILLIAM, 49
FOWLE, REV. ROBERT, sketch of,
  308
FOWLER, CALEB, 110
FOWLER, EDWARD, BP., 6; Design
  of Christianity, 260?
FOWLER, JOHN, 61, 63-64, 73, 77,
  91, 93
FRANCE, 82, 218, 247, 273, 281
FRANK, THOMAS, 7
FRAYSSE, PAUL, 33
FRAZIER, DANIEL, 173-174
FRAZIER, THOMAS, 173-174
FRAZIER, WILLIAM, 146
FREDERICKSBURG, N.Y., 208, 246,
  289
FREEMAN, SAMUEL, 12
FRENCH, CAPT., 278
FRENCH, CHRISTIAN, 38
FRENCH, JEREMIAH, 50
FRENCH, JOHN, 50, 152
FRENCH, JONATHAN, 50, 152
FRENCH, JOSEPH, 152
FRENCH, SAMUEL, 50
FRENCHFIELD, ELIHU, 29
FRINK, JEDIDIAH, 49
FRONTIER TOWNS, 100
FROST, CAPT., 226
FROST, MILLER, 50
FROST, STEPHEN, 50
FULHAM PALACE, 288
FULLAR, JOHN, 63
FULLER, ELIJAH, 245
FULLER, JOHN, 183
FULSOM, ISRAEL, 49
FUND FOR THE RELIEF OF THE
  WIDOWS AND CHILDREN OF
  CLERGYMEN, 200
FURNITURE. See Communion Furni-
  ture.
FURNIVAL RIVER, 152
FUTURE JUDGMENT, 154

copy of an I. deed at New London, 187; I. corn, 201; I. tribes, 188

INDIANS, 13, 33-34, 40, 54, 58, 67, 69, 71, 77-79, 95, 130, 136-137, 146, 155-156, 185, 187, 279; of the Narraganset tribe, 40, 140, 156; instruction of, 21; 200 in Johnson's Stratford, 34; plans for conversion of, 36; stole and barbarously abused a child, 142; their loyalty and gifts to the Church, 148; Prayer Book in Mohawk tongue, 188; small village of I. near Newtown, 36; Sir Wm. Johnson appointed over His Majesty's I., 130; prejudice against the I., 142; instructions concerning the I. in North America, 148; plan for promoting the gospel among the I., 159; Gen. Lyman is no friend to the plundered I., 150; Micmac I., 267; Mohawk I., 298; Mohegan tribe, 270; Narraganset I., 150; see also: Heathen, Iroquois, Nahantic Tribe, and Narraganset.

INDIES, 194

INFANT BAPTISM, 154

INFANT BAPTISM (WALL)

INFANTS are refused baptism by the Dissenters, 171

INFIDELITY, 6, 85, 135, 142, 144; is coming in like a flood, 283

INFIDELS, 18, 33, 46, 57, 59-60, 76, 80, 83, 86, 89, 91, 123, 130, 155

INFLUENZA, 280

INGERSOL, MR., 244; attorney for Godfrey Malbone, 170

INGERSOL, RALPH T., 264

INGERSOLL, JARED, attorney representing the Colony of Connecticut in England, 103-105

INGERSOLL, JONATHAN, 247-248, 251, 254-255, 261-262, 302

INGHAM, NORTH, 50, 57

INGHAM, SAMUEL, 49

INGLIS, REV. CHARLES, later Bishop of Nova Scotia, 136, 146, 206, 230, 246, 268, 272, 279-280, 282, 285, 288; suggests that Bp. Seabury write the English bishops about his diocese, 236

INGLIS, JACK, 235

INGLIS, PEGGY, 234

INGRAHAM, MR., 170

INGRAHAM, NATHANIEL G., 153

INNER TEMPLE, LONDON, 177

INOCULATION of missionaries before sailing for England, 149; against small pox, 103, 225

INSURANCE on organ sent from England, 277

INVESTMENTS: depreciation of Church i., 200

IPSWICH, MASS., 268

IRELAND, 305

IRISH-JEANS, 64

IRISH TOWN in Connecticut, 59

IROQUOIS, 181

ISAAC, JOHN, SR., 27

ISAAC, RALPH, 51

ISAACS, ABIGAIL, 310

ISAACS, BENJAMIN, 265

ISAACS, ELIZABETH, 274

ISHAM, ZACHEUS, 7

ISLAND, 123

ISLIP, LONG ISLAND, 301

ISRAEL, EPHRAIM, 49

ITHACA, N.Y., 310

ITINERANT MISSIONARIES, need for, 37

IVES, EDWARD J., 307

IVES, PHINEAS, 57

IVES, REV. REUBEN, 237, 252, 282, 291, 293, 295; sketch of, 292, 307

IVES, THOMAS, 50, 57

IVES, ZACHARIAH, 292

J

JACKSON, DANIEL, 50

JACKSON, GABRIEL, 92

JACKSON, RICHARD, merchant in New Haven, 139; late of Stamford, 145

JACKSON, SILAS, 62

JACOBITES or NON-JURORS: esp. the Scottish bishops who remained loyal to the superseded Jacobean line of kings, 225, 231, 271

JACOBS, REV. ALEXANDER, 145

JAILS, 56, 60, 62, 137, 171, 173, 183

JAMAICA, B.W.I., 67

JAMAICA, LONG ISLAND, 294; Grace Church, 288, 290, 301

JAMES, HENRY, 48, 52

JANES, MR., 28

JARVIS, MR., 217

JARVIS, ABRAHAM, BP., 125-126, 128-129, 133, 145, 151, 153, 198-200, 205-210, 214-216, 227-230, 236-239, 250-254, 271, 273?-275, 277, 280?-283, 286, 288, 293, 296, 299-301; married Hannah (Peck) Farmar, 283; questioned by the S.P.G. secretary, 146; on the loyalty of Episcopal clergymen to the State of Conn., 248; Abp. Secker spoke to him of the wisdom of not pushing the matter of American bishops until the bitterness might be diminished, 127; letter to him from Wm. Rivet concerning books, 133; clergy ordained by, 310ff.; sketch of, 288

JARVIS, HANNAH (PETERS), 286; see also Hannah Delavan Peters.

JARVIS, ISAAC, 281

JARVIS, LEVINA, 286

JARVIS, MARTHA (SEYMOUR), 279

JARVIS, NANCY, 281

JARVIS, NAOMI (BRUSH), 288

JARVIS, SAMUEL, 51, 72-73, 77, 98, 246-247, 279

JARVIS, CAPT. SAMUEL, 288

JARVIS, REV. SAMUEL FARMAR, D.D., 216, 289, 293; sketch of, 313; Chronological Harmony of the Four Gospels, 314; Church of the Redeemed, 314

JARVIS, WILLIAM, husband of Hannah Delavan Peters, 51?, 231, 271, 279, 281-282, 286-287

JEANES, WILLIAM, 28

JEFFERY, JOHN, 12

JEFFIRES, GEORGE, 49

JEFFREY, JOHN, 49

JENCKS, CHARLES, 260

JENNINGS, DAVID, 262

JENNINGS, ISAAC, 77

JENNINGS, JOHN, 51

JENNINGS, JOSHUA, 51

JENNINGS, NATHAN, 51

JENNINGS, SAMUEL, 51

JENNINGS, SOAME, 300

JENNINGS, ZECHARIAH, 92

JERSEY, 140

JERUM, ROBERT, 243

JERVOIS, THOMAS, 7

JESSUP, JAMES, 255-256

JESUITS at work in the colonies, 6; English J. are the equals of those of France and Spain, 285

JEWETT, BENJAMIN, 163-164, 169

JEWETT, REV. STEPHEN, sketch of, 314

JEWS, 34; converted to the Church in Stratford, 33

JOHNSON, CAPT., on the Church in Guilford, 250

JOHNSON, MR., carries Samuel Seabury's letter to Andrew Millar, Bookseller, 96; a lawyer in Newport--faithless to the Indians, 150

JOHNSON, ANNE (BEACH), 270

JOHNSON, ASAHEL, 153

JOHNSON, CHARITY (FLOYD), 270

JOHNSON, CLARISSA, 304

JOHNSON, JOHN, 28, 48, 52

JOHNSON, NATHANIEL, 50

JOHNSON, CAPT. NATHANIEL, 274

JOHNSON, SIR NATHANIEL, 12

JOHNSON, ROBERT, 49, 64

JOHNSON, SAMUEL, of Guilford, 304; a teacher in the Presbyterian Method, 34

JOHNSON, REV. SAMUEL, D.D., of Stratford, 29-32, 35, 39, 41, 44-45, 54, 57, 67, 77, 83, 85, 89, 96, 106, 109, 115, 120-121, 124-126,

OGDEN, REV. JOHN COSINS, 282; sketch of, 306

OGDEN, JONATHAN, 110

OGDEN, MARY WOOSTER, 307

OGDEN, REV. UZAL, D.D., 217, 298

OGILVIE, CATHARINE (SYMES), 298

OGILVIE, REV. GEORGE, 282; sketch of, 298, 308

OGILVIE, REV. JOHN, 136, 146, 150, 156, 298, 308

OHIO, 311, 313; O. College, 311

OLD JEWRY, LONDON, 216

OLD TESTAMENT: Robert Lowth's commentary upon the Prophets, 154

OLIVER, ALDERMAN, in the Tower of London for contempt of the House of Commons, 172

OLIVER, REV. THOMAS FITCH, 228; sketch of, 304

OLMSTED, NATHAN, 51

OMISSIONS from the Liturgy, 224, 269; see also Liturgy and Prayer Book.

ON JUSTIFICATION (WOLSELEY)

ONDERDONK, BENJAMIN TREDWELL, BP., 296, 306, 309

ORANGE, CONN.: See Oyster River.

ORANGE COUNTY, VT., 268-269

ORANGE RANGERS, 268

ORDINANCES of the Church of England, 27

ORDINATION: Episcopal vs. Presbyterian o., 29; death toll among those seeking o., 88; candidates must go a thousand leagues for every o., 135; Seabury's first o. of candidates, 228

ORGAN in and for American churches, 276, 296; qualities desired in the o. intended for Trinity Church, New Haven, 275-277

ORGANIST wanted by Trinity Church, New Haven, 276

ORTHODOXY, standard of, 287

OSBALDESTON, RICHARD, BP., 267, 288; arranged for Abraham Jarvis' ordinations, 127

OSBORN, JOHN, 153

OSBURN, DAVID, 50

OSBURN, RICHARD, 50

OSBURN, WILLIAM, 51

OSTERVALD, J. F., 12

OVID: Metamorphoses, 135

OWEN, SIR ARTHUR, 7

OWEN, ELIZABETH, 279

OWEN, HANNAH, 279

OWEN, JOHN, 30, 107?

OWEN, SILAS, 279

OXFORD, CONN., 98, 193-194, 300, 303-304, 307; St. Peter's Church, 291, 293

OXFORD, ENGLAND, 312; University of, 30, 268-269, 280, 288; Dean of Christ Church, 46

OYSTER PONDS, LONG ISLAND, 195

OYSTER RIVER: part of the boundary between New Haven and Orange, in which the ancient parish of Christ Church, West Haven, was situated.

P

PADDOCK, REV. SETH BIRDSEYE, 271

PAGE, DR., 303

PAGET, THOMAS, 12

PAINE, DR., 201

PAINE, MR., Apothecary, 203

PAINE, SETH, 165, 168-169

PAINE FARM, 162

PALL, MATHEW, 74

PALMER, JOEL, 245

PALMER, JOHN, 245

PALMER, JONATHAN, 245

PALMER, LEVI, 260

PALMER, MARY (MRS. SOLOMON), married again--to a Dissenter in good circumstances and in a space of four months after P's death, 180; married again because of poverty, 186

PALMER, REV. SOLOMON, 101, 103, 104-105, 107, 109-111, 114-115, 121, 123, 125-126, 129, 133-134, 139, 142, 144, 151, 153-155, 158, 170, 226, 230, 289, 291; was a Dissenting teacher at Cornwall, Conn., for fourteen years, 101; sustained damages when he left his Dissenting congregation, 124; lives amicably with the dissenters of every denomination, 133; his removal to Litchfield, 145; strong request for his continuance at Litchfield and Cornwall, 116; assigned to Rye, N.Y., 120; left the S.P.G. library in New Haven when transferred, 154; his son-in-law is Dr. George Hurd of New Milford, 189; his widow and orphans, 223; Mary, his widow, became Mrs. Buel, 189; the death of his widow, Mary Palmer Buel, 189; his children, now settled in New Milford, are described, 186; S.P.G. donation for his now fatherless children, 184; his youngest children deserve the S.P.G. charitable donation, 187

PALMES, GUY, 49

PAMPHLETS, 172

PANTON, REV. GEORGE, 206

PAPISTS, 43, 57, 60, 74-76, 80, 83, 86, 89-91, 118, 123, 130; prohibited from holding real estate, 78

PARAPHRASE AND COMMENTARY ON THE NEW TESTAMENT (WHITBY)

PARAPHRASE...UPON THE EPISTLES AND GOSPELS (STANHOPE)

PARDEE, REV. AMOS, sketch of, 310

PARISH, JOSEPH, 49

PARISH REGISTERS to be maintained, 18

PARK, ADAM, 49

PARK, JACOB, 49

PARK, JOSIAH, 49

PARKE, JOHN, 38

PARKER, JAMES, 49

PARKER, JOHN, 49

PARKER, SAMUEL, BP., 212, 216, 227-228, 240, 249

PARLIAMENT, 147; authority of, 143; acted to permit consecration of American bishops, 235

PARNELL, MOSES, 33

PAROCHIAL LIBRARY. See Libraries.

PAROCHIAL SCHOOLS. See Schools.

PARROT, WILLIAM, 12

PARSONS, AARON, 258

PARSONS, CURTIS, 258

PARTRICK, JOHN, 51

PARTRICK, RICHARD, 51

PASTIMES, 16

PASTORAL MATTERS, 136

PATRICK, SIMON, BP., 6

PATRICK, SYMON + ROBERT LOWTH: Commentary upon the Old and New Testaments (vols. 1-3: The Prophets), 154

PATRIOTISM, 192-193

PATTEN, 112; difficulty in holding the p., 89

PATTERSON, JOHN, 100

PAUG, CONN., alias for Northford, a parish belonging to Branford, 129, 134

PAUL, MATTHEW, 74-75, 80

PAWLET, MR., 32

PAXTON, MR., 177

PAYNE, SETH, 164; Dissenting Teacher in Stafford conforms to church, 66

PEACE SOCIETY, EAST HADDAM, 308

PEACOCK, JOHN, 27

PEARCE, BENJAMIN, 50

PEARS, THOMAS, 50

PEARSON, EDWARD, Treasurer of the S.P.G., 101, 106, 109, 112, 118, 120, 124-125, 130, 132, 138-139, 141, 145, 154, 157, 172; succeeded by Mr. Symondson, 151

PEARSON, JOB, 44

PEARSON, WILLIAM, 51

PEASE, SIMON, 177, 179

PEAT, BENJAMIN, 27

PEAT, DAVID, 50

PEAT, ELNATHAN, 77

PEAT, JOHN, 27

PEAT, JOSEPH, 50

PECK, ELIZABETH, 283

SCIOTA COMPANY, 311
SCOTLAND, 162, 283, 288-289, 306;
continues to aid American Presby-
terians, 145; Episcopal Church of,
229, 246-247
SCOTT, EDMUND, 64
SCOTT, GERSHOM, 64
SCOTT, JONATHAN, 50, 64
SCOTT, ZEBULON, 64
SCOVIL, ANNA, 292
SCOVIL, REV. JAMES, 102, 133, 140,
142, 199-200, 205-206, 212, 227,
232, 237, 275-276, 278?, 281-282,
290, 293
SCRANTON, ICHABOD, 258
SCRIPTURES, 39; see also Bible.
SCUDAMORE, THOMAS, 50
SEABURY, MR., New York merchant,
223, 226
SEABURY, ABIGAIL (MUMFORD), 288
SEABURY, REV. CHARLES, youngest
son of Bp. Seabury, 235, 252, 296;
sketch of, 300, 309
SEABURY, JOHN, 49
SEABURY, MARY (HICKS), wife of
Bp. Seabury, 300
SEABURY, NATHANIEL, 49
SEABURY, REV. SAMUEL, SR., father
of Bp. Seabury, 44, 46, 57, 84, 288,
299, 301; list of his parishioners in
New London, 49; removal from New
London, 63
SEABURY, SAMUEL, BP., 95, 110, 146,
206-207, 210, 214-215, 217, 219,
221, 225-226, 228, 231, 234, 237-
238, 267-269, 271, 273, 283-284,
289-300, 303ff.; appointed to New
Brunswick, N.J., 93; threatened by
an English bookseller with an attachment of his S.P.G. salary, 96; his
wise and prudent conduct, 247; if he
fails to become a bishop, he will settle in Nova Scotia, 214; alarmed Parker by the circumstance of his being
a refugee and absentee, 212; will not
enjoy any allowance from the English
Episcopal Fund, 214; consecrated
Bp. of Conn., 223; talked of a visit to
Philadelphia, 226; to meet the clergy
at Middletown, 227; his reply to the
Conn. clergy, 229; how Conn. clergy
elected him, 272; his carefulness in
the matter of ordinations, 231; clergy
ordained by him, 303; details re. his
mitre, 235; urged to write the English
bishops about his diocese, 236; application for trust funds for his support,
247-248; problem of securing help
from the General Assembly toward
establishing a trust fund for his support, 249; Jeremiah Leaming asked
to become his Coadjutor Bishop, 283;
Bishops White and Provoost refuse

to unite with him in constituting a
Bishop for Va., 286; "continues
to conduct with propriety," 286;
sundry of his disciples cannot find
cures, 287; they court him but will
never coalesce with him in the consecration of a Bishop, 287; "...you
will never be considered...Mem-
bers of the British Church after you
submit to the Episcopal Power of
Bishop S.," 223; sketch of, 288;
Letters of a Westchester Farmer,
288
SEABURY, REV. DR. SAMUEL, III,
son of Rev. Charles Seabury, 301
SEABURY, REV. DR. WILLIAM JONES,
grandson of Rev. Charles Seabury,
301
SEA-CAPTAIN: case of the old s-c.
discussed (Capt. Durfey), 87
SEAGAR, SAHDRICK, 57
SEAL of the S.P.G., 8
SEAMAN, DUTTON, 7
SEARLE, REV. ROGER, sketch of, 312
SEARS' MILL, 152
SEBLY, JOSEPH, 92
SECKER, THOMAS, ARCHBP., 103-
104, 133, 142, 271, 274, 279?; John-
son writes him re. Solomon Palmer,
122; speaks to Abraham Jarvis and
Bela Hubbard about not wishing to
hurry the matter of American bish-
ops, 127; discoursed freely upon ec-
clesiastical affairs in America, 128;
his correspondence postponed be-
cause of gout, 128; wisely did not
present to the King the petition of
the Conn. clergy for a resident
bishop, 141
SECTARIES, 142, 287
SECULARIZATION, 309
SEELY, GIDEON, 152
SEELY, JOHN, 50
SEELY, JOSEPH, 92
SEELY, NEHEMIAH, 50, 67, 73
SEELY, OBADIAH, 72
SEELY, ROBERT, 50, 67, 73
SELBY, JOSEPH, 92?
SELKRIG, J. SAMUEL, 64
SELLECK, MAJOR, 28
SELLECK, JOANNA, 284
SEPARATISTS, 245
SERMONS, 17, 31, 56, 97, 123, 140,
180, 200, 216; read by lay readers,
35, 134; borrowed from the Whole
Duty of Man, 64; demand for printed
s., 123; candidates for Orders should
not compose their own s. except un-
der the direction of a clergyman, 215
SETAUKET, LONG ISLAND, 309; Caro-
line Church, 301
SEVEN TOWNSHIPS, 47, 56-57
SEYMOUR, MR., 273; Mayor of Hart-

ford, 218
SEYMOUR, JOHN Y., 258
SEYMOUR, MARTHA, 279
SEYMOUR, THOMAS, 248, 250
SEYMOUR, CONN., orig. Hum-
phreysville, 295; Trinity Church,
295; Union Church, 295
SHALER, ABIGAIL, 153
SHALER, NATHANIEL, 153
SHARKMAPLE, JOHN, 33
SHARON, CONN., contiguous with
Salisbury, 104-105, 110, 115-116,
121, 125, 127, 135, 143, 145, 151,
153, 157-158, 165, 171, 173, 175,
180, 184, 195, 199, 211, 225, 238,
281, 303, 313; its church building
now completed, 134; desires folio
Bible and Prayer Book, 114; Epis-
copal Church there, 284
SHARP, GRANVILLE: tract on the
ancient legal division of the people
into tithings and hundreds, 216
SHARP, JOHN, BP., 6, 12
SHARP, THOMAS, 92
SHARPE, REV. JOHN: his journal of
1710, 28
SHATTOCK, TOBIAS, 150
SHECHEN INDIANS, 69
SHEFFIELD, MASS., 122
SHELBURN, VT., 307
SHELBURNE, NOVA SCOTIA, 213,
282
SHELDON, MR., 77
SHELFIELD, ELISHA, 201
SHELTON, ABIJAH, 152
SHELTON, ANNA (WHEELER), 269
SHELTON, BENJAMIN, 255
SHELTON, DANIEL, 152, 290
SHELTON, EBENEZER, 152
SHELTON, ELISHA, 255
SHELTON, HAMILTON, 290
SHELTON, HANNAH, 269
SHELTON, JAMES, 152, 269
SHELTON, JOHN, 152
SHELTON, JOSIAH, 152
SHELTON, LUCY (NICHOLS), 304
SHELTON, REV. PHILO, 228, 237-
239, 251, 282, 290, 293, 297; en-
tered on the Convention minutes
as a candidate for Orders, 206;
sketch of, 304
SHELTON, SAMUEL, 152, 290
SHELTON, THADDEUS, 152
SHELTON, VICTORY, 255
SHELTON, WILLIAM, 152
SHELTON, REV. WILLIAM, D.D.,
290
SHERLOCK, THOMAS, BP., 81-82,
85-86, 88-90, 93, 95, 98, 279,
284, 288; Letter to the Clergy
and People of London and West-
minster on Occasion of the Late
Earthquakes (London, 1750), 82;

To the Wardens and Veſtry of the Church in *Hartford*

GENTLEMEN,

AGreeable to a reſolve of the Convention of this State, I tranſmit to you the ſum to be collected in your Society for the uſe of the Epiſcopal Academy.—Upon a calculation, it appears that your proportion of the ſum contemplated to be raiſed is *Five Dollars*

You will be pleaſed to tranſmit the money collected, to the Rev'd Doctor Bowden by the firſt day of January next.

$5

With reſpect,

Your obedient ſervant,

Aſhbel Baldwin.

Stratford, November 1ſt, 1800.

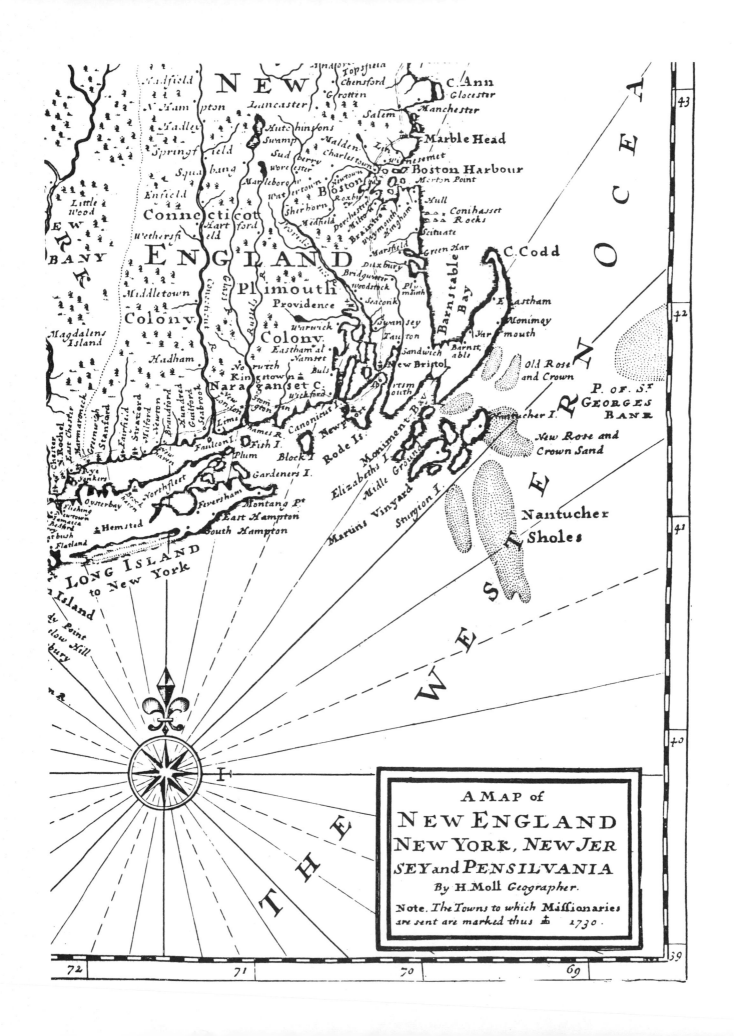

THE SEAL OF THE S. P. G.